A COURSE OF LECTURES

ON

NATURAL PHILOSOPHY

AND THE

MECHANICAL ARTS.

BY THOMAS YOUNG, M.D.

FOR. SEC. R.S. F.L.S. MEMBER OF EMMANUEL COLLEGE, CAMBRIDGE,
AND LATE PROFESSOR OF NATURAL PHILOSOPHY IN THE
ROYAL INSTITUTION OF GREAT BRITAIN.

IN TWO VOLUMES.

VOLUME II.

LONDON:

PRINTED FOR JOSEPH JOHNSON, ST. PAUL'S CHURCH YARD,
BY WILLIAM SAVAGE, BEDFORD BURY.

1807.

PREFACE.

THE first part of this volume, consisting of the mathematical elements of natural philosophy, is in part reprinted from the syllabus of the lectures, but considerable additions have been made to it, both of elementary matter and of original investigations. These elements are perfectly independent of every other work introductory to any branch of the mathematics, and they comprehend all the propositions which are required for forming a complete series of demonstrations, leading to every case of importance that occurs in natural philosophy, with the exception of some of the more intricate calculations of astronomy. It was therefore absolutely necessary that they should be expressed in the most concise manner that was possible; yet except a few propositions which have been cursorily introduced in some of the scholia, no essential step of a demonstration has ever been omitted. The best use, that a student could make of these elements, would be to read over each theorem or problem superficially, then to endeavour to form for himself a more particular demonstration, and to compare this again with that which is here given: for the exertion of a certain degree of invention is by far the surest mode of fixing any principle of science in the mind.

The catalogue of references has been methodically subdivided, as far as it was possible to do it with convenience and accuracy, and the works and passages belonging to each subdivision have in general been arranged in chronological order; except that the different productions of the same author have been placed together. The divisions of the catalogue follow very nearly the same order as the text of the lectures, so that there has been no occasion for any references from one to the other. This arrangement may be the most conveniently understood from the table of contents prefixed to the catalogue; and the method of classing the subdivisions and titles, which become more and more particular, has been as much as possible such, that if sufficient information cannot be found under the head to which the subject immediately belongs, there may always be a chance of obtaining it from some more extensive work, under the last head, of a more general nature, which may be found, in the catalogue, by looking back for a change of type, or in the table of contents, by recurring to a column situated one degree more to the left. On the other hand, in order to facilitate, in some measure, the labour of selection, such works, as appeared to possess superior merit and originality, have been distinguished by asteriscs; and those, on the contrary, that have been thought either erroneous or unimportant, have been marked with an obelisc. It must not however be understood, that all the other works mentioned are considered as deserving neither commendation nor censure, since with respect to the greater number of them the evidence must necessarily be imperfect. The extracts occasionally inserted, as well as the original remarks which are sometimes introduced, are not so much intended for the general reader, as for those who make any single department their particular study; many of them being only brief hints, which may serve to direct their attention to a further pursuit of the subjects. In the mathematical and astronomical parts, all references to the transactions of foreign societies have in general been omitted; partly because they would have been too numerous for insertion, and partly because they may be found at large in the copious works of Murhard and of Reuss. The references to periodical publications have been continued, where it was possible, to the beginning of the year 1805.

For the convenience of those who have access to the libraries of the Royal Institution, of the Royal Society, of its most liberal and illustrious President, and of the British Museum, such works as are to be found in these collections are marked respectively, R. I, R. S, B. B, and M. B: and where the same book is contained in more than one of them, it has generally been marked as belonging to that which is most accessible to the public, the preference being given to the library of the Royal Institution. The articles printed in Italics are intended to form, if taken separately, a complete catalogue of the books which are quoted, without repetitions. The capital Roman numerals refer to volumes, the smaller ones to divisions or sections, and the figures to pages or years.

The miscellaneous papers are reprinted with some corrections and additions, but with no other alterations, of any kind, than might have been made at the time when they were first published: except the insertion of the last section of the essay on the cohesion of fluids, which consists of comparative extracts from a later memoir of Laplace, and of remarks on the method of investigation which he has employed. The abstract of the papers read before the Royal Society consists of such notes, as have in general been inserted in their places among the references; but as they constitute a continued account of the proceedings of the society for the whole of one season, it has been thought most eligible to preserve them united in order of time.

Welbeck Street, 30th March, 1807.

SOLD BY MR. JOHNSON.

1. De corporis humani viribus conservatricibus, dissertatio, auctore Thoma Young, M. D. 8vo. Price 2s.

2. A Reply to the animadversions of the Edinburgh Reviewers on some papers published in the Philosophical Transactions. By Thomas Young, M. D. 8vo. Price 1s.

CONTENTS.

MATHEMATICAL ELEMENTS OF NATURAL PHILOSOPHY; P. 1.

Part I. Pure Mathematics.
  Section 1. Of quantity and number; 1.
    Powers of numbers; 4. Table of reciprocals; 5. Logarithms of prime numbers; 6.
  2. Of the comparison of variable quantities; 7.
  3. Of space; 8.
  4. Of the properties of curves; 22.

Part II. Mechanics. Of the motions of solid bodies.
  Section 1. Of motion; 27.
  2. Of accelerating forces; 28.
  3. Of central forces; 30.
  4. Of projectiles; 32.
  5. Of motion confined to given surfaces; 33.
  6. Of the centre of inertia, and of momentum; 35.
  7. Of pressure and equilibrium; 37.
  8. Of the attraction of gravitating bodies; 45.
  9. Of the equilibrium and strength of elastic substances; 46, 83.
  10. Of collision, and of energy; 51.
  11. Of rotatory power, 52.
  12. Of preponderance, and the maximum of effect; 54.
  13. Of the velocity and friction of wheelwork; 55.

Part III. Hydrodynamics. Of the motions of fluids.
  Section 1. Of hydrostatic equilibrium; 57.
  2. Of floating bodies; 59.
  3. Of specific gravities; 59.
  4. Of pneumatic equilibrium; 60.
  5. Of hydraulics; 60.
  6. Of sound; 65, 84.
  7. Of dioptrics and catoptrics; 70.
  8. Of optical instruments; 76.
  9. Of physical optics. To p. 80, Art. 461.

A SYSTEMATIC CATALOGUE OF WORKS RELATING TO NATURAL PHILOSOPHY AND THE MECHANICAL ARTS; WITH REFERENCES TO PARTICULAR PASSAGES, AND OCCASIONAL ABSTRACTS AND REMARKS; 87.

Contents of the catalogue; 89.

MISCELLANEOUS PAPERS; 521.

I. Observations on vision; 523.
  Theories of the accommodation of the eye; 523. New explanation; 525. Solution of optical queries; 527. Explanation of plate 1; 530.

II. Outlines of experiments and inquiries respecting sound and light; 531.
  Subjects of the paper; 1. Of the quantity of air discharged through an aperture; 531. 2. Of the direction and velocity of a stream of air; 532. 3. Ocular evidence of the nature of sound; 536. 4. Of the velocity of sound; 5. Of sonorous cavities; 537. 6. Of the divergence of sound; 538. 7. Of the decay of sound. 8. Of the harmonic sounds of pipes. 9. Of the vibrations of different elastic fluids;

10. Of the analogy between light and sound; 541. 11. Of the coalescence of musical sounds; 544. 12. Of the frequency of vibrations constituting a given note; 545. 13. Of the vibrations of chords; 546. 14. Of the vibrations of rods and plates. 15. Of the human voice; 549. 16. Of the temperament of musical intervals; 551. Explanation of plate 2..7; 553.

III. An essay on cycloidal curves, with introductory observations; 555.

1. On mathematical symbols; 555. 2. On cycloidal curves; 558.

IV. An essay on music; 563.

1. Of music in general; 563. 2. Of the origin of the scale; 566. 3. Practical application of the scales; 568. 4. Of the terms expressive of time; 571.

V. The Bakerian Lecture for 1800. On the mechanism of the eye; 573.

1. Changes of opinions respecting the crystalline lens; 573. 2. Division of the subjects to be investigated. 3. General consideration of the sense of vision; 574. 4. Description of an optometer; 575. 5. Dimensions and powers of the author's eye; 578. 6. Extent of the changes required for the accommodation of the eye; 585. 7. Examination of the state of the cornea; 586. 8. Examination of the length of the axis; 589. 9. Examination of the changes of the lens; 592. 10. Anatomical remarks on the eyes of different animals; 597. Explanation of plate 8..13; 604.

VI. A letter to Mr. Nicholson, respecting sound and light, and in reply to some observations of Professor Robison; 607.

Heads of the paper on sound and light; 607. Remarks on Smith's harmonics; 609. On temperament; 610.

VII. The Bakerian lecture for 1801. On the theory of light and colours; 613.

Excellence of Newton's experiments; 613. Hypothesis of an elastic ether; 614. Undulations; 615. Colours; 616. Constitution of material bodies; Transmission of impulses; 618. Spherical divergence; 619. New divergence; 620. Partial reflection; 622. Refraction; Total reflection; Dispersion; 623. Combination of undulations; 624; Striated surfaces; 625. Thin plates; 626. Thick plates; 628. Inflection; General conclusion respecting the nature of light; Iceland crystal; 629. Momentum of light; Solar phosphori; 630. Heat; Experiment proposed; 631. Plate 14; 632.

VIII. An account of some cases of the production of colours not hitherto described; 633.

General law of double lights; Colours of fibres; 633. Colours of mixed plates; 625. Internal reflection; 636. Dispersion; Dr. Wollaston's experiments; 637. Blue light of a candle; Dispersive powers of the eye; 638.

IX. The Bakerian lecture for 1803. Experiments and calculations relative to physical optics; 639.

1. Experimental demonstration of the general law of the interference of light; 639. 2. Comparison of measures deduced from various experiments; 640. 3. Application to the supernumerary rainbows; 643; 4. Argumentative inference respecting the nature of light; 645. 5. Remarks on the colours of natural bodies; 646. Experiment on the dark rays of Ritter; 647.

X. An essay on the cohesion of fluids; 649.

1. General principles; 649. 2. Form of the surface of a fluid; 649. 3. Analysis of the simplest forms; 650. 4. Application to the elevation of particular fluids; 651. 5. Of apparent attractions and repulsions; 655. 6. Physical foundation of the law of superficial cohesion; 657. 7. Cohesive attraction of solids and fluids; 658. 8. Additional. Extracts from Laplace, with remarks; 660. Plate 15; 670.

ACCOUNT OF THE PROCEEDINGS OF THE ROYAL SOCIETY, FROM NOVEMBER 1801 TO JULY 1802; 671.

INDEX; 683.

ADDITIONS AND CORRECTIONS.

P. 2. Art. 20, last line, for $\frac{a}{b}$ read $a:b$.

P. 20. Art. 179, l. 2, for "planes" read "parallel planes."

P. 23. Col. 2. L. 35, for "being opposite to them" read since these lines have the same side A B opposite to them in the triangles A B C, A B I, and their equals B C, B I are opposite to the same angle B A C.

P. 35, after article 265, insert,

265. B. THEOREM. Supposing the force retarding a pendulum or balance to be to the force of gravitation or of elasticity at the extreme point of each vibration as f to 1, the circumference of a circle to its diameter being as c to 1, the time of each vibration will be increased in the ratio of 1 to $1 + \frac{2ff}{c}$, or $1 + .64 ff$ very nearly.

The impulse being supposed to be momentary, and to be given at A, the pendulum, will move to B as if completing a vibration of which C is the middle point, A C being to A B as f to 1: in its return the middle point will be D, and the extent of the vibration being B E, the space D A, which is equal to C A, will be described in a time as much longer than would have been required for describing C A, as D E or D B is shorter than C B, that is, in the ratio of $1-2f$ to 1, very nearly. But the whole time of describing C A is less than if the velocity were equable, in the ratio of the diameter of a circle to its semicircumference, or of 1 to $\frac{c}{2}$, and is therefore to that of a semivibration as f to $\frac{c}{2}$, and to that of a complete vibration as f to c; consequently we have for the retardation $\frac{2ff}{c}$, the time of a vibration being unity.

SCHOLIUM. If the propelling force of a balance or pendulum, and the friction which retards it, be increased in the same proportion, the extent of the vibration will remain unaltered, and the motion will be retarded in proportion to the square of the fraction expressing the friction. But if the propelling force be increased in a greater proportion than the friction, the extent of the vibration will be increased in the ratio of this excess, and the value of the fraction f will be diminished in the same proportion. Thus, if the friction were doubled, and the propelling force quadrupled, the extent of vibration would be doubled, and the time would remain unaltered; but if the propelling force were only tripled, the fraction f would on the whole be increased $\frac{1}{2}$, and the retardation $\frac{2}{4}$.

P. 54, after art. 359, insert,

359. B. THEOREM. Every compound body has at least three axes of permanent rotation, at right angles to each other.

When a body revolves round any axis, it is necessary, in order that the revolution may be permanent, that the centrifugal forces on all sides balance each other, so that the axis may not be urged to revolve round the centre of gravity. The centrifugal force of each particle being proportional to its distance from the axis, its tendency to turn the axis, in a given direction, being represented by the force reduced to that direction, will be proportional to its distance from a plane passing through the axis, perpendicular to the supposed direction; and its effect will also be the greater as its distance from the equatorial plane is greater; since the axis may be considered as a lever, and the centre of gravity as its fulcrum. Now if a plane be made to revolve on a line passing through the centre of gravity, it is obvious that there is a position in which the sums of all the products of the particles into their distances from this plane and from a plane perpendicular to it, passing through the same line, will be equal on both sides of the plane; and the plane remaining in this position, if another plane be supposed to turn round any line out of the first plane until it acquire a similar property with it, it may easily be understood that the intersection of these planes will be an axis of permanent rotation, since any other plane passing through it will possess the same property with respect to the parts of the solid on each side of it. If then two planes perpendicular to each other be supposed to revolve round this axis, until they acquire that position in which either of them

VOL. II.   b divides the solid into parts possessing equal powers to turn the axis, the other will also divide it in a similar manner, and their intersections with the equatorial plane of the first axis will also be permanent axes of rotation: for the same sums will express the action of the particles in both cases, the distance from either plane being equally concerned in the effect of each particle, and the effects of those particles which are in contiguous sections of the solid either way counteracting each other, and cooperating with the effects of the sections diagonally opposite. And in the same manner it may be shown that the equatorial plane divides the solid in such a manner with respect to both these axes as to enable the body to maintain a permanent rotation round them.

359. C. THEOREM. If a body, revolving freely round any axis, be caused for a moment to revolve at the same time round another, the joint result of both motions will be a revolution round a third axis, in an intermediate position, which will continue to be the axis of rotation, provided that the body be capable of revolving permanently round it.

If the angle formed by the axes be divided into two parts, of which the sines are inversely proportional to the velocity of revolution round the contiguous axes, it is obvious that the line thus dividing the angle will remain at rest, in consequence of the equal velocities of the two motions, the angle divided being supposed to be one of those in which the revolutions are in opposite directions: and the angular velocity of rotation round the new axis will be to the greater of the former velocities as the sine of the whole angle to the sine of the greater portion thus determined, as may be inferred from considering the motion of the poles of either of the primitive revolutions. The position of the new axis, and the motion of any other point of the body, is obviously sufficient to determine the velocities and directions of the motions of every other part, since the form of the body is supposed to be unchangeable; so that it is unnecessary to demonstrate that the motion resulting from the separate motions of each point is such as belongs to its place with respect to the new axis of rotation; and the body, beginning once to revolve upon this axis, will continue its rotation exactly in the same manner as if it had arisen from a simpler cause.

P. 55. Col. 2, after art. 364, insert,

SCHOLIUM. In the same manner it may be shown, that if B E D be any circle, or in general any curve, rolling on the wheel A, and describing the line C D, and if the same curve, rolling within the circle of which B is the centre, and which touches A, describe the line B D, whether straight or curved, the force will still be directed to the point of contact E, and the motion of the wheels will be uniform.

P. 58. Col. 2. L. 29, for "C D" read C B.

P. 64. Col. 2. L. 15, for "$70\tfrac{10}{3}$" read $160\tfrac{10}{3}$.

P. 64. At the end,

SCHOLIUM 2. It may be demonstrated that an impulse communicated to a liquid at any point of the margin of a reservoir, of which the bottom is an inclined plane, terminated by that margin, will advance every way in a cycloidal direction; by reasoning similar to that which is employed for the demonstration of the property of the cycloid, as the curve of swiftest descent (261). The form of the wave will be that of a curve cutting an infinite number of cycloids at right angles; and any number of points in it may be found, by drawing on any points in a parabola as centres, a number of circles touching the vertical tangent of the parabola, and laying off on each from the point of contact an arc equal to the distance of that point from the vertex of the parabola. The truth of this may easily be shown from the properties of cycloidal pendulums, (259).

P. 76. Col. 2. L. 5, omit "or."

P. 79. Col. 2. L. 6, for "differs .. in" read, scarcely differs from this except in.

P. 80. Before art. 451, insert, SECTION IX. OF PHYSICAL OPTICS.

P. 122. Col. 1, after l. 20, insert, Such solids of revolution are generally called spindles, where the curve is convex outwards; in this case, where it is concave, they might be called trochi.

P. 139. Col. 2, after l. 14, insert,

Pressure of Bodies in Motion.

Hée on the pressure of weights in machines, Ph. tr. 1755.1.

P. 144. Col. 1, after l. 28, insert,

From the British Magazine for March, 1801

The pinacographic instrument resembles in its construction a musical pen, but is much broader, so as to draw parallel lines at one or two strokes over the whole surface of any page. Its use is to manufacture an index. It is to be accompanied by inks of nine different colours, such as are the most easily distinguished from each other at first sight. In order to construct an index, procure two copies of the best edition of your work;—cover each page with parallel lines, expressive of its number, drawing them vertical for units, horizontal for tens, and oblique for hundreds, denoting each figure by the ink of the bottle on which you find it marked; then, with the assistance of your wife and daughters, cut the pages first into lines, and then into words; distribute all the words into little boxes, marked with the two initial letters, and then paste them on the pages of a blank book in the precise order of the alphabet. The index being thus completed,—if you print it, a very little habit will enable the compositors to read off the references as correctly from this method of notation as if they were written out at length. If the number of colours be found too great, the difficulty may be easily removed by using only five, and supplying the deficiency either by providing two instruments of different constructions, or by drawing the lines in a greater variety of positions.

P. 166. Col. 2, at the end, insert,

The work of a coalheaver on the river Thames is considered as very laborious, but the effect produced is not comparatively great. Four men are employed in filling baskets in the hold of the lighters, and four in "whipping" or elevating them from 12 to 20 feet, which is performed by ascending three or four steps, and standing on a stage, which descends while the baskets are raised; and the labour of filling and raising them is nearly equal. The usual work of a day is to raise 42 chaldrons, weighing about 126000 pounds, that is, 31 500 pounds for each labourer, to the height of 16 feet, making 504000 pounds, raised 1 foot, instead of 3 600 000, or .14

But it is not difficult to do twice or twice and a half as much, and 105 chaldron are often raised, or .35

There have even been instances in which 195 chaldron have been raised, or .65

P. 167. Col. 1. L. 4 from the bottom, for "Cazand" read Cazaud.

P. 198. Col. 1. L. 2, for "barculus" read barulcus.

P. 256. Col. 1. L. 12, for "aerostation," read aerostatation.

P. 278. Col. 2. L. 17, for " v ", read U.

P. 319. Col. 1. L. 11 from the bottom, for "170" and "180", read $\frac{1}{70}$ and $\frac{1}{75}$.

Col. 2. L. 7, after "case" insert as.

L. 22, for "specimen" read spectrum.

L. 24, after " in," insert a.

P. 330. Col. 1. L. 3. from the bottom, for "3553", read .3553.

P. 354. Col. 1. l. 29. for "1" read nearly $\frac{1}{4}$.

P. 356. Col. 2. After l. 3 from the bottom, insert,

Observations on the Sun's Light.

Heliostate. S'Gravesande's Natural Philosophy.

P. 362. Col. 2, last Line, for "56707°.. Snellius," read, 56070 to 56802 Klostermann.

$-22°$ 18' S. 57037 Lacaille, 1752.

$$\begin{pmatrix} 56746 \\ \text{or } 57070 \text{ Fernelius} \\ 55021 \text{ Snellius.} \end{pmatrix}$$

P. 364. Col. 1. L. 2 from the bottom, for " or" read the diameters.

P. 367. Col. 1. L. 29. for $\frac{x^s}{}$ read $\frac{1}{4}^w$.

P. 367. Col. 2. L. 12, for "$73\frac{1}{4}$," read 39, or perhaps 40.

P. 387. Col. 2. L. 11. from the bottom, for "areometry" read acrometry.

P. 452. Col. 2, after l. 2, insert.

According to Kirwan's theorem, the mean temperature of the year, and that of the month of April, is 84°—26. 5 v. s. 2 l. The greatest mean heat of the summer months may be found very nearly, according to Kirwan's table, by this formula, 86—18 v. s. 2 l—1.7 v. s. 12 $(l+15°)$, and the mean heat of the month of January, which is the coldest month by 80—29. 5 v. s. 2 l—v. s. ^{2} 4 l—v. s. 18 $(l+7°)$. The error seldom amounts to more than a degree.

P. 455. Col. 1, after l. 20, insert,

Laplace Exp. du syst. du monde, 267. Asserts that " the attraction of the sun and moon does not produce, either in the sea, or in the atmosphere, any constant motion from east to west."

P. 455. Col. 2. after l. 7 from the bottom, insert,

Remarks on the Effects of the Sun's Heat on the Atmosphere.

It is very difficult to demonstrate conclusively that the sun's relative motion from east to west has or has not such a tendency as Halley attributed to it, to cause an easterly wind in the neighbourhood of the equator; it appears however to be possible to show that no effect of this kind can be produced in any sensible degree.

The immediate effect of the expansion of the air at any place must be to cause a partial elevation of the surface of the atmosphere: for the instant that this elevation remains, the lateral pressure will be unequal at every part of the height of the column except the basis, and the inequality must become greater in ascending, being always proportional to the difference of the weights of the columns contiguous on each side to any given point. The elevation may therefore be considered as the beginning of a wave, which will be propagated each way with a certain velocity; and this velocity must at first be less than that of a similar wave in a fluid perfectly homogeneous, but will approach to it as it spreads, the inequality of temperature soon disappearing. If the cause of expansion continues, new waves will continually succeed each other, so that the surface will remain horizontal. Hence will arise a pressure; forcing the lower parts of the air towards the point of expansion, and a current will be produced, which will cause a continual circulation. But it is obvious that no parts of the atmosphere can be urged towards the place of expansion, until the first wave has reached them, and if the velocity of this wave be greater in one direction than in another, the effect must be more extensive on that side. Now in the case of the successive expansion of the air by the sun, all the points of expansion move westwards with a velocity of about 1500 feet in a second, which is considerably greater than that of a wave moving upon the atmosphere, or that of sound propagated through it, which is more immediately comparable to that of the effect in question; consequently the wave cannot precede the point of expansion, so as to produce any current in the more westerly parts; the current from east to west must, therefore, prevail. But, at the opposite part of the globe, the refrigeration must produce an effect precisely contrary to that of the heat; the air tending to descend and flow from the parts which are coolest; the depression not being transmitted to the more westerly parts with sufficient velocity, to produce a current from east to west by these means, the easterly parts only will be affected by a current from west to east, which will probably exactly counterbalance the easterly tendency produced at the opposite part of the globe, so that the breezes thus excited must be merely transitory, and in opposite directions.

P. 463. Col. 2. L. 4 and 5 from the bottom must be transposed.

P. 471. Col. 1. L. 2 after the table, for "above" read about.

P. 481. Col. 2. L. 6. for "charged", read charred.

P. 509. In the columns "Refractive force" and "simple refractive power", the numbers opposite to "White wax" and "Oak" should be opposite to "Olive oil" and "White wax", respectively.

P. 560. Col. 1. L. 39, after "purpose", insert, Mr. Giddy has observed that an equiangular spiral may impel another similar curve without friction: it is indeed easy to see that two such spirals must always touch each other in the line joining their centres.

P. 562. Col. 1. L. 11, for "$\frac{1}{4}$", read, $\frac{1}{5}$.

L. 5 from the bottom, for "concentrating", read generating.]

MATHEMATICAL ELEMENTS

OF

NATURAL PHILOSOPHY,

DEDUCED FROM AXIOMATICAL PRINCIPLES.

MATHEMATICAL ELEMENTS

OF

NATURAL PHILOSOPHY.

PART I.

PURE MATHEMATICS.

SECTION I. OF QUANTITY AND NUMBER.

1. DEFINITION. The letters of the alphabet are employed at pleasure for denoting any quantities, as algebraical symbols or abbreviations. But, in general, the first letters in order are used to denote known quantities, and the last to denote unknown quantities; and constant quantities are often distinguished from variable quantities in the same manner.

2. DEFINITION. Quantities are equal when they are of the same magnitude.

SCHOLIUM. The abbreviation $a = b$ implies that a is equal to b; $a > b$ that a is greater than b; and $a < b$ that a is less than b.

3. DEFINITION. Addition is the joining of magnitudes into one sum.

SCHOLIUM. The symbol of addition is an erect cross: $a + b$ implies the sum of a and b, and is called a more b.

4. DEFINITION. Subtraction is the taking as much from one quantity as is equal to another.

SCHOLIUM. Subtraction is denoted by a single line, as $a - b$, or a less b, which is the part of a remaining when a part equal to b has been taken from it.

5. DEFINITION. A negative quantity is of an opposite nature to a positive one, with respect to addition or subtraction; the condition of its determination being such, that it must be subtracted where a positive quantity would be added, and the reverse.

SCHOLIUM. A negative quantity is denoted by the sign of subtraction: thus if $a + b = a - c$, $b = -c$ and $c = -b$. A debt is a negative kind of property, a loss a negative gain, and a gain a negative loss.

6. DEFINITION. A unit is a magnitude considered as a whole complete within itself.

SCHOLIUM. When any quantities are enclosed in a parenthesis, or have a line drawn over them, they are considered as one quantity with respect to other symbols; thus $a - (b+c)$ or $a - \overline{b+c}$ implies the excess of a above the sum of b and c.

7. DEFINITION. A whole number is a number composed of units by continued addition.

Thus one and one compose two, $2+1=3$, $3+1=4$, or $2+2=4$. Such numbers are also called multiples of unity.

8. DEFINITION. A simple fraction is a number which by continual addition com-

poses a unit, and the number of such fractions contained in a unit, is denoted by the denominator, or number below the line.

Thus $\frac{1}{3}+\frac{1}{3}+\frac{1}{3}=1$.

9. DEFINITION. A number composed of such simple fractions by continual addition, may properly be termed a multiple fraction; the number of simple fractions composing it is denoted by the upper figure or numerator.

In this sense $\frac{2}{3}$, $\frac{3}{3}$, $\frac{4}{3}$, are multiple fractions, and $\frac{3}{3}=1$, $\frac{4}{3}=\frac{3}{3}+\frac{1}{3}=1+\frac{1}{3}$, or $1\frac{1}{3}$.

10. DEFINITION. Such quantities as are expressible by the relations denoted by whole numbers, or fractions, are called commensurable quantities.

SCHOLIUM. All quantities may, in practice, be considered as commensurable, since all quantities are expressible by numbers, either accurately, or with an error less than any assignable quantity.

11. DEFINITION. Multiplication is the adding together so many numbers equal to the multiplicand as there are units in the multiplier, into one sum, called the product.

SCHOLIUM. Multiplication is expressed by an oblique cross, by a point, or by simple apposition; $a \times b = a.b = ab$.

12. DEFINITION. Division is the subtraction of a number from another as often as it is contained in it; or the finding of that quotient, which, when multiplied by a given divisor, produces a given dividend.

SCHOLIUM. Division is denoted by placing the dividend before the sign $\div$ or :, and the divisor after it; as $a \div b = a : b$.

13. AXIOM. When no difference can be shown or imagined between two quantities, they are equal.

14. AXIOM. Quantities equal to the same quantity, are equal to each other.

If $a=b$ and $c=b$, then $a=c$.

15. AXIOM. If to equal quantities equal quantities be added, the wholes will be equal.

If $a=b$, then $a+c=b+c$; if $a=b=c$, then adding b, $a=b+c$; if $a+b=c=d$, then adding e, $a+b=c+d$.

16. AXIOM. If from equal quantities equal quantities be subtracted, the remainders will be equal.

If $a=b$, $a-c=b-c$, if $a+b=b+c$, $a=c$.

17. AXIOM. If equal quantities be multiplied by equal numbers, the products will be equal.

If $a=b$, $3a=3b$; if $a=b:3$, $3a=b$; and if $a=b$, $ca=cb$.

18. AXIOM. If equal quantities be divided by equal numbers, the quotients will be equal.

If $5a=10b$, $a=2b$; and if $ca=cb$, $a=b$.

SCHOLIUM. Articles 16, 17, 18, might have been deduced from art. 15, but they are all easily admitted as axioms.

19. THEOREM. A multiple fraction is equal to the quotient of the numerator divided by the denominator.

Or, $\frac{a}{b}=a:b$, for $\frac{a}{b}=\frac{1}{b}.a$ (9); and $b.\frac{a}{b}=b.\frac{1}{b}a$ (17); but $b.\frac{1}{b}=1$ (8); and $b.\frac{1}{b}.a=1.a=a$, therefore $b.\frac{a}{b}=a$ (14), and $a:b=\frac{a}{b}$ (12).

SCHOLIUM. Hence $\frac{a}{b}$ is a common symbol for $a:b$.

20. THEOREM. A quantity multiplied by a simple fraction, is equal to the same quantity divided by its denominator.

Or $a.\frac{1}{b}=a:b$; for $a.\frac{1}{b}=\frac{a}{b}$ (9), and $\frac{a}{b}=a:b$ (19), therefore $a.\frac{1}{b}=\frac{a}{b}$ (14).

21. THEOREM. A quantity divided by a simple fraction, is equal to the same quantity multiplied by its denominator.

Or $a:\frac{1}{b}=ab$, for if $a:\frac{1}{b}=c, a=c.\frac{1}{b}$ (12)$=\frac{c}{b}=c.b$ (20), and multiplying by b, $ab=c=a:\frac{1}{b}$.

22. THEOREM. A quantity multiplied by a multiple fraction is equal to the same quantity multiplied by the numerator, and then divided by the denominator.

Or $a.\frac{b}{c}=ab:c$; for $a.\frac{b}{c}=a.b.\frac{1}{c}=ab.\frac{1}{c}=ab:c$ (20).

23. **Theorem.** A quantity divided by a multiple fraction is equal to the same quantity multiplied by the denominator, and divided by the numerator.

Or $a : \frac{b}{c} = ac : b$; for $a : \frac{b}{c} = a : \left(b . \frac{1}{c}\right) = a : b : \frac{1}{c} = a : b.c\,(21), = ac : b$.

Scholium. A beginner may perhaps render these demonstrations more intelligible by substituting any numbers at pleasure for the characters. For example, the demonstration of the first theorem may be written thus. Twelve fourths, $\frac{12}{4}$, are equal to 12 divided by 4; for, by the definition of a multiple fraction, $\frac{12}{4} = 12.\frac{1}{4}$, and multiplying these equals by 4, $4.\frac{12}{4} = 4.12.\frac{1}{4}$; but by the definition of a simple fraction $4.\frac{1}{4} = 1$, therefore $4.12.\frac{1}{4} = 12$, whence $4.\frac{12}{4} = 12$, and by the definition of division, $12 : 4 = \frac{12}{4}$. But, in fact, the proposition is too evident to admit much demonstrative confirmation.

24. **Theorem.** A positive number or quantity being multiplied by a positive one, the product is positive.

For the repeated addition of a positive quantity must make the result actually greater. What is true of numbers, may practically be affirmed of quantities in general (10).

25. **Theorem.** A negative number or quantity being multiplied by a positive one, the product is negative.

For since adding a negative quantity is equivalent to subtracting a positive one, the more of such quantities that are added, the greater will the whole diminution be, and the sum of the whole, or the product, must be negative.

26. **Theorem.** A negative number or quantity being multiplied by a negative one, the product is positive.

Or $-a . -b = ab$. For $a . -b = -ab\,(25)$: that is, when the positive quantity a is multiplied by the negative b, the product indicates that a must be subtracted as often as there are units in b: but when a is negative, its subtraction is equivalent to the addition of an equal positive number; therefore in this case an equal positive number must be added as often as there are units in b.

27. **Definition.** If the quotients of two pairs of numbers are equal, the numbers are proportional, and the first is to the second, as the third to the fourth; and any quantities expressed by such numbers, are also proportional.

If $a : b = c : d$, a is to b as c to d, or $a : b :: c : d$.

28. **Theorem.** Of four proportionals, the product of the extremes is equal to that of the means.

Since $a : b = c : d$, $a . \frac{1}{b} = c . \frac{1}{d}$, $bd . \frac{a}{b} = c : d . bd\,(17)$, or $ad = cb$.

29. **Theorem.** If the product of the extremes of four numbers is equal to that of the means, the numbers are proportional.

If $ad = cb$, $ad : bd = cb : bd\,(18)$, and $a : b = c : d$; also $ad : cd = cb : cd$, and $a : c = b : d$.

30. **Theorem.** Four proportionals are proportional alternately.

If $a : b :: c : d$, $ad = bc\,(28)$, therefore $a : c :: b : d\,(29)$.

31. **Theorem.** Four proportionals are proportional by inversion.

If $a : b :: c : d$, $ad = bc$, $ad : ac = bc : ac$, and $d : c = b : a$.

32. **Theorem.** Four proportionals are proportional by composition.

If $a : b :: c : d$, $a + b : b :: c + d : d$; for since $ad = bc$, $ad + bd = bc + bd\,(15)$, or $(a + b) . d = (c + d) . b$, therefore $a + b : b :: c + d : d\,(29)$.

33. **Theorem.** Four proportionals are proportional by division.

If $a : b :: c : d$, $a - b : b :: c - d : d$; for since $ad = bc$, $ad - bd = bc - bd\,(16)$, $(a - b) . d = (c - d) . b$, and $a - b : b :: c - d : d\,(29)$.

34. **Theorem.** If any number of quantities are proportional, the sum of the antecedents is in the same ratio to the sum of the consequents.

If $a : b :: c : d$, $a : b :: a + c : b + d$; for since $ad = bc$, $ab + ad = ab + bc$, $a . (b + d) = b . (a + c)$, and $a : b :: a + c : b + d\,(29)$.

35. **Theorem.** If any number of antecedents and any number of consequents be added together, the ratio of the sums will be less than the greatest of the single ratios, when those ratios are unequal.

Let $\frac{a}{b} > \frac{c}{d}$, then $\frac{a+c}{b+d} < \frac{a}{b}$; for if $\frac{a}{b} = \frac{e}{d}$, $e > c$, and $\frac{a+e}{b+d} > \frac{a+c}{b+d}\,(34)$; consequently $\frac{a}{b} > \frac{a+c}{b+d}$. The same demonstration may be extended to any number of ratios.

36. DEFINITION. A series of numbers formed by the continual addition of the same number to any given number, is called an arithmetical progression.

2, 5, 8, 11, 14, 17, 20, by adding 3.
20, 17, 14, 11, 8, 5, 2, by adding —3.
$a, a+b, a+2b, a+3b, \ldots \ldots a+(n-1).b$, in general.

SCHOLIUM. It may be observed that the sum of each pair of the numbers of these equal progressions is $22 = 2+20 = a+a+(n-1).b = 2a+(n-1).b$; the whole sum $22 \times 7 = (2a+(n-1).b).n$, and the sum of each, $na + \frac{nn-n}{2}.b$, a being the first term, b the difference, and n the number of terms.

37. DEFINITION. A series of numbers formed by continual multiplication by a given number, is called a geometrical progression.

As 2, 6, 18, 54; multiplying 2 continually by 3.
$a, ab, abb, abbb$; multiplying a by b.

38. DEFINITION. If one of the terms of a geometrical progression is unity, the other terms are called powers of the common multiplier.

As $\frac{1}{32}, \frac{1}{16}, \frac{1}{8}, \frac{1}{4}, \frac{1}{2}, 1, 2, 4, 8, 16, 32$. Each term is denoted by placing obliquely over the common multiplier a number expressive of its distance from unity, as $8 = 2^3$: negative numbers, implying a contrary situation to positive ones, denote that the term precedes instead of following the unit, as $\frac{1}{4} = 2^{-2}$.

By reversing the series it is obvious that $\frac{1}{2} = (\frac{1}{2})^3$, and $2 = (\frac{1}{2})^{-1}$.

It appears that the addition of the indices denoting the places of any terms will point out a term which is their product, as $2^3 \times 2^2 = 2^5$, or $8 \times 4 = 32$; and that the subtraction of the index is equivalent to division by the term. Hence if $a^2 = b = b^1$, a^1 must be equal to $b^{\frac{1}{2}}$ in order that $b^{\frac{1}{2}} + b^{\frac{1}{2}}$ may make $b^1 = a^2$. So that simple fractional numbers serve as indices of the number of times that the quantity must be multiplied together, in order that the product may be the common multiplier of the series, or the simple number b.

SCHOLIUM. Fractional powers are sometimes denoted by the mark $\sqrt{}$, meaning root: thus $\sqrt{a} = a^{\frac{1}{2}}, \sqrt[3]{a} = a^{\frac{1}{3}}$. The second power of a number a, being called its square, and the third its cube, the fractional powers are called square and cube roots.

The sums of geometrical progressions may be thus computed, if $a+ab+ab^2 \ldots +ab^{n-1} = x$, $ab+ab^2+ab^3 \ldots +ab^n = bx$, and subtracting the former equation from the latter $ab^n - a = bx - x$, therefore $x = \frac{ab^n - a}{b-1}$. Which, when $b < 1$ and $n = \infty$, or infinite, becomes $\frac{a}{1-b}$.

The binomial theorem, for involution, is $(a+b)^n = a^n + n.a^{n-1}b + n.\frac{n-1}{2}.a^{n-2}b^2 + n.\frac{n-1}{2}.\frac{n-2}{3}.a^{n-3}b^3 + \ldots$
In simple cases, its truth may be shown by induction.

POWERS OF NUMBERS.

1st	2d	3d.	4th.	5th.	6th.	7th.	8th.
2	4	8	16	32	64	128	256
3	9	27	81	243	729	2187	6561
4	16	64	256	1024	4096	16384	65536
5	25	125	625	3125	15625	78125	390625
6	36	216	1296	7776	46656	279936	1679616
7	49	343	2401	16807	117649	823543	5764801
8	64	512	4096	32768	262144	2097152	16777216
9	81	729	6561	59049	531441	4782969	43046721

$2^{\frac{1}{2}} = 1.414213$; $3^{\frac{1}{2}}, 1.732$; $5^{\frac{1}{2}}, 2.236$; $6^{\frac{1}{2}}, 2.449$; $7^{\frac{1}{2}}, 2.646$; $8^{\frac{1}{2}}, 2.828$; $10^{\frac{1}{2}}, 3.162$.

$2^{\frac{1}{3}} = 1.26$; $3^{\frac{1}{3}}, 1.442$; $4^{\frac{1}{3}}, 1.587$; $5^{\frac{1}{3}}, 1.71$; $6^{\frac{1}{3}}, 1.817$; $7^{\frac{1}{3}}, 1.913$; $9^{\frac{1}{3}}, 2.08$; $10^{\frac{1}{3}}, 2.154$.

39. DEFINITION. In decimal arithmetic, each figure is supposed to be multiplied by that power of 10, positive or negative, which is expressed by its distance from the figure before the point.

Thus 672.53 means $6 \times 10^2 + 7 \times 10^1 + 2 \times 10^0$, or 2×1, $+ 5 \times 10^{-1}$, or $\frac{5}{10}$ or $\frac{50}{100} + 3 \times 10^{-2}$, or $\frac{3}{100}$, together $672\frac{53}{100}$.

SCHOLIUM. On some occasions other numbers are substituted for 10 in calculations: particularly 12, which has many advantages, and is used in operations respecting carpenter's work; and sometimes the number 2 facilitates computations; and it may be employed where it is inconvenient to multiply characters; since two different marks, or a mark and a vacant place, are sufficient, when continually repeated, to express all numbers. The powers of 60 are also used in the subdivisions of time, and of angles.

40. DEFINITION. The reciprocal of a number is the quotient of a given unit divided by that number.

TABLE OF RECIPROCALS.

No.	Recipr.	No.	Recipr.	No.	Recipr.	No.	Recipr.	No.	Recipr.	No.	Recipr.
1	1000000	54	0185185	107	0093458	160	0062500	213	0046948	266	0037594
2	5000000	55	0181818	108	0092592	161	0062112	214	0046729	267	0037453
3	3333333	56	0178571	109	0091743	162	0061728	215	0046512	268	0037313
4	2500000	57	0175439	110	0090909	163	0061350	216	0046296	269	0037175
5	2000000	58	0172414	111	0090090	164	0060975	217	0046083	270	0037037
6	1666666	59	0169490	112	0089286	165	0060606	218	0045872	271	0036900
7	1428571	60	0166666	113	0088496	166	0060241	219	0045662	272	0036765
8	1250000	61	0163934	114	0087719	167	0059880	220	0045454	273	0036630
9	1111111	62	0161290	115	0086957	168	0059524	221	0045249	274	0036496
10	1000000	63	0158730	116	0086207	169	0059172	222	0045045	275	0036363
11	0909090	64	0156250	117	0085470	170	0058824	223	0044843	276	0036232
12	0833333	65	0153846	118	0084745	171	0058480	224	0044643	277	0036101
13	0769230	66	0151515	119	0084034	172	0058141	225	0044444	278	0035971
14	0714285	67	0149254	120	0083333	173	0057803	226	0044248	279	0035842
15	0666666	68	0147059	121	0082645	174	0057471	227	0044053	280	0035714
16	0625000	69	0144928	122	0081967	175	0057143	228	0043860	281	0035587
17	0588235	70	0142857	123	0081300	176	0056818	229	0043668	282	0035461
18	0555555	71	0140845	124	0080645	177	0056497	230	0043478	283	0035336
19	0526316	72	0138888	125	0080000	178	0056180	231	0043290	284	0035211
20	0500000	73	0136986	126	0079365	179	0055866	232	0043103	285	0035088
21	0476190	74	0135135	127	0078740	180	0055555	233	0042918	286	0034965
22	0454545	75	0133333	128	0078125	181	0055249	234	0042735	287	0034843
23	0434783	76	0131579	129	0077519	182	0054945	235	0042553	288	0034722
24	0416666	77	0129870	130	0076923	183	0054645	236	0042373	289	0034602
25	0400000	78	0128205	131	0076336	184	0054348	237	0042194	290	0034483
26	0384615	79	0126582	132	0075757	185	0054054	238	0042017	291	0034364
27	0370370	80	0125000	133	0075188	186	0053763	239	0041841	292	0034246
28	0357143	81	0123457	134	0074627	187	0053476	240	0041666	293	0034130
29	0344828	82	0121950	135	0074074	188	0053191	241	0041494	294	0034014
30	0333333	83	0120482	136	0073529	189	0052910	242	0041322	295	0033898
31	0322581	84	0119048	137	0072993	190	0052632	243	0041152	296	0033783
32	0312500	85	0117647	138	0072464	191	0052356	244	0040984	297	0033670
33	0303030	86	0116279	139	0071942	192	0052083	245	0040816	298	0033557
34	0294118	87	0114943	140	0071429	193	0051813	246	0040650	299	0033445
35	0285714	88	0113636	141	0070922	194	0051546	247	0040486	300	0033333
36	0277777	89	0112360	142	0070423	195	0051282	248	0040323	301	0033223
37	0270270	90	0111111	143	0069930	196	0051020	249	0040161	302	0033113
38	0263158	91	0109890	144	0069444	197	0050761	250	0040000	303	0033005
39	0256410	92	0108696	145	0068966	198	0050505	251	0039841	304	0032895
40	0250000	93	0107527	146	0068493	199	0050251	252	0039683	305	0032787
41	0243902	94	0106383	147	0068027	200	0050000	253	0039526	306	0032680
42	0238095	95	0105263	148	0067567	201	0049751	254	0039370	307	0032573
43	0232558	96	0104166	149	0067114	202	0049504	255	0039216	308	0032468
44	0227272	97	0103093	150	0066666	203	0049621	256	0039063	309	0032362
45	0222222	98	0102041	151	0066225	204	0049020	257	0038911	310	0032258
46	0217391	99	0101010	152	0065789	205	0048750	258	0038760	311	0032154
47	0212766	100	0100000	153	0065359	206	0048544	259	0038610	312	0032051
48	0208333	101	0099009	154	0064935	207	0048309	260	0038462	313	0031949
49	0204082	102	0098039	155	0064516	208	0048077	261	0038314	314	0031847
50	0200000	103	0097087	156	0064103	209	0047847	262	0038168	315	0031746
51	0196078	104	0096154	157	0063694	210	0047619	263	0038023	316	0031646
52	0192308	105	0095238	158	0063291	211	0047393	264	0037878	317	0031546
53	0188679	106	0094340	159	0062893	212	0047170	265	0037736	318	0031447

41. DEFINITION. The harmonic mean of two quantities is the quantity of which the reciprocal is the half sum of their reciprocals.

Thus, the harmonic mean of 3 and 6 is 4; for $\frac{1}{2}(\frac{1}{3}+\frac{1}{6})=\frac{1}{4}$. And the harmonic mean is equal to the product divided by the half sum. Thus $\frac{18}{4\frac{1}{2}}=4$.

42. DEFINITION. The common logarithm of a number is that power of 10 which expresses it.

For instance, l. 1000$=$3, since $10^3=1000$. l. 2$=$.30103, for $10^{.30103}=2$. The principal use of logarithms is derived from that property of indices by which their addition and subtraction is equivalent to the multiplication and division of the respective numbers.

TABLE OF LOGARITHMS.

Including all Prime Numbers under 1000, without the Indices.

No.	Logar.	No.	Logar.	No.	Logar.	No.	Logar.	No.	Logar.	No.	Logar.
1	0000000	67	8260748	227	3560259	401	6031444	599	7774268	797	9014583
2	3010300	71	8512583	229	3598355	409	6117233	601	7788745	809	9079485
3	4771213	73	8633229	233	3673559	419	6222140	607	7831887	811	9090209
4	6020600	79	8976271	239	3783979	421	6242821	613	7874605	821	9143432
5	6989700	83	9190781	241	3820170	431	6344773	617	7902852	823	9153998
6	7781513	89	9493900	251	3996737	433	6364879	619	7916906	827	9175055
7	8450980	97	9867717	257	4099331	439	6424645	631	8000294	829	9185545
8	9030900	101	0043214	263	4199557	443	6464037	641	8068580	839	9237620
9	9542425	103	0128372	269	4297523	449	6522463	643	8082110	853	9309490
10	0000000	107	0293838	271	4329693	457	6599162	647	8109043	857	9329808
11	0413927	109	0374265	277	4424798	461	6637009	653	8149132	859	9339932
12	0791812	113	0530784	281	4487063	463	6655810	659	8188854	863	9360108
13	1139434	127	1038037	283	4517864	467	6693169	661	8202015	877	9429996
14	1461280	131	1172713	293	4668676	479	6803355	673	8280151	881	9449759
15	1760913	137	1367206	307	4871384	487	6875290	677	8305887	883	9459607
16	2041200	139	1430148	311	4927604	491	6910815	683	8344207	887	9479236
17	2304489	149	1731863	313	4955443	499	6981005	691	8394780	907	9576073
18	2552725	151	1789769	317	5010593	503	7015680	701	8457180	911	9595184
19	2787536	157	1958997	331	5198280	509	7067178	709	8506462	919	9633155
20	3010300	163	2121876	337	5276299	521	7168377	719	8567289	929	9680157
23	3617278	167	2227165	347	5403295	523	7185017	727	8615344	937	9717396
29	4623980	173	2380461	349	5428254	541	7331973	733	8651040	941	9735896
31	4913617	179	2528530	353	5477747	547	7379873	739	8686444	947	9763500
37	5682017	181	2576786	359	5550944	557	7458552	743	8709888	953	9790929
41	6127839	191	2810334	367	5646661	563	7505084	751	8756399	967	9854265
43	6334685	193	2855573	373	5717088	569	7551123	757	8790959	971	9872192
47	6720979	197	2944662	379	5786392	571	7566861	761	8818847	977	9898946
53	7242759	199	2988531	383	5831988	577	7611758	769	8859263	983	9925535
59	7708520	211	3242825	389	5899496	587	7686381	773	8881795	991	9960737
61	7853298	223	3483049	397	5987905	593	7730547	787	8959747	997	9986952

43. PROBLEM. To solve a quadratic equation.

Reduce the equation to the form $xx \pm ax = b$, add the square of half a; then $xx \pm ax + \frac{aa}{4} = b + \frac{aa}{4}$, whence $x \pm \frac{a}{2} = \pm \sqrt{\left(b+\frac{aa}{4}\right)}$ and $x = \pm \sqrt{\left(b+\frac{aa}{4}\right)} \pm \frac{a}{2}$.

SECT. II. OF THE COMPARISON OF VARIABLE QUANTITIES.

44. DEFINITION. The quantities by which two variable magnitudes are increased or decreased in the same time, are called their increments or decrements, or their increments positive or negative.

SCHOLIUM. They are denoted by an accent placed over the variable quantity; thus x' and y' are the simultaneous increments of x and y.

45. DEFINITION. The ratio which is the limit of the ratios of the increments of two quantities, as they are taken smaller and smaller, is called the ratio of the velocities of their increase or decrease.

SCHOLIUM. It would be difficult to give any other sufficient definition of velocity than this. If both the quantities vary in the same proportion, the ratio of x' and y' will be constant (18), and may be determined without considering them as evanescent; but if they vary according to different laws, that ratio must vary, accordingly as the time of comparison is longer or shorter: and since the degree of variation, at any instant of time, does not depend on the change produced at a finite interval before or after that instant, it is necessary, for the comparison of this variation, that the increments should be considered as diminished without limit, and their ultimate ratio determined; and it is indifferent whether these evanescent increments be taken before, or after the given instant, or whether the mean between both results be employed.

46. DEFINITION. Any finite quantities in the ratio of the velocities of increase or decrease of two or more magnitudes, are the fluxions of those magnitudes.

SCHOLIUM. They are denoted by placing a point over the variable quantity, thus, $\dot{x}$, $\dot{y}$. And $\frac{x'}{y'}$ is always ultimately equal to $\frac{\dot{x}}{\dot{y}}$. The variable quantity is called a fluent with respect to its fluxion, as x is the fluent of $\dot{x}$, or $x = \int \dot{x}$. On the continent the term fluxion is not used, but the evanescent increment is called a difference, and denoted by d or ∂, and the variable quantity is conceived to consist of the entire sum or integral of such differences, and marked $\int$, as $x = \int dx$, or $\int \partial x$. This mark has the advantage of differing in form from the short s, which is used as a literal character.

47. THEOREM. When the fluxions of two quantities are in a constant ratio, their finite increments are in the same ratio.

For if it be denied, let the ratios have a finite difference; then if the time in which the increments are produced be continually divided, the ratio of the parts may approach nearer to the ratio of the fluxions than any assignable difference, for that ratio is their limit (46), and this is true, by the supposition, in each part; therefore the sums of all the increments will be to each other in a ratio nearer to that of the fluxions than the assigned difference (35).

48. THEOREM. The fluxion of the product of two quantities is equal to the sum of the products of the fluxion of each into the other quantity.

Or $(xy)^{\cdot} = y\dot{x} + x\dot{y}$. Let the quantities increase from x and y to $x+x'$ and $y+y'$, then their product will be first xy and afterwards $xy+yx'+xy'+x'y'$, of which the difference is $yx'+xy'+x'y'$ and the ratio of the increments of x and xy is that of x' to $yx'+xy'+x'y'$; or, when the increments vanish, to $yx'+xy'$ since in this case $x'y'$ vanishes in comparison with xy'. But $x' \cdot (yx'+xy') :: \dot{x} \cdot (y\dot{x}+x\dot{y})$, and the fluxion is rightly determined (46); for since $\frac{y'}{x'} = \frac{\dot{y}}{\dot{x}}$, $\frac{xy'}{x'} = \frac{x\dot{y}}{\dot{x}}$ (18); but $\frac{yx'}{x'} = \frac{y\dot{x}}{\dot{x}}$ (18), and $\frac{yx'+xy'}{x'} = \frac{y\dot{x}+x\dot{y}}{\dot{x}}$ (15).

49. THEOREM. The fluxion of any power of a variable quantity is equal to the fluxion of that quantity multiplied by the index of the power, and by the quantity raised to the same power diminished by unity.

Or $(x^n)^{\cdot} = nx^{n-1}\dot{x}$. Let $n=2$, then $(xx)^{\cdot} = x\dot{x}+x\dot{x}$ (48) $= 2x\dot{x} = nx^{n-1}\dot{x}$. If $n=3$, $x^n = (xx).x$, and its fluxion is $x(xx)^{\cdot} + (xx)\dot{x} = 2xx\dot{x}+xx\dot{x} = 3x^2\dot{x} = nx^{n-1}\dot{x}$. And the same may be proved of any whole number. If n is a fraction, as $\frac{1}{p}$, put $y=x^n$, then $x=y^p$, and $\dot{x}=py^{p-1}\dot{y}, \dot{y}=\frac{\dot{x}}{py^{p-1}} = \frac{1}{p}.y^{1-p}\dot{x}$ (38) $= \frac{1}{p}y.y^{-p}\dot{x} = nx^{n-1}\dot{x}$, as before; and in the same manner the proof may be extended to all possible cases.

50. THEOREM. When the logarithm of a quantity varies equably, the quantity varies proportionally.

Or, if $l. x = y$, $\frac{\dot{y}}{a} = \frac{\dot{x}}{x}$. For $x = b^y$ (42), and when y becomes $y + y'$, $x + x' = b^{y+y'} = b^y.b^{y'} = x.b^{y'}$, and $x' = x.b^{y'} - x = x.(b^{y'} - 1)$; but y' being constant by the supposition, $b^{y'} - 1$ is constant, and may be called $\frac{y'}{a}$, and $x' = \frac{xy'}{a}$; therefore $\dot{x} = \frac{x\dot{y}}{a}$, and $\frac{\dot{x}}{x} = \frac{\dot{y}}{a}$.

SCHOLIUM. Numerical logarithms do not, strictly speaking, vary by evanescent increments; but other quantities may flow continually, and be always proportionate to logarithms: in either case the proposition is true. In Briggs's logarithms, commonly used, b is 10, and a, the modulus, is .4342944819; dividing all the system by a, or multiplying by 2.302585093, we have Napier's original hyperbolical logarithms, where $\dot{y}$ becomes $= \frac{\dot{x}}{x}$, and $a = 1$.

51. THEOREM. The fluxion of any power of a quantity, of which the exponent is variable, is equal to the fluxion of the same power considered as constant, together with the fluxion of the exponent multiplied by the power and by the hyperbolical logarithm of the quantity.

If $x^y = z$, $\dot{z} = yx^{y-1}\dot{x} + (\text{h. l. } x). x^y \dot{y}$; for h. l. $z = y$. (h. l. x), (42); now (h. l. $x)^{\cdot} = \frac{\dot{x}}{x}$, (50); and $\dot{z} = z.$ (h. l. $z)^{\cdot}$ $= z. (y. (\text{h. l. } x))^{\cdot} = z. (\frac{y\dot{x}}{x} + (\text{h. l. } x).\dot{y})$, (48, 50) $=$ $yx^{y-1}\dot{x} + (\text{h. l. } x) z\dot{y}$.

52. THEOREM. When a variable quantity is greatest or least, its fluxion vanishes.

For a quantity is greatest when it ceases to increase, and before it begins to decrease; that is, when it has neither increment nor decrement; and it is least when it has ceased to have a decrement and has not yet an increment.

53. PROBLEM. To solve a numerical equation by approximation.

The most general and useful mode of solving all numerical equations is by approximation. Substitute for the unknown quantity a number, found by trial, which nearly answers to the conditions; then the error will be a finite difference of the whole equation; which, when small, will be to the error of the quantity substituted, nearly in the ratio of the evanescent differences, or of the fluxions; and this ratio may be easily determined.

Thus, if $x^3 - 6x^2 + 4x = 6699$, call 6699, y, then $3x^2\dot{x} - 12x\dot{x} + 4\dot{x} = \dot{y}$, and $\dot{x} = \frac{\dot{y}}{3x^2 - 12x + 4}$, and $x' = \frac{y'}{3x^2 - 12x + 4}$ nearly; now assume $x = 20$, then $y = 5680$, and $y' = 1019$, whence $x' = 1.05$, and x corrected is 21.05; by repeating the operation we may approach still nearer to the true value 21.

If $x^n = y$, $\dot{x} = \frac{\dot{y}}{nx^{n-1}}$, whence the common rule for the extraction of roots is derived. In order to find the nearest integer root, the digits must be divided, beginning with the units, into parcels of as many as there are units in the index, and the nearest root of the last or highest parcel being found, and its power subtracted, the remainder must be divided by its next inferior power multiplied by the given index, in order to find the next figure, adding the next parcel to the remainder before the division. There are also in particular cases other more compendious methods.

SECTION III. OF SPACE.

54. DEFINITION. A solid is a portion of space limited in magnitude on all sides.

SCHOLIUM. Space is a mode of existence incapable of definition, and supposed to be understood by tradition.

55. DEFINITION. A surface is the limit of a solid.

56. DEFINITION. A line is the limit of a surface.

57. DEFINITION. A point is the limit of a line.

SCHOLIUM. The paper of which this figure covers a part, is an example of a  solid, the shaded portion represents a portion of surface: the boundaries of that surface are lines, and the three terminations or intersections of those lines are points. In conformity with this more correct conception, these definitions are illustrated by representations of the respective portions of space of which the limits are considered; and also by the more usual method of denoting a line by a narrow surface, and a surface by such a line surrounding it.

58. DEFINITION. A line joining two points is called their distance.

59. DEFINITION. When the distance of any two or more points remains unchanged, they are said to be at rest; and a space of which all the points are at rest, is a quiescent space.

60. DEFINITION. A line which must be wholly at rest with respect to any quiescent space when two of its points are at rest in that space, is a straight line.

61. DEFINITION. A line which is neither a straight line, nor composed of straight lines, is a curve line.

62. DEFINITION. A plane is a surface, in which if any two points be joined by a straight line, the whole of the straight line will be in the surface.

63. DEFINITION. An angle is the inclination of two lines to each other.

SCHOLIUM. An angle is sometimes denoted by this mark ∠, and is described by three letters placed near the lines, the middle letter at the angular point.

64. DEFINITION. When a straight line standing on another straight line makes the adjacent angles equal, they are called right angles.

65. DEFINITION. A straight line between two right angles is called a perpendicular to the line on which it stands.

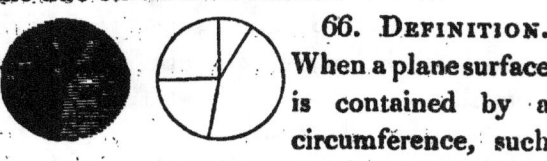

66. DEFINITION. When a plane surface is contained by a circumference, such that all straight lines drawn to it from a certain point in the plane are equal, the surface is a circle.

67. DEFINITION. The point equally distant from the circumference, is called the centre.

68. DEFINITION. Any straight line drawn from the centre to the circumference, is called a radius.

69. DEFINITION. The term circle also often implies the circumference, and not the circular surface.

70. DEFINITION. A portion of the circumference of a circle is called an arc.

71. DEFINITION. A straight line joining the extremities of an arc, is its chord.

72. DEFINITION. The surface contained between an arc and its chord is called a segment of a circle.

73. DEFINITION. A chord passing through the centre is a diameter.

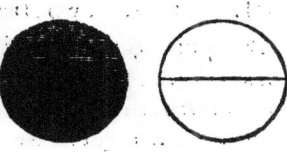

74. DEFINITION. A triangle is a surface contained between three lines; and these lines are understood to be straight, unless the contrary is expressed.

75. DEFINITION. When two straight lines, lying in the same plane, may be produced both ways indefinitely, without meeting, they are parallel.

SCHOLIUM. The parallelism of lines is sometimes denoted by this mark ||.

76. POSTULATE. It is required that the length of a straight line be capable of being identified, whether by the effect of any object on the senses, or merely in imagination, so that it may remain invariable.

SCHOLIUM. This is practically performed by making visible marks on a material surface; although, strictly speaking, no such marks remain at distances absolutely invariable, on account of changes of temperature, and of other circumstances.

77. POSTULATE. That a straight line of indefinite length may be drawn through any two given points.

78. POSTULATE. That a circle may be described on any given centre with a radius equal to any given straight line.

79. AXIOM. A straight line joining two points is the shortest distance between them.

SCHOLIUM. With respect to all straight lines, this axiom is a demonstrable proposition; but as the demonstration does not extend to curve lines, it becomes necessary to assume it as an axiom.

80. AXIOM. Of any two figures meeting in the ends of a straight line, that which is nearer the line has the shorter circumference, provided there be no contrary flexure.

81. AXIOM. Two straight lines coinciding in two points, coincide in all points.

SCHOLIUM. If they did not coincide in all points, the two points of coincidence being at rest, and one of the lines being made the axis of motion, the other must revolve round it, contrarily to the definition of a straight line. Although this is sufficiently obvious, it can scarcely be called a formal demonstration.

82. AXIOM. All right angles are equal.

83. AXIOM. A straight line, cutting one of two parallel lines, may be produced till it cut the other.

84. PROBLEM. From the greater of two right lines, AB, to cut off a part equal to the less, CD.

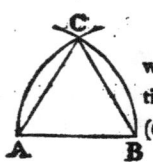

On the centre A describe a circle with a radius equal to CD (78), and it will cut off AE=CD (66).

85. PROBLEM. On a given right line, AB, to describe an equilateral triangle.

On the centres A and B draw two circles, with radii equal to AB, and to their intersection C, draw AC and BC; then AB=AC=BC (66), and the triangle ABC is equilateral.

86. THEOREM. Two triangles, having two sides and the angle included, respectively equal, have also the base and the other angles equal.

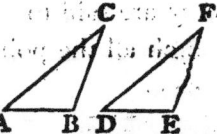

In the triangles ABC, DEF, let AC=DF, BC=EF, and ∠ACB= DFE. Now supposing a triangle equal to DEF to be constructed on AC, the side equal to FE must coincide in position with CB, because ∠ACB=DFE, and also in magnitude, for they are equal, therefore the point B will be an angular point of the supposed triangle; and since the base of both triangles must be a right line, it must be the same line AB (81), and the supposed triangle will coincide every where with ABC; therefore ABC=DEF, and the angles at A and B are equal to the angles at D and E.

87. THEOREM. If two sides of a triangle are equal, the angles opposite to them are equal.

In the sides AB and AC produced, take at pleasure AD=AE, and join BE, CD; then since AD=AE, and AC=AB, and the angle at A is common to the triangles ADC, AEB, those triangles are equal (86), and ∠ACD=ABE, ∠ADC=AEB, and CD=BE; but BD=CE (16), therefore ∠BCD=CBE (86), and ∠ACD−BCD=ABE−CBE (16), or ∠ACB= ABC.

88. THEOREM. If two angles of a triangle are equal, the sides opposite to them are equal.

Let ∠ABC=ACD; then AC=AB. If it be denied, take in the greater AC, CD equal to the less AB; then, since ∠ ABC=DCB, AB=DC, and BC is common, the triangle ABC=DCB (86), the whole to a part, which is impossible.

89. THEOREM. If two triangles have their bases equal, and their sides respectively equal, their angles are also respectively equal.

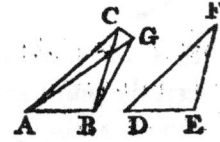

If a triangle be supposed to be constructed on AB, the base of ABC, equal to DEF, the vertex of the triangle must coincide with C, and the whole triangle with ABC. For if it be denied, let G be the vertex of the triangle so constructed; join CG; then since AC=AG, ∠ACG=AGC (87), and in the same manner ∠BGC=BCG; but BGC>ACG, therefore BGC>ACG; and ACG>BCG, therefore much more BGC>BCG, to which it was shown to be equal. And the same may be proved in any other position of the point G; therefore the triangle equal to DEF, supposed to be described on AB, coincides with ABC.

90. PROBLEM. To bisect a given angle.

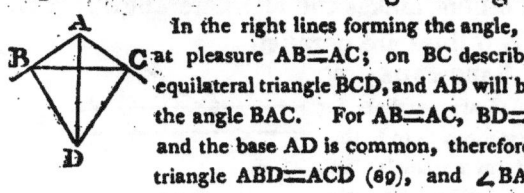

In the right lines forming the angle, take at pleasure AB=AC; on BC describe an equilateral triangle BCD, and AD will bisect the angle BAC. For AB=AC, BD=CD, and the base AD is common, therefore the triangle ABD=ACD (89), and ∠BAD=CAD.

91. PROBLEM. To bisect a given right line, AB.

Describe on it two equilateral triangles, ABC, ABD, and CD, joining their vertices, will bisect AB in E. For since AC=CB, AD=BD, and CD is common to the triangles ACD, BCD, ∠ACD=BCD (89); but CE is common to the triangles ACE and BCE, therefore AE=EB (86).

92. PROBLEM. To erect a perpendicular to a given right line at a given point.

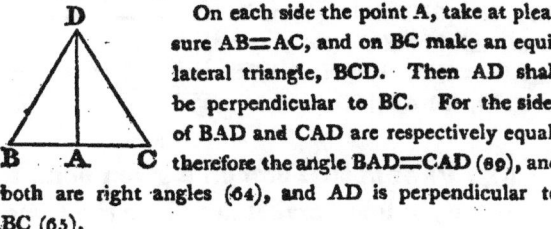

On each side the point A, take at pleasure AB=AC, and on BC make an equilateral triangle, BCD. Then AD shall be perpendicular to BC. For the sides of BAD and CAD are respectively equal, therefore the angle BAD=CAD (89), and both are right angles (64), and AD is perpendicular to BC (65).

93. PROBLEM. From a point, A, without a right line, BC, to let fall a perpendicular on it.

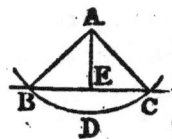

On the centre A, through any point D, beyond BC, describe a circle, which must obviously cut BC; join AB and AC, and bisect the angle BAC by the line AE; AE will be perpendicular to BC. For ∠BAE=CAE, AB=AC, and AE is common to the triangles BAE, CAE; therefore ∠AEB=AEC (86), and both are right angles (64).

94. THEOREM. The angles which any right line makes on one side of another, are, together, equal to two right angles.

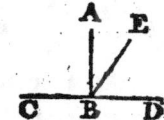

Let AB be perpendicular to CD, and EB oblique to it, then CBE+EBD= CBA+ABE+EBD=CBA+ABD (14).

95. THEOREM. If two right lines make with a third, at the same point, but on opposite sides, angles together equal to two right angles, they are in the same right line.

If it be denied, let AB, which together with AC, makes with AD, the angles BAD, DAC equal to two right angles, be not in the right line CAE. Then BAD +DAC, being equal to two right angles, is equal to EAD +DAC (94), and BAD=EAD, the less to the greater, which is impossible.

96. THEOREM. If two right lines intersect each other, the opposite angles are equal.

From the equals, ABC+ABD and ABD +DBE (94, 82), subtract ABD, and the remainders, ABC, DBE, are equal. In the same manner ABD=CBE.

97. THEOREM. If one side of a triangle be produced, the exterior angle will be greater than either of the interior opposite angles.

Bisect AB in C, draw DCE; take CE =CD, and join BE, then the triangle ACD=BCE (96, 86), and ∠CBE= CAD; but ABF>CBE, therefore ABF> CAD. And in the same manner it may be proved, by producing AB, that ABF is greater than ADB.

98. THEOREM. The greater side of any triangle is opposite to the greater angle.

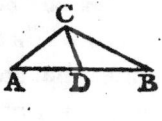

Let AB>AC, then ∠ACB>ABC. For taking AD=AC, and joining CD, ∠ACD =ADC (87). But ∠ADC>CBD (97), and ACB>ACD, therefore much more ∠ACB>CBD, or ABC.

99. Theorem. Of two triangles on the same base, the sides of the interior contain the greater angle.

Produce AB to C, then ∠ABD > ACD (97), and ∠ACD > AEC, therefore much more ABD > AED.

100. Problem. To make a triangle, having its sides equal to three given right lines, every one of them being less than the sum of the other two.

Take AB equal to one of the lines, and on the centres A and B describe two circles with radii equal to the other two lines; draw AC and BC to the intersection C, and ABC will be the triangle required.

101. Problem. At a given point in a right line, to make an angle equal to a given angle.

In the lines forming the given angle ABC, take any two points, A and C, join AC, and taking DE=BC, make the triangle DEF, having DF=BA and FE=AC (100), then ∠FDE=ABC (89).

102. Theorem. If two triangles have two angles and a side respectively equal, the whole triangles are equal.

Let the equal sides be AB and CD, intervening between the equal angles, then if on AB a triangle equal to CDE be supposed to be constructed, the points A and B, and the angles at A and B being the same in this triangle and in ABF, the sides must coincide both in position and in length; therefore ABF=CDE.

If the equal sides are AF and CE, opposite to equal angles, then AB=CD, and the whole triangles are equal. For if AB is not equal to CD, let it be the greater, and let AG=CD; then, by what has been demonstrated, the triangle AFG=CED, and ∠AGF=CDE=ABF, by the supposition; but AGF > ABF (97), which is impossible.

103. Theorem. The shortest of all right lines that can be drawn from a given point to a given right line is that which is perpendicular to the line, and others are shorter as they are nearer to it.

Let AB be perpendicular to CD, then AB is shorter than AD. Produce AB, take BE=AB, and join DE; then the triangle ABD=EBD (86), and AD=DE. But AB+BE or 2AB is less than AD+DE or 2AD (79), therefore AB < AD (18). In a similar manner 2AD < 2AF (80), and AD < AF.

104. Theorem. If a right line cutting two others, makes the alternate angles equal, the two lines are parallel.

If ∠ABC=ADE; BC and DE are parallel: for if they meet, as in F, they will form a triangle BDF, and ∠ADE > ABC (97).

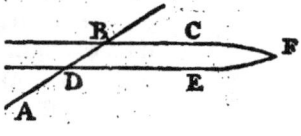

105. Theorem. A right line cutting two parallel lines, makes equal angles with them.

Let AB cut the parallels BC, DE; then if ∠ABC is not equal to ADE, let it be equal to ADF, then BC and DF are parallel (104), and DE, which cuts DF, will also, if produced, cut BC (83), contrarily to the supposition.

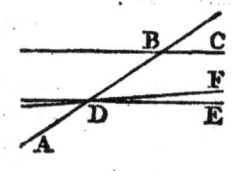

106. Theorem. Right lines, parallel to the same line, are parallel to each other.

Let AB and CD be parallel to EF; draw GHI cutting them all, then ∠KGB=KIF (105), and ∠KHD=KIF, therefore ∠KGB =KHD, and AB∥CD (104).

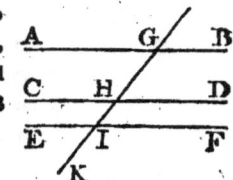

107. Problem. Through a given point to draw a right line parallel to a given right line.

From A draw, at pleasure, AB, meeting BC in B, and make ∠BAD=ABC (101), then AD∥CB (104).

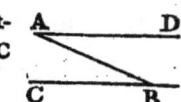

108. Theorem. The angles of any triangle taken together, are equal to two right angles.

Produce AB to C, and draw BD parallel to AE. Then ∠EBD=AEB (105), and ∠DBC=EAB; therefore the external angle EBC is equal to the sum of the internal opposite angles, AEB, EAB, and

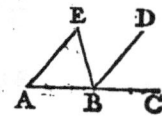

adding ABE, the sum of all three is equal to ABE+EBC, or to two right angles (94).

109. THEOREM. Right lines joining the extremities of equal and parallel right lines, are also equal and parallel.

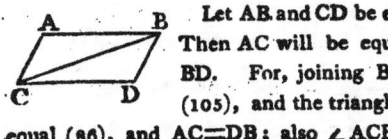 Let AB and CD be equal, and parallel. Then AC will be equal and parallel to BD. For, joining BC, ∠ABC=BCD (105), and the triangles ABC, DCB, are equal (86), and AC=DB; also ∠ACB=DBC, therefore AC ‖ BD (104).

110. DEFINITION. A figure of which the opposite sides are parallel, is called a parallelogram.

111. DEFINITION. A straight line joining the opposite angles of a parallelogram is called its diagonal.

112. DEFINITION. A parallelogram, of which the angles are right angles, is a rectangle.

113. DEFINITION. An equilateral rectangle is a square.

114. THEOREM. The diagonal of a parallelogram divides it into two equal triangles, and its opposite sides are equal.

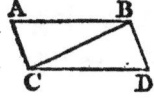 For ABC is equiangular with DCB (105), and BC is common, therefore they are equal (102), and AB=CD, and AC=BD.

115. THEOREM. Parallelograms on the same base, and between the same parallels, are equal.

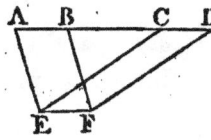 Since AB=CD, both being equal to EF, AC=BD (15, or 16), and the triangle AEC is equiangular (105) and equal (102) to BFD; therefore deducting each of them from the figure AEFD, the remainder ED is equal to the remainder AF.

116. THEOREM. Parallelograms on equal bases, and between the same parallels, are equal.

For each is equal to the parallelogram formed by joining the extremities of the base of the one, and of the side opposite to the base of the other (115).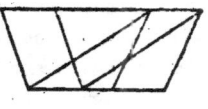

117. THEOREM. Triangles on equal bases, and between the same parallels, are equal.

Take AB and CD equal to the base EF or GH, and join BF and DH. Then EB and GD are parallelograms between the same parallels (109), and on equal bases, therefore they 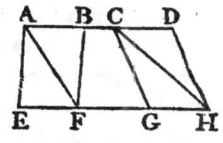 are equal (116), and their halves, the triangles AEF, CGH (114), are also equal (18).

118. THEOREM. In any right angled triangle, the square described on the hypotenuse is equal to the sum of the squares described on the two other sides.

Draw AB parallel to CD the side of the square on the hypotenuse, then the parallelogram CB is double any triangle on the same base and between the same parallels (114, 117), as ACD; but ACD=FCG, their angles at C being each equal to ACG increased by a right angle, FC to AC, and GC to DC. Again, GAH is a 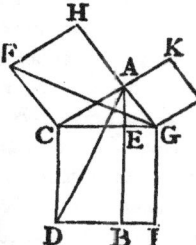 right line (95), parallel to CF, therefore the triangle FCG is half of the square CH on the same base, and CH=CB, since they are the doubles of equal triangles. In the same manner it may be shown that GK=GB; therefore the whole CDIG is equal to the sum of CH and GK.

119. PROBLEM. To find a common measure of any two quantities.

Subtract the less continually from the greater, the remainder from the less, the next remainder from the preceding one, as often as possible, and proceed till there be no further remainder; then the last remainder will be the common measure required. For since it measures the preceding remainder, it will measure the preceding quantities in which that remainder was contained, and which, increased at each step by the remainders, makes up the original quantities.

For example, if the numbers 54 and 21 be proposed, 54−21−21=12, 21−12=9, 12−9=3, 9−3−3=3.

$=0$, therefore 3 is the common measure, for it measures 9, and $9+3$ or 12, and $12+9$ or 21, and $2 \times 21 + 12$ or 54.

SCHOLIUM. Hence it is obvious, that there can be no greater common measure of the two quantities than the quantity thus found; for it should measure the difference of the two quantities, and all the successive remainders down to the last, therefore it cannot be greater than this last. It must also be remarked, that in some cases no accurate common measure can be found, but the error, or the last remainder, in this process, may always be less than any quantity that can be assigned, since the process may be continued without limit. That there are incommensurable quantities, may be thus shown: every number is either a prime number, that is, a number not capable of being composed by multiplication of other numbers, or it is composed by the multiplication of factors, which are primes. Let the number a be composed of the prime numbers bcd, or $a = bcd$, then $aa = bcd.bcd = bb.cc.dd$ and each prime factor of aa occurs twice; so that every square number must be composed of factors in pairs; and a square number multiplied by a number which is not composed of factors in pairs cannot be a square number: for instance, $2aa$ or $3aa$ cannot be a square number, since the factors of 2 are only 1.2, and of 3, 1.3, and not in pairs: therefore the square root of 2 or 3 cannot be expressed by any fraction, for the square of its numerator would be twice or thrice the square of its denominator. But the ratio of the hypotenuse of a triangle to its side may be that of $\sqrt{2}$ or $\sqrt{3}$ to 1; so that quantities numerically incommensurable may be geometrically determined.

120. THEOREM. Triangles and parallelograms of the same height are proportional to their bases.

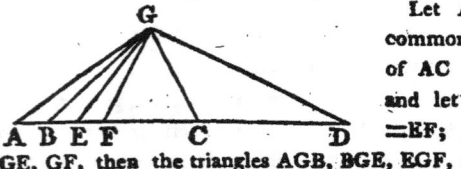

Let AB be a common measure of AC and AD, and let $AB = BE = EF$; join GB, GE, GF, then the triangles AGB, BGE, EGF, are equal, and the triangle AGD is the same multiple of AGB that AD is of AB; and AGC is the same multiple of AGB that AC is of AB, or $AGD : AGB = AD : AB$, and $AGC : AGB = AC : AB$; hence, dividing the first equation by the equal terms of the second (18), $AGD : AGC = AD : AC$, and $2AGD : 2AGC = AD : AC$, therefore the parallelograms which are double the triangles, are also proportional.

SCHOLIUM. The demonstration may easily be extended to incommensurable quantities. For if it be denied that $AC : AD = AGC : AGD$, let $AC : AD$ be the greater, and let the difference be $\frac{1}{n}$, then $\frac{AC}{AD} - \frac{1}{n} = \frac{AGC}{AGD} = \frac{n.AC}{n.AD} - \frac{AD}{n.AD} = \frac{n.AC - AD}{n.AD}$. Let $m.AD$ be that multiple of AD which is less than $n.AC$, but greater than $n.AC - AD$, then a triangle on the base $m.AD$ will be equal to $m.AGD$, which will be less than $n.AGC$, the triangle on $n.AC$; now multiplying the former equation by $\frac{n}{m}$, $\frac{n.AGC}{m.AGD} = \frac{n.AC - AD}{m.AD}$, and $n.AGC.m.AD = m.AGD.(n.AC - AD)$; but the first factors have been shown to be respectively greater than the second, therefore their products cannot be equal, and the supposition is impossible.

121. THEOREM. The homologous sides of equiangular triangles are proportional.

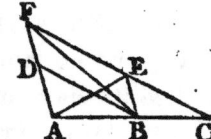

Let the homologous sides AB, BC, of the equiangular triangles ABD, BCE, be placed contiguous to each other in the same line, then $AD \parallel BE$, and $BD \parallel CE$; produce AD, CE, till they meet in F, and join AE and BF. Then the triangles FAE, EAC, are proportional to their bases FE, EC, and the triangles AFB, BFC, to AB, BC (120). But $FAE = AFB$ (117), and $EAC = EBC + EAB = EBC + EFB = BFC$, therefore $FAE : EAC = AFB : BFC$, and $FE : EC = AB : BC$; but $FE = DB$ (114). In the same manner it may be shown that the other homologous sides are proportional.

SCHOLIUM. Hence equiangular triangles are also called similar.

122. THEOREM. Equal and equiangular parallelograms have their sides reciprocally proportional.

If $AB = BC$ then $DB : BE = BF : BG$. For $DB : BF = AB : GF$ (120) $= BC : GF = BE : BG$ (120); or $DB : BE = BF : BG$.

123. THEOREM. Equiangular parallelograms, having their sides reciprocally proportional, are equal.

For they may be placed as in the last proposition, and the demonstration will be exactly similar.

SCHOLIUM. Hence is derived the common method of finding the contents of rectangles; let a and b be the sides of a rectangle, then $1 : a :: b : ab$, and the rectangle is equal to that of which the sides are 1 and ab, or to ab square units. Hence the rectangle contained by two lines is equivalent to the product of their numeral representatives.

124. THEOREM. Equiangular parallelograms are to each other in the ratio compounded of the ratios of their sides.

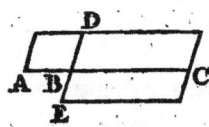

Or in the ratio of the rectangles or numeral products of their sides. For since AB : BC=AD : DC (120), and DC : CE=DB : BE, multiplying the former equation by the terms of the latter, AB.DB : BC.BE=AD.CE.

125. THEOREM. Similar triangles, and figures composed of similar triangles, are in the ratio of the squares of their homologous sides.

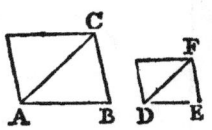

Since similar triangles are the halves of equiangular parallelograms, which are in the ratio compounded of the ratios of their sides (124), the triangles are in the same ratio, or ABC : DEF=AB.BC : DE.EF; but AB : DE=BC : EF (121), therefore ABC : DEF=AB.AB : DE.DE, or ABq : DEq. And the same may be proved of similar polygons, by composition (32).

126. DEFINITION. An indefinite right line, meeting a circle and not cutting it, is called a tangent.

127. THEOREM. A right line, passing through any point of a circle, and perpendicular to the radius at that point, touches the circle.

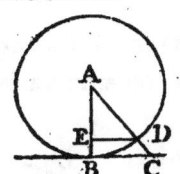

Since the perpendicular AB is shorter than any other line AC that can be drawn from A to BC (103), it is evident that AC is greater than the radius AD, and that C, as well as every other point of BC, besides B, is without the circle; therefore BC does not cut the circle, but touches it.

128. DEFINITION. BC is called the tangent of the arc BD, or the angle BAD.

129. DEFINITION. AC is the secant of BD, or BAD.

130. DEFINITION. DE perpendicular to AB, is the sine of BD or BAD.

131. DEFINITION. AE is the cosine of BD or BAD.

132. DEFINITION. EB is the versed sine of BD or BAD.

SCHOLIUM. The circle is practically supposed to be divided into 360 equal parts, called degrees, each of these into 60 minutes, a minute into 60 seconds; and the division may be continued without limit; thus 60″=1′, 60′=1°, 90° make a right angle. Some modern calculators divide the quadrant into 100 equal parts, and subdivide these decimally.

133. THEOREM. The angle subtended at the centre of a circle by a given arc, is double the angle subtended at the circumference.

Let ABC and ADC be subtended by AC. Draw the diameter DBE, then ∠ ABE= ADB+BAD(108)=2ADB (87). Also ∠ CBE=2CDB, therefore ABE−CBE= 2ADB−2CDB, or ABC=2ADC. In a similar manner it may be proved in other positions.

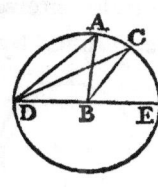

134. THEOREM. The angle contained by the tangent and any chord at the point of contact, is equal to the angle contained in the segment on the opposite side of the chord.

Draw the diameter AB, and join BC; then ∠ BCA is equal to half the angle subtended at the centre by the semicircle AB, or to a right angle, and ABC and BAC make together another right angle (93), therefore deducting BAC, ABC= CAD. And it appears also from the last proposition that the angle contained in the lesser segment CA is equal to the complement of ABC to two right angles, or to CAE.

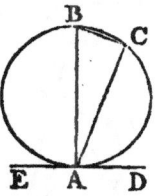

135. PROBLEM. To draw a tangent to a circle from a given point without it.

Join AB, bisect it in C, and on C draw a circle, with the radius CB, intersecting the former circle in D, then AD shall touch the circle. For the angle ADB, in a semicircle, is a right angle (134, 127), and BD is the radius of the given circle.

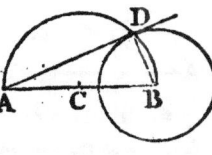

136. THEOREM. In equal circles, equal angles stand on equal arcs.

For the chords of equal angles are equal (86), and the segments cut off by them contain equal angles (133); and if a segment equal to AB be supposed to be described on the chord CD, and on the same side with CED, it must coincide with CED, for since, at each point of each arc, CD subtends the same angle, the points of one arc can never be within those of the other (99); the arcs are therefore equal.

SCHOLIUM. Hence it may easily be shown, that multiple and proportionate angles are subtended by multiple and proportionate arcs.

137. THEOREM. If two chords of a given circle intersect each other, the rectangles contained by the segments of each are equal.

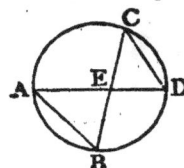

Join AB and CD. Then $\angle AEB=DEC$ (96), and $\angle BAE=DCE$ (133), both standing on BD, therefore the triangles AEB, CED, are similar, and $AE:CE::EB:ED$ (121), therefore $AE.ED=CE.EB$ (123).

138. THEOREM The rectangle contained by the segments of a right line intercepted by a circle and a given point without it, is equal to the square of the tangent drawn from that point.

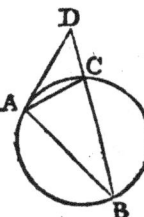

Join AB, AC; then $\angle ABC=CAD$ (134), and the angle at D is common, therefore the triangles ABD, CAD, are similar, and $BD:AD::AD:CD$ (121), whence $BD.DC=ADq$ (123).

139. THEOREM. In every triangle the sides are as the sines of their opposite angles, the radius being given.

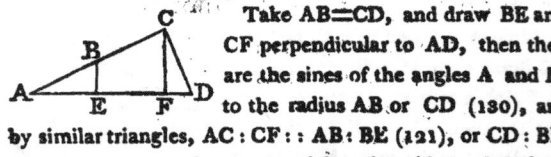

Take $AB=CD$, and draw BE and CF perpendicular to AD, then they are the sines of the angles A and D, to the radius AB or CD (130), and by similar triangles, $AC:CF::AB:BE$ (121), or $CD:BE$. And the same may be shown of the other sides and angles.

140. THEOREM. The sine of the sum of any two arcs, is equal to the sum of the sines of the separate arcs, each being reduced in the ratio of the radius to the cosine of the other arc.

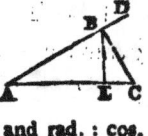

Let AB and BC be the sines of any two angles, ACB, BAC, then AC will be the sine of their sum CBD, or of ABC. Now making BE perpendicular to AC, $AC=AE+EC$, and rad. : cos. BAC :: AB : AE, and rad. : cos. ACB :: BC : CE (139).

141. THEOREM. The ratio of the evanescent tangent, arc, chord, and sine, is that of equality.

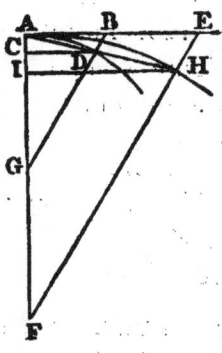

Let AB be the tangent, and CD the sine of the arc AD. Let AE be taken at pleasure in the tangent, and EF be always parallel to DG, the radius of AD, and on the centre F, draw the circle. AH; join AH, then since $\angle EAD=\frac{1}{2}AGD=\frac{1}{2}AFH$, the chord AH will coincide with the chord AD (133, 134). And when DA vanishes, DG coinciding with AG, EF will be parallel to AF, and the angle EAH will vanish, therefore AH will coincide with AE and with IH parallel to the sine CD; and by similar triangles the ratio of AB, AD, and CD, is the same as that of AE, AH, and IH, and is ultimately that of equality. But the arc AD is nearer to the chord AD than the figure ABD, and it has no contrary flexure, therefore it is longer than the line AD (70), and shorter than ABD (80), until their difference vanishes, and it coincides with both.

SCHOLIUM. The same is obviously true of any curve coinciding at a given point with any circle; and all the elements agree as well in position as in length.

142. THEOREM. The fluxion of the arc being constant, the fluxion of the sine varies as the cosine.

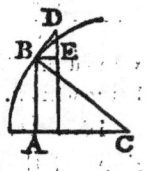

The fluxion of the arc is equal to that of the tangent, since their evanescent increments coincide (141). Let AB be the sine, AC the cosine, BD the increment of the tangent, DE that of the sine: then $\angle ABC=EBD$ (16), and the triangles ABC, EBD, are similar, and BD is to DE as BC to AC; but the ultimate ratio of the increments is that of the fluxions, therefore the fluxion of the tangent, or of the arc, is to that of the sine as the radius to the cosine. The same may easily be inferred from the theorem for finding the sine of the sum of two arcs (140).

143. THEOREM. The area of a circle is equal to half the rectangle contained by

the radius and a line equal to the circumference.

Suppose the circle to be described by the revolution of the radius: the elementary triangle to which the fluxion of the circle is proportional (141), is equal to the contemporaneous increment of the rectangle, of which the base is equal to the circumference, and the height to half the radius: consequently the whole areas are equal (47).

144. THEOREM. The circumferences of circles are in the ratio of their diameters.

Supposing the circles to be concentric, and to be described by the revolution of different points of the same right line, the ratio of the fluxions, and consequently that of the whole circumferences, will be the ratio of the radii, or of the diameters (47).

SCHOLIUM. The diameter of a circle is to its circumference nearly as 7 to 22, and more nearly as 113 : 355, or $1 : 3.14159265359$; hence the radius is equal to $57.29578°$ $=3437.7467'=206264.8''$; and, the radius being unity, $1° = .017453293$, $1' = .000290888$, and $1'' = .000004848$.

145. DEFINITION. A straight line is perpendicular to a plane, when it is perpendicular to every straight line meeting it in that plane.

146. DEFINITION. A plane is perpendicular to a plane, when all the straight lines drawn in one of the planes perpendicular to the common section, are perpendicular to the other.

147. DEFINITION. The inclination of a straight line to a plane is the angle contained by that line, and another straight line drawn from its intersection with the plane to the intersection of a perpendicular let fall from any point of the line upon the plane.

148. DEFINITION. The inclination of two planes is the inclination of two lines, one in each plane, perpendicular to the common section.

149. DEFINITION. Parallel planes are such as never meet, although indefinitely produced.

150. DEFINITION. A solid angle is made by the meeting of two or more plane angles, in different planes.

151. DEFINITION. Similar solid figures are such as have all parts of their surfaces similar and similarly placed: and which have all their sections, in similar directions, respectively similar.

152. DEFINITION. A pyramid is a solid contained by a plane basis and other planes meeting in a point.

153. DEFINITION. A prism is a solid contained by planes of which two that are opposite, are equal, similar, and parallel, and all the rest parallelograms.

154. DEFINITION. A cube is a solid contained by six equal squares.

155. DEFINITION. A solid of revolution is that which is described by the revolution of any figure round a fixed axis.

156. DEFINITION. A sphere is described by the revolution of a semicircle on its diameter as an axis.

157. DEFINITION. A cone is a solid described by the revolution of an indefinite right line passing through a vertex and moving round a circular basis.

158. DEFINITION. A cylinder is a solid described by the revolution of a right angled parallelogram about one side.

159. THEOREM. Two straight lines cutting each other are in one plane.

For a plane passing through one of them may be supposed to revolve on it as an axis until it meet some point of the other; and then the second line will be wholly in the plane (62).

160. THEOREM. If two planes cut each other, their section is a straight line.

For the straight line joining any two points of the section must be in each plane (62), and must therefore be the common section of the planes.

161. THEOREM. A straight line, making right angles with two other lines at the point

of their intersection, is at right angles to the plane passing through those lines.

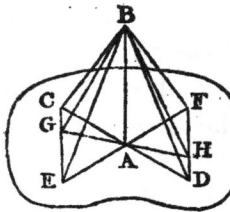

Let AB be perpendicular to CD and EF intersecting each other in A: take AC at pleasure and make AC=AD=AE=AF; draw through A any line GH, and join CE, DF; then the triangles ADH, ACG are equal and equiangular, AH=AG and DH=CG; but since the triangles CBE, DBF, are equal, and equiangular, the angles BCG and BDH are equal, and the triangle BCG= BDH, BG=BH, and the triangles ABG, ABH, are equal and equiangular: consequently the angle BAG=BAH, and both are right angles: and the same may be proved of any other line passing through A; therefore AB is perpendicular to the plane passing through CD and EF (145).

162. THEOREM. Three straight lines which meet in one point and are perpendicular to one line, are in one plane.

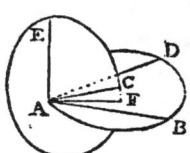

Let AB, AC, and AD meet in A, and be perpendicular to AE, then they are all in one plane. For if either of them AC is out of the plane which passes through the other two, let a plane pass through AE and AC, and let it cut the plane of AB and AD in AF then the angle EAF is a right angle (161), and EAF=EAC, the greater to the less: which is impossible.

163. THEOREM. Two straight lines which are perpendicular to the same plane, are parallel to each other; and two parallel lines are always perpendicular to the same planes.

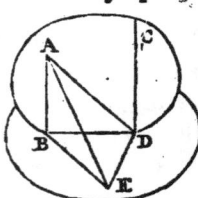

Let AB, CD, be perpendicular to the plane BED: draw DE at right angles to BD, and equal to AB, then the hypotenuses AD, BE, will be equal, and the triangles ABE, EDA, having all their sides equal, will be equiangular, and the angle ADE will be a right angle: consequently DE is perpendicular to the plane BC (161), and to DC (162), and AB is in the same plane with DC: and ABD and BDC being right angles, AB || CD.

Again, if AB || CD, and AB is perpendicular to the plane BED, the triangles ABE and EDA being equiangular, ADE is a right angle: therefore CDE is a right angle (161); but CDB is a right angle (105), therefore CD is perpendicular to BED.

164. THEOREM. Straight lines which are parallel to the same straight line, not in the same plane, are parallel to each other.

From any point in the third line, draw perpendiculars to the two first, and let a plane pass through these perpendiculars: then the third line is perpendicular to this plane (161); consequently the first and second are perpendicular to it, and therefore parallel to each other (163).

165. THEOREM. If the legs of two angles not in the same plane are parallel, the angles are equal.

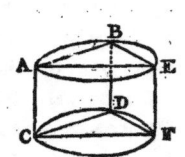

Let AB || CD, and BE || DF, then ∠ ABE=CDF. Take AB=BE=CD=DF: then AC ||=BD ||=EF (109), and AE =CF (109); therefore ABE and CDF are equal and equiangular.

166. PROBLEM. To draw a line perpendicular to a plane from a given point above it.

From the point A let fall on any line BC in the given plane a perpendicular AD; draw DE perpendicular to BC in the same plane, and from A draw AE perpendicular to DE: then AE will be perpendicular to the plane BEC; for if EF be parallel to BC, it will be perpendicular to the plane ADE (163), and consequently to AE; therefore AE, being perpendicular to DE and EF, will be perpendicular to the plane passing through them.

167. PROBLEM. From a given point in a plane, to erect a perpendicular to the plane.

From any point above the plane let fall a perpendicular on it, and draw a line parallel to this from the given point: this line will be the perpendicular required.

168. THEOREM. If two parallel planes are cut by any third plane, their sections are parallel lines.

For if the lines are not parallel, they must meet, and if they meet, the planes in which they are situated must meet, contrarily to the definition of parallel planes.

169. DEFINITION. A parallelepiped is a solid contained by six planes, three of which are parallel to the other three.

170. THEOREM. The opposite planes of

every parallelepiped are equal and equiangular parallelograms.

The opposite sides of all the figures are parallel, because they are the sections of one plane with two parallel planes (168): the corresponding sides of two opposite planes being, for the same reason, parallel to each other, contain equal angles (165), and they are also equal, as being the opposite sides of parallelograms; consequently the opposite figures are the doubles of equal triangles, and are therefore equal parallelograms.

171. THEOREM. If a prism be divided by a plane parallel to its two opposite surfaces, its segments will be to each other as the segments of any of the divided surfaces or lines.

Let the prism AB be divided by the plane CDE parallel to AFG and BHI. Find FK a common measure of FD and DB (119), make KL=FK, and let the planes KMN, LOP be parallel to AFG; then the prisms AK, ML may be shown to be contained by similar and equal figures similarly situated, in the same manner as it is shown of parallelepipeds, and there is no imaginable difference between these prisms: they are therefore equal; and the prism AD is the same multiple of AK that FD is of FK, and AB the same multiple of AK that FB is of FK, or AD : AK=FD : FK, and AB . AK=FB : FK, whence AD : AB=FD : FB, and the prisms are in the same ratio as the segments of the line FB, or of the parallelogram GB (27).

If the segments are incommensurable, they are still in the same ratio, for it may be shown that the ratio of the prisms is neither greater nor less than that of the lines.

172. THEOREM. Parallelepipeds on the same base and contained between the same planes, are equal.

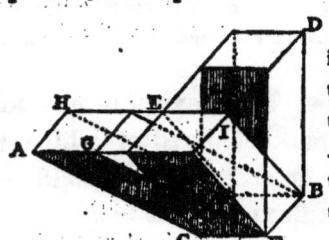

The parallelepiped AB is equal to CD standing on the same base BC, and terminated by the plane AED. For each is equal to the parallelepiped EF; since the triangular prism GB is similar and equal to the triangular prism HC, and deducting these from the solid HCI, the remainders AB and EF are equal.

And in the same manner it may be shown that CD=EF; therefore AB=CD.

173. THEOREM. Parallelepipeds on equal bases and of the same height are equal.

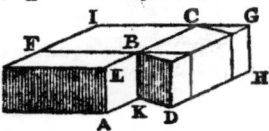

Each parallelepiped is equal to the erect parallelepiped on the same base. Let one of these be so placed that the plane of one of the sides AB may coincide with the plane BC of the other parallelepiped CD, and that EBC may be a straight line. Then producing FB, and making CG parallel to it, the parallelepiped BH will be equal to CD (172). Now completing the parallelepiped IK, as the parallelogram CF is to EF, so is KI to AF (171); and as CF to BG, so is KI to BH, but EF is equal to the base of AF, and BG to the base of CD, they are therefore equal, and the parallelepipeds AF and BH are equal, and AF=CD.

174. THEOREM. Parallelepipeds of the same height are to each other as their bases.

For one of them is equal to a parallelepiped of the same height on an equal base which forms a single parallelogram with the base of the other; and this is to the other in the ratio of the bases (171); consequently the first two are in the same ratio.

175. THEOREM. Parallelepipeds are to each other in the joint ratio of their bases and their heights.

For one of them is to a third parallelepiped of the same height with itself, but on the basis of the second, in the ratio of the bases, and the third is to the second in the ratio of the heights, consequently the first is to the second in the joint ratio of the bases and the heights. Thus, a and b being the bases, c and d the heights, $e, f,$ and g the three parallelepipeds, $a : b :: e : g$, and $c : d :: g : f$; $ac : bd = e : f$.

SCHOLIUM. Hence is derived the common mode of finding the content of a solid, by multiplying the numerical representatives of its length, breadth and height, and thus comparing it with the cubic unit of the measure.

176. THEOREM. Similar parallelepipeds are in the triplicate ratio of their homologous sides.

For the joint ratio of the bases and heights is the same as the triplicate ratio of the sides.

177. THEOREM. A plane passing through the diagonals of two opposite sides of a parallelepiped, divides it into two equal prisms.

The diagonals are parallel, because the lines in which they terminate are parallel and equal, and every line and 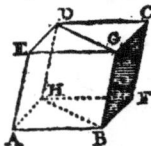 angle of the one prism is equal to the corresponding line and angle of the other prism; consequently the prisms are equal. Thus AB=CD, AE=CF, DE=BF, the angle EAB=DCF, EAH=GCF, and BAH=DCG.

178. Theorem. Prisms are to each other in the joint ratio of their bases and their heights.

Triangular prisms are in the same ratio as the parallelepipeds on bases twice as great, of which they are the halves; and all prisms may be divided into triangular prisms, by planes passing through lines similarly drawn on their ends, and they will be equal together to the half of a parallelepiped on a basis twice as great; consequently two such prisms are in the same ratio as the parallelepipeds.

179. Theorem. All solids of which the opposite surfaces are planes, and the sides such that a straight line may be drawn in them from any point of the circumference of the ends parallel to a given line, are to each other in the joint ratio of their bases and their heights.

For if they are terminated by rectilinear figures, the solids are prisms; and if they are terminated by curvilinear figures, they will always be greater than prismatic figures, of which the bases are inscribed polygons, and less than figures of which the bases are circumscribed polygons; and if the proposition be denied, it will always be possible to inscribe a prism in one of the solids which shall be greater than any solid bearing to the other solid a ratio assignably less than the ratio determined by the proposition, and to circumscribe a prism less than any solid bearing a ratio assignably greater. Such solids may not improperly be called cylindroids.

180. Theorem. The fluxion of any solid described by the revolution of an indefinite line passing through a vertex, and moving round any figure in a plane, is equal to the prismatic or cylindroidal solid, of which the base is the section parallel to the given plane, and the height the fluxion of the height.

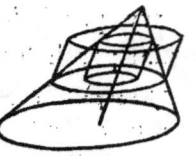

In any increment of the solid, which is cut off by planes determining the increment of the height, suppose a prismatic or cylindroidal solid to be inscribed, of which the base is equal to the upper surface of the segment, and the sides such that a line may always be drawn in them parallel to a given line passing through the vertex and the basis of the solid: and let another solid be similarly described on the lower surface of the segment as a basis: then it is obvious that the increment is always greater than the inscribed solid, and less than the circumscribed; and that when the increment is diminished without limit, its two surfaces are ultimately in the ratio of equality, and the increment coincides with the cylindroid described on its basis. Such solids may be termed in general pyramidoidal.

181. Theorem. All pyramidoidal solids are equal to one third of the circumscribing prismatic or cylindroidal solids of the same height.

The area of each section of such a figure parallel to the basis, is proportional to the square of its distance from the plane of the vertex. For each section is either a polygon similar to the basis, or it may have polygons inscribed and circumscribed, which are similar to polygons inscribed and circumscribed in and round the basis, and which may differ less from each other in magnitude than any assignable quantity, consequently each section is as the square of any homologous line belonging to it, or, by the properties of similar triangles, as the square of the distance from the vertex, or from the plane of the vertex. If then the area of the base be a, the whole height b, and the distance of any section from the plane of the vertex x, the area of the section will be $\frac{xx}{bb}.a$, and the fluxion of the solid $\frac{a}{bb}x^2\dot{x}$, of which the fluent is $\frac{1}{3}\frac{a}{bb}x^3$, and when $x=b$, the content is $\frac{1}{3}ax$, which is one third of the content of the whole prismatic or cylindroidal solid. Hence a pyramid is one third of the circumscribing prism, and a cone one third of the circumscribing cylinder.

182. Theorem. The fluxion of any solid is equal to the parallelepiped of which the base is equal to the section of the solid, and the height to the fluxion of its height.

For every part of a solid may be considered as touching some pyramidoidal solid, and having the same fluxion:

and the fluxion expressed by a cylindroid is equal to a parallelepiped on the same base and of the same height.

183. THEOREM. *The curve surface of a sphere is equal to the rectangle contained by its versed sine and the sphere's circumference.*

The fluxion of the surface is obviously equal to the rectangle contained by the fluxion of the circumference and the circumference of the circle of which the radius is the sine; it varies therefore as the sine; but the fluxion of the cosine or of the versed sine varies as the sine, consequently the surface varies as the versed sine. Now where the tangent becomes parallel to the axis, the fluxion of the surface becomes equal to the rectangle contained by the sphere's circumference, and the fluxion of the versed sine: hence the whole surface of any segment is equal to the whole rectangle contained by its versed sine and the sphere's circumference; and the surface of the whole sphere is four times the area of a great circle.

184. THEOREM. *The content of a sphere is two thirds of that of the circumscribing cylinder.*

The fluxion of the sphere is to that of the cylinder as the square of the sine to the square of the radius; or if the fluxion of the cylinder be $aa\dot{b}\dot{x}$, that of the sphere will be $(2ax - xx)\dot{b}\dot{x}$, or $2a\dot{b}x\dot{x} - \dot{b}xx\dot{x}$, of which the fluent is $abx^2 - \frac{1}{3}bx^3$; which, when $x = a$, becomes $\frac{2}{3}a^3b$, while the content of the cylinder is a^2b.

185. THEOREM. *When a picture is projected on a plane, by right lines supposed to be drawn from each point to the eye, the whole image of every right line, produced without limit, is a right line drawn from its intersection with the plane of projection, to its vanishing point, or the point where a line drawn from the eye, parallel to the given line, meets the plane of projection; and this image is divided by the image of any given point in the ratio of the portion of the line intercepted by that point and the picture, to the line drawn from the eye to the vanishing point; so that if any two parallel lines be drawn from the ends of the whole image, and the distances of the eye and of the given point be laid off on them respectively, the line joining the points thus found, will determine the place of the required image of the point.*

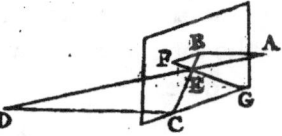

For A being the eye, and B the vanishing point of the line CD; AB and CD being parallel, are in the same plane, and AD is also in that plane (62); and BC is the intersection of this plane with that of the picture; therefore E, the image of the point D, is always in the line BC; and AB : CD :: BE : EC; and taking the parallel lines BF, CG, in the same ratio, FG will also cut BC in E. When AB is perpendicular to the plane, B is called the point of sight, and is the vanishing point of all lines perpendicular to the plane of the picture: and the vanishing point of any other line may be found by setting off from B a line equal to the tangent of its inclination to the perpendicular line, the radius being AB.

SCHOLIUM. When a line becomes parallel to the plane of the picture, the distance of its vanishing point becomes infinite, and the image is therefore parallel to the original. In this case, the magnitude of the image may be determined by means of lines drawn in any other direction through the extremities of the original line. In the orthographical projection, the images of all parallel lines whatever become parallel, the distance of the eye, and consequently that of the vanishing point, becoming infinite.

186. DEFINITION. *The subcontrary section of a scalene cone is that which is perpendicular to the triangular section of the cone passing through the axis, and perpendicular to the base, and which cuts off from it a triangle similar to the whole, but in a contrary position.*

187. THEOREM. *The subcontrary section of a scalene cone is a circle.*

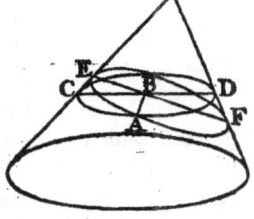

Through any point A of the section, let a plane be drawn parallel to the base; then its section will be a circle, as is easily shown by the properties of similar triangles; and the common section of the planes will be perpendicular to the triangular section of the cone to which they are both perpendicular; consequently, $ABq = CB.BD$; but since the triangles CBE, FBD are equiangular and similar, CB : BE :: BF : BD, and $CB.BD = BE.BF = ABq$; therefore EAF is also a circle.

188. THEOREM. The stereographic projection of any circle of a sphere, seen from a point in its surface, on a plane perpendicular to the diameter passing through that point, is a circle.

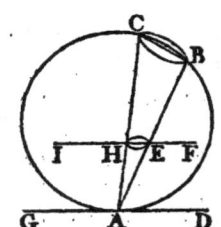

Let ABC be a great circle of the sphere passing through the point A and the centre of the circle to be projected, then the angle ACB=BAD=BEF, and ABC=CAG=CHI, and the triangle AHE is similar to ABC, and the plane ABC is perpendicular to the plane BC and the plane HE, therefore HE is a subcontrary section of the cone ABC, and is consequently a circle.

SECTION IV. OF THE PROPERTIES OF CURVES.

189. DEFINITION. Any parallel right lines intercepted between a curve and a given right line, are called ordinates, and each part of that line intercepted between an ordinate and the curve, is the absciss corresponding to that ordinate.

190. THEOREM. The fluxion of the area of any figure is equal to the parallelogram contained by the ordinate and the fluxion of the absciss.

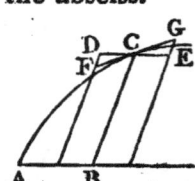

Let AB be the absciss, and BC the ordinate, through C draw DCE∥AB, and take DC=DE=half the increment of AB, then the simultaneous increment of the figure ABC will ultimately coincide with the figure FCGEB, since the curve ultimately coincides with its tangent (141), but the triangles CDF, CEG, are equal, therefore the parallelogram DBE is ultimately equal to the increment of ABC. And if any other line than DE represent the fluxion of AB, as DE is to this line, so is the parallelogram DBE to the parallelogram contained by BC and this line; therefore that parallelogram is the fluxion of ABC (46).

SCHOLIUM. Those who prefer the geometrical mode of representation, may deduce from this proposition a demonstration of the theorem for determining the fluxion of the product of two quantities (48); for every rectangle may be diagonally divided into two such figures as are here considered, and the sum of their fluxions, according to this proposition, will be the same with the fluxion of the rectangle determined by that theorem.

191. DEFINITION. A flexible line being supposed to be applied to any curve, and to be gradually unbent, the curve described by its extremity is called the involute of the first curve, and that curve the evolute of the second.

192. DEFINITION. The radius of curvature of the involute is that portion of the flexible line which is unbent, when any part of it is described.

193. THEOREM. The radius of curvature always touches the evolute, and is perpendicular to the involute.

If the radius of curvature did not touch the evolute, it would make an angle with it, and would therefore not be unbent; and if the evolute were a polygon composed of right lines, each part of the involute would be a portion of a circle, and its tangent therefore perpendicular to the radius: but the number of sides is of no consequence, and if it became infinite, the curvature would be continued, and the curve would still at each point be perpendicular to the radius of curvature.

194. THEOREM. The chord cut off in the ordinate by the circle of curvature, is directly as the square of the fluxion of the curve, and inversely as the second fluxion of the ordinate, that is, as the fluxion of its fluxion.

The constant fluxion of the absciss being equal to AB, the fluxion of the ordinate at A, is BC, at D, DE, consequently its increment is CD+BE, or CD+AF, twice the sagitta of the arc AD: and the chord is equal to the square of AC divided by CD, and it is therefore always in the direct ratio of the square of the fluxion of the curve, and the inverse ratio of the second fluxion of the ordinate.

195. THEOREM. When the curve approaches infinitely near to the absciss, the cur-

vature is simply as the second fluxion of the ordinate.

For the fluxion of the curve becomes equal to that of the absciss, and the perpendicular chord to the diameter.

196. DEFINITION. If the sum of two right lines drawn from each point of a curve to two given points, is constant, the curve is an ellipsis, and the two points are its foci.

197. DEFINITION. The right line passing through the foci, and terminated by the curve, is the greater axis, and the line bisecting it at right angles, the lesser axis.

198. THEOREM. A right line passing through any point of an ellipsis, and making equal angles with the right lines drawn to the foci, is a tangent to the ellipsis.

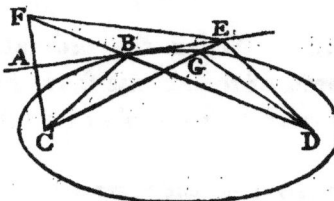

Let AB make equal angles with BC and BD, then it will touch the ellipsis in B. Let E be any other point in AB. Produce DB, take BF=BC, and join CF, then AB bisects the angle CBF, and CAB is a right angle. Join EC, ED, EF, GD, then EC=EF, and EC+ED=EF+ED, and is greater than DF (79), or BC+BD, or GC+GD, therefore E is not in the ellipsis, and AB touches it.

199. THEOREM. The right lines drawn from any point of the ellipsis to the foci, are to each other as the square of half the lesser axis to the square of the perpendicular from either focus, on the tangent at that point.

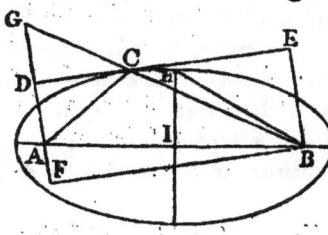

Let A and B be the foci, C the point of contact, and AD the perpendicular to the tangent CD, draw BE and BF parallel to AD and CD, produce AD each way, and let it meet BF and BC in F and G. Then since ∠ACD=BCE =DCG, CG=AC; and BG=AC+BC. And BFq=BGq −FGq=BAq−FAq (118), therefore BGq−FAq=FGq −FAq; but (FG+FA).(FG−FA)=FGq−FAq; and FG+FA=2FD=2BE, and FG−FA=AG=2AD; also BG=2BH, and BA=2BI, whence BGq−BAq=4HIq, therefore BE.AD=HIq, and $BE = \frac{HIq}{AD}$, but BE : BC : : AD : AC, and $BE = AD \cdot \frac{BC}{AC} = \frac{HIq}{AD}$, or $\frac{BC}{AC} = \frac{HIq}{ADq}$.

200. THEOREM. The chord of the circle of equal curvature with an ellipsis at any point, passing through the focus, is equal to twice the harmonic mean of the distances of the foci from the given point, or to the product of the distances divided by one fourth of the greater axis.

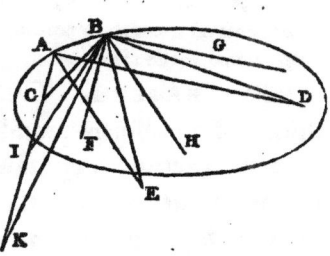

Let AB be an evanescent arc of the ellipsis coinciding with the tangent, then the radius of curvature bisecting always the angle CAD or CBD, the point E where the radii AE and BE meet will ultimately be the centre of the circle of equal curvature. Let BF, BG, be parallel to AC, AD, then BH, bisecting FBG, will be parallel to AE: but EBH=CBF+FBH−CBE= CBF+½FBG−½CBD=CBF−½CBF+½DBG=½(CBF+ DBG)=½(ACB+ADB). Now in the triangles ABC, ABD, as AC is to the sine of ABC, so is AB to the sine of ACB, and as AD is to the sine of ABD, so is AB to the sine of BDA; but the sines of ABC and ABD are ultimately equal; consequently ACB and ADB are inversely as AC and AD, or as their reciprocals, and EBH or AEB, which is the half sum of ACB and ADB, is as the mean of those reciprocals: let BI be the reciprocal of that mean, or the harmonic mean of AC and AD, then the angle AIB=AEB; for the evanescent angles ACB, AIB, or their sines, are reciprocally as AC, AI, being opposite to the same angle BAE and having AB opposite to them; for the same reason taking BK=2BI, AKB is half of AEB; consequently K is in the circle of curvature, and BK is its chord.

201. THEOREM. The square of the perpendicular falling on the tangent of an ellipsis from its focus, is to the square of the distance of the point of contact from the focus, as a third proportional to the axes is to the focal chord of curvature.

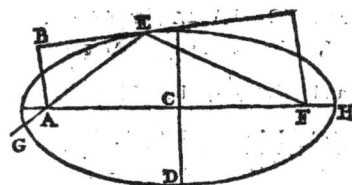

It has been shown that $ABq : CDq :: AE : EF$ (199), therefore $ABq : AEq :: CDq : AE.EF$; but the chord of curvature EG is $\frac{2AE.EF}{CH}$, and $AE.EF = \tfrac{1}{2} EG.CH$, therefore $ABq : AEq :: CDq : \tfrac{1}{2} EG.CH :: 2\frac{CDq}{CH} : EG$.

SCHOLIUM. It may easily be demonstrated that a perpendicular to the normal of the curve, or to the line perpendicular to its tangent, passing through the point where it meets the axis, bisects the focal chord of curvature, and that a perpendicular falling from the same point on the chord, cuts off a constant portion from it, equal to the third proportional to the semiaxes.

202. THEOREM. The square of any ordinate of an ellipsis parallel to the lesser axis, is to the rectangle contained by the segments of the greater axis, as the square of the lesser axis to the square of the greater.

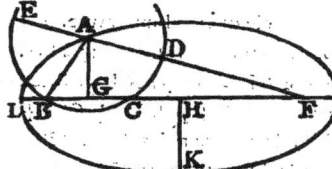

On the centre A describe the circle BCDE passing through the focus B; then $EF : BF :: CF : DF$ (138). Call HI, a, HB, b, AB, x, GH, z, then $EF = 2a$, $BF = 2b$, $CF = 2BH = 2BG = 2GH = 2z$, $DF = EF - ED = 2a - 2x$, and $2a : 2b :: 2z : 2a - 2x$, $a : b :: z : a - x$, $a : a+b :: z : z+a-x :: a+z : 2a-x+b+z$ (32); also $a : a - b :: z : z - (a-x) :: a - z : 2a - x - (b+z)$, and by multiplying the terms, $aa : aa - bb :: (a+z).(a-z) : (2a-x)^2 - (b+z)^2$, or $HIq.HKq :: IG.GL : AFq - GFq$, or AGq.

203. THEOREM. The area of an ellipsis is to that of its circumscribing circle, as the lesser axis to the greater.

For since the square of the ordinate is to the rectangle contained by the segments of the axis, or to the square of the corresponding ordinate of the circle (187), as the square of the lesser axis to that of the greater, the ordinate itself is to that of the circle in the constant ratio of the lesser axis to the greater. For if four quantities are proportional, their squares are proportional, and the reverse. But the fluxions of the areas are equal to the rectangles contained by these ordinates and the same fluxion of the absciss (190), they are therefore in the constant ratio of the ordinates, and the corresponding areas are also in the same ratio (47).

204. DEFINITION. If the square of the absciss is equal to the rectangle contained by the ordinate and a given quantity, the curve is a parabola, and the given quantity its parameter.

SCHOLIUM. Thus $ABq = P.BC$. If the axes of an ellipsis are supposed infinite it becomes a parabola; for since $\frac{b^2}{a^2} = \frac{y^2}{ax-xx}$, if a becomes infinite, xx vanishes in

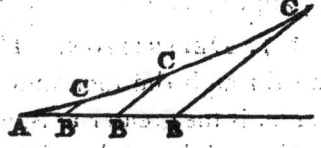

comparison of ax, and $\frac{b^2}{a^2} = \frac{y^2}{ax}, \frac{b^2}{a} x = y^2$, and $\frac{b^2}{a}$ is the parameter of the parabola; and the distance from the focus is in a constant ratio to the square of the perpendicular falling on the tangent.

205. DEFINITION. When the ordinate is as any other power of the absciss than the second, the curve is still a parabola of a different order.

Thus when the ordinate is as the third power of the absciss the curve is a cubic parabola.

206. THEOREM. If any figure be supposed to roll on another, and any point in its plane to describe a curve, that curve will always be perpendicular to the right line joining the describing point and the point of contact.

Suppose the figures rectilinear polygons; then the point of contact will always be the centre of motion, and the figure described will consist of portions of circles meeting each other in finite angles, so that each portion will be always perpendicular to the radius, though no two radii meet in the point of contact. And if the number of sides be increased without limit, the polygons will approach infinitely near to curves, and each portion of the curve described will still be perpendicular to the line passing through the point of contact.

207. DEFINITION. A circle being supposed to roll on a straight line, the curve described by a point in the circumference is called a cycloid.

208. THEOREM. The evolute of a cycloid

is an equal cycloid, and the length of its arc is double that of the portion of the tangent cut off by the vertical tangent.

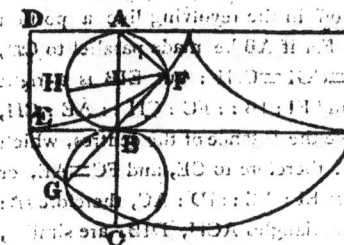

Let two equal circles AB, BC, rolling on the parallel bases DA and EB, at the distance of a diameter of the circles, describe with the points F and G the equal cycloids EF and EG. Draw the diameter FH; then H will be the point that coincided with D, and HA=DA=EB= arc BG, and the remainders AF and GC are equal, therefore ∠AEF=CBG (132), and FBG is a right line (96). But FG is perpendicular to AF (134), therefore it touches EF (206), and it is always perpendicular to EG (206); therefore EG will coincide with the involute of EF, for they set out together from E, and are always perpendicular to the same line FG (184), which they could not be if they ever separated. Consequently the curve EF is always equal to FG (192), or 2FB, twice the portion of the tangent cut off by EB.

209. THEOREM. The fluxion of the cycloidal arc is to that of the basis, as the evolved radius to the diameter of the generating circle.

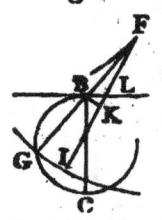

For the increment GI=2BK, and BK : BL :: BG : BC, and 2BK : BL :: FG : BC, which is therefore the ratio of the fluxions.

SCHOLIUM. If the fluxion of the base be constant, that of the curve will vary as the distance of the describing point from the point of contact.

210. DEFINITION. If the absciss be equal to the arc of a given circle, and the perpendicular ordinate to the corresponding sine, the curve will be a figure of sines.

211. DEFINITION. If a second figure of sines be added, by taking ordinates equal to the cosines, the pair may be called conjugate figures of sines.

212. THEOREM. The radius of curvature of the figure of sines at the vertex is equal to the ordinate.

For the fluxion of the base becoming ultimately equal to that of the absciss in the corresponding circle, while the ordinates are also equal, the curve ultimately coincides with a portion of that circle.

213. THEOREM. The area of each half of the figure of sines is equal to the square of the vertical ordinate.

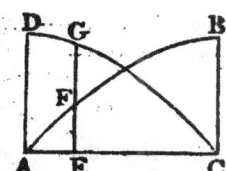

For the fluxion of the absciss being constant, that of the sine varies as the cosine (142), therefore the fluxion of the ordinate of the figure of sines may always be represented by the corresponding ordinate of the conjugate figure. Let AB, CD, be the conjugate figures, then EF will represent the fluxion of EG, and, since the arc and sine are ultimately equal, the fluxion of EG at C will be equal to that of the absciss, therefore BC will always represent the constant fluxion of the absciss, But the fluxion of the area AEF, is the rectangle under the fluxion of the absciss AE and the ordinate EF; that is, the rectangle under BC and the fluxion of EG, and the fluent BC.(AD—EG) is therefore equal to the area, which at C becomes BCq.

214. DEFINITION. Each ordinate of the figure of sines being diminished in a given ratio, the curve becomes the harmonic curve.

SCHOLIUM. The ordinates being diminished in a constant proportion, their increments and fluxions are diminished in the same proportion, the fluxion of the base remaining constant.

215. THEOREM. The radius of curvature at the vertex of the harmonic curve is to that of the figure of sines, on the same base, as the greatest ordinate of the figure of sines to that of the harmonic curve.

For taking any equal evanescent portions of the vertical tangents the radii will be inversely as the sagittae, which are similar portions of the corresponding ordinates, and are therefore to each other in the ratio of those ordinates.

216. THEOREM. The figure, of which the ordinates are the sums of the corresponding ordinates of any two harmonic curves, on equal bases, but crossing the absciss at different points, is also a harmonic curve.

The absciss of the one curve being x, that of the other will be $a+x$, and the ordinates will be $b.(\sin. x)$ and $c.(\sin$

$a+x$); now $\sin. a+x = (\cos. x).(\sin. a) + (\cos. a).(\sin. x)$ and the joint ordinate will be $(b+c.(\cos. a)).(\sin. x) + c.(\sin. a).(\cos. x)$; if therefore d be the angle of which the tangent is $\dfrac{c.(\sin. a)}{b+c.(\cos. a)}$ its sine and cosine will be in the ratio of $c.(\sin. a.)$ to $b+c(\cos. a)$, and $(\cos. d).(\sin. x)+(\sin. d).(\cos. x)$, will be to the ordinate in the constant ratio of $\sin. d$ to $c.(\sin. a)$; but $(\cos. d).(\sin. x)+(\sin. d).(\cos. x)$ is the sine of $d+x$; consequently the newly formed figure is a harmonic curve.

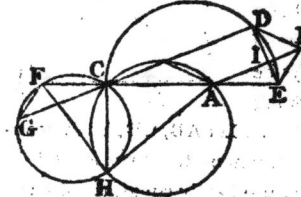

The same may be shown geometrically, by placing two circles, having their diameters equal to the greatest ordinates of the separate curves, so as to intersect each other in an angle equal to twice the angular distance of the origin of the curves: then a right line revolving round their intersection with an equable velocity will have segments cut off by each circle equal to the corresponding ordinate, and the sum or difference of the segments will be the joint ordinate: and if a circle be described through the point of intersection, touching the common chord of the two circles, and having its radius equal to the distance of their centres, this circle will always cut off in the revolving line a portion equal to the ordinate. For if AB be made parallel to CD, and EB to FG, $\angle$ ABE=CGF=CHF: but EIB is a right angle, as well as HCF, and EI : IB : : FC : CH : : AE : CH, since AF is equal to twice the distance of the centres, which bisect AH and FH, and therefore to CE, and FC=AE, or EI : AE : : IB : CH; but EI : AE : : ID : AC, therefore IB : CH : : ID : AC, and the triangles ACH, DIB, are similar, and $\angle$ DBI=CHA=DKA, and AD is a parallelogram, consequently, KD=AB=CG.

If the circle CG be supposed to revolve round C, the intersection H will always show the angular distance of the point in which the curve crosses the axis; and the distance of the centres will be equal to the greatest ordinate. If therefore the circles are equal, the greatest ordinate will also vary as the chord of an arc increasing equably, or as the ordinate of the harmonic curve.

MATHEMATICAL ELEMENTS

OF

NATURAL PHILOSOPHY.

PART II.

MECHANICS.

OF THE MOTIONS OF SOLID BODIES.

SECTION I. OF MOTION.

217. **Axiom.** Like causes produce like effects, or, in similar circumstances, similar consequences ensue.

218. **Definition.** Motion is the change of rectilinear distance between two points.

219. **Definition.** A space or surface, of which all the points remain spontaneously at equal distances from each other, is said to be quiescent, or at rest within itself.

Scholium. The term " spontaneously" is introduced, in order to exclude from the definition of a quiescent space any surface, of which the points are only retained at rest by means of a centripetal force, while they revolve round a common centre; for with respect to such a revolving space or surface, the motions of any body will deviate from the laws which govern them in other cases.

220. **Definition.** When a point is in motion with respect to a quiescent space, the right line joining any two of its proximate places is called its direction; such a point is often simply denominated a moving point.

221. **Theorem.** A moving point never quits the line of its direction without a new disturbing cause.

A right line being the same with respect to all sides, no reason can be imagined why the point should incline to one side more than another. Let AB be the direction of the motion of A in the plane ABC, and let CB and DB be equal, and perpendicular to AB, then the triangles ABC and ABD are equal (86), and A is similarly related to C and D. Then if A depart from AB, and be found in any point out of it, as E, ED will be greater than EC (103), and A will be no longer similarly related to C and D, contrarily to the general law of induction (217).

222. **Definition.** The times in which a point, moving without disturbance, describes equal parts of the line of its direction, are called equal times.

223. **Theorem.** The equality of times being estimated by any one motion, all other points, moving without disturbance, will describe equal portions of their lines of directions in equal times.

A C E B D F   G Let A and B be moving in the same line, and while A describes AC, let B describe BD; then while A describes CE=AC, B will describe DF=BD. For suppose AC=2BD, and let AG=2AB, then AB and BG have been equally decreased in one instance, and the relations remaining the same, they will still be equally decreased (217); for the relative motion of A and B is equal to that of B and G, and any absolute motion being no way determinable, there can be no reason why the one should be otherwise affected than the other; therefore CE will be twice DF: and a similar proof might be given in cases more complicated.

224. THEOREM. If any number of points move in parallel lines, describing equal spaces in equal times, they are quiescent with respect to each other; and if all the points of a plane move in this manner on another plane, either plane will be in rectilinear motion with respect to the other.

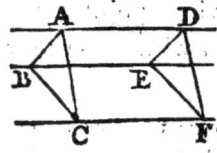

Let A, B, and C, describe, in a given time, the equal parallel lines AD, BE, CF, then AB=DE, EF=BC, and DF=AC (109), and the points are mutually quiescent (218, 219).

225. DEFINITION. If a plane be in rectilinear motion with respect to another, and if, besides this general motion of the plane, any point be supposed to have a particular motion in it, it will have two motions with respect to the other plane, one in common with its plane, and the other peculiar to itself; and the joint effect of these motions with respect to the other plane, is called the result of the two motions.

226. THEOREM. The result of two motions with respect to a quiescent space is the diagonal of the parallelogram of which the sides would be described by the separate motions; and any motion may be considered as the result of any other motions thus composing it.

Let A, B, and C, be three quiescent points, and let Z, Y, and X, be three points in another plane which moves in the direction AZ, BY; then the point A has a rectilinear motion with respect to the plane ZYX; now while AZ is described by Z, let A have a motion in its own plane equal to AB; then it will have two motions with respect to ZYX, by the joint effect of which it will arrive at X in that plane; and if the motions are both equable, it may be shown by the properties of similar triangles, that it describes the diagonal ZX. Now it is of no consequence to the relative motion of A and ZXY, which, or whether either, be imagined to be absolutely at rest; therefore, in general, the result of two motions in a quiescent space, is the diagonal of the parallelogram of which the sides would be described by the separate motions. And the motion thus produced is precisely the same as if derived from a simpler cause.

227. THEOREM. Any equable motions represented by the sides of a triangle or polygon, supposed to take place in the same moveable point, in directions parallel to those sides, and in the order of going round the figure, destroy each other, and the point remains at rest.

For two sides of the triangle, AB, BC, are sides of the parallelogram ABCD, therefore by the motions AB, BC, or AB, AD, A would arrive at C, while by the motion CA it would be brought back to A in the same time; and all the motions being equable, it will always remain in A. In the same manner the proof may be extended to any number of sides; and the truth of the proposition will also appear by considering several successive planes as moving on each other, and the point A as moving in the last.

SECT. II. OF ACCELERATING FORCES.

228. DEFINITION. Any immediate cause of a change of motion is called a force.

SCHOLIUM. The essential nature of force is unknown to us: even in cases of apparent impulse, the bodies are not actually in contact. When a body is once in motion, it needs no foreign power to sustain its velocity (223); and the action of such a cause in the direction of its motion can only increase or diminish that velocity.

229. DEFINITION. When the increase or diminution of the velocity of a moving body is uniform, its cause is called a uniform force: the increments of space which would be described in any given time with the initial velocities, being always equally increased or diminished.

SCHOLIUM. The power of gravitation acting at the earth's surface, in a direction perpendicular to it, may, without sensible error, be considered as such a force.

230. THEOREM. The velocity produced by any uniformly accelerating force is proportional to the magnitude of the force, and the time of its operation, conjointly.

For the time and the velocity flow equably (229, 47). Calling the accelerating force a, the time t, and the velocity v, $at : v$ is a constant quantity; or making this quantity unity, $at = v$. It may be shown by the composition of motion that a double action produces a double velocity.

231. THEOREM. The increment of space described is as the increment of the time, and as the velocity, conjointly.

This is evident from the definition of velocity (45); calling the space described x, $x' = vt'$. If the velocity is variable, the increment must be considered as evanescent.

232. THEOREM. The space described by means of a uniformly accelerating force, is as the square of the time of its action; it is also equal to half the space which would be described in the same time with the final velocity; and if the forces vary, the spaces are as the forces, and the squares of the times, conjointly.

Since $v = at$ (230), and $x' = vt'$ (231), $x' = att'$ also $\dot{x} = att$ (46), of which the fluents are $x = \frac{att}{2}$ (49) $= \frac{tv}{2}$. Therefore x varies as tt, or as att, and v being the velocity acquired in the time t, tv instead of $\frac{1}{2}tv$ would be described with that velocity in the same time.

SCHOLIUM. The space described by the fall of a heavy body in one second is 16.0916 feet.

233. THEOREM. The times are as the square roots of the spaces directly, and of the forces inversely; they are also as the spaces directly, and the final velocities inversely: the final velocities are also as the spaces directly, and the times inversely.

Since $x = \frac{att}{2}$, $t = \sqrt{\left(\frac{2x}{a}\right)}$, and if $a = 1$, $t = v = \sqrt{(2x)}$; and since $x = \frac{tv}{2}$, $t = \frac{2x}{v}$, and $v = \frac{2x}{t}$.

234. THEOREM. The forces are as the spaces directly, and the squares of the times inversely, beginning from the state of rest.

For $2x = att$, and $a = \frac{2x}{tt}$.

235. THEOREM. The fluxions of the squares of the velocities are as the fluxions of the spaces, and as the forces, conjointly, whether the forces be uniform or variable.

In the evanescent time t', the variation of the force vanishes in comparison with the whole, and $v' = at'$ (230), whence $\dot{v} = a\dot{t}$; but $\dot{x} = v\dot{t}$ (231), therefore $a\dot{x} = v\dot{v}$, $a\dot{x} = v\dot{v} = \frac{1}{2}(vv)$. (49).

236. THEOREM. In considering the effects of a retarding force, the body may be supposed to be at rest in a moveable plane, and the motion generated by the force may be deducted from that of the plane.

For $\dot{x}$ becomes $-\dot{x}$, and, if $a = 1$, $-x = \frac{1}{2}tt$, that is, the diminution of the space which would be described varies as the square of the time. It is also obvious, that the degrees by which an ascending body is retarded, being the same as those by which it is accelerated in descending, the velocities will be the same at the same heights.

237. THEOREM. If two forces act in the same right line on a moveable body, varying inversely as the square of its distance from two given points, of which the distance is a, their magnitudes being expressed by b and c at the distance d, the square of the velocity generated in the passage of the body from any two points of which the distances from the first centre are successive values of x, is the difference of the corresponding values of

$$2dd\left(\frac{b}{x} + \frac{c}{a \pm x}\right)$$

The sum of the forces acting on the body is $\frac{bd^2}{xx} \pm \frac{cd^2}{(a\pm x)^2}$, and since $v\dot{v} = f\dot{x}$, $v\dot{v} = \frac{bd^2\dot{x}}{xx} \pm \frac{cd^2\dot{x}}{(a\pm x)^2}$, and $\frac{vv}{2} = -\frac{bd^2}{x} - \frac{cd^2}{a\pm x}$, $vv = \mp\left(\frac{2bd^2}{x} + \frac{2cd^2}{a\pm x}\right)$; and if $c=0$, $v=\sqrt{\left(\frac{2b}{x}\right)}d$.

SCHOLIUM. In the case of a body projected from the moon towards the earth, $d=20,900,000$ feet, $a=60d$, $b=32.2$ feet, the velocity produced in $1''$ at the earth's surface; $c=\frac{1}{70}b$, nearly; then taking $x=\frac{219}{220}a$, at the moon's surface, and $\frac{84}{94}a$, at the point where the force becomes neutral, we have $\frac{2bdd}{a}\left(\frac{1}{219}+\frac{1}{70}\right) \times 220$ and $\frac{2bdd}{a}\left(\frac{1}{84}+\frac{1}{700}\right) \times 94$, of which the difference is $\frac{5.788bdd}{a}$, or $.09640bd$, and its square root about 8070 feet. Hence, if the velocity of a projectile from the moon exceed 8070 feet, it may pass the neutral point, and descend to the earth; where its velocity will become more than 36000 feet in a second.

SECTION III. OF CENTRAL FORCES.

238. DEFINITION. An accelerating force tending to a point out of the line of direction of a moving body, deflects it from that line, and is then usually called a central force.

239. THEOREM. The force, by which a body is deflected into any curve, is directly as the square of the velocity, and inversely as that chord of the circle of equal curvature, which is in the direction of the force; and the velocity in the curve is equal to that which would be generated by the same force, during the description of one fourth of the chord by its uniform action.

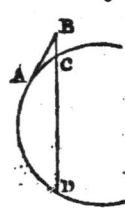

For the force is as the space described by its action, beginning from a state of rest, or as the evanescent sagitta through which the body is drawn from the tangent of the curve in a given instant of time: but the portion AB of the tangent described in a given instant is as the velocity, and $BC = \frac{AB q}{BD}$, or ultimately $\frac{ABq}{CD}$, which is as the square of the velocity directly, and inversely as the chord of the circle of curvature of the arc AC.

Now the velocity generated during the description of BC is expressed by twice BC, since the force may be considered for an instant as constant: consequently it is to the orbital velocity as twice BC to AB, or as twice AB to BD, or as AB to half CD; and if the time of the action of the force were continued during the time that half CD would be described with the orbital velocity, it would generate a velocity equal to that velocity; but in this time one fourth of CD only would be described by its action.

240. THEOREM. When a body describes a circle by means of a force directed to its centre, its velocity is every where equal to that which it would acquire in falling by the same uniform force through half the radius; and the force is as the square of the velocity directly, and as the radius inversely.

For in this case the chord, passing through the centre, becomes a diameter.

241. THEOREM. In equal circles the forces are as the squares of the times inversely.

For the velocities are inversely as the times, and the deflective chords are equal.

242. THEOREM. If the times are equal, the velocities are as the radii, and the forces are also as the radii, and, in general, the forces are as the distances directly, and the squares of the times inversely; and the squares of the times are directly as the distances, and inversely as the forces.

For the velocities are as the distances directly, and as the times inversely; and the squares of the velocities are as the squares of the distances directly, and as the squares of the times inversely; consequently the forces are as the radii directly, and the squares of the times inversely; and the squares of the times are as the radii directly, and as the forces inversely.

243. THEOREM. If the forces are inversely as the squares of the distances, the squares of the times are as the cubes of the distances.

For the squares of the times are as the distances directly, and as the forces inversely (242); that is, in this case, as the distances and as the squares of the distances, or as the cubes of the distances.

244. THEOREM. The right line joining a revolving body and its centre of attraction, always describes equal areas in equal times, and the velocity of the body is inversely as the perpendicular drawn from the centre to the tangent.

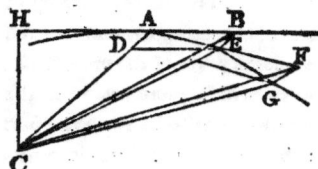

Let AB be a tangent to any curve in which a body is retained by an attractive force directed to C, and let AB represent its velocity at A, or the space which would be described in an instant of time without disturbance, and AD the action of C in the same time; then completing the parallelogram, AE will be the joint result (220); again, take EF=AE, and EF will now represent its spontaneous motion in another equal instant of time, and by the action of C it will again describe the diagonal of a parallelogram EG; but the triangles ABC, AEC; AEC, ECF; ECF, ECG, being between the same parallels, are equal (117); and if they be infinitely diminished, and the action of C become continual, they will be the evanescent increments of the area described by the revolving radius, while the body moves in the curvilinear orbit; and the whole areas described in equal times will therefore be equal. And since the constant area ABC=AB.½CH (117, 114), $AB = 2ABC.\frac{1}{CH}$, therefore AB, representing the velocity, is always inversely as CH, or $v = \frac{1}{u}$.

245. THEOREM. Two bodies being attracted towards a given centre, with equal forces, at equal distances, if their velocities be once equal at equal distances, they will remain always equal at equal distances, whatever be their directions.

Let one of the bodies descend in the right line AB, towards C, and let the other describe the curve AD, and let the velocities at B and D be equal; let DE in the tangent of AD be the space which would be described in an evanescent portion of time by the velocity at D, FG the arc of a circle on the centre C, and GE its tangent; and while BF would be described by the velocity at B, let FH be added to it by the attractive force; draw the arc HI and its tangent IK, and EL||DC, and KL perpendicular to DK, then DG : DE :: GI : EK :: EK : EL, by similar triangles; therefore, GI is to EL in the duplicate ratio of DG to DE, or as the square of DG to the square of DE (124): therefore EL will be the space described by the attractive force, while DE would be described by the velocity at D; for the force may be considered as uniform during the description of the evanescent increments; and the spaces described by means of such a force are as the squares of the times: hence the joint result will be DL, which is ultimately equal to DK, and the whole velocity will be increased in the ratio of DK to DE, or DI to DG, or BH to BF; consequently, since H, I, and K, are ultimately equidistant from C, the velocities in AB and AD, being always equally increased at equal distances, will therefore always remain equal at equal distances.

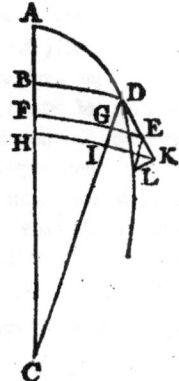

246. THEOREM. If a body revolves in an elliptic orbit, by a force directed to one of the foci, the force is inversely as the square of the distance.

The force is directly as the square of the velocity, and inversely as the deflective chord; but the velocity is inversely as the perpendicular falling on the tangent; therefore the force is inversely in the joint ratio of the square of the perpendicular and of the deflective chord; now in the ellipsis, the focal chord varies directly as the square of the distance, and inversely as the square of the perpendicular (201), consequently this joint ratio is that of the square of the distance, and the force is always inversely as the square of the distance.

247. THEOREM. The velocity of a body revolving in an ellipsis is equal, at its mean distance, to the velocity of a body revolving at the same distance in a circle; and the whole times of revolution are equal.

For the focal chord of curvature at the mean distance

becomes equal to twice that distance, or to the diameter of the circle (800); therefore the velocities are equal (239). But since the perpendicular height of the triangular element of the area, of which the base is the element of the orbit at the mean distance, is equal to the lesser axis, this element is to the contemporaneous element in the circle as the lesser to the greater axis, or as the whole ellipsis to the whole circle (203), consequently both areas being uniformly described, the times of revolution are equal.

248. THEOREM. If a body describes an equiangular spiral round a given point, the force must be inversely as the cube of the distance, and the velocity equal to that with which a circle might be described at the same distance.

For the orbit of a body projected in any direction with a velocity equal to that with which a circle may be described at the same distance, will initially coincide with an elliptic orbit as its mean distance; and the inclination of the orbit to the revolving radius is constant at the mean distance; for if it were either increasing or diminishing, the two halves of the ellipsis could not be equal and similar, since the angles contained between the tangent and the lines drawn to the foci (198) would be different at equal distances on each side of the lesser axis. It follows therefore that the velocity must always be equal to the velocity in a circle, in order that the equiangular spiral may be described; but in this curve, the perpendicular on the tangent is by its fundamental property always proportional to the radius: the velocity must therefore be always inversely as the radius; and the velocities of bodies revolving in circles must be inversely as the radii, and the forces inversely as the squares of the radii and the radii conjointly (240), or inversely as the cubes of the radii.

249. THEOREM. When a body revolves round a centre by means of a force varying more or less rapidly than in the inverse ratio of the squares of the distances, the apsides of the orbit, or the points of greatest and least elongation, will advance or recede respectively.

In an elliptic orbit, when the body descends from the mean distance, the velocity continually prevails over the central force, so as to deflect the orbit more and more from the revolving radius, until, at a certain point, it becomes perpendicular to it: but, if the central force increase in a greater proportion than in the ellipsis, the point where the velocity prevails over it will be more remote than in the ellipsis, and the apsis will move forwards. This becomes more evident by considering the extreme cases: supposing the central force to vanish, the lower apsis would recede to the point where a perpendicular falls from the centre on the tangent; but, supposing the force to increase as the cube of the distance decreases, the curve would be an equiangular spiral, and the lower apsis would be infinitely distant.

SCHOLIUM. The action of a second force, varying in the inverse ratio of the squares of the distances, and directed to a second centre, tends in some parts of the orbit to deduct a portion of the first force which increases with the distance of the body, and in other parts to increase the first force in a similar manner: but the former effect is considerably greater than the latter, so that on the whole, the joint force decreases more rapidly than the square of the distance increases, and the apsides advance. Thus the apsides of the planetary orbits have direct motions, in consequence of their mutual perturbations.

SECTION IV. OF PROJECTILES.

250. DEFINITION. The force of gravitation, as far as it concerns the motions of projectiles, is considered as a uniformly accelerating force, acting in parallel lines, perpendicular to the horizon.

251. THEOREM. The velocity of a projectile may be resolved into two parts, its horizontal and vertical velocity: the horizontal motion will not be affected by the action of gravitation perpendicular to it, and will therefore continue uniform; and the vertical motion will be the same as if it had no horizontal motion.

For a uniformly accelerating force is supposed to act equally on a body in motion and at rest, so that the vertical motion will not be affected by the horizontal motion; and the diagonal motion resulting from the combination will terminate in the same vertical line as the simple horizontal motion; therefore the horizontal motion will remain unaltered.

252. THEOREM. The greatest height to which a projectile will rise may be determined by finding the height from which a body must fall in order to gain a velocity equal to its vertical velocity; and the horizontal range may be found by calculating the distance described by its horizontal velocity in twice the time of rising to its greatest height.

This is evident from the equality of the velocity of ascending and descending bodies at equal heights, and from the independence of the vertical and horizontal motions of the projectile.

253. THEOREM. With a given velocity, the horizontal range is proportional to the sine of twice the angle of elevation.

The time of ascent being as the vertical velocity, or the sine of the angle of elevation, the range is as the product of the vertical and horizontal velocities, or as the product of the sine and cosine; that is, as the sine of twice the angle (140).

254. THEOREM. The path of a projectile moving without resistance, is a parabola.

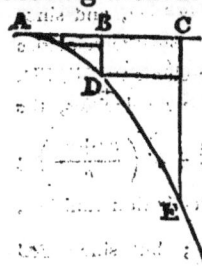

Since the horizontal velocity is uniform, the times of describing AB, AC, or x, are as their lengths, and the spaces BD, CE, described by the accelerating force of gravitation, as the squares of these times, or as x^2, whence $x^2 = ay$, and ADE is a parabola, of which a is the parameter (204).

SCHOLIUM. In practical cases the resistance of the atmosphere renders this theory of little use, except when the velocity is very small.

SECT. V. OF MOTION CONFINED TO GIVEN SURFACES.

255. THEOREM. When a body descends along an inclined plane, without friction, the force in the direction of the plane is to the whole force of gravity as the height of the plane is to its length.

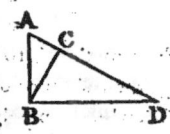

For if AB represent the motion which would be produced by gravity in a given time, this may be resolved into AC and CB (226); by means of AC the body arrives at the line CB in the same time as if it were at liberty; but the motion CB is destroyed by the resistance of the plane; and as AB to AC so is AD to AB (121). But forces are measured by the spaces described in the same time (230).

256. THEOREM. When bodies descend on any inclined planes of equal height, their times of descent are as the lengths of the planes, and the final velocities are equal.

Since $t = \sqrt{\left(\frac{2x}{a}\right)}$ (233), and here $a = \frac{1}{x}$, $t = \sqrt{(2xx)} = \sqrt{2x}$; and the times vary as the spaces, but the times being greater in the same proportions as the forces are less, the velocities acquired are equal (230).

257. THEOREM. The times of falling through all chords drawn to the lowest point of a circle are equal.

The accelerating force in any chord AB is to that of gravity as AC to AB, or as AB to AD (121), therefore the forces being as the distances, the times are equal; for their squares are as the spaces directly and the forces inversely (233).

258. THEOREM. When a body is retained in any curve by its attachment to a thread, or descends along any perfectly smooth surface of continued curvature, its velocity is the same, at the same height, as if it fell freely.

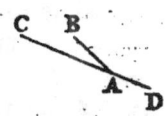

Since the velocity is the same at A, whether the body has descended an equal vertical distance from B or C, it will proceed in AD with the same velocity in both cases, provided that no motion be lost in the change of its direction, and therefore its velocity will be the same after passing any number of surfaces as if it had fallen perpendicularly from the same height. But where-

A the curvature is continued, no velocity is lost in the change of direction; for let AB be the thread or its evolved portion, the body B, if no longer actuated by gravity, would proceed in the circular arc with uniform motion (240), consequently no velocity is destroyed by the resistance of the thread, nor by that of the surface BC, which can only act in the same direction, perpendicular to the direction of the moving body.

259. THEOREM. If a body be suspended by a thread between two cycloidal cheeks, it will describe an equal cycloid by the evolution of the thread (208); and the time of descent will be equal, in whatever part of the curve the motion may begin, and will be to the time of falling through one half of the length of the thread, as half the circumference of a circle is to its diameter. And the space described in the cycloid will be always equal to the versed sine of an arc which increases uniformly.

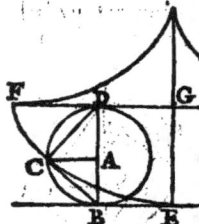

For since the accelerating force, in the direction of the curve, is always to the force of gravity as AB to BC, or as BC to the constant quantity BD, it varies as BC, or as its double, CE, the arc to be described (208). If therefore any two arcs be supposed to be equally divided into an equal number of evanescent spaces, the force will be every where as the space to be described; and it may be considered for each space, as equable, and the increments of the times, and consequently the whole times, will be equal. Supposing the generating circle to move uniformly, the velocity of the describing point C will always be as CD (209), or, since $AD : CD :: CD : BD$, and $CD = \sqrt{(AD.BD)}$, as $\sqrt{AD}$; but the velocity of a body falling in DA, or descending in FC, varies in the same ratio (232, 230, 258); therefore if the velocity at E be equal to that which a body acquires by falling through GE, the describing point C will always coincide with the place of a heavy body descending in FCE; and the velocity of the point of contact D is half that of C at E (209), it would therefore describe a space equal to GE in the time of the fall through GE (232), and will describe FG in a time which is to that time as FG to GE, or as half the circumference of a circle to its diameter,

and this will be the time of descent in the cycloidal arc. And since $FC = 2DB - 2BC$, FC is equal to the versed sine of the angle CBD, to the radius 2DB; but $\angle CAD$ increasing uniformly, its half, CBD, increases uniformly. And if the motion begin at any other point, the velocity will be in a constant ratio to the velocity in similar points of the whole cycloid. It is also obvious that the arc of ascent will be equal to the arc of descent, and described in an equal time, supposing the motion without friction.

260. THEOREM. The times of vibration of different cycloidal pendulums are as the square roots of their lengths.

For the times of falling through half their lengths are in the ratio of the square roots of these halves, or of the wholes.

261. THEOREM. The cycloid is the curve of swiftest descent between any two points not in the same vertical line.

Let AB and CD be two parallel vertical ordinates at a constant evanescent distance, in any part of the curve of swiftest descent, and let a third, EF, be interposed, which is

always in length an arithmetical mean between them, and which, as it approaches more or less to AB, will vary the curvature of the element BFD. Call AB, a; EF, b; $b - a$, c; AE, x; and EC, v; then $BF = \sqrt{(uu + cc)}$, and since $CD - EF = EF - AB$, $FD = \sqrt{(vv + cc)}$. But the velocities at B and F are as $\sqrt{a}$ and $\sqrt{b}$, and the elements BF, FD, being supposed to be described with these velocities, the time of describing BD is $\sqrt{\left(\frac{uu+cc}{a}\right)} + \sqrt{\left(\frac{vv+cc}{b}\right)}$, which must be a minimum; therefore its fluxion vanishes, or $\frac{2u\dot{u}}{2\sqrt{(a(uu+cc))}} + \frac{2v\dot{v}}{2\sqrt{(b(vv+cc))}} = 0$; but since AC or $u + v$ is constant, $\dot{u} + \dot{v} = 0$, or $\dot{u} = -\dot{v}$; therefore $\frac{u}{\sqrt{(a(uu+cc))}} = \frac{v}{\sqrt{(b(vv+cc))}}$. Let the variable abscissa GA be now called x; the ordinate AB, y; and the arc GB z; then u and v are increments of x, and BF and FD of z, when y becomes $= a$ and b respectively; and $\frac{\dot{x}}{\sqrt{y\dot{z}}}$ is the same in both cases, and is therefore constant, or $= \frac{1}{a}$, and $\frac{\dot{x}^2}{\dot{z}^2 y} $ or $\frac{\dot{x}^2}{\dot{z}^2} = \frac{y}{a}$. Now in the cycloid $\sqrt{y}$ is always the

 chord of the generating circle, the diameter being 1; and the arc being perpendicular to that chord, its fluxion, by similar triangles, is to that of the abscissa as the diameter to $\sqrt{y}$: therefore the cycloid answers the conditions in every part, and consequently in the whole curve.

SCHOLIUM. The demonstration implies that the origin of the curve must coincide with the uppermost given point: now only one cycloid can fulfil this condition and pass through the other point, and it will often happen that the curve must descend below the second point and rise again.

262. THEOREM. The time of vibration of a simple circular pendulum in a small arc is ultimately the same as that of a cycloidal pendulum of the same length; but in larger arcs the times are greater.

For in small cycloidal arcs the radius of curvature is nearly constant, but, at greater distances from the lowest point, the circular arc falls without the cycloidal, and is less inclined to the horizon.

263. THEOREM. If a body suspended by a thread revolve freely round the vertical line, the times of revolution will be the same when the height of the point of suspension above the plane of revolution is the same, whatever be the length of the thread.

For by the resolution of forces, the force urging the body towards the vertical line is to that of gravity as the distance from that line to the vertical height; the other part of the force being counteracted by the effect of the thread; and when the forces are as the distances, the times are equal (242).

264. THEOREM. The time of a revolution of a body suspended by a thread is equal to the time occupied by a cycloidal pendulum of which the length is equal to the height of the point of suspension above the plane of revolution, in vibrating once forwards and once backwards to the point at which its motion began; and if the revolutions be small, and the thread nearly vertical, they will be nearly isochronous, whatever be their extent.

For, supposing the distance equal to the height, the central force will be equal to the force of gravity, and while the body describes a distance equal to the radius, another body would fall through half that radius (240), and the whole time of revolution is therefore to this time as the circumference to the radius, and is therefore equal to the time of four semivibrations of a cycloidal pendulum of which the length is equal to the given height. And since the time varies, in the same revolving pendulum, only as the square root of the cosine of the angle of inclination, it will be nearly constant for all small revolutions.

265. THEOREM. The vibrations of a cycloidal pendulum will be performed in the same time, whether they be without resistance, or retarded by a uniform force.

Let the relative force of gravity, at the distance AB in the curve from its lowest point, be always represented by the ordinate 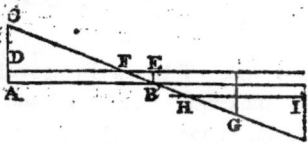 AC; then CB will be a right line: now the resistance may always be represented by the equal ordinates AD, BE, and DC will express the remaining force, which becomes neutral at F, and then negative: therefore the force is always the same at equal distances on each side of F, as in the simple pendulum on each side of B, and the vibration will be perfectly similar to the vibration of the simple pendulum in a smaller arc; but it will extend only to G. In the return of the body from G, the neutral point will be determined by the intersection of HI parallel to AB, and as much below it as DE was above it: this vibration will terminate in a point as much above H as G is below it: so that the extent of each vibration will be less than that of the preceding one by twice the length of FE, until the whole force is exhausted, the time remaining unaltered.

SECTION VI. OF THE CENTRE OF INERTIA, AND OF MOMENTUM.

266. DEFINITION. A moveable body is to be imagined as a point, composed of single points or particles equally moveable, which, as they differ in number, constitute the proportionally different mass or bulk of the body.

267. DEFINITION. A reciprocal action between two bodies is an action which affects

the single particles of both equally, increasing or diminishing their distance.

268. DEFINITION. The centre of inertia of two bodies is that point in the right line joining them, which divides it reciprocally in the ratio of their magnitudes.

269. THEOREM. The centre of inertia of two bodies, initially at rest in any space, remains at rest, notwithstanding any reciprocal action of the bodies.

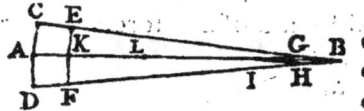

Suppose the bodies equal, and consisting each of a single particle, then it is obvious that both will be equally moved by any reciprocal action, and the centre of inertia will still bisect their distance (217). Again, let one body A be double the other B, and suppose A to be divided into two points placed very near each other, as C, D. Join BC, BD, take any equal distances CE, DF, BG, BH, and they will represent the mutual actions of B on C and D, and of C and D on B, and the motions produced by these equal actions; complete the parallelogram BGIH, and the diagonal BI will be the joint result of the motions of B; which, when C and D coincide in A or K, becomes equal to 2BG, 2CE, or 2AK; but L being the centre of inertia, BL=2AL (268), therefore IL remains equal to 2KL (15), and L is still the centre of inertia. And in the same manner the theorem may be proved when the bodies are in any other proportion.

270. DEFINITION. The joint ratio of the masses and velocities of any two bodies is the ratio of their momenta.

271. THEOREM. The momentum of any body is the true measure of the quantity of its motion.

For the same reciprocal action produces in a double body half the velocity, the common centre of inertia remaining at rest (269); and, the cause being the same, the effects must be considered as equal: and when the reciprocal force varies, the velocity of both bodies varies in the same ratio.

272. DEFINITION. The centre of inertia of three or more bodies is found by considering the first and second as a single body, equal to their sum, and placed in their common centre of inertia, determining the centre of inertia of this imaginary body and the third, and proceeding in the same manner for any greater number of bodies.

273. THEOREM. The centre of inertia of three or more bodies will be the same by whatever steps it be determined.

Let a, b, and c, denote the masses of the three bodies A, B, and C; let D be the centre of inertia of A and B, and take ED : EC :: c : $a+b$; draw AEF, then F will be the centre of inertia of 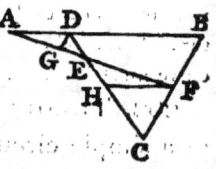 B and C, and AE to EF as $b+c$ to a. Draw DG and FH parallel to BC and BA, then (121) AD : AB :: DG : BF= DG. $\frac{AB}{AD}$=DG.$\frac{a+b}{b}$ (32); and DE : EC :: DG : CF=DG. $\frac{EC}{DE}$=DG.$\frac{a+b}{c}$, therefore BF : CF :: $\frac{1}{b}$: $\frac{1}{c}$ :: c : b, and F is the centre of inertia of B and C. Again, CB : CF :: BD : FH=BD.$\frac{b}{b+c}$, but AD=BD.$\frac{b}{a}$, and FH : DA :: $\frac{b}{b+c}$: $\frac{b}{a}$ :: a : $b+c$ :: FE : EA (121), and E is the same point as if determined from A and F. And from this demonstration the proposition may be shown to be true in cases where the number is greater, following the changes step by step. For instance, that in 4 bodies the order 1, 2, 3, 4, will give the same result as 3, 1, 4, 2; since (1, 2, 3), 4, is shown to be the same as (3, 1, 2), 4; and (3, 1), 2, 4, the same as (3, 1), 4, 2, or 3, 1, 4, 2.

274. THEOREM. The velocity and direction of the motion of the centre of inertia of any system of bodies, are the same as those of a single body equal to their sum, to which momenta equal to those of the several bodies, and in parallel directions, are communicated at the same time.

Let A be the common centre of inertia of B, C, and D, and E the centre of inertia of C and D. Let B move in a given time to F; then joining EF, and drawing AG parallel to BF, G will now be the common centre of inertia; but 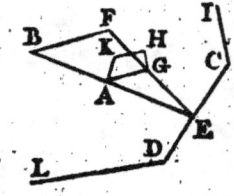 BF : AG :: AB+AE : AE :: B+C+D : B ; therefore the momentum of the single body B+C+D in describing AG is equal to that of B in describing BF (270, 28). And in the same manner if the common centre be transferred from G to H by the motion of C in CI, and then to K by that of D in DL, K will still be the place to which the single body would be removed by equal momenta successively communicated to it. If the motions of the separate bodies be not successive but simultaneous, K will nevertheless be their common centre of inertia; and if the motions of the single body be communicated to it at the same instant, their joint result will still transfer it to K, since AK is the result of the motions AG, GH, HK (226). Therefore the motion of the single body always coincides with that of the common centre of inertia of the system.

275. THEOREM. The centre of inertia of a system of bodies moving without disturbance is either at rest, or moving equably and rectilinearly.

For the result of any number of equable and rectilinear motions being also an equable rectilinear motion, as may easily be shown, by combining them in pairs, from the properties of similar triangles, the motion of the centre of inertia will also be equable and rectilinear (274).

276. THEOREM. If parallel lines be drawn from each of a system of bodies, and from their common centre of inertia, to a given plane, the sum of the products of all the bodies into the segments of their respective lines, will be equal to the product of the sum of all the bodies into the line drawn through the centre of inertia.

Suppose each body to describe its segment in the same time, then when they arrive at the plane, their centre of inertia will also be in the plane, and the product of each body into its segment will represent its momentum; and the product of their sum into the distance described by the centre of inertia will be the momentum of a single body equal to their sum, and coinciding always with that centre; but these momenta have been shown to be equal (274). The theorem may also be more directly demonstrated.

277. THEOREM. The distance of the centre of inertia of any triangle from the vertex is two thirds of the line that bisects the base.

The triangle being supposed to be divided by lines parallel to the base into evanescent portions, it is obvious that the centre of gravity must be in the line which bisects them all; and the sum of the products of each portion of the line into the corresponding element, divided by the whole area, will be the distance required; but the whole area being $\frac{1}{2}axx$, the area of each portion is axx', and the product $ax'x'$, the fluxion $ax^2\dot{x}$, and the fluent $\frac{1}{3}ax^3$; which, divided by the area, gives $\frac{2}{3}x$ for the distance required.

278. THEOREM. The place of the centre of inertia of three or more bodies is not affected by any reciprocal action among them.

For since, in all reciprocal actions between two bodies, equal momenta are communicated in opposite directions (269, 270), the joint effect of each pair on a single body supposed to be placed in the centre of inertia of the system, will be to destroy each other, therefore its place, and that of the centre of inertia (274), will be the same as if no reciprocal action existed.

279. THEOREM. When bodies of the same kind attract or repel each other, the force is in the compound ratio of their bulks.

For each particle of A, being actuated by each particle of B with a force equal to unity, is actuated by the whole of B with a force equal to B, and the whole of A with a force equal to A.B.

280. THEOREM. If two bodies act on each other with forces proportional to any power of their distance, the forces will also be proportional to the same power of either of their distances from their common centre of inertia; hence the reciprocal forces of two bodies may be considered as tending to their common centre of inertia as a fixed point.

For x, the distance of either body from the common centre of inertia, being in a constant ratio to the whole distance y, may be called ay, and the force $y^n = \left(\frac{x}{a}\right)^n = x^n : a^n$, which is to x^n in the constant ratio of 1 to a^n.

SCHOLIUM. It is observed that all known forces are reciprocal. This circumstance is generally expressed by the third law of motion, that action and reaction are equal; but it often happens that the difference of the magnitudes of the two bodies being very great, the motion of the greater may be disregarded.

SECT. VII. OF PRESSURE AND EQUILIBRIUM.

281. DEFINITION. A pressure is a force

counteracted by another force, so that no motion is produced.

282. DEFINITION. Equal and proportionate pressures are such as are produced by forces which would generate equal and proportionate momenta in equal times.

283. THEOREM. Two contrary pressures will balance each other when the momenta, which the forces would separately produce in contrary directions, are equal; and one pressure will counterbalance two others when it would produce a momentum equal and contrary to the joint momenta which would be produced by the other forces.

Conceive the forces to act alternately during equal evanescent intervals of time, then the one will at each step destroy the preceding effect of the other; let this action be doubled, and the forces will become a continual pressure, the total effects still destroying each other. If this reasoning be thought unsatisfactory, the proposition may be assumed axiomatically, or may be deduced from the equality of the effects of equal causes.

284. THEOREM. If a body remain at rest by means of three pressures, they must be related in magnitude as the sides of a triangle parallel to the directions.

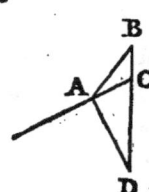

Suppose the body A to be suspended by the thread AB, on the inclined plane AC, to which AD is perpendicular, BD being the direction of gravity, then that the force BD may be destroyed, it must be opposed by an equal force DB, and if DB be composed of forces in the directions DA, AB; the forces must be as those sides, or as the sides of the parallelogram of which DB is the diagonal; and the same is true of any other pressures.

285. THEOREM. If two gravitating bodies be suspended at constant distances from each other and from a given point, they will be at rest when their centre of inertia is in the vertical line passing through the point of suspension: and the equilibrium will be stable when the centre of inertia would ascend in quitting the vertical line, tottering when it would descend, and neutral when it cannot quit it.

Suppose the bodies A and B, of which C is the centre of inertia, to be suspended from D by the threads AD, DB, and to be retained at the distance AB by the rod AB, and let C be in the vertical line DC. Let the force of gravity be represented by DC, then AD will represent the action of the thread, and AC the pressure exerted by A on any obstacle at C (284); and in the same manner BC will represent the pressure of B in the direction BC, supposing the weights A and B equal; but since they are unequal, the ratio of their masses must be compounded with that of the forces, and A.AC will represent the actual force of A, and B.BC that of B; but A : B=BC : AC, and A.AC=B.BC; therefore the pressures are equal, and the bodies will remain in equilibrium. But if the centre of inertia ascended towards either weight, as A, the segment AC, which determines the action of A, would be increased, and BC lessened; therefore the weight of A would prevail, and the centre would return to the vertical line. But supposing C above D, the rod and threads must change places, and the same demonstration will hold good; and since in this case the weights pull against each other, the prevalence of A when the centre of inertia descends towards its place will draw it still further from the vertical line, and the equilibrium will be lost. Now the distance of C above or below D is of no consequence to the equilibrium; therefore

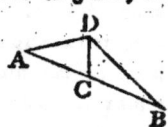

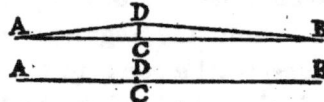

when that distance vanishes, and the thread and rod are united into one inflexible right line or lever, those points will coincide, and there will still be an equilibrium; which may properly be termed neutral, since no change of the position of the bodies will create a tendency either to return to their places, or to proceed further from them. But the case of an inflexible right line is perfectly out of the reach of experiment, since the strength necessary for the inflexibility of a mathematical line becomes infinite, and that in an infinitely small quantity of matter. If any other mode of connexion by inextensible and incompressible lines be imagined, there will still be an equilibrium; for instance, if AC, BC, DC, be rods; and AD, DB, threads; and C the centre of suspension; or if AE, BE, DE, be rods; and AD, BD, threads.

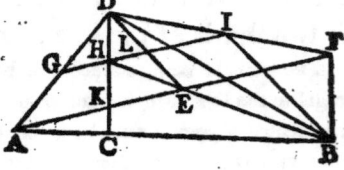

This case is somewhat intricate, and may be thus demonstrated. Draw BF parallel to CD, and GHI to AE produced to F, then HE : KE :: BE : FE (121), and DE : DL :: KE : HL :: FE : IL, therefore HE : HL :: BE : IL (17), and BI is parallel to ED. Now A : B :: BC : AC :: FK : AK :: IH : GH, and A.GH=B.HI. But by what has been already demonstrated, the pressure of A and B in the directions AE, BE, are A.GH and B.HB, DH representing the force of gravity, since the lines are parallel to the forces exerted; and A.GH=B.HI : therefore the forces of A and B at E being B.HI and B.BH, their result will be parallel to BI, or in the direction ED, and will therefore be wholly counteracted by the rod DE, without any tendency to turn it round D.

There is another simple and elegant mode of demonstrating the property of the lever, which deserves to be noticed. Supposing the arms to be a little bent, and the forces to act perpendicularly to them, so that their directions may meet in a distant point; then if their actions be imagined to be concentrated in that point, it will be easy to show that in order that the resulting force may pass through the point of suspension, and that an equilibrium may be thus produced, the forces must be inversely as the perpendiculars falling from that point on their directions; that is, as the arms of the lever inversely; and this will be true whether the lever be more or less bent, and consequently even if it be not bent at all. It is not however strictly shown in this demonstration, that the effect of the forces must be the same as if they were applied in the point where their directions meet, and a link appears to be still wanting in the chain.

286. THEOREM. A system of any number of gravitating bodies, or a mass composed of such bodies, will remain in equilibrium when its centre of inertia is in the vertical line, passing through the point of suspension.

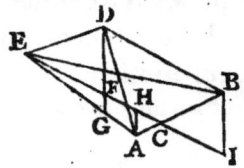

Let us first suppose the number of bodies to be three; let A and B be so connected as to remain in equilibrium on their centre of inertia C; and let this centre and the third body E be in any way connected with the point of suspension D: then since C supports the weight of A and B, it will retain E in equilibrium whenever the common centre of inertia F is in the vertical line. And the same may be demonstrated if the bodies be connected in any other manner: for instance, if all the bodies be suspended from D, and retained in their places by the lines AB, AE, BE. Then A will counterpoise a body at E of which the weight is to its own as AG to GE (78), or HF to FE, and B a weight in the proportion of IF to FE, and both, a weight
$$= \frac{A.HF + B.IF}{FE} = \frac{A.(CF-HC) + B.(CF+CI)}{FE} = \frac{(A+B).CF}{FE} + \frac{B.CI - A.HC}{FE};$$
but A : B :: CB : CA :: CI : HC, and B.CI=A.HC; therefore the last term vanishes, and A and B support a weight at E equal to $(A+B).\frac{CF}{FE}$, or equal to E : and the effect is the same as if they were united in C. Therefore either of the bodies may be divided into two, and the equilibrium will remain, provided their centre of gravity be in the place of the single body : and thus the number of the bodies may be increased without limit.

The proposition may also be more generally and compendiously demonstrated from other properties of the centre of inertia. Imagine the fulcrum itself to be suspended by a vertical thread, and let the centre of inertia of the system of bodies be so placed, as to be in the same right line with this thread; there will then be a perfect equilibrium: for the motion of each of the bodies in consequence of the action of gravitation, and of course the motion of their common centre of inertia, would, if they were wholly at liberty, be in vertical lines; and since the mutual connexion of the bodies suspended, causes only a reciprocal action between them, it can have no effect on the motion of their common centre of inertia: consequently the thread acting in a vertical line directed to that centre, will render its descent impossible, and completely counteract the whole force of gravitation, so that no force will remain to produce any other motion. Now since the fulcrum suspended by a thread would remain at rest, it is obvious that it may be fixed in any other manner, and the equilibrium of the system will remain undisturbed, as long as the centre of inertia is in the same vertical line.

SCHOLIUM. Hence the place of the centre of inertia of any body may be practically found by determining the intersection of any two positions of the vertical line.

287. DEFINITION. The centre of inertia is also called, on account of these properties, the centre of gravity.

288. THEOREM. If a sphere or cylinder be placed on another, the equilibrium will be either stable or tottering, accordingly as the height of the centre of gravity above the

point of contact is less or greater than a fourth proportional to the sum of the radii, and the radii taken separately.

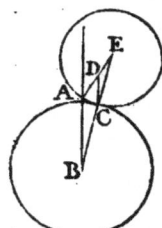

Let the sphere or cylinder roll from the vertical position into a position infinitely near to it on either side: then the point A of the upper cylinder, which was originally in contact with the lower, may still be considered as in the vertical line BA: and if CD be the vertical line passing through the actual point of contact, BE : AE :: BC : AD, and if the centre of gravity be at D in the line AE, the point of support being immediately under it, the equilibrium will remain : but if the centre of gravity be below D, the sphere will return towards AB; if above, it will retire further from it.

For example, if CE be infinite, and the lower surface of the moveable body be a plane, the equilibrium will remain stable, while the height of the centre of gravity above the point of contact is less than the radius of the sphere. If the fixed body have its upper surface horizontal, the equilibrium of any body will be determined by its radius of curvature, as the equilibrium of an egg placed on one end is tottering, but stable when placed on one side.

289. THEOREM. If any other equivalent forces be substituted for weights, acting at the same distance from the fulcrum, and with the same inclination to the rods or levers, the phenomena of equilibrium will be precisely the same. Also if either of the forces be transferred to an equal distance on the other side of the point of suspension or fulcrum, and act there in a contrary direction, the equilibrium will still remain.

For the arguments derived from the composition of pressures are equally applicable to all these cases.

290. THEOREM. If a force be applied obliquely to a lever, its effect in turning the lever will be diminished, in the ratio of the sine of the inclination to the radius.

For instance, if two levers be connected by a rope, two forces applied perpendicularly to the levers, at the ends of the rope, will be in equilibrium when the forces are as the perpendiculars let fall on the respective levers from the opposite ends of the rope. For the action of each force in the direction of the rope, and its absolute strength, are as the sides of the triangle formed by the lines of direction, or as the length of the rope and the perpendicular falling from its end on the lever : therefore,  each perpendicular representing the absolute force, the length of the rope will in both cases express the relative action. The forces are represented in the figure by arrow heads, and the fulcrums by little circles.

291. THEOREM. If two threads, or perfectly flexible and inextensible lines, be wound in contrary directions round two cylinders, moveable on the same axis, there will be an equilibrium when the weights attached to them are inversely as the radii of the cylinders.

For every section of the cylinder perpendicular to the axis, is a circle, and the threads being tangents to the circles, will be at the distances of the radii from the vertical plane ; therefore, by similar triangles, the right line 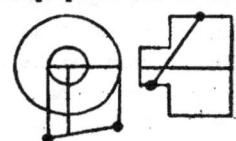 joining the weights will be divided in the ratio of the radii, and the centre of gravity will be in the vertical plane ; and the point of the axis immediately over it is a centre of suspension ; therefore there will be an equilibrium (285).

292. THEOREM. When the direction of a thread is altered by passing over any perfectly smooth curve surface, it communicates the whole force acting on it.

For the resistance of the curve is always in a direction perpendicular to that of the thread, and therefore does not impair its action, as is obvious from the composition of forces.

293. DEFINITION. A pulley is a cylinder moving on an axis, in order to change the direction of a thread without friction.

SCHOLIUM. The comparison of a pulley to a lever is both unnecessary and imperfect.

294. THEOREM. By means of a single moveable pulley, each portion of the thread being vertical, a weight may be supported by two forces, each equivalent to half the weight; or by two threads, each passing over a fixed pulley, and connected with ano-

ther weight equal to half the first; or one of them connected with such a weight, and the other to a fixed point.

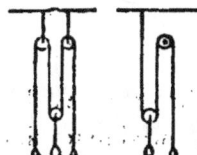

For it is obvious that each thread supports an equal part of the weight (217, 292,) and the substitution of equivalent weights, or of a fixed point, will not impair the equilibrium.

295. THEOREM. If several moveable pullies be connected with a weight, and parallel portions of the same thread act upon them all, there will be an equilibrium when the weight attached to the thread is to the weight attached to the pullies, as one to the number of threads at the lower block.

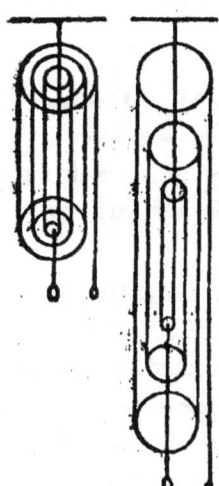

For the force being equably communicated throughout the length of the thread, each portion will co-operate equally in supporting the weight, and will support that portion of it which is to the whole as 1 to the number of threads; consequently a weight equal to that portion will retain any part of the thread in equilibrium, and with it the whole thread, and the whole weight. And if the radii of the pullies be taken in arithmetical progression, their angular velocity may be made equal, and they may be fixed to the same axis.

296. THEOREM. If one end of a thread, supporting a moveable pulley, be fixed, and the other attached to another moveable pulley, and the threads of this pulley be similarly arranged, the weight will be counterpoised by a power which is found by halving it as many times as there are moveable pullies.

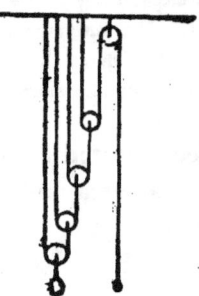

The proposition is obvious from a consideration of the figure, and the law of the single moveable pulley.

297. THEOREM. If two threads be attached to a weight and passed over fixed pullies, there will be an equilibrium when the distance of the weight from the horizontal line is to its distance from either pulley, as the weight to the sum of the equal forces acting on the threads.

By producing the oblique lines, and crossing them with a vertical one, a triangle will be formed of which the sides will represent the forces (264); whence the truth of the proposition will appear. And if the weights are unequal, their situation may be determined by the same general law. In the same manner the force may be

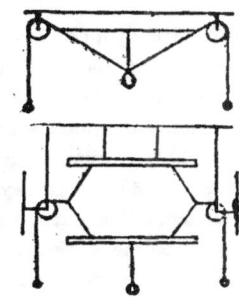

found, which is requisite for sustaining a weight, by inflecting a thread connected in any manner with it, as by means of a lever or a bar.

298. THEOREM. If two threads are wound in contrary directions round a cylinder, the first perpendicularly, the second obliquely, there will be an equilibrium when the forces are as the perpendicular distance of any point of the oblique thread from the axis, to its distance from the point of contact.

Since AB, which is equal to the distance of C from the axis, is the portion of the force BC, which is efficient in turning the cylinder, it will be counteracted by an equal force acting on the direct thread.

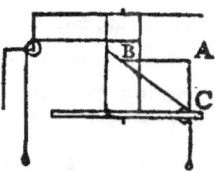

The force AC is lost in the direction of the cylinder; but this is the force which tends to shorten a twisted rope.

299. THEOREM. When a thread is coiled round a cylinder, the pressure on any part of the circumference is to the tension as its length to the radius; when the direction of the line is oblique, the pressure on the whole circumference is to the tension as the circumference to the radius; and the tension of the oblique line is to a force straining it in the direction

of the cylinder, as the length of a coil to the length of the axis.

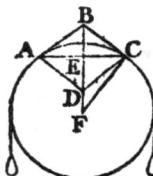

Let AB and BC be tangents of the small arc AC; then if BC, and BA represent the force of tension, at A and C, the diagonal of the parallelogram BD will be the joint result; but BD=2BE, and by the properties of similar triangles BE : BC :: EC : CF, BD : BC :: AC : CF. If the position of the thread be oblique, we shall find by the composition of forces, supposing it uncoiled, and its extremities retained in a line parallel to the axis, that its tension is to a force acting in the direction of the axis, as the oblique length of any portion to its height. Now this tension produces on any small oblique portion of the circumference, a pressure equal to that which would be produced on the corresponding transverse portion by an equal force acting transversely; for the versed sine of the arc is the same in both cases; consequently the pressure on the whole circumference is equal to that which would be produced by the same tension acting transversely.

300. THEOREM. The perpendicular pressure of a weight resting on an inclined plane, and retained in its situation by a resistance in the direction of the plane, is to the weight, as the horizontal length of the plane to its oblique length, and to the resistance, as the horizontal length to the height.

The truth of the proposition is evident from the proportions of the sides of the triangle corresponding to the directions of the forces.

SCHOLIUM. Hence the proportion of the friction to the weight may be determined by measuring the tangent of the angle at which the weight begins to slide down the plane.

301. DEFINITION. A wedge is a solid included by two equal triangles joined by three rectangles; and we shall suppose the surfaces to be perfectly smooth.

302. THEOREM. Three forces acting directly on the sides and base of a wedge will be in equilibrium when each force is proportional to the side on which it acts; provided that they be all applied at such parts, that their directions may meet in one point.

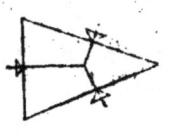

For the triangle formed by three lines perpendicular to the sides of another triangle, is equiangular with it, and if the forces act completely on any point, it will remain in equilibrium (284).

303. THEOREM. Supposing a moveable inclined plane, or a rectangular wedge to slide without friction on a horizontal plane, it will remain in equilibrium with a weight acting vertically, when the horizontal force is to the weight as the height to the horizontal length.

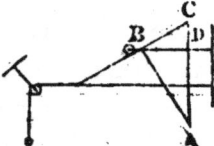

The triangle ABC is similar to ADB, and to BDC; and if AD represent the weight, its perpendicular pressure on the plane will be AB (284), which will be held in equilibrium by a force on the base, which is to it, as BD to AB (302); and this force will be to the weight, as BD to AD, or as CD to BD.

304. DEFINITION. By rolling a thin and flexible wedge round a cylinder, we form a screw.

305. THEOREM. A force acting in the direction of the circumference of a screw, supposed to move freely round its axis, will counterbalance a weight pressing vertically on the screw, which is to it as the circumference is to the height of one spire.

For when the horizontal length of the wedge becomes equal to the circumference of the circle, its height is the height of the first spire of the screw, or the distance between any two spires or threads.

SCHOLIUM. The cylinder may be either convex or concave, making a cylindrical or a tubular screw, together sometimes called a screw and a nut. The nut acts on the screw as a single point would do, only dividing the pressure. In general the screw is applied in combination with a lever.

306. THEOREM. If it be required to find the position of four equal beams capable of supporting each other in equilibrium, two of them fixed at the extremities of the base of

a given isosceles triangle, and the other two meeting in its vertex, a circle being circumscribed round the triangle, and perpendiculars erected from the quadrisections of the base, the lower beam on each side must be directed to the nearest intersection of the perpendiculars with the circle, and the upper one must be in a chord of equal length.

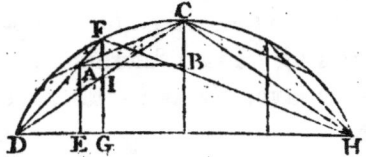

The two upper beams act against each other in a horizontal direction only, consequently the horizontal thrust of the lower beams must be equal to that of the upper beams, produced by their own weight only, while the thrust of the lower beams is derived not only from their own weight, but also from that of the upper beams, acting at their extremities; but the horizontal effect of the weight of the upper beam is to its weight as half AB to BC, since the centre of gravity may be supposed to act on a lever of half the length of AB, and the horizontal force on a lever of the length BC (290); but the horizontal thrust of AD is equal to that of AC, and is to the force acting vertically at A as DE to AE; and the force acting vertically at A is the whole weight of AC and half the weight of AD, which is three times as much as the weight acting vertically at C; consequently $\frac{DE}{AE}$ must be equal to $\frac{AB}{3BC}$; now the triangle ADE is similar to FDG, and ABC to HFG, since the angle DFH=DCH, and GFH=DFH−DFG=DFH−(DIG−IDF)=DCH−(BCH−ACD)=DCB+ACD=ACB, therefore $\frac{DE}{AE} = \frac{DG}{FG}$, and $\frac{AB}{3BC} = \frac{GH}{3FG} = \frac{3DG}{3FG} = \frac{DG}{FG}$, as is required for the equilibrium.

307. THEOREM. When an arch is composed of blocks acting on each other without friction, the weight of the arch must increase at each step as the portion of the vertical tangent cut off by lines drawn from a given point in a direction parallel to that of the joints.

The thrust in the direction AB, by which the block A is supported, must be to its weight as AB to BC, or as DE to EF, and to the horizontal thrust, as AB to AC, or DE to DF: and for the same reason the weight of any other part FG must be to the horizontal thrust as HI to IG, or as FK to FD: but the horizontal

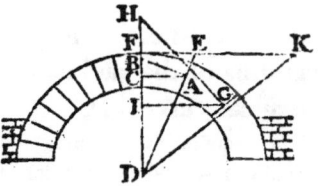

thrust is equal throughout the arch, being propagated from the abutments, since the weight of the blocks, acting in a vertical direction, can neither increase nor diminish it; and it may therefore always be represented by the line DF, while FE, EK, represent the weight of the arch and of its parts; and it will be equal to the weight of a portion of the length of the radius DF and of the depth of the block AC, as is obvious from considering the effect of the upper block acting as a wedge.

308. THEOREM. A spherical dome of equable thickness, having its joints in the direction of the radii, may remain in equilibrium if its height do not exceed 392 thousandths of the radius.

The action of the weight of the dome resembles that of a wedge, pressing on each horizontal course with a force which is to its weight as the radius to the sine of the angular distance from the vertex x, and its pressure is supported by the weight of the course, acting also as a wedge; this weight is first reduced by the inclination of the joint in the ratio of the cosine of the angular distance from the vertex y, to the radius, and its effect is increased in the ratio of the length of the wedge to its base, or of the radius to the breadth of the course: the effect will therefore be equal to the weight of a portion equal in breadth to the radius, reduced by the obliquity of the joint in the ratio of 1 to the cosine y. While therefore the weight of a circumference of the breadth y is greater than that of the dome increased in the ratio of 1 to x, the course will retain the incumbent dome in equilibrium; but when it is in a smaller proportion, the course will be forced outwards, unless it be restrained by external pressure; and the limit will be when the weight of the dome is equal to that of a cylindrical surface of the breadth xy, and of the radius x. Now the spherical surface is equal to a cylindrical surface of the breadth $1-y$ and of the radius 1, therefore $xy=1-y$, $(1-yy)y=1-y$, $(1+y)y=1$, $y+yy+\frac{1}{4}=\frac{5}{4}$, $y=\sqrt{\frac{5}{4}}-\frac{1}{2}$ $=\frac{\sqrt{5}-1}{2}=.61803$.

309. THEOREM. In order that a spherical dome of the span $2r$, may stand without external pressure, the thickness must be in-

creased, where x is greater than 786 thousandths of the radius, so as to be every where inversely as $x-x^3$.

The equilibrium requiring that xxy should be at least equal to $1-y$, where the thickness is equable, if the thickness at any part be to the mean thickness of the superincumbent portion as q to r, the equilibrium may be preserved while $qxxy$ is equal to $r.(1-y)$, or $q = \frac{r(1-y)}{xxy}$. Now the whole weight being p, the mean thickness r is $\frac{p}{c(1-y)}$, c being the circumference of the circle of which the radius is 1, hence $q = \frac{p}{cxxy}$ and the increment $\dot{p}$ is expressed by the increment of the circular circumference $\dot{z}$, multiplied by cxq; therefore $\dot{p} = cq x \dot{z}$; but $\dot{z} = \frac{\dot{x}}{y}$, and $\dot{p} = \frac{cqx\dot{x}}{y} = \frac{p\dot{x}}{xyy}$, and $\frac{\dot{p}}{p} = \frac{\dot{x}}{xyy} = \left(\text{h.l.}\frac{x}{y}\right)^{\cdot}$, since $\left(\frac{x}{y}\right)^{\cdot} = \frac{\dot{x}}{y} - \frac{x\dot{y}}{yy}$, which divided by $\frac{x}{y}$ is $\frac{\dot{x}}{x} - \frac{\dot{y}}{y} = \frac{y\dot{x} - x\dot{y}}{xyy}$; but $x\dot{x} + y\dot{y} = 1$, therefore $x\dot{x} = -y\dot{y}$, and the expression becomes $\frac{y^2\dot{x} + x^2\dot{x}}{xyy} = \frac{\dot{x}}{xyy}$; consequently h.l.$p = $ h.l.$\frac{x}{y} \pm a$, and $p = \frac{x}{y}$, or $\frac{bx}{y}$; then $q = \frac{p}{cxxy} = \frac{b}{cxyy}$. Therefore the thickness must be inversely as xyy, or as $x-x^3$; but if we estimate the thickness in a vertical direction, it becomes $\frac{b}{cxy^2}$. If we wish to give a certain degree of stability to the dome, we must make $q = \frac{dr(1-y)}{xxy} = \frac{dp}{cxxy}$, d being some constant multiplier greater than unity; then $\frac{\dot{p}}{p} = \frac{d\dot{x}}{xyy}$, and h.l.$p = d\left(\text{h.l.}\frac{x}{y}\right) \pm a$ and $p = b\left(\frac{x}{y}\right)^d$, therefore if $d = 1 + e$, $q = \frac{db}{cxyy}\cdot\left(\frac{x}{y}\right)^e$. And the constant quantities may be so determined as to correspond to the weight at any particular part, whether the centre of the dome be closed or open, b being $\left(\frac{y}{x}\right)^d p$, and the stability will be secure if all the lower parts be made of the thickness q; for the lower parts can never force up the higher, however they may be loaded, since their pressure will always be resisted by the collateral parts of the course. By making q a minimum, we find that the thickness is least where $x = \sqrt{\left(\frac{2-d}{3}\right)}$, or, if $d = 1$, when $x = .578$, if $d = 1.5$, when $x = .408$, if $d = 2$, when $x = 0$, so that in this case the dome must become gradually thicker from the vertex. In practice, considering the friction of the materials, it will be amply sufficient to make $d = 1.5$, or even $\frac{1}{4}$, and in this case q is least when $x = .5$, consequently the thickness of the lower parts must begin to be augmented at the distance of 30° from the vertex, at 60° it must become 2.28 times as great, and if the dome be continued much lower, it will be proper to employ a chain to confine it, since at 80° from the vertex a thickness 50 times as great as at 30° would be required for the equilibrium.

310. THEOREM. *When a weight is supported by a bar resting on two fulcrums, the pressure on each is inversely as its distance from the weight.*

For, by the property of the lever, it is to the whole weight, as the distance of the weight from the other fulcrum to the whole length of the lever.

311. THEOREM. *The strain on a given point of a bar, supported at the ends, from a weight placed on it, is proportional to the rectangle of the segments into which the point divides the bar.*

For, considering A as the fulcrum of the lever, the weight B produces at C a pressure $= \frac{AB}{AC}$, and the strain at B is as the length of the lever by which it is applied, or as $\frac{AB.BC}{AC}$; it is therefore equal to the strain produced by the weight applied at the end of a lever of which the length is $\frac{AB.BC}{AC}$.

312. THEOREM. *The strain produced by the weight of an equable bar at any point of its length is equal to the strain produced by half the weight of one segment acting at the end of a lever equal to the other segment.*

The strain produced at any point A by a weight B on either side is equal to the strain of the same weight acting at the distance $\frac{BC.AD}{DC}$; therefore the strain produced by the portion AC of the bar, of which the weight may be imagined to be collected into its centre of gravity, is as $AC.\frac{AC}{2}.\frac{AD}{DC}$; and for the same reason the weight of AD produces a strain. $AD.\frac{AD}{2}.\frac{AC}{DC}$; therefore both together produce a strain of $\frac{AC.AD}{2}$, which is equal to the effect of half the weight of AC, acting at the distance AD.

313. THEOREM. In all cases of equilibrium one general law prevails; if motion were imparted to the weights, their momenta in the direction of gravity would be equal and contrary.

Taking the lever for an example, it is obvious that the velocity of the bodies must be as their distances from the fulcrum; and their weights being inversely in the same ratio, their momenta must be equal, and always in directions perpendicular to the same line; so that if the one ascend vertically, the other must descend vertically. This has been considered by some as a sufficient foundation for the demonstration of all cases of equilibrium, since it appears to be an absurdity to suppose, that any cause should so act as to produce two equal effects, of which the one must be contrary to the other, and to the operation of the common cause. But it is more satisfactory to have direct demonstrations in every case, and to deduce the general law from all.

SCHOLIUM. This principle was extended still further by John Bernouilli, under the name of the law of virtual velocities. Where the forces acting on the different bodies are different, there is always an equilibrium when the sum of all the products of the masses into the forces by which they are actuated, and then into the initial velocities with which they would be obliged to move, referred to the direction of these forces, becomes equal to nothing.

SECTION VIII. OF THE ATTRACTION OF GRAVITATING BODIES.

314. DEFINITION. Gravitating bodies are those of which the particles attract each other with forces varying inversely as the squares of the distances.

315. THEOREM. All parallel sections of a given cone or pyramid, supposed to be gravitating surfaces, of a given evanescent thickness, attract a particle of gravitating matter placed at the vertex with equal force.

The sections being considered as composed of evanescent rectilinear figures terminated by the same right lines, meeting in the vertex, their areas are in the duplicate ratio of their homologous sides, or of their distances from the vertex (125, 121); and the whole areas, and the number of material particles are in the same ratio; therefore the increase of the number exactly compensates for the increase of the distance, and the forces acting in each line are the same; therefore the attractions of the whole sections are the same.

316. THEOREM. A gravitating point placed within a gravitating spherical surface, remains at rest.

Conceive one half of the surface to be divided into evanescent areolas, and cones or pyramids to stand on them all, and to be continued through the given point as a vertex, till they reach the surface on the opposite side: then the inclination of each of two opposite cones to its base is the same, and the magnitude of the section is the same as if the sections were parallel, consequently the two opposite and equal attractions destroy each other, and the same is true of each particle of the surface, and of the whole surface.

317. THEOREM. A gravitating point, placed without a gravitating spherical surface, or sphere, is attracted towards its centre with the same force as if the whole matter of the surface or sphere were collected there.

Call the radius unity, and the distance of the ordinate of the sphere from the centre, x, then the fluxion of the curve, $\dot{z}$, will be $\frac{\dot{x}}{\sqrt{(1-xx)}}$ (142), and if the ratio of the circumference of a circle to its diameter be that of p to 1, the circumference corresponding to x will be $2p\sqrt{(1-xx)}$, the fluxion of the surface $2p\dot{x}$, and the superficial area itself $2px$, and, when $x=1$, $2p$. The distance of the given point from the centre being a, the absolute attraction of the circular element of the superficies will be $\frac{2p\dot{x}}{(a+x)^2+1-xx}$ $=\frac{2p\dot{x}}{aa+2ax+1}$, and the effect in the direction of the axis being diminished in the ratio of $a+x$ to $\sqrt{(aa+2ax+1)}$, the fluxion of the attraction in that direction will be $\frac{2p.(a+x).\dot{x}}{(aa+2ax+1)^{\frac{3}{2}}} = \left(\frac{2p}{aa} \cdot \frac{ax+1}{\sqrt{(aa+2ax+1)}}\right)$, and while x increases from -1 to 1, the fluent increases from $\frac{-2p}{aa}$ to

$\frac{2p}{aa}$, therefore the whole effect is $\frac{4p}{aa}$, which represents the attraction of the whole surface at the distance a.

SECTION IX. OF THE EQUILIBRIUM AND STRENGTH OF ELASTIC SUBSTANCES.

318. DEFINITION. A substance perfectly elastic is initially extended and compressed in equal degrees by equal forces, and proportionally by proportional forces.

319. DEFINITION. The modulus of the elasticity of any substance is a column of the same substance, capable of producing a pressure on its base which is to the weight causing a certain degree of compression, as the length of the substance is to the diminution of its length.

320. THEOREM. When a force is applied to an elastic column, of a rectangular prismatic form, in a direction parallel to the axis, the parts nearest to the line of direction of the force exert a resistance in an opposite direction; those particles, which are at a distance beyond the axis, equal to a third proportional to the depth and twelve times the distance of the line of direction of the force, remain in their natural state; and the parts beyond them act in the direction of the force.

The forces of repulsion and cohesion are initially proportional to the compression or extension of the strata, and these to their distance from the point of indifference: the forces may therefore be represented by the weight of two triangles, formed by the intersection of two lines in the point of indifference; and their actions may be considered as concentrated in the centres of gravity of the triangles, which are at the distance of two thirds of the length of each from the vertex, and at the distance of two thirds of the depth from each other. This distance constitutes one arm of a lever, which is of constant length, while the distance of the line of direction of the force from the centre of gravity of the nearest triangle constitutes the other arm; and calling the distance of the line of direction of the force from the axis, a, and the depth, b, the length of this arm, on the supposition that the point of indifference is at the assigned distance, will be $a + \frac{bb}{12a} - \frac{1}{3}\left(\frac{1}{2}b + \frac{bb}{12a}\right)$, or $a + \frac{bb}{36a} - \frac{1}{6}b$, that of the constant arm being $\frac{1}{3}b$. The cohesive and repulsive forces must therefore be as $a + \frac{bb}{36a} - \frac{1}{6}b$ to $a + \frac{bb}{36a} + \frac{1}{6}b$, since that which serves as the fulcrum of the lever must bear a force equal to the sum of the two forces applied at the ends, which are proportional to the opposite arms of the lever; or as $36aa - 12ab + bb$ to $36aa + 12ab + bb$, that is, as $(6a-b)^2$ to $(6a+b)^2$: but these forces are actually as the squares of the sides of the similar triangles which represent them, that is, as $\left(\frac{1}{2}b - \frac{bb}{12a}\right)^2$ to $\left(\frac{1}{2}b + \frac{bb}{12a}\right)^2$, or as $(6a-b)^2$ to $(6a+b)^2$, which is the ratio required: there will therefore be an equilibrium under the circumstances of the proposition.

321. THEOREM. The weight of the modulus of the elasticity of a column being m, a weight bending it in any manner f, the distance of the line of its application from any point of the axis, a, and the depth of the column, b, the radius of curvature will be $\frac{bbm}{12af}$.

Supposing first the force to act longitudinally, and $a = \frac{1}{6}b$, the point of indifference will be in the remoter surface of the column, and the compression or extension of the nearer surface will be twice as great as if the force had been applied equally to all the strata; and will therefore be to the length of any portion as $2f$ to m; but as this distance is to the length, so is the depth to the radius of curvature, or $2f : m :: b : \frac{bm}{2f}$, which is the radius of curvature when $a = \frac{1}{6}b$. But when a varies, the curvature will vary in the same ratio; for the curvature is proportional to the angle of the triangles representing the forces, and the angle of either triangle to its area divided by the square of its length; but the force exerted by the remoter part of the column is to f as $a + \frac{bb}{36a} - \frac{1}{6}b$ to $\frac{1}{3}b$, or as $(6a-b)^2$ to $24ab$, and is equal to $\frac{f}{24ab} \cdot (6a-b)^2$, but the square of the side of the corresponding triangle is $\left(\frac{1}{2}b - \frac{bb}{12a}\right)^2$, or $(6a-b)^2 \cdot \left(\frac{b}{12a}\right)^2$; consequently the force, or the area, divided by this square becomes $\frac{aaf}{b^3}$, and the curvature varies directly as a, and as f, and inversely as b^3: but since m varies as b, we must make the expression for the radius of curvature $\frac{bbm}{12af}$, which becomes $\frac{bm}{af}$ when $a=\frac{1}{2}b$, and which varies as b^3 directly, and as a and f inversely.

If the force be applied obliquely, its effect may be determined by finding the point at which it meets the perpendicular to the axis, and resolving it into two parts: that which is in the direction of this perpendicular will be counteracted by the lateral adhesion of the substance, the other will always produce the same curvature as if the force had been originally in a direction parallel to the axis: but the place of the point of indifference will be determined from the point of intersection already mentioned, and when the force becomes perpendicular to the column, the neutral point will coincide with the axis.

SCHOLIUM. If one surface of the column were incompressible, and all the resistance of its strata were collected in the other, the radius of curvature would evidently be $\frac{bbm}{af}$, a being the distance from the incompressible side, which is ultimately 12 times as great as in the natural state of an elastic substance.

322. THEOREM. The distance of the point of greatest curvature of a prismatic beam, from the line of direction of the force, is twice the versed sine of that arc of the circle of greatest curvature, of which the extremity is parallel to that of the beam.

Supposing the curve, into which the beam is bent, to be described with an equable angular velocity, its fluxion will be directly as the radius of curvature, or inversely as a, the distance of the force from the axis of the beam; this we may still call a at the point of greatest curvature, and y elsewhere, the corresponding arc of the circle of curvature being z; then the fluxion of the curve will be $\frac{a\dot{z}}{y}$; but this fluxion is to $\dot{y}$ as the radius r to the sine of the angle or arc z, or $\mp\dot{y}=\frac{a\dot{z}}{y}\cdot\frac{\sin.z}{r}$, but $\frac{(\sin.z)\dot{z}}{r}=\dot{v}$, v being the versed sine of the arc z, $\mp y\dot{y}=a\dot{v}$, and $yy=b\mp 2av$, b being a constant quantity: when $y=a$, $v=0$, and $aa=b$, therefore $yy=aa-2av$, and when $y=0$, $aa=2av$, and $a=2v$.

SCHOLIUM. When the force is longitudinal, and the curvature inconsiderable, the form coincides with the harmonic curve, the curvature being proportional to the distance from the axis: and the distance of the point of indifference from the axis becomes the secant of an arc proportional to the distance from the middle of the column.

323. THEOREM. If a beam is naturally of the form which a prismatic beam would acquire, if it were slightly bent by a longitudinal force, calling its depth, b, its length, e, the circumference of a circle of which the diameter is unity, c, the weight of the modulus of elasticity, m, the natural deviation from the rectilinear form, d, and a force applied at the extremities of the axis, f, the total deviation from the rectilinear form will be $a=\frac{bbccdm}{bbccm-12eef}$.

The form being originally a harmonic curve, the curvature and length of the ordinate added at each point by the action of the force will also be equal to those of a harmonic curve, of which the vertical radius of curvature must be $\frac{bbm}{12af}$, and the basis the length of the beam; but the vertical ordinate of the harmonic curve is a third proportional to its radius of curvature and that of the figure of sines on the same basis, which in this case would be $\frac{e}{c}$, the additional vertical ordinate must therefore be $\frac{ee}{cc}\cdot\frac{12af}{bbm}$, and this added to the deviation d, must become equal to a, and $a=d+\frac{ee}{cc}\cdot\frac{12af}{bbm}$, $a-\frac{ee}{cc}\cdot\frac{12af}{bbm}=d=\frac{abbccm-12aeef}{bbccm}$, and $a=\frac{bbccdm}{bbccm-12eef}$.

SCHOLIUM. It appears from this formula, that when the other quantities remain unaltered, a varies in proportion to d, and if $d=0$, the beam cannot be retained in a state of inflection, while the denominator of the fraction remains a finite quantity: but when $bbccm=12eef$, a becomes infinite, whatever may be the magnitude of d, and the force will overpower the beam, or will at least cause it to bend so much as to derange the operation of the forces concerned. In this case $f=\left(\frac{bc}{e}\right)^2\cdot\frac{m}{12}=.8225\frac{bb}{ee}m$, which is the force capable of holding the beam in equilibrium in any inconsiderable degree of curvature. Hence the modulus being known for any substance, we may determine at once the weight which a given bar nearly straight is capable of supporting. For instance, in fir wood, supposing its height 10,000,000 feet, a bar an inch square and ten feet long may begin to bend with the weight of a bar of the same thickness, equal in length to $.8225 \times \frac{1}{120 \times 120} \times 10,000,000$ feet, or 571 feet; that is, with a weight of about 120 pounds; neglecting the effect of the weight of the bar itself. In the same manner the strength of a bar of any other substance may be determined, either from direct experiments on its flexure, or from the sounds that it produces. If $f = \frac{m}{n}$ $\frac{ee}{bb} = .8225n$, and $\frac{e}{b} = \sqrt{(.8225n)} = .907\sqrt{n}$, whence, if we know the force required to crush a bar or column, we may calculate what must be the proportion of its length to its depth, in order that it may begin to bend rather than be crushed. The height of the modulus of elasticity for iron or steel is about 9,000,000 feet, for wood, from 4,000,000 to 10,000,000, and for stone probably about 5,000,000: its weight for a square inch of iron 30,000,000 pounds, of wood from 1,500,000 to 4,000,000, and of stone about 5,000,000: and the values of n are in the two first cases from 200 to 250, and in the third about 2500, and $\sqrt{n}$ becomes 15 and 50, and $\frac{e}{b}$ 12.3 and 41.1 respectively; so that a column of iron or wood cannot support without being crushed a longitudinal force sufficient to bend it, unless its length be greater than 12 times its depth, nor a column of stone, unless its length be greater than 40 times its depth.

324. THEOREM. When a longitudinal force is applied to the extremities of a straight prismatic beam, at the distance a from the axis, the deflection of the middle of the beam will be $a.(\sec.\mathrm{arc}(\sqrt{(\frac{3f}{m})} \cdot \frac{e}{b}) - 1)$.

If we suppose the length to be increased until $f = (\frac{bc}{e})^2 \cdot \frac{m}{12}$, or $e = bc\sqrt{(\frac{m}{12f})}$, the beam might be retained by the force f in the form of a harmonic curve, of which a might be an ordinate, and the vertical ordinate would be as much greater than a as the radius is greater than the sine of the arc corresponding to its distance from the origin of the curve, or as the secant of the arc corresponding to its distance from the middle of the curve is greater than the radius, and the excess of this secant above the radius will express the deflection produced by the action of the force; but this arc is to the quadrant $\frac{c}{2}$ as e to $bc\sqrt{(\frac{m}{12f})}$, and is therefore equal to $\sqrt{(\frac{3f}{m})} \cdot \frac{e}{b}$.

SCHOLIUM. Hence it appears that when the other quantities are constant, the deflection varies in the simple ratio of a. The radius of curvature at the vertex is $\frac{bbm}{12af.(\sec.\mathrm{arc}\sqrt{(\frac{3f}{m})} \cdot \frac{e}{b})}$, from which the degree of extension and compression of the substance may be determined.

325. THEOREM. The form of an elastic bar, fixed at one end, and bearing a weight at the extremity, becomes ultimately a cubic parabola, and the depression is $\frac{2}{3}$ of the versed sine of an equal arc, in the smallest circle of curvature.

The ordinate of the cubic parabola being ax^3 its fluxion is $3ax^2\dot{x}$, and its second fluxion $6ax\dot{x}\dot{x}$, which varies as x the absciss. If the curvature had been constant, the second fluxion would have been $b\dot{x}\dot{x}$, the first fluxion $bx\dot{x}$, and the ordinate $\frac{1}{2}bxx$; but as it is $b x\dot{x} - x\dot{x}\dot{x}$, the first fluxion is $bx\dot{x} - \frac{1}{2}x^2\dot{x}$, and the fluent $\frac{1}{2}bx^2 - \frac{1}{6}x^3$, which, when $b = x$ becomes $\frac{1}{3}b^3$, instead of $\frac{1}{2}$.

326. THEOREM. The weight of the modulus of the elasticity of a bar is to a weight acting at its extremity only, as four times the cube of the length to the product of the square of the depth and the depression.

If the depression be d, the versed sine of an equal arc in the smallest circle of curvature will be $\frac{3}{2}d$, and the radius of curvature $\frac{ee}{3d}$, e being the length; but the radius of curvature is also expressed by $\frac{bbm}{12af}$, a being here equal to e, therefore $\frac{ee}{3d} = \frac{bbm}{12ef}$, $12e^3f = 3bbdm$, and $m = \frac{4e^3}{bbd} \cdot f$. If f be the weight of a portion of the beam of which the length is g, the height of the modulus will be $\frac{4e^3}{bbd} \cdot g$.

SCHOLIUM. In an experiment on a bar of iron, mentioned by Mr. Banks, e was 18 inches, b and d each 1, f 480 pounds, and g about 150 feet: hence the height of the modulus could not have been less than 2,500,000 feet. But d was probably much less than this, as the depression was only measured at the point of breaking, and m must have been larger in the same proportion.

327. THEOREM. If an equable bar be fixed horizontally at one end, and bent by its own weight, the depression at the extre-

mity will be half the versed sine of an equal arc in the circle of curvature at the fixed point.

The strain on each part is here equal to the weight of the portion beyond it, acting at the end of a lever of half its length: the curvature will therefore be as the square of the distance from the extremity. And if the second fluxion at the vertex be $a a \dot{x} \dot{x}$, it will be every where $(a-x)^2 \dot{x} \dot{x} = a a \dot{x} \dot{x} - 2 a x \dot{x} \dot{x} + x^2 \dot{x} \dot{x}$; the first fluxions of these quantities are $a a x \dot{x}$ and $a a x \dot{x} - a x^2 \dot{x} + \frac{1}{3} x^3 \dot{x}$, and the fluents $\frac{1}{2} a^2 x^2$, and $\frac{1}{2} a^2 x^2 - \frac{1}{3} a x^3 + \frac{1}{12} x^4$; or, when $x = a$, $\frac{1}{2} a^4$ and $\frac{1}{12} a^4$; therefore the depression is in this case half of the versed sine.

328. THEOREM. The height of the modulus of the elasticity of a bar, fixed at one end, and depressed by its own weight, is half as much more as the fourth power of the length divided by the product of the square of the depth and the depression.

The weight of the bar operates as if it were concentrated at the distance of half the length, or as if it were reduced to one half, acting at the extremity: we have therefore $\frac{e}{2}$ for the length of a portion equivalent to the weight, and $\frac{ee}{4d} = \frac{bbm}{12ef}$, whence $m = \frac{3e^3}{bbd} f$, and the height $\frac{3e^4}{2bbd}$.

329. THEOREM. The depression of the middle of a bar supported at both ends, produced by its own weight, is five sixths of the versed sine of half the equal arc in the circle of least curvature.

The curvature varies as $a a - x x$, and the second fluxion is therefore represented by $a a \dot{x} \dot{x} - x x \dot{x} \dot{x}$, while that of the versed sine is $a a \dot{x} \dot{x}$; the first fluxions are $a a x \dot{x}$ and $a a x \dot{x} - \frac{1}{3} x^3 \dot{x}$, and the fluents $\frac{1}{2} a^2 x^2$ and $\frac{1}{2} a^2 x^2 - \frac{1}{12} x^4$, or, when $x = a$, $\frac{1}{2} a^4$, and $\frac{5}{12} a^4$, which are in the ratio of 6 to 5.

330. THEOREM. The height of the modulus of the elasticity of a bar, supported at both ends, is $\frac{5}{32}$ of the fourth power of the length, divided by the product of the depression and the square of the depth.

For the strain at the middle is equal to the effect of the weight of one fourth of the bar acting on a lever of half the length (329); and the radius of curvature there is $\frac{5ee}{48d} = \frac{bbm}{6ef}$, and $m = \frac{5e^3 f}{8bbd}$, and the height $\frac{5e^4}{32bbd}$, substituting $\frac{e}{4}$ for f.

SCHOLIUM. From an experiment made by Mr. Leslie on a bar in these circumstances, the height of the modulus of the elasticity of deal appears to be about 9,328,000 feet. Chladni's observations on the sounds of fir wood, afford very nearly the same result.

331. THEOREM. The weight under which a vertical bar not fixed at the end, may begin to bend, is to any weight laid on the middle of the same bar, when supported at the extremities in a horizontal position, nearly in the ratio of $\frac{514}{10000}$ of the length to the depression.

For the weight laid on the bar being f, the pressure on each fulcrum is $\frac{f}{2}$, and the length of the lever $\frac{a}{2}$, so that the weight of the modulus becomes $\frac{a^3 f}{4bbd}$; but the force capable of keeping the column bent is $\left(\frac{bc}{e}\right)^2 \cdot \frac{m}{12}$, or since $e = a$, $\frac{acc}{48d} f = .0514 \frac{a}{d} f$. The effect of the weight of the bar in the depression may be separately observed and deducted.

332. DEFINITION. The stiffness of bodies is measured by their resistance at an equal linear deviation from their natural position.

333. THEOREM. The stiffness of a beam is directly as its breadth, and as the cube of its depth, and inversely as the cube of its length.

Since $m = \frac{4e^3}{bbd} f$ (326), and m varies as bh, h being the breadth, $b^3 d h$ varies as $e^3 f$, and f as $\frac{b^3 d h}{e^3}$, that is, when d is given, as h, as b^3, and inversely as e^3.

334. THEOREM. The direct cohesive or repulsive strength of a body is in the joint ratio of its primitive elasticity, of its toughness, and the magnitude of its section.

Since the force required to produce a given extension is as the extension, where the elasticity is equal, the force at the instant of breaking is as the extension which the body will bear without breaking, or as its toughness. And the force of each particle being equal, the whole force must be as the number of the particles, or as the section.

SCHOLIUM. Though most natural substances appear

in their intimate constitution to be perfectly elastic, yet it often happens that their toughness with respect to extension and compression differs very materially. In general, bodies are said to have less toughness in resisting extension than compression.

335. THEOREM. The transverse strength of a beam is directly as the breadth and as the square of the depth, and inversely as the length.

The strength is limited by the extension or compression which the substance will bear without failing; the curvature at the instant of fracture must therefore be inversely as the depth, and the radius of curvature as the depth, or $\frac{bbm}{12f}$ as b, consequently bm must be as af, and f as $\frac{bm}{a}$, or, since m is as bh, as $\frac{bbh}{a}$.

SCHOLIUM. If one of the surfaces of a beam were incompressible, and the cohesive force of all its strata collected in the other, its strength would be six times as great as in the natural state; for the radius of curvature would be $\frac{bbm}{af}$, which could not be less than twice as great as in the natural state, because the strata would be twice as much extended, with the same curvature, as when the neutral point is in the axis; and f would then be six times as great.

336. DEFINITION. The resilience of a beam may be considered as proportional to the height from which a given body must fall to break it.

337. THEOREM. The resilience of prismatic beams is simply as their bulk.

The space through which the force or stiffness of a beam acts, in generating or destroying motion, is determined by the curvature that it will bear without breaking; and this curvature is inversely as the depth; consequently, the depression will be as the square of the length directly, and as the depth inversely: but the force in similar parts of the spaces to be described is every where as the strength, or as the square of the depth directly, and as the length inversely: therefore the joint ratio of the spaces and the forces is the ratio of the products of the length by the depth; but this ratio is that of the squares of the velocities generated or destroyed, or of the heights from which a body must fall to acquire these velocities. And if the breadth vary, the force will obviously vary in the same ratio; therefore the resilience will be in the joint ratio of the length, breadth, and depth.

338. THEOREM. The stiffest beam that can be cut out of a given cylinder is that of which the depth is to the breadth as the square root of 3 to 1, and the strongest as the square root of 2 to 1; but the most resilient will be that which has its depth and breadth equal.

Let the diameter or diagonal be a, and the breadth x; then the depth being $\sqrt{(aa-xx)}$, the stiffness is $(aa-xx)^{\frac{3}{2}}x$, and the strength $aax-x^3$, which must be maximums; and $(aa-xx)^2xx$ must be a maximum; so that $3(aa-xx)^2 . (-2x\dot{x}).xx+(aa-xx)^3(2x\dot{x})=0$, $aa-xx=3xx$; and the squares of the breadth and depth are as 1 to 3; also $aa\dot{x}=3x^2\dot{x}$, $x=\sqrt{\frac{1}{3}}a$, and the depth $\sqrt{\frac{2}{3}}a$, for the strongest form. It is evident that the bulk, and consequently the resilience, will be greatest when the depth and breadth are equal.

339. THEOREM. Supposing a tube of evanescent thickness to be expanded into a similar tube of greater diameter, but of equal length, the quantity of matter remaining the same, the strength will be increased in the ratio of the diameter, and the stiffness in the ratio of the square of the diameter, but the resilience will remain unaltered.

For the quantity of matter remaining the same, its action is in both cases simply as its distance from the fulcrum, or from the axis of motion, and this distance is simply as the diameter, since the section remains similar in all its parts: the tension at a given angular flexure being also increased with the distance, the stiffness will be as the square of the distance, and the force in similar parts of the space described being always inversely as the space, the square of the velocity produced or destroyed will remain unaltered.

SCHOLIUM. When a beam of finite thickness is made hollow, retaining the same quantity of matter, the strength is increased in a ratio somewhat greater than that of the diameter, because the tension of the internal fibres at the instant of breaking is increased.

340. THEOREM. If a column, subjected to a longitudinal force, be cut out of a plank or slab of equable depth, in order that the extension and compression of the surfaces may be initially every where equal, its outline must be a circular arc.

Neglecting the distance of the neutral point from the axis,

the curvature must be constant, in order that the tension of the superficial fibres may be equal; and the breadth must be as the distance of the line of application of the force; that is, as the ordinate of a circular arc, or, when the curvature is small, it must be equal to the ordinate of another circular arc, of which the chord is equal to the axis.

341. THEOREM. If a column be cut out of a plank of equable breadth, and the outline limiting its depth be composed of two triangles, joined at their bases, the tension of the surfaces produced by a longitudinal force, will be every where equal, when the radius of curvature at the middle becomes equal to half the length of the column; and in this case the curve will be a cycloid.

For in the cycloid, the radius of curvature varies as the distance, in the curve, from its origin, or as the square root of the ordinate a, and if the depth b be as this distance, a will vary as bb, and the curvature, which is proportional to $\frac{a}{b^3}$, will be always as $\frac{1}{b}$, and the tension will be equable throughout. In every cycloid the radius of curvature at the middle point is half of the length.

SCHOLIUM. When the curvature at the middle differs from that of the cycloid, the figure of the column becomes of more difficult investigation. It may however be delineated mechanically, making both the depth of the column and its radius of curvature proportional always to $\sqrt{a}$. If the breadth of the column vary in the same proportion as the depth, they must both be every where as the cube root of a.

SECT. X. OF COLLISION, AND OF ENERGY.

342. THEOREM. When two elastic bodies approach each other with a uniform motion, until at a certain point a repulsive force commences, their relative velocities, in their return back from that point, will again be uniform, and equal to what they were, but in a contrary direction.

For according to the definition of elastic bodies, their forces are always the same at the same distances from the centres, since they depend on the degree of compression. And if two bodies act reciprocally, so as to change the direction of each other's motions, by any forces which are always the same at the same distance, their relative velocities in approaching and receding will be equal at equal distances. For since the velocity generated in describing each element of the distance in returning, is equal to that which was destroyed while the same element of space was described in approaching, the whole velocities at any equal distances must also be equal.

SCHOLIUM. Bodies which communicate motion without a permanent repulsive force, or in circumstances which more or less prevent its action, are called more or less inelastic.

343. THEOREM. When two elastic bodies meet each other directly, their velocities after collision are equal to twice the velocity of the common centre of inertia, diminished by their respective velocities.

For the motion of the centre of inertia remains unaltered, and the motions of the bodies with respect to each other and with respect to the centre of inertia being, after collision, equal and in contrary directions, the velocity of each must be changed by twice the difference of its velocity and that of the centre of inertia, and will therefore become equal to twice the velocity of the centre of inertia diminished by its own velocity.

344. THEOREM. When two equal elastic bodies meet each other directly, their motions will be exchanged.

For twice the velocity of the centre of inertia is here the sum of the velocities; therefore either deducted from this will leave a remainder equal to the other, for the motion of the body to which it belongs.

345. THEOREM. An elastic body striking a larger one at rest, is partially reflected, and a body striking a smaller one, continues to move forwards.

For the velocity in the first case is greater than twice that of the centre of inertia, in the second smaller.

346. THEOREM. When the impulse of an elastic body is communicated to another through a series of bodies differing infinitely little from each other in bulk, the momentum of the last is to that of the first in the subduplicate ratio of their bulks.

Let the first be $1-x$, the second $1+x$, and the velocity of the first 1; then the velocity of the centre of gravity will be $\frac{1-x}{2}$, and the velocity of the second after the impulse will be $1-x$; and its momentum $(1-x).(1+x)$, therefore the momentum is increased in the ratio of 1 to $1+x$, or in the subduplicate ratio of 1 to $1+2x+xx$, which as x is diminished, approaches infinitely near to the subduplicate ratio of $1-x$, to $1+x$, or 1 to $1+2x+2x^2+2x^3...$ since all the succeeding terms vanish in comparison with the preceding: and in the same manner it may be shown that at every succeeding step the momentum will be increased in the subduplicate ratio of the bulk; therefore the joint ratio of all the changes of momentum will be the subduplicate ratio of the corresponding change of bulk.

SCHOLIUM. The first body will also have a retrograde motion after the collision, with the velocity x, and the subsequent bodies will recoil with velocities gradually smaller, in the same proportion as their progressive velocities have been smaller. If a second impulse be communicated to the first body, it will impel the second with a velocity infinitely near to that which the first impulse produces, and will itself recoil with a double velocity.

347. DEFINITION. The product of the mass of a body into the square of its velocity may properly be termed its energy.

SCHOLIUM. This product has been called the living or ascending force, since the height of vertical ascent is in proportion to it; and some have considered it as the true measure of the quantity of motion; but although this opinion has been very universally rejected, yet the force thus estimated well deserves a distinct denomination.

348. THEOREM. In two bodies perfectly elastic, the joint energy, with respect to any quiescent space, is unaltered by collision.

Let the bodies A and B have a relative motion; then their velocities towards the centre of inertia will be reciprocally as their masses; and the momenta in opposite directions will be A.B and B.A. Now if the centre of inertia have also a motion C with respect to a quiescent space, in the direction of A, the velocities will be C+B and C—A respectively, and the joint energies will be $A.(C+B)^2 + B.(C-A)^2$. But after collision, the velocities B and A relative to the centre of inertia are in a contrary direction, the motion of that centre remaining the same (269), therefore the velocities are C—B and C+A respectively, and the energies $A.(C-B)^2 + B.(C+A)^2$; but $A.(C+B)^2 - A.(C-B)^2 = 2ABC = B.(C+A)^2 - B.(C-A)^2$, and the two sums are equal.

SCHOLIUM. The energy must be estimated in the respective directions of the velocities before and after collision, while the sum of the momenta, which also remains unaltered, requires to be reduced to the same direction. The reason of this difference is, that the square of a negative quantity is the same as that of the same quantity taken positively.

SECTION XI. OF ROTATORY POWER.

349. THEOREM. When a system of bodies has a rotatory motion round any centre, the effect of each body in turning the system round a given point must be estimated by the product of its momentum into the distance of the body from that point; and the power of each body, with respect to the original centre of rotation, will be expressed by the product of the mass into the square of the distance.

Suppose the bodies A and B, fixed to the ends of two equal levers, to meet each other, and simply to communicate their motion, and let B be twice A, and moving with half its velocity, then the motion of A will exactly destroy the motion of B, and this effect is therefore the measure of the motion of A: but if the bodies A and B be connected with the arms of an inflexible line, and move with equal velocities in the same direction, they will be totally stopped by the application of a fulcrum at the centre of gravity; for the propositions respecting equilibrium are as well deducible from the computation of motion as from that of force, and the motion of A is here equivalent to the motion of B, moving with equal velocity at half the distance: but it was before shown to be equal to the motion of B with half the velocity at its own distance: therefore these two motions of B are equivalent with respect to effect in producing rotatory motion; and the same may be shown in other cases. And the distance from the centre of rotation being as the velocity, the power is as the square of the velocity.

350. DEFINITION. The centre of gyration is a point into which if all the particles of a revolving body were condensed, it would retain the same degree of rotatory power.

351. THEOREM. The centre of gyration of two equal points is at the distance of the square root of half the sum of the squares of the separate distances from the axis.

The distance of the points from the axis being a and b, the whole rotatory power will be $a^2 + b^2$, which is equal to the sum of the particles multiplied by the square of $\sqrt{\left(\frac{aa+bb}{2}\right)}$.

352. THEOREM. *The distance of the centre of gyration of a right line from an axis at its extremity, is to its length, as 1 to $\sqrt{3}$.*

The fluxion of the rotatory power is $x^2 \dot{x}$, consequently the whole rotatory power is $\frac{1}{3}x^3$, which is equivalent to the effect of x at the distance of $\sqrt{\frac{1}{3}x}$. But if the centre of motion does not coincide with the end of the line, the rotatory power will be the sum or difference of the two values of x at the end of the line, as $\frac{1}{3}(a^3 \pm b^3)$, and the distance of the centre of gyration becomes $\sqrt{(\frac{1}{3}(a^3 \pm b^3))}$, divided by $a \pm b$.

353. THEOREM. *The distance of the centre of gyration of a circle or any circular sector from its centre of rotation and of curvature is to the radius as 1 to $\sqrt{2}$.*

The area of any increment of the circle, of which the radius is x, will be as $x \dot{x}$, and its rotatory power $x^3 \dot{x}$, the fluxion $x^3 \dot{x}$ and the fluent $\frac{1}{4}x^4$; but the whole area will be as $\frac{1}{2}x^2$, and the rotatory power the same as if the whole were at the distance $\sqrt{(\frac{1}{2}x^2)}$.

354. DEFINITION. *The centre of percussion is a point in which an obstacle must be placed in order to receive the whole effect of the motion of a revolving body, without producing any pressure on the axis.*

355. DEFINITION. *The centre of oscillation of a body is a point of which the distance from the axis of motion is equal to the length of a pendulum vibrating in the same time with the body.*

356. THEOREM. *The centres of percussion and of oscillation coincide always in the same point.*

The effect of the velocity of every part of the body, reduced to the direction in which the obstacle opposes it, is expressed by the product of each particle, into its distance from the line drawn through the axis, parallel to that direction: now the joint effect of all these reduced momenta is equal to the resistance of the obstacle, since the axis is supposed to be free from any pressure in consequence of the percussion; and the resistance of the obstacle acting at the given distance is also equivalent to the rotatory power of the whole body. But the sum of the reduced momenta is also expressed by the product of the whole mass into the distance of the centre of gravity from the line drawn through the axis (276) which is equal, acting at the distance of the centre of percussion, to the whole rotatory power, or the sum of the products of all the particles by the squares of their distances, and the distance of the centre of percussion from the centre of suspension is found by dividing the rotatory power by the mass and the distance of the centre of gravity.

In the same manner, when a body is suspended as a pendulum, the tendency of the weight of each particle, to turn it round the axis, is proportional to the distance from the vertical line passing through the point of suspension; and the sum of the forces of all the particles is expressed by the product of the whole weight into the distance of the centre of gravity from the same line; and the rotatory mass to be moved is to be estimated by the joint products of the particles into the squares of their distances: and in order that the angular velocity of the equivalent pendulum may be equal, its distance from the vertical line must be to the square of its distance from the centre, in the same ratio, as the product of the distance of the centre of gravity into the whole weight, to the rotatory mass; but the distance of these points from the vertical line is as the distance from the centre, therefore the distance of the centre of oscillation is expressed by the rotatory mass divided by the weight and the distance of the centre of gravity from the point of suspension; consequently it is equal to the distance of the centre of percussion from the same point.

SCHOLIUM. It may also be shown that the distance of the centre of oscillation from the centre of gravity varies inversely as the distance of the centre of suspension from the same point.

357. THEOREM. *The centre of oscillation of two equal points in a right line passing through the axis is found by dividing the sum of the squares of their distances by the sum or difference of their distances.*

For the rotatory power is $a^2 + b^2$, and the weight multiplied by the distance of the centre of gravity is $a \pm b$.

358. THEOREM. *The centre of oscillation of a right line suspended at its extremity is at the distance of two thirds of its length.*

The fluxion of the rotatory power is $x^2 \dot{x}$, the fluent $\frac{1}{3}x^3$, the distance of the centre of gravity $\frac{1}{2}x$, the product $\frac{1}{2}x^2$, and the quotient $\frac{2}{3}x$.

359. THEOREM. The centre of oscillation of a triangle, suspended at its vertex, and vibrating in a direction perpendicular to its plane, is at the distance of $\frac{3}{4}$ of its height from the vertex.

Calling, for the sake of simplicity, the base of the triangle unity, the fluxion of the rotatory power is $x^2\dot{x}$, the fluent $\frac{1}{3}x^3$, the distance of the centre of gravity $\frac{2}{3}x$, the product $\frac{1}{4}x^3$, and the quotient $\frac{3}{4}x$.

SECTION XII. OF PREPONDERANCE, AND THE MAXIMUM OF EFFECT.

360. THEOREM. In order that a smaller weight may raise a greater to a given height on an inclined plane in the shortest time possible, the length of the plane must be to its height as twice the greater weight to the smaller.

Let the descending weight be 1, the ascending a, and the length of the plane to its height as x to 1, the weights being simply connected by a thread and pulley; then the portion of the power employed in maintaining the equilibrium is $\frac{a}{x}$ (255), and the remaining portion $1-\frac{a}{x}$; and the weight to be moved being constantly $a+1$, the velocity produced by the acting power $1-\frac{a}{x}$ will vary as $1-\frac{a}{x}$, and the square of the time of describing x, as $x : \left(1-\frac{a}{x}\right)$ (233), or $\frac{xx}{x-a}$, the fluxion of which vanishes when it is a minimum; therefore $\frac{2x\dot{x}}{x-a} - \frac{x^2\dot{x}}{(x-a)^2} = 0$; and multiplying by $\frac{(x-a)^2}{x\dot{x}}$, $2(x-a)-x=0$, $x-2a=0$, and $x=2a$.

361. THEOREM. If a given weight, or any equivalent force, be employed to raise another given weight by means of levers, wheels, pullies, or any similar powers, the greatest effect will be produced, if the acting weight be able to sustain in equilibrium a weight about twice as great as the weight to be raised, when this weight is very large; or about twice and a half as great, when the weights are nearly equal.

Suppose the two weights fixed at opposite ends of a lever, and let it be required to determine their respective distances from the fulcrum, so that the velocity of the ascending weight may be the greatest possible; let this weight be called a, and its distance from the fulcrum unity, the descending weight being 1, and its distance x. Then, if the weights were in equilibrium, a would be $=x$; and the difference of x and a, or $x-a$, is the force tending to raise a; but the mass to be raised is equivalent to $a+xx$, for the mass of the weight 1 acts in the duplicate ratio of its distance from the fulcrum (349), and the velocity of a will be $\frac{x-a}{a+xx}$, and its fluxion $\frac{\dot{x}}{a+xx}-\frac{(x-a)2x\dot{x}}{(a+xx)^2}=0$, hence $a+xx-2xx+2ax=0$, $a=xx-2ax$, and adding aa, $xx-2ax+aa=a+aa$, $(x-a)^2=a+aa$, $x-a=\sqrt{(a+aa)}$, $x=a+\sqrt{(a+aa)}$. Hence if $a=1$, $x=1+\sqrt{2}$; if $a=\infty$ $x=2a$. And the same reasoning is applicable to any other mechanical power. If the mass of the machine be also considered, let the weight of each of its parts be reduced to the place of a (349), and let b be equivalent to their sum, then the velocity will become $\frac{x-a}{a+b+xx}$, and $x=a+\sqrt{(a+b+aa)}$.

362. THEOREM. If the heights of descent and ascent, and the descending weight be given, the operation being supposed to be continually repeated, the effect will be greatest in a given time when the ascending weight is to the descending weight as 1 to 1.618, in the case of equal heights; and in other cases, when it is to the exact counterpoise in a ratio which is always between 1 : 1.5 and 1 : 2.

Let the height of descent be 1, that of ascent a, the descending weight 1, and the ascending $\frac{1}{x}$; then the equilibrium would require $x=a$ (313), and $1-\frac{a}{x}$ is the force acting on 1; but the mass, reduced, as before, is $1+\frac{aa}{x}$, and the relative force $\frac{x-a}{x+aa}$, and the space being given, the time is as $\sqrt{\left(\frac{x+aa}{x-a}\right)}$ (233); and the whole effect in a given time being directly as the weight raised, and inversely as the time of ascent, will be as $\frac{1}{x}\sqrt{\left(\frac{x-a}{x+aa}\right)}$; but when this is a maximum, its square is a maximum, and

$\left(\frac{1}{xx} \cdot \frac{x-a}{x+aa}\right) = 0$, $\frac{\dot{x}}{x^3+aaxx} - (x-a) \cdot \frac{3xx\dot{x}+2aax\dot{x}}{(x^3+aaxx)^2} = 0$,
$x^2 + a^2x - (x-a).(3x^2 = 2a^2) = 0$, $x^2 + a^2x - 3x^3 - 2a^2x + 3ax + 2a^3 = 0$, $2x^2 + (a^2 - 3a).x = 2a^3$, $x = \sqrt{(a^3 + \frac{1}{16}(a^2-3a)^2)}$
$- \frac{1}{4}(a^2-3a) = \frac{a}{4}.(\sqrt{(aa+10a+9)} - a + 3)$. Hence, if $a =$
1, $x = \frac{1+\sqrt{5}}{2}$, and when a is diminished without limit,
$x = \frac{3}{2}a$; when it is increased without limit, $x = 2a$; for in
this case $\sqrt{(aa+10a+9)}$ approaches infinitely near to
$a + 5$. This proposition has not always been sufficiently
distinguished from the preceding one.

SCHOLIUM. If the force accumulated during the operation of the machine, as that of a stream of water collected continually in a reservoir, there would be no limit to the advantage of a slow motion.

363. THEOREM. If a weight be drawn along a horizontal surface by a given force, with a resistance in the direction of the surface which is always a certain portion of the pressure, the force will act with the greatest advantage when the tangent of its inclination is to the radius as the resistance to the pressure.

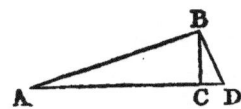

Let AB represent the force, and let BC be to CD as the pressure to the friction, then AD will represent the sum of the horizontal forces, AC being the efficient portion of the force AB, and CD the diminution of the friction. But the angle D is given, since the proportion of BC to CD is given, and BCD is a right angle; and AB being given, AD will vary as the sine of the angle ABD, which is greatest when ABD is a right angle; and ACB is then similar to BCD; but BC is the tangent of the angle BAC, AC being the radius. The angle BAC is also the same at which the weight would begin to slide along the given surface if it were inclined to the horizon (300).

SECTION XIII. OF THE VELOCITY AND FRICTION OF WHEEL WORK.

364. THEOREM. The angular motion of two wheels may be made uniform at the same time by means of a right line sliding on an epicycloidal surface, or by two surfaces which are involutes of circles, acting on each other.

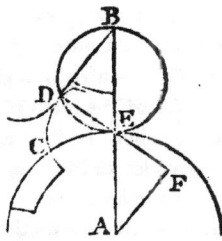

Let A and B be the centres of the wheels, and CD a portion of an epicycloid, described by the point D of the circle BDE, equal in diameter to the radius of the wheel B, in rolling on the wheel A: then if the tooth of the wheel B be terminated by the right line BD, and touch CD in D, the line DE perpendicular to BD, will pass through the point of contact of the circles, E (206); and the force will be communicated in the direction DE, so that the angular motion of each wheel will be the same, as if it acted immediately at the end of the perpendicular AF, and the angular motion of A will be to that of B, in the constant ratio of BD to AF, or BE to AE. It is obvious, that BD cannot act in the same manner on CD beyond the line BA, unless its extremity be made epicycloidal, and the corresponding part of the tooth of A a right line. Let each tooth now terminate in the curve described by the evolution of a thread from its respective circle: then the curve will be always perpendicular to the thread (193), which is the tangent of the circle, and the force will always act in the direction of the circumference of the circles at E and G, and the motion will be uniform as before.

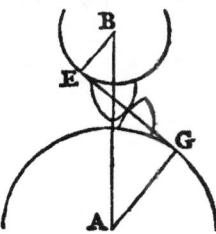

365. THEOREM. The relative velocity of the teeth of two wheels, or the velocity with which the surfaces slide on each other, varies ultimately as the sum of the angular distances of the point of contact from the line joining the centres.

Let A and B be the two centres, C the point of contact, and CD the common tangent there; and suppose the teeth to move to the positions E, F, and G to be the new point of contact; and let BD and BH be perpendicular to CD and to AC produced; then CE and CF, the elements of the paths of the points which were at C, will be perpendicular to AC and BC; and the difference of EG and FG, which represents the friction, ultimately equal

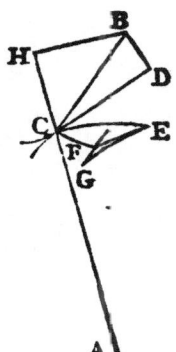

to EF, EFG becoming a right line parallel to CD, and the angle CFG=DCF=DBC; but the angle ECF=BCH, and in the triangle ECF, sin. CFE : sin. ECF : : CE : EF (139) : : sin. CBD : sin. BCH : : CD : BH. For the substance of this demonstration I am indebted to Mr. Cavendish. In the epicycloidal tooth, CD coincides with CB, and CBD is a right angle, so that the friction is to the motion CE of the tooth of A, as the sine of BCH, or of ACB, to the radius. In the involute, CD is constant, and the friction varies as BH, supposing the motion in CE constant. If the pinion acted within the concave surface of a cylindrical wheel, the friction would be as the sine of the difference, instead of the sum, of the angular distances from the line of junction.

SCHOLIUM. The immediate quantity of the force of friction does not appear to be materially altered by the relative velocity of the surfaces: but its mechanical effect in resisting the motion of a machine is so much the greater as the relative velocity is greater.

366. THEOREM. If a given number of teeth are to be disposed on an unlimited number of wheels and pinions, so as to increase or diminish the velocity of the last wheels of the series as much as possible, the proportion of each pinion to its wheel must be nearly that of 1 to 3.59.

In order to increase the angular velocity in the ratio of 1 to a, with the least possible number y of wheels, each having to its pinion the ratio of x to 1, we must make x the number of which the hyperbolical logarithm exceeds the reciprocal by unity. For $x^y = a$, $x = a^{\frac{1}{y}}$; and $y.(x+1)$, the number of teeth, must be a minimum: but $y.(x+1) = a^{\frac{1}{y}}y + y$, and $a^{\frac{1}{y}}\dot{y} - y(h.l.\ a)a^{\frac{1}{y}}\frac{\dot{y}}{yy} + \dot{y} = 0$, $a^{\frac{1}{y}} + 1 = a^{\frac{1}{y}}\frac{h.l.\ a}{y}$, or $x + 1 = x(h.l.x)$ since $h.l.a = y(h.l.x)$; therefore $1 + \frac{1}{x} = h.l.x$, and x is found $= 3.59$. This is therefore the most advantageous proportion for producing the greatest velocity with a given number of teeth.

MATHEMATICAL ELEMENTS

OF

NATURAL PHILOSOPHY.

PART III.

HYDRODYNAMICS.

OF THE MOTIONS OF FLUIDS.

SECTION I. OF HYDROSTATIC EQUILIBRIUM.

367. DEFINITION. A fluid is a collection of particles considered as infinitely small spheres, moving freely on each other without friction.

SCHOLIUM. Some have defined a fluid, as a substance which communicates pressure equally in all directions; but this appears clearly to be a property derivable from a simpler assumption, although, from the deficiency of our analysis, all attempts to investigate mathematically the affections of fluids, have hitherto been so unsuccessful, that even this fundamental law can scarcely be strictly demonstrated.

368. THEOREM. The surface of a gravitating fluid at rest, is horizontal.

Suppose two minute straight tubes differently inclined to the horizon, and joined at the bottom by a curved portion, and let them be filled with evanescent spherules: then the relative force of gravity is inversely as the length, when the height is the same (255), and the number of particles is directly as the length: consequently the absolute pressures will be equal, and there will be an equilibrium; and if the fluid in either arm be higher, it will preponderate. The pressure on the tube at any part is only the effect of the particle immediately in contact with it, and is communicated in the direction perpendicular to the tube, therefore if another similar row of particles in equilibrium were placed on the first, this pressure, acting in the same direction, would not disturb the equilibrium of the particles among themselves, however they might be situated with respect to the first. And conceiving any fluid to be divided into an infinite number of tubes, bent or straight, in which the particles form a continuous series, there can be no force to preserve the equilibrium in each of them, unless the height of each portion be equal. Yet some may perhaps hesitate to admit the conclusiveness of this reasoning, without an appeal to our experience of the phenomenon as observed in nature: it may however be admitted by such as an illustration of that phenomenon.

SCHOLIUM. In the equilibrium of fluids, there is some analogy to the general law of mechanical equilibrium (313); thus, supposing the whole body of the fluid to begin to move either way, the initial momenta of the particles in the surfaces of the unequal portions of a bent tube will be equal. For instance, if one surface be ten times as large as the other, its subsidence will raise the other ten times as much as it sinks.

369. THEOREM. The surface of a gravitating fluid, revolving round an axis, is parabolic.

The centrifugal force is simply as the distance from the axis, and may be represented by the ordinate, while the constant force of gravity is represented by the subnormal, or the portion of the axis intercepted between the ordinate and the perpendicular to the curve, the perpendicular or normal being the result of the two forces. But the curve in which the subnormal is constant is a parabola; for the triangle composed by the increments of the curve, the ordinate and the absciss, is similar to that which is formed by the normal, the subnormal, and the ordinate, consequently $y' : x' :: s : y$, $\dot{y} : \dot{x} :: s : y$, $y\dot{y} = s\dot{x}$, and $s = \frac{y\dot{y}}{\dot{x}}$; but in the parabola, since $ax = yy$ (204), $a\dot{x} = 2y\dot{y}$, $\dot{x} = \frac{2y\dot{y}}{a}$, and $s = \frac{a}{2}$, which is constant.

370. THEOREM. The pressure of a fluid on every particle of the vessel containing it, or of any other surface, real or imaginary, in contact with it, is equal to the weight of a column of the fluid of which the base is equal to that particle, and the height to its depth below the surface of the fluid.

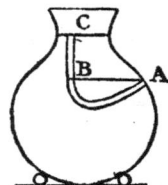

Imagine an equable tube to be so bent that one of its arms may be vertical, and the other perpendicular to the given surface: then drawing a horizontal line AB, the fluid in the portion of the tube AB will remain in equilibrium, and will only transmit the pressure of BC to the surface at A, and this will be true whatever be the position of the imaginary tube; and since some particles of the fluid may be so arranged as to be no more disturbed in their initial tendency to motion than the fluid in such a tube would be, the equilibrium can never be permanent unless the pressures be such as are here assigned.

SCHOLIUM. If therefore any portion of the superior part of a fluid be replaced by a part of the vessel, the pressure against this from below will be the same which before supported the weight of the fluid removed, and, every part remaining in equilibrium, the pressure on the bottom will be the same as if the horizontal section of the vessel were every where of equal dimensions. In this manner the smallest given quantity of a fluid may be made to produce a pressure capable of sustaining a weight of any magnitude, either by diminishing the diameter of the column and increasing its height, or by increasing the surface which supports the weight.

371. THEOREM. The pressure on any vertical or oblique plane surface is equal to the weight of a column of a fluid of which the base is equal to the surface, and the height to the distance of its centre of gravity below the level surface of the fluid.

Suppose the surface to be divided into a number of equal evanescent portions, then the number of particles in each column standing on the same base being as its length, the weight will be as the length and the base conjointly, or as the numerical product of the base and length: but from the property of the centre of gravity or of inertia, the sum of the products of each particle of the surface into its depth, is equal to the product of the whole into the distance of the centre of gravity (276), which represents a column of the same height, and on the same base.

372. THEOREM. A hemisphere or semi-cylinder of uniform density, having its axis fixed in the surface of a fluid, and remaining in equilibrium in any one position, will remain in equilibrium when its position is changed by the increase or diminution of the quantity of the fluid.

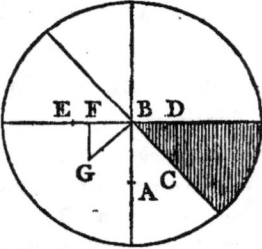

The pressure of the fluid on the convex surface of the solid will have no effect in turning it round its axis, consequently we have only to consider the pressure exerted on its plane surface. The centre of gravity of this surface AB or CD being at A or C, the pressure of the fluid will be always as the depth AB, CD: but the effect of the weight of the solid will be always as EB, FB, the distance of the centre of gravity E, G from the vertical line AB: but the triangle BDC is always similar to the triangle GFB, consequently CD varies always as FB, and if the forces are once equal, they will remain always equal in any position of the solid.

SCHOLIUM. If the surface of the fluid be below the axis, and there be an equilibrium, for instance when the surface is at A, there will be an equilibrium, for a similar reason, when the fluid rises to C in the oblique position of he solid.

373. THEOREM. If fluids are of different specific gravities, that is, if equal bulks of them have different weights, they will counterbalance each other in a bent tube, when

their heights above the common surface are inversely as their specific gravities.

For if the tube be equable, and its arms similar, the actual weights above the common surface will be equal; and if otherwise, the efficient weights will be equal, since, in either fluid, the pressures on the common surface are simply as the heights.

SECTION II. OF FLOATING BODIES.

374. THEOREM. If any body floats on a fluid, it displaces a quantity of the fluid equal to itself in weight.

For since the body is supposed to remain at rest, and to retain the pressure of the fluid below it in equilibrium, it must exert by its weight a pressure downwards, equal to that of the quantity of fluid which would retain the same pressure in equilibrium, or to the quantity displaced.

375. THEOREM. When the centre of gravity of the floating body is in the same vertical line with the centre of gravity of the fluid displaced, the body remains in equilibrium.

If a uniform fluid, of the same specific gravity as the fluid, occupied the place of the portion removed, it would remain at rest, in consequence of the contrary actions of the fluid and of gravity. Now the effect of any forces on the motion of the centre of gravity of a compound body, is the same as if they were applied to the same mass placed in the centre of gravity; therefore since the direction of gravitation is vertical, the result of the combined pressures of the fluid which counteract it, would, if united at the centre of gravity, be also vertical: and if the actual centre of gravity of the body of equal weight be placed in this line, there will be an equilibrium; but if otherwise, the centre of gravity will descend towards this line, and a part of the immersed portion will in the mean time be somewhat raised by the pressure of the fluid.

376. THEOREM. If a floating body have its section, made by the surface of the fluid, a parallelogram, its equilibrium will be stable or tottering, accordingly as the height of its centre of gravity, above that of the portion of the fluid displaced, is smaller or greater than one twelfth of the cube of the breadth, divided by the area of the transverse vertical section of the immersed part.

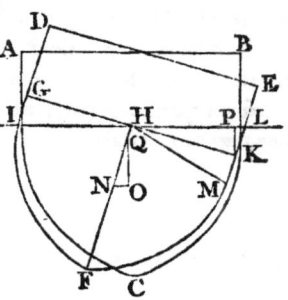

Let the body be inclined in a small degree from the position of equilibrium ABC, into the position DEF; then the triangles GHI and KHL will be equal, since the area of the section immersed must remain constant, and GK and IL will ultimately bisect each other in H. Now the centre of gravity of the section ILF, is the common centre of gravity of its parts IHMF and LHM, making KM=GI; but N the centre of gravity of IHMF is in the line HF bisecting it, and the common centre of gravity may be found by making NO parallel to HK or to HL, in the same ratio to the distance of the centre of gravity of LHM from H that LHM bears to IFL. Now the distance of the centre of gravity of any triangle from the vertex is two thirds of the line which bisects the base (277); that is in this case $\frac{2}{3}$HK, and the area of the triangle LHM is HK.KP, therefore NO : $\frac{2}{3}$HK :: HK.KP : LFI, NO= $\frac{\frac{2}{3}\text{HKq.KP}}{\text{IFL}}$; but drawing OQ vertically through O, NO : NQ :: KP : HK and NQ=$\frac{\text{NO.HK}}{\text{KP}}=\frac{\frac{2}{3}\text{HK cub.}}{\text{IFL}}=\frac{1}{12}\frac{\text{ILcub}}{\text{IFL}}$.

If therefore the centre of gravity be in Q, the body will remain in its position in any small inclination; since the result of the pressure of the fluid acts in the direction OQ, if the centre of gravity be below Q, it will descend towards the line QO, and the body will recover its situation; if above Q, the body will overset. Hence the point Q is sometimes called the centre of pressure, or the metacentre. The theorem may be easily accommodated to bodies of other forms.

SECTION III. OF SPECIFIC GRAVITIES.

377. THEOREM. If a body is immersed in a fluid, it loses as much of its weight as is equivalent to an equal bulk of the fluid.

For if the body were of the same specific gravity with the fluid, it would remain at rest, without any tendency to ascend or to descend, the pressure of the fluid counteracting its whole weight: but that pressure will be the same whatever may be the weight of the body, and will support an equal weight in both cases.

SCHOLIUM. Hence the specific gravity of any fluid may be determined by finding how much weight it deducts from a body of known dimensions immersed in it. And the dimensions of a solid may be found by weighing it in a fluid of known specific gravity, and thence its specific gravity may also be ascertained.

SECTION IV. OF PNEUMATIC EQUILIBRIUM.

378. DEFINITION. Elastic fluids are such as have a tendency to expand when at liberty, with a force which is proportional to their density.

Atmospheric air, gases, and vapours, are examples of such fluids.

379. THEOREM. Supposing the force of gravitation constant, the logarithm of the rarity of the atmosphere must be in a constant ratio to the height.

Let the length of a column of air increase equably in descending, then the densities at each point being as the pressures which counteract the expansive force (378), and the increments of the pressures being as these densities, the pressures vary proportionally while the heights vary equably; therefore the heights are in a constant ratio to the logarithms of the numbers representing the pressures (50): and in ascending, the same logarithms, taken negatively, are the logarithms of the reciprocals of the densities (38), or of the rarities. So that if $a, b; h, r;$ be corresponding heights and rarities, $a : l.b :: h : l.r.$ Suppose a 7 miles, and $l=4$, then $7 : 1.4 :: h : l.r,$ and $l.r=\frac{1.4}{7}h=\frac{h}{1.1626}$, and $h=1.1626$ (l.r), also since $l.r=(1.4).\frac{h}{7}$, $r=(4)^{\frac{h}{7}}$. Practically $h=10000$ (l.r), in fathoms.

380. THEOREM. The height of a column of air, of equal density with the atmosphere at any part, capable of producing a pressure equal to the atmospheric pressure at that part, is the same at all distances above the earth's surface.

The height of such a homogeneous atmosphere must be directly as the pressure to be produced, and inversely as the density, and since the density varies as the pressure, the result will be constant. This height is found to be somewhat more than 5 miles: in very great elevations it probably varies.

381. THEOREM. If a fluid be contained in a tube closed at the top, it will be supported by the pressure of the atmosphere at such a height, that its weight will be equal to that of a column of air on the same base, and of the height of the atmosphere.

For if an upright tube be partly immersed in a fluid, a heavier fluid will be sustained in it at a proportionate height, provided that the access of the fluid to its upper part be prevented; and in this case, the pressure of the atmosphere is as effectually removed from the upper surface of the fluid in the tube, as if the tube were continued throughout the height of the atmosphere.

SECTION V. OF HYDRAULICS.

382. THEOREM. The velocity of a small jet of water issuing in any direction from a reservoir, is nearly equal, in favourable circumstances, to the velocity acquired by a body in falling through the height of the surface of the reservoir above the orifice.

Supposing a very small plate of water immediately within the orifice, to be put in motion at each instant by means of the whole pressure of the fluid, which is equal to the weight of a column on the same base, of the height of the reservoir, and supposing the whole pressure to be employed in generating the velocity of the thin stratum, neglecting the motion of the surrounding fluid, this stratum would be urged by a force as much greater than its own weight as the column is higher than its thickness, through a space which is shorter than the height of the column in the same ratio. But the spaces being inversely as the forces, the final velocities are equal; and the velocity thus generated would be equal to that of a body falling through the height of the column. And although a part of the pressure of the column is expended in producing motion in its own particles, this part is not wholly lost, because the velocity of these particles renders them more easily actuated by the pressure of the succeeding column. Still, however, some deduction must be made for the lateral motions of the neighbouring particles, which tend rather to diminish the quantity of the discharge, than to lessen the actual velocity of the jet: the particles approaching and even passing through the orifice obliquely, contract the diameter of the stream nearly in the ratio of 4 to 5, when the aperture is in a thin plate; but the velocity in the contracted part is only one fortieth or one fiftieth less than that which is due to the height.

SCHOLIUM. The velocity of the discharge through different kinds of apertures may be found by multiplying the square root of the height in feet by a certain coefficient; this, for the undiminished velocity, is 8.0229; for an orifice imitating the form of the contracted stream 7.8; for bridges with pointed piers 7.7; for bridges with square piers 6.9; for short pipes, from two to four times as long as their diameter, 6.6; for orifices in a thin plate, and for weres, about 5. When the orifice is made between two reservoirs, the discharge is nearly in the same relation to the difference of their heights.

383. THEOREM. A jet of water issuing from an orifice of a proper form, and directed upwards, rises nearly to the height of the head of water in the reservoir.

For it has been shown, that the velocity is nearly equal to that which is produced by the fall of a body through the height, and each of the particles may be considered nearly as a separate projectile.

384. THEOREM. If a jet issue horizontally from any part of the side of a vessel standing on a horizontal plane, and a circle be described having the whole height of the fluid for its diameter, the fluid will reach the plane at a distance from the vessel, equal to that chord of the circle in which the jet initially moves.

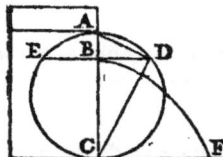

The horizontal velocity of the jet, being equal to that which is acquired by a body falling through the distance AB below the surface, would describe in the time of falling through AB, a distance equal to 2AB (232), and in the time of falling through BC, in which the jet will reach the horizontal plane (251), a distance greater in the ratio of those times, or of the square roots of the spaces (233). Call AC, 1, then (121) 1 : AD :: AD : AB, $ADq = AB$, and $AD = \sqrt{AB}$; in the same manner $CD = \sqrt{BC}$, therefore the times are as AD and CD: but AD : CD :: AB : BD, and 2BD, or DE will be equal to the space CF described by the horizontal velocity (251) in the time of falling through BC.

385. THEOREM. When a cylindrical or prismatic vessel empties itself by a small orifice, the velocity at the surface is uniformly retarded; and in the time which it occupies in emptying itself, twice the quantity would be discharged if it were kept full by a new supply.

For the velocity of the surface is in a constant ratio to that at the orifice; and since the velocity varies as the square root of the height, or of the space to be described, the law of the motion will be the same as in the ascent of a projectile (230, 233, 236), and the space described by every such motion is half the space that would be described by the initial velocity.

386. THEOREM. The quantity of a fluid discharged through an aperture of equal breadth, continued from the bottom of a reservoir to the surface, is two thirds of that which would be discharged with the velocity at the bottom.

For the velocity at the distance x below the surface is $a\sqrt{x}$, and the fluxion of the discharge $a\sqrt{x}\dot{x}$ or $ax^{\frac{1}{2}}\dot{x}$, of which the fluent is $\frac{2}{3} ax^{\frac{3}{2}}$, which is $\frac{2}{3}$ of what would be discharged with the velocity $a\sqrt{x}$.

387. THEOREM. The friction of fluids varies nearly as the square of the velocity.

The friction appears to depend principally on the centrifugal force of the particles of the fluid moving in certain curves in order to surmount minute obstacles; hence it may be compared with the force of a revolving body, which always varies as the square of the velocity. The identity of the curves in all cases could however scarcely be inferred from theory only, if it were not supported by experience. The viscidity of the fluid seldom adds much to the resistance.

388. DEFINITION. The hydraulic mean depth of a river is the quotient of the area of its section, divided by the length of the outline of the section in contact with the bottom.

389. THEOREM. When a river flows with a uniform motion, its velocity varies as the square roots of the hydraulic mean depth and of the sine of the inclination conjointly.

For since the relative weight produces no acceleration, it must be exactly balanced by the friction: but the friction is as the square of the velocity, therefore the relative weight must be as the square of the velocity, and the velocity as the square root of the relative weight, or of the sine of the inclination. And since the friction produced by the bed of the river is for any given portion of water, as the extent of the bed directly and inversely as the quantity of water, that is inversely as the hydraulic mean depth, the square of the velocity must vary in the direct ratio of the depth in order to produce a given friction, and the velocity must be as the square root of the mean depth.

SCHOLIUM. It is found by experience that the mean velocity of a river in a second is nearly nine tenths of a mean proportional between the hydraulic mean depth, and the fall in two English miles. And if this velocity be expressed in inches and increased by its square root, it will give the velocity of the surface, if diminished by its square root, the velocity at the bottom. It appears however that the velocity increases a little more rapidly than the square root of the fall. The discharge of a were may be found by determining the velocity due to the sum of its height, and the height corresponding to the velocity with which the water arrives at it.

390. THEOREM. The square of the velocity of a fluid discharged through a pipe varies directly as the height multiplied by the diameter, and inversely as the diameter increased by a certain constant fraction of the length.

The height of the reservoir above the orifice of the pipe may be considered as divided into two parts, the one employed in overcoming the friction, the other in producing the velocity. Now the whole friction varies directly as the length of the pipe, inversely as its hydraulic mean depth, which is one fourth of its diameter, and directly as the square of the velocity; or calling the height employed on the friction, f, $f = \frac{al}{d} \cdot v^2$, a being a constant quantity. But the height employed in producing the velocity v, is $\frac{v^2}{b^2}$, b being the proper coefficient for determining the velocity from the height; consequently $\frac{al}{d} \cdot v^2 + \frac{v^2}{b^2} = h$; h being the actual height, and $(alb^2 + d) \cdot v^2 = b^2 dh$, and $v^2 = \frac{b^2 dh}{ab^2 l + d}$.

SCHOLIUM. The coefficient b is in this case 6.6, and ab^2 is nearly .0211, where the velocity is moderate: but it is more accurate to make $v = 50 \sqrt{\left(\frac{dh}{l + 50d}\right)}$; all the measures being expressed in English feet. When the pipe is bent, we may find the height employed in overcoming the additional resistance, by multiplying the square of the velocity by the sine of the angle of inflection, and by .0038. We may also deduce the velocity of a river from the same formula, supposing the pipe to be in train, or so constituted, that its velocity is independent of its length; for making $h = c + kl$, we have $\frac{(a + kl)d}{l + 50d}$ constant, whatever may be the magnitude of l, and if $l = \infty$, $v = 50 \sqrt{(kd)}$; but (k) is the sine of the inclination, and e being the mean depth, $d = 4e$ and $v = \sqrt{(10000 ke)}$; or, if we employ .0211 as the value of ab^2, $v = \sqrt{(8280 ke)}$; while the rule deduced from observation is equivalent to $v = \sqrt{(8553 ke)}$.

391. THEOREM. The hydraulic pressure of a jet acting directly on a plane surface, so as to lose its whole progressive motion, is equal to twice the weight of a column on the same base, and of the height corresponding to the velocity.

For in the time required for a body to fall through this height, each particle of the jet would lose its velocity by the immediate action of gravitation; but in this time the same number of particles lose their velocity by the reaction of the surface as are contained in a column on the same base, and of twice the height: therefore the effects being equal, the causes must also be equal.

392. THEOREM. The resistance of a fluid to a body moving through it, is as the square of the velocity.

For the relative motions are nearly the same as in the impulse of a jet; and the height of the column varies as the square of the velocity.

SCHOLIUM. When the impulse is oblique, the resistance may be calculated from the laws of the decomposition of force; but the results are not accurate enough to be of any use without a comparison with experiments.

393. THEOREM. When the whole of a

given quantity of a fluid acts upon a body, its effect is simply as the relative velocity.

For the length of the stream being given, the time of its operation will be inversely as the relative velocity, and the effect being as the pressure and the time, or as the square of the velocity directly, and inversely as the velocity, will be simply as the velocity. If the fluid acts in such a manner that the time does not vary, the proposition may be proved from considering simply the quantity of motion that the fluid loses, which must be the measure of the force with which it acts on the solid.

394. THEOREM. *The rotatory power of a limited stream is greatest when it impels an obstacle moving with half its own velocity.*

For the rotatory power is as the force and the velocity conjointly; now the length of the stream being limited, its force is simply as the relative velocity, or as $a-v$, a being the velocity of the stream, and v that of the obstacle; but $av-vv$ is a maximum when $a\dot{v}=2v\dot{v}$, or $2v=a$.

395. THEOREM. *When the surface of an incompressible fluid, contained in a narrow prismatic canal, is elevated or depressed a little at any part above the general level, if we suppose a point to move in the surface each way with a velocity equal to that of a heavy body falling through half the depth of the fluid, the surface of the fluid at the part first affected will always be in a right line between the two moveable points.*

The particles constituting any column of the fluid are actuated by two forces, derived from the hydrostatic pressures of the columns on each side, and these pressures are supposed to extend to the bottom of the canal, with an intensity regulated only by the height of the columns themselves; and this supposition would be either perfectly or very nearly true if the particles of the fluid were infinitely elastic, or absolutely incompressible. The difference of these forces constituting a partial pressure, is the immediate cause of the horizontal motion, and the vertical motion is the effect: and this difference is every where to the weight of the column, or of any of its portions, as the difference of the heights to the thickness of the column, or as the fluxion of the height to that of the horizontal length of the canal. Such therefore is the force acting horizontally on any elementary column: but the elongation or abbreviation of the column depends on the difference of the velocities with which its surfaces are made to advance, and this elevation or depression is therefore to the whole height, as the variation of the fluxion of the length, produced by the operation of the force, is to the whole fluxion of the length. While therefore one of the supposed moveable points describes a given elementary arc, and the column is elevated or depressed through its versed sine, which expresses half the second fluxion of the height, its limits will approach each other horizontally through a space as much less, as the fluxion of the length is less than the whole height, and the whole horizontal velocity being as much greater than this relative velocity, as the force is greater than its fluxion, or as the first fluxion of the height is greater than its second fluxion, it follows that the whole horizontal velocity will describe a space equal to half the first fluxion of the height, diminished in the ratio of the fluxion of the length to the height; but if the force were altered so as to become equal to that of gravity, or in the ratio of the fluxion of the height to that of the length, the space described would become equal to half the fluxion of the length, diminished in the ratio of the fluxion of the length to the height; and if the time were increased in the ratio of the elementary arc, or the fluxion of the length, to the height the space described would be increased in the duplicate ratio, and would become equal to half the height: since therefore the moveable point describes a space equal to the depth, in the time that half that space would be described by the action of gravity, its velocity is equal to that which is acquired by a heavy body in falling through half the depth, and the surface of the fluid will initially describe a space equal to the versed sine of an arc thus described by the moveable point.

In this manner the initial change of situation of every part of the given surface may be determined, and the figure which it will have acquired at the end of any instant may be considered as determining the acceleration of the motion for a successive instant, which will always be such as to add to the space described with the velocity acquired at the beginning of the instant, a space equal to the mean of the versed sines of the equal elementary arcs of the new curve on each side of the point. But the sum of these versed sines is always half the sum of the second fluxions of the height of the original surface at equal distances on each side, corresponding to the place of the moveable points, for the extremities of the new elementary arcs being determined by the bisections of two equal chords, removed to the distance of the arc on each side, the sagitta at each end is half of the excess of the increment on one side above the increment adjoining to the corresponding one on the other side, and the sum of the sagittas is therefore half of the sum of the differences of the increments from the contiguous increments on the same side, and the mean of the sagittas is half of the mean of the second fluxions: but the second fluxion of the space may always be expressed by twice its second increment; the second fluxion of the space is therefore equal to the mean of the second fluxions of the sagittas corresponding to the places of the moveable points, and the space to the mean of the sagittas themselves, since the same mode of reasoning may be extended step by step throughout the length of the surface.

The actions of any two or more forces being always expressed by the addition or subtraction of the results produced by their single operations, it may easily be understood that any two or more impressions may be propagated in a similar manner through the canal, without impeding each other, the inclination of the surface, which is the original cause of the acting force, being the joint effect of the inclinations produced by the separate impressions, and producing singly the same force as would have resulted from the combination of the two separate inclinations; and the elevation or depression becoming always the sum or difference of those which belong to the separate impressions. If then we suppose two similar impulses, waves, or series of waves, to meet each other in directions precisely opposite, they will still pursue their course, but the point, in which their similar parts meet must be free from all horizontal motion, since the motions peculiar to each, destroy each other: consequently a solid obstacle fixed in a vertical direction would produce precisely the same effect on either series, as is produced by the opposition of a similar series, and would reflect it in a form similar to that of the opposite series.

SCHOLIUM. The limited elasticity of liquids actually existing produces some variations in the phenomena of waves, which have not yet been investigated; but its effect may be in some degree estimated by approximation. For a finite time is actually required in order for the propagation of any effect to the parts of the fluid situated at any given depth below the surface, and for the return of the impulse or pressure to the superficial parts: so that the summit of every wave must have travelled through a certain portion of its track before the neighbouring parts of the fluid can have partaken in the whole effects which its pressure would produce by means of the displacement of the lower part of the fluid. This cause probably cooperates with the cohesion of the liquid in rounding off any sharp angles which may originally have existed; it limits the effect that an increase of depth can produce in the velocity of the transmission of waves of a finite magnitude, and diminishes the velocity of all waves the more as the depth approaches more to this limit. If the surface was originally in the form of the harmonic curve, it may be shown that the force acting at any time on a given point in consequence of the sum of the results of the forces derived from the effect of a given portion of a wave which has already passed by, will still follow the law of the same curve: but the force will be diminished in the ratio of the arc corresponding to half the space described by the wave while the impulse returns from the bottom, to its sine, the whole distance of the wave being considered as the circumference; and the velocity will be diminished in the subduplicate ratio; but the arc which, when diminished in the subduplicate ratio that it bears to the sine, is the greatest, is that of which the length is equal to the tangent of its excess above a right angle, or an arc of about $70°\frac{1}{4}$, its sine is .94 and its length 2.8, the subduplicate ratio that of 1 to .57, and the velocity will be so much less than that which is due to the height: but with this velocity the wave will describe a portion equal to $\frac{211}{140}$ of its breadth, while the effect descends and reascends to the depth concerned; and supposing the velocity with which the impulse is transmitted through the fluid to be equal to that which is acquired by a body falling through a space equal to $\frac{1}{4}m$, and calling the depth h, and the breadth of the wave a, while $\frac{211}{140}a$ is described by v, $2h$ is described by that which is due to $\frac{1}{4}m$, or by $b\sqrt{\left(\frac{m}{2}\right)}$; and v being $.57b\sqrt{\left(\frac{h}{2}\right)}$, as $.57b\sqrt{\left(\frac{h}{2}\right)}$ to $\frac{211}{140}a$, so is $b\sqrt{\left(\frac{m}{2}\right)}$ to $2h$, and $1.14h^{\frac{3}{2}} = \frac{211}{140}a\sqrt{m}$, whence $h = .5(a^2m)^{\frac{1}{3}}$. For water, according to Mr. Canton's experiments, m is not more than 750,000 feet, but we may venture to call it a million; then if a, the breadth of the wave, were 1 foot, h would be 50, and the velocity nearly 23 feet in a second. If a were 1000 feet, h would be 5000; and the addition of a greater depth could not increase the velocity. Where the depth is given, the correction may be made in a similar manner. For h being in this case given, we must find the arc which is to its sine in the duplicate ratio of the velocity due to the height to the diminished velocity, represented by that arc, while that of the impulse propagated in the medium is expressed by twice the depth. Thus if h were 8 feet, and a 1 foot, the velocity being v, the arc must be to its sine as 256 to vv, and v to 5660 as twice the arc to twice the depth and the arc $\frac{10}{1125}$, or in degrees .51v; but this arc is somewhat more than 8°, and exceeds its sine so little that the velocity is scarcely diminished one thousandth by the compressibility of the water. The friction and tenacity of the water must also tend in some degree to lessen the velocity of the waves.

SECTION VI. OF SOUND.

396. THEOREM. When a uniform and perfectly flexible chord, extended by a given weight, is inflected into any form, differing little from a straight line, and then suffered to vibrate, it returns to its primitive state in the time which would be occupied by a heavy body in falling through a height which is to the length of the chord as twice the weight of the chord to the tension; and the intermediate positions of each point may be found by delineating the initial figure, and repeating it in an inverted position below the absciss, then taking, in the absciss, each way, a distance proportionate to the time, and the half sum of the corresponding ordinates will indicate the place of the point at the expiration of that time.

We may first suppose the initial figure of the chord to be a harmonic curve: then the force impelling each particle will be proportional to its distance from the quiescent position, or the base of the curve. For the force acting on any element z' is to the whole force of tension p, as the element z' to the radius of curvature r (299), therefore the force is inversely as the radius of curvature, or directly as the curvature, that is, in this case, as the second fluxion of the ordinate (195); but the second fluxion of the ordinate of the harmonic curve is proportional to the ordinate itself; for the fluxion of the sine is as the cosine, and its fluxion again as the sine: the force being therefore always as the distance from a certain point, as in the cycloidal pendulum, the vibrations will be isochronous, and the ordinates will be proportionally diminished, so that the figure will be always a harmonic curve. Now calling the length of the chord a, and the greatest ordinate y, the ordinate of the figure of sines being to the length as the diameter of a circle to its circumference, or $=\frac{a}{c}$, the radius of curvature of the harmonic curve will be $\frac{aa}{ccy}$, and the force acting on the element z' will be $\frac{ccypz'}{aa}$; but the weight of the chord being q, that of z' is $\frac{qz'}{a}$, and the force is to the weight as $\frac{ccyp}{a}$ to q, or as $\frac{ccyp}{aq}$ to 1: therefore the time of vibration will be to that of a pendulum of the length y as 1 to $\sqrt{\left(\frac{ccyp}{aq}\right)}$ and to that of a pendulum of the length a in a ratio as much less as $\sqrt{y}$ is less than $\sqrt{a}$, or as 1 to $c.\sqrt{\frac{p}{q}}$. But the time of the vibration of a pendulum of the length a is to the time in which a body would fall through half a, as c to 1, consequently a single vibration of the chord will be performed in the time of falling through $\frac{a}{2}\cdot\frac{q}{p}$, and a double vibration in the time of falling through $2a.\frac{q}{p}$. Now the element z', moving according to the law of the cycloidal pendulum, describes spaces which are the versed sines of arcs, increasing equably (259), and the difference of the sine at any point from the half sum of the sines of two equidifferent arcs, is in a constant ratio to the versed sine of the difference, therefore, by taking the half sum of two equidistant ordinates, we find the space remaining to be described, after a time proportionate to the absciss. If the base be divided into two equal parts, and a harmonic curve be described on different sides of each part, the same demonstration is applicable to both parts, as if they were two separate chords: since the middle point will always be retained at rest by equal and opposite forces: and nothing prevents us from combining this compound vibration with the original one, since, by adding together the ordinates, we increase or diminish the fluxions and increments, in proportion to the spaces that are to be described, and the same construction of two equidistant ordinates, will determine the motion of each part. Such a compound figure may be made to pass through any two points at pleasure, and it may easily be conceived, that by subdividing the chord still further, and multiplying the subordinate curves, we may accommodate it to any greater number of points, so as to approximate infinitely near to any given figure; by which means the proposition is extended to all possible forms.

SCHOLIUM. If the initial figure consist of several equal portions crossing the axis, the chord will continue to vibrate like the same number of separate chords; and it is sometimes necessary to consider such subordinate vibrations as compounded with a general one. It usually happens also that the vibration deviates from its plane, and becomes a rotation, which is often exceedingly complicated, and may be considered as composed of various vibrations in different planes.

397. THEOREM. The chord and its tension remaining the same, the time of vibration is as the length; and if the tension be changed, the frequency will be as its square root: the time also varies as the square root of the weight of the chord.

It has been shown, that the time varies in the subduplicate ratio of the force, that is, of the tension directly, and of the weight inversely; and since the weight varies as the length, the equivalent space will vary as the square of the length, and the time of describing it simply as the length.

SCHOLIUM. The properties of vibrating chords have been demonstrated in a more direct and general manner by means of a branch of the fluxionary calculus which has been called the method of variations, and which is employed in comparing the changes of the properties of a curve existing at once in its different parts, with the variations which it undergoes in successive portions of time from an alteration of its form. An example of this mode of calculation has already been given in the investigation of the motions of waves (395), and it may be applied with equal simplicity to the vibrations of chords, and to the propagation of sound, notwithstanding the intricacy and prolixity with which it has been always hitherto treated. It may be shown that every small change of form is propagated along an extended chord with a velocity equal to that of a heavy body falling through a height equal to half the length of a portion of the chord, of which the weight is equivalent to a force producing the tension, and which may be called the modulus of the tension; and that the change is continually reflected when it arrives at the extremities of the chord; and from this proposition all the properties of vibrating chords may be immediately deduced.

For the force, acting on any small portion of the chord, being to the tension as its length to the radius of curvature, and its weight being to the tension as its length is to the modulus of tension, the force is to the weight as the length of the modulus to the radius. By this force the whole portion is initially impelled, since the change of curvature in its immediate neighbourhood is inconsiderable with respect to the whole: and it will describe a space equal to its versed sine, which is to the arc as the arc to the diameter, in the time in which a body falling by the force of gravity would describe a space as much less, as the modulus of tension is greater than the radius, that is, a space which is to the arc as the arc to twice the modulus; and if the time be increased in the ratio of the arc to the modulus, the space described by the falling body will be increased in the duplicate ratio, and will become equal to half the modulus:

If therefore a point move in the original curve with such a velocity as to describe the arc, while its versed sine is described by the motion of the chord, it would describe the length of the modulus while a heavy body would descend through half that length, and its velocity will therefore be equal to that which is acquired by a body falling through half the length: and supposing a point to move each way with such a velocity, the successive places of the given point of the chord will be initially in a straight line between these moving points. The place of the given point will also remain in a straight line between the two moving points as long as the motion continues. For the figure of the curve being initially changed in a small degree according to this law, each of the points of the chord will be found in a situation which is determined by it, and its motion will be continued in consequence of the inertia of the chord, and will receive an additional velocity from the effect of the new curvature. The space described in the first instant being equal to the mean of the versed sines of the arcs included by the two moveable points, the velocity, as well as the second fluxion of the versed sine, may be represented by twice that mean: the increment of this velocity in the next succeeding position of the curve will be represented by the new mean of the versed sines, which is always half of the mean of the second fluxions of the ordinates on each side; for the extremities of the new elementary arcs being determined by the bisections of two equal chords removed to the distance of the arc on each side, the versed sine of each is half of the excess of the increment on one side above the increment adjoining to the corresponding one on the other side, and the sum of the versed sines is therefore half the sum of the differences of the increments from the contiguous increments on the same side, consequently the fluxion, or rather the variation of the velocity, which is represented by twice the mean versed sine, is equal to the half sum of the second fluxions of the original curve at the parts in which the moveable points are found, and the second fluxion or variation of the space, which is as the variation of the velocity, is equal to the mean of the second fluxions of the ordinates; therefore the space described is always equal to the diminution of the mean of the ordinates. And the same mode of reasoning may be extended through the whole curve. If the initial figure be such that two of its contiguous portions, lying on opposite sides of the absciss, are similar to each other, and placed in an inverted position, it is obvious that the point in which they cross the axis must remain at rest, consequently its place may be supplied by a fixed point, and either portion of the curve will continue its motion, when vibrating separately, in the same manner as if the chord were prolonged without end by a repetition of similar portions, of which the alternate ones are in an inverted position.

398. THEOREM. *The times, occupied by the similar vibrations of elastic rods, are directly as the squares of their lengths, and inversely as their depths.*

If the length vary, the force at a given depression will vary inversely as its cube, and the weight will vary as the length, consequently the relative force will be inversely as the fourth power of the length; and where the spaces are given, the times are as the square roots of the forces. The weight is also directly as the depth, and the force as its cube; the accelerating force is therefore as the square of the depth, and the time inversely as the depth.

SCHOLIUM. It may be shown that the accelerating force, which acts on any point of an elastic rod, is as the difference of the curvature at the given point from the sum of the curvatures at equal small distances on each side, that is, as the second fluxion of the curvature, or ultimately, as the fourth fluxion of the ordinate. In the harmonic curve, the second fluxion of the curvature, as well as the second fluxion of the ordinate, is proportional to the ordinate itself; hence it follows that a rod infinitely long being bent into a series of harmonic curves, each of its points would reach the basis at the same instant; that a finite rod, loosely fixed at both ends, might vibrate in a similar manner; and that a ring is also capable of similar vibrations, if it be divided into any even number of vibrating portions. The time of such a vibration may be thus determined. The extremities of the rod, when loosely fixed, may be considered as simply subjected to a transverse force, since the curvature ultimately disappears: the sum of these transverse forces being equal to the whole of the forces which urge the rod towards the basis, and each of them being expressed by the area of one half of the curve. Now the curvature of a bar fixed at one end, and depressed a little by a weight at the other, increases uniformly in advancing towards the fixed point, until the radius of curvature there becomes $\frac{bbm}{12af}$ (321); and this curvature may be represented by the ordinate of the harmonic curve produced until it meets the tangent at the origin; so that the radius of curvature at the vertex of the harmonic curve will be greater than $\frac{bbm}{12af}$ in the same ratio as the produced ordinate is longer than the original ordinate, that is, as the quadrant of a circle is greater than the radius, and will therefore be equal to $\frac{bbcm}{24af}$; but the radius of curvature is also $\frac{ll}{ccy}$ (396), l being the length, and y the ordinate, therefore $y = \frac{24afll}{bbc^3m}$, or, since $l = 2a$, $\frac{12fl^3}{bbc^3m}$. The weight of the element of the rod x' is to m as x' to the height of the modulus h, and is therefore $= \frac{x'}{h}m$, and the force urging it is to f, as the area corresponding to x', is to half the area of the curve, that is, as yx' to $\frac{yl}{c}$, or as x' to $\frac{l}{c}$, and is equal to $\frac{cfx'}{l}$; but $f = \frac{bbc^3my}{12l^3}$, and $\frac{cfx'}{l}$ is to the weight as $\frac{bbc^4my}{12l^4}x'$ to $\frac{m}{h}x'$, or as $\frac{bbc^4hy}{12l^4}$ to 1; the time of vibration is therefore as much less than that of a pendulum of which the length is y, as $\frac{bc^2}{l^2}\sqrt{\left(\frac{hy}{12}\right)}$ is greater than unity, and as much less than that of a pendulum of which the length is $12h$, as $\frac{bc^2h}{l^2}$ is greater than unity, and the time of a complete vibration is to the time of falling through $6h$ as $2l^2$ to bch.

399. DEFINITION. *A sound, of which the number of vibrations in a second is any integer power of 2, is denoted in music by the letter c.*

SCHOLIUM. Hence we may form a table of the number of vibrations of each note in a second.

Scales of C.	256		288	307	320	341		384	409	427	451	480 512.
Equal temperament.	256	271	287	304	323	342	362	384	406	431	456	483 512.
Progressive temperaments.	256	270	287	303	321	341	360	383	405	427	455	481 512.

400. THEOREM. All minute impulses are conveyed through a homogeneous elastic medium with a uniform velocity, equal to that which a heavy body would acquire by falling through half the height of the medium causing the pressure.

If a moveable point be urged through a small space by the difference of two forces, varying inversely as its distance from two equidistant fixed points, in the same right line, the times of describing that space will be ultimately equal, whatever be its magnitude. For, calling the distance of each point a, and the space to be described x, the forces will be $\frac{1}{a-x}$ and $\frac{1}{a+x}$, and their difference $\frac{2x}{aa-xx}$, which is to $\frac{1}{a}$ as $2x$ to $a-\frac{xx}{a}$; but since x is evanescent, this ratio becomes that of $2x$ to a, and the force varies as the space to be described, consequently the times are equal. If therefore all the particles of an elastic medium contiguous to any plane, be agitated at the same time by a motion varying according to any law, they will communicate a motion to the particles on each side, and this motion will be propagated in each direction with a uniform velocity, and so that each particle shall observe the same law in its motion. For, as in the collisions of elastic balls (344), each ball communicates its whole motion to the next, and then remains at rest, so each particle of the medium will communicate its motion to the next in order; the common centre of inertia of two neighbouring particles supplying the place of a fixed point; and the retrograde motions will also be similarly communicated by the expansive force and pressure of the medium; and since the magnitude of the motion, while it is considered as evanescent, does not affect the time of its communication from one particle to the next, the velocity will not be affected by this magnitude, and the whole successive motions will be transferred to the neighbouring particles in their original order and proportion.

For computing the velocity, it is convenient to assume a certain law for the motion of each particle, and it is simplest to suppose it moving according to the law of the cycloidal pendulum.

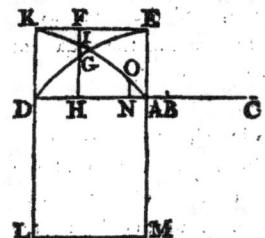

Let AB be the minute space described by the particle A, in one semi-vibration, while the undulation is transmitted through AC = DA, and let DE be a figure of sines, of which DA is the half basis; then if EF flow uniformly with the time, that is, if it increase with the velocity of the undulation, the versed sine FG will be in a constant ratio to the motion of A (259); the velocity of A will be as the fluxion of the space, or of FG, that is, as the conjugate ordinate HI (142); the force will be as the fluxion of the velocity, or as FG; and the force being as the change of density, or as its fluxion, the density, or rather the excess above the natural density, will be again as HI, and the fluent of the product of HI into the fluxion of the base, will give the whole excess of density in DA, which will therefore be represented by the figure DAK (190). But when A arrives at B, the beginning of the undulation reaches C, and the whole fluid which occupied A is condensed into BC, so that its mean density is increased in the ratio of AC to BC, and AB represents the excess above the natural density; therefore let the rectangle DLMA be to DAK, or DKq (203), as BC to AB, or ultimately as AC or DA to AB; that is, let DA.DL : DKq :: DA : AB, or $DL = \frac{DKq}{AB}$, then DL will represent the natural density, while the ordinates HI everywhere represent its increase. Let NA be the evanescent length of the particle A, then the force actuating it will be as the difference of the densities at its extremities, or as NO, which is equal to NA (141); therefore the force impelling A, is to the whole elasticity, as NA to DL. Now if h be the height of a column of the fluid, equal in weight to the whole elasticity, this weight will be to the weight of A as h to NA; and the force impelling A being $h.\text{NA} : \text{DL}$, this force will be to the weight of A as h to DL, or as $h.\frac{\text{AB}}{\text{DKq}}$ to 1. Let there be two pendulums, of which the lengths are h and AB, then with the same force, they will vibrate in times which are as $\sqrt{h}$ and $\sqrt{\text{AB}}$, and if the force in AB become $h.\frac{\text{AB}}{\text{DKq}}$, the time being inversely in the subduplicate ratio of the force, the vibrations will be as $\sqrt{h}$ to $\sqrt{\text{AB}}. \sqrt{\left(\frac{\text{DKq}}{h.\text{AB}}\right)}$ or as h to DK; and in the time of this semivibration in AB, the undulation will be transmitted through DA, therefore in a semivibration of h, it will be transmitted through a space greater in the ratio of h to DK, which will be to h as DA to DK, or as half the circumference of a circle to its diameter; and while a heavy body falls through half h, the undulation will describe h (259), its velocity will therefore be equal to the final velocity of the body falling through half h (232). According to this theorem the mean velocity of sound should be 946 feet in a second, h being 27880 feet, but it is found to be nearly 1130, which is one fifth greater than the computed velocity. The most probable reason that has been assigned for this difference is the partial increase of elasticity occasioned by the heat and cold produced by condensation and expansion.

401. THEOREM. *The height of the barometer will not affect the velocity of sound; but, if the density vary, the pressure remaining the same, the velocity will vary in its subduplicate ratio.*

For the velocity varies in the subduplicate ratio of the height of a homogeneous atmosphere, and that height remains the same while the density is only varied by means of pressure.

SCHOLIUM. The velocity of the transmission of an impulse through an elastic medium of any kind may be more generally determined without the consideration of any particular law for the variation of the density; and it may be directly demonstrated, that the velocity, with which any impulse is transmitted by an elastic substance, is equal to that which is acquired by a heavy body in falling through half the height of the modulus of its elasticity. The density of the different parts of the medium, throughout the finite space, which is affected by the impulse at any one time, may be represented by the ordinates of a curve; that which corresponds to the natural density being equal to the height of the modulus of the elasticity. The force acting on any small portion will be expressed by the difference of the ordinates at its extremities, that is, by the weight of a portion of the modulus equal in height to that difference; this force is to the weight, which is to be moved, as the fluxion of the ordinate to that of the absciss; and the velocity with which the density increases will be as the difference of the forces at the extremities of the portions, or as the second fluxion of the ordinate of the curve; and the increment of the ordinate expressing the density will be to the whole, as half of its second fluxion to its first fluxion; while therefore the density varies so as to be represented by the mean of two ordinates at a small distance on each side of the first ordinate, the increment of the ordinate being represented by the mean versed sine of the arcs, or half the second fluxion of the mean ordinate, the decrement of the space occupied by the particles will be as much less as the fluxion of the absciss is less than the ordinate, and the whole velocity being as much greater than the difference of the velocities, as the force is greater than its fluxion, or as the first fluxion of the ordinate is greater than its second fluxion, it follows that, in the same time, the particles will actually describe a space equal to half of the first fluxion of the ordinate, diminished in the ratio of the fluxion of the absciss to the ordinate; but if the force were altered in the ratio of the fluxion of the ordinate to that of the absciss, so as to become equal to that of gravity, the space described would become equal to half the fluxion of the absciss, diminished in the ratio of the fluxion of the absciss to the ordinate; and if the time were increased in the ratio of the fluxion of the absciss to the ordinate, the space described would be increased in the duplicate ratio, and would become equal to half the ordinate: and if a point move each way through the curve so as to describe an arc while the variation of density causes the ordinate to be diminished by a space equal to the mean versed sine, it would describe a space equal to the ordinate or the height of the modulus, while half that space would be described by the action of gravity; consequently the velocity of the points would be initially equal to that of a heavy body falling through half the height of the modulus. And that it would always remain equal to this velocity, so that the density of the medium might always be expressed by the mean ordinate, may be shown exactly in the same manner as has already been done with respect to the motions of waves and of vibrating chords. The variation of the velocity, and the change of place of the particles may be easily deduced from the successive forms of the curve representing the density; and the whole effect may also be considered as arising from the progressive motion of the same curves which express the cotemporary affections of the different parts of the medium, and which will also show the successive states of any one portion of it at different times.

SECTION VII. OF DIOPTRICS AND CATOPTRICS.

402. DEFINITION. Light is an influence capable of entering the eye, and of affecting it with a sense of vision. A ray of light is considered as an evanescent element of a stream of light; and a pencil as a collection of such rays accompanying each other.

403. DEFINITION. Light is distinguished by its effect on the sense of vision, into white and coloured light; and coloured light into a great number of various hues: but they may all be referred to the three primitive colours, red, green, and violet.

404. DEFINITION. Those substances, through which light passes uninterrupted in straight lines, are called homogeneous transparent mediums.

405. PHENOMENON. When rays of light arrive at a surface, which is the boundary of two mediums not homogeneous, they continue in the same planes; but a part of them, and sometimes nearly the whole, is reflected, making with the perpendicular an angle of reflection equal to the angle of incidence; and another part is transmitted, making such an angle of refraction, that at the same surface, and for rays of the same kind, the ratio of the sines of incidence and refraction is constant, whatever may be their magnitude.

406. PHENOMENON. If the same refracted ray return to the surface in an opposite direction, it will be transmitted back in the direction of the incident ray.

406. DEFINITION. The medium, in which the ray is nearer to the perpendicular, is said to have the greater refractive density; and a ray of light being supposed to pass from an empty space into a transparent medium, the index of the refractive density of the medium is that number which is to unity as the sine of incidence to the sine of refraction.

408. PHENOMENON. When, between two transparent mediums, a third is interposed, terminated by parallel surfaces, the whole angular refraction remains unchanged.

SCHOLIUM. The proportions of the sines of the angles of incidence and refraction may be deduced from the mechanical laws of motion, whether we consider refraction as produced by a constant attractive force, acting in a given small space on the particles of light as projected corpuscles, or by the change in the velocity with which an undulation is transmitted through mediums of different densities. For when a moving body approaches a surface obliquely, its velocity may be resolved into two parts, one in a direction parallel, and the other perpendicular to the surface; and the attractive force, being supposed to be perpendicular to the surface, will not affect its lateral motion. Now, since the fluxion of the square of the velocity varies as the fluxion of the space, and as the force, conjointly (235), the space and the force remaining the same, the finite increments of the squares of any two perpendicular velocities will also be equal. Calling the whole velocity in the hypotenuse a, and the perpendicular velocity x, the lateral velocity will be $\sqrt{(aa-xx)}$; and after refraction, we have $\sqrt{(xx+bb)}$ for the perpendicular velocity, and $\sqrt{(aa+bb)}$ for the whole velocity, which is therefore in a constant ratio to the former velocity a. But the lateral velocity remaining, in any one refraction, constant, may be made radius, and the whole velocities will be the cosecants of the angles, which, by similar triangles, are inversely as the sines of the same angles, and the ratio of the sines is therefore constant. In the undulatory system, the distance between any two points of the surface being made radius, the perpendicular distance which the same undulation passes over, while it travels from the first to the second, is the sine of the respective angle in each medium, and these distances, being described 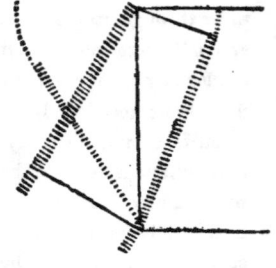 in the same time, must be in the constant ratio of the velocities appropriate to the mediums.

409. THEOREM. The index of refraction

at the common surface of two mediums is the quotient of their respective indices.

For the indices being r and qr, if the sine of incidence from a vacuum be 1, the sine of refraction in the first medium will be $\frac{1}{r}$, and this interposed medium being terminated by parallel surfaces, the sine of refraction in the second medium will be the same as in the absence of the first, or $\frac{1}{qr}$, which is to $\frac{1}{r}$ as 1 to q.

410. THEOREM. The angle of deviation being given, the angles of incidence and refraction will be equal to the angles at the base of any triangle, of which the sides are as 1 to the index of refraction, including an angle equal to the angle of deviation.

For the sines of the angles of a triangle are proportional to the sides opposite to them.

411. DEFINITION. The point of intersection of the directions of any two or more rays of light is called their focus; and the focus is either actual or virtual, accordingly as they meet in it, or only tend to or from it.

412. DEFINITION. When the divergence or convergence of rays is altered by refraction or reflection at any surface, the foci of the incident and refracted or reflected rays are called conjugate to each other; and the new focus is called the image of the former focus.

413. THEOREM. In reflections at a plane surface, the conjugate foci are at equal distances from the surface, and in the same perpendicular.

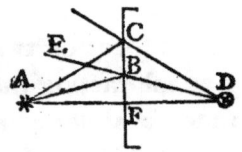

For in the triangles ABC, DBC, ∠ABC=DBC, since EBC=ABF=DBF; and ∠ACB=DCB, and CB is common to both triangles; therefore BD=AB, and the triangle BDF=BAF, and DF=AF.

414. THEOREM. For rays falling on a spherical surface nearly in the direction of the axis, the reciprocal of the radius being increased by the reciprocal of the distance of the focus of incident rays, the sum, divided by the index of refraction, is equal to the sum of the reciprocals of the radius, and of the distance of the focus of refracted rays: the distances being considered as negative when the respective foci are on the concave side of the surface.

Let AB be the axis, and AC a ray infinitely near it; let D be the centre, and E the focus conjugate to A. Call BD, a, AB, d, BE, e, the index of refraction, r, and the angle CAB, or its sine, s. 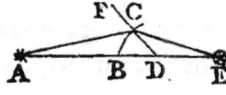 Then CD : CA : : ∠CAB : ∠CDB, the arcs coinciding ultimately with their sines, and ∠CDB$=\frac{d}{a}s$, and the angle of incidence ACF$=\frac{d}{a}s+s$, whence DCE$=\frac{1}{r}$ ACF$=(d+a).\frac{s}{ra}$. But sin. DCE : sin. CDE : : DE : CE, or $(d+a).\frac{s}{ra} : \frac{d}{a}s :: e-a : e$, $\frac{d+a}{r} : d :: e-a : e$, $\frac{de+ae}{r}$ $=de-da$, $rda=rde-de-ae$, $e=\frac{rda}{rd-d-a}$, $\frac{1}{e}=\frac{1}{a}-\frac{1}{ra}$ $-\frac{1}{rd}$, and $\frac{1}{ra}+\frac{1}{rd}=\frac{1}{a}-\frac{1}{e}$. But since E is on the concave side, we must substitute $-e$ for e to make the theorem general, and $\frac{1}{ra}+\frac{1}{rd}=\frac{1}{a}+\frac{1}{e}$, or $\frac{1}{e}=\frac{1}{ra}+\frac{1}{rd}-\frac{1}{a}$.

415. THEOREM. The distances of the conjugate foci from a plane refracting surface are in the ratio of the sines; and both are on the same side.

For here $a=\infty$, and $\frac{1}{e}=\frac{1}{rd}$, or $rd=e$, and both distances are positive, or both negative.

416. DEFINITION. When the focus of incident rays becomes infinitely distant, the rays are parallel, and the conjugate focus of such rays is called the principal focus of a surface or substance.

417. THEOREM. The principal focus of a spherical reflecting surface is at the distance of half the radius.

By making $r=-1$, we accommodate the general theorem for refraction to reflecting surfaces, and $-\frac{1}{a}-\frac{1}{d}=\frac{1}{a}+$

$\frac{1}{e}$, or $\frac{1}{e} = -\frac{2}{a} - \frac{1}{d}$; and when $d = \infty$, $\frac{1}{e} = -\frac{2}{a}$, and $e = -\frac{1}{2}a$.

418. THEOREM. When diverging rays fall on a concave mirror, the reciprocal of the distance of the focus of reflected rays is the difference of the reciprocals of the principal focal length and the distance of the focus of incident rays; and the same is true when converging rays fall on a convex mirror; and in either case, when the focus of incident rays is within the principal focal distance, the focus of reflected rays is on the convex side of the surface.

The distance d being negative, $\frac{1}{e} = \frac{1}{d} - \frac{2}{a}$, and when $\frac{1}{d} > \frac{2}{a}$, $\frac{1}{e}$ being positive, the focus is on the convex side.

419. THEOREM. When converging rays fall on a concave mirror, or diverging rays on a convex mirror, the reciprocal of the focal distance of reflected rays is the sum of the reciprocals of the principal focal length, and of the focal distance of incident rays; and the focus of reflected rays is in either case within the sphere.

Here d remains positive, and $\frac{1}{e} = -\left(\frac{2}{a} + \frac{1}{d}\right)$.

420. DEFINITION. A lens is a detached portion of a transparent substance, of which the opposite sides are regular polished surfaces, of such forms as may be described by a line revolving round an axis. In general, one of the sides is a portion of a spherical surface, and the other, either a portion of a spherical surface, or a plane; whence we have double convex, double concave, planoconvex, planoconcave, and meniscus lenses. It is simplest to suppose the lens of evanescent thickness, and denser than the surrounding medium.

421. THEOREM. The reciprocal of the principal focal length of any lens, is equal to the sum or difference of the reciprocals of the radii, multiplied by the index lessened by unity: and when diverging rays fall on a convex lens, or converging rays on a concave one, the reciprocal of the principal focal length is equal to the sum of the reciprocals of the distances of the conjugate foci; but to their difference, when converging rays fall on a convex lens, or diverging rays on a concave one.

For the focus after the first refraction we have $\frac{1}{e} = \frac{1}{ra} + \frac{1}{rd} - \frac{1}{a}$, and changing the signs, on account of the change of direction of the convexity, $\frac{1}{e} = \frac{1}{a} - \frac{1}{ra} - \frac{1}{rd}$ to be substituted for $\frac{1}{d}$ in the second refraction, where the radius is b, and the index $\frac{1}{r}$; hence $\frac{1}{e} = \frac{r}{b} + \frac{r}{a} - \frac{1}{a} - \frac{1}{d} - \frac{1}{b} = (r-1) \cdot \left(\frac{1}{b} + \frac{1}{a}\right) - \frac{1}{d}$; and when $d = \infty$, $\frac{1}{d}$ vanishes, and $\frac{1}{e} = (r-1) \cdot \left(\frac{1}{b} + \frac{1}{a}\right) = \frac{1}{f}$. In the concave lens, d being negative, $\frac{1}{e} = \frac{1}{f} + \frac{1}{d}$. In the meniscus, the signs not being changed, $\frac{1}{e} = \frac{r}{b} - \frac{r}{a} + \frac{1}{a} + \frac{1}{d} - \frac{1}{b} = (r-1) \cdot \left(\frac{1}{b} - \frac{1}{a}\right) + \frac{1}{d}$.

SCHOLIUM. If the index be $\frac{3}{2}$, as in some kinds of glass, the focal length of a double convex or a double concave lens, will be equal to the common radius; and of a planoconvex or planoconcave, equal to the diameter: if the index be $\frac{4}{3}$, as in water, the focal length will be to that of an equal lens of glass, as 3 to 2.

422. THEOREM. The joint focus of two lenses is found by adding or subtracting the reciprocals of their separate focal lengths, accordingly as they agree or differ with respect to convexity and concavity; or by dividing their product by their sum or difference.

For it may be shown in the same manner as for two surfaces, that $\frac{1}{e} = \frac{1}{f} + \frac{1}{d}$, or $\frac{1}{e} = \frac{1}{f} - \frac{1}{d}$ (421); and $e = \frac{fd}{f \pm d}$

423. DEFINITION. The centre of a lens is a point, between which and the centres of the surfaces, segments of the axis are intercepted, proportional to the respective radii, and lying on the concave or convex sides of both surfaces.

424. THEOREM. All rays, which in their passage through the lens, tend to the centre, are transmitted in a direction parallel to their original direction.

Let AB pass through the centre C, and join AD and BE; then since CD : E :: AD : BE, AD is parallel to BE; and the surfaces at A and B being also parallel, the ray is equally refracted in contrary directions at A and B.

SCHOLIUM. In some cases, the optical centre may be without the lens, but no practical inconvenience results from considering it as always within the lens, especially when the thickness is evanescent; and then the two parallel directions of the rays passing through it must coincide in the same line. Now when the focus of incident rays is removed a little from the axis, the inclination of each ray to the surface being increased or diminished nearly alike, their mutual inclination after refraction or reflection remains but little changed, and the conjugate focus is nearly at the same distance as before. Hence we may find the place of the conjugate focus of a point without the axis; for since the ray, which passes through the centre of the surface or lens, preserves its rectilinear direction, the focus must necessarily be in this line, and at the distance already determined for rays in the direction of the axis: and thus we have the magnitude, as well as the place, of the image of any object, sufficiently near the truth for common purposes.

425. THEOREM. When a ray of light is refracted at the surface of a sphere, the intersections of the incident ray with a concentric sphere of which the diameter is greater in the ratio of the index of refraction to unity, and of the refracted ray with another concentric sphere which is smaller in the same proportion, are in the same radius.

Let AB : AC :: AC : AD :: 1 : r; then the triangles ABC, ACD are equiangular, and ∠ACD=ABC. But sin. ABC : sin. ACB :: AC : AB :: r : 1, and ACB is the angle of refraction corresponding to the angle of incidence ACD. This theorem affords an easy method of constructing problems relative to spherical refraction.

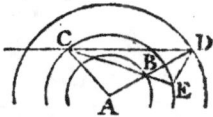

SCHOLIUM. It may easily be shown, that if the ray CD were reflected at D, it would meet the ray CE at E; and supposing the velocity greater in the rarer medium, in the ratio of the densities, it would arrive there in the same time; and if DE were again reflected at E, it would coincide with CE again refracted.

426. DEFINITION. When a pencil of rays falls obliquely on the surface of a sphere, the point towards which those rays, which are situated in any plane passing through the axis, are made to converge, may be called the peripheric focus.

SCHOLIUM. These points form a line of concourse, which is a part of the circumference of a circle; and this is the focus at which the image of a circular circumference becomes most distinct. It has hitherto been in general exclusively considered, under the name of the geometrical focus of oblique rays.

427. DEFINITION. The focus of collateral rays, situated in a conical surface having the same axis with the sphere, may be called the radial focus.

SCHOLIUM. It is obvious that the rays of the collateral planes, which are always perpendicular to the surface of the sphere, can only meet in the axis: therefore the points in which the collateral rays of a pencil meet, constitute a portion of the axis. The image of any radiating lines, crossing the axis, must evidently be most distinct at the radial focus.

428. THEOREM. When rays fall obliquely on a spherical surface, the index of refraction being r, the actual cosine of incidence t, the cosine of refraction u, and the

focal distance of the incident rays d, the distance of the peripheric focus of refracted rays will be $\dfrac{rduu}{rdu-dt-tt}=e$.

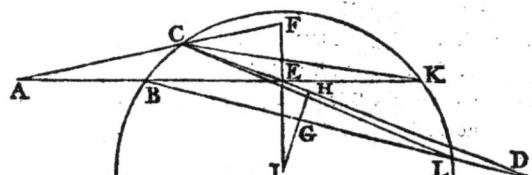

Let AB and AC be two incident rays infinitely near to each other, refracted into the positions BD, CD; then EF, GH, will be the increments of the sines EI, GI, which are in the constant ratio of r to 1. Now the angle at A being to the radius unity as EF to AE, is $=\dfrac{EF}{AE}$, and the angle at $D=\dfrac{GH}{GD}$, and $\angle A : \angle D :: \dfrac{r}{AE} : \dfrac{1}{GD} :: r.GD : AE$. But $\angle A : \angle BKC :: BK : AB$, and $\angle BKC(=BLC) : \angle D :: BD : BL$, therefore $\angle A : \angle D :: BK.BD : AB.BL :: BE.BD : AB.BG :: r.GD : AE$, or $te : du :: r(e-u) : d+t$, $det+ett=dure-duru$, $rdue-dte-tte=rduu$, and $e=\dfrac{rduu}{rdu-dt-tt}$. If for t and u we substitute at and au, taking t and u the cosines to the radius unity, we have $e=\dfrac{rduu}{rdu-dt-att}$, which, when $a=\infty$, becomes $\dfrac{rduu}{-tt}$; and if $d=\infty$, $e=\dfrac{rauu}{ru-t}$.

429. Definition. The relative centre is the point of intersection of the right lines joining any two pairs of conjugate peripheric foci of pencils of oblique rays, falling on the same point of a curved surface in the same direction.

Scholium. For the radial foci, the relative centre is always the centre of the sphere.

430. Theorem. The relative centre is situated in the bisection of that chord of the circle of curvature which bisects the two chords cut off from the incident and refracted rays.

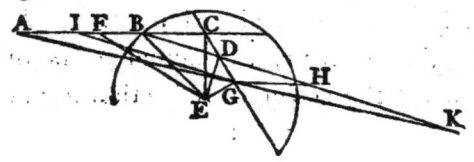

Let AB be d, BC, t; BD, u, then CE and DE being the sines of incidence and refraction, are to each other as r to 1, or making $EF=r.EB$, as EF to EB, and since CEF becomes equal to the angle of refraction, or BED, $\angle BEF= CBD=CED$, and BEF, DEC are equiangular, and DEG is also similar to BEC, and FB : BC :: CD : DG; and if $GH \parallel BC$, $:: BC : GH=\dfrac{BCq}{FB}$; also FB : FC :: CD : CG :: BD : BH$=\dfrac{BD.FC}{FB}$, and AI : BH $(=IG) :: AB : BK$, or AB : $\dfrac{BCq}{FB} : \dfrac{BD.FC}{FB} :: AB : BK=\dfrac{AB.BD.FC}{AB.FB-BCq}$. But since $FE=r.BE$, $FC=r.BD=ru$, and $FB=ru-t$, whence $BK=\dfrac{duru}{rdu-dt-tt}=e$. And it is obvious that AI and HK are the distances of the conjugate foci from the foci of parallel rays coming in a contrary direction, and that their product is always equal to IB.BH.

431. Theorem. For parallel rays falling obliquely on a double convex or double concave lens of inconsiderable thickness, of which the radii are a and b, the distance of the peripheric focus is $e=\dfrac{ab}{a+b} \cdot \dfrac{tt}{ru-t}$; t and u being the cosines corresponding to the radius unity.

This expression is obtained by substitution and reduction, from $e=\dfrac{raduu}{rdu-dt-att}$, taking for r, $\dfrac{1}{r}$; for a, $-b$; for u, t; for d, $-\dfrac{rauu}{ru-t}$; and for t, u.

432. Theorem. The radius of a sphere being a, the actual cosine of incidence t, that of refraction, u, the distance of the focus of incident rays from the given point d, from the centre of the sphere c, the distance of the radial focus from the point of incidence is $\dfrac{rdaa}{d.(ru-t)-aa}$, and from the centre $\dfrac{caa}{d.(ru-t)-aa}$.

Let AB be $=r.AC$, then $\angle BAC$ will be the angle of deviation, and $BC=ru-t$; and if $DE \parallel CF$, the triangles

ABC and DEC are similar, and AC : BC :: DC : CE = $\frac{DC.BC}{AC}$, and AE $= \frac{DC.BC}{AC} - AC$; but AE : AD :: AC : AF $= \frac{AD.ACq}{DC.BC - ACq} = \frac{caa}{d.(ru-t) - aa}$; also $1 : r :: CA : BA ::$ CD : DE $= rd$; and AE : DE :: AC : CF $= \frac{DE.ACq}{DC.BC - ACq}$ $= \frac{rdaa}{d.(ru-t) - aa} = f$. When $a = \infty$, $f = rd$; when $d = \infty$, $f = \frac{raa}{ru - t}$. If t and u denote the tabular cosines, $f = \frac{rda}{d.(ru-t) - a}$, and when $d = \infty$, $f = \frac{ra}{ru - t}$.

433. Theorem. For parallel rays, falling obliquely on a double convex or double concave lens, the distance of the radial focus is $\frac{ab}{(a+b).(ru-t)}$; u and t denoting the cosines corresponding to the radius unity.

This expression is obtained from $f = \frac{rda}{d.(ru-t) - a}$, substituting $\frac{1}{r}$ for r, $\frac{-rn}{ru-t}$ for d, $-b$ for a, t for u, and u for t.

434. Theorem. The longitudinal aberration of rays refracted at a spherical surface is ultimately $\frac{qc^2(ra+c)}{rb.(qb-a)^2}.y$, q being $r-1$, a the radius, b the focal distance of incident rays, $a + b = c$, and y the versed sine of the arc of the surface; and, for parallel rays, $\frac{y}{qr}$.

The focus of the rays next the axis being A, the longitudinal aberration will be AB. Now

AC is $\frac{caa}{b.(qa) - aa}$, and BC $= \frac{caa}{d.(ru-t) - aa}$, d being DE, and AB $= \frac{caa.(d.(ru-t) - qab)}{(qab - aa).(d.(ru-t) - aa)}$ but EB $= \frac{rdaa}{d.(ru-t) - aa}$ and AB $=$ EB . $\frac{c(d(ru-t) - qab)}{rd(qab - aa)} =$ EB . $\frac{c}{r(qab - aa)} . \left(ru-t - qa\frac{b}{d}\right)$; but FD : ED :: GD : HD, and $\frac{b}{d} = \frac{d+2t}{b+2a}$, and AB $=$ EB . $\frac{c}{r(qab - aa)} . \left(ru-t - qa.\frac{d+2t}{b+2a}\right)$, and AI : EI :: AB : AK, which is ultimately $=$ EI . $\frac{c}{r(qab - aa)} . \left(ru-t - \right.$

$\left. qa.\frac{d+2t}{b+2a}\right)$. If we substitute for EB its ultimate value FA $= \frac{rab}{qb - a}$, AB will become $\frac{bc}{(qb-a)^2}.\left(ru - t - qa.\frac{d+2t}{b+2a}\right)$. Now, when x' is small, $x' = \frac{(xx)'}{2x}$, since $(xx)' = 2x\dot{x}$, therefore since EI $= \sqrt{(2ay - yy)}$, or $\sqrt{(2ay)}$, DE or $d = \sqrt{((b+y)^2 + 2ay)} = b + \frac{c}{b}y$; and since the small angle ACEG is equal to EDC + ECD, its sine may be considered as the sum of their sines, and $s = \sqrt{(2ay)} . \left(1 + \frac{a}{b}\right)$, $ss = 2ay.\frac{cc}{bb}$, $\sqrt{(aa-ss)} = t = a - \frac{cc}{bb}y$, $\frac{ss}{rr} = 2ay.\frac{cc}{rrbb}$, and $u = a - \frac{cc}{rrbb}.y$, whence $ru = ra - \frac{cc}{rbb}.y$, and $ru-t = qa + \frac{qcc}{rbb}y$; but $d + 2t = b + 2a + \left(\frac{c}{b} - \frac{2cc}{bb}\right).y$, $\frac{d+2t}{b+2a} = 1 + \frac{cb-2cc}{(b+2a)bb}.y = 1 - \frac{2cc-cb}{(c+a)bb}.y = 1 - \frac{cc+ca+cc-ca-cb}{(c+a)bb}.y = 1 - \frac{c}{bb}.y$; and AB $= \frac{bc}{(qb-a)^2}.\left(qa + \frac{qcc}{rbb}.y - qa + \frac{qac}{bb}.y\right) = \frac{qbc}{(qb-a)^2}$ $\left(\frac{cc+rac}{rbb}\right)y = \frac{qc^2(ra+c)}{rb(qb-a)^2}.y$. This, when $b = \infty$, becomes $\frac{y}{qr}$. When $c = -ra$, the aberration vanishes, the point D being in the circumference of the outer circle employed for determining the refraction (425).

435. Theorem. The longitudinal aberration of parallel rays refracted by a double convex or double concave lens of inconsiderable thickness, and of equal radii, the refractive density being 1.5, is to the thickness of the lens as 130 to 81.

The effect of the aberration at the first surface is modified by the refraction of the second, and instead of $\frac{y}{qr}$, or $\frac{4y}{3}$, becomes $\frac{8}{81}y$; for the first focal length is $\frac{ra}{q}$ which may be called $-d$, and $\frac{1}{e} = \frac{1}{ra} + \frac{1}{rd} - \frac{1}{a}$, whence $\frac{e'}{ee} = \frac{rd'}{rrdd}$, nearly, and $e' = \frac{ee}{rdd}d'$; but $dd = \frac{rraa}{qq} = qaa$ and $e = a$, whence $e' = \frac{2}{27}d' = \frac{8}{81}y$. Then substituting in the formula $\frac{qc^2(ra+c)}{rb(qb-a)^2}.y$, for r, $\frac{3}{2}$; for q, $-\frac{1}{2}$; for b, $\frac{ra}{q} = 3a$; and for c, $4a$, we have $\frac{-\frac{1}{2}16a^2(\frac{3}{2}a + 4a)}{2a(2a)^2}.y = \frac{16.14}{72}.y = \frac{28}{9}y$, which added to $\frac{8}{81}y$, makes $\frac{260}{81}$, or $\frac{130}{81}$ of the thickness.

SCHOLIUM. In a similar manner it may be shown, that if the radii are a and b, and the versed sines y and z, the aberration will be $\frac{bb}{qr^4(a+b)^4} \cdot y + \frac{ra+qb}{(a+b)^4} \cdot \left(\frac{qr+q}{rra}tb + \frac{2r+1}{r}b + \frac{ra}{q} \right) \cdot z$. Hence, by proper substitutions, the aberration may be expressed in terms of the focal length and one of the radii, and by making its fluxion vanish, the form of the lens of least aberration may be determined. The aberration of a system of lenses may be found in a similar manner, and their proportions may be so determined that the whole aberration may be destroyed.

436. THEOREM. The radial image of an object infinitely distant, formed by a double convex lens of equal radii, is a portion of a spherical surface of which the radius is to the focal length of the lens as r to $r+1$; and the peripheric image coincides at the axis with a surface of which the radius is to the focal length as r to $3r+1$.

The focal length for oblique rays is $AB = \frac{a}{2(ru-t)}$; but if $CD = r.AC$, C being the centre of curvature, AD is $(ru-t)a$ (432), and drawing the circle DE, $AE = \frac{AF.AG}{AD} = \frac{(rq+q)aa}{(ru-t)a} = rq+q\frac{a}{ru-t} = 2(rq+q).AB$. The point B will therefore always be situated in a figure similar to DE, that is, in a circle, and the radius of this circle will be $\frac{CD}{2rq+2q}$ or $\frac{ra}{2rq+2q}$; but the focal length of the lens being $\frac{a}{2q}$, the radius will be to the focal length as $\frac{r}{r+1}$ to 1, or as r to $r+1$. Now the distance of the peripheric focus is $\frac{att}{2(ru-t)} = AB \cdot tt$, and the curvature of the image may be found by adding the sagitta of any small arc x in the circle BH to the difference of AB and AB.tt. The sagitta belonging to BH is $\frac{xx(r+1)}{2re}$ and ultimately AB.$(1-tt) = AH$. $(2-2t) = \frac{xx}{e}$, and the sum is $\frac{xx.(3r+1)}{2re}$, and xx divided by this becomes $\frac{2re}{3r+1}$, therefore $\frac{re}{3r+1}$ is the radius of curvature, which is to the focal length e as r to $3r+1$.

SCHOLIUM. Hence the mean radius of curvature of the image at the axis may be called $\frac{re}{2r+1}$, which is to e, when $r=\frac{1}{2}$, or as 3 to 8. It has hitherto been usual to neglect the effect of the obliquity, and to consider the focal length as the radius of curvature of the image; but it is obvious that this estimation is extremely erroneous. By similar calculations it may be found that the radius of curvature of the image of a right line, formed by a single spherical surface, with a diaphragm placed at its centre, so as to exclude all oblique rays, is equal to the principal focal length of the surface, whatever may be the distance of the line.

SECTION VIII. OF OPTICAL INSTRUMENTS.

437. THEOREM. When an angle is measured by means of Hadley's quadrant, and the ray proceeding from one of the objects is made to coincide, after two reflections, with the ray coming immediately from the other, the inclination of the reflecting surfaces is half the angular distance of the objects.

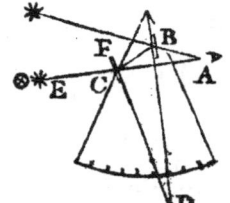

The angle $ABC = 2CBD$, and $BCE = 2BCF$; therefore $BAC = 2BCF - 2CBD = 2CBD$ (108).

438. THEOREM. When an image of an actual object is formed by any lens or speculum, it is inverted if the rays become convergent to an actual focus, but erect if they diverge from a virtual focus; and the object and image subtend equal angles at the centre of the lens; so that a convex lens and a concave mirror form an image smaller than the object, when the object is at a greater distance than twice the principal focal length; but larger, when the object is within this dis-

tance; and when it is within the principal focus, the magnified image is virtual, and erect: but a concave lens and a convex mirror, always form a virtual image, which is erect, and smaller than the object.

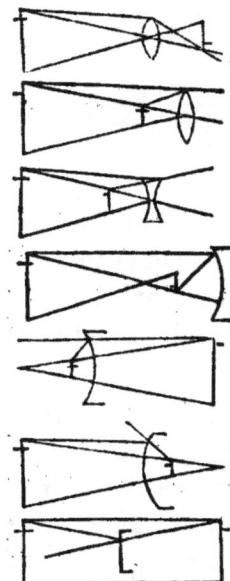

For in a lens, if the rays converge after refraction, it must be to a point beyond the centre, and the rectilinear rays will decussate in the centre; and if hey diverge, it must be from a point on the same side of the centre with the object, and the rectilinear rays have not crossed. In the concave mirror the foci are always on opposite sides of the centre of the sphere, since the sum of the reciprocals of their distance is equal to twice the reciprocal of the radius (418), except when the object is within the principal focus, and then there is an erect virtual image beyond the surface. In the convex mirror the image is always virtual and erect, being between the surface and the principal focus (419); and in the plane mirror the image is obviously erect and equal to the object.

439. THEOREM. The image of any object formed by a spherical reflecting surface subtends the same angle as the object both from the surface and from its centre.

It is obvious that the rays which pass through the centre must remain in the same right line; and since in this case $\frac{1}{e} = \frac{1}{d} - \frac{2}{a}$, and $e = \frac{ad}{a - 2d}$, or $\frac{ad}{2d - a}$, $e - a = \frac{aa - ad}{a - 2d}$, $\frac{d}{e} = 1 - \frac{2d}{a} = \frac{a - 2d}{a} = \frac{a - d}{e - a}$, and $d : e :: a - d : e - a$, but the distances from the centre are $a - d$ and $e - a$, and d and e are the distances from the surface; consequently the image and object are in both cases the bases of similar triangles.

440. AXIOM. The intensity of light is inversely as the surface on which any given portion of it is spread.

SCHOLIUM. Hence the illumination is said to decrease as the square of the distance increases.

441. THEOREM. The illumination of the image, formed by any lens or mirror, is equal to that which would be produced by the immediate effect of the surface of the lens or mirror, if equally illuminated with the object.

Supposing the whole quantity of light that falls on the lens or mirror to be collected into the image, the condensation is in the ratio of the surface of the lens to that of the image. Now the illumination produced by a surface equal to the image at the distance of the lens or mirror, is equal to the illumination produced by the object at its actual distance, supposing the brightness equal, since the linear magnitudes of the object and image are proportional to their distances from the lens or mirror, and the surfaces are as the squares of the distances; the intensity of the light falling on the lens is therefore such as the supposed surface would produce; and when this is increased in the ratio of the surface of the lens to that of the image, it becomes equal to the illumination produced by the surface of the lens, supposing it similar to that of the luminous object.

442. THEOREM. The intensity of illumination of the image of a luminous point, formed by a spherical surface, is inversely as the fourth power of the cube root of the distance from the centre.

The quantity of light which falls on any portion of the surface is as the square of its sine xx, or as the versed sine y; and the lateral aberration varies as the longitudinal aberration and as the aperture conjointly, that is as xy or as x^3; now the intensity of light is as the fluxion of the quantity of light, divided by the fluxion of the surface, or as $\frac{2x\dot{x}}{6x^5\dot{x}}$, or as $\frac{1}{x^4}$, or inversely as the fourth power of the aperture, or of the cube root of the radius of the circle of aberration.

SCHOLIUM. This is not the least circle of aberration but it is probably the circle in which the aberration has the least effect in producing indistinctness, and therefore it must be considered as determining the degree of distinctness of the image.

443. THEOREM. If the whole of the light falling uniformly on an infinitely small sphere were regularly reflected, it would be scattered equally in all directions.

The quantity of parallel rays falling on a ring, of which the breadth is z', the evanescent increment of the circle, and represented by a hollow cylinder, must be as xx', x being the sine, or as xyz', y being the cosine: but the angular dissipation after reflection is as the product of twice z' and the sine of twice the arc z, since the light forms twice as great an angle with the axis after reflection as before. But the sine of twice the arc z is $2yx$, and the product $4xyz'$ is always proportional to the former product xyz', expressing the space in which the light was uniformly spread before reflection; it will therefore be uniformly spread after reflection.

SCHOLIUM. If the quantity of light reflected varied according to any given function of the obliquity, the density of the reflected light would vary according to the same law, considering the obliquity as determined by half the angular distance of the reflected light from the axis. The density of the light reflected by a cylinder varies as the cosine y, supposing none to be lost.

444. DEFINITION. In telescopes and compound microscopes, the image formed by one lens or mirror stands in the place of a new object for another.

445. DEFINITION. In the astronomical telescope, the object glass first forms an actual inverted image nearly in the principal focus of the eyeglass, and the eyeglass a second virtual and inverted image of the first.

446. THEOREM. The magnifying power of the astronomical telescope is expressed by the quotient of the focal lengths of the glasses.

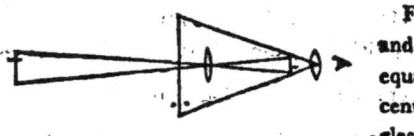

For the object and image subtend equal angles at the centre of the object glass; and the angles subtended by the image at the centre of the eyeglass and object glass are ultimately in the inverse ratio of the distances (139, 141).

447. DEFINITION. The double microscrope resembles in its construction the astronomical telescope, excepting that the distance of the lenses much exceeds their joint focal length.

448. THEOREM. The angular magnitude of an object viewed through a double microscope is greater than when viewed through the eyeglass alone, in the ratio of the distances of the object and first image, from the object glass.

For the first image may be considered as a new object in the focus of the eyeglass (424).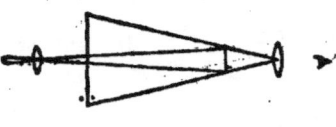

449. DEFINITION. In the Galilean telescope, or opera glass, a concave eyeglass is placed so near the object glass, that the first image would be formed beyond it, and near its principal focus.

450. THEOREM. In the Galilean telescope, the second virtual image, formed by the eyeglass, is inverted with respect to this image, and erect with respect to the object; and the magnifying power is the quotient of the focal lengths.

Since, for a concave lens $\frac{1}{e} = \frac{1}{d} - \frac{1}{f}$ (421), when d is little greater than f, e becomes very large; and the two images are on different sides of the eyeglass. The magnifying power is ultimately the quotient of the distances of the glasses from the first image.

451. DEFINITION. In day telescopes, one or more eyeglasses are added, in order to restore the image to its natural position.

SCHOLIUM. In the common day telescopes of Rheita, two eyeglasses are employed, of nearly equal focus, and so placed, as scarcely to affect the magnifying power; but in either case, they may be so disposed as to vary it at pleasure; for such an eye piece is a species of compound microscope.

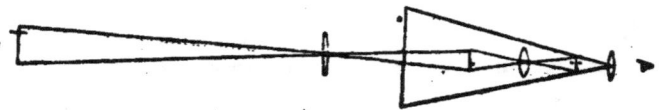

452. DEFINITION. Dr. Herschel's reflecting telescopes resemble, in their effects, the simple astronomical telescope: but the principal rays are received and reflected somewhat obliquely, in order to allow the light free access to the speculum.

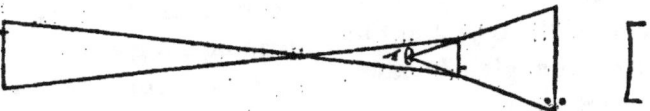

453. DEFINITION. The Newtonian reflector has a plane speculum placed in its axis, at the inclination of half a right angle, for the convenience of fixing the eyeglass in the ide of the tube.

SCHOLIUM. Dr. Herschel's construction differs from this only in the omission of the plane speculum.

454. DEFINITION. In the Gregorian telescope, the object speculum is perforated, and the image formed by it, is transmitted through the aperture, after reflection from a smaller concave speculum, which also reverts it: it is afterwards submitted to one or more eyeglasses.

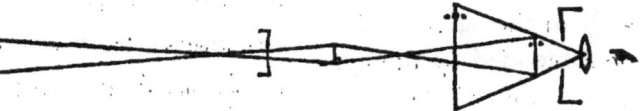

455. DEFINITION. The telescope of Cassegrain has a convex speculum instead of Gregory's smaller concave, placed within the focal distance of the large speculum, so that the first image falls near its principal focus, and the second is thrown back into the focus of the eyeglass.

SCHOLIUM. The image is here inverted.

456. DEFINITION. Dr. Smith's reflecting microscope resembles Cassegrain's telescope, but the rays of light are first admitted through a perforation in the small speculum, and prevented by a screen from falling immediately on the eye. The radii of the surfaces are equal.

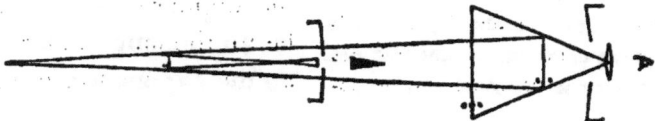

OF OPTICAL INSTRUMENTS.

457. THEOREM. In all refracting telescopes and microscopes, the diameter of the object glass is to that of its image formed beyond the eyeglass, as the angle subtended by the magnified image of the object at the place of this image, is to the angle subtended by the object at the object glass.

Supposing all the rays to be collected in their foci, those which proceed from the centre of the object glass will meet in each of its images; and those rays coincide in direction with the rays from different parts of the distant object which cross in that centre, therefore these will also meet in the same point, and with the same inclination, determining the angular magnitude of the ultimate image at an infinite distance. But the inverse ratio of these angles is the same as that of the magnitude of the object glass to its image, and the successive images to each other: for the images and objects are always as the distance from the centre, and the angles are inversely as the distances.

458. THEOREM. The field of view, or the angular magnitude of the part of the object of which the telescope forms an ultimate image, is nearly equal, in the astronomical telescope, to the angle subtended by the eyeglass at the object glass; the whole image comprehending somewhat more, and its brightest part somewhat less.

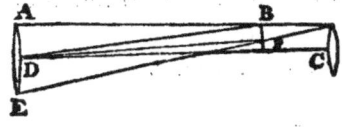

The extreme ray being AB, the angle CDB limits the whole image: but no rays coming to the eyeglass from E fall above F, therefore CDF limits the part fully illuminated.

SCHOLIUM. If a lens be added at the place of the first image, it will have no effect on the distance of any subsequent image, nor on the magnifying power, but it will enlarge the field of view, by throwing more rays on the original eyeglass. But, if the image fell exactly on such a lens, a particle of dust attached to the lens, or any accidental opacity, would intercept a portion of the image, since all the rays belonging to each point of the object are collected in the respective points of the image: the field glass is therefore generally placed somewhat nearer to the object glass, both in telescopes, and in the common compound microscopes. The best places for the various lenses in an eyepiece are partly determined from similar considerations.

459. DEFINITION. Mr. Dollond's achromatic object glasses are composed of two or more lenses, of different kinds of glass, which produce equal dispersions of the rays of different colours, with different angular deviations: the joint deviation being employed to produce an image, while the equal dispersions are opposed to each other in such a manner as to prevent a separation of colours.

460. THEOREM. The focal lengths of the two lenses of an achromatic object glass must be in the ratio of the dispersive powers of the respective substances, at an equal deviation.

If the ratios of the sines be for one glass $1+m : 1$, and $1+m+n : 1$, and for the other $1+p : 1$, and $1+p+q : 1$; then the dispersive powers will be as $\frac{n}{m}$ and $\frac{q}{p}$. Let the focal lengths of the lenses for the first kind of rays be therefore $\frac{n}{m}$ and $\frac{q}{p}$, then for the second they will be $\frac{n}{m+n}$ and $\frac{q}{p+q}$ respectively (421); and the reciprocal of the joint focus in the first case $\frac{m}{n} - \frac{p}{q}$, and in the second $\frac{m+n}{n} - \frac{p+q}{q}$ (422) $= \frac{m}{n} - \frac{p}{q}$; therefore the focal length will be the same for rays of both kinds.

SCHOLIUM. The chromatic aberration is also sometimes partially corrected in an eyepiece, by causing the image formed by the least refrangible rays to subtend, at the eyeglass, nearly the same angle with the image formed by the most refrangible rays.

461. THEOREM. If the refractive density of a medium vary as a given power of the distance from a certain central point, the angular deviation of a ray of light will be to the angle described round the centre as the exponent of the power to unity.

Since the densities are supposed to be equal at equal distances from the centre the radius must always be perpendicular to the direction of the refracting surface, and two perpendiculars falling on the direction of the ray in any two points infinitely near each other, will be the sines of incidence and refraction for the intervening surface: this perpendicular will therefore always vary inversely as the refractive density; and if the density be as the power q of the distance x, the perpendicular u will be as x^{-q}, or $u = ax^{-q}$. Now $\sqrt{(ax\dot{x}-u\dot{u})}:u::\dot{x}:\dfrac{-u\dot{x}}{\sqrt{(xx-uu)}}$ which is the increment of the arc described by the radius accompanying the ray, and $\dfrac{-bu\dot{x}}{x.\sqrt{(xx-uu)}}$ is the fluxion of a similar arc of which the radius is b. But the fluxion of the arc in the same circle of which $\dfrac{b}{x}u$ is the sine, that is, of the arc corresponding to the inclination of the ray to the radius, is $\dot{\left(\dfrac{u}{x}-\dfrac{u\dot{x}}{xx}\right)}\cdot\dfrac{x}{\sqrt{(xx-uu)}}$; and since $u = ax^{-q}$; $\dot{u} = \dfrac{-qu\dot{x}}{x}$, $\dfrac{\dot{u}}{x} = -q\dfrac{u\dot{x}}{xx}$, and the fluxion of this arc becomes $-(q+1).\dfrac{bu\dot{x}}{x.\sqrt{(xx-uu)}}$, which is to the fluxion of the arc described as $(q+1)$ to 1: therefore the finite increments of these arcs are in the same proportion. But the difference between the angle described, and the change of the inclination to the radius, is the angle of deviation, which is therefore to the angle described as q to 1, and to the change of inclination as q to $q+1$.

SCHOLIUM. It is found that the circumstances of atmospherical refraction agree nearly with such a constitution of the medium, supposing $q = -\frac{1}{5}$; but from particular circumstances which take place near the earth's surface, the terrestrial refraction, instead of being $\frac{1}{5}$ of the arc intervening between two places, is seldom more than $\frac{1}{10}$. If any two values of x are given, the ratio of the corresponding values of u is also given, and the ratio of the sines of inclination to the radius will be constant for any rays passing through the same depth of the medium; and the angle of inclination being determined, the angle of deviation will be to this angle in the ratio of q to $q+1$. For the whole height of the atmosphere, the logarithm of the ratio of the sines of inclination is .0007200, and $q:q+1::1:6$; so that if we deduct this logarithm from the logarithmic sine of the apparent zenith distance, we shall find an angle, which differs from the zenith distance by six times the refraction, at a mean height of the barometer and thermometer. At the horizon the refraction is 33'; at the altitude 45°, 57''.

462. DEFINITION. The rainbow is produced by a combination of refractions and reflections, which cause the sun's rays of different colours, to be transmitted most copiously to the spectator, from the spherical drops of rain or dew, under different angles of incidence. In the interior rainbow the rays are once reflected at the posterior surface of the drop; in the exterior they are twice reflected.

463. THEOREM. In the interior rainbow, the tangent of the angle of incidence is twice, in the exterior three times, that of the angle of refraction.

When parallel rays fall on a sphere, and after refraction at their entrance, are reflected again from the posterior concave surface, and refracted a second time in their passage out of the sphere, the ray in the direction of the axis emerges in the same line, but the lateral rays deviate more and more from their former direction, till, at a certain distance from the axis, the deviation is again lessened; and, as in other maximums and minimums, the change of the deviation being slowest when it becomes a maximum, the light being most dense where this change is smallest, the conical surface formed by the rays most inclined to the axis, determines the direction of the strongest light; we must therefore compute the magnitude of the greatest deviation. Now $\angle$ ABC $= 2$ABD (405) and ABD $=$ EFD $-$ BEF $=$ DEF $-$ BEF, therefore the difference between the angles of refraction and of deviation at E, must be a maximum, and their fluxions must be equal, therefore the fluxions of their sum DEB must be double that of DEF. 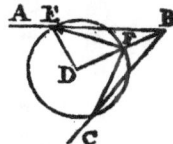 Now, when the sines of two arcs are in a constant ratio, the fluxions of the sines are in the same ratio as the sines themselves: and the fluxion of the sine is to that of the arc, as the cosine to the radius (142), or as the sine to the tangent (121), therefore the fluxions of the two arcs are as the tangents. Hence the tangent of DEB must be twice the tangent of DEF. Let their sines be rx and x; then their cosines will be $\sqrt{(1-r^2x^2)}$ and $\sqrt{(1-x^2)}$, and their tangents $\dfrac{rx}{\sqrt{(1-r^2x^2)}}$ and $\dfrac{x}{\sqrt{(1-x^2)}}$;

and $\frac{rx}{\sqrt{(1-r^2x^2)}} = \frac{2x}{\sqrt{(1-x^2)}}$, or $\frac{r^2}{1-r^2x^2} = \frac{4}{1-x^2}$; $r^2 - r^2x^2 = 4 - 4r^2x^2$, $3r^2x^2 = 4 - r^2$, and the square of the sine of incidence DEB, $r^2x^2 = \frac{1}{3}(4-r^2)$. The whole angle of deviation in a sphere of water, is thus found to be for red rays, 42°, and for violet $40\frac{1}{2}°$; so that the external part of the rainbow is red. When there are two intermediate reflections, we have for the ultimate inclination, first the deviation at the first surface, then at each reflection two right angles, lessened by twice the angle of refraction, and again, the deviation at the transmission; so that the four right angles destroying one another, the whole inclination is twice the difference of the angle of deviation, and twice the angle of refraction, and the tangent of the angle of incidence must be three times the tangent of the angle of refraction; whence we have $r^2x^2 = \frac{1}{8}(9-r^2)$. The whole deviation of red rays, twice reflected, is about 51°, and of violet rays, 54°; so that in this rainbow the violet colour is external.

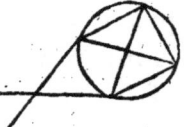

464. THEOREM. In the eye of an animal, the image which is formed on the retina is inverted with respect to the object.

The eye is an irregular spheroid, composed of transparent substances of various refractive densities, calculated to collect the rays of light, diverging from each point of an object, on a distinct point of its posterior concave surface, according to the angular place of the object. The first refraction is at the surface of the cornea; but the cornea, being very nearly of equable thickness, has little effect by its own refractive power. Its concavity is filled and distended by the aqueous humour, which is partially divided by the uvea or iris, perforated by the pupil. Immediately behind the uvea, and connected to its base by the ciliary processes, is the crystalline lens, a substance much more refractive than the aqueous humour, and increasing in density towards its centre. The remaining cavity is filled by an aqueous fluid, lodged in a texture of extremely fine membrane, and called the vitreous humour. The retina which is capable of transmitting to the sensorium the impression of the colour and intensity of the light, together with a distinction of the precise situation of the focal point, lines the whole posterior part of this cavity, it is semitransparent, and supported by the choroid, a very opaque black or brown membrane, continued from the uvea and ciliary processes: but immediately where the retina is connected with the optic nerve, the choroid is necessarily perforated; and at this part a small portion of the retina is insensible. The whole is surrounded by an opaque continuation of the cornea, called the sclerotica.

An image is formed on the retina according to the common laws of refraction, it is therefore inverted with respect to the object; but this inversion has no relation to the transmission of impressions constituting vision.

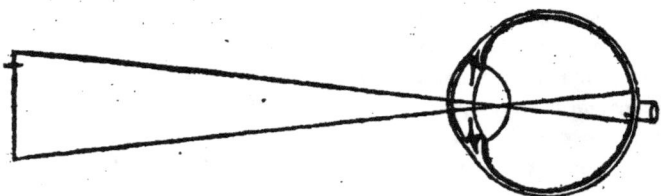

465. THEOREM. If a sphere, of which the radius is a, have a nucleus of uniform density, its radius being b, and its refractive density to that of the surrounding medium as r to 1, and if the external parts of the sphere vary in density according to a certain power of the distance from the centre, until they become at the surface similar to the surrounding medium, the distance of the principal focus of the sphere from the centre will be $\frac{q+1}{2q} \cdot \frac{rab}{rb-a}$, q being $\frac{l.r}{l.b-.la}$; and if a lens consist of two equal portions of such a sphere, the principal focal length of the lens will be less by one fourth of the thickness of the portion removed.

Since the density varies as a certain power q of the distance, $1 : r :: a^q : b^q$, and $r = \left(\frac{b}{a}\right)^q$, whence $q = $ log. r : log. $\frac{b}{a}$, or $\frac{l.r}{l.b-.la}$. Now let AB be the path of the

ADDITIONS.   83

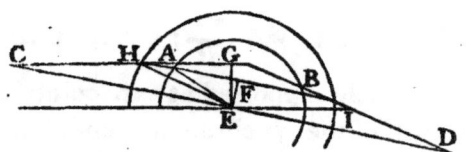

ray within the nucleus, and CD a diameter parallel to AB; call EF, s, then EG perpendicular to CH will be rs, and the sine of EHG to that of EAF as $\frac{rs}{a}$ to $\frac{s}{b}$; and since the angles are evanescent, they will be in the same ratio as their sines, and the deviation ECH is $\frac{q}{q+1}\left(\frac{rs}{a} - \frac{s}{b}\right)$ (461): but ECH : EH .. : EHC : EC $\frac{q+1}{q} \cdot \frac{ab}{s.(rb-a)}$, and if EI ∥ CH, it is obvious that the focal distance EI is half CG or CE; and that if AB be diminished by the removal of a part of the nucleus, CG will be dimi-half as much, and EI one fourth.

SCHOLIUM. If $q = -1$, or $rb = a$, this expression fails, the numerator and divisor vanishing: in such cases the value of a fraction is evidently equal to the quotient of the evanescent increments, or of the fluxions. Now $\frac{q+1}{2q}$. $\frac{rab}{rb-a} = \frac{rab}{2q} \cdot \frac{q+1}{rb-a}$, of which the latter factor only fails; and its value may be found by substituting for r, and making the exponent q variable; thus $rb = \left(\frac{b}{a}\right)^q b$ and the fluxion of $\left(\frac{b}{a}\right)^q$ is $\left(h.\, l.\, \frac{b}{a}\right) r\dot{q}$, which is to $\dot{q}$ as $\left(h.\, l.\, \frac{b}{a}\right) r$ to 1; and the focal distance becomes $\frac{a}{2q.(h.\, l.\left(\frac{b}{a}\right))}$ or $\frac{a}{2(h.\, l.\, r)}$.

ADDITIONS.

After article 331.

331. B. THEOREM. The force acting on any point of a uniform elastic rod, bent a little from the axis, varies as the second fluxion of the curvature, or as the fourth fluxion of the ordinate.

For if we consider the rod as composed of an infinite number of small inflexible pieces, united by elastic joints, the strain, produced by the elasticity of each joint, must be considered as the cause of two effects, a force tending to press the joint towards its concave side, and a force half as great as this, urging the remoter extremities of the pieces in a contrary direction; for it is only by external pressures, applied so as to counteract these three forces, that the pieces can be held in equilibrium. Now when the force, acting against the convex side of each joint, is equal to the sum of the forces derived from the flexure of the two neighbouring joints, the whole will remain in equilibrium: and this will be the case whether the curvature be equal throughout, or vary uniformly, since in either case the curvature at any point is equal to the half sum of the neighbouring curvatures; and it is only the difference of the curvature from this half sum, which is as the second fluxion of the curvature, that determines the accelerating force.

After article 339.

339. B. THEOREM. The stiffness of a cylinder is to that of its circumscribing prism as three times the bulk of the cylinder to four times that of the prism.

The force of each stratum of the cylinder may be considered as acting on a lever of which the length is equal to its distance x from the axis: for although there is no fixed fulcrum at the axis, yet the whole force is exactly the same as if such a fulcrum were placed there, since the opposite actions of the opposite parts would remove all pressure from the fulcrum. The tension of each stratum being also as the distance x, and the breadth being called $2y$, the fluxion of the force on either side of the axis will be $2x^2 y\dot{x}$, while that of the force of the prism is $2x^2\dot{x}$, and its fluent $\frac{2}{3}x^3$. But the fluent of $2x^2 y\dot{x}$, or $2\sqrt{(1-xx)}x^2\dot{x}$, calling the radius unity, is $\frac{1}{4}(z - y^3 x)$, z being the area of the portion of the section included between the stratum and the axis, of which the fluxion is $y\dot{x}$; for the fluxion of $z - y^3 x$ is $y\dot{x} - y^3\dot{x} - 3y^2 x\dot{y} = y\dot{x} - y^3\dot{x} - 3y^2 x.\left(\frac{-x\dot{x}}{y}\right) = y\dot{x} + 3y x^2\dot{x} = 4yx^2\dot{x}$; and when $x = 1$, and $y = 0$, the fluent becomes $\frac{1}{4}z$; while the force of the prism is expressed by $\frac{2}{3}$.

SCHOLIUM. It is obvious that the strength and resilience are in this case in the same ratio as the stiffness. The strength of a tube may be found by deducting from the strength of the whole cylinder that of the part removed, reduced in the ratio of the diameters.

After article 371.

SCHOLIUM. The strain produced by the pressure of a fluid on an elastic substance which confines it, may be determined from the principles which have been already laid down respecting the flexure of such substances. Thus if a plank placed in a vertical situation, be supported at its two extremities only, and exposed to the pressure of a cistern of water of which the surface coincides with its upper end, the curvature will be every where as $ax - x^3$, x being the distance from the surface, and will be greatest where the depth is to the length of the plank as 1 to $\sqrt{3}$. If we wish to find the strength of a circular plate, simply supported at its circumference, we must consider the effect of the curvatures in two directions at right angles to each other; and we shall find that the second fluxion of the curvature in a direction perpendicular to a radius of the circle at any point, is simply as the curvature in the direction of the radius. The curvature may therefore be represented by the difference between a constant quantity and the ordinate of an elastic curve, the ordinate itself representing the force immediately arising from the curvature; and since this curve is supposed to deviate but little from a right line, its ordinates become equal to the mean of the ordinates of two logarithmic curves, and the position of its tangent may be determined accordingly. Hence it may be shown, that in order to break such a plate, the height of the fluid must be to the height which would break a square plate of the same length, supported at the ends only, as $\sqrt{3}$. h.l. $(2 + \sqrt{3})$ or 2.2811 to 1. The height required to break a square plate is twice as great, as if the weight of the fluid were collected in the middle of the length of the square (312).

For article 398.

398. THEOREM. When a prismatic elastic rod is fixed at one end, its vibrations are performed in the same time with those of a pendulum of which the length is $\frac{.9707 l^4}{ddh}$ l being the length, d the depth, and h the height of the modulus of elasticity: also if n denote the number of complete vibrations in a second, the measures being expressed in feet, h will be $1.1907 \frac{n^2 l^4}{d^2}$; and if a prismatic rod be loosely supported at two points only, the length of the synchronous pendulum will be $\frac{.023976 l^4}{ddh}$, and $h = .02941 \frac{n^2 l^4}{d^2}$, or $\frac{n^2 l^4}{34 d^2}$; and in this case, for a cylindrical rod of which d is the diameter, $h = \frac{2 n^2 l^4}{51 d^2}$, the time of vibration being to that of the circumscribing prismatic rod as 2 to the square root of 3.

We must suppose the form of the curve, in which the rod vibrates, to be such, that all its points may perform their vibrations in a similar manner, and arrive at the line of rest at the same time; on this supposition we may determine the time in which the rod is capable of vibrating; and if the time of vibration is the same in all cases, the determination will hold good in all; if not, the problem is not capable of a general resolution; but there appears to be little or no difference in the simple sounds excited in various manners, this variety arising principally from a combination of secondary sounds. The form of the curve must therefore be such, that the fourth fluxion of the ordinate may be proportional to the ordinate itself; its equation may be found either by means of logarithmic and angular measures, or more simply by an infinite series.

The conditions of the vibration must determine the value of the coefficients: supposing the loose extremity to be the origin of the curve, the curvature and its fluxion must begin from nothing: for the curvature at the end cannot be finite, nor can its fluxion be finite, since in these cases an infinite force, or a finite force applied to an infinitely small portion of the rod, would be required, and the force could not be proportional to the ordinate; the initial ordinate must also be independent of the absciss; in the case of a rod fixed at the end, the ordinate and its fluxion must both vanish at the fixed point; and in the case of a rod not fixed, the second and third fluxions of the ordinate must also vanish at the remoter end, and the centre of gravity of the curve must remain in the quiescent line, the whole area, considered as belonging to either side of the basis, becoming equal to nothing; a condition which will be found identical with that of the third fluxion vanishing at the remoter end.

The series for a curve, in which the fourth fluxion of the ordinate is to be as the ordinate, can only be of this form,
$$y = a + \frac{bax^4}{2.3.4.l^4} + \frac{b^2 ax^8}{2.3.4.5.6.7.8 l^8} + \ldots + \frac{cax}{l} + \frac{bcax^5}{2.3.4.5 l^5}$$

$+\frac{b^2cax^9}{2..9l^9}+\ldots+\frac{bdax^6}{l^6}+\frac{bdax^8}{3..6l^8}+\ldots+\frac{cax^3}{l^3}+\frac{bcax^7}{4..7l^7}$
$+\ldots$, for the fourth fluxion of this expression, divided by b, is of the same form with the expression itself; and the number of terms allows it to fulfil all the conditions that may be required. In both the cases here proposed, the coefficients d and e vanish, because the second and third fluxions are initially evanescent, and the equation becomes
$y = a + \frac{bax^4}{2..4l^4} + \frac{b^2ax^8}{2..8l^8} + \frac{b^3ax^{12}}{2..12l^{12}} + \ldots + \frac{cax}{l} + \frac{bcax^5}{2..5l^5}$
$+ \frac{b^2cax^9}{2..9l^9} + \frac{b^3cax^{13}}{2..13l^{13}} + \ldots$. In the first case, when $x=l$, or $\frac{x}{l}=1$, $y=0$, and $\dot{y}=0$, whence $1 + \frac{b}{2..4}$
$+ \frac{b^2}{2..8} + \frac{b^3}{2..12} + \ldots + c + \frac{bc}{2..5} + \frac{b^2c}{2..9} + \frac{b^3c}{2..13}$
$+\ldots = 0$, and $\frac{b}{2.3} + \frac{b^2}{2..7} + \frac{b^3}{2..11} + \ldots + c + \frac{bc}{2..4}$
$+ \frac{b^2c}{2..8} + \frac{b^3c}{2..12} + \ldots = 0$; therefore $-c =$

$$\frac{1 + \frac{b}{2..4} + \frac{b^2}{2..8} + \frac{b^3}{2..12} + \ldots}{1 + \frac{b}{2..5} + \frac{b^2}{2..9} + \frac{b^3}{2..13} + \ldots}, \text{ and } =$$

$$\frac{\frac{b}{2.3} + \frac{b^2}{2..7} + \frac{b^3}{2..11} + \ldots}{1 + \frac{b}{2..4} + \frac{b^2}{2..1} + \frac{b^3}{2..12} + \ldots}.$$

Hence, by multiplying the numerator of each fraction by the denominator of the other, and arranging the products according to the powers of b, we obtain the equation $1 - \frac{1}{3.4}b + \frac{4}{3..8}b^2 -$
$\frac{16}{3..12}b^3 + \ldots = 0$, which has an infinite number of roots; the first two being $b = 12.3623$, and $b = 489.4$. In a similar manner we obtain, for the second case, making the second fluxion of y, and either its third fluxion, or the area, vanish when $x = l$, the equation $\frac{1}{3.4} - \frac{4}{3..8}b + \frac{16}{3..12}$
$b^2 - \frac{64}{3..16}b^3 + \ldots = 0$; and of this the first two roots are $b = 500.5$ and $b = 3803$. From these values of b, those of c may be readily found; and for each value after the first, the rod has an additional quiescent point.

In order to determine the time of vibration, we must compare the force acting on a particle x' at the end of the rod with its weight. The force is $\frac{bbm}{12ar}$ (321), a being equal to $\frac{1}{2}x'$, r to $\frac{\ddot{x}\dot{x}}{\dot{y}}$ (194), and b being the depth, which we may

here call d: but the weight of the particle x' is $\frac{m}{h}x'$, and the force is to that of gravity as $\frac{ddh}{6x'x'}\cdot\frac{\ddot{y}}{\dot{x}\dot{x}}$ is to unity. Now $\frac{\ddot{y}}{\dot{x}\dot{x}} = \frac{bax'^2}{2l^4}$; for, when x is evanescent, the subsequent terms are inconsiderable in comparison with this, and the force is $\frac{baddh}{12l^4}$, the space to be described being a; and if the space became $\frac{12l^4}{bddh}$, and the force equal to that of gravity, the vibration would be performed in the same time: this is therefore the length of the synchronous pendulum; that is, for the fundamental sound, in the first case $\frac{.9707l^4}{ddh}$, and in the second $.023976\frac{l^4}{ddh}$.

A pendulum, of which the length is $\frac{.9707l^4}{ddh}$ feet, makes $\frac{d}{l^2}\sqrt{\left(\frac{h}{.9707}\cdot\frac{39.13}{1.2}\right)}$ vibrations in a second, and $\frac{d}{2l^2}\sqrt{\left(\frac{h}{.9707}\cdot\frac{39.13}{12}\right)} = n$ double vibrations, such as are considered in the estimation of musical sounds. Hence $h = 1.1907\left(\frac{nll}{d}\right)^2$. And in the same manner, for a rod loosely supported at two points, $h = .02941\left(\frac{nll}{d}\right)^2$.

When the rod is loosely fixed at both ends, the figure coincides with the harmonic curve, (398. SCHOLIUM), and the length of the equivalent pendulum is $\frac{12l^4}{c^4d^2h}$, c being 3.1416, and c^4, or b, 97.41.

If a prismatic bar supported at the extremities, be depressed by a weight equal to a portion of itself of which the length is gl, the depression being e, h will be $\frac{gl^4}{4dde}$, and when $h = \frac{n^2l^4}{34d^4}$, $n^2 = 8.5\frac{g}{e}$, e being expressed in feet. The weight under which the bar may begin to bend, (323) will be equal to that of a portion of which the length is $.0242n^2l^2$.

The stiffness of a cylinder being to that of its circumscribing prism as three times its mass to four times that of the prism, the relative force will be $\frac{3}{4}$ as great as in the prism, and the time will be increased in the subduplicate ratio, or as 1 to .866. If a cylinder be compared with a prism of the same length and weight, its vibrations will be less frequent in the ratio of 300 to 307, or nearly of 43 to 44.

The second values of b show the proportion of the first harmonic or secondary sounds of the rods, the length of the synchronous pendulum being diminished in the ratios of 1 to 39.59, and 1 to 7.6, and the times of vibration in the ratios of 1 to 6.292, and of 1 to 2.757.

SCHOLIUM. All these results are amply confirmed by experiment, and they afford an easy method of comparing the elasticity of various substances. In a tuning fork of steel, l was 2.8 inches, d .125, and $n = 512$, hence h is about 8 530 000 feet. In a plate of brass, held loosely about one fifth of its length from one end, l was 6.2 inches, $d = .072$, and $n = 273$, whence $h = 4 940 000$; in a wire of inferior brass, l being 20 inches, d .225, and $n = 74$, h appears to be 4 700 000. A plate of crown glass, 6.2 inches long and .05 thick, produced a sound consisting of 284 vibrations in a second, whence $h = 9 610 000$ feet. A box scale .012 f. thick, and 1.01 f. long, gave 154 vibrations, hence $h = 5 050 000$ feet. When these substances were held in the middle, the note became higher by an octave and somewhat more than a fourth. Riccati found the difference between the elasticities of steel and brass somewhat greater than this. For ice, h appeared to be about 850 000.

Two small rods of deal, one foot in length, produced sounds, consisting of 270 and 384 vibrations in a second; their weights were 153 and 127 grains respectively: hence the formula $.0242 n^2 l^3$ gives nearly 35 and 65 pounds for the force under which they would bend; the experiment, which was made somewhat hastily, gave 36 and 50.

A CATALOGUE OF WORKS

RELATING TO

NATURAL PHILOSOPHY,

AND THE

MECHANICAL ARTS.

WITH REFERENCES TO PARTICULAR PASSAGES

AND

OCCASIONAL ABSTRACTS AND REMARKS.

CONTENTS

OF

THE CATALOGUE.

	Page
CATALOGUES	105
Collections relating to the Sciences	105
Collections of the Works of single Authors	111
Mathematics in General	113
Of Quantity and number, or Algebra	113
Proportion	114
Fractions	114
General Theorems	114
Impossible Quantities	114
Equations	114
Equations with radical quantities	115
Impossible Roots of Equations	115
Cubic and Biquadratic Equations	115
Limits of Equations	115
Machines for Equations	115
Arithmetic	115
Series	116
Interpolations, and Reduction of Observations	116
Logarithms	116
Tables of Logarithms	117
Combinations and Chances	117
Interest and Annuities	117
Geometry. Of Space in General	117
Mensuration	118
Trigonometry and Polygonometry	118
Spherical Trigonometry	119
Comparison of Variable Quantities	119
Particular Fluents	120
Properties of Curves	120
Tangents of Curves	120
Curvature	120
Quadrature of Curves	120
Length of Curves	121
Construction of Equations	121
Conic Sections in General	121
Circle	121
Ellipsis	122

CONTENTS OF THE CATALOGUE.

	Page
Hyperbola	122
Algebraical Curves of higher orders	122
Mechanical Curves	122
Cycloid	122
Involute of a Circle	122
Figures of Sines and Tangents	122
Logarithmic Curve	123
Quadratrix of the Hyperbola	123
Tractory	123
Curved Surfaces and Solids	123
Maxima of Curves	123
History of Mathematics	124
Natural Philosophy and Mechanical Arts in General	124
Mechanics in General	129
Motions of a Point in General	130
Composition of Motion	131
Accelerating Forces	131
Central Forces	132
Compound Central Forces	132
Projectiles	132
Confined Motion	132
Variable Pendulums and Elastic Surfaces	133
Motions of Simple Masses	134
Centre of Inertia	134
Momentum	134
Equilibrium of Systems, or of Compound Bodies	134
Pressure and Composition of Force	134
Mechanical Powers	135
Lever	135
Cylinders	135
Wedge	135
Screw	135
Props or Shores	135
Compound Machines	135
Centre of Gravity	135
Equilibrium of Heavy Systems	135
Equilibrium of Elastic Bodies	136
Motions of Systems, or of Compound Bodies	136
Collision	136
Rotatory Power, and Centres of Gyration, Percussion, and Oscillation	137
Constrained Revolution	138
Rotation with Progression and Resistance	138
Motions of Connected Systems	138
Bodies acting on each other	139
Pendulous Bodies	139
Vibrations independent of Gravity	139
Propagation of Motion in Solids	139
Measure of Force	139
Maximum of Mechanical Effect	140
General Derivative Laws of Mechanics	140
Practical Mechanics, and Theory of Machines	141
Projects for a Perpetual Motion	142

CONTENTS OF THE CATALOGUE.

	Page
Mathematical and Preliminary Mechanics	142
Drawing and Painting	142
Writing, Characters, Signals	143
Geometrical Instruments in General	144
Pens and Rules	144
Compasses	144
Proportional Compasses	144
Pantographs	144
Triangles	145
Measurement of Angles in General, and Construction of Instruments	145
Micrometer	145
Theodolites, Quadrants, and Sextants	145
Protractors, and Compasses for measuring Angles	146
Angular Surveying	146
Levels	146
Mathematical Machines	146
Measures	146
Modes of obtaining a Standard	146
Comparison of Measures	147
Tables of Measures. Standards	148
English Measures	150
Scotch Measures	151
Old French Measures	151
New French Measures	152
Ancient Measures	152
Modern Measures	153
Modern Measures of Surface and Capacity	155
Measuring Instruments	155
Rods	155
Chains	155
Scales	155
Micrometers	155
Hodometers. Machines for measuring Distances	156
Instruments for observing Distances	156
Surveying	156
Maritime Surveying	156
Gauging, and Measurement of Solids	156
Modelling	157
Casting	157
Sculpture	157
Perspective	157
Perspective Instruments	157
Projections of the Sphere	158
Engraving and Etching	158
Printing	158
Types	158
Musical Types	159
Copper plate Printing	159
Copying	159
Paper	159
Bookbinding	159

CONTENTS OF THE CATALOGUE.

	Page
Statics	159
Effect of the Air	159
Balances	159
Weighing Machines	159
Steelyards	160
Bent Levers	160
Spring Steelyards	160
Standard Weights	160
English Weights	161
Scotch Weights	161
Old French Weights	161
New French Weights	162
Ancient and Modern Weights	162
Ancient Weights	162
Modern Weights	162
Apothecaries' Grains	164
Sources of Motion	164
Animal Mechanics	164
Animal Force	164
Immediate Force of Men	165
Performance of Men by Machines	166
Force of Horses	167
Work of Mules	167
Inanimate Force	167
Passive Strength	168
Friction	169
Architecture in General	172
Columns and Walls; their strongest Forms	173
Particular Structures	174
Materials. Masonry, Bricks, Pavements	174
Mortars, Cements, and Stuccos	175
Security from Fire	175
Arches, Domes, and Bridges	175
Carpentry in General	178
Beams and Floors	178
Wooden Bridges and Centres	178
Roofs	178
Slating and Tiling	179
Furniture	179
Particular Edifices	180
Inclosures and Gates	180
Painting and Preservation of Wood	180
Tools	181
Machinery, or Modification of Motion	181
Regulation of Descent	181
Fire Escapes	181
Jacks	181
Application of Moving Forces	181
Economy of Motion	182
Springs	182
Jointed Work	182
Production and Rectification of Rotatory Motion	182

	Page
Wheelwork	183
Particular Kinds of Wheels	183
Structure and Proportions of Wheels	183
Wheelwork with Appendages	184
Friction of Wheelwork	184
Machinery for Entertainment	184
Union of Flexible Fibres	184
Materials	184
Animal	184
Vegetable	184
Mineral	185
Preparations for Spinning or Winding	185
Spinning	186
Winding, Reeling, and Simple Twisting	186
Ropemaking	186
Manufacture of Cloth. Weaving	187
Looms and their Parts	187
Operations subsequent to Weaving	188
Textures not regularly woven	188
Knots	189
Sewing	189
Appendages to Clothes	189
Felting	189
Papermaking	190
Papermills	190
Timekeepers in General	191
Particular Construction of Clocks and Watches	191
Parts of Timekeepers	193
Maintaining Power	193
Fusee	193
Wheels	193
Escapements, or Scapements	193
Pendulums and Balances	194
Hands and Bells	194
Compensations and Corrections	194
Sympathy of Clocks	195
Supports for Clocks, and Management of Timekeepers	195
Sandglasses	196
Measures of Time not simply Mechanical	196
Raising Weights in General	196
Levers	196
Wheel and Axis	196
Capstans	196
Pullies	197
Fixed Inclined Planes	197
Wedge	197
Screws	197
Jacks, Crics, Fr.	198
Cranes and Gins	198
Modes of Raising Weights of particular Descriptions	199
Lowering Weights	200
Removing Weights, Diminishing Friction	200

CONTENTS OF THE CATALOGUE.

	Page
Removing Weights without Wheel Carriages	200
Theory of Wheel Carriages	201
Particular Kinds of Carriages	201
Parts of Carriages	203
Appendages to Carriages, Drags, Harnesses, Sadlery	203
Roads	203
Compression	204
Presses, strictly so called	204
Vices, Pincers, and Pliers	204
Calender Mills and Mangles, with Rollers	205
Compression between Rollers	205
Compression by Percussion	205
Extension	205
Simple Extension	205
Extension by Pressure	205
Extension by Percussion	205
Arts depending principally on Extension	206
Penetration and Division	206
Theory of Penetration	206
Instruments of Penetration in General, and Substances of which they are composed	207
Penetration by Pointed Instruments	207
Cutting Instruments or Edge Tools	208
Lathes	209
Division, or Separation without Sharp Instruments	210
Sawing	210
Wheelcutting, Filing, and cutting Screws	210
Grinding and Polishing	210
Boring	211
Digging	211
Mining, and Subterraneous Work in General	211
Ploughing, Sowing, and Harrowing	212
Trituration, Pulverisation, Levigation, Mills	213
Parts of Mills	215
Appendages to Mills, Preparation, of Corn and Flour	215
Machines for Agitation, nearly allied to Mills	216
Demolition	216
History of Mechanics	216
Particular Dates	217
Hydrodynamics in General	219
Hydrostatics	219
Equilibrium of Floating bodies	220
Pneumatostatics, or Pneumatic Equilibrium	220
Theory of Hydraulics	221
Oscillations of Fluids, and of Floating Bodies	223
Phenomena of Rivers	224
Resistance of Fluids, or Hydraulic Pressure	225
Hydrostatic Instruments	231
Levels	231
Determination of Specific Gravities	231
Hydrometers	231
Hydraulic Architecture in General	232

CONTENTS OF THE CATALOGUE.

	Page
Thrust of Earth	232
Building in Water	232
Cisterns. Casks	233
Dikes and Embankments	233
Harbours	233
Docks	233
Sluices	233
Management of Rivers	234
Bridges	234
Weres	234
Canals	234
Locks	235
Conveyances substituted for Locks	235
Aqueducts. Irrigation	235
Drains	235
Modification or Application of Hydraulic Forces	235
Hydrodynamic Measures	235
Force of Water	236
Air or Wind	238
Wind and Water combined. Seamanship in General	239
Effects of Wind and Water	240
Naval Architecture, and Forms of Ships	240
Parts of Ships and of their Rigging	241
Masts	241
Rudders	241
Sails	241
Blocks	241
Cables	241
Anchors	241
Oars	242
Particular Kinds of Ships and Boats	242
Bridges of Boats	242
Modes of Rowing and Impelling Boats and Ships	242
Towing	243
Modes of Raising and removing Ships	243
Preservation of Ships and their Crews	243
Swimming and Diving	243
Instruments subservient to Seamanship	244
Measuring a Ship's Way	244
Sounding	244
Measures of the Wind	244
Marine Quadrants	245
Hydraulic Instruments and Machines, for Producing Motion in Fluids	245
Regulations of Discharge	245
Pipes and Simple Fountains	245
Appendages to Pipes. Valves, Stopcocks, and Filters	246
Machines for Raising Water. Pumps of all Kinds, Fire Engines, and Fountains not simple	247
Pneumatic Machines	252
Machines simply Pneumatic	252
Bellows, Fans, and other Mechanical Ventilators	252
Air Pumps, Condensers, and Air Guns	253

CONTENTS OF THE CATALOGUE.

	Page
Pneumatic Machines and Apparatus, connected with Hydraulics	254
Bellows and Gasholders	254
Submarine Apparatus	255
Pneumatic Machines connected with Heat	256
Aerostation, either by heated Air or by Gases	256
Ventilation by Heat	257
Steam Engine	257
Steam Air Pump	259
Inflammable Vapours	259
Gunnery	259
Theory of Gunnery, and Operation of Powder	259
Particular Constructions of Guns and their Parts	262
Rockets and other Fireworks	263
History of Hydraulics and Pneumatics	263
Particular Dates	263
Acustics. Sound in General	264
Propagation of Sound	264
Decay of Sound	266
Echos	266
Sources of Sound	266
Vibrations of Fluids	266
Vibrations of Solids	267
Vibrations from Tension	267
Chords	267
Surfaces	268
Vibrations from Elasticity	268
Lateral Vibrations	268
Longitudinal Vibrations	269
Spiral Vibrations	269
Effects of Sound	269
Sympathetic Sounds	270
Ear and Hearing. Instruments for Hearing	271
Theory of Music	272
Musical Instruments	274
Stringed Instruments	274
Drums	274
Elastic Instruments	274
Wind Instruments	275
Voice and Speech	275
Organs of the Human Voice	275
Speech	275
A Description of Articulate Sounds, with appropriate Characters	276
Examples, with the Mode of Writing the Words in these Characters	277
Teaching the Deaf	278
Peculiarities of Speech	278
Speaking Trumpet	279
Voices of different Animals	279
Instruments subservient to Music	279
History of Acustics	279
Optics in General	280

CONTENTS OF THE CATALOGUE.

	Page
Theory of Dioptrics and Catoptrics	280
Optical Instruments in General	281
Photometers	282
Measurement of Refractive Powers	282
Measurement of Transparency	282
Catoptric Instruments	282
Lenses	283
Optical Scenery	284
Microscopes, Simple and Compound	285
Telescopes	286
Micrometers	289
Physical Optics	290
Sources of light	290
Light from Combustion	290
Light attending Decomposition without sensible Heat	291
Spontaneous Light	291
Solar Phosphori	292
Light from Friction	293
Velocity of Light	293
Aberration	294
Decay of Light	294
Interception and Partial Reflection of Light	294
Refractive Powers	294
Dispersion of Colours by Refraction	295
Total or internal Reflection	296
Tables of Refractive and Dispersive Powers	296
Table of the Order of Dispersive Powers	298
Wollaston's comparative Table	299
Atmospheric Refraction	299
Ordinary Atmospheric Refraction, Celestial or Terrestrial	299
Irregular Atmospheric Refraction	301
Horizontal Refraction	301
Irregular Refraction at Various Altitudes	302
Beams of Light from Atmospherical Refraction or Reflection	303
Observations of Parhelia, or Paraselenes, and Halos	303
Particular Accounts	303
Theory of Halos and Parhelia	305
Glories, or coloured Anthelia	308
Simple Rainbows	308
Double Refraction	309
Vision in General	310
Structure of the Human Eye	311
Comparative Anatomy of the Eye	311
Immediate Functions of the Eye	312
Perception of external Objects	313
Shadows	313
Colours, as affecting the Eye	314
Aerial Perspective, and Management of Colours	314
Ocular Spectra, and Coloured Shadows	314
Imperfections of Sight	315

CONTENTS OF THE CATALOGUE.

	Page
Defects of focal Distance	315
Imperfection of Focus	315
Squinting	315
Confusion of Colours	315
Debility of Sight	316
Cataract	316
Employment for the Blind	316
Production of Colours in Double Lights	316
Nature of Light and Causes of Colours	318
History of Optics	323
Dates	323
Physics	324
Astronomy	324
Fixed Stars in General	325
Stars visible in London	327
System of Stars, Nebulae, and Double Stars	328
Distance and Magnitude of the Stars	329
Proper Motion of the Stars	330
Changeable Stars and new Stars	330
Twinkling of the Stars	331
Sun	331
Solar Atmosphere, or Zodiacal Light	332
Planets in General	332
Particular Planets	333
Mercury	333
Venus	333
The Earth, in its Relations to the Celestial Bodies	333
Mars	334
Juno	334
Pallas	334
Ceres	334
Jupiter	335
Saturn	335
Georgian Planet	335
Secondary Planets	335
Supposed Satellite of Venus	335
Moon	335
Satellites of Jupiter	337
Satellites of Saturn	337
Satellites of the Georgian Planet	337
Comets	337
Laws of Gravity in General	338
Equilibrium and Figure of Gravitating Bodies	339
Orbits of the Primary Planets	339
Orbits of the Secondary Planets	340
Orbits of Comets	341
Projectiles from the Moon	341
Rotation of the Earth and Planets	341
Theory of the Tides	342
Celestial Appearances in General, with Reference to the Earth	344
Appearances of the Stars	344
Appearances of the Sun	344

CONTENTS OF THE CATALOGUE.

	Page
Appearances of the Primary Planets	344
Appearances of the Secondary Planets	345
Moon	345
Appearances of the Sun and primary Planets jointly	345
Transits	345
Appearances of the fixed Stars and Moon	345
Appearances of the Sun and Moon jointly	345
Eclipses	345
Appearances of the Primary and Secondary Plants conjointly	346
Eclipses of Jupiter's Satellites	346
Appearances of Comets	346
Planetary Worlds. Appearances with respect to different Planets	346
Practical Astronomy in General	346
Astronomical Apparatus in General	347
Observatories	347
Time	347
Equation of Time	347
Equation Clocks, for Solar Time	347
Observations of Time, in General	348
Dialling, or Gnomonics	348
Chronology and Calendars	349
Instruments for Observation	349
Reflecting Instruments for Angles	350
Astronomical Telescopes, and Telescopic Sights, Micrometers, and Photometers	351
Theodolites	352
Fixed Instruments	352
Transit Instruments	352
Mural Quadrants	352
Zenith Sectors	352
Equatorial Instruments	353
Levels, Mechanical or Hydrostatical	353
Modes of fixing Insrruments	354
Observations in General	354
Corrections	354
Refraction	354
Aberration of Light	355
Parallax in General	355
Dip	355
Azimuths and Altitudes in General	355
Observations of the Stars	355
Corrections	355
Aberration	355
Annual Parallax	355
Places of the Stars	355
Altitudes of the Stars	355
Observations of the Sun	355
Parallax, and Modes of determining it	355
Observations of the Solstice	356
Observations of Solar Altitude	356
Observations of the Planets	356
Aberration	356

		Page
Observations of the Places of the Planets		357
Observations of the Secondary Planets		357
Lunar Observations		357
Corrections: Refraction, and Parallax		357
Moon's Appearance		358
Observations of the Earth's Motion		358
Geography		358
Figure and Magnitude of the Earth		358
Tabular Comparison of Observations		362
Length of a Degree on the Level of the Sea		362
Length of the Pendulum		363
Ellipticity, or Excess of the Equator above the Axis		363
Density of the Earth		364
Observations for finding the Situation of Places		364
Latitudes		365
Longitudes		365
Particular Geography		365
Table of Heights		367
Observations of the Tides		368
Navigation		370
Collections of Observations and Tables		371
Corrections		371
Elements and Epochs		371
Tables of Places of the Heavenly Bodies		373
Projections, Charts, Globes, Orreries, and other Instruments, illustrative of Astronomy and Geography		374
History of Astronomy and Geography		376
Properties of Matter in General		377
Divisibility of Matter		378
Repulsion, or Impenetrability		378
Inertia		379
Nature of Gravitation		379
Cohesion in General		380
Cohesion and Capillary Action of Fluids		380
Fluidity of Liquids, and firmness of Solids		383
Heat and Cold		383
Sources of Heat and Cold		385
Sources simply Mechanical; Friction, Compression		385
Combustion		385
Spontaneous Combustion		385
Effects of Heat		385
Temporary Effects and Measures of Heat.		385
Expansion. Pyrometers, Thermometers		385
Expansions of different Substances		390
Effects of Heat on the Form of Aggregation		394
Freezing, Thawing, and Melting		394
Degrees of Fluidity		396
Boiling, Simple Evaporation, Sublimation, Volatilisation and Deposition		396
Construction of Thermometers		398
Comparative Table of Thermometers		399

CONTENTS OF THE CATALOGUE.

	Page
Table of the Effects of Heat	399
Table of the elasticity of Steam, in Inches of Mercury	400
Chemical and Physiological Effects	403
Permanent Effects of Heat and Cold	403
Communication of Heat by Contact, and in General	404
Radiant Heat	406
Capacity for Heat	408
Natural Zero	409
Heat denominated latent	409
Economy of Heat and Cold	410
Extinction of Fires	413
Nature of Heat	413
Electricity. Literature of Electricity	414
Electricity in General	414
Theory of Electricity	417
Equilibrium of Electricity	418
Induced Electricity	418
Charge	418
Electric Attraction and Repulsions	419
Conducting Powers	419
Table of Conductors, in Order, chiefly from Cavallo	421
Motions of the Electric Fluid.	421
Velocity	421
Simple Communication	421
Lateral Explosions	422
Discharge	422
Immediate Effects	422
Chemical Effects	423
Physiological Effects	424
Mechanical Changes	422
Electric Heat	423
Congelation	423
Supposed Transmission of Odours	423
Secondary Effects of the Communication of Electricity	424
Streams of Air	425
Excitation, or Destruction of the stable Electric Equilibrium	425
Excitation by simple Contact	425
Excitation by Friction	426
Lichtenberg's Table of Excitation, transposed	426
Excitation by Change of Form of Aggregation	427
Electricity from Chemical Changes. Galvanism	427
Electrical Apparatus, in General	430
Excitation. Electrical Machines for applying Friction	431
Amalgams	432
Electrophorus	432
Conductors	433
Coated Jars and Batteries	433
Electrical Measures in General	433
Measures of Tension. Simple Electrometers	433
Microelectrometers. Condensers, Multipliers, and Galvanometers	434

CONTENTS OF THE CATALOGUE.

	Page
Regulators and Dischargers	434
Distinguishers	434
Spontaneous Electricity	435
Of Inanimate Substances	435
Atmospherical Electricity	435
Mineral Electricity. Tourmalin and other Crystals	435
Animal Electricity	435
Raia Torpedo	435
Gymnotus Electricus	436
Silurus Electricus	436
Trichiurus Indicus	436
Tetrodon, as supposed	436
Magnetism in General	436
Theory of Magnetism	437
Magnetic Substances	438
Supposed Magnetism of Animals	439
Particular Experiments and Phenomena	439
Terrestrial Magnetism. Declination, Dip, and Variation	440
Magnetical Apparatus	443
Artificial Magnetism	443
Compasses and Dipping Needles	444
Magnetical Observations	445
Magnetical Measures	446
Meteorology. Literature of Meteorology	446
Meteorology in General	446
Meteorological Apparatus, and Modes of observing	448
Meteorological Journals	448
General Effects of the Sun and Moon	449
Climate in General	450
Particular Observations of Temperature	452
Meteorological Thermometers	454
Winds	454
Winds in General	454
Regular Winds	454
Measures of Wind	455
Intensity of Wind	457
Particular Observations of Storms	457
Particular Kinds and Effects of Winds	458
Currents of the Sea	458
Barometers	459
Mercurial Barometers, and Barometers in General	459
Statical Baroscopes, Air Barometers, and Manometers	461
Variations of the Barometer in General	462
Particular Barometrical Observations	463
Mean Height of the Barometer	464
Atmospherical Evaporation, or Hygrology	464
Hygrometers	468
Barometrical Measurements	472
Clouds and Mists	474
Dew	474
Rain in General	475
Rain Gages	476
Particular Registers of Rain	476

CONTENTS OF THE CATALOGUE.

	Page
Annual Fall of Rain	477
Storms of Rain	478
Snow and Hail	478
Springs, Rivers, Lakes, and Seas: Water and Ice	479
Sweetening Sea Water, and Preserving Fresh	481
Atmospherical Electricity in General	481
Particular Accounts of Storms	483
Measures of Atmospherical Electricity	485
Preservation from Lightning. Conductors and Precautions	485
Waterspouts	486
Aurora Borealis	488
Earthquakes and Agitations. In order of Time	490
Subterraneous Fires and Volcanos	493
Geology	495
Luminous Meteors	499
Exhalations	499
Atmospherical Meteors and Shooting Stars	499
Meteors which have fallen to the Ground	501
Natural History in General	502
Density of Particular Substances	503
A Table of Specific Gravities	503
A Table of the Capacity of different Substances for Heat	508
A Comparative Table of the Physical Properties of Various Substances	509
General Effects of Mixture	510
Affinities and Combinations	510
Mineralogy in General	510
Systems	511
Philosophy of Mineralogy	511
Forms of Primary Aggregation. Crystallization	511
Botany in General	511
Systems	511
Vegetable Anatomy and Physiology	512
Zoology. In General	516
Systems	516
Physiology	516
Cultivation of Natural Productions, including Agriculture and Horticulture	519
History of Terrestrial Physics	519

A CATALOGUE OF WORKS
RELATING TO
NATURAL PHILOSOPHY,
AND THE
MECHANICAL ARTS.

CATALOGUES.

Morhofii Polyhistor, 1695. 1714. M. B. Ed. 4. 2 v. 4. Lubeck, 1747.

*Monthly Review. 8. London, 1749... R. I.

Boerhaave Methodus studii medici, a Haller. 2 v. 4. Amst. 1751. M. B.

Rohrs physikalische bibliothek, von Kästner. 8. Leipz. 1754.

Scheibels einleitung in die mathematische bücherkenntniss. Bresl. 1777.

Weigel, Grundriss der chemie. 2 v. 8. Greifsw. 1777.

*Allgemeines repertorium der literatur. 6 v. 4. 1785 .. 1795. Jen. 1793... B. B.

Murhards literatur der mathematischen wissenschaften. vol. 1, 2. 8. Leipz. 1798. R. I.

*(B. B.) Dryander Catalogus bibliothecae Banksianae. 5 v. 8. Lond. 1798.

*Reuss Repertorium commentationum a societatibus litterariis editarum. 4. Gott. 1801...

A systematical index, not yet completed.

Dutens Bibliothèque choisie. 8. Lond. 1802. R. I.

COLLECTIONS RELATING TO THE SCIENCES.

Royal Society of London, originating from the Society instituted at Oxford in 1645.

(Ph. tr.) Philosophical transactions, giving some account of the present undertakings, studies and labours of the ingenious in many considerable parts of the world.

    Vol. 1. n. 1 .. 22. 1665—6
        2. 23 .. 32. 1667.
        3. 33 .. 44. 1668.

Vol. 4.	n. 45 .. 56.	1669.
5.	57 .. 68.	1670.
6.	69 .. 80.	1671.
7.	81 .. 91.	1672.
8.	92 .. 100.	1673.
9.	101 .. 111.	1674.
10.	112 .. 122.	1675.
11.	123 .. 132.	1676.
12.	133 .. 142.	1677—8.
13.	143 .. 154.	1683.
14.	155 .. 166.	1684.
15.	167 .. 178.	1685.
16.	179 .. 191.	1686—7.
17.	192 .. 206.	1691—3.
18.	207 .. 214.	1694.
19.	215 .. 235.	1695—7.
20.	236 .. 247.	1698.
21.	248 .. 259.	1699.
22.	260 .. 276.	1700—1.
23.	277 .. 288.	1702—3.
24.	289 .. 304.	1704—5.
25.	305 .. 312.	1606—7.
26.	313 .. 324.	1708—9.
27.	325 .. 336.	1710—2.
28.	337.	1713.
29.	338 .. 350.	1714—6.
30.	351 .. 363.	1717—9.
31.	364 .. 369.	1720—1.
32.	370 .. 380.	1722—3.
33.	381 .. 391.	1724—5.
34.	392 .. 398.	1726—7.
35.	399 .. 406.	1727—8.
36.	407 .. 416.	1729—30.
37.	417 .. 426.	1731—2.
38.	427 .. 435.	1733—4.
39.	436 .. 444.	1735—6.
40.	445 .. 451.	1737—8.
41.	452 .. 461.	1739—41.
42.	462 .. 471.	1742—3.
43.	472 .. 477.	1744—5.
44. i.	478 .. 481.	1746.

Vol. 44. ii. n. 482 .. 484.	1747.
45. 485 .. 490.	1748.
46. 491 .. 497.	1749—50.
47.	1751—2.
48. i.	1753.
ii.	1754.
49. i.	1755.
ii.	1756.
50. i.	1757.
ii.	1758.
51. i.	1759.
ii.	1760.
52. i.	1761.
ii.	1762.
53.	1763.
54.	1764.
55.	1765.
56.	1766.
57.	1767.
58.	1768.
59.	1769.
60.	1770.
61.	1771.
62.	1772.
63.	1773.
64.	1774.
65.	1775. R. I.

Philosophical transactions of the Royal Society of London.
    Vol. 66. .. 81, 1776 .. 1791.
    For the year   1792 ... 4. London. R. I.

Maty's general index to the philosophical transactions, to the end of the 70th volume. 4. Lond. 1787. R. I.

*Philosophical transactions to 1750, abridged by Lowthorp, Jones, Eames, and Martin. 11 v. 4. Lond. (Vol. i. to vii. R. I.)

Abregé des transactions philosophiques, redigé par M. Gibelin. 13 v. 8. Par. 1787—91. R. I.

Sprat's history of the Royal Society. 4. Lond. 1687.

**Birch's* history of the Royal Society, as a supplement to the philosophical transactions; to 1687. 4. v. 4. Lond. 1756—7. R. I.

**Hooke's* philosophical collections, n. 1..7, 1679—82. 4. Lond. R. I.

Derham's miscellanea curiosa, being the most valuable discourses read and delivered to the Royal Society 3 v. 8. Lond. 1723. R. I.

Philosophical transactions abridged by Hutton, Shaw, and Pearson. 4. Lond. 1803. B. B.

Imperial Academy der Naturforscher, 1652.

Miscellanea curiosa. Decur. I..III. 4. Nuremb. 1670..1706. B. B.

Ephemerides academiae Caesareae. Cent. I. X. 1712..1722. B. B.

Acta physicomedica academiae Caesareae. 10 v. 1727..1754. B. B.

Nova acta academiae Caesareae. Nuremb. 1757... B. B.

Abhandlungen der Kaiserlichen academie. 4. Nuremb. 1755...

Kellneri index rerum memorabilium in E. N. C. 4. Nuremb. 1739. B. B.

Büchneri historia academiae naturae curiosorum. 4. Hal. 1756. B. B.

Archiducal Academy del Cimento, 1657.

*Saggi di naturali esperienze fatte nel' academia del Cimento. f. Flor. 1667. 1691. R. I.

With additions, in *Tozzetti* Aggrandimenti delle scienze fisiche. 4. 1780. II. B. B.

Tentamina academiae del Cimento, a Musschenbroek. 4. L. B. 1731. M. B.

Experiments of the academy del Cimento, translated by Waller. 4. Lond. Extr. Ph. tr. 1684. XIV. 757.

Journal des savans. 12. Paris. 1665... R. I.

Royal Academy of Sciences at Paris, 1666.

*(A. P.) *Histoire* et mémoires de l'Académie royale des sciences depuis 1666, jusq'a 1699. 11 v. 4. Par. 1733.
Année 1699... Par. 1702... R. I.
Reprinted 12. Amst. 1692...(To 1754. R. I.)

Recueil des pièces qui ont remporté le prix. Par. 1721... 1771. M. B.

*(S. E.) *Mémoires* de mathématique et de physique presentés à l'Académie. 11 v. 4. Par. 1750.... R. I.

*(Mach. A.) *Machines* et inventions approuvées par l'Académie. 7 v. 4. 1735..1777. Vol. I. 1666... II. 1702... III. 1713... IV. 1720... V. 1727... VI.... 1732. VII. 1734..54. R. I.

Rozier Table des articles, depuis 1666 jusqu'en 1770. 4 v. 4. 1775—6. R. I.

Duhamel Historia academiae regiae scientiarum. 4. Par. 1698. B. B.

Acta eruditorum Lipsiensia. 4. Leipz. 1682... 1731. B. B.

Nova acta eruditorum. 4. Leipz. 1732..1776. B. B.

Academy of Sciences at Siena, 1691.

*Atti dell' academia di Siena. 1760. 4. Siena. 1761... B. B.

Harris Lexicon technicum. f. Lond. 1699. 1704. M. B.
Extr. Ph. tr. 1704. XXIV.

Royal Society of Sciences at Berlin, 1700. Academy, 1743.

*Miscellanea Berolinensia. 7 v. 4. Berl. 1710..1743. B. B.

*Histoire et mémoires de l'académie royale des sciences et belles lettres de Berlin. 25 v. 4. Berl. 1746..1771. B. B.

*Nouveaux mémoires de l'académie royale. 16 v. 4. Berl. 1770..1787. B. B.

*Mémoires de l'académie royale. 1792... B. B.

Histoire de l'académie royale depuis son origine jusqu' à present. 4. Berl. 1752. B. B.

Institute of Bologna, 1712.

*(C. Bon.) *Commentarii* de Bononiensi scientiarum et artium instituto atque academia. 4. Bologn. 1731 ... B. B.

Imperial Academy of Sciences at Petersburgh, 1725.

*(C. Petr.) *Commentarii* academiae Petropolitanae. 14 v. 4. Petersb. 1726 .. 1752. B. B.

*(N. C. Petr.) *Novi* commentarii academiae Petropolitanae. 20 v. 4. Vol. I. 1747—8 ... Petersb. 1750 ... 1776. B. B.

*(A. Petr.) *Acta* academiae Petropolitanae. 1777 ... 1782. B. B.

*(N. A. Petr.) *Nova* acta academiae Petropolitanae. Praecedit historia academiae, ad annum 1783. 4. Vol. I ... Petersb. 1787 ...

Royal Academy of Sciences at Upsal, 1725.

Acta literaria Sueciae. 4 v. 4. Ups. 1720 .. 1739. B. B.

Acta societatis regiae Upsaliensis. 5 v. Ups. 1744 .. 1751. B. B.

Nova acta societatis Upsaliensis. 4. Ups. 1773 ... B. B.

Commercium litterarium Norimbergense. 15 v. Nuremb. 1731 .. 1745. B. B.

Royal Academy of Sciences at Stockholm, 1739.

Kongl. Svenska vetenskaps academiens handlingar, 1739 ... 8. Stockh. 1740 .. 1779. B. B.

Nya handlingar. Vol. I ... 1780 ... B. B.

*(Schw. Abh.) *Abhandlungen* der königlichen Schwedischen akademie, von Kästner und andern. 40 v. 8. Hamb. 1749 ...

Neue Abhandlungen, 1780 ... 8. Leipz. 1784 .. (To 1790. R. I.)

Physical Society at Danzig.

Versuche und Abhandlungen der naturforschenden Gesellschaft in Danzig. 3 th. Danz. 1747 .. 1756. B. B.

Neue sammlung. 8. Danz. 1778.

Royal Society of Denmark.

Skrifter, som udi det Kiobenhavnske Selshab ere fremlagde. 12 v. 4. Copenh. 1745 .. 1779. B. B.

In Latin, Scripta societatis Hafniensis. 3 v. 1745 .. 1747.

Acta literaria universitatis Hafniensis. 1778. 4. Copenh.

Nye Samling af det kongelige Danske videnskabers selskabs skrifter. Cop. 1781 ... B. B.

Abhandlungen die von der D. G. den preis erhalten. Copenh. 1781.

Hamburgisches Magazin. 26 v. 8. Hamb. 1747 .. 1763.

Neues Hamburgisches magazin. 8. Hamb. 1767 .. 1781. B. B.

Royal Society of Sciences at Gottingen, 1750.

*(C. Gott.) *Commentarii* societatis regiae scientiarum Gottingensis. 4 vol. 4. Gott. 1752, 1755. B. B.

*(N. C. Gott.) *Novi* commentarii societatis Gottingensis. 8 v. 4. 1769 .. 1778. B. B.

*(Commentat. Gott.) *Commentationes* societatis Gottingensis. 4. 1778 ... B. B.

Deutsche schriften von der königlichen societat zu Göttingen. 8. Gotting. 1771. B. B.

Assemblée publique de l'académie de Montpelier. 1751.

Physikalische Belustigungen. 50 st. 8. Berl. 1751 .. 1756. B. B.

Society of Basle.

Acta Helvetica physicomathematicobotanicomedica. 4. Basil. 1751 .. 1777. B. B.

Nova acta Helvetica. Vol. I. Bas. 1787. B. B.

Society of Edinburgh.

**Essays* and observations, physical and literary, of a society in Edinburgh. 3 v. 8. Ed. 1754 .. 1771. R. I.

*(Ed. tr.) *Transactions* of the Royal Society of Edinburgh. 4. v. 1788 ... R. I.

Dutch Society of Sciences at Haarlem, 1752.

Verhandelingen uitgegeeven door de Hollandse maatschappy der weetenschappen te Haarlem. 8. Haarl. 1775 ...

In German, by Kästner. Altenb. 8. 1785.

Allgemeines Magazin. 2 v. 8. Leipz. 1753 .. 1767.

Electoral Academy of useful Sciences at Erfurt, 1754.

Acta academiae electoralis Moguntinae scientiarum utilium quae Erfordiae est. 8. Vol. I .. Erf. 1751 ... B. B.

Dresdnisches Magazin. 2 v. 8. Dresd. 1759 ... B. B.

Physical Society at Zurich.

Abhandlungen der naturforschenden gesellschaft zu Zürich. 3 v. 8. Zurich, 1761 .. 1766 ... B. B.

Electoral Bavarian Academy of Sciences, 1759.

Abhandlungen der Baierischen academie. 4. Munich. 1763 ... B. B.

Royal Society of Sciences at Turin, 1760.

*(M. Taur.) *Miscellanea* philosophicomathematica societatis privatae Taurinensis. 4. Tur. 1759. B. B.

*(M. Tur.) *Mélanges* de la société royale de Turin. 4. Vol. 2 .. 5. Tur. 1761 .. 1776. (To vol. 3. B. B.)

**Mémoires* de l'académie de Turin. 5 v. (Vol. 3 .. 5. B. B.)

Bremisches magazin. 7 v. 8. Bremen, 1760 .. 1764.

Neues Bremisches magazin. 8. Brem. 1676 ...

Royal Society of Norway.

Trondhiemske selskabs skrifter. Copenh. 1761 .. 1774. B. B.

In German, Copenh. 1765 .. 1767. 3 v. 8.

Det Kongelige Norske videnskabers selskabs skrifter. v. 4, 5. 8. Copenh. 1768 .. 74. B. B.

Nye Samling af det kongelige Norske videnskabers selskabs skrifter. 8. Copenh. 1784. B. B.

Electoral Palatine Academy of Sciences, 1763.

Historia et commentationes academiae scientiarum et elegantiorum literarum Theodoropalatinæ. 4. Manh. 1776 ... B. B.

Zealand Society at Vliessingen, 1765.

Verhandelingen uitgegeeven door het Zeeuwsch genootschap der wetenschappen te Vlissingen. 8. Middelb. 1769. B. B.

Berlinisches magazin. 8. Berl. 1765—7. B.B.

Berlinische sammlungen. 8. Berl. 1768—79. B. B.

Stralsundisches magazin. 8. Berlin. 1767 ... B. B.

Mannichfaltigkeiten. 8. Berl. 1769 ...

Batavian Society of Experimental Philosophy at Rotterdam, 1769.

Verhandelingen van het Bataafsch genootschap der proefondervindelyke wisbegeerte. 4. Rotterd. 1774 ... B. B.

Hessian Academy of Sciences at Giessen.

Acta philosophicomedica academiae scientiarum principalis Hassiacae. 4. Giessae, 1771. B. B.

American Philosophical Society at Philadelphia, 1769.

(Am. tr.) *Transactions* of the American philosophical society for promoting useful knowledge. 4. Philad. 1771 ... R. I.

Neue physikalische Belustigungen. 8. Prag. 1770 ...

Imperial and Royal Academy of Sciences at Brussels.

Mémoires de l'académie des sciences et belles lettres de Bruxelles. 5 v. 4. 1777—88. B. B.

Journal de physique.

**Rozier*, Introduction aux observations sur

la physique, sur l'histoire naturelle, et sur les arts. 2 v. 4. Paris, 1777. B. B.

*Observations sur la physique, par Rozier, Mongez, et Lametherie. Paris, 1773—92. B. B.

Lamétherie, Journal de physique, de chimie, et d'histoire naturelle. 4. Par. an 2 ... R. I.

Physical Society of Friends at Berlin, 1773.

Beschäftigungen der Berlinischen Gesellschaft naturforschender Freunde. 4 v. 8. Berl. 1775—9. B. B.

Schriften, 11 v. 1787—93. B. B.
Vol. 7. is also entitled Beobachtungen, vol. 1.

Neue Schriften. 4. Berl. 1795. B. B.

Hutton's diarian miscellany, from 1704 to 1773. 5 v. 12.

Hutton's mathematical and philosophical dictionary. 2 v. 4. R. I.

The Preceptor. 2 v. 8. London.

Erxlebens physikalische bibliothek. 4 v. 8. 1. Gottingen, 1774—79. B. B.
A review.

Mathematical Society of Bohemia.

Abhandlungen einer privatgesellschafft in Böhmen. 6 v. 8. Prag. 1775—84. B. B.

Abhandlungen der Böhmischen gesellschafft der wissenschaften. 4. Prag. 1785 ... B. B.

Eberhard's philosophisches magazin.

Bernisches Magazin. 8. Bern, 1775.

Scelta di opuscoli interessanti, 36 v. 12. Mil. 1775—7. B. B.

Opuscoli scelti sulle scienze e sulle arti. 4. 18 v. Mil. 1778—95. B. B.

Brugnatelli biblioteca fisica d'Europa. 8. Pavia.

Crells chemisches journal. 8. Lemgo, 1778—81. B. B.

Crells neueste entdeckungen in der chemie. 8. Leipz. 1781—4.

Crells chemische annalen. 8. Helmstadt, 1784 ... B. B. R. I.

Genevan Society for Arts and Agriculture.

Mémoires de la societé établie à Genève. Gen. 1778. R. I.

Sammlungen zur physik und naturgeschichte, 4 v. 8. Leipz. 1778—92. B. B.

Göttingisches magazin der wissenchaft und litteratur, von G. C. Lichtenberg und G. Forster. 8. Gött. 1780—5. B. B.

Leipziger magazin zur naturkunde, mathematik, und ökonomie, von Funk, Leske, und Hindenburg. Leipz. 1781—4. B. B.

Leipziger magazin zur naturkunde und ökonomie, von Leske und andern. Leipz. 1786—8. B. B.

Leipziger magazin der reinen und angewandten mathematik, von Bernoulli und Hindenburg. 1786...

Gothaisches magazin für das neueste aus der physik und naturgeschichte, von L. C. Lichtenberg und J. H. Voigt. 8. Gotha, 1781 ... B. B.

* Memoire di mathematica e fisica della società Italiana. Veron. 4. 1782 ... B. B.

Nouveaux mémoires de l'académie de Dijon, pour la partie des sciences et arts. 1782... Dijon, 1783 ... B. B.

* (E. M.) Encyclopédie methodique. 4. Paris, 1782 ... R. I.

(E. M. A.) Arts et metiers. 8 v.

(E. M. M.) Manufactures et arts. 4 t.

(E. M. Pl.) Plates of the Encyclopédie.

These have sometimes been quoted merely to save the labour of referring to the text.

*(S. A.) Transactions of the society for the encouragement of arts, manufactures, and commerce. 8. London, 1783 ... R. I.
Began to distribute premiums, 1751.

Physikalische arbeiten der einträchtigen freunde in Wien, aufgesammelt von Born. 4. Vienn. 1783—87. B. B.

Mémoires de la societé des sciences physiques de Lausanne. 4. Vol. 1. Laus. 1784. B. B.

*Memoirs of the literary and philosophical society of Manchester. 8. Vol. 1 .. Warrington, 1785... Repr. Lond. R. I.

(Am. Ac.) *Memoirs* of the American academy of arts and sciences. 4. Boston, 1785. B. B.

*(Ir. Tr.) *Transactions* of the Royal Irish academy. 3 v. 4. Dubl. 1787—9. R. I. Vol. 4. Dubl.

(As. Res.) *Asiatic* researches of the society of Bengal. 4. Calcutta. 1788 ... B. B.

Annales de chimie, par Morveau, Lavoisier, Monge, Berthollet, Fourcroy, Dietrich, Hassenfratz, et Adet. 20 v. 8. Par. 1789... R. I.

Annales de chimie, par Guyton, Monge, Berthollet, Fourcroy, Adet, Seguin, Vauquelin, Pelletier, Prieur, Chaptal, et Van Mons. Vol. 21 ... Par. 1797 ... R. I.

*Grens journal der physik. 8. Halle, 1790...

*Gilberts journal der physik. 8. Halle, 1799 ... R. I.

*Mémoires de l'Institut national. 4. Paris, 1798 ... R. I.

*Bulletin de la societé philomatique. 4. Paris. R. I.

Monthly magazine. London. (From Vol. 9. R. I.)

*Repertory of arts. London, 1794 ... R. I.

Magazin encyclopédique, par Millin, Noel, et Warens. 8. Par. an 3 ... B. B.

Hindenburgs archiv der mathematik. 2 v. 8. Leipz. 1795 ... R. I.

Pictet, Bibliothèque Britannique. Geneva, 1796 ... R. I.

Beckmann's history of inventions and discoveries, by Johnson. 3 v. Lond. 1797. R. I.

Auswahl der neuesten abhandlungen. 2 v. in 1. Quedlinburg, 1797. R. I.

*(Enc. Br.) Encyclopaedia Britannica. 18 v. 4. Supplement. 2 v. Edinburgh, 1797 .. 1800. R. I.

*(Nich.) *Nicholson's* journal of natural philosophy, chemistry, and the arts. 5 v. 4. London, 1797—1801. R. I.

(Nich. 8.) New series. 8. London, 1802 ... R. I.

*(Ph. M.) *Tilloch's* philosophical magazine. Lond. 1798 ... R. I.

Annals of philosophy. 8. London, 1800 ... R. I.

Annales des arts et manufactures. 8. Paris. R. I.

Journal polytechnique. 4. Paris. R. I.

Gehlers physikalisches wörterbuch. 5 v. 8. Leipz. 1798. R. I.

Anderson's recreations. 6 v. 8. Lond. 1799... R. I.

Commercial and agricultural magazine. 8. Lond. 1799 ... R. I.

Mémoires sur l'Egypte. 8. Par. an 8 ... R. I.

Mémoires du musée de Paris. Sciences. Vol. 1. 8. Par. an 8. R. I.

Décade litéraire et politique. 8. Par. an 8 ... R. I.

Willich's domestic encyclopaedia. 4 v. 8. Lond. 1802 ... R. I.

COLLECTIONS OF THE WORKS OF SINGLE AUTHORS.

*Aristotelis opera omnia. f. Lyons, 1590. B. B.

*Archimedes. f. Oxf. 1792. R. I.

**Bacon's* works. 5 v. 4. London, 1765. R. I.

Bacon's works, by Shaw. 3 v. 4. Lond. 1733. R. I.

Galilaei Galilaei opera. 4. Bologna. R. I.
Barrow's works. 3 v. f. Lond. 1683. M. B.
Cartesii opera omnia. 4 v. 4. Amst. 1692. Mostly M. B.
Dechales Cursus mathematicus. 3 v. f. Lyons, 1674. M. B.
 Extr. Phil. Trans. 1674. IX.
Boyle's works. 5 v. f. Lond. 1665, 1744. M. B.
Torricellii opera mathematica. M. B.
Hugenii opera varia, a Gravesande. 2 v. 4. Leyden, 1724. R. I.
Hugenii opera reliqua. 2 v. 4. Amst. 1728. R. I.
Hooke's posthumous works, by Waller. f. Lond. 1705. R. I.
Hooke's Cutlerian lectures. 4. R. I.
Mariotte Oeuvres. 2 v. 4. Leyden, 1717. Vol. 1. M. B.
Wallisii opera, 3 v. f. Oxf. 1713. R. I.
**Newtoni* opera, edente Horsley. 5 v. 4. Lond. 1779. R. I.
Leibnitii opera, a Dutens. 6 v. 4. Genev. 1768. R. I.
Pascal Oeuvres. R. I.
Vossii opera. R. I.
Leeuwenhoek's select works. 4 v. 4. Lond. 1798. R. I.
Joannis Bernoullii opera. 4 v. 4. Laus. 1742. R. I.
Jacobi Bernoullii opera. 2 v. 4. Genev. 1744. R. I.
Leonardi Euleri opuscula varii argumenti. 3 v. 4. Berlin, 1746—51.
Maupertuis Oeuvres. 4 v. 8. Lyons, 1756. R. I.

Robins's mathematical tracts. 2 v. 8. Lond. 1761. R. I.
Hollmanni commentationum sylloge. 4. Gott. 1764. R. S.
 Sylloge altera. 1784.
Franklin's works. 2 v. 8. London. R. I.
Ferguson's tables and tracts on arts and sciences. 8. R. S.
Emerson's cyclomathesis.
Emerson's miscellanies.
Mayeri opera inedita, a Lichtenberg. 4. Gott. 1774. R. S.
Pringle's six discourses. 8.
Kaestneri dissertationes mathematicae et physicae. 4. Altenb. 1776.
Achards chymisch physische schriften. 8. Berl. 1780.
Fontana Opuscoli scientifici. Flor. 1783.
Sénébier Essais de physique et de chimie.
Bergmann Opuscula physica et chemica. 6 v. 8. B. B.
Garnett's tracts. 2 v. 8. R. I.
Ingenhousz Vermischte schriften physischen und medicinischen inhalts, von Molitor. 2 v. 8. Vienn. 1785.
Hutton's tracts, mathematical and philosophical. 4. London, 1786. R. S.
Busse, Kleine beiträge zur mathematik und physik. Leipz. 1786.
Links beytrage zur physik und chemie. Vol. I. 8. Bostoch, 1797.
Rumford's essays, political, economical, and philosophical. 3 v. 8. Lond. 1800. R. I.
Rumford's philosophical papers. Vol. I. 8. London, 1802. R. I.

MATHEMATICS IN GENERAL.

The numerous papers purely mathematical, contained in the memoirs of foreign academies, are in general omitted in this catalogue.

Mathematici veteres. f. 1693. R. I.

Pappi collectanea mathematica.

Pellii idea Matheseos, about 1638. Hooke Ph. coll. V. 127.

Mersennus in Pellii ideam. 1639. Hooke Ph. coll. V. 135.

Cartesius de Pellii idea. Hooke Ph. coll. v. 144.

Pellii responsio. Hooke Ph. coll. V. 137.

Barrow Lectiones opticae et geometricae. 4. Lond. 1669.
   Extr. Ph. tr. 1671. IV. 2258, 2264.

Papers on mathematics. Ph. tr. abr. I. i. 1. ii. 120. IV. i. 1. VI. i. 1. VIII. i. 1. X. i. 1.

Dechales Cursus mathematicus.

Wallis's mathematical works. 2 v. f.
   Extr. Ph. tr. 1695. XIX. 73.

Jones Synopsis palmariorum matheseos. Lond. 1706.
   Extr. Ph. tr. 1713.

*Simpson's mathematical dissertations and tables. 4. 1743. R. I.

Simpson's exercises for young proficients. 8. 1752. R. I.

Simsoni opera reliqua. 4. R. I.

Simpson's essays. 4.

Stewart's mathematical tracts. 8.

Stewart's general theorems.

Dodson's mathematical repository. 3 v. 12.

Emerson's cyclomathesis, or introduction to the mathematics. 10 v. 8. Lond. 1770. R. I.

Emerson's miscellanies. 8. Lond. 1771.

Hendon's six mathematical tracts. 8. R. S.

Lockie's military mathematics. 2 v. 8. R. S.

Gherli elementi teoricoprattici delle mathematiche pure. 7 v. 4. R. S.

Karstens Anfangsgründe der mathematik. 2 v. 8. Greifsw. 1780.

Unterbergers anfangsgründe der mathematik. 1781.

Vegas vorlesungen über die mathematik. 3 v. 8. Vienna, 1782. R. I.

Sturms kurzer begriff der gesammten mathesis.

Encyclopédie methodique. Mathématiques. 3 v. By D'Alembert, Bossut, and others.

Amusemens de mathématique. 1 v.

Klügels encyclopädie. 1784.

Waring Excerpta mathematica. 4.

Tables to be used with the nautical almanac. 8. B. B.

Hutton's mathematical tables. 8. Lond. 1785. R. S.

Hutton's miscellanea mathematica. 12.

Hutton's translation of Montucla's recreations. 4 v. 8. Lond. 1803. R. I.

Landen's mathematical memoirs. 2. v. 4. London. R. I.

Hellins's mathematical essays. 4. Lond. 1788. R. S.

OF QUANTITY AND NUMBER, OR ALGEBRA.

Wallis's algebra.

*Newton's universal arithmetic.
   Extr. Ph. tr. 1685. XV. 1095.

Demoivre Miscellanea analytica. 4. 1730. R. I.

Saunderson's algebra. 2 v. 4. 1740. R. I.

*Maclaurin's algebra. 8. 1788. R. I.

Emerson's cyclomathesis. IV.
Condorcet, Essai d'analyse. 4. R. S.
Davison's algebra. 8.
Davis Miscellanea analytica. 4.
Waring Meditationes algebraicae. 4.
Waring Miscellanea analytica. 4. R. S.
*Waring meditationes analyticae. 4. Cambr. 1785. R. S.
Nicolai analyseos elementa. 4. Pad. 1786. R. S.
Euler's elements of algebra. 2 v. 8. Lond. 1797. R. I.
Lacroix Elémens d'algebre. R. I.
Lacroix Complément des élémens d'algebre. Paris, an 7. R. I.
Prony's mechanical algebra. Journ. Polyt. II. 92.
**Donna Agnesi's* analytical institutions, by Colson. 2 v. 4. Lond. 1801. R. S.
Woodhouse on the independence of algebra and geometry. Ph. tr. 1802. 85.
**Woodhouse's* principles of analytical calculation. 4. Cambr. 1803. R. S.

PROPORTION.

Glenie on the laws of proportion. Ph. tr. 1777. 450.
Glenie on universal comparison. 4. Lond. 1789. R. S.
Glenie on the antecedental calculus. Ed. tr. IV. 65. Separate. Lond. 1793. R. S.
Slusii mesolabum. 4. Liege, 1688. Acc. Ph. tr. 1699. IV. 903.

FRACTIONS.

Demoivre de fractionibus algebraicis reducendis. Phil. tr. 1722. XXXII. 102.
Landen on the resolution of fractions by the circle. Ph. tr. 1754. 566.

GENERAL THEOREMS.

Castillioneus de formula polynomia Newtoni. Ph. tr. 1742. XLII. 91.
On the binomial theorem.
Demoivre's multinomial theorem. Ph. tr. 1697. XIX. 610.
Hindenburg über den polynomial-lehrsatz. 8. Leipz. 1795.
Roberts on the binomial theorem. Ph. tr. 1795. 292.
Sewell on the binomial theorem. Ph. tr. 1796. 882.
Brougham's general theorems. Ph. tr. 1798. 378.

IMPOSSIBLE QUANTITIES.

Playfair on the arithmetic of impossible quantities. Ph. tr. 1778. 318.
Woodhouse on the truth of conclusions from imaginary quantities. Ph. tr. 1801. 89.

EQUATIONS.

Collins on some defects in algebra. Ph. tr. 1684. XIV. 575.
Halley on finding the roots of equations. Ph. tr. 1674. XVIII. 210.
Demoivre Aequationum superiorum resolutio. Ph. tr. 1707. XXV. 2368.
Maclaurin on the roots of equations. Ph. tr. 1729. XXXVI. 59.
Mallet Analysis aequationum. 4. R. S.
Hayles Analysis aequationum. 4.
Waring's problems on equations. Ph. tr. 1763. 294.
Waring on the general resolution of equations. Ph. tr. 1779. 86.
Waring on the method of corresponding values. Ph. tr. 1789. 166.
Lord Stanhope on the roots of equations Ph. tr. 1781. 195.

Wales on the use of angular tables in solving equations. Ph. tr. 1781. 459.

Hellins on the equal roots of equations. Ph. tr. 1782. 417.

Wood on the roots of equations. Ph. tr. 1798. 369.

Wilson on algebraic equations. Ph. tr. 1799. 265.

Equations with Radical Quantities.

Demoivre de reductione radicalium. Ph. tr. 1738. XL. 463.

Simpson on equations involving radical quantities. Ph. tr. 1751. 20.

Mooney on clearing equations from radicals. Ir. tr. VI. 221.
<small>Removes 5 or 6 quadratic surds.</small>

Impossible Roots of Equations.

Maclaurin on equations with impossible roots. Ph. tr. 1726. XXXIV. 104.

Campbell on the impossible roots of equations. Ph. tr. 1728. XXXV. 515.

Cubic and Biquadratic Equations.

Colson Aequationum cubicarum et biquadraticarum resolutio. Ph. tr. 1707. XXV. 2353.

Maseres on the irreducible case of a cubic equation. Ph. tr. 1778. 902.

Maseres on the extension of Cardan's rule. Ph. tr. 1780. 85.

Hutton on cubic equations. Ph. tr. 1780. 387.

Meredith on cubic equations. Ir. tr. VII. 69.

Ivory on cubic equations. Ed. tr. V. 99.

Limits of Equations.

Milner on the limits of algebraic equations. Ph. tr. 1778. 380.

Machine for Equations.

Rowning on a machine for solving equations. Ph. tr. 1770. 240.

ARITHMETIC.

Archimedis Psammites Wallisii. Oxf. 1676. Acc. Ph. tr. 1676. XI. 567.

Archimedes's Arenarius, by Anderson. 8.

Diophantus Bacheti et Fermatii. f. Toulouse, 1670.
Acc. Ph. tr. 1671. VI. 2185.

Collins on the resolution of numerical equations. Ph. tr. 1669. IV. 929.

Tabula numerorum quadratorum. Lond. 1672.
Acc. Ph. tr. 1672. VII. 4050.

†Wood on infinite fractions. Hooke Ph. coll. n. iii. p. 45.

Wallis on the extraction of roots. Ph. tr. 1695. XIX. 2.

Taylor on approximation in numerical equations. Ph. tr. 1717. XXX. 610.

Leupold Theatrum arithmeticum. f. Leipz. R. I.
<small>Reckoning by the fingers. Tab. 1.</small>

Colson's negativo-affirmative arithmetic. Ph. tr. 1726. XXXIV. 161.

Emerson's cyclomathesis. I. II.

Robertson on circulating decimals. Ph. tr. 1768. 207.

Horsley's sieve of Eratosthenes. Ph. tr. 1772. 327.

Hutton's table of powers and products. f. R. S.

Clarke's rationale of circulating numbers. 8. R. S.

M. Young on the extraction of roots. Ir. tr. 1787. 59.

Waring on the sums of divisors. Ph. tr. 1788. 388.

Goodwyn on the reciprocals of primes. Nich. IV. 402.

Lagrange de la resolution des equations numeriques. Par. 1798. R. I.

Werneburg's reine zahlen system. 8. 1800.
Duodecimal arithmetic. Calls 12 taun.

Gough on primes and factors. Nich. 8. I. 1.

The African nations employ a quinary arithmetic, calling six five and one. Winterbottom's Sierra Leone.

Numerical equations may often be easily resolved by finding the result of two conjectural values of the quantity sought; then the difference or sum of the errors will be to the difference of the supposed values nearly in the same proportion as either of the errors to the error of the corresponding supposed value.

SERIES.

Demoivre on the roots of an infinite equation. Ph. tr. 1698. XX. 190.

Monmort et Taylor de seriebus infinitis. Ph. tr. 1717. XXX. 633.

Simson on Gerard's remark upon series and fractions. Ph. tr. 1753. 368.

Simpson on the partial sum of a series. Ph. tr. 1758. 757.

Landen on the sums of series. Ph. tr. 1760. 553.

Landen on converging series. 4. R. S.

Landen's observations on converging series. 8. R. S.

Lorgna specimen de seriebus convergentibus. 4. R. S.

Clarke's translation of Lorgna on series. 4. R. S.

Hutton on quickly converging series. Ph. tr. 1776. 476.

Hutton on infinite series. Ph. tr. 1780. 387.

Maseres on a slowly converging series. Ph. tr. 1777. 187. 1778. 895.

Vince on infinite series. Ph. tr. 1782. 389. 1785. 32. 1786. 1791. 295.

Waring on infinite series. Ph. tr. 1784. 385. 1786. 81. 1787. 71.

Rotheram on geometrical series. Manch. M. III. 330.

L'Huilier on series. Ph. tr. 1796. 142.

Brinkley on the transformation and reversion of series. Ir. tr. VII. 321.

Hellins on a converging series. Ph. tr. 1798. 183.

INTERPOLATIONS, AND REDUCTION OF OBSERVATIONS.

Emerson's miscellanies. 199.

*Lagrange on taking the mean of observations. M. Taur. V. ii. 167.

Waring on interpolations. Ph. tr. 1779. 59.

Euler on Lagrange's mode of taking a mean. N. A. Petr. III. 1785. 289.

LOGARITHMS.

Mercatoris Logarithmotechnia. Extr. Ph. tr. 1668. III. 753.

Halley on logarithms. Ph. tr. 1695. XIX. 58.

Craig Logarithmotechnia generalis. Ph. tr. 1710. XXVII. 191.

Long's new method for making logarithms. Ph. tr. 1714. XXIX. 51.

Taylor's method of computing logarithms. Ph. tr. 1717. XXX. 610.

Dodson on a series for computing logarithms. Ph. tr. 1753. 273.

Bayes on a logarithmic series. Ph. tr. 1763. 260.

Emerson's miscellanies. 189.

Jones on logarithms. Ph. tr. 1771. 455.

Ferroni theoria magnitudinum exponentialium. 4. R. S.

Hellins's theorems for computing logarithms. Ph. tr. 1780. 307. 1796. 135.

Maseres scriptores logarithmici. 3 v. 4. 1791. 6. R. I.

Allman on logarithms. Ir. tr. VI. 391.
Murray on Halley's series for logarithms. Ir. tr. IX. 3.

Tables of Logarithms.

Sherwin's tables of logarithms. 8.
Dodson's antilogarithmic canon. f. 1742. R. I.
Bernoulli's sexcentenary tables for proportions below 10′. 4. R. S.
Vega's tafeln und formuln. 8. R. S.
Vega Logarithmische tafeln. f. Leipz. 1794. R. I.
*Taylor's tables of logarithms. 4.
*Callet, tables de logarithmes, edition stéreotype. 8. Par. 1795.
*Errors of Callet's tables. Zach Mon. corr. VI. 398.
Borda et Delambre tables trigonometriques decimales. 4. Par. 1801. R. S.
Account of the new decimal tables of logarithms. M. Inst. V. 49.

COMBINATIONS AND CHANCES.

On the credibility of human testimony. Ph. tr. 1699. XXI. 359.
Robertson on the chances of lotteries. Ph. tr. 1693. XVII. 677.
Thornycroft on combination. Ph. tr. 1706. XXV. 1961.
*Demoivre de mensura sortis. Ph. tr. 1711. XXVII. 213.
Demoivre problematis solutio combinatoria. Ph. tr. 1714. XXIX. 145.
Demoivre's doctrine of chances. 4.
N. Bernoulli de problemate Moivraei. Ph. tr. 1714. XXIX. 133.
Simpson's laws of chance. 4.
Combinations. Emerson's cyclomathesis. X.
Laws of chance. Emerson's miscellanies. I.
Bayes on a problem on chances, with Price's letter. Ph. tr. 1763. 370.
Price's continuation of Bayes's paper. Ph. tr. 1764. 296.
S. Clark's laws of chance. 8.
*Several papers of Laplace and Condorcet. A. P. 1781, and elsewhere.
Lambert on lotteries at cards. Hindenb. Arch. III.
Hindenburg on the combinatorial analysis. Hindenb. Arch.

INTEREST AND ANNUITIES.

Martindale on compound interest. Hooke Ph. coll. n. 1. 34.
Halley on the value of annuities. Ph. tr. 1693. XVII. 596. 653.
Watkinson on interest. Ph. tr. 1714. XXIX. 111.
Demoivre on the calculation of annuities. Ph. tr. 1744. XLIII. n. 473. p. 65.
Emerson's miscellanies. 49. 121. 226.
Price on the expectations of lives. Ph. tr. 1769. 89.
Price on survivorships. Ph. tr. 1770. 268.
Price on life annuities. Ph. tr. 1776. 109.
Price on reversionary payments. 8. 2 copies. R. S.
*Price on annuities, by Morgan. 8. London.
*Robertson on compound interest. Ph. tr. 1770. 508.
Morgan on the value of a contingent reversion. Ph. tr. 1789. 40.

GEOMETRY. OF SPACE IN GENERAL.

*Euclides Gregorii. f. Oxford, 1703. R. I. Extr. Ph. tr. 1704.
*Barrow's Euclid. 8. London.
Cunn's Euclid. 8. London, 1762. R. I.
*Simson's Euclid. 8. 1801. London, R. I.
Cowley's appendix to Euclid. 4.
Apollonii inclinationum libri a Horsley. 4. R. S.
Apollonii loci plani, a Simson. 4.

Apollonius on tangencies, by Lawson. 4. R. S.
Apollonius de sectione rationis et spatii. 8.
Burrow's restitution of Apollonius on inclinations. 4. R. S.
Archimedes a Barrow. 4. London, 1675.
    Extr. Ph. tr. 1675. X.
*Archimedes. f. Oxford. R. I.
Gregorii geometriae pars universalis. Pavia, 1668.
    Extr. Ph. tr. 1668. III. 685.
Pardies elémens de géometrie. 12. Par. 1671.
    Extr. Ph. tr. 1671. VI. 3064.
Brackenridge exercitatio geometrica. 4.
Ash's demonstration of some propositions of Euclid. Ph. tr. 1684. XIV. 672.
Simson de Pappi et Euclidis porismatis. Ph. tr. 1723. XXXIII. 330.
Stewart on a geometrical proposition of Pappus. Ed. ess. L. 141.
Stewart Propositiones geometricae. 8.
Simpson's geometry. 8. Lond. 1768. R. I.
Emerson's cyclomathesis. II.
Bossut Elémens de géometrie.
    Acc. A. P. 1775. H. 55.
Lelyveld sur la proportion de la diagonale au coté. 8. R. S.
Glenie on the division of lines, surfaces, and solids. Ph. tr. 1776. 73.
Bonnycastle's geometry. 8. London.
Playfair on porisms. Ed. tr. III. 154.
Wallace on porisms. Ed. tr. IV. 107.
Hauff on parallel lines. Hind. Arch. III. 74.
    Employs Eucl. X. I.
Mascheroni Géometrie du compas, par Carette. Par. 1797.
Lacroix Elémens de géometrie. 8. Par. 1799. R. I.
Carnot Géometrie de position. 4. Par. 1803. R. I.
Limrick on the 12th axiom of Euclid. As. Res. VII. 449.

MENSURATION.

See geometrical instruments.

†Collins on a chorographical problem. Ph. tr. 1671. VI. 2087.
Chorographic problems. Ph. tr. 1685. XV. 1231.
Perks, Gregory, and Wallis, on squaring portions of lunes. Ph. tr. 1699. XXI. 411.
Robarts on the comparative magnitude of points. Ph. tr. 1712. 470.
Euler on dikes. N. C. Petr. IX. i. 362.
Stedman on triangles described in circles. Ph. tr. 1775. 296.
Horsley de polygonis circulo inscriptis. Ph. tr. 1775. 301.
Hutton's treatise on mensuration. 4. Newcastle, 1770. R. I.
Bonnycastle's mensuration. 12.
    S. E. IX. 80. The square of the area of any plane surface is equal to the sum of the squares of any three orthogonal plane projections of the surface.

TRIGONOMETRY AND POLYGONOMETRY.

See Circle.

Murdoch's trigonometry abridged. Ph. tr. 1758. 538.
Simson's Euclid.
Emerson's cyclomathesis. III.
Lexell's polygonometrical theorem. Ph. tr. 1775. 281.
Hutton's demonstration of the polygonal theorem. Ph. tr. 1776. 200.
Hutton's project for a new division of the quadrant, in parts of the radius. Ph. tr. 1784. 21.
Cagnoli Trigonometria piana e sferica. 4. Par. 1786. R. S.
Cagnoli Traité de trigonometrie. 4. R. I.
Cagnoli's trigonometrical propositions. Soc. Ital. VII. 1.

L'Huilier Polygonometrie. 4. Genev. 1789. R. S.

Lorgna on the variations of triangles. Soc. Ital. VII. 346.

Schubert's spherical trigonometry, from Ptolemy. N. A. Petr. 1794. XII. 165.

Lacroix Traité de trigonometrie. 8. R. I.

Spherical Trigonometry.

See Nautical Astronomy.

Lacaille on the differences of spherical triangles. A. P. 1741. 238. H. 115.

Blake on spherical trigonometry. Ph. tr. 1751. 441.

Lambert on the simplification of spherical trigonometry by hyperbolic sectors. A. Berl. 1768. 327.

Pemberton's three problems. Ph. tr. 1772. 434.

*Lyons on spherical trigonometry. Ph. tr. 1775. 470.

Euler on spherical trigonometry. A. Petr. III. i. 72.

Gua on spherical trigonometry. A. P. 1783. 291.

Kelly's spherics and nautical astronomy. 8. London.

Trembley essai de trigonometrie spherique. 8. R. S.

Spheroidical Trigonometry. See Figure of the earth.

COMPARISON OF VARIABLE QUANTITIES.

Halley on infinite quantity. Ph. tr. 1693. XVII. 556.

Demoivre's specimen of the method of fluxions. Ph. tr. 1695. XIX. 52.

Taylor Methodus incrementorum. 4. Extr. Ph. tr. 1715. XXIX. 339.

Stirling Methodus differentialis illustrata. Ph. tr. 1719. XXX. 1050.

Stirling on the differential method. 4.

*Newton's fluxions, by Colson. Extr. Ph. tr. 1736. XXXIX. 320.

Fontenelle's geometry of infinites. A. P. 1725. Suite.

**Maclaurin's fluxions. 2 v. 4. Lond. 1742. R. I.
Extr. Ph. tr. 1743. XLII. 325.

Bossut on the differentiation of parameters. S. E. II. 435.

Arithmetic of infinites. Emerson's cyclomathesis. V.

Emerson's fluxions. 8. London, 1757. R. I.

Emerson's method of increments. 4.

Lyons's fluxions. 8. London, 1758.

Rowe's fluxions. 8.

Euler's elements of the method of variations. N. C. Petr. X. 51. XVI. 35.

*Lagrange on the method of variations. M. Taur. IV. ii. 163.

Euleri calculus integralis. 4 v. 4. Petersb. 1792.

Condorcet on partial differences. A. P. 1770. 151.

Cousin Leçons de calcul differentiel. 2 v. 8. Par. 1777. R. S.

Caluso sur les manieres de traiter le calcul differentiel. 4. R. S.

Caluso proposes different marks over letters, like those of fluxions. M. Tur. III.

Arbogast sur les differences partielles. 4. Petersb. 1791. R. S.

Arbogast du calcul des derivations. 4. Strasb. 1800. R. I.
Acc. Lalande's Montucla. IV. 659.

Ferronius de calculo integralium. 4. Flor. 1792. R. S.

Ditton on fluxions. 8.

Lacroix Traité du calcul differentiel. 2 v. 4. Par. 1797. R. I.

Lacroix Traité des différences. 4. Par. 1800. R. I.
Brinkley. Ir. tr. VII. See Series.
Carnot on the infinitesimal calculus, by Dickson. Ph. M. VIII. 222.
Variations of Triangles. See Trigonometry.

PARTICULAR FLUENTS.

Simpson on the fluents of polynomials. Ph. tr. 1748. 328.
Table of Fluents. Emerson's fluxions. 75.
Landen on fluents expressed by arcs. Ph. tr. 1771. 298.
Vince on finding fluents by continuation. Ph. tr. 1786. 432.

PROPERTIES OF CURVES.

Problematis de curva alias secante solutio generalis. Ph. tr. 1710. XXVI. 399.
Cotesii logometria. Ph. tr. 1714. XXIX. 5.
Cotesii harmonia mensurarum, a Smith. 4. Cambr. 1722. R. I.
  Extr. Ph. tr. 1722. XXXII. 139.
Taylor on the Leibnitzian problem of a curve cutting others. Ph. tr. 1717. XXX. 695.
Maclaurin de curvarum constructione et mensura. Ph. tr. 1718. XXX. 803.
Maclaurin methodus describendi curvas. Ph. tr. 1718. XXX. 934.
*Maclaurin geometria organica. 4. 1720. R. I.
  Extr. Ph. tr. 1720. XXXI. 38.
Maclaurin's further remarks on the description of curves. Ph. tr. 1735. XXXIX. 143.
Solutio problematis de curvis inveniendis. Ph. tr. 1722. XXXII. 106.
Brackenridge on describing curves by intersections. Ph. tr. 1735. XXXIX. 25.
Emerson's cyclomathesis. V.
Goudin sur les courbes. 4. Par. 1800. R. I.

TANGENTS OF CURVES.

Apollonius on tangencies. See Geometry.
Wallis's method of tangents. Ph. tr. 1672. VII. 4010.
Slusius's mode of drawing tangents. Ph. tr. 1672. VII. 5143. 1673. VIII. 6059.
Duttonus de curvarum tangentibus. Ph. tr. 1703. XXIII. 1333.

CURVATURE.

Krafft on curves which are their own evolutes. C. Petr. II. 216.
Euler on curves similar to their evolutes. C. Petr. XII. 3.
Riccati on determining curves from the radius of curvature. C. Bon. II. iii. 159.
Landerbeck Methodus inveniendi curvas e variatione curvaturae. Ph. tr. 1783. 456. 1784. 477.

QUADRATURE OF CURVES.

D. Gregory de dimensione figurarum.
  Extr. Ph. tr. 1684. XIV. 730.
Wallis on a quadrable portion of a spherical surface. Ph. tr. 1697. XVII. 584.
Wallis on easy measurements of figures. Ph. tr. 1700. XXII. 1697.
Gregory on a quadrable portion of a surface. Ph. tr. 1694. XVIII. 25.
Craig Methodus figurarum quadraturas determinandi. London, 1685.
  Extr. Ph. tr. 1686. XVI. 185.
  Addition by Craig. 186.
Craig de quadraturis. Ph. tr. 1694. XVIII. 113. 1697. XIX. 708, 785.
Craig Specimen methodi quadraturarum. Ph. tr. 1705. XXIII. 1346.
Demoivre's method of quadrature and reduction. Ph. tr. 1702. XXII. 1113.

*Newton Tractatus de quadratura curvarum, in optices ed. lat. 4. 1706.
Newton's quadrature of curves, by Stewart. 4.
Robins on a proposition of Newton's quadratures. Ph. tr. 1727. XXXIV. 230.
Waring's problems on quadratures. Ph. tr. 1763. 294.
Landen's new mode of computing areas. Ph. tr. 1768. 174.
Landen's new theorems for areas. Ph. tr. 1770. 441.
M. Young on the quadrature of curves. Ir. tr. 1787. 31.

LENGTH OF CURVES.

Craig de linearum curvarum longitudine. Ph. tr. 1708. 64.

CONSTRUCTION OF EQUATIONS.
See Equations.

Baker's geometrical key.
  Acc. Ph. tr. 1684. XIV. 549.
Halley de constructione problematum solidorum. Ph. tr. 1686. XVI. 335.
Euler on the construction of equations by the tractory. C. Petr. VIII. 66.

CONIC SECTIONS IN GENERAL.

*Apollonius Pergaeus et Serenus Halleii. f. Oxf. 1710. R. I.
  Acc. Ph. tr. 1717. XXX. 732.
L'hospital on conic sections. 4.
Demoivre proprietates sectionum conicarum. Ph. tr. 1717. XXX. 622.
*Simson sectiones conicae. 4. Edin. 1750.
Hamilton de sectionibus conicis. 4. 1758. R. I.
Emerson's cyclomathesis. V.
Waring's new properties of conic sections. Ph. tr. 1764. 193.

Waring's two theorems in conics. Ph. tr. 1765. 143.
Jones's properties of the conic sections. Ph. tr. 1773. 340.
**Vince's* elements of conic sections. 8. Camb. 1781. R. S.
Mallet de planis diametralibus in cono. 4. Ups. 1784. R. S.
Hutton's conic sections. 8. Lond. 1787. R. S.
Robertson Sectiones conicae. 4. Oxf. 1792. R. I.
Robertson's conic sections. 8. Oxf. 1802. R. I.
Walker's conic sections. 4. Lond. 1794. R. S.
Hellins on the rectification of the conic sections. Ph. tr. 1802. 448.

Circle.

Gregorii circuli et hyperbolae quadratura. 4. Pav.
  Acc. Ph. tr. 1668. III. 640.
Leibnitz on the quadrature of the circle. Hooke, Ph. coll. n. 6. p. 204.
Demoivre de sectione anguli. Ph. tr. 1722. XXXII. 228.
Jones on the relation of goniometrical lines. Ph. tr. 1747. XLIV. 560.
Vega, N. A. Petr. 1791.
  <small>Gives the proportion of the circumference to the diameter as far as 140 or 143 places.</small>
Hellins's improvement of Halley's quadrature of the circle. Ph. tr. 1794. 217.
Klügel on the rectification of the circle. Hind. Arch. II. 308.
Bürmann on the rectification of the circle. Hind. Arch. II. 487.
Pizzati sulla trisezione dell angolo. 8. Ven. 1795. R. S.
  <small>Gauss has discovered a mode of dividing the circle into any prime number of parts expressible by adding 1 to an integer power of 2.</small>

Brinkley on the sines of multiple arcs. Ir. tr. VII. 27.
Brinkley on Cotes's property of the circle. Ir. tr. VII. 151.
Montucla and Lalande. IV. 619.

Ellipsis.

Euler on finding the axes of an ellipsis from its diameters. N. C. Petr. III. 224.
Vince on the oval lathe. Ph. tr. 1780. 378.
Ivory on the rectification of the ellipsis. Ed. tr. IV. 177.
Wallace on elliptic arcs. Ed. tr. V. 251.

If a and b be the diameters, the circumference will be nearly equal to that of a circle of which the diameter is $\frac{1}{2}(a+b+\sqrt{2(aa+bb)})$. Hutton.

Hyperbola.

Brouncker's squaring of the hyperbola. Ph. tr. 1668. III. 645.
Wren on a hyperbolic cylindroid. Ph. tr. 1669. IV. 961.
Gregory on the hyperbola, in answer to Huygens. Ph. tr. 1668. III. 732. 882.
Klingenstierna Curvarum hyperbolicarum quadratura. Ph. tr. 1731. XXXVII. 45.
Landen on the arc of the hyperbola. Ph. tr. 1775. 283.

ALGEBRAICAL CURVES.

Viviani de locis solidis. f. 1701.
   Extr. Ph. tr. 1704. XXIV. 1607.
*Newton de lineis tertii ordinis. 4. With the Optice. 1706.
Demoivre on a curve of the third order. Ph. tr. 1715. XXIX. 329.
†Grandi flores geometriae. Ph. tr. 1723. XXXII. 355.
Bragelonge on lines of the fourth order. A. P.
Stone on two lines of the third order, omitted by Newton and by Stirling. Ph. tr. 1740. XLI. 318.
Castilioneus de curva cardioide. Ph. tr. 1741. XLI. 778.
Pemberton on the locus for three and four lines. Ph. tr. 1763. 496.
Waring proprietates algebraicarum curvarum. 4. R. S.

MECHANICAL CURVES.

Emerson's cyclomathesis. V.

Cycloid.

Roberval squared the cycloid in 1634. Montucla II. 9.
Wallis on quadrable portions of the cycloid. Ph. tr. 1695. XIX. 111.
Caswell's quadrature of a portion of the epicycloid. Ph. tr. 1695. XIX. 113.
Halley's general quadrature of epicycloidal spaces. Ph. tr. 1695. XIX. 125.
Hermann on spherical epicycloids. C. Petr. I. 210.
Clairaut's cycloidal description of the spiral of Archimedes. A. P. 1740. 148.
Lexell on spherical epicycloids. A. Petr. III. i. 49.
Euler on the double generation of epicycloids and hypocycloids. A. Petr. 1781. V. i. 48.
The concavity of a larger circle rolling on a smaller.

Involute of a Circle.

On the involute of a circle. Ph. tr. 1700. XXII. 445.
Fantoni on a mechanical curve. Ph. tr. 1767. 358.

Figures of Sines and Tangents.

Emerson's miscellanies. 232.

Logarithmic Curve.

Craig's quadrature of the logarithmic curve. Ph. tr. 1698. XX. 373.

Quadratrix of the Hyperbola.

Perks on a quadratrix of the hyperbola. Ph. tr. 1706. XXV. 2253.
  The sum of the tangent and subtangent is constant: the logarithmic curve may be organically described nearly in the same manner.

Tractory.

Hugens, Leibnitz, Grandi, Poleni, Bomie, Bernoulli, Clairaut, and Fontaine.

Perks on the tractrix. Ph. tr. 1715. XXIX. 331.

Cotes, logometria.

Clairaut on the tractories of curves. M. Berl. 1739. V. 33.

Riccati on the tractory and on syntractories. C. Bon. III. 479.

Emerson's fluxions.

Euler on simple and compound tractories. N. A. Petr. II. 1784. 3, 28.
  The mechanical tractory of a right line, without friction, is a cycloid.

Brougham. Ph. tr. 1798. 378.

British Magazine. April 1800.

CURVED SURFACES AND SOLIDS.

Wren on a hyperbolic cylindroid. Ph. tr. 1669. IV. 961.

Cowley's solid geometry, by Jones. 4.

Demoivre on the solids formed by lunes. Ph. tr. 1700. XXII. 624.

Euler's elements of the doctrine of solids. N. C. Petr. IV. 109.

Euler on the curvature of surfaces. A. Berl. 1760. 119.

Euler on the inverse method of tangents applied to solids. N. A. Petr. 1788. VI. 77.

Brackenridge on a solid not yet considered. Ph. tr. 1759. 446.
  A locus of right lines.

On the arrangement of spheres in a space. Emerson's miscellanies, 438.

Monge on stereotomy. Journ. Polyt. I. i. 1.

Kästner on the screw. Commentat. Gott. 1795. 1797.

Brinkley on certain portions of a sphere. Ir. tr. VIII. 513.

Brinkley on the surface of an oblique cylinder. Ir. tr. IX. 145.

Woodhouse on certain portions of a sphere. Ph. tr. 1801. 153.

MAXIMA OF CURVES.

Solution of Bernoulli's isoperimetrical problems. Ph. tr. 1697. XIX. 334.

Craig on curves of equal lengths. Ph. tr. 1704. XXXIV. 1527.

Euler on the general isoperimetrical problem. C. Petr. VI. 123.

Euler on the maxima and minima of curves. C. Petr. VIII. 159.

Euler Methodus inveniendi curvas maximi minimive proprietate gaudentes. 4. Lausanne, 1744.

Euler on isoperimetrical curves. N. C. Petr. VI. 3.

Simpson on isoperimetrical problems. Ph. tr. 1755. 4, 623.

De quibusdam maximis et minimis. 4. R. S.

Frisi on isoperimetrical problems. N. C. Petr. VII. 227.

Borda on the maxima of curves. A. P. 1767. 551. H. 90.

*Lagrange on isoperimetrical problems. M. Taur. II. ii. 173.

L'Huilier de maximis et minimis. 4. Wars. 1782. R. S.

HISTORY OF MATHEMATICS.

Wallis, Brouncker, and Wren on Neile's rectification of a parabolic curve in 1657, and Wren's of the cycloid in 1658. Ph. tr. 1673. VIII. 6146, 6149.

Wallis on the history of the cycloid. Ph. tr. 1697. XIX. 561.

<small>Wallis affirms that he extracted the square root of a number of 53 figures, to 27 places, by memory, in bed.</small>

Gregory on the true authors of some inventions. Ph. tr. 1694. XVIII. 233.

Vindiciae matheseos Gregorianae. Ph. tr. 1706. XXV. 2336.

Commercium epistolicum Collinsii et aliorum. R. I.

Extr. Ph. tr. 1715. XXIX. 173. On the invention of fluxions.

Conti and Leibnitz on the method of fluxions. Ph. tr. 1718. XXX. 923.

Taylor Apologia contra J. Bernoullium. Ph. tr. 1719. XXX. 955.

History of the quadrature of the circle, by Montucla, 1754.

Extr. in Hutton's recreations. I.

Maseres on the discovery of Cardan's rules. Ph. tr. 1780. 221.

Montucla, Histoire des mathématiques, par Lalande. 4 v. 4. Par. 1799.

Kästner Geschichte der mathematik. 8. Gotting. 1796—7.

<small>It is said that figures were employed by the Arabs in 813, in Europe in 991, in England 1253; that decimal arithmetic was introduced in 1402, Napier's logarithms in 1614.</small>

NATURAL PHILOSOPHY AND MECHANICAL ARTS IN GENERAL.

<small>Some works belonging to this class are arranged under the article Mathematics.</small>

*Aristotelis naturalis auscultationis libri.

Lucretius de rerum natura. 4. Lond. 1722.

Lucretius de rerum natura, a Creech. 8. Oxf. 1695. Basil, 1770.

Mathematici veteres.

Senecae quaestiones naturales. Ven. 1522. R. I.

R. Bacon Opus majus, by Jebb. 1733. R. I.

Ramelli Artificiose machine. f. Par. 1588. R. I.

Baconis scripta in philosophia. 12. Amst. 1653.

*Bacon's philosophical works, methodized by Shaw. 3 v. 4. Lond. 1733. R. I.

On induction. Bacon's novum organum.

Sennerti philosophia naturalis. 4. Wittemb. 1618.

Epitome Sennerti. 12. Amst. 1651.

Mersenni cogitata physicomathematica. Par. 1644. M. B.

B. Porta Magia naturalis. 8. 1650. M. B.

Descartes Principia philosophiae. Opp. II.

Schotti magia universalis. 4 v. 4. Wurtzb. 1657. M. B.

Schotti technica curiosa. 4. Nur. 1664. M. B.

M. of Worcester's scantlings of inventions. 24. Lond. 1663. B. B.

Repr. Ph. m. XIII. 43.

Jungii doxoscopiae physicae minores. 4. Hamb. 1668.

Power's experimental philosophy. 4. 1664. M. B.

Claubergii physica. 4. Amst. 1664.

Hooke's micrographia. f. Lond. 1665. R. I.

Hooke's experiments and observations, by Derham. 8. Lond. 1726. R. I.

Duchess of Newcastle on experimental philosophy. f. 1666. M. B.

Boyle on the usefulness of experimental philosophy. 4. Oxf. 1671.
  Extr. Ph. tr. 1671. VI.
Rohault Traité de physique. Par. 1671.
  Extr. Ph. tr. 1671. VI. 2138.
*Rohaulti physica Clarkii. 2 v. 8. Lond. 1711. 1729.
Rohault's natural philosophy. 2 v. 8. 1728. R. I.
Petty on the use of the duplicate proportion in natural philosophy. Birch. III. 156.
Dechales mundus mathematicus.
Duhamel philosophia vetus et nova. 4. Par. 1681. M. B.
Senguerdi Philosophia naturalis. 4. Leyd. 1685. M. B.
**Newtoni philosophiae naturalis principia mathematica. 4. Lond. 1687.
  Extr. Ph. tr. 1687. XVI. 297.

  " It may be justly said, that so many valuable philosophical truths as are herein discovered and put past dispute, were never yet owing to the capacity and industry of any one man."

*Newtoni principia, a Jaquier et Le Seur. 3 v. 4. Genev. 1739. R. I.
Newtoni principia, a Tssanek. 4. P. 1. Prague, 1780.
Newton's mathematical principles. 2 v. 8. Lond. 1729. R. I.
Newton's mathematical principles, by Davis. 8. Lond. 1803. R. S.
Emerson's commentary on Newton's principia. 8. Lond. 1770. R. I.
Sturmii physicae conamina. 12. Nuremb. 1687. M. B.
Sturmii physica electiva. 4. Nuremb. 1697. 1722. M. B.
Sturmii collegium experimentale. 2 v. 4. 1676. 1685. M. B.
Amontons Remarques et expériences de physique. Par. 1695. M. B.

Hofmanni lexicon universale. 4 v. f. Leyd. 1698. R. I.
Keillii introductio ad veram physicam. 8. Oxf. 1700. Lond. 1719.
Keil's natural philosophy. 8. 1726. R. I.
Hawksbee's mechanical experiments. 4. Lond. 1709. 8. 1719. R. I.
Muys Elementa physices. 4. Amst. 1711. M. B.
Scheuchzers naturwissenschaft. 2 v. 8. Zur. 1711.
Derham's physicotheology. 8. Lond. 1754. R. I.
Nieuwentyt regt gebruyk der wereltbeschouwingen. 4. Amst. 1716. B. B.
Nieuwentyt's religious philosopher. 3 v. 8. 1719. R. I.
Whiston on Newton's philosophy. 8. 1716. M. B.
Servière, Recueil d'ouvrages curieux. Lyons, 1719. R. I.
S'Gravesande Physices elementa mathematica. 2 v. 4. Leyd. 1742. M. B.
S'Gravesande's natural philosophy, by Desaguliers. 2 v. 4. Lond. 1747. R. I.
S'Gravesande's explanation of Newton. 8.
Verdries Conspectus philosophiae naturalis. 8. Giess. 1720. M. B.
Wolff's nützliche versuche. 3 v. 8. Halle, 1721—43.
Wolff's vernunftige gedanken. 3 v. 8. Halle, 1723—5.
*Leupolds theatrum machinarum. 9 v. f. Leipz. 1724 ... R. I.
*Pemberton's Newtonian philosophy. 4. 1728. R. I.
Musschenbroek dissertationes physicae. 4. Leyd. 1729. M. B.
Muschenbroek Elementa physices. 8. Leyd. 1734.
Musschenbroek's natural philosophy, by Colson. 2 v. 8. 1744. R. I.

*Musschenbroek Introductio ad philosophiam naturalem. 2 v. 4. Leyd. 1762. R. I.

Molières Recueil de leçons de physique. M. B. Abstr. A. P. 1734, 1736—8. H.

Teichmeyeri elementa philosophiae naturalis. 4. Jena, 1733. M. B.

Vanderzyl Theatrum machinarum. f. Amst. 1734.

Hambergeri elementa physices. 8. Jen. 1735. M. B.

Voltaire Philosophie de Newton. 8. Amst. 1738. M. B.

Helsham's lectures on natural philosophy. 8. 1739. R. I.

Martine's medical and philosophical essays. 8. 1740. R. I.

Institutions de physique. 8. Amst. 1741.

Bülfingeri elementa physices. 8. Leipz. 1742.

*Maclaurin's account of Newton's discoveries. 4. Lond. 1743. 8. 1750. R. I.

Nollet Leçons de physique experimentale. 6 v. 12. Par. 1743... M. B.
  Abstr. A. P. 1743, 1745, 1748, 1755, 1764, H.

Nollet Art des experiences. 3 v. 12. Par. 1770.

Segners einleitung in die naturlehre. 8. 1746. 1770.

Rutherforth's natural philosophy. 2 v. 4. 1748. R. I.

Crusius über natürliche begebenheiten. 8. Leipz. 1750.

Kraftii praelectiones in physicam theoreticam. 3 v. 8. Tubing. 1750.

Krügers naturlehre. 8. Halle, 1750.

Gordon Physicae elementa. 2 v. Erfurt. 1751.

Khell physica. 2 v. 4. Vienn. 1751.

Eberhards erste gründe der naturlehre. 8. Halle, 1752—67.

Eberhards sammlung der ausgemachten wahrheiten. 8. Halle, 1755.

Eberhards beiträge zur mathesi applicatae.

Saverien Dictionnaire de mathématique et de physique. 2 v. 4. Par. 1753.

Winklers anfangsgründe der physik. 8. Leipz. 1753. 1754.

Winkler's natural philosophy. 2 v. 8. 1757. R. I.

Desaguliers's course of experimental philosophy. 2 v. 4. Lond. 1763. R. I.

Martin's philosophia Britannica. 3 v. 8. 1759. R. I.

Martin's young gentleman and lady's philosophy. 3 v. 8. 1781. R. I.

Boscovich Philosophiae naturalis theoria redacta ad unicam legem. 4. Vienn. 1759. R. S.

Suckow Entwurf einer naturlehre. 1761.

Jones's first principles of natural philosophy. 4. 1762. R. I.

Jones's physiological disquisitions. 4. Lond. 1781.

Guyton de Morveau Essais de physique. 12. Dijon, 1762. R. I.

Euler Briefe an eine Deutsche prinzessinn. 3 v. 8. Leipz. 1769—74.

Euler Lettres a une princesse d'Allemagne, 3 v. 8. Mitau, 1770—4.
  Avec les additions de Condorcet et de Lacroix. 2 v. Par. 1787—8.

Euler's letters to a German princess, by Hunter. 2 v. 8. Lond. 1795. 1802. R. I.

Hanovii philosophia naturalis. 4. Hal. 1763.

Lovett's elements of natural philosophy. 8.

Handmaid to the arts. 8. London, 1764. R. I.

Emerson's remarks on the rules of philosophizing. Em. misc. 405.

Kästners einleitung in die mathematik. 4 v. 8. Gott. 1764—86.

Kaestneri dissertationes mathematicae et physicae. 4. Altenb. 1776.

From the transactions of the R. S. Gott.

Karstens Lehrbegriff der gesammten mathematik. Greifsw. 1764.
Karstens Anfangsgründe der naturlehre. 8. Halle, 1790. R. I.
Karstens Anleitung zur kenntniss der natur. 8. Halle, 1783. R. I.
Karstens Kurzer entwurf der naturwissenschaft. 8. Halle, 1785.
Rowning's natural philosophy. 2 v. 8. 1765. R. I.
Malers physik. 8. Carlsruhe, 1767.
Sigaud de la Fond Leçons de physique élémentaire. 2 v. 8. Paris, 1767. R. I.
Sigaud de la Fond Elémens de physique. 4 v. 8. Par. 1771.
Sigaud de la Fond Description d'un cabinet de physique. 2 v. 8. Par. 1785. R. I.
Silberschlags ausgesuchte versuche. 8. Berl. 1768.
Stattleri physica. 8 v. 8. Augsb. 1772.
Die natur der dinge erklärt. 8. Hannov. 1773.
Beyträge zur allgemeinen naturlehre. 4. Erf. 1773.
Hambergers allgemeine experimental naturlehre. 8. Jen. 1774.
Titii physicae dogmaticae elementa. 8. Wittemb. 1774.
Titii physicae experimentalis elementa. 8. Leipz. 1782.
Böckmanns naturlehre. 8. Carlsr. 1775.
  Maler improved.
Sénébier Art d'observer. 2 v. 8. Genev. 1775.
Eberts naturlehre für schulen. 8. Leipz. 1775.
Ferguson's lectures on natural philosophy. 8. London, 1776.
Goldsmith's survey of experimental philosophy. 2 v. 8. Lond. 1776. M. B.
Gablers naturlehre. 4 v. 8. Munich, 1778.
Richter Lehrbuch einer naturlehre. 1779.
Horsley's treatise on the power of God.
Turner's introduction to arts and sciences. 12.

Physique du monde, par Marivetz et Goussier. 5 v. Planches. 3 v. 4. Paris, 1780—7. R. I.
Achards chemisch physische schriften. 8. Berl. 1780.
Bailey's plates of machines approved by the society for the encouragement of arts. 2 v. f. Lond. 1782.
Atwood's description of experiments. 8. R. S.
Atwood's analysis of a course of lectures. 8. R. S.
Funks naturliche magie. 8. Berl. 1783.
Wieglebs sammlung von kunststücken. 2 v. 8. Leipz. 1784.
Wieglebs magie, von Rosenthal. 8. Berl. 1793 . . .
*Jacobsons technologisches wörterbuch. 4 v. Rosenthals fortsetzung. 4 v. 8. Berl. 1784 ...
Beckmanns beiträge zur geschichte der erfindungen. 6 v. Leipz. 1784 . . .
Percival on the pursuit of experimental philosophy. Manch. M. II. 326.
Bruchhausen Institutiones physicae. Münster, 1785—7.
Bruchhausens anweisung zur physik, von Bergmann. 3 v. 8.
Cancrins bergmaschinenkunst. Mayence, 1790.
Hallens magie. 4 v. 8. Vienna, 1785—7. R. I. 9 v. 8. Berl. 1793.
Decremps Magic blanche devoilée. Supplément. 8. Par. 1785.
Chambers's cyclopaedia, by Rees. 5 v. f. Lond. 1786. R. I.
Priestley's experiments relating to natural philosophy. 3 v. 8. Birm. 1786. R. S.
Priestley on airs. 3 v. 8. 1790. R. S.
Schurer Elémens de physique, en tables. 8. Strasb. 1786.
Deloys Abrégé chronologique. 4 v. 8. Strasb. 1786—9. R. I.

*Van Swinden Positiones physicae. 2 v. Harderwyck, 1786.
*Nicholson's introduction to natural philosophy. 2 v. 8. Lond. 1787. 1796. R. I.
Serrati Lettere di fisica sperimentale. 12. Flor. 1787. R. S.
Herz Grundlage zu vorlesungen. 8. Berl. 1787.
Kratzensteins vorlesungen über die physik. Copenh. 1787.
King's morsels of criticism. 4. Lond. 1788. R. S.
Delairas Physique nouvelle. 8. Par. 1788. R. S.
St. Pierre Etudes de la nature. 4 v. 12. Bruss. 1788. R. S.
Hellmuths volksnaturlehre. Brunsw. 1788.
Nicolai Anfangsgründe in der naturlehre. 1788.
*Grens grundriss der naturlehre. 8. Halle, 1788. 1801. R. I.
Ingenhousz nouvelles expériences. 8. Par. 1789. R. S.
Hoberts grundriss der naturlehre. 8. Berl. 1789.
Abr. tr. ph. Physique, par Reynier. 2 v. 8. Par. 1790.
Gütle Maschinen kabinet. Leipz. 1790.
Wolfs compendium der naturlehre. 8. Gott. 1791.
Ciscàr Maquinas y maniobras. f. Madr. 1791. B. B.
De Luc Lettres physiques et morales. 5 v. 8. R. I.
Vausenville Essai physicogeometrique. 8.
Krünitz Oeconomisch technologische encyclopädie, von Flörken. Berlin.
Klügels grundriss der naturlehre. 8. Berlin, 1792.
Klügels encyclopädie.
Hutton's dissertations in natural philosophy. 4. Edinb. 1792. R. I.

Geisslers beschreibung der neuesten instrumenten. 3 v. 8. Zittau. 1792—7. R. I.
Hube Unterricht in der naturlehre. 2 v. 8. Leipz. 1793.
Vince's plan of a course of lectures. 8. Cambr. 1793.
E. M. Amusemens des sciences. 1 v.
E. M. Mathématique. A . . Buf.
E. M. Physique, par Monge, Cassini, Bertholon . . . Vol. I. Par. 1793.
*Erxlebens naturlehre, von Lichtenberg. 8. Gott. 1794.
Hooper's rational recreations. 12. Lond. 1794. R. I.
Robison. Enc. Br. Art. Philosophy. Physics.
Robison's elements of mechanical philosophy. 8. Edinb. 1804.
*Repertory of arts and manufactures. 8. London. 1794 . . . R. I.
Anderson's institutes of physics. 8. Glasgow. 1795. R. I.
Gregory's economy of nature. 3 v. 8. Lond. 1796. R. I.
Kunze Schauplatz der maschinen. 8. Hamburg, 1796 . . .
*Barruel La physique réduite en tableaux. 4. Paris, an 7. R. I.
*Reports of the late Mr. Smeaton. 4. 1797. B. B.
Gehlers physicalisches wörterbuch. 5 v. 8. Leipz. 1798. R. I.
*Enfield's institutes of natural philosophy. 4. London, 1799. R. I.
Adams's lectures on natural and experimental philosophy. 4 v. 8. Lond. 1799. R. I.
Brehm's inquiries. 8. Glocester, 1799. R. I.
Walker's system of familiar philosophy. 4. Lond. 1799. R. I.
Brisson Dictionnaire de physique. 6 v. 8. Planches. 4. Par. an 8. R. I.

Brisson Principes de physique. 3 v. 8. Par. R. I.
Büsch Mathematik zum nützen und vergnügen. 2 v. 8. Hamb. 1800. R. I.
Bérard Mélanges physicomathématiques. 8. Par. an 9. R. I.
Jacotot Cours de physique expérimentale et de chimie. 2 v. 8. Pl. 1 v. 4. Paris, an 9. R. I.
Libes Traité élémentaire de physique. 3 v. 8. Par. 1801. R. I.
Willich's domestic encyclopaedia. 4 v. 8. Lond. 1802. R. I.
*Rees's cyclopaedia. 4. Lond. R. I.
*Cavallo's natural or experimental philosophy. 4 v. 8. Lond. 1803. R. I.
Imison's elements of science and art. 2 v. 8. Lond. 1803. R. I.
Kett's elements of general knowledge. 2 v. 8. 1803.
Hutton's recreations in mathematics and natural philosophy, from Montucla. 4 v. 8. 1803.
M. *Young's* analysis of the principles of natural philosophy. 8. Lond. 1803. In the form of a text book.
*Haüy Traité élémentaire de physique. 2 v. 8. Par. 1803. R. I.
  Acc. Journ. phys. LVII. 412.
**Dictionnaire des sciences naturelles. 8. Par. 1804 ...
Scientific dialogues for young people. 6 v. 12. London, 1800—5.

MECHANICS IN GENERAL.

Aristotelis mechanica.
Extracts from manuscripts of Vinci. Nich. II. 84.
Galileo della scienza mecanica. Op. I. 597.
Galileo Discorso intorno a due nuove scienze. Op. II. i. 79.
Torricellius de motu gravium. 4. Flor. 1644.

Cartesii mechanica. Op. Posth.
Mechanics. Ph. tr. Abr. I. v. 457. IV. iv. 346. VI. v. 275. VIII. v. 281. X. iv. 160.
Wallisii mechanica. 4. Lond. 1670. Op. I. 571.
  Extr. Ph. tr. 1669. IV. 1085.
Pardies La statique. 12. Par. 1673.
  Extr. Ph. tr. 1673. VIII. 6042.
Wilkins's mathematical magic. 8. 1680. B.B.
Roberval's project of a work on mechanics. A. P. VI. 68.
Lahire Mécanique. A. P. IX. 1.
**Newtoni principia. L. i. ii.
Leibnitii hypothesis physica. Op. II. ii. 3.
Leibnitii theoria motus abstracti. Op. II. ii. 35.
Parent Elémens de mécanique. M. B.
Parent Nouvelle statique. 1704.
Jean Bernoulli du mouvement. Op. III. 1.
*Hermanni phoronomia. 4. M.B. Amst. 1716.
Camus Traité des forces mouvantes. 8. Par. 1722.
Varignon Nouvelle mécanique. 2 v. 4. Par. 1725. R. I.
D. Bernoulli on the principles of mechanics. C. Petr. I. 126.
Pluche Spectacle de la nature. 4 v. 8. 1732. M. B.
Clairaut's dynamical problems. A. P. 1736. 1. H. 105.
Clairaut's dynamical principles. A. P. 1742. 1. H. 125.
Belidor. Arch. Hydr. I. i. 1.
Euleri mechanica. 2 v. 4. Petersb. 1736. M. B. Greifsw. 1790.
Euler on the general principles of motion and rest. A. Berl. 1751. 169, 199.
Euler on the mechanical knowledge of bodies. A. Berl. 1758. 131.
*Euleri theoria motus corporum solidorum. 4. Rostock. 1765. R. S.

Lacaille Leçons de mécanique.
Acc. A. P. 1743. H. 164.
Dalembert Traité de dynamique. 4. Par. 1743.
D'Arcy's dynamical problems and theorems. A. P. 1747. 344. 1750. 107.
Courtivron's statical and dynamical researches. A. P. 1748. 304. 1749. 15. H. 177.
Bossut's dynamical researches. S. E. III. 473.
Bossut Traité élémentaire de mécanique et de dynamique.
Acc. A. P. 1763. H. 135.
Bossut Traité de mécanique statique.
Acc. A. P. 1772. i. H. 99.
Foncenex on the fundamental laws of mechanics. M. Taur. II. ii. 299.
Kraft Forelæsninger over mechanik. 2 v. 4. Soroe. 1762—4.
Kraftii mechanica, a Tetens. 4. Bütz. 1772.
Krafts mechanik, von Steingrüber. Dresd. 1787.
Karstens Lehrbegriff.
Emerson's cyclomathesis. VII.
Emerson's mechanics. 4. 1794. R. I.
Ferguson's mechanics. 8. 1799. R. I.
Clark's theory of mechanics. 4.
Kästner Anfangsgründe.
Marie Traité de mécanique. 4.
Klügel grundsätze der reinen mechanik. Eberhards Phil. mag. I. iv. II. i.
Unterberger Anfangsgründe der mathematik. 1781. III.
E. M. Pl. VII. Mécanique.
Parkinson's mechanics. 4. Cambr. 1785. R. S.
Delangez on the motion of solids. Soc. Ital. III. 1.
Frisii cosmographia.
Lagrange Mécanique analitique. 4. Par. 1788. R. I.
Pasquich von der bewegung. Leipz. 1789.

Ciscar Maquinas y maniobras.
Busse's remarks on Euler and others. Hind. arch. II. 30.
**Laplace* Mécanique celeste. 4 v. 4. Par. an 6. R. I.
*Robison, Enc. Br. Suppl. art. Dynamics.
Robison's elements.
Francoeur Traité de mécanique élémentaire. 8. Par. an 9. R. I.
Eytelweins handbuch der mechanik und hydraulik. 8. Berl. 1801. R. I.
Prony Mécanique philosophique. Journ. polytechn. III. vii. R. I.

MOTIONS OF A POINT, IN GENERAL.

Wallis on the laws of motion. Ph. tr. 1668. III. 864.
Boyle's philosophical essays, ed. 2. Lond. 1669.
Extr. Ph. tr. 1669. IV. 1069. On the universality of motion.
A discourse on local motion, from the French. 12. Lond. 1670.
Extr. Ph. tr. 1670. V. 2010.
Mariotte on motion. A. P. I. 120. 132.
Lahire on motion. A. P. IX. 150.
Varignon's laws of motion. A. P. X. 153.
†On the continuation of motion. A. P. 1701. H. 14.
Carré on the laws of motion. A. P. 1706. 442. H. 124.
Hermann's general theory of motion. C. Petr. II. 139.
Crousaz on the nature of motion. A. P. Pr. I. i.
Riccati on the laws of motion. C. Bon. V. i. C. 171. 212.
Home on the laws of motion. Ed. Ess. I. 1.
Stewart on motion and inertia. Ed. Ess. I. 70.

Camus on motion, and on the elements of matter. Roz. VI. 420.
David on the cause of motion. Roz. XVIII. 192, 267.
Watson on time. 8. Lond. 1785.
Sack on motion, Geologie, 1785.

Composition of Motion.

Aristotle Mech. probl. I. 722.
Barrow Lectiones geometricae.
Roberval on the composition of motion. A. P. VI. 1.
Illustrations of the composition of motion. S'Gravesande and Musschenbroek.
Zanotti on compound motion. C. Bonon. I. 515.
Riccati on the cause of the composition of forces. C. Bon. II. ii. 305.
Euler on the motions of solids in all directions. N. C. Petr. XX. 188. 208.
Pistoi on the composition of motion and force. Acc. Sienn. III. 107.
Gr. Fontana on the resolution of force. Soc. Ital. III. 519.

Accelerating Forces.

Torricellius de motu gravium. 1641.
Riccioli almagestum novum. ii. c. 21.
Hooke on falling bodies. Birch. I. 195.
Borellus de motionibus a gravitate. 4. Reg. Jul. 1670.
    Abstr. Ph. tr. 1671. VI. 2210.
Halley on gravity. Ph. tr. 1686. XVI. 3.
On force. Act. erud. Lips. 1686. 161. 1696. 145.
Mariotte on the fall of heavy bodies. A. P. I. 249.
Varignon on the space described by falling bodies. A. P. II. 96. On accelerated motion. X. 231. 242. On arbitrary acceleration. 1709. 69. H. 97. On accelerated motion with resistance. 1709. 267. H. 97. On the velocity caused by various forces. 1719. 195. H. 77. On constant and variable forces. 1720. 107. H. 97.
Machines for measuring the fall of bodies. Leup. Th. M. G. t. 70.
Camus on motion accelerated by springs. A. P. 1728. 159. H. 73.
Riccati on the effects of attraction. C. Bon. II. iii. 143.
Manfredi and Zanotti on the impulse of springs. C. Bon. II. iii. 383. 413.
Euler on the effects of forces. A. Berl. 1748. 184.
Euler on the rectilinear motion of three bodies. N. C. Petr. XI. 144.
Kurdwanowski on the fall of bodies. A. Berl. 1755. 394.
J. A. Euler on the fall of a body towards a centre. A. Berl. 1760. 250.
Riccati on rectilinear motion towards a centre. C. Bon. VI. O. 138.
Kästner, Karstens, Kraft.
Vega Vorlesungen über die mathematik. III.
Frisi on the laws of gravity.
*Atwood on rectilinear motion and rotation. 8. R. I.
Flauguergues on a mechanical problem of forces with resistance. N. A. Petr. 1790. VIII. H. 31.
Anstice on the laws of falling bodies. 8. Lond. 1794. R. S.
Benzenberg's experiments on falling bodies. Gilb. XII. 367. XIV. 222.
Benzenbergs versuche über die gesetze des falles. Hamb.
Fischer's simplification of Atwood's machine. Gilb. XIV. 1.

Central Forces.

Hooke on central forces. Birch. II. 90.
*Huygens de vi centrifuga. Op. Posth.
Varignon on central forces. A. P. 1700. 83. H. 78. 1701. 20. H. 80. 1703. 140. 212. H. 65. 73. 1706. 178. H. 56. 1710. 533. H. 102.
Bomie on central forces. A. P. 1707. 477. H. 97.
Keill on central forces. Ph. tr. 1708. XXVI. 174.
*Keill de inverso problemate virium centripetarum. Ph. tr. 1714. XXIX. 91.
Hermann and Bernoulli on the converse problem of central forces. A. P. 1710. 519. H. 102.
*Demoivre de viribus centripetis. Ph. tr. 1717. XXX. 622.
*Maclaurin Geometria organica.
Montigny on the motion of bodies round a centre. A. P. 1741. 280. H. 143.
Emerson's fluxions.
Riccati on curvilinear motions. C. Bon. IV. O. 139.
Zanotti. C. Bon. V. i. C. 184.
David. Roz. XIX. 229.
Waring. Ph. tr. 1788. 67.
Cesaris. Soc. Ital. II. 325.
*On the inverse method of central forces. Manch. M. IV. 369. V. 101.
Trembley on trajectories. A. Berl. 1797. 36.
Brinkley. Ir. tr. VIII. 215.

Compound Central Forces.

Euler. A. Berl. 1760. 228. N. C. Petr. X. 207. XI. 152.
Euler on central forces in curves not lying in a plane. N. A. Petr. 1785. III. 144.
Lagrange. M. Taur. II. ii. 196. IV. iv. 188.
Riccati. C. Bon. V. ii. 421.
Jones's demonstration of Machin's law of equal solids. Ph. tr. 1769. 74.
Lexell. A. Petr. 1782. VI. i. 157.
Waring on the resolution of attractive forces. Ph. tr. 1789. 185.

Projectiles.

Halley on gunnery. Ph. tr. 1686. XVI. 3. 1695. XIX. 68.
Taylor de projectilium motu. Ph. tr. 1726. XXXIV. 151.
Maupertuis's arithmetical balistics. A. P. 1731. 297. H. 72.
Simpson on projectiles, independently of conic sections. Ph. tr. 1748. 137.
Casali's machine for measuring the motions of projectiles. C. Bon. V. i. C. 121. ii. 71.
Bernoulli on a balistic machine. A. Berl. 1781. 847.
Tennis. E. M. A. Art. Paumier.
*Robison. Enc. Br. Art. Projectiles.

Confined Motion.

Hugenii horologium osciliatonum. f. Par. 1653.
On the isochronism of vibrations in a cycloid. Ph. tr. 1673. VIII. 6032.
On descent in a cycloid. Ph. tr. 1697. XIX. 424.
Sault on the curve of swiftest descent. Ph. tr. 1698. XX. 425.
Varignon on the motion of bodies on united planes. A. P. X. 301.
Varignon on certain curves of descent. A. P. 1699. 1. H. 68. 1703. 140. H. 65.
Varignon on Sebastian's machine. A. P. 1699. H. 116.
Craig on the curve of swiftest descent. Ph. tr. 1701. XXII. 746.

Carré on pendulums. A. P. 1707. 49. V. 58.

Parent on the descent of a body producing a constant pressure. A. P. 1708. 224. H. 84.

Saurin on the shortest descent to a given line. A. P. 1709. 257. H. 68. 1710. 203.

Machin de curva celerrimi descensus vi data. Ph. tr. 1718. XXX. 86.

Bernoulli on isochronous and brachistochronous curves. A. P. 1718. 136. H. 55.

Louville on a difficulty respecting the evanescent arc and chord. A. P. 1722. 128. H. 82.

Euler on brachistochronous curves. C. Petr. II. 126. IV. 49. V. 143. VI. 28. VII. 135. N. C. Petr. XVII. 488. A. Petr. I. ii. 70.

Euler on vibrations in finite arcs. A. Petr. I. ii. 159.

Euler on a rotatory pendulum. A. Petr. 1780. IV. ii. 133. 164.

Euler Theoria motus solidorum.

Euler on the pressure upon the pivot of a pendulum. N. A. Petr. VI. 145.

Krafft on the conical paradox. C. Petr. VI. 389.

Krafft on descent upon an inclined plane. C. Petr. XII. 261. XIII. 100.

Krafft on circular pendulums. N. A. Petr. 1791. IX. 225.

Fontaine on tautochronous curves. A. P. 1734. 371. 1768. 460.

Courtivron on a circular pendulum. A. P. 1744. 384. H. 30.

Näcker on a tautochronous curve. S. E. IV. 99.

Lagrange on isochronous curves. A. Berl. 1765. 361. 1770. 97.

Dalembert on isochronous curves. A. Berl. 1765. 381.

Borda on the maxima of curves. A. P. 1767. 551. H. 90.

Landen's properties of the circular pendulum. Ph. tr. 1771. 308. 1775. 287.

Kästner on the cylinder rolling up a plane. D. Schr. S. Gott. 113.

Maseres's series for a circular pendulum. Ph. tr. 1777. 215.

Fontana on the descent of bodies in convex lines. Soc. Ital. I. 174.

Legendre on the cycloid. A. P. 1786. 30.

Legendre's example of a circular pendulum. A. P. 1786. 637.

Riccati on the tension of the thread of a pendulum. Soc. Ital. IV. 81.

Malfatti on circular descent. Soc. Ital. VII. 462.

Montucla Hist. math. IV. i. 5.

Biot on tautochronous curves. B. Soc. Phil. n. 73.

Brunings on the motion of a double cone. Hind. Arch. II. 321.

Bunce's governor for steam engines. Nich. II. 46. A conical pendulum.

Variable Pendulums and Elastic Surfaces.

Bossut on a pendulum of variable length. A. P. 1778. 199.

Euler on pendulums hanging by an elastic thread. A. Petr. III. ii. 95.

Bernoulli on a rotatory pendulum with an extensible thread. N. A. Petr. 1783. I. 213. 1784. II. 131. 1785. III. 162. 1786. IV. H. 102.

Fuss on the descent of a body on an inclined plane, with one or more elastic supports. N. A. Petr. 1791. IX. 252. 1792. X. 91.

Confined Motion with Resistance.

Krafft on the inclined plane. C. Petr. XII. 261. XIII. 100.
Euler on descent upon an inclined plane with resistance. C. Petr. XIII. 197.
Euler on a rotatory pendulum with resistance. A. Petr. 1780. IV. ii. 164.
Näcker. S. E. IV. 95.
Kästner on the inclined plane. Leipz. Mag. II. 1.
See Hydraulic Resistance.

MOTIONS OF SIMPLE MASSES.

Centre of Inertia.

See Centre of Gravity.

Lahire on the motion of the centre of inertia. A. P. IX. 175.
Laura Bassi on the motion of the centre of inertia. C. Bon. IV. O. 74.
Robison Enc. Br. Suppl. Art. Position.

Momentum.

Bulfinger on momentum. C. Petr. I. 43.

EQUILIBRIUM OF SYSTEMS OR OF COMPOUND BODIES.

Pressure and Composition of Force.

See Composition of Motion.

Stevin Oeuvres mathématiques. 4. 1634. M. B.
Varignon's machine not admitting equilibrium. A. P. II. 76.
Unstable equilibrium.
Varignon on a combination of forces. A. P. 1714. 280. H. 87.
Leupold. Th. St. t. 1. 2.
Krafft on the apparent ascent of a double cone. N. C. Petr. VI. 389.
Kotelnikow. N. C. Petr. VIII. 286.
Maupertuis on the laws of rest. A. P. 1740. 170.
Riccati on equilibrium, and on the composition of forces. C. Bon. II. ii. 305. iii. 215. V. ii. 186.
Bernoulli. C. Petr. I. 126.
Kaestner de vecte et compositione virium. 4. Leipz. 1753.
Kästner on a cylinder appearing to roll upwards. D. Schr. Soc. Gott. 113.
Foncenex M. Taur. II. ii. 299.
Journal des sav. 1764.
Dalembert, Dynamique.
Dalembert A. P. 1769.
Euler on the effect of friction in equilibrium. A. Berl. 1762. 265.
Euler on the distribution of pressure on a plane. N. C. Petr. XVIII. 289. Hind. Arch. I. 74.
Euler on some cases of equilibrium. A. Petr. III. ii. 106.
Belidor Ingénieur François.
Matteucci. C. Bonon. VI. O. 286.
Gr. Fontana on the resolution of force. Soc. Ital. III. 519.
Frisii cosmographia.
Fuss on the equilibrium of weights on curved surfaces. N. A. Petr. 1788. VI. 197.
Burja Grundlehren der statik. 1789.
Delangez on a case of pressure. Soc. Ital. V. 107.
Salimbeni's elements of statics. Soc. Ital. V. 426.
Paoli on the distribution of pressure. Soc. Ital. VI. 534.
Lorgna on the pressure of a body on its supports. Soc. Ital. VII. 178.
Laplace Mécanique céleste. I.
*Robison Enc. Br. Suppl. Art. Dynamics.

Mechanical Powers.

Archimedes.
Hamilton. Ph. tr. 1763. 103.
  His demonstration of the property of the lever is deduced from that of Archimedes.
Landen's essay on the mechanical powers.
Edgeworth's panorganon. Nich. IV. 443.

Lever.

Lahire on the lever. A. P. IX. 6. 152.
Roberval's paradox. Leup. Th. St. 4. t. 17.
Desaguliers on a paradoxical balance. Ph. tr. 1731. 125.
Aepinus on a new property of the lever. N. C. Petr. VIII. 271.
  A peculiar maximum.
Kaestner vectis theoria.
Vince on the lever. Ph. tr. 1794. 33. Repert. X. 49.
Schwab and Burja on the lever. A. Berl. 1797. 137.
Robison Enc. Br. Art. Statics. Steelyard.

Cylinders.

Hotchkiss's patent mechanical power. Repert. XIV. 24.
  A double capstan.

Wedge.

Bärmann de cuneo. 4. Wittemb. 1751.
Ludlam's essays.

Screw.

Leupold Th. Machinarium. t. 6. 7.
C. Bon. III. 131. 304.
Hunter on a new way of applying the screw. Ph. tr. 1781. 58.
Kästner on the screw. Commentat. Gott. XIII. 1795. M. 1, 47. XIV. 1797. M. 3.
Kaestner de theoria cochleae. Diss. vi. 38. Nich. I. 158.

Props.

Desaguliers's new statical experiments, on props. Ph. tr. 1737. 62.

Compound Machines.

Marcorelle on the statics of the human body. S. E. I. 191.

Centre of Gravity.

See Centre of Inertia.
Wallis de centro gravitatis hyperbolae. Ph. tr. 1672. VII. 5074.
Roberval on the centres of gravity of solids. A. P. VI. 270. 282.
Varignon on the centre of gravity of spheres. A. P. X. 508.
Clairaut on finding the centre of gravity. A. P. 1731. 159.
Bossut on the centres of gravity of cycloidal surfaces and solids. S. E. III. 603.
Illustrations of the centre of gravity. E. M. Pl. VIII. Amusemens de mécanique.
Gr. Fontana on the axis of equilibrium and the centre of gravity. Ac. Sienn. VI. 177.
L'Huilier's theorem respecting the centre of gravity. N. A. Petr. 1786. IV. H. 39.
Kramp on the centre of gravity of spherical triangles. Hind. Arch. II. 296.

Equilibrium of heavy Systems.

See Architecture.
D. Gregorii catenaria. Ph. tr. 1697. XIX. 637. 1699. XXI. 419.
Clairaut on catenariae. M. Berl. 1743. VII. 270.
Krafft on catenariae. N. C. Petr. V. 145.
Canterzani on the catenaria. C. Bon. VI. O. 265.
Legendre on the catenaria. A. P. 1786. 20.
Kästner on chains of unequal thickness. Hind. Arch. I. 69.

Fuss on the equilibrium of flexible threads, loaded with weights. N. A. Petr. 1794. XII. 145.

Equilibrium of Elastic Bodies.

Jo. Bernoulli on the elastic curve. Acta Lips. 1694. 1695.
Bernoulli on the cohesion and resistance of beams fixed at one end. A. Berl. 1766. 78.
Euler on the elastic curve. C. Petr. III. 70.
Euler on the equilibrium of elastic bodies. N. C. Petr. XV. 381. XX. 286. A. Petr. III. ii. 188.
Euler on the rectangular elastic curve. A. Petr. 1782. VI. ii. 34.
Lexell. A. Petr. 1781. V. ii. 207.

MOTIONS OF SYSTEMS, OR OF COMPOUND BODIES.

Collision.

Of impulsion. Galileo. Op. I. 957. II. 479.
Borellus de vi percussionis.
    Abstr. Ph. tr. 1667. II. 626.
Wallis, Wren, and Huygens. Ph. tr. 1668, III. 1669. IV.
Huygens, Journal des savans. Mars. 1669. A. P. X. 341. Op. II. 73.
Huygens Opusc. posth.

_{Huygens was the earliest in discovering the laws of collision, but not in publishing them.}

Mariotte Traité de la percussion. Op. I. 1.
Lahire on percussion. A. P. IX. 168.
Leibnitz Hypothesis physica.
Leibnitz Theoria motus abstracti.
Hermanni phoronomia.
Saulmon on the collision of elastic bodies. A. P. 1721. 126. H. 86. 1723. H. 101.
Mairan on the reflection of bodies. A. P. 1722. 6. H. 109. 1723. 343. H. 107. 1738. 1. H. 82. 1740. 1. H. 89.
Molières on the collision of elastic bodies. A. P. 1726. 7. H. 53.
Eames on the forces of moving bodies. Ph. tr. 1726. 183.
N. Bernoulli on percussion. C. Petr. I. 121.
Jean Bernoulli sur les loix de la communication de la motion. Par. 1727. Op. III.
*Maclaurin's demonstration of the laws of collision. A. P. Pr. I. iii.
*Maclaurin's fluxions.
*Maclaurin's Newtonian philosophy.
Mazières on the collision of bodies more or less elastic. A. P. Pr. I. v.
Bernoulli on the communication of motion. A. P. Pr. I. vii.
Euler on collision. C. Petr. V. 159.
Euler on oblique collision. C. Petr. IX. 50.
Euler on percussion. A. Berl. 1745. 21.
Euler on the impulse of a bullet on a plane. N. C. Petr. XV. 414.
Euler on the oblique collision of revolving pendulums. N. C. Petr. XVII. 315.
Euler Theoria motus corporum solidorum.
Louville's comparison of gravity and percussion. A. P. 1732. H. 100.
Hamberger. El. phys.
Gravesande on triple collision. Nat. Phil. Sect. 1257.
Rizzetti. C. Bon. I. 497.
Zanotti. C. Bon. I. 557. IV. O. 219.
Zanotti on elastic springs. C. Bon. III. iii. 413.
Manfredi on the impulse of springs. C. Bon. II. iii. 383.
Eberhard. Roz. Introd. I. 159.
Milner on the communication of motion by impact. Ph. tr. 1778. 344.
Lamberts gedanken über das gleichgewicht. Beyträge. II. 363.

Billiards. E. M. Pl. IV. Art. Paulmerie, pl. 4. 5. E. M. Amusemens de mécanique.

Kästner Höhere mechanik.

Ja. Bernoulli on the stroke of a ball on a board. N. A. Petr. IV. 1786. 148.

Gr. Fontana. Soc. Ital. III. 509. 513.

Büsch Mathematik.

Bruchhausen Anweisung, I. 81.

Bernstorff's problem relating to billiards. Journ. Phys. XLV. (II.) 45.

*Robison. Enc. Br. Suppl. Art. Impulsion. Percussion.

Rotatory Power, and Centres of Gyration, Percussion, and Oscillation.

Lahire on the effect of weights striking a lever. A. P. IX. 175.

Huygens on the centres of oscillation and agitation. A. P. X. 446. 462.

Parent on the centres of conversion and friction. A. P. 1700. H. 149.

Bernoulli on the centres of agitation and percussion. A. P. 1703. 78. 272. H. 114. 1704. 136. H. 89.

Taylor de centro oscillationis. Ph. tr. 1713. XXVIII. 11.

D. Bernoulli on mechanical centres. C. Petr. II. 208.

D. Bernoulli on eccentric percussion. C. Petr. IX. 189.

D. Bernoulli on oscillation. C. Petr. XVIII. 245.

Clairaut on the oscillations of a suspended body. A. P. 1735. 281. H. 92.

Camus on a problem respecting weights on a wheel. A. P. 1740. 201. H. 103.

Montigny on the motion of a system of bodies round an immoveable centre. A. P. 1741. 280. H. 143.

Euler on a new principle of mechanics. A. Berl. 1750. 185.

Euler on rotation upon a variable axis. A. Berl. 1758. 154. 1760. 176.

Euler on the collision of revolving bodies. N. C. Petr. XVII. 272.

Euler on the mechanical centres of triangles. A. Petr. III. ii. 126.

Euler on the momentum of rotation with respect to any axis. N. A. Petr. 1789. VII. 191. 205.

Short on Serson's horizontal top. Ph. tr. 1751. 35.

It spun in vacuo 2 h. 16'.

Bouguer on the forms fittest for rotation. A. P. 1751. 1.

Segner de motu turbinum. Halle, 1755.

First pointed out the three natural axes of rotation of all bodies: their existence was demonstrated by Albrecht Euler in 1760.

Mechanical centres. Emerson's fluxions. Emerson's mechanics. vi.

D'Alembert Opuscules.

Lagrange on the free rotation of a body of any figure. A. Berl. 1773. 85.

Frisi de rotatione corporum. 4. R. S.

Frisi on rotation. C Bon. VI. O. 45.

Frisii Cosmographia.

Smeaton on mechanic power. Ph. tr. 1776. 450.

Landen's new theory of rotatory motion. Ph. tr. 1777. 266.

Landen's mathematical memoirs.

Landen on the rotatory motion of a body of any form. Ph. tr. 1785. 311.

Asserts, in contradiction to Euler and D'Alembert, that the angular velocity must always be constant.

Milner. Ph. tr. 1779. 505.

Vince on progressive and rotatory motion. Ph. tr. 1780. 546.

Treats only of symmetrical bodies.

Atwood on motion.
Pasquich von der bewegung.
Wildbore on spherical motion. Ph. tr. 1790. 496.

> Defends Euler and D'Alembert, and attributes to Landen some confusion respecting motive and accelerative forces.

*Robison, Enc. Br. Art. Rotation.
M. Young's analysis.

> Contains several propositions copied from other authors, in which motion and force appear to be confounded.

Constrained Revolution.

Bernoulli on the rotation of a pipe and ball. A. Berl. 1745, 54.

Rotation with Progression and Resistance.

D. Bernoulli on the descent of spheroids on inclined planes. C. Petr. XIII. 94.
Euler on motions upon a horizontal plane. C. Petr. XIII. 220.
Euler on the motion of flexible bodies. C. Petr. XIV. 182. A. Berl. 1745. H. 54. N. C. Petr. XX. 286.
Euler on the motion of a body tied on a horizontal plane. A. Petr. II. ii. 162.
Euler on the descent of a rod upon a cylinder. A. Petr. 1782. VI. i. 117.
Euler on the motions of bodies rolling on a plane. A. Petr. 1781. V. ii. 131. 1782. VI. ii. 107. N. A. Petr. 1783. I. 119.
Euler on the motion of a cylinder with a thread round it. N. A. Petr. 1787. V. 149.
J. A. Euler on the motion of a globe upon a horizontal plane. A. Berl. 1758. 284. 1760. 261.
Chabanon de Maugris on the motion of a rod between two planes. S. E. IV. 646.
Vince on friction. Ph. tr. 1785. 165.
Fuss on the motion of a cylinder drawn up a plane. N. A. Petr. 1787. V. 176.
Fuss on the descent of a rod leaning against a wall. N. A. Petr. 1788. VI. 172.
Riccati on compound rotatory motion. Soc. Ital. IV. 96.
Kononov on the motion of a double cone. N. A. Petr. 1789. VII. 220.
Delangez on rotation upon inclined planes. Soc. Ital. V. 278.
Charles on the effects of rotation in billiard balls. Roz. XL. 19.
Bernstorff on billiards. Journ. Phys. XLV. (II.) 45.
Brünings on the motion of a double cone. Hind. Arch. II. 321.
Prony sur le mouvement d'un corps sollicité par des puissances quelconques. 4. Par. 1800. R. S.
Prony on the rotation of a body actuated by various forces. Journ. Polyt. II. vi. 297. IV. xi. 87.

Motions of connected Systems.

Parent on the track of bodies tied together. A. P. 1703. H. 110.
D. Bernoulli on the motion of an inclined surface. C. Petr. V. 11.
Euler on the equilibrium and motion of bodies with elastic joints. N. C. Petr. XIII. 250.
Euler on oscillations upon pulleys. A. Petr. II. ii. 137.
Euler on the motion of connected bodies on a plane. A. Petr. 1780. IV. i. 107.
Euler on the motion of a perfectly flexible thread. N. A. Petr. 1784. II. 108.

> The problem can only be solved in a few cases, and then by indirect methods.

Euler on the motion of connected cylinders. N. A. Petr. 1785. III. 142.

Lexell on the motion of connected bodies on a plane. A. Petr. 1781. V. i. 196.

Ja. Bernoulli on the motion of two irregular bodies connected together. N. A. Petr. 1788. VI. 154.

Fuss on the motion of a cylinder suspended by a thread wound round it. N. A. Petr. 1790. VIII. 256.

Bodies acting on each other.

See Laws of Gravity.

Euler on the rectilinear motion of three bodies. N. C. Petr. XI. 144.

Pendulous Bodies.

Bernoulli on the oscillations of a system of bodies. C. Petr. VI. 108. VII. 162. XV. 97. XVIII. 245.

Bernoulli on the coexistence of simple vibrations. N. C. Petr. XIX. 239.

A double pendulum, and the oscillations of two scales.

Euler on the oscillations of a flexible thread. C. Petr. VIII. 30.

Euler on a new kind of oscillations. C. Petr. XI. 128.

Euler on the motion of bodies perfectly flexible. C. Petr. XIV. 182.

Euler on isochronous compound pendulums. N. C. Petr. III. 286.

Euler on the oscillation of bodies divided or suspended by a thread. N. C. Petr. XVIII. 269.

The flexure of the thread produces no perceptible perturbation, when its length is greater than three times the radius of the ball.

Euler on a loaded pendulum. N. C. Petr. XIX. 285.

Euler on the vibrations of two scales. N. C. Petr. XIX. 302.

Euler on the equilibrium and motion of flexible bodies. N. C. Petr. XX. 286.

Euler on mixed oscillations. A. Petr. III. i. 89.

Euler on the oscillations of a suspended thread. A. Petr. 1781. V. i. 157.

Euler on the pressure of the pivot of a pendulum. N. A. Petr. 1788. VI. 145.

Krafft on a new species of oscillation. C. Petr. X. 200.

On the motion of flexible bodies. A. Berl. 1745. H. 54.

Riccati on compound confined motion. C. Bon. V. i. O. 150.

Fuss on a pendulum of two threads. N. A. Petr. 1783. I. 184. 203.

Vibrations independent of Gravity.

See Acoustics.

Lagrange on the force of springs. A. Berl. 1769. 167.

A spiral spring may be so fixed as to exert a force nearly constant. Supposing the number of convolutions infinite, the law of its motion approaches to that of a circular pendulum.

Propagation of Motion in Solids.

See Acoustics.

The whole of acoustics, except the sounds of some kinds of pipes, might be introduced here.

MEASURE OF FORCE.

Louville on the force of moving bodies. A. P. 1721. H. 81.

Pemberton on the force of moving bodies, against Poleni. Ph. tr. 1722. XXXII. 57.

Desaguliers's experiments to show that force is proportional to velocity. Ph. tr. 1723. XXXII. 269. 285.

Eames on the forces of moving bodies. Ph. tr. 1726. XXXIV. 188.

Clarke on velocity and force. Ph. tr. 1728. XXXV. n. 401. p. 381.

Mairan on the estimation of moving force. A. P. 1728. 1. H. 73.

Camus on the force of bodies in motion. A. P. 1728. 159. H. 73.

Hermann on the measure of force. C. Petr. I. 1.

S'Gravesande on the force of moving bodies. Ph. tr. 1733. XXXVIII. 143.

Explanation of the experiments on springs.

Jurin de vi motrice. Diss. 9.

Abstr. by Eames. Ph. tr. 1741. XLI. 607.

Jurin on the measure of force. Ph. tr. 1745. XLIII. 423.

Insists on Maclaurin's illustration by supposing a moveable space.

Jurin Principia mechanices metaphysica. Ph. tr. 1746. XLIV. 103.

Voltaire on moving force. A. P. 1741. XLI. H. 149.

Reid on quantity. Ph. tr. 1748. XLV. 505.

Richardson on percussion. Ph. tr. 1768. 17.

Smeaton on mechanic power. Ph. tr. 1776. 450.

Smeaton's fundamental experiments on collision. Ph. tr. 1782. 337.

Smeaton says, that, in the common hypothesis, the change of form in inelastic bodies must be an effect without a cause, since the quantity of motion remains the same. The fallacy lies in the definition of motion: the relative motion of the two bodies, which is destroyed, is the cause of the change.

Milner on the communication of motion by impact and gravity. Ph. tr. 1778. 344.

Against Bernoulli.

Lambert on the effect of the square of the velocity. A. Berl. 1783. 266.

Zuliani Sperimenti sopra l'effetto della caduta di gravi nelle materie cedenti. 4. Pad. 1798. R. S.

MAXIMUM OF MECHANICAL EFFECT.

S'Gravesande's natural philosophy. I. c. 21.

Euler on maxima and minima in the action of forces. A. Berl. 1748. 149.

Blake on the greatest effect of engines. Ph. tr. 1759. 1.

*Lambert on machines moved by a winch. N. Act. Helv. 1787. I. 75.

Lambton on the maximum of effect. As. res. VI. 137.

Langsdorfs hydraulik. c. 34.

Banks on mills.

Young. Journ. R. I. I. Nich. VI. 56. Rep. ii. II. 48.

GENERAL DERIVATIVE LAWS OF MECHANICS.

Jo. Bernoulli on living force. C. Petr. II. 200. Act. erud. 1735. 210. Op. III. n. 145.

D. Bernoulli on living force. C. Petr. X. 116. A. Berl. 1748. 356.

Maupertuis's principle of motion. A. Berl. 1746. 267.

D'Arcy on Maupertuis's minimum of action. A. P. 1749. 531. H. 179. 1752. 503.

Boscovich on living forces. C. Bon. II. iii. 289.

Euler on the general principles of motion and rest. A. Berl. 1751. 169. 199. On König's law of equilibrium. 219. 240. A. Berl. 1751. 246.

Bertrand on the least action. A. Berl. 1753. 310.

Dalembert on the principles of mechanics. A. P. 1769. 278.

Lexell's general theorems for the motion of solids. N. C. Petr. XX. 239.

Lagrange on a property of the centre of gravity. Ac. Berl. 1783. 290.

Lagrange on virtual forces. Journ. Polyt. II. v. 115.

Malvezio on the principle of Maupertuis. C. Bon. VI. O. 315.

Fossombroni sul principio delle velocità virtuali. 4. Flor. 1796. R. S.

Essay on the principle of virtual forces. Journ. Phys. XLVIII. 210.
Fourrier and Prony on the principle of virtual forces. Journ. Polyt. II. v. 20. 191.
Laplace Exposition du système du monde.
Laplace on determining a fixed plane. Journ. Polyt. II. v. 155.
Montucla and Lalande. III. 626.

PRACTICAL MECHANICS AND THEORY OF MACHINES.

Vitruvius.
Vitruve, par Perrault. f. Par. 1673.
Newton's Vitruvius. 2 v. f. R. I.
Marquis of Worcester's inventions.
Moxon's mechanic exercises. Lond. 1677. 8. 1703. R. I.
  Abstr. Ph. tr. 1678. XII. 967. 1006.
Papin Recueil de pièces touchant quelques machines. 8. Cass. 1695.
  Acc. Ph. tr. XIX. 1697.
Amontons on the force of machines. A. P. 1703. H. 100.
Leibnitz on the resistance of machines. M. Berl. I. 307.
Parent on the perfection of machines. A. P. 1714. H. 93.
Cabinet de M. de Servière.
Leupold Theatrum machinarum.
Tielen en Vander Horst Theatrum machinarum.
*Euler on the theory of machines. C. Petr. X. 67. N. C. Petr. III. 254. VIII. 230. A. Berl. 1747. 1752.
Vanderzyl Theatrum machinarum.
Pitot on the effects of machines. A. P. 1737. 269.
Polley Theatrum machinarum. Amst. 1737.
Krafft on simple machines. C. Petr. XI. 274.
Ferguson's select mechanical exercises. 8. Lond. 1790. R. S.

Belidor Ingénieur François.
Bossut Traité de mécanique.
Halle Werkstätte der künste. 6 v. 4. Brandenb. 1760—86.
Berthelot Mécanique appliquée aux arts. 2 v. 4. 1773.
Silberschlag on the instruments of the mechanical school at Berlin. 8. 1777.
*Coulomb on simple machines. S. E. X. Extr. Roz. XXVII. 204. 282.
E. M. Arts et Métiers. 8 v. By Roland de la Platrière.
E. M. Manufactures et Arts. 3 v. By Pilatre de Rozier.
Allgemeines repertorium der literatur.
  Account of various books on machines and manufactures.
Beckmann Anleitung zur technologie. 8. Gott. 1787.
*Jacobsons technologisches wörterbuch, von Rosenthal. Berl. 1787.
Justi Abhandlungen von manufacturen. 8. Berl. 1789.
Jungs lehrbuch der fabrikenwissenschaft. Nuremb. 1794.
Cancrins Bergmaschinenkunst.
Fenwick's four essays on practical mechanics. Newcastle.
*Smeaton's reports.
Langsdorff's maschinenlehre. 4.
*Robison, Enc. Br. Suppl. Art. Machinery. Mechanics.
Lempe Begriff der maschinenlehre. Leipz. 1797.
Rinmann and Nordwall on the mechanics of mining. 4. Stockholm.
  Acc. Ph. M. XIII. 76.
Dictionnaire des arts et métiers. 5 v. 8. Lyons, 1801. R. I.
Person Recueil de mécanique. 4. Paris, an 10. 1802. R. I.

*Banks on the power of machines. 8. Kendal, 1803. R. I.

Projects for a Perpetual Motion.

Papin on a pretended perpetual motion. Ph. tr. 1685. XV. 1240. 1686. XVI. 138, 267.
Lahire on the impossibility of a perpetual motion. A. P. X. 426.
Parent on the impossibility of a perpetual motion. A. P. 1700. H. 159.
Desaguliers on attempts towards a perpetual motion. Ph. tr. 1721. XXXI. 234.
Leupold. Th. M. G. t. 7. Hydr. ii. t. 15.
Emerson's mechanics. pr. 118.
On the impossibility of a perpetual motion. A. P. 1775. H. 65.
Apparent perpetual motions. E. M. Pl. VIII.
Amusemens de mécanique. Pl. 8.
Duplessis sur une machine à oscillations croissantes. 8. R. S.
Gr. Fontana. Soc. Ital. III. 502.
Montucla and Lalande. III. 813.
Nicholson. I. 375.
†Shivier's patent. Repert. VII. 165.
Balls to be raised, as usual.
†Varley's perpetual moving power. Repert. X. 9.
†Thiville's patent hydraulic moving power. Repert. XIV. 289.
Deduced from the oscillations of fluids, and from their capillary ascent.

Mathematical and preliminary Mechanics.

Drawing and Painting.

*Vinci on painting, by Rigaud. 8. London, R. I.
Dufresnoy's art of painting, by Dryden. 12.
On painting. Ph. tr. abr. I. ix. 593. VI. ix. 469.
Lahire on the practice of painting and drawing. A. P. IX. 425, 431, 464.
Depiles's principles of painting. 8.
Muzels and Parsons on encaustic painting. Ph. tr. 1756. 652—5.
Handmaid to the arts. 8. Lond. 1758.
On the materials for drawing and painting.
Colebrooke on encaustic painting. From Vitruvius. Ph. tr. 1759. 40, 53.
Draughtsman's assistant. 4.
Caylus on encaustic painting. 8. Lond.
Magellan on the use of caoutchouc. A. P. 1772. i. H. 10.
*Reynolds's discourses. 8.
Russel on painting in crayons. 4.
Drawing and painting. E. M. Beaux Arts. 2.
Painting. E. M. A. VI. Art. Peinture.
Brushes and pencils. E. M. M. I. Art. Crin.
Crayons. E. M. A. VI. Art. Pastel.
Mosaic work. E. M. A. V. Art. Mosaïque.
Prangens schule der mahlung. 8. Halle, 1782.
*Cooper on the painting of the ancients. Manch. M. III. 510.
Bayley's proportional scale for drawing. S. A. IX. 156. Repert. I. 144.
Lorgna on painting with compound oil. Soc. Ital. VI. 560.
Conté's crayons. Ann. Ch. XX. 370.
Lomet on crayons. Ann. Ch. XXX. 284. Nich. III. 416.
Neveu on design. Journ. Polyt. i. 78. ii. 107. iv. 698. v. 119. vi. 419.
Salmon's method of transferring pictures. Repert. VIII. 257.
Fabbroni on encaustic painting. Ph. M. I. 23, 141. Gilb. V. 357.
Fabbroni on cleaning prints. Repert. XI. 141.

Tatham on encaustic paintings, with hard resins. Ph. M. I. 406.
Blackman's oil colour cakes. S. A. XII. Ph. M. XVIII. 268.
Sheldrake on the Venetian painting. Ph. M. II. 302. Repert. X. 56.
Dayes on colouring. Ph. M. VIII. 1.
Inlaying marble. Repert. X. 326.
On mosaic work. Ph. M. IX. 289.
*Mechanics of drawing. Imison's elements. II. 240. Copying drawings. 327.
Davy on Wedgwood's mode of copying by a metallic solution. Journ. R. I. I. 173. Nich. 8. III. 167.
Gill on Indian ink. Ph. M. XVII. 210.
Malton's portfolios. Nich. IX. 128. Gilb. XIII. 113.

Writing, Characters, Signals.

Caneparius de atramentis.
On the Chinese characters. Ph. tr. 1686. XVIII. 63.
Chaumette's knife for making a pen at a stroke, with an inkstand for a handle. A. P. 1715. H. 66. Mach. A. III. 57. 61.
On speaking with the hands. Leup. Th. Ar. t. 2.
Clerk de stylis veterum et chartarum generibus.
  Acc. by Gale. Ph. tr. 1731. XXXVII. 157.
Jeake and Byron on short hand. Ph. tr. 1748. XLV. 345, 388.
Byron's short hand. 8.
Lalande Art de faire le papier. f. Par. 1761.
Lalande Art du parcheminier. 1762.
Cotteneuve's polygraph. A. P. 1763. H. 147.
Vaussenville on ruling paper. A. P. 1766. H. 162.
Lambert on ink and paper. A. Berl. 1770. 58.

*Büttner on the alphabets of all nations. N. C. Gott. 1776. VII. 106.
Holdsworth and Aldridge's short hand. 8.
Essay on signals. 8.
*Characters. E. M. A. I. Art. Caractères. With 25 plates by Deshauterayes.
Writing. E. M. A. II. Art. Ecriture.
Multiplying copies. E. M. A. VI. Art. Polygraphe.
Signals. E. M. A. VII. Art. Signaux.
Tablets for writing with silver. E. M. A. VIII. Art. Tabletier.
Short hand. E. M. A. VIII. Art. Tachygraphe.
Astle's origin and progress of writing. 4. R.I.
Blanchard's short hand. 4.
Gurney's short hand. 12.
Wakefield on the origin of alphabetical characters. Manch. M. II. 278.
Grenville's reckoning board for the blind. S. A. IV. 129, 144.
Blagden on ancient inks. Ph. tr. 1787, 451. Repert. II. 389.
<small>The letters may be made visible by moistening them first with a prussiated alkali, and then with a diluted acid.</small>
Report on Coulon's tachygraphy. A. P. 1787. H. 9.
Harvey on alphabetical characters. Manch. M. IV. 135.
Thicknesse on decyphering.
Thornton on the elements of written language. Am. tr. III. 262.
On intelligible signals. Am. tr. IV. 162.
Cooke on signals. Ir. tr. VI. 77.
Edgworth on the telegraph. Ir. tr. VI. 95. 319. Nich. II. 319.
On writing. Nich. I. 18.
On pasigraphy. Nich. II. 342.
Chappe, Breguet, and Bétancourt on the telegraph. B. Soc. Phil. n. 16.
Coquebert's mode of copying. B. Soc. Phil. n. 50.

Fry's pantographia. 8. Lond. 1799. R. S.
On a telegraph. M. Inst. III. H. 22.
Telegraph. Ph. M. I. 312.
A telegraph with lamps. Repert. I. 382.
Northmore on the pangraph, or universal character. Repert. II. 307. III. 91.
Ribaucourt on ink. Repert. IX. 125.
<small>Galls, logwood, gum, sulfate of iron and of copper, and sugarcandy.</small>
Nocturnal telegraph. Repert. X. 28.
Brunel's patent double pen. Repert. XIII. 153.
Boaz's patent telegraph. Repert. XVI. 223. Ph. M. XII. 84.
Enc. Br. Art. Signals. Telegraph.
Anderson on a universal character. Manch. M. V. 89. Anderson's Recreations. VI. 1.
Brown on a written character. Manch. M. V. 275.
Bérard's palpable mathematics. Mélanges. 182. Nich. 8. III. 189.
Close's writing ink. Nich. 8. II. 145.
Sheldrake's indelible ink. Nich. 8. II. 237.
Edelcrantz on telegraphs. Journ. Phys. LVI. 468. Nich. 8. V. 193.
Gough's scotiography. Nich. VII. 53.
<small>For the blind.</small>
A simple telegraph. Nich. VIII. 164.

Geometrical Instruments in general.

Digges's pantometria. Lond. 1571.
Schotti organum mathematicum. 2 v. Würtzb. 1668.
Varignon on the utility of mechanics in geometry. A. P. 1714. 77. H. 45.
Leupold. Th. Ar. Th. Suppl.
Mayer on geometrical instruments. C. Gott. II. 325.
Bion on mathematical instruments. f. 1758. R. I.

Fletcher's universal measurer.
Robertson on the use of mathematical instruments. 8. London.
E. M. A. III. Art. Instrumens de mathématique.
Fontana's account of the grand duke's cabinet. Roz. IX. 41.
Barrow on mathematical instruments.
Adams's geometrical and graphical essays, by Jones. 2 v. 8. London.

Pens and Rules.

Steel pens. Leup. Th. Ar. t. 24.
Parallel rules. Leup. Th. Ar. t. 21. a.
<small>Among others the scales made of late by Marquois.</small>

Compasses.

Duval's new compasses. A. P. 1717. H. 83.
Compasses. Leup. Th. Ar. t. 20. a. b.
Triangular compasses. Leup. Th. Ar. t. 28.
Gallonde's wheel and pinion compasses. A. P. 1745. H. 83.
Tilière's spiral compasses. A. P. 1742. H. 150. Mach. A. VII. 163.
Elliptic compasses. Vince Ph. tr. 1780.
Lorgna on the organic description of the conic sections. C. Bon. VII. O. 32.
Beam compasses. Shuckburgh, Ph. tr. 1798.

Proportional Compasses.

Vinci's M.SS.
Leup. Th. Ar. p. 121.
Toussaint de St. Marcel's proportional compasses. A. P. 1768. H. 131.

Pantographs.

Pantometer. Leup. Th. Ar. t. 26.
Langlois's pantograph. Mach. A. VII. 207.
Compound pantograph. Leup. Th. Suppl. t. 14. 15. Enc. Br. Art. Pantograph.
Sike's pantograph. A. P. 1778.

Triangles.

Triangle. Leup. Th. Ar. t. 18.
Cramer's trigonometrical instrument. Leup. Th. A. t. 31.
Bouffer's trigonometrical instrument. A. P. 1758. H. 101.

Measurement of Angles in general, and construction of Instruments.

Hooke's dividing engine with a screw. Animadv. on Hevelius.
Mayer on goniometrical instruments. C. Gott. II. 325.
Passement's mode of dividing the quadrant. Mach. A. VII. 341.
Duc de Chaulnes on the dividing machine. A. P. 1765. H. 140.
Duc de Chaulnes Art pour diviser les instrumens de mathematique. A. P. Arts. f. Acc. A. P. 1768. H. 127.
Pattier's dividing tools. A. P. 1771.
*Ramsden's description of a dividing engine. Lond. R. S.
Roz. I. 147.
Romain on the division of an angle. Roz. VIII. 55.
Rochon. A. P. 1777. H. 64.
Castillon on modes of division employed by Bird and by the D. de Chaulnes. A. Berl. 1780. 310.
Perez Trilichanon goniarithmetron. 4. Flor. 1781. R. S.
Perez sopra il suo stromento goniometro triplindice. 4. Bologna, 1786. R. S.
Carangeot's goniometer. Roz. XXII. 193. XXXI. 204.
Hutton's proposal for a new division of the quadrant. Ph. tr. 1784. 21.
Into parts of the radius.
Smeaton on the graduation of instruments. Ph. tr. 1786. 1.

Hindley's method was to drill equidistant holes in a brass plate, and then to make a hoop of it. Smeaton recommends to take from a scale the chord of 16°, and then to bisect it continually. He thinks divisions can only be ascertained to $\frac{1}{7000}$ of an inch, even by microscopes; and proposes several indices to be employed at once.

Ludlam on Bird's method of dividing. 4. Lond. 1786. R. S.
Hill's machine for measuring angles. S. A. VI. 183.
A simple instrument for measuring heights. Repert. III. 234.
Komarzewski on a subterraneous graphometer. Par. 1803. R. S. Nich. 8. V. 283.

Micrometer.

Hooke's lectures. Anim. on Hevelius.
Lambert über die Branderschen micrometer. 12. Augsb. 1769.
Hunter's screw. Ph. tr. 1781. 58.
Enc. Br. Art. Micrometer.
Austin's mode of cutting fine screws. Ir. tr. IV. 145. Repert. II. 399.
On the use of the screw. Nich. I. 158.
Hornblower on the micrometer screw. Nich. VI. 247.
Huddart's station pointer. Nich. VII. 1.
See also optical instruments.

Theodolites, Quadrants, and Sextants.
See Practical Astronomy.

Protractors, and Compasses for measuring Angles.

Calibers. Leup. Th. Suppl. t. 24. Enc. Br. Robertson Math. instr.
Mechanical trisection of an angle, by Ceva. 1694. Leup. Th. Ar. p. 167. t. 27.
Duval. Mach. A. III. 113.
Carangeau's graphometer for crystals. Nich. 8. I. 132.

Angular surveying.

See Figure of the Earth.

Pothinot on determining the position of a place concealed from view. A. P. X. 150.

Beighton's new plotting table. Ph. tr. 1741. XLI. 747.

On the height of the ascent of rockets. Robins. Ph. tr. 1749. XLVI. 131. Ellicott. Ph. tr. 1750. XLVI. 578.

Gensanne's machine for measuring small distances from a single station. Mach. A. VII. 111.

Langlois's machine for fixing instruments. A. P. 1751. H. 174.

Michell on the use of Hadley's quadrant in surveying. Ph. tr. 1765. 70.

Enc. Br. Ar. Circumferentor.

Meister on Meyer's scale for reducing angles to the horizon. Commentat. Gott. 1785. VIII. 75.

The white lights were found the best object by night. Ph. tr. 1790.

Levels.

See Astronomical Instruments.

Mathematical Machines.

Hooke in Birch III. 85.

Leibnitz's arithmetical machine. M. Berl. I. 317.

Napier's reckoning rods. Leup. Th. Ar. t. 4. 5.

Biler's logarithmic circle. 1696. Leup. Th. Ar. t. 13.

Reckoning machines. Leup. Th. Ar. t. 6..9.

Perrault's rhabdological abacus. Mach. A. I. 55.

Lepini's arithmetical machine. A. P. 1725. H. 103. Mach. A. IV. 131.

Pascal's machine. Mach. A. IV. 137. E. M. Pl. VII. Algèbre 2.

Clairaut's trigonometrical instrument. Mach. A. V. 3.

Clairaut's circular instrument. A. P. 1727. H. 142. Nich. V. 40.

Hillerin de Boissandeau's arithmetical machine. A. P. 1730. H. 116. Mach. A. V. 103.

Méan's arithmetical tarif. Mach. A. V. 165.

Gersten's arithmetical machine. Ph. tr. 1735. XXXIX. 79. Fig.

Smethurst's shwanpan, or account table. Ph. tr. 1749. XLVI. 22.

Robertson on Gunter's scale. Ph. tr. 1753. 96.

Description of Robertson's improved Gunter's scale. R. S.

Rowning's machine for finding the roots of equations. R. S.

Described Ph. tr. 1770. 240.

Nicholson's logistic circle and scales. Ph. tr. 1787. 246. Nich V.

Lorgna Fabrica delle squadre. 4. R. S.

Pearson on Gunter's scale. Nich. I. 45.

Measures.

Modes of obtaining a Standard.

Condamine on an invariable measure. A. P. 1747. 489. H. 83.

Blakey on a universal measure. 8. R. S. Rozier XV. 59.

Hatton's machine for finding a standard. S. A. I. 238.

Whitehurst's attempt to obtain measures of length from the measurement of time. 4. London, 1787.

Fordyce bought his apparatus: when well fixed it kept time very accurately. Ph. tr. 1794. 2.

Whitehurst on pendulums. 1792. R. I.

Boscovich on finding the length of the pendulum. Op. ined. V. 179.

Report on the choice of a unit of measures.

By Borda, Lagrange, Laplace, Monge, and Condorcet. A. P. 1788. H. 7. 17.
<small>The preference is given to the measurement of the meridian.</small>
Brisson on uniformity of measures, and on standards. A. P. 1788. 722.
<small>Recommends the pendulum as a standard, and measures of wood.</small>
Bonne Principes sur les mésures. 8. Paris, 1790. R. S.
Cotte on standards and universal measures. Roz. XXXVIII. 171. XXXIX. 89.
Boulard's invariable toise. Roz. XL. 198.
†Cooke on a standard. Am. tr. III. 328.
<small>Deduced from the discharge of water.</small>
*Reports to the National Institute on the measurement of the meridian. Roz. XLIII. 169. Journ. phys. XLIV. (I.) 81. B. Soc. Phil. n. 28. Nich. III. 316.
Account of the measurement of a base in France, and of the standards of platina. Ph. M. I. 269.
Prony on the reduction of observations of the pendulum. B. Soc. Phil. n. 44.
Leslie on a standard pendulum. Repert. I. 170.
*Remarks on experiments with pendulums. Nich. III. 29.

Comparison of Measures.

Bernardus de ponderibus et mensuris. Oxf. 1685.
   Acc. Ph. tr. 1685. XV. 1242. With a comparative engraving.
Cumberland on the Jewish weights and measures. 8. Lond. 1686. M. B.
   Acc. Ph. tr. 1686. XVI. 33.
Cassini on some Italian measures. A. P. VII. i. ii. 37.
Picard de mensura liquidorum et aridorum. A. P. VII. i. 321.

Cassini on ancient itinerary measures. A. P. 1702. 13. H. 80.
Delisle on the ancient geographical measures. A. P. 1714. 175. H. 80.
Lahire on the old Roman foot. A. P. 1714. 394.
Arbuthnot on antient coins. 4. Lond. 1727.
*Folkes on the standards in the capitol at Rome. Ph. tr. 1736. XXXIX. 262.
D'Ons en Bray on measures. A. P. 1739. XLI. 51.
Barlow on the analogy between English weights and measures of capacity. Ph. tr. 1740. XLI. 457.
*Comparison of English and French measures. Ph. tr. 1742. XLII. 185.
*Comparison of English standards. Ph. tr. 1743. XLII. 541.
Hellot and Camus on the standard ell. A. P. 1746. 607. H. 109.
*Gray on the measures of Scotland. Ed. ess. I. 200.
Berk on the Swedish measures. Swedish transactions.
Raper on the Roman foot. Ph. tr. 1760. 774.
<small>From monuments and buildings.</small>
*Christiani delle misure. 4. Ven. 1760.
Tillet on measures of corn and liquids. A. P. 1765. 452. H. 128.
Emerson's cyclomathesis. X.
La Condamine on the toise of the Chatelet. A. P. 1772. ii. 482. H. 8.
Norris's inquiry into the ancient English weights and measures. Ph. tr. 1775. 48.
*Paucton Metrologie. 1780.
E. M. A. VII. Superficies. E. M. Commerce. 3 v.
Howard on lazarettos. 5.
Romé de l'Isle Metrologie des anciens. Roz. XXXIV. 471.

Rennel on the travelling of camels. Ph. tr. 1791. 129.
Carney sur les poids et les mesures. 8. Montp. 1792. R. S.
Cotte on measures. Journ. phys. XLIV. (I.) 291.
Dawes's pantometry. 12. Lond. 1797. R. S.
Coquebert on the old and new measures. B. Soc. Ph. n. 5. Nich. I. 193.
*Shuckburgh on a standard of weights and measures. Ph. tr. 1798. 133. Nich. III. 97.
Fair's tables. R. S.
Eytelwein on the Prussian weights and measures.
Goodwyn's tables of English and French measures and weights. R. S. Nich. IV. 163.
Colebrooke on Indian weights and measures. As. Res. V. 91.
Tables of measures. Nich. I. 332. Ph. M. I. 245.
On the metre. Journ. Phys. XLVIII. 460.
Burja on the length of the pendulum at Berlin. A. Berl. 1799. 3.
On the cubit of the Nile. Nich. III. 330.
Vega and von Zach on measures and weights. Zach. Mon. corr. I. 610.
Beigel on the weights and measures of Bavaria. Zach. Mon. corr. I. 610.
Metrologie constitutionelle. 2 v. 4. Par. 1801. B. B.
Lesparat Metrologie. 2 v. 4. Par. 1801. R. S.
Brillat Metrologie Française. 1802. R. I.
Reports to the National Institute. M. Inst.
Egyptian measures. Nouet. Ph. M. XII. 208.
Pictet on the English and French measures. Bibl. Brit. n. 148. Journ. R. I., I. Ph. M. XII. 229. Nich. 8. II. 244. Repert. ii. III. 444.
Cavallo Exp. Ph. IV.
Hutton's recreations. I. 434.
On the Parisian pint. M. Inst. V. 29.
Gérard on the Egyptian measure. To be printed. S. E.

Tables of Measures. Standards.

The English yard is said to have been taken from the arm of King Henry I. in 1101.

Graham found the length of the pendulum vibrating seconds accurately equal to 39.13 inches. Desaguliers.

Bird's parliamentary standard is considered as of the highest authority: it agrees sufficiently with Sir George Shuckburgh's and Professor Pictet's scales made by Troughton.

The Royal Society's standard by Graham is perhaps about a thousandth of an inch longer than Bird's: but it is not quite uniform throughout its length. Maskelyne. Ph. tr.

The standard in the exchequer is about .0075 inch shorter than the yard of the Royal Society. Ph. tr. 1743. 541.

General Roy employed a scale of Sisson, divided by Bird. He says, that it agreed exactly with the Tower standard on the scale of the Royal Society. Ph. tr. 1785. 385.

Taking Troughton's scales for the standard, Sir G. Shuckburgh finds the original Tower standard 36.004, the yard E. on the Royal society's scale by Graham 36.0013 inches, the yard Exch. of the same scale 35.9933, Roy's scale 36.00036, the Royal Society's scale by Bird 35.99955, Bird's parliamentary standard of 1758, 36.00023.

The English standards are adjusted and employed at the temperature of 62° of Fahrenheit's thermometer: the French at the freezing point of water.

The French metre, the ten millionth part of the quadrant of the meridian, is 39.37100 English inches. Pictet, and Journ. R. I., I. 129. Y.

The metre has been found to contain 36.9413 French inches, or 3 feet 11.296 lines.

Hence the French toise of 72 inches is equal to 76.736 English inches. One of Lalande's standards measured by Dr. Maskelyne, was 76.732, the other 76.736. Ph. tr. 1765. 327.

In latitude 45°, a pendulum of the length of a metre would perform in a vacuum 86110.5 vibrations in a day. Borda. The length of the second pendulum is .993827 at Paris. M. Inst. II.

Prony's Report to the National Institute of Sciences and Arts. 6 Nivose, year 10, (27th December, 1801). Journ. R. I., I. 125.

A member read, in the name of a committee, the following report on the comparison of the standard metre of the Institute, with the English foot.

Mr. Pictet, Professor of Natural Philosophy at Geneva, submitted to the inspection of the class in the month of Vendémiaire, an interesting collection of objects relative to the sciences and arts, which he collected in his journey to England.

Among them was a standard of the English linear measure, engraved on a scale of brass, of 49 inches in length, divided by very fine and clear lines into tenths of an inch.

It was made for Mr. Pictet by Troughton, an artist in London, who has deservedly the reputation of dividing instruments with singular accuracy, it was compared with another standard made by the same person for Sir George Shuckburgh, and it was found that the difference between the two was not greater than the difference between the divisions of each; that is, it was a quantity absolutely insensible. This standard may therefore be considered as identical with the standard described by Sir George Shuckburgh in the Philosophical Transactions for 1798.

M. Pictet also exhibited to the Institute a comparer, or an instrument for ascertaining minute differences between measures, constructed also by Mr. Troughton. It consists of two microscopes with cross wires, placed in a vertical situation, the surface of the scale being horizontal, and fixed at proper distances upon a metallic rod. One of them remains stationary at one end of the scale, the other is occasionally fixed near to the other end; and its cross wires are moveable by means of a screw, describing in its revolution $\frac{1}{100}$ of an inch, and furnished with a circular index, dividing each turn into 100 parts; so that having two lengths which differ only one tenth of an inch from each other, we may determine their difference in ten thousandths of an inch. The wires are placed obliquely with respect to the scale, so that the line of division must bisect the acute angle that they form, in order to coincide with their intersection. General Roy has described, in the 75th volume of the Philosophical Transactions, a similar instrument made by Ramsden, for measuring the expansion of metals.

M. Pictet offered to the class the use of the standard, with the micrometer described, for the determination of the comparative length of the metre, and the English foot: the offer was accepted with gratitude, and MM. Legendre, Méchain, and Prony, were appointed to cooperate with M. Pictet in the comparison of the standard metre of platina and the English foot.

The first meeting was on the 28th Vendémiaire (21st of October), at the house of Mr. Lenoir.

At first a difficulty occurred from the different manner in which the measures were defined: the English scale was graduated by lines; the French standards were simply cut off to the length of a metre: hence the length of the metre could not easily be taken by the microscopes; nor could the English scale be measured by the method employed for making new standard metres, which consists in fixing one end against a firm support, and bringing the other into contact with the face of a cock or slider, adjusted so as barely to admit the original standard between it and the fixed surface.

Mr. Lenoir attempted to overcome this difficulty by reducing to a thin edge the terminations of a piece of brass of the length of a metre; so that it was compared with the standard metre in the usual manner; and its extremities, when placed on the English scale, constituted two lines parallel to those which were really engraved on the scale, and capable of being viewed by the microscopes.

The standard metre of platina, and another standard of iron, belonging also to the Institute, were thus compared with the English foot; each of these two measures being equal, at the temperature of melting ice, to the ten millionth part of the quadrant of the meridian. At the temperature of 15.3° of the decimal thermometer, or 59.5° of Fahrenheit, the metre of platina was equal to 39.3775 English inches; and that of iron to 39.3788, measured on Mr. Pictet's scale.

These first experiments showed, however, that the method employed was liable to some uncertainty, arising from the difficulty of placing the cross wires precisely at the extremity of the thin edge of the plate of brass employed in the comparison; a reflection or irradiation of light, which took place at that extremity, prevented its being distinctly observed if the optical axis of the microscope was precisely a tangent to the surface exactly at the termination.

In order to remove this inconvenience, another arrangement was proposed by one of the committee. (It was Mr. Prony that suggested this ingenious method, and M. Paul of Geneva, who happened to be present, that executed it. B. B.) A line was traced on a small metallic ruler, perpendicular to its length; the end of the ruler was fixed against a solid obstacle, and the cross wires made to coincide with the line: the standard metre was then interposed between the same obstacle and the end of the piece, and the line traced on it, which had now obviously advanced the length of the metre, was subjected to the other microscope. The microscopes, thus fixed, were transferred to the graduated scale; one of them was placed exactly over one of the divisions, and the micrometer screw was turned in order to measure the fraction, expressing the distance of the other microscope from another division.

The comparison was repeated in the same manner the 4th Brumaire (26th October) last, at the house of one of the committee, and after several experiments, agreeing very satisfactorily with each other, it was found that at the temperature 12.75°, or 55° of Fahrenheit, the standard of platina was 39.3781, and that of iron 39.3795 English inches.

The two metres being intended to be equal at the temperature of melting ice, these operations may be verified by reducing their results to that temperature. For this determination we are provided with the accurate experiments made by Borda, and the committee of weights and measures, on the dilatation of platina, brass, and iron; from which it appears, that for every degree of the decimal thermometer, platina expands .00000856; iron .00001156; and brass .00001783; for Fahrenheit's scale these quantities become 476,642, and 990 parts in a hundred millions. From these data we find, that, at the freezing point, the standard metre of platina was equal to 39.38280, and that of iron to 39.38265 English inches of M. Pictet's scale. The difference is less than the 500th of a line, or the 200000th of the whole metre, and is therefore wholly inconsiderable.

The result of the whole comparison is therefore this. Supposing all the measures at the temperature of melting ice, each of the standard metres is equal to the 10000000th part of the quadrant of the meridian, and to 39.38272 English inches of M. Pictet's scale. Paris, 16. Jan. 1802.

On examining the reduction of the standards of platina and iron to the freezing point, it appears that they differ somewhat less than is stated in the report, and that they coincide within a unit in the last place of the decimals expressing their magnitudes, or one ten thousandth of an inch. The standard of platina at the freezing point becomes equal to 39.37380, and that of iron to 39.37370 English inches on the scale of brass at 55°, and the mean of these to 39.37100 English inches at 62°, which is the temperature that has been universally employed in the comparison of British standards, and in the late trigonometrical operations in particular. This result agrees surprisingly with Mr. Bird's determination of the lengths of the toises sent by Mr. Lalande to Dr. Maskelyne, of which the mean was 76.734 inches: hence the metre, having been found to contain 36.9413 French inches, appears to be equal to 39.3702 English inches: or rather to be either 39.3694 or 39.3710, accordingly as the one or the other of the two toises happens to have been the more correct; we may therefore give the preference to that which measured 76.736 inches.

Allowing the accuracy of the French measurements of the arc of the meridian, the whole circumference of the globe will be 24855.43 English miles, and its mean diameter 7911.73. Journ. R. I., I. 129.

In the Bibliothéque Britannique, Vol. 19, No. 4. we find a description of the comparer of Lenoir, by Mr. Prony. Its peculiarity consists in the application of a bent lever, of which the shorter arm is pressed against the end of the substance to be measured, while the longer serves as an index, carrying a vernier, and pointing out on a graduated arch the divisions of a scale, which by this contrivance is considerably extended in magnitude. It does not, however, at first sight, appear to be certain that the difficulty of fixing the axis of the lever with perfect accuracy, and of forming a curve for the surface of the shorter arm, or of reducing the graduation of the arc to equal parts of the right line in the direction of the substance to be measured, might not in practice more than counterbalance the advantage of this mechanical amplification of the scale, over the simpler optical method employed in the English instruments. Journ. R. I., I. 180.

English Measures.

A foot is	12 inches.
A yard	36
A pole or rod	198
A furlong	7920
A mile	63360
A link	7.92
A chain	792
A nail of cloth	$2\frac{1}{4}$
A quarter	9
A yard	36
An ell	45
A hand	4
An acre	4840 square yards.

By an act of Queen Anne, the wine gallon is fixed at 231 cubic inches.

Hence, A pint is	28.875 cubic inches.
A quart	57.75
A barrel	7276.5
A hogshead	14553.

A pint, beer measure, ale measure, and country measure, is 35.25 cubic inches.

A quart 70.5 cubic inches.
A gallon 282.
A barrel, beer measure, is 10152
A barrel, ale measure, is 9024
A barrel, country measure, is 9588
A hogshead, beer measure, is 15228
A hogshead, ale measure, is 13336
A hogshead, country measure, is 14382

A pint, dry measure, is 33.6 cubic inches.
A quart 67.2
A pottle 134.4
A gallon 268.8
A peck, 537.6
A Winchester bushel 2150.42
A heaped bushel is one third more.
A quarter 17203.36

Five quarters make a way or load; two loads, a last of wheat.

A bushel of wheat, at a mean, weighs 60 pounds, of barley 50, of oats 38.

A chaldron of coals is 36 heaped bushels, weighing about 2988 pounds.

Ten yards of inch pipe contain exactly an ale gallon, weighing 10⅜ pounds. Emerson.

The old standard wine gallon of Guildhall contains 224 cubic inches.

It is conjectured, that some centuries before the conquest, a cubic foot of water weighing 1000 ounces, 32 cubic feet weighed 2000 pounds or a ton; that the same quantity was a tun of liquids, and a hogshead 8 cubic feet, or 13824 cubic inches, one sixty-third of which was 219.4 inches, or a gallon. A quarter of wheat was a quarter of a ton, weighing about 500 pounds, a bushel one eighth of this, equivalent to a cubic foot of water. A chaldron of coals was a ton, and weighed 2000 pounds. Barlow.

At present, 12 wine gallons of distilled water weigh exactly 100 pounds avoirdupois.

Scotch Measures.

An ell is 37.2 E. inches.
A fall 223.2
A furlong 8928.
A mile 71424.
A link 8.928
A chain, or short rood 892.8 E. inches.
A long rood 1339.2

An acre is 55353.6 square feet, English, or 1.27 English acre.

A gill is 6.462 cubic inches E.
A mutchkin 25.85
A choppin 51.7
A pint 103.4
A quart 206.8
A gallon 827.23
A hogshead 13235.7, or 16 gallons.

By the act of union, 12 Scotch gallons are reckoned equal to an English barrel, or 9588 cubic inches, instead of 9927.

A lippie or feed is 200.345 cubic inches English.

Old French Measures.

A point is .0148025 E. inch, or nearly $\frac{2}{135}$.
A line .088815, or nearly $\frac{8}{90}$.
An inch 1.06578, or $\frac{1}{93828}$, or $\frac{81}{76}$.

Thus, if a tall man were six feet four, French measure, he would be precisely six feet nine, English. And $\frac{81}{76} = \frac{9 \times 9}{4 \times 19}$.

A foot 12.78933.
An ell 46.8947, or 44 French inches; or, according to Vega, 43.9.
A sonde 63.9967, or 5 French feet, about $\frac{3}{5}$ E. fathom. Bonne, E. M.
A toise 76.7360, or 6 French feet.

A former comparison made it 76.71. Ph. tr. 1742. 185. The Bothnian toise was found too short by $\frac{1}{10}$ or $\frac{1}{12}$ line; but this was supposed to be from its having been accidentally injured. Lacondamine.

A perche 230.2080, or 18 French feet.
A perche, mesure royale, 22 French feet.
A league, 2282 toises, or $\frac{1}{25}$ of a degree.
A square inch, 1.13582 square inches, E.
An arpent was 100 square perches, about

$\frac{5}{6}$ E. acre, in the measure commonly used about Paris. An arpent, mesure royale, was about $1\frac{1}{4}$ E. acre.

A cubic inch is 1.21063 cubic inches, E.
A litron   65.34
A boisseau 1045.44, or 16 litrons.
A minot   2090.875, or 3 boisseaux, or nearly an E. bushel.
A mine   4181.75, or 2 minots.
A septier   8363.5, or 2 mines, or 6912 inches, Fr. For oats the septier was double.
A muid   100362. or 12 septiers.
A ton of shipping contains 42 cubic feet.

New French Measures. Journals R. I., I. 130.

The barbarous terms of the new nomenclature are here reduced to a form more consistent with their etymology.

	English Inches.
Millimetre	.03937
Centimetre	.39371
Decimetre	3.93710
Metre 3.281 feet	39.37100
Decametre	393.71000
Hecatometre	3937.10000
Chiliometre	39371.00000
Myriometre	393710.00000

A metre is 1.09364 yards, or nearly 1 yard, 1½ nail, or 443.2959 lines Fr. or .513074 toise.
A decametre is 10 yards 2 feet 9.7 inches.
A hecatometre   109 y. 1 f. 1 in.
A chiliometre 4 furl. 213 y. 1 f. 10.2 in.
A micrometre 6 miles 1 f. 156 y. 0 f. 6 in.
8 chiliometres are nearly five miles.
An inch is .0254 m. 2441 inches 62 metres, 1000 feet nearly 305 metres.

An are, a square decametre, is 3.95 perches, E.

A hecatare, 2 acres 1 rood, 35.4 p.

	Cubic Inches, E.
Millilitre	.06103
Centilitre	.61028
Decilitre	6.10280
Litre, a cubic decimetre	61.02800
Decalitre	610.28000
Hecatolitre	6102.80000
Chiliolitre	61028.00000
Myriolitre	610280.00000

A litre is nearly 2⅛ wine pints; 14 decilitres are nearly 3 wine pints; a chiliolitre is 1 tun, 12.75 wine gallons.

A decistere for fire wood is 3.5317 cubic feet, E.

A stere, a cubic metre,   35.3171

Various Measures, ancient and modern.

From Folkes, Raper, Shuckburgh, Vega, Hutton, Cavallo, and others.

Ancient Measures.

Arabian, foot	1.095 Engl. H.
Babylonian, foot	{ 1.144 H. { 1.135 H.
Drusian, foot	1.090 H.
Egyptian, foot	1.421 H.
Egyptian, stadium	730.8
Greek, foot	1.009 H.
	1.006 } Folkes, $1\frac{1}{24}$
	1.007 } Roman f.
	1.007 C.
Greek, phyleterian foot	1.167 H.
Hebrew, foot	1.212 H.
Hebrew, cubit	1.817 H.
Hebrew, sacred cubit	2.002 H.
Hebrew, great cubit = 6 common cubits. H.	
Macedonian, foot	1.160 H.
Natural foot	.814 H.
Ptolemaic = Greek foot.	H.
Roman, foot	.970 Bernard.
	.967 { Picard and { Greaves.
	.966 } Folkes. .967 }
	.970 before Titus. Raper.
	.965 after Titus. Raper.

Roman, foot	.9672 from rules. Sh.	Brussels, foot	.902 H.
			.954 V.
	.9681 from buildings. Sh.	Brussels, greater ell	2.278 V.
		Brussels, lesser ell	2.245 V.
	.9696 from a stone, Sh.	Castilian, vara	2.746 C.
		Chambery, foot	1.107 H.
	.967 H.	China, mathematical foot	1.127 H.
Roman mile of Pliny	4840.5 C.	China, imperial foot	1.051 H.
Roman mile of Strabo	4903.		1.050 C.
Sicilian foot of Archimedes	.730 H.	Chinese, li	606. C.
		Cologne, foot	.903 H.
		Constantinople, foot	2.195 ⎱ H.
			1.165 ⎰ H.

Modern Measures.

Altdorf, foot	.775 Engl. H.	Copenhagen, foot	1.049 H.
Amsterdam, foot	.927 H.	Cracau, foot	1.169 H. V.
	.930 C.	Cracau, greater ell	2.024 V.
	.931 Howard.	Cracau, smaller ell	1.855 V.
Amsterdam, ell	2.233 C.	Dantzic, foot	.923 H.
Ancona, foot	1.282 H.	Dauphiné, foot	1.119 H.
Antwerp, foot	.940 H.	Delft, foot	.547 H.
Aquileia, foot	1.128 H.	Denmark, foot	1.047 H.
Arles, foot	.888 H.	Dijon, foot	1.030 H.
Augsburg, foot	.972 H.	Dordrecht, foot	.771 H.
Avignon = Arles.		Dresden, foot	.929 Wolfe, Ph. tr. 1769. V.
Barcelona, foot	.992 H.		
Basle, foot	.944 H.	Dresden, ell = 2 feet	1.857 V.
Bavarian, foot	.968 Beigel. See Munich.	Ferrara, foot	1.317 H.
		Florence, foot	.995 H.
Bergamo, foot	1.431 H.	Florence, braccio	1.900 ⎱ C.
Berlin, foot	.992 H.		1.910 ⎰
Bern, foot	.962 Howard.	Franche comté, foot	1.172 H.
Besançon, foot	1.015 H.	Frankfort = Hamburg	H.
Bologna, foot	1.244 H.	Genoa, palm	.812 H.
	1.250 C.		.800 ⎱ C.
Bourg en Bresse, foot	1.030 H.		.817 ⎰
Brabant, ell, in Germany	2.268 V.	Genoa, canna	7.300 C.
Bremen, foot	.955 H.	Geneva, foot	1.919 H.
Brescia, foot	1.560 H.	Grénoble = Dauphiné	H.
Brescian, braccio	2.092 C.	Haarlem, foot	.937 H.
Breslau, foot	1.125 H.	Halle, foot	.977 H.
Bruges, foot	.749 H.	Hamburg, foot	.933 H.

Heidelberg, foot	.903 H.	Paris, metre	3.281 Y.
Inspruck, foot	1.101 H.	Parma, foot	1.869 H.
Leghorn, foot	.992 H.	Parmesan, braccio	2.242 C.
Leipzig, foot	1.034 H.	Pavia, foot	1.540 H.
Leipzig, ell	1.833 H. Journ. R. I.	Placentia = Parma	C.
Leyden, foot	1.023 H.	Prague, foot	.987 H.
Liege, foot	.944 H.		.972 V.
Lisbon, foot	.952 H.	Prague, ell	1.948 V.
Lucca, braccio	1.958 C.	Provence = Marseilles	
Lyons = Dauphiné.		Rhinland, foot	(†1.023 H.)
Madrid, foot	.915 H.		1.030 V. Eytelwein.
	.918 Howard.	Riga = Hamburg	
Madrid, vara	3.263 C.	Rome, palm	.733 H.
Maestricht, foot	.916 H.	Rome, foot	.966 Folkes.
Malta, palm	.915 H.	Rome, deto, 1/12 f.	.0604 F.
Mantua, brasso	1.521 H.	Rome, oncia, 1/12 f.	.0805 F.
Mantuan, braccio = Brescian. C.		Rome, palmo	.2515 F.
Marseilles, foot	.814 H.	Rome, palmo di architet-	
Mechlin, foot	.753 H.	tura	.7325 F.
Mentz, foot	.988 H.	Rome, canna di architet-	
Milan, decimal foot	.855 H.	tura	7.325 F.
Milan, aliprand foot	1.426 H.	Rome, staiolo	4.212 F.
Milanese, braccio	1.725 C.	Rome, canna dei mercanti	6.5365 F. 8 palms
Modena, foot	2.081 H.	Rome, braccio dei mer-	
Monaco, foot	.771 H	canti	2.7876 F. 4 palms.
Montpelier, pan	.777 H.		2.856 C.
Moravian, foot	.971 V.	Rome, braccio di tessitor	
Moravian, ell	2.594 V.	di tela	2.0868 F.
Moscow, foot	.928 H.	Rome, braccio di archi-	
Munich, foot	.947 H.	tettura	2.561 C.
Naples, palm	.861 H.	Rouen = Paris.	H.
	.859 C.	Russian, archine	2.3625 C.
Naples, canna	6.908 C.	Russian, arschin	2.3333 Ph. M. XIX.
Nuremberg, town foot	.996 H.	Russian, verschock, 1/16 ar-	
	.997 V.	schin	.1458
Nuremberg, country foot	.907 H.	Savoy = Chambery	H.
Nuremberg, artillery foot	.961 V.	Seville = Barcelona	H.
Nuremberg, ell	2.166 V.	Seville, vara	2.760 C.
Padua, foot	1.406 H.	Sienna, foot	1.239 H.
Palermo, foot	.747 H.	Stettin, foot	1.224 H.
Paris, foot	1.066 H.	Stockholm, foot	1.073 H.

Stockholm, foot	(.974 Celsius Ph.tr.)
Strasburg, town foot	.956 H.
Strasburg, country foot	.969 H.
Toledo = Madrid	H.
Trent, foot	1.201 H.
Trieste, ell for woollens	2.220 H.
Trieste, ell for silk	2.107 H.
Turin, foot	1.676 H.
	1.681 C.
Turin, ras	1.958 C.
Turin, trabuco	10.085 C.
Tyrol, foot	1.096 V.
Tyrol, ell	2.639 V.
Valladolid, foot	.908 H.
Venice, foot	1.137 H.
	1.140 Bernard, Howard, V.
	1.167 C.
Venice, braccio of silk	2.108 C.
Venice, ell	2.089 V.
Venice, braccio of cloth	2.250 C.
Verona, foot	1.117 H.
Vicenza, foot	1.136 H.
Vienna, foot	1.036 H.
	1.037 Howard, C.V.
Vienna, ell	2.557 V.
Vienna, post mile	24888. V.
Vienne in Dauphiné, foot	1.058 H.
Ulm, foot	.846 H.
Urbino, foot	1.162 H.
Utrecht, foot	.741 H.
Warsaw, foot	1.169 H.
Wesel = Dordrecht	H.
Zurich, foot	.979 H.
	.984 Ph. M. VIII. 289.

Modern Measures of surface and capacity.

In Austria, a yoke of land contains 1600 square fathoms; 1 metz or bushel 1.9471 cubic feet, 1 eimer = 40 kannen = 1.792 cubic feet, of Vienna; 1 fass = 10 eimer. Vega.

In Sweden; a kanne contains 100 cubic inches Swedish. C.

Measuring Instruments.

For their expansion see Heat.
Ph. tr. 1790. 121.

Rods.

Lemonnier on the increase of length of two rods. A. P. 1761. H. 26.

Boulard's invariable toise. Roz. XL. 198.

Roy found that deal rods, not varnished, were lengthened about half an inch in 300 feet by exposure for one night to moisture. Glass tubes were substituted for them, with caps of bell metal at the ends, connected with them by springs, which were brought in each operation to a certain mark on the rods; in order that unequal compression of the rods might be avoided. The French have employed rods of metal not brought perfectly into contact, measuring the short distance by a micrometer.

Chains.

Ramsden's steel chain. Ph. tr. 1785. 394.

The chain was found in the course of the trigonometrical survey began by General Roy not only the most convenient but also the most accurate measure. It was extended, when used, by a considerable weight, which was always equal. See Figure of the earth.

A chain of 40 links each $2\frac{1}{2}$ feet long. Ph. tr. 1795. 423.

Scales.

Hooke on diagonal divisions. Animadv. on Hevelius.

Wallis on diagonal divisions. Ph. tr. 1674. IX. 243.

Calibers. Leup. Th. Suppl. t. 24. Robertson on instruments.

Ramsden's description of a machine for dividing straight lines. 4. R. S.

Beam compasses. See compasses.

Enc. Br. Art. Calibers.

Micrometers.

See Measurement of Angles.

Hodometers, Machines for Measuring Distances.

Vitruvius describes a hodometer which told the miles by the fall of a pebble into a bason.
A. P. I. 45.
Leup. Th. Suppl. t. 3 .. 6.
Meynier. A. P. 1724. H. 96. Mach. A. IV. 93. 101. 105. For carriages.
Outhier. A. P. 1742. H. 143. Mach. A. VII. 175. For carriages.
Boistissandeau. A. P. 1744. H. 61.
Edgeworth's perambulator. Bailey's mach. I. 59.

A long screw serves as an axis to several spokes or radii with which it revolves, and carries an index hanging always vertically.

Enc. Br. Art. Perambulator.
Tugwell's pedometer. Repert. VI. 249. Edgeworth's improved.
Gout's patent watch pedometers. Repert. XIII. 73.

Instruments for observing Distances.
See Practical Astronomy.

Gensanne's machine. Mach. A. VII. 111.
Pantometrum Pauccianum. 4. For a single station. R. S.
Wenz on measuring distances from a single station. Act. Helv. 1760. IV. 55.
An instrument for measuring distances. Soc. Lausanne. Roz. XXXII. 95.
Peacock's reflecting instrument for measuring distances. Repert. I. 163.
Pitt's dendrometer. Repert. II. 238. With and without reflection.
Fallon's reflecting engymeter. Zach. mon. corr. VI. 46.

Surveying.

Ph. tr. abr. I. ii. 120. VI. iv. 271. VIII. iv. 228.
E. M. Pl. VII. Art. Arpentage.
Emerson's cyclomathesis. X.
Wild on subterraneous surveying, and on surveying mountainous countries. M. Laus. 1789. II. 328. 333.
Meagher. Ir. tr. V. 325.
Drallet on surveying hilly ground. Journ. Phys. XLVIII. 321.
Pfleiderer on determining 8 points from 4 stations, after Lambert. Hind. Arch. III. 190.
Davis's surveying. 8. Lond. 1802.
Burckhardt on a problem in surveying. Zach. mon. corr. IV. 359. 653.
Lomet on the use of balloons in surveying. Nich. VI. 194.

b. Maritime Surveying.

Murdoch Mackenzie on maritime surveying. 4. R. S.
Sounding line. E. M. A. VII. Art. Sonde.
Cooke on measuring a ship's way. Nich. V. 48.

Gauging, and Measurement of Solids.

On the tonnage of ships. A. P. I. 243.
Varignon on the tonnage of ships. A. P. 1721. 44. H. 43.
Mairan on the tonnage of ships. A. P. 1721. 76. H. 43. 1724. 227.
Gamaches on gauging casks. A. P. 1726. H. 74. Mach. A. IV. 223.
Pezénas on gauging casks. A.P. 1741. H. 100.
Camus's instrument for gauging. A. P. 1741. 385. H. 105.
Chatelain on gauging casks. A. P. 1759. H. 237.
Tillet's two machines for determining measures of capacity. A. P. 1765. 452. H. 128.
Emerson's cyclomathesis. X.
Hutton's mensuration.
Dès on the theory of gauging. S. E. 1773. xvi.
E. M. A. VIII. Art. Veltage.
E. M. Pl. VII. Mathématique Pl. 8.

Say's instrument for measuring volumes. Ann. Ch. XXIII. 1.

Farey on measuring timber. Ph. M. XIX. 213.

Modelling.

Aurum musivum for bronzing. Birch. I. 103.
Moulage. E. M. A. V.
Porcelaine. E. M. A. VI.
Artificial gems. E. M. A. VI. 739.
Papier maché. E. M. A. VI. Art. Pâtes moulées.
Beads. E. M. A. VI. Art. Paternotrier.
E. M. Beaux Arts.
Impressions in wax. Duhamel Art du cirier. f. Par. p. 93.
On multiplying copies in relief. Wilson. Nich. II. 60.
Gray. Nich. IV. 286.
Wedgwood's patent for ornamented porcelain. Repert. VII. 309.
Yates's patent for multiplying engravings. Repert. XII. 309.
<small>Thin plates filled up with lead.</small>

Casting.

Modelling for foundery. Valvasor on casting statues. Ph. tr. 1686. XVI. 259. E. M. A. III. Art. Fondeur. E. M. Pl. II. Art. Fer. iii. Pl. 3..9. Maullin's patent for casting screws. Repert. XIII. 6.
Imison's elements. II. 555.
Lenormand on moulding carvings. Ph. M. XVI. 247.

Sculpture.

Ph. tr. Abr. I. ix. 598. E. M. A. VII. Art. Sculpture. E. M. Beaux Arts.
On the use of steatite for gems. Ph. M. XVIII. 83.
<small>To be hardened by heat.</small>

Perspective.

Aleaume Perspective speculative et pratique. 4. Paris, 1643. R. S.
La perspective practique. 3 v. 4. Par. 1647.. M. B.
Jesuit's perspective. 4. Lond.
Perspective. Ph. tr. abr. I. ix. 598.
Huret Optique de portraiture. f. Par. 1670. Acc. Ph. tr. 1672. VII. 5048.
*Brook Taylor's linear perspective. 8. Lond. R. I.
Acc. Ph. tr. 1719. XXX. 300.
Zanotti's general theorem for perspective. C. Bon. III. 169.
Emerson's cyclomathesis. VI.
Malton's perspective. 4. R. I.
Martin's graphical perspective. 8. 1771.
Priestley's perspective. 8.
Kirby's perspective.
Kirby's perspective of architecture.
Clark's practical perspective. 8. R. S.
Perspective. E. M. Pl. VII. E. M. Pl. VIII. Art. Amusemens d'optique.
Torelli Elementa perspectivae. 4. Veron. 1788. R. S.
Lambert on perspective. Hind. Arch. III. 1.
Valenciennes Elémens de perspective pratique. 4. Par. an 7. R. I.
*Monge Géometrie descriptive. 4. R. I.
Edwards on perspective. 4. Lond. 1803. R. S.

Perspective Instruments.

Wren's instrument for drawing in perspective. Ph. tr. 1669. IV. 898.
Saint Clare Parallelogrammum prosopographicum. Ph. tr. 1673. VIII. 6079.
L'ouvrier's instrument for drawing from nature. A. P. 1753. H. 301.
Edgeworth's instrument for drawing. Nich. 8. I. 281.

Hettlinger's machine for drawing. Roz. XXIV. 389.
With glass.

Peacock's instruments for drawing in perspective. Repert. I. 313.

†Storer's patent delineator. Repert. IV. 289.
A camera obscura.

A frame for drawing in perspective. Hutton's recreations. II. 208.

Edgeworth's instrument for drawing. Nich. 8. I. 281.

Bérard's steganographic scale. Nich. 8. IV. 246.

Projections of the Sphere.
See Geography.

Engraving and Etching.

Evelyn's art of engraving. 8. Lond. 1662. M. B.

Mortimer on an antique metal stamp. Ph. tr. 1798. XL. 388.

Gravure. E. M. A. III. E. M. Beaux Arts.

Jackson on engraving in chiaro scuro. 8. B. I.

Cutting letters in copper. E. M. A. VI. Art. Plaques de cuivre.

Etching. E. M. A. VI. Art. Pinceau.

Rochon's mode of engraving by a machine. Rochon Recueil de mécanique. Journ. Phys. XLVII. (IV.) 365. Nich. III. 61. Enc. Br. Art. Type.

Nicholson's instrument for drawing parallel lines. Nich. II. 429.

Lowry's ruling machine. Nich. II. 523.

Accum upon etching on glass. Nich. IV. 1.

Puymarin on engraving upon glass. Repert. V. 210.

Longhi's moveable table for engravers. Repert. V. 354.

The aquatinter. 4. London.

Imison's elements. II. 345.

The ground for etching is made of white wax and asphaltum, each 40 parts, black pitch and Burgundy pitch, each one part: the wax and pitch are melted together, and the asphaltum is added; the whole is then kept simmering, till it becomes of a proper consistence. The plate is to be heated over a chafing dish, so as to melt the ground. The margin is surrounded with a mixture of one part of bees wax with two of pitch. Turpentine varnish, mixed with lamp-black, is occasionally used during the progress of the work. Imison.

Printing.

For Presses, see Compression.

Fournier Manuel typographique. 2 v. 8. Par. 1764. R. I.

Printing cards. *Duhamel* du Monceau Art de faire les cartes à jouer. f. Paris.

Luckombe on printing 8. 1771. R. I.

Anisson on printing, and on a new press, with figures. S. E. 1785. X. 613.

E. M. A. III. Art. Imprimerie. Imprimerie en taille douce. Imprimerie en couleurs.

Printer's grammar. 8. 1787. R. I.

Nicholson on printing with rollers. Nich. I. 18.

On stereotype printing. M. Inst. Nich. III. 43.

Rochon on typography. See Engraving.

Niebuhr on the Babylonian bricks. Zach. mon. corr. VII. 435.

Tilloch on stereotype printing. Ph. M. X. 267.

Magrath's Printers' Assistant. 8. 1805.

Types.

Moricherel's new matrixes for types. A. P. 1751. H. 171.

Types. E. M. A. I. Art. Caractères d'imprimerie.

Luce's vignettes for printing. A. P. 1772. i.

†Barclay's patent types. Repert. II. 4.

Sage on type metal. Repert. VIII. 418.

Ashby on printing types. Repert. XI. 18.

Enc. Br. Art. Printing press.
Rusher's patent types. Repert. ii. I. 91.

Musical Types.

Fournier's musical types. A. P. 1762. H. 192.
Gando on printing music. A. P. 1765. H. 184.

Copying.

Watt's patent for copying writings. Repert. I. 13.
Coquebert's simple method of copying. B. Soc. Phil. n. 50. Nich. 8. I. 147.
_{By putting sugar in the ink, and passing a hot iron over unsized paper laid on the writing.}
Toplis's method of multiplying copies. Repert. IV. 111.
_{Printing ink is applied to the block, and the corresponding parts of the impression remain white.}

Paper. See Union of Fibres.

Bookbinding.

Dudin Art du relieur doreur de livres. f. Par.
E. M. M. III. Art. Relieur.
Williams's patent for bookbinding. Repert. XII. 89.
Palmer's patent for binding books, with hinges of metal. Repert. XIV. 305.
Unrolling old books. E. M. A. VI. 732.

Statics.

Effect of the Air.

Fuss on the application of statics to geometry. N. A. Petr. 1793. XI. 220.
Homberg on the difference of weight in the air and in a vacuum. A. P. X. 257. See Hydrostatics.

Balances.

Lahire on balances. A. P. IX. 42.
Roberval's new balances. A. P. X. 343.
Illustrations of balances. Leup. Th. Stat. 5, 6..9.
Euler on balances. C. Petr. X. 3.
Emerson's mechanics. Fig. 188. 205. 206.
Brander Beschreibung einer hydrostatischen wage. 8. Augsburg, 1771.
Magellan's balances. Roz. II. 253. XVII. 44. 432.
Scanegatty's hydrostatic balance. Roz. XVII. 82.
E. M. A. I. Art. Balancier. E. M. Physique. Art. Balance.
Ramsden's balance. Roz. XXXIII. 144.
_{Turns with $\frac{1}{1000000}$ of the weight, and weighs ten pounds.}
Ramsden's hydrometrical balance. Roz. XL. 432.
Shuckburgh on a balance. Ph. tr. 1798.
Lüdicke's balance. Gilb. I. 123.
Troughton's balance. Nich. III. 233.
Andrews's patent balance. Repert. XI. 16.
Prony's universal support for balances. Ann. Ch. XXXVI. 3. Nich. V. 313. Repert. XV. 51.
Guyton's report on a balance. Ann. Ch. XLII. 23.
Atwood on balances. Gilb. IV. 148.
Dillon's balance approved. M. Inst. IV.
Wilson's patent weights. Repert. ii. II. 100.
_{Studer remarks, that beams of steel become sometimes erroneous by acquiring magnetic polarity. Gilb. XIII. 124.}
_{For weighing air or gases, the apparatus may be plunged in water, to lessen the pressure on the beam. Robison.}
_{Money is sometimes weighed by a simple lever with a fixed weight: by flattening it, it might be made to preponderate.}

Weighing Machines.

Weighing machines. Leup. Th. Stat. t. 45. 10..19. Th. M. G. t. 33. 34.

Desaguliers. p. 23.
Emerson's mechanics. f. 312.
   A weighing machine with chains.
Salmon's patent weighing machine. Repert. VI. 73.
   A weight acting on a spiral.
Whitmore's patent weighing machine. Repert. IX. 103.
   Secured from rust.
Weighing machine. Rees Cyclop. II. Pl. Engine.

Steelyards.

Hooke's steelyard. Birch. IV. 242.
Roëmer's Danish balance. Mach. A. I. 79.
Lahire on the steelyard. A. P. IX. 46.
†Emerson's mechanics. F. 190. Compound steelyard. F. 288.
Lambert. Act. Helv. III. 13.
Steelyard for iron. E. M. Pl. II. Art. Fer. ii. Pl. X.
   Cassini's steelyard shows the price of goods weighed.
Pictet on Paul's steelyard. Ph. M. III. 408.
   A coarse steelyard with a moveable fulcrum is sometimes made of wood.

Bent Levers.

Lahire on the bent lever balance. A. P. II. 9.
Lambert. Act. Helv. III. 13.
Desaguliers on the balance with an oblique thrust. Ph. tr. 1729. XXXVI. 128.
Ludlam's bent lever balance for yarn. Ph. tr. 1765. 205.
   A balance with a curved surface as a fulcrum is a bad substitute for a bent lever balance.

Spring Steelyards.

A spring steelyard. Musch. Introd. I. Pl. 4.
   Formed like a pair of shears.
Hanin's spring steelyard. A. P. 1765. H. 135. S. A. IX. 151. Roz. XXXIX. Enc. Br.
Regnier's spring steelyard, approved. M. Inst.

Standard Weights.

See Standard Measures.

Rhemnius Fannius Palaemon de ponderibus et mensuris.
   Commonly published with Priscian.
Norris's inquiry into the ancient English weights and measures. Ph. tr. 1775. 48.
Desaguliers on the French and English weights. Ph. tr. 1720. XXXI. 112.
*Barlow on the analogy between English weights and measures of capacity. Ph. tr. 1740. XLI. 457.
Comparison of English and French weights. Ph. tr. 1742. XLII. 185. 1743. XLII. 541.
*Reynardson on English weights and measures of capacity. Ph. tr. 1749. XLVI. 54.
   Considers the avoirdupois as the true standard, and the ounce as equal to the old Roman ounce.
Christiani delle misure d'ogni genere. 4. Ven. 1760.
Tillet on French and foreign weights. A. P. 1767. 300. H. 175.
Raper on the Greek and Roman money. Ph. tr. 1771. 462.
Brookes on East Indian weights.
Colebrooke on Indian weights. As. res. V. 91.
E. M. Commerce. 3 v.
Coquebert on the Chinese weights. B. Soc. Phil. n. 1.
Coquebert on the Dutch weights. B. Soc. Phil. n. 74.
Fair's tables. R. S.
Shuckburgh's experiments on standards. Ph. tr. 1798.
Studer on the weight of water. Gilb. XIII. 122.
Eytelwein. See Journ. R. I., I. 150.
Cavallo's Philosophy. IV.

Hutton's recreations. II. 152.
Fletcher on Shuckburgh's experiments. Nich. 8. IV. 35.

A gramme, the standard of the new French weights, is the weight of a cubic centimetre of pure water, at its maximum of density, =.0610280 cubic inches, English. The cubic decimetre was found to weigh in a vacuum 18827.15 grains of the marc of Charlemagne, which differed a little from Tillet's. The chiliogramme of platina was adapted for a vacuum, that of brass for the air. The cubic foot of water weighed 70 pounds 223 grains, at its maximum; 70 pounds 130 grains at the freezing point. M. Inst. II. 701. Hence a pound is 489.5058 grammes, a gramme 18.82715 grains French. According to Coquebert Montbret, a pound is only 489.147 grammes. B. Soc. Phil. n. 74.

It may be inferred from Sir George Shuckburgh's experiments, that the diameter of a sphere being 6.00745 inches, it loses 28715.85 grains of Troughton in water, reduced to 39°, or the maximum of density of water, the air at 39°, the barometer at 30., the standard brass scale employed at 62°. Hence, under these circumstances, the weight of a cubic inch of water, weighed against brass in air, is 252.8033 parliamentary grains: in vacuo 253.094; of a cubic foot in air 43684.41 grains=998.5 oz. av.=62.4063 pounds av.; in vacuo 43735.6 grains=999.67 ounces=62.48 pounds.

If we reduce these measures to more usual temperatures, the barometer being still at 30, the weight of a cubic inch at 52° will be found 252.68 grains; of a cubic foot 998 ounces; at 60°, the temperature employed by Gilpin, 252.56 grains, and 997.6 ounces; at 62°, the standard temperature of English measures, 252.52 grains, and 997.4 ounces. At this temperature, four cubic inches make 1010 grains, and 12 gallons exactly 100 pounds avoirdupois.

Mr. Fletcher finds some other experiments of Sir G. Shuckburgh more accurate than the author supposed them, and therefore takes a mean of the whole. After all corrections, the barometer standing at 29.5, the temperature 60°, the cubic inch of water appears to weigh in air 252.519 grains from the experiments on the cube, 252.432 from the cylinder, and 252.568 from the sphere; the mean being 252.506; in a vacuum 252.806. If the barometer be at 30, the weight from the sphere will be 252.563, nearly, as already stated, and the mean 252.501; we may therefore call it accurately 252.50; in a vacuum 252.77; for we must not add .3, which is the whole weight of a cubic inch of air, but only the difference between the weight of air and of brass. The French experiments, reduced to the same circumstances, give 252.56, and 252.83, agreeing with the sphere; taking the gramme=15.44403 gr. If we prefer Mr. Fletcher's mean, we must make the gramme=15.440 grains.

Professor Robison found a cubic foot at 55° weigh 998.74 ounces. Enc. Br. Art. Specific gravity. Hence, a cubic inch is equal to 252¼ at 50°; but his weights were not so well authenticated as Sir G. Shuckburgh's. Atkins on Specific Gravity.

Jacquin found a cylinder, 1 inch in diameter, 2 inches long, lose, in distilled water, 393.6 grains apothecaries weight of Vienna, the thermometer being at 43°, the barometer 28¼ inches of Vienna; it was weighed in air.

English Weights.

The avoirdupois ounce is supposed by Barlow to be the thousandth part of a cubic foot of water. The avoirdupois pound has been found to weigh 7001.5 or 7000.5 grains troy. Ph. tr. 1743.

A pennyweight, troy is 24 gr.
An ounce, or 20 pennyweights, 480
A pound, or 12 ounces, 5760

A drachm, avoirdupois, is 27.35 gr. troy.
An ounce, or 16 drachms, 437.5
A pound, or 16 oz. about 7000.

A stone is 14 pounds; a quarter 28 pounds; a hundred weight 112 pounds; a ton 20 hundred weight, or 2240 pounds.

A scruple, ℈j, apoth. weight, is 20 gr. troy.
A drachm, ʒj, or ℈iij, 60
An ounce, ℥j, or ʒviij, 480
A pound, ℔j, or ℥xij, 5760

Ten ounces troy are nearly equal to 11 avoirdupois, and 17 pounds troy to 14 avoirdupois.

Scotch Weights.

An ounce is 476 grains troy.
A pound trone is 20 ounces; a stone 16 pounds.

Old French Weights.

A grain is .8203 gr. Eng.
A denier, 24 gr. French, 19.69
A gros, 3 deniers, 59.06
An ounce, 8 gros, 472.5, 6¾/24 oz. troy.
A marc, 8 ounces, 3780.

162 CATALOGUE.—PHILOSOPHY AND ARTS, PRACTICAL MECHANICS.

A pound, 2 marcs, 7560. $\frac{21}{16}$ lb. troy.
1.08 lb. av.

New French Weights.

Milligramme	.0154 grains Eng.
Centigramme	.1544
Decigramme	1.5444
Gramme	15.4440 = $\frac{10000}{647}$, or 18.827 gr. Fr.
Decagramme	154.4402, or 5.65 dr. av.
Hecatogramme	1544.4023, or 3 oz. 8.5 dr. av.
Chiliogramme	15444.0234, or 2 lb. 3 oz. 5 dr. av.
Myriogramme	154440.2344, or 22 lb. 1.15 oz. av.

A hundred myriogrammes are nearly a ton. The sous and the franc weigh each 5 grammes. The franc contains one tenth of copper.

Ancient and Modern Weights.

Ancient Weights, from Hutton.

Greek Weights, in English grains.

Attic obolus	8.2	Christiani.
	9.1	Arbuthnot.
Attic drachma	51.9	Christiani.
	54.6	Arbuthnot.
Attic lesser mina	3892.	= 75 drachms. Chr.
Attic greater mina	5189.	= 100 dr. Chr.
	5464.	Arbuthnot.
Attic medical mina	6994.	Arbuthnot.
Attic and other talents = 60 minae.		
Old Greek drachm	146.5	Arbuthnot.
Another Gr. drachm	62.5	= Roman denarius. Arbuthnot.
Old Greek mina	6425.	Arbuthnot.
Egyptian mina	8326.	
Ptolemaic mina of Cleopatra	8985.	
Alexandrian mina of Dioscorides	9992.	

Roman Weights.

Denarius	51.9	Christiani, $\frac{1}{7}$ oz.
	62.5	Arbuthnot, $\frac{1}{7}$ oz.
Ounce	415.1	Christiani.
	437.2	Arbuthnot.
Pound of 10 ounces	4151.	Christiani.
Pound of 12 ounces	4981.	Christiani.
	5246.	Arbuthnot.

Various Modern Weights, from Hutton, Cavallo and Vega.

Pounds.	E. grains.	
Aleppo, rotolo	30985.	H.
Alexandria	6159.	H.
Alicant	6909.	H.
Amsterdam	7461.	H.
Amsterdam, commercial pound	7636.	= 10280 ases = 494.048 grammes. Coquebert. = 493.93 grammes. Vega.
Amsterdam, troy pound	7602.	Adjusted at Brussels 1553, = 10240 ases = 491.96 gram. Coquebert, = 492.0044 gram. Vega. A stone is 16 pounds, a pound 16 ounces, an ounce 16 drops.
Amsterdam, apothecaries pound, 369 gram. Vega.		
Antwerp	7048.	H.
Avignon	6217.	H.
Basle	7713.	H.
Bayonne	7461.	H.
Bergamo	{ 4664.	H.
	{ 11660.	H.
Bergen	7833.	H.

Pounds.	E. grains.	Pounds.	E. grains.
Berlin	7232. Eytelwein.	Genoa	{4426. H. / 6638. H.

A cubic foot Fr. of water, weighing 65.9368 pounds.

Bern	6722.	Germany, apoth. pound	5523.=357.66 grammes. Vega.
Bilboa=Bayonne.	H.		
Bois le Duc	7105. H.		
Bourdeaux=Bayonne		Hamburg	7315. H.
Bourg	7074. H.	Konigsberg	5968. H.
Brabant pound of Amsterdam	7249.=469.12 grammes. Coquebert.	Leghorn	5146. H.
		Leyden	7038. H.
		Liege	7089. H.
Brescia	4497. H.	Lille	6544. H.
Brussels, heavy pound=Troys. V.		Lisbon	7005. H.
Brussels, light pound	7201.=466.3 grammes. V.	London, avoirdupois	7000.=453.61 grammes. Vega.
Cadiz	7038. H.		
China, kin	{9223. H. / 5802.=375.708 grammes. =12 oz. 2 gros 24 gr. Fr.=10 leangs =100 tsiens. Coquebert.	London, troy	5760. H.=373.14gram.V.
		Lucca	5273. H.
		Lyons, silk	6946. H.
		Lyons, town weight	6432. H.
		Madrid	6544. H.
		Marseilles	6041. H.
Cologne	{7220. H. / 7218. Eytelwein.	Mélun	4441. H.
		Messina	4844. H.

A cubic foot Fr. of water, making 66.0656 pounds.

7223.=467.74 grammes.
Vega.

A cubic inch Fr. of water, at 59°, weighs 330.94 grains of Cologne. Studer, in Gilb. XI. 11. 122.

		Montpelier	6218. H.
		Namur	7174. H.
		Nancy	7038. H.
		Naples	4952. H.
Constantinople	7578. H.	Nuremberg	7871.=509.78 grammes. Vega.
Copenhagen	6941 H.		
Cracau, commercial pound	6252. H.=404.85 gram. Vega.	Paris	7561. H.=489.5 gram.V.
		Prague, commercial pound	7947.=514.35 grammes. Vega.
Cracau mint mark 3071.=198.82 grammes. Vega.			
		Revel	6574. H.
Damascus	25613. H.	Riga	6149. H.
Dresden	7210.=468.83grammes.V.	Rome	5257. H.
Dantzic	6574. H.	Rouen	7772. H.
Dublin	7774. H.	Saragossa	4707. H.
Florence	5287. H.	Seville=Cadiz.	
Geneva	9407. H.	Smyrna	6544. H.

Pounds.	E. grains.
Stettin	6782. H.
Stockholm	9211. H.
Strasburg	7277. H.
Toulouse	6323. H.
Troys. See Amsterdam.	
Turin	4940. H.
Tunis	7140. H.
Tyrol	8693.=562.92 grammes.V.
Venice	{ 4215. H.
	{ 6827. H.

Venice, libra sottile of 12 ounces=302.03 grammes. Vega.

Venice, pound of 12 ounces=358.1 grammes. Vega.

Venice, pound of 12 ounces, peso grosso= 468.17 grammes. Vega.

Venice, libra grossa=477.49 grammes. Vega.

Verona	5374. V.
Vicenza	{ 4676. H.
	{ 6879. H.

Vienna, commercial pound 8648.=560.01 grammes. Vega.

Vienna, apoth. pound=420.01 grammes. Vega.

Vienna, mint mark=280.64 grammes. V.

The jeweller's carat at Vienna is .206083 grammes. Vega.

Apothecaries Grains of different countries, from Vega.

Austria	1.125=$\frac{9}{8}$
Bern	.956
France	.981
Genoa	.850
Germany	{ .958
	{ .959=$\frac{71}{74}$ Gilbert.
Hanover	.978
Holland	.989
Naples	.860
Piemont	.824
Portugal	.864
Rome	.909
Spain	.925
Sweden	.955
Venice	.809

Sources of Motion.

For the application, see Machinery.

Deschamps on the force of machines. A. P. 1723. H. 120.

*Leup. Th. M. G. t. 33. 34.

On the measure and expense of first movers. Nich. II. 459.

Animal Mechanics.

*Borelli de motu animalium. R. I.

Perrault on animal mechanics. A. P. I. 181.

Parent on animal mechanics. A. P. 1702. H. 95.

D. Bernoulli on the muscles and the nerves. C. Petr. I. 297.

Mairan on the position of the legs in walking. A. P. 1721. H. 24.

Bourgelat on the motions of a horse. S. E. III. 531.

Motions of animals, flying, and swimming. Emerson's mechanics, f. 222..226, p. 206.

Horses. E. M. A. IV. Art. Maréchal ferrant.

Pinel on animal mechanics. Roz. XXXI. 350. XXXIII. 12. XXXV. 457.

Barthez Elémens de la science de l'homme. Extr. Journ. Phys. XLVII. (IV.) 271.

Imison's elements. I. 73.

Animal Force.

On the strength of men and horses. A. P. I. 47.

Lahire on the strength of men and horses. A. P. 1699. 153. H. 96.

Amontons on moving powers. A. P. 1703. H.

Camus Traité des forces mouvantes. 8. Par. 1722. M. B.

Instances of human strength. Desag. Lect. I. 289.

Deparcieux on the draught of horses. A. P. 1760. 263. H. 151.

Emerson's mechanics.

Ferguson's mechanics.

Lambert on human strength and its application. A. Berl. 1776. 19.

Cazaud on sugar mills. Ph. tr. 1780. 318.

Horses. E. M. A. I. Art. Chevaux.

Schulze on the strength of men and horses. A. Berl. 1783. 333.

Rennel on the rate of travelling of camels. Ph. tr. 1791. 129.

About 2¼ miles an hour.

Regnier's dynamometer. Journ. Polyt. II. v. 160. Gilb. II. 91. Ph. M. I. 399.

Coulomb on the daily labour of men. B. Soc. Phil. n. 16. M. Inst. II. 380. Nich. III. 416.

Buchanan on human labour. Repert. XV. 319.

The comparative force exerted in the action of pumping was 1742, by a winch 2856, in ringing 3883, in rowing 4095.

On the powers of horses and steam engines. Nich. IX. 214.

According to Schulze's experiments, the force which a man or a horse can exert with the velocity v, is $= f \left(1 - \frac{v}{a}\right)^2$, f being the force in equilibrium, and a the velocity without resistance. This is a formula of Euler: another of his expressions $f \left(1 - \frac{vv}{aa}\right)$ does not agree so well with Schulze's experiments. But Euler's theory is founded on assumptions wholly arbitrary. According to the first formula, the greatest mechanical effect would be when $v = \frac{1}{3}a$; according to the second, when $v = \sqrt{\frac{1}{3}a}$.

In order to compare the different estimates of the force of moving powers, it will be convenient to take a unit which may be considered as the mean effect of the labour of an active man, working to the greatest possible advantage, and without impediment; this will be found, upon a moderate estimation, sufficient to raise 10 pounds 10 feet in a second, for 10 hours in a day: or to raise 100 pounds, which is the weight of 12 wine gallons of water, 1 foot in a second, or 36000 feet in a day; or 3600000 pounds, or 432 000 gallons, 1 foot in a day. This we may call a force of 1. continued 36000″.

Immediate Force of men, without deduction for friction.

	Force.	Continuation.	Days work.
A man weighing 133 pounds Fr. ascended 62 feet Fr. by steps, in 34″, but was completely exhausted. Amontons.	2.8	34″	
A sawyer made 200 strokes of 18 inches Fr. each in 145″, with a force of 25 pounds Fr. He could not have gone on above 3 minutes. Amontons.	.6	145″	
A man can raise 60 pounds Fr. 1 foot Fr. in 1″, for 8 hours a day. Bernoulli.	.69	8h.	.552
A man of ordinary strength can turn a winch, with a force of 30 pounds, and with a velocity of 3¼ feet in 1″, for 10 hours a day. Desaguliers.	1.05	10h.	1.05
Two men working at a windlass, with handles at right angles, can raise 70 pounds more easily than one can raise 30. Desaguliers.	1.22		1.22
A man can exert a force of 40 pounds for a whole day, with the assistance of a fly, " when the motion is pretty quick, as about 4 or 5 feet in a second." Desaguliers, Lect. 4. But from the annotation it appears to be doubtful whether the force is 40 pounds or 20.	2.		2.
For a short time, a man may exert a force of 80 pounds, with a fly, " when the motion is pretty quick." Desaguliers.	3.	1′	
A man going up stairs ascends 14 metres in 1′. Coulomb.	1.192	1′	
A man going up stairs for a day raises 205 chiliogrammes to the			

	Force.	Continu-ation.	Days work.
height of a chiliometre. Coulomb.			.412
With a spade a man does $\frac{12}{10}$ as much as in ascending stairs. Coulomb.			.391
With a winch a man does $\frac{1}{3}$ as much as in ascending stairs. Coulomb.			.253
A man carrying wood up stairs raises, together with his own weight, 109 chiliogrammes to 1 chiliometre. Coulomb.			.219
A man weighing 150 pounds Fr. can ascend by stairs 3 feet Fr. in a second for 15″ or 20″. Coulomb.	5.22	20″	
For half an hour 100 pounds Fr. may be raised 1 foot Fr. in a second. Coulomb.	1.152	30′	

According to Mr. Buchanan's comparison, the force exerted in turning a winch being made equal to the unit, the force in pumping will be .61

In ringing 1.36

In rowing 1.43

Allowing the accuracy of Euler's formula confirmed by Schulze, supposing a man's action to be a maximum when he walks $2\frac{1}{2}$ miles an hour, we have $7\frac{1}{2}$ for his greatest velocity, $.04 (7\frac{1}{2}-v)^2$ for the force exerted with any other velocity, and $.016v(7\frac{1}{2}-v)^2$ for the action in each case: thus, when the velocity is one mile an hour, the action is .676

When two miles .964

Three .972

Four .784

And when five .5

And the force in a state of rest becomes $2\frac{2}{3}$, or about 70 pounds, with a velocity of two miles, 36 pounds, with three, 24 pounds, and with four, 15. It is obvious that in the extreme cases, this formula is inaccurate; but for moderate velocities it is probably a tolerable approximation.

Coulomb makes the maximum of effect, when a man weighing 70 chiliogrammes carries a weight of 53 up stairs. But this appears to be too great a load: he considers 145 chiliogrammes as the greatest weight that can be raised. He observes that in Martinique, where the thermometer is seldom below 68°, the labour of Europeans is reduced to one half.

Harriot asserts, that his pump with a horizontal motion enables a man to do one third more work than a common pump with a vertical motion. See hydraulic machines.

Porters carry from 200 to 300 pounds at the rate of 3 miles an hour; chairmen walk 4 miles an hour with a load of 150 pounds each; and it is said, that in Turkey there are porters who by stooping forward carry from 700 to 900 pounds placed very low on their backs.

The most advantageous weight for a man of common strength to carry horizontally is 111 pounds, or if he returns unladen, 135. With wheel barrows, men will do half as much more work as with hods. Coulomb.

Performance of Men by Machines.

	Force.	Continu-ance.	Days work.
A man raised by a rope and pulley 25 pounds Fr. 220 feet Fr. in 145″. Amontons.	.436	145″	
A man can raise by a good common pump a hogshead of water 10 feet high in a minute for a whole day. Desaguliers.	.875		.875
By the mercurial pump, or another good pump, a man may raise a hogshead 18 or 20 feet in a minute, for one or two minutes.	1.61	2′	
In a pile engine $55\frac{1}{4}$ pounds Fr. were raised 1 foot Fr. in 1″, for 5 hours a day, by a rope drawn horizontally. Coulomb.	.64	5h.	.32
Robison says, that a feeble old man raised 7 cubic feet of water $11\frac{1}{4}$ feet in 1′ for 8 or 10 hours a day, by walking backwards and forwards on a lever. Enc. Br.	.837	9h.	.753
A young man weighing 135 pounds, and carrying 30, raised $9\frac{1}{4}$ cubic feet $11\frac{1}{4}$ feet high for 10 hours a day without fatigue. Robison.	1.106	10h.	1.106
Wynne's machine enables a man to raise a hogshead twenty feet in a minute. Y.	1.75	3′	

Force of Horses.

	Force.	Continu-ance.	Days work.
Two horses attached to a plough in moderate ground exerted each a force of 150 Fr. Amontons. We may suppose that they went a little more than 2 miles an hour, for 8 hours.	5.4	8h.	4.32
A horse can draw with a force of 200 pounds 2½ miles an hour for 8 hours in the day.	7.33	8h.	5.87
With a force of 240 only 6 hours. Desaguliers.	8.8	6h.	5.28
The mean draught of 4 horses was 36 myriogrammes each, or 794 pounds. Regnier. This must have been momentary. Supposing the velocity 2 feet in a second, the action would have been	15.88	1″	
By means of pumps a horse can raise 250 hogsheads of water 10 feet high in an hour. Smeaton's reports.	3.64	1h.	

A horse can in general draw no more up a steep hill than three men can carry, that is from 450 to 750 pounds, but a strong horse can draw 2000 pounds in a cart up a steep hill which is but short. Desaguliers.

The diameter of a walk for a horse mill ought to be at least 25 or 30 feet. Desaguliers.

Some horses have carried 650 or 700 pounds 7 or 8 miles without resting, as their ordinary work; and a horse at Stourbridge carried 11 hundred weight of iron, or 1232 pounds, for 8 miles. Desaguliers.

A horse was exhibited in London, Jan. 1805, which was stated in the advertisement to be 20 hands high, 16 feet 5 inches long, and 8 feet 2 inches in girt: it was a coarse cart horse, bred at Denham in Middlesex. As nearly as I could measure it, its real height was 19¾ hands, or 6 feet 7 inches. It appeared to be very sluggish in its motions.

Work of Mules.

	Force.	Continu-ance.	Days work.
Cazand says, that a mule works in the West Indies 2 hours out of about 18, with a force of about 150 pounds, walking 3 feet in 1″	4.5	2h 40′	1.2

Inanimate Force.

Beale's remarks on mills. Ph. tr. 1677. XII. 841.

Cassini and Lahire on the water required for a mill. A. P. I. 286.

Kratzenstein's thermometrical power for a clock. N. C. Petr. II. 221.

*Smeaton on the powers of wind and water. Ph. tr. 1759. 100. Reprinted 8. Lond.

Loriot on raising weights by the tide. A. P. 1761. H. 159.

Stedman on the degrees of wind required for machines. Ph. tr. 1777. 493.

Heavy machines can only work about 10 of the year.

Coulomb on windmills. A. P. 1781. 65.

A windmill with 4 sails measuring 66 feet Fr. from one extremity to that of the opposite sail and 6 feet wide, or a little more, was capable of raising 1000 pounds Fr. 218 feet in a minute, and of working on an average 8 hours in a day. This is equivalent to the work of 34 men as it has been above estimated, 25 square feet of canvass performing about the daily work of a man.

On a perpetual motion by barometers. Nich. III. 126.

Robison says, that a hundred weight of coals burned in a steam engine will raise at least 20000 cubic feet of water 24 feet high: this effect is equivalent to the daily labour of 8.32 men. A steam engine in London, with a 24 inch cylinder, does the work of 72 horses, and burns a chaldron of coals in a day; each bushel being equivalent to two horses, and each square inch of the cylinder performing nearly the work of a man.

If we calculate the quantity of motion produced by gunpowder, we shall find that this agent, though extremely convenient, is far more expensive than human labour. But the advantage of powder consists in the great rarity of the active substance: a spring or a bow can only act with a moderate velocity on account of its own weight; the air of the atmosphere, however compressed, could not flow into a vacuum with a velocity so great as 1500 feet in a second; hydrogen gas might move more rapidly; but the elastic substance produced by gunpowder is capable of propelling a very heavy cannon ball with a much greater velocity.

It is said that 9 tons of water, falling 10 feet, will grind and dress a bushel of wheat; consequently a man might do the same in 33′ 36″.

Passive Strength.

Marchetti de resistentia solidorum. 4. Flor. 1665.
   Extr. Ph. tr. 1672. VII. 4050.
Plott on felling timber. Ph. tr. 1693. XVII. 455.
Leeuwenhoek on felling timber. Ph. tr. 1694. XVIII. 224.
Blondel on the forms of greatest strength. A. P. V. 116.
Lahire on the resistance of solids. A. P. IX. 203.
Varignon on the resistance of solids. A. P. 1702. 66. H. 102.
Parent on hollow cylinders. A. P. 1702. H. 120.
On the resistance of solids. A. P. 1705. 176. H. 130.
Parent on the strength of beams. A. P. 1707. 512. 1708. 17. H. 116.
Parent on the points of rupture. A. P. 1710. 177. H. 126.
Deschamps's machine for measuring the force of springs. A. P. 1723. H. 120. Mach. A. IV. 49.
Leup. Th. Pontif. t. 8.
Pitot on the strength of centres. A. P. 1726. 216. H. 65.
Bulfinger on the resistance of solids. C. Petr. IV. 164.
   Makes some mistakes. Robison.
Musschenbroek. Dissert. Phys.
*Musschenbroek Introductio. cap. 21. I. 390.
Musschenbroek Systeme de physique par Lafond. Par. 1760.
Buffon on increasing the strength of timber. A. P. 1738. 169. H. 54.
Buffon on the strength of timber. A. P. 1740. 453. 1741. 292.
Duhamel on the strength of timber. A. P. 1742. 335. 1768. 534. H. 29.
Duhamel on water imbibed by wood. A. P. 1744. 475. H. 1.
Duhamel Exploitation des arbres. R. I.
Account of Duhamel's work on felling timber. A. P. 1764. H. 68.
Account of Duhamel's work on the preservation and strength of wood. A. P. 1767. H. 81.
Jurin on the action of springs. Ph. tr. 1744. XLIII. n. 472. p. 46.
Krafft de corporum cohaerentia, a Neuffer. 4. Tubing. 1752.
Emerson's fluxions. 343.
Emerson's mechanics. viii.
   Shows that the force exerted by a spring is as its curvature. 104.
Euler. N. C. P. 1757. A. Petr. 1778.
Belidor Architecture hydraulique. I. ii. 92.
Jo. Bernoulli on the extension of threads, and on the resistance of beams. A. Berl. 1766. 78. 108.
Coulomb. S. E. VII. See Architecture, Columns.
Coulomb on the force of torsion. A. P. 1784. 229.
Gauthey on the strength of stones. Roz. IV. 402.
Fougeroux on the oak and the chesnut. A. P. 1781. 49. H. 14. Daubenton. 205.
Ximenes delle resistenze dei solidi. 2 v. 4. Flor. 1782. Pisa, 1784. R. S.
Sickingen über die platina. 8. Manh. 1782.
On timber. E. M. A. IV. Art. Marchand de bois. V. Suppl.
On timber fit for knees, E. M. Pl. V. Marine. Pl. 97. 103.
On iron. E. M. A. IV. Art. Marchand de fer.
Coach springs. E. M. Pl. IV. Serrurerie. pl. 29.
Ropes. E. M. Pl. V. Marine. pl. 24.
Gazeran on the strength of iron. Ann. Ch. VII. 97.
*Robison. Enc. Br. Art. Strength.

Girard Traité de la résistance des solides. Paris, 1797.

The historical part of the preface is the only thing of value that the work contains.

On the strength of beams. Banks on machines. 73.

On steel. Nich. I. 468. II. 64. Stodart, Nich. IV. 127.

A wire of $\frac{1}{10}$ inch of lead breaks with $29\frac{1}{4}$ pounds; of tin with $49\frac{1}{4}$; of copper with $299\frac{1}{4}$; of brass with 360; of silver with 370; of iron with 450; of gold with 500. Emerson.

A yard of oak an inch square will bear in the middle for a very short time 330 pounds. But, according to Emerson, a third or a fourth of this is as much as can be applied in practice. Mech. p. 114. It is in fact much more; for in general the weight supported ought not to produce a sensible bending; and this practical limit requires more attention than it has hitherto received. Allowance must also be made for the occasional depredations of insects.

Wood is from 7 to 20 times weaker transversely than longitudinally. It becomes stronger both ways when dry.

Proportional strength of various substances in bearing pressure. Fine freestone 1: alder, asp, birch, white fir, willow, 6: lead, $6\frac{1}{4}$: beech, cherry, hasel, $6\frac{1}{2}$: red fir, holly, elder, plane, apple, 7: walnut, thorn, $7\frac{1}{2}$: elm, ash, $8\frac{1}{4}$: box, yew, plumbtree, oak, 11: bone, 22: brass, 50: iron, 107. These results however differ materially from some others.

A cylinder an inch in diameter will bear, when loaded to $\frac{1}{4}$ of its whole strength, if of fir 8.8 cwt., if of rope 22 cwt., if of iron 6.75 tons, or 135 cwt. Emerson.

Count Rumford found the cohesive strength of a cylinder of iron an inch in diameter 63466 or 63173 pounds; the mean 63320. Ph. tr. 1797. This is only $\frac{1}{10}$ more than Emerson.

Sickingen makes the comparative cohesive strength of gold 150955, of silver 190771, of platina 262361, of copper 304696, of soft iron 362927, of hard iron 559880. Gilb. Journ. Guyton makes platina a little stronger.

In Buffon's experiments, b, d, and l being the breadth, depth, and length of a beam of oak in inches, the weight which broke it, in pounds was $bd^2\left(\dfrac{54.25}{l}-10\right)$. Robison.

A piece of sound oak an inch square bears 8000 pounds directly, and is broken transversely by 200 at the distance of 12 inches from the fulcrum. Iron is not cheaper than wood of equal strength. The immediate transverse strength of lateral adhesion of most substances exceeds their direct cohesive strength, but the difference is less in fibrous substances than in others. Robison. Coulomb found them nearly equal.

Six of the pieces of oak employed in Girard's experiments broke under the pressure of 2710 pounds on a square inch at a mean; but 15 others supported a much greater load.

A rib of cast iron with abutments of $29\frac{1}{2}$ feet span, 11 inches high in the centre, supported 11130 pounds, but sunk $3\frac{7}{8}$ inches, and rose again $\frac{3}{4}$ inch: without abutments it broke with 6174 pounds. Bars of iron 1 inch square and 3 feet long, weighing 9 pounds, sunk about an inch, and broke with 960 pounds. In general iron is about 4 times as strong as oak, and 6 times as strong as deal. Banks on machines, 93.

The hardness of metals follows this order, iron, platina, copper, silver, gold, tin, lead. Cavallo. II. 147.

When a body is broken by means of an impulse of any kind, there is a certain velocity which is sufficient to produce fracture, whatever may be the bulk of the impelling body. Thus, supposing any body to be capable of being compressed or extended one hundredth part of its length, this effect will require the pressure of the hundredth part of the weight of the modulus of elasticity, or the impulse of the same weight falling through $\frac{1}{200}$ of the length, or the impulse of a weight equal to its own, falling through $\frac{1}{20000}$ of the height of the modulus, and acquiring a velocity equal to one hundredth of that which is due to half the height of the modulus: this is therefore the utmost velocity that the particles of such a body can receive without exceeding the limit at which a separation takes place; and it is for this reason that a body, moving very rapidly, carries before it only the part of the substance which is in immediate contact with it, and does not extend its effects any further. The same limit may also be derived from a consideration of the velocity with which an impulse is transmitted through any substance.

A body being broken by a force directed to a point at the distance a from the axis of a beam, of which the depth is b, the strength is to the direct cohesive or repulsive strength as b to $6a\pm b$, accordingly as the beam gives way on the side next to the force or on the opposite side.

Friction.

Amontons on the resistance of machines. A. P. 1699. 206. H. 104. 1700. 47. 1703. H. 105. 1704. 173. 206.

Allows about $\frac{1}{3}$ of the weight.

Parent on the centre of friction. A. P. 1700. H. 149.

Parent's statics with and without friction. A. P. 1704.
Sauveur on the friction of ropes coiled round a cylinder. A. P. 1703. 305.
Sturm on friction. M. Berl. I. 294.
Leibnitz on the resistance of machines. M. Berl. I. 307.
Varignon on the pressure of solids round which ropes are coiled. A. P. 1717. 195. H. 68.
Leupold. Th. M. G. t. 30 .. 32.
Bülfinger on friction. C. Petr. II. 403.
Makes it $\frac{1}{4}$ of the weight.
Desaguliers on friction. Ph. tr. 1732. 292. 394.
Allows about $\frac{1}{4}$.
Euler on friction. A. Berl. 1748. 122. 133.
Euler on the friction of revolving bodies. N. C. Petr. VI. 233.
Euler on the pressure and friction of ropes. N. C. Petr. XX. 304. 327.
Musschenbroek Introductio. I. 145.
Schober Versuch einer theorie von der überwicht. 1752.
*Bernoulli on friction. N. C. Petr. XIV. i. 249.
Emerson's mechanics. Pr. 118.
Meister. N. C Gott. I. 181.
Lambert on friction. A. Berl. 1771. 9. 1776. 3.
Thinks it not constant, as commonly supposed, but varying as the square of the velocity.
Belidor. Arch. Hydr. l. 70.
Machine for experiments on the friction of pivots. E. M. Pl. III. Horlogerie.
Langez Esperienze intorno alla resistenza del fregamento. 8. Verona, 1782.
Ximenes Resistenze dei solidi.
*Coulomb. S. E. X. Account in Journ. Phys. Sept. 1785.
*Vince on friction, and on the centre of friction. Ph. tr. 1785. 165. Ph. M. XVII. 47.

The friction of hard bodies is a uniform force, that of cloth increases with the velocity. The friction is greater as the surface is greater, but not in any regular proportion.
Metternich de frictione. 4. Erfurt, 1786.
Metternich von dem widerstande der reibung. Maynz. 1789.
Burrow on friction. As. Res. I. 171.
Prony Architecture hydraulique.
Cavallo. N. Ph. I. 275.
A block of 5 pullies, which with 150 pounds should raise 1500, will barely draw up 500.
Southern on friction. Ph. M. XVII. 120.
In confirmation of Vince's observations.

Abstract of Coulomb's memoir on friction. S. E. 1785. X. 161.

This memoir received a prize from the academy of sciences in 1781; the experiments were made on a large scale, at Rochfort, in 1779.

Amontons thought that friction was nearly independent of the extent of the surfaces. Musschenbroek found it otherwise.

At a maximum, that is, after resting some time, the friction, or rather the adhesion, is found to be, for oak on oak, from $\frac{1}{2.28}$ to $\frac{1}{2.39}$ of the weight, according to the magnitude of the surface; for oak on fir $\frac{1}{1.5}$; for fir on fir $\frac{1}{1.78}$; for elm $\frac{1}{2.18}$: the fibres moving longitudinally. When they cross at right angles, the friction of oak is $\frac{1}{3.76}$. For iron on oak, $\frac{1}{5.5}$; for iron on iron $\frac{1}{3.5}$: in this case the time of rest had no effect. For iron on brass $\frac{1}{6}$ when the surfaces are well polished; when larger, and not quite so smooth, $\frac{1}{3.8}$.

With tallow or grease on oak, some days were required to obtain the maximum of friction or adhesion, when the surfaces were large: but when they were small it was very soon acquired. This maximum was nearly the same as without grease; sometimes a little greater. The addition from rest varied at first as the fifth root of the time. For iron or copper with tallow, the increase during rest is less considerable: at first the friction is $\frac{1}{11}$ of the weight, besides a small force, of a pound for every 30 square inches, independent of the weight. After some time the friction becomes $\frac{1}{10}$ or $\frac{1}{9}$. When olive oil is used, the friction becomes at once $\frac{1}{6}$, with old soft grease about $\frac{1}{7}$.

In order to examine the friction of bodies in motion, the adhesion was destroyed by shaking the apparatus a little. When oak moved on oak in the direction of its fibres, the friction was nearly the same in all degrees of velocity; but when the surfaces were large, the friction increased a little with the velocity, and was diminished as the velocity increased when they were small. For a pressure from 100 to 4080 pounds on a square foot, the friction is about $\frac{1}{9.5}$, besides a resistance of about 1¼ pound for each square foot, independent of the pressure, increasing a little with the velocity, occasioned perhaps by a down on the surfaces. When the surface is very small, the friction is somewhat diminished. The narrow surface being cross grained, the friction was invariably $\frac{1}{10}$. For oak on fir, the friction was $\frac{1}{6.2}$; for fir on fir $\frac{1}{6}$, for elm on elm $\frac{1}{19}$, but varying according to the extent of surface; for iron or copper on wood $\frac{1}{13}$, which was at first doubled by increasing the velocity to a foot in a second, but after continuing the operation for some hours, was again diminished. For iron on iron $\frac{1}{3.55}$, on copper, $\frac{1}{4.15}$, after long attrition, $\frac{1}{6}$, in all velocities.

When an unctuous substance was interposed between surfaces in motion, the hardest was found to diminish the friction most, where the weight was great. Tallow being applied fresh from time to time to oak, the friction was $\frac{1}{28}$ of the pressure, besides an adhesion of 1 pound for every 36 square inches, when the velocity was insensible, or for every 20 or 24 inches, when the velocity was a foot in a second. When the surfaces are very small, the tallow loses its effect, and the friction becomes $\frac{1}{17}$ or $\frac{1}{16}$; it is also increased by an increase of velocity, and by the substitution of soft grease for tallow. When the surfaces were soaked in grease, and wiped, the friction was about $\frac{1}{14}$, the adhesion 7 pounds for a square foot. The narrow surface being placed across the fibres of the fixed board, and drawn in their direction, the effects were nearly the same, but more regular. The interposition of tallow has the greatest effect where wood and metal move slowly on each other; thus the friction of iron on oak becomes $\frac{1}{35}$, of brass on oak $\frac{1}{47}$; but after 15 experiments, more than three times as much force was necessary to continue the motion; so that tallow not frequently renewed appears to be injurious: when the surfaces are small, it has little effect. For narrow surfaces of wood, moved on iron across the grain, the friction was $\frac{1}{14}$ in all velocities. In cases also where the operation has been long continued, as in all machines, the friction is independent of the velocity. For iron on iron, with tallow, the friction was $\frac{1}{10}$, the adhesion 1 pound for 15 square inches; on copper $\frac{1}{11}$, the adhesion 1 pound for 13 square inches; with oil or soft grease, the friction of iron or copper was $\frac{1}{8}$, without any addition for adhesion. When the surface of iron, moving on copper, was small, the friction was $\frac{1}{9}$ with tallow, $\frac{1}{8}$ with oil, in all velocities. On the whole it appears, that in the case of most machines, $\frac{1}{8}$ of the pressure is a fair estimate of the friction.

The next subject investigated is the rigidity of ropes. This was supposed by Amontons and Desaguliers to vary as the diameter, as the curvature, and as the tension. Coulomb finds the power of the diameter expressing the rigidity to be generally 1.7 or 1.8, never less than 1.4, and that a constant quantity must be supposed to be added to the weight. Wet ropes, if small, are a little more flexible than dry; if large, a little less flexible. Tarred ropes are stiffer by about ¼, and in cold weather somewhat more. The stiffness of ropes increases after a little rest.

A rope of three strands, each of 2 yarns, 12⅔ lines in circumference, 6 inches of which weighed 2¼ gros, and consequently 125 grains E., being bent on a fixed axis 4 inches in diameter, required a constant force of $\frac{1}{10}$ pound Fr., and $\frac{1}{54.3}$ of the weight, to overcome its rigidity. The same rope tarred required ⅛ pound, and $\frac{1}{50}$ of the weight. The strands being of 5 yarns, the circumference 20 lines, and the weight 6¼ gros, the rigidity was equal to ½ pound, and $\frac{1}{23.1}$ of the weight; when tarred, the rope required 1 pound and $\frac{1}{21.4}$ of the weight to move it. With strands of 10 yarns, a circumference of 28 lines, and a weight of 12½ gros for 6 inches, the untarred rope showed a rigidity of a pounds, and $\frac{1}{13.33}$ of the weight, and the tarred rope, of 2.3 pounds and $\frac{1}{10.34}$ of the weight.

These results were confirmed by experiments on a roller allowed to move on a horizontal plane, while a rope was coiled completely round it. Here it becomes necessary to make an allowance for the friction of the roller on the plane, which varies as its weight, and inversely as its diameter. For a roller of guaiacum or lignum vitae, 2.6 inches in diameter, moving on oak, it was $\frac{1}{100}$ of the weight; for a roller of elm $\frac{2}{3}$ more.

Mr. Coulomb proceeds to relate experiments made immediately on a simple pulley, where the friction of the axis and the rigidity of the rope produce a joint resistance. When guaiacum moved on iron, the friction was $\frac{1}{5.4}$ or $\frac{1}{6.4}$ of the weight in all velocities, besides the rigidity of the rope; the mean was $\frac{1}{6.1}$, or, with a small weight, a little greater. For axes of iron on copper $\frac{1}{11}$ or $\frac{1}{11.5}$, where the velocity was small: the friction being always a little less than for plane surfaces. With grease, the friction was about $\frac{1}{7.5}$.

With an axis of green oak, or ilex, and a pulley of guaiacum, the friction with tallow was $\frac{1}{26}$; without it $\frac{1}{17}$; with a pulley of elm, these quantities became $\frac{1}{33}$ and $\frac{1}{20}$. An axis of box, with a pulley of guaiacum, gave $\frac{1}{23}$ and $\frac{1}{14}$; with a pulley of elm, $\frac{1}{29}$ and $\frac{1}{20}$. An axis of iron, and a pulley of guaiacum gave, with tallow, $\frac{1}{20}$.

The velocity had little effect on the rigidity of ropes, except to increase the resistance slightly, when the pressure was small.

Mr. Coulomb suggests that the lower surface of a dray ought to be a little convex, in order to facilitate a slight agitation, and to diminish the friction. For launching ships, he recommends oak sliding on elm, previously well rubbed with tallow, by means of heavy weights; and observes that the velocity ought not to be so great as to melt the tallow.

In the pulley, the friction on the axis is somewhat modified by the situation of the surface of contact, which is not perfectly horizontal, but the difference may be neglected in practice. This excellent memoir is concluded by a calculation of the force requisite to raise 8000 pounds by a capstan, and a rope of 120 strands, with a purchase of 12 to 1; and it appears, by inferences from the experiments already stated, that about one ninth of the force employed would in this case be lost.

Architecture in General.

Vitruvius.
Vitruve par Perrault. f. Par. 1673.
Newton's Vitruvius. 2 v. f. R. S.
Palladio. f. 1721. R. I.
Ph. tr. Abr. I. viii. 588. VI. viii. 465.
Blondel's resolution of the four principal problems of architecture. A. P. V. ii. 1.
Aldrich's elements of civil architecture. 8. Oxf. 1789.
Krafft's theory of the orders of architecture. C. Petr. XI. 288.
Nollet's observations on architecture in Italy. A. P. 1749. 473. H. 15.
Emerson's mechanics.
Emerson's miscellanies, 322.
Vitruvius Britannicus. 3 v. f. Continued. 2 v. f. London.
Kent's Inigo Jones. f. 1770. R. I.
Pini dialoghi dell' architettura. 4. Milan, 1770. R. S.
Huths bürgerliche baukunst.
*Coulomb's application of the rules of maxima and minima to problems of architecture. S. E. 1773. 343.
E. M. Architecture, 1¼ vol. to Es. R. I.
Chambers on civil architecture. f. 1791. R. I.
Rudiments of antient architecture. London.
Essays on Gothic architecture. 8. London. R. I.
Stuart's ruins of Athens. f. London. R. I.
P. *Nicholson's* student's instructor. 8. Lond. R. I.

P. Nicholson's principles of architecture. 3 v. 8. 1795. R. I.
> The plates by Lowry. Chiefly on architectural drawing.

Labaume, Lamblardie, and Ballard on architecture. Journ. Polyt. I. i. 15. ii. 124. iv. 577.

Prony on the declination of the columns of the Pantheon. B. Soc. Phil. n. 57.

Sammlung die baukunst betreffend. Berlin.

Hall on Gothic architecture. Ed. tr. IV. ii. 3.

Büsch Practische darstellung der bauwissenschaft. 2 v. 8. Hamb. 1800. R. I.

Rees's cyclopaedia. I. II.
> Beautiful plates.

Columns and Walls; their strongest forms.

See Hydraulic Pressure.

Blondel on the diminution of columns. A. P. V. ii. 7.

Couplet on the thrust of earth against walls. A. P. 1726.

Euler on the strength of columns. A. Berl. 1757. 252. A. Petr. II. i. 121. 146. 163.

Lambert on the fluidity of sand and earth. A. Berl. 1772. 33.

Lorgna on the resistance of walls to the pressure of earth. A. Sien. II. 155.

Emerson's mechanics.
> Does not sufficiently consider the compressibility.

Belidor on the thickness of walls. Arch. hydr. II. i. 420.

*Coulomb. S. E. VII.

Lagrange on the figure of columns. M. Tur. V. ii. 123.
> Refers the resistance to flexure; makes a cone stronger than any conoid; but a cylinder the strongest form of all.

Account of a memoir on the pressure of earth. N. A. Petr. 1793. XI. H. 3.

Girard Traité de la résistance des solides, et des solides d'égale résistance.
> Contains a general determination of the strongest forms.

Lambton on the theory of walls. As. res. VI. 93.

Prony on the lateral pressure of earth. B. Soc. Phil. n. 24.

Prony sur la poussée des terres. 4. Par. 1802. R. S.

Prony sur les murs de revêtement. 4. Par. 1802. R. S.

The strongest form of a substance included by horizontal surfaces, or cut out of a horizontal plank, for supporting a weight at its extremity, is that of a triangle. The same form is also the stiffest. For supporting a weight distributed uniformly throughout its length, the form must be that of a parabola, with its convexity turned inwards.

For a vertical plank, bearing a weight at its extremity, the strongest and stiffest form is that of a common parabola, with its convexity outwards. If the weight is equally divided, it must be a triangle. To support its own weight, it must have for its outline a common parabola, with its convexity inwards. If such a plank were supported by its lateral adhesion only, its outline must be a logarithmic curve, to sustain its own weight.

A horizontal column turned in a lathe, or having all its transverse sections similar, must have its outline a cubical parabola, convex outwards, in order to support the greatest weight at its extremity. The same form is also the stiffest. To support a weight equally distributed through the length, the curve must be a semicubical parabola. To support its own weight, the outline must be a common parabola, convex towards the axis, having its vertex at the extremity.

A triangular prism fixed at one end, with its edge uppermost, is weaker than if its depth were reduced to eight ninths, by cutting away the edge. With a certain force, such a beam would crack at its edge, and not break off.

If a beam, cut out of a vertical plank, be supported at both ends, and bear a weight at any one given point, its portions must be bounded by two common parabolas. If the weight be equally applied throughout the length, or if it be applied at a point variable at pleasure, the outline must be an ellipsis.

If a beam, supported at both ends, have all its transverse

sections similar, the two portions must have their outlines cubic parabolas. For a weight equally divided, or applied to any point at pleasure, the cube of the diameter must be as the square of the segments.

A wall, turning a vertical face to the wind, ought to have the other face an inclined plane, in order to resist the force of the wind to the greatest advantage, if made of cohesive materials; but if of loose materials, it ought to be convex and parabolic behind. Emerson.

A cohesive wall, supporting a bank of earth or a fluid with its vertical face, ought to be concave behind, in the form of a semicubical parabola, with its vertex at the top of the wall: but if the materials are loose, the back of the wall should be an inclined plane. Emerson.

A pillar or column of cohesive materials, formed to resist the wind, must be a cone or a pyramid; of loose materials, a parabolic conoid; to support its own weight only, a pillar must have the logarithmic curve for its outline. Emerson.

A mortise hole should be taken out of the middle of a beam, not from one side; but if it is on the concave side, and is filled up with hard wood, it does not diminish the strength. For similar reasons, a piece spliced on, to strengthen a beam, should be on the convex side. If a cylinder is to be supported at two points with the least strain, the distance between the points should be .5858 of the length. Emerson.

If a piece be spliced on a divided beam, equal in depth to half the depth of the beam, the strength is greater than that of the entire beam, in the ratio of 1 to 1.054, very nearly.

Coulomb found the lateral cohesion of brick and stone only $\frac{1}{12}$ more than the direct cohesion, which, for stone, was 215 pounds for a square inch; for good brick from 280 to 300. Supposing the lateral cohesion constant, a pillar will support twice as much as it will suspend, and its angle of rupture will be 45°. From the same supposition it may be inferred, that the strongest form of a body of given thickness for supporting a weight, is that of a circle, since the power of the weight in the direction of every section varies as the length of that section; and the strength is therefore equal throughout the substance. But if the cohesion is increased, like friction, by pressure, and supposing, with Amontons, that this increase, for brick, is three fourths of the weight, the plane of rupture of a prismatic pillar will form, according to Coulomb, an angle of 63° 26' with the horizon, and the strength will be doubled. On both suppositions the strength is simply as the section. It is of the less consequence to investigate the lateral pressure of soft materials, as they are generally liable to be penetrated by water, which acts according to the laws of hydrostatics.

Particular Structures.

Barville's turning parapets for defence. Mach. A. II. 23.

Godefroi's staircase. A. P. 1716. H. 78. Mach. A. III. 99.

Lahire on keeping out rain from windows. A. P. 1716. 326.

Belidor on lighthouses. Arch. Hydr. II. ii. pl. 18.

Meister on the pyramids of Egypt. N. C. Gott. V. 192. On fortifications. Commentat. Gott. II. M. 20. III. 30. 52.

Report of a committee on prisons. A. P. 1780. 409. H. 8.

Tessier on stables. Roz. XV. 114.

*Smeaton on the Edystone lighthouse. f. Lond. 1793. R. I.

Lighthouses. Smeaton's reports.

Saunders on theatres. Vol. 1. 4. London.

Bentham's panopticon.

Beatson, Hunt, Crocker, and Sinclair on farm buildings. Board Agr. I. 1.

Lord Brownlow on cottages. Board Agr. I. 85.

Baillet sur les theatres. 4. 1801.

Plaw's rural architecture. 4. 1802. R. I.

Chimnies. See pneumatic machines.

Materials. Masonry, Bricks, Pavements.

See Passive Strength. Roofs.

Fourcroy et Gallon Art du tuilier briquetier. f. Paris.
Extr. A. P. 1763. H. 139.

Duhamel Art du couvreur. f. Par.
Extr. A. P. 1766. H. 156.

Jars on making bricks and tiles. A. P. 1768. H. 127.

Masonry. Belidor. Arch. Hydr. I. ii.

Bricks. Roz. Introd. I. 433.

E. M. A. I. Art. Ardoisier, Briquetier, Carreleur. II. Art. Couvreur. IV. Art. Maçonnerie. Marbrier. VI. Art. Paveur.

On the disposition of stones in masonry. Roz. XXX. 401.

Mongez on Roman buildings. Roz. XL. 143.

On brickmaking. Bergman's essays. Nich. II. 498.

Georgi on artificial slate. Ph. M. III. 148.

Cartwright's patent bricks. Repert. III. 84.
To tie together.

Walker's patent houses, baked in a mass. Repert. III. 369.

Richter's patent for inlaying marble. Repert. X. 326.

Brodie's hollow iron bars for building. S. A. XXII. 256.
The Romans sometimes built with pitchers, or hollow bricks, as in the upper part of Caracalla's circus. A nobleman has lately employed hollow bricks for arches in a magnificent edifice in this country.

Mortars, Cements, and Stuccos.

Perrault on a hard mortar. A. P. I. 199.

Pike on a mortar made in the East Indies. Ph. tr. 1792. XXXVII. 231.

Macquer on lime and plaster. A. P. 1747. 678. H. 65.

Machy Art du distillateur des eaux fortes. f. Paris, p. 102.

Mortar for water. Roz. Intr. I. 237.

Pisé. Roz. Intr. I. 682.

Lafaye on Roman mortar. Roz. IX. 437.

On plastering walls. Roz. XIV. 417.

Higgins on cements. 8. London, 1780.

Higgins's patent cement. Repert. II. 289.

Mortar. E. M. A. I. Art. Ciment. V. Art. Mortelier.

Plastering. E. M. A. IV. Art. Marbrier. VI. Art. Plafonneur, Pouzzolane.

Mud walls. E. M. A. VI. Art. Plaqueur en argile.

A new kiln for plaster. Roz. XXXVI. 470.

Smeaton's Edystone.

Williams's patent stucco. Repert. II. 1.

Guyton on mortars. Ann. Ch. XXXVII. 253. Nich. V. 109. Repert. XV. 132.

Holland and Jacour on pisé. Board Agr. I. 387.

Puymarin's new mortar. Ph. M. XIV. 125.

Fulcher's patent stucco. Repert. III. ii. 329.

Anderson on lime as a cement. 8. London.

Anderson's recreations.

See mills.

Parker's patent stucco is said to stand extremely well.

Security from Fire.

See Machinery.

Hales on checking the progress of fires. Ph. tr. 1748. XLV. 277.

A fire ladder. A. Petr. I. i. H. 67.
Supporting itself.

Lord Mahon on securing buildings from fire. Ph. tr. 1778. 884.

Krafft on Lord Mahon's incombustible house. A. Petr. III. ii. H. 9.

Mann on preserving buildings from fire. Roz. XII. 149.

On safety from fire. Roz. XIII. 306. 356.

Hartley's prevention of fire. E. M. A. VI. Art. Preservatif.

Repert. VIII. 233.
A patent for interposing plates of metal.

Cartwright's patent incombustible substitute for wood work. Repert. VIII. 155.

Audibert's machine for fires approved. Mem. Inst. IV.

Arches, Domes, and Bridges.

Robinson on the Roman bridge at St. Esprit. Ph. tr. 1684. XIV. 583.

Abeille's flat arch. A. P. I. 159.
Sebastien's flat arch. A. P. I. 163.
Lahire on curves used in architecture. A. P. 1702. 94. H. 119. On arches. 1712. 69. H. 74.
Senès on arches and vaults. A. P. 1719. 363.
Leupold Theatrum Pontificiale.
Couplet on the thrust of arches. A. P. 1729. 79. H. 75. 1730. 117. H. 107.
Chardon on arches. A. P. 1731. H. 53.
Bouguer on arches and domes. A. P. 1734. 149.
Frézier Coupe des pierres pour les voûtes. 3 v. 4. Strasb. 1737.
Labelye on Westminster bridge. 1739. R. I.
Aepinus on the abutments of an arch. A. Berl. 1755. 386.
Emerson's fluxions, 325. Mechanics. F. 307. 311.
Emerson's miscellanies, 148.
Euler on the effect of friction in equilibrium. A. Berl. 1762. 265.
Euler's mode of judging of the strength of a bridge from a model. N. C. Petr. XX. 271.
Belidor. Arch. hydr. II. ii. 415.
A quadruple vaulted bridge. Belidor. Arch. hydr. II. ii. pl. 56.
Perronet on preventing the sliding away of ground. A. P. 1769. 233. H. 112.
Perronet on the forms of bridges. A. P. 1777. 553. H. 51.

Recommends that the arch should begin at high water mark: remarks, that the breadth of the piers may be made much less than one fifth of that of the arches.

Perronet is sometimes too ostentatious of art, but his bridge at Orleans is a masterpiece; the bridge at Neuilly can scarcely stand long. Robison.

Perronet sur les ponts. f. Par. 1782. 3. Supplément. 1789. R. S.
† Krafft. N. C. Petr. IV. 199.

Giral sur les constructions des ponts. 4. R. S.
Baldwin's plates relative to Blackfriars bridge. London. R. I.
Regemotte on the bridge at Moulins. Abstr. A. P. 1771. H. 66.
Lambert on the fluidity of sand and earth. A. Berl. 1772. 33.
Bossut on the equilibrium of arches. A. P. 1774. 534. H. 59. 1776. 587.
Coulomb. S. E. 1773. 343.

Observes, that in the plates bandes, or flat arches, over windows, the planes of the joints should converge to a single axis; and that the stones will fall unless the perpendicular to the lowest point of the abutment meet the vertical, passing through the centre of gravity of the half arch, within its substance. This may be easily understood by considering the arch as composed of two pieces.

Centres of earth. Roz. III. 67.
Arches tied across with iron. Roz. VIII. 158.
Effect of temperature on a bridge. Roz. VIII. 399.
Nordstern's model of a bridge. A. Petr. II. ii. 85.
Lorgna on the curve of an arch. A. Petr. III. ii. 156.
Ferrari on arches. A. Sienn. VI. 193.
Arrow's oval dome for avoiding fires. Bailey's mach. II. 62.
†Cazeneuve's plan of a bridge. Roz. XVIII. 407.
* Fuss on the strains of carpentry. A. Petr. II. i. 194.
Arch in equilibrium. E. M. Pl. VIII. Amusemens d'architecture.
Foundations of bridges. E. M. A. VI. Art. Ponts.
Plan of an iron bridge of 400 feet span, with a pyrometer. E. M. Pl. V. Voutes.
Arches for cielings. E. M. A. VIII. Art. Voutes.

Bunce's plan and elevation of a dome. Lond. 1792. R. I.

Southern on the equilibrium of arches. Ph. M. XI. 97.

Note of Bossut's memoir on arches. Ph. M. XI. 179.

Tatham's bricks for circular arches. Ph. M. XV. 143.

Mascheroni sull' equilibrio delle volte. 4. Bergam. 1785.

Montpetit on the theory of iron bridges. Roz. XXXII. 430.

Trembley on arches. Roz. XXXIII. 132.

Hutton's principles of bridges. R. I.
  Hutton recommends an elliptical arch.

M. Young on the gothic arch. Ir. tr. 1789. III. 55.

Kästner on cylindrical vaulting. Commentat. Gott. X. M. 30. 104.

Prévost Dacier on the iron bridge at Coalbrook Dale. Roz. XXXV. 16.

Bridges. Smeaton's reports.

Arches. Langsdorff's hydraulik. pl. 8. 9.

Burdon's patent cast iron blocks and tubes for arches, with an account of the bridge at Wearmouth. Repert. V. 361.
  The arch is a segment of a circle, its span 236 feet, its versed sine 34, making about 84°. Its weight is 900 tons, 260 of them are iron. The height from the level of the water is 61 feet.

Plates of the bridge at Wearmouth. R. I.

Jordan's patent for bridges. Repert. VI. 220.
  A path suspended from an arch.

Nash's patent bridges, of hollow iron and earth. Repert. VI. 361.

Wyatt's bridges without wood. Repert. XIV. 145.
  Hollow pieces of cast iron.

Robison. Enc. Br. Suppl. Art. Arch.

Atwood on arches, with a supplement. 4. 1801. R. I.

Review of Atwood, said to be by Robison. British critic. XXIII. 6.

Person's pumps to be used in building bridges. Recueil, pl. 4.

Iron bridges. Fulton on canals.

Tatham's circular architecture. 8. Lond. 1803. R. I.

Tatham's patent clumps. Ph. M. XV. 143. Repert. ii. II. 333.

Wilson's patent for uniting iron blocks. Repert. ii. III. 87.

Rees's cyclopaedia. Art. Arch.

New bridge at Paris. B. Soc. Phil. n. 78.

Reports on the port of London. f. R. I.

Supposing the pressure of the materials vertical only, a quadrant of a circle will support a horizontal road in equilibrium, if the depth of the bridge in the middle be to the radius as 1 to 6¼, that is, about one ninth of the span. Emers. Mech. But this appears to be only an approximation.

A catenaria will support a horizontal road 100 feet above it, if the height and half the span are each 159. A logarithmic curve will form a half arch of equilibrium if the road be horizontal. Emerson. But all these proportions would make the bridge too heavy.

Perronet thinks that a bridge of 500 feet span might stand, the bridge of Mantes having sunk to a radius of 500 feet.

In the construction of bridges, Professor Robison observes, that something is to be allowed for the lateral pressure of the materials; and that the cohesive strength of the arch, and its resistance to any force in the manner of a lever, ought to be taken into the calculation. These remarks are extremely just, but they do not appear to have been practically considered, except so far as theory has been modified by experience.

If there be an arch composed of stones of a given magnitude considered as perfectly solid, the effect of a weight bearing on the key stone will be a displacement of the pressure on the abutment: the centre of pressure on the abutment will be removed to a distance, which is to the height of the arch nearly as the tangent of the immediate change of the direction of the new compound thrust of the key stone to the radius. It seems to be desirable that this displacement should never exceed the limits of the abutments themselves.

Supposing the pressure of the materials vertical only, the curve may be constructed mechanically without difficulty, by making the centre of each portion of it at a distance below the arc which is inversely as the distance of the arc from the road. In the case of a horizontal road, the greatest curvature will be where this distance is a mean proportional between the radius of curvature at the vertex and the depth of the materials at the same point.

Carpentry in General.

Moxon's mechanic exercises.
Account, Ph. tr. 1677. XII. 967. 1006.
The three first numbers treat of smith's work, the three next of joiner's work.

Roubo Art du ménuisier. f. Paris. Acc. A. P. 1769. H. 124. 1770. H. 111.

*Fuss on the strains of framed carpentry. A. Petr. 1778. II. i. 194.

E. M. A. I. Art. *Charpentier. IV. Art. Ménuiserie.

Pain's practical house carpenter. 4. Lond.

P. *Nicholson's* carpenter's new guide. 4. London.

P. *Nicholson's* carpenter's and joiner's assistant. 4. Lond. 1797. R. I.

Robison. Enc. Br. Suppl. Art. Carpentry.

Hassenfratz Art de la charpenterie.
Approved by the Institute.

Beams and Floors.

Morveau on increasing the strength of beams. Roz. IV. 157.

Panseron and Bonnin on floors. Roz. XXXV. 211.

Upton's barn floor. S. A. XIV. 305. Repert. VI. 111.

Wilson's patent for combining timbers. Repert. IX. 100.

Smart's patent masts and beams. Repert. XIV. 17.

Woart's mode of securing decayed beams. S. A. XX. 258. Nich. VI. 120. Repert. ii. II. 346.

Wooden Bridges and Centres.

Perrault's wooden bridge of a single arch. Mach. A. I. 59.

Perrault's drawbridge. Mach. A. II. 51.

Hebert's turning bridge. Mach. A. II. 68.

A wooden bridge. Ph. tr. 1684. XIV. 714.

Wooden bridges, drawbridges, centres, a bridge of ropes. Leup. Th. Pontif.

Pitot on the strength of centres. A. P. 1726. 216. H. 65.

Gallon's falling drawbridge. A. P. 1733. H. 120.

Meyzeray's model of a bridge of ropes. A. P. 1748. H. 120.

Emerson's mechanics, f. 212.

Perronet on the centres of bridges. A. P. 1773. 33. H. 72.

Perronet sur les ponts.

Drawbridge. Belidor. Arch. Hydr. II. ii. pl. 53.

Turning bridge. Belidor. Arch. Hydr. II. ii. pl. 54. 55. Enc. Br. Art. Drawbridge.

Robison. Enc. Br. Suppl. Art. Arch, Carpentry, Centre.

Plans of Grubenmann's bridge at Schaffhausen. R. I.

A wooden bridge. Person Recueil. Pl. 10.

Roofs.

Couplet on roofs. A. P. 1731. 69. H. 62.

Salimbeni on roofs inclined one way. Soc. Ital. IV. 249.

Robison. Enc. Br. Art. Roof.

Woart's mode of raising a sunk roof. S. A. XXI. 374.

Robison and others recommend that the abutment of a rafter should be an arch having the other end of a rafter for its centre; but this can be of no use unless we suppose the lower end of the rafter to slide upwards on the abutment when the other end sinks.

Slating and Tiling.

See Masonry.

Fourcroy et Gallon, Art du tuilier briquetier. f. Par. Acc. A. P. 1763. H. 139.
Duhamel Art du couvreur. f. Par. Acc. A. P. 1766. H. 156.
Meister on the best forms for tiling a roof with economy. Commentat. Gott. 1781. IV. M. 57.
E. M. A. I. Art. Ardoisier. II. Art. Couvreur.
Georgi on artificial slate. N. A. Petr. 1786. IV. 266.
M'Carthy's patent compound for covering houses. Repert. XI. 14.
Elliott's patent slate. Repert. XII. 385.
Loffler on increasing the durability of tiles. Repert. XIII. 212.
Cathala's tiles hanging diagonally. Repert. ii. III. 479.

Furniture.

Roubo Art du ménuisier en meubles. Art du ménuisier ébèniste.
Roubo Art du treillagure. f. Paris, 1775.
E. M. A. IV. Art Ménuiserie. P. 1. Furniture. P. 4. Trellis work.
Ince and Mayhew on furniture. f.
Upholstery. E. M. A. VIII. Art. Tapissier.
Inlaid work. E. M. A. II. Art. Ebèniste.
Tortoiseshell and ivory work. E. M. A. II. Art. Ecaille.
Coarse work in bone. E. M. A. IV. Art. Layetier.
Doors and Hinges. See Ironmongery.
Windows. Godefroi's window protected from wind. Mach. A. II. 21. E. M. A. VIII. Art. Vitrier. Fontanieu's machine for shutting windows. A. P. 1771. H. Playfair's patent sashes, drawn through rollers. Repert. VIII. 158.
Beds. Chaumette's ciel de lit. Mach. A. III. 67. St. John on the arcuccio. Ph. tr. 1732. XXXVII. 256. Hanot's bed for invalids. A. P. 1742. H. 155. Mach. A. VII. 121. Hanot's bed without posts. A. P. 1745. H. 81. Fresnel's military bed. A. P. 1746. H. 120. Mach. A. VII. 321. Garat's bed for the sick. A. P. 1771. H. 68. Tranoy's jointed bed. A. P. 1772. i. H. †Thoelden's patent spring bed. Repert. ii. II. 104.
Cabinets. Guyot's cabinet for curiosities. Mach. A. VI. 169.
Trunks. E. M. A. I. Art. Coffretier. E. M. M. III. Art. Malle. Aughtie. Repert. X. 73. Boxes of sheet lead. Repert. ii. I. 133.
Hangings. *Fougeroux* Art de faire des tapisseries de cuir. f. Paris. Acc. A. P. 1762. H. 187. Eckhardt's patent cloth and paper hangings. Repert. II. 87, 90. Nicholson's patent for printing paper. Repert. V. 145.
Ironmongery. Aumont's lock. A. P. 1721. H. 98. Mach. A. IV. 21, 23. *Duhamel* Art du Serrurier. f. Paris. Acc. A. P. 1768. H. 126. Boissier's locks. A. P. 1778. H. 56. Delivetz's screw hinge. Bailey's Mach. I. 165. Gascoigne's falling hinge. Bailey's Mach. II. 68. E. M. A. I. Art. Cloutier. VII. Art. Serrurier. Marshall's secret

escutcheon. S. A. III. 163. A spring staple for horses. Repert. II. 17. *Bramah's patent for locks. Repert. V. 217. Clifford's patent nails. Repert. VII. 217. 377. Spears's patent locks. Repert. VIII. 91. Bentham's patent fire irons. Repert. VIII. 145. Finch's patent nails. Repert. IX. 390. Arkwright's door lock. S. A. XVIII. 242. Repert. XIV. 372. Bullock's lock, not closing till the door is shut. S. A. XIX. 282. Nich. 8. II. 204. Holomberg's patent locks. Repert. XV. 366. Bérard's lock. Mélanges. 107. Nich. 8. III. 216. An old secret lock. Nich. 8. V. 203. Regnier's padlock of combination. Nich. VI. 43. Pritty's patent hinges. Repert. ii. I. 321. Opening on either side of the doorway. Smith's patent alarm bell. Repert. ii. III. 182. An Egyptian lock. Nich. VIII. 115.

Cooper's work. *Fougeroux* Art du tonnelier. f. Paris. Acc. A. P. 1763. H. 140. Levec's bathing tub. A. P. 1767. H. 186. Hoops. E. M. A. VI. 721. E. M. A. VIII. Art. Tonnelier.

Buckets, measures, and turnery ware. E. M. A. I. Art. Boisselier. Emerson's mechanics. F. 261. 262.

Beehives. Saintefois's beehive. A. P. 1772. i. H. v. E. M. A. VII. Art. Ruches. A beehive. Bailey's Mach. I. 65. Harasti's beehive. Repert. XI. 342.

Umbrellas. Navarre's umbrella. A. P. 1759. H. Marius's umbrella. Mach. A. II. 87, 89, 145, 161. E. M. A. V. Art. Parasols. E. M. M. I. Art. Boursier.

Snuff boxes. Chaumette. A. P. 1715. H. 66. Mach. A. III. 55.

Cases. E. M. M. III. Art. Gainier.

Machine for drawing lotteries. Daubicourt. Mach. A. II. 109. 163.

Tennis. *Garsault* Art du paumier raquetier. f. Paris. Acc. A. P. 1767. H. 182.

Particular Edifices.

Tents. Marius. Mach. A II. 93, 97, 147.
Granaries. E. M. A. III. Art. Grainier.
Dobson's barn. Repert. VI. 319.

Inclosures and Gates.

Sluice gates. Belidor. Arch. Hydr. I. ii.
Orme's field gate. Bailey's machines. II. 7.
 Raised by inclined planes. Produces a great strain.
Underwood's patent railing. Repert. VII. 167.
*Haddington on inclosures. Board Agr. II. 1.
Parker on gates. 8. London, 1801. R. I. Repert. ii. II. 50.
Waistell's gates. S. A. XXII. 73.
Dickson's practical agriculture. R. I.

Painting and Preservation of Wood.

See Drawing.

Grinding paint. See trituration.
Colebrooke on encaustic painting. Ph. tr. 1759. 40.
Ward on preventing the bad effects of white lead. S. A. XIII. 229.
Batson on the dry rot. S. A. Repert. II. 112.
 Recommends that the wood be charred, and kept very dry.
Ludicke's substitute for oil paint. Ph. M. I. 22.
Worth's patent preparation for preserving ships. Repert. V. 177.
Fabbroni on encaustic painting. Ph. M. I. 23, 141.
Beevor on the duration of wood. Repert. VIII. 57.
Pattenson's preservation of weatherboards. Repert. VIII. 126.
Atkinson's patent white paint, from zinc. Repert. VIII. 309.

Nystrom's amber varnish. Repert. XIV. 391.
Cadet de Vaux on painting with milk. Repert. XV. 411. Ph. M. X. 338. Nich. V. 247.
Darcet on painting with milk. Nich. 8. I. 212.
Carbonel on painting with serum. Journ. Phys. LVI. 228. Ph. M. XV. 240. Repert. ii. II. 373.
Johnson on the dry rot. S. A. XXI. 284.
<small>Said to be the boletus lacrymans.</small>

Tools.

See Penetration and Division.

E. M. A. IV. Art. Menuiserie.
Makingglue. E. M. M. III. Art. Colle.
Rich's bolt drawer. S. A. Repert. I. 246.
Bentham's patents for working in wood and metal. Repert. V. 293. X. 250.
<small>Chiefly by rotatory machines.</small>
Phillips's tubes for driving copper bolts without flattening the heads. S. A. XIX. 274. Nich. 8. III. 35.

Machinery, or Modification of Motion.

Perrault's hand. Mach. A. I.
†Lespiniere's assemblage of machines. A. P. 1726. H. 73. Mach. A. IV. 221.
On communicating motion by ropes, rods, endless ropes with knots, endless chains, wheels, systems of levers, and racks. Emerson's mech. Prop. 110. On equalising or accelerating motion. Pr. 111. On changing its direction. Pr. 112.
Lowndes's gymnasticon, for exercising the body. Repert. VI. 88.
*Imison's elements. I. 78.

Regulation of Descent.

See Cranes.

Fire Escapes.

Leup. Th. Machinarium. t. 54. 55.
Stay on a rope by friction. Emerson's mech. f. 228. 229.
Varcourt. A. P. 1761. H. 158.
Collins. Am. tr. IV. 143. Repert. XV. 35.
Audibert's machine approved. M. Inst. IV. Repert. ii. I. 439.

Jacks.

Emerson's mechanics. f. 258.

Application of Moving Forces.

Walking wheels for horses, oxen, and goats, vertical and oblique. Leup. Th. M. G. t. 35. 36.
Employment for invalids. Leup. Th. Hydrot. 2. t. 14.
Application of weights. Leup. Th. M. G. t. 86.
Emerson's mechanics. Pr. 119.
Churchman. Ph. tr. 1734. XXXVIII. 402.
<small>Harnesses his horses to a fixed point, and makes them walk in or on a wheel.</small>
†Sarrebourg's new moving power. A. P. 1753. H. 300. Mach. A. VII. 461.
<small>Mercury descending in a spiral tube.</small>
Bernoulli on the application of force to machines. N. C. Petr. XIII. 242.
Lambert on the winch. N. Act. Helv. I. 75.
Baillet de Belloy on applying the draught of horses in a perpendicular direction. Roz. XLII. 129. Repert. III. 422.
Buchanan's improved cattle mills, with a catch. Repert. II. 19.
Eckhardt's patent for applying animal force. Repert. II. 361.
<small>By external walking wheels, and flexible roads.</small>

Lambie's patent for applying force to machinery. Repert. XI. 371.
  A man standing on a moveable foot board.
Person's mill worked by a lever. Recueil. pl. 3..5.
Walker's familiar philosophy. Lect. 3.
  Mills are sometimes driven in military service by the wheels of waggons. Fig.
R. B. on a barometrical perpetual motion. Nich. IX. 212.
For the forces of wind and water, see hydraulic machines.

Economy of Motion.

Hooke's centrifugal regulator. Hooke. Lect. Cutl. Lampas. p. 43.
On fly wheels. Leup. Th. M. G. t. 22. 23.
Emerson's mechanics. Pr. 113.
On fly wheels. Langsd. Hydr. c. 35.
Burgess's patent rotatory motion by a catch and fly. Repert. V. 11.
Fly wheels. Imison's elements. I. 65.
†Prony's condenser of force. B. Soc. Phil. n. 85. Nich. IX. 275.
  Nicholson justly observes, that wherever a weight is wound up there is a loss of force.

Springs.

Emerson's mech. 177.
  Springs are weakened by use, but recover their strength if they are laid by.
Hopkinson's spring block. Am. tr. III. 331. Repert. L. 44.
  To prevent the heeling of the ship, which might be caused by too sudden an impulse,
On springs. Ph. M. II. 67.
  Metal springs, if allowed to vibrate freely, soon break or change their form, and take a set: wooden springs are more liable to break if stopped and not suffered to vibrate. Red deal is the fittest wood for springs.
  Springs must be thin in order to be flexible; and must derive their strength either from their breadth, or from the addition of different plates.

Jointed Work.

Hook's universal joint. Lect. Cutl. Helioscopes. p. 14. Birch. IV. 216.
Martenot's endless chain. Mach. A. II. 115.
Loriot's endless chain. A. P. 1761. H. 161.
Kästner on suspended systems of rods. N. C. Gott. 1770. II. 132.
Chains. E. M. A. I. Art. Chainetier.
Vaucanson's chain. E. M. Pl. VIII. Tirage des soies.
Giraud on the best forms of chains and cords. Roz. XXXV. 42.
Jointed levers and frame work. Langsdorffs hydr. Pl. 33. 40.
Hancock's chain. S. A. XIV. 313. Repert. VI. 241.
Fussell's patent chain for lessening friction. Repert. XII. 303.
King's patent joint. Repert. XIII. 297.

Production and Rectification of Rotatory Motion.

Lahire on winches and cranks. A. P. IX. 99, 164.
Auger's machine for producing perpendicular motion by a jack. A. P. 1721. H. 97.
Leup. Th. M. G. t. 13, 21...27, 71. Th. Hydr. ii. t. 26, 27.
Belidor. Arch. Hydr. I. i. 36.
Garousse's lever. Mach. A. II. 15. 17. Belidor. Arch. Hydr. I. i. 122.
  A lever with a double catch to turn wheels.
Ellipses instead of cranks. Belidor. Arch. Hydr. II. i. Pl. n. 13, 14.
Cranks. Emerson's mechanics, f. 238. Undulating rollers. F. 247.

Lambert on the winch. N. Act. Helvet. I.
Kästner on the velocity of a crank or winch. N. C. Gott. 1774. V. 119.
Triple crank. Corn mill. Am. tr.
Alternate racks. Langsdorffs hydr. Pl. 32.
Fulton's patent cylinder for working pumps. Repert. III. 220.

A double screw.

Landen's patent mode of moving pump rods. Repert. XII. 145.
Prony on converting rotatory into alternate motion. M. Inst. II. 216.
Cranks. Banks on machines. 46.
Jones on Wolff's equalised crank. Nich. VII. 133.

Nearly resembling a fly in its effect.

R. B. Nich. IX. 212.

The distance of two centres being 3, two levers move on them of which the lengths are 2 and 4: the shorter supports a third of which the length is 5, receiving the end of the longer in a joint at the distance 1; the motion of the end will be initially almost rectilinear.

The truth of this may be shown from the properties of the ellipsis, and from the comparison of the sines of the evanescent angles. But, more correctly, the length of the second lever being to the same length increased by the short portion of the third as x to 1, the distance of the fixed points must be to the same whole length as $4x - 4xx$ to 1. Thus if $x = .8$, as in the case proposed, the distance of the fixed points must be to the whole length as .64 to 1, and to the short lever as .64 to .36 or as 16 to 9, and not as 3 to 2.

Wheelwork.

Leup. Th. M. G. t. 14. Belidor. Arch. Hydr. I. i. 119. E. M. A. Pl. III. Horlogerie. E. M. A. VII. Art. Roue.

Particular kinds of Wheels.

Hook's perfection of wheelwork. Animadv. on Helvetius.

Several wheels on the same axis.

Bevilled wheels. Enc. Br. Art. Mechanics.
Wheels without cogs. Nich. I. 328.
On lantern pinions. Nich I. 522. 546.
†Kelly's instrument for bevilling wheels. Repert. VI. 106.

Says that the angles should be as the diameters of the wheels: in reality the tangent of the angle must be to the radius as one diameter to the other.

Walking wheels. See application of force.

When a strap runs on a revolving cone, and is sufficiently tight, it advances towards the base of the cone, and does not slide towards the point: for the edge of the strap nearest the base is drawn more rapidly than the other, and the part advancing towards the wheel is bent towards the base. Hence, in order that the strap may remain on the middle of a wheel, it must consist of two portions of cones joined at their bases, and if rounded, must be convex, not concave, at its circumference, as may be seen in many manufactories. Y.

Structure and Proportions of Wheels.

Lahire on the teeth of wheels. A. P. IX. 90. 283. 292.
*Camus on the teeth of wheels. A. P. 1733. 117. H. 81.
Blakey's mode of drawing wire for pinions. Mach. A. VII. 255.
Gallonde's compass for wheelwork. Mach. A. VII. 315.
*Euler on the teeth of wheels. N. C. Petr. V. 299. XI. 207.

A form without friction is perfectly impracticable, although for a single tooth possible.

Cutting engine for wheels. Emers. mech. f. 304.
Lecerf on the proportion of wheels and pinions. Ph. tr. 1778. 950.
Kästner on the teeth of wheels. Commentat. Gott. 1781. IV. M. 3. 1782. V. M. 1. Dissert. Math.
*†Enc. Br. Suppl. Art. Machinery.
Imison's elements. I. 78.

Haynam's gage for cutting wheels. S. A. XVII. 325.

Donkins's table of the radii of wheels. Nich. VI. 86.

Wheelwork with Appendages.

See Jointed Work, Cranks.

Deparcieux on the form of the undulations for raising stampers. A. P. 1747. 243. H. 121.

Garousse's tooth wheeled lever. Mach. A. II. 15. 17. Lever with a hook. 19.

Gensanne's lantern substituted for cranks. Mach. A. VII. 105.

Friction of Wheelwork.

See removing weights.

Coulomb on the friction of pivots. A. P. 1790. 448.

> The friction varies nearly as the pressure. Pivots run with less friction on garnet than on agate: a perfect polish reduces the friction to $\frac{1}{2}$ or $\frac{1}{3}$ of what is usual in ordinary work. For the point of a cone of steel bearing less than 100 grains, the best angle is $10°$ or $12°$; when the weight is 4 or 500 or more, about $45°$.

Machinery for Entertainment.

Maillard's artificial swan. Mach. A. VI. 133. Gondola with an artificial horse. 137.

Tumbling figures. Mussch. Introd. I. pl. 11.

Ferguson's mechanical paradox. Mech. exerc. 44.
> Wheels moving in contrary directions.

Automatons. E. M. Physique. Art. Automate.

Vaucanson's flute player, piper, and duck. Montucla and Lalande. III. 802. 803.
> These machines were purchased by Professor Bayreuss of Helmstadt. Raisin's automaton harpsichord was found to contain an infant performer.

Union of Flexible Fibres.

(E. M. M.) Various manufactures. E. M. Manufactures, arts, et métiers, par Roland de la Platière. III. t. 1785—91.

Materials.

Animal.

Aglionby on the nature of silk. Ph. tr. 1699. XXI. 183.

Bon on the silk of spiders. Ph. tr. 1710. XXVII. 2.

Daubenton on the magnitude of the fibres of wool. A. P. 1779. 1. H. 1.
> The fibres of superfine wool are $\frac{1}{10}$ of a line in diameter, or $\frac{1}{171}$. E. I.

Daubenton on the new wool. A. P. 1785. 454.

Silkworms. E. M. A. VIII. Art. Vers à soie.

Silk. E. M. M. II. Art. Soie.

Wool. E. M. M. I. Art. Moutons. Laine.

Hair. E. M. M. I. Art. Poil.

Intestines. E. M. M. III. Art. Boyaudier.

Leather. E. M. M. III.

Swayne's apparatus for rearing silkworms. S. A. VII. 148.

Chappe on a transparent texture derived from the silkworm. Ann. Ch. XI. 113.

Silk gut. Hochheimer. Ph. M. I. 368.

Des Lozieres on animal cotton. Nich. 8. IV. Ph. M. XIX. 120.

Vegetable.

Cloth of the bark of the genista. C. Bon. IV. O. 349.

Cerati on the bark of the broom. A. P. 1763. H. 52.

Ironside on the son, or crotalaria juncea, used for ropes. Ph. tr. 1774. 99.
Antill on hemp. Roz. XIII. Suppl. 97. Repert. V. 384.
Flax and hemp. E. M. M. I. Art. Lin. Chanvre. II. Suppl. Art. Lin et Chanvre.
Cotton. E. M. M. I. Art. Coton.
Stipa tenacissima, lime-tree bark, reeds, straw, and agave or tree aloe. E. M. M. II. Art. Sparte.
Apocynum Syriacum. Möller on the Syrian silk plant. Ph. M. VIII. 149.
Guthrie on the cotton tree. Manch. M. V. 214.
Labillardière on the flax of New Zealand. B. Soc. Phil. n. 75. Journ. R. I. II. Ph. M. XVII. 374.
Roxburgh on the strength of various vegetables. S. A. XXII. 363.

Finds hemp the strongest of all, except the agave and the aletris: the agave $\frac{1}{7}$ stronger, the aletris nervosa $\frac{1}{4}$.

From the Journals of the Royal Institution. II. 104. Extract from a Memoir of Mr. Labillardière, on the Strength of the Fibres of the Flax of New Zealand. Read before the National Institute. B. Soc. Phil. n. 75.

This flax, the phormium tenax, was procured from the inhabitants of New Zealand, by Mr. Labillardière himself, in the voyage he made in search of La Peyrouse.

In these experiments particular care was taken to employ substances of a diameter as equable as possible throughout their lengths. The inferences are, that the strength of the fibres of the great aloe, agave Americana, being equal to 7, that of common flax is represented by $11\frac{2}{3}$; that of hemp, by $16\frac{1}{4}$; that of the flax of New Zealand by $23\frac{7}{12}$; and that of silk by 34. If we call the strength of flax 1000, that of the aloe will be 596, of hemp 1390, of the phormium 1996, and of silk 2894.

The degree of extension of these fibres, before they break, is in a different proportion. Supposing it 1 for flax, it is 2 for hemp, 3 for the flax of New Zealand, 5 for the agave, and 10 for silk. It is well known that the strength of cords depends as well on their elasticity, as on the ultimate force required to break them.

The experiments and reflexions of Mr. Labillardière show,

beyond contradiction, that many advantages may be obtained from the cultivation of this flax on a large scale; and that it may be attempted with a prospect of success in the southern parts of France.

Mineral.

Ciampini on asbestus. Ph. tr. 1701. 911.
Gold thread. E. M. Pl. IV. Tireur d'or.

Preparations for Spinning or Winding.

Chopitel's machine used in making cards. A. P. 1747. H. 127.
Preparation of silk. Roz. Intr. II. 227.
Comb pots. Bailey's mach. I. 111.
Antill on hemp. Roz. XIII. Suppl. 97. Repert. V. 384.
Machine for hackling flax. E. M. Art Aratoire.
Enc. Br. Art. Woolcombing. E. M. M. I. Art. Peignage.
E. M. M. I. Art. Cardes.
Collomb on the varnish of silk. Roz. XXVII. 95.
Hughes's machine for twitching wool. S. A. VII. 193. Repert. I. 93.
Prozet on dressing hemp. Roz. XXIX. 241.
Cartwright's patent machine for combing wool. Repert. I. 228.
Wright's patent machine for combing wool. Repert. II. 217.
Daniel's comb pot. Repert. VII. 199.
Hawksley's patent for combing wool. Repert. VIII. 217.
Varley's patent for carding and spinning. Repert. XI. 217.
Foden's size for dressing cotton. Repert. XIII. 5.
Bowden's patent machine for batting cotton. Repert. XVI. 5.
Before carding.

Walmsley's patent machine for batting cotton. Repert. ii. I. 401.
Berthollet on imitating cotton with hemp. Nich. VI. 252. Repert. ii. III. 388.
Barker's machine for preparing wool. S. A. XXI. 323.

Spinning.

Ciampini on spinning asbestus. Ph. tr. 1701. XXII. 911.
André's spinning wheel. A. P. 1745. H. 82. Mach. A. VII. 293.
Spinning wheel. Emers. mech. F. 191.
Brisout's spinning machine. A. P. 1761. H. 154.
A wheel that spins and reels at once. Roz. XIV. 415.
Spinning wheels. Bailey's mach. I. 111.
Spinning and spinning machines. E. M. M. I. Art. Filature.
Antis's spinning wheel, the bobbin moving backwards and forwards. S. A. XI. 157. Repert. I. 37. Further improved. Repert. IV. 173.
Kendrew's patent spinning machine. Repert. XVI. 73.

Thread has been sold for 4l. an ounce.

Winding, Reeling, and simple Twisting.

Grieser's machine for doubling and twisting silk. A. P. 1743. H. 170.
Rouvière's reel for silk. A. P. 1744. H. 62. Mach. A. VII. 265.
Vaucanson's machine for winding silk. A. P. 1749. 142.
Vaucanson's machines for doubling and twisting silk. A. P. 1751. 121. 1757. 155. H. 160.
*Vaucanson on winding silk. A. P. 1770. 437. H. 106. 1773. 445. H. 74.
Vaucanson on the construction of silk mills. A. P. 1776. 156. H. 46.
Twisting mill. Emers. Mech. F. 300.
Pullein's new silk reel. Ph. tr. 1759. 21.
Paulet Art du dévidage des soies. f. Paris.
Vaussena's machine for winding silk. A. P. 1767. H. 184.
An Italian silk reel. Bailey's mach. I. 104.
Reels. Bailey's mach. I. 111.
Cruger's machine for doubling yarn. Bailey's mach. II. 31.
Spoules for winding thread. E. M. M. I. Art. Canons.
Twisting silk. E. M. M. II. Art. Rétordre.
Twisting bowstrings. E. M. M. III. Art. Boyaudier.
Descharmes on twisting. Roz. XXV. 466.

Ropemaking.

Hooke's experiments on cordage, 1669. Birch. II. 393.

Showed that twisting diminished its strength.

Réaumur on the strength of ropes compared with that of their parts. A. P. 1711. 6. H. 82.
Depontis on cords. A. P. 1739. H. 56.
Duhamel Traité de la corderie perfectionnée. 4. Paris. R. S.
E. M. M. I. Art. Corderie. E. M. Pl. V. Marine, 26, 27, 31 .. 91.
Belfour's patent ropes and cordage. Repert. II. 145.
Chapman's patent for laying cordage. Rep. IX. 1.

With an account of the whole process of ropemaking.

Chapman's patent preservative of cordage. Repert. ii. II. 91.
Curr's patent flat rope. Repert. X. 361.

*Robison. Enc. Br. Art. Ropemaking.
Möglich's woven rope. Ph. M. III. 331.
Mitchell's patent for cordage. Repert. XI. 302. Repert. ii. I. 19.
  More divided than usual.
*Huddart's patent registered cordage. Rep. XII. 80.
Huddart's patent for tarring cordage. Rep. XIV. 231.
Huddart's remarks on the patent registered cordage. 4. Lond. 1800.
  With 3 yarns in a strand, nothing is lost in the common way; with 6, ¼ or less; with 100, about ½; the registered cordage of 96 yarns loses nothing, according to the author's theory; but in the experiment it appeared to lose an eighth. The registered cordage stretches also much less than the common.

Manufacture of Cloth. Weaving.

Petty's history of cloth making. Birch. I. 55.
Cerati on cloth made of the bark of the broom. A. P. 1763. H. 52.
Paulet Art de fabriquer les étoffes de soie. f. Paris.
Duhamel Art du drapier. f. Paris. Acc. A. P. 1765. H. 132.
Duhamel Art de faire des tapis. f. Paris. Acc. A. P. 1766. H. 157.
Cloths. Roz. Intr. I. 236.
Fine muslins are woven wet in India. Vaucanson. A. P. 1776. 161.
La Platrière Art du fabriquant des étoffes en laine. f. R. S.
La Platrière Art du fabriquant de velours de coton. f. R. S.
Improvements in weaving. Bailey's mach. I. 124.
Woollen cloths. E. M. M. I. Art. Draperie.
Cloth of linen and hemp. E. M. M. II. Art. Toile.
Gauzes and crapes. E. M. M. I. Art. Gazes.
Ribbons. E. M. M. II. Art. Ruban.
Velveret. E. M. Pl. VI. Toilerie. E. M. Pl. VIII. Velours de coton.
Borders of cloths. E. M. M. I. Art. Lisière.
Carpets. E. M. M. II. Art. Tapis.
Drawing patterns. E. M. M. I. Art. Dessins.
Preparation for weaving. E. M. M. I. Art. Chaîne. Ourdir.
Size for weaving. E. M. M. I. Art. Colle.
Daubenton on the first superfine cloth of France. A. P. 1784. 76.
Rochon's varnished wire cloth, as a substitute for horn. Journ. Phys. XLVI. (III.) 272. Nich. II. 412. Repert. X. 207.
Miller's patent for weaving. Repert. VIII. 148.
  With wheelwork for winding up the cloth.
Holland's patent fleecy hosiery. Repert. XV. 17.
Enc. Br. Art. Weaving.
Fryer's patent cotton goods. Repert. ii. I. 257.
Haden's patent nail bagging. Repert. ii. III. 13.
Cobb's patent shag or plush. Repert. ii. III. 14.

Looms and their parts.

Genné's machine looms. Ph. tr. 1677. XII. 1007.
  From the Journal des Savans.
Vaucanson's tapestry loom. A. P. 1758. 245. H. 96.
Délier's mode of making the combs of looms. A. P. 1767. H. 185.
Combs. *Paulet* Art du Peignier. Paris, 1776.
Almond's loom for woollen cloth. Bailey's mach. I. 99. Other looms. 111.
Looms. E. M. M. I. Art. Métier.

Combs or reeds. E. M. A. V. Art. Parfaiseur de peignes. E. M. M. I. Art. Peigne ou Ros.
Heavels or harnesses. E. M. M. I. Art. Lisse.
Shuttles. E. M. M. I. Art. Navette.
Shott's loom for slight silk. S. A. VIII. 172. Repert. V. 322.
Enc. Br. Art. Ribbon loom, Silk loom, Weaving loom.
Clulow's loom for figured ribbons. S. A. Repert. XIV. 374.
Clulow's improved loom, applicable to weaving sacks. S. A. XX. 347. Repert. ii. III. 35.

Operations subsequent to weaving.

Moulin's machine for folding stuffs. A. P. 1737. H. 107.
Durand's mill for fulling and raising a nap. A. P. 1744. H. 160. Mach. A. VII. 223.
Fulling mill. Emers. mech. F. 255.
Vaucanson's machine for laminating stuffs. A. P. 1757. 155. H. 161.
Vaucanson's machine for cording silk stuffs. A. P. 1769. 5. H. 109.
A printing press for stuffs. Roz. Intr. I. 74.
Duhamel Art de friser et de ratiner les étoffes de laine. f. Par.
  Acc. A. P. 1766. H. 156.
La Platrière Art d'imprimer les étoffes en laines. f. R. S.
Raising a nap. E. M. M. I. Art. Frise.
Teazles. E. M. M. I. Art. Chardon-bonetier.
Printing woollen stuffs. E. M. Pl. VIII. Impression des étoffes.
Descharmes on the dressing of stuffs. Roz. XXXIV. 381.
A cylinder of paper for calendering. Journ. Phys. XLVII. (IV.) 389.
Nicholson's patent for printing linen. Rep. V. 145.

Jeffrey's machine used in dying. Rep. VIII. 296.
Gillispie's patent for printing calicos. Rep. XI. 365.
Chaptal on cleaning cloths. Rep. XII. 56.
Harmar's patent machine for raising a shag. Repert. XII. 289.
Harmar's cropping and shearing machine. Repert. XV. 1.
Hornblower's patent machine for glazing calicos. Repert. XIII. 289.
Newman's patent for embossing cloth. Rep. XIII. 295.
Fryer's patent for dressing cloth. Repert. ii. I. 335.
Fryer's patent for cutting cloth. Repert. ii. II. 23.
Vauquelin on water-proof cloths. B. Soc. Phil. n. 87.
  Thinks the operation is performed by means of soap, glue, alum, and a little sulfuric acid.

Textures not regularly woven.

Bedeau's stocking machine. A. P. 1737. H. 118.
Unwin's stocking frame. Bailey's mach. I. 93.
Hairwork. *Garsault* Art du perruquier et du barbier. f. Paris.
  Acc. A. P. 1767. H. 183.
Knitting and stocking weaving. E. M. A. I. Art. Bas. E. M. M. I. Art. Bas.
Lace. E. M. M. I. Art. Dentelles.
Hairwork. E. M. A. VI. Art. Perruquier.
Rushwork and matting. E. M. M. II. Art. Sparte.
Mats and straw work. E. M. A. V. Art. Nattier.
Basket work. E. M. A. VIII. Art. Vannier.
Beehives. See Carpentry.
Sieves. E. M. M. III. Art. Cribles.

Wire gratings. Duhamel Art. de l'épinglier. 55.
Fishing nets. E. M. A. II. Art. Filets. E. M. Pêches. Pl. 36.
Whips. E. M. M. III. Art. Fouets.
Boswell's loom for fishing nets. S. A. XIV. 275.
Stocking loom. Nich. III. 229.
Woven ropes. Möglich. Ph. M. III. 331.
Eaton's patent stocking frame for cross-stitch. Repert. XI. 361.

Knots.

Knots. Emers. Mech. Pr. 114. E. M. Pl. V. Marine. Pl. 15. E. M. Pl. VI. Soierie. Pl. 113.

Sewing.

Umbrellas. See Carpentry.

La Chaumette's matrass. A. P. 1717. H. 83. Mach. A. II. 117.
Cay's coat of six pieces. A. P. 1720. H. 114. Mach. A. IV. 9.
Garsault Art. du tailleur. f. Paris. Acc. A. P. 1769. H. 124.
Garsault Art du cordonnier. f. Paris. Acc. A. P. 1768. H. 127.
Garsault Art de la lingère. f. Paris.
Dudin Art du relieur doreur de livres. f. Paris.
Anisson on bookbinding. M. S. f. R. S.
Bookbinding. See printing.
Clothes. E. M. M. I. Art. Habit. Modes. II. Art. Tailleur.
Linen. E. M. M. I. Art. Couturière. Linge.
Embroidery. E. M. M. I. Art. Broderie.
Fringes. E. M. M. I. Art. Passementier.
Belts. E. M. M. III. Art. Ceinturon.
Gloves. E. M. M. III. Art. Gant.
Shoes. E. M. M. III. Art. Cordonnier.
Lasts. E. M. A. III. Art. Formier.
Brushes. E. M. M. I. Art. Crin.
Needles. E. M. A. I. Art. Aiguillier.
Camper sur la meilleure forme des souliers. 8. R. S.
Dunnage's waterproof hats. Repert. IV. 302.
Bell's patent needles. Repert. IX. 47.
Boileau's patent straw hats. Repert. XI. 97.
Broussonet on morocco leather. Repert. XI. 282.
Simpson's patent straw plat. Repert. XV. 19.
The straw is folded instead of platting; hats are made by sewing the plat together.
Holden's improvements in shoemaking. S. A. XXII. 304.

Appendages to Clothes.

Chaumette's buckle. Mach. A. III. 61.
Duhamel Art de l'épinglier. f. Paris. Acc. A. P. 1761. H. 152.
Pins. E. M. A. II. Art. Epinglier.
Button moulds. E. M. A. I. Art. Boutonnier.
Bell's patent buckles. Repert. I. 149.
Cheston's patent buckles. Repert. V. 19.
Clay's patent buttons. Repert. XII. 241.
Harris's patent pins. Repert. XIII. 217.
Hornblower's patent pattens. Repert. XIII. 236.
Barnett's patent buttons. Repert. XIII. 368.
Longman's patent pattens. Repert. XVI. 145.
Ross's expanding ring. S. A. XXI. 370.

Felting.

Nollet Art du chapelier. f. Paris. Acc. A. P. 1765. H. 132.
Gerard on felts. A. P. 1770. H. 116.
Hats. E. M. M. I. Art. Chapellerie. III. Suppl. Art. Chapeau.
Trousier on beaver hats. Roz. XXVII. 71.

Monge on felting. Ann. Ch. VI. 300. Repert. III. 351.
<small>Thinks the hairs are united by projecting serratures or filaments. But this supposition is not necessary for explaining the adhesion of felts, which may be deduced from the force of friction only.</small>
Chaussier on hatmaking. Journ. Polyt. I. 162. Nich. I. 399. Repert. X. 275.
On hatmaking. Nich. II. 467. 509. III. 22. 23. 73. IV. 236.
Tilstone's patent for making hats. Repert. I. 1.
Burns's patent for hats. Repert. IX. 167.
Dunnage's patent for ventilating hats. Repert. X. 149.
Chapman's patent for taking off the fur from sealskins. Repert. XI. 374.
Ovey and Jepson's patent for hats. Repert. XIII. 373.
Walker's patent waterproof hats. Repert. XVI. 217.

Papermaking.

Guettard on the materials for making paper. A. P. 1741. H. 159.
Lalande Art de faire du papier. f. Paris.
Desmaret on the mode of making paper in Holland. A. P. 1771. 335. H. 65. 1774. 599. H. 64.
Ironside on the mode of making paper in India. Ph. tr. 1774. 99.
Papermaking. Bailey's mach. I. 124.
E. M. A. V. Art. Papier.
Cards. E. M. A. I. Art. Cartier.
Pasteboard. E. M. A. I. Art. Cartonnerie.
Franklin on papermaking in China. Am. tr. III. 8. Repert. I. 41.
Faujas on paper of mulberry bark. Roz. XLII. 239.
Broussenel on mulberry paper. Roz. XLIII. 394.

On regenerated paper. Journ. Phys. XLIV. (I.) 303.
Deyeux on regenerated paper. Ann. Ch. XIX. 237. Repert. X. 136.
Eckhardt's patent paper hangings. Repert. II. 90.
Cunningham's patent preparation of rags. Repert. II. 222.
Hooper's patent printing paper. Repert. III. 377.
<small>With a mixture of plaster or of talc.</small>
Carpenter's patent for bleaching paper. Repert. V. 369.
Bigg's patent for bleaching paper. Repert. VI. 235.
Koop's patent for regenerated paper. Repert. XIV. 225.
Koop's patent straw paper. Repert. ii. I. 241.
<small>With quicklime.</small>
Sewel's specimen of paper made of gunny bags or paut, corchorus. 8. Lond. 1801.
Straw paper. Journ. Phys. LII. 376.
Loysel on bleaching pulp for paper. Ann. Ch. XXXIX. 137. Nich. 8. I. 118. Repert. XVI. 200. Ph. M. XI. 273.
Winter's patent animal floor paper. Repert. XVI. 361.
Campbell on the state of papermaking. Nich. 8. II. 6.
Plus's patent paper. Repert. ii. II. 406.
<small>Paper of cotton is said to have been used about the year 1000, of rags in 1319; the manufacture was introduced into England in 1588.</small>

Papermills.

A paper and corn mill. Mach. A. I. 121.
Pannetiers stampers of cast iron. A. P. 1772. i.
Enc. Br. Art. Papermill.
See Mills.

Timekeepers in General.

*Hugenii horologium oscillatorium. f. Par. 1673.
  Acc. Ph. tr. 1673. VIII. 6068.
Huygens on the invention of watches. A. P. X. 381.
Hooke's centrifugal regulator. Hooke. L. C. Lampas. 43.
Hooke on timepieces. Nich. IV. 287.
Lahire on clocks. A. P. 1700. 161. H. 144. 1703. 285. H. 130.
Lahire on the invention of pendulum clocks. A. P. 1717. 78.
*The artificial clockmaker, by W. D. F. R. S. (Derham). 12. Lond. 1714. M. B.
Saurin on clocks. A. P. 1720. 208. H. 106.
Kratzenstein on marine timekeepers. N. C. Petr. III. 381.
Cumming's elements of clock and watch work. 4. Edinb. 1766. R. I.
Hatton on clock and watch work. 8.
Berthoud Traité des horloges marines. 4. R. S.
Berthoud éclaircissemens. 4. R. S.
*Berthoud histoire de la mesure du temps par les horloges. 2 v. 4. Par. Acc. Journ. Phys. XLVIII. 461. ed. 2. 1802. R. I.
  With an account of works on the subject, at the end.
Harrison on the mensuration of time. Lond. 1767.
Harrison on clockwork and music. 8. 1775. R. S.
Schulze on clocks. A. Berl. 1780. 349. 359.
Chabert on marine watches. A. P. 1783. 49.
Chabert Extrait. 4. Par. 1785. R. S.
*E. M. A. III. Art. Horlogerie.
Whidby on marine timekeepers. Papers on Nav. Arch. II. iii. 54.
Enc. Br. Art. Clock.
Rittenhouse on timekeepers. Am. tr. IV. 26.
*Robison. Enc. Br. Suppl. Art. Watchwork.

Pearson on watches. Nich. III. 49. 189. V. 46.
E. Walker on Barraud's improved timekeepers. Nich. VII. 203.
  Disapproves of jewelling.
*J. Haley on the wear of timekeepers. Nich. VIII. 46.
  Watches were made at Nuremberg in 1477. Hooke's watch with a spring in 1658.

Particular Constructions of Clocks and Watches.

On the watches of Hugens and Lord Kincardine. Ph. tr. I. 1665—6.
Hooke's spring watches. Hooke on helioscopes. 4. Lond. 1675.
  Acc. Ph. tr. 1765. X. 440.
Hugens's portative watches. Ph. tr. 1675. X. 272.
  With a spiral spring, and a pinion on the axis of the balance.
Wheeler on a rolling clock. Ph. tr. 1684. XIV. 647.
Baufré's watch with a balance making several revolutions. A. P. I. 288.
Harquin's new watch. A. P. II. 68.
Perrault's clock moved by water. Mach. A. I. 39.
Lebon's clock with a weight. A. P. 1714. H. 128.
Sully's watch. A. P. 1716. H. 77. Mach. A. IV. 93. 95.
Sully's marine clock. A. P. 1724. H. 94. Mach. A. IV. 75.
Massy on marine timekeepers. A. P. Prix. I. ii.
Leroy's repeating clock. A. P. 1728. H. 110. Mach. A. V. 61.
Leroy's flat watches. A. P. 1751. H. 174.
Leroy's clock of two wheels. A. P. 1752. H. 149. Mach. A. VII. 423.

Leroy's clock with one wheel in each part. A. P. 1755. H. 140.

Leroy's night watch. A. P. 1761. H. 157.

Leroy's simplified watches. A. P. 1763. 420. H. 127.

Leroy's marine watches. A. P. 1767. H. 125.

Cassini on Leroy's watches. A. P. 1769. H. 102.

Voyage pour éprouver les montres de Leroy. 4. Paris. R. S.

His watches determined the longitude within 15' after six weeks.

Collier's repeating clock. A. P. 1728. H. 110. Mach. A. V. 75. 77.

Dutertre's marine clock with a double pendulum. Mach. A. V. 79.

Outhier's spring clocks. Mach. A. VI. 65.

Larçay's repeating clock. A. P. 1734. H. 106. Mach A. VI. 191.

Thiout's repeating watch and clock. A. P. 1737. H. 107. Mach. A. VII. 61.

Gallonde's clock with few wheels. A. P. 1740. H. 110. Mach. A. VII. 79.

Gourdain's portable watch and clock without fusee. A. P. 1742. H. 161. Mach. A. VII. 147.

Gourdain's half minute watch for the log. A. P. 1743. H. 172. Mach. A. VII. 217.

Jodin's watch with two balances. A. P. 1754. H. 140.

Charmy's clock. A. P. 1754. H. 141.

Mesurier's clock resembling Leroy's. A. P. 1755. H. 141.

Romilly's watch. A. P. 1755. H. 143.

Ridreaut's repeating clock. A. P. 1756. H. 131. 1758. H. 103.

Clock. Emerson's mech. F. 302, 303.

Mason on the rate of Ellicott's clock. Ph. tr. 1762. 534.

Millot's half second clock. A. P. 1762. H. 189. 190.

Lespine's repeating watch. A. P. 1763. H. 140.

Biesta's watches. A. P. 1764. H. 182.

Coupson's watch without a fusee. A. P. 1764. H. 183.

Nioux's watches. A. P. 1764. H. 183.

Tosembach's striking watch of 26 pieces. A. P. 1769. H. 128.

Franklin's clock with three wheels and two pinions. Ferguson's mech. exerc. 1. Another similar clock. 4.

Wollaston on the rate of a clock of Holmes. Ph. tr. 1771. 559. 1773. 67. 1775. 290.

It varied but 2" or 3" a day for a whole year.

Ferin's watches. A. P. 1772. i.

Robin's clock. A. P. 1778. H. 56.

Robin on turret clocks. Roz. XXXII. 45.

Magellan's clock. Roz. XVII. 283.

Hill's repeating timepiece. Bailey's mach. II. 63.

With large plates.

Fleurieu Voyage pour éprouver les horloges de Berthoud. 4. R. S.

Count de Bruhl's registers of a watch. 4. R. S.

Sampson's chime clock. S. A. IV. 177.

Maskelyne on Mudge's timekeepers. 8. Lond. 1792. R. S.

Leslie's patent nautical watch. Repert. II. 91.

Henry's sentinel register. Repert. V. 32.

Haley's patent timekeeper. Repert. VI. 145.

Desaguliers's chronometer. Enc. Br. Art. Chronometer.

Day's patent noctuary for a watchman. Nich. 8. V. 133. Repert. ii. III. 161.

Marquis of Exeter on a timepiece for registering the attendance of a watchman. Nich. 8. V. 158.

Clock. Imison's elements. I. pl. 5.

Prior's simple striking part. S. A. XXI. 400. Nich IX. 92.

Massey's clock with a striking part regulated by a pendulum. S. A. XXI. 402. Nich. VIII. 162. Ph. M. XVIII. 303.

Elliott's simple repeater. S. A. XXII. 319. Nich. VII. 157.

Parts of Timekeepers.

Maintaining Power.
See Machinery.

Lebon's clock winder. Mach. A. III. 23.

On making springs. Leup. Th. M. G. t. 69.

Kratzenstein's thermometrical power for a clock. N. C. Petr. II. 221.

Leplat's mode of winding up clocks by a current of air. A. P. 1751. H. 171. Mach. A. VII. 401.

A weight hung on an endless cord. Emers. mech. f. 230.

Galloys's machine for winding up continually the weights of a clock. A. P. 1766. H. 159.

Thorowgood on a new watch key. 8. R. S.

On the maintaining power in clocks and watches. Nich. I. 429. II. 49.

Fusee.

Lahire on the figure of fusees. A. P. IX. 102.

Varignon on the fusee. A. P. 1702. 192. H. 122.

Leroy on a new situation of the fusee. A. P. 1763. 420. H. 127.

Chains for fusees. E. M. Pl. I. Chainetier. Pl. 2.

Wheels.
See Machinery.

Ridley's sector and deepening tool. S. A. VI. 188. 196.

Escapements, or Scapements.

Sully's escapement without friction. Mach. A. III. 95.

Leroy's and Sully's clock escapement. Mach. A. VI. 83.

Leroy's escapement of repose for watches. A. P. 1742. H. 158. Mach. A. VII. 127.

Leroy's detent escapement. Mach. A. VII. 385.
<small>The first detached escapement.</small>

Leroy's new dead beat escapement. A. P. 1748. H. 120.

Volet's watch escapement. A. P. 1742. H. 162. Mach. A. VII. 139.

Gourdain's watch escapement. A. P. 1742. H. 158. Mach. A. VII. 141.

Galonde's clock escapement with rollers. A. P. 1742. H. 165. Mach. A. VII. 159.

Soumille's crank escapement. Mach. A. VII. 325.
<small>For a pendulum of 19 feet, with a weight of 50 pounds.</small>

Caron's dead beat escapement. A. P. 1754. H. 139.

Christin's watch escapement. A. P. 1755. H. 138.

Lagrange on escapements. A. Berl. 1777. 173.

Magellan's escapement. Roz. XX. 376.

Howell's detached escapement. S. A. X. 216.

Robin's watch escapement. Roz. XLIII. 342.

Prior's detached escapement. S. A. XVI. 307. Nich. II. 363.

Goodrich's crank escapement for clocks. S. A. XVII. 333. Nich. III. 342.

Reid on escapements. Nich. V. 55.

Delafons's watch escapement. S. A. XIX. 331. Repert. XVI. 241. Nich. 8. I. 251.
<small>Seems to resemble Mudge's and Haley's: but the locking is said by the inventor to be simpler.</small>

Breguet's escapements. Montucla and Lalande. III. 794.
<small>With a figure.</small>

Massey's escapement for clocks. S. A. XXI. 414. Nich. VIII. 161. Ph. M. XVIII. 305.

The scape wheel of Arnold's and of Earnshaw's pocket timekeepers has 15 teeth: those of the box timekeepers 13. Arnold makes the impelling teeth of the scape wheel cycloidal, acting against a point. His detent unlocks inwards, or towards the axis of the wheel; Earnshaw's outwards.

Pendulums and Balances.

Baufré's watch with a balance making several revolutions. A. P. I. 288.
Leibnitz's proposal for regulating motion by springs alternately wound up. Ph. tr. 1675. X. 285.
Lahire on second pendulums. A. P. 1715. 130.
Derham's experiments on pendulums. Ph. tr. 1736. XXXIX. 201.
Euler on a new kind of oscillation. C. Petr. XI. 128.
Rivaz on a pendulum moving in small arcs. A. P. 1749. H. 182.
Godin's watch with a double balance. A. P. 1754. H. 140.
Grenier's pendulum. Roz. XVI. 139.
Magellan on the advantage of a large vibration. Roz. XX. 376.
Crossthwaite's pendulums. Ir. tr. 1788. II. 7. Repert. III. 254.

One of them supported by a diamond.

Mackay. Enc. Br. Art. Pendulum.
Atwood on the vibrations of watch balances. Ph. tr. 1794. 119.

An isochronous combination of springs. Approves Mudge's escapements.

Leslie's patent short pendulum. Repert. II. 91.
Benzenberg on a centrifugal pendulum. Gilb. XVI. 494.

For avoiding the alternation of motion.

E. Walker on the effect of the arc of vibration of a pendulum. Nich. 8. II. 76. 273. III. 35.
Hardy's mode of banking or checking the motions of a balance. S. A. XXII. 311.
Length of the pendulum. See Geography, and Rozier's Index. A. P. Art. Pendule.

For every minute that a clock varies in a day, a second pendulum must be altered $\frac{1}{3}$ or .054 inch; a half second pendulum, $\frac{1}{12}$ or .00134.

Bernoulli observes, that the time of vibration in a circular arc may be found very nearly, by adding to the radius one 8 millionth of the versed sine.

Six balance springs weigh a grain, and are worth 2l. 5s.; a grain of gold only 2d.

Springs may be made of gold with $\frac{1}{3}$ or $\frac{1}{4}$ its weight of copper; they are more elastic and more brittle than hard drawn steel wire, but less so than spring tempered wire.

Hands and Bells.

Molard's mode of moving hands at a distance. Mach. A. II. 159.
Fouchy on applying small clocks to large bells. A. P. 1740. 122.
Dupont's enamelled dialplates. A. P. 1755. H. 138.
Ridrot's striking part. A. P. 1758. H. 103.
Courtois's changeable chimes. A. P. 1769. H. 129.

Compensations and Corrections.

Picard on clocks gaining in summer. A. P. I. 73.
Lahire on the inequalities of clocks. A. P. 1703. 285. H. 130.
Derham on pendulums in a vacuum. Ph. tr. 1704. XXIV. 1785.

A half second pendulum lost 2″ in an hour, when placed in a vacuum: when the arc of vibration was increased to the same extent in the open air, it lost 6″ in an hour.

Williamson's general correction. Ph. tr. 1719. XXX. 1080.

An equated clock, including a correction for temperature.

Graham's correction for temperature. Ph. tr. 1726. XXXIV. 40.

> Mercury in a tube of glass or of varnished brass.

Thiout's new corrections for timekeepers. A. P. 1737. H. 107.

Cassini's compensation pendulum. A. P. 1741. 363. H. 147.

Ellicott's two compensations. Ph. tr. 1751. 479.

> One of them is effected within the weight of the pendulum.

Short's history of compensation pieces. Ph. tr. 1751. 517.

Guinette's compensation. A. P. 1760. H. 155.

Lemonnier on the increase of length of two rods. A. P. 1761. H. 26.

Leroy's compensation. A. P. 1769. H. 131.

Lambert on the resistance of the air to pendulums. Berl. Ephem. 1776.

Bernoulli on compensations. A. Petr. I. ii. 109.

Grenier's pendulum. Roz. XXIX. 114.

Crossthwaite. Ir. tr. 1788. II. 7. Repert. III. 254.

Fordyce on a new pendulum. Ph. tr. 1794. 2.

> The fixed cheeks which embrace the spring are raised by a bar of the same materials as the pendulum; but as much longer as to compensate for the expansion of the fixed substance.

Pine's new pendulum. Repert. III. 15.

> The method resembles Fordyce's; but the expanding bar is made too short.

Rittenhouse. Am. tr. IV. 26. Nich. III. 522. Repert. XIV. 323. Ph. M. IX. 298.

On compensations for temperature. Nich. I. 56, 575. III. 205.

Varley on the errors arising from magnetism. Ph. M. I. 16.

> A difference of 12' in 24 h. was observed in the different positions of a watch.

Döhler's compensation for clocks. Gilb. VII. 318.

Two rods which carry a cross bar supporting a bob or weight. Cavallo, N. Ph. III. Pl. 18. f. 10.

Benzenberg's gridiron pendulum. Gilb. XIV. 315. Nich. VII. 300.

> The balances of brass and steel, carrying a weight at the end, are best made by immersing the steel into melted brass, and turning it afterwards into a proper form.
>
> Sometimes the compensation is made by the flexure of a compound bar, which only widens or contracts the distance of the two pins between which the spring plays.
>
> Earnshaw professes to make the vibrations of the balance in short arcs more rapid than in larger, in order that the contraction of the arc by the increased tenacity of the oil may compensate for the unavoidable diminution of force of the balance spring, which is relaxed by continual action.

Sympathy of Clocks.

Hague on the invariable agreement of two clocks. Coll. Acad. I. 252.

Ellicot on the mutual influence of two clocks. Ph. tr. 1739. 126.

> The clocks resting against the same rail agreed for several days, without varying a second: when separate, they varied 1' 36" in 24 h. The slower, having a longer pendulum, set the other in motion, by the intervention of the rail, in 16¼', and stopped itself in 36¾': when the cases were connected by a bar of wood, the shorter pendulum was set in motion in 6', and the longer stopped in 6' more. On a stone floor the effects were slower. The shorter pendulum could not put the longer one in motion, because, as its vibrations became wider, they were still slower.

Supports for Clocks, and Management of Timekeepers.

Instructions for the use of pendulum watches at sea. Ph. tr. 1669. IV. 937.

Massy on using clocks at sea. A. P. Prix. I. ii.

Biesta's suspension for a clock. A. P. 1770. H. 114.

> Arsandaux's suspension was judged injurious. A. P.
>
> Cumming recommends that a watch or clock be fixed to a block of marble.
>
> Berthoud found that a clock lost 207" in a day, by being more firmly fixed; and Bernoulli, in the memoirs of the

Academy of Petersburg, calculates, that according to theory, it ought to have lost 2″ only. But Bernoulli's theory appears to be erroneous; he says, that the compound vibrations can only exist in such a manner that the point of suspension shall move in a direction opposite to that of the weight. Nicholson asserts, with more apparent truth, that the vibrations are more rapid as the fulcrum is firmer. The fulcrum must not be considered as a weight, but as a portion of an elastic substance.

Sandglasses.

Lahire's new hourglasses. A. P. X. 472.
Prosper's hourglass. A. P. 1727. H. 143. Mach. A. V. 23.
Soumille's sandglass of 30 hours. S. E. I. 80.
Sand is said to flow equably. Cooke. Ph. M. XII. 312.
Gould's patent log glass. Rep. ii. III. 242.

Measures of Time not simply mechanical.

See Hydraulics and Practical Astronomy.

Bernoulli on marine clepsydras. A. P. Pr. I. 4.
Duguet's clepsydra. Mach. A. VI. 131.
Arderon on the weaver's alarm. Ph. tr. 1745. XLIII. 555.
   A candle burning a thread passed through it.
Hamilton's clepsydra. Ph. tr. 1746. XLIV. 171.
   Supplied from a cistern running over. Too complex.
Enc. Br. Art. Chronometer.
   The motion of air, the consumption of oil, and the burning of a candle may be employed as measures of time.
   King Alfred is said to have used six wax tapers burning in a lantern. Hero's clepsydra was a siphon, supported by a float, and bent over the side of the vessel.

Raising Weights in general.

Leup. Th. M. G. Th. Machinarium. Th. Hydraul. Th. Hydrost. t. 18. 29.
Belidor. Arch. hydr. I. i. 25.
Loriot on raising weights by the tide. A. P. 1761. H. 159.
A fire ladder. A. Petr. I. i. H. 67.
   Supporting itself.
Brooks's buoyant machine for raising weights. Repert. VII. 361.
Harriott's engine for raising and lowering weights by water. Nich. 8. IV. 41.

Levers.

Levers. Leup. Th. Machinarium. t. 16.
Levers on a large scale. Leup. Th. Hydrot. t. 11. Th. Hydraul. I. t. 56.
Compound Levers. Leup. Th. Machinarium. t. 17. 18.
Levers with ratchets. Leup. Th. Machinarium. t. 17.
†Emerson's mech. f. 186.
Liftingstock, a lever with a double fulcrum. Emers. mech. 295.
Lever with a counterpoise, for raising a bucket. Musschenbr. Introd. I. Pl. 5.
Lever with ratchets. Musschenbroek. Introd. Pl. 6.
Mrs. Wyndham's lever. S. A. XIV. 296. Repert. VI. 246.
   With a cross bar.

Wheel and Axis.

Lahire. A. P. IX. 90.
Debelloy on reducing the weight of chains and ropes. Roz. XXXII. 375.
   Observes, that if they are to be always vertical, the lower part may have its weight diminished.
Featherstonehaugh's counterpoise to the chain of an axis. S. A. XVII. 338. Repert. XII. 105.

Capstans.

Leup. Th. Machinarium. t. 19. 20.
Madelaine's capstan. Mach. A. II. 3.

Bourgès's lantern capstan. Mach. A. II. 7.
J. Bernoulli on the capstan. A. P. Pr. V. i.
On the capstan. A. P. Pr. V. ii.
Polen on the capstan. A. P. Pr. V. iii.
Ludot on the capstan. A. P. Pr. V. iv.
Depontis on the capstan. A. P. Pr. V. v.
Fenel on the capstan. A. P. Pr. V. vi.
Lorme on the capstan. A. P. Pr. V. vii.
†Emerson's mechanics. f. 248.
Eckhardt's double capstan with a catch. A. Petr. 1781. V. i. H. 38.
Ximenes on the capstan. Soc. Ital. I. 613.
Hotchkis's patent mechanical power. Rep. XIV. 24.
  A double capstan.
Lalande's capstan. Montucla and Lal. IV. 585.
Hamilton's capstan. Rep. ii. II. 126.
  The obliquity of the surface to the axis is 9° 30′, so that the messenger easily slides up.
On the compound capstan. Nich. VII. 50.
Hawkins on the compound capstan. Nich. VII. 267.
  Plucknett's patent capstan has levers and inclined planes " to surge the messenger."

Pullies.

Lahire on pullies. A. P. IX. 116.
Parent on the friction and equilibrium of pullies. A. P. 1704. 206. H. 96.
Leup. Th. M. G. t. 8 .. 10. Th. Machinarium. t. 35 .. 39.
Bessonius's complicated pullies. Leup. Th. Machinarium. t. 37.
Smeaton's new tackle. Ph. tr. 1751. p. 494.
Emerson's mechanics. F. 196 .. 198.
E. M. A. VI. Art. Poulieur.
Taylor's patent pullies. Repert. VI. 93.
  Of metal or cross grained wood.

Garnett's pullies. Cavall. N. Ph. I. pl. 8. f. 2.
  A pulley with ropes not parallel is called by seamen a swigg.

Fixed Inclined Planes.
See Roads.

Inclined plane with a series of carriages. Leup. Th. Hydrot. t. 22.
Belidor. Arch. Hydr. II. ii. pl. 27.
Fulton's patent machine for conveying boats. Repert. VII. 222.
Fulton on canal navigation.
Egerton on the Duke of Bridgewater's inclined plane. S. A. XVIII. 288. Nich. IV. 486. Ph. M. IX. 30. Repert. XVI. 153.

Wedge.

Varignon on the wedge. A. P. II. 117.
Lahire on the wedge. A. P. IX. 120.

Screws.
See Presses.

Lahire on the screw. A. P. IX. 129. 141.
Varignon on the screw. A. P. 1699. 91. H. 111.
Leup. Th. M. G. t. 18 .. 20. Th. Machinarium. t. 45 .. 48.
Lemaire on raising weights by the screw. A. P. 1726. H. 71. Mach. A. IV. 179.
Hunter's way of applying the screw. Ph. tr. 1781. 58. Nich. VII. 50.
E. M. A. VIII. Art. Vis.
Making screws. E. M. Pl. IV. Tourneur. pl. 8.
On the construction and uses of the screw. Nich. I. 158.
Pocock's patent machine for raising heavy bodies. Repert. XIII. 79.

Jacks. Crics, Fr.

Heronis barulcus, from a manuscript translation from the Arabic. Brugmans Commentat. Gott. 1784. VII. M. 75.
Perrault's balance jack. Mach. A. I. 5.
Thomas's circular jack. Mach. A. I. 209. II. 37.
Thomas's jack applied to a cart. Mach. A. II. 39.
Gobert's jack. Mach. A. I. 213. 215.
Dalesme's jacks. A. P. 1717. 301.
Leup. Th. Machinarium. t. 16.
Emerson's mech. f. 249.
Staghold's screw jack. Bailey's mach. I. 168.
E. M. Pl. I. 30. E. M. Pl. III. Maréchal grossier. Pl. 4.
Mocock's jack. S. A. VIII. 180. Roz. XXXIX.
Person's jack moved by a lever. Pers. Recueil. Pl. 6.

Cranes and Gins.

Perrault's rope crane without friction. Mach. A. I. 13. Leup. Th. Machinarium. t. 14. 15.
Thomas's jack applied to a crane. Mach. A. II. 41.
Thomas's machine for raising weights. Mach. A. II. 131.
Resson's invention for lowering weights. Mach. A. III. 25.
Crane with screws. Leup. Th. Machinarium. t. 48.
Crane with a chain. Leup. Th. Machinarium. t. 40.
Crane with a perpetual screw. Leup. Th. Machinarium. t. 49.
Henry's machine. A. P. 1725. H. 103. Mach. A. IV. 141.
Auger's machine. A. P. 1726. H. 71.
Montigni's machine. A. P. 1728. H. 109. Mach. A. V. 55.
Desaguliers on the crane. Ph. tr. 1729. 194.
Desaguliers on Perrault's crane and axis. Ph. tr. 1730. 222.
Guyot's crane. Mach. A. VI. 167.
Loriot's safe crane. A. P. 1755. H. 144.
Loriot's crane acting by the tide. A. P. 1761. H. 159.
Loriot's tumbler crane. A. P. 1761. H. 160.
Emerson's mech. F. 193 .. 195, 227, 233, 242 .. 244, 250, 257, 298.
Vaucanson's weighing crane. A. P. 1763. 326. H. 131.
Ferguson's crane with four powers. Ph. tr. 1764. 24.
Berthelot's crane. A. P. 1768. H. 130.
Pinchbeck's walking wheel crane. Bailey's mach. I. 146.
Bailey's mach. I. 183.
E. M. Pl. II. 30.
Braithwaite's crane. S. A. III. 159.
A portable crane. Ph. tr. 1790. Pl. 11.
Andrews's weighing crane. S. A. X. 221.
White's crane, with an oblique walking wheel and a break. S. A. X. 230. Repert. III. 113. Enc. Br.
Johnson's double gibbed crane for letting down the weight on different places. S. A. XI. 173.
Dixon's bar for supporting the labourers in a crane. S. A. XI. 201. Repert. I. 34.
Hall's expanding crane, with a spiral groove. S. A. XII. 284. Ph. M. XVIII. 270.
Davis's portable cart crane. S. A. XV. 278. Ph. M. V. 392. Repert. X. 273.
A perpetual screw for cranes. Repert. II. 312.
Collins's elevator. Am. tr. IV. 519. Repert. XV. 26.
A lever with pullies.

Millington's double capstan crane. Repert. XIII. 299.

Inclined plane with cranes. Fulton on canals.

Gent's crane. S. A. XIX. 293. Repert. ii. I. 418.
With a quadrant for raising or lowering the gib.

Keir's crane at Ramsgate. Nich. 8. III. 124.

Harriott's engine. Nich. 8. IV. 41.

Bramah's jib for a crane. Nich. VIII. 99.
With a rope in the axis, which is perforated.

Modes of raising Weights of particular Descriptions.

See seamanship.

Blondel on raising marshes. A. P. I. 234.

Labalme's machine for clearing harbours. A. P. 1718. H. 74.

Gouffe's machine for clearing harbours. Mach. A. II. 63.

Ressin's mode of raising materials in building. Mach. A. III. 27.

Ressin's mode of loading and unloading ships. Mach. A. III. 29.

A machine for clearing harbours. Mach. A. III. 167.

Perpoint's jack for pump rods. Mach. A. IV. 33.

Machine for pulling up trees. Leup. Th. Hydrot. t. 11.

Mode of raising scaffolding or shears. Leup. Th. Machinarium. t. 35.

Pump rods raised by screws or by oblique circles. Leup. Th. Hydrot. ii. t. 36.

Mairan's jack for telescopes. Mach. A. V. 31.

Dubois's machine for clearing harbours. A. P. 1726. H. 70.

Guyot's machine for clearing harbours. A. P. 1733. H. 98. Mach. A. VI. 163.

Briandferés machine for raising stones. A. P. 1737. H. 106.

Macary's machine for clearing harbours. A. P. 1744. H. 62. Mach. A. VII. 259.

Lavier's machine for clearing harbours. A. P. 1745. H. 81.

Lonce's machine with revolving buckets for raising ballast. Mach. A. VII. 449.

Clearing harbours. Belidor. Arch. Hydr. II. ii. 131. 156.

Machine employed for clearing the port of Toulon. Belidor. Arch. Hydr. II. ii. Pl. 20.

Walking wheel for raising a sluice board. Belidor. Arch. Hydr. II. ii. Pl. 54..56.

Robertson's account of the raising of the Royal William. Ph. tr. 1757. 288.

Jurine's machine for pulling up trees. A. P. 1765. H. 136.

Redelykheid Machine a creuser les pores. f. Hague, 1774.

Chatel's machine for clearing harbours. A. P. 1777. H.

Frazer's tongs for fishing up goods. Bailey's mach. II. 72.

Mode of climbing up a steeple. E. M. Pl. I. Couvreur. 2.

Suspended scaffolding. E. M. Pl. IV. Peintre en bâtimens.

Cranes used in glass houses. E. M. Pl. II. Glaces. Pl. 16.

Machine for clearing harbours. E. M. Pl. I. 27. E. M. Pl. V. Marine. Pl. 76.

Machine for pulling up trees. E. M. Art. Aratoire.

Bertrand's machine for clearing harbours. Journ. Phys. XLVIII. 373.

Ellicott's corn mill with buckets for raising flour. Repert. IV. 319.

Sparrow's patent machine for raising earth. Repert. V. 77.

Davis's cart crane. See cranes.

A machine for pulling up trees. Enc. Br. Art. Bern machine.

Arkwright's machine for raising ore. S. A. XIX. 278. Nich. 8. I. 303. Repert. ii. I. 261.
  Buckets connected by frames.
Raising and lowering boats. Fulton on canals.
Whidbey on the recovery of the Ambuscade. Ph. tr. 1803. 321.
Machine for raising floating wood out of the water. Person Recueil. Pl. 11.
Ponti's stone gatherer. Repert. IV. 137. Willich Dom. Enc. Art. Stones.
Saint Victor's machine for rooting up trees. Nich. 8. IV. 248.
Antis's register for the draughts from a mine. S. A. XXI. 380. Nich. IX. 114.

Lowering Weights.

Most machines for raising weights are also employed for lowering them; some are appropriated to this purpose only. See regulation of descent.

Removing Weights. Diminishing Friction.

Lahire on lessening friction. A. P. IX. 119.
Hermand's mode of diminishing friction. Mach. A. III. 7.
Mondran's machine for diminishing friction. A. P. 1725. H. 102. Mach. A. IV. 119.
Fitzgerald on friction wheels. Ph. tr. 1763. 139.
  By means of friction quadrants a steam engine was enabled to do the work of 6 hours in 5, the friction of its beams being reduced from 95 pounds to $\frac{4}{5}$ of a pound, and from 425 pounds to 2½ pounds.

Removing Weights without Wheel Carriages.

Duncombe's patent sedan chairs. 1634.
Blondel's mode of raising marshes. A. P. I. 234.
Perrault's machine for drawing weights. Mach. A. I. 31.
Machine for drawing weights. Mach. A. I. 129.
Willin's sedan chair. Mach. A. II. 137.
Hermand's dray on connected rollers. 1713. H. 76. Mach. A. III. 7.
  Such a carriage was lately made in London.
Alix's machine for drawing weights. Mach. A. III. 193.
Sebastien's machine for moving trees. Mach. A. IV. 107.
Coetaisan's machine for moving trees. Mach. A. IV. 109.
Rollers. Leup. Th. Machinarium. t. 8. 9.
Buckets hung on a rope for moving earth. Leup. Th. Hydrot. t. 20.
Fenel on the alternate tensions of cords drawing a load. A. P. 1741. H. 155.
Pullies. Emers. mech. f. 239.
Carburi Travaux pour transporter un rocher. 8. Paris, 1777. R. I.
Riding. E. M. Equitation. 1 vol.
Monge on the best mode of moving a given quantity of matter into a given situation, déblais et remblais, Fr. A. P. 1781. 666. H. 34.
Screws for removing flour. Ellicott's corn mill. Repert. IV. 319.
Coulomb on carrying weights. See sources of motion.
  Coulomb observes, that the surface of drays ought to be made convex, in order that they may be more shaken, and that the friction may be diminished. See Friction.
Removing goods in fires. Person's parafeu. Recueil. Pl. 12..15.
  Heavy blocks may be removed on rollers mounted upon wheels, so as to avoid the friction on the axles. But this is not great.
  In Holland, when wooden drays are employed, it is usual to carry water for moistening them, in order to prevent their taking fire.

Theory of Wheel Carriages.

On the benefit of high wheels. Ph. tr. 1685. XV. 856.

Lahire on the magnitude of wheels. A. P. IX. 116.

Parent on the friction upon axles. A. P. 1712. 96.

Réaumur on the axles of wheels. A. P. 1724. 300.

Couplet on the draught of carriages. A. P. 1733. 49. H. 82.

Dupin de Chenonceau on fourwheeled carriages. A. P. 1753. H. 301.

Emerson's mech. 194.

<small>The axis is conical, that it may not wear loose; and it must be a little inclined in order to avoid its working against the linch pin.</small>

Deparcieux. A. P. 1760. 263. H. 151.

Boulard and Margueron on broad wheels. Roz. XIX. 424.

Jacob on the draught of wheel carriages. 4.

Anstice on wheel carriages. 8.

Rizzetti Riforma de' carri di quattro ruote. 8. Trevigi, 1785. R. S.

Edgeworth's experiments on wheel carriages. Ir. tr 1788. II. 73. Repert. I. 101.

Lamber on four wheeled carriages. Hind. Arch. II. 51.

<small>The axes of the wheels should be as their diameters, the centre of gravity should divide the distance in the ratio of the cubes of the diameters. A good proportion for the wheels is 4 to 5, the centre of gravity being twice as near the hind as the fore wheels. This is not very remote from the usual practice.</small>

Grobert sur les voitures a deux roues. 1797.

Enc. Br. Art. Mechanics.

A. Young, annals of agr. XVIII.

<small>Strongly in favour of carts.</small>

Fuss Versuch einer theorie des widerstandes zwey-und-vier-rädiger fuhrwerke. Copenh. 1798.

<small>Extr. Ph. M. XIII. 115.</small>

<small>On muddy roads, four wheels have the advantage, if they run in the same ruts. On harder roads, whether smooth or rough, if not very steep, two wheels have the advantage, and sometimes on soft roads, where there is much lateral friction on the flat surfaces of the wheels.</small>

Anderson's institutes of physics. Mech. xvii. quoted by Cavallo. N. Phil.

<small>A horse can draw 25 cwt. on a level road in a cart weighing 10 cwt. with wheels 6 feet high. In a common cart 2 horses easily draw 30 cwt. In a common waggon 6 horses draw 80 cwt.: in 3 carts they might draw 90, in 6, 150 cwt.: and 3 carts cost less than a waggon.</small>

Cumming on the effect of conical wheels. Board Agr. II. 351. Repert. XIII. 256.

<small>Would have the axis straight and the wheels cylindrical, but somewhat dished.</small>

Montucla and Lalande. III. 732.

Imison's elements. I. 129.

Ferguson's lectures by Brewster. 3 v. 1805.

<small>With many useful additions, yet not without mistakes.</small>

<small>The great advantage of broad wheels is in deep roads, where the resistance is derived from the depth of immersion.</small>

Particular kinds of Carriages.

Sailing carriages. Wilkins's mathematical magic.

Cusset's cart for moving great weights, binard Fr. Mach. A. I. 99.

Thomas's cart with a windlass. Mach. A. II. 39.

Bezu's chair on castors. Mach. A. II. 173.

Girard's machine for moving a chair. Mach. A. II. 187.

Descamus's coach suspended in the middle. A. P. 1713. H. 76.

Descamus's improvements in coaches. A. P. 1717. H. 83. Mach. A. III. 65. 109.

Godefroy's inversable chair. Mach. A. III. 97.

Lelarge's jointed car. A. P. 1719. H. 81. Mach. A. III. 197.

Tanney de Gourney's inversable coach. A. P. 1719. H. 82. Mach. A. III. 207.

Réaumur's carriages for narrow streets. A.P. 1721. 224.

Mondran's carriage with little friction. Mach. A. IV. 123.

Coetnisan's machine for moving trees. A. P. 1724. H. 96.

Maillard's chairs driven by winches. A. P. 1731. H. 92. Mach. A. V. 171. 173.

Maillard's chair with an artificial horse. Mach. A. VI. 141.

Lievre's landaulet. A. P. 1732. H. 118. Mach. A. VI. 3.

Duquet's inversable coach. Mach. A. VI. 7.

Brodier's chair for driving one's self. S. E. IV. 351. E. M. Pl. VII. Mécanique. Pl. 3.

Chenonceaux's carriage. Mach. A. VII. 439.
The lowest wheels 4 feet high.

Loriot's machine for moving statues. A. P. 1755. H. 144.

Loriot's jointed cart for barrels. A. P. 1761. H. 161.

Garsault's new berline. A. P. 1756. H. 127.

Cart. Emerson's mech. f. 201.

Waggon, driven within. Emerson's mech. f. 202.

Brethon's carriage remaining horizontal. A. P. 1763. H. 147.

Brethon's chaise for bad roads. A. P. 1766. H. 159.

Roubo Art du ménuisier carossier. f. Paris. Acc. A. P. 1770.

Ferry's arm chair on wheels. A. P. 1770. H. 117.

La Gabrielle, a cart for sculpture. Roz. XI. 522.

Carriages. Bailey's mach. I. 185.

Bailey's waggon for short turnings. Bailey's mach. II. 59.
The axles connected diagonally.

Waggons and carts. E. M. A. I. Art. Charron.

Carriages. E. M. A. IV. Art. Ménuiserie. Part 3.

Carriages for casks. E. M. Pl. IV. Tonnelier. Pl. 8.
With a windlass.

Scavenger's carts. E. M. A. VIII. Art. Vuidangeur.

Carriages used in glass houses. E. M. Pl. II. Glaces. Pl. 16.

Wheelbarrows. E. M. Art. Aratoire.

Boulard's cart. Roz. XXVII. 426.

Hatchett's plates of the coach of safety. R.S.

Besant's high wheeled timber carriage. S. A. VI. 203.

Anderson's conveyance for boats. Repert. II. 21.

Weldon's patent machine for conveying vessels. Repert. II. 235.

Middleton's machine for dragging hay. S. A. XIV. 197. Repert. VI. 27.

Beatson's mode of avoiding deep ruts. Repert. VIII. 26.

Jeffrey's patent for conveying coals. Repert. XI. 145.

Overend's patent carriage on castors. Repert. XI. 159.

Bakewell's improved car. Repert. XIV. 110.

Reddel's patent land and water carriages. Repert. XIV. 369.

†A coach. Walker's philosophy. Lect. iii.

Lord Somerville's dray cart. Board Agr. II. 415. Repert. XVI. 49.
Capable of elevation, so as to bear more or less on the horses; with Mr. Cumming's drag, applied laterally to the wheels.

Improved Irish car. Board Agr. II. 417.
Low and easily laden, the wheels cylindrical and under it.

Lord R. Seymour's cart. Willich's Dom. Enc. Art. Cart.

Wheelbarrows. Person Recueil. Pl. 6, 7.

Bauer's patent carriages. Repert. ii. I. 250.
With small axles.

Mason's patent waggon making two carts. Repert. ii. III. 249.

For deep roads, a dray may be combined with a cart, so as to support the weight when the wheels sink too much.

Parts of Carriages.

Thomas's suspension of carriages. Mach. A. II. 43.

Godefroi's mode of hanging post chaises. A. P. 1716. H. 78.

Zacharie's suspension for coaches. A. P. 1761. H. 156.

Reynal on carriage springs. A. P. 1765. H. 134.

Maillard's suspension for chairs with wheels. Mach. A. VI. 95.

Jacob's spiral carriage springs. Bailey's mach. I. 167.

Jacob's patent box for axles. Repert. ii. III. 170.

Wheelwright's work. E. M. A. IV. Art. Maréchal grossier. VII. Art. Roue.

Coach springs. E. M. Pl. IV. Serrurerie. Pl. 29.

Dodson's patent naves of wheels. Repert. XII. 235.
With rollers.

Appendages to Carriages. Drags, Harnesses, Sadlery.

Horses. See Statics.

Dalesme's simple mode of stopping horses. A. P. 1708. H. 141. Mach. A. II. 153.
By blindfolding them.

Lahire's machine for unlocking horses. A. P. 1712. 242.

Ressin's mode of facilitating descents to carriages. Mach. A. III. 31.

Harness and sadlery. *Garsault* Art du Bourrelier et du Sellier. f. Par. E. M. M. III. Art. Sellier.

Accoutrements and harness. E. M. A. II. Art. Eperonnier.

Black's Roman yoke. S. A. II. 87.

Colley's locking pole for a carriage. S. A. XI. 198.

Jones's patent woman's saddle. Repert. IV. 9.

Kneebone's wheel drag. S. A. XIII. 262. Repert. IV. 25.

Hesse's elastic stirrups. Repert. XIII. 371.

Inglis's patent saddle. Repert. XV. 217.

Snart's alexippus, or sliding lever for a cart S. A. XVIII. 230. Repert. XV. 110.

Davis's mode of unlocking horses and stopping the wheels. S. A. XVIII. 256. Repert. XV. 166.

Dickinson's patent saddles. Repert. XVI. 294.

Dickinson's patent saddle straps. Repert. ii. I. 247.

Cumming's drag. See Lord Somerville's cart.

Williams's patent for disengaging horses. Repert. ii. I. 86.

Pottinger's patent for disengaging horses. Repert. ii. III. 96.

Bowler's gripe for carriages. S. A. XXI. 358. Nich. IX. 177.

Meyer has a patent for a method of stopping horses by winding up the reins on an axis turned by a wheel of the carriage.

Roads.

See Inclined Planes. Agricultural Instruments.

Lelarge's mode of paving roads. Mach. A. III. 129.

Considerations on roads. 8. Lond. 1734. R. S.

Lambert on the best ascent of roads. A. Berl. 1776. 19.

Meister on the shortest roads to different places. N. C. Gott. 1777. VIII. 124.

Pinchbeck's road plough. Bailey's mach. II. 21.

Harriott's road harrow. S. A. VII. 205.
With sweeps.

Beatson's roller for preventing deep ruts. Repert. VIII. 26.

Edgeworth on rail roads. Nich. 8. I. 221.

Roads. Board Agr. I. 119.

Harrows and rollers for roads. Board Agr. I. 150.

Wilkes, Board Agr. I. 199.
> Concave roads are much approved in Leicestershire.

Wilkes on iron railways. Board Agr. II. 474. Repert. XIII. 167.

Iron roads. Board Agr. I. 203.
> A horse drew 3 tons up a railway rising 7 inches in 144. The draught was 327 pounds besides friction.

Woodhouse's patent rail roads. Repert. ii. III. 15.

Woodhouse on concave iron roads. Repert. ii. III. 17.

Wyatt on a railway. Repert. ii. III. 283.

Hollister's patent machinery for making roads. Repert. ii. III. 401.

Winterbottom's machine for clearing roads from mud. S. A. XXI. 334. Nich. VIII. 29.

Compression.

Presses, strictly so called.

See Printing.

Leupold. Th.

Moulins's machine for folding stuffs. A. P. 1737. H. 107.

Cheese press. Emers. mech. f. 189.

Lloyd's cyder press. Bailey's mach. II. 5.
> Without a screw.

Hunter's screw. Ph. tr. 1781. 58. Nich. VII. 50.

Press with a water wheel. E. M. Pl. I. Charpentier. t. 18.

Cheese press. E. M. A. III. Art. Fromage.

Printing press. E. M. A. III. Art. Imprimerie.

Simple press with a windlass. E. M. Pl. IV. Parfumeur. Pl. 2.

Tobacco and snuff presses. E. M. A. VIII. Art. Tabac.

An oil press with screws. E. M. Pl. VIII. Moulin à huile.

Wine press. E. M. Art Aratoire.

Anisson Déscription d'une presse d'imprimerie. 4. R. S. S. E. X. 613.
> Many figures; somewhat complicated.

Haas Déscription d'une presse d'imprimerie. 4. Basle. 1791. R. S.

Ridley's printing press with a lever. S. A. XIII. 243. Repert. V. 26.

Peck's packing press. S. A. XV. 267. Rep. VIII. 46.

Sabatier's patent mode of packing. Repert. VIII. 73.

Prosser's patent printing press. Repert. VIII. 368.
> With springs.

Whieldon's patent press. Repert. IX. 217.
> With wheelwork.

Enc. Br. Art. Cyder Press. Press. Printing Press.

Buschendorf's packing press. Repert. ii. III. 362.

Bowler's press with a spiral spring. S. A. XXI. 363.
> To continue an active pressure.

Vices, Pincers, and Pliers.

Hullot's new vice. A. P. 1756. H. 127.

E. M. Pl. III. Horlogerie. E. M. Pl. IV. Taillanderie.

Clamp vice. E. M. Pl. II. Doreur. Pl. 2. f. 20.

Wooden vices. E. M. Pl. II. Ebéniste. Pl. VI.

Calender Mills and Mangles, with Rollers.

Bunting's calender mill, worked by a crank supported on rollers. S. A. XV. 269. Repert. VIII. 176.

Jee's mangle worked by a crank. S. A. XVI. 303. Repert. XIV. 109. Ph. M. II. 419.

Calendering is usually performed by a polishing stone or glass pressed down by a spring, and moved backwards and forwards by a mill.

Compression between Rollers.

Rolling press. Emers. mech. f. 273.

Cazaud connaissances pour juger des moulins a cannes. Ph. tr. 1780. 318.

The work of 36 mules produces 80 or 100 gallons of liquor in an hour: making 120 to 150 hogsheads in a season; the immediate resistance being about 19,000 pounds; a good water mill should do twice as much.

Sugar mill. E. M. Pl. IV. Sucrerie.

Watt's patent for copying writings. Repert. I. 13.

Kirkwood's patent copperplate printing press. Repert. ii. III. 245.

Compression by Percussion.

Dubois's rams or stampers for beating the earth. A. P. 1726. H. 70. Mach. A. IV. 163, 169, 171.

Extension.
Simple Extension.

Glass blowing and drawing threads of glass. E. M. A. VIII. Art. Verre.

Réaumur thinks that glass as fine as spider's webs might be woven.

Extension by Pressure.

A. P. 1714. H.

Dalesme proposed to draw leaden pipes with a core, in the way that the patent pipes are now made.

Fayolle's machine for laminating lead. A. P. 1728. H. 108. Mach. A. V. 43.

Blackey on drawing steel wire. A. P. 1744. H. 61. Mach. A. VII. 255.

Chopitel's machine for laminating iron. A. P. 1752. H. 148.

Vaucanson's machine for laminating silver and gold thread. A. P. 1757. 155. H. 161.

Plating mill. Emers. mech. f. 251.

Glazier's vice. Emers. mech. f. 305.

Duhamel Art de réduire le fer en fil d'archal. f. Par.

Acc. A. P. 1768. H. 128. 1770. H. 110.

E. M. A. IV. Art. Laminage.

Wire drawing. E. M. A. VIII. Art. Tireur-fileur. Trefilerie.

Drawing rods for bolts. E. M. Pl. IV. Serrurerie. Pl. 24.

Glazier's vice. E. M. Pl. V. Vitrier. Pl. 3.

Wilkinson's patent pipes, drawn on a core. Repert. XVI. 92.

Extension by Percussion.

Compagnot's forge hammer. A. P. 1730. H. 115. Mach. A. V. 101.

Forge hammer. Emers. mech. f. 236. 237.

Courtivron et Bouchet Art des forges à fer. f. Paris.

Acc. A. P. 1761. H. 153. 1762. H. 187.

Duhamel Art de forger les enclumes. f. Par. Acc. A. P. 1762. H. 188.

Forges. Roz. Introd. II. 76.

Forges. E. M. A. II. Art. Fer.

Hand forge. E. M. Pl. IV. Serrurerie. Pl. 32.

Gold and silver leaf. E. M. A. I. Art. Batteur.

Forges at Carron. Smeaton's reports.

On hammering metals into plates. Nich. I. 131.

Hand forge. Pesron Recueil. Pl. 9, 17.

Walby's forge hammer worked by a man. S. A. XXII. 335.

A hammer of 70 pounds making 300 strokes in a minute.

Arts depending principally on Extension.

See Appendages to Clothes.

Plumbery. Fayolle's machine for casting lead pipes. Mach. A. V. 53.

Coining. Dubuisson's machine for preventing accidents in coining. A. P. 1731. H. 91. Mach. A. V. 155.

Gold and silver plate. Dufay on applying reliefs of gold to gold or silver plate. A. P. 1745. H. 45.

Horn plate work. D'Incarville on the Chinese lanterns. S. E. II. 350.

Plumbery. *Art* du plombier. f. Paris.

Pipemaking. *Duhamel* Art de fabriquer les pipes. f. Paris.

Porcelain. *Milli* Art de la porcelaine. f. Par.

Pottery. *Duhamel* du Monceau Art du potier de terre. f. Paris.

Anchors. *Duhamel* Art de la fabrique des ancres.
Acc. A. P. 1761. H. 152.

Baking pottery. Roz. Intr. II. 266.

Pottery. Bosc d'Antic on pottery. S. E. VI. 372.

Defensive arms. E. M. A. I. Art. Armurier.

Coppersmith's work. E. M. A. I. Art. Chaudronnier.

Brass work. E. M. A. II. Art. Cuivre jaune.

Pewter ware. E. M. A. II. Art. Etain.

Pottery. E. M. A. II. Art. Fayencerie. VI. Art. Poterie.

Tin plate work. E. M. A. II. Art. Ferblantier.

Blacksmith's work. E. M. A. IV. Art. Maréchal-grossier.

Coining. E. M. A. V. Art. Monnoyage.
With an account of the coins of different nations.

Goldsmith's work and jewellery. E. M. A. V. Art. Orfevre.

Resingue is an elastic anvil, which rebounds, and acts as a hammer in the inside of a vessel. Vocab. Art. Resingue.

Pipemaking. E. M. A. VI. Art. Pipes à fumer.

Plumber's work. E. M. A. Art. Plomb.

Pewter. *Salmon* Art du potier d'étain. f. Par. 1788. R. S.

Coining. Montu's coining press, with a swing lever. B. Soc. Phil. n. 14.

Pottery. Lasteyrie on the alcarraza, for cooling water. Ph. m. I.

Smith's work. Moorcroft's patent horse shoes. Repert. VI. 157.
Made by machinery.

Porcelain. Dechemant's patent paste for teeth. Repert. VI. 379.

Porcelain. Turner's patent. Repert. XII. 294.

Nails. Spencer's patent horse nails. Repert. XV. 316.

Coining. Hatchett and Cavendish on the wear of gold. Ph. tr. 1803. 43. Nich. 8. V. 286. Journ. R. I. II.

Penetration and Division.

Theory of Penetration.

Camus on a board pierced by a bullet, and scarcely moved. A. P. 1738. 147. H. 98.

Euler on the strokes of bullets on a board. N. C. Petr. XV. 414.

Ja. Bernoulli on the stroke of a bullet upon a board. N. A. Petr. 1786. IV. 148.

Gough on the motion of a cylinder urged by a falling block. Manch. M. IV. 273.
Merely speculative. Observes, that in driving piles, the resistance is neither uniform nor proportional to the depth.

The velocity of a carpenter's hammer is about 25 feet in a second. Robison.

Instruments of Penetration in general, and Substances of which they are composed.

Military engines. Mathematici veteres Vegetius, and Ammianus Marcellinus.

Réaumur Art de convertir le fer en acier. 4. Paris.

Silberschlag on the warlike machines of the ancients. A. Berl. 1760. 378.

Perret Art du coutelier. f. Paris. Acc. A. P. 1769. H. 131.

Fougeroux Art du coutelier en ouvrages communs. f. Paris.

Duhamel Art du serrurier. f. Paris.

Cutlery. E. M. A. II. Art. Coutelier.

Sword cutlery. E. M. A. III. Art. Fourbisseur.

Coarse tools, files, and ironmongery. E. M. A. VIII. Art. Taillanderie.

Agricultural instruments. E. M. Agriculture. $3\frac{1}{2}$ volumes to Ey.

Instruments of agriculture and horticulture. E. M. Art Aratoire. 1 vol.

Little on making steel. Am. Ac. I. 525.

Vandermonde on steel and cutlery. Ann. Ch. XIX. 13.

Frankland on welding cast steel. Ph. tr. 1795. 296. Repert. V. 327.

Pearson on wootz. Ph. tr. 1795. 322.

Pearson on some ancient arms. Ph. tr. 1796. 395. 422.

<small>Consisting of copper with some tin, from 9 to 14 per cent. The ancients sometimes also employed cast steel, of which some specimens were examined. A mixture of copper and iron was less hard than an alloy with tin.</small>

On steel. Nich. I. 468. II. 64. Ann. Ch. XXVII. 186.

Stodart on steel. Nich. IV. 127.

Wild's patent for uniting steel and iron. Repert. II. 368.

Cort's patent for preparing iron. Repert. III. 289, 361.

Dizé on the copper cutting instruments of the ancients. Repert. IV. 62.

Hartley's patent for tempering instruments. Repert. IV. 310.
<small>By a thermometer.</small>

Clouet on cast steel. B. Soc. Phil. n. 14.

Varley on steel and its preparation. Ph. M. II. 92. 178.

Mushet on iron and steel. Ph. M. II. 155. 340.

Collier on iron and steel. Manch. m. V. 109. Repert. X. 97.

<small>Saws are quenched in oil; penknives are tempered till they become light yellow; scissors light brown; table knives, swords, and watch springs, blue.</small>

Edgill's patent steel. Repert. XI. 157.

Gazéran on steel. Ann. Ch. XXXVI. 61.

On gilding cutlery. *Accum's* chemistry. II. 172. Nich. VI. 142.

<small>Conté says, that oil varnish with half its weight of spirit of turpentine, is a good preservative from rust.</small>

Stodart on Damascus sword blades. Nich. VII. 120.

Penetration by Pointed Instruments.

Taking whales. Birch. I. 325.

Pile engine. Mach. A. I. 125.

Lahire's pile engine. A. P. 1707. 188.

Camus's pile engine. A. P. 1713. H. 76. Mach. A. III. 3.

Vergier's machine for driving piles. Mach. A. III. 189.

Driving piles. Leup. Th. Hydrot. t. 24, 25, 29.

Raucourt's invention for shooting with cross bows. Mach. A. VI. 157.

Martin's pile engine. A. P. 1742. H. 156.

Bond on killing whales by means of a balista. Ph. tr. 1751. 429.

L'Herbette's pile engine. A. P. 1759. H. 236, 256.

Arrows. Emers. mech. f. 220.
<small>Revolving in order to move more steadily.</small>

Old pile engine. Emers. mech. f. 245.

Loriot's pile engine. A. P. 1763. H. 142.

Vauloué's pile engine. Belidor. Arch. hydr. I. ii. 107.

Fish hooks. *Duhamel* Art de pêche. f. Par. p. 12.

Piles. Bugge Theoria sublicarum. Ph. tr. 1779. 120.

Staghold's gun harpoon. Bailey's mach. II. 61.

Needles. E. M. A. Art. Aiguillier.

Pile engines. E. M. Pl. I. Charpente. Pl. 11.

Balistas, Bows. E. M. Pl. VII. Art. Militaire. Pl. 2, 4.

A gun harpoon. S. A. II. 191.

Moore's harpoon gun. S. A. IX. 164.

Bell's harpoon gun. S. A. XI. 191.

Enc. Br. Art. Balista. Bow.

<small>Kirby's fish-hooks are of an improved form, the point being turned more inwards, so as to be in the direction of the line.</small>

Cutting Instruments, or Edge Tools.

Duverger's machine for cutting files. Mach. A. I. 155.

Chaumette's flexible knives. Mach. A. II. 117.

Cutting machine. Leup. Th. M. G. t. 15.

Fardouel's machine for cutting files. A. P. 1725. H. 103. Mach. A. IV. 125.

Focq's plane for iron. A. P. 1751. H. Mach. A. VII. 407.

Brachet's machine for cutting files. A. P. 1756. H. 128.

Messier's chaff cutter. A. P. 1758. H. 100.

Mury's machine for pruning large trees. A. P. 1760. H. 159.

Razors. Garsault Art du perruquier. f. Par. *Perret* Pogonotomie.

A machine for cutting files. Am. tr. I. 365.

Ringrose's thistle cutter. Bailey's mach. I. 26.

Edgill's chaffcutter, with a spiral knife. Bailey's mach. I. 42.

Edgill's machine for slicing turnips. Bailey's mach. I. 65.

Scythes from Brabant and Hainault. Bailey's mach. I. 65.

Smith's machine for cutting straw, with a double knife. Bailey's mach. II. 24.

Cork cutting. E. M. A. I. Art. Bouchonnier.

Engraving plate. E. M. A. I. Art. Ciseleur.

Slitting mill. E. M. Pl. II. Fer. v. pl. 1..8.

Razors. E. M. A. VI. Art. Perruquier. From Perret.

Working stones. E. M. A. VI. Art. Pierres.

Sword blades. E. M. VII. Art. Sabres.

Stone cutting. E. M. A. VIII. Art. Tailleur de Pierres.

Shears. E. M. M. I. Art. Forces.

Potatoe cutter, scythes, chaff cutter, root cutter, and compound chaff cutter with knives placed side by side. E. M. Art. Aratoire.

Pike's chaff cutter, with a revolving knife. S. A. V. 63.

Bétancourt Molina's machine for cutting weeds. S. A. XIV. 317. Repert. VI. 175.

Salmon's chaff cutter, with two knives, cutting to 20 different lengths. S. A. XV. 281. Repert. VII. 401. Ph. M. III. 292.

Choumert's machine for splitting hides. Repert. IV. 104.

Scythe of Milan. Repert. V. 62.

Sandilands's sward cutter. Repert. X. 329.

Enc. Br. Art. Chaff cutter.
On a machine for cutting files. Nich. II. 309. Repert. V. 179.
Bentham's patent modes of working. Repert. X. 250. 293.
Willich's Dom. Enc. Art. Scythes.
Riesch's straw cutter. Willich's Dom. Enc. Art. Straw.
Sward cutter. Willich's Dom. Enc.
Reaping wheelbarrow. Person Recueil, Pl. 8.
Nicholson on razors. Nich. 8. I. 47, 210. Gilb. XVII. 453.
Nicholson's patent for cutting files. Repert. ii. II. 258.
Sawdon's patent straw cutter. Repert. ii. I. 409.
Bramah's patent machinery for planing. Repert. ii. II. 165.
Brown's patent machine for slicing turnips and tallow. Repert. ii. III. 405.

Lathes.

Plumier Art de tourner. Fr. Lat. f. 1710. M. B.
Lahire's machine for turning polygons. A. P. 1719. 320.
Leup. Th. Suppl. t. 26.
Grandjean de Fouchy's lathe for screws. Mach. A. V. 83, 89, 91.
La Condamine on the lathe. A. P. 1734. 216, 295.
Balzac on turning silver plate. A. P. 1756. H. 129.
Roubo Art du ménuisier ébéniste. f. Paris. p. 902.
Arquier's wheel lathe. A. P. 1769. H. 128.
Hullot Art du tourneur mécanicien. 1776.
Ludlam on the oval lathe. Ph. tr. 1780. 378.
Lathe for ornamental plate. E. M. Pl. IV. Orfèvre grossier. Pl. 11.

Turning ivory and snuff boxes. E. M. A. VIII. Art. Tabletier.
E. M. A. VIII. Art. Tourneur.
Common spring lathe. E. M. Pl. IV. Tourneur. Pl. 2.
Tournant's lathe for mouldings. Roz. XLII. 215.
Ridley's foot lathe. S. A. XV. 273. Repert. VIII. 395.
Bentham's patent. Repert. X. 250.
Cook's mode of turning spheres. Repert. XIV. 260.
Healy on turning screws. Ph. M. XIX. 172.

Division, or Separation without sharp Instruments.

Lahire on separating millstones from their blocks. A. P. IX. 327.
Parent on the force of the wedge in separation. A. P. 1704. 186. H. 96.
On the wedge. Leup. Th. M. G. t. 16. Ph. tr. 1729. XXXVI.

Stones are sometimes divided by drawing lines on them with fat or oil, and then exposing them to heat. It may be doubted whether the oil, by preventing the evaporation of moisture, allows the stone to be more heated at the part oiled, and by the irregularity of the expansion produces a separation; or on the contrary, the oil, having insinuated itself, is converted into vapour at a high temperature, and forces the stone asunder.

†Slitting mill for iron. Emers. mech. f. 251.
Working slate. Fougeroux de Bondaroy Art de l'ardoisier. f. Paris.
Acc. A. P. 1762. H. 186.
Stonequarries and limekilns. E. M. A. I. Art. Carrier.
Slitting whalebone. E. M. A. II. Art Fanons de Baleine.
Slitting mill for iron. E. M. Pl. II. Fer. v. Pl. 1 .. 8.

Working stones. E. M. A. VI. Art. Pierres. E. M. A. VIII. Art. Tailleur de Pierres.
Unrolling old books. E. M. A. VI. 732.
P. Nicholson on the wedge. Ph. M. I. 316.

Sawing.

Lahire's machine for moving saws. A. P. IX. 159.
Sawing machine. Mach. A. I. 115.
Duguet's saw for curved work. Mach. A. I. 169.
Fonsjean's machine for sawing marble. Mach. A. I. 199.
Guyot's sawing machine. A. P. 1720. H. 114. Mach. A. IV. 3, 7.
Chambon's mode of making saws act. A. P. 1740. H. 111.
Pommyer's machine for sawing off piles under water by the force of the stream. A. P. 1753. H. 302. Mach. A. VII. 453.
Euler on saws. A. Berl. 1756. 267.
Sawing machine. Emers. mech. f. 263.
Sawing mill. Belidor Arch. Hydr. I. i. 321.
Machine for sawing piles. Belidor Arch. Hydr. II. ii. Pl. 60.
Model of a sawing mill. A. Petr. I. i. H. 65.
Standfield's saw mill. Bailey's mach. I. 136.
Saw under water. E. M. Pl. I. Charpente. Pl. 9.
Sawing mill. E. M. Pl. I. Charpente, Pl. 21.
Mill for sawing stones. E. M. Pl. III. After Maçonnerie.
Saws and sawing. E. M. A. VII. Art. Scie.
Bentham's patent rotatory saw. Repert. X. 250.
Fould's semicircular and circular saws for piles. S. A. XIII. 241. Repert. XI. 171.
An improvement on the old method of working a saw backwards and forwards by a lever, with ropes and pullies.
Bundy's patent for cutting combs. Repert. XI. 227.
Wilde's patent saws. Repert. XVI. 389.

Wheelcutting, Filing, and Cutting Screws.

Wheelcutter. See Machinery, Structure of Wheels.
Files. See Cutting Instruments.
Zeiher's two machines for cutting screws. N. C. Petr. VIII. 279.
On files. Repert. XVI. 66.

Grinding and Polishing.

Jenkins's machine for grinding spherical lenses. Ph. tr. 1741. XLI. 555.
Jeffries on diamonds and pearls. 8. 1751. R. I.
Polishing iron and steel. Perret Art du coutelier. Duhamel Art du serrurier.
Songy's polishing machines. A. P. 1763. H. 143.
Coné's composition for whetstones and razorstraps. A. P. 1766. H. 160.
Polishing gems. E. M. A. II. Art. Diamantaire.
Polishing looking glasses. E. M. A. III. Art. Glacerie.
Working stone. E. M. A. VI. Art. Pierres. VIII. Art. Tailleur de Pierres.
Polishing. E. M. A. VI. Art. Poliment.
Polishing gunpowder. E. M. Pl. IV. Poudre à canon, Lissoir.
Grindstones. E. M. Pl. IV. Tourneur, Pl. 10.
Tripoli. E. M. A. VIII. Art. Tripoli.
Cutting glass. E. M. A. VIII. Art. Verre tourné.
Pajot's machine for polishing glass and copper. Roz. XXXIII. 430.
Lambert on the velocity of vessels in which balls are rounded. Hind. Arch. II. 287.
Grinding glass. Enc. Br. Art. Burrough's machine, Glass, Lens.

On grinding. Nich. I. 131.
Person's grindstone. Pers. Recueil. Pl. 18.
F. Cuvier on an oxid of iron. B. Soc. Phil. n. 67.
Guyton on an oxid of iron for polishing. Ph. M. XIV. 276.
<small>Made from old hats.</small>
<small>Looking glasses are polished by a block moved by a crank; sometimes one glass is made to slide on another. See optical instruments.</small>

Boring.

Leup. Th. Hydrot. t. 12, 25.
Boring mills. Belidor Arch. Hydr. I. i. 321.
Boring for coals. Morand Art d'exploiter les mines de charbon. II. ii. 388.
Boring small cannon. Roz. Introd. I. 157.
Bailey's auger with wheelwork. Bailey's mach. I. 159.
Cook's spiral auger. Bailey's mach. I. 163.
Boring for coals. E. M. Pl. I. Charbon de terre. Pl. 1.
Boring gun barrels. E. M. Pl. I. Pl. 17.
Boring cannon. E. M. Pl. I. 58.
<small>Old method.</small>
Drill with a bob or weight. E. M. Pl. II. Pl. 7. f. 34.
Boring. E. M. A. VII. Art. Sonde.
Boring mill. Smeaton's reports.
Enc. Br. Art. Pipe borer.
Baillet's borer and sounding instrument. B. Soc. Phil. n. 39. Nich. IV. 227.
Howell's patent for boring wooden pipes. Repert. IX. 45.
<small>By a hollow cylindrical borer.</small>
Eccleston's peat borer. S. A. XIX. 168. Repert. XVI. 317. Nich. 8. V. 28.
Poterat's boring mill approved. M. Inst. IV.
Billingsley's patent boring machine. Repert. ii. II. 321.

Digging.

See Clearing Harbours.

Leup. Th. Hydrot. t. 7 ...
Laplatrière, Art du tourbier. 4. R. S.
Digging trenches. E. M. A. VII. Art. Sapeur.
Cutting turf. E. M. A. VIII. Art. Tourbe.
Cook's hoe. E. M. Art. Aratoire.
Stone quarries and lime kilns. E. M. A. I. Art. Carrier.
Macdougall's turnip hoe. S. A. XI. Frontisp.
Eckhardt on a machine for deepening canals. f. R. S.
Ducket's hand hoe. Board Agr. II. 424. Repert. XIV. 112.
Horse hoes. See ploughing.

Mining, and Subterraneous Work in general.

Moray on the mines at Liege, and on blasting rocks. Ph. tr. 1665..6. I. 79, 83.
Leup. Th. Hydrot.
Belidor on military mining. A. P. 1756. 1. 184. H. 11.
Leach on navigation and mines. 8.
Coal mines. *Duhamel* Art du charbonnier. f. Paris. Acc. A. P. 1761. H. 152. *Morand* Art d'exploiter les mines de charbon de terre. f. Paris. Acc. A. P. 1768. H. 129.
Calvör vom Oberharze. Brunsw. 1763.
Delius Anleitung zur bergbaukunst. Vienna, 1773.
Coal mines. E. M. A. I. Art. Charbon mineral.
Bituminous coal. E. M. A. III. Art. Houille.
E. M. A. VIII. Art. Travaux des mines.
White on the quarries under Paris. Manch. M. II. 361.

Kirwan on coal mines. Ir. tr. 1788. II. 157.
Proposal for a tunnel under the Thames. Ph. M. I. 223.
Lefebure on the French coal mines. Ph. M. XVI. 15.
Taylor on mining in Devonshire and Cornwall. Ph. M. V. 357.
Marescot on military mines. M. Inst. III. 370.
Props used in mining. Rees's Cyclop. II. pl. Art. Mineralogy.

Ploughing, Sowing, and Harrowing.

Evelyn on the Spanish sembrador, for ploughing, sowing, and harrowing. Ph. tr. 1670. V. 1055.
Lassisi's windmill for ploughing. A. P. 1726. H. 69. Mach. A. IV. 157.
Jaravaglia's plough without cattle. Mach. A. V. 35.
Tull's horse hoeing husbandry. 8.
Clark and Lord Kaimes on shallow ploughing. Ed. ess. III. 56, 68.
Knowles's open drain plough. Bailey's mach. I. 3.
With three coulters, and with wheels.
Makin's drain plough. Bailey's mach. I. 4.
Without wheels.
Gee's six furrow plough. Bailey's mach. I. 8.
Ducket's three furrow plough. Bailey's mach. I. 13.
Ducket's trenching plough. Bailey's mach. I. 16.
Willey's drill plough. Bailey's mach. I. 19.
Hewit's horse hoe and harrow. Bailey's mach. I. 22.
Ringrose's plough for turning up heath. Bailey's mach. I. 26.
Arbuthnot's double furrow plough. Bailey's mach. I. 29.
Clarke's plough, with adjustments for the direction of the draught. Bailey's mach. I. 32.
Lloyd's horse hoe and harrow. Bailey's mach. I. 39.
Various ploughs described. Bailey's mach. I. 68.
Clark's drain plough. Bailey's mach. I. 68.
Chateau Veaux's cultivators. Bailey's mach. I. 71.
Baker's scarificator. Bailey's mach. II. 9.
Peters's plough. Bailey's mach. II. 11.
With a circular coulter, for ploughing up furze.
Brand's iron plough. Bailey's mach. II. 13.
Hope and Clare's drill plough. Bailey's mach. II. 17.
Pinchbeck's road plough. Bailey's mach. II. 21.
Blanchard's drill plough. Bailey's mach. II. 30.
Meister on the best direction for ploughing. Commentat. Gott. 1781. IV. 26.
Drills. E. M. A. VII. Art. Sémoir.
Ploughs, drills, and harrows. E. M. Art. Aratoire.
Harrows and rollers for roads. Board Agr. I. 150.
Snow plough. Board Agr. I. 198.
Halcott on the oriental drill plough. Board Agr. I. 352.
A figure of the plough long used in the east.
Close's frame for setting wheat. S. A. IV. 8.
Harriott's road harrow. S. A. VII. 205.
With sweeps.
A mould board. Am. tr. IV. 313.
Coquebert on the arrangement of ploughs, with an account of a plough with two shares. B. Soc. Phil. n. 6. Journ. Phys. XLV. (II). 311.
Knight's harrow with wheels. S. A. XIV. 201. Repert. VI. 311.
Knight's drill machine. S. A. XIX. 128. Repert. XVI. 319. Ph. M. XII. 271.
For turnips.
Kirkpatrick's instrument for transplanting turnips. Repert. VII. 196.

Duke of Bridgewater's drain plough. S. A. XIX. 128. Repert. ii. I. 340. Ph. M. XII. 269.

Scott's mole plough. S. A. XVI. 234. Rep. VIII. 316.

Watt's patent implement for draining. Rep. VIII. 225.
<small>A mole plough.</small>

Sandilands's harrows. Repert. X. 329.

Enc. Br. Art. Agriculture, Brakes, Drill-plough, Harrow, Plough.

Wynne's harrows and drag. Repert. XIII. 102.

François de Neufchateau sur les charrues. 8. Par. 1801. R. S.

Munning's drill machine. S. A. XIX. 168. Repert. XVI. 306.

Lester's cultivator. S. A. XIX. 168. Repert. XVI. 314. Ph. M. XIII. 20.
<small>With seven shares, for pulverising fallows.</small>

Wright's patent machine for sowing wheat. Repert. XV. 369.

Jackson's patent turnip drill. Repert. XVI. 220.

Harrows and rollers for roads. Board Agr. I. 150.

Lord Somerville's two furrow plough. Board Agr. II. 418.
<small>With and without wheels.</small>

Willich. Dom. Enc. Art. Drill, Plough.

Green's hand drill. S. A. XXI. 230. Nich. VIII. 19.

Charles's machine for levelling lands. S. A. XXI. 272. Nich. VIII. 181.
<small>A kind of plough.</small>

Ploughs and other instruments. Dickson's practical agriculture.

Cartwright's three furrow plough. Nich. VIII. 24.

Trituration, Pulverisation, Levigation, Mills.

Langelot's philosophical mill. Ph. tr. 1672. VII. 5056, 5058.

Beale's remarks on mills. Ph. tr. 1677. XII. 846.

Garouste's four corn mills united. Mach. A. II. 143.

Moralec's powder mills. A. P. 1722. H. 122. Mach. A. IV. 41.

Windmills. Leup. Th. M. G. t. 39 .. 47.

Auger's bark mill. A. P. 1726. H. 71.

La Gache's little mill. Mach. A. IV. 37.

Dubuisson's machine for beating plaster. Mach. A. VI. 129.

Limperch Architectura mechanica of Moeleboek. f. Amst. 1727. R. I.

Snuff mills. Mach. A. VI. 161.

Soumille's snuff mill. A. P. 1735. 103. Mach. A. VII. 37.

Mansard's portable mill. A. P. 1741. H. 167.

D'Ons en Bray's snuff mill. A. P. 1745. 31.

Gensanne's paper mill. Mach. A. VII. 201.

Mill for grinding madder. *Duhamel* sur la Garance.
Acc. A. P. 1767. H. 50.

Jodin's washing mill for goldsmiths. A. P. 1759. H. 233.

Mills in general. Emerson's mech. Windmill. f. 203. Common grist mill. f. 260. Horse mill. f. 294. Powder mill. f. 297.

Corn mills. Belidor Arch. Hydr. I. i. 276.

Windmills, handmills, and horsemills. Belidor Arch. Hydr. I. i. Pl. n. 26.

Powder mills. Belidor Arch. Hydr. I. i. 348.

Belidor Arch. Hydr. I. i. 359.
<small>Mill for grinding mortar.</small>

Loriot's machine for grinding ore. A P 1761 H. 159.

A machine for washing and stamping. A. P. 1761. H. 161.
Flour mills. *Malouin* Art du meûnier. f. Par. Acc. A. P. 1767. H. 182.
Chamoy's watermill for snuff. A. P. 1767. H. 184.
Leather mill. *Lalande* Art du chamoiseur. p. 7.
Kästner on the lifters of stamping mills. N. C. Gott. 1770. II. 117.
On oil mills. Roz. VIII. 417. XII. 399.
Dutch oil mills. Roz. X. 417.
Mortar mill. Roz. XIII. 199.
Quatremère Dijonval on a handmill for grinding indigo. S. E. IX. 78. Pl. 7.
A machine for grinding colours. Roz. XIX. 314.
Evers's windmill for threshing and grinding corn. Bailey's mach. I. 54.
Various mills. Bailey's mach. I. 175.
Lloyd's cider and maltmill. Bailey's mach. II. 1.
Lloyd's handmill. Bailey's mach. II. 44.
Verrier's windmill. Bailey's mach. II. 47.
Malt mills. E M. Pl. I. Brasserie. Pl. 45.
Cider mill. E. M. Pl. I. Cidre.
Coffee mills. E. M. Pl. II. Distillateur. Pl. 4.
Mills for pottery. E. M. Pl. II. Fayencerie. Pl. 9.
Washing and stamping mills for ore. E. M. Pl. II. Fer. i. Pl. 7 .. 10. vi. Pl. 1, 2.
Some mills. E. M. Pl. III. Art. Instrumens de mathématique.
Stamping mills. E. M. A. IV. Art. Lavage.
Corn mills. E. M. A. V. Art. Meûnier.
Hesiod's pestle worked by the foot. E. M. A. VI. Art. Piler.
E. M. A. VI. Art. Pulvérisation.
Stamping and rolling mills for gunpowder. E. M. Pl. IV. Poudre à canon.
Tobacco and snuff mills. E. M. A. VIII. Art. Tabac.
Stamping mill for bark. E. M. Pl. V. Tanneur. Pl. 7.
Handmill, and mill driven by an ox in a walking wheel. E. M. Art. Aratoire.
Baumé on potatoe mills. A. P. 1786. 689. Repert. III. 62.
Boulard's mode of preserving the health of colourgrinders. Roz. XXXVII. 353. Repert. V. 138.
Mills and millstones. Langsdorfs Hydraulik. Pl. 44 .. 46, 48 .. 50.
Stamping mills. Langsdorfs Hydr. Pl. 52.
Banks on mills. 8. London, 1795.
Nancarrow on mills. Am. tr. IV. 348.
A paper mill. Kunze. I. f. 110.
Howard's engine for beating tanning materials.
Lastérie's machine for powdering bones. B. Soc. Phil. n. 14.
A corn mill at Kilrie. Board Agr. I. 52.
Ellicott's corn mill. Repert. IV. 319.
Grenet's machine for granulating potatoes Repert. IV. 353.
Ward's prevention of injury from grinding white lead. S. A. XIII. 229. Repert. V. 249.
Dearman's patent malt mill. Repert. V. 247.
Weldon's patent bark mill. Repert. X. 77. XV. 90.
Rustall's family mill and bolter. S. A. XVIII. 222. Repert. XIV. 197.
Terry's mill for hard substances. S. A. XIX. 282. Nich. 8. II. 206. Repert. ii. II. 182.
<small>With a spring regulator.</small>
Bagnall's machine for chopping and pounding bark. Repert. XV. 145.

Barratt's patent machine for grinding corn. Repert. XVI. 79.
    A windmill.
Enc. Br. Art. Levigation, Oil mill, Paper mill.
Rasping mill. Bérard Mélanges. 147.
Pounding mill. Bérard Mélanges. 161.
Powder mill. Person Recueil. Pl. 5.
    Moved by a lever.
Hand mill. Person Recueil. Pl. 16.
    With a fly.
Stamping mill. Person Recueil. Pl. 17.
    By hand.
The Indian hand mill. Nich. 8. III. 186.
On the Scotch querns or hand mills. Nich. 8. IV. 220.
Hawkins's patent floating mill. Repert. ii. I. 162.
Table for the construction of mills. Imison's elements. I. 90.
Corn mill. Imison's elements. I. Pl. 3.
Mills of all kinds. *Gray's* experienced millwright. London.
    With plates.
Rawlinson's colour mills. S. A. XXII. 260.
*Ferguson's lectures by Brewster.
    Enters much into the form of the teeth of wheels.
Paper mills. See union of fibres.
    Pearl barley is prepared by first pounding the barley, to separate the husks, then grinding the corns between mill stones set wide, and separating them by sieves of different sizes.

Parts of Mills.

Millstones. E. M. A. V. Art. Meulier.
Pratt's patent composition for millstones. Repert. VII. 1.
Bowes on a quarry of millstones. Repert. XIV. 189.

Appendages to Mills. Preparation of Corn and Flour.

Threshing machine with flails. M. Berl. I. 325.
Descamus's machine for working several sieves. A. P. 1711. H. 101.
Knopperf's fan for corn. A. P. 1716. H. 78. Mach. A. III. 101, 103.
Duquet's threshing machine. A. P. 1722. H. 121. Mach. A. IV. 27, 31.
Meiffren's threshing machine. A. P. 1737. H. 108.
Malassagny's threshing machine. A. P. 1762. H. 193.
Loriot's threshing machine. A. P. 1763. H. 141.
Poix's cylindrical sieve for corn. A. P. 1763. H. 145.
Gambier's sieve for corn. A. P. 1768. H. 131.
Munier's winnowing machine. Roz. Intr. II. 79.
Krünitz Dreschkunst. 8. Berl. 1776.
Threshing, threshing mills, wooden fan. E. M. Art. Aratoire.
Evers's winnowing machine. Bailey's mach. I. 51.
Evers's mill for threshing by stampers. Bailey's mach. I. 54.
Stedman's bolting mill. Bailey's mach. II. 57.
Bolting mills. Langsdorfs hydraulik. Pl. 47.
Desmazi's machine for dressing corn. Journ. Phys. XLIV. (I.) 314.
    Cranks connected by rods.
Threshing mills. Board Agr. I. 51, 52.
Wardrop's threshing machine with elastic flails. Repert. IV. 243.
Steedman's patent threshing machine with flails. Repert. VII. 305.

Meikle's patent machine for separating corn from straw. Repert. X. 217.
Tunstall's hand engine for threshing. Repert. XIII. 361.
Machine to thresh, sift, and winnow at once. Person Recueil. Pl. 1, 2.
Threshing machines. Willich's Dom. Enc. Art. Thrashing.
Polfreeman's winnowing machine. Willich's Dom. Enc. Art. Winnow.
Winnowing. See Pneumatic Machines.
Bolting. See Mills.

Machines for Agitation, nearly allied to Mills.

Solignac's machine for kneading dough. A. P. 1760. H. 156.
Churns. E. M. Pl. II. Fromage.
Bowles's pendulum churn. S. A. XIII. 252. Repert. IV. 107. Ph. M. XIX. 56.
Machine for kneading dough with horses. Journ. Phys. LI. 64. Nich. IV. 281. Rep. III. 283. Ph. M. VII. 261.
Raby's patent churn. Repert. VII. 289.
Jones's machine for mixing malt. Repert. IX. 242.
Fischer's washing machine. Willich's Dom. Enc. Art. Washing.
Jumilhac on churning. Nich. 8. IV. 241.
Machines for bleaching and washing. Rees Cyclop. III. Pl. Art. Bleaching.

Demolition.

Military engines. Mathematici veteres, Vegetius, and Ammianus Marcellinus.
Beaumont on blasting rocks. Ph. tr. 1685. XV. 854.
Dubois's spoon for the removal of earth beaten down by a ram. A. P. 1726. H. 70. Mach. A. IV. 165.
Lavier's machine for breaking ice. A. P. 1743. H. 167.
Belidor on military mining. A. P. 1756. 1, 184. H. 11.
See mining.
Machine for drawing piles. Belidor Arch. Hydr. I. ii. Pl. 12.
Silberschlag on the military engines of the antients. A. Berl. 1760. 378.
Loriot's machine for breaking ice. A. P. 1763. H. 141.
Saverland's machine for levelling land. Bailey's mach. I. 61.
Rollers for breaking clods of earth. E. M. Art. Aratoire.
Rich's nail drawer. S. A. IX. 156. Repert. I. 246.
Hill's nail drawer. S. A. X. 224.
Bolton's bolt drawer. S. A. XVI. 315. Repert. XI. 39. Ph. M. III. 189.
Enc. Br. Art. Catapulta, Shipbolt drawer.
Knight's apparatus for blasting wood. S. A. XX. 258. Repert. ii. II. 342. Nich. 8. V. 31. Gilb. XIV. 342.
Baillet on blasting rocks under water. Ph. M. XIII. 268.
Sonnini's machine for blasting. Gilb. XIV. 345.
Common crow. Cavall. N. Ph. I. Pl. v. f. 19.
Charles's machine for levelling land. S. A. XXI. 272.
 A kind of plough.
See Pneumatic machines.

HISTORY OF MECHANICS.

Diogenes Laertius Meibomii. 2 v. 4. Amst. 1692. R. I.
P. Vergilius de inventoribus rerum. Basle, 1521. R. I.
Hooke on Hevelius.
 Claims the invention of the circular pendulum in 1665.

Hooke Lect. Cutl. on Helioscopes.
Claims the invention of the balance spring.
Huygens on the invention of watches. A. P. X. 381.
Bagford on the invention of printing. Ph. tr. 1707. XXV. 2397.
Pancirollus's history of memorable things. 3 v. 12. 1715. R. I.
Lahire on the invention of clocks. A. P. 1717. 78.
Derham's artificial clockmaker.
Leup. Th. Arithm.
Says, that proportional compasses were invented by Justus Byrgius in 1600. Perhaps reinvented after Vinci.
Regnault Origine ancienne de la physique nouvelle. 3 v. Amst. 1735.
Mairan on Des Piles's balance of painters. A. P. 1755. 1. H. 79.
Mattaire, Marchand, Bowyer, Ames, and Lemoine's works on the history of printing. R. I.
Bowyer and Nichols's origin of printing. 8. R. S.
Rollin's history of the arts and sciences of the ancients. 3 v. 8. 1768. R. I.
Luckombe's history of printing. 8. 1771. R. I.
Luckombe's tablet of memory. 12. London.
Waring's prefaces to his mathematical works.
De Loys Abrégé chronologique.
Degoguet's origin of laws, arts, and sciences. 3 v. 8. 1775. R. I.
*Priestley's chart of biography. R. I.
Dictionnaire des origines des inventions utiles. 6 v. 12. Par. 1777. R. I.
*Astle's origin and progress of writing.
Brugmans on the mechanics of the antients. Commentat. Gott. 1784. VII. M. 75.
Lord Charlemont on the antiquity of the woollen manufacture in Ireland. Ir. tr. 1787. I. Ant. 17.
Burja on the mathematical knowledge of Aristotle. A. Berl. 1790. 257.

*Cooper on the art of painting among the ancients. Manch. M. III. 510.
Shows that it was highly improved.
Mongez on ancient coining. Roz. XL. 426.
Dutens on the origin of discoveries. 4. R. I.
Beckmann's history of inventions. 3 v. 8. Lond. 1797. R. I.
Camus Histoire du polytypage et de la stereotypie. 1801.
Poppe Geschichte der uhrmacherkunst. 8. 1801.
*Montucla et Lalande Histoire des mathematiques. 4 v. 4. Par. R. I.
Fischer sur les monumens typographiques de Gutenberg. 4. Mentz, 1802. R. S.
Account of Newton. Turnor's collections for the history of Grantham. 4. Lond. 1806. B. B.
Contains the original papers sent by Mr. Conduit to Fontenelle, and some other documents.

Particular Dates, chiefly from Luckombe's Tablet of Memory.

Scipio Nasica's clepsydra.	B. C. 159
Scissors invented in Africa.	
Diophantus employed some algebraic symbols. Montucla.	
Pens made from quills.	A. D. 635
Glass introduced into England	674
Silk worked in Greece about	700
Paper of linen introduced about	1100
Glass commonly used in England	1180
Some Greek weavers settled at Venice	1207
Linen first made in England	1253
A clock at Westminster Hall about	1288
A clock at Canterbury	1292
Faenza's earthern ware invented	1299
Two weavers from Brabant settled at York	1331
Wire invented at Nuremberg	1351
Engraving on metal and rolling press printing invented	1423

Printing invented by Faust	1441
Delft ware invented at Florence	1450
Printing made public by Gutenberg	1458
Wood cuts invented	1460
Casts in plaster, by Verocchio	1470
Watches made at Nuremberg	1477
Diamonds polished at Bruges	1489
Hats made at Paris	1504
Etching on copper invented	1512
Proportional compasses invented by L. da Vinci, before	1519
Spinning wheel invented by Jürgen of Brunswick	1530
Pins brought from France	1543
Needles made in England	1545
Stockings first knit in Spain about	1550
Many Flemish weavers were driven to England by the Duke of Alva's persecution	1567
Three clockmakers came to England from Delft	1568
Log line used	1570
Coaches used in England	1580
Stocking weaving invented by Lee of Cambridge	1589
A slitting mill erected at Dartford	1590
The dimensions of bricks regulated	1625
Vernier's index made known	1631
Clocks and watches generally used about	1631
Bows and arrows still used in England, and artillery with stone bullets	1640
Newton born	1642
Fromantil is said to have applied pendulums to clocks in	1656
Hooke's watch with a balance spring	1658
Threshing machines with flails invented	1700
China made at Dresden	1702
China made at Chelsea	1753
Wedgwood's improvements in pottery	1763
Muslins made in England	1781

In 1787 about 23 million pounds of cotton were manufactured in Britain; about 6 were imported from the British colonies, 6 from the Levant, and 10 from the settlements of other European nations. Half the quantity was employed in white goods, one fourth in fustians, one fourth in hosiery, mixtures, and candle wicks; giving employment to 60 000 spinners, and 360 000 other manufacturers. In 1791, the quantity was increased from 23 millions to 32.

The value of the wool annually manufactured in England is about 3 millions sterling; it employs above a million persons, who receive for their work about 9 millions.

Thread has been spun so fine as to be sold for L.4 an ounce; lace for L.40.

The premiums annually proposed by the society for the encouragement of arts, enable us to form some opinion of the present state of our machinery and manufactures. Some of their objects are, a substitute for white lead paint, a red pigment, a machine for carding silk, cloth made from hop stalks, paper made from raw vegetables, transparent paper, the prevention of accidents from horses falling, cleaning turnpike roads, machines for raising coals, and for making bricks, instruments for harpooning whales; machines for reaping or mowing corn, for dibbling wheat, for threshing; a family mill, a gunpowder mill, a quarry of millstones; and a mode of boring and blasting rocks 1802.

HYDRODYNAMICS IN GENERAL.

Schotti mechanica hydraulico-pneumatica. 4. 1657. M. B.
Ph. tr. Abr. I. vi. 515. IV. v. 423. VI. vi. 326. VIII. vi. 321. X. v. 247.
*Newtoni principia.
Ditton on fluids. 8. Lond. 1719. M. B.
**D. Bernoulli* Hydrodynamica. 4. 1738. R. I.
Cotes's hydrostatical and pneumatical lectures. 8. 1747. R. I.
S'Gravesande. Nat. Phil.
Musschenbroek Introd.
Belidor Architecture hydraulique. 4 p. 4. Par. 1782. R. I.
D'Alembert de l'equilibre et du mouvement des fluides.
    Acc. A. P. 1744. H. 55.
Lecchi Idrostatica e Idraulica. Mil. 1765.
Kästner Anfangsgründe der hydrodynamik. 8. Gott. 1769.
**Bossut* Traité d'hydrodynamique. 2 v. 8. Paris, 1771. R. I.
    Acc. A. P. 1771. H. 61.
    German by Langsdorf. Frankf. 1792.
*Buat Traité d'hydraulique. 2 v. 8.
E. M. Pl. VII. Mathématique. Hydrostatique.
Emerson's hydrostatics.
Cousin on the mathematical theory of fluids. A. P. 1783. 665.
Lambert on fluids. A. Berl. 1784. 299.
Karstens Lehrbegriff. V. VI.
Langsdorfs theorie der hydrodynamischen grundlehren. Frankf. 1787.
Langsdorfs hydraulik. 4. Altenb. 1794.
Klügel's remarks on Langsdorf. Hind. Arch. II. 221.
Parkinson's hydrostatics. 4. 1789. R. I.
*Lagrange Mécanique analitique.
Prony Architecture hydraulique. 4. Paris, 1790.
Burja Grundlehren der hydrostatik. 1790.
Büsch Mathematik. II.
Enc. Br. Art. Hydrostatic Amusements.
Venturi Recherches experimentales. 8. Par. 1797.
Rinmann and Nordwall's essay on the mechanics of mining. 4. Stockholm.
    Abstr. Ph. M. XIII. 76.
Eytelweins mechanik und hydraulik. 8. Berlin, 1801.
Trembley on the uncertainty of hydrodynamics. A. Berl. 1801. Ph. 33.

HYDROSTATICS.

Stevini hydrostatica.
Boyle's hydrostatical paradoxes.
    Acc. Ph. tr. 1665—6. I.
Boyle on the weight of water in water. Ph. tr. 1669. IV. 1001.
Sinclari ars gravitatis et levitatis. Rotterdam, 1669.
    Acc. Ph. tr. 1669. IV. 1017.
Lamy Mécanique. 12. Par. 1674. M. B.
Mariotte on hydrostatics. A. P. I. 69.
On the equilibrium of liquids. A P. II. 78.
Lahire. A. P. IX. 144.
<small>Describes an arrangement of levers by which a single weight is made to produce a pressure on each side of a box equal to the hydrostatic pressure.</small>
Varignon on conical vessels. A. P. X. 10.
Saulmon on the principles of the actions of fluids. A. P. 1717. H. 73.
Leup. Th. M. G. t. 55, 56. Th. Hydraul. I. t. 1, 41.
Switzer's hydrostatics. R. I.
Belidor. Arch. hydr. I. i. 126.
Nollet's experiments on the affections of

fluids in a revolving globe. A. P. 1741. 184. H. 1.

Nollet's new hydrostatical phenomena. A.P. 1766. 431. H. 150.

Gulielmini on hydrostatics. C. Bon. I. 545.

†Segner on the surfaces of fluids. C. Gott. 1751. I. 301.

Euler's principles of hydrostatics. A. Berl. 1755. 217.

Euler on the equilibrium of fluids. N. C. Petr. XIII. XIV. XV.

Lambert on the fluidity of sand and earth. A. Berl. 1772. 33.

Meister on oil swimming upon water. Commentat. Gott. 1778. I. 35.

Matteucci on a principle of statics and hydrostatics. C. Bon. VI. O. 286.

Gr. Fontana on the pressure of fluids. Soc. Ital. II. 142.

J. Bernoulli's hydrostatical considerations. N. Act. Helv. I. 229.

*Delangez on the statics and mechanics of semifluids. Soc. Ital. IV. 329.

Kästner on the pressure of a fluid covering a sphere. Hind. Arch. I. 424.

Equilibrium of Floating Bodies.

Regulating counterpoise. See Hydraulic Instruments.

**Archimedes de insidentibus humido.

Parent on floating bodies. A. P. 1700. H. 154.

D. Bernoulli on the equilibrium of floating bodies. C. Petr. X. 147. XI. 100.

Bouguer on the oscillations of floating bodies. A. P. 1755. 481. H. 135.

E. M. Pl. V. Marine. Pl. 152. 153.

English on floating bodies, from Chapman. N. Svensk. Handl. 1787. Ph. M. I. 371, 393.

PNEUMATOSTATICS, OR PNEUMATIC EQUILIBRIUM.

See Properties of Matter.

Boyle on the spring and weight of the air. 4. Oxf. 1663.
   Acc. Ph. tr. 1668. III. 845.

Boyle's statical baroscope. Ph. tr. 1665. I. 231.

Boyle on air. 4. Lond. 1670.
   Acc. Ph. tr. 1670. V. 2052.
   See airpumps.

Boyle on the effects of atmospherical pressure. Ph. tr. 1672. VII. 5155.

Guericke Experimenta nova Magdeburgica. f. Amst. 1670.
   Acc. Ph. tr. 1672. VII. 5103.

Table of the compression of air. Ph. tr. 1671. VI. 2191, 2239.

Hooke on the elasticity of the air. Birch. III. 384, 387.

Mariotte sur la nature de l'air. 1676.

Mariotte and Homberg on the weight of air. A. P. II. 41.

Homberg on the spring of air in vacuo. A.P. II. 105.

Wallis on the air's gravity. Ph. tr. 1685. XV 1002.

Lahire on the condensation and dilatation of the air. A. P. 1705. 110. H. 10.

Wolfii elementa aerometriae. 12. Leipz. 1706.

Amontons on the rarefaction of air. A. P. 1705. 119. H. 10.

†Hauksbee on condensing the air permanently. Ph. tr. 1708. 217.

Carré's experiment on the spring of air. A.P. 1710. 1. H. 1.

Varignon on the densities of elastic fluids from pressure, according to given laws of compression. A. P. 1716. 107. H. 40.

Pressure of the atmosphere. Leup. Th. Aerostaticum.

Bédaut's atmospherical machines. Mach. A. VI. 27.

Elasticity of the air. C. Bon. I. 208.

Richmann on the compression of the air by ice. N. C. Petr. II. 162.

<small>The air was compressed mechanically to $\frac{1}{120}$, without much deviation from Hooke's law; by freezing it was reduced to $\frac{1}{100}$ of its bulk.</small>

Lowitz Versuche über die luft. 4. Nuremberg, 1754.

Belidor. Arch. Hydr. II. i. 1.

Achard on the properties of gases. A. Berl. 1778. 27.

Beds of air or bladders. E. M. A. VI. 731.

E. M. Physique. Art. Air.

Cavallo on air and elastic fluids. 4. R. I.

Fontana on the elasticity of gases. Soc. Ital. I. 83.

Gerstners luftwage. Gren. IV. 172.

Hutton's recreations. IV. 135.

Dalton's theory of mixed gases. See Meteorology.

*Barometers and manometers. See Meteorology.

<small>According to Lavoisier 1 cubic inch Fr. of air weighs 48 grains. A. P. 1774. 364. According to Fouchy a cubic foot weighs 10 gros. A. P. 1780. 3. A hundred English wine gallons weigh a pound avoirdupois.</small>

<small>Roy thinks that there are some exceptions to the law of Boyle and Mariotte. Ph. tr. 1777. Others attribute these irregularities to the presence of water.</small>

THEORY OF HYDRAULICS.

Baliani de motu gravium. 4. Genev. 1646. M. B.

Davis and Papin on the siphon. Ph. tr. 1685. XV. 846.

Papin on the air rushing into a vacuum. Ph. tr. 1686. XVI. 193.

<small>Assumes the specific gravity of air equal to $\frac{1}{840}$ of that of water, and deduces thence a velocity of 1305 feet in a second.</small>

*Mariotte Traité du mouvement des eaux. 8. Par. 1686.

Acc. Ph. tr. 1686. XVI. 119.

<small>Contains a good account of ajutages.</small>

Newtoni principia. L. ii.

Varignon on the principle of the motion of water. A. P. II. 162.

Varignon on the motion of fluids. A. P. 1703. 238. H. 125.

Picard de aquis effluentibus. A. P. VII. 323.

Lahire on the motion of fluids. A. P. X. 162.

Lahire on the motion of waves. A. P. X. 264.

Hauksbee's experiment illustrative of the effects of wind. Ph. tr. 1704. XXIV. 1629.

<small>A blast produced by a condensation to 3 or 4 times the natural density caused a column of mercury connected with a vessel through which the blast passed to fall two inches or more.</small>

†Carré on the discharge of long pipes. A. P. 1705. 275. H. 135.

Saulmon's experiments on bodies in a vortex. A. P. 1712. 279. H. 77. 1714. 381. H. 102. 1715. 61. H. 61. 1716. 244. H. 68.

<small>Bodies floating on the surface of water in an eddy are impelled either towards the centre or towards the circumference, according to circumstances; they are not made to approach the centre on account of their levity, since they only displace as much water as is equal to their own weight, but probably because the resistance of the air causes them to move more slowly, and to have less centrifugal force than the water. When they move towards the circumference, it is probably because of the greater retardation of the water from the friction of the vessel. Y.</small>

Hermanni phoronomia.

Poleni de motu aquae mixto. 4. Pad. 1717. Extr. Ph. tr. 1717. XXX. 723.

Polenus de castellis.

†Jurin de motu aquarum fluentium. Ph. tr. 1718. XXX. 748. 1739. XL. 1, 5.

<small>Follows Newton, with some inconclusive and erroneous inferences.</small>

Jurin de motu cordis. Ph. tr. 1718. XXX. 863, 929. 1719. XXX. 1039.

Jurin defensio contra Michelottium. Ph. tr. 1722. XXXII. 179.

Keill de viribus cordis contra Jurinum. Ph. tr. 1719. XXX. 995.

Raccolta di autori chi trattano del moto dell' acque. 3 v. 4. Flor. 1723.

<small>Contains Archimedes, Albici, Galileo, Castelli, Michelini, Borelli, Montanari, Viviani, Cassini, Guglielmi, Grandi, Manfredi, Picard, and Nanducci.</small>

Eames on the estimation of force in hydraulic experiments. Ph. tr. 1727. XXXIV. 343.

D. Bernoulli on the motion, action, and lateral pressure of fluids. C. Petr. II. 111, 304. IV. 194.

Pitot on the motion of fluids. A. P. 1730. 336. H. 110.

Couplet on the motion of fluids. A. P. 1732. 113. H. 107.

Dufay on two streams crossing each other. A. P. 1736. 191. H. 118.

Mairan on the analogy of sound and waves. A. P. 1737. 45. H. 97.

S'Gravesande. Nat. Phil.

Clare on the motion of fluids. 8. 1737. R. I.

Jo. Bernoulli on the motion of water in pipes. C. Petr. IX. 3, 19. X. Op. IV.

Krafft on hydraulics. C. Petr. X. 207.

Wolf Cursus mathemat.

On cataracts or weres. C. Bon. II. i. 413.

Mackenzie. Ph. tr. 1749. 149.

<small>Says, that eddies with a cavity of 2 or 3 feet, which sometimes swallow up small boats, may be broken and filled up by throwing in an oar.</small>

Petit Vandin on hydraulics. S. E. I. 261.

Euler on the motion of water in pipes. A. Berl. 1752. 111.

Euler's principles of hydraulics. A. Berl. 1755. 274, 316. N. C. Petr. VI. 271.

Euler on the reaction of water in pipes. N. C. Petr. VI. 312.

Euler on the equilibrium of fluids, and the effects of heat. N. C. Petr. XIII. 305. XIV. i. 270. X. 1. 210, 219.

Emerson's fluxions. iii.

Robertson on weres. Ph. tr. 1758. 492. See Hydr. Architect.

Belidor. Arch. Hydr. I. i. 165.

Laura Bassi on a hydraulic problem. C. Bon. IV. O. 61.

Batarra and Pistoi on the descent of water in bent pipes. A. Sienn. III. 85.

*Borda on the discharge of fluids. A. P. 1766. 579. H. 143.

Nuovo raccolta. 7 v. 4. Parm. 1766. . .

Kästner on hydraulics, after Bernoulli. N. C. Gott. 1769. I. 45.

Michelotti Sperienze idrauliche. 2 v. 4. Turin, 1771. R. S.

Stattleri physica.

*D'Alembert Opuscules. VI. Acc. A. P. 1773. H. 87.

Lagrange on the motion of fluids. A. Berl. 1781. 151.

*Lagrange Mécanique analitique.

*Bossut.

Buat Principes d'hydraulique. Ed. 2. Paris, 1786. R. I.

Ximenes Nuove sperienze idrauliche.

Riccati on the cavity of a fluid in a funnel. Soc. Ital. III. 238.

Lametherie on the motion of fluids. Roz. XXVIII. 283.

M. Young on spouting fluids. Ir. tr. 1788. II. 81. VII. 53. Repert. XV. 95.

<small>Shows by experiments on a long pipe through which mercury runs in a vacuum, that the pressure of the atmosphere increases the discharge in some cases in the ratio of 26 to 19.</small>

Jo. Bernoulli on the reaction of water in pipes. N. A. Petr. 1788. VI. 185.

Lateral friction. Saint Martin's ventilator. Roz. XXXIII. 161.

Bernhard Hydraulique. Germ. by Langsdorf, Leipz. 1790.

Prony Archit. hydraulique.
Lorgna on spouting fluids. Soc. Ital. IV. 369.
Lorgna on the discharge of weres. Soc. Ital. V. 313.
Lorgna on the principles of Castelli. Soc. Ital. VI. 218.
Lempe Begriff der maschinenlehre. Leipz.
Vince on the motions of fluids. Ph. tr. 1798. Gilb. II. 399. IV. 34.
*Gerstner on the discharge of water at different temperatures. Böhm. Gesellech. 1798. Gilb. V. 160.
Bonati on the discharge of a vessel with diaphragms, and of a lengthened pipe. Soc. Ital. V. 501.

With experiments on the lateral communication of motion. 1790.

Stratico on the pressure of fluids, Soc. Ital. V. 525.

On the lateral friction.

Girard on the pressure of running water. Roz. XLII. 429.

Shows that it is not perceptibly diminished by any common velocity.

Venturi sur la communication latérale du mouvement dans les fluides. Par. 1798. R. S. Journ. Phys. XLV. (II.) 362. B. Soc. Phil. n. 8. Gilb. II. 418. III. 35. Nich. II. 172.

Venturi found the discharge of a pipe greatest when the ajutage diverged in an angle of 3°: when the angle became 11°, the augmentation ceased. The diameter of the external orifice of a conical pipe may be to that of the vena contracta as 18 to 10.

Busse's remarks on Venturi. Gilb. IV. 116.
Eytelwein's experiments with Venturi's apparatus. Gilb. VII. 295.

Afterwards published in his Handbuch.

Robison. Enc. Br. Art. River.
Banks on the velocity of air. Manch. M. V. 398. Nich. 8. II. 269. Repert. ii. I. 342.

The area of an aperture being .0046, 425.1 cubic inches of air were expelled in 33" by a pressure of 30 inches of water; by a pressure of 6 feet in 21.3". This gives .634 to 1 for the contraction of the stream: the velocities being 233.3 and 361.6. Hence a pressure of a foot gives 147½, of an inch 42, or 20 miles an hour.

Young's summary of hydraulics from Eytelwein. Journ. R. I., I. Nich. 8. III. 25.
Young on the discharge of a vertical pipe. Journ. R. I., I. Rep. ii. II. 45. Nich. VI. 56.

Leslie found that hydrogen gas admitted through an aperture filled a given space in an inverted jar in 45"; common air in 130"; hence he infers that the densities were as 1:8¼. Lesl. on heat. The same mode might be applied to steam.

Michelotti found a stream of water a little more contracted as the velocity was greater. Robison.

Air is subject to friction in pipes in the same manner as water.

Oscillations of Fluids, and of Floating Bodies.

Mairan on the analogy of sound and waves. A. P. 1737. 45. H. 97.
D. Bernoulli on the oscillation of floating bodies. C. Petr. 100.
Franklin's works.

Franklin observed, that when oil swimming on water was contained in a vibrating vessel, the water was agitated while the oil remained still.

Meister on the effect of oil swimming on water. Commentat. Gott. 1778. I. 35.

On the oscillations observed by Franklin.

Achard on calming the agitation of a fluid. A. Berl. 1778. 19.
†Percival on attraction and repulsion. Manch. M. II. 429.
Bennet on Franklin's experiment. Manch. M. III. 116.

Shows, that if the lower part of a vessel of water be tinged with any colour, it may be made to exhibit the same appearance with water on which oil is swimming. The fact is easily explained by considering the distance of the different parts of the fluid from the axis of vibration.

Stratico on the agitation of fluids in oscillating vessels. Ac. Pad. I. 242.

Flaugergues on waves. Journ. Sav. Oct. 1789. Montucla and Lal. III. 717.

<small>Found the velocity of waves independent of their magnitude.</small>

Paterson on Franklin's experiments upon the oscillations of a fluid. Am. tr. III. 13.

<small>Dr. Wollaston observed, that a bore or large wave, 800 feet wide, moved a mile in a minute, where the depth of the water was said to be 50 fathoms. Lagrange's theorem gives about 40 fathoms for the depth with this velocity. I have also observed the waves or oscillations of water in a cistern, moving with a velocity smaller than that of a body falling through half the height, and nearly in the same proportion.</small>

Phenomena of Rivers.

From Mann.
" *Frontinus* Poleni. 1722. M. B.
Aleotti.
*Castelli de mensura aquarum currentium. M. B.
Baratteri dell architettura d'acque lib. vi. Piacenz. 1656. M. B.
Beltinzoli.
Cabaeus in Aristotelis meteora. M. B.
Galileo.
*Baliani de motu liquidorum.
Riccioli geographia et hydrographia reformata. M. B.
*Deschales de fontibus et fluminibus.
Varennius by Jurin and Shaw. 1765. I. 295—358. M. B.
Jurin. Ph. tr. n. 355. p. 748.
Mariotte Traité du mouvement des eaux.
Varignon. A. P. 1699. 1703.
Newton Princip. ii. 7. ed. 1726.
*D. Bernoulli hydrodynamica. 4. Strasb. 1738.
*Guglielmini della natura dei fiumi. 4. Bologn. 1697.
*Polenus de castellis et de motu aquae mixto. Patav. 1697. 1718. 1723.
*Raccolta d'autori. 3 vol. 4. Fiorenz. 1723.
Hermanni phoronomia. X. 226.
Wolf cursus mathem. Hydraul. c. vi. 4. Genev. 1740.
Buffon Hist. Nat. II. 38. ed. in 12.
Pitot and others. A. P. 1730. 1732.
S'Gravesande Elementa physices. I. ii. c. 10.
*Lecchi hydrostatica. Milan, 1765. With some pieces of Boscovich.
Stattleri physica. III. 232. 8 vol. 8. Augsb. 1772.
Frisius de fluviis.
Lalande's history of canals. fol.
Forfait on clearing canals. Mantua." †Mann on rivers and canals. Ph. tr. 1779. 555.

<small>Marks the best with asterisks.</small>

Danubius illustratus.
Grandi de castellis.
Guglielmini de fluviis et castellis.
Guglielmini on running water. M. Berl. I. 188.
Pitot on the confluence of rivers. A. P. 1738. 299. H. 101.
Belidor Arch. Hydr. II. ii. 273.
Condamine's voyage on the river Amazons. A. P. 1745. 391. H. 63.
Euler on the motion of rivers. A. Berl. 1760. 101.
Carena on the course of the Po. M. Taur. II.
Ximenes on the velocity of rivers. A. Sien. III. 16. VI. 31.
Ximenes on the effect of obstacles in a river. A Sienn. VII. 1.
Ximenes Nuove sperienze idrauliche.
Bacialli on the mouths of rivers. C. Bon. V. ii. 99.
Michelotti Sperienze idrauliche

Zendrini de motu aquarum.
Bossut.
Genetté Tableau des rivières.
Buat.
Measurement of the depth of a river. Roz. III. 64.
Lespinasse and Frisi on the velocity of rivers. Roz. IX. 145, 398. XI. 58.
Lorgna Memorie intorno all' acque correnti. Veron. 1777.
Lorgna Ricerche intorno alla distributione delle velocità nella sectione de fiumi. 4. R. S.
Rennel on the Ganges. Ph. tr.
Brünings über die geschwindigkeit des fliessenden wassers, von Kronke. Frankf.
Woltmann's beiträge zur hydr. arch. III.
Aubry on the force of torrents. Roz. XIV. 101.
Bernhard Hydraulique.
Stratico on rivers. Ac. Pad. III. 333. IV. 114.
Trembley on the course of rivers. A. Berl. 1794. 3. 1798. 62. 1799. 8.
Hennert on the velocity of water in rivers. Hind. Arch. I. 1.
Smeaton's reports.
Fabre sur les torrens et les rivières. Par. 1797. R. I.
Robison Enc. Br. Art. River.
Silberschlag Théorie des fleuves.
   Acc. Montucl. and Lalande. III. 712.
Venturi on the motions of fluids.
On friction in watercourses. Nich. III. 252.
Edelbrooke on the Ganges. As. Res. VII. 1.
Cavallo Nat. Phil. II. 173.
   Chiefly from Venturi.

The friction of rivers is not quite proportional to the square of the velocity, the velocity increasing somewhat more rapidly than the square root of the fall. The excess of the superficial velocity v above the velocity at the bottom, is $2\sqrt{v} - 1$, v being expressed in French inches. The mean velocity is $v - \sqrt{v} + \frac{1}{2}$. Buat.

Gerstner finds Buat's formula not perfectly accurate at any temperature, for small pipes. But in fact the formula can by no means have been intended to be applied to such pipes. Buat's theorems are $b = \frac{478 l}{478 h - v^2}$, b being the length of the pipe which employs the pressure of an inch of the head of water in overcoming its friction, l the length of the pipe, h the whole height of the head, and v the velocity, all in French inches; but for the number 478 Langsdorf substitutes 482; then $v = \frac{297(\sqrt{e} - .1)}{\sqrt{b} - \text{h.l.} \sqrt{(b + 1.6)}} - .3(\sqrt{e} - .1)$, e being the hydraulic mean depth, or one fourth of the diameter d; and for the determination of v, b may be taken $= \frac{l + 45d}{h}$. In English measures, we may use the same value $\frac{l + 45d}{h}$ for b, and $v = (\sqrt{e} - .1) \cdot \left(\frac{307}{\sqrt{b} - \text{h.l.} \sqrt{(b+1.6)}} - .3 \right)$.

Instead of $\text{h.l.} \sqrt{(b + 1.6)}$, we may substitute $.85 b^{\frac{11}{25}}$ which is nearly the same, for moderate velocities. The expression $v = 307(\sqrt{e} - 1) \cdot \left(\frac{1}{\sqrt{b}} + \frac{1.6}{b^{.88}} - .001 \right)$ will also be found to agree extremely well with Buat's formula, and will perhaps be in many respects more useful; and we may employ, with very little inaccuracy, $b^{.675}$ instead of $b^{.88}$, the term $\frac{1.6}{b^{.88}}$ becoming $\frac{1.6 b^{\frac{1}{8}}}{b}$, which may be determined without logarithms, and the whole formula may be thus expressed: $v = 153(\sqrt{d} - .2) \cdot \left(\sqrt{\frac{h}{l + 45d}} + 1.6 \left(\frac{h}{l + 45d} \right)^{\frac{7}{8}} - .001 \right)$. These formulas may also be employed for rivers $\frac{1}{b}$ being the sine of their inclination.

When the pipe is bent in one or more places, the effect of the flexure may be found by adding into one sum s the squares of the sines, then $l = \frac{l}{h - \left(\frac{v^2}{482} + \frac{v^2 s}{3000} \right)}$, or more simply $v = \sqrt{\left(\frac{482 dh}{d + \frac{1}{45} l + .16 ds} \right)}$. Langsdorf, from Buat.

A floating log descends faster than a chip, its own weight tending to accelerate it. Robison.

Resistance of Fluids, or Hydraulic Pressure.

See Seamanship.

Newton's Principia.

Mariotte.

†Wallis on the air's resistance. Ph. tr. 1686. XVI. 269.

Lahire on the elevation of bubbles of water. A. P. IX. 315.

L'Hopital on the solid of least resistance. A. P. 1699. 107. H. 95.

Craig on the solid of least resistance. Ph. tr. 1701. XXII. 746.

Carré on the refraction of balls in water. A. P. 1702. H. 14. 1705. 211.

Derham on pendulums in vacuo. Ph. tr. 1704. XXIV. 1785.

Parent. A. P. 1704.

Hawksbee on bodies falling in vacuo. Ph. tr. 1705. XXIV. 1946, 1948.

Hawksbee on the descent of balls in air. Ph. tr. 1710. XXVII. 196.

Varignon on motions in a resisting medium. A. P. 1707. 382. H. 139. 1708. 212, 250, 302, 419. H. 123. 1709. 1710. 1711. 248. H. 87.

Bernoulli on central forces in resisting mediums. A. P. 1711. 47. H. 84.

Fatii problema de solido minimae resistentiae. Ph. tr. 1713. XXVIII. 172.

Lahire on the fall of bodies in the air. A. P. 1714. 333.

Bomie on the densities of resisting mediums. A. P. 1714. H. 52.

Desaguliers on the resistance of the air, from experiments in St. Paul's cathedral. Ph. tr. 1719. XXX. 1071. n. 362.

Desaguliers on the motion of a pendulum in fluids. Ph. tr. 1721. XXXI. 142.

Pitot on the oblique impulse of fluids. A. P. 1727. 49. H. 137.

Molières on motion in a spherical vortex. A. P. 1728. 245. H. 97.

Molières on the resistance of ether. A. P. 1731. H. 66.

D. Bernoulli on hydraulic pressure. C. Petr. III. 214. VIII. 99, 113.

D. Bernoulli on projectiles with resistance. C. Petr. IV. 136.

D. Bernoulli on pendulums with resistance. C. Petr. V. 106.

Euler on tautochronous curves with resistance. C. Petr. IV. 67. N. C. Petr. X. 156. XVII. 333, 349, 362.

Euler on the motions of projectiles in the air. A. Berl. 1753. 34.

<small>Less elegant in theory than Bernoulli, but more convenient for practice. Robison.</small>

*Euler on the friction of fluids. N. C. Petr. VI. 338.

Euler on the resistance of fluids. N. C. Petr. VIII. 197.

Euler on the figure of a fluid exposed to the wind. A. Petr. I. i. 190.

<small>According to the law of resistance, the surface may be a cycloid, or a tractory, or a curve of an intermediate nature.</small>

Euler on the vibrations of a board exposed to the wind. N. A. Petr. 1786. IV. 131.

Maupertuis on the curve of equable descent in a resisting medium. A. P. 1730. 233. H. 94.

Maupertuis on the ascent of a bubble of air. A. P. 1733. 255. H. 90.

Bouguer on curvilinear motion in moving media. A. P. 1731. 390. H. 76.

Bouguer on the solid of least resistance. A. P. 1733. 85. H. 86. 1767. 504. H. 110.

Bouguer on the impulse of fluids on pyramidical prows. A. P. 1746. 237. H. 289.

Pendulum for experiments on resistance. S'Graves. N. Ph. by Desagul. Ph. tr. 1748. 332.

Krafft on the impulse of a vein of water. C. Petr. VIII. 253. XI. 233.

Krafft on tables for the motions of projectiles. A. Petr. IV. i. 154. ii. 175.

Clairaut on the centre of oscillation in resisting mediums. A. P. 1738. 159.

D'Arcy on the curve of equal pressure in a resisting medium. A. P. 1742. H. 56. S. E. I. 73.

St. Jacques de Silvabelle on the solid of least resistance. S. E. III. 639.

Necker on curves of descent in a resisting medium. S. E. IV. 96.

D'Alembert's theory of the resistance of fluids.
Acc. A. P. 1753. H. 289.

Adami de resistentia corporum in fluidis motorum. 4. Berl. 1753.

Sulzer on the resistance of the air to a musket ball. A. Berl. 1755. 104.

Sulzer on the resistance of fluids. A. Berl. 1761. 41.

Euler junior on kites. A. Berl. 1756. 322.

Emerson on the solid of least resistance. Pap. on N. A. II. i. 39.

Kites. Emers. mech. f. 209.

Robins's gunnery.

*Borda on the resistance of fluids. A. P. 1763. 358. H. 118. 1767. 495. H. 145.

*Borda on the curve described by balls. A. P. 1769. 247.

Lambert on the resistance of fluids to projectiles. A. Berl. 1765. 102.

Lambert on a balistic scale. A. Berl. 1773. 34.

Lambert on the resistance of pendulums of clocks. Berl. Ephem. 1776.

Lambert on the constitution of fluids. A. Berl. 1784. 299.

Molinelli on the descent of bodies in water. C. Bon. V. i. O. 280.

Bossut Experiences sur la résistance des fluides.
Acc. A. P. 1777. H. 61. Extr. Bossut Hydrod.

Bossut's experiments. A. P. 1778. 353. H. 38.

Mann's experiments on the resistance in shallow canals. Ph. tr. 1779. 629.

J. and J. Bernoulli on a balistic machine. A. Berl. 1781. 347.

Komarzewski's curves of projectiles. M. S. R. S.

E. M. Pl. V. Marine. pl. 152, 153.

Edgeworth on the resistance of the air. Ph. tr. 1783. 136. Repert. X. 87.

A vertical axis was made to revolve with a given velocity, bearing a horizontal arm. Alone, it required a weight of 40 ounces. With a parallelogram 9 inches by 4, fixed to the arm, the longer side being horizontal, 112 ounces; the shorter horizontal, 121. With a piece of tin 4 inches square, $80 = 40 + 40$ ounces, with a piece 8 inches square $262 = 40 + 222$, instead of $40 + 160$. The parallelogram being bent into an arch with a chord of 8 inches, the shorter side being horizontal, the weight required was 128, instead of 121; when the chord was only $7\frac{1}{4}$ inches, 133 ounces. Hence it is inferred that sails act best when bent. The difference of the effect in different positions must have been derived from the effect of the rotatory motion.

Marguerie Mém. de l'Acad. Royale de marine.

Riccati on rectilinear motion towards a centre. C. Bon. VI. O. 138.

Coulomb on the force of torsion. A. P. 1784. 229.

Finds the constant friction of water only 1 grain in 255 square feet; from the oscillations of a cylinder sustained by a wire.

Coulomb on the cohesion and resistance of fluids. M. Inst. III. Ph. M. VII. 183.

Examined by the force of torsion. Pressure does not augment the friction; on the contrary, the resistance is greater when the immersion is only partial. Greasing wood does not lessen the friction. The friction of oil is $17\frac{1}{4}$ times as great as that of water. A part of the friction is proportional to the velocity: the constant part is almost insensible. A circle .195 metre in diameter, turning in water with a velocity of .14 m. in 1″, meets a resistance equivalent to a weight of 1 gramme acting on a lever of .143 m. The portion proportional to the velocity is equivalent to .042 gr. for a surface equal to twice such a circle moving in its own direction with a velocity of .01 m.

Ulloa.

Juan Examen maritime.

Buat Hydraulique.

Legendre's example of the solid of least resistance. A. P. 1786. 21.

Tempelhoff on the motion of a projectile in a resisting medium. A. Berl. 1788. 216.

Michelotti on the impulse of the vein of a fluid. M. Tur. 1788. IV. App. 121.

Produces some experiments not agreeing with the common theory.

Lorgna on the impulse of fluids. Soc. Ital. IV. 418.

Saint Martin's ventilator acting by lateral friction. Roz. XXXIII. 161.

Hydraulic pressure. Langsdorfs hydraulik. pl. 5, 6.

Resistance of fluids. Langsdorfs hydraulik. pl. 7, 8.

Zuliani on the impulse of a vein of a fluid. A. Pad. III. 337.

Zuliani sperimenti sopra l'effetto della caduta de' gravi nelle materie cedenti. 4. Pad. 1798. R. S.

Vince on the motion and resistance of fluids. Ph. tr. 1795. 24.

A machine for measuring the resistance of the air.

Vince on the resistance of fluids. Ph. tr. 1798.
1. Nich. III. 506. Papers on nav. arch. II. iii. 12.

The resistance to a globe moving in water was $\frac{4}{5}$ of the resistance to a cylinder. The force acting in the direction of a plane struck by a stream of water, varied considerably according to the part of the plane impelled.

Hutton's abstract of experiments on the resistance of the air. Ed. tr. II. 29. Hutt. Math. dict. II. 365.

Gerstner's theory of the impulse of water. Böhm. Abh. 1795. II.

Prony Arch. Hydr.

*Experiments of the society for the advancement of naval architecture. 4. Lond. R. I.

Avanzini on the resistance of fluids. A. Pad. IV. 96.

On bodies falling in serpentine lines.

Extract from Schober's experiments on the impulse of the air. Kunzes Schauplatz. I. 312.

Trembley on motion in resisting mediums. A. Berl. 1798. 60.

Eytelwein's experiments with the hydraulic quadrant. Samml. zur Baukunst. 1799.

Otto on the effect of oil on waves. Zach. Ephem. II. 516. III. 242.

Seems to depend on the friction of the air.

Benzenberg's experiments on falling bodies. Gilb. XII. 367. XIV. 222.

A body fell 144 feet Fr. in 186.93‴, instead of 186.86‴. When the velocity exceeds 100 feet in 1″, the resistance increases faster than its square. Robins says 200.

Benzenberg Versuche über den gesetz des falles. Hamb.

Lacroix on the resistance of fluids. B. Soc. Phil. n. 69.

Robison's table of elevations and ranges. Enc. Br. Art. Projectiles.

Moreau on projectiles in resisting mediums. Journ. Polyt. IV. xi. 204.

Borda found the resistance of a sphere to that of a circle, as 1 : 2.45 in air, in water as 1 : 2.5. Hutton found the resistance of the flat side of a hemisphere moved in air to that of the convex side 2.45:1. Ed. tr.; to that of the whole globe as 2¼:1. Math. dict. Whence we might conclude, that the resistance of a globe is greater than that of a hemisphere. This, however, cannot be the fact.

The experiments of the society for naval architecture contain some valuable remarks on the different effects of the form of the different parts of a body moving in water. The form nearest to the shape of a fish appears to move with least resistance. Soaked planks were more resisted than planks not soaked.

A surface of 46 square feet, moving in its own direction with a velocity of 1 nautical mile per hour, produced a friction of .563 pounds, with a velocity of 2 miles 1.992, of 4, 6.642, of 6, 12.839, of 8, 19.856.

The direct resistance appeared to vary as $v^{2.106}$. The same body having prows differently inclined, the resistance at different angles was thus.

9°	44'	10"	30.67
14	28	40	35.34
19	28	15	41.71
30			51.44
90			148.25

Hutton makes the resistance $\frac{1}{22}av^{2.04}s^{1.84?}c$, c being the cosine, s the sine. Thus, for 32 square inches or $\frac{2}{9}$ foot moving 12 feet per second, $.840^{1.84?}c$.

Angle.	Observ.	Form.	Sine.
10°	.044	.035	.146
20	.133	.131	.287
30	.278	.278	.420
40	.448	.450	.540
50	.619	.613	.643
60	.729	.736	.727
70	.803	.808	.789
80	.835	.836	.827
90	.840	.840	.840

Calculations from the resistance to plane surfaces make the resistance to curved surfaces in general greater than experiments; the particles gliding more easily along these surfaces. The resistance calculated from the curves in which the particles of a fluid were observed in Sir Charles Knowles's experiments to move, was $\frac{1}{16}$ less than the observed resistance; perhaps on account of the adhesion, which was not calculated. A quadruple velocity had no effect on these curves. Robison.

In Bossut's experiments, the resistance was nearly (cos. $x)^2 + 3.153\left(\frac{x}{6}\right)^{9.25}$, x being the complement of half the angle at the prow, in degrees. Robison.

The direct impulse of the wind on a surface of a square foot in pounds is nearly $\frac{v^2}{500}$, v being the velocity in a second in feet; or more nearly $.00229v^2$, when v is 10, $.002287v^2$ when 100. In grains $16v^2$. Robison.

Remarks on the Resistance of Fluids. By Dr. Young.
See Journ. R. I., II. 14, 78.

The first approximation to a determination of the effect of the resistance to a body of a given section, terminated by oblique planes, is to suppose each particle of the fluid to impinge once on the surface, and then to retire for ever: on this supposition, the resistance ought to vary as the square of the cosine of the angle of incidence.

Another part of the resistance is occasioned by the adhesion of the particles of the fluid; this may be supposed to vary, as the product of the secant and the sine of the angle of incidence; that is, as its tangent. This portion appears in fact to be but small, it may however be taken into consideration, in order to facilitate the computation.

A third part depends on the form of the posterior surface of the body, and upon the unknown irregularities produced in the motions of the particles of the fluid, by the difference of the forms of its anterior part. It may be expected, that this negative pressure will be nearly uniform, when the shape of the posterior part of the body remains unaltered, as in Bossut's experiments; but that, when a thin surface is employed, as in Mr. Vince's apparatus, it will be somewhat diminished by the obliquity of that surface, even supposing the transverse projection of the surface to remain unaltered. This portion, however, may naturally be expected to be liable to great irregularities; and it appears to be somewhat increased, when the thin surface is inclined in a small angle only.

Mr. Romme has remarked, that the facility, with which the particles of the fluid can escape before the moving body, is proportional to the angular space of the fluid which remains open to admit them, and that therefore the resistance must vary in proportion to this angle. Without allowing the truth of the observation in its whole extent, we may with propriety inquire, whether or no the portion of the pressure derived from impulse may not in part depend on some simple function of the angle of incidence; and whether the whole resistance to an oblique surface may not be considered, as composed of a constant portion, a portion varying with the tangent of the angle of incidence, and a third portion proportionate to the square of the cosine, diminished in the ratio of a power, or other function, of the angle of incidence. And it will appear upon inquiry, that if we take one fifth of the radius, increased by one twenty-fifth of the tangent, and add to it four fifths of the square of the cosine, diminished in the ratio of the circumference of a circle increased by the angle of incidence, to the simple circumference, we may approach always within about one fiftieth, to the number expressing the oblique resistance, until the angle of incidence becomes greater than 60°. Thus, the direct resistance being unity, and a the angle of incidence, the oblique resistance will be $.2 + .04 t.a + .288 (\cos.a)^2 : (360 + a^o)$. A formula, somewhat more accurate than this, deduced from experiment only, is $r = (\cos.a)^2 + .00000004217 a^{3.16}$; the quantity added to the square of the cosine being a little less than the millionth of the cube of the angle of incidence, expressed in degrees. The results of these and other formulas are compared, in the following table, with various experiments.

Angle	(Cos.a)²	T.a	Eytelw.	Form. A.	Form B.	Form. C.	Bossut.	N. Arch.
0°	1.0000	.000	1.0000	1.0000	1.0000	1.0000	1.0000	
6	.9890	.105	.9910	.9995	.9824	.9891	.9893	
12	.9568	.212	.9656	.9780	.9492	.9580	.9578	
18	.9045	.325	.9241	.9370	.9022	.9086	.9084	
24	.8346	.445	.8690	.8791	.8438	.8449	.8446	
30	.7500	.577	.8036	.8077	.7769	.7710	.7710	
36	.6544	.726	.7308	.7270	.7049	.6919	.6925	
42	.5523	.900	.6551	.6423	.6317	.6135	.6148	
48	.4478	1.111	.5802	.5589	.5606	.5414	.5433	
54	.3455	1.376	.5103	.4831	.4985	.4816	.4800	
60	.2500	1.732	.4500	.4232	.4407	.4403	.4404	.347
66	.1654	2.246	.4026	.4000	.3924	.4231	.4240	
72	.0955	3.078	.3719	.4033	.3869	.4344	.4142	.269
78	.0432	4.705	.3600	.5137	.4166	.4816	.4063	.222
84	.0109	9.514	.3693	(.9623)	.5875	.5658	.3999	

Eytelwein's formula is $(\cos.a)^2 + .4$ v. s. a. Formula A is $(\cos.a)^2 + .1 t.a$. Formula B is the first, and C the second, of those which have been mentioned. The experiments of the society for the encouragement of naval architecture have been reduced by interpolation to the angles employed by Bossut: but the society appears to have made some deductions which cause a part of the apparent difference.

M. Romme found, by numerous experiments, that when the magnitude of the greatest section of a floating body, and its distance from the angular points, were constant, the form of the outline of any section of the body, whether composed of right lines, or of curves of any kind, was either wholly, or very nearly, indifferent to the magnitude of the resistance: hence he infers, that in the construction of ships, the curve of the sides ought to be determined from considerations independent of the resistance.

In experiments like those of Mr. Vince, the circumstances are materially different: but the accuracy of Mr. Vince's experiments on water is, in some measure, confirmed, by a comparison with those of Schober, which were made in a similar manner on air. The results of both these investigations are here exhibited in a table, and compared with a coarse approximation from this formula $r = .4 + .6 (\cos a)$. Dr. Hutton's experiments on air, when reduced, like the rest, to surfaces of given transverse projections, indicate at first an increase of resistance as the surface becomes more oblique.

Angle.	Cos. a	Form. D.	Schober.	Vince.	Hutton.
0°	1.0000	1.0000	1.0000	1.0000	1.000
10	.9848	.9909	.9854	.9787	1.010
20	.9397	.9638	.9808	.9743	1.068
30	.8660	.9196	.9200	.9463	1.003
40	.7660	.8596	.8308	.8729	.968
50	.6428	.7857	.7568	.7869	.830
60	.5000	.7000	.6738	.6610	.662
70	.3420	.6052	.6359	.4913	.453
80	.1736	.5042	.5833	.2779	.304

HYDROSTATIC INSTRUMENTS.

Levels.

See Geometrical Instruments, and Astronomical Instruments.

Determination of Specific Gravities.

Boyle's works. Ed. 1772. IV. 204.

Homberg on the difference of weight in the air and in a vacuum. A. P. X. 257.

Jurin on weighing bodies. Ph. tr. 1721. XXXI. 223.

<small>Observes, that wood becomes heavier than water, when the air is extricated from it.</small>

Fahrenheit on specific gravities. Ph. tr. 1724. XXXIII. 114.

Dalibard on the weight of bodies in different liquids. S. E. I. 212.

Baumé Elemens de pharmacie.

Baumé's hydrometer. Avantcoureur. 1768, 9. Nich. I. 37.

Ramsden on the specific gravities of fluids. 4. Lond. 1792. Roz. XL. 432. Ann. Ch. XIII. 243.

Schmeisser's instrument for determining specific gravities. Ph. tr. 1793. 165.

Robison. Enc. Br. Art. Specific Gravity.

Prony Architecture hydraulique. § 614.

Say's instrument for measuring volumes. Ann. Ch. XXIII. 1.

Hassenfratz and Schmidt on specific gravities. Ann. Ch. XXXIX. 193.

<small>H. prefers weighing in a bottle to a hydrometer.</small>

Atkins on specific gravities. 4. Lond. 1803. R. I.

Extr. Ph. M. XV. 277.

<small>Leslie measures the specific gravity of gases by the velocity with which they are discharged. Lesl. on heat.</small>

Hydrometers.

Boyle's hydrometer for solids. Ph. tr. 1675. X. 329.

Monconi's hydrometer. Birch. I. 257.

Hooke's waterpoise for liquids. Ph. tr. 1693. XVII. 63.

Hooke's hydrometer. Birch. III. 344, 348, 364.

<small>A bulb nearly of the weight of water.</small>

Homberg's areometer. A. P. 1699. 46.

Fahrenheit areometri descriptio. Ph. tr. 1724. XXXIII. 140.

<small>With a cup on the stem for weights.</small>

Leupold Th. hydrostaticum. Th. hydrotechn.

Desaguliers on Clarke's hydrometer. Ph. tr. 1730. XXXVI. 277.

<small>Clarke substituted copper for glass, and screwed on weights at the bottom of the instrument.</small>

Gesner de hydroscopio. Zurich, 1754.

Gesner von den hydroscopen. Vien. 1771.

Montigny on comparative areometers. A. P. 1768. 435.

Le Roy on comparable areometers. A. P. 1770. 526.

De Luc's comparable areometer. Ph. tr. 1778. 509.

Casbois on the areometer. Roz. XV. 228.

E. M. A. VI. Art. Pese-liqueurs.

E. M. Physique. Art. Areometre.

On the oenometer. Roz. XXII. 89. XXIII. 55.

Nicholson's hydrometer. Manch. M. II. 370.

<small>Boyle's hydrometer was chiefly for guineas. Clarke's had weights that were screwed on below. Quin's had a conical stem, making the degrees more equal. Nicholson's has a dish below, as well as above, and may be employed for examining solids.</small>

Weigel de historia barylliorum. 4. Greifsw. 1785.

Brisson's areometer, requiring no calculation. A. P. 1788. 582.

Vallet on areometers. Roz. XXXIII 241.

On the hydrometer. Ph. tr. 1790 342.

Quin's hydrometer. S. A. VIII 98.

Schmidt's areometer. Gren. VII. 186.
Schmidt's remarks on Hassenfratz. Gilb. IV. 194.
Sanmartini on the areometer. Soc. Ital. VII. 79.
Guyton's gravimeter. Ann. Ch. XXI. 3. Nich. I. 110.
Hassenfratz on the areometer. Ann. Ch. XXVI. 3, 132. XXVIII. 3, 282. XXXI. 125. XXXIII. 3. Journ. Phys. XLVII. (IV.) 274. Nich. IV. 128. Gilb. I. 158, 396, 515. IV. 2.
Arnim on the areometer. Gilb. I. 412.
Nicholson. I. III.
Barré on graduating areometers. Journ. Phys. LVII. 433.
Speer on the hydrometer. 8. London. 1802. R. S. Ph. M. XIV. 151.
Speer's patent hydrometer. Repert. ii. III. 81.
Atkins on specific gravities.
Fletcher on Atkins's hydrometer. Nich. 8. II. 276.
On Atkins's hydrometer. Nich. 8. III. 50.
Richter's areometer. Gilb. XVII. 485.

HYDRAULIC ARCHITECTURE IN GENERAL.

Leup. Th. hydraulicum. Th. hydrotechnicum.
*Belidor Architecture hydraulique. 4 parts. 4. Par. 1782. R. I.
  Acc. A. P. 1737. H. 105. 1750. H. 157. 1753. H. 294.
Hydraulic architecture in a strict sense. Bel. I. ii.
Woltmann Beiträge zur hydraulischen architectur. Gotting.
Prony Architecture hydraulique.
Gilly Grundriss zu den vorlesungen über wasserbaukunst. Berl. 1795.

Wiebeking und Kronke Wasserbaukunst. 2 v. 4. Darmst. 1798. B. B.
Smeaton's reports.

Thrust of Earth.

Couplet on the thrust of earth. A. P. 1726. 106. H. 58. 1727. 139. H. 132. 1728. 113. H. 103.
Lambert on the fluidity of sand and earth. A. Berl. 1772. 33.
Delangez on the statics and mechanics of semifluids. Soc. Ital. IV. 329.
Account of a memoir on the pressure of earth. N. A. Petr. 1793. XI. H. 3.
Prony on the lateral pressure of earth. B. Soc. Phil. n. 24.
Prony sur la poussée des terres. 4. Par. 1802. R. S.
Prony sur les murs de revêtement. 4. Par. 1802. R. S.

Building in Water.

See Architecture.

Machine for digging foundations in water. Belidor Arch. Hydr. II. ii. pl. 25. Building in water. p. 168.
Perronet on subaqueous buildings. A. P. 1766. 139. H. 137.
A mortar for water. Roz. Intr. I. 237.
On Loriot's mode of building in water. Roz. IV. 162. 416.
Essai de batir sous l'eau. 4. Stockholm.
Leyritz on Building in water. Roz. XXX. 88.
Semple on building in water. London.
On the cones at Cherbourg. Roz. XXXIII. 246. XXXIV. 133. Fig.

Cisterns. Casks.

See Carpentry.

Cisterns and reservoirs. Belidor Arch. Hydr. II. i. pl. n. 47.

F. de Bondaroy on cisterns for wine. Roz. XXIV. 301.

<small>Meux's porter cask is 65½ feet in diameter, 25½ high, containing 20 000 barrels of porter, worth 30 shillings each. It cost 10,000l. Luckombe.</small>

Dikes and Embankments.

Stevini hydrostatica.

†*Bleiswyck* de aggeribus.

Bourgeois's dike. Mach. A. II. 81.

Chamberlayne on a sunk island in the Humber, recovered from the sea. Ph. tr. 1719. XXX. 1014.

Leup. Th. Suppl.

Euler on dikes. N. C. Petr. IX. 362.
<small>Merely on the area included by a certain outline.</small>

Dugdale on embanking. f. Lond.

Hales on fencing banks with furze. Ph. tr. 1761. H. 137.

Bossut et Viallet sur les digues.

Silberschlag on the rupture of dikes. A. Berl. 1786. 71.

Lee on inclosing a salt marsh. S. A. VIII. 114.

Corbet's embankment. S. A. XII. 249.

Beatson and others on embankments. Board Agr. II.

Taylow on an embankment. Repert. XV. 326.

Dudley on gaining land from the sea. Rep. XVI. 45.

Brémontier on fixing the downs near Bayonne.
Extr. Journ. Polyt. II. v. 61.

Harbours.

Belidor Arch. Hydr. II. ii. 53.

Sluices for clearing harbours. Belidor Arch. Hydr. I. ii. pl. 35.

Description of Dunkirk. Belidor Arch. Hydr. I. ii. 25.

Romain on improvements of the port of Toulon. Roz. VI. 71.

On jettées. Roz. IX. 291.

On the port of Havre. Roz. XVI. 42.

Smeaton on Ramsgate harbour. 8. Lond. 1791. R. I.

Smeaton's reports.

Reports on the port of London. 2 v. f. 1796. R. I.

Proposed improvements of the port of London. Ph. M. X.

Pape's improvement of Rye harbour. S. A. XXII. 245.

Clearing harbours. See Mechanics, Raising Weights.

Docks.

Gaillon's dock. Mach. A. V. 135.

Tracts on wet docks. 8. Lond. 1797. R. I.

Sluices.

Stevin sur les écluses.

Grandi de castellis.

Desbillettes's sluice. A. P. 1699. 63. H. 114.

Bourgeois's sluice gate. Mach. A. II. 81.

Leupold Th. Suppl.

Four new sluices. Mach. A. VI. 105 .. 111.

Belidor Arch. Hydr. I. ii. 54. Sluices for clearing harbours. pl. 35.

Guglielmini de fluviis et castellis.

Zacharie's sluice gate. A. P. 1763. H. 146.

On the forms of sluices. Roz. X. 153.

Boulard on sluices. Roz. XVI. 186.

Boulard Traité des éclures.

Solage's sluice. B. Soc. Phil. n. 52.

Management of Rivers.

Belidor Arch. Hydr. II. ii. pl. 35, 42. Navigable rivers. p. 14.
Scheibel on the means of contracting rivers. A. Berl. Deutsch. Abh. 1788. 81.
Crawley on gaining ground by rivers. S. A. XIII. 140.
Forfait on the navigation of the Seine. M. Inst. I. 120.

Bridges.

See Architecture.

Mezeray's bridge of ropes. A. P. 1748. H. 120.
Robertson on the fall of water under bridges. Ph. tr. 1758. 492.

The breadth of the river in feet being b, the breadth between the piers c, the velocity in a second v, the fall of a heavy body in $1''$ $a(=16.0899)$, the fall of the river will be $\left(\left(\frac{25b}{21c}\right)^2 - 1\right).\frac{vv}{4a}$. Thus at London bridge $b=926$, $c=236$, reduced by the piles to $196\frac{1}{4}$, $v=3\frac{1}{4}$; hence the fall is 4.739; by observation 4.75. At Westminster bridge, $b=994$, $c=820$, $v=2\frac{1}{4}$, and the fall becomes about an inch.

Bridges of boats. See shipbuilding.

Weres.

Comm. Bon. II. i. 413.
Baciallo on weres. C. Bon. IV. O. 98.
Lorgna on the discharge of weres. Soc. Ital. V. 313. 330.
    Whether open or submerged.
Lorgna's regulator for a were. Soc. Ital. V. 397.

Canals.

Petit on a proposed canal in the South of France. Ph. tr. 1665—6. I. 41.
Account of the canal of Languedoc. Ph. tr. 1669. IV. 1123.
On the canal of Languedoc, from Froidour. Ph. tr. 1672. VII. 4080.
Perrault's machine for measuring the inclination of water in a canal. Mach. A. I. 163.
Map of the canal of Languedoc. 1774. R. S.
Perronet on bringing part of the Yvette to Paris. A. P. 1775. 21. H. 1.
Forfait on clearing canals. Mantua.
Frisi de canali navigabili.
Lalande sur les canaux. M. B.
Lalande on a canal. Roz. XXIII. 28.
Geoffroy on improving a canal. Roz. XIV. 140.
Dazay on a proposed canal. Roz. XXII. 36. 93.
Fer de la Noverre Science des canaux navigables. 8. Par. 1785.
Report on the interior navigation in Britanny. A. P. 1785. 111.
Eckhardt on a machine for deepening canals. R. S.
On the junction of the Red Sea to the Mediterranean. Journ. Phys. XLVI. (III.) 338.
Enc. Br. Art. Canals.
Phillips's history of inland navigation. 4. 1795. R. I.
Fulton on canal navigation. 4. 1796. R. I.
Tatham on inland navigation. R. I.
Smeaton's reports.
Leach on inland navigation. 8.
Vallancey on inland navigation. 4.
Chapman on canal navigation. 4. Lond. 1797. R. I.
Pitt on saving water. Repert. I. 376.
Rowland and Pickering's patent canals without locks. Repert. I. 81.
Longbotham's patent method of supplying canals with water. Repert. IV. 145.

Green's patent for canals without locks. Rep. V. 11.
Telford on canals. Ph. M. XV. 77.
Andreossy Histoire du canal du Midi. 8. Par. 1800. R. I.
Digging. See mechanics.

Locks.

Leupold. Th. Suppl.
Belidor Arch. Hydr. II. ii.
Enc. Br. Art. Locks.
Smeaton's reports.
Playfair's patent locks. Repert. III. 303.

Conveyances substituted for Locks.

Huddlestone's mode of conveying boats by plungers. Repert. XV. 81. Nich. 8. IV. 336.
See mechanics. Raising and removing weights.

Aqueducts. Irrigation.

Belidor Arch. Hydr. II. i. Pl. n. 46.
Perronet on the Yvette. A. P. 1775. 21. H. 1.
Ferrari on the distribution of waters. Soc. Ital. VII. 157.
Davies on irrigation. Repert. III. 43, 123.
Pitt on irrigation. Repert. III. 239.
Tatham on irrigation. 8. Lond. 1801.

Drains.

On draining. Belidor Arch. Hydr. II. ii. Valves for drains. I. ii. Pl. 58.
Deparcieux's traps for drains. A. P. 1767. H. 133.
Turner on draining bogs. 8.
Keysell's drains. S. A. X. 123.
Higgins on draining ponds by digging. Am. tr. III. 325.
Moore on drains. S. A. XII. 234.
Corbet's drains. S. A. XII. 250.
Elkington on draining. 4.
His method is to cut off the springs.
Draining. Smeaton's reports.
Wedge on draining land. Repert. III. 405.
Drains for houses. Repert. VII. 234. XI. 237. XV. 73.
Moyle on draining a marsh. Repert. XV. 321.
Sir J. Banks on the effect of the equisetum palustre in choking drains. Board Agr. II. 350.
Willich's domest. enc. Art. Drains.
Fraser's stopper for drains. Am. tr. V. 148. Repert. ii. III. 214.
The common air trap.
Bayley on draining. Repert. ii. III. 99.
Curwen's drains. S. A. XXII. 47.
Dickson's agriculture.
Drain ploughs and mole ploughs. See Mechanics. Ploughing.

MODIFICATION, OR APPLICATION OF HYDRAULIC FORCES.

Hydrodynamic Measures.

Perrault's machine for measuring the inclination of water in a canal. Mach. A. I. 63.
Huygens's machine for measuring the force of the air. Mach. A. I. 71.
Leupold. Th. M. G. t. 59, 60.
Pitot's machine for measuring the velocities of fluids. A. P. 1730. 1732. 363. H. 103.
Brouckner's machine for measuring velocities. A. P. 1750. H. 169.
By the revolution of a fly.

Measurement of the depth of a river. Roz. III. 64.
Windgages. E. M. A. VI. 645. E. M. Pl. VII. Hydrostatique. Pl. 3.
Woltmann Theorie des hydrometrischen flügels. Hamb. 1790. Also in Langsd. Hydr. p. 631. Pl. 51.
Tubes for measuring the velocity of water. Langsd. Hydr. Pl. 25.
Eytelwein's experiments with the hydraulic quadrant. Samml. zur Bauk. 1799.
Prony sur le jaugeage des eaux courantes. 4. Par. 1802. R. S.
Banks's air gage. Manch. M. V. 398.
See instruments subservient to seamanship, and meteorological instruments.

Force of Water.

Parent on the perfection of machines moved by fluids. A. P. 1704. 323. H. 116.
Duquet's mill for ships' pumps. II. 136
Joué's waterwheel. Macn. A. III. 123, 127.
Waterwheels. Leupold. Th. M. G.
Horizontal waterwheel. Leupold Th. M. G. t. 64, 65.
Bead pump as a power. Leupold Th. Hydraul. 2. t. 54.
Pitot on the force of machines moved by water. A. P. 1725. 78. H. 80.
Pitot on the floatboards of waterwheels. A. P. 1729. 253, 385. H. 81.
Martin on the preservation of watermills. A. P. 1737. H. 106.
Gensanne's acting pump. Mach. A. VII. 99.
Amy's hollow levers. Mach. A. VII. 277.
Dubost's spiral wind or watermill. A. P. 1741. H. 165. Mach. A. VII. 369.
Dubost's new watermill. A. P. 1747. H. 127.
*Maclaurin's fluxions.

Arderon on a waterwheel. Ph. tr. 1746. 1.
With oblique floatboards.
Segner exercitationes hydraulicae. 4. Gott. 1747.
A mill turned by counterpressure.
Waterwheels. Belidor Arch. Hydr. I. i. Pl. n. 19.
Horizontal spoon wheels used in Provence. Belidor Arch. Hydr. I. i. Pl. n. 22.
Tide mills. Belidor Arch. Hydr. I. i. Pl. n. 25.
A horizontal acting pump. Belidor. Arch. Hydr. II. i. Pl. n. 33.
Denisard and La Deuille's machine, with improvements. Belidor Arch. Hydr. II. i. Pl. n. 37.
Acting pumps, with air vessels.
Buckets raising each other. Belidor Arch. Hydr. II. i. Pl. n. 38.
Deparcieux on the advantages of a slow motion in overshot wheels. A. P. 1754. 603. H. 134.
Deparcieux on floatboards inclined to the radius. A. P. 1759. 288, 477. H. 123, 223.
Euler on Segner's hydraulic machine. A. Berl. 1750. 311. 1751. 271.
Euler on machines moved by the reaction of water. A. Berl. 1754. 227.
J. A. Euler enodatio quaestionis de molis. Gott. 1754.
J. A. Euler on moving vessels without wind. A. Berl. 1764. 240.
By oars, vanes, or the reaction of water.
Lambert on mills. A. Berl. 1755.
Lambert on waterwheels. A. Berl. 1775. 49, 70, 82.
Veltmann's waterwheel. A. P. 1756. H. 129.
A waterwheel for raising weights. Emers. mech. f. 192.
An overshot spiral waterwheel with a vertical axis. Emers. mech. f. 306.

*Smeaton on the powers of wind and water. Ph. tr. 1759. 100.

Mallet on waterwheels. Ph. tr. 1767. 372.

Finds, that at the moment that one of the floatboards is vertical, their number is indifferent to the effect; but that at other times, the number 6, 9, or 36, has an advantage, accordingly as the position is more or less remote from a vertical one.

*Borda on hydraulic wheels. A. P. 1767. 270. H. 149.

Bossut's general determination of the effect of wheels. A. P. 1769. 288, 477. H. 121.

Well's machine for pumping vessels. Am. tr. I. 353. Roz. I. 228. Repert. V. 38.
With a waterwheel.

On a machine moved by a counterpressure. Roz. V. 73. VI. 166.

Collection des arts et métiers. f. Paris.

Tide mills described. Bailey's mach. I. 178. E. M.

A watermill on a boat. E. M. Pl. I. Charpenterie. Pl. 19.

Trough or spoon pump. E. M. Art. Aratoire.

Westgarth's statical engine. Bailey's mach. II. 52. S. A. V. 192.
An acting pump.

Fenwick on practical mechanics.

Dransy sur les moulins a eaux. Pr. A. P. 1787.

Klügel on undershot waterwheels. Commentat. Gott. 1787. IX. M. 26.

Quayle's pentrough for equalising the flow of water. S. A. XI. 166. Repert. III. 343.
The water running over a float.

†Waring's theory of watermills. Am. tr. III. 144, 319. Hutton's dictionary. Art. Mills.

Observes, that the number of floatboards impelled being proportional to the velocity of the wheel, the relative velocity ought for this reason to be half of the absolute velocity for the greatest effect. But the time of action on each floatboard being as much smaller as their number is greater, this consideration cannot in any degree affect the calculation.

Waring on Barker's mill. Am. tr. III. 185.

Krafft on the employment of Segner's machine in mines. N. A. Petr. 1792. X. 137.

*On the force of wind and water. Langsdorfs hydraulik.

Waterwheels. Langsdorfs hydr. Pl. 9..13, 53.

Euler's machine for rotation from counterpressure. Langsdorfs hydr. Pl. 16.

Kempele's rotatory machine. Langsdorfs hydr. Pl. 20.

Höll's acting pumps. Langsdorfs hydr. C. 20. Pl. 18, 21, 22.
Eight of these have been erected at Schemnitz.

Oblique float boards. Langsdorfs hydr. Pl. 50. f, 286.

Langsdorfs maschinenlehre.

Gerstner Böhm. Abh.

Eckhardt on the advantages of wheels with inclined floatboards. f. R. S.

Eiselen on undershot wheels. Samml. zur bauk. 1798.

On waterwheels. Nich. II. 497, 544.

Leslie's tidewheel. Repert. I. 385.

Bramah's patent hydraulic power. Repert. VI. 289. Nich. I. 29.

Bramah's compound piston giving a great force. Nich. VII. 50.

Brooks's buoyant machine for raising weights. Repert. VII. 361.

A greasing machine for waterwheels. Repert. VIII. 97.

Luccock's patent hydrostatical machine. Repert. XI. 73.
An acting pump.

Sir T. Hanmer's waterwheel. S. A. XVII. 350. Repert. XII. 176.
The water turned back on the wheel.

Buchanan on the velocity of waterwheels. Ph. M. X. 278.

The velocity of a cotton mill was found to be as the water expended; the effect being as the square of either. Y.

Buchanan's breast wheel. Ph. M. XI. 79.

West's pump turned by a spiral pipe. Ph. M. XI. 166.

Sargeant's machine for raising water by a reservoir as a moving power. S. A. XIX. 260. Ph. M. XII. 14. Nich. 8. II. 60. Repert. ii. I. 109.

Besant's undershot waterwheel. S. A. XIX. 274. Ph. M. XIII. 22. Nich. 8. III. 49. Repert. ii. I. 40. Gilb. XV. 194.

Intended for diminishing the resistance of the water in running off.

Johnson's patent for a perpetual motion. Repert. XIV. 73.

By a tide wheel.

Close's apparatus worked by a siphon. Nich. 8. I. 27.

Trevithick's acting pump. Nich 8. I. 161.

Norton's patent watermill. Repert. ii. III. 327.

A spiral wheel.

On Barker's rotatory mill, on Westgarth's machine, and on horizontal waterwheels. Banks on machines. 1, 20, 38.

Robison says, that there is no limit to the advantage derived from a slow motion in an overshot wheel. But the advantage is in fact trifling, within any moderate limits.

Waterwheels are sometimes made of cast iron.

The Dutch camels are machines for raising weights by the buoyant power of water.

Some authors make the force of water as the quantity and the square of the velocity conjointly; this is true of the mechanical power, which is proportionate to the product of the quantity and the height, but not of the immediate force.

In the Mathematical Elements, Art. 393, p. 62 of this volume, the word effect is used in too vague a sense: the whole article must be considered only as a part of the following.

See hydraulic machines.

Air or Wind.

Sailing carriages. Wilkins's mathematical magic.

Hooke on the sails of mills and ships. Hooke. Ph. Coll. n. 3, 61.

Describes a horizontal windmill in which the sails are moved by machinery during each revolution into the best possible condition; but does not approve it.

Lahire on wind mills. A. P. IX. 96.

†On the position of the axis of a windmill with respect to the wind. A. P. 1701. H. 138.

Couplet's horizontal mill. Mach. A. I. 105.

Duquet's horizontal mill. Mach. A. I. 107.

Windmills. Leup. Th. M. G.

Self regulating windmill. Leup. Th. Hydraul. 2. t. 32.

Gallon's horizontal mill. Mach. A. VI. 75.

Du Bost's horizontal windmill. Mach. A. VII. 117.

Euler on windmills. N. C. Petr. VI. 41.

Makes the best angle about 63° 26', for a moderate velocity.

Euler on windmills. A. Berl. 1756. 165.

Belidor Arch. Hydr. II. i. 30.

Windmills. Emers. mech. f. 203, 266.

Sailing chariots. Emers. mech. f. 213, 214, 234.

A horizontal windmill, from Wilkins, of which the sails unfurl when the wind acts on their concave side.

*Smeaton on the powers of wind and water. Ph. tr. 1759. 100.

Bourrier's horizontal mill. A. P. 1762. H. 190.

Maizières's windmill. A. P. 1767. H. 185.

Maizières's horizontal windmill. Roz. Intr. I. 306.

Gilpin's horizontal windmill. Am. tr. I. 405.

Windmills described. Bailey's mach. I. 180.

Verrier's windmill with eight sails. Bailey's mach. II. 47.

Four of the sails are turned according to the strength of the wind.

Coulomb on windmills, and the figure of their sails. A. P. 1781. 65. H. 41.

Each pair of the 4 sails of a windmill being 66 feet Fr. long from top to top, and 6 feet wide, or a little more, and being inclined from 60° to 78° or 84°, the wind blowing 20 feet in 1", about 15 miles E. an hour, 1000 pounds Fr. were raised 218 feet Fr. in a minute: and this, on an average, could be performed eight hours in the day. The whole force without impediment would raise the same weight 253 feet in a minute.

Mills. E. M. A. V. Art. Meunier.
Essay on windmills. 8. R. I.
Enc. Br. Art. Smokejack.
Langsdorfs hydr. Pl. 14, 15, 50.
Wiseman's patent sails with horizontal levers. Repert. IV. 12.
 The sails of a horizontal windmill changing their position in different parts.
Maunsel's horizontal windmill. Repert. VII. 6.
 With moveable wind boards.
Gower on the vanes of vertical windmills. Ph. M. IV. 174.
 Recommends an inclination between 80° and 20°.
Beatson on vertical and horizontal windmills. 8. Lond. 1798. R. I.
Beatson's patent horizontal mills. Repert. ii. II. 13.
Brayshay's patent horizontal windmill. Rep. ii. I.
 It is an advantage that the sails should be short and wide. The axis is placed obliquely to the horizon, so as to allow a space between the sails and the lowest part of the mill, both for convenience, and in order to give the wind room to act on the sails when near the ground.

Wind and Water combined. Seamanship in general.

Navigation. See astronomy.
Renaud Manoeuvre des vaisseaux.
Groignard.
Bernoulli's theory of the manoeuvres of ships. A. P. 1714. H. 107.
Pitot Theorie de la manoeuvre des vaisseaux. Acc. A. P. 1731. H. 81.
Bouguer's problems relative to the manoeuvres of ships. A. P. 1754. 342. H. 91. 1755. 355, 481. H. 83, 135.
Bouguer Manoeuvre des vaisseaux. M. B. Acc. A. P. 1757. H. 165.
 Extract in Bézout Cours de mathématiques.
Clairaut's problems on the manoeuvres of ships. A. P. 1760. 171. H. 141.
Euler Scientia navalis. 4. Petersb. 1749. M. B.
Euler Theorie de la construction et de la manoeuvre des vaisseaux. 8. R. S.
Euler on the construction of vessels. 8. Lond. 1790. R. I.
Bourdé de Villehuet Theorie des mouvemens du navire. Acc. A. P. 1765. H. 91. Engl. 4. Lond.
Franklin's maritime observations. Am. tr. II. 294. Roz. XXXI. 224.
Leroy's letters on maritime affairs. Roz XXXII. 209, 288. XXXIII. 136. XXXVII. 42.
Blondeau Science du navigateur. 4. R. S.
Juan Examen maritimo. 2 v. 4. Madr. 1771. French, by Levêque. Paris, 1783.
E. M. Marine. 3 v. By Blondeau and Vial du Clairbois.
Elements of rigging and seamanship. 2 v. 4.
Lescailler Vocabulaire de marine.
Romme Art de la marine. 4. Paris, 1787. Extract. Pap. on N. A. II. i. 46.
Papers on naval architecture. 2 vol. 8. Lond. R. I.
 *Literature of shipbuilding, by Captain Muller. I. ii. 1.
 Petty's outline of naval philosophy. I. i. 30.
Falconer's marine dictionary. 4. 1789. R. I.
Ciscàr Maquinas y maniobras. f. Madrid, 1791. B. B.
Hutchinson's seamanship and naval architecture. 4. 1794. R. I.

Robison. Enc. Br. Art. Seamanship.
Böttcher on ships. Gilb. VI. 448.
Charnock's history of marine architecture. 3 v. 4. Lond. 1800. R. I.
Clarke's history.

Effects of Wind and Water.

On the effect of a sail. Emers. mech. f. 200.
Euler on the resistance to a ships bows. A. P. 1778. 597. H. 40.
Euler on the swinging of a ship at anchor. A. Petr. II. ii. 150.
Edgeworth's remark on bent sails. See resistance of fluids.
On the point vélique. Pap. on N. A. II. i. 19.

According to theory, if lines were drawn parallel to the directions of a ship's course, the wind, and the sails respectively, so as to form a triangle, a circle being drawn round the triangle, the ship ought to arrive at any part of the circle in an equal time. But the fact is far otherwise. Robison.

The lee way is found to remain nearly the same in various directions of the wind. Robison.

When the sails are taken in, the ship is found to have a tendency to turn her head to the wind. Robison.

Greasing a ship's bottom is supposed to lessen the friction, and the experiments of the society for naval architecture show, that a watersoaked plank is more resisted than a dry one. Coulomb however found little or no effect from oiling or greasing wood.

Effect of oars. See modes of rowing.

Naval Architecture, and forms of Ships.

Docks. See hydraulic architecture.
Ph. tr. abr. I. viii. 588. VI. viii. 465.
Witsen's scheeps bouw en bestier. f. Amsterd. 1671. M. B.
Acc. Ph. tr. 1671. VI. 3006.
Meibomius de triremium fabrica. 4. Amst. 1671. M. B.
Acc. Ph. tr. 1671. VI. 3071.

Dalesme on sheathing with lead. A. P. 1716. H. 140.
Mairan's method of gauging ships. A. P. 1724. 227.
Boats. Leup. Th. Pontif. t. 1, 2.
Gallon's mode of launching vessels. A. P. 1731. H. 90.
Duhamel Architecture navale. 4. Par. 1758. R. I.
Acc. A. P. 1752. H. 141.
Boat. Emers. mech. f. 199.
Parts of a ship. Emers. mech. f. 276.
Bouguer Traité du navire.
Extr. in Bézout Cours de math.
Cay on Cumberland's method of bending planks. Ph. tr. 1775. 22.
Gordon's principles of naval architecture. 8.
Murray on shipbuilding. 4. M. B.
Stalkart's naval architecture. f.
Pallas on wood for shipbuilding. A. Petr. III. ii. H. 7.
Dumaitz Traité de la construction des vaisseaux.
Elements of rigging and seamanship. 2 v. 4.
Boats. E. M. Pl. I. Charpentier. Pl. 28, 29. E. M. Physique. Art. Bateau.
Preservation from worms. E. M. A. VII. Art. Sud.
Euler on the construction of vessels, by Watson.
Mackay. Enc. Br. Art. Shipbuilding.
Randall on training oaks for naval purposes. S. A. XIII. 212. Repert. V. 101.
*Atwood on the stability of ships. Ph. tr. 1796. 46. Papers on Naval Arch. II. iii. 1. Ph. tr. 1798. 201.

Considers the inclination of a body when equal to a given angle, and not as evanescent; shows by the example of a square beam, that the effect of a finite inclination must in practice be of consequence; examines the actual stability of various forms in different circumstances, and applies the theory to the dimensions of the ship Cuffnells. Corrects some errors relative to the metacentric curve.

On increasing the velocity of ships. Papers on nav. arch. I. iii. 164.

On the forms and properties of ships. Papers on nav. arch. II. i. 1.

Chapman on finding the centres of gravity of ships. Papers on nav. arch. II. ii. 85.

Chapman on the measurement of ships. Papers on nav. arch. II. iii. 76.

Donithorne's patent metal for sheathing. Repert. VI. 308.
A mixture of tin and zinc.

Sir. G. Shee on the construction of ships. Ir. tr. VI. 15. Repert. IX. 339.

Bosquet's patent for improving ships. Rep. IX. 381.
A composition for keeping off rats.

Charnock's history of marine architecture.

Phillips's tubes for driving copper bolts. S. A. XIX. 274. Nich. 8. III. 35.
To prevent their heads being flattened.

Montucla and Lalande. IV. 381.

Penneck's patent for improvements in shipbuilding. Repert. ii. I. 325.

Brindley's patent for securing ship's beams. Repert. ii. III. 1.

Boswell's patent for triangular framing. Nich. IX. 166.

Elements and practice of naval architecture. f. London, 1805.
Coulomb recommends, that when ships are launched, oak should be made to slide on elm, previously well rubbed with tallow by drawing heavy weights over it; and that care should be taken to avoid too great a velocity, which melts the tallow and increases the friction.

A man of war of 74 guns requires about 3000 loads of timber, of 50 cubic feet each, worth, at L.5 a load, L.15000. A tree contains about 2 loads, and 3000 loads would cover 14 acres. The value of shipping in general is estimated at L.9 or L.10 a ton.

It is said that 180 000 pounds of hemp are required for the rigging of a first rate man of war.

Masts.

Bouguer. A. P. 1745. 309. Pr. I. viii. II.

A. P. Prix. II. i.

Camus. A. P. Prix. II. ii.

Romme Art de la mâture. 1778.

E. M. Pl. V. Marine. Pl. 20, 139.

Pakenham's temporary masts. S. A. X. 214.

Smart's patent for hollow masts. Repert. XIV. 17.

Levêque's masts. M. Inst. V. 16.

Rudders.

Pakenham's temporary rudder. S. A. VII. 218.

Pakenham's mode of preserving a rudder. S. A. XI. 183.

Bolton's patent rudder. Repert. XVI. 152.
Captain T. Hamilton hangs his rudder so that it may be raised when it strikes, without being unshipped, and fixes the tiller on the head of the rudder, instead of putting it into a mortise of the rudder.

Sails.

Sailmaker's assistant. Lond.

Blocks.

Hopkinson's spring block. Am. tr. III. 331.
To prevent the ship's heeling, from too sudden an impulse of the wind.

Cables. See Cordage.

Mode of securing cables. A. P. I. 287.

Perrault's machine for the preservation of cables. M. A. I. 45.

Anchors.

J. Bernoulli. A. P. Prix. III. iv.

Trésaquet. A. P. Prix. III. v.

D. Bernoulli. A. P. Prix. III. vi.

Poleni. A. P. Prix. III. vii.

Duhamel Art de la fabrique des ancres. f. Paris.
  Acc. A. P. 1761. H. 152.
E. M. A. I. Art. Ancres.
Enc. Br. Art. Anchor.
Smeaton's reports.
  Suggests cast iron for anchors.
Stuard's patent anchors. Repert. V. 380.
Chapman on anchors. Gilb. VI. 81.

Oars.
E. M. A. VI. 702. Art. Avirronnier.
Pott's patent oars. Repert. VI. 160.

Particular kinds of Ships and Boats.
Sir W. Petty's boats. Birch. I. 183.
Duquet's vessel impelled by mechanism. Mach. A. III. 41.
Drouet's ferry boat. Mach. A. IV. 39.
Schank's sketch of boats with sliding keels. R. S.
Rafts. E. M. A. III. Art. Flottage.
A life boat for frozen rivers. Roz. XXXIX. 245.
Patterson's improved river boats. Am. tr. IV. 298.
Wheel boats. Chapman on canals.
Lukin's patent boats that will not overset. Repert. III. 10.
Miller's patent vessel that cannot founder. Repert. VI. 18.
Thomason's fireship. Repert. X. 399.
Ice boat. Willich's dom. enc. Art. Boat.
Boswell's patent vessels. Repert. ii. II. 81. Nich. II. 166.
Greathead's life boat. S. A. XX. 320. Ph. M. XV. 331. Repert. ii. II. 409.
Account of Greathead's life boat. 8. 1804. R I.

Bridges of Boats.
Camus's floating bridge. Mach. A. III. 13, 15.
D'Hermand's floating bridge. A. P. 1713. H. 77. Mach. A. III. 17.
Dubois's opening bridge of boats. A. P. 1727. H. 142. Mach. A. V. 13.
Gallon's floating bridge. Mach. A. VI. 101.
Guillaute's floating bridge. A. P. 1748. H. 121.
Pommier's bridge of boats. A. P. 1752. H. 150. Mach. A. VII. 431.
Flying bridge on a rapid river. E. M. Pl. I. Charpentier. Pl. 17.

Modes of rowing and impelling Boats and Ships.

Duquet's revolving oars. Mach. A. I. 173.
Chazelles on Duquet's mode of rowing. A. P. 1702. 98.
Duquet and Chazelles on revolving oars. Ph. tr. 1721. XXXI. 239.
Lahire on the force required for moving boats. A. P. 1702. 254. H. 126.
Camus's modes of applying oars. Mach. A. II. 45, 47, 49.
Martenot's union of several oars. Mach. A. II. 65.
De Saxe's machine for impelling a galley. Mach. A. V. 127.
Limousin's mode of working the oars of a galley. Mach. A. VI. 103.
Euler on Ja. Bernoulli's mode of impelling vessels. N. C. P. I. 106.
Euler on the action of oars. A. Petr. X. 22. A. Berl. 1747. 180.
Euler on forcing ships against a stream by its own force. A. Petr. 1780. IV. i. 119.
  Possible, but not advantageous.
Masson's revolving oars. Mach. A. VII. 297.
Babut's oars for galleys. A. P. 1762. H. 192.
On the improvement of oars for galleys. Act. Helv. V. 205.

Kratzenstein's mode of propelling boats. N. C. Petr. II. 214.

Krafft on the force of a new kind of oars. N. C. Petr. XX. 343.

Invented by Bernoulli; to be drawn backwards and forwards under water: supposed from theory to be very advantageous.

Franklin. Am. tr. II. 294. Roz. XXXI.

Bache's patent propeller. Repert. VI. 163.

A kind of pump.

Thomason's fire ship to be rowed by steam. Repert. X. 399.

With machinery for steering it.

Lorgna on the motions of ships with oars. Soc. Ital. II. 457.

Fussel's machine for moving boats. Repert. XI. 7.

Symington's steam boat. Journ. R. I., I.

Towing.

Lahire. A. P. 1702. 254. H. 126.

Dalesme's ropes for towing boats. A. P. 1706. 139.

Martenot's machine. Mach. A. II. 25.

Duquet's machine. Mach. A. II. 31. V. 95.

Chabert's machine. Mach. A. II. 177.

Drouet's machine. Mach. A. IV. 43.

Boulogne's machine. A. P. 1726. H. 72. Mach. A. IV. 203.

Caron's machine. Mach. A. IV. 213.

Comte de Saxe's machine. Mach. A. VI. 37.

Duvivier's machine. Mach. A. VI. 195.

Machine for towing. E. M. Pl. I. Charpentier. Pl. 25, 26.

Modes of raising and removing Ships.

Redingues's manner of weighing vessels. Mach. A. I. 203.

Du Mé's machine for drawing ships on shore. Mach. A. II. 9.

Blanchart's machine for drawing ships on shore. Mach. A. II. 55, 57.

Lahire's modes of raising vessels. A. P. 1703. 299. Mach. A. II. 69.

Ressin's mode of loading and unloading ships. Mach. A. III. 29.

Tremel's machine for floating boats. A. P. 1717.

Goubert's mode of weighing the ship Tajo. A. P. 1742. H. 135. S. E. II. 501.

Bonvoux's mode of raising a hulk. S. E. V. 394.

Barnard on the removal of damaged ships. Ph. tr. 1780. 100.

By building false bottoms.

Whidbey on the recovery of the Ambuscade. Ph. tr. 1803. 321.

Sepping's mode of suspending ships under repair. S. A. XXII. 276.

Preservation of Ships and their Crews.

Huygens's mode of saving vessels that strike. Mach. A. I. 73.

Figuières's preservation of boats passing bridges. A. P. 1717. H. 84. Mach. A. III. 119.

Mode of stopping holes. Pap. on N. A. II. iii. 51.

On saving lives by shooting a rope. Ph. M. IV. 247.

On sweetening salt water. See Meteorology, Water.

Swimming and Diving.

Borelli and Mersennus on submarine navigation. Hooke. Ph. coll. n. 2. p. 36.

Air jackets. Leup. Th. Pontif. t. 1, 2.

Bachstrom's Kunst zu schwimmen. 8. Berl. 1742.

Bazin on swimming. Hamb. Mag. I. III. and XXI.

Robertson on the specific gravity of men. Ph. tr. 1757. 30.

Gelacy's jacket for supporting men. A. P. 1757. H. 179.

Franklin's works. Letter 55.

Wilkinson on the buoyancy of cork. Ph. tr. 1765. 95.

La Chapelle's scaphander, or swimming dress. A. P. 1765. H. 139.

Thévenot Art de nager. Par. 1781.

Diving. E. M. A. VI. Art. Plongeur. Art. Nacre.

Bernardi Arte ragionata del noto. 2 v. 4. Napl. 1794. R. S.

Klingert on a new diving machine. Ph. M. III. 59.

Spencer's marine spencer. Ph. M. XVI. 172.

Lawson on saving lives. Ph. M. XX. 362.
By means of a common hat tied up in a handkerchief.

Instruments subservient to Seamanship.

Measuring a Ship's way.

Hooke's waywiser for a ship. Birch. IV. 230.
Revolving.

Pourchef's watch. Mach. A. III. 203.

Saumarez's marine surveyor. Ph. tr. 1725. XXXIII. 411.
A revolving Y fixed to a rope as an axis, and making a turn in every ten feet.

Saumarez's further account of his marine surveyor. Ph. tr. 1729. 45.
Substitutes sometimes a wheel with oblique floatboards for the fly or Y. The fly revolved somewhat oftener in a given space as the motion was more rapid.

Dubuisson's machine. Mach. A. VI. 87.

Bouguer's log. A. P. 1747. 644. H. 96.

Bouguer on the corrections of the pilots. A. P. 1752. 1. H. 125.

Poleni. A. P. Pr. II. viii.

Smeaton's experiments on measuring a ship's way. Ph. tr. 1754. 532.
By a revolving plate.

Hopkinson's machines. Am. tr. II. 159. III. 239. Repert. I. 49. Papers on nav. arch. II. i. 33.
One by the inclination of an oar, the other by a tube with oil.

Cooke's instrument with a spring. Ir. tr. 1789. III. 117. Nich. V. 265. Ph. M. XII. 311.

Gould's patent logs, with wheelwork. Rep. XIII. 225. XV. 227.

Hamilton's substitute for a log. Papers on nav. arch. Repert. ii. I. 355.
A reservoir with an orifice constantly discharging.

See hydrodynamic measures.

Sounding.

Hooke's sounding instrument. Birch. I. 307. III. 397.
With an apparatus for bringing up water.

Cook's machine for sounding the sea. Ph. tr. 1746. XLIV. 146.
By observing the time of its descent and ascent.

Charnock's sea gage. Repert. II. 180.
With a fly and wheelwork.

Ph. M. XI. 359.
Humbolt has observed that the sea is colder near shallows.

Massey's patent for sounding at sea. Repert. ii. III. 171.
With rotatory motion.

See measuring instruments.

Measures of the Wind.

D'ons en Bray's machine for showing the direction of the wind at sea. A. P. 1731. 236.

Bouvet's machine for measuring the force of the wind at sea. Mach. A. VI. 153.

See meteorological instruments.

Marine Quadrants.

E. M. Pl. V. Marine. Pl. 106.
Enc. Br. Art. Quadrant.
See astronomical instruments.

HYDRAULIC INSTRUMENTS AND MACHINES, FOR PRODUCING MOTION IN FLUIDS.

Regulations of Discharge.

*Hero.

Hero's clepsydra was a siphon supported by a float and bent over the side of the vessel.

Boyle's lamp. Hooke. Ph. Coll. n. 2. p. 33.

Kept full by a supply from an inverted reservoir at a distance.

A lamp by Hooke. Birch. II. 155.

The second of his Lampas.

Hooke's lampas. 4. Lond. 1677. Lect. Cutl.

Proposes a variety of methods for keeping a lamp full. 1. A moveable vessel with a partition, of half the specific gravity of oil, balanced so that the surface of the oil in one of the compartments is always at the same heigh. 2. A semicylindrical or hemispherical counterpoise of half the specific gravity of oil, moveable on its axis. 3. A float on a hinge at the edge of a moveable vessel. 4. A simple float within a glass vessel. 5. A float supporting a lamp at a distance. 6. 7. A counterpoise acting on a spiral fusee. 8. A vessel with oil suspended by a counterpoise below a fixed plug which fits it.

Observes, that an equable discharge from an orifice may be thus produced, and employed for the measurement of time by the graduation of the counterpoise: and that two such cavities may be made to discharge their fluids into each other, and to be alternately raised and depressed by the preponderance.

A lamp kept full by water dropping into a branch of the vessel. Ph. tr. 1698. XX. 378.

Varignon's mode of making clepsydras. A. P. 1699. 51. H. 99.

Bernoulli on clepsydras, or hour glasses. A. P. Pr. I. iv.

Perronnier's float regulator. Mach. A. VII. 395.

Supporting a cone or conoid, which passes through the orifice, and regulates its magnitude.

Preigney's oil candle, or lamp of Amiens, with a pump. Mach. A. VII. 395.

Keir's hydrostatic lamp. Repert. VIII. 289. Nich. III. 467. Gilb. VI. 96.

Edelcrantz's statical lamp. Nich. 8. V. 93.

Steevens on equalising the discharge of fluids. Ph. M. XX. 289.

See sources of light.

Pipes and Simple Fountains.

The ancients did not use leaden pipes, because they thought them unwholesome. Palladius Mens. August.

Vitruvius.

Papin's siphon always full. Birch. IV. 350.

Papin found that a siphon stopped after a quarter of an hour, from the extrication of air. Birch. IV. 400.

Mariotte on the resistance of waterpipes. A. P. I. 69.

Cassini on the waters and fountains at Modena. A. P. I. 93.

Mariotte on the supply of fountains, and on the resistance of pipes. A. P. I. 170, 225.

Observation on conduits. A. P. I. 284.

Lahire on springs and cisterns. A. P. 1703. 56. H. 1.

Leupold Th. hydrotechn.

Desaguliers on the running of water in pipes. Ph. tr. 1726. 77.

Found the discharge of a long pipe only $\frac{1}{7}$ of the full quantity, and attributed the difference to air in the pipe. This may have had some little effect, but Buat's simplest rule gives only $\frac{1}{7}$ in the case of the experiment.

Pitot on the distribution of water. A. P. 1735. 244. H. 70.

Waterpipes and fountains. Belidor Arch. Hydr. II. i. 265. pl. n. 54, 55.

Deparcieux on conduits. A. P. 1750. 39. H. 153.

Euler on fountains. N. C. Petr. VI. 379.
Bossut Hydrodynamique.
Pipes and fountains. E. M. A. III. Art. Fontainier.
Finding springs. E. M. A. VII. Art. Sources.
Siphon. E. M. A. VII. Art. Syphon.
Pipes. E. M. A. VIII. Art. Tuyaux.
Darwin on an artificial spring. Ph. tr. 1785. 1.

Some pipes being fixed so as to pass through a stratum of clay into a lower stratum, they brought the water above the surface, and discharged 3 or 4 hogsheads in 24 hours.

Ferrari on the distribution of waters. Soc. Ital. VII. 157.
On pipes. Leipz. Intelligenz blatt. 1794. 159.
Langsdorfs Hydr. Pl. 4.
Grossart on manufacturing elastic gum. Repert. I. 70, 131.
Vulliamy on the means employed to obtain an overflowing well. Ph. tr. 1797. 325. Nich. II. 276. Repert. X. 181.

The water ran at first mixed with sand, which hardened and stopped it; and when this was removed, the same happened again. At last by raising the sand out of the water by means of an iron box, the water was made to overflow, so that 40 gallons were discharged in a minute.

Venturi on the motion of fluids.
Hornblower's mode of laying waterpipes. Repert. X. 251.
Wilkinson's patent pipes. Repert. XVI. 92.
Wright on preventing the freezing of water in pipes. Ph. M. XIX. 147.
Barber on preventing the freezing of water in pipes. Ph. M. XX. 209.

The best aperture for a jet is about 1¼ inch: such a jet rises 79 feet when the height of the reservoir is 100. Cavallo N. Ph.

At Petersburg there are two jets 9 inches in diameter that rise 60 feet. Robison.

Desaguliers says, that 140 feet of 7 inch lead pipe require a thickness of ⅜ inch. Belidor, that 60 feet Fr. of 18 inch pipe require half an inch. If we multiply the length in feet by the diameter in inches, the thickness must be about 1/100 of the product, in inches.

Appendages to Pipes. Valves, Stopcocks, and Filters.

Papin's pneumatic filter. Birch. IV. 966.
Amontons on valves. A. P. 1703. H. 95.
Amy's filtering machines. A. P. 1745. H. 82. 1748. H. 121. Mach. A. VII. 280.
Desaguliers. Ph. tr. 1726. XXXIV.

Describes the apparatus for discharging air by tall pipes: objects to a valve with cork, supposing that it will not open: but the orifice may be made very small.

Valves. Belidor Arch. Hydr. II. i. 122. Pl. n. 8. Valve unequally divided by an axis. Pl. n. 31.
Préaux's tap for drawing wine. A. P. 1763. H. 146.
Deparcieux's traps for drains. A. P. 1767. H. 133.
Westgarth's valve. S. A. V. 192.
Bramah's patent watercock. Repert. I. 561.
Bramah's patent apparatus for drawing off liquors. Repert. IX. 361.
Hempel's patent filtering vessels. Repert. II. 230.
Strong's patent for improved pistons and valves. Repert. VII. 373.

T valves and screws.

Collier's apparatus for filtering. Ph. M. VI. 240.
Peacock's patent for filtering. Repert. XI. 221.

By ascent.

Filtering wells. Repert. XVI. 331.
Filtering machines. Gilb. XIII. 108.
A joint for steam tubes. Nich. 8. IV. 107.
Harman's filter. Nich. VIII. 126.
Parrot's filter. Nich. IX. 40.
Sir H. Englefield's filter, with sand. Nich. IX. 95.

The perforation of a valve, as well as the aperture of an air vessel, might with advantage be trumpet shaped. Robison.

Machines for raising Water. Pumps of all kinds, Fire Engines, and Fountains not simple.

Vitruvius.
Ramelli.
Strada Wasserkünsten. f. Frankf. 1617. M. B. Cologne, 1623.
De Caus Inventions hydrauliques. f. M. B.
Cavalleri's hydracontisterium and Prince Rupert's engine. Birch. I. 285.
   Both made by one cylinder revolving within another, the internal one having a sliding valve, like Bramah's patent.
†Moreland's undertaking to raise water. Ph. tr. 1674. IX. 25.
Description of a fire engine. Ph. tr. 1676. XI. 679.
Conyers's cheap pump. Ph. tr. 1677. XII. 888.
   Made of wood, square and tapering: the bottom 6 inches square.
†Papin's secret way of raising water, with various conjectures upon it. Ph. tr. 1685. XV. 1093, 1254, 1274.
   A trick, a communication being formed by means of air; which the author proposes to extend to a great distance.
Papin's engine for raising water. Ph. tr. 1686. XVI. 263.
Papin Recueil de pièces touchant quelques machines. 8. Cassel, 1695.
   Acc. Ph. tr. 1697. XIX. 481.
   Describes the centrifugal or Hessian pump.
†Rule for judging of the goodness of hydraulic machines. A. P. I. 170.
Perrault's new piston for pumps. A. P. I. 249. Mach. A. I. 9.
Perrault's hydraulic machine. Mach. A. I. 27.
Cusset's hydraulic pendulum. A. P. II. 20. Mach. A. I. 95.

Lahire's hydraulic machine with little friction. A. P. IX. 161.
Lahire's application of the epicycloid to pumps. A. P. IX. 284.
Lahire's perpetual pump. A. P. 1716. 322.
Of jets. Mariotte Oeuvres. Traité des mouvemens des eaux.
Joly's hydraulic invention. Mach. A. I. 75.
Amontons's pump. Mach. A. I. 103.
A hydraulic machine. Mach. A. I. 113.
Francini's hydraulic machine. Mach. A. I. 145.
A fire engine. Mach. A. I. 151.
Cordamoy's hydraulic machine. Mach. A. I. 205.
Billettes's two hydraulic wheels. A. P. 1699. 184. H. 114.
Gay's hydraulic machine. Mach. A. II. 13.
L'heureux's hydraulic machine. Mach. A. II. 191.
Lafaye's hydraulic machine. A. P. 1717. 67. H. 70.
Joué's hydraulic wheel. A. P. 1717. H. 84. Mach. A. III. 123, 127.
Martenot's hydraulic machine. Mach. A. III. 157.
Marchand's artificial fountain. Mach. A. III. 191.
Auger's pump rods. A. P. 1721. H. 97. Mach. A. IV. 19.
Auger's hydraulic machine. Mach. A. IV. 181.
Cabinet de M. de Servière.
Desaguliers's improvement of Haskins's mercurial pump. Ph. tr. 1722. XXXII. 5.
   The objection is, that the mercury becomes oxidated.
Ublemann's fire engine. A. P. 1722. H. 122. Mach. A. IV. 35.
†Perpoint's piston moving always in a parallel direction. A. P. 1722. H. 121. Mach. A. IV. 33.

Hydraulic machines. Leupold. Theatr. Hydraul.

Tielen en Van der Horst theatrum machinarum.

Dufay's pump to be used as a fire engine. A. P. 1725. 35. H. 78.

Laesson's pump. Mach. A. IV. 145.

Mey and Meyer's hydraulic machine. A. P. 1726. H. 71.

Beighton on the waterworks at London bridge. Ph. tr. 1731. XXXVII. 5.

_{They raised about 35000 hogsheads 120 feet high in a day.}

Denisart and de la Deuille's hydraulic machine. Mach. A. V. 159.

Lebrun's hydraulic machine. A. P. 1731. H. 91.

Ledemoust's hydraulic machine. A. P. 1732. H. 118. Mach. A. VI. 9.

Churchman's engine for raising water. Ph. tr. 1734. XXXVIII. 402.

_{Worked by horses walking in and on a wheel, harnessed to a fixed point: disapproves of cranks.}

Centrifugal pump. Mach. A. VI. 13.

Boulogne's hydraulic machine. Mach. A. VI. 15.

Boulogne's piston without friction. Mach. A. VI. 85.

Saulm's hydraulic machine. Mach. A. VI. 19.

Gallon's hydraulic machine. Mach. A. VI. 173.

Deparcieux's hydraulic machine. A. P. 1735. H. 101. Mach. A. VII. 29.

Lebrun's new piston A. P. 1735. H. 102.

Drussen's pump. A. P. 1735. H. 102.

Renou's hydraulic machine. A. P. 1735. H. 103.

Bertier's hydraulic machine. A. P. 1735. H. 103.

Pitot's new theory of pumps. A. P. 1735. 327. H. 72. 1739. 393. 1740. 511.

Pitot on the screw of Archimedes. A. P. 1736. 173. H. 110.

Polley theatrum machinarum. Amst. 1737.

Bernoullii hydrodynamica.

_{Screw of Archimedes.}

Bernoulli on the spiral pump. N. C. Petr. XVII. 249.

Camus on the best application of buckets. A. P. 1739. 157. H. 49.

Camus on the best proportions of pumps. A. P. 1739. 287. H. 49.

Gensanne's improvements of pumps. A. P. 1741. H. 163.

Gensanne's fire engine. Mach. A. VII. 95.

Geffrier's hydraulic machine. A. P. 1743. H. 168.

Dupuy's pump. Mach. A. VII. 85.

Amy's hydraulic machine. A. P. 1745. H. 82. Mach. A. VII. 277.

Thillay's fire engine. A. P. 1746. H. 120.

Bonnet's fire engine. A. P. 1749. H. 182.

Euler on Demours's mode of raising water by centrifugal force. A. Berl. 1751. 305.

Euler on pumps. A. Berl. 1752. 149, 185.

Euler on the screw of Archimedes. N. C. Petr. V. 259.

Preigney's oil candle, with a pump. Mach. A. VII. 395.

Jacquet's piston for sucking pumps. A. P. 1752. H. 148.

Bélidor Arch. Hydr. Chain pumps. I. i. 360. Chain piston pumps and square pumps. Pl. n. 58. Bucket wheel. Pl. n. 39. Chained buckets. Pl. n. 39, 40. Water shovel. Pl. n. 41. Troughs with a valve. Pl. n. 41. Quadrant pump. Pl. n. 41. Hand buckets. Pl. n. 42. Zigzag or swinging troughs. Pl. n. 43. Swinging bucket wheel. Pl. n. 44. System of spiral pipes. Pl. n. 44. Pumps. II. i. 53. Pistons. 114. Machines appplied to pumps. 132. Fire engine. 186. Machine at Marly. 198. Machine of the Pont Notre Dame. 204. Various hydraulic machines. 235, 308. Artificial fountains. 389. Windmills for draining and watering. Pl. n. 2..4. Balance pump for treading. Pl. n. 10. Ellipses instead of cranks. Pl. n. 13, 14. Buckets for deep mines. Pl. n. 44, 45. On watering. II. ii. l. 4.

<small>Belidor's piston has too much friction. Robison.</small>

Darcy on hydraulic machines. A. P. 1754. 679. H. 138.

Veltman's hydraulic wheel. A. P. 1756. H. 129.

Emerson's mechanics. Rag pump or chain pump for cleaning foul water. f. 254. Forcing pump. f. 267. Lifting pump. f. 268. Archimedes's screw. f. 272. Fire engine. f. 275. Waterworks. f. 281. Pumps with arched beams, called a bob gin. f. 296. Horse pump. f. 299.

Hell's hydraulic siphon. A. P. 1760. H. 160.

Varau's hydraulic machine. A. P. 1760. H. 162.

Limbourg's hydraulic machine. A. P. 1761. H. 154.

Loriot's endless chain for wells. A. P. 1761. H. 161.

Van Zyl Theatr. mach. Amst. 1761.

<small>Throwing wheels.</small>

Wolfe's description of Hero's fountain at Schemnitz. Ph. tr. 1762. 547.

Deparcieux's piston with little friction. A. P. 1762. 1. H. 182.

Calvör vom oberharze. Brunsw. 1763.

Nollet's pumps for raising water 55 feet. A. P. 1766. H. 150.

Ziegler on the spiral pump. Gesellsch. zu Zürich. III.

Mezieres's windmill for drawing water. A. P. 1767. H. 185.

Hennert sur la vis d'Archimede. Berl. 1767.

*Borda on pumps. A. P. 1768. 418. H. 122.

Jars on the machine at Schemnitz. S. E. V. 67.

Quentin's forcing and sucking pump. A. P. 1769. H. 130.

Ferguson's mech. exerc. Machine at Schemnitz. 102. Lahire's pump. 109.

Bertier's machine for raising water by mercury. A. P. 1770. H. 117.

Poda Beschreibung der Maschinen zu Schemnitz. Prag. 1771.

Delius Anleitung zur Bergbaukunst. 4. Vienna, 1773.

Karstens Abhandlung über die Feuerspritzen. Greifsw. 1773.

Karstens lehrbegriff der mathematik.

Meister on the machine at Schemnitz. N. C. Gott. 1773. IV. 169.

<small>With a plan for multiplying it.</small>

Klügel über die Feuerspritzen. Berl. 1774.

Whitehurst's account of the machine executed at Oulton in Cheshire in 1772, for raising water by its momentum. Ph. tr. 1775. 277. Repert. VIII. 338.

<small>Since called in France the hydraulic ram.</small>

Venel on a new hydraulic machine at Orbe. M. Laus. II. 81.

<small>A long chain of small leathern buckets moved by a water wheel.</small>

Buat Hydraulique.

Fougeroux Art de l'ardoisier.

Wright on watering meadows. 8.

Dugdale on embanking and draining fens. f.

Turner on draining bogs. 8.

B. Martin on pump work. Reprinted Ph. M. XX. 223, 291.

<small>With a description of a patent pump; the pistons working in bags, to avoid friction.</small>

Würtz's spiral pump. Bailey's mach. I. 151.

Merryman's plunger pump. Bailey's mach. I. 154.

<small>The sails bad.</small>

Blandford's piston. Bailey's mach. I. 163.

Pumps compared. Bailey's mach. I. 188.

Collier's windmill with a scoop wheel and ladle. Bailey's mach. II. 37, 43.

Westgarth's hydraulic machine. Bailey's mach. II. 52.

Water whimsey. E. M. Pl. I. Pl. 14.

Waterworks. E. M. Pl. I. Pl. 23, 24.

Some hydraulic machines. E. M. A. III. Art. Instrumens de Mathématique.

Pumps. E. M. A. VI. Art. Pompes.

Chain buckets used at Rochfort. E. M. Pl. V. Marine. Pl. 89.

Ship pump. E. M. Pl. V. Marine. Pl. 156. xii.

Machine at Marly. E. M. Pl. VII. Hydraulique.

Hydraulic amusements. E. M. Pl. VIII. Pièces hydrauliques.

Watering engine, trough pumps, screw of Archimedes, and forcing pump. E. M. Art. Aratoire.

Rozier on Vera's rope machine. Roz. XX. 132.

Landriani description d'une machine. 8. R. S.
A rotatory pump.

Fabre sur les machines hydrauliques. 4. Par. 1783.

Hydraulic machines, Perronet Description des projets des ponts de Neuilly. Par. 1783.

Nicander on the spiral pump. Schwed. Abh. 1783, 1784.

Throwing wheels. Büsch mathematik zum nützen. II.

Bianchi's breast pump. Roz. XXVII. 198.

Ja. Bernoulli on a centrifugal hydraulic machine. N. A. Petr. 1786. IV. 158.
Finds that ⅔ of the force is lost.

Descharmes on raising water by centrifugal force. Roz. XXX. 192.

Wex Machine hydraulique. 8. Nantes, 1787. R. S.

Dansey's machine for draining ponds. S. A. VIII. 191.

Detrouville's hydraulic machine. Roz. XXXVIII. 299.
A compound pneumatic apparatus. A similar apparatus is described in Darwin's phytologia, and in Willich's dom. enc. Art. Water.

Hydraulic wheel. Enc. Br. Art. Moss.

Centrifugal pump. Enc. Br. Pl. 136.

*Robison. Enc. Br. Art. Pumps, Waterworks.

Butler's bucket and machine for raising water. S. A. XII. 289.

Russel's bucket for deep water. S. A. Ph. M. XVIII. 271.

Centrifugal pumps. Langsdorfs Hydr. Pl. 17.
Once supposed to be capable of producing a perpetual motion. A double one. Pl. 50.

*Forcing pumps of various kinds and all their parts. Langsd. Hydr. Pl. 26 .. 33.

*Fire engine. Langsd. Hydr. Pl. 41, 42, 45.

Chains of buckets, bead pumps, and cellular pumps. Langsd. Hydr. Pl. 43.

Water screws. Langsd. Hydr. Pl. 44, 48.

Montgolfier's hydraulic ram, approved by the Institute. Journ. Phys. XLVI. (III.) 143. Bull. Soc. Phil. n. 8. Montucla and Lal. III. 769. Gilb. I. 363.
Like Whitehurst's and Bolton's.

Viallon on the hydraulic ram.
With various combinations.

Extr. Journ. Phys. XLVI. (III.) 288.

Skey's patent pump. Repert. II. 301.
With smoke jack fans.

Bramah's rotatory hydraulic machine. Rep. II. 73.

Bramah's patent fire engine. Repert. III. 368.

Spiral pump. Lempe Magazin der Bergbaukunst. xi. Dresd. 1795.

Dearborn's pump engine and fire engine. Am. Ac. I. 520. Repert. III. 119.

Davies on irrigation. Repert. III. 43, 123.

Pitt on irrigation. Repert. III. 239.

Busse on fire engines, against Karstens. Hind. Arch. III. 237.

Buchanan's patent pump. Repert. V. 236. Ph. M. X. 192.

Sylvestre on watering gardens. Repert. V. 423.

Wright on drying marshes. Am. tr. IV. 243.

Smeaton's reports. Hydraulic machines; a ship pump; a fire engine.

Baader Théorie der pumpen. 4. Bayr. 1797. R. I.

Harriott's pump capstan. Papers on Nav. Arch. II. ii. 93.

†Richmond's patent combination of pumps. Repert. VI. 22.

Noble's patent pump. Repert. VII. 107. Gilb. XV. 71.
With two pistons in each chamber, the one perforated.

Simpkin's patent fire engines. Repert. VII. 301.
The valves in chambers.

Strong's patent for improved pistons. Rep. VII. 373.
With screws.

Clarke's method of working ships' pumps. Repert. IX. 105.
By a lever and rope.

Boulton's patent apparatus for raising water. Repert. IX. 145.
Whitehurst's improved.

Bramah's patent apparatus for drawing off liquors. Repert. IX. 361.

Prony's theory of Detrouville's hydraulic siphon. B. Soc. Phil. n. 36. Nich. IV. 283.

On the machine at Schemnitz. Nich. IV. 8.

Boswell's improvements of the machine at Schemnitz, and history of the pressure engine. Nich. IV. 117. Nich. 8. II. 1.

Goodwyn's barometrical machine. Nich. IV. 162. Improved. 342.

Close's mode of raising water by lateral friction. Nich. IV. 293, 493. Nich. 8. I. 145.

Close's application of the siphon. Nich. IV. 547. V. 22. Nich. 8. I. 27.

A mercurial hydraulic engine. Nich. IV. 326.

A new rotatory hydraulic engine. Nich. IV. 466.

Wood's patent hand pump. Repert. X. 321.
A common pump with a rod in collars.

Landen's patent mode of moving pump rods. Repert. XII. 145.

Staton's patent apparatus for raising fluids by the pressure of air. Repert. XIV. 217.

Berger's marine pump approved. M. Inst. IV.

West's centrifugal pump, turned by a spiral pipe. Ph. M. XI. 166.

Eytelwein's handbuch der mechanik und hydraulik.

Chassiron on draining lands. Mem. Soc. d'agric. du dép. de la Seine.

Account of the machine at Marly. Montucla and Lalande. III. 744.

Person's pumps. P. Recueil. Pl. 4.

On Erskine's centrifugal pump. Banks on machines. 41.

Imison's elements. I. Pl. 9.
Good figures.

Van Marum's portable pumps for fires. Ann. Ch. XLVI. 3.

Sarjeant's hydraulic machine. See hydraulic force.

Trevithick's forcer for a pump. Nich. 8. II. 216.

Bailey on draining. Rep. ii. III. 99.

Rope pump. Cavall. N. Ph. II. 441.
With a rope pump, the wheel being 3 feet in diameter, the rope half an inch, the depth of the well 95 feet, a labouring man could produce but 60 revolutions in a minute,

and could not continue the exertion long: this raised 6 gallons in a minute. Much water was raised with 50 turns, but very little with only 30 turns in a minute. The rope soon decays, especially if it is not made of hair.

Sharples on raising water by the fall of waste water. Nich. VII. 298.

A hydraulic machine from Servière's cabinet. Nich. VIII. 35.

Two pinions fitted tight and revolving within a box.

Draining. Dickson's practical agriculture.

Harriott's patent pump capstan is preferred to Dodgson's patent double headed ship pump. The lever works horizontally by means of wheelwork, and this motion is said to be less fatiguing to the men, so that they can work for an hour or more: and a rope may be applied so that any number may work together. The friction is said to be diminished to $\frac{1}{L}$ by applying a guide to the pistons.

A pump should have a valve near the moveable piston, and another below the level of the water. Robison.

A bag like a powder puff with valves makes a good simple pump. Robison.

Quantity of water raised by pumps. See animal force.

PNEUMATIC MACHINES.

*Heronis spiritalia.
Leupold. Th. M. G.
E. M. Pl. VIII. Amusemens de physique.

Machines simply Pneumatic.

Bellows, Fans, and other Mechanical Ventilators.

Papin on the Hessian or rotatory bellows. Ph. tr. 1705. XXIV. 1990.

Knopperf's fan for corn. A. P. 1716. H. 78. Mach. A. II. 101, 103.

Barrières's leathern ventilator. A. P. 1723. H. 120. Mach. A. IV. 53.

Desaguliers's pump ventilator. Ph. tr. 1727. XXXV. 353.

Desaguliers on the centrifugal ventilator. Ph. tr. 1735. XXXIX. 40.

Raynes's bellows. A. P. 1728. H. 108.

Terral's bellows for founderies and forges. A. P. 1729. H. 92. Mach. A. V. 41, 93. VI. 121.

Farel's mode of working bellows. A. P. 1733. H. 99.

Hales on ventilators. 8. 1743. R. I. 2 v. 8. Lond. 1758.

Hales on ventilation. Ph. tr. 1748. XLV. 410.

Hales's ventilator. Bailey's mach. I. 170.

Ellis on the effect of ventilation. Ph. tr. 1751. 211.

A ventilator erected in the Hotel des Invalides. Mach. A. VII. 379.

Pommier's ventilator improved after Hales. Mach. A. VII. 413.

Bellows moved by water. Emers. mech. f. 240, 241.

Smith's bellows. Emers. mech. f. 244.

Blowing wheel. Emers. mech. f. 284.

The Hessian or centrifugal bellows of Papin.

Gensanne's bellows for ventilating mines. S. E. IV. 158.

Jars on the circulation of air in mines. A. P. 1768. 218. H. 18.

Bellows. Gauger Mécanique du feu.

Munier's winnowing machine. Roz. Introd. II. 79.

De Bory on purifying the air of vessels. A. P. 1780. 111. H. 13.

Leroi's simple ventilation by windsails. A. P. 1780. 598. H. 13.

Evers's winnowing machine. Bailey's mach. I. 51.

Fitzgerald's ventilator. Bailey's mach. I. 172.

Hill's ventilator for mercurial vapours. Bailey's mach. II. 70.

Wilson's patent for applying vapours. Rep. XII. 1.

Elastic tubes.

Fans. E. M. A. II. Art. Eventailliste.
Wooden bellows. E. M. Pl. II. Pl. 3.

Ventilation. E. M. A. VIII. Art. Tuyaux aériques, Ventilateur.
Bellows. E. M. M. III. Art. Soufflet.
Ventilators for ships. E. M. Pl. V. Marine. Pl. 156. n. 2.
Wooden fan for corn. E. M. Art. Aratoire.
Hassenfratz's bellows for a blowpipe. Roz. XXVIII. 345.
Rozier's apparatus for breathing in cellars. Roz. XXVIII. 418.
Leblond on the blow pipe. Roz. XXX. 92.
Saint Martin's ventilator. Roz. XXXIII. 161.
Acting by lateral friction.
On antimephitic pumps. Ann. Ch. VI. 86.
Whitehurst on ventilation. 4. Lond. 1794.
Robins on ventilation. Am. tr. III. 324. Repert. I. 119.
Lambert on the theory of bellows. Hind. Arch. III. 1.
Blast machine at Carron. Smeaton's reports.
Böbert von luftwechsel maschinen. 4. Petersb. 1797. R. S.
Salmon's ventilator. Repert. IX. 252.
Boswell's blast ventilator. Nich. IV. 4. Gilb. V. 364.
Roebuck on blast furnaces. See economy of heat.
South's ventilator for corn on shipboard. Repert. XI. 397. Ph. M. V. 393.
Mushet on an airvault. Ph. M. VI. 362.
Sir G. O. Paul's stoves and windows for ventilating hospitals. S. A. XIX. 330. Rep. ii. II. 268.
Polfreeman's winnowing machine. Willich's dom. enc. Art. Winnow.
Bellows. Banks on machines. 9.
Gardner's patent ventilator. Repert. ii. II. 241.
Dobson's patent zephyr. Repert. ii. II. 404.
Haas's blowpipe. Nich. 8. III. 119.

The pistons of large bellows are sometimes fitted with wool and black lead, but Laurie's hydraulic bellows are much preferable. Robison.

We can draw mercury 2 or 3 inches by the lungs, 25 by the mouth; we can force it 5 or 6 inches, but not without pain. Robison.

Air Pumps, Condensers, and Air Guns.

Casp. Schotti mechanica hydraulicopneumatica. 4. 1657.
Boyle's new experiments touching the spring of the air. 8. Oxf. 1660. Works. I. 1.
Boyle's continuation of experiments. Oxf. 1669. Works. III. 1.
Boyle on the rarefaction of air. 4. London, 1671. Works. III. 202.
Boyle's second continuation. 8. Lond. 1681. Works. IV. 96.
Boyle's general history of the air. 4. Lond. 1692. Works. V. 105.
Guericke experimenta nova Magdeburgica. f. Amst. 1672.
Acc. Ph. tr. 1672. VII. 5103.
Papin nouvelles expériences du vuide. 4. Par. 1674.
Papin on shooting by rarefaction. Ph. tr. 1686. XVI. 21.
Gallois on an air gun remaining charged 16 years. A. P. II. 146.
Varignon on the exhaustion of air pumps. A. P. X. 285.
Mariotte de la nature de l'air. 12. Par. 1699. Oeuvr. I. 148.
Senguerd de aeris natura. 4. Lond. 1699.
Leupolds Beschreibung der luftpumpe. 4. Leipz. 1707. 1712.
Leupold. Th. Aerostat.
Hauksbee's physicomechanical experiments.
S'Gravesande's natural philosophy.
Desaguliers's natural philosophy.

Nollet on pneumatic experiments. A. P. 1740. 385, 567. 1741. 338. H. 145.
Smeaton's air pump. Ph. tr. 1751. 415.
Lowitz über die eigenschaften der luft. 1754.
Emers. mechanics. Air pump. f. 277.
Leistens Beschreibung einer luftpumpe. 4. Wolfenb. 1772.
Nairne's experiments on the pear gage, with Smeaton's pump, explained by Cavendish. Ph. tr. 1777. 614.

There still remained some anomalous experiments, in which the pear gage indicated a less complete exhaustion than the barometrical gage.

On Nairne's pneumatic experiments. Roz. XI. 159.
Coulomb on condensing with an air pump of any kind. Roz. XVII. 301.
Greppin and Billiaux on a condenser. Roz. XIX. 438.
Cavallo on Haas and Hurter's pump with a stopcock. Ph. tr. 1783. 435.

The pump when in good order rarefied to $\frac{1}{1000}$.

Cavallo on Nairne's improved air pump. Roz. XXV. 261.

With a figure.

Cuthbertson's description of an air pump. 1783.

Is said to rarefy to $\frac{1}{10000}$.

Ingenhousz Vermischte schriften. 197.

Ingenhousz has proposed to make a vacuum by the absorption of air into ignited charcoal while acting.

Mode of boiling mercury in a gage. Ph. tr. 1785. 276.
Hindenburg de antlia Baaderiana. 4. Leipz. 1787.

A mercurial pump.

Hindenburg de antlia nova. 4. Leipz. 1789. Goth. Mag. V. ii. 81.
Cazalet's air pump. Roz. XXXIV. 334.

A Torricellian vacuum made by means of water.

Hervieu's air pump. Roz. XXXV. 60.
Michel's mercurial air pump. Roz. XXXV. 209.

Schrader's air pump. Gren. III. 357.
On the imperfections of gages. Brook on electricity.
Lichtenberg's account of Smeaton's air pump. Licht in. Erxleb. p. xxxvi.
*Robison. Enc. Br. Art. Pneumatics.
Jones's note on air pumps. Adams's lectures. I. 153.
Prince's air pump. Am. Acad. I. 497.
Prince and Cuthbertson's air pump. Nich. I. 119. Gilb. I. 352.
Prince's improved air pump. Nich. VI. 235.
Sadler's air pump. Nich. I. 441. Gilb. I. 352.
Van Marum's simple air pump. Gilb. I. 379.

With a stopcock turned by external force. Gilbert thinks it preferable to Cuthbertson's, which is said to be liable to become clogged by the thickening of the oil.

Little's air pump. Ir. tr. VI. 319. Nich. II. 501. Gilb. V. I.
Mackenzie's air pump. Nich. II. 28.
On the air pump with metallic valves. Nich. II. 370.
Clare's two air pumps. Nich. IV. 261.

One of them mercurial.

Smith's air pump vapour bath. Ph. M. XIV. 293.
Cuthbertson's air pump, Air gun. Rees's cyclop. II. Plates. Art. Pneumatics.
Edelcrantz's mercurial air pump. Nich. VII. 188.

Swedenberg made a mercurial air pump.

Pneumatic Machines and Apparatus, connected with Hydraulics.

Bellows and Gasholders

Shower bellows. Belidor. Arch. Hydr. II. i. Pl. n. 24.
Bellows and gasholders.
Triewald's water bellows, worked by troughs as a beam. Ph. tr. 1738. XL. 231.

Barthès on shower bellows. A. P. 1742. H. 132. S. E. III. 378.

Stirling on shower bellows. Ph. tr. 1745. XLIII. 315.

Guignon's machine for breathing vapour. Mach. A. VII. 467.

Cavendish. Ph. tr. 1766. 141.

Pneumatic apparatus.

Meusnier on the gazometer. A. P. 1782. 466.

Shower bellows. E. M. Pl. II. Fer. ii. Pl. 34. Trompes.

Venturi's inquiry. Prop. 8.

Boulard's gasholder for making hydrogen. Roz. XXIX. 172.

Saluce on pneumatic apparatus. Mem. Tur. 1788. IV. 83.

Bonati on shower bellows. Soc. Ital. V. 501.

Tries's gazometer. Roz. XL. 116.

Van Marum sur un gazometre. 4. Harl. 1796.

Van Marum's gazometer. Ann. Ch. XII. 113. XIV. 313. Ph. M. II. 85.

Lüdicke on Baader's hydraulic bellows. Gilb. I. 1.

Cavallo's pneumatic apparatus. Ph. M. I. 305.

Robison. Enc. Br. Art. Pneumatics.

Seguin's gazometer. B. Soc. Phil. n. 10.

On gazometers. Gilb. II. 185.

Pepys's mercurial gazometer. Ph. M. V. 154.

Pepys's apparatus for gases. Ph. M. XI. 253.

Pepys's new gasholder. Ph. M. XIII. 153.

Willson's patent for applying vapours. Rep. XII. 1.

Hindmarsh's stream bellows. Repert. XII. 217.

Clayfield's mercurial air holder. Ph. M. VII. 148.

Warwick's gasholder. Ph. M. XIII. 256.

Hornblower's hydraulic bellows. Nich. 8. I. 219.

Read's cheap pneumatic apparatus. Nich. 8. III. 55.

On pneumatic apparatus. Nich. 8. IV. 4.

Edelcrantz's mode of extracting air from boilers supplied by siphons. Nich. VII. 81.

Michelotti's gazometer. Journ. Phys. LIII. 284.

Submarine Apparatus.

Hooke on measuring the depth of the sea. Ph. tr. 1665 .. 6. I. n. 9. n. 14. n. 24.

Boyle and Ray on the bladders of fish. Ph. tr. 1675. X. 114, 310, 349.

On the pressure of water upon sunk bottles. Ph. tr. 1693. XVII. 504.

Halley's art of living under water. Ph. tr. 1716. XXIX. 492. 1721. XXXI. 177.

Halley was one of five that were 9 or 10 fathom under water for an hour and a half. Describes a cap for submarine excursions.

Diving bells. Leup. Th. Pontific. t. 26.

D'Achery on a corked bottle let down 130 fathom. A. P. 1725. H. 6.

Says, that the water forced into it was much less salt than common sea water.

Hales and Desaguliers's machine for measuring the depth of the sea. Ph. tr. 1728. XXXV. 559.

Letting go a weight at the bottom.

Triewald on the diving bell. Ph. tr. 1736. XXXIX. 377.

With a pipe for breathing the cooler part of the air.

Cossigny on an experiment of sinking a corked bottle. A. P. 1737. H. 8.

Krafft on a bottle sunk 60 fathom without effect. A. P. 1745. H. 19.

E. M. Pl. V. Marine. Pl. 159.

Enc. Br. Art. Diving Bell, Sea Gage.

Spalding's diving bell. S. A. I. 236.
Bushnell on submarine vessels. Am. tr. IV. 303. Repert. XV. 385. Nich. IV. 229.
    Like two tortoise shells combined.
Diving bell. Walker's philosophy. Lect. vi.
Fulton's diving boat. Montucla and Lalande. III. 782.
Healy on diving bells. Ph. M. XV. 9.
    Succeeded in supplying the air by a condenser.

Aerostation, either by heated Air, or by Gases.

Lichtenberg suggests the term aerostation.
Lohmeier de artificio navigandi per aerem. 1676. Repr. 4. R. S.
    Lohmeier was of Rinteln.
Rosnier's mode of flying. Hooke. Ph. Coll. n. 1. p. 15.
    Rosnier is said to have descended obliquely over some houses.
Francesco Lana on exhausted globes; after Albertus de Saxonia and Wilkins. Hooke. Ph. Coll. n. 1. p. 18.
Mongez on imitating the flight of birds. Roz. II. 140.
Euler on the ascent of balloons. A. P. 1781. H. 40.
    This paper was found on his slate after his death.
E. M. A. VIII. Théorie des aérostats. E. M. Physique. Art. Ballon.
Report of a committee on Montgolfier's machine. A. P. 1783. H. 5. Roz. XXIV. 81.
Saint Fond sur les expériences de Montgolfier. 8. R. S.
L'Art de faire les ballons. 8. Amst. 1783.
Reneaux sur les machines aérostatiques. 4. R. S.
Galvez sur un moyen de donner la direction aux machines aérostatiques. Ph. tr. 1784. 469.
    An experiment tried with a boat. Three pairs of wings each worked by a man, impelled a boat 95 feet long, at the rate of 303 feet in about 2 minutes, about 2¼ miles an hour.
Martin's hints on aerostatic globes. 8. Lond. 1784.
Robert frères sur les expériences aérostatiques. Par. 1784.
L'Art de voyager dans les airs. 8. Par. 1784.
Bertholon sur les globes aérostatiques. Montpel. 1784.
Parachute. Bertholon's essays.
Krump Geschichte der aerostatik. 2 Parts. 8. Strasb. 1784. Anhang, 1786.
Hallens Magic. II.
Milly on aerostatic experiments. Roz. XXIV. 64, 156.
Cavallo's history and practice of aerostation. 8. Lond. 1785.
Cavallo's N. Ph. IV. 316.
Southern on aerostatic machines. 8. Birm. 1785. R. S.
Meusnier on aerostatic machines. Roz. XXV. 39.
Baldwin's aeropaidie. 8. Chester, 1786.
Burja hydrostatik. ix.
Henzion sopra le machine aerostatiche. 4. Flor. 1788. R. S.
Prieur on parachutes. Ann. Ch. XXXI. 269.
Le Normand on parachutes. Ann. Ch. XXXVI. 94.
On the parachute. Nich. I. 523.
Wright on aerostation. Ph. M. XIV. 357.
On Garnerin's voyages. Nich. 8. III. 57.
Gilbert on the ascent of Garnerin, Robertson, and others. Gilb. XVI. 1. 164, 257.
    Hydrogen gas is seldom procured more than 5 or 6 times as rare as common air.
On the parachute. Gilb. XVI. 156.
Balloons. Rees's cyclop. III. Plates. Art. Pneumatics.
Aerial excursions. Ph. M. XVII. 188.

Ventilation by Heat.

Chimnies and furnaces. See Physics, Economy of Heat.

Sutton on extracting foul air from ships. 8. M. B.

Sutton's ventilator. Ph. tr. 1742. XLII. 42.

Watson on Sutton's ventilator for ships. Ph. tr. 1742. XLII. 62.
  Thinks it preferable to windsails or funnels.

Lomonosow on the currents of air in mines. N. C. Petr. I. 267.

Euler on the equilibrium of fluids, with the effects of heat. N. C. Petr. XI. XIII. XIV. XV.

Steam Engine.

Force of steam. See Physics, Heat.

Marquis of Worcester's century of inventions.

Papin Recueil de pieces. 8. Cassel, 1695. Acc. Ph. tr. 1697. XIX. 481.
  Proposes a mode of employing the force of steam by removing the fire continually from one part of the machine to another.

Savery's steam engine. Ph. tr. 1699. XXI. 228.
  The model was exhibited 16 June 1699.

Amontons's mode of employing the force of fire. A. P. 1699. 112. H. 101. Leup. Th. M. G. t. 53.

Newcomen's patent.
  Dated 1705. Robison. He introduced the piston.

Mey and Meyer's steam engine for raising water. Mach. A. IV. 185.

Bosfrand's steam engine. Mach. A. IV. 191, 199.

Leupold's fire wheel. Th. M. G. t. 50.

Steam engine. Leup. Th. M. G. Th. Hydraul. 2.

Belidor. Arch. Hydr. II. i. 308.

Desaguliers. N. Ph. II.

Dupuys's steam engine, with Moura's improvements. A. P. 1740. 111.

Payne's new invention of expanding fluids. Ph. tr. 1741. 821.
  Thinks that much may be saved by making the boilers red hot. Makes steam in specific gravity $\frac{1}{1000}$.

Gensanne's steam engine. A. P. 1744. H. 60. Mach. A. VII. 227.

Blake on steam engine cylinders. Ph. tr. 1751. 197.

Smeaton on De Moura's improvement of Savery's steam engine. Ph. tr. 1751. 436.

†Fitzgerald on increasing steam by ventilation. Ph. tr. 1757. 53, 370.

Fitzgerald's ventilators worked by steam engines. Ph. tr. 1758. 727.

Emers. mech. f. 274.

Beighton's steam engine. Bossut Hydrodynamique.

Morand Art d'exploiter les mines de charbon. f. Paris, p. 408.

Cancrins Bergmaschinenkunst.

Falck on the steam engine.

Lavoisier on the expense of steam engines. A. P. 1771. 17. H. 63.

A. P. 1771. 20.

Blackey sur les pompes a feu. 4. Amst. 1774.

Maillard sur la théorie des machines mues par la force de la vapeur.

E. M. Mathématique. Art. Hydraulique, pompe à feu.

François's steam engine without a piston. M. Laus. I. 51. Repert. IV. 203.
  Working the cocks by a tumbler.

Langsdorfs Hydr. und pyr. grundl. c. 11.

Langsdorf's proposal for a steam engine. L. Hydr. Pl. 19, 20. A tumbler. Pl. 40.

Kempel's rotatory eolipile. Langsdorfs Hydr. Pl. 22. f. 129.

Beighton's and Watt's steam engines. Langsd. Hydr. Pl. 23, 24.

Cooke's rotatory steam engine. Ir. tr. 1789. 113. Repert. III. 401.
Driving a wheel with falling flaps.

Gehler's phys. wörterb.

Prony. Arch. hydr.

Burja Grundlehren der hydrostatik. II. §. 28.

*Watt's patent for saving fuel in steam engines. Repert. I. 217.

Robison. Enc. Br. Art. Steam. Steam engine.

Nancarrow on the dimensions of a steam engine. Am. tr. IV. 348. Repert. XIV. 329. Nich. IV. 545. Ph. M. IX. 300. Gilb. XVI. 152.
On Savery's construction, with a condenser.

Thomson's furnace for steam engines. Rep. IV. 316.
For burning smoke.

Droz's steam engine without a beam, approved by the Institute. B. Soc. Phil. n. 3. Gilb. XVI. 356.

Curr's coal viewer and engine builder. 4. Sheffield, 1797. R. S.

Nicholson on the steam engine without a piston. Nich. I. 44. Gilb. XVI. 129. With a piston. Nich. II. 228. Gilb. XVI. 336.

On Cartwright's patent steam engine. Ph. M. I. 1. Repert. X. 1.
After Watt. Retains the water of injection for the boiler, without exposing it to the air; proposes to apply the vapour of spirits during distillation to the purposes of a steam engine; and describes a rotatory engine.

Cartwright's patent improvements on steam engines. Repert. XIV. 361.
For making them more compact. The cylinder is placed within the boiler, as in some other engines.

Remarks on Cartwright's piston. Nich. II. 364, 476. Reply. Ph. M. II. 221.

Hornblower's patent steam engine. Repert. IV. 361.

Hornblower's patent rotatory steam engine. Repert. IX. 289.
Producing a rotatory motion by diaphragms.

Hornblower's beams for engines. Nich. 8. II. 68.

On the boiler. Nich. III. 86.

Boulton's steam engine. Walker's philosophy. Lect. vi.

Walker's improved steam engine. Walker's philosophy. Lect. vi.

Sadler's patent rotatory steam engine. Rep. VII. 170.

Murray's patent steam engine. Repert. XI. 309.
A horizontal cylinder and a piston with rocks.

Murray's patent steam engine. Repert. XVI. 298.

Murray's patent rotatory steam engines. Repert. ii. II. 175. Repeated. III. 235.

Keir's improved boiler. Nich. V. 147.

Nieuwe Verhandelingen van het Bataafsch Genootschap. I. Rotterd. 1800.
On steam engines.

Murdock's patent for manufacturing steam engines.

Hase's patent improvement in steam engines. Repert. XV. 220.
For saving the heated water.

Roberton's patent steam engines. Repert. XVI. 366.

Savery's Newcomen's, and Watt's engines. Imis. elem. I. Pl. 10, 11.
Good figures.

Woolf's apparatus for employing waste steam. Nich. 8. II. 203.

Woolf on equalising the motion of steam engines. Nich. VI. 218.

Woolf's steam regulator. Nich. VI. 249.
A bent lever.

Woolf's boiler consisting of several cylinders. Ph. M. XVII. 40.

Woolf's steam valve. Ph. M. XVII. 164.

Woolf's improvements in steam engines. Nich. VIII. 262. Ph. M. XIX. 133.

Account of the explosion of Trevithick's steam engine. Repert. ii. III. 394. Ph. M. XVI. 372.

Saint's patent steam engines. Repert. ii. III. 408.
The flue carried through the boiler.

On the force of steam engines. Nich. IX. 214.

Perier on the employment of the steam engine in coal mines. M. Inst. V. 360.

Edelcranz's safety valve for emitting steam or admitting air. S. A. XXII. 329.

In the original form of the steam engine, the pressure of steam, and not that of the atmosphere, forced down the piston. Robison. Enc. Br.

Mr. Watt finds it most advantageous to work his engine at a high temperature. Robison. Enc. Br.

The whole force obtained from steam stopped when it has filled one fourth of the cylinder, appears from calculation to be twice as great as when it is continually admitted. Robison. Enc. Br. But perhaps a greater quantity of heat would be required.

The boiler should contain about ten times as much steam as the cylinder. M. Young.

An account of Mr. Symington's new Steam Boat. From the Journals of the Royal Institution. I. 195.

Several attempts have been made to apply the force of steam to the purpose of propelling boats in canals, and there seems to be no reason to think the undertaking by any means liable to insuperable difficulties. Mr. Symington appears already to have had considerable success, and the method that he has employed for making a connexion between the piston and the water wheel is attended with many advantages.

By placing the cylinder nearly in a horizontal position, he avoids the introduction of a beam, which has always been a troublesome and expensive part of the common steam engines: the piston is supported in its position by friction wheels, and communicates, by means of a joint, with a crank, connected with a wheel, which gives the water wheel, by means of its teeth, a motion somewhat slower than its own; the water wheel serving also as a fly. The steam engine differs but little with respect to the condensation of the steam, from those of Boulton and Watt now in general use; there is an apparatus for opening and shutting the cocks at pleasure, in order to revert the motion of the boat whenever it may be necessary. The water wheel is situated in a cavity near the stern, and in the middle of the breadth of the boat, so that it becomes necessary to have two rudders, one on each side, connected together by rods, which are moved by a winch near the head of the boat; so that the person who attends the engine may also steer. It has been found most advantageous to have a very small number of float boards in the water wheel.

Another material part of the invention consists in the arrangement of stampers, at the head of the boat, for the purpose of breaking the ice on canals, an operation which is often attended with great labour and expense. These stampers are raised in succession by means of levers, of which the ends are depressed by the pins of wheels, turned by an axis communicating with the water wheel.

Mr. Symington calculates, that a boat capable of doing the work of twelve horses may be built for eight or nine hundred pounds. An engine of the kind has been actually constructed at the expense of the proprietors of the Forth and Clyde navigation, and under the patronage of the governor, Lord Dundas: it was tried in December last, and it drew three vessels, of from 60 to 70 tons burden, at the usual rate of two miles and a half an hour. Mr. Symington is at present employed in attempting still further improvements, and when he has completed his invention, it may, perhaps, ultimately become productive of very extensive utility.

Steam Air Pump.

Carradori on Berretray's steam air pump. Roz. XXXVIII. 150.

Inflammable Vapours.

Street's patent inflammable vapour force. Repert. I. 154.

†Barber's patent for procuring motion by inflammable air. Repert. VIII. 371.
A stream of ignited air impelling a fly wheel.

Gunnery.

Theory of Gunnery, and Operation of Powder.

See Projectiles. Resistance of Fluids.

Hooke's powder proof. Birch. I. 302. Fig.

Greaves on the force of guns. Ph. tr. 1685. XV. 1090.

Blondel on throwing bombs. A. P. I. 150, 165.

Mariotte on the recoil of fire arms. A. P. I. 233.

Perrault's machine for increasing the effect of fire arms. A. P. I. 272. Mach. A. I. 11.

Lahire on projectiles. A. P. IX. 187, 198. 1700. 205. H. 147.

Lahire on the theory of the air in powder. A. P. 1702. H. 9.

Cassini on the recoil. A. P. 1703. H. 98.

Cassini on the effect of different charges. A. P. 1707. H. 3.

Guisnée's Galilean theory. A. P. 1707. 140. H. 120.

Chevalier on the effect of powder. A. P. 1707. 526. H. 152.

Ressons on throwing bombs. A. P. 1716. 79.

Ressons on the force of powder. A. P. 1719. H. 20. 1720. H. 112.

Maupertuis on throwing bombs. A. P. 1731. 297. H. 72.

Bélidor on gunpowder. M. Berl. 1734. IV. 116.

Bigot de Morogue on the effects of powder, according to the laws of accelerating forces. A. P. 1735. H. 98.

Leutmann on gunnery. C. Petr. IV. 265.

Dulacq's theory of the mechanism of artillery. A. P. 1740. H. 108.

Deidier on throwing bombs. A. P. 1741. H. 153.

Report of a committee on gunnery. Ph. tr. 1742. 172.

Found that the whole of the powder is not fired, that the ball is moved before all that is fired takes effect; and that the longest chamber is the most efficacious.

Robins's new principles of gunnery. R. I. Extr. Ph. tr. 1743. 437.

In support of the opinions controverted by the committee, as allowable approximations. Attributes the whole effect to fluids permanently elastic.

Missiessy on the escape of powder at the touch hole. A. P. 1748. H. 28.

Duhamel on the escape of powder at the touch hole. A. P. 1750. 1. H. 30.

D'Arcy on the theory of artillery. A. P. 1751. 45. H. 1.

D'Arcy Essai sur la théorie de l'artillerie. Acc. A. P. 1760. H. 142.

Montalembert on the rotation of balls. A. P. 1755. 463. H. 34.

Montalembert on proving cannon. A. P. 1759. 358. H. 227.

Vandelli on the force of steam in gunpowder. C. Bon. III. 92. IV. 106.

Saluce on the elastic fluids produced from gunpowder. M. Taur. I. II.

Casali on the force of powder. C. Bon. V. ii. 345, 357.

Simpson's exercises.

Euler's gunnery, by Brown. 4. R. S.

Anderson's gunnery.

Fortification and gunnery. Emers. misc. 242, 277.

Treatise on gunpowder and fire arms. 8.

Glenie's history of gunnery. 8. R. S.

St. Auban sur les nouveaux systêmes d'artillerie. 8. R. S.

*Borda on projectiles. A. P. 1769. 247. H. 116.

Devalliere on the superiority of long and heavy pieces of cannon. A. P. 1772. ii. 77. H. 44.

Examen de la poudre. 8. 1773. R. I.

Hutton on the force of fired gunpowder. Ph. tr. 1778. 50.

The powder appears to fire almost instantaneously, for the force is nearly in the direct proportion of the powder, the velocity in its subduplicate ratio, and in the subduplicate ratio of the ball inversely. The height and the range are therefore as the weight of powder.

Two ounces of powder impelled a ball of 28¼ oz. with a velocity of 613 feet in a second: this would carry it to a height of 5930 feet, producing an effect equal to the labour of a man continued 105 seconds, and 10 hours of such labour would produce an effect equal to that of 43 pounds of powder. This force is therefore not comparatively cheap, supposing the whole effort of the powder to be consumed; but it would be almost impossible to find mechanical means so convenient for producing velocity. Air, compressed in an air gun, would never move even into a vacuum with a velocity greater than about 1400 feet in a second: much less could it carry before it the weight of a cannon ball with a velocity of 2000 feet: and a bow or a spring of any kind would have a still greater disadvantage. The great rarity of the heated elastic fluids disengaged from powder, combined with their great elasticity, gives them the faculty of imparting so prodigious a velocity. Hydrogen gas, sufficiently condensed, would escape with a velocity 3 times as great as common air. Hutton thinks the force equal to 1500 or 1600 atmospheres. Y.

Ingenhousz. Ph. tr. 1779.

Robins found the force of gunpowder equal to 1000 atmospheres, and observed, that a red heat made air expand to 4 times its bulk; hence he inferred that powder produced 250 times its bulk of air. Hauksbee, Amontons, Bélidor, and Saluces agree that it yields 222 times its bulk.

Thompson's experiments on gunpowder. Ph. tr. 1781. 229.

Count Rumford observes, that the piece is heated sooner when fired without than with balls, perhaps because the great velocity of the air excites more heat by friction. When the piece is become warm, a smaller quantity of powder serves. The operation of ramming increases the force of powder in the ratio of 6 to 5, or more: the velocity is nearly in the subduplicate ratio of the weight of the powder, at least for musket bullets. The situation of the vent has very little effect; the cavity of the piece should have a hemispherical termination. The velocity is more accurately determined by measuring the recoil of the piece when suspended than by the motion of a pendulum struck by the ball, deducting always that which would be produced without any ball. The velocity was sometimes greater than 2000 feet in a second. Robins makes the force of gunpowder equal to 1000 atmospheres; but, upon his own principles, it is equal at least to 1308. The velocity is very nearly in the subtriplicate ratio of the weight of the ball, increased by half that of the powder, inversely. The force of aurum fulminans appears to be but one fourth of that of gunpowder. The experiments were made with a bore of about ¾ inch. It is surprising that there should be so much difference between these experiments and others, that a quadruple weight in the one case should have produced the same effect with an octuple weight in the other. It may be questioned whether the difference of the squares of the velocities ought not rather to be taken in making the correction for the recoil. Y.

Rumford on the force of fired gunpowder. Ph. tr. 1797. 222. Nich. I. 459. Gilb. IV. 257, 377.

Bernoulli makes the expansive force of gunpowder equal to 10 000 atmospheres; Rumford, from the bursting of a barrel of iron, 50 000, from some more direct experiments, from 20 000 to 40 000. The utmost that can be justly inferred from the bursting of the barrel is in reality about 30 000, since the tension could by no means be equal through every part of its substance. The force was, in atmospheres $1.841(1000x)^{1+.4x}$, x being the quantity of powder, the whole capacity of the cavity being unity. In some other experiments the multiplier, instead of 1.841, appears to be 6.37; giving 101 021 atmospheres instead of 29 178, when x becomes 1. A cubic inch of gunpowder contains nearly 11 grains of water of crystallization, and 5 of moisture, which Count Rumford thinks, would be sufficient for furnishing the steam. This is however a great mistake: a heat of 1200 would scarcely more than double, or at most quadruple, the expansive force of a given portion of steam, consequently the density of steam at this temperature, exerting a pressure of 50 000 atmospheres, ought to be more than 10 000 times as great as under the usual pressure, that is, probably, almost 4 times as great as the density of water. Count Rumford finds that much of the powder is discharged unfired.

E. M. A. VI. Art. Poudre à canon.

Massey on saltpetre. Manch. M. I. 184. Rep. I. 248.

S. E. XI.

A collection of memoirs on saltpetre. At first there were 38 unsuccessful attempts; in the second instance Thouvenel gained the first prize of 8000 livres, among 28 competitors. A few of the best memoirs only are printed at large.

Napier on gunpowder. Ir. tr. 1788. II. 97. Rep. II. 276.

Robison. Enc. Br. Art. Projectiles, Resistance.

Bullion on saltpetre and gunpowder. Repert. VI. 49.

Howard on a fulminating mercury. Ph. tr. 1800. 204.

On increasing the effects of powder. Journ. Phys. Repert. VII. 135.
<small>By leaving a vacant space behind the wadding. Thus a bomb if but partly filled breaks into a larger number of pieces; but they are not scattered so far as when it is quite filled.</small>

Regnier's powder proof. Nich. III. 198. Ph. M. IV. 394. Gilb. IV. 400.
<small>With a spring.</small>

†Vandelli on the force of gunpowder. Rep. X. 286.

Griffith on mixing lime with gunpowder. Repert. XII. 341.

Coleman on gunpowder. Ph. M. IX. 355.

Jessop on blasting rocks. Nich. IX. 230.

Farey on blasting rocks. Ph. M. XX. 208.
<small>The best charge of powder is about ¼ or ⅓ of the weight of the ball, for battering ½. A 24 pounder with 16 pounds of gunpowder at an elevation of 45° ranges 20 250 feet, about ⅓ of the range that would take place in a vacuum. The resistance is at first 400 pounds or more, and reduces the velocity in a second from 2000 to 1200 feet in the first 1500 feet. Cavallo, from Robins.

It has been found, that the velocity of a ball is not materially affected by increasing the weight or firmness of a piece of ordnance, beyond very moderate limits.</small>

Particular Constructions of Guns and their Parts.

Chaumette's horse pistols. Mach. A. I. 201. Jointed carbine. A. P. 1715. H. 66. Mach. A. II. 27. Guns loaded at the breech. A. P. 1715. H. 66. Mach. A. II. 79, 99, 101. III. 53. Jointed powder horn. Mach. A. III. 49. Powder horn with balls. Mach. A. III. 51. Appendages to locks. Mach. A. III. 59.

Bedaut's machine for red hot balls. Mach. A. II. 61.

†Destau's rolling battery of muskets. Mach. A. II. 75.

Villon's machines for making gunbarrels and cannons. A. P. 1716. H. 77. Mach. A. III. 71, 73, 77, 79.

Machine for boring cannons. Mach. A. III. 81.

Deschamps's improvements of guns. A. P. 1718. H. 74. Mach. A. III. 171, 177, 181, 183.
<small>Rifle muskets and cannons.</small>

Leutmann on rifle barrels. C. Petr. III. 156.

D'Arcy's light cannons. A. P. 1733. H. 70.

Raucourt's inventions for throwing bombs. Mach. A. VI. 157.

Lacq on the mechanism of artillery. A. P. 1740. H. 108.

Ladoyreau on cannons of wrought iron. A. P. 1742. H. 141.

Reinier's double barrelled gun. A. P. 1742. 155.
<small>Fusil tournant à deux coups.</small>

Pas de Loup's machine for charging artillery. A. P. 1742. H. 157.

Maty's gunpowder air gun. Condamine. A. P. 1757. 405. Ingenhousz. Ph. tr. 1779.
<small>Shot a bullet 60 paces with the air of 2 ounces, which served 12 times.</small>

Montalembert on priming cannons. A. P. 1759. 358. H. 227.

Challier's gun lock. A. P. 1762. H. 192.

Descourtieux's gun barrels. A. P. 1765. H. 133.

Boullet's gun acting by the circular motion of the barrel. A. P. 1767. H. 186.

Delaunay's gun easily primed. A. P. 1771. H. 68.

E. M. A. I. Art. Arquebusier. Canons.

Watts's patent for making small shot. Rep. III. 313.

On shot. Nich. I. 260, 380.

Aitken's patent for loading fire arms. Rep. VI. 239.

Many changes introduced at once.

Wilson's patent fire arms, Repert. VI. 304.
Preserved from rust.

Marescot on shooting grenades. M. Inst. II. 242.

Dodd's safe gun lock. S. A. XXII. 296.

Haycraft's patent gun carriage, Repert. XII. 16.

Dolomieu on the art of cutting gun flints. M. Inst. III. 348. Nich. 8. I. 89.

Prosser's patent guns and pistols. Repert. XV. 224.

On casting shot. Gilb. VIII. 250.

A wheelbarrow for throwing grenades. Person, Recueil. Pl. 7.

De Poggi's patent ordnance. Repert. ii. I. 169.

Webb's safe gun lock. S. A. XX. 247. Nich. 8. V. 29.

A magazine pistol. Nich. 8. IV. 250.
From Lord Camelford, who had "used it in various parts of the world."

Two muskets for quick firing. Nich. 8. V. 116.

On a gun for throwing double shot. Nich. VII. 146.

Rockets, and other Fireworks.

Pasdeloup's machine for loading fireworks. Mach. A. I. 125.

Buffon on rockets. A. P. 1740. H. 105.

Robins on the height of the ascent of rockets. Ph. tr. 1749. 131.
A rocket of a pound ascended 450 or 500 yards, in 7″; a rocket of 4 pounds remained 14″.

Ellicott on the height of the ascent of rockets. Ph. tr. 1750. 578.
Rockets two inches and a half in diameter a proper size. A rocket fired at Hackney was seen at Barkway. Some of three inches in diameter rose 1200 yards.

HISTORY OF HYDRAULICS AND PNEUMATICS.

Balloons. See Aerostatics.

Lowther examined inflammable air in 1733. Ph. tr. 1733.

Bélidor's history of antient and modern canals. Arch. Hydr. II. ii. 348, 357.

Leroy sur les navires des anciens. 8. R. S.

Luckombe's tablet of memory.

Glenie's history of gunnery. R. S.

Kepler Bergm. Journal. 1791.
Matthesius is said to have mentioned a steam engine in his Sarepta before 1568.

Phillips's history of inland navigation. 4. R. I.

On the Chinese canal. Staunton's voyage. R. I.

Charnock's history of marine architecture. 3 v. 4. Lond. 1800.

Montucla and Lalande. Hist. Mathém. History of shipbuilding. IV. 381.

Prieur and Lenormand on parachutes. Ann. Ch. XXXI. 269. XXXVI. 94. Gilb. XVI. 156.

Beckmann on the invention of fire engines. Ph. M. XI. 238.

Gilb. XVI. 385.
Erman observes, that Aristotle weighed the carbonic acid gas exhaled from the lungs, when he found that a blown bladder was heavier than an empty one.

Wiegleb on the antiquity of gunpowder. Nich. VI. 71.

Hints towards a steam engine in 1627. Nich. VII. 311. Brunau.

Particular Dates.   A. D.

The Chinese canal 806 miles long, finished by 30 000 men in 43 years — 980
The first canal in England, from the Trent to the Witham — 1134
Windmills invented — 1299
Cannons invented — 1330
Gunpowder used according to Langlais — 1338

Battle of Cressy	1346
Gunpowder used at Lyons in Brabant. Wiegleb	1356
Muskets used at the siege of Arras	1414
Shipping improved, and port holes invented by Decharges	1500
Air guns made at Nuremberg	1560
Bombs invented at Venloo	1588
New River brought to London	1614
Guericke invented the air pump	1654
Hooke finished his air pump	1658
Savery had erected steam engines	1696
Chain shot invented by Dewit	1666
Balloons invented by Montgolfier	1783
Lunardi ascended in Moorfields	1784

The Society for the encouragement of arts still offer premiums to the inventors of new hydraulic machines for irrigation and other purposes, as well as for the improvement of ventilators.

ACUSTICS. SOUND IN GENERAL.

*Aristotle.

Bacon Sylva sylvarum.
   Contains many experiments.

*Mersenne Harmonie universelle. f. Paris, 1636. M. B.

Mersenni cogitata physicomathematica. 4. Par. 1644. M. B.

*Galilei Discorsi mathematichi. 1638.

Acustics. Ph. tr. Abr. I. v. 457. IV. iv. 346. X. iv. 160.

Bartoli del sono. 1680. M. B.

Bishop of Ferns on sound. Ph. tr. 1684. XIV. 471.

Perrault on sound. A. P. I. 145.

Carré on the production of sound. A. P. 1704. H. 88.

Lahire's experiments on sound. A. P. 1716. 262, 264 H. 66.

On numbering the vibrations of sound. C, Bon. I. 180.
   From the sound of a wheel with teeth, striking the air only.

Haller Elementa physiologiae. V.

*Lagrange on sound. M. Taur. I. II.

Britz vom schalle. 4. Berl. 1764.

Euler. A. Berl. 1765.

Burdach de vi aeris in sono. 4. Leipz. 1767.

Hales Doctrina sonorum. 4. Lond. 1778.

Funccius de sono et tono. 4. Leipz. 1779. Germ. in Leipz. Mag. 1781.

Jones's physiological disquisitions. 4. Lond. 1781.

M. Young on sounds and musical strings. 8. Dubl. 1784.

Busse kleine beyträge zur math. und phys. 131.

*Chladni Entdeckungen über die theorie des planges. 4. Leipz. 1787. R. I.

Chladni. Berl. naturf. fr.

Chladni promises a general work on acustics. Hind. Arch. III. 234.

†Perrolle on the vibrations of sounding bodies. Roz. XXXV. 423.

*Forkel Allgemeine literatur der musik. 8. Leipz. 1792.

Suremain Missery theorie acousticomusicale. 8. Par. 1793.
   Extr. by Lalande. Roz. XLII. 161.

*Robison. Enc. Br. Art. Sound. Trumpet. Suppl. Art. Temperament Trumpet.

T. Young on sound and light. Ph. tr. 1800. 106. Nich. V. 72. 161.

Terzi del suno. 8. R. S.

Propagation of Sound.

See Longitudinal Vibrations.

Papin's whistle fitted to the mouth of the tube of an air pump. Birch. IV. 379.
   To show the effect of the air on the force of sound.

Walker on the velocity of sound. Ph. tr. 1698. XX. 433.

Observed the time occupied in the return of an echo. Found the velocity from 1150 to 1526 feet in a second.

Hawksbee on sound in condensed and rarefied air. Ph. tr. 1705. XXIV. 1902. 1709. XXVI. 367.

A bell was heard at the distance of 30 yards when the air was in its common state, at 60 with the force of two atmospheres, at 90 with the force of three: beyond this the intensity did not much increase. A vacuum was made between two receivers, the bell being within the innermost, and the sound was not transmitted.

Hawksbee on the propagation of sound through water. Ph. tr. 1709. XXVI. 371.

*Derham de soni motu. Ph. tr. 1708. XXVI. 2.

Velocities observed by different persons.

Roberts. Ph. tr. n. 209	1300
Boyle. Essay on motion	1200
Walker. Ph. tr.	1338
Mersennus, Balistica	1474
Flamsteed and Halley	1142
Florentine academicians	1148
Cassini and others, Duhamel. H. A.	1172
Derham	1142

Derham found the effect of the wind, but not of any changes of weather.

Mairan. A. P. 1737. H. 1.

Cassini on the propagation of sound. A. P. 1738. 128. H. 1.

Makes the velocity 1107 feet.

Cassini. A. P. 1739.

Bianconi della diversa velocità del suono. Venice.

Bianconi on the velocity of sound. C. Bon. II. i. 365.

In summer, the thermometer being at 20°, 76 vibrations of the pendulum elapsed while a sound passed over 13 miles; in winter 79 seconds, the thermometer being at —1.2°. In a cloud or mist 155" elapsed while the sound passed and repassed. Hence the air should expand $\frac{1}{76}$ for 21.2°, or $\frac{1}{76 \times 6}$ for 1° of the thermometer employed, probably Reaumur's, which is $\frac{1}{450}$ for 1° of Fahrenheit. The mean difference of the temperature of the air was probably somewhat less than is supposed, perhaps 17° or 18°.

Zanotti on the intensity of sound in air of different densities. C. Bon. II. Coll. Ac. X.

†Euler on the propagation of pulses. N. C. Petr. I. 67.

Euleri conjectura physica circa propagationem soni et luminis. 4. Berl. 1750. Opusc.

Euler on the propagation of sound. A. Berl. 1759.

Euler on the propagation of agitations. M. Taur. II. ii. 1.

Euler on the generation and propagation of sound. A. Berl. 1765. 335.

Winkler Tentamina circa soni celeritatem. 4. Leipz. 1763.

Lagrange. M. Taur. I. II.

†Lambert on the velocity of sound. A. Berl. 1768. 70. 1772. 103. Roz. XVIII. 126.

Thinks that the air contains about $\frac{1}{3}$ of foreign matter.

Blagden. Ph. tr. 1784. 201.

Observes, that many witnesses agreed that they heard the whizzing of a very distant meteor at the instant of its appearance; but that this was probably a fallacy.

Perrolle on the propagation of sound in gases. M. Tur. 1786. III. Corr. 1. 1790. V. Corr. 195. Roz. XXIII. 378. Journ. Phys. XLIX. 382. Nich. I. 411. Gilb. III. 167. IV. 112.

Found it very weak in hydrogen gas.

Wunsch on the velocity of sound in wood. A. Berl. Deutsch. abh. 1788. 87.

Sound was conveyed instantaneously through 36 connected laths of 24 feet each, or 864 feet, if not through 72, which was the whole number employed.

Robison. Enc. Br. XVIII. Art. Trumpet articulate.

Alleges many facts in favour of the nondivergence of sound and waves. He observes, that "all the general corollaries respecting the lateral divergence of waves are little more than sagacious guesses."

†Lamarck on the medium of sound. Journ. Phys. XLIX. 397.

Thinks it a medium more subtile than air.

*Chladni on the propagation of sound. Gilb. III. 159, 177, 182, 184.

Its velocity in different mediums.

Chladni infers from the longitudinal vibrations of different substances, a velocity of 7800 feet in a second in tin, 9300 in silver, 12500 in copper, 17500 in glass and iron, 11000 to 18000 in wood, and 10000 to 12000 in tobacco pipes. His observations are fully confirmed by calculations from different grounds. According to the elasticity of fir, as inferred from an experiment of Mr. Leslie, the velocity of an impulse should be 17300. The velocity may be easily calculated from the sound of a loose rod; if the number of vibrations of the gravest sound in a second be n, the velocity will be $.978 \frac{nl^2}{d}$, l being the length, and d the depth in feet.

From an experiment of this kind, I find the velocity 17700 in crown glass, and 11800 in brass.

Von Arnim on the propagation of sound. Gilb. III. 167. IV. 112.

Gough. Manch. M. V. 622.

Observes, that sound does not diverge equally.

Englefield and Young on the effect of sound on the barometer. Journ. R. I., I. Repert. ii. I. 111. Nich. 8. II. 181. Gilb. XIV. 214.

Biot on the effect of heat in the propagation of sound. B. Soc. Phil. n. 63. Journ. Phys. LV. 173.

It will appear under the article Capacity for Heat, that some of Dalton's experiments agree more nearly with Biot's calculations than his own conclusions from others warranted us to suppose. See Journ. R. I., I.

At first sight, it might be imagined, that a loud sound ought to be more accelerated by heat than a weak one; but, on a more accurate examination, we shall find that the law of isochronism of small vibrations will remain unimpaired.

Parseval on the propagation of sound in all directions. To be printed, S. E.

Cassini makes the velocity of sound 1107 feet, Meyer 1195, Müller 1169, Pictet about 1130.

See Vibrations of Fluids.

Sound conveyed by pipes. See Hearing.

Decay of Sound.

The human voice has been heard more than ten miles at Gibraltar. Derham.

Echos.

On an echo in Gloucester cathedral. Birch. I. 120.

Quesnet on an echo. A. P. II. 87. X. 127.

Grandi de sono. Ph. tr. 1709. XXVI. 270.

Echo from two towers. A. P. 1710. H. 18.

Southwell on echos. Ph. tr. 1746. XLIV. 219.

A building with projecting wings produced 60 repetitions.

Euler on echos. A. Berl. 1765. 335.

Guynet on an echo repeating 14 syllables. A. P. 1770. H. 23.

Actis on an echo at Girgenti. M. Tur. 1788. IV. App. 43.

From the parabolic form of a church.

An echo in Woodstock park repeats 17 syllables by day, and 20 by night. An echo on the north side of Shipley church in Sussex repeats 21 syllables. Cavallo, from Plot and Harris.

Sources of Sound.

Vibrations of Fluids.

Mariotte on the sounds of the trumpet. A. P. I. 209.

Bernoulli on organ pipes. A. P. 1762. 431. H. 170.

Extr. Haüy Traité de Phys. I. 316.

Euler on the motion of air in pipes. N. C. Petr. XVI. 281.

Equal and unequal, hyperbolical and conical. All shut pipes are unmusical, except cylindrical ones.

On the sounds of gases. Nich. III. 43.

Chladni on the tones of an organ pipe in different gases. Ph. M. IV. 275.

The sound of carbonic acid gas, nitrous gas, and oxygen gas, agreed with the theory; but azote, of which the specific gravity was .985, common air being unity, gave a note half a tone lower than common air. Hydrogen gas produced a note an octave or a minor tenth higher.

Delarive on the sounds from hydrogen gas. Journ. Phys. LV. 165. Nich. 8. IV. 23. Ph. M. XIV. 24.

Higgins on the sound from hydrogen gas. Nich. 8. I. 129.

A harmonica. Gilb. XVII. 482.

A glass tube sounding while hot.

The air in a flute is like a slow river with waves moving rapidly along it.

Account of M. Delarive's Memoir on the Sounds produced by burning Hydrogen Gas. Journ. R. I., I. 259.

It is well known, that when a stream of hydrogen gas passes through a small tube, and is inflamed at its orifice, if a large tube be held over the flame so as partially to inclose it, an agreeable sound is frequently produced. The frequent failure of the experiment, and the impossibility of producing the same effect with other kinds of flame, left considerable obscurity with respect to the immediate cause of the sound. M. Delarive appears to have been very successful in his attempts to remove these difficulties. He supposes the continual production and condensation of aqueous vapour to cause a brisk vibratory motion, which must be able, in order to produce a sound, to harmonize with the dimensions of the tube, and is then regulated and equalised by the regular reflections from the tube, so as to constitute together a clear musical sound: he observes, that for this purpose there must be a great difference of temperature in the air and the tube near the flame; hence the failure of the vapour of ether, which produces too slight a degree of heat, and the difficulty of succeeding in a warm room, for want of a sufficient supply of cool air. This explanation is confirmed by a curious experiment on tubes with bulbs resembling that of a thermometer, in which a small particle of water or mercury is exposed to a considerable heat, so as to be wholly converted into vapour, while the upper part of the tube remains cool; in this case a sound is produced somewhat similar to that of hydrogen gas, but much fainter. Brugnatelli has obtained a sound from phosphorus burnt in a tube; and M. Delarive supposes that the phosphorous acid, in the form of a vapour, possesses a high degree of elasticity, and that it is condensed with sufficient rapidity for the production of the sonorous effects. Y.

Vibrations of Solids.

Chords.

Lahire on the trumpet Marigni. A. P. IX. 330.

Taylor de motu nervi tensi. Ph. tr. 1713. XXVIII. 26.

Sauveur on the sounds of chords. A P. 1713. 324. H. 68.

Jo. Bernoulli on vibrating chords. C. Petr. III. 13.

D. Bernoulli on the curvature of an extended chord. C. Petr. III. 62.

D. Bernoulli on vibrating chords. A. Berl. 1753. 147, 173.

Bernoulli on the vibrations of unequal chords. A. Berl. 1765. 281.

Some may be harmonious though unequal; others inharmonious.

Bernoulli on the vibrations of compound chords. N. C. Petr. XVI. 257.

Euler on the vibrations of flexible and rigid bodies. C. Petr. VII. 99.

Euler on the oscillations of flexible bodies. C. Petr. XIII. 124. XIV. 182.

On the motion of flexible bodies. A. Berl. 1745. H. 54.

Euler on the vibration of chords. A. Berl. 1748. 69.

Euler's remarks on Bernoulli. A. Berl. 1753. 196.

Euler on the vibrations of a loaded thread. N. C. Petr. IX. 215.

Euler on the vibrations of unequal chords. N. C. Petr. IX. 246.

Euler on the propagation of agitations. M. Taur. II. ii. 1.

Euler on the agitations of chords. A. Berl. 1765. 307, 335.

Euler on equal and unequal chords. M. Taur. III. ii. 1, 27.

Euler on the equilibrium and motion of flexible and elastic bodies. N. C. Petr. XV. 381. XX. 286.

Euler on unequal vibrating chords. N. C. Petr. XVII. 381. A. Petr. 1780. IV. ii. 99.

Euler finds, that a chord composed of two parts, of which the length is reciprocally as the thickness, will sound like a single one. A chord composed of two parts equal in length, one four times as heavy as the other will produce sounds related as .30408, .69591, 1.30408, 1.69591, 2.30408, and will therefore be very discordant.

Euler on the vibrations and revolutions of extended musical chords. N. C. Petr. XIX. 340. XX. 304. A. Petr. III. ii. 116. 1782. VI. ii. 148.

Observes, that the revolutions may be reduced to compound vibrations.

Euler on the perturbation of the motion of a chord from its weight. A. Petr. 1781. V. i. 178.

When the chord is horizontal the perturbation vanishes.

Dalembert on the curve of a vibrating chord. A. Berl. 1747. 214, 220. 1750. 355.

Dalembert's remarks on vibrating chords. A. Berl. 1763. 235. M. Taur. III. ii. 389.

Riccati on elastic force. C. Bon. I. 523.

M. Young on sounds and musical strings.

J. Bernoulli on the problem of vibrating chords. Hind. Arch. III. 266.

Montucla and Lalande. III. 659.

Voigt on the nodes of chords. Ph. M. IV. 347.

Surfaces.

Euler on the vibrations of drums. N. C. Petr. X. 243.

Riccati on the vibrations of drums. Ac. Pad. I. 419.

Biot on the vibrations of surfaces. M. Inst. IV. 21.

Extr. B. Soc. Phil. n. 43.

Says, that the time of vibration depends on the initial figure. This does not however appear to agree with experiment.

Vibrations from Elasticity.

Lateral Vibrations.

Birch. II. 475.

Hooke explained the vibrations of a glass bell by putting flour on it, which moved differently, according to the difference of the sounds.

Blondel on the sound of a glass full of water. A. P. I. 209.

Carré on the sounds of cylinders. A. P. 1709. 47. H. 93.

†Lahire on the extinction of sounds at the ends of a cylinder. A. P. 1709. H. 96

Bernoulli on the curvature of an elastic rod. C. Petr. III. 62.

Bernoulli on the vibrations of plates. C. Petr. XIII. 105, 167.

The sounds are related as 1, 6.82, 17.63, 34.54, 57.1, 86.3. The length of a pendulum vibrating with equal frequency is to the linear deflection by a given weight at the end of a rod fixed at the extremity, as 12 times the weight of the rod to 49 times the deflecting weight; thus a knitting needle weighing 15.5 grains was deflected by a weight of 1000 grains $\frac{1}{17}$ of the length of the second pendulum: hence the length of the synchronous pendulum is .1025, and it makes 175 or 176 vibrations in a second, the note being G, as it was found. The length was $\frac{17}{11\frac{1}{2}}$; half the length gave the double octave, the time of vibration being always as the square of the length. At the standard concert pitch the note would be nearly F.

Bernoulli. N. C. Petr. XV. 361.

Euler on the vibrations of rigid bodies. C. Petr. VII. 99.

Euler on bells. N. C. Petr. X. 26.

Makes the sounds as 1, $\sqrt{6}$, $\sqrt{20}$, $\sqrt{50}$; considering the bell as composed of rings.

Euler on the vibrations of plates. N. C. Petr. XVII. 449.

The progression of sounds as 1.192, 6.9977, 19.6888.

Euler on the vibrations of plates. A. Petr. III. i. 103.

The sounds of rings are as the squares of the natural numbers.

Riccati on elastic force. C. Bon. I. 523.

*Riccati on the sounds of cylinders. Soc. Ital. I. 444.

With many experiments, and tables for forming the scale. Corrects some material errors of Euler.

Lexell on the vibrations of rings. A. Petr. 1781. V. ii. 185.

Lambert on the sounds of elastic bodies. N. Act. Helv. I. 42.

With experiments. Makes the series 1, 6.267, 17.547, 34.38. An approximation only.

*Chladni Entdeckungen über die theorie des klanges.

Finds the vibrations generally agreeing with theory; that is, nearly as the squares of the odd numbers in most cases; in one, as the squares of the natural numbers. The sounds of rings do not agree with either of Euler's suppositions, but are nearly as the squares of the odd numbers.

Acccount of Chladni's figures. Journ. Phys. XLVII. (IV.) 390. Ph. M. II. 315, 391.

Jo. Bernoulli on the vibrations of rectangular plates. N. A. Petr. 1787. V. 197.

Compared with Chladni's experiments.

Perrolle. M. Tur. 1790. 1. App. 209.

Voigt on Chladni's figures. Ph. M. III. 389.

Parseval on the complete integration of the formulae for the vibrations of plates. To be printed in the Mém. des sav. étr. of the Institute.

See page 84.

Longitudinal Vibrations.

Chladni über die longitudinal schwebungen der stäbe. 4.

From the transactions of the society at Erfurt.

On Chladni's longitudinal sound. Ph. M. IV.

Spiral Vibrations.

Chladni on spiral vibrations. Gilb. II. 87. Ph. M. XII. 259.

From the memoirs of the Naturf. Fr. These vibrations are found to be a fifth lower than the longitudinal vibrations.

Effects of Sound.

Remarks on the Effect of Sound upon the Barometer. By Sir HENRY C. ENGLEFIELD, Bart. F. R. S. Journ. R. I., I. 157.

During the time I spent at Brussels in the years 1773 and 1774, it occurred to me, that the effect of sound on the barometer had not, to my knowledge, been attended to; and that it was by no means certain, whether that instrument was capable of being sensibly affected by those elastic vibrations caused in the atmosphere, by the percussion of a sonorous body. I thought the idea worthy of being pursued, and the means of making satisfactory experiments were most opportunely in my power.

The sound of a very large bell appeared to me the most powerful, and, at the same time, to be approached with the greatest security and ease to the observer. The explosion of artillery, besides the very disagreeable smoke and danger of the recoil, might be objected to, on account of the sudden production of elastic and heated vapour, which might, independent of the sound, instantaneously alter the state of the atmosphere, and thereby lead the observer into very great and unavoidable errors.

Every one who has been in the Low Countries must know, that very large bells, and immense numbers of them, are the pride of their churches, and that they are rung quite out, not tolled, on every great festival. The great bell of the collegiate church of St. Gudula, at Brussels, weighs, as I was told, sixteen thousand pounds, and on this I determined to found my experiment.

Two objections only could be made to the result of this trial, the one, that the motion of the bell might cause a vibration in the walls of the building, which would hinder the placing the barometer in a state of repose; the other, that the swinging so large a mass with a considerable degree of velocity, might of itself agitate the air so as to cause vibrations in the mercury, totally independent of sound.

The strength of the walls of the steeple, and manner of hanging the bell, which was contained in a frame of timber, founded on a strong vault, and totally independent of the walls of the steeple, might alone have answered the first of these objections, but happily a most complete and satisfactory answer to both of them was furnished by the manner in which the bell was rung.

As the bell was to ring out full in an instant, at a signal given from below; it is necessary to have it in motion some time beforehand; and during that time, the clapper is fixed to one side by a strong stick crossing the mouth of the bell, which, at the signal, is pulled out by the hand of a person placed for that purpose. If, then, our barometer showed no variation during all this time; we were absolutely certain, that whatever motion was perceived afterwards, was wholly owing to the sound.

Mr. Pigott, who was then at Brussels, was kind enough to lend me one of his barometers, made by Ramsden, and his son made the following observations jointly with myself.

At two o'clock in the afternoon of the first of November, 1773, we went into the northwest tower of St. Gudula's church, and having fixed the barometer firmly in the opening of a window, not above seven feet from the bottom of the bell, we waited quietly for its ringing.

The height of the mercury before the bell began to swing, as observed by Mr. Pigott, was 29.478 inches. The bell being in full swing no alteration whatever was perceptible.

The instant that the clapper was loosed, the mercury leaped up, and continued that sort of springing motion at every stroke of the clapper, during the whole time of the ringing of the bell. These were our observations.

During the ringing of the bell, Mr. P.	29.469
During the ringing, by myself	
Highest	29.480
Lowest	29.474
Highest	29.482
Lowest	29.472

These observations were made with the greatest attention; and considering their delicacy and the difficulty of observing, agree very nearly. They appear to give from 6 to 10 thousandths of an inch for the effect of this sound on the barometer. It is to be observed, that Mr. Pigott in general, estimated the height of the mercury about five thousandths lower than myself, which brings our observations to a very near agreement. The following observations prove this.

On the top of the tower, Mr. P.	29.424
Ditto, by me	29.430
At the foot of the tower, Mr. P.	29.639
Ditto, by me	29.642
In the court of the English Nuns, by Mr. Pigott	29.676
Ditto, by me	29.682

And I should think, that the difference of eyes may frequently cause such a variation among different observers; at least, in delicate observations, it will be always prudent to make the experiment.

Note by Dr. Young.

These observations appear to agree too well with each other, to allow us to doubt of their accuracy. It therefore becomes necessary to inquire after the cause of the different heights of the barometer. It is indeed barely possible, that a sudden stroke of the clapper of the bell might produce a greater agitation of the building than the preceding alternate motion of the bell itself; but this explanation cannot be called satisfactory. It is certain, that there was neither more nor less air in the tower while the bell was sounding, than while it was silent; the mean density of the air could therefore not have been changed; and if the alternate motions of the particles of air which constitute sound, had taken place by equal degrees and with equal velocities in each opposite direction, there is no reason to suppose that the increase of pressure on the surface of the mercury, at one instant, could have tended to raise it, more than the decrease of pressure, in the opposite state of the undulation, would have depressed it. But the same consequence does not follow, if we conceive the motion of the air in advancing to be more rapid, but of shorter continuance, than its retrograde motion. For if the wind blew for one hour with a velocity of four, and the same air returned in the course of two hours with a velocity of two, an obstacle upon which it had acted in both directions, would not be found in its original place; for the action of the wind upon an obstacle, is as the square of the velocity, and the time would not compensate for the difference of force. It is therefore easy to suppose, that the law of the bell's vibration was in this experiment such, that the air advanced towards the barometer with a greater velocity than it receded, although for a shorter time, and that hence the whole effect was the same as if the mean pressure of the air had been increased. Such a law might easily result from a combination of a more regular principal vibration with one or more subordinate ones, in different relations; and similar cases may sometimes be observed in the vibrations of chords.

Sympathetic Sounds.

Morhofii stentor hyaloclastes, de scypho vitreo fracto. Kiel, 1662. 1683.

Wallis on the partial sympathetic tremors of chords. Ph. tr. 1677. XII. 839.

Shown by bits of paper laid on the chords.

Lahire on a buttress at Rheims that vibrates when one of the bells is rung. A. P. II. 87.

Probably from being capable of vibrations equally frequent with the swinging of the bell.

*Ellicott on the mutual influence of two clocks. Ph. tr. 1739. 126.

A curious instance of sympathetic vibration; the motion of one of the clocks put the pendulum of the other in motion, even when they stood on a stone pavement near each other: the effects were accelerated when the communication was more direct. See Timekeepers.

*Huddlestone's observations on sound. Nich. 8. I. 329.

Showing the sympathy of chords and even of organ pipes, materially influencing the frequency of each others vibrations.

Ear and Hearing. Instruments for Hearing.

Perrault on the organ of hearing. A. P. I. 158.
Duverney on hearing. A. P. I. 256.
Duverney de l'ouie. 12. M. B.
Valsalva de aure. 4. Bologn. 1704. M. B.
  Acc. by Douglas. Ph. tr. 1705. XXIV. 1978.
Duquet's hearing trumpet. Mach. A. II. 119.
Duquet's chair for the deaf. Mach. A. II. 129.
Blair on the organ of hearing in elephants. Ph. tr. 1718. XXX. 885.
Mairan on the effect of sound on the ear. A. P. 1737. 49. H. 97.
Leprotti on the perforation of the membrana tympani. Coll. Acad. X. 518.
On a perforated membrana tympani. C. Bon. I. 350.

The hearing unimpaired. Rivinus called it his foramen.

Martiani's model of the ear. A. P. 1743. H. 85.
Nollet on the hearing of fishes. A. P. 1743. 199.
Brocklesby's extract from Klein on the hearing of fishes. Ph. tr. 1748. 233.
Arderon on the hearing of fish. Ph. tr. 1748. 149.

Thinks that river fish have no hearing: observes, that sound is transmitted but faintly through water. A hand grenade bursting under water produced prodigious tremors.

Geoffroy on the hearing of reptiles. S. E. II. 164.
Haller. Physiol. V.
Camper on the hearing of fishes. S. E. VI. 177.
Elliot on vision and hearing. 8.
Vicq D'Azyr on the ear of birds. A. P. 1778. 381. H. 5.
Hunter on the organ of hearing in fish. Ph. tr. 1782. 379.

Shows that they hear.

Galvani on the ear of birds. C. Bon. VI. O. 420.
*Scarpa de auditu et olfactu. f. Pav. 1789.
Comparetti de aure interna. 4. Pad. 1789. R. S.
  Extr. Roz. XLII. 344.
Brunelli on the hearing of reptiles. C. Bon. VII. O. 301.
Lentin on deafness. Commentat. Gott. 1791. XI. Ph. 39.
Caldani sulla membrana del timpano. 8. Pad. 1794. R. S.
Home on the membrana tympani. Ph. tr. 1800. 1. Nich. V. 93.
Cooper on the destruction of the membrana tympani. Ph. tr. 1800. 151. Nich. 8. I. 102.
Cooper on an operation for deafness. Ph. tr. 1801. 435.
On hearing by the teeth. B. Soc. Phil. n. 41. Nich. IV. 383.
Beaumont's hearing instrument approved. M. Inst. IV.
Gilb. X. 567.

The deaf sometimes hear acute sounds.

Gough on the method of judging of the position of sonorous bodies. Manch. M. V. 622.

Thinks the bones of the head assist us in forming the judgment. A sound just audible at 240 feet was distinguished as being nearer at 40 feet than at 42. A horizontal angular difference of 8° was perceptible, an elevation of 10°.

On the invisible girl. Nich. 9. III. 56.

Sound conveyed by pipes, which open in a crevice of the moulding of a frame.

E. Walker's apparatus for conducting sound. Nich. 8. IV. 69. Gilb. XIV. 220.

Vieth's acustic observation. Gilb. XVII. 117.

Asserts, that there is a point precisely in the axis of hearing where the sound is not audible.

Darwin's zoonomia. II. 487.

"The late blind Justice Fielding walked for the first time into my room, when he once visited me, and after speaking a few words said, this room is about 22 feet long, 18 wide, and 12 high; all which he guessed by the ear with great accuracy." Darwin.

Theory of Music.

Musicae antiquae scriptores, Meibomii. 4. Amst. 1652. R. I.

Cl. Ptolemaei harmonica a Wallis. 4. Oxf. 1682. Op. III.

Zarlino Istitutioni harmoniche. f. Ven. 1558. 1573. M. B.

Salinas de musica. f. Salamanc. 1577. M. B.

Mersenni harmonica. f. Par. 1635.

Mersenne Harmonie universelle. f. Paris, 1636.

Kircheri musurgia. 2 v. f. Rom. 1650. M. B.

Kircheri phonurgia. f. 1673. M. B.

Cartesii musicae compendium. Utr. 1650. M. B.

Dechales mundus mathematicus. Ph. tr. abr. I. x. 606. IV. vii. 469.

Menzoli Musica speculativa. 4. Bologna, 1670.
Acc. Ph. tr. 1673. VIII. 6194.

Salmon on music. 8. London, 1672. M. B.
Acc. Ph. tr. 1671. VI. 3095.

Wallis on the division of the monochord. Ph. tr. 1698. XX. 80.

Wallis on the imperfections of the organ. Ph. tr. 1698. XX. 249.

Wallis's Works, vol. 3. f. Oxford, 1699.
Acc. Ph. tr. 1699. XXI. 259.

Sauveur's general system of intervals. A. P. 1701. 299. H. 121.

Sauveur on the organ. A. P. 1702.

†Salmon's music reduced to proportions. Ph. tr. 1705. XXIV. 2069.

Henfling's musical system. M. Berl. I. 265.

Malcolm on music. 8. Edinb. 1721. R. I.

Rameau Traité de l'harmonie. 4. Par. 1722. M. B.

Rameau systême de musique. 4. Par. 1726.

Rameau du principe d'harmonie.
Acc. A. P. 1750. H. 160.

Rameau on the principles of music. Mém. Trév. Aug. 1762.

Rameau's other musical works. See Forkel.

†*Euler* tentamen novae theoriae musicae. 4. Petersb. 1729. M. B.

Euler on some discords, and on the character of modern music. A. Berl. 1764. 165, 175.

Euler on the true principles of harmony. N. C. Petr. XVIII. 330.

Euler's speculum musicum.

F   C   G   D
  A   E   B   F#
C# G# D# Bb

Montvallon on musical intervals. A. P. 1742. H. 117.

On numbering vibrations. C. Bon. I. 180.

By the teeth of a wheel striking the air only.

Smith's harmonics. 8. Cambr. 1749. 1759. R. I.

Estève sur l'harmonie.
Acc. A. P. 1750. H. 165.

Estève on the best system of music, and on temperament. S. E. II. 113.

Romieu on grave harmonics. Ac. Montpel. 1751.

Romieu on tempered systems of music. A. P. 1758. 483.

Agrees nearly with the progressive temperament.

Avison on musical expression. 12. 1752.
Dalembert Elémens de musique. 8. Paris, 1752.
†*Tartini* della vera scienza dell' armonia. 4. Pad. 1754. M. B.
Rousseau Dictionnaire de musique.
Rousseau's musical dictionary.
Marpurg Anfangsgründe der theoretischen musik. 4. Leipz. 1757.
On ratios and temperaments.
Marpurgs versuch über die temperatur. 8. Bresl. 1776.
Jamard sur la théorie de la musique. 8. Par. 1768.
Emerson's miscellanies. 353.
*Holden on a rational system of music. 4. Lond. 1770. M. B.
*Kirnberger Kunst des reinen satzes. 4. Berl. 1771 ...
Sulzers theorie der schönen künste. 4 v. 8. Leipz. 1772.
Lambert on musical temperament. A. Berl. 1774. 55.
Harrison on clockwork and on music. 8. 1775. R. S.
Gedanken über Kirnbergers temperatur. 8. Berl. 1775.
Vandermonde Système d'harmonie. 8. R. S. Acc. A. P. 1778. H. 51.
Bemetzrieder Essai sur l'harmonie. 8. R. S.
Bemetzrieder Méthode de musique. 8. R. S.
Bemetzrieder Traité de musique. 8. R. S.
Steele's prosodia rationalis. 4. Lond. 1779.
Good theory, but inaccurate declamation.
Essay on tune. 8. Edinb. 1782. M. B.
Jones's treatise on music. f.
E. M. Musique, ½ vol to Cyt. by Framery and Ginguené.
Barca on a new theory of music. A. Pad. I. 365. II. 329. IV. 71.
Cavallo on temperament. Ph. tr. 1788. 238.

Recommends the equal temperament.
Sacchi's theory of music. C. Bon. VII. O. 139.
*Forkel Allgemeine litteratur der musik. 8. Leipz. 1792.
Jones on the musical modes of the Hindoos. As. Res. III. 55.
Suremain Missery Théorie acousticomusicale.
Patterson's notation of music. Am. tr. III. 139.
Young. Ph. tr. 1800.
Additional remarks. Nich. V. 141.
Young on compound sounds, in answer to Gough. Nich. 8. II. 264. III. 145. IV. 72.
Young's harmonic sliders. Journ. R. I. Nich. 8. IV. 101.
Robison. Enc. Br. Suppl. Art. Temperament, Trumpet.
Enc. Br. Suppl. II. 650.
"The perception of harmonious sound is the sensation produced by another definite form of the agitation. This is the composition of two other agitations; but it is the compound agitation only that affects the ear, and it is its form or kind which determines the sensation, making it pleasant or unpleasant." Robison.
Chladni on finding the velocity of vibrations. Gilb. V. 1.
Proposes to number the vibrations of a long rod, and to observe the sound of a portion of it. Suggests Sauveur's last pitch as a new idea.
Gough on the theory of compound sounds. Manch. M. V. 653. Nich. 8. IV. 152.
Defends Smith against Dr. Young, but misunderstands both.
Gough on compound sounds and grave harmonics, in reply. Nich. 8. III. 39. IV. 1, 139.
Mrs. M. Young's patent for teaching music. Repert. XVI. 9.

Musical Instruments.

Mersenne Harmonie universelle.
Kircheri musurgia et phonurgia.
Schotti mechanica hydraulicopneumatica. 4. Würzb. 1657.
Carré on musical instruments. A. P. 1702. H. 136.
Miller's harmonic gate. Ac. Sienna. II. 132.
E. M. A. IV. Art. Instrumens de musique.
Cavallo. N. Ph. II. 384.

The note A was found by experiment to consist of 107 vibrations in a second.

The A of the progressive temperament, derived from Sauveur's pitch, consists of $106\frac{3}{4}$, which agrees within the possible limits of error.

Stringed Instruments.

Roberts on the trumpet marine. Ph. tr. 1693. XVII. 559.
Lahire on the trumpet marine. A. P. IX. 330.
Molyneux on the ancient lyre. Ph. tr. 1703. XXIII. 1267.
Marius's harpsichords. Mach. A. I. 193. A. P. 1716. H. 77. Mach. A. III. 89.
Marius's pianoforte. Mach. A. III. 83, 85, 87.
Cuisinier's harpsichord. Mach. A. II. 153.
Cuisinier's harpsichord or vielle. A. P. 1734. H. 105.
†Maupertuis on the form of musical instruments. A. P. 1724. 215. H. 90.
Thevenart's single stringed harpsichord. A. P. 1727. H. 142. A. Mach. A. V. 11.
Bellot's harpsichord. A. P. 1732. H. 118.
Levoir's harpsichord. A. P. 1742. H. 146. Mach. A. VII. 183.
Domenjoud's head for violins. A. P. 1756. H. 130.
Weltmann's harpsichord. A. P. 1759. H. 241.
Laborde Clavecin electrique. 12. Par. 1761.
A play thing.

Legay's keyed instrument with harp strings. A. P. 1762. H. 191.
Berger's organized harpsichord. A. P. 1765. H. 138.
Vireboy's harpsichord. A. P. 1766. H. 161.
Joubert's organized vielle. A. P. 1768. H. 130.
Gosset's division of the finger board. A. P. 1769. H. 131.
Lepine's pianoforte. A. P. 1772. i. H.
A pianoforte. E. M. A. VII. Supplement.
M. Young on the harp of Eolus. Y. on sound. Nich. III. 310.
Bagatella regole per la costruzione de' violini. Pad. 1786.
A prize essay.

Hopkinson on quilling a harpsichord. Am. tr. II. 185.
Pérolle on the resonance of musical instruments. M. Tur. 1790. V. Corr. 195. Nich. I. 411.
Against Maupertuis.

Fowke on the Indian lyre. As. Res. I. 295.

Drums.

E. M. M. III. Art. Tambour.
Riccati. Ac. Pad. I.

Elastic Instruments.

Franklin's harmonica. A. P. 1773. H. 81.
On the harmonica. Roz. VII. 462.
Golovin on the theory of the harmonica. A. Petr. 1781. V. ii. 176.
Bells. E. M. A. I. Art. Cloches.
Deudon's harmonica. Roz. XXXIII. 183.
Lalande on the weight of bells. Journ. Phys. XLIV. (I.) 85.

Burja on musical instruments of glass. A. Berl. 1796 i. 3.

Chladni's euphon. Ph. M. II. 315, 391.
  Made of glass cylinders.

Chladni's clavicylinder. Gilb. IV. 494.

Wind Instruments.

Roberts on the trumpet. Ph. tr. 1693. XVII. 559.

*Sauveur on the composition of organ pipes. A. P. 1702. 308. H. 90.

Marius's organ, with bellows to each pipe. Mach. A. III. 91.

Organ. Emerson's mech. f. 313.

*Bédos Art du facteur d'orgues. f. Par. 1766 .. 1778.
  Acc. A. P. 1767. H. 180.

Meister on the antient hydraulum. N. C. Gott. 1770. II. 152.
  With good figures.

Steele on musical instruments from the South Seas. Ph. tr. 1775. 67.

Engramelle Tonotechnie. 8. Par. 1775.
  On hand organs.

Lambert on flutes. A. Berl. 1775. 13.

Halle Kunst des orgelbaues. 4. Brandenb. 1779.

Trumpets. E. M. Pl. I. Chaudronnier. Pl. 4.

Organs. E. M. Pl. III. Luthier.

E. M. Pl. III.
  Bagpipes have drones with reed mouth pieces.

Pini pantaulo. 8. Milan, 1783. R. S.

Fitzgerald's patent signal trumpet. Repert. XI. 100.
  For conveying the sound of a pistol.

Close on the properties of wind instruments. Nich. V. 213.

Longman's patent barrel organs. Repert. XIV. 367.
  For a more steady connexion of the parts.

Godfry's patent barrel organs with a tabor and pipe. Repert. XV. 361.

†Beyer on the glass chord. Journ. Phys. XLVIII. 408.

On silk strings. Nich. I. 328.

Lüdicke's micrometer for wires. Gilb. I. 137.

Becker's patent harps. Repert. XVI. 146.
  Making the half notes by a change of tension.

Bemetzrieder's patent pianoforte. Repert. ii. III. 324.

Langguth's Eolian harp. Gilb. XV. 305.

Robison. Enc. Br. Suppl. Art. Pianoforte, Trumpet.
  Euler's clavichord produced the twelfth of each string that was struck, dividing it into three parts; and had a very sweet tone. Robison.

Voice and Speech.

Organs of the Human Voice.

*Dodart on the human voice. A. P. 1700. 244. H. 17. 1706. 136, 388. 1707. 66. H. 18.

*Ferrein on the human voice. A. P. 1741. 409. H. 51.

Vicq d' Azyr on the organs of voice. A. P. 1779. 178. H. 5.

Speech.

Holder's elements of speech. 8. Lond. 1669.
  Acc. Ph. tr. 1669. IV. 958.

Vossius de poematum cantu. 8. Oxf. 1673.
  Acc. Ph. tr. 1673. VIII. 6024.

Amman de loquela.

Lodwick's universal alphabet. Ph. tr. 1686. XVI. 126.

Byrom on Lodwick's universal alphabet. Ph. tr. 1748. XLV. 401.

Debrosses Formation mécanique des langues.

Steele on the melody and measure of speech. 4. 1779. R. S.
  Good theory, but bad declamation.

*_Kratzenstein_ Tentamen coronatum de voce. Kratzenstein on the imitation of the human voice. A. Petr. 1780. IV. ii. H. 16.

<small>Made pipes imitating the vowels.</small>

*Kratzenstein on the vowels. Roz. XXI. 358.

<small>Figures of the different pipes.</small>

Gough on the variety of voices. Manch. M. V. 58.

<small>Deduces the variety of tones from different combinations of imperfect unisons.</small>

Gough on ventriloquism. Manch. M. V. 650. Nich. 8. II. 122. V. 247.

<small>Attributes the effect to the reflection of sound.</small>

Nicholson on ventriloquism. Nich. 8. IV. 202. V. 247.

<small>Shows that the effect is in general only a fallacy.</small>

Gibbon's life, quoted by Cavallo. N. Ph. I.

<small>" A rapid orator pronounces about two English words in a second."</small>

A Description of Articulate Sounds, with Appropriate Characters.

Classes of Letters.

Class 1. Pure vowels consist of a vocal sound formed in the larynx, not interrupted by the tongue and lips, nor passing in any degree through the nose.

Class 2. Nasal vowels consist of a vocal sound, passing without interruption through both the mouth and the nose.

Class 3. Pure semivowels consist of a vocal sound, much impeded in its passage, yet capable of being prolonged, not passing through the nose.

Class 4. Nasal semivowels consist of a vocal sound, stopped in the mouth, and passing only through the nose.

Class 5. Mixed semivowels consist of a vocal sound, much impeded in its passage through the mouth, and passing partly through the nose.

Class 6. Explosive letters consist of a vocal sound, stopped in its passage.

Class 7. Susurrant or whispering letters have no vocal sound, but are capable of being continued.

Class 8. Mute letters have no vocal sound, and are incapable of being sounded alone or continued.

Class 1. Pure vowels.

E. The tongue and lips in their most natural position, without exertion.

A. The tongue drawn backwards, and a little upwards, so as to contract the passage immediately above the larynx.

O. The contraction of the mouth greatest immediately under the uvula. The lips must be also somewhat contracted.

U. The contraction continued below the whole of the soft palate.

I. The contraction formed by bringing the tongue nearly into contact with the bony palate.

From these principal vowels all others may be deduced by considering them as partaking more or less of the nature of each, accordingly as they are situated nearer to them in this scheme.

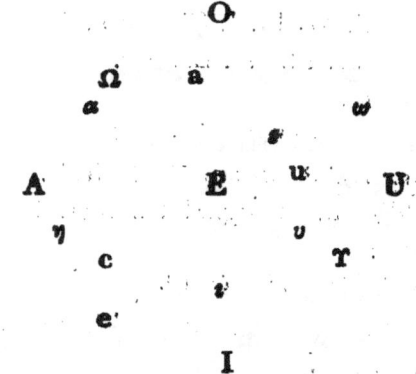

Class 2. Nasal vowels.

The nasal vowels are derived from the pure vowels by lowering the soft palate so as to suffer the sound to pass in part through the nose: they may be marked by the same characters as denote the pure vowels, with the addition of the grave accent.

Class 3. Pure semivowels.

L. The point of the tongue is pressed against the palate, the sound escapes laterally.

Λ. The point of the tongue is brought very near to the palate, but the contact is closer a little behind the point, the sound still escaping further back.

Π. The point and middle of the tongue press against the palate, the sound escaping at the base, but not without difficulty.

R. The middle and point of the tongue strike the palate with a vibrating motion, the point being drawn back.

r. The point of the tongue is drawn backward, and is brought very near to the palate, but without a distinct vibration.

V. The lower lip presses on the upper teeth.

Δ. The tongue presses against the upper teeth.

Γ. The middle of the tongue is brought nearly into contact with the palate, the point being a little depressed.

Z. The point of the tongue is brought nearly into contact with the upper teeth, the air being forced against the edges of the teeth with violence.

J. The air is forced with violence against the teeth, being first confined between the tongue and palate immediately behind the upper teeth.

Class 4. Nasal semivowels.

M. The passage of the mouth is closed by the lips.

N. The passage of the mouth is closed by the point of the tongue.

n. The passage of the mouth is closed by the middle of the tongue.

Class 5. Mixed semivowels.

v. The passage of the mouth is very nearly closed by the approach of the base of the tongue to the soft palate.

Class 6. Explosive letters.

B, D, G. The tongue is placed as in M, N, n, respectively.

Class 7. Susurrant letters.

H. The breath is forced through the mouth, which is every where a little contracted.

F, Θ, X, S, Σ. Differ from V, Δ, Γ, Z, J, respectively, only in the absence of the vocal sound.

Class 8. Mutes.

P, T, K, are distinguished from B, D, G, by the absence of the sound formed in the larynx.

Examples, with the mode of writing the words in these characters.

1. E. The man, eye, a window. E. ΔE MAN, EI. E UɪNDE. Le, repos. Fr. LE, REPO.

2. A. Father. E. FAΔEr.

3. α. Ame, femme. Fr. $\bar{\ }$M, F$_a$M. Dank. G. DαnK.

4. Ω. All, not, joy, owl. E. ΩL, NŎT, DJ$\overline{Ω\iota}$, $\overline{ΩU}$L.

5. a. Homme de robe. Fr. aM DE RaB.

6. O. Old. E. OLD. Eaux. Fr. O.

7. ε. Jeu, oeil, Fr. Jε, εIΛ.

8. ω. Jeux, noeuds. Fr. Jω. Nω.

9. u. But, shut. E. BuT, ΣuT.

10. U. Too full. E. TU FUL. Vous. Fr. VU.

11. v. Lügen. G. LvrEN.

12. ϒ. Une laitue. Fr. ϒN LETϒ. In Norfolk and in Devonshire the English U is sometimes pronounced ϒ.

13. I. Ye see. E. $\bar{\iota}$I SI. Ici. Fr. ISI.

14. ι. Lip. E. LιP. Mit. G. MιT. When 'lip' is lengthened in singing, it does not become 'leap.'

15. e. Hate. E. HēT. Nez, eclat. Fr. Ne, eKLɑ.
16. c. Met, pen. E. McT, PcN. Glèbe, peine, père. Fr. GLcB, PcN, PcR.
17. η. Blême, seize, mes, mets, mais. Fr. BLηM, SηZ, Mη, Mη, Mη.
18. ɑ̀. An, camp, tems. Fr. ɑ̀, Kɑ̀, Tɑ̀.
19. ò. Mon nom. Fr. Mò Nò.
20. ἰ. Un parfum, à jeun. Fr. ἰ PaRFἰ, a Jἰ.
21. ʋ. The Erse term for a calf is πʋE, as pronounced in Rossshire.
22. ὴ. Main, chemin. Mὴ, ΣEMὴ.
23. L. Love. E. LuV. Loi. Fr. LŪη.
24. Λ. Fille. Fr. FIΛ. Ciglio It. ΤΣΙΛΙΟ.
25. Π. Llangollen. W. ΠANGΩΠeN.
26. R. Rouge. Fr. RUJ. The Scotch and Irish give this sound to the English r.
27. r. Round, under. E. rΩ̄UND. uNDEr.
28. V. Vow. E. VΩ̄U. Vous. Fr. VU.
29. Δ. Though. E. ΔO. The δ of the modern Greeks.
30. Γ. Sagen. G. ZaΓEN. Gemir. Sp. ΓeMIR.
31. Z. Zeal. E. ZIL. Oser. Fr. Oze.
32. J. Measure, judge. E. McJEr, DJuDJ. Juge. Fr. JɤJ.
33. M. Man. E. MAN. Mort. Fr. MaR.
34. N. Nine. E. NĒN. Nonne. Fr. NɑN or NɑNNE.
35. n. Thank. E. ΘAnK. Denken. G. DcnKEN or DcnKN.
36. ν. Regner. Fr. Rcνe.
37. B. Bow. E. BO. Beau. Fr. BO.
38. D. Dark. E. DArK. Dame. Fr. DɑM.
39. G. Good. E. GŪD. Gueux. Fr. Gw.
40. H. Home. E. HOM. Hameau. Fr. HɑMO.
41. F. Fall. E. FΩL. Foi. Fr. FŪη.
42. Θ. Think. E. ΘinK. Luz. Sp. LUΘ.
43. X. Nach. G. NɑX. Ax, ojo. Sp. ɑx,

OXO. The Scotch give this sound to gh in 'night.'
44. S. Sing. E. Sɪn. Sage. Fr. SAJ.
45. Σ. Shun. E. ΣuN. Chou. Fr. ΣU. Mucho. Sp. MUTΣO.
46. P. Pump. E. PuMP. Peur. Fr. PɛR.
47. T. Tongue. E. Tun. Tout. Fr. TU.
48. K. Call. E. KΩL. Courir. Fr. KURIR.

SPECIMEN.

HŪcN LuVLɪ ŪuŪMEN STŪPS TE
    FΩ̄Lɪ,
END FEiNDZ TU LēT ΔET McN
    BɪTreɪ,
¿HŪΩT TΣArM KEN SUΔ Hcr
    McLENKΩLɪ?
¿HŪΩT ArT KEN ŪEɪP HEr GɪLT
    Evcɪ?

Some would read in the first line TŪ, and not TE.

Teaching the Deaf.

Wallis on teaching the deaf to speak. Ph. tr. 1698. XX. 353.
Amman Surdus loquens.
Ernaud on the deaf and dumb. S. E. V. 233.
Pereire on conversing with the dumb. A. P. 1749. H. 183. S. E. V. 500.
Pereire's machine for making the deaf speak. A. P. 1750. H. 169.
E. M. A. V. Art. Muets et Sourds.
*Vox oculis subjecta, with an account of Braidwood's academy. S. R. S.
Thornton on teaching the dumb to speak. Am. tr. III. 262.
Sicard Grammaire pour les sourds muets. Paris.

Peculiarities of Speech.

Jussieu on speech without a tongue. A. P. 1718. 6.

Account of a woman who spoke fluently without a vestige of a tongue. Ph. tr. 1742. 143.

Parsons's account of M. Cutting, who had lost her tongue. Ph. tr. 1747. 621. Ph. M. IV. 214.

Maunoir and Paul observed, that hydrogen gas inspired made their voices shrill. From Prévost's Journal. Perhaps rather harsh than shrill. Y.

Speaking Trumpet.

Kircher.
Moreland on the speaking trumpet. London, 1671.
Acc. Ph. tr. 1671. VI. 3056.
Conyers's improved speaking trumpet. Ph. tr. 1677. XII. 1027.
With an internal tube.
Haasius de tubis stentoreis. 4. Leipz. 1719.
*Lambert on some acustic instruments. A. Berl. 1763. 87.
E. M. Pl. V. Marine. Pl. XIII.
Hassenfratz on speaking trumpets. Ann. Ch. Nich. IX. 233.
Considers the effect as similar to that of a trumpet, or of a reed organ pipe, and thinks that reflection is not concerned.

Voices of different Animals.

Duverney on the voice of the fowls. A. P. II. 4.
On the organ of voice of the horse, ass, and mule. Coll. Acad. VIII. App. 24.
Herissant on the organs of voice in quadrupeds and birds. A. P. 1753. 279. H. 107.
Parsons on the windpipes of birds. Ph. tr. 1766. 204.
Barrington on singing birds. Ph. tr. 1773. 249.
Camper on the organs of speech of the oran outang. Ph. tr. 1779. 139.
Observes, after Galen, that it is impossible for these animals to speak. But had they intellect sufficient, they might certainly whisper.

Vicq d'Azyr on the organs of voice. A. P. 1779. 178. H. 5.
Daubenton on the tracheae of birds. A. P. 1781. 369. H. 12.
Ballanti on the organ of voice in animals. C. Bon. VI. C. 50.
Cuvier on the voice of birds. B. Soc. Phil. n. 15. Journ. Phys. I. 426.
Latham Trans. Linn. Soc.

Instruments subservient to Music.

Loulié's sonometer. Mach. A. I. 187, 189.
A monochord.
Sauveur's echometer. A. P. 1701. 317. H. 121.
A tabular instrument.
Demotz's mode of writing music. A. P. 1726. H. 73.
Ons en Bray's metrometer. A. P. 1732. 182.
For beating time.
Creed's proposal for a method of writing voluntaries. Ph. tr. 1747. 445.
Sulzer's instrument for writing voluntaries. A. Berl. 1771. 538. Fig.
Ungers entwurf einer maschine. 4. Brunsw. 1774.
For writing voluntaries.
Burja Beschreibung eines zeitmessers. 8. Berl. 1790.
For measuring time.
Weisskens tactmesser. Leipz. 1790.
Montu's sonometer. Ph. M. XII. 187.

History of Acustics.

Dodart on antient and modern music. A. P. 1706. 388.
Pepusch on the genera and species of music among the ancients. Ph. tr. 1746. 266.
Styles on the modes of the antients. Ph. tr. 1760. 695.
Burney on an infant musician. Ph. tr. 1779. 183.

Crotch, who played "God save the King" at the age of
2 years and 3 weeks.
Burney's history of music. 4 v. 4. R. I.
Hawkins's history of music, 5 v. 4. M. B.
Dalberg on the music of the Hindoos. Ph.
 M. II. 105.
Forkels Geschichte der musik. 4.
J. Bernoulli on the problem of vibrating
 chords. Hind. Arch. III. 266.
Montucla and Lalande. IV. 644.

Guido lived 1025; the present notes were introduced
1334; chimes were applied to bells at Alost 1487; Franklin invented the Harmonica 1760.. Luckombe.

OPTICS IN GENERAL.

Heliodorus de opticis. 4. Par. 1657. M. B.
Risneri opticae thesaurus. f. Bas. 1585. M. B.
Faulhaberi descriptio instrumentorum geo-
 metriae et opticorum. 4. Frankf. 1610.
De Dominis de radiis visus et lucis. 4. Ven.
 1611. M. B.
Rhodi Optique. 8. 1612.
Eskinard's century of optical problems. 1615.
Kircheri ars magna lucis et umbrae. f. Rom.
 1646. M. B.
Zucchii optica philosophia. 1652. M. B.
J. Gregorii optica promota. Lond. 1663. M.B.
Grimaldi physicomathesis de lumine. 4. Bo-
 logna, 1665. M. B.
 Acc. Ph. tr. 1671. VI. 3068.
 Ph. tr. abr. I. iii. 128. IV. ii. 173. VI. ii. 110.
 VIII. ii. 111. X. ii. 29.
*Newton's optics. 4. Lond. 1701.
Bouguer Traité d'optique. Par. 1729. En-
 larged. 1760. M. B.
*Newtonianismo per le donne. 4. Napl. 1737.
 By Algarotti.
Smith's optics. 4. Cambr. 1738. R. I. Germ.
 by Kästner. 4. Altenb. 1755.
Courtivron Traité d'optique.
 Acc. A. P. 1752. H. 131.
La Caille lectiones opticae. 4. Vienn. 1757.

Langebacks der ganzen optik. Alt. 1757.
Emers. cyclomathesis. VI. Misc. 453.
Lambert Photometria. 8. Augsb. 1760. R.I.
Priestley's history and present state of disco-
 veries relating to vision, light, and colours.
 4. London, 1772. R. I. Germ. by Klügel.
 4. Leipz. 1776.
Harris's optics. 4. Lond. 1775. R. I.
Boscovich opera pertinentia ad opticam et
 astronomiam. 5 v. 4. Bassano, 1785. R. I.
Göthe Beytrage zur optik. 8. Weimar, 1792.
Traité d'optique par les élèves de l'école po-
 lytechnique. 8. Par.
Haüy. Phys. II. 144.

Theory of Dioptrics and Catoptrics.

Euclidis optica. Gr. L. 4. Par. 1557.
Alhazen et Vitellio. f. Bale, 1572. M. B.
Kepleri paralipomena ad Vitellionem. 4.
 Frankf. 1604. M. B.
Kepleri dioptrice. 4. Augsb. 1611. M. B.
Descartes dioptrica. Opusc. II.
Barrow lectiones opticae. 4. Lond. 1669.
Hugens and Sluslus on the problem of Al-
 hazen. Ph. tr. 1675. VIII. 6119. 6140.
Hugenii dioptrica. Op. rel. II.
Halley on the foci of optical glasses. Ph. tr.
 1693. XVII. 960.
Hartsoeker Essai de dioptrique. 4. Par. 1694.
 M. B.
Gregorii catoptrices et dioptrices elementa. 8.
 Oxf. 1695. M. B.
 Acc. Ph. tr. 1696. XIX. 214.
Gregory's elements of catoptrics and dioptrics.
 8. 1735.
Picard's fragments of dioptrics. A. P. VII. 325.
Lahire on the caustic of a circle. A. P. IX.
 294. 363.
L'Hopital on caustics by refraction. A. P. X.
 260.
Carré's rectification of caustics by reflection.
 A. P. 1703. 183. H. 69.

Carré's abridgement of catoptrics. A. P. 1710. 46. H. 112.

Guisnée on the focus of lenses. A. P. 1704. 24. H. 76.

Rolle on foci. A. P. 1706. 284.

Ditton theorema catoptricum universale. Ph. tr. 1705. XXIV. 1810.

Krafft on a catoptrical problem. C. Petr. V. 82.

Krafft on the caustic of the cycloid. C. Petr. VII. 3.

Krafft on the image of a point. C. Petr. XII. 243.

Krafft on foci. N. C. Petr. II. 39.

Mairan on anaclastics. A. P. 1740. 2.

Kaestner on the aberrations of lenses. C. Gott. I. 185. II. 183.

Kaestner on Alhazen's problem. N. C. Gott. 1776. VII. 92.

> Employs tables of sines and tangents.

Klingenstierna on refraction. Schw. Abh. 1754. 300.

Klingenstierna on aberration. Schw. Abh. 1760. 79.

*Klingenstierna de aberrationibus luminis in superficiebus sphaericis. Ph. tr. 1760. 944.

Klingenstierna de aberrationibus luminis. 4. Petersb. 1762.

Redern on dioptrics. A. Berl. 1759, 1760, 1761.

Maskelyne's theorem for spherical aberration. Ph. tr. 1761. 17.

Euler on the confusion of dioptric glasses. A. Berl. 1761. 1762.

Euler on vision through spherical segments. N. C. Petr. XI. 185.

Euleri dioptrice. Petersb. 1771.
Acc. A. P. 1765. 555. H. 124.

Euler. N. C. Petr. XVIII.

> Supersedes his dioptrics. Klügel.

Lagrange's dioptrical formulae. M. Taur. III. ii. 152. A. Berl. 1778. 162.

Boscovich on the improvement of dioptrics. C. Bon. V. i. O. 169.

Boscovich Dissertationes dioptricae. 4. R. S.

Meister on the effect of oil swimming on water. Commentat. Gott. 1781. I. 35.

Klügels analytische dioptrik. 4. Leipz. 1778.

Wales's example of a tentative calculation in Alhazen's problem. Ph. tr. 1781. 472.

Gr. Fontana on refraction. Soc. Ital. III. 498.

Fuss on the caustic of a parabola. N. A. Petr. 1790. VIII. 182.

M. Young on Newton's theorem for aberration. Ir. tr. IV. 171.

Mallet on the construction of problems concerning refraction. Schw. Abh. XII. 238.

Bürja on lenses not spherical. A. Berl. 1797. ii. 3.

Bürja on the track of light in a prism. A. Berl. 1798. 3.

Hällström on refraction. Gilb. III. 235. VI. 431.

On the place of the image of a mirror. Nich. VII. 71.

> Klingenstierna gives for the lens of least aberration $\frac{a}{b} = \frac{(r+4-2rr)d+(2rr+r)e}{(r+4-2rr)e+(2rr+r)d}$, a and b being the first and second radii, r the index of refraction, d the focal distance of incident, and e of refracted rays; this expression, when $r = \frac{3}{2}$ and $d = \infty$, becomes $\frac{1}{6}$ when $r = 1686$, $\frac{1}{\infty}$, or a plano-convex.

See Telescopes.

Optical Instruments in general.

Lehrgebaüde der ganzen optik. Altona, 1757.

D. de Chaulnes's dioptrical experiments. A. P. 1767. 423. H. 162.

Fontana's account of the Grand Duke's cabinet. Roz. IX. 41...

E. M. Pl. VIII. Amusemens d'optique.

Photometers.

Bouguer Traité d'optique.

Bouguer on the measurement of light. A. P. 1757. 1. H. 145.

Celsius on the measure of light. A. P. 1735. H. 5.
  Confirms Bouguer's estimate of the moon's light as 1/300000 of that of the sun.

*Lambert Photometria. 8. R. I.

Nux's mode of determining the magnitude of the stars. A. P. 1762. H. 135.
  By viewing them through semitransparent substances of different thicknesses.

Priestley's optics, vi. §. 7.

Fontana on the measurement of light. Soc. Ital. I. 111.

Count Rumford's photometer. Ph. tr. 1794. 67. Repert. IV. 255.

Leslie's photometer. Nich. III. 461, 518. Gilb. V. 286.
  A thermometer.

Measurement of Refractive Powers.

Clairaut on the measurement of refrangibility. A. P. 1756. 408.

Martin's optics.

Euler on the examination of refraction by prisms. A. Berl. 1766. 202.

Duc de Chaulnes. A. P. 1767. 429. H. 162.

Priestley's optics. v. §. 8. c. 2.

Venturi on measuring dispersion. Soc. Ital. III. 268.

Rochon Recueil de mémoires sur la mécanique et la physique. Mém. sur la mesure de la dispersion et de la réfraction.
  His diasporometer is a compound prism.

*Wollaston's mode of examining refractive and dispersive powers. Ph. tr. 1802. 365. Nich. a. IV. 29.

Measurement of Transparency.

Murhard on Saussure's diaphanometer, for measuring the transparency of the air. Ph. M. III. 377.

Catoptric Instruments.

Account of Vilette's concave, 30 inches in diameter, 3 feet focus. Ph. tr. 1665—6. I. 95.

Vilette's second concave of metal, 34 inches in diameter. Ph. tr. 1669. IV. 986.

A speculum 3 Leipzig ells in diameter, of thin copper plate. Ph. tr. 1686. XVI. 352.
  Not very good.

†Gray on specula nearly parabolic. Ph. tr. 1697. XIX. 787.
  In the form of the catenaria.

Lagarouste on a burning mirror. A. P. I. 276.

Lahire on the multiplication of images by plane glasses. A. P. 1699. 75. H. 86.

Leupold Anamorphosis nova. 4. Leipz. 1713.

Harris and Desaguliers on Vilette's concave, 47 inches in diameter, 38 inches focus. Ph. tr. 1719. XXX. 976.
  They say, that it burnt less powerfully when it grew hot. Perhaps for the same reason as Herschel's glasses transmitted more heat when they were hot, and reflected less.

Dufay's catoptrical experiments. A. P. 1726. 165. H. 47.
  Observes how much culinary heat is intercepted by glass.

Leutmann's anamorphosis. C. Petr. IV. 202.

Cal. Smith's glass speculums. Ph. tr. 1739. XLI.

Newton's paper on a reflecting instrument like Hadley's. Ph. tr. 1742. 155.

Speculums. Smith's optics. iii. c. 2.

Chateau Blanc's reflecting lamps. A. P. 1744. H. 62. Mach. A. VII. 273.

Cassini on burning mirrors. A. P. 1747. 25. H. 113.

Courtivron's comparison of plane and spherical mirrors. A. P. 1747. 449. H. 117.

Needham on Buffon's mirror, burning at the distance of 66 feet Fr. Ph. tr. 1747. 493.

Nicolini on Buffon's mirror. Ph. tr. 1747.
   Composed of 168 plane mirrors each 6 inches square; burning wood at the distance of 150 feet; melting a silver plate at 10 feet.

Buffon's account of his burning speculum. Ph. tr. 1748. 504.
   It was 6 feet broad and of the same height; burnt wood at the distance of 200 feet, melted tin and lead at 120, silver at 50.

Parsons on the burning instrument of Archimedes. Ph. tr. 1754. 621.

Lievreville's reflecting lamps. A. P. 1759. H. 234.

Zeiher on burning mirrors. N. C. Petr. VII. 237.

On mirrors. Abat Amusemens philosophiques. 1763. Montucla and Lalande. III. 554.

Reflecting lamps. Art du Vitrier. f. Paris. ii. 224.

Wolfe de speculis Dni. Hoesen. Ph. tr. 1769. 4.
   They are made of brass plates, fixed on wood of a parabolic form; one 9 Dresden feet 7 inches in diameter, 4 feet in focus; the diameter of the focus being not more than half an inch. Melted in Hoffman's experiments a large nail in 3″, a pistole in 2″. Hoffman used the two opposite each other, as Dufay had done before and Pictet has done since. They reflected very powerfully the heat of a strongly heated stove. 2 Sept. 1766.

Lambert on portelumieres. A. Berl. 1770. 51.
   Cones of tin for directing light.

On speculum metal. Roz. Introd. I. 435.

Alat on looking glasses. Roz. III. 328.

Kaestner on the multiplication of images in looking glasses. Dissert. ii. 8.

Kaestner on the magnitude of images in a spherical mirror. N. C. Gott. 1777. VIII. 96.

Mudge on the composition and formation of speculums. Ph. tr. 1777. 296.

Castillon on conductors of light. A. Berl. 1777. 42.

E. M. A. V. Art. Métal blanc. Miroitier.

Miroirs de métal. VI. 742. Reflecting lamps.

E. M. Physique. Art. Ardent.

Edwards on metal for speculums. Nautical almanac. 1787. Nich. III. 490. Gilb. XII. 167.

Sickingen on platina.
   Recommends 6 parts platina, 3 iron, and 1 gold. Lichtenb. in Erxleb.

Rochon on platina. Gilb. IV. 282.

Klaproth on an ancient mirror. A. Berl. 1797. 14.
   Copper 62, tin 32, lead 6.

On Descharmes's art of soldering glass. Journ. Phys. XLIX. 305. Gilb. V. 232.

Bernard on the manufactory of looking glasses. Journ. Polyt. II. 71. Repert. X. 351.

Bérard's photophorus. Mélanges. 1.

Benzenberg on speculums. Gilb. XII. 496.

Herschel on the action of mirrors. Ph. tr. 1803. 214. Nich. 8. V. 304.

See Radiant Heat.

Lenses.

Son's parabolic glasses. Ph. tr. 1665—6. I. 119.

Smethwick's lenses not spherical. Ph. tr. 1668. III. 631.

On grinding glasses on a plane. Ph. tr. 1668. III. 837.

Wren's mode of grinding hyperbolic glasses. Ph. tr. 1669. IV. 1059.
   Two cylinders revolving in contact across each other, become hyperbolic cylindroids, and form the glass revolving below them into a hyperbolic conoid.

Cherubin Dioptrique oculaire. f. Paris, 1671. Acc. Ph. tr. 1671. VI. 3045.

Butterfield on making glass globules. Ph. tr. 1677. XII. 1026.
   Of pounded glass held on a pin, in the flame of a spirit lamp with a wick of wire.

Borelli on finding the focus of an object glass. A. P. X. 457.

Compares the focal image formed by oblique rays to the profile of Saturn with his ring.

Lahire on centering lenses. A. P. 1699. 139. H. 86.

Borrichius on burning glasses three or four feet in diameter. A. P. 1699. H. 90.

Tschirnhaus's large lens, of 32 feet focus. A. P. 1700. H. 131.

Parent on a tool for hyperbolic glasses. A. P. 1702. H. 92.

Cassini on centering glasses. A. P. 1710. 223.

Homberg on the ancient burning glasses. A. P. 1711. H. 16.

Bianchini and Reaumur's support for large lenses. A. P. 1713. 299.

Hertel on grinding lenses. M. Berl. III. 146.

Nollet's machine for grinding lenses. Mach. A. VI. 127.

Deparcieux's machine for grinding glasses. A. P. 1736. H. 120. Mach. A. VII. 50.

Jenkins's machine for grinding spherical lenses. Ph. tr. 1741. XLI. 555.

A cup and ball both revolving.

Short's method of working object glasses truly spherical. Ph. tr. 1769. 507.

Delivered sealed 1752.

Zeiher on burning lenses. N. C. Petr. VII. 237.

Euler on polishing lenses. N. C. Petr. VIII. 254.

For preserving the form.

Euler on optical glasses. A. Berl. 1761. 107, 147. 1762. 117, 195.

Antheaulme on polishing object glasses. S. E. VI. 465.

Libaude on making flint glass. S. E. 1773.

Cadet and Brisson on Trudaine's lens. A. P. 1774. 62. H. 1.

Made of plate glass bent, with 140 pints of spirit of wine.

On a spherometer for measuring lenses. Roz. VII. 484. Fig. VIII. 398.

Burrows's machine for grinding glass. Bailey's mach. I. 142.

E. M. A. IV. Art. Lunettier.

Water lens. E. M. A. VI. 733.

Canterzani on grinding lenses. C. Bon. VI. O. 382.

Achard on optical glass. A. Berl. 1788. 14. 1790. 40.

Enc. Br. Art. Burroughs's machine, Glass polishing, Lens.

Dick Anweisung vergrösserungsgläser zu schleifen. Hamb. 1793.

Macquer on flint glass. Repert. VII. 211.

Globules for microscopes. Nich. I. 131.

On optical glass. Nich. I. 180.

On achromatic lenses. Nich. II. 233.

Benzenberg on the improvement of flint glass. Gilb. XI. 255.

Dr. Benzenberg warmly recommends, that the glass be suffered to cool in the pots without stirring, and that the mass be then divided in a horizontal direction, so that the variation of density may be regular, and then, by a proper form of the glasses, the errors of refraction may be corrected. The idea is not new, but it does not appear to have been carried into practice. Dr. Benzenberg considers achromatic telescopes as promising much more than reflectors, and thinks that they intercept much less light.

The dishes in which lenses are sometimes ground are of bell metal; the emery is prepared by elutriation. The large clumps now used for lamps are first formed in hemispherical ladles. This mode was proposed by Gessner in 1726.

Optical Scenery.

Hook on forming pictures on a wall. Ph. tr. 1668. III. 741.

Nollet's camera obscura. Mach. A. VI. 125.

Euler's improved magic lantern and solar microscope. N. C. Petr. III. 363.

†Storer's patent delineator. Repert. IV. 239.

A camera obscura.

On the phantasmagoria. Montucla and Lalande. III. 551.

Nicholson on the phantasmagoria. Nich. 8. I. 147.

Philipsthal's patent phantasmagoria. Rep. XVI. 303.

R. B.'s perspective instrument. Nich. IX. 122.

Panorama. See Vision, Aerial perspective.

Microscopes, Simple and Compound.

Hooke's Micrographia. f. Lond. 1665. R. I. Acc. Ph. tr. 1665. I. 27.

On a microscope of Fabri. Ph. tr. 1668. III. 842.

Leeuwenhoek's microscopes. Ph. tr. 1673. VIII. 6037.

†Gray on microscopes of water. Ph. tr. 1696. XIX. 280, 353, 539.

Some of the images thus seen are shadows. Y.

Huygens on a microscope. A. P. X. 427.

Wilson's description of his pocket microscopes. Ph. tr. 1702. XXIII. 1241.

Adams on microscopes. Ph. tr. 1710. XXVII. 24.

Globules.

Folkes on Leeuwenhoek's microscopes. Ph.tr. 1723. XXXII. n. 380.

Baker's catoptric microscope. Ph. tr. 1736. XXXIX. 442.

Like the Gregorian telescope.

Baker on Leeuwenhoek's microscopes. Ph. tr. 1740. XLI. 503.

The deepest $\frac{1}{12}$ of an inch focal length. A Wilson's microscope made by Cuff for Folkes, had a lens of $\frac{1}{16}$. Account of Lieberkuhn's opaque and solar microscope, p. 516.

Lieberkuhn's anatomical microscope. A. Berl. 1745. 14.

Euler's solar microscope. N. C. Petr. III. 363.

Euler on microscopes. A. Berl. 1757. 283, 323. 1761. 191, 201. 1764. 105, 117. N. C. Petr. XII. 195, 224.

Wideburg de microscopio solari. Erlang. 1755.

Wideburg Beschreibung eines sonnenmikroscops. Nuremb. 1758.

Aepinus's solar microscope. N. C. Petr. IX. 316.

For opaque objects.

Aepinus on an achromatic microscope. N. A. Petr. II. 1784. H. 41.

Aepinus Déscription des nouveaux microscopes. 8. Petr.

Zeiher's double solar microscope for opaque objects. N. C. Petr. X. 299.

Stiles on some microscopes made at Naples. Ph. tr. 1765. 246.

These globules were made by Father Latorre, one of them was $\frac{1}{12}$ of an inch in diameter, magnifying 2560 times. Describes, among many other objects, the globules of the blood, as articulated rings.

Baker's report of Latorre's globules. Ph. tr. 1766. 67.

Found them useless.

Baker on microscopes. 2 v. 8. 1785. R. I.

D. de Chaulnes's dioptrical experiments. A. P. 1767. 423. H. 162.

Selva's catoptric microscope. A. P. 1769. H. 129.

Dallebarre's microscope. A. P. 1771. H.

Dallebarre Mémoire sur le microscope. R. S.

Gleichen vom sonnenmikroscop. 4. Nuremb. 1781.

Beguelin's remark on Aepinus's microtelescope. A. Berl. 1784. H. 46.

Ph. tr. 1785. See Telescopes.

Ramsden applied to his pyrometer a microscope calculated for an equable enlargement of the image. The microscopes that he at first applied to Roy's theodolite were afterwards much improved.

Enc. Br. Art. Microscope.

Custance's machine for preparing sections of plants for microscopical inspection. Ph. M. III. 302.

Adams on the microscope, by Kanmacher. 4. Lond. 1798.

Microscopes of varnish. Ferguson's lectures, by Brewster.
> The eyepiece of a telescope makes a good solar microscope. Robison.

Telescopes.

Hooke, Auzout, and Campani on telescopes. Ph. tr. 1665—6. I. 2, 55, 56, 63, 68, 74, 131, 123, 203. A. P. VII. part. 2. i.

*Newton's new telescope. Ph. tr. 1672. VII. 4004, 4032. Birch. III. 2, 5.

Newton's remarks on Cassegrain's telescope. Ph. tr. 1672. VII. 4051.
> Thinks Cassegrain's telescope no improvement on Gregory's.

Hugens's aerial telescope. Ph. tr. 1684. XIV. 668.

Hugens on Newton's telescope. A. P. X. 351.

Huygens's telescopic level. A. P. X. 439.

Molineux on the telescope with four glasses. Ph. tr. 1686. XVI. 169.

Gray on telescopes. Ph. tr. 1697. XIX. 539.

Lahire on colours seen in telescopes. A. P. IX. 390.

Lahire's telescopes without tubes. A. P. 1715. 4.

Borelli on large telescopes. A. P. X. 393.

Cassini on telescopic glasses. A. P. X. 492.

Perrault's mirror for a telescope. Mach. A. I. 35.

Sebastian's machine for a telescope of 100 feet. Mach. A. I. 98.

Derham on Gascoigne's telescopic sights. Ph. tr. 1717. XXX. 603.

Hadley's account of a catadioptric telescope. Ph. tr. 1723. XXXII. 303.
> A Newtonian telescope 5½ feet long, equal to one of Hugens of 123 feet.

Pound on Hadley's telescope. Ph. tr. 1723. XXXII. 382.

Mairan's jacks for telescopes. Mach. A. V. 31.

Smith's optics.

Caleb Smith on catadioptrical telescopes with glass speculums. Ph. tr. 1740. XLI. 326.
> From theory only.

Le Maire's reflecting telescope. Mach. A. VI. 61.
> Like Dr. Herschel's.

Construction d'un télescope par réflexion. 8. Amst. 1741.

Euler on telescopes and object glasses. A. Berl. 1747. 274. 1757. 283, 323. 1761. 107, 147, 181, 201, 212. 1762. 117, 143, 185, 195, 226, 249. 1764. 200. 1766. 119, 171. M. Taur. III. ii. 60, 90. A. Berl. 1767. 131. N. C. Petr. XII. 195, 224. XVIII. 377 . . .

Kratzenstein on the management of long tubes. N. C. Petr. I. 291.

Kratzenstein and Euler on the iconantidiptic telescope. A. Petr. III. i. 192, 201.

Hertel Anweisung telescopia zu verfertigen. 8. Halle, 1747.

Kaestner on the aberration of lenses. C. Gott. See Theory of Dioptrics.

J. Dollond on an improvement of refracting telescopes. Ph. tr. 1753. 103.
> Adding a sixth lens.

Dollond and Euler on chromatic corrections. Ph. tr. 1753. 287.

*Dollond on the different refrangibility of light. Ph. tr. 1758. 733.

Klingenstierna on refraction. Schw. Abh. 1754. 300.

*Clairaut on the improvement of telescopes. A. P. 1756. 380. H. 112. 1757. 524. H. 153. 1762. 578. H. 160.

Finds the index of refraction of plate glass from 1.54 to 1.56: of flint 1.585 to 1.615; the dispersion of water equal to that of plate glass: thinks the colours differently distributed by different mediums.

Legentil on the aberration of light passing through two lenses. A. P. 1757. 545.

Legentil on binocular telescopes. A. P. 1787. 401. Roz. XXXI. 3.

Recommending them.

Redern on object glasses. A. Berl. 1759. 89. 1760. 3. 1761. 3.

J. A. Euler on object glasses with water. A. Berl. 1761. 231.

Beguelin on achromatic prisms. A. Berl. 1762. 66.

Beguelin on the improvement of telescopes. A. Berl. 1762. 343.

*Beguelin on telescopes. A. Berl. 1769. 1.

Beguelin on Aepinus's achromatic microtelescope. A. Berl. 1784. H. 40.

Murdoch on achromatic refraction. Ph. tr. 1763. 173.

Defends Newton.

Fougeroux on Campani's object glasses. A. P. 1764. 251. H. 169.

P. Dollond on achromatic telescopes with triple object glasses. Ph. tr. 1765. 54.

D'Alembert on achromatic telescopes. A. P. 1764. 75. H. 175. 1765. 53. H. 119. 1767. 43. H. 153.

D'Alembert Opuscules, vol. I. A. Berl. 1769. 254.

Acknowledges some mistakes of his own and of Clairaut.

Lagrange's dioptrical formulae. M. Taur. III. ii. 152.

Lagrange on the theory of telescopes. A. Berl. 1778. 162.

Cotes's theorem.

Boscovich on achromatic glasses. C. Bon. V. ii. 265. Germ. 8. Vienn. 1765.

Duc de Chaulnes on achromatic lenses. A. P. 1767. 423. H. 162.

Scherfer on dioptrical telescopes, by Hardy. 8. 1768.

Darquier on the focus of telescopes. S. E. V. 367.

Zeiher de novis dioptricae augmentis. 4. Wittenb. 1768.

Jeaurat on the refraction and dispersion of crown glass and flint glass, with tables for object glasses. A. P. 1770. 461. H. 103.

Lambert on achromatic telescopes of one kind of glass. A. Berl. 1771. 388.

Rochon's achromatic telescope. A. P. 1773. 299. Gilb. IV. 300.

Rochon on reflecting telescopes. Ph. M. II. 19. 170.

Navarre's telescope. A. P. 1778. H. 56.

Fuss sur les telescopes. Germ. by Klügel. 4. Leipz. 1778.

Telescopic appearances of the stars. Herschel, Ph. tr. 1782. 82.

Herschel on the magnifying powers of his telescopes. Ph. tr. 1782. 173.

Herschel on the front view of the reflecting telescope. Ph. tr. 1786. 499.

Herschel on the magnitude of the optic pencil. Ph. tr. 1786. 500.

A pencil of $\frac{1}{50}$ of an inch was sufficient for distinct vision with a high magnifying power. Suspects that the aperture ought to be in a certain ratio to the focal length, even in a large telescope.

*Herschel on his forty feet telescope. Ph. tr. 1795. 347.

Herschel on darkening telescopes. Ph. tr Nich. 8. I. 224.

Herschel on the action of mirrors. Ph. tr. 1803. 214. Nich. 8. V. 304.

Ramsden on the eyeglasses of telescopes applied to mathematical instruments. Ph. tr. 1783. 94.

Corrects the chromatic aberration nearly in the manner of Euler and Boscovich, and proposes to remedy the curvature of the first image, by placing a planoconvex lens a little beyond it, with the flat side towards it. By completing the investigation, it will be found, that in order to produce the greatest effect, the distance of the first image from the lens should be between a half and the whole of its radius; and in this case the centre of curvature of the mean image formed by the lens will be about the length of the radius beyond the lens, supposing it to have been at first a plane. Thus, for an object glass of 2 feet focal length, the radius of curvature of the mean image being about 9 inches, if the image be about 2 inches distant from a planoconvex lens of 4 inches radius, the effect of the curvature of a circle of 6 inches will be produced, which will make the mean image a little concave towards the eyeglass, as it ought to be. The radial focus is little affected by this arrangement. Y.

Adams's auzometer. Roz. XXII. 65. Fig.

For measuring the magnitude of the pencil of rays.

Oriani on the improvement of telescopes. Soc. Ital. III. 664.

Cassini on the interposition of a resinous substance between the lenses of an object glass, by Rochon and Grateloup. 1785. A. P. 1787. 30.

In order to lessen the partial reflection.

An eyeglass with a prism for observations near the zenith. Ph. tr. 1790. 155.

Schröter on a telescope of Schrader. Commentat. Gott. 1791. XI. M. 32.

Klügel's new double object glass. Commentat. Gott. 1795. XIII. M. 28.

Free from all aberration. Taking the mean refractive powers 1.53175 and 1.58121, and the dispersive powers .00586 and .00937, after Beguelin, the focal distance from the posterior surface being 10000, the focal length of the convex lens is 2123, of the concave 4397, the radius of the anterior surface of the first is 2168, of the posterior 7092, its thickness 79; that of the anterior of the second 4606, of the posterior 5740, the thickness 31; the distance of the lenses 31, their aperture 937.

Klügel Hind. Arch. II. 191.

Klügel here gives, for the same refractive powers, in 10000ths of the focal length of the convex lens, the first radius 6943, the second 22712, the thickness 250, the distance of the lenses 100, the focal length of the second 14074, the first radius 14850, the second 18211, the thickness 100, the joint focus 32056, the aperture 3216; and this he says is correct at a considerable distance from the axis.

Bürja. A. Berl. 1797. ii. 8.

Thinks that where much light and a small field is wanted, object glasses not spherical may be employed with advantage.

Bürja on achromatic glasses. A. Berl. 1798. 3.

Blair on achromatic telescopes. Ed. tr. III. 3. Nich. II. 1. Gilb. VI. 129.

Blair's patent refracting telescopes. Repert. VII. 15.

*Robison. Enc. Br. Art. Telescopes.

Says, that Blair's object glass with fluids performs admirably.

Nicholson's iris. Nich. I. 180.

Nicholson's remarks on Grateloup's object glasses. Nich. Gilb. VI. 151.

Account of Schrader's 26 feet reflecting telescope. Ph. M. I. 113.

Varley on the magnifying powers of telescopes. Ph. M. IV. 87.

Browne's telescope with a perforated plane mirror. Repert. XI. 21.

After Martin.

Adams's patent portable telescope tubes. Repert. XV. 156.

Cavallo. Nat. Ph.

Dimensions of two object glasses of Dollond. Two double convex lenses, with a double concave interposed, radii 28, 40, 20.9, 28, 28.4, 28.4 inches, beginning from the object; focal length 46; and 28, 35.5, 21.1, 25.75, 29,28; focal length 46.3.

Böckmann on the colours of sun glasses. Gilb. X. 359.

Mr. Böckmann recommends, for viewing the sun, an eyeglass composed of four pieces, a light violet, a light green, a dark green, and a dark blue.

Hornblower on the eye stop of a telescope. Nich. VI. 247.

On the usual principle.

Eyepieces for telescopes. Ferguson's lectures by Brewster.

A cask filled with sand is one of the best supports for a telescope. Robison.

Abstract of Dr. Herschel's Observation of the Transit of Mercury, with Remarks on the Action of Mirrors. Journ. R. I. II. 64.

The planet appeared, when viewed with Dr. Herschel's ten feet reflector, and with other telescopes, much darker than any of the solar spots, and perfectly well defined; no irregularity of form was perceptible at the moment of contact; but the observation appears to have been intermitted at the instant of the approach of the planet to the sun's limb. Dr. Herschel could not perceive the slightest degree of ellipticity in the form of the planet's disc. Nothing was gained by employing a higher magnifying power than 130; a circumstance which Dr. Herschel attributes to the effect of the heat of the sun's rays in distorting the figure of the speculums, by partial alterations of their temperature; and this supposition he supports by several experiments on the effects of the neighbourhood of heated bodies on their focal lengths.

Dr. Herschel has also found that, in general, " In order to see well with telescopes, it is required that the temperature of the atmosphere and mirror should be uniform, and the air fraught with moisture." Thus a frost after a thaw, or a thaw after a frost, will impair the perfection of the focus: a telescope brought out of a warm room into a cold air, or even directed through an aperture of any kind, acts but imperfectly: windy weather is unfavourable to distinct vision, from a mixture of air of different temperatures: an aurora borealis sometimes affects the distinctness of the view, as well as the air ascending from the warm roof of a house: dampness, fogs, and the neighbourhood of moisture, are very favourable to distinct vision with telescopes, except when a fog is so opaque as totally to intercept it. Dr. Herschel remarks, that some of these obstacles are insuperable; but that the effect of heat may sometimes be remedied by the application of a heated body near the opposite surface of the mirror. Y.

In a paper read to the Royal Society, Dec. 1804, Dr. Herschel shows, that the central part of a mirror produces a greater aberration in the image of a fixed star than the whole mirror, and the whole mirror a greater aberration than an annular portion remote from the centre: and that this is true of all good mirrors.

See Theory of Optics, Lenses, Micrometers.

Micrometers.

See Astronomical Instruments.

Auzout and Hook. Ph. tr. 1665—6. I. 123.

Townley on Gascoigne's micrometers. Ph. tr. 1667. I. 457.

Hook on Gascoigne's screw micrometer. Ph. tr. 1667. II. 541.

Lefevre's micrometer. Mach. A. II. 103.

Kirckius's micrometer. M. Berl. I. 202.

Cassini's universal micrometer. A. P. 1724. 347.

Fouchy's micrometer. Mach. A. VI. 45.

Smith's optics.

Hollmann de micrometro. Ph. tr. 1745. XLIII. 239.

Of crape.

Segner on extending the field of a micrometer. C. Gott. 1751. I. 27.

Segner on the parallax of a micrometer. C. Gott. 1752. II. 200.

Short on Servington Savery's micrometer, in 1743. Ph. tr. 1753. 165.

A double object glass.

Dollond's divided object glass micrometer. Ph. tr. 1753. 178. 1754. 551.

Bevis on Gascoigne's micrometer in 1640. Ph. tr. 1753. 190.

Aepinus on micrometers. A. Berl. 1756. 365.

Maskelyne on Dollond's micrometer. Ph. tr. 1771. 536.

Maskelyne's prismatic micrometer. Ph. tr. 1777. 799.

An achromatic prism, sliding along the axis of the telescope. Shows the defects of the divided object glass.

Wilson on flattening the cross wires of telescopes. Ph. tr. 1774. 105.

Boscovich's micrometer. Ph. tr. 1777. 789.

A prism of glass; or of rock crystal, divided by a spherical surface, and moveable also along the axis of the telescope.

Ramsden on two new micrometers. Ph. tr. 1779. 419.

Finds the divided object glass insufficient. The first method is to divide the small speculum of a telescope of Cassegrain's construction, and to give it a motion round a point near the centre: the second is to divide the eyeglass. The aberration of the telescopes of Cassegrain is about ⅔ of the aberration of the Gregorian telescopes: the error of the eyeglass has much less effect than that of the object glass employed as a micrometer; the divided glass is placed in the focus of that lens in the eyepiece, which is nearest to the object glass.

Herschel's lamp micrometer. Ph. tr. 1782.

Herschel's improvement of his angular micrometer. Ph. tr. 1785. 46.

Smeaton's equatorial micrometer. Ph. tr. 1787.

Rochon on telescopes with micrometers of rock crystal. N. A. Petr. 1788. VI. H. 37. Nich. 8. IV. 110.

Rochon's prismatic micrometer. Recueil de méc.

Rochon's achromatic micrometer. Journ. Phys. LIII. 169.

Kästner on micrometers. Astronomische abhandl. II. 263.

Kästner on terrestrial micrometers. Commentat. Gott. 1789. X. M. 1.

Cavallo on a micrometer. Ph. tr. 1791. 283.

Made of semitransparent mother of pearl. A table for estimating distances from apparent magnitudes of a man. Perhaps the bricks of a house would afford a more certain measure.

Cavallo on a micrometer. 4. Lond. 1793.

*Enc. Br. Art. Micrometer.

Rand's patent military telescope. Repert. XII. 152.

With a micrometer and a table.

Physical Optics.

Sources of Light.

Lomonosow de origine lucis. 4. Petersb. 1758.

Light from Combustion.

Boyle's lamp. Hooke. Ph. Coll. n. 2.

Hooke's lamp. Birch. II. 155.

Hooke's lampas. Lect. Cutl.

A lamp with water dropping in. Ph. tr. 1698. XX. 378.

Bouguer's comparison of the light of the sun and moon with the light of candles. A. P. 1726. H. 11.

Confirmed by Celsius, in the ratio of 300000 to 1.

Virgile's subaqueous lantern. Mach. A. VI. 77.

Bourgeois de Chateaublanc's reflecting lamp. A. P. 1744. H. 62.

Preigney's lamp of Amiens. Mach. A. VII. 395.

Lievreville's reflecting lamps. A. P. 1759. H. 234.

Fordyce on light from inflammation. Ph. tr. 1776. 504. Roz. XIII. Suppl. 115.

Thinks that all light arising from decomposition is blue, and attributes other colours to ignition.

A night lamp. Roz. XI. 56.

On lighting theatres. A. P. 1781. 409.

Morgan on the light of bodies in combustion. Ph. tr. 1785. 190.

Thinks that the more refrangible rays are always first thrown off in combustion; but that they are often extinguished by the surrounding vapour, so that the flame may thus become even at first yellow, green, or even red. Melted brass exhibits a fine green vapour. Rotten wood burning exhibits only the orange and red rays.

Villiers's lamp for reading at night. Roz. XXVIII. 54.

On illumination. M. Tur. IV. 1788. lix.

Wedgwood. Ph. tr. 1792. 279.

Found that air not luminous made a wire red hot.

Count Rumford on the light of luminous bodies. Ph. tr. 1794. 67.

In order to produce a given quantity of light, we must burn of wax 100, of tallow 101, of oil, in Argand's lamp, 110, in a common lamp, 129, of an ill snuffed tallow candle, 229 parts by weight. Flame is very transparent.

Hassenfratz on the light produced in combustion. Ann. Ch. XXIV. 78.

Differs from Count Rumford in not preferring Argand's lamp.

Keir's patent hydrostatic lamp. Repert. VIII. 289. Nich. III. 467. Gilb. VI. 96.

Thiville's patent lamp. Repert. XIV. 9.

Smethurst's patent lamp, with lenses. Rep. XIV. 84.

White's patent lamp. Repert. XV. 93.

More easily cleaned than Argand's.

Argand's lamp. Montucla and Lal. III. 564.

Thermolamp. Montucla and Lal. III. 565. Gilb. X. 491.

Thilorier's phloscope. Montucla and Lal. III. 565.

The flame is led through a tube of glass.

Guyton's report on Carcel's lamp. Ann. Ch. XXXVIII. 135. Nich. 8. II. 108.

With a pump and a contracted chimney; produced a heat of $7°$ Wedgwood, $505.6°$ cent. or $942°$ F.

Davy on light produced under water. Journ. R. I., I. Gilb. VI. 109.

Kretschmar's thermolamp. Gilb. XIII. 498.

Bünger's thermolamp. Gilb. XV. 231.

Hermstadt on the light of candles. Repert. ii. 1. 59.

Dawson's patent lamp for carriages. Repert. ii. II. 401.

A photophorus. Repert. ii. III. 372. See Catoptric Instruments.

E. Walker on the light of candles. Nich. 8. III. 272. IV. 40. VI. 90. Gilb. XIII. 240.

Finds it nearly proportional to the quantity of tallow consumed, when the combustion is perfect. Recommends that candles be burnt in an inclined position.

Edelcrantz's statical lamp. Nich. 8. V. 93.

Paul's lamps with reflectors. Nich. 8. V. 133.

On the light of wax candles of different dimensions. Nich. 8. V. 219.

A small candle gave about $\frac{1}{17}$ more light from the same weight than a large one.

Boswell's lamp for tallow. Nich. IX. 105.

Lambert found, that the light emitted by a shining surface in any direction is as the sine of the angle of inclination; so that the density is equal in every direction. He adds an illustration from theory. Photometr. § 81.

Lambert thinks, that the moon's light cannot exceed $\frac{1}{100000}$th of the sun's, from theory; Leslie makes it much greater, and thinks, with some of the ancients, that the moon must have the property of a solar phosphorus.

The solar light has been attributed to an atmosphere by Gascoigne, by the author of Experiments and Observations on light and colours. 8. Lond. 1786. p. 162. by King, and by Herschel.

Light attending Decomposition without sensible Heat.

Spontaneous Light.

Bartholinus de luce animalium. 1669. M. B.

Beale on the light of fish. Ph. tr. 1665—6. I. 226. on the light of flesh. Ph. tr. 1676. XI. 599.

Flesh that had been killed but a day, in February, became luminous.

*Boyle on the light of fish, wood, and flesh. Ph. tr. 1667. II. 581, 605. 1672. VII. 5107. Works. III. 304.

Found that the light was extinguished in a vacuum.

Marsigli Storia del mare. Histoire de la mer.

Bourzes on the light in the wake of ships. Ph. tr. 1713. XXVIII. 230.

Réaumur on the spontaneous light of some fish. A. P. 1723. 198. H. 8.
C. Bon. II. i. 248, 274.
Nollet on luminous insects. A. P. 1750. 54, 57. H. 7.
Untersuchungen vom meere. 4. Frankf. 1750.
Riville and Leroy on the light of the sea. S. E. III.
Rigaud on the light of the sea. A. P. 1765. H. 26.
Fougeroux on a luminous insect of Cayenne. A. P. 1766. 339. H. 29.
Fougeroux on the light of the sea. A. P. 1767. 120. H. 6.
Legentil voyage aux Indes Orientales. I. 685.
Canton on the light of sea water, when putrefying. Ph. tr. 1769. 446.
Haller Physiol. V. 446.
Priestley's optics.
On the light of sea water. Roz. III. 106.
Dicquemare on the light of the sea. Roz. VI. 319. XII. 137.
Dombey on the light of the sea. Roz. XV. 212.
Borch on the light of the sea. A. Sienn. VI. 317.
Achard on the light of rotten wood. A. Berl. 1783. 98.
On the light of the Baltic. Roz. XXIV. 56.
Forster on physical geography. Germ.
With an account of other authors.
Razumowsky on the glowworm. M. Laus. II. 240.
Spallanzani. Leipz. Samml. IV. 289.
Spallanzani on phosphoric medusae. Soc. Ital. VII. 271.
Goth. Mag. II. iv.
Account of a luminous potatoe. Roz. XXXVI. 225.

Beckerhielm on the light of glowworms. Ann. Ch. IV. 19.
Tingry on animal light. Journ. Phys. XLVII. (IV.) 287.
Carradori on spontaneous light. Ann. Ch. Gilb. I. 205. Nich. II. 132.
Carradori on the lampyris Italica. Ann. Ch. Ph. M. II. 77.
The light was restored by moisture after a short dryness.
Wasström on the light of the sea. Gilb. II. 352.
*Hulme on spontaneous light. Ph. tr. 1800. 161. 1801. 403. Nich. IV. 421. Nich. 8. II. 31. Gilb. XII. 129, 224.
It is not increased by oxygen gas, but disappears in a vacuum.
On the light of the sea. Montucla and Lal. III. 567.
Blumhoff on the luminous appearance of the sea. Ph. M. VIII. 97.
Mitchill on the luminous appearance of sea water. Ph. M. X. 20. Gilb. XII. 161.
From the phosphorescence of animalcules.
Böckmann on wood shining in gases. Ph. M. XVI. 18.

Solar Phosphori.

Bodies shining after having been exposed to the light, without decomposition.

Baldwin's phosphorus. Ph. tr. 1676. XI. 788.
Nitrate of lime. Ph. tr. 1746.
Cellio la pietra Bolognese preparata. Rom. 1680. M. B.
Acc. Hooke. Ph. Coll. n. 3.
The stone burnt with charcoal in a close furnace.
Marsigli dissertazione del fosforo minerale. 4. Leipz. 1698.
Acc. Ph. tr. 1698. XX. 306. A. P. I. 234.
Homberg on the Bolognan stone. A. P. II. 12, 138.
Chemical.

Wall on the phosphorescence of diamonds.
Ph. tr. 1708. 73.

Bourgues on a phosphorescent stone. A. P.
1724. H. 58.
By heat.

Nollet on the Bolognan stone. A. P. 1743.
H. 105.

On the Bolognan stone. C. Bon. I. 184.

*Beccari de phosphoris. 4. Bologna, 1744.
*Extr. by Watson. Ph. tr. 1746. 81.
Found that the light was brightest when the surfaces were rough; smooth ones retained no light. This does not look like chemical attraction.

Beccari Comm. Bonon. II. ii. 136. iii. 498.
V. 106.

Beccaria on Canton's phosphorus. Ph. tr.
1771. 212.
Emitting only the colour that it receives.

Wilson and Beccari on phosphori. 4. Lond.
1775. R. I.

Euler on Wilson's experiments. A. Petr. I. i.
H. 71.

Canton on a phosphorus. Ph. tr. 1768. 337.
Oyster shells burnt.

Krafft on Canton's phosphorus. A. Petr. I.
H. 77.

*Grösser on the light of the diamond. Roz.
XX. 270.
Even such phosphori, as emitted red light only, were made to shine most by exposure to blue light.

Morgan. Ph. tr. 1785.
An oyster shell emitting green light will emit red light when warmed.

Morozzo on the appearance of the Bolognan
spar in gases. Soc. Ital. III. 420.

Marchetti on solar phosphori. C. Bon. VII.
O. 289.

*T. Wedgwood on the production of light by
heat and by attrition. Ph. tr. 1792. 28.
Almost all bodies when powdered emit heat at a temperature from 400° to 600° F. An account of the authors who have treated on solar phosphori.

Brugnatelli on the modifications of light.
Extr. Ann. Ch. XII. 188. XXVI. 107.
Ph. M. VII. 285.

On the phosphorescence of the diamond.
Journ. Phys. LV. 60.

Accum on the light from borax. Nich. II.
28.
Ph. M. III. 321.
Carradori thinks putrescent wood a solar phosphorus.

Dizé on heat as the cause of shining. Journ.
Phys. XLIX. 177. Gilb. IV. 410.

Hulme's improvement on Canton's phosphorus. Ph. tr. 1801. 426.

On the light of diamonds. Gilb. XII. 259.

Light from friction.

Philonis belopoeica.
Mentions the light produced by Ctesibius's air gun.

Nollet on the illumination of ice. A. P. 1766.
H. 2.

See Electricity.

Razumowsky on light from friction. M.
Laus. II. 39.

*Giobert on the phosphorescence of vitriolated tartar. Mem. Tur. 1788. IV. 73. Roz.
XXXVI. 256.
Under water; not an electric phenomenon.

T. Wedgwood on the production of light by
heat and by attrition. Ph. tr. 1792. 28.
Thinks that light from attrition is produced by a heat of about 400° or 600° F., since almost all bodies emit some light at this temperature.

Severgyne on the light of stones. N. A. Petr.
1793. XI. 12.

Light from an air gun. Ph. M. XIV. 363.
Gilb. VIII. 366.
Remer could find no electricity in the light of an air gun. The gun must be highly laden, and, as some say, made of iron.

Light from electricity. See Electricity.

Velocity of Light.

Römer on the motion of light. A. P. X. 399.
Ph. tr. 1677. XII. 893. Journ. des savans.

Homberg on the force of light. A. P. 1708. H. 21.

Mairan on the velocity of light. A. P. 1738. 37. H. 82.

Aberration.

Bradley on a newly discovered motion of the stars. Ph. tr. 1728. XXXV. 637.

Clairaut on the aberration of the stars, planets, and comets. A. P. 1737. 205. H. 76. 1746. 539. H. 101.

Euler on the phenomena arising from the progressive motion of light. C. Petr. XI. 150.

Assumes the projectile hypothesis of light for its simplicity, but observes, that in some cases the phenomena are different on the different suppositions.

Winthrop and Price on planetary aberration. Ph. tr. 1770. 358, 536.

Boscovich on the aberration of light. Op. ined. V. 417.

†Jeaurat on the planetary aberration of light. A. P. 1786. 572.

Robison on the motion of refracting mediums. Ed. tr. II. 83.

Corrects some errors of Boscovich.

Some mistakes appear to have been made respecting this subject; they may be avoided by attending to one general principle; that is, when a body moves uniformly forwards, the relative situation of another body, whether quiescent or in motion, appears at all times to be such as it really was at the moment of the emission of the light of the second body: in other words, neglecting the changes in the earth's motion, during the passage of the light, the apparent place of the sun, or of any star or planet, is its true geocentric place for the instant at which the light was emitted by the sun or star, or reflected by the planet. Y.

Decay of Light.

Ph. tr. 1794.

Light is found to diminish in intensity as the squares of the distances increase, or a little faster. Rumford.

Interception and partial Reflection of Light.

See Shadows.

Gregory on oblique reflection. Birch. III. 79.

Bouguer Optique.

The moon reflects about 1/3 of the light that falls on it. Bouguer found that water reflected 1/4 of the light falling perpendicularly, quicksilver 11 or .683. At an inclination of 50° quicksilver reflected only 32 times as much as water.

Kurdwanowski's problems respecting light. Acc. A. P. 1732. H. 95.

On the degree of illumination.

Krafft on the reflection of light by a transparent medium. C. Petr. X. 183.

†Edwards on reflection. Ph. tr. 1763. 229.

On the reflection of light by transparent mediums. Roz. III. 27. 116.

Dionis du Séjour on the quantity of light falling on the moon in eclipses, and on the faint light of the new moon. A. P. 1776.

The faint light is a minimum at 48° elongation, a maximum at 0° and at 69°: at 90° it is about half the greatest quantity.

Count Rumford found that a pane of plate glass stopped .1972 parts of the light; another .1869; two together .3184; a piece of thin window glass stopped .1268. In reflection from a glass mirror .35 was lost, .65 being reflected: this is but little less than was reflected in Bouguer's experiment by quicksilver only.

Refractive Powers.

J. A. Porta de refractione. 4.

Lahire on the refraction of ice. A. P. IX. 328. X. 172.

Less refractive than water.

Lahire on the refraction of oil and water. A. P. IX. 382.

Lowthorp on the refraction of air. Ph. tr. 1699. XXI. 339.

Cassini on the refraction of air. A. P. 1700. 78. H. 112.

Hauksbee's experiments. 4. 1709. Fr. by Desmarest.
Acc. A. P. 1754. H. 34.
Hauksbee on the refraction of fluids. Ph. tr. 1710. XXVII. 204.
  With the specific gravities.
Delisle on the refraction of air. A. P. 1719. 330. H. 71.
Euler on the refractive powers of liquids. A. Berl. 1756. 235.
Euler on refraction. A. Petr. I. i. 174.
J. A. Euler on the refraction of fluids. A. Berl. 1762. 279.
J. A. Euler on the effects of heat in refraction. A. Berl. 1762. 328.
  The focus of a lens of glass was shortened from $16\frac{1}{4}$ to 16 inches or less by an addition of 66° of Reaumur to the temperature: each degree reducing it about $\frac{1}{2500}$ or $\frac{1}{1600}$. The refractive power was changed from 1.550 to 1.5578.
Jeaurat on the refraction and dispersion of different kinds of glass. A. P. 1770. 461.
Cadet and Brisson on the refractive powers of fluids. A. P. 1777. 541. H. 9.
  In lenses.
†Fabroni on the refractive powers of fluids. Journ. Phys. XLVIII. 215. Gilb. VI. 149.
*Wollaston. Ph. tr. 1802.
Cavallo's tables. N. Phil. III. 176.
  From Newton, Euler, Zeiher, Hauksbee, Martin, Rochon, and others.

Dispersion of Colours by Refraction.

Newton's theory of light and colours, with various illustrations and explanations. Ph. tr. 1671. VI. 3075. 1672. VII. 4059, 4091. 5004, 5014, *5084. 1673. VIII. 6087. 6108. 1674. IX. 217. 1675. X. 500, 503. 1676. XI. 511. 698. Birch. III. 272, 280, 296.
  The experiments were first made in the beginning of 1666.
Hooke on the refraction of colours. Birch. III. 52.
Experiments proposed to Newton. Ph. tr. 1672. VII. 4059.
Pardies's remarks on Newton's theory of light. Ph. tr. 1672. VII. 4087, 5012, 5018.
Considerations on Newton's doctrine of colours. Ph. tr. 1673. VIII. 6086.
  Allowing only yellow and blue.
Answer from Paris to a letter of Newton. Ph. tr. 1673. VIII. 6112.
†Linus on the theory of light and colours. Ph. tr. 1674. IX. 217. 1675. X. 499.
Lucas's exceptions to Newton's experiments. Ph. tr. 1676. XI. 692.
†Mariotte on colours. A. P. I. 189.
Desaguliers's optical instruments in confirmation of Newton's theory. Ph. tr. 1716. XXIX. 336. 448. 1722. XXXII. 206.
Desaguliers's experiments on occasion of Rizzetti's optics. Ph. tr. 1728. XXXV. 596.
Castelli optica colorum. 1740.
  In favour of three colours.
Euler on a controversy respecting refraction. A. Berl. 1753. 294.
Euler on the refraction of rays of different colours. N. C. Petr. XII. 166.
Euler on dispersion. A. Petr. I. i. 174.
Nollet's opinion of three colours, orange, green, and indico. Leçons de physique. V. 388.
D'Alembert on three colours. Opuscules. III. 393.
Jeaurat on the dispersive powers of glass. A. P. 1770. 461.
Lambert's farbenpyramide. 4. Berl. 1772.
Rochon Recherche sur la nature de la lumière des étoiles fixés.
Rochon Recueil de mécanique.
Camparetti de luce et coloribus. 4. Pad. 1787. R. S.

Grüber über strahlenbrechung und abprallung. 4. Dresd. 1787.

†*Marat* sur la lumière. 8. Par. 1788. R. S. Extr. Roz. XXXII. 140.

Marat denies the different refrangibility of light; attributes the appearance of colours to inflection by the margin of the sun, or by other objects.

Dree on Marat's experiments. Roz. XVIII. 402.

Achard on the prismatic composition of colours. A. Berl. 1788. 14.

Obbiezzioni alla teoria di Newton intorno a' colori. Piacenz. 1791.
Acc. A. Berl. 1792. H. 19.

The anonymous author is probably Mr. Consonni: he maintains, that there are but three colours, but that each is spread a little over the adjoining one in refraction.

Nordmark on dispersion. Sv. Vetensk. N. H. XV. 113.

Blair on the unequal refrangibility of light. Ed. tr. III. 3. See Telescopes.

M. Young on the number of colorific rays. Ir. tr. VII. 119. Nich. IV. 395.

Makes only red, yellow, and blue rays, and some of each scattered through the spectrum.

Lüdicke on showing the composition of white light. Gilb. V. 272.

*Herschel on heat and light. Ph. tr. 1800. Gilb. VII. 137.

†Leslie on light and heat. Nich. IV. 344, 416. Gilb. X. 88.

Ritter's invisible rays. Gilb. VII. 527. XII. 409.

Vicktred on Ritter's invisible rays. B. Soc. Phil. n. 75. Nich. 8. V. 255.

Englefield on the separation of light and heat by refraction. Journ. R. I. I. Nich. 8. III. 125.

*Wollaston on the division of the spectrum. Ph. tr. 1802. 365.

Total or internal Reflection.

†Brougham. Ph. tr. 1796. 227. 1797. 352. Nich. I. 551.

*Prévost's remarques d'optique. Ph. tr. 1798. 311. Journ. Phys. XLIX. 273. Nich. III. 222. Gilb. V. 129.

In defence of Newton, against Mr. Brougham.

Prévost's further remarks. Journ. Phys. XLIX. Gilb. V. 147.

Tables of Refractive and Dispersive Powers.
Principally from Wollaston and from Cavallo's tables.

A Chemical Appendix to Physical Optics.

	Index of refraction
A vacuum	1.00000
Atmospheric air. Lowthorp	1.00036
Hawksbee	1.00032
From Bradley B. 29.6, Th. 50°	1.000276
Ice, by observation. W.	
Ice, by calculation from halos. Y.	1.310
Water. W. H.	
Vitreous humour. W.	1.336
Lime water. C.	(1.334)
Well water. C.	1.336
Spirit of hartshorn. C.	1.337
Solution of caustic ammonia. C.	1.349
Solution of soda. C.	1.352
Ether. W.	1.358
French brandy. C.	1.360 / (1.368)
Albumen. W.	1.36
Hawksbee	(1.351)
Alcohol. W.	1.37
C.	1.371
Distilled vinegar. Hawksbee.	1.372
Euler	(1.344)
Saturated solution of salt. C.	1.375
Salt 1, water 27. C.	(1.348)
Solution of sal ammoniac	1.382

CATALOGUE.—PHYSICAL OPTICS.

	Index of refraction.		Index of refraction.
Solution of potash. C.	1.390	Gum arabic. C.	(1.477)
Nitric acid, sp. gr. 1.48. W.	1.410	Human cuticle. W.	
Nitric acid. C.	1.412	Dutch plate glass. W.	1.517
Fluor spar. W.	1.433	Gum lac. W.	
Sulfuric acid. W.	1.435	Caoutchouc. W.	1.524
C.	(1.426)	Nitre. C.	1.524
Spermaceti, melted. W.	1.446	Selenite. W.	1.525
Crystalline lens of an ox. W.	1.447	Crown glass, common. W.	1.525
	(to 1.380)	Canada balsam. W.	1.528
C.	(1.463)	Centre of the crystalline of fish, and dry crystalline of an ox. W.	1.530
Oil of wax. C.	1.452		
Alum. W.	1.457	Pitch. W.	
C.	1.458	Crown glass, sp. gr. 2.52. C.	1.532
Tallow, melted. W.	1.460	Yellow plate or Venetian glass, sp. gr. 2.52. C.	1.532
Borax. C.	1.467		
Oil of lavender. W.	1.467	Brazil pebble, sp. gr. 2.62. C.	1.532
C.	(1.469)	Radcliffe crown glass. W.	1.533
Oil of peppermint. W.	1.468	Anime. W.	1.535
Oil of olives. W.	1.469	Copal. W.	1.535
C.	(1.465)	Oil of cloves. W.	1.535
Oil of almonds. W.		White wax, cold. W.	
Oil of turpentine, rectified. W.	1.470	Elemi. W.	
Oil of turpentine, common. W.	1.476	Mastic. W.	
C.	(1.482)	Arseniate of potash. W.	
Essence of lemon. W.	1.476	Sugar, after fusion. W.	
Butter, cold. W.	1.480	Sugar, 1, water 27. C.	(1.346)
Linseed oil. W.	1.485	Spermaceti, cold. W.	
Camphor. W.	1.487	Red sealing wax. W.	
C.	(1.500)	Oil of sassafras. W.	1.536
Iceland spar, weakest. W.	1.488	C.	(1.544)
strongest. W.	(1.657)	Bees wax. W.	1.542
Tallow, cold. W.	1.49	Boxwood. W.	
Sulfate of potash. W.	1.495	Colophony. W.	1.543
Oil of nutmeg. W.	1.497	Glass of St. Gobin. C.	1.543
French plate glass. W.	1.500	Old plate glass. W.	1.545
English plate glass. W.	1.504	Rock crystal (double). W.	1.547
Oil of amber. W.	1.505	C.	{(1.568) (1.575)}
C.	(1.501)		
Balsam of capivi. W.	1.507	Amber. W.	1.547
Gum arabic. W.	1.514	C.	(1.556)

Index of refraction.

Opium. W.	
Mica. W.	
Plate glass, or coach glass, sp. gr. 2.76. C.	1.573
Phosphorus. W.	1.579
Horn. W.	
Flint glass. W.	{ 1.583 { 1.586 }
Benzoin. W	
Guaiacum. W.	1.596
Balsam of Tolu. W.	1.60
White flint glass, sp. gr. 3.29. C.	1.600
A yellow pseudotopaz. C.	1.642
Sulfate of barytes (double). W.	1.646
Iceland spar, strongest. W.	1.657
Glass, of lead 1, flint 4. C.	1.664
Gum dragon. W.	
Glass, tinged red by gold. C.	1.715
Glass, of lead 1, flint 2. C.	1.724
Glass, of lead 3, flint 4. C.	1.732
White sapphire. W.	1.768
Glass, of lead 1, flint 1. C.	1.787
Muriate of antimony, variable. W.	
Arsenic. W. (A good test).	1.811
Spinelle ruby. W.	1.812
Glass, of lead 2, flint 1. C.	1.830
Jargon. W.	1.95
Glass of antimony. W.	1.98
C.	(1.89)
Glass, of lead 6, sand 1. W. Doubtful.	1.987
Glass, of lead 3, flint 1. C.	2.028
Native sulfur (double). W.	2.04
Scaly oxid of iron. Y. About	2.1
Oxid of lead, by induction. Y.	2.15
Plumbago. W.	
Diamond. Newton.	2.44
Rochon.	2.755

From Dr. Wollaston's mode of observation, it may be inferred that his numbers belong correctly to the extreme red rays.

Table of the order of Dispersive Powers, from Wollaston, the Numbers from Rochon and from Cavallo's table.

Sulfur. W.		
Glass, of lead 6, sand 1. W.		
Glass, of lead 3, flint 1. r.2.028.		7.09
Glass, of lead 2, flint 1. r.1.830.		5.24
Glass, of lead 1, flint 1. r.1.787.		4.82
Glass, of lead 3, flint 4. r.1.732.		3.25
Glass, tinged by gold. r.1.715.		2.90
Glass, of lead 1, flint 2. r.1.724.		2.65
Glass, of lead 1, flint 4. r.1.664.		2.00
Balsam of Tolu. W.		
Oil of sassafras. W.		
Muriate of antimony. W.		
Guaiacum. W.		
Oil of cloves. W.		
Flint glass. r.1.6.		1.80
Flint glass. W.		
Colophony. W.		
Canada balsam. W.		
Oil of amber. W.		
Jargon. W.		
Oil of turpentine. W.		
Copal. W.		
Balsam of capivi. W.		
Anime. W.		
Iceland spar. W.		
Iceland spar	r.1.562 1.625	{ 1.69 { 2.33
Amber. W.		
Diamond. W.		
Diamond. r.2.755.		2.86
Alum. W.		
Plate glass. r.1.573		1.65
Brazil pebble. r.1.532.		1.59
Nitric acid. r.1.412.		1.54
Plate glass. Dutch. W.		

Plate glass, English. W.
Glass of St. Gobin. r.1.543.   1.49
Crown glass. W.
Crown glass. r.1.532.   1.48
Solution of sal ammoniac. r.1.382. 1.34
Ruby, spinelle. W.
Saturated solution of salt. r.1.375. 1.22
Water. W. - - 1.00
Sulfuric acid. W.
Alcohol. W.
Sulfate of barytes. W.
Selenite. W.
Rock crystal. W.
Rock crystal. r.1.560.   { 1.21
             1.575.   { 1.24
Sulfate of potash. W.
White sapphire. W.
Fluor spar. W.

It is obvious, that many of the results of these observations cannot be reconciled; and it is probable, that the numbers are frequently inaccurate.

Wollaston's Table of the Refractive Powers of solutions equal in Dispersive Powers to Plate Glass.

	In water.	In alcohol.
Nitromuriate of gold.	1.364	1.390
Nitromuriate of platina.	1.370	
Nitrate of iron.	-	1.375
Sulfuret of potash.		1.375
Red muriate of iron.		1.385
Nitrate of magnesia.		
Nitric acid.		1.395
Nitrate of jargon.		
Balsam of Tolu		1.400
Acetite of litharge.	1.400	
Nitrate of silver.		
Nitrate of copper.		
Oil of sassafras	-	1.405
Muriate of antimony	-	1.410
Nitrate of lime	1.410	1.422
Nitrate of zinc		
Green muriate of iron	1.415	
Muriate of magnesia	1.416	
Essence of lemon	-	1.430
Muriate of lime	1.425	1.440
Muriate of zinc	1.425	
Balsam of capivi	-	1.440

Hence it seems to follow, that the dispersion of the nitric acid is a fourth more than that of plate glass: a disproportion much greater than appears in the numbers of Cavallo's table.

With crown glass the nitric acid was diluted to 1.375, and the muriatic from 1.39 to 1.382.

Ordinary Atmospheric Refraction, Celestial or Terrestrial.

See Meteorology, to which this subject partly belongs.

Refractio solis inoccidui. See Irregular Refraction.

Cassini on refraction. Bologn. 1672.
   Acc. Ph. tr. 1672. VII. 500.

Cassini on refractions. A. P. I. 103. 1700. 39. H. 112. 1714. 33. H. 61. 1742. 203. H. 72. 1743. 249. H. 140.

Cassini on the dip. A. P. VIII. 71. 1707. 195. H. 89.

Lahire on the atmospheric refraction at Toulon. A. P. VII. i. 174.

†Lahire on the path of light in the atmosphere. A. P. 1702. 32. 182. H. 54.

Laval on refractions. A. P. 1708. H. 105. 1710. H. 109.

Delisle on the refraction of the air. A. P. 1719. 330. H. 71.

Halley on atmospherical refraction, with Newton's table. Ph. tr. 1721. XXXI. 169.

Taylor Methodus incrementorum.

Bouguer on refraction in the torrid zone. A. P. 1739. 407. H. 45. 1749. 75. H. 152.

Mairan on the refraction of the air. A. P. 1740. 32. H. 89.

Euler on atmospheric refractions at different temperatures. A. Berl. 1754. 131.

Euler on terrestrial refraction. A. Petr. I. ii. 129.

La Caille on refractions. A. P. 1755. 547. H. 111.

Thinks that it is nearly the same throughout the temperate zones.

Lambert Route de la lumière par les airs. 8. Hague, 1758.

Lambert on the density of the air. A. Berl. 1772. 103. Roz. XVIII. 126.

Heinsius on northern refraction. N. C. Petr. VII. 411.

At Olenek, lat. 73° 4', certainly not greater than in Cassini's tables, which give 6' 23" at 8° 30' altitude.

*Simpson Math. dissert.

Lemonnier's proposal for observations on refraction. A. P. 1766. 608. H. 104.

Lemonnier on horizontal refraction at sunset. A. P. 1773. 77. H. 53.

Lemonnier. A. P. 1781.

Found a horizontal refraction of 50' in very cold weather.

Lagrange on astronomical refractions. A. Berl. 1772. 259.

A formula like Simpson's.

Kästner on refraction. N. C. Gott. 1772. III. 122.

Cassini on refractions. A. P. 1773. 323. H. 54.

Thinks that they are somewhat greater at equal altitudes on the south side of the zenith than on the north.

Legentil on atmospherical refraction in the torrid zone. A. P. 1774. 330. H. 47.

Legentil. A. P. 1789. 224.

Finds the horizontal refraction 2'.5 less in India than in France.

Table of refraction for the coast of Coromandel. A. P. 1774. 399.

Dionis du Sejour on the effects of refraction in eclipses. A. P. 1775. 265.

Attributes a refraction of about 5" to the lunar atmosphere.

Dionis du Sejour on the curve described by light in the atmosphere; upon the optical hypothesis of its density. A. P. 1776. 273.

Maskelyne. Ph. tr. 1777. 722.

The terrestrial refraction is equal to the angle subtended by about $\frac{1}{10}$ of the distance of two objects; in order to correct for the joint effect of curvature and refraction, we may divide the square of the distance by $\frac{1}{4}$ of the diameter of the earth.

Bradley's rule for refraction. Maskelyne. Ph. tr. 1787. 156.

At 45° 3' 57", correcting for the temperature in the ratio of 400 to 350+f°, and for the barometer in the ratio of its height to 29.6 inches. But even from some observations here inserted, this correction for temperature appears to be too great. At 45°, Maskelyne makes the refraction 56".5, from another comparison of observations 55".8; Lord Macclesfield 54".6, which agrees exactly with Hawksbee's experiment; La Caille 66".6, which is much too great. Maskelyne recommends that a table of refractions be made for each instrument by immediate observation.

Herschel. Ph. tr. 1785. 88.

Found that ε, 20, Sagittarii appeared to form a spectrum measuring 16" 9'" vertically, 8" 35'" horizontally, the difference 7" 34'", near the meridian, 4th May 1783.

The altitude must have been about 4°, and the refraction 21', the declination being 34° 27'$\frac{1}{4}$.

A. P. 1787. 355.

The terrestrial refraction was found equal to $\frac{1}{14}$ of the angular distance.

Roy on terrestrial refraction. Ph. tr. 1790. 233. Gilb. III. 281.

Found it vary from $\frac{1}{4}$ to $\frac{1}{22}$ of the angular distance. Bouguer made it $\frac{1}{4}$, Maskelyne $\frac{1}{10}$, Lambert $\frac{1}{14}$. A correction for temperature is given in a note by Dr. Maskelyne, but there is some mistake in it.

Oriani Ephem. Milan.

Cagnoli on refraction. Soc. Ital. V. 259.

At Verona $\frac{1}{71}$ less than in Bradley's tables, and agreeing with those of Oriani.

Zanotti. C. Bon. VII. O. 1.

Finds the barometrical and thermometrical corrections of little use.

Deluc on refractions. Roz. XLIII. 422.

Principally on the correction for temperature.

Dalby. Ph. tr. 1795. 581. Gilb. III. 281.

The terrestrial refraction varied from $\frac{1}{5}$ to $\frac{1}{17}$, but was generally $\frac{1}{10}$ of the arc.

Mayer. Op. ined.

*Hennert on refraction, and on its corrections. Hind. Arch. II. 1, 129.

Gives .0007205 for the logarithmic difference to be employed in the calculation.

Piazzi's table. Bode Jahrb. 1798.

Makes the refraction 57.2″ at 45°.

Kramp on refractions. Hind. Arch. II. 380, 499.

Calculates them according to the true constitution of the atmosphere, and finds that they agree with Newton's table, and with Bradley's as far as 86° zenith distance, below this they differ sometimes 30″, but agree at the horizon. Assumes for the effect of temperature a correction far too great, so as to agree with the Refractio solis inoccidui.

Kramp Analyse des réfractions. 4. 1798.

Kramp. Hind. Arch. III. 228.

Mayer's rule agrees in principle with Bradley's. He employs Shuckburgh's expansions instead of Bradley's.

Ph. tr. 1797.

The terrestrial refraction was in general $\frac{1}{11}$ of the angle, in one case $\frac{1}{14}$.

Mudge. Ph. tr. 1800. 716, 724.

Found the terrestrial refraction from $\frac{1}{5}$ to $\frac{1}{16}$ of the arc, but generally from $\frac{1}{10}$ to $\frac{1}{11}$.

*Laplace Mécanique céleste. IV.

Brandes on terrestrial refraction. Gilb. XVII. 129.

Takes $\frac{1}{16}$ as a mean.

Irregular Atmospheric Refraction.

Near the horizon, or some heated surface.

Horizontal Refraction.

Hevelius. See Beams of Light.

Cassini on two mock suns. A. P. II. 103. and X. 159.

January 1693, 34′ above and below the sun's centre.

Cassini on a double sun. A. P. VII. 2. P. ii. 18.

Supposes reflection and refraction.

Cassini on the irregularities of the dip. A. P. 1707. 195. H. 89.

Malézieux on three suns seen at Sceaux. A. P. 1722. H. 13.

In October, touching each other vertically.

Conti on the elevation of the sea on certain coasts. A. P. 1743. H. 40.

Minasi sopra la Fata Morgana. 8. Rome, 1773. R. S. Gilb. XII. 20. R. S.

Legentil on atmospherical refraction. A. P. 1774. 330. H. 47.

The horizontal refraction at Pondicherry was usually 2′ greater in summer than in winter.

Boscovich. Gilb. III. 302.

Büsch tractatus duo optici argumenti. Hamb. 1788. R. S.

Gilb. III. 290.

Ellicott on terrestrial refraction. Am. tr. III. 62. Nich. I. 152. Gilb. III. 302.

Ph. tr. 1795. 581.

Dalby found a difference of 9′ 28″ in two measures of the elevation of St. Ann's hill.

Another case of irregular refraction was observed where the sun was warm, and there was much dew.

Fata Morgana at Reggio. Nich. I. 298.

Huddart on horizontal refractions. Ph. tr. 1797. 29. Nich. I. 145.

Attributes them to vapours less dense than the air. The curvature of the rays is justly delineated, for the simplest cases.

Latham on atmospheric refraction. Ph. tr. 1798. 357. Ph. M. II. 232. Nich. II. 417. Gilb. IV. 147.

The cliffs of France fifty miles off were seen distinctly at Hastings, much magnified, and even Dieppe was said to be visible from 5 to 6 in the afternoon; in July, the weather hot and no wind.

Monge on the mirage in Egypt, Ann. Ch. XXIX. 207. Ph. M. II. 427. Gilb. III. 302.

Vince on horizontal refraction. Ph. tr. 1799. 13. Ph. M. VII. 54. Nich. III. 141. Gilb. IV. 129.

Additional appearances of inverted images.

*Wollaston on double images. Ph. tr. 1800. 239. Nich. IV. 298. Gilb. XI. 1.

Caused by atmospherical refraction. With satisfactory experiments. The refraction being greatest where the change of density is the most rapid, and less on each side of this point, the whole effect must be similar to that of a convex lens.

Wollaston on horizontal refraction and on the dip. Ph. tr. 1803. 1. Repert. ii. III. 419. Nich. VI. 46.

Mudge. Ph. tr. 1800. 720.
  Looking over Sedgmoor, after a warm day, Glastonbury tor was depressed 29' 50".

Deluc on the apparent elevation of horizontal objects. Ph. M. XII. 148.

Horizontal refraction at Youghal. Beauford. Ph. M. XIII. 336.

Gruber on refraction near a warm surface. Gilb. III. 377, 439.

Woltmann on terrestrial refraction. Gilb. III. 397.

Heim on an unusual refraction. Gilb. V. 370.

Dangos on a horizontal refraction at Malta. Ph. M. XIV. 176.

Gorsse on mirage. Ann. Ch. XXXIX. 211.

Wrede on an atmospherical refraction by the walls of Berlin. Gilb. XI. 421.

Giovene on the fata morgana. Gilb. XII. 1. Gilb. XVII. 129.
  Brandes found the terrestrial refraction diminished whenever the air cooled suddenly.

Castberg on the fata morgana at Reggio. Gilb. XVII. 183.
  Thinks it a shadow.

It may frequently happen in a medium gradually varying, that a number of different rays of light may be inflected into angles equal to the angles of incidence, and in this respect the effect resembles reflection rather more than refraction. Y.

Abstract of the Bakerian Lecture, by Dr. Wollaston, consisting of observations on the quantity of horizontal refraction, and the method of measuring the dip at sea. Journ. R. I.

Dr. Wollaston notices Mr. Monge's memoir on the "mirage" observed in Egypt, as containing facts, which fully agree with his own theory formerly published. From his observations on the degree of refraction produced by the air near the surface of the Thames, it appears that the variations derived from changes of temperature and moisture in the atmosphere, are by no means easily calculable; but that a practical correction may be obtained, which, for nautical uses, may supersede the necessity of such a calculation. Dr. Wollaston first observed an image of an oar at a distance of about a mile, which was evidently caused by refraction, and when he placed his eye near the water, the lower part of distant objects was hidden, as if by a curvature of the surface. This was at a time when a continuation of hot weather had been succeeded by a colder day, and the water was sensibly warmer than the atmosphere above it. He afterwards procured a telescope, with a plane speculum placed obliquely before its object glass, and provided with a micrometer, for measuring the angular depression of the image of a distant oar, or other oblique object; this was sometimes greatest when the object glass was within an inch or two of the water, and sometimes when at the height of a foot or two. The greatest angle observed was somewhat more than nine minutes, when the air was at 50°, and the water at 63°; in general the dryness of the air lessened the effect, probably by producing evaporation, but sometimes the refraction was considerable, notwithstanding the air was dry. Dr. Wollaston has observed but one instance which appeared to encourage the idea, that the solution of water in the atmosphere may diminish its refractive power.

In order to correct the error, to which nautical observations may be liable, from the depression of the apparent horizon, in consequence of such a refraction, or from its elevation in contrary circumstances, and at the same time to make a proper correction for the dip, Dr. Wollaston recommends, that the whole vertical angle between two opposite points of the horizon, be measured by the back observation, either before or after taking an altitude; and that half its excess above 180° be taken for the dip: or if there be any doubt respecting the adjustment of the instrument, that it be reversed, so as to measure the angle below the horizon, and that one fourth of the difference of the two angles, thus determined, be taken as extremely near to the true dip. It is indeed possible, that the refraction may be somewhat different at different parts of the surface, but Dr. Wollaston is of opinion that this can rarely happen, except in the neighbourhood of land. Y.

Irregular Refraction at various Altitudes.

Refractio solis inoccidui. 4. Stockh. 1695. Engl. 8. London.
  Acc. Ph. tr. 1697. XIX. Lahire's remarks. A. P. 1700. 37. H. 112.

In lat. 66° 43′ the sun was three diameters above the horizon, 14 June at midnight. The Dutch are said to have seen it 4° too high in Nova Zembla. At Stockholm the horizontal refraction is sometimes 47′.

Mairan on the sun appearing oval at 10° altitude. A. P. 1733. 329. H. 23.

Elliptic appearance of the sun at a considerable height. A. P. 1741. H. 134.

Dicquemare on a distorted iris. Roz. X. 136.
Probably by irregular refraction.

Beams of Light from Atmospherical Refraction or Reflection.

Hevelius on a mock sun and a vertical train of light seen in Russia. Ph. tr. 1674. IX. 26.
A red mock sun below the real sun, and a vertical train from the sun upwards. At first the mock sun was at the distance of a few degrees, at last the sun descended and united with it. A severe frost followed.

Derham on a pyramidal light. Ph. tr. 1707. 2411.
April 7, 1707, after sunset, perpendicular to the horizon, succeeded by a halo. I have also observed such a beam in June. Y.

Messier on two vertical cones of light attached to the moon. A. P. 1771. 434.
The moon being covered with thin clouds.

Gilbert on a singular meteor. Gilb. III. 360.
A perpendicular beam of light above the sun after sunset, in August.

Remarks on the zodiacal light. Zach. Mon. corr. VII.

Observations of Parhelia, or Paraselenes, and Halos of about 22° or 44°, in general.

Zahn Mundi oeconomia. 2 v. f. M. B.

Lycosthenis chronicon prodigiorum. f. Bas. 1557. M. B.

Fritsch on meteors.

Particular Accounts.

In order of time, with the angles, where they have been measured.

Roman parhelia. Descartes meteorol. C. X.

Journal des savans. 1666. Ph. tr. 1665—6. I. 219.

Brown on parhelia in Hungary. Ph. tr. 1669. IV. 953.

Observation of the French academy. Ph. tr. 1670. V. 1065.
A halo 22° 0′.

Petto on parhelia at Sudbury. Ph. tr. 1699. XXI. 107.

Stephen Gray on parhelia at Canterbury. Ph. tr. 1699. XXI. 126.
H. 23° 0′.

Lahire. A. P. II. 208.

Lahire. A. P. X. 47.
H. n. 1. 21° 30′. n. 2. 23° 20′. n. 3. 22° 45′. n. 4. 21° 0′.

Cassini and Grillon. X. 152, 168, 273, 454.
A circle 22° above and 23° below the sun, 168.

A. P. X. 411.

Chazelles and Feuillée. A. P. 1699. H. 82.

St. Gray on a parhelion and halo. Ph. tr. 1700. XXII. 535.

*Halley. Ph. tr. 1702. XXIII. 1127.
The arches touching the halo appeared to be portions of circles having their centres near the opposite side of the halo: the upper one was continued across the horizontal circle, and at the intersections were parhelia 31°¼ distant from the sun. The sun's altitude was from 40° to 45°. The clouds were seen to drive under the circles: they were therefore formed high in the atmosphere.

A circle at Clermont. A. P. 1708. H. 109.

Cassini. A. P. 1713. H. 67.

Halley. Ph. tr. 1721. XXXI. 201.
The air apparently replete with snowy particles. Observes, that an explanation " seems wanting."

Whiston. Ph. tr. 1721. XXXI. 212.
An inverted arch not much bent touched the halo. The external tangent arch was without a halo, it seemed 90° long: its centre near the zenith; sun's altitude 23°¼, distance of the external arch from the zenith 20°. The halo became

oval; its horizontal diameter the shorter; the parhelia a degree or two beyond it.

Maraldi on two meteors. A. P. 1721. 231. H. 4.

The internal tangent arc appeared like two portions having their centres in the lateral parhelia. Observes, that there are always delicate and almost invisible clouds when they appear: the wind N. E. or E. and a little frost, succeeded by a milder air. Some slender melting snow fell two days after.

Dobbs on a parhelion seen in Ireland. Ph. tr. 1722. XXXII. 89.

Three parhelia without halos. Two inverted arches above.

Whiston. Ph. tr. 1727. XXXV. 257.

The halo was touched by two curves above and by one below: the lateral parhelia were without the halo, but not in the intersection of either of the tangent arches produced with the horizontal circle: there was a small portion of a secondary halo about one third larger than the primary: perhaps belonging to the tangent arch. There were two anthelia, further apart than the parhelia. March 1, ¼ after 10. Kensington. The two tangent curves appeared to be independent of each other, one only appearing at first.

Academy of Bezières. A. P. 1729. H. 2.

June, from 10 to 12. H. 20° 31′.

Musschenbroek. Ph. tr. 1732. XXXVII. 357.

A white horizontal circle above the sun, 58° 15′ in diameter, crossed by the coloured halo. At 50° 30′ from this crossing was a parhelion in the horizontal circle. Apr. 28, from ½ p. 10 to ¾ p. 11. H. 45° 30′, externally.

Schultz. Coll. Acad. VI. 270. Mentzelius. 301. Others. 445.

Frisch on a halo. M. Berl. 1734. IV. 64.

Some anomalous arcs passing through the sun.

Dufay. A. P. 1735. 87.

Chiefly from 27 observations of Musschenbroek in 1734. The thin clouds forming them are always higher than the common clouds. N. 1. H. 23° 12′ internally, lunar. N. 2. H. 23°. A second arc was seen near the zenith, its diameter varying from 24° to 30°, 28°½, and 27°¾, being greatest at 11 o'clock, in January. The halo changed also from 23° distance to 19° 50′, 19°, and 18° 30″. N. 3. More than half the circumference of an inverted arc touching the first halo, and of the same curvature with it: the circle about the zenith appeared of a constant diameter while the sun's altitude varied; this altitude was about 14°¼. N. 4. A train of light ascended from the sun. N. 7. Lasted all day, June 17, exactly 23°½ radius. N. 8. Exactly 23°½, from the red edge to the centre of the sun, about 1°¼ broad. N. 9. H. 22°.

Grandjean de Fouchy on a paraselene. A. P. 1735. 585.

The moon in a cross, 20° altitude.

Neve. Ph. tr. 1737. XL. 50.

At Petersburg.

Weidler. Ph. tr. 1737. XL. 54.

Sun's altitude 15°¼. Ext. H. 45°½. Lateral parhelion at 20° exactly.

Folkes on three mock suns. Ph. tr. 1737. XL. 59.

Weidler de parheliis anni 1736. 4. Wittemb. 1738. M. B.

Acc. by Stack. Ph. tr. 1740. XLI. 459.

Bad theory.

Weidler de anthelio. Ph. tr. 1739. XLI. 209.

This was an appearance in the north, at ½ p. 9. 18 Jan. 1738, of two arcs crossing at an angle of 60°, with a halo 2°½ horizontally, and 1°¼ vertically in diameter, red within. Snow fell soon after. A similar appearance is related by Hevelius de Mercurio in sole viso.

Mills on parhelia seen in Kent. Ph. tr. 1742. XLII. 47.

Gostling. Ph. tr. 1742. 60.

December. From sunrise till noon.

Halos and parhelia seen once or twice a week in Hudson's bay. Middleton. Ph. tr. 1742. XLII. 157.

Lacroix. A. P. 1743. H. 33.

Says the horizontal band was coloured; the tangent arc nearly straight.

Two suns at Wilna. A. P. 1745. H. 19.

Grischow on lunar circles and paraselenae. Ph. tr. 1748. XLV. 524.

The two inverted arches concentric with the zenith.

Arderon. Ph. tr. 1749 XLVI. 203.

A halo surrounding the zenith, 11 July, 5 P. M. Appears from the figure to be about 5° or 6° in diameter; the sun's rays were seen shining through the cloud.

Macfait. Ed. ess. I. 297.
October.

Musschenbroek. A. P. 1753. H. 75.
A parhelion about 30° from the sun, with arcs crossing in it.

Boscovich on a halo. A. P. 1754. H. 32.
No clouds were visible, but the sun was obscure.

Nollet. A. P. 1755. H. 37.

Braun's observations in Siberia. N. C. Petr. VI. 425. X. 375.
One March 1760, 21° above the sun 25° below it; another in August, the thermometer 65.6° F. in the shade: thin clouds floating from 8 o'clock to two.

Pingré. A. P. 1758. H. 23.

Moeren. Coll. Acad. VI. 299.

Barker on a halo. Ph. tr. 1761. 3.
H. 22°¼. Vertical diameter of the external halo 45°, with an elliptical curve 4° narrower or wider horizontally, coinciding with it at the summit, without parhelia. May 20, 1737, ¾ before 11.

Aepinus. N. C. Petr. VIII. 392.
An ellipsis, including the interior halo, touching it above and below; another with the horizontal diameter of the ellipsis about 31°, the vertical 45°.

Swinton on an anthelion. Ph. tr. 1761. 94.
July 24, very cold.

Dunn on a parhelion. Ph. tr. 1763. 351.
Many days in September and October.

*Wales. Ph. tr. 1770. 129.
There are constant parhelia in Hudson's Bay, the sun's rising being preceded by two streams of light about 20° distant from him; these accompany the sun the whole day in the winter, with three parhelia.

Saint Amans. Roz. XI. 377.

Atkins. Ph. tr. 1784. 59.
Terminating in a field of snow.

Rozières on a paraselene. A. P. 1786. 44.
With a tail. In a halo 7° or 8° in diameter, but not essentially connected with it.

Hamilton. Ir. tr. 1787. I. 23.
An obscure light at 90°. Parh. 26°.

*Baxter on halos seen in North America. Ph. tr. 1787. 44. Fig.
H. 22° 24'. An anthelion in the horizontal circle, like a St. Andrew's cross: A second and third anthelion about half way between the first and the halo.

Reynier. Roz. XXXVII. 308.
22 Jul. 7 evening.

Ussher on two parhelia. Ir. tr. 1789. III. 143.

Parhelia at Caumont. Ph. M. I.

Hall. Ed. tr. IV. 174. Nich. II. 485. Gilb. III. 257.
A large circle not horizontal. Scheiner's was also oblique.

Wrede on a paraselene. Ph. M. XII. 346.
Elliptic, the horizontal diameter being about 60°.

*Lowitz. N. A. Petr. 1790. VIII. 384.
At Petersburg, 18 June 1790; the most complicated halos and parhelia that have been observed.

Sargeant on parhelia in Cumberland. Nich. IV. 178.

A third concentric halo. Ph. M. XII. 373.
Not very circumstantially described.

Englefield. Journ. R. I. II. 1. Nich. VI. 54.
H. 24°, 48°.

Brandes. Gilb. XI. 414.
H. 21° to 22°.

See Weigels grundriss der chemie.
May 14, 1804, ¾ before 12 at night, I observed a lunar halo, the internal limit passed nearly through gamma leonis, but more accurately half way between gamma and Regulus. Hence the distance from the middle of the illuminated part of the moon was accurately 21° 20' or 22', without a probability of an error of more than a few minutes.
June 16, 1804. I saw a portion of a halo in the evening, the clouds were light and high.
Out of 52 of these observations 2 only were in July, 3 in August, 4 in January, 4 in September, 5 in March, 5 in June, 6 in February, 6 in October, 6 in December, 8 in April, and 9 in May.

Theory of Halos and Parhelia.

†Hugens. Ph. tr. 1670. V. 1065.

Hugenius de coronis et parheliis. Op. rel. II.

*Mariotte Traité des couleurs. Paris, 1686. Oeuvr. I. 272.

Wood's theory of halos. Manch. M. III. 336.

Supposes them produced by vesicles of which the thickness is $\frac{1}{71}$ of the diameter.

Brandes on parhelia. Gilb. XI. 414.

Supposes vesicles filled with a medium of a certain density, producing the halos as the drops of water produce the rainbow.

Mariotte Phenomenon 12. The great Coronæ.

"Sometimes when the air is pretty serene, a circle of about 45° diameter is seen round the sun or moon: the colours are not in general very lively, the blue is without and the red within, their breadth is nearly as in the common external rainbow. Explanation. I take for the cause of this appearance small filaments of snow, moderately transparent, having the form of an equilateral triangular prism. I conjecture that the small flat flakes of snow, which fall during a hard frost, and which have the figure of stars, are composed of little filaments like equilateral prisms, particularly those which are like fern leaves, as is easily seen by the microscope. I have often looked at the filaments which compose the hoar frost, that appears like little trees or plants in the cold mornings of spring and autumn: and I have found them cut into three equal facets; and when viewed in the sunshine they exhibited rainbow colours. Now it is very probable, that before these little figures of trees or stars are formed, there are floating among the thin vapours in the air, some of these separate prisms, which when they unite form the compound figures. These little stars are very thin, and very light, and the little filaments, which compose them, are still more so, and may often be supported a long time in the air by the winds: hence when the air is moderately filled with them, so as not to be much darkened, many of them, whether separate or united, will turn in every direction as the air impels them, and will be disposed to transmit to the eye for some time, a coloured light nearly like to that which would be produced by equilateral prisms of glass."

The angles are then calculated, and 16' being deducted for the semidiameter of the sun, and 30' for the deviation of the red rays, there remains 22° 30' for the ultimate angular distance of the halo.

P. 276. *Phenomenon 13. Parhelia or mock suns.*

"The most usual are at the same altitude as the sun. Among the prisms of snow there are often many heavier at one end than at the other, and consequently situated in a vertical direction: these cause a bright parhelion, with a tail, which cannot be above 70° long. I have read an account of a halo seen in May, soon after sunrise, with parhelia in its circumference, which after two or three hours were more than a degree distant from it. This appearance arises from the coincidence of the sun's rays with the transverse section of the prism when they are nearly horizontal, and from their obliquity when the sun is elevated, causing a greater deviation, and throwing the parhelia outwards, as may be shown by an experiment on two prisms. There are also accounts of parhelia above and below the sun, of anthelia, and of a white horizontal circle. I do not undertake to explain these appearances, because I have never seen any of them, and I have not certain information of the circumstances attending them."

Remarks on halos. See Journ. R. I. II. 4.

The explanation of the primary and secondary rainbow begun by De Dominis, and completed by Descartes and Newton, derives an entire and satisfactory confirmation, from the perfect coincidence of the observed angular magnitudes, with the result of calculations of the effect of spherical drops. We know that drops of water, either accurately, or very nearly spherical, exist in great abundance in every cloud, and in every shower of rain; and whatever their dimensions may be, they must necessarily conspire in the same general effect, of producing the same rainbow, whenever a spectator is placed in a proper situation for observing it; consequently such rainbows are of very frequent occurrence.

I have attempted to show, that for producing the phenomena of variable halos or coronae, often observable in hot climates, it is only necessary that a considerable part of the spherules of a cloud or mist, be either accurately, or very nearly, of equal magnitude, a condition, of which the possibility is easily admitted from analogy, and the probability is favoured by the apparent uniformity of the different parts of such mists as we can examine.

The hypotheses, by which Huygens attempted to explain the production of halos and parhelia, are both arbitrary and improbable. He imagined the existence of particles of hail, some globular, others cylindrical, with an opaque part in the middle of each, bearing a certain ratio to the whole; and he supposed the position of the cylinders to be sometimes vertical, and sometimes inclined to the horizon in a given angle.

It has already been objected, that no such particles have ever been observed to accompany halos; and it is, besides, highly improbable, that such an opaque part should bear the same proportion in all the hailstones, and that the cylinders should have terminations so peculiar as is supposed; and the most incredible circumstance of all is, that all these proportions should be commonly such, as always to produce a halo at the distance of 23° or 22° from the sun or moon. We may explain all these phenomena in a much more simple and natural manner, by reverting to the theory long ago proposed by Mariotte, but of late years almost entirely abandoned and forgotten.

It is well known, that the crystals of ice and snow tend always to form angles of 60°; now a prism of water or ice, of 60°, produces a deviation of about 23°½, for rays forming equal angles with its surfaces, and the angle of deviation varies at first very slowly, as the inclination changes, the variation amounting to less than 3°, while the inclination changes 30°.

Now if such prisms were placed at all possible angles of inclination, differing equally from each other, one half of them would be so situated, as to be incapable of transmitting any light regularly by two successive refractions directed the same way; and of the remaining two fourths, the one would refract all the light within these three degrees, and the other would disperse the light in a space of between 20° and 30° beyond them.

In the same manner, we may imagine an immense number of prismatic particles of snow to be disposed in all possible directions, and a considerable proportion of them to be so situated, that the plane of their transverse section may pass within certain limits of the sun and the spectator. Then half of these only will appear illuminated, and the greater part of the light will be transmitted by such as are situated at an angular distance of 23°½, or within 3° of it: the limit being strongly marked internally, but the light being externally more gradually lost. And this is precisely the appearance of the most common halo. When there is a sufficient quantity of the prismatic particles, a considerable part of the light must fall, after one refraction, on a second particle; so that the effect will be doubled: and, in this case, the angle of refraction will become sufficient to present a faint appearance of colour, the red being internal, as the least refrangible light, and the external part having a tinge of blue.

These concentric halos of 23°½ and 47°, are therefore sufficiently explicable, by particles of snow, situated promiscuously in all possible directions. If the prisms be so short as to form triangular plates, these plates, in falling through the air, will tend to assume a vertical direction, and a much greater number of them will be in this situation than in any other. The reflection from their flat surfaces will consequently produce a horizontal circle of equal height with the sun: and their refraction will exhibit a bright parhelion immediately over the sun, with an appearance of wings, or horns, diverging upwards from the parhelion.

For, all such particles as are directed nearly towards the spectator, will conspire in transmitting the light much more copiously than it can arrive from any other part of the circle; but such as are turned more obliquely, will produce a greater deviation in the light, and at the same time a deflection from the original vertical plane. This may be easily understood, by looking at a long line through a prism held parallel to it: the line appears, instead of a right line, to become a curve, the deviation being greater in those rays that pass obliquely with respect to the axis of the prism; which are also deflected from the plane in which they were passing.

The line viewed through the prism has no point of contrary flexure, but if its ordinates were referred to a centre, it would usually assume a form similar to that which has often been observed in halos.

The form of the flakes of snow, as they usually fall, is indeed more complicated than we have been supposing, but their elements in the upper regions of the air are probably more simple. It happens however not uncommonly, that the forms of the luminous arches are so complicated as almost to defy all calculation. The coincidence in the magnitude of the observed and computed angles is so striking, as to be nearly decisive with respect to the cause of halos; and it is not difficult to imagine that many circumstances may exist, which may cause the axes of the greater number of the prisms to assume a position nearly horizontal, which is all that is required for the explanation of the parhelia with their curved appendages. Perhaps also, the effect may sometimes be facilitated by the partial melting of the snow into conoidal drops: for it may be shown, by the light of a candle transmitted through a wine glass full of water, that such a form is accommodated to the production of an inverted arch of light, like that which is frequently observed to accompany a parhelion.

If the refractive power of ice were precisely equal to that of water, the angle of deviation of an equilateral prism would be 23° 50′, but the average of 22 of the most accurate observations gives 22° 29′, and that of 20 less accurate ones 22° 10′. Now an angle of 22°½ corresponds to a refractive power of 1.32. Lahire found the refractive power of ice less than that of water; but Krafft in his oration on northern climates makes it greater. It was therefore desirable to ascertain its powers by direct experiment, and Dr. Wollaston was so good as to try it by his excellent method, which showed that the refractive power was in fact no greater than 1.31, giving a deviation of 21° 50′. Perhaps a partial melting of crystals may sometimes cause a difference in the actual magnitude of the deviation. In the lunar halo, which I observed, the angle was certainly not greater than this, and there could scarcely have been any material error in the observation.

The situation of the lateral parhelia, without the halo, is very satisfactorily explained by Mariotte; and the diversified forms of the tangent arches may probably all be deduced from the suppositions laid down in the Journals of the Royal Institution. As an instance, we may take the case there described by Sir Henry Englefield, where the sun's altitude was about 15°. The horizontal prisms will then cause an appearance of an arch with a contrary curvature, exactly as Sir Henry has described it.

The calculation is somewhat intricate: Its principal steps are these, taking the refractive power $\frac{4}{3}$.

Deviation of transverse rays 22° 37'.

For rays inclined 20°, the inclination of the planes of the rays is 29° 32', the deviation 26° 12'; the altitude being 15°, the angle with the horizon is 25° 8' more than the altitude.

For rays inclined 25°, the inclination of the planes is 34°, the deviation 27° 47'; the angle with the horizon 25° 47' more than the altitude 15°.

For rays inclined 30°, the inclination of the planes is 120°, that is, the rays are in the planes of the surfaces; the deviation 38° 56'; the angle with the horizon 6° 4' less than the altitude 15°.

When the altitude increases, the tangent arch descends so as to approach considerably to the halo, as in the halos observed by Halley and by Barker. For, calculating upon the true refractive power of ice, the angles become these.

For rays inclined 25°, the inclination of the planes 30° 55', the deviation 25° 40' = 21° 50' + 3° 50', the angle with the horizon 56° 24' = 45° + 11° 24'. For altitude 15°, 38° 57' = 15° + 23° 57'.

It may also become double, the inferior arch being visible: thus the angle with the horizon becomes 21° 18' or 45° — 23° 42', as well as 56° 24'.

The mode of calculation is this; A being the inclination within the prism, and r the index. Sec. $B = \frac{\text{Sec. A}}{\sqrt{\frac{4}{3}}}$ for the incidence; S.C = r, S.B, D = C — B. As S.C : Sec. A :: S:D: x, $\sqrt{\frac{4}{3}} = y$, $1 - y : \frac{1}{2}z$; Rad : T. E, 2 E is the mutual inclination of the planes passing through the rays and the axis of the prism, $\frac{\text{T.A}}{r}$: $\frac{1}{2}z$ :: Rad : S. F; 2 F is the whole deviation: $1 - \frac{1}{y^2} \cdot \frac{1}{2}x = sz$; $z = \frac{\text{T.A}}{r}$ :: S. Altitude : S. G, the elevation of the plane of the incident ray; $G \pm 2E = H$ the elevation of the plane of the emergent ray; $\frac{\text{T.A}}{r}$: z :: S. H : S. I, the depression of the emergent ray.

Mr. Cavendish has suggested, with great apparent probability, that the external halo may be produced by the refraction of the rectangular termination of the crystals, rather than by two successive refractions through the angles of different crystals: which, with the index 1.31, would produce a deviation of 45° 44'. If this supposition is true, the index cannot be greater than 1.31; for 1.32 would give 47° 56'; which is more than appears to have ever been assigned.

The mean of 4 accurate observations is about 45° 50', that of 4 of the best estimations 46°.

The lateral anthelia may be produced by the rays refracted after two internal reflections, which will have a constant deviation 60° greater than those which form the halo; these anthelia ought therefore to be about 82° from the sun; they are however usually represented as much more distant.

Glories, or coloured Anthelia.

See Colours from Interference.

Ulloa's Voyage. I.
Mentions several coloured circles of different sizes, and a white one 67° in diameter.

Macfait. Ed. ess. I. 197.
Halos with a glory.

Mongez on a glory. Roz. XII. 223.
8 June, by moonshine.

Haygarth on a glory. Manch. M. III. 463.
In a cloud, which was probably icy. The shadow was surrounded by coloured coronae, next to these were bright arches, wider than those of a rainbow.

Simple Rainbows.

De Dominis de radiis visus et lucis.
Primary rainbow.

Rainbows crossing each other, by the river, at Chartres. Ph. tr. 1665—6. I. 219.

†Linus on the rainbow. Ph. tr. 1675. X. 386.

Mariotte on the rainbow. A. P. I. 189.

Lahire on a red iris seen at Angers in 1690. A. P. II. 53.

Cassini on a rainbow in the twilight. A. P. X. 275.

Halley on an iris by reflection. Ph. tr. 1698. XX. 193.
A very accurate account.

Halley de iride. Ph. tr. 1700. XXII. 714.

Makes the angles 41° 30′ and 51 55′ for the usual rainbows: the ternary and quaternary would be 40° 20′ and 45° 33′ from the sun.

A red rainbow. A. P. 1708. H. 109.

Thoresby on a lunar rainbow. Ph. tr. 1711. XXVII. 320.
With all the colours.

Langwith on a hyperbolic rainbow on the ground. Ph. tr. 1721. XXXI. 229.

Sturmii iridis admiranda.

Pemberton's optical porisms. Ph. tr. 1723. XXXII. 245.

Smith's optics.

Jo. Bernoulli. Op. IV. 197.

Celsius on a rainbow seen in Dalecarlia. A. P. 1743. H. 35.

Berthier on a singular rainbow. A. P. 1747. H. 52.
On the banks of the Loire.

Webb on an inverted iris on the grass. Ph. tr. 1751. 248.

Edwards on a rainbow after sunset. Ph. tr. 1757. 293.

Legentil on two singular rainbows. Ph. tr. 1757. 39.

Kotelnikow on the iris. N. C. Petr. VII. 252.
The tertiary iris, after 3 reflections, would be very broad, and partly covered by the secondary.

Bergmann on the rainbow. Schw. Abh. 1759. 231.

Boscovich on the secondary rainbow. S. E. III. 321.
In order to avoid a difficulty deduced from the imaginary fits of reflection, is obliged to suppose the drops imperfectly spherical.

Boscovich. Hamb. Magaz. X. 531.

Mallet on the rainbow. Schw. Abh. 1763. 239.

Singular rainbows. Coll. Acad. VI. 253, 265, 286, 296, 299, 356, 433.
On the ground, red, and lunar.

Séjour on a lunar rainbow. A. P. 1770. H. 22.
White.

Roz. II. 296.
A third iris between the common ones, not concentric with them. Probably by reflection.

An entire rainbow. Roz. III. 416.

A lunar rainbow. Roz. X. 81.

Dicquemare on a distorted iris. Roz. X. 136.
Probably by refraction.

E. M. Physique. Art. Arc-en-ciel.

Tunstall on lunar irides. Ph. tr. 1783. 100.

L'*Abbé* P. sur l'arc en ciel. 8. Par. 1788. R. S.

A lunar rainbow. Roz. XXXIV. 60.

Hellwag N. Deutsch. Merkur. 1790. ii. 420.

Sturges on two rainbows. Ph. tr. 1793. 1.
One by reflection from the sea.

A lunar rainbow. Ph. M. XI. 96.

Bouvier on a lunar rainbow. Journ. Phys. LVII. 472.

A lunar rainbow. Gilb. XI. 480.
Seen by Professor Seyffer of Gottingen. The red, green, orange, and violet colours were very lively and distinct. The editor remarks that this phenomenon is not so rare as is sometimes supposed, for that Mr. Alfeld has collected accounts of 30 lunar rainbows which had been seen before 1750. This observation is only of consequence as it tends to destroy the opinion of the existence of a difference in the colours of the lunar and solar rainbows.

THEOREM. The angular distance of the primary and secondary rainbow being given, if a unicuspidate and a bicuspidate epicycloid be described in a circle, touching it in points at the given angular distance; the distance of their point of intersection from the centre will be to the radius as unity to the index of refraction. Y.

Double Refraction.

Bartholin on Iceland crystal. Ph. tr. 1670. V. 2039.

*Hugens Traité de la lumière.

On Iceland crystal. A. P. I. 186.

Lahire on Iceland crystal. A. P. 1710.

Beccaria on the double refraction of rock crystal. Ph. tr. 1762. 486.

The separation appears to be greatest when the rays pass most transversely with respect to the axis; hence it may be inferred that this is an unusual refraction.

Rochon's artificial doubling spar. Goth. Mag. I. 184.

Plates of different densities cemented together.

†Haüy on the double refraction of Iceland crystal. A. P. 1788. 34.

Haüy on double refractions. Ann. Ch. XVII. 140.

Haüy on the double refraction of sulfur. B. Soc. Phil. n. 16. Ph. M. I. 221.

Haüy Traité de phys. II. 347.

Thinks that the carbonate of lime, and the sulfate, have unusual refractions, because they are composed of obliquangular parallelepipeds: other crystals have only the usual refraction, being derived from rectangular forms.

Haüy on double refractions, noticed. Ph. M. VI. 131.

Ph. tr. 1797. 352.

Brougham denies the polarity of the particles of light with respect to Iceland crystal.

Linck on double refraction. Crell Ann. 1797. vii. B. B.

Extr. Ann. Ch. XXVIII. 84.

Hind. Arch. II. 74.

Kramp attributes the double refraction to reflection from the sides of a primitive crystal, and appears to be fully satisfied with the explanation.

*Wollaston on the oblique refraction of Iceland crystal. Ph. tr. 1802. 381. Nich. 8. IV. 148.

Narcl on the optical properties of rock crystal. Ph. M. XIV. 306.

A certain prism cut out of it simply changes right to left, without displacing the image: this must be from some reflection. Y.

Diffraction and Irradiation, as affecting Astronomical Observations.

See Eclipses.

Legentil on the apparent diameter of the sun. A. P. 1755. 437. H. 93.

Distinct marks of an atmosphere, or of inflection, or of both, in the transit of Venus, 1760.

Legentil on the apparent magnitude of opaque bodies. A. P. 1784. 469.

Observes, that it is diminished 5" of 6" when they are viewed on a light ground: from experiments on a parallelogram enlightened half behind and half before: and on two contiguous images of circles.

Maskelyne. Ph. tr. 1768. 355.

Dunn's figure of the appearances of Venus on the sun. Ph. tr. 1770. 65.

Lalande on the elongation of the disc of Venus in the transit. A. P. 1770. 406. H. 80.

Says, that the aberrations of the rays of light in the telescope make the sun's diameter appear too large by about 6".

A. P. 1773. 265.

Dionis du Séjour attributes an inflection of about 5" to the refraction of the lunar atmosphere. Observes, that a star appears to enter on the moon's disc in an occultation.

A. P. 1780. 237.

Dionis du Séjour considers a solar irradiation of 3"½, and a lunar inflection of the same quantity, as absolutely demonstrable.

Herschel. Ph. tr. 1783. 4.

A light circle being viewed, together with a dark one placed on a light ground, the light circle appears the larger.

Irradiation is generally, and perhaps always, an affection of vision, but perhaps it may sometimes be occasioned by a deviation of light from a direction perfectly rectilineal, and its effects are not any time easily distinguished from those of diffraction.

See Telescopes.

Vision in general.

Fabricius ab Aquapendente de visione. f. Ven. 1600. M. B.

De Dominis de radiis visus et lucis.

Scheineri oculus. 4. Rom. 1652. M. B.

Traner nervus opticus. f. Vienn. 1690.

Berkeley's theory of vision. 8. Dubl. 1709. M. B.

Porterfield on the eye. 2 v. 8. Edinb. 1759.
On vision. C. Bon. V. i. C. 110.
Scarella on vision. C. Bon. V. ii. 446. VI. O. 344.
Bonati's theory of vision. Soc. Ital. II. 676.
Adams on vision. 8. Lond. 1792. R. I.
Comparetti observationes dioptricae et anatomicae. 4. Pad. 1798. R. S.

Structure of the Human Eye.

Leeuwenhoek on the crystalline lens. Ph. tr. 1684. XIV. 780. A. P. I. 68.
Duverney on the organ of vision. A. P. I. 161.
Lahire on the eye. A. P. IX. 355. X. 478.
  Describes the obliquity of the lens.
Zahn oculus artificialis. f. Nuremb. 1702.
Méry on the iris. A. P. 1704. 261. H. 12. 1710. 274. H. 33.
Winslow on the muscles of the eye. A. P. 1721. 310.
Petit on the chambers of the eye. A. P. 1723. 38. H. 19. 1728. 206, 289. H. 17.
Petit on the capsule of the crystalline. A. P. 1730. 435. H. 33.
Lecat on the coats of the eye. A. P. 1739. H. 19.
Haller disputationes anatomicae selectae. 6 v. 4. Gott. 1746... M. B.
Demours on the vitreous humour, the cornea, and the uvea. A. P. 1741. H. 60, 68. S. E. II. 586.
Zinn on the external parts of the eye. C. Gott. 1753. III. 115.
*Zinnii oculus. 4.
*Albinus on the eye. Mussch. Introd. II. 744.
Portal on the muscles of the eye. A. P. 1770. 246. H. 44.
Wrisberg on the membrana pupillaris. N. C. Gott. 1770. H. 108.
This membrane disappears about the end of the 8th month: it seems to have been known to Albinus; and was described about the same time by Haller and Hunter.
Häseler über das menschliche auge. 8. Hamb. 1771.
Sömmering on the foramen of the retina. Commentat. Gott. 1795. XIII. Ph. 3.
Léveillé on the foramen of the retina. B. Soc. Phil. an. 5. n. 54.
Home on Sömmering's orifice in the human retina. Ph. tr. 1798. 332.
  Home denies the existence of the fold which Sömmering describes as covering it; thinks it the entrance of a lymphatic, and that it is too small to produce any inconvenience in vision.
†Chenevix on the analysis of the humours of the eye. Ph. tr. 1803. Nich. VI. 21. Ph. M. XVI. 268.

Comparative Anatomy of the Eye.

Leeuwenhoek on the eyes of insects. Ph. tr. 1698. XX. 169.
Leeuwenhoek on the eyes of whales and fishes. Ph. tr. 1704. XXIV. 1723.
Méry on the cat's pupil. A. P. I. 260. X. 461.
Méry on the bony circle in the eye of the eagle and the raven. A. P. II. 15.
Lahire on the cat's eyes. A. P. IX. 406. 1712. H. 73.
Lahire on the eyes of insects. A. P. X. 429.
Poupart on the eyes of the libella. Ph. tr. 1700. XX. 676.
†On the crystalline of a serpent. A. P. 1706. H. 8.
Ranby on an ostrich. Ph. tr. 1725. XXXIII. 223.
Warren. Ph. tr. 1726. XXXIV. 115.
  The ring consists of 13 bones in water fowls, and 14 in land fowls.
*Petit on the crystalline lens in different animals. A. P. 1730. 4. H. 33.

*Petit on the eye of the turkey. A. P. 1735. 123.

*Petit on the eye of the owl. A. P. 1736. 121.

*Petit on the eyes of the frog and the tortoise. A. P. 1737. 142.

Stancari on the eyes of insects. C. Bon. I. 301.

Zinn on the comparative anatomy of the eye. C. Gott. 1754. IV. 247. Commentat. Gott. 1778. I. App. 47.

Haller on the eyes of some fishes. A. P. 1762. 75. H. 42.

Brown. Ph. tr. 1778. 794.
  The cornea of the flying fish is very flat.

André on the eye of the monoculus polyphemus. Ph. tr. 1782.

Hey on the eye of the seal. Manch. M. III. 274.
  Shows that the nerve does not enter in the axis.

Bonvicini on the blindness of snails. Soc. Ital. VII. 291.

†P. Smith on the eyes of birds. Ph. tr. 1795. 263.

Home's Croonian lecture. Ph. tr. 1796. 1.

La Cepède on the eyes of the anableps. M. Inst. II. 372. B. Soc. Phil. n. 8.
  A double iris and a divided cornea, but only one lens.

Young. Ph. tr. 1801.

Immediate Functions of the Eye.

Hooke Animadv. on Hevelius.
  Makes the minimum of vision .5'.

Mariotte and Pecquet on the insensible spot of the retina, and on the seat of vision. Ph. tr. 1668. III. 668. 1670. V. 1023. A. P. I. 66.

Briggs on the theory of vision. Ph. tr. 1683. XIII. 171. Hooke. Ph. coll. n. 6. 167.

Lahire on vision. A. P. IX. 355.
  Thinks no change of conformation possible.

Méry on the principal organ of vision. A. P. 1704. 261. H. 12.

Petit on the vision of infants. A. P. 1727. 246. H. 10.

*Porterfield on the external and internal motions of the eye. Edinb. med. essays. III. IV.

Porterfield on the eye. 2 v. 8.

Weitbrecht on the motions of the pupil. C. Petr. XIII. 349.

Leroy on the accommodation of the eye to different distances. A. P. 1755. 594.

Mayer on the powers of sight. C. Gott. 1754. IV. 120. Roz. Intr. I. 241.
  The minimum .5' for detached objects, 1' for contiguous objects in common day light: and in a different degree of illumination the angle varies as the 6th root of the light.

Dalembert. A. P. 1765.
  Maintains that the eye is not achromatic.

Darcy on the duration of the sensation of sight. A. P. 1765. 439.

Fontana dei moti dell' iride. 4. R. S. Roz. X. 25.

On the changes of the eye. Nich. I. 505.

Olbers de oculi mutationibus internis. 4. Gott. 1780. R. S.

Herschel on the magnitude of the optic pencil. Ph. tr. 1786. 500.
  A pencil of 1/50 of an inch was sufficient, with a high magnifier.

Herschel on the powers of the prismatic colours to heat and illuminate. Ph. tr. 800. 255. Ph. M. VII. 311.
  The greenish yellow rays the most effective.

Venturi's optical considerations. Soc. Ital. III. 268.
  Finds the dispersion of the eye nearly equal to that of glass.

Maskelyne on the effect of the different refrangibility of light in vision. Ph. tr. 1789. 256.
  Thinks the effect too small to be perceived.

Young on vision. Ph. tr. 1793. 169.

Young on the mechanism of the eye. Ph. tr. 1801. 23.
Home's facts relative to Hunter's intended Croonian lecture. Ph. tr. 1794. 21.
On the muscularity of the crystalline lens of the sepia,
Home's Croonian lecture. Ph. tr. 1795. 1.
Attributes the change of the eye to the cornea.
Home's Croonian lecture. Ph. tr. 1796. 1.
Abandons a part of the effect of the cornea.
Home's experiments on persons deprived of the crystalline lens. Ph. tr. 1802. 1.
Ph. tr. 1796.
Brougham shows, after Musschenbroek, the effect of the refraction of light by the moisture of the eyelids.
Mollweide on the dispersion of the eye. Gilb. XVII. 328.

Perception of external Objects.

On the apparent form of the heavens. Descartes, Desaguliers, Rowning, Smith, Priestley, Ferguson.
Hooke on the horizontal moon. Birch. III. 503, 507.
The true explanation.
Molineux and Wallis on the apparent magnitude of the sun and moon. Ph. tr. 1686. XVI. 314, 323.
Chesselden's account of a person who was couched. Ph. tr. 1728. XXXV. 447.
Desaguliers on the horizontal moon. Ph. tr. 1736. XXXIX. 390.
As Molineux.
Mairan on the apparent curvature of the heavens. A. P. 1740. 47.
Gmelin de visione fallaci per microscopia. Ph. tr. 1745. XLIII. 387.
The effect was probably owing to the inversion of the image by the microscope, causing the lights to fall on the contrary side with respect to external objects, so that the image appeared convex instead of concave. Y.
*Berkeley on vision.
A good theory of erect vision, p. 312.
Dutour on single vision. S. E. III. 514. VI. 241. H. 88.

Euler on vision through spherical segments. N. C. Petr. XI. 185.
†Dunn on the horizontal sun and moon. Ph. tr. 1762. 462.
Jetze's remarks on the estimation of distance. Leipz. Mag. 1783.
Gr. Fontana on the apparent brightness of objects. Ac. Sienn. V. 103.
After Buffon.
Robinson on single vision. Roz. XII. 329.
Rittenhouse on an optical deception. Am. tr. II. 37.
A true explanation of Gmelin's experiment.
Walter on erect vision. A. Berl. Deutsche abh. 1788. 3.
Wells on single vision with two eyes. 8. Lond. 1792. R. S.
Atkins on the horizontal moon. 8. Lond. 1793.
Lambert on the place of images. Hind. Arch. III. 61.
Explains some difficulties suggested by Barrow and others.
Ware on a recovery of sight. Ph. tr. 1801. 382. Nich. 8. I. 57.
Nicholson on the horizontal moon. Nich. VII. 236.
†Walker on the horizontal moon, with remarks by C. L. Nich. IX. 164, 235.
The apparent distance of the horizontal moon is increased by its faintness.

Shadows.

Picard on shadows. E. P. VII. i. 185.
Lahire on the strength of a penumbra. A. P. 1711. 157. H. 74.
Maraldi on shadows. A. P. 1723. 111. H. 90.
On shadows and penumbras. Lambert Photometria. §. 1218.
Monge on shadows and penumbras. S. E. IX. 1780. 400.
Mathematical.
Fourcroy on the shadow of a lattice. A. P. 1784. 355.

The lights appeared to answer to the shades of a perfect shadow, except when part of the sun's disc was covered by clouds. Hence the effect must have been owing to the penumbra. Y.

Jordan on the spectre of the Brocken. Ph. M. I. 232.

A shadow falling on clouds.

Gilb. XVII. 183.

Castberg thinks the fata morgana at Reggio a shadow thrown on a mist.

Colours, as affecting the Eye.

Waller's catalogue of simple and mixed colours. Ph. tr. 1686. XVI. 24.

With specimens annexed, many of which now only serve as tests of the want of permanence of the colours employed.

Ph. tr. 1716. XXIX. 449, 451.

A different colour being viewed with each eye at the same time, the result is not a mixed colour, but a contemporaneous sensation of both. Sometimes the colours appear to succeed each other alternately. Y.

Lambert's farbenpyramide. 4. Berl. 1772.

Dicquemare on the vision of colours. Roz. VIII. 64.

Prangens farben lexicon. 4. Halle, 1782.

Opoix on colours. Roz. XXIII. 402.

Opitz sur les couleurs. MS. R. S.

Mayer de affinitate colorum. Op. ined. I. 31.

Saussure on the light required for viewing different colours. Mem. Tur. 1788. IV. 441.

Legentil on objects viewed through coloured glasses. Ann. Ch. X. 225.

Herschel on the illumination of different colours. Ph. tr. 1800. 255.

The greenish yellow rays the brightest.

Aerial Perspective, and management of colours.

Lambert on photometry, as subservient to painting. A. Berl. 1768. 80.

Lambert on aerial perspective. A. Berl. 1774. 74.

Pfannenschmid über das mischen der farben. 8. Hann. 1781.

Prangens schule der mahlung. 8. Halle, 1782.

Morgan. Ph. tr. 1785.

Says, that an electric spark in a Torricellian vacuum with a few drops of ether appears green to an eye near it, and red at the distance of a few yards. Probably some imperfection of the focus was concerned.

Analytical determination of tints in painting. Journ. polyt. I, i 167.

Barker's patent panorama. Repert. IV. 165.

Montucla and Lalande. III. 565.

Ocular Spectra, and coloured shadows.

Jurin in Smith's optics.

Buffon on accidental colours. A. P. 1743. 147. H. 1.

Aepinus's optical observations. N. C. Petr. X. 282. Roz. XXVI.

Darcy. A. P. 1765.

Beguelin on coloured shadows. A. Berl. 1767. 27.

Beguelin on a description of sight with respect to colour. A. Berl. 1771. 8.

Franklin's experiments and observations. Lond. 1769. 470. Roz. II. 383.

Mongez on ocular spectra. Roz. VI. 491.

Mongez on blue shadows. Roz. XII. 127.

Godard on ocular spectra. Roz. VII. 309. VIII. 1, 269, 341. XXV. 219.

Dicquemare on illusions of sight. Roz. XI. 403.

Observations sur les ombres colorées. 8. Par. 1782.

Scherffer and Aepinus on accidental colours. Roz. XXVI. 175, 273, 291.

*R. W. Darwin on ocular spectra. Ph. tr. 1786. 313.

Explains some phenomena very satisfactorily from the contrast of sensations; but others might be better understood from the analogy of coloured shadows, especially the direct spectra. Darwin thinks, that the stimulus of light accordingly as its intensity becomes greater, produces, first simple spasmodic action; 2, intermitting spasmodic action; 3, opposite spasmodic action; 4, various successive actions; 5, fixed spasmodic action; 6, paralysis. Mentions the effect of light coming through the eyelids, and a mode of observing the circulation of the blood in the eye.

On accidental colours. Roz. XXX. 407.
Marat sur la lumière.
Monge on coloured shadows. Ann. Ch. III. 131.
Rumford on coloured shadows. Ph. tr. 1794. 107. Nich. I. 101.
Shows that they are mere fallacies.

Hassenfratz on coloured shadows. Journ. polyt. IV. xi. 272. Nich. VI. 282. VII. 23.

Imperfections of sight.

Defects of focal distance.

†Myopibus juvamen. R. H. Hooke. Ph. coll. n. 3. p. 59.
Lahire on the use of spectacles. A. P. IX. 366. 417.
Desaguliers on telescopes for myopic persons. Ph. tr. 1719. XXX. 1017.
On the effect of glasses upon the flexibility of sight. A. P. 1770. H. 50.
Spectacles. E. M. A. IV. Art. Lunettier.
Henry on a person becoming short sighted in advanced age. Manch. M. III. 182.
At 50, probably from reading a small print frequently without much light.

Richardson's patent spectacles. Repert. X. 145.
With additional glasses, which may be turned back at pleasure.

Wollaston's improved periscopic spectacles. Nich. VII. 143, 241. Ph. M. XVII. 327. XVIII. 165.
Meniscus lenses.

Jones on Wollaston's spectacles. Nich. VII. 192. VIII. 38. Ph. M. XVIII. 65, 273.
†E. Walker on spectacles. Nich. VII. 291.

Imperfection of focus.

Lahire on the obliquity of the crystalline lens. A. P. IX. 399.

Aepinus on the apparent diameter of a small hole. N. C. Petr. VII. 303.
Telescopic appearances of stars. Herschel. Ph. tr. 1782.
Stack on improving defective sight. Ir. trans. 1788. II. 27.
Supposes myopia to depend on aberration.

Irradiation. See diffraction, as affecting astronomical observations.

Squinting.

Buffon. A. P. 1743. 231. H. 68.
Dutour. S. E. VI. 479.
Darwin. Ph. tr. 1778. 86.
Arnim on a case of double vision. Gilb. III. 249.

Confusion of colours.

Ph. tr. 1738.
All objects appeared red to some persons who had eaten henbane roots.

Huddart on persons who could not distinguish colours. Ph. tr. 1777. 260.
Harris, a shoemaker, could only tell black from white; had two brothers equally defective: one of them mistook orange for green.

Scott's imperfection of sight. Ph. tr. 1778. 613.
Full reds and full greens appeared alike; but yellows and dark blues were very nicely distinguished.

Roz. XIII. 86.
Monge. Ann. Chim. III. 131.
Dalton on some facts relating to the vision of colours. Manch. M. V. 28.
His own case, agreeing with those of several other persons. He cannot distinguish blue from pink by daylight, but by candlelight the pink appears red; in the solar spectrum the red is scarcely visible, the rest appears to consist of two colours, yellow and blue, or of yellow, blue, and purple. He thinks it probable that the vitreous humour is of a deep blue tinge: but this has never been observed by anatomists, and it is much more simple to suppose the absence or paralysis of those fibres of the retina, which are calculated to perceive red; this supposition explains all the phenomena,

except that greens appear to become bluish when viewed by candlelight; but in this circumstance there is perhaps no great singularity.

Debility of sight.

Taper tubes assisting weak sight. Ph. tr. 1668. III. 727, 765.

Briggs's case of indistinct vision at night. Ph. tr. 1684. IV. 559.

Dale on a blindness at night. Ph. tr. 1694. XVIII. 158.

Cataract.

Young on the extraction of the cataract. Ed. ess. II. 324.

Employment for the Blind.

Cheese's musical machine for the blind. S. A. V. 125.

Bew on employment in blindness. Manch. M. I. 159.

Bérard's palpable mathematics for the blind. B. Mélanges. 182.

Some books have been printed in Paris in palpable characters.

Production of Colours in Double Lights.

See diffraction.

Hooke on the colours of a bubble. Birch. III. 29.

Newton on the colours of thin plates. Birch. III. 247, 278.

Lahire on the iris round candles. A. P. IX. 364.

Langwith and Pemberton on supernumerary rainbows. Ph. tr. 1723. XXXII. 241, 245.

Mairan on diffraction. A. P. 1738. 53. H. 82.

Daval on an extraordinary rainbow. Ph. tr. 1749. XLVI. 193.

Confirming Langwith's account. "Within the purple of the common rainbow there were arches of the following colours. 1. Yellowish green, darker green, purple. 2. Green, purple. 3. Green, purple." These colours were not visible near the horizon, although the bow was very bright there.

Boscovich on a halo near the sun. A. P. 1754. H. 32.

Mazéas on the colours produced by friction. A. Berl. 1752. 248. S. E. II. 26.

Euler on the colours of thin plates. A. Berl. 1752. 262.

Duc de Chaulnes on some experiments of Newton. Book 2, part 4. A. P. 1755. 136. H. 130.

Gives an explanation, which is confuted by his own suggestion, that the same effect ought to be expected from a lens as from a mirror.

N. C. Petr. VI. 420.

Bülfinger saw in 1741 three supernumerary rainbows within the primary one, the first red, the second blue, green, and red, the third dark and red. There are also three other similar observations.

Dutour on coloured rings and on diffraction. S. E. IV. 285. V. 635. VI. 19.

Dutour on the phenomena of thin plates, flaws, and thick plates. Roz. I. 368. II. 11, 349. V. 120, 230. VII. 330, 341.

Dutour on fringes of colours. Roz. VI. 135, 412.

Delaval on the colours produced by metals. Ph. tr. 1765. 10.

Benvenuti de lumine. 4. Vienn. 1766.

Boscovich's theory.

Diequemare. Roz. VII. 300.

Observed a third iris beyond the second, as much weaker than the second as the second was than the first; and at the distance of its breadth, or at ½ of the distance of the first from the second: the red was internal, as in the secondary rainbow.

Cockin on an extraordinary appearance in a mist. Ph. tr. 1780. 157.

An oblong shadow, surrounded by two luminous and coloured arches: the centre being dark, yellow next, then dark, then a rainbow. Quotes Priestley and others for three parallel cases.

Barker. Ph. tr. 1783. 245. 1787. 370.
Some coronae.

Stratico on the diffraction of light. Ac. Pad. II. 185.

Hopkinson and Rittenhouse on inflection through cloth. Am. tr. II. 201. Nich. I. 13.

Comparetti **de luce inflexa et coloribus. 4. Pad. 1787. R. S.**
Contains some curious experiments, but generally in very complicated circumstances.

Brougham on inflection and colours. Ph. tr. 1796. 227. 1797. 352. Nich. II. 147.

Jordan's **observations on light and colours. 8. Lond. 1799. 1800. R. I.**
Acc. Nich. IV. 78.

Colours produced by distant glasses. Nich. II. 312.
Probably from a slight difference in the thickness of the glasses, the rays twice reflected within the first glass only, interfering with the rays twice reflected in the second only. The analogy with the colours of thin plates is wholly foreign to the subject.

Colours of steel. Nich. IV. 127.

Young on some cases of the production of colours. Ph. tr. 1802. 387. Nich. 8. IV. 180.

Young on the colours of thin plates shown by the solar microscope. Journ. R. I., I. 241. Nich. 8. III. 283.

Young on physical optics. Ph. tr. 1804. 1. Nich. IX. 63.

Messier on a lunar corona. M. Inst. V. 130.

Anthelia. See Glories, Parhelia.

Description of Dr. Young's *Apparatus for exhibiting the Colours of thin Plates, by means of the Solar Microscope. Journ. R. I. I. 241.*

The colours of thin plates were observed by Boyle and Hooke, and more accurately analysed by Newton: but little or nothing was added to the account that Newton gave of them, until some attempts were lately made to explain them, and to build at the same time on the explanation, the principal arguments in favour of a new system of light and colours. The phenomena themselves were very little known, except from Newton's description; it had happened but to few to observe them: and they had never been made conspicuous to a public audience in a form equally beautiful and interesting.

It appeared, however, that there would be little difficulty in applying the apparatus for representing opaque objects in the solar microscope, to the exhibition of these colours on a large scale: but several precautions were necessary, in order to obtain the most advantageous representation; and, these precautions having been completely successful, it may be of some utility to give a detached account of them.

The colours of thin substances must often have been seen in bubbles of water or of other fluids, and in the film produced by a drop of oil spreading on water; they were more particularly observed in the plates of talc, or of selenite, into which those substances readily divide. Sir Isaac Newton made his experiments principally on the colours of soap bubbles, and on those which are produced by the contact of two lenses. For inspecting the colours of soapy water, the most convenient method is that of Mr. Jordan. He dips a wine glass into a weak solution of soap, and then holds it in a horizontal position against an upright substance, for example, a window shutter; the film covering the glass being in a vertical position, the gravity of the fluid tends to make it thicker at the lower part, and it becomes every where gradually thinner and thinner, till at length it bursts at the uppermost point. The colours assume, in this case, the form of horizontal stripes, similar to the rings which are to be more particularly described.

It has been observed by Newton, that the colours thus reflected from a plate of a denser medium, are more vivid than when a plate of a rarer medium is interposed between two denser mediums. But the cause of this apparent difference is, probably, the quantity of foreign light that is generally present in the experiment, reflected as well from the upper surface of the superior medium as from the lower surface of the inferior, both these surfaces being often nearly parallel to the surfaces in contact. It becomes therefore desirable to remove this foreign light: this may be done effectually, by employing one glass in the form of a prism, and coating the lower surface of the other with black sealing wax: the light reflected by the oblique surface of the first is thus thrown into another direction; and the reflection of the inferior surface of the second is either destroyed or rendered imperceptible. And, with these precautions, the rings of colours, produced in the reflected light, may be rendered a very beautiful object by means of the solar microscope.

The most perfectly plane glasses are those which are used for Hadley's quadrants: one of these may be ground in the direction of the diagonal of its transverse section, so as to make a thin wedge or prism; and the surface of the lens employed must be a portion of a sphere of from five to ten feet radius. The two glasses must be retained in their position by means of three screws; for, as soon as the pressure is removed, they repel each other with considerable force; and, for this reason, neither of them ought to be very thin, otherwise they will bend before they are sufficiently near.

For adjusting the glasses of the microscope, it is convenient to fix them in a cylinder of sufficient size to project beyond the glasses and their screws, in order that they may be readily turned so as to reflect the light coming from the speculum, into the direction of the axis of the microscope: it is obvious, that in this case, they must be somewhat inclined to the light, so that the focus of the whole image will never be equally perfect; and, instead of being circular, like the rings themselves, their images on the screen will be oval. In this manner, eight or ten alternations of colours may easily be observed; but their order and sequence is too complicated to be easily understood; for they are really composed of an infinite number of series of rings of different magnitude, each series being formed by each of the gradations of light in the prismatic spectrum, which, near the centre, are sufficiently separate to form distinct appearances, either alone or in combination; but, after eight or ten alternations, are lost in the common effect of white light. For, when the glasses are illuminated by homogeneous light only, separated from the rest by the refraction of a prism, or otherwise, the rings of each colour occupy, together with the dark spaces, the whole visible surface, their number being only limited by the power of the eye in perceiving objects so minute as the external ones become, in consequence of the rapid increase of the thickness of the plate of air near the edges of the curved surface. This circumstance being once understood, it is also capable of being illustrated in a manner still more elegant, by placing a prism a few feet from the microscope, leaving only a narrow line of its surface exposed to the incident rays, and then throwing the rings of colours on it, in such a direction, that this line shall pass through their centre. Care being taken to exclude from the prismatic spectrum thus formed all extraneous light, it exhibits a most interesting analysis of these colours; for the line consists of portions of the rings of all possible gradations of colour, each forming a broken line, but not of the same dimensions; and, by the prismatic refraction, all these broken lines are separated and placed parallel to each other, on account of the different refrangibility of the light of which they consist. Thus the broken line of the extreme red, which consists of the longest portions, is least refracted; the other reds follow, and are placed in contact with the first, and with each other, but, on account of the different magnitude of the portions, somewhat obliquely. The dark spaces also are in contact, and form a separation between each portion of light. In the same manner, the green follows the red, with little or no visible yellow. The blue and violet are somewhat mixed: for these two colours are much less widely separated by thin plates than by the prism: for this reason, each portion of light formed by the contiguous lines of the different colours is bounded not by straight but by curved lines.

It is evident, that, by drawing a line across this compound spectrum at any part, we may learn the component parts of the light constituting the rings at that part; for the prism only spreads the colours in a direction transverse to this spectrum: and it may be observed, that after the eighth or tenth alternation, the light transmitted at each point is so mixed, that we may easily understand how it appears white.

The colours of thin plates, as seen by transmission, are also easily exhibited in the solar microscope; but, since it is utterly impossible to exclude the very great proportion of the light which does not appear to be concerned in their formation, they are never so brilliant as the colours seen by reflection.

Account of Dr. Young's *Experiments and Calculations relative to Physical Optics. From the Journals of the Royal Institution, II.*

Dr. Young divides this paper into six sections. 1. Experimental demonstration of the general law of the interference of light. 2. Comparison of measures, deduced from various experiments. 3. Application to the supernumerary rainbows. 4. Argumentative inference respecting the nature of light. 5. Remarks on the colours of natural bodies. 6. Experiment on the dark rays of Ritter.

The object of the first section is to demonstrate in a simple and elementary manner, by the direct evidence of the senses, the truth of the general principle, which appears to connect an extensive class of phenomena by a clear analogy. This principle is, that where two portions of light arrive at any point by different routes very nearly in the same direction, they sometimes destroy and sometimes corroborate each other, according to the different lengths of their respective paths. This is proved by placing a slip of card in a sun beam admitted through a small aperture, its shadow being divided by alternate lines of light and shade when the light is allowed to pass by both of its parallel edges; but when the light on either side is intercepted, the fringes disappear. The crested fringes observed by Grimaldi within the rectangular termination of a shadow, are also shown to depend on the mixture of the two portions of light inflected at the two edges of the object, which form the angle.

In the second section, the appropriate interval for the brightest light is calculated from experiments of Newton, and from others which are new, and made under a variety of circumstances; and the measure deduced from each observation agrees with the mean without an error of more than a fourth or a fifth: if the principle had been erroneous, there is no reason why this distance should not have varied at least as much as the measures of the fringes, which were changed in the ratio of 7 to 1, or even in a much greater ratio. There is still, however, some doubt with respect to the cause of the slight difference observed, the measure of the interval being always a little larger in these experiments than in the observations of Newton on thin plates; and the error is the greater as the track of the light is the more rectilinear. The proportions of the intervals for the different colours are also shown to be the same here as in the colours of thin plates: and it is observed that the form of Grimaldi's crested fringes, ought according to the calculation to be that of an equilateral hyperbola.

The law being thus established, is in the third place applied to the supernumerary rainbows observed by Dr. Langwith and others, which Dr. Pemberton has attempted to explain by a comparison with the colour of thin plates.

The advantage which Dr. Young's explanation possesses is this, that he refers the colours to the light regularly reflected, and Dr. Pemberton employs the light irregularly dissipated, of which the effect must be perhaps some hundred times weaker. Comparing the two portions of light of which the extreme terminations constitute the common rainbow, he finds that they must cause, by their interference at other parts, rings of colours, agreeing perfectly with those which were observed in a particular instance by Dr. Langwith, if the drops of rain concerned were all between 170 and 180 of an inch in diameter.

Hitherto, Dr. Young observes in the fourth section, he has advanced in this Paper no general hypothesis: and he attempts to infer, by a chain of experimental arguments, that refraction is not produced by an attractive force: since from the smaller length of the appropriate intervals of interference in a denser medium, it may be concluded that light moves more slowly as the medium has a greater refractive density. He remarks that the existence of the intervals of interference in an arithmetical progression, agrees so well with the nature and properties of a musical sound, which consists in the succession of motions in contrary directions at intervals which are also in arithmetical progression, that we can scarcely avoid concluding that the nature of sound and of light must have a very strong resemblance.

It was conjectured by Newton that the colours of all natural bodies are similar to some of the series of colours produced by thin plates. In this case Dr. Young has observed in a former paper they ought to be divided into two, three, or more portions, by prismatic refraction, as the colours of thin plates necessarily are; and he has pointed out an instance of the kind in the blue light of a candle, which consists, as Dr. Wollaston discovered, of five separate portions. He now describes the effect of the prism on the light transmitted by the blue glass sold in the shops, which appears to be divided in a similar manner into seven portions. But he confesses that the analogy suspected by Newton is imperfect in more than one respect.

In the last section an experiment is related by which the effects of thin plates and the general laws of interference are shown to extend to the dark rays discovered by Ritter, and hitherto only known by their effects on metallic oxids. The specimen of rings, which has been repeatedly exhibited in the theatre of the Royal Institution, was thrown on a paper dipped in solution of the nitrate of silver, and the blackening effect was distinctly observable in the portions of three rings, which were marked on the paper nearly of the same dimensions as the violet rings, but apparently a little smaller. The same mode of analysis, Dr. Young observes, might be extended with great advantage to the rays of invisible heat discovered by Dr. Herschel, if we had thermometers of sufficient delicacy to assist us in its application.

Nature of Light, and Causes of Colours.

Aristoteles de anima. L. xi. c. 7.

Zucchii optica philosophia. 1652.
   Maintains the colours are exhibited by transmission only: Kepler showed the same by experiments. Wells.

Hooke's micrographia.

Hooke's considerations on light. Birch. III. 10.

Hooke's opinion of light. Birch. III. 194.

Newton's hypothesis of light. Birch. III. 247, 278. See Refraction.

Mariotte de la nature des couleurs. Oeuvres. I. 195.

Halley's queries respecting the nature of light. Ph. tr. 1693. XVII. 998.
   Follows Huygens, but with some misconceptions. Observes, that the ether is generally supposed to penetrate all bodies with full liberty.

Huygens's system of light. A. P. I. 184.

*Huygens Traité de la lumière. 4. Leyd. 1690.

Duclos on the properties and extension of light. A. P. IV. 27.

Malebranche on light and colours. A. P. 1699. 22. H. 17.

Lahire's remarks on some colours. A. P. 1711. 78.

Mairan on colours and sound, on the figure and rotation of the particles of light, and on their different refrangibility. A. P. 1720. H. 11. 1737. 22. H. 97. 1738. 8. H. 82.

Rizzetti de luminis affectionibus. Trevis. 1727. R. S.
   Remarks. Ph. tr. 1728. XXXV.
   Explains refraction and total refraction as Euler and others.

J. Bernoulli on the propagation of light. A. P. Pr. III. iii.

Clairaut on the Cartesian and Newtonian theory of refraction. A. P. 1739. 259.

Clairaut on Courtivron's calculation of the velocity of light. Ph. tr. 1754. 776.
   Making the required difference greater than Melvil.

Clairaut on the hypothesis of different velocities of different colours. A. P. 1756. 422.

Segner de raritate luminis. 4. Gotting. 1740.

Krüger on ocular music. M. Berl. 1743. VII. 345.

On light and colours. A. Berl. 1745. H. 13.

Euler on the propagation of light. A. Berl. 1746. 141.

Euleri nova theoria lucis et colorum. Opusc. I. 179.

Euleri conjectura physica circa propagationem soni et luminis. 4. Berl. 1750. Opusc.

Euler on the colours of thin plates. A. Berl. 1752. 262.

Euler on the nature of colours, and the refrangibility of different rays. A. Berl. 1754. 200.

Euler on the refraction of different rays. N. C. Petr. XII. 166.

Euler on refraction and dispersion. A. Petr. J. i. 174.

Melvil on the refrangibility of light. Ph. tr. 1753. 261.
   Supposing a difference of velocity.

Melvil on light and colours. Ed. ess. II. 12.
   Its nature, tenuity, and different velocity.

Short on the eclipses of Jupiter's satellites. Ph. tr. 1753. 268.
   Proving the velocities of all kinds of light equal.

On the effects of light. C. Bon. IV. C. 76.
   Changes of colour and of texture.

Boscovich's difficulty respecting the secondary rainbow. S. E. III. 321.

Boscovich theoria philosophiae naturalis.

Eberhard über die natur der farben. 8. Halle, 1762.

Eberhard on the colour of the air. Roz. Introd. I. 618.

Westfeld über die erzeugung der farben. 8. Gott. 1767.

Horsley on difficulties respecting light. Ph. tr. 1770. 417. 1771. 547.

Beguelin's proposal for experiments on the propagation of light. A. Berl. 1772. 152. Roz. XIII. 38.
   Inclines to the Huygenian theory.

Objections to Beguelin's proposal. Allgem. Deutsche bibl. XXIV. 18.

On ocular music. Mendelsohn's briefe. ii.

Saboureux on ocular music. Roz. II. 78.

On the immediate cause of refraction. Roz. II. 271.

Delaval on changes of colour. A. Berl. 1774. 154.

Delaval on the colours of opaque bodies. 4. R. S.

Delaval on the permanent colours of opaque bodies. Manch. M. II. 131.

<small>Maintains, that all light is reflected by white particles, and coloured in its transmission. No transparent coloured medium reflects any light when examined within a blackened bottle; this is shown by experiments on 68 kinds of fluids and on many kinds of glasses. Vegetable extracts also appeared black, earth being the only reflective substance in vegetables. Fibrous animal substances are white, the extractive juices black. Supposes that coloured metals consist of yellow transparent matter mixed with white reflective particles. Glass tinged with a little arsenic is yellow or orange by transmitted, and blue by reflected light, like the atmosphere: for this, and for the colours of the sea Mr. Delaval proposes a very improbable theory. It appears that bodies acquire this property as they lose their transparency: thus glass tinged with gold and rendered opaque by heat transmits violet light, and appears by reflection brown. Infusions of woods, used in dying red, transmit yellow or red light according to their thickness. Sap green digested in alcohol transmits green light when thin, dull yellow and then bright red when thicker: other vegetable greens have the same property, and the aqueous infusion in some degree. Infusion of litmus appears to be blue when thin, then purple, and when still thicker, bright red. Mr. Delaval supposes that these colours are produced by inflection: the colours of thin plates, he says, are produced by the reflection of light from their posterior surfaces.</small>

Higgins on light. 8. Lond. 1776. R. I.
On colours. Roz. X. 66.

Arena Physicae quaestiones. 4. Rom. 1777.

Sénébier sur l'influence de la lumière solaire pour modifier les êtres des trois regnes de la nature. 3 v. 8. Genev. 1782.

Sénébier on light, in answer to Marivetz. Roz. XXV. 74.

Sénébier on the effect of light in bleaching wax. M. Laus. III. 362.

Sénébier on the effect of light in bleaching. Roz. XXXVIII. 56.

Answer to Sénébier's remarks on light. Roz. XIII. Suppl. 281.

VOL. II.

Bonnet on the effects of light upon colours. Roz. XIII. 462.

Wilson's proposed experiment on the aberration of the fixed stars. Ph. tr. 1782. 58.

Fontana on light. Soc. Ital. I. 104. Crell. Chem. ann. 1784.

Fontana on the path of light during refraction. Soc. Ital. III. 498.

Marat sur la lumière.

Marivetz on the propagation of light in an elastic medium. Roz. XXIII. 340. XXIV. 40, 230, 275. In answer to Sénébier. Roz. XXVI. 140.

Remarks on Marivetz. Roz. XXIII. 380. Ph. tr. 1784. 35.

<small>Michel observes, that the attraction of large stars should produce a difference in the velocity of light.</small>

†Bowdoin on the nature and waste of light. Am. Ac. I. 187, 208.

<small>Supposes a solid orb to surround the whole universe and to preserve the light emitted from the sun and stars.</small>

Experiments and observations on light and colours. 8. Lond. 1786.

<small>Suggests, that light constitutes a scale of rays extending considerably on each side of the spectrum, the middle part only being visible to us: but forms no conjecture respecting the nature of the extremes.</small>

Berthollet on the influence of light. Roz. XXIX. 81.

Chaptal on the effect of light in crystallization. Roz. XXXIII. 297.

Deluc on light and heat. Roz. XXXVII. 54, 116.

Comparetti de luce et coloribus.

Saussure on the chemical effects of light. M. Tur. 1788. IV. 441.

<small>Finds the effect increased on a high mountain.</small>

Dorthes on the effects of light. Ann. Ch. II. 92.

Robison on the motion of refracting mediums. Ed. tr. II. 83.

<small>Corrects the errors of Boscovich.</small>

Vassalli's comparison of solar light with the light of fire. M. Tur. 1790. VI. 186, 287.
  Producing the same chemical effects.
Gehlers physic. wörterb. Art. Licht.
Wedgwood. Ph. tr. 1792. 270.
  Air not visible made a wire red hot.
Ph. tr. 1792. 81.
  Bennet could discover no momentum in light by a very delicate test.
Burja on colours. A. Berl. 1792. 23.
Franklin on light and heat. Am. tr. III. 5.
  The Huygenian theory.
Bancroft on the philosophy of permanent colours. 8. Lond. 1794. R. S.
  On dying.
Hutton's dissertation on light, heat, and fire. 8. Edinb.
Acc. Ed. tr. IV. H. 7.
  Calls radiant heat obscure light.
Tingry on the effect of light on oils. Journ. Phys. XLVI. (III.) 161.
Dizé on the matter of heat and light. Journ. Phys. XLIX. 177. Gilb. IV. 410.
Brougham on inflection, reflection, and colours. Ph. tr. 1796. 227. 1797. 352. Nich. I. 551. II. 147. See double Refraction.
Engel on light. A. Berl. 1796. ii. 194.
  Thinks it an element, but not tangible matter.
Prévost Remarques d'optique. Ph. tr. 1798. 311. Nich. III. 222.
*Prévost on the reflexibility of the rays of light. Journ. Phys. XLIX. 273. Gilb. V. 129, 147.
  In answer to Mr. Brougham's two papers.
Prévost on the impulse of light, with objections. Ph. M. I. 421.
Rumford on the chemical properties attributed to light. Ph. tr. 1798. 449. Gilb. II. 273.
  Attributes them to an intense heat, excited in a small space, but without any satisfactory evidence.

On Parr's theory of light and heat. Nich. II. 547.
Laplace on the attraction of bodies to light. Zach. Ephem. IV. 1.
  A star, 250 times as great in diameter as the sun, ought to overcome the velocity of light and draw it back; such a star would therefore be invisible.
T. Young on sound and light. Ph. tr. 1800. 106. Nich. V. 72, 161.
Young on the theory of light and colours. Ph. tr. 1802. 12. Nich. 8. II. 78.
Young on the production of colours. Ph. tr. 1802.
Young on physical optics. Ph. tr. 1804. 1.
Herschel on light and heat. Ph. tr. 1800. 255.
Messier on the effect of light on the evaporation of mercury. M. Inst. II. 473. Gilb. XII. 96.
Le Sage on the chemical effects of light. Gilb. II. 273.
†Brugnatelli on the forms of the matter of light. Gilb. IV. 438.
Hermstädt on the colours of natural bodies. A. Berl. 1801. 83. Ph. M. XVIII. 201.
Ritter on the blackening rays. Gilb. VII. 527. XII. 409. Journ. Phys. LVII. 409. Nich. VIII. 214.
Ocular music. Montucla and Lalande. III. 566.
Montucla and Lalande. III. 604.
  Lalande concludes with Dalembert " La lumière se propage suivant une ligne droite d'une manière qui nous est inconnue."
Von Charpentier on the evaporation of mercury. Gilb. XII. 365. See Heat, Evaporation.
†Heron on the nature of light. Ph. M. VIII. 161.
†Pownall on light. Ph. M. XII. 42.
  Makes only one colour.

†Regner on the propagation of light. Zach. Mon. corr. VI. 348.

Scheele's experiments on the chemical effects of light. Ph. M. XIII. 42.

Englefield on the separation of light and heat by refraction. Journ. R. I., I. Nich. 8. III. 125.

Wollaston on some chemical effects of light. Nich. VIII. 293.

Found that invisible heat deoxidated as well as the red rays.

Wollaston. Ph. tr. 1804. 428.

Observes, that the crystals of palladium, and some tourmalins, are of a deep red when viewed in the direction of the axis, and of a yellowish green when viewed in a transverse direction. Some crystals are greenish in the first direction, and reddish in the second.

Effects of light on vegetation. See Vegetable Physiology.

Besides the salts of silver and the gums, the martial flowers of sal ammoniac are much affected by light.

See Double Refraction, Telescopes.

When a ball 1 strikes a ball r so as to be reflected at an equal angle with respect to a given surface, the ball r is propelled in such a direction that $s.2I : s.2R :: r : 1$. The velocity of 1 is $\frac{s.(I-R)}{s.(I+R)}$; that of r, $\frac{2\cos.(I-R)}{r+1}$. I and R being the angles of incidence and of refraction. Y.

History of Optics.

Ph. M. XVIII. 245.

Recorde, in 1551, mentions a wonderful glass of Roger Bacon, agreeing to the description of a telescope, and professes to understand its construction.

Digges's pantometria. Lond. 1571. Ph. M. XVIII. 245.

Contains some hints of a telescope.

Borellus de vero telescopii inventore. 4. Hague, 1655.

Derham on Gascoigne's invention of telescopic sights. Ph. tr. 1717. XXX. 603.

Lahire on the invention of telescopes and of the micrometer. A. P. 1717. 78.

*Priestley's history of optics.

Meister on the optical knowledge of the ancients. N. C. Gott. 1774. V. 141. 1775. VI. 129.

Particularly in painting.

Pringle on the invention of the reflecting telescope. 4. Lond. 1778.

Account of discoveries relating to solar phosphori. T. Wedgwood. Ph. tr. 1792.

Hind. Arch. III. 95.

Pfleiderer attempts to show, that Descartes did not borrow his law of refraction from Snellius.

Rochon on achromatic glasses. Gilb. IV. 300.

On Hall's achromatic glasses. Ph. M. II. 177.

*On the invention of the telescope and other optical instruments. Ph. M. XVIII. 245. XIX. 66, 176, 232, 344. XX. 14.

Dates.

R. Bacon's magic lantern	1252
Spina invented spectacles at Pisa	1299
Armati at Florence before	1300
Looking glasses made only at Venice	1300
Telescopes discovered by Jansen	1590
A reflecting telescope mentioned by Eskinard	1615
Snellius discovered the laws of refraction. Died	1626
Descartes published on refraction	1629
Hall invented achromatic glasses	1729
Ritter discovered the blackening rays	1801

PHYSICS.

Gilbert Philosophia nova de mundo. 4. Amst. 1631.
Physics. Ph. tr. Abr. II. i. 1. IV. pt. 2. i. 1. VIII. pt. 2. i. 377. X. pt. 2. i. 269.
Miscellanea curiosa. 3 v. 8. 1716.
Keil Tentamina physicomedica. 8. 1718. M. B.
Rackstrow's miscellaneous observations. 8. Lond. 1748.
Kant Allgemeine naturgeschichte. 8. Königsb. 1755.
Trembley Instructions d'un père a ses enfans. 3 v. 8. R. I.
Bonnet Contemplation de la nature, 2 v. 8. Amst. 1764. R. I.
Buffon Histoire naturelle. 4.
Deluc Lettres physiques.
Dakar's description of the universe. 4. R. S.
Darwin's botanic garden. Notes.
Philibert Histoire naturelle. 8.
Barruel on general physics. Journ. Polyt. I. i. 120. ii. 128. iii. 337. ii. 623.
Hassenfratz on general physics. Journ. Polyt. II. vi. 372.
Gren's account of authors on physics. Gilb. I. 167.

ASTRONOMY.

Ptolemaei magna syntaxis, cum Theone. f. Basle, 1538. 1551. R. I.
Ptolemy, by Bode. 8. Berl. 1795. R. S.
Manilius a Pingrè. 2 v. 8. Par. 1786. R. S.
Copernicus de revolutionibus orbium coelestium. f. 1543. M. B. Basle, 1566. 1543. M. B.
Copernici astronomia reformata. 4. Amst. 1617.
Tychonis de Brahe astronomiae instauratae progymnasmatu. 4. Prag. 1603.
Tycho de Brahe de mundi aetherei phaenomenis. 4. Prag. 1610.
Tychonis de Brahe epistolae astronomicae. 4. 1610. M. B.
Tychonis de Brahe historia coelestis. f. Augsb. 1666. M. B.
Galilaei dialogus de systemate mundi. 4. 1635.
Kepleri epitome astronomiae. 8. Francf. 1635. M. B.
Riccioli almagestum novum. f. 1651. M. B.
†*Riccioli* astronomia reformata. f. Bologn. 1665.
Extr. Ph. tr. 1665—6. I. 394.
Astronomy. Ph. tr. abr. I. iv. 216. IV. iii. 206. VI. iii. 147. VIII. iii. 152. X. iii. 32.
Hevelii machina coelestis. f. Dantz. 1673. 1679. M. B.
D. Gregorii elementa astronomiae. f. Oxf. 1702. M. B.
Flamsteedii historia coelestis. 3 v. f. Lond. 1725.
Acc. Ph. tr. 1725. XXXIII. 350.
Delisle sur l'astronomie. 4. Petersb. 1738.
Baxter's matho. 2 v. 12. 1740. M. B.
Cassini Élémens d'astronomie. 2 v. A. P. 1740. Suite. 4 v. 4. Par. 1742.
Weidleri historia astronomiae. 4. Wittemb. 1741. R. I.
*Keil's introduction to astronomy. 8. 1769. R. I.
Clairaut on the system of the world. A. P. 1745. 329.
La Caille Leçons d'astronomie. 8. Par. 1746. 1755. R. I. Par Lalande. 1780.

La Caille's elements of astronomy, by Robertson.
Wright's theory of the universe. 4. London, 1750.
Derham's astrotheology. 8. London, 1758. R. I.
Dieterichs schöpfung und schöpfer.
Emerson's cyclomathesis. VIII. IX.
Lambert Cosmologische briefe. 8. Augsb. 1761.
Lambert Système du monde. 8. Bouillon, 1770.
Lalande Exposition du calcul astronomique. 8. Par. 1762.
   Acc. A. P. 1762. H. 136.
*Lalande Astronomie. 3 v. 4. Paris, 1792. R. I.
   Acc. A. P. 1771. H. 86. Journ. Phys. XLIV. (I.) 126.
Lalande Astronomie des dames. 8. 2 ed. Par. 1795.
*Lalande Bibliographie astronomique. 4. Par. 1805. R. I.
Long's astronomy. 2 v. 4. R. I.
Ferguson's introduction to astronomy. 8. R. S.
Ferguson's astronomy. 8. R. I.
Röhl Einleitung in die astronomische wissenschaften. 8. Greifsw. 1768. 1779.
J. Bernoulli Ephemerides astronomicae. 8. R. S.
J. Bernoulli Recueil pour les astronomes. 8. Berl. 1771... R. S.
J. Bernoulli Lettres astronomiques. 8. Berl. 1771. R. S.
Schmid von den weltkörpern. 8. Leipz. 1772.
Kaestner Astronomische abhandlungen. 8. Gott. 1772—4. 2 p.
Segner Astronomische vorlesungen. 4. Halle, 1775—6.
Hellmuth Sternwissenschaft. 8. Brunsw. 1776.
Frisii cosmographia.
E. M. Physique. Art. Astronomie.

Boscovich opera inedita. 5 v. 4. Bassano, 1785. Notice abregée de l'astronomie. V. 270.
Bonnycastle's introduction to astronomy. 8. 1803. R. I.
Cousin Astronomie physique. 4. Par. 1787. R. S.
   Extr. Roz. XXXI. 25.
Schröters beyträge zur erweiterung der sternkunde. 8. Gotting. R. S.
_{Several parts.}
Bode Erläuterung der sternkunde. 8. Berl. 1793.
Bode Sammlung astronomischer abhandlungen. 8. Berl. 1795. R. S.
*Robison. Enc. Br. Art. Precession. Suppl. Art. Astronomy.
*Robison's elements.
Melanderhjelm Astronomie. 2 v. Stockh. 1795. R. S.
Vince's astronomy. 3 v. 4. Cambridge, 1797.
Vince's introduction to astronomy, in Pinkerton's geography.
Von Zachs geographische ephemeriden. 4 v. 8. Monatliche correspondenz. 8. Weimar, 1798... B. B.
**Laplace Exposition du système du monde. 4. Par. an. 7. R. I.
**Laplace Mécanique céleste. 4 v. 4. Par. an. 7—13. R. I.
Hassenfratz Physique céleste. 8. Par. 1803. R. S.
   Acc. Ann. Ch. XLIV. 285.
   _{A commentary on Laplace.}
O. Gregory's astronomy. 8. Cambr.
   Acc. Ph. M. XII. 87.
See History of Astronomy.

Fixed Stars in General.

Baieri uranometria. Augsb. 1603. M. B.
Bernard on the places of the principal fixed stars. Ph. tr. 1684. XIV. 567.

Zimmermans coniglobium. 8. 1692. Hamb. 1770.

Flamsteedi historia coelestis. M. B.
Herschel finds that 111 stars are inserted without observations, and 5 or 600 observed are omitted. Ph. tr. 1797. 293.

Flamsteed Atlas coelestis. Lond.

Doppelmaieri atlas coelestis. Nuremb. 1742.

Barker. Ph. tr. 1760.
Arcturus, Aldebaran, Pollux, Antares, and Orion's shoulder have always been reddish.

Funkens kenntniss der gestirne vermittelst zweener sternkegel. 8. Leipz. 1770.

Hellmuth's gestirn beschreibung. 8. Brunsw. 1774.

Bode Vorstellung der gestirne auf 34 kupfertafeln. Berl. 1782.

Bode Anleitung zur kenntniss des gestirnten himmels. 8. Berl. 1788. R. I.

Bode Beschreibung einer himmelscharte. Berl. 1786. R. I.

Bode Friedrichs sternendenkmal. 4. Berl. 1787. R. S.

Bode on the distribution of the stars. A. Berl. 1794. 179.

*Bode Uranographia. f. Berl. 1801. R. I.
Contains above 17000 stars.

Valentin Beschreibung der sternbilder. 8. Kiel, 1785.

Herschel on the construction of the heavens. Ph. tr. 1785.

Herschel on the brightness of stars, with a catalogue. Ph. tr. 1796. 166.
Compared with the neighbouring stars.

Herschel's second catalogue of the brightness of stars. Ph. tr. 1796. 452.

Herschel's third catalogue of the brightness of stars. Ph. tr. 1797. 293.

Herschel's catalogue of stars omitted by Flamsteed. f. 1798. R. I.

Herschel's fourth catalogue of the brightness of stars. Ph. tr. 1799. 121.

On Herschel's numbers of the stars. Goth. M. V. ii. 171.

Deguignes's Chinese planispheres. Fig. S. E. 1785. X. App.

**Wollaston's* astronomical catalogue, in zones. f. R. S.

Lalande's 8000 stars. A. P. 1789. 187. 1790. 345.

Lemonnier on the Arsacides. A. P. 1790. 1.

Burja on the constellations. A. Berl. 1792. 337.

*Piazzi Stellarum inerrantium positiones. f. Palermo, 1803. R. S.

Ph. M. XI. 361.

Comparative brightness of the stars ascertained by Humboldt, by means of diaphragms, in Herschel's manner, Sirius 1. Canopus .98, α Centauri .96, Achernar, .94, α Indi .50, β .47, α Toucan .70, α Phoenicis .65. α Pavonis .78. α Gruis .81, β .75, γ .58.

STARS VISIBLE IN LONDON,

INCLUDING ALL OF THE FIRST AND SECOND MAGNITUDE.

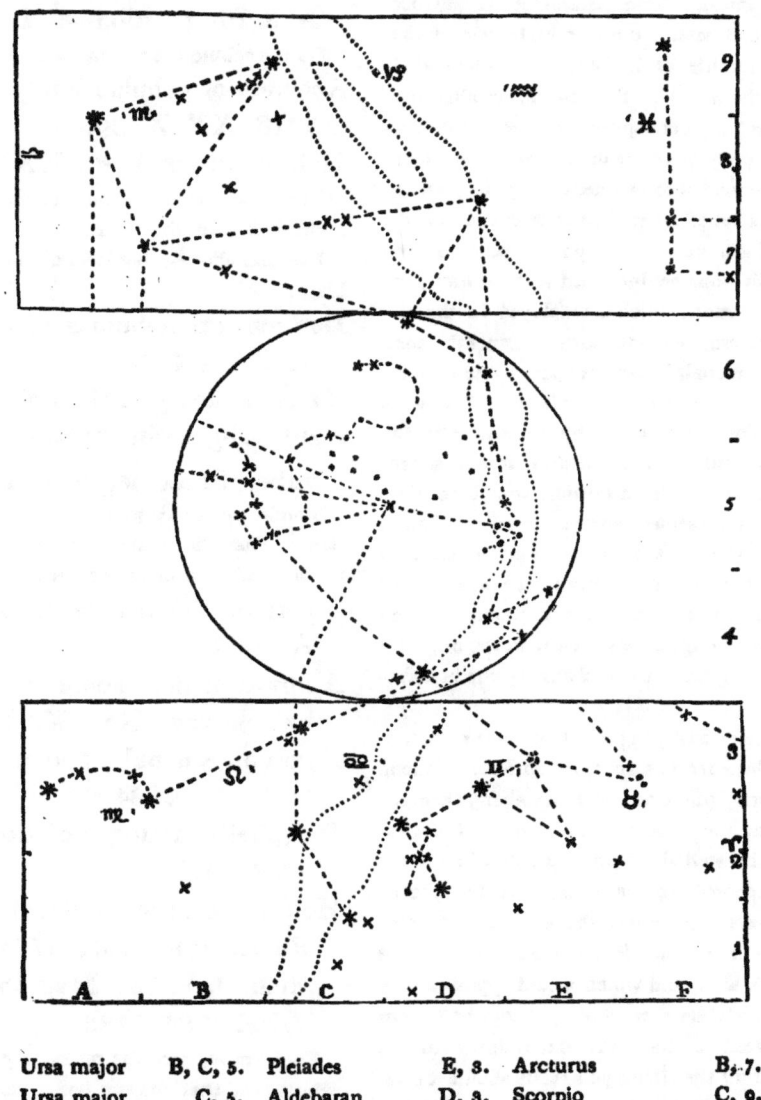

Ursa major	B, C, 5.	Pleiades	E, 3.	Arcturus	B, 7.
Ursa major	C, 5.	Aldebaran	D, 3.	Scorpio	C, 9.
Cassiopeia	E, 5.	Menkar	E, 2.	Libra	B. 8, 9.
Capella	D, 4.	(Canopus)		Corona borealis	B, 7.
Algenib	D, 4.	Aries	F, 3.	Hercules	C, 7.
Algol	E, 4.	Orion	D, 2.	Serpentarius	C, 7.
Cygnus	D, 6.	Castor	C, 3.	Aquila	D, 8.
Lyra	D, 8.	Procyon	C, 2.	Pegasus	F, 7.
Draco	C, D, 5, 6.	Sirius	C, 1.	Fomalhaut	F, 9.
Cepheus	D, 5.	Regulus	B, 2.	(Centaurus	**).
Andromeda	E, 4, F, 3, 7.	Spica	A, 3.	(Crux	†).

When a spherical surface has been projected on a plane, it has been usual to consider it as viewed from a particular point, either infinitely remote, as in the orthographical projection, or situated in the opposite surface of the sphere, as in the stereographical. The latter method produces the least distortion, and is the most commonly used, but even here, at the extremities of the hemisphere, the scale is twice as great as in the middle. Sometimes, another principle is employed, and the hemisphere is divided into segments, by omitting portions in the directions of their radii, as if the paper were intended to be fixed on a globe; and in the same form as if a spherical surface were cut in the direction of its meridians, and spread on a plane. If the number of these divisions be increased without limit, the result will be the projection, which is employed in the circular part of this diagram, and in the same manner the zone on each side the equinoctial, being cut open by innumerable divisions, so as to be spread on a plane, will coincide with the two remaining portions. By these means the distortion becomes inconsiderable. In the common stereographical projection indeed, the distortion would be of no consequence, if it represented always those stars only, which are at once above the horizon of a given place, for we actually imagine the stars in the zenith to be much nearer together, than when they are nearer the horizon, and the picture would appear to agree very well with the original: but their positions being continually changing, the inconvenience remains.

It is not however necessary, in projections of the stars, to refer them in any instance to a spherical surface. Among Doppelmayer's charts, published at Nuremberg, there are six, which represent the sides of a cube, on which the various parts of the constellations are represented: the eye being probably supposed to be situated in the centre. Funck and others have represented the stars as projected on the inside of two flat cones. But the most convenient representation of this kind, and which would approach very near to the projection here employed, would be to consider the eye as placed in the centre of a hollow cylinder, so proportioned that all the circumpolar stars should be represented on one of its flat ends, and all those which rise and set on its concave surface; or if it were desired to have a division without referring to any particular latitude, the circular part might extend to the limits of the zodiac, and the parallelogram, into which the cylinder unfolds, might comprehend all the stars to which the planets approach. The horizon, and other great circles, would form lines of various and contrary curvatures.

Systems of Stars, Nebulae, and Double Stars.

Bullialdi monita duo.
Acc. Ph. tr. 1665—6. I. 387.
On the nebulosa Andromedae.

Account of nebulae lately observed. Ph. tr. 1716. XXIX. 390.

Halley. Ph. tr. 1720. XXXI. 22.
Says, that it would be hard to place 13 points on a sphere at the distance of the radius.
Kaestner shows, that it would be impossible. Dissertat. Math.

Derham on nebulous stars. Ph. tr. 1733. XXXVIII. 70.

Wright's theory of the universe.

Kants Allgemeine naturgeschichte.

Lambert Photometria. §. 1139. 1140.
Thinks the milky way as it were the ecliptic of the fixed stars. That the greater stars belong to the solar nebula, the other nebulae being confused together in the milky way.

Figure of the nebula in Orion, by Messier. A. P. 1771. 458.

A figure of the nebula in Orion, supposed to be changed. Roz. XXII. 34.

Pigott on a nebula, and on double stars. Ph. tr. 1781. 82, 84.

Herschel's catalogue of double stars. Ph. tr. 1782. 112.

Herschel on the construction of the heavens. Ph. tr. 1784. 437. 1785. 213. 1802. 477. Nich. 8. V. 75. Magnified figures of nebulae. 1784. 1785.

Conjectures, that the milky way is the projection of our nebula, and that the sun has a motion towards its node, near Cepheus, and Cassiopeia, 1784. In a circle of 15' diameter 588 stars were counted; if these were at equal distances in a cone, the length of the cone must have been 497 times their distance. From calculations of this kind a figure of the nebula is drawn, showing a section passing through its poles at right angles to the line of the nodes. The right ascension of the pole is 186°, its polar distance 56°; 1785.

Herschel's second catalogue of double stars. Ph. tr. 1785. 40.

Herschel's 1000 new nebulae. Ph. tr. 1786. 457.

Herschel's second thousand of new nebulae. Ph. tr. 1789. 212.

Herschel on nebulous stars. Ph. tr. 1791. 71.

Stars surrounded by a faint light, which Dr. Herschel thinks must be a shining fluid.

Herschel. Ph. tr. 1795. 46.

Found 600 stars in a circle 15' in diameter. This statement has been much mistaken by some authors.

Herschel's 500 new nebulae. Ph. tr. 1802. 477.

Herschel on the changes of double stars. Ph. tr. 1803. 339. 1804. 353. Nich. VII. 210.

Cassini's verification of Herschel's double stars. A. P. 1784. 331.

Asks if they are satellites. Differs a little from Herschel respecting the colour of the stars.

Michell. Ph. tr. 1784. 35.

Conjectures that some stars revolve round others.

Lemonnier on the nebula in cancer. A. P. 1789. 610.

A catalogue of the stars. The double star zeta lyrae sometimes appears accompanied by several little stars.

Account of Dr. HERSCHEL's *paper on the changes that have happened, during the last twenty five years, in the relative situation of double stars; with an investigation of the cause to which they are owing. From the Journals of the Royal Institution. II.*

Dr. Herschel devotes this paper principally to the consideration of the second class of the systems into which he has divided the sidereal world. After cursorily remarking, with respect to the solar system, as a specimen of the first class, which, among the insulated stars, comprehends the sun, that the affections of the newly discovered celestial bodies extend our knowledge of the construction of this insulated system, which is best known to us; he proceeds to support, by the evidence of observation, the opinion, which he has before advanced, of the existence of binary sidereal combinations, revolving round the common centre of gravity. Dr. Herschel first considers the apparent effect of the motion of either of the three bodies concerned, the two stars, and the sun with its attendant planets; and then states the arguments respecting the motions of a few only

out of the fifty double stars, of which he has ascertained the revolutions. The first example is Castor, or alpha Geminorum: here Dr. Herschel stops to show how accurately the apparent diameter of a star, viewed with a constant magnifying power, may be assumed as a measure of small angular distances; he found that ten different mirrors, of seven feet focal length, exhibited no perceptible difference in this respect. In the case of Castor no change of the distance of the stars has been observed, but their angular situation appears to have varied somewhat more than 45° since it was observed by Dr. Bradley, in 1759; and they have been found by Dr. Herschel in intermediate positions at intermediate times. Dr. Herschel allows that it is barely possible that a separate proper motion, in each of the stars and in the sun, may have caused such a change in the relative situation, but that the probability is very decidedly in favour of the existence of a revolution. Its period must be a little more than 342 years, and its plane nearly perpendicular to the direction of the sun. The revolution of gamma leonis is supposed to be in a plane considerably inclined to the line in which we view it, and to be performed in about 1200 years. Both these revolutions are retrograde; that of epsilon Boötis is direct, and is supposed to occupy 1681 years, the orbit being in an oblique position with respect to the sun. In zeta Herculis Dr. Herschel observed, in 1802, the appearance of an occultation of the small star by the larger one: in 1782 he had seen them separate; the plane of the revolution must therefore pass nearly through the sun; and this is all that can at present be determined respecting it. The stars of delta serpentis appear to perform a retrograde revolution in about 375 years: their apparent distance is invariable, as well as that of the two stars which constitute gamma virginis, the last double star which Dr. Herschel mentions in this paper, and to which he attributes a periodical revolution of about 708 years. Y.

Distance and magnitude of the Stars.

See Practical Astronomy.

Gregory on the annual parallax of the stars. Birch. III. 225.

Suggests the observation of the distance of two neighbouring stars.

Roberts on the distance of the fixed stars, after Hugens. Ph. tr. 1694. XVIII. 101.

Flamstead. Ph. tr. 1701. XXII. 815.

Fancied he had found an annual parallax of 40″ or 45″; the polar distance being greatest in June.

Cassini on the magnitude and distance of the fixed stars. A. P. 1717. 256. H. 62.

Halley. Ph. tr. 1720. 1.

Says, that the apparent diameter of Sirius cannot be several seconds, as Cassini makes it.

Halley on the infinity of the sphere of fixed stars. Ph. tr. 1720. XXXI. 22.

Asserts that the equilibrium could not be maintained without an infinite number.

Bradley. Ph. tr. 1728. XXXV. 637.

Thinks he would have perceived an annual parallax if it had amounted to 1″.

Clairaut on the best determination of the parallax of the stars. A. P. 1739. 358. H. 42.

Maskelyne on finding the annual parallax of Sirius. Ph. tr. 1760. 889.

Conjectures, from La Caille's observations, that it may be 8″ or 9″.

Lambert's Photometria.

Supposing Saturn to reflect ¼ of the light that falls on him, and to be equal in brightness to a star as large as the sun, the distance of the star will be 425100 times as great as that of the sun, and its apparent diameter 0‴ 16⁗. Hence we may assume the distance about 500000.

Michell on the probable parallax of the stars. Ph. tr. 1767. 234.

From their light.

Michell on the distance and magnitude of the fixed stars. Ph. tr. 1784. 35.

Observes, that a star of 500 times the diameter of the sun ought to recall the particles of light from an infinite distance, and thinks that a sensible effect might be produced by a star 22 times as large in diameter as the sun: the attraction of the sun ought to retard it $\frac{1}{497000}$ in an infinite distance. The light of a star of the sixth magnitude is to that of the sun as one to 100 billions.

Herschel on the parallax of the fixed stars. Ph. tr. 1782. 82.

With figures of their telescopic appearances. Makes Lyra subtend 3553″.

Herschel on the sun and fixed stars. Ph. tr. 1795. 46.

Some stars, if as remote from each other as Sirius is from the sun, should be 42000 times as far off as Sirius. At this distance Sirius would scarcely be visible.

Herschel on the power of penetrating into space by telescopes. Ph. tr. 1800. 49. Nich. IV. 496.

A cluster of 5000 stars barely visible as a mass, by the 40 feet telescope, must be above 11 millions of millions of millions of miles off.

Proper motion of the Stars.

Bernard's chronology of the places of the stars. Ph. tr. 1684. XIV. 567.

Delisle on the proper motion of the stars. A. P. 1727. 19.

Cassini on the proper motion of the stars. A. P. 1738. 273. H. 70.

Hornsby on the proper motion of Arcturus. Ph. tr. 1773. 93.

Mayer de motu fixarum proprio. Op. ined. I. 175.

Herschel on the motion of the sun and solar system. Ph. tr. 1783. 247.

Supposes the motion not slower than that of the earth in its orbit.

Changeable Stars and new Stars.

Hevelius's new star in the swan. Ph. tr. 1665. I. 372. A second of the third magnitude. Ph. tr. 1670. V. 2087. Further accounts Ph. tr. 1671. VI. 2197, 2198.

Bullialdi ad astronomos monita duo. Acc. Ph. tr. 1665-6. I. 381.

A new star in the whale.

Anthelme's new star in the swan. Ph. tr. 1670. V. 2092. A. P. I. 87.

Cassini on the changeable star in the whale's neck. A. P. I. 87. X. 422.

Kirchius de stella nova in collo cygni. Misc. Berl. Ph. tr. 1715. 226.

History of new stars observed within 150 years. Ph. tr. 1715. XXIX. 354.

Maraldi on the changeable star in the whale. A. P. 1719. 94. H. 66.

Maupertuis on the changes of stars. Ph. tr. 1732. XXXVII. 240. A. P. 1732. H. 85.

Barker on the mutations of stars. Ph. tr. 1760.

Produces 5 authorities to show that Sirius was formerly reddish, and even redder than Mars, and proves that it is now white.

Herschel on the periodical star in the whale's neck. Ph. tr. 1780. 338.

The change was before observed to happen about seven times in six years.

Herschel on changeable stars. Ph. tr. 1792. 24.

Herschel on the changes of stars. Ph. tr. 1795. 166.

Herschel on the changes of alpha Herculis, and on the rotation of stars. Ph. tr. 1796. 452.

Its period 60 ¼ days.

Goodricke on the variation and period of the light of Algol. Ph. tr. 1783. 474. 1784. 287.

The period 2d. 20h. 48' 56".

Goodricke on the changes of beta lyrae. Ph. tr. 1785. 153.

Varies from the 3d magnitude to the 4th or 5th: the period 12d. 19h.

Goodricke on the changes of delta Cephei. Ph. tr. 1786. 48.

It varies from 3½ to 4½ or the 5th magnitude. The period 5d. 8h. 37'¼. The variation of Algol is not always equal in degree.

Englefield, Palitch, and Bruhl on the star Algol. Ph. tr. 1784. 1, 4, 5.

Pigott on the changes of eta Antinoi. Ph. tr. 1785. 127.

From the third or fourth to the fourth or fifth magnitude: period 7d. 4h. 38'.

Pigott on changeable stars in general. Ph. tr. 1786. 189.

Pigott on the changes of two stars. Ph. tr. 1797. 193.

In Sobiesky's shield, and in the northern crown.

Huber on the star Algol. N. Act. Helv. I. 307.

Lalande on the star Algol. A. P. 1788. 240.

Assigns 2d. 20h. 49' 2" as its period.

Wurm on Algol. Zach. Ephem. II. 210.

Its period 2d. 20h. 48'. 58".7 from 15 years observation.

Twinkling of the Stars.

Garcin on the twinkling of the stars. A. P. 1743. H. 28.

Observes, that at Bender Abassi in Asia, where the air is very pure and dry, the stars have a light absolutely fixed.

Michell. Ph. tr. 1767. 234.

Attributes the twinkling to the irregularity of the emission of light.

Sun.

Joh. Fabricius de maculis in sole observatis. Wittemb. 1611. M. B.

The discoverer.

Epistolae ad Velserum de solis maculis. 4. Augsb. 1612.

Scheineri rosa ursina. f. 1630. M. B.

Cassini on the sun's motion. Bologna. Acc. Ph. tr. 1672. VII. 5001.

Derham on the solar spots. Ph. tr. 1711. XXVII. 270.

Thinks them the clouds of volcanos, afterwards becoming faculae.

Crabtrie, in 1640, calls them exhalations like clouds. 281.

Hausen Theoria motus solis. 4. Leipz. 1726.

Krafft de distantia macularum a sole. Comm. Petr. VII. 279.

A. Euler de motu solis determinando. C. N. P. XII. 273.

†Horsley on the sun's atmosphere. Ph. tr. 1767. 398.

Kaestner formulae ad motum solis. C. N. Gott. I. 110.

Spots. A. P. Index. Art. Soleil.

A. Wilson on the solar spots. Ph. tr. 1774. 1. 1783. 144.
Maintains, that they are excavations, against Lalande.

Marshall on the solar spots. Ph. tr. 1774. 194.

Wollaston on the solar spots. Ph. tr. 1774. 329.

Lalande on the sun. Brugnatelli Bibliot. fisic. I. 55.

Lalande's answer to Wilson. Ph. tr. 1776.

Bode Anleitung. Sect. 616.

Mayer on the sun's motion. Ac. Palat. IV.

Herschel on the sun's motion. Ph. tr. 1783. 247.

Herschel on the sun and fixed stars. Ph. tr. 1795. 46. Nich. I. 8. Ph. M. V.
Thinks the sun an opaque body, possibly inhabited, covered with an atmosphere in which clouds of a luminous matter are floating, and the spots interruptions of these clouds; of these clouds he thinks there are two strata, of which the upper only is luminous, and the under stratum he supposes to protect the body of the sun from their heat.

Herschel on the nature of the sun. Ph. tr. 1801. 265, 354.
Endeavours to show that the variation of heat of different years is owing to the more or less copious supply of fuel in the sun, which constitutes his spots.

Prévost on the motion of the whole solar system. A. Berl. 1781. 418.
Towards the corona borealis. The idea was first suggested by Mayer.

King's morsels of criticism. 4. Lond. 1786. R. S.
On the sun, as surrounded by luminous matter.

Schröter über die sonne. 4. Erf. 1789.

Fischer on the sun's spots. Bode. Jahrb. 1791.

Wurm on the degree of certainty of the sun's motion. Bode. Jahrb. 1795.

Lichtenberg. Erxleb. naturl.
Appears to doubt of the sun's motion.

Von Hahn on the sun and its light. Bode. Jahrb. Ph. M. XI. 39.

Woodward on the substance of the sun. 8. Washington. 1801. R. S.
Dr. Herschel thinks, that the motion of the sun is probably directed towards a point, of which the right ascension is 245° 52′ 30″, and the north polar distance 40° 22′, 1805.

Solar Atmosphere, or zodiacal Light.

Cassini. A. P. VII. 119. VIII. 193.

Derham on a glade of light. Ph. tr. 1706. XXV. 2220.
March 20. Moving with the heavens.

Mairan Traité de l'aurore boreale. 1731. A. P. 1747. 371. H. 32.

Lemonnier. A. P. 1757. 88.

Lalande. Astronom. Sect. 845.

Dicquemare on a zodiacal light. Roz. III. 330.

Murhard on the atmospheres of the sun and planets. Ph. M. VI. 166.

Melanderhielm on solar and planetary atmospheres. Gilb. III. 96.

†Regnier on the zodiacal light. Zach. Mon. corr. VI. 14.

Planets, in general.

Kepleri astronomia nova. f. Prag. 1609.
Lays down his great laws.

Cassini on the atmospheres of the heavenly bodies. A. P. VIII. 193.

Maupertuis on the figures of planets. Ph. tr. 1732. XXXVII. 240. A. P. 1732. H. 85.

Euler on the contraction of the orbits of the planets. Ph. tr. 1749. 203. 1750. 357.
Maintains that such a contraction has taken place, attributes it to resistance, hence argues, that the world has had a beginning, and must have an end.

Lemonnier on the planetary atmospheres. A. P. 1757. 88.

Herschel on the rotation of the planets. Ph. tr. 1781. 115.

Ducarla on the rings of the planets. Roz. XIX. 386.

Ximenes on the density of the planets. Soc. Ital. III. 278.

Schröter on the planetary atmospheres. Bode Jahrb. 1793. Gotting. Anz. 1792. n. 86.

*Murhard on the planetary atmospheres. Ph. M. VI. 166.

Melanderhielm on planetary atmospheres. Gilb. III. 96.

†Voigt on the rotation of the planets. Gilb. VII. 232.

†On Ophion. Gilb. XI. 482.
> Supposes that the comet of 1759 may be considered as a planet beyond the Georgian planet.

Benzenberg on a law of planetary distances. Gilb. XV. 169.

On the progressive distances of the planets. Zach. Mon. corr. VII. 74.

Particular Planets.

Mercury.

Wallot sur le passage de Mercure. Ph. tr. 1784. 312.
> Attributes a horizontal refraction of .276″ to Mercury, equivalent to 26″.4 in time.

Olbers on Schröter's observations of Mercury. Zach. Mon. corr. I. 574.
> Schröter thinks it revolves in 24h. or 24h. 5′.

Lalande on the motion of Mercury. M. Inst. V. 442.
> In the transit of Nov. 1802, Mr. Bugge could find no traces of an atmosphere. Journ. R. I., I.
> Von Zach says, that the mean apparent diameter of Mercury is not so much as 7″, probably little more than 5″.

Venus.

Bianchini Hesperi phaenomena. f. Rom. 1728.

Acc. Ph. tr. 1729. XXXVI. 158.
> Makes the period of diurnal rotation 25 days.

Larcher Mémoire sur Venus. 8. R. S.

Maskelyne. Ph. tr. 1768. 355.
> Distinct marks of an atmosphere, or of inflection, or of both.

Wallot. Ph. tr. 1784. 312.
> Attributes to Venus a horizontal refraction of .205″, equivalent to 8″ or 9″ in time.

Schröter on the atmosphere of Venus. Ph. tr. 1792. 309. Ph. M. IV.
> Asserts, that Venus has a twilight of more than 4°; and mountains 4 or 5 times as high as ours.

Schröter über die Venus. 4. Erfurt. 1793.

Schröter's further observations on Venus. Ph. tr. 1795. 117.
> Seems to have made very numerous observations; persists in the rotation of 23h. 21′; says, that the mountains are generally obscured by the atmosphere.

Schröters Aphroditographische fragmenten. 4. Helmst. 1796. R. S.

Schröter's plate of the height of the mountains in the earth, the moon, and Venus. Journ. Phys. XLVIII. 459.

Herschel's observations on Venus. Ph. tr. 1793. 201.
> Denies the existence of high mountains, and the accuracy of Schröter's observations on this planet in general. Allows that Venus revolves, and not slowly; that its atmosphere must be considerable, from the excess of its cusps above a semicircle, which Schröter first observed; but remarks, that Schröter, in considering it, has neglected the effect of the sun's penumbra. Thinks Venus a little larger than the earth: her disc appears brightest at the margin.

Lalande on the motion of Venus. M. Inst. V. 350.

The Earth, in its relations to the Celestial Bodies.

Figure of the earth. See Geography.

Precession of the equinoxes. See Laws of Gravity.

Gregory on the controversy of Angelis and Riccioli, respecting the motion of the earth Ph. tr. 1668. III. 693.

Bernard's history of the obliquity of the ecliptic. Ph. tr. 1684. XIV. 721.

Louville on the change of place of the ecliptic. A. P. 1716. H. 48. Act. Lips. 1719. 281.

Halley on the change of latitude of some stars. Ph. tr. 1718. XXX. 736.
<small>Most stars indicate a change of about 20′ since the time of Hipparchus.</small>

Godin on the diminution of the obliquity of the ecliptic. A. P. 1734. 491.

Legentil on the obliquity of the ecliptic. A. P. 1743. 67. H. 121. 1757. 180.

Lemonnier on the nutation of the earth's axis. A. P. 1745. 512. H. 58.
<small>Bradley's discovery.</small>

Bradley on an apparent motion of the stars. Ph. tr. 1748. XLV. 1.
<small>The nutation of the earth's axis.</small>

Euler on the approach of the earth to the sun. Ph. tr. 1749. XLVI. 203.

Euler. Ph. tr. 1750. XLVI. 357.
<small>Queries if the earth's rotation is uniform: says, that the action of Jupiter accelerates its motion in its orbit, and infers, that its rotation must probably also be accelerated.</small>

Lalande on the change of latitude of the stars. A. P. 1758. 339. H. 87.

Lalande on the obliquity of the ecliptic. A. P. 1762. 267. H. 130. 1780. 285.
<small>Diminishing about 66″ in a century.</small>

Lalande. Ph. M. IX. 11.
<small>Makes the secular change 36″, 38″, or 41″, the obliquity 1 Jan. 1800, 23° 27′ 58″.</small>

Smeaton and Maskelyne on the menstrual parallax. Ph. tr. 1768. 154.

Maskelyne on the nutation of the earth's axis. Astron. observ. 1776.

Hornsby on the obliquity of the ecliptic. Ph. tr. 1773. 93.
<small>Diminishing about 58″ in a century.</small>

Kästner on the obliquity of the ecliptic. Astron. abh. iii.

Wallot sur l'obliquité de l'écliptique. 4. R. S.

Mars.

Herschel. Ph. tr. 1781. 115.
<small>Siderial rotation of Mars 24 h. 39′ 22″.</small>

Herschel on Mars. Ph. tr. 1784. 223.

Juno.

<small>Harding's Juno is supposed to be somewhat nearer to the sun than Ceres. Dr. Herschel finds that neither this body nor either Ceres or Pallas, subtends any measurable angle. Dec. 1804. It was discovered 1 Sept. 1804.</small>

Pallas.

Olbers's planet, discovered 28 March 1802. Ph. M. XII. 287.

Lalande on Olbers's planet. Journ. Phys. LV. 65. Ph. M. XIII. 279. Nich. VIII. 222.

Burckhardt's parabolic orbit of Pallas. Ph. M. XII. 371.

Burckhardt's elements of Pallas. Ph. M. XIV. 186.

On Olbers's Pallas. Nich. 8. II. 20. Journ. R. I., I. 93.

See Ceres.

Ceres.

On a new planet. Zach. Mon. corresp. IV. 53.
<small>Discovered 1 Jan. 1801.</small>

On the planet Piazzi. Journ. Phys. LIV. 165, 469.

On the nature of Ceres and Pallas. Zach. Mon. corr. VI. 290.
<small>Olbers thinks they may be fragments of some larger planet.</small>

Von Zach on Ceres. Nich. 8. II. 213. Ph. M. XVI. 49.

Accounts of Piazzi's Ceres. Nich. 8. I. 72, 193, 284, 317. II. 48. Ph. M. XII. 62.

Bode on Piazzi. A. Berl. 1801. M. 132.

Herschel on the two lately discovered celestial bodies. Ph. tr. 1802. 213. Nich. 8. IV. 126.

Lalande's orbits of the new planets. Nich. VIII. 222.

Journ. R. I., I. 69, 93.

Jupiter.

Cassini on Jupiter's rotation. Ph. tr. 1665-6. I. 143.
Period 9h. 56'.
Maclaurin on the changes of Jupiter. Ed. ess. I. 184.
Herschel. Ph. tr. 1781.
Schröter on Jupiter. Beyträge. I.
Schröter on the rotation of Jupiter. Roz. XXXII. 108.

Saturn.

Pound. Ph. tr. 1718. 773.
Observed that the ring was double.
Maupertuis. Ph. tr. 1732. 240.
Derives Saturn's ring from the tails of comets.
Heinsius de annulo Saturni. 4. Leipz. 1745.
Varelaz on the disposition of Saturn's ring. Ph. tr. 1774. 113.
The west end appeared always the more luminous: some bright points were seen at the extremities.
Messier's observation of points in the ring of Saturn. A. P. 1774. 49. H. 55.
On the ring of Saturn. Roz. XI. 77. 381.
Bugge on the node of Saturn. Ph. tr. 1787. 37.
Laplace on Saturn's ring. A. P. 1787. 249.
A figure of Saturn with his ring. Herschel. Ph. tr. 1790. 1.
Herschel on the rotation of Saturn's ring. Ph. tr. 1790. 427.
Herschel on the ring of Saturn. Ph. tr. 1792. 1.
A good figure of the ring with its division.
Herschel on a quintuple belt of Saturn. Ph. tr. 194. 28. Fig.
Herschel on the rotation of Saturn. Ph. tr. 1794. 48.
In 10h. 16' 0".4.
Herschel. Ph. tr. 1805.
Makes the figure of Saturn not an elliptic spheroid, but a little inclined to a cylindrical form.
Deluc on the ring of Saturn. Roz. XL. 101.
Robison. Enc. Br.
Observes, that the inner edge of the ring of Saturn should revolve in 11h. 16', the outer in 17h. 10'.
Schroeter doubts the rotation of the ring.

Georgian Planet.

Herschel's account of a planet. Ph. tr. 1781. 492.
Herschel on the magnitude of the Georgian planet. Ph. tr. 1783.
Apparent diameter 4".
Herschel on the Georgian planet and its satellites. Ph. tr. 1788. 364.
Boscovich on the new planet. Soc. Ital. I. 55.
Bode von dem neu entdeckten planeten. 8. Berl. 1784.
Lexell Recherches sur la nouvelle planete. Petersb.
Wurm, Geschichte des neuen planeten. 8. Gotha, 1791.

Secondary Planets.

Supposed Satellite of Venus.

Short. Ph. tr. 1741. 646.
A. P. 1741. H. 124.
Mairan. A. P. 1762. 161.
Lambert. Ac. Berl. 1773. 222.
Bode Jahrbuch. 1777, 1778.
Chambers's Cyclopaedia, by Rees.

Moon.

Lunar atmosphere. See eclipses.
Hooke's micrographia. Ch. 70.
Hevelii selenographia. f. Dantz. 1667. R. I.
Cassini Carte de la lune. Paris. R. S.
Is 19 inches in diameter. Remained long unpublished.
Louville on a lunar atmosphere. A. P. 1715. 89. Cassini. 137. H. 54. Delisle. 147. H. 47.
Liesmann Bresl. Samml. 1722. Goth. Mag. I. i. 189.
On a perforation.

Fouchy. A. P. 1734. H. 68.

Fouchy de atmosphaera lunari. Ph. tr. 1739. XLI. 261.
> Thinks that there is not enough to produce a refraction of 1″ or 2″.

Lemonnier Sélénographie.

Acc. A. P. 1735. H. 65.

Weidler. Ph. tr. 1739. XLI. 228.
> Observed lightning in a lunar eclipse. After Halley.

Mylius Gedanken über die atmosphäre des mondes. 4. 1746.

Mayers cosmographische nachrichten. 1748. 379.
> On the lunar rotation and atmosphere.

Mayer von den Nürnbergischen mondkugeln. 4. 1750. Nuremb.

Mayer's map of the moon. Op. ined. I.

Euler on the moon's atmosphere. Ac. Berl. 1748. 103.

Dunthorne on the acceleration of the moon's motion. Ph. tr. 1749. XLVI. 162.
> About 10″ in 100 years.

Short on a gap in the mountains surrounding the lunar spot Plato. Ph. tr. 1751. 164.

Boscovich de lunae atmosphaera. 4. Rom. 1753. Vienn. 1766.

Dunn on a lunar atmosphere. Ph. tr. 1762. 578.
> Infers an atmosphere from a haziness, seen about Saturn emerging from behind the moon.

Murdoch's comparison of the sun and moon. Ph. tr. 1768. 24.
> Attributes great density to the moon.

Ulloa on a perforation in the moon. Ph. tr. 1779. 105. Rozier 1780. See eclipses.

Herschel on the mountains in the moon. Ph. tr. 1780. 507.
> Makes the highest only a mile and three quarters.

Herschel on lunar volcanos and other changes. Bode Jahrbuch, 1782, 1789.

Herschel on three volcanos in the moon. Ph. tr. 1787. 229.
> Looking like a coal covered with a thin coat of ashes: one of them 3 miles in diameter. The inequalities of the moon are easily visible by the light reflected from the earth.

Herschel. Ph. tr. 1792. 27.
> Luminous points in the moon seen in an eclipse.

Herschel. Ph. tr. 1794. 39.
> Few or no signs of a lunar atmosphere in an eclipse.

Beccaria on Ulloa's eclipse. Roz. XVII. 447.
> Thinks the spot volcanic; himself observed a spot in 1772.

Aepinus on volcanos in the moon. N. A. Petr. 1784. II. H. 50. Goth. mag. I. iv. 155.
> Quotes Hooke.

Girtanner on Herschel's lunar volcanos. Roz. XXX. 472.

Schröters Beyträge. 8. Berl. 1788.

Schröter on a spot in the moon. Roz. XXXIII. 313.

Schröters Selenotopographische fragmenten. 2. v. 4. Gott. 1791. 1802. R. S.

Schröter on the lunar atmosphere. Ph. tr. 1792. 309.
> Observed a very faint appearance of twilight.

Schröter on the mountains of the moon. Roz. XLVIII. 459. Fig. Ph. M. IV. 393.

Schröter. Ph. M. XV.
> Finds lunar mountains 4000 toises, or nearly 5 miles high, and such a twilight as indicates an atmosphere 300 toises high.

Bode on a luminous point in the dark part of the moon. A. Berl. 1788. 204.

On lunar volcanos. Bode Jahrbuch, 1792.

Lichtenberg on the lunar spots. Goth. Mag. I. i.

Kant on the lunar spots. Berl. Monathschr. März, 1793.

Russel's globe of the moon. Lond. R. I.

Maskelyne on Wilkins and Stretton's observations of a light in the dark part of the moon. Ph. tr. 1794. 429.
> Stretton might have seen only Aldebaran, which was eclipsed by the moon at the time; Wilkins could scarcely have been so much mistaken.

Kästner. Hind. Arch. II. 8.
> Averroes and Bacon thought of the moon, as Euler did of all opaque bodies, that its substance was made luminous by the sun's rays.
> Mr. Leslie has lately advanced the same opinion.

*Murhard. Ph. M. VI. 166.
> Rather inclines to suppose a very rare lunar atmosphere. Laplace and Delambre have found from the latest calculations that the moon's mass is $\frac{1}{68.5}$ of the earth. Zach. Mon. corr. Lapl. Méc. cel.
> The moon's distance varies from 54 to 78 semidiameters.

Satellites of Jupiter.

Galilei nuntius sidereus. Op. II. i.
Marii mundus Jovialis. 4. Nuremb. 1614.
Herschel on the magnitude and rotation of Jupiter's satellites. Ph. tr. 1797. 332.
> The third is by much the largest, the first and fourth equal, the second a little smaller. They all present the same face to Jupiter throughout their revolutions.

Satellites of Saturn.

For the ring, see Saturn.
Hugenii systema Saturninum. 4. Hague, 1659.
Cassini's discovery of two of Saturn's satellites. Ph. tr. 1673. VIII. 5073.
Pound on the satellites of Saturn. Ph. tr. 1718. XXX. 768.
A sixth satellite announced. Herschel. Ph. tr. 1789.
Herschel on a sixth and seventh satellite of Saturn. Ph. tr. 1790. 1.
Herschel on Saturn's satellites and ring. Ph. tr. 1790. 427.
Herschel on the rotation of Saturn's fifth satellite. Ph. tr. 1792. 1.
> Presents always the same face to Saturn.

Satellites of the Georgian Planet.

Herschel on two satellites of the Georgian planet. Ph. tr. 1787. 125. 1788. 364.
Herschel on four additional satellites of the Georgian planet. Ph. tr. 1798. 47.

Comets.

Senecae quaestiones naturales. vii.
Bartholinus de cometis. 4. Copenh. 1665. M. B.
Lubinietz Theatrum cometicum. f. Amst. 1668. M. B.
Hevelii cometographia. f. Dantz. 1668. M. B.
Hooke's lectures and collections. 4. 1678. Cometa. Figures, p. 2, 3.
Halleii astronomiae cometicae synopsis. Ph. tr. 1705. XXIV. 1882.
Lord Paisley on the comet of 1723, with figures. Ph. tr. 1724. XXXIII. 50.
Heinsius über den cometen. 4. Petersb. 1744.
Mairan on the tails of comets. A. P. 1747. 411.
Dunthorne against the identity of the comets of 1106 and 1680. Ph. tr. 1751. 281.
Winthrop on the tails of comets. Ph. tr. 1767. 132.
Wiedeburg über den cometen. Jena, 1769.
Williamson on comets. Am. tr. I. 133.
Oliver on comets. 8. Salem, 1772.
Laplace on the orbits of comets. S. E. 1773. 503.
Dionis du Séjour sur les cometes. A. P. 1774. H. 78.
Dionis du Séjour Essai sur les cometes. Par. 1775. R. S.
Euler on the effects of comets. N. C. Petr. XIX. 499.
Lexell on the comet of 1770. A. P. 1776. 638. Ph. tr. 1779. 68.
> Calculates that it moves, as Prosperia supposed, in an elliptic orbit, its period about 5½ years, its aphelion a little beyond the orbit of Jupiter.

*Pingré cometographie. 2 vol. Par. 1783. R. I.

Deguignes. S. E. X. 1785. App. 39.
  Enumerates two or three hundred comets mentioned by Chinese authors.
Maskelyne on the comet expected in 1788. Ph. tr. 1786. 426.
  Halley admitted doubts respecting this comet in his second edition.
Bode. Ac. Berl. 1786. 1787.
Bode on comets, with a map. 8. 1791. R. I.
Bode's Jahrbuch. 1795.
Bode's plate reduced. Rees's cyclop. I. Art. Astronomy.
Kästner's gedichte. Vermischte Schriften. 69.
Miss Herschel and Dr. Herschel on a new comet. Ph. tr. 1787. 1, 4.
Miss Herschel on a comet. Ph. tr. 1794. 1.
Olbers on the comet expected in 1788. Leipz. Mag. 1787. iv. 430.
Von Zach on the expected comet. Goth. gel. zeit. 1788. xiii.
Deluc on comets. Journ. Phys. LIV. 253.
Rüdiger on the tails of comets. Gilb. II. 99.
O. Gregory's astronomy. c. 21.
  The comet of 1680 had a tail at least 100 millions of miles long.

Laws of Gravity in General.

See Central Forces.

Hooke on gravity in wells. Birch. II. 70.
**Newtoni principia.
Keill de legibus virium centripetarum. Ph. tr. 1708. XXVI. 174.
De maximis et minimis in motibus coelestibus, secundum Demoivre. Ph. tr. 1719. XXX. 952.
Cassini on vortices. A. P. 1720.
Bülfinger on bodies moving in a vortex. C. Petr. I. 245.
Molières on the resistance of ether. A. P. 1731. H. 66.
Maupertuis on the law of attraction. A. P. 1732. 343. H. 112.
Sigorgne on the impossibility of vortices. Ph. tr. 1740. XLI. 409.
Boscovich on attraction to a centre. C. Bon. II. iii. 262.
Euler de resistentia aetheris. Opusc. I. 295.
Euler on perturbations. A. Berl. 1763. 141.
Euler on the problem of three bodies. A. Berl. 1763. 194.
Euler on the motion of three bodies in a right line. N. A. Petr. 1785. III. 126.
Clairaut on the system of the world according to gravitation. A. P. 1745. 329.
Clairaut on the law of attraction, in answer to Buffon. A. P. 1745. 529, 578, 583.
Buffon on the law of attraction. A. P. 1745. 493, 551, 580.
A. P. 1745. 557.
  Clairaut fancied, from the motion of the moon's apogee, that a part of the force of gravitation varied inversely as the fourth power of the distance. Buffon endeavoured to confute the opinion. Clairaut afterwards found his mistake, by a more accurate calculation.

Kratzenstein's spring steelyard, for measuring the force of gravity. N. C. Petr. II. 210.
Lalande Exposition du calcul astronomique. 8. Par. 1762.
  Acc. A. P. 1762. H. 136.
Simpson's miscellanies.
Dalembert Opuscules.
Bossut sur la resistance de l'ether. 4. Charleville, 1766.
Condorcet on the motions of three attractive bodies. A. P. 1767. H. 93.
Frisi on the laws of gravity. C. Bon. V. i. ii.
Frisi de gravitate universali. 4. R. S.
Lambert on the problem of three bodies. A. Berl. 1767. 353.

Laplace on the system of the world. A. P. 1772. ii. 267. H. 87. 1775. 75. H. 39.

Berthier's opinions. Roz. Intr. I. 658. IV. 340, 433, and elsewhere. His retraction. Roz. IX. 460.

On gravitation. Roz. I. 245.

Mayeri opera inedita. R. S.

Lexell on Lambert's theorem respecting central force. N. A. Petr. 1783. I. 140.

Ximenes on the density of the planets. Soc. Ital. III. 278.

Melanderhielm on the diminution of the sun and the resistance of ether. N. Act. Helv. I. 98.
Supposes that they compensate each other.

Hellins on a problem in physical astronomy, with an appendix. Ph. tr. 1798. 527.
On perturbations.

Hellins's second appendix. Ph. tr. 1800. 86.

Benzenberg on falling bodies. Gilb. XI. 169, 470. XIV. 222. XVII. 476.
Found that 144 feet, Fr. were described in 186′′.95, instead of 186′′.86.

Woodhouse on problems in physical astronomy. Ph. tr. 1804. 219.

See Primary Planets.

Equilibrium and Figure of Gravitating Bodies.

Maupertuis sur les figures des astres. 8. Par. 1732.

Clairaut Traité de la figure de la terre. 8. Paris. M. B.
Acc. A. P. 1742. H. 86.

Clairaut's explanation in answer to Frisi. Ph. tr. 1753. 77.

St. Jaques de Silvabelle on the solid of the greatest attraction. S. E. I. 175.

D'Arcy on the attraction of spheroids. A. P. 1758. 318.

Canterzano on the attraction of a sphere. C. Bon. V. ii. 66.

Laplace on the equilibrium of a gravitating fluid in rotation. S. E. 1773. 524.

Laplace on the attraction of spheroids and the figures of the planets. A. P. 1782. 113. H. 43.

Lagrange on spheroids. A. Berl. 1773. 121. 1775. 273. 1792. 258.

Hutton's determination of the point of greatest attraction of a solid. Ph. tr. 1780. 1.

Legendre on the figure of the planets. A. P. 1784. 370.

Legendre on the attraction of homogeneous spheroids on a distant point. S. E. X. 1785. 411.

Legendre's example of the attraction of a spheroid. A. P. 1788. 463.

Legendre on the figure of the planets. A. P. 1789. 372.

Krafft upon Lagrange's researches on elliptic spheroids. N. A. Petr. 1784. II. 148.

Euler on the centrifugal force of the earth. N. A. Petr. 1784. II. 121.
Says, that if the whole earth were fluid it could not remain at rest without intestine motion. But would there not then be friction, and must it not be retarded?

Waring on infinite series. Ph. tr. 1791. 146.
Examples of the attraction of circles and spheroids.

Gerlach on the figure of the earth, and on the motion of its axis. 8. R. S.

Trembley on the attraction of spheroids. A. Berl. 1799. 68.

Pasquich on the effect of ellipticity on pendulums. Zach. Mon. corr. II. 3.

See also Geography.

Orbits of the Primary Planets.

Halley's direct mode of determining the planetary orbits. Ph. tr. 1676. XI. 683.

Varignon on the central forces of the planets. A. P. 1700. 224. H. 78.

Gregory de orbita Cassiniana. Ph. tr. 1704. XXIV. 1704.

Keill problematis Kepleriani solutio. Ph. tr. 1713. XXVIII. 1.

Cassini on the reconciliation of vortices with the Keplerian laws. A. P. 1720.

Machin's solution of Kepler's problem. Ph. tr. 1738. XL. 205.

Euleri theoria motuum planetarum. 4. Berl. 1744.

Dalembert on the planetary orbits. A. P. 1745. 365.

Determination of the apsidal angle. Ph. tr. 1748. XLV. 355.

Silvabelle on the nodes and inclinations of the planetary orbits. Ph. tr. 1754. 385.

†Maclaurin on the variation of the obliquity of the ecliptic. Ed. ess. I. 173.

Walmesley on perturbations. Ph. tr. 1756. 700. 1761. 275.

Stewart's solution of Kepler's problem. Ed. ess. II. 105.

J. A. Euler on the planetary perturbations. A. Berl. 1759. 358.

Jeaurat's direct determination of the place of a planet. S. E. IV. 601.

Lagrange on Kepler's problem. A. Berl. 1764. 204.

Lagrange on the secular variations of the nodes and inclinations. A. P. 1774. 97. H. 89.

The obliquity of the ecliptic has diminished for 2000 years, and will diminish for at least 2000 more, reckoning from 1760.

Laplace on the secular equations of the planets. A. P. 1772. i. 343. H. 67. 1784. 1. 1787. 267.

Laplace on the theory of Jupiter and Saturn. A. P. 1785. 33. 1786. 201.

Lalande on the diminution of the obliquity of the ecliptic. A. P. 1780. 285. H. 38. Makes it 1" annually.

Fuss on finding the true anomaly. N. A. Petr. 1785. III. 302.

Robison on the orbit of the Georgian planet. Ed. tr. I. 305.

Duséjour on Kepler's problem. A. P. 1790. 401.

Schubert on the obliquity of the ecliptic. N. A. Petr. 1792. X. 433.

Schubert finds the mean obliquity of the ecliptic 24° 11′; its limits 20° 34′, and 27° 49′: that it will continue to diminish for 4900 years, and will then be 22° 58′; but he observes that some little inaccuracy has been introduced into the calculation, the mass of Venus having been made too great.

Wurm on the perturbations of Mars. Zach. Mon. corr. VI. 549.

Ivory on Kepler's problem. Ed. tr. V. 203.

Brinkley's series for the Keplerian problem. Ir. tr. VI. 349.

Brinkley on the Keplerian problem. Ir. tr. IX. 83.

A new mode of calculation, and a comparison of all former methods.

Robison thinks, that Laplace's data are determined too arbitrarily, in his calculations respecting the Georgian planet.

Orbits of the Secondary Planets.

Clairaut on the lunar orbit. A. P. 1743. 17. H. 123. 1748. 421.

Clairaut Théorie de la lune. 4. Petersb. 1752. M. B.

Dunthorne on the moon's motion. Ph. tr. 1747. 412.

A correction for the sun's anomaly.

Walmesley on the effect of ellipticity on a satellite. Ph. tr. 1758. 800.

The distance of the sun deduced from the theory of gravity. Edinb. 1763. By Stewart.

Euler on the lunar motions. A. Berl. 1763. 180, 221.

Euler on the satellites of Saturn. A. Berl. 1763. 311.
Mayer Theoria lunae. 4. Lond. 1767. R. S.
Euleri theoria motuum lunae. 4. R. S.
J. A. Euler on the variation of the moon. A. Berl. 1766. 334.
Lunar motions. Emerson's miscellanies. 139.
Pemberton on the computation of the lunar parallax. Ph. tr. 1771. 437.
Lagrange's prize memoir on the secular equation of the moon. S. E. 1773. 1.
  Rather doubts the fact; thinks an ether would explain it, if it existed. Laplace suspects a small irregularity in the action of gravity, p. 37.
Laplace on the secular equations of the planets and satellites. A. P. 1784. 1. 1785. Errata page. 1786. 235.
  Shows the true cause, 1785.
Laplace on the satellites of Jupiter. A. P. 1788. 249. 1789. 1, 237.
Laplace on the lunar motions. Zach. Mon. corr. II. 157. IV. 113. VI. 272.
Ph. M. IX. 7.
  Laplace has deduced a nutation of the lunar orbit, from the oblate figure of the earth, amounting to 6″ or 7″, and an inequality of 6″ depending on the longitude of the node.
Note of Laplace's two lunar equations of 180 years. Ph. M. XII. 278.
Krafft on Euler's lunar tables. N. A. Petr. 1787. V. 289.
Bürg on the lunar motions. Zach. Mon. corr. IV. 275.
  The sun's place differs about 8″ at the moon's quadratures.

Orbits of Comets.

Halleii astronomiae cometicae synopsis. Ph. tr. 1705. XXIV. 1882.
Bouguer. A. P. 1733. 331. H. 71.
Clairaut Théorie du mouvement des comètes.
Clairaut on the planetary perturbations of comets. A. P. 1760. H. 128.

Dalembert Opuscules. II.
Boscovich on the orbits of comets. S. E. VI. 198, 401.
Laplace on the orbits of comets. S. E. 1773. 503. A. P. 1780. 13. H. 41.
Fuss on the perturbations of comets. S. E. X. 1785. 1.
Lagrange on the perturbations of comets. S. E. X. 1785. 65.
Sir H. Englefield on the orbits of comets. 4. Lond. 1793. R. S.

Projectiles from the Moon.

Biot on the velocity of bodies falling from the moon. B. Soc. Phil. n. 68.
Poisson on the velocity of a body thrown from the moon. B. Soc. Phil. Gilb. XV. 329.

Rotation of the Earth and Planets.

Wallis on the possible change of the meridian. Ph. tr. 1699. XXI. 285.
†Parent on the direction of rotation to the left. A. P. 1703. H. 14.
Euler on the precession of the equinoxes. A. Berl. I. 749, 289.
Euler on the rotation of the heavenly bodies. A. Berl. 1759. 265.
St. Jacques de Silvabelle on the precession of the equinoxes. Ph. tr. 1754. 385.
Dalembert on the effects of a dissimilitude of meridians. A. P. 1754. 413. H. 116. 1768. 1. 332. H. 95.
Dalembert on the motion of heavy bodies, combined with the rotation of the earth. A. P. 1771. H. 10.
Dalembert sur la précession des equinoxes.
Walmesley on precession. Ph. tr. 1756. 700.
Walmesley on the effect of the tides on the earth's rotation. Ph. tr. 1758. 809.

Simpson on the horary displacement of the earth's equator. Ph. tr. 1757. 486.
  Correcting Silvabelle and Walmesley.
Lalande on the change of latitude of the stars. A. P. 1758. 339. H. 87.
Darcy on the precession of the equinoxes. A. P. 1759. 420.
J. A. Euler on perturbations from want of sphericity. A. Berl. 1765. 414.
Murdoch's comparison of the sun and moon. Ph. tr. 1768. 24.
  Makes the moon very dense.
Precession of the equinoxes. Emerson's miscellanies. 180.
Gerlach on the figure of the earth, and on the motion of its axis. 8. R. S.
Laplace on the precession of the equinoxes. A. P. 1777. 329.
Laplace on the rotation of the heavenly bodies. M. Inst. I. 301.
Laplace on the fall of a body from a great height. B. Soc. Phil. n. 75. See Practical astronomy.
Milner on the precession of the equinoxes. Ph. tr. 1779. 505.
  Finds it by a simple method 21" 6'" for the effect of the sun. There seems to be some confusion respecting compound rotation.
Hennert et Frisius de uniformitate motus diurni terrae. 4. Petersb. R. S.
Acc. N. A. Petr. 1783. I. 132.
Vince on the precession of the equinoxes. Ph. tr. 1787. 363.
  The solar portion 21" 6'", supposing the earth of uniform density, and the ellipticity $\frac{1}{316}$; but in reality about $\frac{1}{334}$.
Bode on the displacement of the earth's axis. A. Berl. 1797. 100. Ph. M. XI. 310.
Trembley on the precession of the equinoxes. A. Berl. 1799. 131.
M. Young on the precession of the equinoxes. Ir. tr. VII. 3.

Von Zach on the precession of the equinoxes. Zach. Mon. corr. II. 500.
  The lunisolar precession 50".2380, the real observed precession 50".054 or rather 50".0982.
  Robison doubts the accommodation of the period of the moon's rotation to that of her revolution, and principally because her axis is not perpendicular to her orbit. Elements, 518.

Theory of the Tides.

Aerial Tides. See Meteorology.
For the particular phenomena, see Practical Astronomy.
Hydrology. Ph. tr. abr. II. IV. VI. VIII. X.
†Wallis on the tides. Ph. tr. 1665-6. I. 263, 297. 1668. III. 652.
  Deducing the tides from the earth's centrifugal force, in revolving round the common centre of gravity of the earth and moon.
Wallis's answer to Childrey. Ph. tr. 1670. V. 2068.
Philips. Ph. tr. 1668. III. 656.
  Observes, that the monthly variations of the tides are as the versed sines of the times.
Childrey's remarks on Wallis's theory. Ph. tr. 1670. V. 2061.
Hooke. Birch. II. 475.
  Illustrated the ascent of a tide in a narrow channel by the agitation of mercury in a triangular vessel.
Newtoni Principia.
Halley's Newtonian theory of the tides. Ph. tr. 1697. XIX. 445.
  Observes, that great variations in the time of the tides may be produced by shoals.
Prize essays on the tides, by Cavalleri, Bernoulli, Maclaurin, and Euler. A. P. Prix. IV. vi. . . ix.
  The last three are also in Le Seur's Newton.
Euler on a new kind of oscillations. C. Petr. XI. 128.
Euler on the equilibrium of the sea. A. Petr. 1780. IV. i. 132.
Wargentin on the tides. Schw. abh. 1753. 165, 249. 1754. 83.

Walmesley on the effect of the tides upon the earth's rotation. Ph. tr. 1758. 809.

Lalande on the tides. A. P. 1772. i. 297. H. 1.

Lalande Traité du flux et réflux. Printed in the Astronomy. Note. Ph. M. VIII. 134.

Lalande Astronomie.

Laplace on the tides. A. P. 1775. 73. 1776. 1790. 45. Mécan. céleste.

Laplace on some high tides. Nich. VI. 239.
Agreeing with the theory.

†Saint Pierre Etudes de la nature.
Deduces the tides from the melting of the circumpolar ice.

Suremain's remarks on St. Pierre. Roz. XLI. 239.

Villeterque on St. Pierre's hypothesis. Journ. Phys. XLIV. (I.) 99.

Chiminelli's researches on the tides. A. Pad. II. 204.

Robison. Enc. Br. Art. Tides.
Observes, that the smallest solar retardation of the tides is to the greatest, as the difference of the solar and lunar influence is to their sum: that is, from Dr. Maskelyne's observations at St. Helena, as 37 to 87; and the sun's effect is therefore to that of the moon as 2 to 4.96.

Woods on St. Pierre's hypothesis. Ph. M. VIII. 134.

A Simple Theory of the Tides. Y.

It has been sufficiently demonstrated by different authors, that the form which the sea would assume, in consequence of the moon's attraction, if the earth were at rest, is that of an oblong elliptic spheroid, of which the axis would exceed the equatorial diameter by about 10 feet, the whole height of the tides being 5 feet; but when the effects of the earth's rotation are considered, the investigation becomes much more difficult.

The spheroid of equilibrium, revolving continually, causes the position of the horizon of any place to vary periodically, so as to perform, in the course of a lunar day, two complete oscillations, resembling those of a cycloidal pendulum; and the surface of any detached portion of the sea, so inclosed by perpendicular and parallel shores, as to be capable of permanent oscillations, is drawn after this variable horizon, in the same manner, as a pendulum suspended from a centre, which is itself performing its own vibrations; the middle of the sea, or lake, remaining nearly at rest.

Now it may easily be shown, that a pendulum suspended from a centre, which performs regular small vibrations of its own, may vibrate in the same time with the centre, provided that the extent of its vibrations be to that of the vibrations of the centre, as the length of the thread carrying the centre is to the difference of the lengths of the two threads; for, in this case, the situation of the thread of the pendulum will be always the same as that of a simple pendulum, of the length of the thread carrying the centre. When this thread is the longer, the vibrations will agree in direction, but, when shorter, their directions must be contrary to each other; and, it appears to be in the latter case only, that the pendulum will always tend to acquire such a state of permanent vibration, whatever may have been its original situation, although it may sometimes approach rapidly to it, even when the thread of the pendulum is the shorter. If the breadth of a lake, or sea, from east to west in miles, be b, and its depth d, the time required for its complete oscillation, or the time, in which a wave might pass over twice its breadth, will be $\frac{b}{140\sqrt{d}}$ in hours, and the lengths of the synchronous pendulums being as the squares of the times, the extent of the oscillations of the lake will be to the extent of those of the temporary horizon, as the square of half a lunar or solar day, to the difference between that time, and the time required for the oscillation of the lake; the motions either agreeing or differing in direction, accordingly as the oscillation of the lake would occupy more or less time than half a day. Supposing the luminary vertical, the extent of the oscillation of the temporary spheroid will be, for the lunar tide $5\ s.c$, c being half the breadth of the lake in degrees; and for the solar tide, $2\ s.c$; whence the height of the tides at the eastern and western shores will be $5\ s.c\ \frac{3030000 d}{3030000 d - bb}$, and $2\ s.c\ \frac{2830000 d}{2830000 d - bb}$ respectively. These become infinite, when $b = 1740\sqrt{d}$, and $1682\sqrt{d}$, and in these cases, the magnitude of the tides would be only limited by the resistances; this must happen, if $d = 1$, when $b = 1740$, or $25°$ for the lunar tide; if $d = 9$, when $b = 5220$, and if $d = \frac{1}{4}$, or 100 fathoms, when $b = 580$, or between 8° and 9°. If d were 1, and b 6000, the lunar tide would be about .46 feet, and if b were 6216, or 90° of the equator, it would be .42.

At the eastern and western shores of a sea or lake, 90° in diameter, the ascent and descent of the water would be precisely the same as in every part of an open ocean, of the same depth; and the tides of such an ocean may, therefore, be calculated, by making $b = 6216$, and the height, h will be $\frac{303d}{303d-3953} - \frac{5d}{d-13} = \frac{2d}{d-14}$, whence $d = \frac{13h}{h-5}$ or $\frac{14h}{h-2}$; and if d is less than 13, h being negative, the place of low water must be immediately below the luminary, and $d = \frac{13h}{h+5}$ or $\frac{14h}{h+2}$.

The same conclusion may be obtained by very different means; considering the tide, in comparison with the surface of the spheroid of equilibrium, as a wave, which is to produce by its propagation, a sufficient velocity of ascent and descent, for the actual motion of the tide upon a sphere. Thus, if d were 52, the height of the tide would be 6 feet, that is 1½ feet above the spheroid; and such a wave being naturally propagated with a velocity twice as great as that of the tide, the water would ascend or descend, with a velocity sufficient for its propagation with a velocity twice as great as the velocity of rotation, and, since it is actually exposed to the same force, for a time twice as great, a quadruple velocity will be generated, which will be equal to the velocity of ascent, or descent, required for the tide of 6½ feet, which is four times as much elevated as the supposed wave.

It appears, therefore, that for any given magnitude of the elevation h, there are two values of d, accordingly as we suppose the time of high water, or of low water to coincide with that of the moon's southing: thus, if $h = 2$, d must be either 8½ or 3½; and it is difficult to determine for the open ocean whether the time of high or of low water, is nearest to the transit of the luminary. For a sea 4000 miles broad, the depth must exceed 5 miles, in order that the time of high water may coincide with that of the greatest elevation of the horizon; and, if it be less than this, the time of high water must be that of the greatest depression, that is, on the eastern shore, about 5 hours after the moon's southing; on the western, about 7; and, if the sea were narrower, these times might vary from the fifth to the third, and from the seventh to the ninth hours, respectively. The effects of resistance will also accelerate the tides of the latter kind, and in this manner, the theory may be perfectly reconciled with observation.

Celestial Appearances in general, with reference to the Earth.

Baxter's matho.
Hugenii cosmotheoros, 4. Hag. 1698.
Fontenelle sur la pluralité des mondes. 12. 1686. Par Lalande. 1800.
Dionis du Séjour Traité analitique des mouvement apparens des corps celestes. 2 v. 4. Par. 1786. R. S.
Euler on the degrees of light of the heavenly bodies. A. Berl. 1750. 280.

Makes the light of the sun equal to that of 6560 candles at 1 foot distance, that of the moon to a candle at 7½ feet, of Venus, to a candle at 421 feet, and of Jupiter to a candle at 1620 feet: partly from Bouguer's experiments. Hence the sun would appear like Jupiter, if removed to 831,000 times his present distance.

Appearances of the Stars.

Twinkling. See Fixed Stars.
Bradley on a newly discovered motion of the fixed stars. Ph. tr. 1728. XXXV. 637.

The aberration. It was observed by Flamstead, but not understood.

Lalande on the change of latitude of the stars. A. P. 1758. 330. H. 287.
Lagrange on the variations of the earth's orbit. A. P. 1774. 97. H. 39.

On the changes of latitude and longitude of the stars. p. 164. The change of obliquity affects the right ascension a little, but not the declination.

Appearances of the Sun.

Seasons, Day and Night, Twilight.

La Caille on the length of twilight at the Cape. A. P. 1751. 544. H. 158.
Bergmann on twilight. Schw. Abh. 1760. 237. Opusc. V. 331. VI. 1.
Lambert Photometria. §. 987.

The limit of visible twilight is when the sun is 6°½ below the horizon. In order to find the time when the twilight is shortest, as Rad : Sin. Lat : : S. 6° 22° : S. Sun's declination, south.

Appearances of the Primary Planets.

Halley on the appearance of Venus in the day time. Ph. tr. 1716. XXIX. 466.
Godin on the apparent motions of the planets in epicycloids. A. P. 1733. 285. H. 67.

Kies on the greatest brightness of Venus. A. Berl. 1750. 218.

Ussher on the disappearance of Saturn's ring. Ir. tr. 1789. III. 135.

Bode on the disappearance of Saturn's ring. Ph. M. XV. 219.

Calkoen on the disappearance of Saturn's ring. Ph. M. XV. 222.

Appearances of the Secondary Planets.

Moon.

Cassini on the libration of the moon. A. P. 1721. 168. H. 53.

Lalande on the lunar libration. A. P. 1764. 555. H. 112.

Dionis du Séjour on the faint light of the new moon. A. P. 1776.

This light is a minimum at 43° elongation, a maximum at 0° and at 69°; at 90° about half the greatest quantity.

Kästner on the phases of the moon. Commentat. Gott. 1780. III. M. I.

Harvest moon. O. Gregory's astronomy. C. xvi. Cavallo. IV. 143.

Appearances of the Sun and primary Planets jointly.

Transits.

See Practical Astronomy.

Appearances of the fixed Stars and Moon.

Occultations. Vince's Astronomy. O. Gregory's Astronomy.

Appearances of the Sun and Moon jointly.

Eclipses.

Flamstead's method of calculating eclipses. Moore's system of Mathematics. I.

Plantade and Clapiers on a lunar eclipse from the earth's penumbra. A. P. 1702. H. 73.

Ph. tr. 1706. XXV. 2240.

In a total eclipse of the sun, 12 May, 1706, a streak of light was observed 6″ or 7″ before the sun's disc: hence Flamstead infers a lunar atmosphere $\frac{1}{105}$th of the moon's diameter in height: but this might have been from oblique reflection.

Duillier on a total eclipse of the sun. Ph. tr. 1706. XXV. 2241.

A whiteness was seen round the moon, one twelfth of her diameter in extent; and a white halo 4 or 5 degrees in diameter beyond it: this vanished soon after the sun reappeared: hence he infers a lunar atmosphere of 130 geographical miles in height, and deduces the halo from the solar atmosphere. Many stars were seen during the eclipse.

Halley on a total eclipse of the sun seen in London. Ph. tr. 1715. XXIX. 245.

A ring of light surrounded the moon, one sixth of her diameter in extent, which seemed to proceed rather from a lunar than from a solar atmosphere: and a line of light was seen lingering behind. Some lightning too was seen.

Lahire on the ring seen in total eclipses of the sun. A. P. 1715. 161. H. 47.

Delisle's experiment on a ring of light like that which appears in eclipses. A. P. 1715. 166. H. 47.

Delisle and Lahire produced an appearance nearly of the same kind, by interposing an opaque substance, as a ball of stone, between the eye and the sun: but here it might be objected, that the earth's atmosphere supplied the light.

Louville's geometrical mode of calculating eclipses. A. P. 1724. 63. H. 74.

Gersten methodus calculi eclipsium. Ph. tr. 1744. XLIII. 22.

Ph. tr. 1748. XLIV. 490. C. Bon. I. 267.

A brown light was seen beyond the sun's cusps, in an eclipse nearly annular.

Lalande on the effect of ellipticity in eclipses. A. P. 1756. 364. H. 96. 1763. 413.

Lalande on a lunar eclipse. A. P. 1789. 89.

Adds 36″ to the earth's shadow for the effect of the atmosphere.

Boscovich de solis et lunae defectibus. 4. 1760. R. I.

Jeaurat on the projection of eclipses. S. E. IV. 818.

Witchell on the shadow of a spheroid. Ph. tr. 1767. 28.

Dionis du Séjour. A. P. 1775.
   Attributes a refraction of about 5″ to the lunar atmosphere.

Dionis du Séjour on the quantity of light falling on the moon in eclipses. A. P. 1776.

Lemonnier on the eclipse of 24 June 1778. A. P. 1778. 62. H. 34.
   With a good figure of Ulloa's spot, and of the whole luminous appearance.

Lemonnier on total eclipses of the sun, and on the lunar atmosphere. A. P. 1781. 243. H. 47.
   Finds a refraction of 24″ ¼.

Marcorelle on the heat of the sun in an eclipse. Roz. XIV. 352.

Ulloa on a total eclipse of the sun. Ph. tr. 1779. 105.
   There was a great appearance of light round the moon, which seemed to be agitated, and emitted rays to the distance of a diameter; it was reddish next the moon, then yellowish. Stars of the first and second magnitude were seen, those of the first for about 4 minutes. A minute and a quarter before the emersion, a small point was visible near the disc of the moon. From the ruddy colour of the light, the ring is referred to the moon's atmosphere: the spot to a fissure in the moon's substance. Such a fissure must have been above 40 miles in depth.

Herschel on an eclipse of the sun. Ph. tr. 1794. 39.

Schröter on the solar eclipse. Ph. tr. 1794. 262.

Goudin sur les éclipses du soleil. 4. Par. 1800.

On calculating eclipses. Vince's Astronomy.

Irradiation and diffraction in eclipses. See **Physical Optics**.

The nodes coincide with the syzygies in 6480 lunations, with an angular error of only 8′ ¼ in 6000 years. Cavallo, from Gregory.

The nodes and apsides return to the same position, after about 83 revolutions of the nodes.

Appearances of the primary and secondary Planets conjointly.

Eclipses of Jupiter's Satellites.

Short. Ph. tr. 1753. 268.

Lalande on the effect of ellipticity in eclipses. A. P. 1756. 364. H. 96. 1763. 413.

Appearances of Comets.

Euler on the effects to be apprehended from a comet. N. C. Petr. XIX. 499.

Lambert on the apparent orbit of comets. A. Berl. 1771. 352.

Planetary Worlds. Appearances with respect to different Planets.

Buffon and others on the heat of the celestial bodies. Roz. IX. 7.

Ducarla on the rings of planets. Roz. XIX. 386.

Practical Astronomy, in general.

Cassini on the precautions necessary in astronomical observations. A. P. 1736. 203.

Simpson's calculation of the advantage of a mean of several observations. Ph. tr. 1755. 82.

Geography. Emerson's cyclomathesis. IX.

Lalande on the use of interpolations in practical astronomy. A. P. 1761. 125. H. 92.

Lalande Exposition du calcul astronomique. 8. Paris, 1762.
   Acc. A. P. 1762. H. 136.

*Rösler*s handbuch der practischen astronomie.

Lagrange on taking the mean of observations. M. Taur. 1770. 3. V. ii. 167.

Lagrange on the simplest mode of expressing a given number of facts. A. P. 1772. i. 513. H. 83.

Euler on Lagrange's mode of taking a mean of observations. N. A. Petr. 1785. III. 289.

Bergmann on interpolations in astronomy. Opusc. VI. 1.

Lorgna Principi di geografia astronomico-geometrica. Verona, 1789. R. S.

Vince's practical astronomy. 4. Lond. 1799. R. S.

Trembley on taking a mean of observations. A. Berl. 1801. M. 29.

Astronomical Apparatus, in general.

See Geometrical Instruments.

Hevelii organographia astronomica. f. Ghent, 1673.
  Acc. Ph. tr. 1673. 6150.

Hooke's animadversions on Hevelius's machina coelestis. 4. London, 1674. Lect. Cutl.

Maskelyne's remarks. Ph. tr. 1764. 348.

Duc de Chaulnes on the improvement of astronomical instruments. A. P. 1765. 411. H. 65.

Magellan Traité sur des instrumens d'astronomie.

E. M. Pl. VII. Astronomie. Pl. 15.

Ludlam on Bird's method of dividing. 4. Lond.

Montucla and Lalande. IV. 334.

Troughton on some astronomical instruments. Zach. Mon. corr. II. 207

Observatories.

Godin's convenient observatory. Mach. A. VI. 49.

Bouin's trap door for an observatory. A. P. 1763. H. 148.

Barker's account of the observatory at Benares. Ph. tr. 1777. 598.

Schulze on the situation of an observatory. A. Berl. 1777. 223.

Williams's particulars of the observatory at Benares. Ph. tr. 1793. 45.

Ussher on the observatory in Dublin. Ir. tr. 1787. I. 3.

Piazzi della specola astronomica de' regi studi di Palermo, f. Palermo, 1792. 4. R. S.

Acc. Hind. Arch. I. 257.

Time.

Equation of time.

Lalande on the equation of time. A. P. 1762. 131. H. 120.

Maskelyne on the equation of time. Ph. tr. 1764. 336.

Pemberton. Ph. tr. 1772. 434.
  A problem relative to the calculation.

Kästner on reductions of time. A. Gott. D. Schr. 101, 194.

Equation Clocks, for Solar Time.

Lahire's clock, showing true time. A. P. 1717. 238.

Leroy's solar clock. A. P. 1717. H. 85. Mach. A. III. 151. A. P. 1728. H. 110. Mach. A. V. 63.

Williamson's claim to the invention of equated clocks. Ph. tr. 1719. XXX. 1080.

<small>Made one in 1693 or 1694; another with an elliptic roller raising the pendulum, which went 400 days: this is still in the palace at Hampton Court. Made one by comparison of the sun's motion with another clock; this of course included a general equation for temperature.</small>

Lebon's solar clock. A. P. 1722. H. 119. Mach. A. III. 21. A. P. 1726. H. 70. Mach. A. IV. 45.
Meynier's solar clock. A. P. 1723. H. 122. Mach. A. IV. 59.
Thiout's solar clock. A. P. 1724. H. 93. Mach. A. IV. 67, 69, 173.
Dufay's machine for showing true time. A. P. 1725. 67.
Kriegseisen's equation clock. A. P. 1726. H. 69. Mach. A. IV. 155. A. P. 1732. H. 117.
St. Cyr's solar clock. Mach. A. IV. 149.
Duchesne's equation clock. Mach. A. IV. 153.
Leroy's equation applied to a striking part. Mach. A. V. 67, 71, 73.
Duterew's equation watch. A. P. 1742. H. 163. Mach. A. VII. 153.
Berthoud's equation clock. A. P. 1752. H. 147. 1754. H. 140. Mach. A. VII. 425, 473.
<small>Going 13 months.</small>
Biesta's equation clock. A. P. 1757. H. 179.
Biesta's equation by a moveable dial plate. A. P. 1770. H. 115.
Ferguson's astronomical and equation clock. Ferg. mech. ex. 11.
Schulze on an equation clock. A. Berl. 1782. 222.

Observations of Time, in general.

Bernoulli on finding the time at sea. A. P. Prix. VI. i.
Delambre on finding the time from corresponding distances. Zach. Mon. corr. IV. 93.

Dialling, or Gnomonics.

Account of dials in the garden at Whitehall. 4. Lond. 1624.
<small>By Gunter.</small>
Hooke's instrument for making dials. Birch. II. 155.
Picard on dialling. A. P. VII. i. 185.
Lahire on dialling. A. P. X. 444.
Parent's instrument for shewing the true shadow. A. P. 1701. H. 116.
Clapies on the angles of dials. A. P. 1707. 569.
Delisle's gnomon for the sun's transit. A. P. 1719. 54.
Gnomonic instruments. Leup. Th. M. G. t. 10, 11.
Méan's compound dial. A. P. 1731. H. 92.
Gensanne's transit instrument and dial. A. P. 1736. H. 120. Mach. A. VII. 55.
Krafft on dialling. C. Petr. XIII. 255.
Lemonnier's obelisc for shewing the time of noon. A. P. 1743. 361. H. 142. 1762. 263.
Emerson's cyclomathesis. IX.
Wenz's dial. Acc. Helv. VI. 167.
La Condamine's gnomonical cane. A. P. 1770. H. 114.
Bertier's globes serving for dials. A. P. 1770. H. 117.
Ferguson's mechanical exercises. 95.
Lalande on a vertical linear gnomon. A. P. 1757. 483.
Ferguson on dials. Ph. tr. 1767. 389.
E. M. Pl. V. Marine. I.
E. M. Pl. VIII. Amusemens de gnomonique.
Carayon's sun dial with wheelwork. Roz. XXIV. 312.
Mignon on Carayon's dial. Roz. XXV. 377.
Castillon on gnomonics. A. Berl. 1784. 259.

Wollaston on a universal meridian dial. 4. Lond. 1793. R. S.

Montucla and Hutton's recreations.

Lefrançois on dialling. Journ. polyt. IV. xi. 261.

See Transit Instruments.

Chronology, and Calendars.

Cassini on the calendar. A. P. II. 198. X. 433, 520. 1701. 367. H. 105.

Richaud on the calendar of the Siamese. A. P. VII. part. 2. iii. 154.

Wallis on altering the calendar. Ph. tr. 1699. XXI. 343.
  Prefers the Julian reckoning.

Lord Burleigh and Greaves on the calendar. Ph. tr. 1699. XXI. 355, 356.

Observations on the calendar. A. P. 1700. H. 127. 1703. H. 91.

Jackman on the rule for finding easter. Ph. tr. 1704. XXIV. 2123.

Newton on a French publication of his chronological index. Ph. tr. 1725. XXXIII. 315.

Halley's defence of Newton's chronology. Ph. tr. 1726. XXXIV. 205. 1727. XXXV. 296.

Sauveur's perpetual calendar. A. P. 1732. H. 94.

*Lord Macclesfield on the solar and lunar years. Ph. tr. 1750. 417.

Emerson's cyclomathesis. X.

Horsefall on a chronological question. Ph. tr. 1768. 100.

Marsden on the Hejera. Ph. tr. 1788. 414.
  The years of the Hejera are lunar, commencing 16 July, 622.

Marsden on the chronology of the Hindoos. Ph. tr. 1790. 560.

Lalande on epacts. A. P. 1789. 95.

Lamétherie on the division of time, and on a general epoch. Roz. XLIII. 296, 315.
  An epoch from the precession of the equinoxes.

Gilchrist on the hours of the Hindoos. As. res. V. 81.

Wurm on the new French calendar. Hind. Arch. II. 15.

Gauss on the computation of easter. Zach Mon. corr. II. 121.

Winter on the solar year. Nich. VII. 116.

Robison's Elements.

  The Egyptians reckoned by years of 365 days: Hipparchus and Ptolemy employ the same method. In A. D. 940, the first day of the Egyptian year, was the first of January; another Egyptian year began 31 December. In the new stile, 10 days were omitted in 1582; before this time, each century contained 36525 days. Robison.

  To find the prime number, sometimes called the solar cycle, add 9 and divide by 28; the indiction, add 3 and divide by 15. Add 1 to the year and divide by 19, the remainder is the golden number, take 1 from the golden number, multiply by 11, and divide by 30, the remainder is the epact, or the moon's age on the first of January. Lalande.

  [In astronomical language, 1 Jan. 1805, 6 o'clock A. M. is 1804, Dec. 31d. 18h. Lichtenberg.

Instruments for Observation.

Simple Astronomical Quadrants. See Geometrical Instruments.
  Now seldom used.

Buot's azimuthal instrument. Mach. A. I. 67.

Lahire's universal astrolabe. A. P. 1701. 257. H. 97.

Parent on the astrolabe. A. P. 1702. H. 70.

Louville's instrument for right ascensions. A. P. 1719. 188.

Meynier's instrument for solar altitudes. A. P. 1724. H. 93. Mach. A. IV. 71.

Montigny's instrument for marine observations. Mach. A. V. 57.

An instrument for marine observations. Mach. A. V. 97.

Godin's mural quadrant. A. P. 1731. 194. 1733. 36.

Elton's instrument for taking altitudes. Ph. tr. 1732. XXXVII. 273.
By the sun's image.

Quereineuf's instrument for marine observation. A. P. 1732. H. 119. Mach. A. VI. 177.

Lecarlier's universal instrument for altitudes and time. Mach. A. VI. 187.

Condamine on an instrument for determining a parallel circle. A. P. 1733. 294. H. 53.

Logan on Godfrey's improvement on Davis's quadrant. Ph. tr. 1734. XXXVIII. 441.
Catching the sun's image on an arch.

Grandjean de Fouchy's machine for managing a quadrant. A. P. 1740. 468. Mach. A. VII. 47.

A quadrant with a reflecting telescope. A. P. 1746. H. 121.

Gersten quadrantis muralis idea nova. Ph. tr. 1747. XLIV. 507.

Art pour diviser les instrumens. f. Paris.

Fouchy on making a quadrant into an azimuthal instrument. A. P. 1781. 254.

E. M. Pl. V. Marine. XV.

Cesaris de quadrante murali Mediolanensi Ramsdeni. 8. R. S.

Enc. Br. Art. Astronomy. Quadrants.

A mural quadrant. Cavallo, N. Ph. IV. pl. 29. fig. 4.

On Synesius's astrolabe. M. Inst. V. 34.

Reflecting Instruments for Angles.

*Hooke's reflecting quadrant. Animadv. on Hevelius. 4. Lond. 1674.

Newton's paper on a reflecting instrument like Hadley's. Ph. tr. 1742. 155.

*Hadley's instrument for taking angles. Ph. tr. 1731. 147. 1732. 32.

Ph. tr. 1734. 442.
Godfrey seems to have made a reflecting quadrant before Hadley.

On a reflecting instrument in the observatory at Berlin. A. Berl. 1749. 370.
It was made by Whitehead, and sent over by Hooke.

Segner's catadioptric sector. N. C. Petr. VI. 399.

Ewing's improvement on Hadley's quadrant. Am. tr. I. 126.

Dollond's addition to Hadley's quadrant for maritime use. Ph. tr. 1772. 95.

*Maskelyne's remarks on Hadley's quadrant. Ph. tr. 1772. 99.
Inverts the instrument, in order to find the correction for the back observation on shore.

Carré's improvement of octants. A. P. 1777.

Magellan Description des octans et sextans Anglais. 4. R. S.

Magellan sur les instrumens circulaires de reflexion. 4. R. S.

Account of Magellan's nautical instrument. N. A. Petr. 1783. I. H. 141.

Atwood's general theory of the inclination of direct and twice reflected rays. Ph. tr. 1781. 395.
Proposes two new arrangements of the specula, for particular purposes: they give a greater extent of arc than Hadley's method, but require a nicer adjustment.

Lexell on Burdett's optical compass. N. A. Petr. 1783. I. H. 111.
A sextant with points.

Cassini. A. P. 1788. 706.
The angles are multiplied.
Borda's circle true within 1"½, or at most 4"½.

Cassini on Borda's circle. A. P. 1790. 617.

Account of Borda's circle. Conn. des tems, 1798.

Ludlam on Hadley's quadrant. 8.

Count Brühl on the investigation of astronomical circles. 8. Lond. 1794. R. S. Germ. with additions by Zach. Hind. Arch. I. 257.

Von Zach on the circles of Borda and Lenoir Hind. Arch. I. 450.

Peacock's reflecting instrument for measuring distances. Repert. I. 163.
Containing a base.

Pitt's dendrometer, with and without reflection. Repert. II. 238.

Patterson's adjustment of the quadrant for the back observation. Am. tr. IV. 154. Repert. XV. 266.

Mendoza y Rios's improved reflecting circle. Ph. tr. 1801. 363. Nich. 8. I. 4.
For multiple measurements. Troughton's circles only multiply the readings: which in some cases must be the best method.

Steinhäuser's catoptric instrument for measuring angles. Gilb. XV. 377.

Fallon's reflecting engymeter. Zach. Mon. corr. VI. 246.

Wollaston on the dip. Ph. tr.

Lomet's addition to the sextant, for arostatic uses. Journ. polyt. IV. xi. 252.

E. Walker's improved quadrant. Nich. 8. IV. 218. VI. 219.

Ward on correcting the sextant for the back observation. Ph. M. XVIII. 123.

Astronomical Telescopes, and Telescopic Sights, Micrometers, and Photometers.

See Optics.

Fouchy on telescopic sights, invented by Morin, 1634. A. P. 1787. 385.

Hooke in favour of telescopic sights. Animadv. on Hevelius. 4. Lond. 1674.

Hooke's helioscopes. 1676. Lect. Cutl.
Using frequent reflections.

Lahire on the places of stars, measured by the micrometer. A. P. 1701. 101. H. 91.

Lahire's wire micrometer for eclipses. A. P. 1701. 119. H. 92.

Lahire's universal micrometer for eclipses. A. P. 1717. 57.

Halley on observations with cross hairs in a telescope. Ph. tr. 1720. XXXI. 112.
Cassini invented an oblique hair, to estimate the difference of declination, by the difference of the times of crossing it.

Godin's mode of using long telescopes, and long tubes of telescopes. Mach. A. VI. 53, 67.

†Hadley's proposition respecting telescopes. Ph. tr. 1736. XXXIX. 185.

Bouguer's heliometer. A. P. 1748. II. H. 87.

Zanotti on a micrometer. C. Bon. II. ii. 347.

Passement's reflecting telescope applied to the quadrant, with a new mode of dividing it. Mach. A. VII. 341.

Nux's mode of determining the magnitude of the stars. A. P. 1762. H. 135.
By the interposition of semitransparent substances of different thicknesses.

Charnières's megameter. A. P. 1767. H. 129.

Novarre's Gregorian telescope for astronomical observations. A. P. 1769. H. 130.

Bradley on the use of the micrometer. Ph. tr. 1772. 46.

Bernoulli on the rhomboid reticle. A. Berl. 1773. 193.

Jeaurat's iconantidiptic telescope. Ph. tr. 1779. 130.
Representing one erect and one inverted image, coinciding at the moment that the object passes the axis.

Jeaurat on diplantidian telescopes. A. P. 1779. 23. H. 33.

Jeaurat on iconantidiptic telescopes. A. P. 1786. 562.

Kästner on the wires of a micrometer. Commentat. Gott. 1779. II. M. 1.

Herschel's micrometer for the angle of position. Ph. tr. 1781. 500.

Herschel's telescopes. See Telescopes, Fixed Stars.

Herschel's lamp micrometer. Ph. tr. 1782. 163.

For ascertaining angular situations, by comparison with two lamps viewed by the other eye, one of them moveable every way. Makes Lyra subtend 3353".

Herschel's dark and lucid disc and periphery micrometers. Ph. tr. 1783. 4.

A light circle being compared with a dark one on a light ground, the light one appears the larger.

Ussher on telescopes for viewing stars in the day. Ir. tr. 1788. 37.

The highest magnifiers the best.

Eaglefield on Bradley's rhomboid micrometer. 4. Bath.

Pigott on the comparative magnitudes of the stars. Ph. tr. 1785. 135.

Suggests, that they may be measured by ascertaining how much light, thrown into the telescope, will efface them.

Wollaston on a system of wires. Ph. tr. 1785. 346.

A rhombus instead of a rhomboid, for ascertaining right ascensions and declinations.

Am. tr. II. 181. Nich. 8. I. 319.

Rittenhouse used spiders' webs instead of wires, for micrometers.

Cavallo on a micrometer. See Optical Instruments.

E. Walker on Bradley's mode of observing transits. Nich. 8. II. 22.

Astronomical micrometers and photometers. Zach. Eph. III. 318.

Burckhardt on a quadrangular system of wires. Zach. Mon. corr. I. 120.

Burckhardt on micrometers. M. Inst. To be printed in the S. E.

Theodolites.

Theodolites with verniers. Leup. Th. Ar. t. 37. 42.

Circles. E. M. Pl. V. Marine. IV.

*Roy's account of the great theodolite, with its microscopes and micrometers. Ph. tr. 1790. 135.

Ramsden's improved theodolite. Ph. tr. 1795. 457.

A small theodolite of Ramsden. Ph. tr. 1797. 507.

Theodolites. Enc. Br. Art. Geometry.

Ofverbom's theodolite. Zach. Mon. corr. IV. 334. Fig.

Bohnenberger on a circle of Baumann. Zach. Mon. corr. VI. 465.

Fixed Instruments.
Transit Instruments.

Derham's transit instrument. Ph. tr. 1704. XXIV. 1578.

Roemer's simple transit instrument. M. Berl. 1727. III. 276.

Gensanne's transit instrument. A. P. 1736. H. 120. Mach. A. VII. 55.

Ussher on illuminating the wires of a transit instrument. Ir. tr. 1788. II. 19.

Wollaston on a transit circle. Ph. tr. 1793. 133.

A transit instrument by Ramsden. Ph. tr. 1795. 419.

Camerer and Pasquich on the errors of a transit instrument. Zach. Mon. corr. VI. 34, 176, 481.

A transit instrument. Cavallo. N. Ph. IV. Pl. 29. f. 6.

Mural Quadrants.

See Quadrants.

Zenith Sectors.

*A zenith sector by Ramsden and Berge. Mudge. Ph. tr. 1803. 383.

Account of a Zenith Sector, described by Major Mudge. *From the Journals of the Royal Institution. II.*

The external frame of the instrument is of mahogany, constituting a truncated pyramid, on a base of six feet square, tapering to a vertex of three. The internal frame, which immediately supports the sector, revolves on a vertical axis, terminating below in a cone, which rests in a conoidal cavity, convex to the axis, and above in a cylinder, passing through an octagonal aperture in the upper frame. As it turns, its motion is indicated by an azimuth circle attached to the lower part of the external frame, and it may be brought into the direction of the meridian by a telescope fixed in the plane of the arch. The telescope of the sector is eight feet long, and its aperture four inches: the axis is like that of a transit instrument, the plumb line passes through two perforations in it, and is adjusted, by means of a screw with a jointed handle, and a long bent microscope with specula, so as to bisect a point marked on a plate of mother of pearl, precisely in the axis of the instrument; this plate is properly illuminated by the same lamp that serves for the micrometer wires of the telescope, its light being reflected downwards upon the wires from an oblique surface covered with plaster of Paris.

The pivots of the sector's axis are of bell metal, they rest in Y's, firmly attached to the frame, their sliding horizontally is prevented by a fixed friction wheel on one side, and a spring supporting a friction wheel on the other: four cylindrical braces are employed to fix the telescope firmly to the axis; and the bending of the axis is still further obviated by levers with counterpoises, acting by means of friction wheels, close to the tube of the telescope, so as to leave so much of the weight only to be supported by the pivots, as is necessary to keep the instrument steady. The telescope is moved by strings and pullies, and is retained in any given situation by weights. A long spirit level is employed for bringing the axis into a position truly horizontal.

The arch is divided into portions of five minutes each, marked by points, on golden pins, let in at each division. A fine line was struck when the telescope was properly supported on the pivots: the instrument being then removed, the diameter of the circle, of which this arc was a part, was ascertained, and one sixteenth of this, being taken as extremely near to the chord of $7° 10'$, was laid off on each side zero; and this arc was verified by comparison with another, obtained, by means of continual bisections, from an arc of $60°$. The micrometer screw carries a head divided into 59 parts, nearly corresponding to seconds; the half of the arc on one side zero was found to contain only a single second more than the other portion.

The greatest error that could ever be observed from a difference of temperature in different parts of the observatory, was found to be little more than half a second for an arc of five degrees. The observations of the zenith distances of the various stars employed were completed in October 1802; and the instrument was brought back to London without having sustained the least perceptible injury.

VOL. II.

Equatorial Instruments.

Short on an equatorial instrument. Ph. tr. 1749. XLVI. 241.

Nairne's equatorial, or portable observatory. Ph. tr. 1771. 107.

Silberschlag's uranometer. A. Berl. 1778. H. 36.

Smeaton on observations out of the meridian with an equatorial micrometer. Ph. tr. 1787. 318.

Haupoin's equatorial instrument. Roz. XLII. 286.

*Shuckburgh on the equatorial instrument. Ph. tr. 1793. 67.

Levels, Mechanical or Hydrostatical.

On levels. Hooke Anim. on Hevelius. Water levels.

Perrault. Mach. A. I. 63.

Picard. A. P. VII. i. 51, 235.

Couplet. A. P. 1699. 127. H. 112.

Verjus. Mach. A. II. 83.

Lahire. A. P. 1704. 251. H. 99.

Leupold. Th. Horizontost. Th. Hydrotechn. Th. Suppl.

Grandjean de Fouchy. Mach. A. VI. 113.

Hadley's spirit level to be fixed to a quadrant. Ph. tr. 1733. XXXVIII. 167.
The spirit to vibrate through a stop cock till it settle.

Soumille. A. P. 1737. H. 109. Mach. A. VII. 71.
With an index enlarging the scale by means of a lever.

Leigh's water level fixed to Davis's quadrant. Ph. tr. 1738. XL. 413.

Leigh's mercurial level for a quadrant. Ph. tr. 1738. XL. 417.
True to 2'.

Gensanne. A. P. 1741. H. 164. Mach. A. VII. 109.
Reflecting.

Mathieu. A. P. 1746. H. 121.

Deparcieux. A. P. 1748. 313. H. 116.
Short on Serson's top. Ph. tr. 1751. 352.
> Remained 15' perfectly horizontal.

Chezy. S. E. V. 254. Nich. III. 396.
Ratenfay. A. P. 1772. i.
Ferguson. Mech. exerc. 115.
Meister on the spirit level. N. C. Gott. 1776. VII. 142.
Deluc. Roz. IX. 204.
Carayon's water level. Roz. XI. 368.
A circular spirit level. Dollond. Ph. tr. 1779. 332.
Inochodsoff. A. Petr. III. i. 188. Roz. XXVI. 461.
Fouchy on a level not requiring adjustment. A. P. 1781. 82. H. 44.
> The surfaces of the liquid in different branches of a tube are viewed through a telescope at the same time with the object.

Ducaila Expression des nivellemens. 1782.
> By drawing horizontal lines on a map.

Jonville's instrument for measuring the inclination of strata. Roz. XXX. 100.
Keith's mercurial levels. Ed. tr. II. 14. IV. H. 17. Repertory. III. 338. IX. 49.
> With sights.

Ph. tr. 1793. 67.
> The level of Shuckburgh's equatorial instrument moves of an inch for each second.

Enc. Br. Art. Levels.
Nicholson. Nich. I. 131.
Anderson's instrument for levelling. Repert. II. 317.
Walker on the plumb line and spirit level. Nich. 8. I. 309.
Little's artificial horizon. Ir. tr. VII. 77. Repert. ii. II. 183.
> With a weight.

Gould's patent artificial horizon. Repert. ii. I. 98.
Churchman on levelling. S. A. XXII. 224.
> After Ducaila.

Modes of fixing Instruments.

Hooke on fixing instruments. Animadv. on Hevelius. Lect. Cutl.
Gray on finding a meridian from the pole star. Ph. tr. 1701. XXII. 815.
Derham. Ph. tr. XXIV. 1578.
> Mentions " the thill horse" of the wain as coming to the meridian at the same time with the pole star and the bright star in Cassiopeia's thigh.

Rittenhouse's mode of fixing a meridian. Am. tr. II. 184.
Patterson on a meridian line. Am. tr. II. 251.
Schubert on fixing a meridian. N. A. Petr. 1788. VI. 301.
Kästner on observations of the pole star. Commentat. Gott. 1791. XI. M. 1.
Henry on adjusting a transit instrument. Zach. Mon. corr. III. 344.
On drawing a meridian line. Zach. Mon. corr. III. 419.
On a meridian drawn at Gottingen by observations on glass globes. Zach. Mon. corr. VII. 558.
> The pole is situated where the line drawn through the pointers meets the line drawn from the last horse of the wain to the pole star.

Observations in general.
Corrections.
Refraction.

Refraction. See Physical Optics.
Kästner on corrections for refraction. N. C. Gott. 1772. III. 122.
Cassini on observations of refraction. A. Berl. 1773. 251.
Dollond's apparatus for correcting refraction. Ph. tr. 1779. 332.
> Two lenses sliding on each other, placed before the object glass. Why better than a table?

Smeaton's mode of correcting for refraction. Ph. tr. 1787. 318.

Numerous observations of the transit of 6 June 1761. Ph. tr. 1761.
Zanotti. C. Bon. VII. O. 1.
Montucla and Lalande. IV. 126.
Wollaston on corrections for horizontal refraction. Ph. tr. 1803. 1.

Aberration of Light. See Physical Optics.

Parallax in general.
Mackay. Enc. Br. Art. Parallax.

Dip.
Huddart on the dip. Ph. tr. Nich. I. 145. Gilb. III. 257.
Wollaston on the dip. Ph. tr. 1803. 1.
E. Walker on the dip. Nich. VII. 62.

Azimuths and Altitudes in general.
Bernoulli on three observations of altitudes. C. Petr. IV. 89.
Mayer on observations of altitudes. C. Petr. V. 33.
Lax on observations of two altitudes. Ph. tr. 1799. 74.
An artificial horizon of mercury covered with gauze. Burrows. As. Res. I.

Observations of the Stars.
See Astronomical Telescopes and Micrometers.
Smeaton on observing by comparison with two stars. Ph. tr. 1768. 170.

Corrections.
Aberration.
Bradley on a newly discovered motion of the stars. Ph. tr. 1728. 637.
Clairaut on the aberration of the stars. A. P. 1737. 205. H. 76.
Winsheim on aberration. N. C. Petr. I. 446.

Annual Parallax.
Hooke's attempt to prove the motion of the earth. 4. 1679. Lect. Cutl.
Acc. Ph. tr. 1679. IX. 12. Cassini's approbation. 90.
Wallis's proposal respecting the annual parallax. Ph. tr. 1693. XVII. 844.
Suggests an observation on two neighbouring stars, as the second horse of the wain, and its rider.
Halley on Cassini's proposal to find the parallax of Sirius. Ph. tr. 1720. XXII. 1.

Places of the Stars.
Lahire on finding the difference of declination. A. P. 1701. 101. H. 91.
Maraldi on finding declinations without refraction. A. P. 1736. 43. H. 85.
Maupertuis on finding the declination of the stars. A. P. 1736. 375.
Wollaston on describing the positions of the fixed stars. Ph. tr. 1784. 181.
By drawing little maps from estimation.

Altitudes of the Stars.
Mairan on finding the latitude without refraction. A. P. 1736. 147. H. 87.
Aubert on equal altitudes. Ph. tr. 1776. 92.
Of a star near the pole.
Kastner on observations of the pole star. Commentat. Gott. 1791. XXI. M. 1.

Observations of the Sun.
Parallax, and Modes of determining it.

For Irradiation and Refraction see Physical Optics.
Halley de parallaxi solis ope Veneris determinanda. Ph. tr. 1716. XXIX. 454.
Boscovich on the approaching transit of Venus. Ph. tr. 1760. 865.

Short's comparison of observations of the transit. Ph. tr. 1762. 611.

Parallax at the time 8".52, mean parallax 8".65. Sun's greatest apparent diameter 32' 32", least 31' 28", mean 32' 0".5.

Short's further investigation of the solar parallax. Ph. tr. 1763. 300.

At the time 8".56, which he thinks true within 1/16 th: hence we have 8".69 for the mean.

Duval on the sun's distance from the earth. Ph. tr. 1763. 1.

Ferguson's scheme of the transit of 1769. Ph. tr. 1763. 30.

Hornsby on the solar parallax. Ph. tr. 1763. 467.

At the time 9".732.

Hornsby on the transit in 1769. Ph. tr. 1765. 326.

Hornsby on the sun's parallax. Ph. tr. 1771. 574.

Makes it 8".72.

The distance of the sun deduced from the theory of gravity. Edinb. 1763.

Pingré's supplement on the transit. Ph. tr. 1764. 152.

Pingré on the solar parallax. A. P. 1772. i. 398. H. 71.

Mean 8".8.

Mallet on parallax. Ph. tr. 1766. 244.

Horsley on the sun's distance deduced from the lunar motions by Stewart's method. Ph. tr. 1767. 179.

Parallax 8" 52"'.4.

Horsley's remark on Stewart's method. Ph. tr. 1769. 153.

Landen's animadversions on Stewart's computation. R. S.

Röhl von den durchgängen den Venus. 8. Greifswald, 1768.

Smeaton and Maskelyne on menstrual parallax. Ph. tr. 1768. 154.

Planman on the solar parallax. Ph. tr. 1768. 107.

At the time 8".28.

Maskelyne on the transit of Venus 1769. Ph. tr. 1768. 355.

Distinct marks of an atmosphere, or of inflection, or of both.

Hirst on the phenomena of the transit. Ph. tr. 1769. 228.

On the transit of Venus. N. C. Petr. XIV. ii. 1.

†Price on the aberration of light as retarding the transit. Ph. tr. 1770. 536.

On Winthrop's principles, he makes the retardation 18' 16" of time: the true retardation is only about 9' 20". See Optics.

Lalande on the solar parallax. A. P. 1771. 776. H. 83.

Mean 8".62, polar 8".58.

Smith on the sun's parallax. Am. tr. I. 162.

Euler on the sun's parallax, computed by Lexell. Ph. tr. 1772. 69.

Makes it 8".55.

A. P. Index. Art. Soleil. Venus.

Ph. M. X. 181.

Laplace makes the parallax 8".6 from the moon's motion.

Observations of the Solstice.

Halley. Ph. tr. 1695. XIX. 12.

A problem applicable to this subject. Pemberton. Ph. tr. 1772. 434.

Observations of Solar Altitude.

†R. Graham's globular instrument for altitudes. Ph. tr. 1734. XXXVIII. 430.

Cassini de Thury on the variation of solstitial altitudes. A. P. 1748. 257. H. 91.

Bouguer on observations of altitudes at sea. A. P. Pr. II. iv.

Lalande on the observation of meridian and corresponding altitudes. A. A. 1757. 516.

Pemberton on two observations for the latitude. Ph. tr. 1760. 910.

Observations of the Planets.

Aberration. See Optics.

Observations of the places of the Planets.

Halley on determining the places of the planets by the fixed stars. Ph. tr. 1721. XXXI. 209.

Observations of the secondary Planets.

Lunar Observations.

Halley on finding the longitude by lunar observations. Ph. tr. 1731. 185.
Thinks he can determine the moon's place within 2'.

Mayer on lunar observations. C. Gott. 1753. III. 375.

Maskelyne's lunar observations and computations. Ph. tr. 1762. 558.

Pigott on the transit of the moon's limb. Ph. tr. 1786. 416.

Burrow on lunar observations. As. Res. I. 433.
Recommends that the internal contact of the limbs be observed, in order to avoid the effects of irradiation.

Corrections. Refraction, and Parallax.

Grischow on the lunar parallax. N. C. Petr. IV. 451.

On the lunar parallax. Ed. ess. II. 91.

Lalande on the elliptical parallax of azimuth. A. P. 1756. 373. H. 96.

Maskelyne's concise rules for calculating refraction and parallax in lunar observations. Ph. tr. 1764. 261.

Pingré on parallax, allowing for ellipticity. A. P. 1764. 362.

Tables to be used with the nautical almanac.

Lexell on correcting lunar observations. A. Petr. I.

Euler on the parallax of a spheroid. A. Petr. III. i. 241.

Euler on the calculation of lunar observations. A. Petr. 1780. IV. ii. 301.

Fuss on the corrections of lunar observations. A. Petr. III. i. 310.

The natural cosine of the true distance is $2(\cos.a).(\cos.b).(\sec.c).(\sec.d).(\cos.e).(\cos.f) - \cos.g$; a being half the sum of the observed altitudes and the distance, b half the difference between the sum of the altitudes and the distance, c and d the observed altitudes, e and f the corrected altitudes, and g their sum. This is the simple trigonometrical solution.

Krafft on correcting lunar observations, with a table. A. Petr. VI. ii. 351. 1789. VII. 365.
Not very simple.

An approximate construction. Kelly's spherics.
Draws two lines including an angle equal to the observed distance, sets off the sines of the observed altitudes from the angular point, erects perpendiculars at the points thus found, and the distance of their intersection from the lunar line is the correction, which is subtractive when it lies on the same side with the solar line, and additive when on the opposite side. This correction is measured on the line of chords, calling each degree a minute; it is then reduced by multiplying it by the horizontal parallax, and dividing by 62 when it is subtractive, but by 53 when additive. This includes the effects of refraction, very nearly.

Elliot on correcting lunar observations. Ed. tr. I. 191.

Burrow on the lunar parallax. As. Res. I. 320.

Garrard's tables for reducing lunar observations. 4. Chelsea, 1800.
A short method, for finding the longitude within half a degree.

Mendoza's tables. 4. Lond. 1801.
Contain a simple method. The author has also lately published some tables for a still more expeditious mode of calculation.

Leveque. M. Inst. IV. 467.

Lowe on finding the longitude by land from the moon's transit. Ph. M. XV. 97.

Andrews's mode of correcting lunar distances. Nich. 8. IV. 43.
A direct solution, deduced from plane trigonometry, employing the squares of the sines.
Richer and some others have invented mechanical methods of correction.

Moon's appearance.

Grandjean de Fouchy on deducing the longitude from the appearance of the lunar mountains. A. P. 1733. H. 76.

Observations of the Earth's Motion.

Hooke and Newton on a falling stone. Birch. III. 516, 519.
  Hooke observes that it should fall south eastwards.

Newton's letters. Commercium epistolicum.

Hooke on the motion of the earth. Nich. II. 84.

Proposal for experiments on a diurnal titubation of the earth. A. P. 1742. H. 104.

Poleni de pendulorum perturbatione. Ph. tr. 1743. 299.
  Thinks there should be a difference according to the direction of the vibration.

Gulielmini's experiments. Nich. II. 84.

Saladini on the declination of falling bodies. Ac. Sienn. VII. 55.

Benzenberg. Ph. M. XV.
  Found in a height of 235 feet Fr. a declination of a falling body 4 lines eastwards and 1¼ line southwards.

Laplace on the fall of a body from a great height. B. Soc. Phil. n. 75.
  Makes the deviation 3.9 lines eastwards at Hamburg for 235 feet: attributes the 1.5 lines southwards observed by Benzenberg to some accidental or meteorological cause.

Geography.

Figure and Magnitude of the Earth.

See Laws of Gravity.

Picart on the measurement of the earth. A. P. VII. i. 46.

Acc. Ph. tr. 1675. X. 261.

Account of Norwood's measurement. Ph. tr. 1676. XI. 636.
  Norwood was "a reader of the mathematics" in London. He measured principally by chains, observing the angles, and partly also by paces.

Birch. Hist. R. S. I. 135.

Eisenschmidius de figura telluris, Strasb. 1691. 4. M. B.

Cassini on Snellius's measurement. A. P. 1702. 60. H. 82.

Cassini de la figure de la terre. 12. Amst. 1723.

Cassini on the figure of the earth. A. P. 1735. 255. 1736. 64. H. 80.

Cassini's measurement of an arc. A. P. 1740. Suite.

A. P. 1718. Suite.

Mairan on the diminution of degrees. A. P. 1720. 231. H. 65.

Desaguliers on the figure of the earth. Ph. tr. 1725. XXXIII. 201, 239, 277.
  Shows the insufficiency of Cassini's measures: observes that a revolution round a larger axis must be unstable.

Musschenbroek. Diss. Phys. 355.

Maupertuis on the figure of the earth. Ph. tr. 1733. 1736. 302. A. P. 1737. 389. H. 90.

Maupertuis on the figures of the heavenly bodies. A. P. 1734. 55. H. 88.

Maupertuis Figure de la terre determinée. 12. Amst. 1738.

Maupertuis on the voyage to Peru. A. P. 1744. 249. H. 35.

La Condamine on an instrument for determining a parallel circle. A. P. 1733. 294. H. 53.

La Condamine's extract of the operations near the equator. A. P. 1746. 618.

La Condamine Journal du voyage à l'équateur. 4. Par. 1751. M. B.

La Condamine Mesure de trois premiers degrés. 4. Par. 1751. M. B.

Clairaut's inferences from the perpendicular to the meridian. A. P. 1733. 406. H. 59.

Clairaut on Cassini's new mode of determination. A. P. 1735. 117. H. 51.

Clairaut on the measurement of the earth by several arcs. A. P. 1736. 116.

*Clairaut de terrae figura. Ph. tr. 1737. 19.

*Clairaut on the figure of planets of unequal density. Ph. tr. 1738. XL. 277.

The earth probably denser at the centre, as Newton hinted; but Newton made a little mistake respecting its effect.

Clairaut sur la figure de la terre. 8. Paris, 1743.

Acc. A. P. 1742. H. 86.

Bradley on observations of pendulums by Graham and Campbell. Ph. tr. 1734. XXXVIII. 302.

Maraldi on the verification of the figure of the earth by the lunar parallax. A. P. 1734. 1. H. 59.

Bouguer's comparison of the supposed figures of the earth. A. P. 1734. 21. H. 83.

Bouguer on the measurement of degrees. A. P. 1736. 302, 443.

Bouguer on the direction of the plumb line. A. P. 1754. 250. H. 1.

Stirling on the figure of the earth, and the variation of gravity. Ph. tr. 1735. XXXIX. 98.

Krafft on the figure of the earth. C. Petr. VIII. 220.

Delisle on a measurement in Russia. Ph. tr. 1737. XL. 27.

Celsius de figura telluris. 4. Upsal, 1738.

Acc. by Eames. Ph. tr. 1740. 371.

Alexander on a plan for measurement in New York. Ph. tr. 1740. 389.

Examen des ouvrages faites pour determiner la figure de la terre. 8. Amst. 1741. M. B.

Wargentin on the figure of the earth. Schw. Abh. 1749. 243. 1750. S. 83.

Lacaille on the true length of the degrees in France. A. P. 1751. 425. H. 158.

Lacaille on the precision of the measures of 1740. A. P. 1755. 53.

Frisii disquisitio de figura et magnitudine telluris. Milan, 1752.

Short's remarks on Frisi. Ph. tr. 1753. 5.

Euler on spheroidical trigonometry. A. Berl. 1753. 258.

Darcy on the attraction of spheroids. A. P. 1758. 318.

Reflections on the figure of the earth. A. P. 1755. H. 47.

*Grischow's experiments on the length of the pendulum. N. C. Petr. VII. 445.

Prefers a simple pendulum, corrected for temperature, to a compensation.

Maskelyne on the going of a clock at St. Helena. Ph. tr. 1762. 434.

Maskelyne. Ph. tr. 1777. 722.

Corrects for curvature and refraction together, by dividing the square of the distance by ⅔ of the diameter of the earth.

†Michell on measuring degrees of longitude. Ph. tr. 1766. 119.

Lambert on the figure of the ocean. A. Berl. 1767. 20.

Liesganig's measurement of 3° in the meridian of Vienna. Ph. tr. 1768. 15.

South of Vienna the degree was 155 toises less than northwards towards Brunn, but at Warasdin 800 toises greater than at Vienna: this is attributed to the attraction of mountains near Gräz.

Mason and Dixon's measurement of a degree in Pennsylvania. Ph. tr. 1768. 270.

Lat. 39° 12'. Cavendish calculates, that the degree may have been diminished 60 or 100 toises from the situation of the Atlantic and the effect of the Allegany mountains; similar causes may have operated in Italy and at the Cape.

Mason and Dixon on the going of a clock in Pennsylvania. Ph. tr. 1768. 329.

Dalembert on the change of axis from a difference of meridians. A. P. 1768. 1. H. 95, 332.

On the length of the pendulum. N. C. Petr. XIV. ii. Summ. 14.

Mallet's observations in Lapland. Ph. tr. 1770. 363.

Mallet's mathematical description of the earth. R. S.

Rumovski on the length of the pendulum. N. C. Petr. XVI. 567.

Roy's remarks on the figure of the earth. Ph. tr. 1777. 766.

*Roy's account of the measurement of a base on Hounslow heath. Ph. tr. 1785. 385.

A base from Hampton poorhouse to Cranford bridge was measured as a foundation for the comparison of the situations of London and Dover: the measurement was in a direction a little inclined to the horizon, but the reduction was only half an inch: the length was found 27404.7 feet by the glass rods.

*Roy on the mode of determining the relative situations of Greenwich and Paris. Ph. tr. 1787. 188.

Comparison of the French observations. Proposes a base of verification in Romney marsh. Table of degrees in various directions according to Bouguer's hypothesis, 228; corrections, 465.

Roy on the meridians of Greenwich and Paris. Ph. tr. 1790. 111.

The French committee consisted of Cassini, Méchain, and Legendre. A base of verification of 38582.92 feet was measured in Romney marsh with the steel chain: differing only 9 inches from the calculation of the triangles founded on the base in Hounslow heath: the chain appears to deserve equal confidence with the glass rods: it was lengthened .022 inch in 100 feet by 6 weeks wear. The white lights were found the best objects for nocturnal observations. The measurements on the different sides of the channel agreed within 7 feet in 39800. The longitude of Paris 2° 19' 42", or 9' 18".8 in time E. of Greenwich.

Roy on spherical and spheroidical triangles. Ph. tr. 1790. 168, 192.

Prony's translation of Roy's memoir on the measurement of a base. 4. Paris, 1787.

Legendre on trigonometrical operations. A. P. 1787. 352.

Legendre Operations pour la junction des observatoires. 4. Paris. R. S.

Dalby on the longitudes of Dunkirk and Paris. Ph. tr. 1791. 236.

The correct longitude of Paris 2° 20' 4".0 according to Newton's ellipsis, or 9' 20".4 in time; according to another, dividing the errors, 9' 19".7. Maskelyne from astronomical observations gives 9' 20".

Account of a survey by Williams, Mudge, and Dalby. Ph. tr. 1795. 414.

The base on Hounslow heath was measured again with a chain, and found 27404.3155 feet: the former measurement, with some corrections which had been omitted, 27404.0843; a mean between both 27404.2; the base in Romney marsh corrected was found 28535.4 f. agreeing thus with the base on Hounslow heath, and within an inch or two, with another of 36574.4 feet measured on Salisbury plain.

Williams, Mudge, and Dalby on the continuation of the survey. Ph. tr. 1797. 432.

Mudge's continuation of the trigonometrical survey. Ph. tr. 1800. 539.

Measurement of a base on Sedgmoor, of 27680 feet.

Mudge on the measurement of an arc from Dunnose to Clifton. Ph. tr. 1803. 383.

A new base of verification measured with the chain at the extreme point of the survey.

Laplace on the figure of the earth. S. E. 1773. 503. A. P. 1783. 17.

Laplace Exposition du système du monde. Mécanique céleste.

Dionis du Séjour on geodetic calculation. A. P. 1778. 73. H. 28.

Hubius de figura telluris. 4. Gott.

Gerlach Bestimmung der gestalt der erde. 8. Vienna, 1782. R. S.

Achard Schriften. 197.

De Luc Lettres physiques et morales. xlv.

Lalande on the ellipticity of the earth. A. P. 1785. 1. Bode's Jahrbuch. 1791.

Lalande on Fernel's measurement of the earth published in 1528. A. P. 1787. 216.

Makes it 57070 toises, only a toise more than the later measures. In Ph. tr. X. it is called 56746.

Klostermann's remarks on different measurements. Gott. anz. 1785. 1786. 1799.

........, that from a comparison of the different angles of the triangles employed, it appears that none of the measurements can be considered as sufficiently accurate to authorise us to attribute any irregularity to the earth's figure. Roy thinks his observations of little importance.

Klostermann sur le degré du méridien. 4. Petersb. 1789. R. S.

Meister on Mayer's scale for reducing angles to the horizon. Commentat. Gott. 1785. VIII. 75.

Williams on the earth's diameters. 4. Lond. 1786. 1788. R. S.

Klugel in Bode's Jahrbuch. 1787. 1788. On the magnitude of the zones. 1790. Goth. Mag. III. ii. 148.

Krafft on the length of the pendulum in different latitudes. N. A. Petr. 1789. VII. 215.

Pictet's proposal for a measurement near Geneva. Ph. tr. 1791. 106.

Topping's measurement of a base in the East Indies. Ph. tr. 1792. 99.

Suremain on the figure of the earth. Roz. XLI. 239.

Cagnoli on determining the figure of the earth. Soc. Ital. VI. 227.

By observing the lunar parallax, and its effect in an occultation, a difference of about 9″ ought to be found in some cases.

Henry on the length of the pendulum at Petersburg. N. A. Petr. 1793. XI. 524.

Kästners mathematische geographie. 8. Gott. 1795.

Acc. Hind. Arch. II. 100.

Prony's formulae for the axes of the earth. B. Soc. Phil. n. 1.

*Report from the committee of weights and measures, on the new measurement of the meridian. M. Inst. II. 23. B. Soc. Phil. n. 28. Journ. Phys. XLIX. 98, 161.

The error of the three angles of 90 of the triangles was between 1″ and 2″. The bases were measured by rods of platina, their ends being placed near each other, and the distances measured by a micrometer. They also served as parts of metalline thermometers for correcting the errors of expansion. The degrees were found to diminish all the way from Dunkirk to Montjouy, in a distance of 9.6737972²; but they decreased at first slowly, then more rapidly, and then slowly again.

Delambre Arc du méridien. 4. Par. 1798. R. I.

Clay on the figure of the earth. Am. tr. V. 312.

Burja on the length of the pendulum at Berlin. A. Berl. 1799. M. 3.

Lambton's mode of geographical survey. As. Res. VII. 312.

With the measurement of a degree in the Mysore country.

Melanderhielm on the measurement of a degree in the north. Zach Mon. corr. I. 372.

Melanderhielm and Svanberg on geographical measurements. Zach Mon. corr. II. 250, 257.

Melanderhielm on the degree measured in Lapland by Svanberg and Ofverbom. Zach Mon. corr. VII. 561. Journ. Phys. LVI. 400.

Pasquich on the use of the French geographical measurements. Zach Mon. corr. I. 435.

Pasquich on the effect of ellipticity on pendulums. Zach Mon. corr. II. 3.

Knogler on the measurement of a degree in China. Zach Mon. corr. I. 589.

Note on the earth's ellipticity deduced from lunar observations. Ph. M. VII. 186.

Nouet's degree measured in Egypt. Ph. M. XII. 208.

Playfair on the figure of the earth. Ed. tr. V. 3. Nich. VII. 102.

P. P. on the figure of the earth, and on spheroidal triangles. Nich. VIII. 12, 151.
Remarks on Playfair.

Spheroidal triangles. See Navigation.

Account of MAJOR MUDGE'S *paper on the Measurement of an Arc of the Meridian, extending from Dunnose, in the Isle of Wight, latitude* 50° 37' 8", *to Clifton, in Yorkshire, latitude* 53° 27' 31", *in course of the operations carried on for the Trigonometrical Survey of England, in the years* 1800, 1801, *and* 1802. *From the Journals of the Royal Institution.* II.

In the course of these operations, a new base had been measured on Misterton Carr, and from its length, compared with the former trigonometrical measurements, Major Mudge was enabled to calculate the magnitude of a degree of the meridian, with well grounded hopes of very great accuracy. The result, however, of these calculations indicates an irregularity, which could not possibly have been foreseen, although it has happened in a still greater degree in some former measurements. The northern part of the arc, which, upon the supposition of the ellipticity of the terrestrial spheroid, ought to be less curved than the southern, and to exhibit the length of the degree greater in the same proportion, appeared from the observations, to be more curved, the mean of the whole arc giving the degree 42 fathoms smaller than the arc between Dunnose and Arbury Hill. Major Mudge thinks it improbable that the error of observation can be one tenth as great as this difference implies, and he conjectures that the plumb line must have been deflected at Clifton as much as 8" or 10" southwards, by the irregularity of the terrestrial attraction. This opinion was confirmed, by a comparison of his observations with those which had been made at Blenheim, giving 60884 fathoms for the length of the degree in latitude 51° 13', deduced from the meridional distance of Blenheim from Dunnose. The arc from Dunnose to Clifton gives 60820, in latitude 52° 2' 20"; from Dunnose to Arbury Hill, 60865, in latitude 51° 35' 18". By comparing the latitudes and distance of Clifton and Barcelona, we have 60795 for the degree in latitude 47° 24', the whole arc being somewhat more than twelve degrees; and at the middle point between the parallel of Clifton and Paris, the degree appears to be 60825 fathoms, in latitude 51° 9'. Major Mudge promises to give to the Royal Society, at a future time, an account of the further prosecution of his operations for continuing the trigonometrical survey, which has hitherto been conducted on so extensive a scale. Y.

Tabular comparison of Observations.

Length of a degree, on the Level of the Sea.

Latitude.	Toises.	Fathoms according to Roy.	
66° 20' N.	(57422	61194.2	Maupertuis, 1736—7.)
66° 20' 12"	57209.28		Melanderhielm and Svanberg, 1802.
(52° 46'	57419		Norwood, published 1636.)
50° 41'		60840	Roy. 1790. The degree perpendicular to the meridian 61182.2 fathoms. Ph. tr. 1795.
50° 9' 27"		60826.6	
49° 23'	57074		Maupertuis and Cassini, 1739—40.
49° 7'	57064.5		Picart.
49° 3'		60833.0	Mean of Maupertuis and Cassini and Liesganig.
48° 43'		60830.4	
47° 40'	57091		Liesganig, 1766. The whole from Sobieschiz to Warasdin, 57077.4. From Sobieschiz and Brunn to Vienna, 57085.2. From Vienna to Gräz, 56899.1. From Gräz to Warasdin, 57365.5. Ph. tr. 1768. 15.
45° 0'	57028	60777.6	Cassini, 1739—40,
44° 44'	57069	60821.2	Beccaria, 1768.
43° 52'		60773.2	Mean of Beccaria and Boscovich.
43° 0'	56979	60725.5	Boscovich and Lemaire. 1752.
39° 12'	56888.2	60686.5	Mason and Dixon, 1764—8.
12° 32'		60494	Lambton, 1803.
1° 9'	56750	60485.5	Bouguer and Condamine, 1736—43. Bouguer 56753, Condamine 56750, other calculations 56707° to 56802.

Latitude.	Toises.	Fathoms according to Roy.	
38° 18′ S.	57037		Klostermann.
	56740		La Caille, 1752.
	(or 57070		Fernelius.)
	55021		Snellius.
In Egypt.	56880		Nouet. Ph. M. XII. 209.

The excess of the degrees of the meridian in an elliptic spheroid is very nearly in the ratio of the square of the sine of the latitude: and the length of the degree at any point, is to the length at the equator, accurately, as the cube of a line drawn parallel to the plumb line from a point in the axis equidistant from the centre with the equator, and terminating in a point of the plane of the equator, to the cube of the line drawn from this point to the true pole: Or, if e be the ellipticity, and x the sine of the latitude, the length of the degree will vary, as $(1 + (2e + ee)xx)^{\frac{1}{2}}$.

Length of the Pendulum.

For 100 000 vibrations at Paris, 98770 were made by the same pendulum at the side of the river of Amazons, 98740 at Quito, 98720 on Pichincha. Condamine and Bouguer.

The length of the pendulum at the equator was found by Bouguer 38,9049 English inches; at Spitzbergen 39,1076; the acceleration being 156″ from the equator to London, and 68″.5 from London to Spitzbergen. Roy. Ph. tr. 1787.

The length of the pendulum at St. Helena, lat. 15° 55′ S. is to that at Greenwich, as 1 to 10.0246. Maskelyne. Ph. tr. 1762. 434.

The pendulum at Paris is 1.5 line longer than at the equator: at Petersburg .45 longer than at Paris, and at Ponoi, lat. 67° 4′, .65 longer. In proportion to the square of the sine of the latitude it should be .48 longer at Petersburg than at Paris. Mallet. Ph. tr. 1770. 365.

According to the observations of the pendulum calculated by Roy, as well as some others, it appears that the length of the pendulum is about 39 inches at the equator, and elsewhere $39 + .221$ (s. lat.)^2, or $1 + .00567$ (s. lat.)^2. Instead of .00567 Dr. Maskelyne's observations give .0046 for a multiplier: the observations mentioned by Mallet .00523: the earth's ellipticity being supposed $\frac{1}{170}$, the multiplier becomes, on Clairaut's principles .00547, or, if $\frac{1}{305}$, .00536. Perhaps .0055 is a good mean, and $39 + .215$ (s. lat.)^2 for the length in inches. Robison makes the variation of the pendulum $\frac{1}{180}$, or .00555, and the ellipticity $\frac{1}{314}$.

Ellipticity, or excess of the equator above the axis.

If the earth's density were uniform, the ellipticity would be $\frac{1}{229}$ Newton.

If infinite at the centre and evanescent elsewhere, it would be $\frac{1}{577}$ Laplace.

In the actual circumstances of a density greater towards the centre than at the circumferences, the polar increase of gravity being $\frac{1}{n}$, it must be $\frac{1}{115.2} - \frac{1}{n}$ Laplace after Clairaut.

†Roy's first elliptic spheroid deduced from observations on the pendulum only, without regard to Clairaut's theory $\frac{1}{176}$

Roy's second spheroid, from a comparison of the six best results of measurements, $\frac{1}{191.5}$

Roy's third spheroid, from the degrees of the equator and the old measurement of the polar circle, $\frac{1}{215.1}$

Roy's fourth elliptic spheroid, approaching the nearest to Bouguer's theory, $\frac{1}{221.5}$
Roy's fifth is Newton's.

Roy's sixth spheroid, from the degrees at the equator and in latitude 45° $\frac{1}{309.2}$

Roy's seventh spheroid, having the least possible ellipticity, $\frac{1}{539}$

Roy's eighth spheroid is not elliptic, the excesses of the degrees varying as the squares of the sines of the latitude; this, however, nearly resembles the fourth.

Roy's ninth spheroid is formed upon Bouguer's theory of the excesses of the degrees varying as the fourth power of the sines. This falls within the ellipsis, and according to Roy, agrees best with observation; he finds the power 3.42 nearer the truth than 3 $\frac{11}{12}$ which Bouguer mentions as more accurate than the fourth; the eccentricity is made $\frac{1}{178.4}$

It was, however, found in the course of the survey, that the degree perpendicular to the meridian in latitude 50°41 was 61182.3 fathoms, which is 88 fathoms less than on Bouguer's hypothesis, nor did this measure agree with any elliptic spheroid. From the comparison of this degree with that of the meridian, the ellipticity appeared to be .006751, or $\frac{1}{148}$ Ph. tr. 1795.

Laplace thinks that different meridians are differently curved, but that in Europe the ellipticity of the osculating spheroid is $\frac{1}{150}$

From the measurements in America and at the equator, the ellipticity appears to be $\frac{1}{493}$

From the greatest number of European measurements, $\frac{1}{178}$

From the new measurements in France compared with the equatorial degree $\frac{1}{334}$

From the variation of the pendulum, taking .00567 as its limit, $\frac{1}{332}$

From the lunar motions $\frac{1}{314}$ Laplace.

From the new measurement in Lapland, compared with the Peruvian degree $\frac{1}{313}$ Melanderhielm.

A minimum of errors in Lapland, France, and Peru, gives $\frac{1}{329.4}$

Lambton's measurement, which was not extremely accurate, gives $\frac{1}{300}$ Nich. VIII. 12.

The variation of gravity being $\frac{1}{110}$ the ellipticity becomes $\frac{1}{319}$ Robison.

Dalby makes the earth's equatorial radius 3480932 fathoms, its semiaxis 3473056. Ph. tr. 1791.

Subsequent measurements 3461620 and 3456007, or 7935 and 7882 miles. Ph. tr. 1795.

Density of the Earth.

Bertrand sur la structure intérieure de la terre. 8. Zurich, 1752. M. B.

Maskelyne's proposal for measuring the attraction of a hill, read 1772. Ph. tr. 1775. 495.

Maskelyne's observations made on Schehallion. Ph. tr. 1775. 501.

The sum of the two deflections 11″.6: on a rough computation, the mean density of the earth appears to be at least twice as great as that of the hill, which seems to be an entire rock.

Pringle on the attraction of mountains. 4. London, 1775. Ph. tr. 1775.

Hutton's calculations for determining the mean density of the earth. Ph. tr. 1778. 689.

Finds the specific gravity $\frac{9}{5}$ of that of Schehallion, and concludes that it is about 4½.

*Cavendish on the density of the earth. Ph. tr. 1798. 469. Nich. II. 446. Gilb. II. 1.

A horizontal arm with two balls was suspended by a wire, so as to vibrate 4 or 8 times in an hour: two leaden weights, applied near to the balls, produced a deflection of about 7 inches in the first case, and about 3 in the second: from a mean of many such experiments, the earth's density is found by calculation 5.48, without a chance of an error of $\frac{1}{14}$, confirming Newton's conjecture of 5½. Magnets in the place of the weights produced no effect.

Cavallo. N. Ph. II. 11.

The deepest mine is not more than 2400 feet deep. According to the investigations detailed in Robison's Elements, it may be calculated, that, supposing the decrease of gravity $\frac{1}{110}$, the ellipticity is such as would be assumed by a coat of water surrounding a sphere of the density 1.6, or as if ⅔ of the attractive force of the spheroid were collected in its centre.

Observations for finding the Situation of Places.

Grischow on latitudes and longitudes. N. C. Petr. V. 417.

Alcalá sobre las observationes di latitud y longitud en el mar. 4. Madr. 1796. R. S.

Latitudes.

See Observations of Azimuths and Altitudes.

†Parent's observation of latitude by the rising or setting of two stars. A. P. 1703. H.

Lexell on finding the latitude from the altitude and velocity of motion. A. Petr. III. i. 300.

Krafft on finding the latitude at sea. N. A. Petr. 1791. XI. 353.

Alcalà Galiano sobre el calculo de la latitud. 4. Madr. 1795. R. S.

Longitudes.

See Lunar Observations, and Navigation.

Lynn on determining longitudes by falling stars. Ph. tr. 1727. XXXV. 351.

<small>Supposes them 20 or 30 miles high, and therefore visible in distant places.</small>

Halley on finding the longitude by lunar observations. Ph. tr. 1731. XXXVII. 185.

Fouchy on deducing the longitude from the appearance of the lunar mountains. A. P. 1733. H. 76.

La Condamine on an instrument for determining a parallel circle. A. P. 1733. 294. H. 53.

La Condamine's mode of finding the longitude of neighbouring places. A. P. 1735. 1.

On the discovery of the longitude by the variation. A. P. 1741. H. 131. See Magnetism.

Pingré Voyage pour vérifier l'utilité des méthodes servant à déterminer la latitude et la longitude. 2 v. R. S.

Acc. A. P. 1770. H 97.

Emerson's Miscellanies. 204.

Leroy sur les longitudes en mer. 4. R. S.

Roy on terrestrial observations of longitude. Ph. tr. 1787. 212.

<small>By the pole star.</small>

Van Swinden over het bepaalen der lengte. Amst. 1789.

Barrow on observing the longitude by chronometers. As. Res. II. 473.

Mackay on finding the longitude. 8. Lond. 1793. R. S.

Wales on finding the longitude by timekeepers. 8. Lond. 1794. 1800. R. S.

Hamilton on finding the longitude from transits. Ir. tr. VI. 193.

Lowe on finding the longitude by land. Ph. M. XV. 97.

<small>From the moon's transit.</small>

E. Walker on observing the longitude at sea. Nich. VIII. 65.

Particular Geography.

See Figure of the Earth.

On the general resemblance of the continents. Bacon. Nov. Org. Op. II. 8.

Riccioli geographia et hydrographia reformata. f. Bologn. 1660. M. B.

Ph. tr. abr. I. vii. 546. IV. vi. 449. VI. vii. 363. VIII. vii. 324. X. vi. 250.

Varenii geographia generalis. 8. Cambr. 1672.

Petty on the magnitude of London and Paris. Ph. tr. 1686. XVI. 151.

On the Pike of Teneriff. Hooke. Lect. Cutl. 42.

Correct map of France. Ph. tr. 1697. XIX. 443.

Gouyé's physical and mathematical observations. A. P. VII. Part 1. iii. 1. Part. 2. iii. 129.

Marsigli Histoire de la mer. Amst. 1725. M. B.

Acc. A. P. 1710. H. 23.

Grew on the number of acres in Britain. Ph. tr. 1711. 265.

In South Britain 46 800 000. In Holland 1 million.
Liebknecht Elementa geographiae. 8. Frankf. 1712.
Delisle on the magnitude of cities. A. P. 1725. 48.
Delisle Astronomie et géographie physique. 4. Petersb. 1738.
Martinière Dictionnaire géographique. 10 vol. f. Ven. 1737. R. I.
Maupertuis Elémens de géographie. 8. Paris, 1742. Oeuvr. III. 1.
Danville's atlas. f. Paris. R. I.
T. Heberden on the pike of Teneriffe. Ph. tr. 1751. 353.
Donati storia dell' Adriatico. 4. Ven. 1750. M. B.
Lulofs Beschouwinge des Aardklotes. 4. Leyd. 1750. Germ. by Kästner. 4. Gott. 1755.
*Buache on physical geography. A. P. 1752. 399.
On submarine mountains.
Buache's comparison of rivers. A. P. 1753. 586.
Buache on antarctic lands. A. P. 1755. 17. 1757. 190. H. 143.
Busching's system of geography. 6 v. 4.
Redern's considerations on the globe. Ac. Berl. 1755. 1. 1757. 1. 1765. 1.
Redern Hemisphére septentrional et méridional. Berl. 1762. Maps.
Brookes's geographical dictionary. 2 v. f. Pekin. Ph. tr. 1758. 704.
Geography. Emerson's cyclomathesis. IX.
Brice's geographical dictionary. 2 v. f. Exeter.
Kraschennicoff's Kamtchatka. 4. Petersb. 1759. Acc. by Dumaresque. Ph. tr. 1760. 477.
Lehmanni specimen chorographiae. 4. Petersb. 1762.
E. Short. Ph. tr. 1763. 158.
Longitude of the observatory at Paris. 9' 16".

Bergmann Physik beskrifning äfwer Jordkloten. 8. Ups. 1766. Germ. by Röhl. 4. Greifsw. 1780.
Derbage on the islands of St. John and Cape Breton. Ph. tr. 1768. 46.
Buffon Histoire naturelle, supplément.
Latitudes and longitudes of places. A. P. Index. Art. Pole. Longitude. II. 385.
Funk Anfangsgründe der mathematischen geographie. 8. Leips. 1771.
Duc de Croy Hemisphere australe. 1773.
Duc de Croy on a northern passage. Roz. XXI. 249.
Gatterer Abriss der geographie. 8. Gott. 1775.
Saussure on the physical geography of Italy. Roz. VII. 19.
Saussure Voyages dans les Alpes. 4. R. I.
Cotte's table of elevations. Roz. VII. 291.
Wiedeburgs einleitung in die kosmologie. 8. Gotha. 1776.
Rocheblave on the heights of the Pyrenees. Roz. XVII. 359.
Guthrie's system of geography. 4. Lond. 1782.
E. M. Géographie. 3 vol. Géographie ancienne. 3 vol. Géographie physique. 1 vol.
E. M. Atlas. 2 vol. Par Bonne.
Wilkinson's atlas. R. S.
Cassini Description géometrique de la France. 4. Par. 1783. R. S.
Pasumot on the heights of mountains. Roz. XXIII. 193. Fig.
Bode's two maps on the horizon of Berlin. Berl. 1783. Beschreibung. 8.
Bode Anleitung zur kenntniss der erdkugel. 8. Berl. 1786.
Krafft on the surface of Russia. N. A. Petr. 1783. I. 389.
Makes it 820 500 square leagues, 16 041 290 wersts, or 1/12 of the hemisphere.
Forster's remarks on physical geography. Germ. 8. Berl. 1783.

Morse's American geography. 8.
Molina's natural history of Chili. Germ. 8. Leips. 1786.
*Rennel on the Ganges and Burrampooter. Ph. tr. 1781. 87.
Rennel on the geography of northern Africa. Nich. II. 253.
Cassini and Maskelyne on the situation of Greenwich and Paris. Ph. tr. 1787. 151.
<small>Maskelyne makes the latitude of Paris 48° 50′ 14″, of Greenwich 51° 28′ 40″, the difference of longitude 9′ 20″.</small>
Cassini on the junction of Paris and Greenwich. A. P. 1788. 706.
<small>Legendre questions the accuracy of some of Roy's calculations.</small>
Observations faites dans les Pyrénées. 2 v. Paris, 1789.
Marsden's history of Sumatra.
Tralles Höhen der berge des cantons Bern. 8. Bern, 1790. R. S.
Mitterpachter Physikalische erdbeschreibung. 8. Vienna, 1790.
Reboul on heights in the Pyrenees. Ann. Ch. XIII. 225.
Brühl on the longitude of Paris and Greenwich. N. A. Petr. 1791. IX. 363.
<small>Makes it $\frac{7}{4}$″ in time different from Maskelyne's determination.</small>
Otto Naturgeschichte des meeres. 2 v. Berl. 1792, 1794.
Plants handbuch einer erdbeschreibung. 8. Leipz. 1793.
Bugge on the geography of Denmark. Ph. tr. 1794. 143.
Whitelaw on ascertaining the areas of countries. Ir. tr. VI. 65.
Swan on the lakes of America. Nich. II. 315.
Humboldt's letters from South America. Journ. Phys. XLIX. Ph. M. XVI. XVIII.
Zach Geographische Ephemeriden.
Ellicott on the western parts of Pensylvania. Nich. III. 539.

On the isthmus of Suez. Zach Ephem. II. 97.
Small maps of the Mediterranean, and of the Red Sea. Zach Ephem. II. 392, 505.
Guérin on heights in the Alps. Journ. Phys. LIII. 290.
Smith's English Atlas. 1801.
**Pinkerton's* geography 2 v. 4. Lond. 1802.
Heights of mountains. Hutton's Recreations. IV. 166.
<small>A table from Zach's journal.</small>
Area and population of England. Ph. M. XIX. 197.
<small>From Smith. England and Wales contain 37 334 400 acres, 8 873 000 inhabitants. Scotland has 1 600 000, and Ireland about 4 250 000 inhabitants. England and Wales have 152 inhabitants for each square mile, Scotland 55, and Ireland 146.</small>
<small>England contains about 73¼ millions of acres: its rents are rated at about 29 millions, but are, in reality, about 50. The stock on the land is estimated at 145 millions, the money in the country 50; the shipping 190; merchandise and manufactures 60; of the land 13 millions of acres are inclosed, 11 arable; 6¼ waste in England, 1¼ in Wales, 14¼ in Scotland. For eight millions of inhabitants, the country produces 11 ounces of wheat and 7½ of meat per day. Luckombe in 1793.</small>

Table of Heights.

Measured by Deluc, Shuckburgh, Roy, Bouguer, and others. In English feet, from the level of the sea.

The Caspian Sea, lower by	306
The Thames at Hampton, Roy	14⅓
The Tiber at Rome	33
The Seine at Paris, mean height	36½
The Thames, at Buckingham Stairs, 15½ feet below the pavement in the left hand arcade	43

<small>By barometrical comparison with the Seine and the Mediterranean, but this height is probably too great. Roy supposes the low water of the spring tides at Isleworth to be only one foot above the mean surface of the ocean. He allows 7 feet for the difference of the low water at the Nore and at Isleworth, taking 18 feet for the height of the spring tide, adds one third of this for the mean height of the sea. At Hampton the Thames is 13½ feet above low water mark at Isleworth.</small>

The pagoda in Kew gardens, from the ground	116½
The west end of the Tarpeian rock	151
The Palatine hill	166
The Claudian aqueduct, bottom of the canal	208
The Janiculum	293
The cross at St. Paul's, from the ground	340
St. Peter's, summit of the cross	535
From the ground 471	
Arthur's seat, from Leith pier head,	803
Lake of Geneva	1230
Its greatest depth 393	
Mount Vesuvius, base of the cone	2071
Saddleback	3048
Ben Lomond	3190
Skiddaw	3270
Halvellyn	3324
Chamouny, ground floor of the inn	3367
Cross fell	3390
Pendle	3411
Table Mount, Cape	3454
Schehallion	3461
Ben Gloe	3472
Snowdon	3555
Ben Muir	3723
Ben Lawers	3858
Pennygant	3930
Mount Vesuvius, mouth of the crater	3938
Ingleborough	3987
Whernside	4050
Ben Nevis	4350
Hecla	4887
Pic Ruivo, Madeira	5141
Summit of Mount Jura	5523
Summit of the Mole	6113
Mont Cenis, à la poste	6261
Pic de los Reyes, Pyrenees	7620
Monte Velino, Apennines	8397
City of Gondar, Abyssinia	8440
Canigou, Pyrenees	8544
Summit of Mount Cenis	9212
Pic du Midi, Pyrenees	9300
Quito	9377
Monte Viso	9907
Glacière de Buet	10124
Etna	10954
Pike of Teneriffe, Borda	11022
Pike of Teneriffe, old estimate	15084
Pic d'Ossano, Pyrenees	11700
Aiguille d'Argentière	13402
Ophir in Sumatra, Marsden	13842
Monte Rosa, Alps	15084
Summit of Mont Blanc	15402
Pichincha	15670
Antisana	19390
Chimborazo	19595

It may be observed with respect to General Roy's calculation of the mean height of the sea, that it does not appear that in rivers, or even in narrow seas, we ought to add one third of the height of the tides only to that of low water, in order to find the level; for it is probable that even the original tides may often resemble those of lakes, where, for want of breadths, the effects of a spheroidical tide cannot take place, and the elevation and depression are very nearly equal.

Observations of the Tides.

The tides are mentioned by Homer, Aristotle, Herodotus, Diodorus Siculus, Plutarch, and other ancient authors.

Hydrology. Ph. tr. abr. II. ii. 257. IV. pt. 2. ii. 183. VI. pt. ii. 163. VIII. pt. 2. ii. 641. X. pt. 2. ii. 567.

Moray on the tides in the Hebrides. Ph. tr. 1665-6. I. 53.

*Moray on observing the tides. Ph. tr. 1665-6. I. 298.

Proposes a pump barrel with a small hole in it, and a float, for measuring the height independently of the waves. Specimens of tide tables.

Moray on the tides about the Orcades. Ph. tr. 1673. VIII. 6139.

†Wallis on the tides. Ph. tr. 1665-6. 1. 263. 297.

Deducing the tides from the earth's centrifugal force in revolving round the common centre of gravity of the earth and moon.

Wallis on the tides. 1668. III. 652. Answer to Childrey. 1670. v. 2063.

Wallis on the junction of tides in the channel. Ph. tr. 1701. XXIII. 1022.

The southern tide extends as far as the Dogger Bank.

Norwood's account of the tides at Bermudas. Ph. tr. 1667. II. 565.

Colepresse's observations at Plymouth. Ph. tr. 1668. III. 632.

Philips on the tides. Ph. tr. 1668. III. 656.

Observes, that the monthly variations are as the versed sines of the times.

Stafford on the tides at the Bermudas. Ph. tr. 1668. III. 792.

Sturmy on the tides near Bristol. Ph. tr. 1668. III. 813.

Babin on the Euripus. Ph. tr. 1671. VI. 2153.
Found a variation of a foot.

Flamstead's tide table. Ph. tr. 1683. XIII. 10. 1684. XIV. 458, 821.
Continued in the following volumes.

Heathcote on the tides in Guinea. Ph. tr. 1684. XVI. 578.
On the 24 November, 1683, it was high water at Cabocors or Cape Coast, at half past 2 p. m. By Flamstead's tide table it was high water at London bridge, the same day, at 49 minutes after 2, whence we may take 8h. 30m. as the time of high water at the full moon.

*Davenport on the tides at Tonqueen. Ph. tr. 1684. XIV. 677.

Halley's theory of the tides at Tonqueen. Ph. tr. 1684. XIV. 685.

Molineux on the tides at Dublin. Ph. tr. 1686. XVI. 191.

Times of high water on the coast of France. Ph. tr. 1686. XVI. 220.

Newton de mundi systemate.

Richer on the tides at Cayenne. A. P. I. 116. VII. 1 part. ii. 88.

Richaud on the tides in Siam. A. P. VII. 2 part. iii. 162.

Cassini on tides. A. P. VIII. 171. 1710. 318, 366. H. 4. 1712. 86. H. 1. 1713. 14. H. 1.

On the manner of observing the tides. A. P. 1701. H. 12.

Gouyé on the tides at Calais, rising during the ebb. A. P. 1712. H. 23.

Hauterive on the tides at Martinique. A. P. 1724. H. 17.

*Jones and Saumarez on the tides in the Thames. Ph. tr. 1726. XXXIV. 68.

At Lambeth the spring tide rises 10 feet, and runs 2 feet in 1″ at 2 hours 30 minutes of the flood: it is highest at 2h 15′, and lowest at 2h 5′; it runs back for 2h 40′. At Shadwell, Jones observed a difference of 20 f. 5½ i. in the height.

Jones on a high tide. Ph. tr. 1736. XXXIX. 198.
It was 6½ i. higher than before.

Mackenzie on the tides in Orkney. Ph. tr. 1749. XLVI. 149.
The spring tides rise from 8 to 15 feet; the neap tides from 2 to 3½; running sometimes 9 miles in an hour. There are sometimes whirlpools with a cavity 2 or 3 feet deep, which swallow up small boats, but may be broken and filled up by throwing in an oar.

Wright on an irregular tide in the Forth. Ph. tr. 1750. XLVI. 412.
A "leaky," which is a temporary ebb interrupting the flowing tide.

La Caille on the tides at the Cape. A. P. 1751. 456. H. 158.

*Belidor. Arch. hydr. II. ii. 1. Tides in the Mediterranean. 16. Table for different ports. 24.

Wargentin on the tides. Schw. Abh. 1753. 165, 249. 1754. 83.

Adanson on the tides at Gorée. S. E. II. 605.

More on the tides in the straights. Ph. tr. 1762. 447.

Maskelyne on the tides at St. Helena. Ph. tr. 1762. 586.

Tucker on a tide at Bristol. Ph. tr. 1764. 83.

*Robertson's navigation.

Cook on the tides in the South Sea. Ph. tr. 1772. 357.
Observes, that the flood comes from the South or South East.

Cook. Ph. tr. 1776. 447.
In Lat. 15° 26′ S. off New Holland, 10 June, 1770, the evening tide was the higher by two feet and remained so for three successive spring tides: at the neaps there was no difference.

Lalande on the tides. A. P. 1772. i. 297. H. 1.
Lalande on the tides at Brest. A. P. 1789. 183.
Lalande Traité du flux et reflux. Astr. ed. 1.
Fourcroy de Ramecourt on the tides at Calais. A. P. 1772. i. 319.
Fourcroy de Ramecourt on the tides in Flanders. S. E. VIII. 1780. 577.
Legentil. A. P. 1773. 243. H. 8.
  The tides about Madagascar scarcely rise more than 3 feet.
Legentil on the tides of Normandy. A. P. 1782. 345. H. 15.
  Finds them greatest at the equinoxes.
Toaldo tabulae barometri aestusque maris. 4. Pav. 1773.
Toaldo on the tides in the Adriatic. Ph. tr. 1777. 144.
  At Venice the rise is from 1½ f. to 2½.
Deslandes Flux et reflux de la mer.
Brunelli on an inundation in South America. Roz. III. 436.
Blagden. Ph. tr. 1793. 168.
  A tide of a foot at Naples.
Baussard on the tides at Teneriffe. M. Inst. III. H. 33. Journ. Phys. XLVI. (III.) 351.
Robison. Enc. Br. Art. Tides.
Coquebert on the tides in high latitudes. B. Soc. Phil. n. 21.
Spallanzani on Scylla and Charybdis. Nich. II. 12. Gilb. V. 98.
Löwenorn on the tides on the northern coasts. Zach. Ephem. III. 121.
Balfour on the diurnal tides at Calcutta. As. Res. Ph. M. VII.
  There are seven tides at once in the river of Amazons.
  Robison recommends a float with a rod for observing the tides. He observes that the flood comes into the Severn in a head ten feet high.

Navigation.

See Seamanship, Tides, Situations of Places, Currents, Winds.

Nunnez de arte navigandi. 1573.
Norwood's seaman's practice. Lond. 1636. M. B.
  Contains an account of his measurement of a degree.
Ph. tr. abr. I. vii. 546. IV. vi. 449. VI. vii. 363. VIII. vii. 324. X. vi. 250.
Mercator's problems in navigation. Ph. tr. 1665-6. I. 215.
Instructions for the use of pendulum watches at sea. Ph. tr. 1669. IV. 937.
Cassini on the use of astronomy in navigation. A. P. VIII. 1.
Duillier's navigation improved. 1728.
Maupertuis on a loxodromic circle on the surface of the sea. A. P. 1744. 462.
Maupertuis Astronomie nautique.
Douwes Haarl. Verh. 1754. I.
Bernoulli on finding the time at sea. A. P. Prix. VI. i.
Bouguer Traité de navigation, par Lacaille. M. B.
Emerson's cyclomathesis. IX.
Emerson's navigation. 12.
Lemonnier Astronomie nautique. 8. Par. 1771.
  Acc. A. P. 1773. H. 95.
Lemonnier Questions dans la navigation. 8. Par. 1772.
*Juan Examen maritimo. 2 v. 4. Madr. 1771. French, Par. 1783.
Bézout Cours de mathématiques.
Levêque Guide du navigateur.
Röding Wörterbuch der marine.
Borda on the operations on board the Flora. A. P. 1773. 258. H. 64.
Pézénas Astronomie des marins.

Murdoch's Mercator's sailing. 4.

**Robertson's* elements of navigation, by Wales. 2 vols. 8. Lond. R. I.

Maskelyne's British mariner's guide.

Nautical almanac, with appendices. 8. Lond.

Tables to be used with the nautical almanac. 8. Lond. 1802. B. B.

Bode Jahrbücher.

Schubert on the loxodromic curve. N. A. Petr. 1786. IV. H. 95.

Bettesworth's naval mathematics. 8.

**Kelly's* spherics and nautical astronomy. Lond.

Moore's seaman's daily assistant. 8. 1785. R. I.

Moore's practical navigator. 8. 1796. R. I.

Nicholson's navigator's assistant. 8.

Mendoza y Rios Tratado de la navegacion. 2 v. 4. Madr. 1787. B. B.

Mendoza y Rios sur les principaux problemes de l'astronomie nautique. Ph. tr. 1797. 43.

Mendoza y Rios's tables for nautical calculations. 4. Lond. 1801. B. B.

Mendoza's new tables. 4. Lond. 1805.

Caluso on navigation upon a spheroid. M. Taur. 1788. IV. 325. 1790. V. 100.

Schubert on navigation upon a spheroid. N. A. Petr. 1790. VIII. 140.

Lalande Abregé de navigation. 4. Par. 1793. Acc. Roz. XLIII. 218.

Mackay, Enc. Br. Art. Navigation.

Mackay's navigation. 2 v. 8. Lond.

South's marine atlas. f. M. S. R. I.

Rochon on nautical astronomy. Journ. Phys. XLVII. (IV.) 85.

Cooke's instrument for calculations in navigation. Ir. tr. Repert. IV. 38.

Instruments for navigation. Montucla and Lal. IV. 509.

Collections of Observations and Tables.

Lalande on the use of interpolations in practical astronomy. A. P. 1761. 125. H. 92.

Lagrange on forming tables from observation only. A. P. 1772. i. 513. H. 83.

Observations made in Cook's voyage. 4. Lond. 1782. R. S.

Bugge Observationes astronomicae. 4 Copenh. 1784. R. S.

**Bradley's* observations. 2 vols. f. Oxf. 1798, 1805. R. S.

Corrections.

Tables for correcting refraction and parallax. 4. R. I.

Elements and Epochs.

See fixed Stars.

Mercator on Cassini's determination of the apogee. Ph. tr. 1670. V. 1168.

Messier. A. P. 1774. 93.

<small>Saturn's ring 3 leagues thick or less: exterior diameter 66737 leagues: breadth 9534.</small>

Burckhardt's elements of Pallas. Ph. M. XIII. 91.

<small>Distance 21 to 35. That of Ceres 27 to 28.

Sun. Short makes the sun's apparent diameter 31′ 28″ to 32′ 33″: mean 32′ 1/4″.

The radius of a sphere equal to the earth is 6369374 metres. Laplace. That is 6965800 yards, the diameter 7915.69 miles. Lalande says, 3268159 toises, that is 6966338 yards, which is the radius at 52° 1/4 latitude.</small>

ELEMENTS OF THE SOLAR SYSTEM.

The sun, ☉, revolves on his axis in 25d. 10h. The inclination of his equator is 7° 20″. The place of its ascending node, ☊, 2s 18°, or 78° from the equinoctial point Aries. His diameter is 883,000 English miles, and his density, to that of the earth, as .255 to 1. His mean apparent diameter is 31′ 57″; his mean parallax 8″.75.

	Mercury ☿	Venus ♀	Earth ⊖	Mars ♂	Juno ⚵	Pallas ⚴	Ceres ⚳	Jupiter ♃	Saturn ♄	Georgian planet ♅
	1801. Jan. 1.				1805. Jan. 1.			1801. Jan. 1.		
INCLINATION OF THE ORBIT.	7°	3° 24′		1° 51′	13° 4′	34° 38′	10° 38′	1° 19′	2° 30′	46′
PLACE OF THE ASCENDING NODE.	1s 15° 58′	2s 14° 58′		1s 18° 2′	5s 21° 4′	5s 22° 31′	2s 21° 7′	3s 8° 25′	3s 21° 57′	2s 12° 51′
MEAN DISTANCE.	3871	7233	10000	15237	26640	27650	27670	52028	95497	191836
ECCENTRICITY.	795	50	168	1418	6770	6800	2170	2501	5364	8956
MEAN DISTANCE IN MILLIONS OF MILES.	37	68	95	144	253	263	263	490	900	1800
PLACE OF THE APHELION.	8s 14° 22′	10s 8° 37′	9s 9° 30′	5s 2° 25′	7s 23° 11′	10s 1° 3′	10s 22°	6s 11° 9′	8s 29° 5′	11s 17° 21′
MEAN PLACE OF THE PLANET.	5s 11° 54′	0s 9° 57′	3s 9° 40′	2s 3° 51′	1s 12° 33′	18° 13′	1s 0° 12′	3s 22° 9′	4s 15° 18′	5s 27° 47′
MOTION OF THE NODE IN LONGITUDE IN 100 YEARS.	1° 12′	52″		47′				1°	53′	26′
MOTION OF THE APHELION IN LONGITUDE IN 100 YEARS.	1° 34′	1° 21′	1° 44′	1° 52′				1° 35′	1° 50′	1° 28′
TROPICAL REVOLUTION.	87d 23h 14′ 33″	224d 16h 41′ 27″	1y 5h 48′ 48″	1y 321d 22h 18′.5	4y 128d	4y 219d	4y 221d	11y 315d 14h 39′	29y 161d 19h 16′	83y 294d 8h 39′
SIDEREAL REVOLUTION.	87d 23h 15′ 44″	224d 16h 49′ 11″	1y 6h 9′ 8″	1y 321d 23h 30′.6				11y 317d 14h 27′	29y 174d 1h 51′	84y 29d 29′
DIAMETER IN MILES.	3180	7600	7916	4120				86000	79000	34200
DIURNAL ROTATION.		23h 21′	23h 56′ 4″	24h 39′ 21″				9h 51′	10h 16′	
PROPORTION OF DIAMETERS.			300:301	15:16				12:13	10:11	
MASS, THAT OF THE SUN BEING UNITY.	1/[illegible]	1/[illegible]	1/[illegible]					1/1067	1/3359	1/19504
DENSITY.			1000					258	104	220
MEAN APPARENT DIAMETER.		16½		9″				40″	18″	4″

The obliquity of the earth's equator to the ecliptic is 23° 28'; its secular diminution 50"; its periodical change in a revolution of the moon's nodes, 9" each way; the annual precession of the equinoxes is 50.25"; the greatest apparent change of place of the stars from the aberration of light, 20" each way.

The mean inclination of the orbit of the moon, ☽, is 5° 9'; the place of the ascending node 13° 56'; the mean distance 240000 miles; the eccentricity 13700 miles; the place of the apogee 2s 26° 7'; the moon's place 3s 15° 2'; the diurnal motion of the node 3' 10", its tropical revolution 18y 228d 4h 52' 52", its sidereal revolution 18y 223d 7h 13' 17"; the tropical revolution of the apogee 8y 311d 2h 34' 57"; its sidereal revolution 8y 312d 11h 11'; the moon's tropical revolution 27d 7h 43' 5"; her synodical revolution with respect to ☉, 29d 12h 44' 3"; her diameter 2163 miles; her mass $\frac{1}{70}$ of the earth's; her density .742; her apparent diameter 29' 22" to 33' 34"; her horizontal parallax 53' 46" to 61' 26"; at the mean distance 57' 1". 1 Jan. 1801.

The sidereal periods of the satellites, and their distances in semidiameters of the planets are, Jupiter's I. 1d 18h 27' 33". D. 5.67. II. 3d 13h 13' 42". D. 9. III. 7d 3h 42' 33". D. 14.38. IV. 16d 15h 32' 8". D. 25.3. The third, which is the largest, is about the size of the moon. Saturn's Ring 10h 32' 15". D. 2.33. I. or VII. 22h 37' 23". D. 3.7. II. or VI. 1d 8h 53' 8". D. 4.2. III. or I. 1d 21h 18' 26". D. 4.9. IV. or II. 2d 17h 44' 51". D. 6.3. V. or III. 4d 12h 25' 11". D. 8.75. VI. or IV. 15d 22h 41' 16". D. 20.3. VII. or V. 79d 7h 53' 43". D. 59.15. The longitude of the nodes of the ring 5s 17° 13', retreating about 25° in a century. The Georgian planet's I. 5d. D. 12.7. II. 8d. D. 16.5. III. 10d. D. 19.5. IV. 13.5d. D. 22. V. 38d. D. 44. VI. 108d. D. 88.

Tables of places of the Heavenly Bodies.

Kepleri tabulae Rudolphinae. f. Ulm, 1627.

*Connaissance des temps. 8. Paris. 1679...

Flamsteed's circle for finding the place of Jupiter's satellites. Ph. tr. 1685. XV. 1262.

Lahire Tabulae astronomicae. 4. Paris. Acc. Ph. tr. 1686. XVII. 443.

Wood's almanac. Hooke Ph. coll. ii. 26.

Halley on Albategni's tables. Ph. tr. 1693. XVII. 913.

Pound's tables of Jupiter's satellites. Ph. tr. 1718. XXX. 776. 1719. XXX. 1021.

Wargentin tabulae satellitium Jovis. Act. Upsal, 1741. 27.

Mayer's solar and lunar tables. C. Gott. 1752. II. 383.

Mayer tabulae motuum solis et lunae. 4. London, 1770. R. S.

Mayer's lunar tables. 4. Lond. 1787. R. S.

Ephemerides astromonicae. 8. Vienna, 1757...

Lacaille tabulae solares. 4. Paris, 1758. By Hell. 8. Vienn. 1763.

Elements of new tables of Jupiter's satellites. Ph. tr. 1761. 105.

Hell tabulae lunares. 8. Vienn. 1763.

Euleri novae tabulae lunares. 8. Petersb. R. S.

A. P. Index. Art. Tables.

*Nautical almanac. 8. Lond.

Bailly on the satellites of Jupiter. Ph. tr. 1773. 185.

Bode Astronomisches Jahrbuch. 8. Berlin, 1776... R. S.

Recueil de tables astronomiques. 8. Berlin. R. S.

Englefield's tables of the expected comet. 4. Lond. 1788. R. S.

Laplace et Delambre Tables de Jupiter et de Saturne. 4. Paris, 1789. R. S.

Zach Tabulae motuum solis. 4. Goth. 1792. Supplementa, 1794...

Von Zach on the place of Ceres. Ph. M. XII. 360.

Report on Burg's lunar tables. Ph. M. XIII. 183.
_{Greatest error about 12".}

Ephemeris of the new planets for 1803. Ph. M. XV. 190.

Projections, Charts, Globes, Orreries, and other Instruments, illustrative of Astronomy and Geography.

See Astronomical Instruments, Navigation.

*Hugenii descriptio automati planetarii. Opp. rel. II. 175.

Wallis on the construction of sea charts. Ph. tr. 1685. XV. 1193.
<small>Also on the figure of secants.</small>

Halley on the meridional parts, or the sum of the secants. Ph. tr. XIX. 1696. 202.

Roemer's planisphere. Mach. A. I. 81.

Roemer's planisphere for eclipses. Mach. A. I. 85.

Roemer's wheel for unequal motion. Mach. A. I. 89. Nich. IV. 404.

Cassini's planisphere. Mach. A. I. 133.

Cassini's globe to show the precession of the equinoxes. A. P. 1708. H. 93.

Allemand's celestial globe. Mach. A. I. 157.

Chazelles on hydrographical charts. A. P. 1702. 150. H. 86.

Lagny on reduced maps. A. P. 1703. 95. H. 92.

Chevalier on taking a map by amplitudes. A. P. 1707. H. 113.

Perks on the meridional line. Ph. tr. 1715. XXIX. 331.

Hasius de projectionibus sphaerarum. 4. Leipz. 1717.

Meynier's sphere of paper. A. P. 1723. H. 121. Mach. A. IV. 55.

Meynier's clock, showing the solar motion. A. P. 1723. H. 122. Mach. A. IV. 59.

Meyer's planisphere. Mach. A. IV. 61.

Desagulier's experiment illustrative of the form of the earth. Ph. tr. 1725. XXXIII. 344.

Brouckner's globe of copper. A. P. 1725. H. 103. Mach. A. IV. 143.

Outhier's celestial automaton. A. P. 1727. H. 143. Mach. A. 15, 19, 21.

Mauny's sphere. Mach. A. VI. 89.

Graham's globular instrument for computing latitudes. Ph. tr. 1734. XXXVIII. 450.

Colson on spherical maps, or segments of globes. Ph. tr. 1736. XXXIX. 204.

Latham and Senex on making the poles of the celestial globe revolve. Ph. tr. 1738. XL. 201. 1741. XLI. 730.

Harris's improvement on the terestrial globe. Ph. tr. 1740. XLI. 321.
<small>Placing the horary circle under the meridian.</small>

Segneri machina ad eclipses repraesentandas. Ph. tr. 1741. XLI. 781.

Maclaurin on the meridional parts of a spheroid. Ph. tr. 1741. XLI. 808.

Richmann on maps. C. Petr. XIII. 300.

Maupertuis on a loxodromic circle on the surface of the sea. A. P. 1744. 462.

Ferguson's orrery for the phenomena of Venus. Ph. tr. 1746. XLIV. 127.

Ferguson's improvement of the globe. Ph. tr. 1747. XLIV. 535.
<small>By marks for the sun and moon.</small>

Ferguson's mechanical illustration of eclipses. Ph. tr. 1751. 520.

Ferguson's orreries. Mach. exerc. 72.

Sur la construction des grands globes. f. Nuremberg, 1746.

Mrs. Senex on Senex's globes for showing the precession. Ph. tr. 1749. XLVI. 290.

Passement's moving sphere. A. P. 1749. H. 183.

Lowitz sur les grands globes. 4. Nuremb. 1749. 1753.

Robertson's explanation of Halley on the analogy of the logarithmic tangents and the meridional line. Ph. tr. 1750. XLVI. 559.

Murdoch on the best form of maps. Ph. tr. 1758. 553.

Mountaine on maps and charts. Ph. tr. 1758. 563.

Dunn and Mountaine's defence of Mercator against West. Ph. tr. 1763. 66, 69.

Chabert on forming charts. A. P. 1759. 484. H. 127. 1766. 384.

Projections of the sphere. Emers. cyclom. VII.

King's electrical orrery. Ferg. Mech. exerc. 132.

Castel's moving sphere. A. P. 1766. H. 162.

Kästner on stereographical projections. N. C. Gott. 1769. I, 138. Diss. phys. 88.

Lowitz and Kästner on covering globes. Commentat. Gott. 1778. I. M. 1. Append.
The common way.

Kästner on celestial maps. Zach. Eph. II. 401.

Bertier's globes serving for dials. A. P. 1770. H. 117.

Rittenhouse's orrery. Am. tr. I. 1.

Euler on projections for maps. A. Petr. 1. i. 107.

Euler on covering globes. A. Petr. II. i. 3.
By 12 pentagons inscribed in a circle having its radius .61961r, with segments of circles, of which the radius is 3.4841r.

Jeaurat's asterometer, for showing the rising and setting of a given object. A. P. 1779. 502. H. 37.

Castillon on a moving globe. A. Berl. 1779. 301.

Van Swinden's planetarium. Roz. XVI. 456.

Globes. E. M. A. III. Art. Globes.

Stereographical projection. E. M. Pl. V. Marine 27.

Ducaila Expression des nivellemens. 1782. Acc. Zach. Mon. corr. II. 148.
By marking out horizontal lines at different heights on a map.

Fuss on the stereographic projection. A. Petr. 1782. VI. ii. 170.
Shows that the projections of all circles are circles.

Harrison on the Globes. 8. 1783. R. I.

Grenet's new spheres. Roz. XXIV. 319.

Schubert on the projection of a sphere on a cone. N. A. Petr. 1784. II. 84.

Schubert on the projection of a spheroid. N. A. Petr. 1787. V. 130. 1788. VI. 123. 1789. VII. 149.

Mackay. Enc. Br. Art. Projection.

Cannebier's geocyclic machine. Roz. XXVII. 192.

Klügel Geometrische entwickelung der stereographischen projection. 8. Berl. 1788.

Smeaton's improvement in the quadrant of altitude. Ph. tr. 1789. 1.
Made more solid and accurate.

Lorgna on maps. Soc. Ital. V. 8.
Lorgna proposes that circles be drawn with their radii equal to the chords, from a given point, so that the areas may every where be true. B. Soc. Phil. n. 29.

Mayer über charten und kugeln. 18. Erlang. 1794.
Acc. Hind. Arch. I. 236.

Pearson's satellitian instrument. Nich. II. 122.

Forster's instrument for placing globes by the sun. Ph. M. XII. 83.

Alison's globe timepiece. Am. tr. V. 82.

Alison's pendent planetarium. Am. tr. V. 87. Repert. ii. III. 331.
The balls hanging by threads.

Pattrick on an improved armillary sphere, and on the patent nautical angle. Nich. 8. V. 143.

Delambre on the stereographic projection. M. Inst. V. 393.

Shows, that all the circles intersect each other in the same angles as those which they represent. After Ptolemy.

A planisphere. R. I.

Equation clocks. See Astronomical Time.

Mr. Arrowsmith generally employs for his maps a globular projection, in which the meridians and parallels are portions of circles, cutting the circumference and diameters of the projection at equal distances; they appear also to cut each other into equal portions, so that the distortion principally arises from their not being perpendicular to each other near the poles, besides the inequality of the scale in different parts, which is perhaps nearly as small as possible.

History of Astronomy and Geography.

Ph. tr. 1665-6. I. 3.

Hooke found in 1664 that Jupiter revolved in about 8 hours.

Cassini on the rotation of Venus. A. P. X. 324.

Observed in 1667.

Ph. tr. 1725.

Newton thinks that the constellations were arranged by Chiron when the solstitial and equinoctial points were in the middle of the respective constellations.

Mairan. A. P. 1727. 63. H. 117.

Alexandre and Baliani thought the earth turned round the moon.

Molières on vortices. A P. 1729. 235. H. 87.

Against Newton.

Frisch on astronomical characters. M. Berl. 1729.

Latham on the antient sphere. Ph. tr. 1741. XLI. 730. 1742. XLII. 221.

Costard on the Chinese chronology and astronomy. Ph. tr. 1747. XLIV. 476.

Against its antiquity.

Costard's history of astronomy. 4. 1767. R. I.

Bailly Histoire de l'astronomie. 4 v. 4. Par. 1781. R. I.

Acc. A. P. 1775. H. 44.

Bailly Traité de l'astronomie Indienne. 4. Par. 1787. R. I.

Raper and Lalande on Norwood's measurement. Ph. tr. 1761. 566, 369.

Hassencamp Geschichte der bemühungen die meereslänge zu finden. 8. Rinteln. 1774.

Lalande on Herschel's planet. A. P. 1779. 520. H. 31.

Legentil on the origin of the zodiac. A. P. 1782. 368. H. 51.

Legentil on the antiquity of the constellations. A. P. 1789. 506.

Herschel on his Georgium sidus. Ph. tr. 1783. 1.

Wall on astronomical symbols. Manch. M. I. 243.

Derives ☿ from the caduceus, ♀ from the sistrum, ♂ from the shield and spear, ♃ from Jr, ♄ from the sickle. Frisch deduces ♃ from lightning with the eagle.

Blair's history of geography. 12. Lond. 1784.

Otto on the discovery of America. Am. tr. II. 263. Nich. I. 73.

Zach on Harriot's observations of the solar spots. Bode Jahrb. 1788.

On the knowledge of the earth's motion. *Eberhard* Neue vermischte schriften. 8. Halle, 1788. 67.

Playfair on the astronomy of the Brahmins. Ed. tr. II. 135.

Supposes some observations 5000 years old.

Davis on the astronomy of the Hindoos. As. res. II. 225.

Davis on the Indian cycle of 60 years. As. res. III. 209.

Jones on the Indian zodiac. As. res. II. 289.

Jones on the lunar year of the Hindoos. As. res. III. 257.

Cavendish on the civil year of the Hindoos. Ph. tr. 1792. 383.

Lalande's history of astronomy for 1795 and 1796. Journ. Phys. XLV. (II.) 325.

Lalande Histoire céleste.

Modern Greek tetrastich on Lalande. Zach. Eph. III.

Bentley on the antiquity of the Hindoo astronomy. As. res. VI. 537.
> Makes the principal tables, the Surya Siddhanta, about 781 years old.

Piazzi's planet. Ph. M. X. 285.

Note on the antiquity of the earth. Ph. M. XI. 286.

Piazzi on the new star. Ph. M. XII. 54.

Deluc on the zodiacs found in Egypt. Ph. M. XIII. 371.

Henley on the zodiac at Dendera. Ph. M. XIV. 107.

History of astronomy, geography, and navigation. Montucl. and Lal. IV.

Small's history of the discoveries of Kepler. 1803. R. I.

Account of Gail's memoir on Synesius's astrolabe. M. Inst. V. 34.
> Maps are attributed to Anaximander, 600 A. C.
> According to Plutarch, Heraclides and Ecphantus attributed to the earth a diurnal motion only.
> Astronomy was introduced into Spain by the Moors, 1201.
> The Mexicans, when discovered by the Spaniards, had years of 365 days, and added 13 days at the end of 52 years. Robison.

PROPERTIES OF MATTER IN GENERAL.

> The opinions of the ancients are found in Aristotle and Plato.

Descartes Princ. phil. II. x.
> On a vacuum.

Boyle on the principles of natural bodies.

*Hooke's lectures of spring. L. C. 1678.
> A curious theory of vibrations.

Bernoulli de gravitate aetheris. 12. Amst. 1683. Op. I. 45.

Bernoulli Nouvelle physique céleste. A. P. Prix. III. i.

Newtoni Principia. L. 2.
> On a vacuum.

Newton's Optics.
> Queries at the end.

Desaguliers's experiment to prove a vacuum. Ph. tr. 1717. XXX. 717.

Woodward's natural history of the earth.

Mazières on the vortices of the subtle matter. A. P. Pr. I. vi.

Holdsworth and Aldridge's short hand.
> Contains a hypothesis resembling that of Le Sage.

Musschenbroek Elem. Phys. §. 61, 83, 383.

Musschenbroek Introductio. I. iii.
> Of a vacuum.

On the cause of gravity. M. Berl. 1743. VII. 360.

Maupertuis on laws of nature supposed incompatible. A. P. 1744. 417. H. 53.
> On Fermat and Leibnitz's minimum.

On atoms. A. Berl. 1745. H. 28.

Eller on elements. A. Berl. 1746. 1, 25. 1748. 3.

Keill's introduction to natural philosophy. Lect. viii.

Cadwallader Colden on the primary cause acting on matter. 1745. M. B.

Euler de resistentia aetheris. Opuscul. I. 245.

Euler on the origin of forces. A. Berl. 1750. 418.

Knight on attraction and repulsion. 4. London, 1748. R. I.

Bossut sur la resistance de l'éther. 4. Charleville, 1766.

Chambers's cyclopaedia. Art. Element.

Hiotzeberg on the cause of attraction. Roz. Intr. I. 527.

On union. Roz. II. 173.

Comus on motion, and on the elements of matter. Roz. VI. 420. VII. 162.

Higgins on light.

Lamétherie on the elements. Roz. XVIII. 224.

Lamétherie on the Kantian system of forces. Journ. Phys. XLVII. (IV.) 383. Ph. M. II. 277.

Le Sage Lucrèce Newtonien. A. Berl. 1782. 404.
<small>In favour of the impulse of atoms.</small>

L'huilier Exposition des principes des calculs. 4. Berl. 1786. 187.

Deluc Idées sur la météorologie.

Wall on attraction and repulsion. Manch. M. II. 439.
<small>In most cases considers apparent repulsion as elective attraction.</small>

Hutton's mathematical dictionary. Art. Element.

Sellé on elements. A. Berl. 1796. ii. 42.

Gilbert on attraction. Gilb. II. 63.

Les causes matérielles de l'attraction dévoilées. 12. Lond. 1801.

Cavallo's natural philosophy.

Divisibility of Matter.

Boyle on effluvia.

Halley on the thickness of gold on wire. Ph. tr. 1693. XVII. 540.
<small>Calculates that it is $\frac{1}{112000}$ of an inch.</small>

Réaumur on ductility. A. P. 1713. 199. H. 9.

Keill de materiae divisibilitate infinita. Ph. tr. 1714. XXIX. 82.

Keill's natural philosophy.

Rohault's physics.

S'Gravesande's natural philosophy.

Musschenbroek Introductio.

Hutton's recreations. IV. 80.

Nicholson. Ph. tr. 1789. 286.
<small>Gold leaf is about $\frac{1}{78000}$ of an inch thick.</small>

Ph. M. IX.

In gilding buttons 5 grains of gold are allotted by act of parliament to 144 buttons; but they may be tolerably gilt by half the quantity. The thickness in this case would be about $\frac{1}{112000}$ of an inch.

Musschenbroek says, that a workman of Augsburg drew a grain of gold into a wire 500 feet long. Its diameter must have been only $\frac{1}{750}$ of an inch. Of a silkworm's thread 360 feet weigh a grain; of a spider's web only $\frac{1}{35}$ as much, consequently 12600 feet weigh only a grain.

In drawing gilt wire, 45 marcs or $22\frac{1}{2}$ pounds of silver are covered to the thickness of $\frac{1}{115}$ of an inch with 6 ounces of gold: but one ounce is sufficient for the purpose: this is drawn into a wire 96 leagues long, and when flattened it becomes 110 leagues: the gold is then $\frac{1}{720000}$ of an inch thick; if one ounce only has been used, $\frac{1}{2200000}$; and probably in some parts $\frac{1}{3300000}$: this may still be flattened again and reduced to the thickness of $\frac{1}{8200000}$ of an inch in all parts, and in some to still less, not exceeding one ten millionth. Montucla and Hutton. A sphere of this thickness would contain about one two thousand million million millionth of an inch.

Repulsion, or Impenetrability.

See Collision.

Hooke on the compression of glass. Birch. I. 129.

Hooke's Lectures of spring. L. C. 1678.
<small>With fundamental experiments.</small>

On the compressibility of water. A. P. I. 139.

Varignon on hardness A. P. II. 70. X. 49.

Homberg on the change of volume of liquids in a vacuum. A. P. II. 183.

Hauksbee on the degree of contact of a body immersed in a fluid. Ph. tr. 1709. XXVI. 306.
<small>Finds that it is very intimate.</small>

Euler on pneumatics. C. Petr. II. 347.

Euler on the nature of the air. A. Petr. III. i. 162.
<small>Supposes molecules of air to revolve within vesicles of water more rapidly as the temperature is higher.</small>

Euler. A. Petr. 1779. i.

Desaguliers on the cause of elasticity. Ph. tr. 1739. XLI. 175.

Molières on elasticity. A. P. 1726. 7. H. 53.

Hausen programmata de reactione. Leipz. 1740, 1741.

Lomonosow on the elasticity of the air. N. C. Petr. I. 230, 305.
_{Derives it from heat or gyration only.}

Richmann on the force of water in freezing. N. C. Petr. I. 276.
_{Remarks on Hales's experiments, in which air is said to have been reduced to $\frac{1}{1717}$ of its bulk. Richmann doubts the accuracy of the estimate, but the force of the ice must have been equal to 1435 atmospheres, if not to 2871.}

Nollet on a glass vessel appearing to be filled by its pores. A. P. 1749. 460. H. 15.

Zanotti on elasticity. C. Bon. IV. O. 233.

Cossigny on the supposed penetration of glass by water. S. E. III. 1.

Hollmannus de experimento Florentino. Sylloge. 34.

Canton on the compressibility of water. Ph. tr. 1762. 640. 1764. 261.

Herbert de aquae elasticitate. 8. Vienn. 1774.

Zimmermann Traité de l'élasticité de l'eau et d'autres fluides. 8. Leipz. 1779. R. S.

Mongez on the compressibility of fluids. Roz. XI. 1.

J. Bernoulli on elasticity. Roz. XXI. 463.

Deluc on expansible fluids. Roz. XLIII. 20.

Barruel on elasticity. Extr. Journ. Phys. XLIX. 251. Ann. Ch. XXXIII. 100. Journ. polyt. IV. xi. 295. Ph. M. VI. 51.

Libes on elasticity. Journ. Phys. XLIX. 413. Ann. Ch. XXXIII. 110.

Dalton's theory of gases. See Meteorology.
_{Emerson says, that springs are weakened by use, but recover their strength when laid by.}

Inertia.

Hausen programmata de reactione.

Euler. Ac. Berl. 1750. 428.

Kratzenstein amolitio vis inertiae et vis repulsivae. 8. Hanov. 1770.

Franklin's miscellanies. 4. Lond. 1779. 479.

Kaestner Anfangsgründe. I. xxi. III. 125, 129. Diss. math. x. 75.

Nature of Gravitation.

See Properties of Matter in general.

On the space described by falling bodies. A. P. I. 49.

Varignon on weight. A. P. I. 63. II. 45.

Huygens on the cause of gravity. Op. rel. I. 93.

Keill de legibus attractionis. Ph. tr. 1708. XXVI. 97.

Saurin on the Cartesian system of weight. A. P. 1709. 131. 1718. 191. H. 7.

Hambergerus de experimento Hugenii. 4. Jen. 1723.

Hamberger on the direction of bodies in a vortex. Com. Petr. I. 245.

Mazières on ethereal vortices. A. P. Pr. I. vi.

Bulfinger on motion in a vortex. C. Petr. IV. 144.

Bulfinger's experiment on the physical cause of gravity. A. P. Pr. II. iii.

Nollet on the motion of fluids within a sphere. A. P. 1741. 184.

Kratzenstein's spring steelyard for measuring gravity. N. C. Petr. II. 210.

Berthier on terrestrial attraction and repulsion. A. P. 1751. H. 38.

Berthier's comparison of attraction with ethereal impulse. A. P. 1764. H. 148.

Van Swinden de attractione. 4. Leyd. 1766.

Hollmann on attraction. Comm. Gott. IV. 215.

Churcol Attractio ad impulsionem revocata. 4. R. S.

Thoughts on general gravitation. London, 1777.

E. M. Physique. Art. Attraction.

Bergmann on universal attraction. Opusc. VI. 38.

Deluc on gravity. Roz. XLII. 88.

Cohesion in general.

Leibnitii theoria motus. 12. Lond. 1671.
  Acc. Ph. tr. 1671. VI. 2213.
  Deriving cohesion from motion.

Desaguliers's experiment on the cohesion of lead. Ph. tr. 1725. XXXIII. 345.
  A circle of contact, about one tenth of an inch in diameter, supported more than 40 pounds.

Triewald's queries respecting cohesion. Ph. tr. 1729. XXXVI. 39.

Hambergerus et Suessmilch de cohaesione et attractione. 4. Jena, 1732.

Hamberger Naturlehre. Vorrede.

Winkler de causis conjunctionis. 4. Leipz. 1736.

Felice de attractione cohaerentiae causa. 4. 1757.

Deluc on cohesion and on affinities. Roz. XLII. 218.

†Libes on molecular attraction. Journ. Phys. LIV. 391.
  Referred to gravitation.

Ritter on cohesion. Gilb. IV. 1.
  Thinks the cohesive force is as the capacity for heat and the distance from the point of fusion conjointly.

†Benzenberg on cohesion. Gilb. XVI. 76.
  From gravitation, a blunder.
  Robison says, that the strength of gold is tripled by drawing it into wire.
  Physiol. disquis. Adams's lect. I.
  Jones deduces cohesion from the pressure of caloric.

Cohesion and Capillary Action of Fluids.

Fabri Dialogi physici. 8. Lyons, 1669.
  Acc. Ph. tr. 1670. V. 2058.

Wallis on the suspension of quicksilver at a great height. De motu. xiv. Ph. tr. 1672. VII. 5160.

Huygens on the suspension of quicksilver at 75 inches, and on the siphon running in a vacuum. Ph. tr. 1672. VII. 5027.

*Boyle on the figure of fluids. Ph. tr. 1676. XI. 775.
  On the common surface of different combinations of fluids, sometimes concave, sometimes convex.

Hooke and Papin on the suspension of mercury and of water in a vacuum. Birch. IV. 300, 301, 307.

Lahire on the contraction of moist ropes. A. P. IX. 157.

Carré on capillary tubes. A. P. 1705. 241. H. 21.

Hauksbee on the effect of capillary tubes remaining in a vacuum. Ph. tr. 1706. XXV. 2223.
  A capillary siphon must have one leg at least as much longer than the other as the length appropriate to its bore, in order to run.

Hauksbee on the ascent of water. Ph. tr. 1709. XXVI. 258.

Hauksbee on the motion of a drop between two plates. Ph. tr. 1711. XXVII. 395.

Hauksbee on the force of attraction of two plates. Ph. tr. 1712. XXVII. 413.
  Measured by the angular elevation at which a drop of oil was held in equilibrium. The force appears to be nearly as the square of the distance inversely. Newton mentions the same law in his queries. At 18 inches from the line of contact the elevation was 15', at 16, 25', at 8, 1° 45', at 4, 6°, at 2, 22°.

Hauksbee on the ascent of water between two plates. Ph. tr. 1712. XXVII. 539.

Hauksbee on the ascent of fluids. Ph. tr. 1713. XXVIII. 151.

The height of spirit of wine was exactly in the inverse ratio of the distance of the plates. When the line of contact of the plates was parallel to the surface of the water, the fluid contained between them bent inwards as the plates were raised, half way between the line of contact and the surface. This curvature may be considered as the vertex of a hyperbola, and the circumstance will be explained. The force of attraction of a drop of spirit was observed more accurately than that of the oil; the inclination of the plates being 18′, at $19\frac{1}{2}$ inches, the elevation was 45′, at $9\frac{1}{2}$, 1° 46′, at $4\frac{1}{2}$, 6°, at $2\frac{1}{2}$, 15°, the inclination being 10′, the distance $19\frac{1}{2}$, the elevation was 1° 30′, at $9\frac{1}{2}$, 3° 36′, at $4\frac{1}{2}$, 14°.

Taylor on the ascent of water between two glass plates. Ph. tr. 1712. XXVII. 538.
The curve is very nearly a hyperbola.

Taylor on the attraction of wood to water. Ph. tr. 1721. XXXI. 204.
An inch square required 50 grains to raise it; the weight was always directly as the surface: the elevation 16 hundredths of an inch, or perhaps more.

Homberg on a capillary siphon running in a vacuum. A. P. 1714. H. 84.

Jurin on capillary tubes. Ph. tr. 1718. XXX. 739.
Denies Hauksbee's remark on a capillary siphon. But both may be right in different circumstances.

Jurin on the action of glass tubes on water and quicksilver. Ph. tr. 1719. XXX. 1083.
Suggests, after Huygens, the pressure of a medium.

Jurin's essay in Cotes's lectures.

Ditton's discourse on the new law of fluids.

Petit's new hypothesis. A. P. 1724. 94. H. 1.

†Petit on the adhesion of the particles of air. A. P. 1731. 50. H. 1.

Bülfinger on capillary tubes. C. Petr. II. 233. III. 281.
With Jurin's experiments.

*Musschenbroek de tubis vitreis. Diss. phys. 271. De speculis, 334.

Weitbrecht on capillary tubes. C. Petr. VIII. 261. IX. 275.

Gellert on lead melted in capillary tubes. C. Petr. XII. 293. " 243."
The appearances resemble those of mercury.

Gellert on prismatic capillary tubes. C. Petr. XII. 302.
Thinks that the height is inversely as the square root of the area.

Lemonnier on fluidity. A. P. 1741. H. 11.

Hollmann on the difference of barometers. C. Gott. 1751. I. 227.
Thinks that in small tubes the nature of the glass has some effect.

*Segner on the surfaces of fluids. C. Gott. 1751. I. 301.
Proceeds on true physical principles, but commits a material error in neglecting the effect of a double curvature: appears also to have made some other mistakes in his calculations. Says that the height of mercury on glass or paper was .1357848 E. i.; half of this he calls the modulus for mercury.

On Taylor's measure of attraction. Misc. Taur. I.

Tetens de fluxu siphonis in vacuo. 4. Bützow. 1763.

Lalande Journ. des sav. 1768.

Lalande sur la cause de l'élévation des liqueurs. 12. Par. 1770.

Morveau on the attraction of water and oils, and on the adhesion of surfaces. Roz. I. 172, 460.

Morveau on apparent adhesion. *Chimie* de l'Acad. de Dijon. I. 63. E. M. Chimie. I. Art. Adhésion.

*Lord C. Cavendish's table of the depression of mercury. Ph. tr. 1776. 382.

Achard on the adherence of solids to fluids. A. Berl. 1776. 149. Schriften I. 355.

*Dutour on capillary tubes, and on adhesion. Roz. XI. 127. XIII. Suppl. 357. XIV. 216. XV. 46, 234. XVI. 85. XIX. 137, 287.
The mean adhesion of a disc of 72 square lines Fr. to water, was 31 gr. Fr. to wine 29, to brandy $22\frac{1}{2}$, to olive oil 22, to spirit of wine 18. A disc of glass, 11 lines in dia-

meter, adhered to mercury with a force of 194 grains, a disc of talc with 119, of tallow 49, of paper $27\frac{1}{2}$, of wax 11; of box, waxed, with a force of 1 only.

Godard on apparent attractions. Roz. XIII. 473.

Meister on oil swimming on water. Commentat. Gott. 1778. I. 35.

Bésile on the cohesion of liquids. Roz. XXVIII. 171. XXIX. 287, 339. XXX. 125.

Gives 82 gr. Fr. for the cohesion of 25 square lines of mercury, $8\frac{1}{4}$ for water. In some cases the apparent adhesion was diminished under the air pump. But this was probably the effect of the extrication of air bubbles.

*Monge on apparent attractions and repulsions. A. P. 1787. 506. Nich. III. 269.

Supposes that the superficial particles of the fluid only act in producing the effects of cohesion, and infers that the curve must be a lintearia. But he has not filled up this true outline with equal success. Spirit of wine, when not too hot, forms floating globules when dropped through a capillary tube. Two dry bodies floating approach each other from an inequality of pressure; even under the surface, as the fingers under mercury. A dry and a moist body repel each other in the same manner as an inclined plane and a body placed on it would separate. Two wet bodies are drawn by the fluid between them as by a chain. But these explanations do not agree with the supposition of the lintearia, which is vertical at its origin. The distance of two plates being $\frac{4}{71}$ of a line, the height of the water was $15\frac{1}{2}$ lines, at $\frac{2}{71}$, the height was $33\frac{1}{2}$, at $\frac{1}{71}$, 74 lines.

Bennet on attraction and repulsion. Manch. M. III. 116.

Shows that the undulations observed by Franklin do not depend on the mutual action of matter.

Banks on the floating of cork balls. Manch. M. III. 178.

Explains the phenomena pretty correctly, after S'Gravesande.

Waterproof cloth. Ph. M. X. 370.

Impregnated with some substance not highly attractive of water. See cloth.

Carradori on the superficial adhesion of fluids. Journ. Phys. XLVIII. 287. Ph. M. XI. 27. Gilb. XII. 108.

Considers it as a mechanical attraction between oils and water.

Otto on the effect of oil on waves. Zach. Eph. II. 516. III. 242. Ph. M. IV. 225.

Leslie on capillary action. Ph. M. XIV. 193.

Hassenfratz on the effect of adhesion in determining specific gravities. Ann. Ch. Gilb. I. 396, 515.

Pounded glass appearing to be specifically lighter.

Schmidt on Hassenfratz's experiments. Gilb. IV. 194.

Denies their accuracy.

B. Prévost on the motions of floating bodies. Ann. Ch. XI. 3.

Milon on capillary tubes. Journ. Phys. LIV. 128. Gilb. XII. Repert. XVI. 427.

Found that the cleanest mercury, when hot, would not rise even in red hot tubes.

Von Arnim. Gilb. IV. 376.

Finds an effect from the length of a capillary tube.

Hällström on the rise of water in tubes. Gilb. XIV. 425.

Attributes the apparent effect of the length of a capillary tube to the circumstance of its being sucked with the lips, which, even when the lips were perfectly clean, appeared to produce a depression. In general it is probable that inequalities in the dimensions of the bore have been the cause of the irregularity, which has never been perceptible in experiments with flat plates. Water rose 11.7 lines Swedish in a tube .2 line in diameter.

Cavallo's Nat. Phil. II. 135, 139.

A small globule of mercury will be drawn away from paper by glass, and from glass by more mercury. An iron ball floating on mercury is surrounded by a depression. A drop of mercury recedes from the line of contact of two glass plates. A needle floats on water when dry, but if any water gets over it, it sinks.

Robison observes that insects, which walk on water, have their feet wetted by a spirituous solution, and sink.

The equation of the surface of a drop of water is $a a x \ddot{x} + a a \dot{y} \dot{y} = x y \dot{y} \dot{z}$, where $\ddot{z} = 0$. Or thus, $a^4 x^2 \dot{x}^2 + 2 a^2 x \dot{y}^2 \dot{x} + (a^1 - x^2 y^1) \dot{y}^4 - x^2 y^2 \dot{x}^2 \dot{y}^2 = 0$. Y. The series given by Euler, A. Petr. III. 188, for the elastic curve, might be applied to the simple lintearia, which is a species of it.

Fluidity of Liquids, and Firmness of Solids.
See heat.
Ductility. See Divisibility.
Boyle fluiditatis et firmitatis historia. Works. I. 240.
Réaumur on the ductility of different substances. A. P. 1713. 199. H. 9.
Réaumur. A. P. 1726. 243.
<small>Lead is rendered less sonorous by hammering.</small>
Fluidity. A. P. 1741. H. 11.
Beguelin on hard bodies. A. Berl. 1751. 331.
On the explosion of grindstones. A. P. 1762. H. 37. 1768. H. 31.
<small>Attributed to the effect of the centrifugal force, and to the expansion of the wooden wedges.</small>
Fontana on solidity and fluidity. Soc. Ital. I. 89.
On hammering. Sickingen über die platina. 115.
Coulomb on the force of torsion. A. P. 1784. 229.
<small>The force varies as the angle of deviation, and as the biquadrate power of the diameter of the wire; a weight of half a pound vibrating twice as fast as a weight of two pounds. Steel wire was $3\frac{1}{2}$ times as stiff as brass; its direct cohesive strength as 12 to 7; it was 18 or 20 times as stiff as a thread of silk: brass wire was less easily deranged by great torsion. The elasticity of annealed wire was the same in quantity as that of unannealed, but its extent of action was reduced from 11 to 6 or 7, in copper: the time of oscillation was exactly the same in both cases. P. 265.</small>
Coulomb's physical theory of friction. S. E. X. 1785. 254.
Lambert on the constitution of fluids. A. Berl. 1784. 299.
*Delangez on the statics and mechanics of semifluids. Soc. Ital. IV. 329.
Hutton on the flexibility of the Brazilian stone. Ed. tr. III. 86.
Fleuriau on elastic stones. Roz. XLI. 86, 91.
On Fleuriau's mode of making marble flexible by heat, producing partial separations. Ph. M. X. 277.
Link on fluidity. Ann. Ch. XXV. 113.
On springs. Ph. M. II. 67.
<small>Springs of metal soon break, or take a set, if suffered to vibrate; wooden springs break if stopped and not suffered to vibrate. Red deal is the best wood for springs.</small>
<small>Crystals slowly formed are the hardest. See Higgins on light.</small>
<small>The cohesive strength depends much on solidity. See cohesion.</small>

HEAT AND COLD.

Boyle on cold. Works II. 228.
  Acc. Ph. tr. 1665-6. I. 3.
Boyle de frigore. 4. Lond. 1683.
Petit sur le froid et le chaud. Par. 1671. M. B.
  Acc. Ph. tr. 1671. VI. 3043.
Dodart on heat and cold. A. P. I. 143.
Mariotte on heat and cold. A. P. I. 174. Oeuvr. I. 183.
Varignon on fire and flame. A. P. II. 171.
Malebranche on fire. A. P. 1699. 22. H. 17.
†Geoffroy on cold. A. P.
  Acc. Ph. tr. 1701. XXII. 951.
Lemery on the matter of fire. A. P. 1709. 400. H. 6.
Boerhaave de igne. Elementa chemiae. I. 116.
Winkler de frigore. 4. Leipz. 1737.
Martine's medical and philosophical essays.
Châtelet Dissertation sur le feu. 8. Par. 1744.
Euler, Du Fiesc, Crequi, Chastelet, and Voltaire on fire. A. P. Prix. IV.
Kraft on cold and heat. C. Petr. XIV. 218.
Bikker de igne. 4. Utrecht, 1756.
Hillary on fire. 8. Lond. 1760.
Belgrado del calore e del freddo. Parma, 1764.
Inquiry into the effects of heat. 8. Lond. 1770.
Herbert de igne. 8. Vienn. 1773.

Bordenave on fire. Roz. IV. 104.

Changeux on heat and cold. Roz. VI. 299, 357.

Marat découvertes sur le feu. 8. Par. 1779.

Marat recherches sur le feu. 8. Par. 1780.

Donnsdorf über Electricität.

Magellan Essai sur la nouvelle théorie du feu élémentaire, 1780.

Magellan on fire. Roz. XVII. 375, 411.

Lavoisier and Laplace on heat. A. P. 1780. 355. H. S.

Scheele Traité de l'air et du feu, par Dietrich. 12. Par. 1781. R. S.

Hopson on fire. 8. Lond. 1781.

Fontana on light, flame, and heat. Soc. Ital. I. 104.

Scopoli, Volta, and Fontana on heat. Crell. N. Entd. XII. 2. Annalen, 1784.

Erxleben on the laws of heat. N. C. Gott. Physik. chem. abh. I. 330.

Experiments on light and colours, with the analogy between heat and motion. 8. Lond. 1786.

Baader vom wärmestoff. 4. Vienn. and Leipz. 1786.

Thompson (Count Rumford) on heat. Ph. tr. 1786, 1787, 1792.

Rumford's institution of a prize. Ph. tr. 1797. 215.

Ducarla sur le feu, R. I.

Carradori Teoria del calore. 2 vol. Flor. 1787.
    Extr. Roz. XXXIV. 271.

Marne über feuer, licht, und wärme. 1787.

Weber über das feuer. 8. Landshut, 1788.

La Serre théorie du feu. Avignon, 1788.

Berlinghieri on heat. Roz. XXXV. 113, 433.

Seguin on heat. Roz. XXXVI. 417.

Seguin sur les phénomènes du calorique. 8. R. S.

Deluc's Letters, cxli.

*Crawford on animal heat. 2 ed. 8. Lond. 1788. R. I.

Lesemelier sur l'air et le feu. 2 v. 8. Par. 1788. R. S.

*Pictet Essais de physique. 8. Gen. 1790.

Pictet on fire. 12. 1791. R. I.

Annales de Chimie, in many parts.

Saussure on heat. Roz. XXXVI. 193.

*Mayer über die gesetze des wärmestoffs. 8. Erlang. 1791. R. I.

Lampadius über electricität und wärme. 8. Berl. 1793.

Dalton's meteorol. obs. 115.

Voigt Theorie des feuers. 8. Jena, 1793.

Lampadius über das feuer. 8. Gott. 1793.

Franklin on light and heat. Am. tr. III. 5.

Göttling Beytrag zur antiphlogistischen chemie. 8. Weimar, 1794.

Gehler's phys. wörterb. II. 207.

Harrington on fire on heat. 8. Lond. 1796, 1798. R. S.

Socquet sur le calorique. Journ. Phys. LII. 214.

On Parr's theory of light and heat. Nich. II. 547.

Mangin Theorie du feu. 8. Paris. 1800. R. S.

Astley on the doctrine of heat. Nich. V. 23.

Von Arnim on heat. Gilb. V. 57.

Prize questions on heat. Ph. M. I. 323.

*Leslie's inquiry into the nature and propagation of heat. 8. Lond. 1804. R. I.

Sources of Heat and Cold.

Sources simply mechanical; friction, compression.

See Capacity for Heat.
Philo Belopoiica.
  Says that fire came out of Ctesibius's airgun.
Friction. Pliny Hist. nat. §. 76, 77.
Of heat and cold in a vacuum. C Bon. II. i. 312.
Of cold from expansion in the machine at Schemnitz. Ph. tr. 1762.
Darwin's frigorific experiments on the expansion of air. Ph. tr. 1788. 43.
  An effect of 4° or 5° was produced in some experiments.
Pictet on heat from friction. Ess. ix.
Pictet on cold produced by exhaustion. Journ. Phys. XLVII. (IV.) 186.
Baillet on ice produced by the expansion of air. Journ. Phys. XLVIII. 166.
Rumford on the heat excited by friction. Ph. tr. 1798. 80. Ess. II. ix. Nich. II. 106.
On heat from compression. Ph. M. VIII. 214.
Dalton on the heat produced by mechanical condensation. Manch. M. V. 515. Nich. 8. III. 160. Repert. ii. II. 118. Ph. M. XIII. 59. Gilb. XIV. 101.
  Estimates, that air under the pressure of two atmospheres absorbs 50° of heat in expanding; and that something more than 50° is produced when air is admitted into an exhausted receiver. See Capacity.
Davy on the collision of steel. Journ. R. I. I. Nich. 8. IV. 103.
On heat in the condenser. Ph. M. XIV. 363. B. Soc. Phil. n. 87.
  Tow was inflamed in an air gun; and light was seen through a strong glass fixed in the substance of the machine.

Combustion.

See Economy of Heat.
Sage on fuel. A. P. 1785. 239. Roz. XXVIII. 57.
Fordyce. Ph. tr. 1787.
  Suspected that fuel differently burnt gave different quantities of heat. Sometimes indeed much is wasted in smoke.
Thomson on combustion. Nich. 8. II. 10.

Spontaneous Combustions.

Albinus et Kletwich de phosphoro. 8. Frankf. an der Oder 1688.
Lefevre on a spontaneous inflammation of serge in a fulling mill. A. P 1725. H. 4.
The Empress and Georgi on spontaneous inflammations with oil, soot, and other substances. A. Petr. III. i. H. 3.
Carette. Roz. XXVII. 92.
Morozzo on spontaneous inflammations. M. Tur. 1786. III. 478. Repert. II. 416.
Humfries on a spontaneous inflammation. Ph. tr. 1794. 426.
  From linseed oil poured on cotton cloth.
Spontaneous inflammations at Spalding and elsewhere. Repert. III. 19, 21, 95.
Supposed spontaneous combustion of a black silk stocking. Ph. M. XVI. 92.
Bartholdi on spontaneous inflammation. Ann. Ch. Nich. VIII. 216.

Effects of Heat.

Temporary Effects and Measures of Heat.

Expansion. Pyrometers, Thermometers.

See Meteorology.
Experiments of the Academy del Cimento. i. With Musschenbroek's additions.
  Spirit thermometers described.

Hooke's statical thermometer. Birch. II. 1.

Wallis and Beale on thermoscopes. Ph. tr. 1669. IV. 1113.

*Croune on the expansion of water before it freezes. Birch. IV. 26.
With Hooke's objections, and Croune's further experiments. Dated 27 Feb. 1684.

Picard on the effect of cold on stones and metals. A. P. I. 77.

Lahire on the effects of heat and cold. A. P. II. 36. IX. 316, 322.

Lahire on thermometers. A. P. 1706. 432. 1710. 546. H. 13. 1711. 144. H. 10.

Lahire on the expansion of air by boiling water. A. P. 1708. 274. H. 1.

Amontons on the effects of heat on air. A. P. 1703. 101. H. 6.
Amontons assumes, that his thermometer is the natural measure of absolute heat: Lambert and Dalton afterwards advanced nearly the same opinion.

Amontons on the apparent fall of the thermometer. A. P. 1705. 75. H. 4.

Hauksbee on the weight of water in different circumstances. Ph. tr. 1708. XXVI. 93. 221.

Brook Taylor on the expansion of fluids in the thermometer. Ph. tr. 1723. XXXII. 291.
He found the expansion proportionate to the increments of heat by mixture.

Leupold. Th. Aerostaticum.

Musschenbroek's pyrometer. Tentam. Exp. and in Desagul. Phil. I. 421.

Leutmann Traité des barometres.

Bulfinger de thermometris. Comm. Petr. III. 196, 242. IV. 216.

Réaumur on thermometers. A. P. 1730. 452. 1731. 250. H. 6.
Réaumur's degrees are thousandths of the bulk of his diluted alcohol.

Delisle on thermometers. M. Berl. 1734. IV. 343.

*Delisle on the mercurial thermometer. Ph. tr. 1736. XXXIX. 221.

Delisle sur l'astronomie et la géographie physique. 4. Petersb. 1738.
Delisle's degrees are ten thousandths of the bulk of the mercury, neglecting the expansion of glass. Fahrenheit's are nearly ten thousandths, without this inaccuracy.

Ellicott's pyrometer. Ph. tr. 1736. 297.

Braun's comparison of scales. C. Petr. VII.

Weitbrecht on thermometers. C. Petr. VIII. 310.

Krafft on thermometers. C. Petr. IX. 241.

Martine on thermometers, heating and cooling. 12.

Segner de aequandis thermometris aereis. 4. Gott. 1739.
Bernoulli's air thermometer was like a barometer, with the reservoir hermetically sealed.

Clayton on the elasticity of steam. Ph. tr. 1739. XLI. 162.
A digester exploded.

Ludolff on thermometers. M. Berl. 1740. VI. 255.

Grischow's comparison of 17 thermometers. M. Berl. 1740. VI. 267.

Description d'un thermometre universel. 8. Par. 1742. M. B.

Celsius on thermometers. Schw. Abh. 1742. 197.
Makes 100 degrees between the freezing and boiling points of water.

Bouguer on the expansion of metals. A. P. 1745. 230. H. 10.

Wheler on the rotation of tubes near the fire. Ph. tr. 1745. XLIII. 341.
By the curvature.

Mortimer on thermometers, and on a metalline thermometer. Ph. tr. 1747. XLIV. 672. n. 484, 485.
Halley suggested mercurial thermometers; Fahrenheit introduced them. A metalline thermometer for multiplying the expansion by means of bars.

Johnson on Fotheringham's metalline thermometer. Ph. tr. 1748. XLV. 128.

Stancari's thermometer of air and mercury. B. Bon. I. 209.

Galeati on an air thermometer. C. Bon. II. ii. 201.

Tabarrani on thermometers. C. Bon. II. iii. 233.

†Miles on thermometers. Ph. tr. 1749. XLVI. 1.

Wargentin on thermometers. Schw. Abh. 1749. 167.

Bourbon's thermometer, with a concave bulb. 1752. H. 148.

Richmann on heat, as measured by thermometers and lenses. N. C. Petr. IV. 277.
Finds the expansion greater in greater heats.

*Smeaton's pyrometrical experiments. Ph. tr. 1754. 598. Errata.

Lambert on expansions. Act. Helv. II. 172.

*Lambert Pyrometrie. 4. Berl. 1779.

Lord Charles Cavendish on thermometers for particular uses. Ph. tr. 1757. 300.
For showing the maximum and minimum.

Recueil de diverses pieces sur le thermometre et barometre. 4. Bâle, 1757. Act. Helvet. III.

Bergen de thermometris. 4. Nuremb. 1757.

Essays on the thermometer. Act. Helv. III. 23.

Sulzer on thermometers. Act. Helv. III. 259. Roz. XI. 371.

Zeiher's metalline thermometer. N. C. Petr. IX. 305.

Zeiher on mending thermometers. N. C. Petr. IX. 314.
By a bulb of iron, adjusted by a screw to the scale.

Fitzgerald's metalline thermometer. Ph. tr. 1760. 823. 1761. 146.
Compound bars.

Titii descriptio thermometri, Loescri. Leipz. 1765.

Musschenbroek. Intr. II.
Copper and brass appear to have expanded more when drawn into wire; lead somewhat less.

Hennert Traité des thermometres. Hague, 1768.

Donnsdorffs Electricität.

Soumille's thermometer of four parts, for enlarging the degrees. A. P. 1770. H. 112.

Haubold de thermometro Reaumuriano. 4. Leipz. 1771.

Meister on the scales of thermometers. N. C. Gott. 1772. III. 144.

Perica's thermometer. Roz. II. 512.

Herbert de igne. Vienna, 1773.

Pasumot's thermometer. Roz. VI. 230.

Strohmeyer über die thermometer. 8 Gott. 1775.

Fontana on the Grand Duke's cabinet. Roz. IX. 41.

*Roy's experiments subservient to the measurement of heights. Ph. tr. 1777. 653.

Roy on Ramsden's pyrometer. Ph. tr. 1785. 461.
The fixed parts were of cast iron, and were kept at the freezing temperature: the object glass of the micrometer was fixed exactly over the ends of the expanding bars, moving with them, and showing a difference of $\frac{1}{1000}$ of an inch. When the adjustment was perfect, the expansion was found not to vary in different parts of the scale.

Report of a committee of the R. S. on thermometers. Ph. tr. 1777. 816.

*Deluc on pyrometry and areometry. Ph. tr. 1778. 419.
Measured the proportions of expansion by ascertaining the quiescent point of a compound bar. Finds a tardiness in most metals to return to their original dimensions after having been heated, when slowly cooled. Attributes an irregularity to the expansion of glass, which later observations have not confirmed.

Deluc observes, that all fluids begin to expand more rapidly as they approach their boiling points. Rech. sur l'atm. II. It appears from Wedgwood's experiments on a silver piece, that in mercury the inequality cannot be very great.

Deluc on expansions. Roz. XLIII. 422.

Van Swinden sur la comparaison des thermometres. Amst. 1778.
Compares 72 scales. Thermometer for a maximum.

Van Swinden on Du Crest's universal thermometer. Roz. XIII. Suppl. 402.

Shuckburgh. Ph. tr. 1779.

Cavallo on the expansion of mercury. Ph. tr. 1781. 511.

Luz über die thermometer. 8. Nuremb. 1781. R. I.

Wedgwood's thermometer for high degrees of heat. Ph. tr. 1782. 305. 1784. 359. 1786. 390. Journ. Phys. XXX. 299. Repert. VI. 255.
By measuring the contraction of pieces of clay exposed to the heat. It was connected with the common thermometers by measuring the expansion of a piece of silver in a gage of earthenware. Found the melting of ice of no use as a test, from the porosity of the ice, and the continuation of the operation of freezing at the same time. Conjectures that vapour freezes at a higher temperature than water. There seem to be many difficulties in being assured of the proper quality of the clay.

Thermometers. E. M. A. VIII. Art. Thermometre.

Pyrometer. E. M. Pl. III. Horlogerie, pl. 50.

Thermometers used by Hutchins. Ph. tr. 1783. 303*.

Zanotti on the effect of immersion on thermometers. C. Bon. VI. O. 83.

Achard on the expansion of fluids. A. Berl. 1784. 3.
On a great variety of fluids and solutions. He seems to neglect the expansion of glass.
Achard's thermometer is of semitransparent porcelain, filled with a composition of 2 parts bismuth, 1 lead, and 1 tin, which melts at the heat of boiling water.

Kirwan on specific gravities, taken at different degrees of heat. Ph. tr. 1785. 267.

Hindenburg Formulae comparandis thermometris idoneae. 4. Leipz.

Rosenthal Meteorologische werkzeuge. I. 38.

Charles on the effect of the expansion of glass. A. P. 1787. 567.

Langsdorf Theorie der hydrodynamischen und pyrometrischen grundlehren.

Blagden. Ph. tr. 1788.
The maximum of density of strong brine, like that of water, is about 8° above its freezing point.

Gaussen sur le thermometre de Réaumur. 8. Bezieres, 1789. Roz. XXXVII. 186.

Gaussen on the expansions of mercury and alcohol. M. Laus. III. 364.
Compares Micheli's and Deluc's experiments, and finds that they agree.

Morveau on the expansion of air. Ann. Ch. I. 256.

Guyton on Wedgwood's thermometer. Ann. Ch. XXXI. 171.

Guyton's metalline thermometer of platina. Repert. ii. III. 458. Nich. VI. 89.

Cotte on thermometers of mercury and of alcohol. Roz. XXXVII. 189. Ph. M. VI. 250.

Ph. tr. 1792. 270.
T. Wedgwood proposes to measure heat by finding the loss of weight of hot water into which the heated substance has been dropped.

Sanmartini's wheel thermometer. Soc. Ital. VI. 71.

Casbois on expansion in barometers. Roz. XLII. 441.

Lemaistre on Six's thermometer. Journ. Phys. XLVII. (IV.) 150.

Enc. Br. Art. Thermometer.

Gilpin's tables of specific gravities. Ph. tr. 1794. 275.

Prony on the expansions of gases and vapours. Journ. Polyt. I. ii. 24. Formulas.

Rutherford's improved thermometer. Ed. tr. III. 247.
For marking the extreme points.

Schmidt on the expansion of air. Gren. IV. 320.

P. Wilson on the motion of lighted wicks when swimming. Ed. tr. IV. 163. Nich. II. 167. With Arnim's remarks. Gilb. III. 447.
From the circulation caused by expansion.

A Drebelian air thermometer, terminating in a ball. Kunze Schaupl. II. 51.
Is a differential thermometer, although perhaps not understood by the inventor.

Rittenhouse on the expansion of wood. Am. tr. IV. 29. Ph. M. X. 343.

Trembley on the dilatation of elastic fluids. A. Berl. 1798. 38.
Remarks on Prony.

Regnier's metalline thermometer. M. Inst. II. 18.
Two arches of brass are confined by iron; their distance is measured by wheelwork.

Lefevre Gineau. M. Inst.
Found, by very accurate experiments, that water is the densest at the temperature of $4°$ C. or $39.2°$ F.

Baumé on thermometers. Extr. by Cotte. Journ. Phys. XLVIII. 282.

Nicholson on the flexure of compound bars by heat. Nich. I. 575.

Gazeran on pieces for Wedgwood's thermometer. Ann. Ch. XXXVI. 100. Repert. XIV. 211. Gilb. VIII. 233.

Rumford on the expansion of cold water. Essays, II. vi. Gilb. I. 436.

Rumford's differential air thermometer. Ph. tr. 1804. 77.

Leslie's photometer. Nich. III. 461, 518.
A differential air thermometer: described also in Leslie on heat.

Pictet's steam thermometer. Gilb. II. 280.
Juch's steam thermometer. Gilb. II. 296. Gilb. V. 64.

Arnim doubts the expansion of water in cooling.

On Wedgwood's thermometer. Ph. M. IX. 153.

Expansion of metals. Ph. M. XI. 271.

Gay Lussac on the expansion of gases. Ann. Ch. cxxviii. 137. Nich 8. III. 207. Gilb. XII. 257.
All gases and vapours that were tried expanded equally.

Nich. 8. I. 34.
Heat appears to give a partial increase of tenacity to a razor's edge. Probably because the edge cools fastest, contracts, and is stretched.

Dalton on the expansion of gases. Manch. M. V. Nich. 8. III. 130. Gilb. XII. 310.
Assuming that the absolute heat is as the distance of the particles, Dalton fixes the natural zero at $1547°$, F. below the freezing point: this Gilbert corrects to $1598°$, or $-1566°$, F.

Dalton on the expansion of water by cold. Manch. M. V. Ph. M. XIV. 355. Nich. 1805.
Dalton says, that in a water thermometer of earthenware, the apparent maximum of density is at $36°$ or $38°$, in queen's ware $40°$, in glass $41.5°$, in iron $42.5°$, in copper $45.5°$, in brass $46°$, in lead $49.5°$. Nich. 1805. Hence, if we compare the expansion of glass with that of iron, copper, brass, and lead, we shall find, according to Dalton's own principles, the maximum at $39.5°$, $38°$, $38°$, and $38.5°$ respectively. The thermometers of earthenware were evidently incapable of great accuracy. The comparison of iron and lead gives about $37.5°$.

Dalton on mercurial thermometers, and on the natural zero. Nich. 8. V. 34.

†Lalande's scale for a thermometer. Journ. Phys. LVII. 454. Gilb. XVII. 102.
Nearly like Delisle's.

Crichton's self registering metalline thermometer. See Meteorology.

*Gilbert on Dalton's expansions. Gilb. XIV. 266.

Hällström on the expansion of fluids. Gilb. XIV. 297.

Hällström on the maximum of density of water, and on the expansion of quicksilver. Gilb. XVII. 107.

Nich. 8. IV. 63.

Speer's hygrometer has 2 scales, for different temperatures.

On air thermometers. Gilb. XV. 57.

Soldner on Dalton's laws of expansion. Gilb. XVII. 44.

*Hope on the contraction of water by heat. Ed. tr. V. 379.

Makes the maximum of density between 39.5° and 40°.

Mushet on the shrinkage of cast iron. Ph. M. XVIII. 3.

Spirit thermometers are very inconvenient for travelling; they are easily deranged by shaking, so that the tube remains constantly full, and the bubble in the ball.

Expansions of different Substances.

According to the Committee of the Royal Society, the apparent expansion of mercury in glass is $\frac{1}{7158}$ for each degree of Fahrenheit: this may be considered as a sufficient definition of those degrees for the present purpose, placing the freezing point of pure water at 32°. Dalton asserts, that all liquids expand with greater rapidity exactly in proportion to the elevation of their temperature above their respective freezing points, making the whole expansions as the squares of the real temperatures; but this does not appear to be by any means true of mercury, nor of alcohol, according to the comparison of thermometers made in Hudson's Bay: nor is it exactly true even in the case of water. It appears, however, that in solids as well as in fluids, equal increments of heat produce somewhat greater expansions as the temperature is higher.

Solids.	For 180°, F.		For 1°, F.		
	In length.	In bulk.	In length.	In bulk.	
Earthenware					Wedgwood says, that earthenware made porous by charcoal, expanded only ½ as much as when solid.
Wood					Much less than glass. Rittenhouse.
Glass tube	.00077615	.002330	.00000431	.00001294	Roy. Ph. tr. 1785. He had before found a glass tube expand 4 times as much as a rod.
	.00083333	.002502	.00000463	.00001399	Smeaton. Ph. tr. 1754.
			.00000046		Deluc's mean. Ph. tr. 1778.
Glass rod	.00080787	.002426	.00000449	.00001347	Roy. The same glass as the tube.
Deal					Roy, 1777. As glass.
Platina	.000856	.002570	.00000476	.00001428	Borda.
Platina, and glass	.0011	.0033	.0000061	.0000183	Berthoud.
Regulus of antimony	.001083	.003253	.00000602	.00001805	Smeaton.
Cast iron prism	.0011094	.003332	.00000617	.00001_85	Roy.
Cast iron	.0011111	.003337	.00000618	.00001853	Lavoisier.
Steel rod	.0011447	.003438	.00000636	.00001907	Roy.
Blistered steel	.001125	.003379	.00000625	.00001875	Ph. tr. 1795. 428.
	.001150	.003454	.00000639	.00001917	Smeaton.
Steel	.0011574	.003476	.00000642	.00001928	Lavoisier.
			.00000661	.00001985	Troughton. Nich. IX.
Hard steel	.001225	.003679	.00000681	.00002042	Smeaton.
Annealed steel	.00122	.00367	.0000068	.0000204	Musschenbroek.
Tempered steel	.00137	.00411	.0000076	.0000228	Musschenbroek.
Iron	.001156	.003472	.00000642	.00001926	Borda.
	.001258	.003779	.00000699	.00002097	Smeaton.
Annealed iron	.00133	.00400	.0000074	.0000222	Musschenbroek.
Hammered iron	.00139	.00417	.0000077	.0000231	Musschenbroek.
Bismuth	.001392	.004180	.00000773	.00002320	Smeaton.
Annealed gold	.00146	.00438	.0000081	.0000243	Musschenbroek.
Gold	.0015	.0045	.0000093	.000025	Ellicott, by comparison.
Gold wire	.00167	.00502	.0000093	.0000279	Musschenbroek.
Copper hammered	.001700	.003109	.00000944	.00002833	Smeaton.
Copper	.00191	.00573	.0000106	.0000318	Musschenbroek.
Brass	.001783	.005359	.00000991	.00002973	Borda.

If glass expanded equally, the expansion of brass at 90° would be about 97 parts for 1°, the mean of the whole scale being 108; but if the inequality of the expansion of glass is so great, as appears from De Luc's experiments, the expansion of brass, at 90°, can be but about 90 parts for 1°.

CATALOGUE.—HEAT, EXPANSION.

Solids.	For 180°, F.		For 1°, F.		
	In length.	In bulk.	In length.	In bulk.	
Brass scale, supposed from Hamburg	.0018554	.005576	.00001031	.00003092	Roy.
Cast brass	.001875	.005635	.00001042	.00003125	Smeaton.
English plate brass rod	.0018928	.005689	.00001052	.00003156	Roy.
English plate brass trough	.0018949	.005695	.00001053	.00003159	Roy.
Brass			.00001066	.00003200	Troughton. Nich. IX.
Brass wire	.001933	.005811	.00001074	.00003222	Smeaton.
Brass	.00216	.00648	.0000120	.0000360	Musschenbroek.
Copper 6, tin 1	.001817	.005461	.00001009	.00003029	Smeaton.
Silver	.00189	.005681	.00001050	.0000315	Herbert.
	.0021	.0063	.00001167	.000035	Ellicott, by comparison.
	.00212	.00636	.0000118	.0000354	Musschenbroek.
Brass 15, tin 1	.001908	.005736	.00001056	.00003168	Smeaton.
Speculum metal	.001933	.005811	.00001074	.00003222	Smeaton.
Spelter solder, brass 2, zinc 1	.002058	.006187	.00001143	.00003430	Smeaton.
Fine pewter	.002283	.006866	.00001238	.00003714	Smeaton.
Grain tin	.002483	.007469	.00001379	.00004137	Smeaton.
Tin	.00284	.00852	.0000158	.0000474	Musschenbroek.
Soft solder, lead 2, tin 1	.002508	.007545	.00001393	.00004179	Smeaton.
Zinc 8, tin 1, a little hammered	.002692	.008095	.00001495	.00004388	Smeaton.
Lead	.002867	.008625	.00001592	.00004776	Smeaton.
	.00344	.01032	.0000191	.0000573	Musschenbroek.
Zinc	.002942	.008850	.00001634	.00004902	Smeaton.
Zinc, hammered out half an inch per ft.	.003011	.009061	.00001673	.00005019	Smeaton.

Liquids.					
Mercury		.01540		.0000855	Cotte. Probably in glass.
		.0165		.0000917	Mean of several experiments. Lichtenberg.
Sp. gr. 13.6 at 45°.		.01655		.000092	Achard, in glass.
		.0185		.000103	Deluc and Laplace.
From 32° to 104°				.0001043.5	Deluc, corrected by Roy.
				.000108	Roy.
Sp. gr. 13.61 at 68°				.000104	Ld.Ch.Cavendish. Mean of Shuckburgh's experiments.
				.00010985	Rosenthal.
		.017583		.000097	Hällström. Seems to allow too little for the glass.

It may be inferred from Deluc's experiments, that the mercurial thermometer may be reduced to a natural scale by adding to the temperature that it indicates $.07\frac{mn}{m+n}$, m being the number of degrees above the freezing point, and n the number below the boiling point, $m + n$ of course 180, 80 or 100, according to the scale employed. These experiments ought, however, to be repeated by mixing various fluids, before we can be confident that their results are perfectly natural. Besides Dr. Crawford, another most able philosopher has found the mercurial scale less at variance with the natural one.

According to this correction, 650° would be reduced to 540° for the boiling point of mercury on the natural scale; but Wedgwood's silver gage makes it about 607°.

TABLE OF THE NATURAL SCALE, ACCORDING TO DELUC. MODIF. DE L'ATM. 309.

Merc. R.	Nat. R.	Form. R.	Merc. R.	Nat. R.	Form. R.
0	0	0	45	46.37	46.35
5	5.43	5.33	50	51.26	51.31
10	10.74	10.61	55	56.15	56.20
15	15.94	15.85	60	60.96	61.05
20	21.12	21.05	65	65.77	65.85
25	26.22	26.20	70	70.56	70.61
30	31.32	31.31	75	75.28	75.33
35	36.40	36.35	80	80.00	80.00
40	41.40	41.40			

Richmann also found the expansion greater than in proportion to the heat; and if the apparent difference in his experiments had arisen from this circumstance only, it would have indicated an inequality more than twice as great as is shown in those of Deluc.

CATALOGUE.—HEAT, EXPANSION.

Water. The degrees of Fahrenheit's thermometer, reckoning either way from 39°, being called f, the expansion of water is nearly expressed by $.0000022 f^2 - .00000004835 f^3$, or, more shortly, $22 f^2 (1 - .002 f)$, in ten millionths; and the diminution of the specific gravity by $.0000022 f^2 - .000000047 2 f^3$.

	Specific gravity.	Diminution of sp. gr.		Expansion.		For 1°.
	Observed.	Observed.	Calculated.	Observed.	Calculated.	
10°	As 69°. Dalton corrected.					
30	.99980 Gilpin, 1794.	20	18	.00020	.00018	.00004
32	.99988 G.	12	11	.00012 (.000144 M.Inst.)	.00011	.00003
34	.99994 G.	6	5	.00006	.00005	.00002
39	1.00000 G.	0	0	.00000	.00000	.00000
44	.99994 G.	6	5	.00006	.00005	.00002
48	.99982 G.	18	16	.00018	.00018	.00004
49	.99978 G.	22	22	.00022	.00022	.00004
54	.99951 G.	49	48	.00049	.00048	.00006
59	.99914 G.	86	84	.00086	.00084	.00008
64	.99867 G.	133	130	.00133	.00130	.00010
69	.99812 G.	188	186	.00188	.00186	.10012
74	.99749 G.	251	250	.00251	.00251	.00014
77		225 De Luc; by comparison.		.00299 Achard.		
79	.99680 G.	320	322	.00321	.00326	.00016
(82)	.99612 Kirwan.	388	368	.00389	.00372	.00017
90	.99511 G. 1790.	489	509	.00491	.00513	.00020
100	.99313 G.	687	711	.00692	.00720	.00024
102	.99246 K.	754	753	.00760	.00763	.00025
122	.98757 K.	1243 1128 De Luc.	1247	.01258 .00949 Achard.	.01264	.00029
142	.98199 K.	1801	1818	.01833	.01859	.00031
162	.97583 K.	2417 2520 De Luc.	2448	.02481	.02512	.00034
167						
182	.96900 K.	3100	3109	.03198	.03219	.00036
202	.96145 K.	3855	3802	.04005	.03961	.00037
212	.95848 K.	4152 4400 De Luc, by comparison.	4140	.04333	.04332	.00038

De Luc's experiments were only comparative; hence the point of coincidence with Gilpin and Kirwan is assumed upon a mean. His expansions vary more nearly as f^2.

Hauksbee says, that water freed from air expands one third less by heat. Ph. tr. 1706. 221.

Saturated brine. One fifth more than water. Robison.

	For 1° F.
Sulfuric acid	.00081 Achard.
Sulfuric acid, sp. gr. 1.7	.00026 At 60° Kirwan. Ir. tr.
Sulfuric acid, sp. gr. 1.84	.00021 At 55° Kirwan.
	.00029 At 60° Kirwan.
	.00037 At 65° Kirwan.
Muriatic acid, sp. gr. 1.185	.00035 At 50° Kirwan.
Nitrous acid, sp. gr. 1.43	.00037 At 53° Kirwan.
	.00055 At 60° Kirwan.
	.00070 At 65° Kirwan.
Spirit of turpentine	.00052 Achard.

CATALOGUE.—HEAT, CHANGES OF FORM.

Spirit highly rectified, specific gr. at 60°.825.

	Comparative Specific Gravity.		Expansion, supposing the unit at 32°.		
	By Observation.	By Formula.			For each Degree.
0° F.		1.0326	0° F.	—.0162	.00047
10		1.0275	12	—.0105	.00050
20		1.0222	32	.0000	.00054
30	1.0169	1.0168	52	.0110	.00057
35	1.0142	1.0141		.0132 Achard.	
40	1.0114	1.0114	72	.0229	.00061
45	1.0087	1.0086	92	.0355	.00065
50	1.0058	1.0057	112	.0489	.00069
55	1.0029	1.0029	132	.0633	.00074
60	1.0000	1.0000	152	.0784	.00078
65	.9971	.9971	172	.0946	.00083
70	.9942	.9941	175	.0971	
75		.9913	.9912		
80 Gilpin. Ph. tr. 1794.	.9882	.9882			
100		.9758			
120		.9630			
140		.9496			
160		.9358			
180		.9214			

The temperature being $f°$, the comparative specific gravity is $113456 - (\frac{1}{4}f + 101)^2$, or reckoning the degrees from 60°, $1 - .00058f - .000\,000\,625 f^2$.

According to Gaussen's comparison of Deluc's experiments, the expansions constitute a series, varying nearly as $f + \frac{1}{110} f^2$, which becomes nearly $.00053f + .000\,000\,6001 f^2$.

Vitriolic ether	.00072	Achard.
Linseed oil	.0009	About 32°. Achard.
Olive oil	.0007	About 100°. Achard.

Deluc found the expansion of olive oil, at 32° to its expansion at 212° as 47 to 54: in middle temperatures there was somewhat less difference in proportion.

Gases.	For 180°.	For 1°.	
Dry air, 1. at 32°	.376	.00209	Mean of 6. Lacaille giving .04, Mayer .046, Bonne .0477, Shuckburgh .0505, Bradley .0544, and Deluc .047, for the expansion. From 32° to 54.8°: the mean .0476. Deluc.
	.377		Mayer's refractions. Gilbert.
	.370	.00206	Lambert.
	.388	.00216	Deluc, reduced by Gilbert.
	.381	.00212	Luz.
		.00214	About 95°. Luz.
		.00210	About 172°. Luz.
	(.484)	(.00243)	Roy: but moisture was admitted.
	.357	.00198	Schmidt: thinks it perfectly uniform, becoming .7 at 392°.
	.400	.00222	Laplace. Syst. du monde.
	*.378	.00210	Gay Lussac, corrected for the expansion of glass, = .003 or .0035.
	.393	.00218	Dalton, reduced by Gilbert.
		.00224	About 95°. Dalton.
		.00212	About 172°. Dalton.
Air, $2\frac{1}{2}$ times as dense as usual	(.434)	(.00241)	Roy.
Moist air, as dry air.			When additional moisture is excluded. Saussure.
Hydrogen gas.			
Oxygen gas.			
Azotic gas.			
Carbonic acid gas.			
Muriatic acid gas.			
Sulfureous gas.			
Nitrous gas.			
Vapour of sulfuric ether			All as air. Gay Lussac, and Dalton.

The inequality of the mercurial scale, as observed by Deluc, is more than equivalent to the inequality of the expansion of air, as observed by Luz, but only half as much as that which is assigned by Dalton.

Robins found that air was expanded by a red heat to 4 times its bulk. This would indicate, according to Schmidt, a temperature of about 1580°.

Effects of Heat on the Form of Aggregation.

Freezing, Thawing, and Melting.

Merret on freezing. Birch. I. 350.

Rinaldini on ice made without air. Ph. tr. 1671. VI. 2169.

Says that it is heavier than common ice.

On the expansion of water in freezing. Ph. tr. 1698. XX. 384.

Desmasters on freezing water. Ph. tr. 1698. XX. 439.

Lahire on the effect of cold on water in a pistol barrel. A. P. I. 14.

Lahire on the figure of ice. A. P. II. 144.

Lahire on ice and on cold. A. P. IX. 313.

Buot on the expansion of water in freezing. A. P. I. 76.

Varignon on ice. A. P. II. 70.

Perrault on the effects of cold on water, boiled or not boiled. A. P. I. 77.

Perrault on congelation. A. P. I. 252.

Homberg on ice. A. P. II. 105. X. 173. 1708. H. 21.

Observes, that it thaws faster in a vacuum than in the air.

Homberg on ice free from air. A. P. X. 173.

Thinks that it is as dense as water.

Mariotte on the congelation of water. A. P. X. 352.

Newton's table of temperatures. Ph. tr. 1701. XXIII. 824.

Amontons on the apparent fall of the thermometer. A. P. 1705. 75. H. 4.

Hauksbee on freezing water freed from air. Ph. tr. 1709. 302.

Found no difference in the density.

Fahrenheit de congelatione in vacuo. Ph. tr. 1724. XXXIII. 78.

Middleton found that the ice of sea water contained $\frac{1}{213}$ of salt, in Hudson's bay.

Triewald on congelation. Ph. tr. 1731. XXXVII. 79.

Produced suddenly by pressure.

Nollet on ice. Ph. tr. 1738. XL. 307.

Gmelin on the cold of ice. C. Petr. X. 303.

Hollmann de subita congelatione. Ph. tr. 1745. XLIII. 239. Sylloge comm. 138.

Experiments on steam. Desaguliers's lect. II. 533.

Bertier on a knife projected from a lump of frozen snow. A. P. 1748. 29.

Richmann on the force of water in freezing. N. C. Petr. I. 276.

Mairan on ice. Acc. A. P. 1749. H. 53.

On the thawing of ice into crystals. A. P. 1751. H. 37.

Braun de frigore artificiali. 4. Petersb. 1760.

Braun on the freezing of fluids. N. C. Petr. VIII. 389.

Braun on the freezing of mercury by artificial cold. N. C. Petr. XI. 268, 302.

Watson's extract. Ph. tr. 1761. 156.

Poissonnier on the congelation of mercury. A. P. 1760. H. 26.

Wilke on freezing. Schw. Abh. XXXI.

Lavoisier on freezing. Roz. Intr. II. 510.

Black on the congelation of boiled water. Ph. tr. 1775. 124.

Takes place at 32°, perhaps from the entrance of air.

Cherna de aqua intra aquam. 4. Groning. 1775.

Hutchins on freezing quicksilver. Ph. tr. 1776. 174.

Hutchins's experiments on the congelation of quicksilver. Ph. tr. 1783. 303*.

Nairne on the freezing of sea water. Ph. tr. 1776. 249. Roz. IX. 361.

Van Swinden sur le froid de 1770. 8. Amst. 1778.

On freezing.

Flauguergues on congelation. Roz. XV. 477.

De Luc Idées sur la metéorologie. I. ccvii. II. dcvi.

On freezing. Pure boiled water may be cooled to $14°$ without freezing.

Wilson's experiments on cold. Ph. tr. 1781. 386.

Snow was observed to evaporate at $27°$ F. without being perceptibly cooled by it. It adhered firmly to glass at $3°$; perhaps the contact of air may cause snow to melt more readily, producing the increased cold which is sometimes observed in it.

*Cavendish on Hutchins's experiments. Ph. tr. 1783. 303.

Makes the point of congelation of mercury — $38\frac{3}{4}°$ of the Royal Society's thermometer.

Cavendish on Macnab's experiments in Hudson's bay. Ph. tr. 1786. 241.

Finds that the sulfuric and nitric acids may be cooled much below their freezing points without congelation; that their strength rather raises than depresses their freezing points, but that when diluted they seem to have two freezing points, one for the acid, the other for the water, both of which however depend on the strength. Thus the nitric acid, its strength being .56, freezes at — $30°$, .53 at — $19°$; .437 at — $4\frac{1}{4}°$; the nitrous acid, strength .54, freezes at — $31\frac{1}{2}°$, .411 at — $1\frac{1}{2}°$, .38 at — $45\frac{1}{4}°$, .243 at $44\frac{1}{4}°$, .21 at — $17°$: the sulfuric acid, strength .98 at — $15°$, .629 at — $36°$, .41 at — $78\frac{1}{2}°$, .35 at — $68\frac{1}{2}°$, .34 at — $66°$, .33 at — $55\frac{1}{2}°$. Diluted alcohol is also similarly affected. Mr. Macnab produced a cold of — $78\frac{1}{2}°$.

Cavendish on Macnab's further experiments. Ph. tr. 1788. 166.

Confirms his former conclusions, and those of Mr. Keir, respecting the sulfuric acid; this has a second point of difficult congelation about the strength of .92, freezing at about — $26°$. Thus at .977 the freezing point was + $1°$, at .918, — $26°$, at .846, + $42°$, at .758, — $45°$. In Keir's experiments the acid of the density of .848 was frozen at $46°$.

Blagden's history of the congelation of mercury. Ph. tr. 1783. 329.

Blagden on the cooling of water below its freezing point. Ph. tr. 1788. 125.

Boiled water is only more readily frozen when it is rendered turbid. Sand, or broken glass, did not promote the congelation, nor even agitation, unless it was minute, as when the inside of the vessel was rubbed with wax, a little water being interposed. A thin film was more easily frozen. The access of air only promotes congelation when it is loaded with frozen particles; the smallest particle of ice producing the effect instantaneously. The contact of metals seems to facilitate congelation, and the rapidity with which the water is cooled. Water expands considerably when thus cooled. The greatest cold supported without freezing was $20°$.

Blagden on the congelation of aqueous solutions. Ph. tr. 1788. 277.

The point of congelation of water with $\frac{1}{n}$ of salt was $32° - \frac{112}{n}$; thus, with $\frac{1}{4}$ it was $4°$, with $\frac{1}{17}$, $28\frac{1}{2}°$. Other salts followed also similar laws. Crystallization did not seem immediately to promote congelation. The maximum of density of water with $\frac{10}{48}$ of salt was about $8°$ above its freezing point.

Euler and Krafft on the congelation of mercury. N. A. Petr. 1785. III. 60.

At about — $36°$ or — $40°$.

Guthrie sur la congélation du mercure. 4. Petersb. 1785.

Keir on the congelation of the vitriolic acid. Ph. tr. 1787. 267.

Found that the sulfuric acid of the specific gravity 1.780, freezes at $45°$ F. into crystals, which are more dense than 1.924, perhaps more than 2, while solid, but which thaw into acid of the specific gravity 1.780, whether the acid was originally a little more or less dense. But when the specific gravity varies as far as 1.75 or 1.81, it will not freeze at $18°$ F.

Chaptal on the congelation of sulfuric acid. Roz. XXXI. 468.

Walker. Ph. tr. 1788. 395.

Cooled water to $10°$ without freezing it.

Walker on the congelation of quicksilver in England. Ph. tr. 1789. 199.

Saussure on liquefaction. Roz. XXXVI. 193.

Williams on the expansive force of freezing water. Ed. tr. II. 23.

Makes the expansion $\frac{1}{17}$ or $\frac{1}{11}$. From the difference of refractive power it might be expected to be $\frac{1}{14}$ or $\frac{1}{15}$.

Priestley on the air evolved in freezing. Am. tr. V. 36.

Heller on the freezing of water. Gilb. I. 474.
† Dickson on water freezing. Ph. M. VII. 69.
† Blanchet on explosions. Ph. M. VII. 71.
Weber on the strength of ice. Gilb. XI. 353.
Driessen on the congelation of water. Ph. M. XV. 249.
Crichton on the melting point of lead and tin. Ph. M. XVI. 48.
Sir J. Hall of the effects of heat with compression. Nich. IX. 98.
See Tables of the Effects of Heat.

Degrees of Fluidity.

*Gerstner on the fluidity of water of different temperatures. Böhm. Gesellsch. 1798. Gilb. V. 160.
  With a tube .0674 inch Fr. in diameter, 33 long, a reservoir was half emptied in 35' 34" at 30° Réaum. in 60' 38" at 10°, in 76' 19" at 4°, the remaining half in 157' 20", 291' 40", and 381' respectively. With a tube .136 in diameter, 7.9 long, the times of the discharge of the first half were 2' 31", 2' 42", and 2' 44": of the second half 7' 16", 7' 55", and 8' 22".

Boiling, Simple Evaporation, Sublimation, Volatilisation and Deposition.

Boyle on fixedness. Birch. III. 144.
  Hooke discovered the permanency of the temperature of boiling water in 1684.
Papin on distilling in vacuo. Birch. IV. 427.
Homberg on the heat of boiling water. A. P. 1703. H. 25.
Fahrenheit de calore liquorum ebullientium. Ph. tr. 1724. XXXIII. 1.
Réaumur on the evaporation of snow. A. P. 1738. H. 36.
Ludolff on the evaporation of mercury. M. Berl. 1741. VI. 109.
Nollet on ebullition, A. P. 1748. 57.
Richmann on evaporation. N. C. Petr. I. 198, 284. II. 134, 145.
  On the effect of the depth of vessels, and on the cold produced.

Baron on the evaporation of ice. A. P. 1753. 250. H. 194.
Cullen on evaporation. Ed. ess. II. 145.
Leidenfrost de aquae qualitatibus. 8. Duisburg, 1756.
  On evaporation at low temperatures.
Franklin's letters. I. 303, 398. Roz. II. 276.
On cold from evaporation. M. Taur. I.
Cigna on evaporation. M. Taur. II. 143.
Cigna on ebullition. Roz. III. 109.
Fourcroy de Ramecourt on the vapour of mercury. A. P. 1768. H. 36.
Wistar on the vapour of melting ice. Roz. VI. 183. Gilb. V. 354.
On water thrown into melted glass. Roz. XI. 30, 411.
Grignon on the effects of a drop of water on hot substances. Roz. XII. 288.
Lavoisier on elastic fluids. A. P. 1777. 420. H. 20.
Lavoisier on fluids becoming aeriform at low temperatures. Roz. XXVI. 142.
Deslandes, Bosc d'Antic, and Grignon on evaporation at low temperatures. Roz. 1778.
Shuckburgh on the temperature of boiling water. Ph. tr. 1779. 362.
Fontana on evaporation in quiescent air. Roz. XIII. 22.
  Finds that evaporation does not take place in closed vessels when the heat is communicated from above. But perhaps the heat was not conveyed to the fluid.
Milon on evaporation in a vacuum. Roz. XIII. 217.
Achard. Berl. Naturf. I. 112. Roz. XVI. 174.
Achard on the heat of boiling fluids. A. Berl. 1782. 3. 1783. 84.
Achard on measuring heights by the boiling point of water. A. Berl. 1782. 54.
Achard on the effect of different substances upon the temperature of boiling water. A. Berl. 1784. 58. With a copious table.

The whole effect of any insoluble substance seldom amounted to a degree of Réaumur. Metallic filings generally lowered the point of ebullition.

Achard on the boiling point of water. A. Berl. 1785. 3.

Finds some irregularities from the nature of the vessels.

Achard on the effect of salts upon the boiling point of water. A. Berl. 1785. 67.

Wilson on cold. Ph. tr. 1781. 386.

Snow was found to evaporate at 27°, but was not perceptibly cooled by it, yet the thermometer was always lower on the snow than in the air, unless very deeply immersed.

Cotte on the evaporations from different vessels. Roz. XVIII. 306.

Cavallo on cold from evaporation. Ph. tr. 1781. 511.

Delessert on the heat of steam. Roz. XXVIII. 170.

Saussure on evaporation. Gren. I. iii. 460. Roz. XXXIV. 443.

Bétancourt sur la force expansive de la vapeur de l'eau. 4 Paris, R. S. Journ. polyt. Prony Arch. hydr. I. 157. Hutton's dictionary II. 755. Ph. M. I. 345.

Deluc on the heat of boiling water. Roz. XLII. 264.

Dalton on the force of steam. Meteor. essays.

* Dalton on the force of steam and on evaporation. Manch. M. V. 5S. Repert. ii. I. 22. Gilb. XV. 1.

Crichton on the boiling point of mercury. Ph. M. XVI. 48.

Lichtenberg. Erxleb. Naturl.

Observes, that pure water may be heated to 234° before it boils, and that it will then sink to 212°.

Table of temperatures. Erxleb. Naturl. 401.

Volta's apparatus for experiments on etherial vapour. Ann. Ch. XII. 292.

Volta's notes. Gilbert. XV.

B. Prévost on the motions of odorous bodies, and on rendering their emanations visible.

Ann. Ch. XXII. 31. XL. 3. B. Soc. Phil. n. 8. S. E. to be printed.

Guyton on odorous emanations. Ann. Ch. XXVII. 218.

Carradori on heat, evaporation, and inevaporable fluids. Ann. Ch. XXIX. 93. XLII. 65. Gilb. XII. 103.

Carradori on Prévost's expansion of odours. Ann. Ch. XXXVII. 38.

Biot on Prévost's experiments. B. Soc. Phil. n. 54.

Klaproth on the evaporation of a drop of water at a high temperature. Journ. Phys. LV. 61. Nich. 8. IV. 202.

Van Marum on the conversion of liquids into gases in a vacuum. Gilb. I. 145.

On the specific gravity of steam. Repert. IX. 249.

Correcting a blunder of Desaguliers.

Messier on the sublimation of mercury. M. Inst. II. 473. Gilb. XII. 96.

Says, that heat would not produce the effect without light, and that bubbles were seen rising, with a glass.

* Bikker and Rouppe on the force of steam. Haarl. Verh. Gilb. X. 257.

The steam was made to press on hot quicksilver; great care was taken to expel the air. Journ. R. I., I. 179.

Von Charpentier Gilb. XII. S65.

Denies the influence of light on the barometer, and the ascent of visible globules; but he does not appear to have excluded all light.

Gilbert's remarks on Dalton's experiments. Gilb. XV. 25.

Soldner on Dalton's laws of expansion. Gilb. XVII. 44.

Mr. Giddy has favoured me with an account of some very accurate observations on the quantity of water employed for supplying a steam engine, by which it appears, that the specific gravity of steam under a pressure of about 30. is nearly $\frac{1}{2400}$, or a little more than one third of that of air; which agrees very well with Desaguliers's experiments.

Professor Robison observes, that, in his experiments, the addition of 30° to the temperature, in most cases, nearly doubled the elasticity both of steam and of the vapour of alcohol. Hence he observes, that the logarithm of the elasticity should vary as the temperature. Encycl. Br. Art. Steam Engine. He could, however, discover no sensible elasticity in alcohol at $32°$; nor could Bétancourt Molina. Dalton pursues Robison's idea of the logarithmic, with some alterations: he made experiments both under the air pump and with the Torricellian column; he found that a difference of $11\frac{1}{4}°$ increased the elasticity 1.4925 times at $32°$, and 1.2425 times at $212°$, hence he infers that .015 is to be deducted from the ratio for every such interval, and continues his table both ways. But it is certain that this cannot be the law of nature, since about $394°$ the elasticity would become uniform, and then decrease, if the law were true. He says that Betancourt and Robison make the elasticity too great in high temperatures from the extrication of air: but the fact is, that when the greatest care has been taken to avoid it, the elasticity has appeared nearly the same, and the circumstance, if it had taken place, would have been very immaterial. Indeed, the only support of Dalton's measures above the boiling point is the law, which he has imagined for the expansion of other vapours; he says, that their elasticity is always equal to that of steam, at a given difference of temperature above or below them: and some experiments, that he adduces, agree exactly with the law; but it is utterly incredible that an expansive force of 7 tenths of an inch which the vapour of alcohol ought to have at the freezing point, should have entirely escaped both Betancourt and Professor Robison. Still, however, his rule for the force of different vapours must be allowed to be a very valuable approximation at temperatures between $50°$ and $220°$.

A much simpler formula will agree extremely well with all Dalton's experiments on water, and with the mean of all the best experiments that have been made by others in higher temperatures. It is this, the elasticity of steam in atmospheres of 30 inches of mercury is $d = (1 + .0029f)^7$, f being the degrees of Fahrenheit above $212°$, whence we have $f = \frac{d^{\frac{1}{7}} - 1}{.0029}$ for the elevation of the boiling point with an increase of pressure. If we reckon f from $32°$, we shall have the elasticity in inches of mercury nearly $.1781 (1 + .006f)^7$; and for the elevation or depression of the boiling point, if e be the elevation of the barometer above 30 in inches, we shall have for small variations $f = \frac{e}{7 \times 30 \times .0029} = \frac{e}{.609} = 1.642e$. Deluc makes the correction $1.59e$, Shuckburgh $1.70e$, the mean is $1.645e$, which agrees very singularly with the calculation. According to Dalton's principles the formula may be accommodated to any other vapour, by reckoning f from some other constant point of the scale; as $-5°$ for alcohol, $50°$ for muriate of lime.

Schmidt's formula is $e = r^{\frac{1.4113 + .005r}{}}$ in hundredths of a French inch of mercury, r being the temperature in degrees of Réaumur. This is nearly equivalent to $f^{1.163 + .0021f}$ in hundredths of an English inch, f being the degrees of Fahrenheit reckoned from $32°$; or to $c^{1.3386 + .004c}$ for the degrees of the centigrade thermometer.

Prony's formula for Bétancourt's experiments, is ridiculously complicated, and yet not at all accurate.

Soldner gives, for expressing Dalton's numbers, the formula $e = 1.30.13 \cdot \frac{(662 - f) \cdot (212 - f)}{52042}$. He accommodates similar formulae to other scales, and deduces from them others for the determination of the heat of boiling water under different pressures.

This however is only an approximation to Dalton's principle, which from the properties of the logarithmic curve, leads to a formula of this kind, $e = .0161373 - (1.0365 - .00008f) \cdot l \cdot (1.0365 - .00008f) - .4343 (.00008f)$.

I have also found several expressions which for particular purposes may possibly be of some use, although they are all superseded in general by the formula first mentioned; these are, reckoning f always from $32°$, $e = .003f^{1.5}$, $e = 10^{.00678 8f}$, $e = 10^{.00678 8f} (f + .00032 9f^2 - .00000001 f^4)$, $e = .2 \left(10^{.0551f - .000019ff} \right)$ $e = \text{numb. l. } .30103 + .01541f - .000017f^2 - .000000008f^3$, in tenths; and for atmospherical temperatures $e = .2 + .007f + .00016f^2$, which is deduced from Dalton's table, but may perhaps be improved by making $e = .18 + .007f + .0001 9f^2$.

Construction of Thermometers.

Braun's comparison of the scales of thermometers. N. C. Petr. VII. pl. 18.

Wentz on dividing thermometers with unequal tubes. Act. Helv. III. 105.

Report of the committee of the R. S. Ph. tr. 1777. 816.

The stem of a thermometer being $100°$ colder than the bulb, the mercury will be about $1\frac{2}{3}°$ lower in $180°$. It ought always to be of the same temperature.

The bulb being immersed an inch under water, the boiling point is raised $.06°$, which is about half as much as the same pressure would occasion if exerted by the air.

The thermometer at a medium stands about .48°, higher immersed in water, than in steam only, which corresponds to a difference of about .3 in the height of the barometer.

The rapidity of boiling makes little difference in the heat, there are, however, sometimes irregularities of half a degree or more, notwithstanding all possible precautions.

The standard thermometer is graduated by immersion in steam, when the barometer is at 29.8: its boiling point is $\frac{1}{4}°$ higher than that of De Luc's, who employs 28.75 for the height of the barometer, immersing the bulb in water. A vessel with a chimney is employed, loosely covered for steam, the bulb being held 2 inches above the water.

When the bulb is immersed, the barometer ought to stand at 29.5, but when an open vessel is used, the barometer must be at 29.8, and the thermometer must be wrapped in cloths, and held upright, and hot water must be frequently poured over it. Rain water or distilled water must be employed.

Corrections are given for the expansion of the scale, and for the coldness of the stem; and a diagonal scale for reducing the effect of the height of the barometer. For each inch $\frac{1}{1000}$ of the interval between the freezing and boiling points must be allowed.

Six on the division of thermometers. Ph. tr. 1782. 72.

Biot's thermometer. See Communication of Heat.

It is simplest and most usual to reduce thermometers to 30. of the barometer.

Comparative Table of Thermometers.

	Degrees from freezing to boiling.	Freezing point.	Boiling point.
Wedgwood	1.484	— 8.142	— 6.658
Poleni	15.6	47.3	62.9
Amontons	21.5	51.5	73
Newton	34.	0.	34
Old Edinburgh	38.8	8.2	47
Del Cimento sometimes	$68\frac{1}{6}$	13.5	$81\frac{2}{3}$
Réaumur	80	0.	80
Sauvages	87	0.	87
Celsius, centigrade	100.	0.	100
Delisle	150	150	0.
Del Cimento sometimes	154	20.	174
Sulzer nearly as Delisle, about	156		
Hales	163	0.	163
Delahire Obs. Par.	$171\frac{1}{3}$	28	$199\frac{1}{3}$
Fahrenheit	180	32	212
Ac. Par. old.	214	25	239
R. S. old	215.5	— $73\frac{1}{2}$	$141\frac{1}{2}$
Fowler	$284\frac{1}{2}$	— 34	$250\frac{1}{2}$
Rosenthal	344	928	1272
Cruquius	440	1070	1510
Hawksbee	490	0	490

Hawksbee's was a spirit thermometer; he found the expansion of air at the freezing point $\frac{1}{1310}$ for each of his degrees: hence his greatest summer heat, of 130°, becomes 80°, F. if we make it 84°, we shall have 450° for the boiling point.

Gaussen's comparison of the thermometers of mercury and alcohol, from the experiments of Deluc and Micheli.

Merc.	R. Alc.	Merc.	Alc.
5°	3.9	45°	40.1
10	7.9	50	45.3
15	12.1	55	50.7
20	16.4	60	56.2
25	20.9	65	61.9
30	25.5	70	67.8
35	30.2	75	73.8
40	35.1	80	80.0

This agrees with the formula $\frac{1}{4}r + \frac{1}{310}rr$.

Micheli found 20° of the spirit thermometer agree to 26.4° of the mercurial, 30° to 36.7°, 40° to 46.4°, 50° to 56.6°, 60° to 64.3°, and 70° to 72.4.

Table of the Effects of Heat.

Wedgwood's greatest heat	240° W.
Nankeen porcelain withstands	160
Best Chinese porcelain softened	156
Pig iron melts completely	150
Bristol porcelain withstands	135
Pig iron begins to melt W.	130 W. 17977 F.
Iron, pure nickel, and pure cobalt melt, Bergman	1601
Smith's forge	125
Plate glass furnace	124
Bow porcelain vitrifies	121
Inferior Chinese porcelain softens	120
Flint glass furnace	114
Derby porcelain vitrifies	112
Chelsea porcelain vitrifies	105
Stone ware, pots de grès, baked,	102
Welding heat of iron	95
Worcester porcelain vitrifies	94
Welding heat of iron begins	90
Cream coloured ware baked	86
Flint glass furnace, weak,	70
Working heat of plate glass	57
Delft ware, baked	41

Fine gold melts, W.	32° W.	5237° F.
Bergman		1301
Settling heat of flint glass	29	
Fine silver melts, W.	28	4717
Bergman		1000
Swedish copper melts, W.	27	4587
Bergman		1450
Brass melts		21
Enamel burnt on		6
Red heat, visible by daylight. W.	0 W.	1077
Bergman		1050
Red heat, visible in the dark	— 1 W.	947
Antimony melts, Bergman		809
Zinc melts, Bergman		699
Mercury boils		660 or 655
Expressed oils boil		600
Sulfuric acid boils		590 / 546
Steel becomes deep blue		580
Oil of turpentine boils		560 / 324.5
Lead melts		540
Biot		504
Bergman		595
Bismuth melts		460
Bergman		494
Steel becomes straw coloured, the best temper for penknives		460
Lead 4, tin 1, melts		460
Tin melts		408
Biot		410
Bergman		415
Crichton. Ph. M.		442
Bismuth 1, tin 1, melts		283
Nitric acid boils		242
Saturated solution of salt boils		218
Water boils, the barometer at 30.		212
Bismuth 5, tin 3, lead 2, melts		212
Bismuth 8, lead 5, tin 3, melts		210
Alcohol boils		174
Serum and albumen coagulate		156
Bees wax melts		142
Heat of tea and coffee		120 to 140
Feverish heat		107 to 112
Heat for incubation		108
A pleasant bath		92° to 106
The interior bath at Edinburgh		100
Blood heat		96 to 100
Temperate air		62
Sulfuric acid. See Cavendish.		

Ice melts	32°F.
Wedgwood thinks the freezing point of vapour a little higher.	
Milk freezes	30
Sea water freezes	28
Alcohol 10, water 14, by weight, freezes	21
Wine freezes	20
Alcohol 1, water 3, freezes	7
Alcohol 1, water 1, freezes	— 7
Alcohol 2, water 1, freezes	— 11
Mercury freezes, contracting about $\frac{1}{11}$,	— 39

Table of the Elasticity of Steam, in Inches of Mercury.

The best formula is $e = .1781 (1 + .006f)^7$; or, secondly, for low temperatures $e = .18 + .007f + .00019f^2$, reckoning f from 32°.

	Formula.	Dalton.	
2°	.044	.068	
12	.073	.096	
22	.115	.139	
23	.120	.144	
24	.126	.150	
25	.132	.156	
26	.138	.162	
27	.144	.168	
28	.150	.174	
29	.157	.180	
30	.164	.186	
31	.171	.193	
32	.178	.200	.0 Schmidt. .18 Form. 2.
33	.186	.207	
34	.193	.214	
35	.202	.221	
36	.210	.229	
37	.219	.237	
38	.228	.245	
39	.237	.254	
40	.247	.263	.1 Robison. .07 Schmidt's formula.
41	.257	.273	
42	.268	.283	.269 Form. 2.
43	.278	.294	.12 Betancourt.
44	.290	.305	
45	.301	.316	
46	.313	.328	
47	.326	.339	
48	.338	.351	
49	.351	.363	
50	.365	.375	
51	.379	.388	
52	.394	.401	.396 Form. 2.
53	.409	.415	
54	.424	.429	
55	.440	.443	Muriate of lime .22. D. as water 18° lower.
56	.456	.458	.4 Van Marum. Alc. 1.3, as water 30° higher. Ammonia 7.7, as water 95° higher. Ether 13.3, as water 118° higher.

CATALOGUE.—HEAT, CHANGES OF FORM.

	Formula.	Dalton.			Formula.	Dalton.	
57°	.474	.474		116°	3.100	3.00	
58	.491	.490		117	3.188	3.08	
59	.509	.507	.407 Schm.	118	3.278	3.16	
60	.528	.524	Alc. 1.45 D. as water 30° higher. Ammonia 4.3 D. as water 69° higher.	119	3.369	3.25	
				120	3.463	3.33	Alc. as water 6° higher. Rob.
				121	3.560	3.42	
61	.547	.542		122	3.658	3.50	3.90 Bet. 3.9 Schm.
62	.567	.560	.561 Form. 2. Ether 12.75, as water 110° higher. Dalt.	123	3.760	3.59	
				124	3.863	3.69	
63	.587	.578		125	3.969	3.79	
64	.609	.597		126	4.078	3.89	
65	.630	.616	Muriate of lime .3 D. as water 19° lower.	127	4.188	4.00	
				128	4.361	4.11	
66	.653	.635		129	4.418	4.22	
67	.676	.655		130	4.536	4.34	
68	.700	.676	.65 Bet. .653 Schm.	131	4.657	4.47	
69	.724	.698		132	4.781	4.60	
70	.750	.721	.55 Rob. Muriate of lime .4 D. as water 18° lower.	133	4.908	4.73	
				134	5.037	4.86	Alc. as water 29° higher. Ach.
71	.776	.745		135	5.171	5.00	
72	.803	.770	.764 Form. 2. .75 Lord C. Cavendish.	136	5.307	5.14	
				137	5.446	5.29	
73	.830	.796		138	5.588	5.44	
74	.858	.823		139	5.732	5.59	
75	.888	.851		140	5.880	5.74	Alc. as water 30° higher. Rob. Ammonia 30, as water 72° higher. Dalton.
76	.918	.880					
77	.949	.910	.96 Bet. .964 Schm.				
78	.980	.940					
79	1.013	.971		141	6.031	5.90	
80	1.047	1.000		142	6.186	6.05	
81	1.082	1.04		143	6.344	6.21	
82	1.117	1.07		144	6.506	6.37	
83	1.154	1.10		145	6.671	6.53	
84	1.192	1.14		146	6.840	6.70	
85	1.231	1.17		147	7.012	6.87	Alc. as water 31.5° higher. Ach. Ether 64.75, D. as water 105° higher.
86	1.270	1.21					
87	1.311	1.24					
88	1.353	1.28		148	7.189	7.05	
89	1.396	1.32		149	7.369	7.23	
90	1.442	1.36		150	7.553	7.42	6.72 Rob. 6.6 Achard.
91	1.487	1.40		151	7.740	7.61	
92	1.533	1.44		152	7.932	7.81	
93	1.580	1.48		153	8.128	8.01	
94	1.629	1.53		154	8.328	8.20	
95	1.680	1.58	Muriate of lime .9 D. as water 18° lower.	155	8.532	8.40	
				156	8.740	8.60	
				157	8.953	8.81	
96	1.732	1.63		158	9.170	9.02	
97	1.785	1.68		159	9.391	9.24	
98	1.839	1.74		160	9.617	9.46	
99	1.895	1.80		161	9.848	9.68	
100	1.953	1.86	1.61 Rob.	162	10.08	9.91	
101	2.012	1.92		163	10.32	10.15	
102	2.073	1.98	Ether 30, as water 110° higher. Dalton.	164	10.57	10.41	
				165	10.82	10.68	
103	2.135	2.04		166	11.07	10.96	
104	2.199	2.11		167	11.33	11.25	11.78 Schm. Alc. as water 33° higher. Ach.
105	2.264	2.18					
106	2.331	2.25	2.38 Bet.	168	11.60	11.54	
107	2.400	2.32		169	11.87	11.83	
108	2.470	2.39		170	12.14	12.13	
109	2.542	2.46		171	12.43	12.43	Alc. as water 36° higher. Ach.
110	2.616	2.53					
111	2.692	2.60		172	12.72	12.72	
112	2.770	2.68		173	13.01	13.02	
113	2.850	2.76		174	13.30	13.32	
114	2.931	2.84		175	13.61	13.62	14. Achard. Alc. 30. Dalt. as water 37° higher.
115	3.015	2.92					

Formula.	Dalton.	Biker.		Formula.	Dalton.	Biker.	
176°	13.92	13.92		237°	48.84		
177	14.24	14.22	14. Kirwan from Deluc.	238	49.76		
178	14.56	14.52	15. Schm. 14.9 Achard.	239	50.71		51.45 Schm.
179	14.89	14.83		240	51.66	52.2	54.9 Rob. Alc. as water
180	15.23	15.15	14.05 Rob. 15.5 Schm. form. Alc. as water 37° higher. Rob.				46° higher. Rob.
				241	52.64		
				242	53.63	(51.34)	53.9
181	15.57	15.50		243	54.63		
182	15.92	15.86		244	55.66		
183	16.27	16.23		245	56.70		
184	16.64	16.61		246	57.75		
185	17.00	17.00		247	58.82		
186	17.38	17.40		248	59.91		60.76 Schm.
187	17.76	17.80		249	61.01		
188	18.16	18.20		250	62.14		62.7 66.8 R.
189	18.55	18.60		251	63.28		
190	18.96	19.00	19.4 Schm.	252	64.43	(60.05)	64.8
191	19.37	19.42		253	65.61		
192	19.79	19.86		254	66.80		
193	20.22	20.32		255	68.02		
194	20.66	20.77	21.47 Achard.	256	69.25		
195	21.10	21.22		257	70.49		71.57 Schm. 76.9 Bet.
196	21.55	21.68		258	71.76		
197	22.01	22.13		259	73.05		
198	22.48	22.69		260	74.36		75.0 80.3 Rob.
199	22.96	23.16		261	75.69		
200	23.44	23.64	22.62 Rob.	262	77.04	(69.72)	77.0
201	23.94	24.12	24.0 Schm.	263	78.41		
202	24.44	24.61		264	79.80		
203	24.95	25.10		265	81.21		
204	25.47	25.61		266	82.65		83.81 Schm. 90. Bet.
205	26.00	26.13		267	84.10		
206	26.55	26.66		268	85.58		
207	27.10	27.20		269	87.08		
208	27.66	27.74		270	88.60		88.6 94.0 Rob.
209	28.23	28.29		271	90.14		
210	28.81	28.84		272	91.70	(79.94)	92.3
211	29.40	29.41		273	93.29		
212	30.00	30.00	Ether 137.6 D. as water 84° higher. Alc. 58.5 D. as water 85° higher.	274	94.91		
				275	96.55		98.53 Schm.
				276	98.21		
213	30.61	31.3		277	99.90		
214	31.23	31.9		278	101.6		105.2
215	31.87	32.5		279	103.3		
216	32.51	33.2		280	105.1		109 Schm. 105.9 Rob. 106 Bet.
217	33.16	33.7					
218	33.83	34.6		281	106.9		
219	34.50	35.1		282	108.7	(90.99)	
220	35.19	35.9	35.8 Rob. Alc. as water 42° higher. Rob.	283	110.6		
				284	112.4		116.98 Schm.
221	35.89	36.4	36.41 Schm.	285	114.3		
222	36.60	(36.25) 37.0		286	116.2		120.5 Schm.
223	37.33			287	118.2		
224	38.07			288	120.1		
225	38.82			289	122.1		
226	39.58			290	124.2		126. Schm.
227	40.35			291	126.2		
228	41.14			292	128.3	(102.45)	
229	41.94			293	130.5		
230	42.75	43.2	43.11 Schm. 44.7 Rob.	294	132.6		
231	43.58		Muriate of lime 30, D. as water 18° lower.	295	134.8		
				296	137.0		
232	44.42	(43.24) 44.8		297	139.2		
233	45.28			298	141.5		
234	46.15			299	143.8		
235	47.03			300	146.2		
236	47.93			301	148.6		

	Formula.	Dalton.
302°	150.9	(114.15)
303	153.4	
304	155.8	
305	158.3	
306	160.9	
307	163.5	
308	166.0	
309	168.7	
310	171.4	
311	174.1	
312	176.2	

The vapour of sulfuric acid ought to have a force of .1 at 390°, that of mercury at 460°, the one boiling at 590°, the other at 660° Dalton.

Chemical and Physiological Effects.

See Economy of Heat.

Richmann on solutions at different temperatures. N. C. Petr. IV. 270.

Blagden's observations made in a heated room. Ph. tr. 1775. 111.

Supported a heat of about 300° in air : and there was no evaporation from the skin to assist in cooling, on the contrary, water was deposited. Tillet found two girls that supported a heat of 280° in an oven. Mercury could not be borne at 120°, nor water at 125°; oil was supportable at 129°, and spirits of wine at 130°.

Harniss on the chemical action of light and heat. Nich. V. 245.

Journ. de phys. LVII. 66.

An account of a Spaniard who washed his hands and face in oil at 224°, put his foot on a red hot iron, and held a lighted candle to his leg. His pulse was 130° or 140°.

See Physiology.

Soda and potash are said to exchange their acids at different temperatures.

In general a bath is pleasantly warm from 90° to 110°; we drink tea about 115° or more, coffee sometimes at 130°

Permanent Effects of Heat and Cold.

*Hooke on glass drops. Micrographia.

Homberg on the Batavian drops. A. P. II. 85. X. 146.

Wolf on brittle bottles. A. P. 1743. H. 43.

Bruni on the Bologna bottles. Ph. tr. 1745. XLIII. 272.

Watson on unannealed glass vessels. Ph. tr. 1745. XLIII. 505.

Casali on unannealed glass. C. Bon. II. i. 321, 328. III. 406. V. ii. 169.

Lecat on glass drops, and on the tempering of steel. Ph. tr. 1749. XLVI. 175.

Observes, that a drop may sometimes be ground away by emery and oil without breaking. Compares tempering to annealing.

Hanow on the Bologna jars. Danz. Gesell. I. 584. III. 328.

Hanow Versuche mit den Springkölbchen. 4. Danz. 1751.

Bosc d'Antic on glass drops. S. E. IV.

Kaestner de lacrymis vitreis. Dissert. viii. 59. 125.

Maupetit on the glass drop. Roz. VI. 394.

*Coulomb. A. P. 1764. 265.

Found that the force of torsion is equally powerful in wires annealed and unannealed: they perfomed their vibrations in equal times. A tempered bar required also as much force to deflect it to a given angle, as a hard one of the same dimensions. A soft bar, a spring tempered, and a hard one, were bent to equal angles by 5 pounds; with 6 the hard bar broke, with 7 the soft one bent, but returned as far from its new position upon the removal of the weight, as if it had not bent. The elastic bar was broken by 18 pounds. Chladni also found the sound of soft iron and steel similar to that of the hardest, and I have observed the same in a tuning fork. This may be inferred from the theory of annealing; the whole cohesive force not being affected by the partial extensions of some strata and the consequent condensation of others.

Nicholson. Manch. M. II. 370.

Observes, that the specific gravity of lead and tin varies in the third figure of the number expressing it, according to the different modes of cooling.

Guyton on tempering steel. Ann. Ch. XXVII. 186.

From Nicholson. See Cutlery.

Cavallo. Nat. Ph. II. 27.

A piece of steel, which measured 2.769 inches when soft, was found, by Mr. Pennington, to measure after hardening, 2.7785, and when again tempered so as to become blue, 2.768. The specific gravity of hammered steel is 7.84, that of hardened steel 7.816. The difference of the length is $\frac{1}{717}$, that of the specific gravity from tempering consequently $\frac{1}{11}$; but the hammering increases it to $\frac{1}{7}$. The expansion of water by freezing presents a similar phenomenon.

On the flexure of wax and metal in cooling. Nich. 8. IV. 176.

Hatchett. Ph. tr. 1803. 118.

Found that gold debased with impure copper became brittle when cast in moulds of sand, but was rendered ductile when cast in moulds of iron. The specific gravity of standard gold when cast in iron was also greater than when cast in sand, in the ratio of 290 to 289, and in one experiment of 61 to 60. The metal cooled more rapidly in sand. In some cases the evolution of gas may, perhaps, be concerned in affecting the specific gravity.

Communication of Heat by contact and in general.

La Chapelle on a bar of steel becoming hot when withdrawn from boiling water. A. P. II. 25.

Homberg on the increased heat of the bottom of a vessel when removed from the fire. A. P. 1703. H. 24.

This appears to be a fallacy: with a clean surface it may easily be detected.

Martine's essay on the heating and cooling of bodies.

Richmann on the laws of the decrement of heat. N. C. Petr. I. 174. II. 172.

Makes its decrement as the surface exposed and as the difference of temperature conjointly.

Richmann on the cooling bodies in air. N. C. IV. 241.

Insists that a ball of metal 4 inches in diameter cannot be heated by boiling water beyond 207°: and the experiments seem to indicate, that even in cooling its temperature is always lower, which indeed is the only point that can affect the theory. Brass and copper retain heat longer than iron, iron than tin, and tin than lead.

Lambert on heating and cooling. Act. Helv. II. 172.

Lambert Pyrometrie.

Darwin. Ph. tr. 1757. 240.

Supposes steam to float in air, and retain its heat.

Musschenbroek's table of the time of heating of different bodies. Introd. II. 678.

Euler on the motions of fluids from heat. N. C. Petr. XI. 232. XIII. 305. XIV. 270. XV. 7, 219.

Braun on the communication of heat. N. C. Petr. XII. 289. Roz. I. 1.

Confirms Richmann's experiments on boiling water and alcohol: but finds the result different with wine and oils. For these, however, the boiling point must be variable, and the result is of no value.

Roy. Ph. tr. 1777. 720.

Observes, that water is a very bad conductor of heat.

Erxleben on the laws of heat. N. C. Gott. 1777. VIII. 74.

Exceptions to the law of Newton, Richmann, and Lambert.

Achard on the conducting powers of gases. A. Berl. 1783. 84.

Achard's comparison of heat and electricity. Roz. XXII. 245.

Achard on the cooling of bodies in air of different densities. A. Berl. 1785. 24.

Makes no general conclusions. The difference between the rates of cooling in air exhausted to $\frac{4}{5}$ and to $\frac{1}{5}$ was sometimes imperceptible, and scarcely in any case $\frac{1}{15}$.

Fordyce's experiment on heat. Ph. tr. 1787. 310.

Two equal cylinders of pasteboard were inclosed in eider down under glass, one was covered with iron, the other with pasteboard, both painted with the same black paint, which was exposed to the sun's rays: the pasteboard never transmitted a heat of more than 110°, the iron 121°: the iron also retained its heat much the longest.

Sir B. Thompson on heat. Ph. tr. 1786. 273. Ess. II. viii. Repert. IV. 30. Gilb. V. 288.

The conducting power of mercury being 1000, that of moist air was 330, of water 313, of common air 80.41, of air $\frac{1}{4}$ as dense 80.23, of air $\frac{1}{14}$ as dense 78, of a vacuum 55. The two last numbers, compared with the conducting power of common air, appear to indicate a formula of this kind, $55 + 25.4 d^{\frac{1}{11}}$, d being the density, compared with that of the atmosphere.

Sir B. Thompson's experiments on heat. Ph. tr. 1792. 48.

Maintains that the attraction of loose substances for air is the principal cause of their impeding the passage of heat: thinks that elastic fluids do not conduct heat like solids and liquids, from particle to particle.

Count Rumford on the propagation of heat in fluids. Ess. I. vi. Ph. M. II. 343. Gilb. 244.

Extends to liquids what he had before suggested respecting elastic fluids. Observes, that water thickened with farinaceous substances is with difficulty heated and cooled, and that fruits have the same property.

Rumford on a phenomenon observed in the glaciers. Ph. tr. 1804. 23. Nich. IX. 58.

The consequence of the expansion of water when it is much cooled, and of the want of conducting power of fluids.

Saussure on collecting heat by glasses. Voyage dans les Alpes. § 932.

Ingenhousz on the heat acquired by metals. Verm. Schr. II. 341. Gren. I. 154. Roz. 1789. i.

Humboldt on the conducting power of various substances for heat. Roz. XLIII. 304.

Lichtenberg in Erxleben.

Silver is the best conductor, platina the worst.

Mayer on the conducting power of metals. Gren. IV. 22.

Mayer on heat communicated by wood. Crell's Journ. Ann. Ch. XXX. 32.

Guyton on the conducting power of charcoal. Ann. Ch. XXVI. 225. Nich. II. 499. Ph. M. II. 182.

Charcoal transmitted in $\frac{3}{4}$ of an hour only $60\frac{1}{4}°$ W. an equal coat of sand $89°$.

Deluc's remarks on Rumford's experiments. Gilb. I. 464.

Socquet on the conducting powers of fluids. Journ. Phys. XLIX. 441. Gilb. VI. 407. Repert. XIII. 277.

Asserts their conducting powers.

Thomson on the conducting powers of fluids. Nich. IV. 529. Nich. 8. I. 81. Gilb. XIV. 129, 146.

* Dalton on the power of fluids to conduct heat. Manch. M. V. 373. Nich. 8. IV. 56. Repert. ii. II. 282. Gilb. XIV. 184.

Shows that fluids actually conduct heat when quiescent, but that their motions are usually the most concerned in its communication. Says that water conducts heat, as it does electricity, more readily than ice: that the maximum of effect of water in thawing ice must be at the maximum of density: which, by neglecting to consider the expansion of glass, he erroneously places at $42\frac{1}{2}°$.

Nicholson's experiment on the conducting powers of fluids. Nich. V. 197.

Murray on the passage of heat through fluids. Nich. I. 165, 242. Gilb. XIV. 158.

Biot on the experiments of Count Rumford and Thomson. B. Soc. Ph. n. 53, 62.

Biot on the propagation of heat in solids. B. Soc. Phil. n. 88. Gilb. XVII. 231.

Confirms Newton's law of decrements proportional to the difference of temperature. A bar of iron was dipped at one end in mercury at $216°$, and 7 holes were made in it at equal distances, in which thermometers were placed: the last was never affected: the next, which was at the distance of 39 inches, was never raised more than $1°$ of Réaumur. Such a rod is recommended as a thermometer for high temperatures: but it is probable that the effect of the air would produce great irregularities. Copper appeared to conduct heat somewhat more readily than iron. The temperatures of thermometers were nearly in geometrical proportion when their distances were in arithmetical proportion.

Leslie's inquiry into the nature of heat.

Maintains that heat is communicated through gases in three ways, by pulsation, by abduction, as in solids, and by regression or circulation: but in liquids he finds that there is no radiation.

Parrot on the propagation of heat in fluids. Gilb. XVII. 257, 369.

Berthollet. Chem. Stat. Nich. VIII. 134.

Thinks that fluids must communicate heat from particle to particle.

Hornblower on the nonconducting power of fluids. Nich. VIII. 169.

Radiant Heat.

Construction of burning lenses and mirrors. See Optical Instruments.

Mariotte on the heat of a burning mirror. A. P. I. 223.

Mariotte observes, that terrestrial heat is intercepted by glass, while light is transmitted. Oeuvres. I.

Homberg on a burning mirror. A. P. 1705. H. 39.

Little effect was produced when the heat of the atmosphere was considerable.

Homberg on the ancient burning glasses. A. P. 1711. H. 16.

†Lahire on the heat of the lunar rays. A. P. 1705. 346.

Harris and Desaguliers on Villette's concave. Ph. tr. 1719. XXX. 970.

It burnt less powerfully as it grew hot.

Segner de speculis Archimedeis. 4. Jen. 1722.

Dufay's catoptrical experiments. A. P. 1726. 115, 165. H. 47.

Courtivron's catoptrical researches. A. P. 1747. 449.

Buffon on burning mirrors. A. P. 1747. 82. 1748. 305.

Burnt wood at 209 feet, by 168 small plane mirrors.

Richmann on the heat of a pencil of rays. N. C. Petr. III. 340. IV. 277.

It was nearly in the inverse ratio of the square of the distance from the focus. See Expansion.

Nollet's experiments with concentrated solar rays. A. P. 1757. 551. H. 23.

Zeiher on burning lenses. N. C. Petr. VII. 237.

Pistoi on the heating of bodies by light. A. Sienn. II. 126.

Franklin on the effect of colours in the admission of heat. Letter lvi. Roz. II. 381.

Wolfe. Ph. tr. 1769. 4.

Hoesen's mirrors melted a wheel nail in 3 seconds, a pistole in 2. Hoffman used them opposite to each other, and collected the heat radiating from a stove strongly heated. 2 Sept. 1768.

Watson on the heat admitted by blackened bodies. Ph. tr. 1773. 40.

Found an elevation from 108° to 118°, by coating the glass bulb of a thermometer with Indian ink.

Lavoisier on the heating of coloured bodies. 1772. ii. 614. 1773. H. 81.

Trudaine on his lens. A. P. 1774. Essai.

It was observed, that the wood caught fire more towards the extremity of the image than in the centre; but this was only from aberration, 70, 71. The diameter was 4 feet, the focal length about 11.

Cavallo's thermometrical experiments. Ph. tr. 1780. 585.

Found that a blackened thermometer rose about 10° higher in the sun's rays, and showed some difference even in the daylight. Found no heat from the moon. When the balls of thermometers were coloured, the colours nearest the violet showed the greatest heat.

Marcorelle on thermometers in different situations. S. E. X. 85.

In August, at Toulon, the sun's rays raised the thermometer 8° or 9°, and twice as much when it was surrounded with other objects. Maitan found that the heat reflected on a thermometer by plane mirrors was proportionate to their number.

Socin on the reflection of heat. Roz. XXVII. 268.

*Pictet on the effect of colours, and on the reflection of invisible heat. Essais de physique.

Pictet's further experiments. Nich. 8. III. 223. Gilb. XIII. 120.

The heat of a candle was intercepted by glass.

Prévost sur l'équilibre du feu. 8. Genev. Gren. VI. Rozier. XXXVIII. 314.

Prévost on heat and its interception. Ph. tr. 1802. 403.

Remarks on Herschel's experiments.

T. Wedgwood. Ph. tr. 1792. 370.

Found that a blackened wire was sooner heated and cooled than a wire not coloured.

Hutton's dissertation on light, heat and fire. 8. Acc. Ed. tr. IV. H. 7. Read 1794.

Calls radiant heat obscure light; observes the greater heat of the red rays, and says that a blackened thermometer is most sensible to the effect of obscure light, as well as to that of visible light.

*Herschel on the heat of the prismatic rays, on the invisible rays of the sun, and on the solar and terrestrial rays that occasion heat. Ph. tr. 1800. 255, 284, 293, 437. Nich. IV. 320, 360. V. 69. Ph. M. VII. VIII. Gilb. VII. 137.

With many experiments on the transmission of heat.

†Leslie's observations on light and heat. Nich. IV. 344, 416. Gilb. X. 88.

*Leslie on heat.

Benzenberg's remarks on Leslie. Gilb. X. 356.

Hermstädt on the effect of heat on different colours. A. Berl. 1801. 83.

Schmidtmüller on the heat communicated to wood by the sun's rays. Gilb. XIV. 306.

Rumford's experiments on radiant heat. Ph. tr. 1804. 77. B. Soc. Phil. n. 87. Gilb. XVII. 33, 218.

On the effects of colours, and on the nature of the surface.

Böckmann's prize essay on the heating of bodies in the solar rays. Note. Gilb. XVII. 122.

On the velocity of radiant heat. Ph. M. XIX. 309.

Parker's was a double convex lens, three feet in diameter, 3 inches thick in the middle: it weighed 212 pounds. Its aperture when set was $32\frac{1}{4}$ inches; its focal length 6 feet 8 inches: the focal length was generally shortened by a smaller lens. The most refractory substance fused was a cornelian, which required 75″ for its fusion; a crystal pebble was fused in 6″; a piece of white agate in 30″. Cavallo. The finger might be placed in the cone of rays within an inch of the focus, without inconvenience. Imison's elements. I. 371. But this remark appears to require confirmation: if it were accurate, we might expect the smallest imperfection in the focal adjustment of the eye to cause a great difference in the apparent brilliancy of an object; which is not the fact: indeed Count Rumford's late experiments appear wholly to confute it.

Leslie discovered, by experiments made in 1802, that the heat emitted by radiation was affected by the nature of the surface exposed. The action of a blackened surface of tin being 100, that of a steel plate was 15, of clean tin 12, of tin scraped bright 16, when scraped with the edge of a fine file in one direction 26, when scraped again across about 13, a surface of lead clean 19, covered with a grey crust 45, a thin coat of isinglass 80, resin 96, writing paper 98, ice 85. Heat as well as light is so projected from a surface as to be equally dense in all directions, consequently from each point in a quantity which is as the sine of the angle of inclination. The radiation is not affected by the quality of the gas, in contact with the surface, but it is not transmitted by water. For the time of cooling of a hollow tin ball 6 inches in diameter, filled with water, in still air, take, in minutes, $L.\frac{h}{i} - L.\frac{a+h}{a+i}$, making the three first decimals integers, h and i being the temperatures on the centigrade scale, and a being 50. And for the same ball painted, make $a = 110$, and take $\frac{1}{11}$ of the result: thus, from 100° C. to 50°, or 212° F. to 122°, metal takes 124′.9, paper or paint 83′.2, to 10° C. or 50° F. 602′ and 844′.1 respectively. For the effect of different gases and different densities, in air the discharge from a vitreous surface is $\frac{1}{7}(3d^{\frac{1}{4}} + 4d^{\frac{1}{10}})$, from a metallic surface $\frac{1}{7}(3d^{\frac{1}{4}} + \frac{1}{2}d^{\frac{1}{10}})$; in hydrogen gas $\frac{1}{7}(12d^{\frac{1}{5}} + 4d^{\frac{1}{10}})$, and $\frac{1}{7}(12d^{\frac{1}{5}} + \frac{1}{2}d^{\frac{1}{10}})$. Thus, if $d = 1$, the abductive power of air is $\frac{3}{7}$, or .4286, the pulsatory energy of a vitreous surface $\frac{4}{7}$, or .5714, of a metallic surface $\frac{1}{14}$, or .0714. In hydrogen gas the pulsatory power the same, the abductive power $\frac{12}{7}$, or 1.7143. If $d = \frac{1}{12}$, the abductive power is .18 for air, .857 for hydrogen, the pulsatory power .48 or .06 in air, .51 or .0637 in hydrogen. If $d = \frac{1}{256}$, the abductive power is .1071 for air, .5655 for hydrogen, the pulsatory power .438 or .054 for air, .475 or .0594 for hydrogen. It would be easy to make an experiment on the velocity with which radiant heat is conveyed to a distance, and there is little doubt but that such an experiment would confute Mr. Leslie's hypothesis of the transmission of heat by a pulsation of the air propagated with the velocity of sound.

Capacity for Heat.

See Natural History.

Compression. See Sources of Heat.

†Desaguliers's experiments on quicksilver and water. Ph. tr. 1720. 81.
> Makes the quicksilver contain most heat in the same bulk.

Richmann on the heat of mixtures. N. C. Petr. I. 152, 168, 174.

Richmann on the heat of quicksilver. N. C. Petr. III. 309.

Richmann on the cooling of bodies. N. C. Petr. IV. 241.

Braun on the phenomena of heat. N. C. Petr. X. 309.

Musschenbroek's table of the time of heating. Introd. II. 678.

Baumé on cold from evaporation. S. E. V. 405, 425.

*Black's experiments on heat.
> Acc. Roz. Intr. II. 428.

Irvine's essays.

Lavoisier and Laplace on a new mode of measuring heat. A. P. 1780. 355. H. 3.
> By the melting of ice.

Cavendish. Ph. tr. 1783. 312.
> Says, that heat is "generated" in freezing, and "disappears" in thawing.

*Wedgwood on the calorimeter. Ph. tr. 1784. 371.

*Crawford on animal heat and combustion. 8. Lond. 2 ed. 1788.

Wilke on specific heat. Roz. XXVI. 256, 381.
> The capacity of water being 1, that of an equal weight of agate is .195, glass .187, iron .126, brass .116, copper .114, zinc 102, silver .082, antimony .063, tin .06, gold .05, bismuth .043, lead .042. But for equal volumes, the proportions are, copper 1.027, water 1, iron .993, brass .971, gold .966, ver .833, agate .517, lead .487, glass .448.

Carette Soyer on the heat excited by lime. Roz. XXIX. 333.

Kirwan's table in Magellan's essay on fire.

Berlinghieri esame della teoria di Crawford. 4. Pisa, 1787.

Espr. des Journ. Mars. 1790.

Gren on Crawford. Journ I.

Morgan on Crawford.

Seguin. Ann. Ch. III. 148. V. 191.

Table of specific heats. Cavallo. N. Ph. III. 70.

From Crawford, Kirwan, and Lavoisier. Specimens.

Water	1.000	Nitrous acid	L. .661
Oxygen	C. 4.749		K. .844
	K. 37.	Spermaceti oil	C. .500
Atmospheric air	C. 1.790		K. .399
	K. 18.670	Iron	C. .127
Aqueous vapour	C. 1.790		K. .125
	Pictet (8.5)		L. .101
Carbonic acid	C. 1.045	Mercury	L. .029
	K. .027		K. .033

Table of capacities for heat. *Thomson's* chemistry. I. R. I.

According to the doctrine which derives many of the variations of sensible heat from the variations of capacity of the substances concerned, the heat extricated by compression, and absorbed in dilatation, must be referred to such a change of capacity, and every substance must have its capacity diminished in proportion as it occupies less space. We may endeavour to ascertain in what ratio this diminution of capacity takes place, supposing, as the most probable ground of calculation, that a condensation in a given degree diminishes the total capacity in a given ratio, whatever the initial density may have been: the capacity must therefore be supposed to vary as a certain power of the rarity; and taking $-1400°$ as the natural zero, we may inquire what that power is. In Mr. Dalton's experiments, 50 degrees of heat, or somewhat more, were produced when the air was readmitted into a space partially exhausted: now it is evident that this cannot be the whole change of temperature of the air so compressed, since it is mixed with the air admitted, which is left in its original state of equilibrium. Suppose the density of the air in the receiver at 50° F. to have been diminished x times, then its capacity will be diminished by compression x^n times, and its temperature will be increased $1450 x^n - 1450$; but this increase of temperature is to be diffused through x times as much air, and it will then become $ax^{n-1} - ax^{-1}$, calling 1450 a, which becomes a maximum when $(n-1).ax^{n-2}\dot{x} + ax^{-2}\dot{x} = 0$, or $(n-1)x^n + 1 = 0$, or $x = (1-n)^{-\frac{1}{n}}$, which, as n becomes small, approaches to 2.718 as its limit. Consequently the greatest heat that can be produced in this manner is when the air has been exhausted to about $\frac{1}{e}$ of the atmospheric density, wherever we place the natural zero. Putting then $\frac{1450 \times 2.7^n - 1450}{2.7} = 50$, we have $2.7^n = \frac{50 \times 2.7}{1450} + 1 = 1.093$, whence n is about $\frac{1}{11.2}$, and the heat produced by compression to x times the density should be $1450 \left(x^{\frac{1}{11.2}} - 1 \right)$, which, if $x = 2$, becomes 93°; and such should have been the degree of cold produced by the return of air of double the natural density to the state of equilibrium. Whether this effect was lost by the difficulty of making the observation with accuracy, or whether the friction produces some heat which is confounded with the effect of expansion, may perhaps be determined by future experiments: but in this case Mr. Dalton observed only a heat of 50°, as in the former experiment. We may, however, deduce from that experiment an acceleration of about $\frac{1}{7}$ to be added to the calculation of the velocity of sound; and since the results of experiments on sound require an acceleration of $\frac{1}{6}$, or only $\frac{1}{4}$ more, which has been ascertained with great accuracy, it may be fair to allow the supposition of Laplace and Biot, that the whole acceleration of sound is owing to this cause, and we may at least assume that acceleration, as affording a limit, which the heat produced by condensation, certainly cannot exceed. We may therefore make the exponent of the density $\frac{1}{6}$, for expressing the change of capacity, and the heat produced $1450 \left(x^{\frac{1}{6}} - 1 \right)$, which, when the density is doubled or halved, becomes 131.2°. A compression of $\frac{1}{15}$ will produce a heat of 1°.

Now it appears from experiments on the sounds of different gases, and from the sound of a pipe in air of densities the most various, that the correction of the velocity of sound is nearly the same in all; hence it may be inferred that the heat produced by condensation follows nearly the same law with respect to all gases. This principle may therefore probably be extended to steam. Supposing the conversion of water into steam to absorb as much heat as would raise its temperature 940°, we may call its capacity at 212° 1.60, and may calculate a table for other temperatures, assuming, with Mr. Dalton, that its simple expansion by heat is equal to that of air. Mr. Watt has shown, by direct experiment, that steam has a greater capacity as its temperature is lower.

	Specific gravity.	Capacity.
182° F.	.56	1.72
192	.68	1.68
202	.83	1.64
212	1.00	1.60
222	1.21	1.56
232	1.44	1.53
242	1.71	1.50
252	2.03	1.47
262	2.38	1.44
272	2.80	1.41

Hence, if a steam engine work with double atmospheres, the heat being about 247°, it will require 1.87 times as much water, of which the capacity is 1.48, its excess above that of water $\frac{4}{5}$ as much as at 212°; it will therefore absorb about 752°, and the heat required for raising water from 100 will be as 1.87 (147 + 752), to 112 + 940, or nearly as 8 to 5, while the effect is doubled.

Robison says, that four ounces of water at 100°, will condense in a second nearly 200 cubic feet of steam, reducing its expansive force to one fifth. If this is correct, it sets at defiance all theories of capacity. The only distant analogy that can be found for it, is the facility with which rarefied air is found to carry off heat, which would induce us to suppose that the capacity of a given bulk of air is much less affected by its density than this calculation appears to demonstrate.

Natural Zero.

Opinions of Amontons, Lambert, and Dalton. See Expansion.

Seguin on heat. Ann. Ch. III. 148. Account of the theories of specific heat. V. 191. Nich. 8. IV. 221.

Observes, that from experiments on the mixture of sulfuric acid and water, it might be inferred that the natural zero is 7292° below the zero of Fahrenheit, but from Kirwan's experiments on ice only 1350°. Other experiments on ice give 1461°, Dalton 1547°.

Dalton on the natural zero. Gilb. XIV. 287.

Gay Lussac's experiments on Dalton's supposition give 1556°. Gilb.

Heat denominated latent.

Landriani. Opusc. fisicoch. viii. Roz. XXVI. 88, 197.

Soycourt against latent heat. Roz. XXXII. 143. Germ. Quedlinburg.
Young in *Higgins's* minutes of a society. 8. Lond. 1795.
Tilloch against latent heat. Ph. M. VIII. 70.
Leslie on heat. Against latent heat.

Economy of Heat and Cold.

Internal fire places in boilers. Birch. I. 173.
Defargues's remedy for smoke. Mach. A. I. 211.
On making ice in the torrid zone. A. P. IX. 320.
Chaumette's mode of preventing smoky chimnies. A. P. 1715. H. 65. Mach. A. III. 47.
Gauger's fire places and stoves. A. P. 1720. H. 114. Mach. A. IV. 11.
Gauger Mécanique du feu.
Smoke Jacks. Leup. Th. M. G. t. 51.
Aeolipile. Leupold. Th. M. G. t. 52.
Fresneau's culinary stove. A. P. 1739. H. 58.
Lagny's fire place with a valve for putting out the fire at pleasure. A. P. 1741. H. 165. Mach. A. VII. 115.
Volckamer on putting out fires in chimnies by gunpowder. Coll. Ac. VI. 281.
Cooke on warming rooms by steam. Ph. tr. 1745. XLIII. 370.
Vannières's portable fire place. A. P. 1752. H. 148.
Pigage's boiler, with a fire in the centre. Mach. A. VII. 307.
Nollet on producing cold without ice. A. P. 1756. 82. H. 1.
Genneté's cover for a chimney. A. P. 1759. H. 232.
Smoke jack, Emers. mech. f. 235.
Montalembert on the conversion of open fire places into stoves. A. P. 1763. 335. H. 7.
J. A. Euler on ovens. A. Berl. 1766. 302.
Euler on the equilibrium of fluids. N. C. Petr. XIII. 305. XIV. i. 270. XV. 1, 219.
With the effects of heat.
Ziegler de digestore Papini. Bâle, 1769.
Gramont on the Chinese stove. Ph. tr. 1771. 59.
Henry's self moving register for a flue. Am. tr. I. 350.
Franklin on smoky chimnies. Am. tr. II. 1.
Franklin on chimnies. Am. tr. II. 231.
Franklin's stove consuming its smoke. Am. tr. II. 57. Roz. XXXV. 356.
The draught going down.
Acc. A. P. 1773. H. 77.
Franklin on smoky chimnies. Lond.
Stoves and fire places. Roz. Introd. I. 615. IX. 49, 162.
Barker on the mode of making ice in the East Indies. Ph. tr. 1775. 252.
By evaporation. Natural ice unknown there. The water perforates through earthen ware pans placed on sugar canes in straw.
On heating rooms. Roz. XV. 148.
Clements's oven. Bailey's mach. II. 55.
Lavoisier on fuel. A. P. 1781. 379.
Furnaces. E. M. Pl. H. Fer. Glaces. E. M. A. III. Art. Fournaliste.
Smoky chimnies. E. M. A. III. Art. Fumiste.
E. M. A. III. Art. Glacière.
Stoves. E. M. A. VI. Art. Poëlier.
A Prussian oven for coals. Roz. XXIII. 433.
Sanches on the vapour baths of Russia. Roz. XXV. 141.
Sage on fuel. A. P. 1785. 239. 1789. 548. Roz. XXXV. 385. Repert. V. 418.
Says that coal gives 7 times as much heat as an equal weight of wood.
Beddoes's account of Walker's experiments on freezing mixtures. Ph. tr. 1787. 282.
Walker on artificial cold. Ph. tr. 1788. 395. 1795. 270. 1801. 120.

Equal parts of muriate of ammonia and nitre, dissolved in water, sink the thermometer about 40°, and may be dried again. Phosphate of soda 9, nitrate of ammonia 6, dilute nitrous acid 4, depress the temperature from 50° to —21°. Muriate of lime 3, snow 2, sink it from 32° to —50°; caustic potash 4, snow 3, to —51°. Ice ground to powder with a centrebit is better than snow, frozen vapour than either.

Rumford on the preparation of food. Ess. I. iii.

*Rumford on fire places. Ess. I. iv.

Rumford on the management of fire and the economy of fuel. Ess. II. vi. Gilb. III. 309. IV. 85, 330.

One pound of pine wood burnt raised the temperature of 20.1 pounds of water 180 degrees: from Kirwan's comparison the same quantity of pitcoal would raise 36 pounds of water in the same degree, and a pound of charcoal 57.6 pounds. According to Lavoisier, equal heats are produced by 403 pounds of coke, 600 of pit coal, 600 of charcoal, and 1089 of oak wood. In general ¾ of the heat of the fuel employed are wasted.

Rumford's perpetual lime kiln. Ess. Journ. Phys. XLIX. 65.

Rumford on increasing the heat of fires by balls. Journ. R. I., I. Repert. XV. 248. Ph. M. X. 42.

Rumford on conveying heat by steam. Journ. R. I., I. Nich. V. 159. Repert. XV. 186. Ph. M. X. 46. Gilb. XIII. 385.

On the cold produced by tattees. Asiatic mirror. May 1789.

See Meteorology, Observations of Climates.

Anderson on smoky chimnies.

*Fossombroni on salt works. Soc. Ital. VII. 57.

Wood produces heat enough in its combustion to evaporate twice its weight of water, and to prepare ¼ of its weight of salt.

Saint Julien on warm baths. Roz. XXXII. 51.

Miché on reverberating furnaces. Roz. XXXII. 385.

Descharmes on a glass house. Roz. XXXVIII. 341.

Williams on the mode of making ice at Benares. Ph. tr. 1793. 56, 129.

It is made when the thermometer is between 35° and 42°.

Blakey on fire machinery. 8. Lond. 1798.

Enc. Br. Art. Furnace.

Brown's evaporator. S. A. XII. 257.

Green's patent for warming rooms. Repert. I. 21.

Stratton's patent kitchen range. Repert. I. 289.

Hoyle's patent for heating buildings. Repert. I. 300.

Ward's patent for employing smoke. Repert. I. 373.

Percival's chamber lamp furnace. Repert. III. 24.

Conway's patent coke oven. Repert. III. 75.

Mode of sweeping chimnies by machinery. Repert. III. 322.

Lowitz on the production of cold. Ann. Ch. XXII. 297.

Percival's lamp furnace. Ir. tr. IV. 91.

Smith's kettle for inflammable fluids. Am. tr. IV. 431. Repert. XV. 327.

On artificial cold. Gilb. I. 479. II. 107.

Pepys on artificial cold. Ph. M. III. 76.

Froze 56 pounds of mercury; produced a cold of —52°. Walker's greatest cold was —63°.

Watt's patent furnaces. Repert. IV. 226.

For burning smoke.

Braithwaite's patent smoke jacks. Repert. VI. 1.

Brodie's patent ship's stove. Repert. VII. 22.

Blast machine at Carron. Smeaton's reports.

Russian stoves. Repert. VII. 63.

Redman's patent portable kitchen. Repert. VII. 105.

Lastérie on the alcarrazas, for cooling liquors. B. Soc. Phil. n. 13.

Collins's patent grate. Repert. VIII. 361.

Peale's improved fireplace. Am. tr. V. 320. Repert. ii. II. 436.
With a sliding frontispiece.

Frearson's patent for evaporation. Repert. IX. 217.

Hassenfratz on the best form of boilers for evaporation. Journ polyt. II. vi. 364.

Chaptal on Schmidt's stove. Ann. Ch. XXXII. 270.

Clavering on chimnies. London.

*Clavelin on chimnies and fire places. Extr. Ann. Ch. XXXIII. 172. Gilb. VI. 293.

Howard's improved air furnaces. Ph. M. V. 190.

*Roebuck on blast furnaces. Ed. tr. V. 31. Nich. IV. 110. Ph. M. VI. 324. Repert. XIII. 19.
Recommends a large quantity of air, supplied with a moderate velocity.

Burns's stoves and grates. Ph. M. V. 204.

Burns's patent grates. Repert. XII. 225. Ph. M. VII. 264.
For preventing accidents.

Blundell's patent machine for saving fuel. Repert. X. 84.

Howard's patent pneumatic kitchen. Repert. X. 147.

Raley's patent furnace. Repert. X. 155.

Kirwan on the carbon in coals. Ir. tr. Repert. XIII. 171.

Fabbroni on the alcarrazas. Gilb. III. 230. Repert. XIII. 274.

Crosbey's patent fire places. Repert. XII. 73.
With tubes, and a false back.

Whittington's patent baking stove. Repert. XII. 78.

Marquard's vapour blowpipe. Repert. XIII. 274.

Rowntree's patent application of fire to boilers. Repert. XIV. 1.
On Rumford's principles, making the smoke descend.

Holmes's family oven, without flues. S. A. XVIII. 230. Repert. XIV. 186.
Heated by a piece of iron projecting into the fire.

Wakefield's steam houses for pines. S. A. XVIII. 398.

Power's patent portable oven. Repert. XIV. 365.

Guyton on Carcel's lamp. Ann. Ch. XXXVIII. 135.
It produced a heat of $7°$ W. or $505.6°$ C. $942°$ F.

Guyton's Swedish stove. Ann. Ch. XLI. 97. Repert. XVI. 254. Nich. 8. II. 24.
With apertures emitting heated air.

Sir G. O. Paul's stoves for ventilating hospitals. S. A. XIX. 330. Repert. ii. II. 268.

Robertson's stove consuming its smoke. Ph. M. XI. 65.

Bérard's stove. B. Mélanges. 57.

Edelcrantz's digester. Journ. Phys. LVI. 147. Nich. VII. 161. Ph. M. XVII. 162.

Anderson's patent hothouses for saving fuel. Anderson's Recreations. Repert. XV. 298.

Cadet de Vaux on cooking with steam. Gilb. XI. 244.

Smith's patent vapour bath. Repert. ii. I. 411.

Thilorier's stove without smoke. Gilb. XI. 241.

Woolf on heating by steam. Gilb. XIII. 395.

A blowpipe by alcohol. Nich. 8. III. 1.

Stephens's patent lime kiln. Repert. ii. III. 89.

On sweeping chimnies. Repert. ii. III. 156.

Wyatt's evaporator. Repert. ii. III. 360.

Hooke's blowpipe by alcohol. Nich. 8. IV. 106.

Black's furnace improved. Nich. VI. 273.

Gilbert on heating fluids by steam. Gilb. XVI. 509.

A furnace for smelting iron. Rees cyclop. II. Pl.

Revolving apparatus for distilling. Rees cyclop. II. Pl. Art. Chemistry.

Hornblower on sweeping chimnies by a blast. Nich. VII. 246.

A mode of heating boilers at Meux's brewery. Ph. M. XVII. 275.

Aikin's portable blast furnace. Ph. M. XVII. 166.

Accum's chemical lamp. Nich. VIII. 216.

Greenough on Melograni's blowpipe. Nich. IX. 25, 143.

Curaudau's evaporating furnace. Nich. IX. 204.

An improved maltkiln. Ph. M. XX. 71.

A good freezing mixture is muriate of lime 5, water 1; or nitrate of ammonia 1, water 1; or muriate of ammonia 5, nitrate of potash 5, water 16. Alcohol and snow produce great cold.

Extinction of Heat.

Bertholon on extinguishing fires. M. Laus. III. 1.

Van Marum's portable pump for extinguishing fires. Repert. ii. III. 461. Nich. 8. V. 103.

Nature of Heat.

Homberg. A. P. 1700. H. 11.
Mentions some effects of motion analogous to those of heat, fixing a vessel to the clapper of a mill.

Lomonosow on the cause of heat and cold. N. C. Petr. I. 206.
Supposes heat to consist in motion.

Whitehurst on the weight of ignited substances. Ph. tr. 1776. 575.

Euler on the nature of the air. A. Petr. III. i. 162.
Supposes the particles of air to revolve within vesicles of water with a velocity of 2150 feet in a second, at $212°$; that this velocity varies as the square root of the expansive force, becoming 1700 at $100°$ of Delisle's thermometer, 1330 at $200°$. This variation is however somewhat too great.

Cavendish. Ph. tr. 1783. 312.
Thinks Sir Isaac Newton's opinion of heat much the most probable.

Achard's comparison of heat and electricity. Roz. XXII. 245.

Achard on the tendency of heat to ascend. A. Berl. 1788. 3. Printed 1793.
The experiments are not conclusive.

Fordyce on the loss of weight in heated bodies. Ph. tr. 1785. 361.
Probably the effect of an ascending current of air.

Fordyce's experiment on heat. Ph. tr. 1787. 310.
Is persuaded that heat is a quality and not a substance.

Romé de l'isle and Marivetz on the matter of heat. Roz. XXXII. 63, 71.

Henry on the increase of weight in heated bodies. Manch. M. III. 174.
Explains it from oxidation.

Henry on the materiality of heat. Manch. M. V. 603. Ph. M. XV. 45. Nich. 8. III. 197.
Thinks that the heat excited by friction may be borrowed from without. But to borrow heat from another body is to be colder than that body, and to cool it.

Reynier on the nature of fire. Roz. XXXVI. 94.

Beddoes. Ph. tr. 1791. 173.
Observes, that heat and flame are produced by oxygen already fixed, in the manufacture of iron.

*Pictet Essais de physique. 8.
The tendency to ascend, which he attributes to heat, may perhaps be partly understood from the great comparative capacity for heat of air highly rarefied.

*Prévost sur l'équilibre du feu. 8. Genev. Roz. XXXVIII. 314.

Young's remarks on the manufacture of iron. Gentl. Mag. 1792.

T. Wedgwood. Ph. tr. 1792. 270.
Air not visible made a wire red hot.

Dizé on heat as the cause of shining. Journ. Phys. XLIX. 177. Gilb. IV. 410.

Rumford on the heat caused by friction. Ph. tr. 1798. 80.
<small>The capacity of chips did not differ from that of any other iron.</small>

Rumford on the weight ascribed to heat. Ph. tr. 1799. 179. Repert. XII. 257. Nich. III. 381. Ph. M. IV. 162.
<small>Weighed water against mercury at different temperatures, and found no difference.</small>

Rumford on the nature of heat. Ph. tr. 1804. 77.
<small>Supposes a radiation of positive cold.</small>

Tilloch on the weight of heat. Ph. M. IX. 158.

Tilloch on the nature of heat. Ph. M. XII. 317.
<small>For caloric.</small>

Leslie on heat.

J. T. Mayer on the nature of heat. Commentat. Gott. 1803. XV. M. 1.
<small>In favour of the existence of caloric.</small>

On the chemical effects of tremors. Nich. VII. 122.
<small>Higgins slacked lime in vessels hermetically sealed, and found no difference in their weight.</small>

LITERATURE OF ELECTRICITY.

Gralath Electrische bibliothek. Danz. Gesellsch. I. 23. B. B.
<small>Copied in Priestley's Hist. Electr. at the end.</small>

Krünitz Verzeichniss der vornehmsten schriften von der electricität. 8. Leips. 1769.

Weigels Grundriss der Chemie.

ELECTRICITY IN GENERAL.

Gilbertus de magnete.

Guerike experimenta Magdeburgica. Ph. tr. abr. X. i. i. 269.

Homberg on the electricity of sulfur. A. P. II. 145.

Hauksbee's electrical experiments. Ph. tr. 1706. XXV. 2277. 1707. XXV. 2313, 2372. 1708. XXVI. 82, 87. 1709. XXVI. 391, 439. 1711. XXVII. 328.

Fr. by Desmarets. Abstr. A. P. 1754. H. 34.

Stephen Gray's electrical experiments. Ph. tr. 1720. XXXI. 104. 1731. XXXVII. 18. 1732. XXXVII. 397.

Dufay's eight memoirs. A. P. 1733, 1734, 1737.

Dufay's letter on electricity. Ph. tr. 1734. XXXVIII. 258.
<small>On vitreous and resinous electricity. Acknowledgements to Hauksbee and Gray.</small>

Schilling on electricity. M. Berl. 1734. IV. 334.

Desaguliers on electricity. Ph. tr. 1739. XLI. 186, 200. 1741. XLI. 634. 1742. XLII. 14, 140.

Desaguliers on electricity. Lond. 1742.

Martenson de electricitate. 4. Upsal, 1740, 1742.

Bose on electricity. A. P. 1743. H. 45.

Winklers Gedanken von der electricität. 8. Leipz. 1744.

Winklers Eigenschaften der electrischen materie. 8. Leipz. 1745.

Winkler Electricitatis recens observata. Ph. tr. 1745. XLIII. 317.

Rose Tentamina electrica. 4. Witteb. 1744.

Nollet on electricity. A. P. 1745, 1746, 1747, 1748, 1749, 1753, 1755, 1760, 1761, 1762, 1764, 1766.

Nollet Essai sur l'électricité. 12. Par. 1746.

Nollet Recherches sur l'électricité. 4. Par. 1749.

Nollet on electricity. Ph. tr. 1748. XLV. 187.

Nollet lettres sur l'électricité. 12. Par. 1753, 1760. M. B.

Extract by Watson. Ph. tr. 1753. 201. 1761. 336.

Watson on electricity. Ph. tr. 1745. XLIII. 481.
> Elementary. Mentions fixed inflammable air.

Watson. Ph. tr. 1746. XLIV. 41. 1747. 695, 704.
> Observes, after Nollet, that electricity is derived from the ground.

Watson on Franklin's theory. Ph. tr. 1751. 202.

Waiz Abhandlung von der electricität. 4. Berl. 1745.

Hollmann de igne electrico. Ph. tr. 1745. XLIII. 239.

Piderit de electricitate. Marburg, 1745.

†Miles's electrical experiments and observations. Ph. tr. 1746. XLIV. 27, 53, 78, 158.

Müller Ursach und nützen der electricitat. 1746.

Boze Recherches sur l'électricité. 1746. M. B.

Boze Tentamina electrica. 4. Wittemb. 1747. M. B.

†Hales on some electrical experiments. Ph. tr. 1748. XLV. 409.

Martin on electricity. 8. Bath, 1748.

Recueil de traités sur l'électricité. 8. Par. 1748.

Jallabert sur l'électricité. 8. Par. 1749. M. B.

Boulanger traité de l'électricité. 12. Par. 1750.

Secondat observations physiques. 12. Par. 1750.

Veratti sur l'électricité. 12. Montpel. 1750.

Dutour's researches on electricity. S. E. I. 345. II. 246, 516, 537. III. 244.

Bina Electricorum effectuum explicatio. 1751.

Wilson on some electrical experiments made at Paris. Ph. tr. 1753. 347. 1763. 436.

Wilson's short view of electricity. 4. London, 1780. R. I.

Canton's electrical experiments. Ph. tr. 1753. 350. 1754. 780.

Leroy on the species of electricity. A. P. 1753. 447. H. 18. 1755. 264. H. 20.

Franklin's electrical experiments. Ph. tr. 1755. 300.

Franklin's letter on electricity. Ph. tr. 1755. 305. 1760. 525.

*Franklin on electricity. 4. Lond. 1769, 1774. R. I.

Klingenstierna Tal om de nyaste rön vid electriciteten. Stockh. 1755.

Lovett's subtile medium. 8. 1756. R. I.

Lovett's philosophical essays. 8. Worcest. 1766. R. I.

Lovett's electrical philosopher. 8. 1777. R. I.

*Aepinus on some electrical experiments. A. Berl. 1756. N. C. Petr. VII. 277.

Musschenbroek Introductio ad Ph. Nat.

Euler junior on electricity. A. Berl. 1757. 125.

Beccaria Lettere dell' elettrismo. f. Bologna, 1758.

Beccaria's experiments. Ph. tr. 1760. 514, 525.

Beccaria dell' elettrismo artificiale. 4. Tur. 1772.

Beccaria on artificial electricity. 4. 1776. R. I.

Symmer's electrical experiments, with a letter of Mitchell. Ph. tr. 1759. 340.

Egelin de electricitate. 4. Utrecht, 1759.

Wesley's electricity made plain. 12. Lond. 1760.

Cigna's electrical experiments. M. Taur. II. 77. III. 31. V. i. 97.

Dalibard Histoire abregée de l'électricité. 2 v. 12. Par. 1766.

Saussure de electricitate. Genev. 1766.
Lullin de electricitate. 8. Genev. 1766.
Hurtmann's Versuche in leeren raüme. 8. Hanov. 1766.
Priestley's introduction to electricity. 8. Lond. 1769. R. I.
Priestley's history and present state of electricity. 4. Lond. 1769.
    Experiments made in 1766. 49.
Bauer von der theorie und dem nützen der electricität. 1770.
Ferguson's introduction to electricity. 8. Lond. 1771. R. S.
Sigaud de la Fond Traité de l'électricité. 12. Par. 1771. R. I.
  Acc. Roz. Intr. I. 89.
Sigaud de la Fond Précis des phénomènes electriques. Par. 1781.
Brydone on some electrical experiments. Ph. tr. 1773. 163.
Jacquet Précis de l'électricité. Vienna, 1775.
Becket on electricity. 8.
Berdoe on the electric fluid. 8.
Gross Electrische pausen. 8. Leips. 1776.
Dubois Lettre sur l'électricité. Tableau des sciences. Par. 1776. 143.
Weber Electrische versuche.
Socin Anfangsgründe der électricität. 1777.
Gallitzin's letters on electricity. A. Petr. I. ii. H. 25.
Le Prince Gallitzin sur l'électricité. 4. Petersb. 1778.
Herbert Theoria phaenomenorum electricitatis. Vienna, 1778.
*Lord Mahon's principles of electricity. 4. Lond. 1779. R. I.
Lord Mahon Principes d'électricité. 8. Lond. 1781. R. I.
Lyons's new system of electricity. 4. Lond. 1780.
Lyons's further proofs. 4.
Marat's electrical discoveries. Roz. XVII. 317, 459.
Marat Recherches physiques sur l'électricité. 8. Par. 1782. Germ. 1784.
On electricity. Roz. XVIII. 157.
La Cépède sur l'électricité. 2 v. 8. Par. 1781. R. S.
Achard's electrical experiments. Roz. XIX. 417. XXII. 245. XXV. 429.
Cuthbertson Eigenschappen van de electricität. 2 parts. Amst. 1782, part 3, 1794. Germ. 8. Leips. 1786.
Cuthbertson über die versuche von Deimann und Troostwyck. 8. Leipz. 1790.
Milner's experiments and observations on electricity.
D'Inarre Anfangsgründe der naturlehre. 8. Frankf. 1783. I.
Kühn Geschichte der electricität. Leipz. 1783.
Van Marum Experiences sur l'électricité. Harl. R. S. Roz. XXXI. 343. Gilb. I. 239, 256. X. 121.
Kunze Neue electrische versuche. 4.
Donndorff's Lehre von der electricität. 8. Erf. 1784.
Tressan sur le fluide électrique. 2 v. 8. Par. 1786. R. S.
Beck Entwurf der lehre von electricität. 1787.
Vassalli and Zimmerman's electrical experiments. Soc. Ital. IV. 264.
Nicholson's experiments. Ph. tr. 1789. 265.
Bennet's new experiments. 8. Derby, 1789. R. S.
On Charles's electrical experiments. Roz. XXX. 433.
Briefe über die electricität, von C. L. 8. Leips. 1789.

Deluc on electricity. Roz. XXXVI. 450.
Brook on electricity. 1790.
Peart on electricity and magnetism. 8. Gainsborough, 1791. R. S.
Peart on electric atmospheres. 1793. R. S.
Adams on electricity, by Jones. 8. London.
Lampadius über electricität und wärme. 8. Berl. 1793.
Cavallo's electricity. 3 v. 8. Lond. 1795. R. I.
Morgan's lectures on electricity. 2 v. 12. Lond.
Acc. Ann. Ch. XXXIV. 95.
Enc. Br. Art. Electricity.
Robison. Enc. Br. Suppl. Art. Electricity.
Von Arnim's electrical experiments. Gilb. V. 33. VI. 116.
Clos on electricity. Journ. Phys. LIV. 316.
Remer's electrical experiments. Gilb. VIII. 323.

Theory of Electricity.

Gray. Ph. tr. 1732. XXXVII. 397.
Found electric attraction in and through a vacuum.

Gordon Versuch einer erklärung der electricität. 8. Erf. 1745.
Rosenberg von der ursachen der electricität. Breslau, 1745.
Kratzenstein Theoria electricitatis. 4 Hal. 1746.
Kratzensteins Vorlesungen. 4. ed. Copenh. 1781.
For two fluids.

Ellicott on the laws of electricity. Ph. tr. 1748. XLV. 195.
An approach to a theory.

J. Euler de causa electricitatis. 4. Petersb. 1755.
J. Euler on the physical cause of electricity. A. Berl. 1757. 125.
Symmer on two electric fluids. Ph. tr. 1759. 340.

Cigna on the analogy of magnetism and electricity. M. Taur. I.
Aepini tentamen theoriae electricitatis et magnetismi. 4. Petersb. 1759. R. I.
Aepinus's comparison of magnetism and electricity. N. C. Petr. X. 296.
Dutour sur la matière electrique. 12. Par. 1760.
Bergmann on the existence of two fluids. Ph. tr. 1764. 84.
*Cavendish on the principal phaenomena of electricity. Ph. tr. 1771. 584.
Herbert Theoria phaenomenorum electricitatis. Vienna, 1778.
Euler's letters. II. 34.
On the identity of the electric fluid with his ether.

Wilke on the existence of two fluids. Schw. Abh. XXXIX. 68.
*Lord Mahon's electricity.
On the law of the force.

Achard on the elasticity of electrified air. A. Berl. 1780.
Perceived no effect.

Achard on the similarity of the excitation of electricity and of heat. Goth. Mag. II. ii. 139.
Achard on the effect of surface. Roz. XXVI. 378.
Karstens Anleitung. ccccxcvii.
For two fluids.

Barletti's theory of electricity. Soc. Ital. I. 1. II. 1.
Laurentii Beraud Theoria electricitatis. Petersb.
Donndorf über electricität. 1783.
Forster. Crells N. Entd. XII. 154.
For two fluids.

*Coulomb. A. P. 1784. A. P. 1785. 578.
Shows that the force varies inversely as the square of the distance.

Coulomb's fourth memoir on electricity. A. P. 1786. 67.

The distribution of electricity is not regulated by elective attractions. The fluid in conductors is accumulated at the surface, and does not penetrate the body, as Cavendish had before observed.

Coulomb on the distribution of the electric fluid. A. P. 1787. 421.

With experiments.

Coulomb on the distribution of the electric fluid in different parts of conductors. A. P. 1788. 617.

With experiments.

In order to avoid the supposed electric repulsion of matter, Coulomb imagines two fluids possessed of equivalent properties, neutralising each other's elasticity like oxygen and hydrogen combined.

Account of Coulomb's memoirs. Roz. XXVII. 116. XLIII. 247. Journ. Phys. XLV. (II.) 235, 448.

Weber Theorie der electricität. Naturf. Fr. xlvi.

Prévost Traité du magnetisme. Preface.

Haüy Théorie de l'électricité et du magnétisme. 8. Par. 1787. R. S.

Haüy Traité de physique.

Extract of Haüy's account of Aepinus's theory. Roz. XXXI. 401.

De Luc Idées sur la meteorologie. R. I.

De Luc Journ. de Physique. Juin, 1790.

Gehlers physicalisches wörterbuch. Art. Flasche.

Chappe on the electric properties of points. Roz. XL. 329.

Voigt Theorie des Feuers.

Schmidt on the weight of the electric fluid. Abhandl. 8. Giessen, 1793. 163.

Biot on the disposition of electricity in a spheroid. B. Soc. Phil. n. 51.

Heidmann Theorie der electricität. 2 v. 8. Vienn. 1799. R. S.

*Robison. Enc. Br. Suppl. Art. Electricity.

From Aepinus and Cavendish, with his own additions. Account of Deluc's theory, near the end.

Tremery against two electric fluids. B. Soc. Phil. n. 63. Journ. Phys. LIV. 357.

Woods on the Franklinian theory of electricity. Ph. M. XVII. 97.

Equilibrium of Electricity.

Induced Electricity.

Guericke Exp. Magdeb. iv. c. 15. art. 3.
Aepinus. N. C. Petr. VI.
Beccaria. Ph. tr. 1770. 277.

Charge.

Gray on the electricity of water. Ph. tr. 1732. XXXVII. 227.

Winklers electrische kraft des wassers in gläsernen gefassen. 8. Leips. 1746.

†Miles on the electricity of water. Ph. tr. 1746. 91.

Wilson's retractation on the Leyden phial. Ph. tr. 1756. 682.

Wilke de electricitatibus contrariis. 4. Rostock, 1757.

Wilke. Schw. Abh. 1758. 241. 1762. 213, 253.

Beccaria's electrical experiments. Ph. tr. 1767. 297.

On combinations of glass plates.

Cavendish. Ph. tr. 1776.

The quantity of electricity is inversely as the thickness of the glass.

Achard on the charge of electricity in proportion to the surface of a body. A. Berl. 1780. 47. Roz. XXVI. 378.

E. W. Gray on the charge of glass. Ph. tr. 1788. 121.

Observes, that glass may receive a certain portion of electricity without discharging any from the other side; and that the capacity of a body is proportional to its surface only.

Barletti on the laws of charged glass. Soc. Ital. IV. 304. VII. 444.

Nicholson. Ph. tr. 1789. 285.

Observes, that some uncompensated electricity is necessary to a charge: that the intensity of the charge, and the explosive distance with a given quantity of electricity, is directly as the thickness of the substance; he found that a piece of Muscovy talc, $\frac{1}{100}$ inch thick, received ten times as much electricity as an equal surface of common glass. Hence a solid inch of such matter must contain at least as much electricity as would charge a conductor 7 inches in diameter, and 135 feet long, so as to give a spark of nine inches; and the bulk of a man more than 5000 times as much.

Wilkinson on the Leyden phial. 8. Lond. 1798.

A double plate of glass takes a higher charge than a single piece of the same thickness.

Electric Attractions and Repulsions.

Gray. Ph. tr. 1732. XXXVII. 397.

Finds that the attraction operates in and through a vacuum.

Dufay on electric attraction and repulsion. A. P. 1733. 475. 1734. 341.

Wheler's experiments on electrical repulsion. Ph. tr. 1739. XLI. 98.

Mortimer on Wheler's experiments. Ph. tr. 1739. XLI. 112.

Desaguliers. Ph. tr. 1742. XLII. 140.

Thinks the attraction between air and water may be electrical, causing the rise of vapour.

Symmer on electrical cohesion. Ph. tr. 1759. 340.

Lichtenberg's figures delineated on electrics by the attraction of dust. N. C. Gott. 1777. VIII. 168. Commentat. Gott. 1778. I. M. 65. Deluc Ideés. xii. Troostwyck en Krayenhoffs verhandling. 8. Germ. Leipz. Samml. xlvi. Goth. Mag. I. iii. 76. V. iv. 176. Cavallo. Ph. tr. 1780. 15.

Sanmartini on the effect of electricity on hydrometers. Soc. Ital. VI. 120.

When the fluid was electrified the hydrometers sometimes rose a few degrees.

Carmoy on the motion of electrified fluids in capillary tubes. Journ. Phys. XLV. (II.) 106.

Thinks the mere presence of electricity has no general effect on this motion.

Miller on electric attraction and repulsion. Ir. tr. VII. 139. Nich. IV. 461.

Gilb. IV. 419. V. 73.

Aldini attributes regular forms, like those of snow, to Lichtenberg's figures. Von Arnim denies their regularity.

On the phenomena of powder thrown on glass. Journ. Phys. LVI. 237.

Von Arnim on terrestrial electricity, as tending to the discovery of springs. Gilb. XIII. 467.

Ritter on an electric polarity. Gilb. XV. 106.

Conducting Powers.

Plot's catalogue of electrics. Ph. tr. XX. 1698. 384.

Gray on the electricity of water. Ph. tr. 1732. XXXVII. 227.

Dufay. A. P. 1733. 73, 233.

Desaguliers. Ph. tr. 1741. XLI. 661.

Watson. Ph. tr. 1746. XLIV. 41.

Found ice a conductor.

Watson on insulation. Ph. tr. 1747. XLIV. 388.

Watson on electricity in a vacuum. Ph. tr. 1751. 362.

Bosc on heated glass. Ph. tr. 1749. XLVI. 189.

Lemonnier on the electricity of the air. A. P. 1752. 233. H. 8.

Dutour on the action of flame upon electrical bodies. S. E. II. 246.

Mazéas on the electricity of the air. Ph. tr. 1753. 377.

Ammersin de electricitate lignorum. 24. Lucern. 1754.

Delaval on electricity. Ph. tr. 1759. 83.

Delaval on the effects of heat. Ph. tr. 1761. 353.

†Wilson and Bergman on the permeability of glass. Ph. tr. 1760. 896, 907.

Canton on Delaval's experiments. Ph. tr. 1762. 457.

Ascribes the increase of conducting power to moisture rather than to cold.

Kinnersley's experiments. Ph. tr. 1763. 84.

†Kinnersley on the conducting power of charcoal. Ph. tr. 1773. 38.

A line drawn by a black lead pencil conducts.

Leroy on the transmission of the spark under different circumstances. A. P. 1766. 451.

Priestley on the conducting power of charcoal. Ph. tr. 1770. 211.

Cotte. A. P. 1772. i. H. 16.

Snow serves as a conductor in storms.

Henley's experiments. Ph. tr. 1774. 389.

Shows that vapour is a conductor, and that an imperfect vacuum conducts.

Henley on the impermeability of glass. Ph. tr. 1778. 1049.

Cavendish. Ph. tr. 1776.

Iron wire conducts 400 million times better than pure water; sea water, with one thirtieth of salt, 100 times better; a saturated solution of salt 720 times better.

Achard on the electricity of ice. Roz. VIII. 364.

Achard on the celerity of electrization. A. Berl. 1777. 25.

Achard on the analogy of conductors of heat and of electricity. A. Berl. 1779. 27. Roz. XXII. 245.

With an instrument for measuring the conducting power.

Achard on the distinction of conductors and electrics. Roz. XV. 117.

Achard Schriften. 246.

Bergman on the conducting power of water. Roz. XIV. 192.

Cavallo. Ph. tr. 1783. 495.

Pith balls electrified did not diverge in the vacuum of an air pump, whether much or little electricity was communicated to them. Perhaps from the perfection of the conductor.

Cavallo on a vacuum. Electr. ed. 4. part 4. c. 8.

Lavoisier and Laplace on the electricity absorbed by vapours. A. P. 1781. 292. H. 6.

Coulomb on the loss of electricity in a given time. A. P. 1785. 612.

Morgan on a vacuum. Ph. tr. 1785. 272.

When the mercury has been boiled for some hours in a gage, neither light nor charge can be procured in it. Air conducts best when the light streaming through it is bluish violet. Acids conduct better than water, and hot water than cold.

Vassalli and Zimmerman's experiments on water and ice. Soc. Ital. IV. 264.

Eandi. M. Tur. 1790. V. 7.

Says that light may be seen in the dark, even when the vacuum is perfect. But it may be said that some mercurial vapour is present.

Volta on the use of the electrometer in hygrometry. Soc. Ital. V. 551.

Volta. Gilb. XIV. 257.

Says that wire conducts a million times better than water. Repeats some of Cavendish's experiments.

Tremery on conductors of electricity, and on the emission of the electric fluid. B. Soc. Phil. n. 19. Journ. Phys. XLVIII. 168.

Bressy on the electricity of water. Gilb. I. 375.

Wood on the permeability of glass. Ph. M. II. 147.

Heller on the conducting power of water. Gilb. VI. 249.

Erman on conducting powers. Gilb. XI. 143.

Shows that ice is a nonconductor.

A thread of gum lac insulates ten times as well as silk. A needle of sealing wax retains for some days its electric polarity. A capillary bore lessens the insulating power of glass. According to Saussure's hygrometer, the dissipation of electricity by the air is nearly in the triplicate ratio of its moisture. A jar will be discharged if sounded like a harmonica. Robison.

Table of Conductors, in order, chiefly from Cavallo.

Conductors.

Gold.	In Henley's experiments, the same charge melted of gold wire 4 inches, of brass 6, of silvered copper 8, of silver 10, of iron 10 or more. Copper is allowed to conduct much more readily than iron. Nairne. Platina is said by some to be a bad conductor.
Silver.	
Copper.	
Platina.	
Brass.	
Iron.	
Tin.	
Mercury.	
Lead.	
Semimetals.	
Metallic ores.	
Charcoal.	Seems to be placed too low.
Animal fluids.	
Acids.	
Saline solutions.	
Hot water.	
Cold water.	
Liquids, excepting oils.	
Red hot glass.	
Melted resin.	
Flame.	
Ice, not too cold.	Snow. Cotte.
Metallic salts.	
Salts in general.	
Earths and soft stones.	
Glass, filled with boiling water.	Kinnersley.
Smoke.	
Steam or vapour.	
An imperfect vacuum.	Yet the electrical machine works in a vacuum.
Hot air.	Read denies that hot air is a conductor.

Nonconductors.

Ice, at — 13° F. Achard.	
Powders, not metallic. Delaval.	
Soft stones, when heated. Delaval.	
Hard stones.	
Dry vegetable substances.	Baked wood requires to be varnished.
Ashes.	
Dry and complete oxids.	
Oils.	
Common air, and other gases.	
White sugar and sugar candy.	
Paper.	
Dry and external animal substances, as feathers, wool, and hair.	White hair conducts less perfectly than black. Henley. Ph. tr. 1776.
Cotton.	
Silk.	
Wax.	
Resins.	
Sulfur.	
Amber.	
Transparent gems.	
Glass of all kinds.	Glass often heated is best for electrical purposes. Bosc.
A perfect vacuum. Morgan.	

Motions of the Electric Fluid. Velocity.

Watson. Ph. tr. 1748. XLV. 49, 491.

No perceptible time was occupied in a circuit of 12276 feet: but the report was not so loud when the circuit was so much extended.

Simple Communication.

Nairne. Ph. tr. 1774. 79.

Observes, that a ball was struck at the distance of nine inches by the same charge that reached a point only at six. Perhaps, however, the point had very rapidly diminished the charge.

On the direction of the electric current. Henley, Ph. tr. 1774. 389. ii.

Flame is driven by a weak charge towards the negative side.

Henley on the long continuance of excitation. Ph. tr. 1777. 85.

Ingenhousz on the motions of electricity. Roz. XVI. 117.

Coulomb on the loss of electricity in a given time. A. P. 1785. 612.

Cavallo's experiments on the escape of electricity. Ph. tr. 1788. 1.

Nicholson found, that a point, projecting more or less from a large ball, produces more or less the effect of a smaller ball, or of a point, and that a smaller projection has the effect of a small ball when it receives than when it emits electricity. Cuthbertson observes, that when the flame of a candle is placed between two balls, the one positive, the other negative, the negative ball only is heated. It may be questioned whether every spark is not rather to be considered as resembling the breaking of a charged jar than as a simple communication.

Lateral Explosions.

*Priestley. Ph. tr. 1769. 57, 63. 1770. 192.
Henley. Ph. tr. 1774. 389. iii.
Cavendish. Ph. tr. 1776.
Electricity spreads even from a wire.

Discharge.

Lemonnier on the communication of electricity. Ph. tr. 1746. 290. A. P. 1746. 497. H. 10.

Bergmann's electrical experiments. Opusc. V. 387.

Immediate Effects.

Mechanical Changes.

On powdering glass by the spark. Roz. XV. 334.

Vacca Berlinghieri. Roz. XL. 133.
Observes, that the electrical fluid has no perceptible momentum.

On Lullin's card. Nich. 8. III. 223.
When the experiment of perforating a card is made in air much rarefied, the perforation is near the negative instead of the positive point.

Perhaps these effects are ultimately referable to heat and expansion.

Light.

See Galvanic Electricity.

Picard on the light of barometers. A. P. II. 125. X. 393.

Bernoulli on the light of barometers. A. P. 1700. 178. H. 5. 1701. 1. H. 1.

Hauksbee on the mercurial phosphorus. Ph. tr. 1705. XXIV. 2129.

The phenomenon is best seen when the air is exhausted to half its density, but is visible in some measure without exhaustion.

Lahire on the barometric light. A. P. 1705. 226.

Wall on the light of diamonds. Ph. tr. 1708. XXVI. 69.

Dufay on electrical light. A. P. 1723. 295. H. 13. 1734. 503. H. 1. 1735. 347. H. 1. 1737. 86, 307.

Beccari on the light of diamonds. Coll. Acad. X. 197.

Gray on electrical light. Ph. tr. 1735. XXXIX. 16.
Opinion respecting thunder. 24.

Miles on luminous emanations from friction. Ph. tr. 1745. XLIII. 441.

Trembley on the electric nature of the barometrical light, 1745. Ph. tr. 1746. XLIV. 58.

Waiz on barometrical light.

Lohier on electric light upon clothes. A. P. 1746. H. 23.

Winkler descriptio pyrorgani electrici. Ph. tr. 1747. XLIV. 497.
A plaything.

Cooke on the sparkling of flannel and hair. Ph. tr. 1748. XLV. 394.

Doppelmayer über das electrische licht. 1749.

Canton's figures of sparks. Ph. tr. 1754. 780.

Fayol on the illumination of a plant. A. P. 1759. H. 36.

Nollet on the illumination of ice. A. P. 1766. H. 2.

Lane. Ph. tr. 1767. 451.
A shock passing through water is visible.

Nairne. Ph. tr. 1777. 614.
Observes that the light is very faint in a moist vacuum.

Deluc Modif. I. lxxxv.
On barometrical light.

Morgan. Ph. tr. 1785. 272.
The more readily a body conducts, the more difficult it is to make it luminous. Gold leaf may be made luminous. The light produced by electricity streaming through very rare air is green: when the air is denser it becomes blue, and then violet, till the air no longer conducts.

Crell on electrical light. Rozier, Feb. 1717.

Good figures of sparks. Nicholson. Ph. tr. 1789. 265.
A ball $\frac{1}{16}$ of an inch in diameter, highly electrified, was surrounded by a steady faint light; a ball of an inch and a half was rendered luminous, with a bright speck moving on its surface.

Eandi. M. Tur. 1790. V. 7.
Says that a faint light may be seen in the dark, in the most perfect vacuum that can be procured.

Erxleben by Lichtenberg. dxxiv.
The lock of a pistol gives light under water.

†Juch on the light of sugar. Ph. M. V. 207.

Electric Heat.

See Galvanic Electricity.

Winkler on firing spirits. Ph. tr. 1744. XLIII. 166.

†Winkler on electrical combustions. Ph. tr. 1754. 772.

Miles on firing phosphorus. Ph. tr. 1745. XLIII. 290.

Roche on a frock set on fire. Ph. tr. 1748. XLV. 323.

Kinnersley on an electrical air thermometer, and on the extension of wire. Ph. tr. 1763. 84.

Priestley on the rings made on metal by explosions. Ph. tr. 1768. 68.
The metals were held near the point of a needle. The battery contained 21 square feet.

Ingenhousz on lighting a candle by electricity. Ph. tr. 1778. 1023.
Employs cotton, with powdered resin.

Nairne on the effect of electricity in shortening wires. Ph. tr. 1780. 334.

Wolf on firing gunpowder. Goth. Mag. II. ii. 70.

Van Marum on the effects of electricity. Nich. II. 527.

Berthollet's comparison of electricity and heat. Nich. VIII. 80.
Thinks that electricity produces heat only by means of chemical changes.
Cuthbertson has observed, that gunpowder is readily fired by a discharge passing through an interrupted circuit, by means of wet tubes and wet twine. He says that a double charge melts a quadruple length of wire.
Ehrmann's electrical lamp consists of an electrophorus, giving a spark, which sets on fire a stream of hydrogen gas.

Congelation.

Robert on the supposed effect of electricity in congelation. Roz. XXXVI. 222.

Supposed Transmission of Odours.

Nollet. Ph. tr. 1750. 368.

Winkler. Ph. tr. 1751. 231.
With Watson's experiments.

Watson against the transmission of odours. Ph. tr. 1756. 348.

Chemical Effects.

Priestley. vii.
Electricity often discolours the leaves of delicate flowers.

Pearson on the gas produced by electricity. Ph. tr. 1797. 142.

Wollaston. Ph. tr. 1801.

Van Marum on decomposing water by electricity. Gilb. XI. 220.

On oxidation by electricity. Gilb. XI. 400.

See Galvanism.

Physiological Effects.

On Vegetables and Animals.

De Bozes on the effect of electricity on an insulated person. Ph. tr. 1745. XLIII. 419.

That it quickens the pulse.

Lallamand's experiment on a glass of water. Ph. tr. 1746. XLIV. 78.

The first time the shock deprived him for some moments of the power of breathing. Musschenbroek repeated his experiment, and says he felt a most terrible pain.

Winkler on the effects of electricity. Ph. tr. 1746. XLIV. 211.

Says, that a shock gave him and his wife convulsions and epistaxis.

Winkler Rei medicae utile electricitatis inventum. Ph. tr. 1748. XLV. 262.

Browning on electrifying trees. Ph. tr. 1747. XLIV. 373.

Perceived no effect from electricity in the operation of phlebotomy.

Watson. Ph. tr. 1751. 231.

Kies et Koestlin de effectibus electricitatis. 4. Tubing. 1775.

Henley on a bullock struck by lightning. Ph. tr. 1776. 463.

The skin was only affected where the hair was white, being there the least perfect conductor.

Cavendish. Ph. tr. 1776.

Says, that the sensible shock depends rather more on the quantity of the electricity than on its force: a double force with half the quantity, producing a shock rather less powerful.

Ingenhousz Versuche mit pflanzen. 3 v. 8. Vienna, 1778.. 1790.

Ingenhousz. Roz. XXXII. 321. XXXV. 81.

Found no effect on vegetation.

Achard on hatching eggs. A. Berl. 1778. 33. Schriften. 241.

Schwankhardt on the influence of electricity upon vegetation. Roz. XXVII. 462. Remarks. XXVIII. 93.

Carmoy on shocks. Roz. XXIX. 194.

Carmoy on the effects of electricity on vegetation. Roz. XXXIII. 339.

Troostwyck et Krayenhoff de l'application de l'électricité. 4. Amst. 1788.

Rouland, Dormoy, Bertholon, and Derozières on the effect of electricity on vegetation. Roz. XXXV. 3, 161, 401. XXXVIII. 351, 427.

Effects of electricity on the hedysarum gyrans. Goth. Mag. V. iii. 13.

Van Marum on death by electricity. Roz. XXXVIII. 62.

Van Marum's experiments. Ph. M. VIII. 193.

A machine capable of fusing 24 inches of wire, $\frac{1}{75}$ of an inch in diameter, produced no effect on the pulse, nor on the perspiration; and did not appear to promote evaporation.

Chappe and Mauduyt on the supposed effects of electricity on the growth of animals. Roz. XL. 62, 241.

Volta. Gilb. XIV. 257.

Says, that only a little more electricity is required to produce an equal shock from a larger surface. A surface 16 times as large required an elevation of the electrometer to one tenth of the number of degrees. But the degrees of the electrometer cannot be an immediate measure of the quantity of electricity, without having regard to its situation with respect to the electrified bodies.

On an insensibility of electricity. Gilb. XIV. 423.

A small charge of a large surface gives a less unpleasant shock than a larger charge of a small one, and may perhaps be fitter for medical purposes. The spark from a long wire is sharper than from a large body. Robison.

Secondary Effects of the communication of Electricity.

Streams of Air.

Lord Mahon's electricity.

Mayer in Gren. VI. vii. §. 208.

Gray on the revolutions of pendulous bodies. Ph. tr. 1736. XXXIX. 280.

†Gray's last experiment on revolutions, related by Mortimer. Ph. tr. 1736. XXXIX. 400.

Gray fancied the motions were naturally directed from west to east.

Wheler on Gray's experiments of revolutions. Ph. tr. 1739. XLI. 118.

According to Lichtenberg, some similar observations have been made by Müller, Delaperriere, Hartmann, and Schäffer.

Henley. Ph. tr. 1774. 389. ii.

Flame is driven by a weak charge towards a negative ball. A tube of glass, surrounding a point, prevents the current of air, and the escape of the fluid. Robison.

Excitation, or Destruction of the stable Electric Equilibrium.

Richmann on excitation. C. Petr. XIV. 299.

Bergmann on the excitation of glass plates, and of ribbons. Opusc. V. 370, 391.

Aubert on electric permutations. Roz. XXXIX. 194.

On excitation. Nich. II. 43.

Vassalli on excitation. Gilb. VII. 498.

Haüy on the excitation of metals. B. Soc. Phil. n. 85. Gilb. XVII. 441.

Bennet found that no electricity was excited by flame, by the explosion of gunpowder, nor by the expansion of condensed air.

Excitation by simple Contact.

Perhaps *Webers* Erfahrungen idioelectrische körper ohne reiben zu electrisiren. 1781.

Bennet's experiments on excitation. Ph. tr. 1787. 26.

Bennet's new experiments on electricity. 1789. Nich. 8. I. 144, 184. Gilb. XVII. 428.

Cavallo's electricity.

Volta's papers on galvanic electricity. See Galvanism.

Excitation by Friction.

See Electrical Machines.

Hauksbee's experiments on attrition in a vacuum. Ph. tr. 1705. XXIV. 2165.

Amber rubbing a woollen cloth produced light and heat: flint and steel only a faint lambent light. Glass rubbed with woollen cloth became electric in a vacuum. Glass rubbed with glass shone both in the open air and in a vacuum, as well as under water.

Gray's experiments on worsteds of different colours. Ph. tr. 1735. XXXIX. 166.

Ludolff on the electricity of barometers. A. Berl. 1745. 1.

Cooke on the electricity of new flannel. Ph. tr. 1747. XLIV. 457.

Symmer. Ph. tr. 1759. 308. Dutour from Symmer. A. P. 1767. H. 34.

Beccaria dell' elettrismo. 4. 1753. Ph. tr. 1766. 105.

Cigna. Misc. Taur. III.

Bergmann. Schw. Abh. XXV. 344. Ph. tr. 1764. 84.

Finds that a body becomes more disposed to negative electricity as it becomes more heated.

Aepinus on the electricity of barometers. N. C. Petr. XV. 303.

On a cat that gave smart sparks. A. P. 1771. H. 37.

Henley. Ph. tr. 1774. 389. v.

*Henley. Ph. tr. 1777. 122.

Socins anfangsgründe der electricität. Hanau, 1778. 66.

Herbert on the excitation of metals. Theoria phaenom. electr. Vienna, 1778. 15.

On metals as electrics. Hemmer in Rozier. XVI. 50, 74.

Nicholson. Ph. tr. 1789.

Wilke de electricitatibus contrariis. Aufsätze. 8. Gott. 1790.

   Finds that the friction of a quill, in different directions, produces different species of electricity.

Lichtenberg in Erxleben. §. 514.

Wilson on the electricity of shavings. Nich. 8. IV. 49. Gilb. XVII. 205.

Gersdorf on the electricity of powder. Gilb. XVII. 200.

Haüy on the electricity of metals. Ph. M. XX. 120.

Lichtenberg's Table of Excitation, transposed.

The marks denote the electricity of the substances under which they stand.

	Polished glass	Hair	Wool	Feathers	Paper	Wood	Wax	Sealing wax	Ground glass	Metals	Resin	Silk	Sulfur
Polished glass	o	—	—	—	—	—	—				—	—	—
Hair								—		—	—		
Wool	+						—		—				
Feathers	+							—					—
Paper	+	+					—	—					—
Wood	+	+	+						—			—	—
Wax	+								—				—
Sealing wax	+	+	+					o	—				—
Ground glass	+		+	+	+	+	+	+				—	—
Metals	+	+						+		o			
Resin	+	+	+						+	+	o		
Silk	+	+							+	+		o	
Sulfur	+			+	+	+	+	+	+				o

   It appears that any substance in this table, rubbed with any of the following substances, becomes positively electric; with any of the preceding, negatively. This proposition is, however, liable to some modifications, according to the mode of applying friction, and the degree of heat; the table requires also some further subdivisions.

   Mr. Henley says, that " a smooth glass tube may be made negative by drawing it crosswise over the back of a cat, or by exciting it with a dry, warm rabbit's skin." Henley made a great number of experiments with a variety of substances rubbed on wool and silk: there are only two instances where the wool produced a positive and the silk negative electricity, and these were probably owing to the greater heat of the wool. There were, however, very great irregularities in the effects produced upon different substances of the same class: thus a guinea, a sixpence, and a piece of tin, became negative; a piece of copper, a steel button, and a silver button, positive, at least when the cloth was warm: animal substances, excepting shells, generally positive: vegetables almost always negative, but the smooth skins of beans positive. common pebbles, marble, coal, and jet, negative: gems and crystals positive: glazed wares and writing paper positive; tobacco pipe, elastic gum, a tallow candle, oiled silk, indian ink, and blue vitriol, negative. Mr. Errington and Mr. Cavallo extended the list to almost 1000 articles.

Excitation by Change of Form of Aggregation.

Gray on melted substances. Ph. tr. 1732. XXXVII. 285.

Kinnersley. Ph. tr. 1763. 84.

   The vapour of electrified water did not carry up electricity.

Henley on the positive electricity of cooling chocolate. Ph. tr. 1777. 85.

Lavoisier and Laplace on the electricity absorbed by vapours. A. P. 1781. 292. H. 6.

Bennet. Ph. tr. 1787.

   Water running through a heated tobacco pipe showed a strong electricity.

Liphardt on the electricity of chocolate. Roz. XXX. 434.

Van Marum and Troostwyck on electricity from melting. Roz. XXXIII. 248.

On electricity from evaporation. Ph. M. XIII. 231.

Electricity from Chemical Changes.

Galvanism.

Gardenii dissertatio de electrici ignis natura.
   Water evaporating from clean iron leaves it negative, from rusty iron, positive.

Al. Galvani de viribus electricitatis in motu musculari commentarius. Bologn. 1791. C. Bon. VII. O. 363.

Mayer Abhandlungen von Galvani und andern. 2 v. 8. Prague, 1793.

Balbo and Valli on Galvani's animal electricity. Roz. XLI. 57, 66, 185...

Vacca Berlinghieri on animal electricity. Roz. XLI. 314.

*Volta on Galvani's discoveries. Ph. tr. 1793. 10. Ph. M. IV. 163, 306.
   The involuntary muscles, even the heart, appeared to Volta to be insensible of the stimulus of Galvanism; insects were affected by it, but not worms. When a piece of zinc was laid on the point of the tongue, and a silver spoon was applied to the tongue further back, and made to touch the zinc, a sour taste was produced by the zinc at the instant of contact.

Volta's remarks. Gren. III. 4. IV. 1. VIII. 303. Ann. Ch. XXIII. 270.

*Volta on electricity excited by contact. Ph. tr. 1800. 403. Ph. M. VII. 289. Journ. Phys. LI. 344.
   Account of the Galvanic pile and series, which he considers as actually producing a perpetual motion from the mechanical powers of electricity.

Volta's letter on the causes of Galvanic effects. Journ. Phys. Nich. 8. I. 135.

Volta's memoir. M. Inst. IV. B. Soc. Phil. n. 58. Ann. Ch. XL. 225. Gilb. X. 421.

Volta's answer to Nicholson's remarks. Bibl. Brit. n. 150.

Volta on charging a battery by the pile. Gilb. XIII. 257.

Volta. Gilb. XV. 86.
   Says, that a battery may be strengthened by the interposition of plates, without a fluid. Gilbert could not, however, succeed in the experiment.

Fowler on animal electricity. 8. Edinb. 1793. R. I.

Desgenettes on animal electricity. Roz. XLII. 238.

On animal electricity. Soc. Philom. Roz. XLII. 292.

Larrey on animal electricity. Roz. XLIII. 461. Gren. VI.

Crève Beytrag zu Galvanis versuchen. 8. Frankf. 1793.

Pfaff de electricitate animali. 8. Stutg. 1790. Acc. in Gren. VIII. 196.

Note of Pfaff's galvanic experiments. Ann. Ch. XXXIV. 307.

Pfaff on Volta's galvanic theory. Gilb. X. 219.

Fabroni on the mutual action of metals. Read, 1793. Nich. Ph. M. V. 268. Gilb. IV. 428.

Achard on the irritation of the nerves by contact. A. Berl. 1790. 3.

Monro's experiments on animal electricity. Ed. tr. III. 231.

Ph. tr. 1794.
   Read finds all noxious vapours in a negative state.

Aldini de animali electricitate. 4. Bologn. R. S. 1794. R. I.

Aldini sopra l'elettricità animale. 8. Pad. 1795. R. S.

Aldini sul galvanismo. 8. Bologn. 1802. R. S.

Aldini on galvanism. 4. Lond. 1803. R. I.

Aldini's experiments. Ph. M. XIV. 88, 191, 364.

Wells on the galvanic contraction of the muscles. Ph. tr. 1795. 246.

On excitation produced by the union of metals and fluids. Observes, that charcoal has a power like that of the metals; and that silver acquires the power of exciting by touching moisture.

Experiments and observations on galvanism, by Nicholson, Cruickshank, Carlisle, Davy, and others. Nich. I.. V.

Hallé's report on galvanism. B. Soc. Phil. n. 17. Journ. Phys. XLVII. (IV.) 392.

Report on galvanism. Ph. M. I. 319.

Vassalli Eandi on galvanism. Journ. Phys. XLVIII. 336. Ph. M. VIII. 171. XV. 38, 310. Nich. 8. V. 109.

Vassalli Eandi on animal electricity. Journ. Phys. L. 148.

Remarks on galvanism and chemical electricity by *Ritter, Böckmann, Pfaff, Hebebrand, Treviranus, Erman, Huet, Simon, Reinhold, Gerboin, Jäger, and others. Gilb. II. VII.

Ritter's galvanic experiments. B. Soc. Phil. n. 53, 76, 79. Ann. Ch. XLI. 208.

*Ritter on galvanism. Gilb. VIII. 386. IX. 1.

Positive electricity gives oxygen, negative hydrogen.

Ritter on the denomination of galvanic poles. Gilb. IX. 212.

Calls the oxygen, or positive side, the true zinc side.

Ritter's experiments with a battery of 600 pieces. Gilb. XIII. 1, 265.

Ritter's galvanic experiments and remarks. Gilb. XVI. 293.

Places conductors in this order of excitation. Some amalgams of zinc and mercury, zinc, lead, tin, iron, bismuth, cobalt, arsenic, copper, antimony, platina, gold, mercury, silver, coal, plumbago, tin crystals, nickel, pyritical substances, palladium, graphite, crystals of manganese. Some experiments on the sensible effects of galvanism.

Ritter's passive battery. Journ. Phys. LVII. 345. Nich. VIII. 176, 184.

Ritter on galvanic phenomena. Nich. VI. 223. VII. 288.

Nicholson, Carlisle, Cruickshank, and others, on galvanic electricity. Ph. M. VII. 337, 347.

Cruickshank on galvanic electricity. Journ. Phys. LI. 164.

On Perkinism. Journ. Phys. XLIX. 232.

Perkins's patent for a mode of curing diseases. Repert. ii. II. 179.

One of the tractors is made of copper, zinc, and gold; the other of iron, silver, and platina.

Hemmer on animal electricity. Ph. M. V. 1.

Davy on galvanic combinations. Ph. tr. 1801. 397. Ph. M. XI. 202.

*Davy's outlines of a view of galvanism. Journ. R. I., I. 49. Ph. M. XI. 326.

Davy's charcoal battery. Journ. R. I., I. Nich. 8. I. 144.

Davy's galvanic experiments. Inst. Nat. B. Soc. Phil. n. 62.

Davy's galvanic experiments. Nich. 8. III. 135.

Wollaston on the chemical production and agency of electricity. Ph. tr. 1801. 427. Gilb. XI. 104.

Experiments made at the Ecole de médecine. B. Soc. Phil. n. 45.

Galvanic experiments. B. Soc. Phil. n. 50.

Robertson's galvanic experiments. Ann. Ch. XXXVII. 132.

Desormes's galvanic experiments. Ann. Ch. XXXVII. 284.

Desormes and Hachette on the principles of galvanism. Ann. Ch. XLIV. 267.

Hachette on galvanism. Journ. Polyt. IV. xi. 284.

Von Arnim. Gilb. V. 465.

Observes, that electricity is only developed by oxidation when no light is produced.

Cuvier's report on galvanism. Journ. Phys. LII. 318.

Report on galvanism. Ph. M. X. 87, 93.

Biot and Cuvier's galvanic experiments. B. Soc. Phil. n. 53. Ann. Ch. XXXIX. 242.

Biot on the motions of the galvanic fluid. B. Soc. phil. n. 54. Journ. Phys. LIII. 264. Gilb. X. 24.

Notes of Biot's experiments. Ph. M. XI. 272, 283.

Biot's reports to the National Institute on Volta's experiments. M. Inst. V. 195. Journ. R. I., I. Ph. M. XI. 301. Gilb. X. 389.

Biot on the effect of oxidation on the pile. B. Soc. Ph. n. 76. Gilb. XV. 90.

Makes the effect little or nothing; but the arguments are inconclusive.

Galvanic experiments by Volta, Nicholson, Carlisle, Grimm, Ritter, Hermbstadt, Hebebrand, Pfaff, Bourguet, Davy, Heidmann, Reinhold, Curtet, Bouvier, Erman, Aldini, Pepys, Buntzen, Brugnatelli, and others. Gilb. VII..XVII.

Galvanic apparatus, by Pfaff, Simon, Hauff, Davy, and others. Gilb. VII. VIII. XI. XII. XV.

Remarks on Volta's galvanic pile, by Gilbert Grüner, Pfaff, Von Arnim, Jäger, Erman, Desormes, Priestley, Biot, Cuvier, Reinhold, and others. Gilb. VII..XV.

Van Marum and Pfaff's comparison of Volta's pile with the Teylerian machine. Nich. 8. I. 154, 173. Ph. M. XII. 161.

Van Marum charged a battery of jars with a pile; its shock was only half as intense as that of the pile.

Van Marum on Pfaff's galvanic experiments. Ann. Ch. XL. 289.

Van Marum on Ritter's experiments. Nich. VIII. 212.

Priestley on Volta's pile. Acc. Nich. 8. I. 198.

Sue Histoire du galvanisme. 2 v. 8. Par. 1802. R. I.

Nauche Journal de galvanisme. Paris.

Lehot on galvanism. Ann. Ch. XXXVIII. 42. Gilb. IX. 188.

Friedlander on some galvanic experiments. Journ. Phys. LII. 101.

Friedlander on the pile. Ph. M. IX. 221.

On medical galvanism. Journ. Phys. LII. 391, 467.

*Fourcroy's galvanic experiments. Ann. Ch. XXXIX. 103.

Gautherot on galvanism. Ann. Ch. XXXIX. 203.

Gautherot on galvanism. Extr. Journ. Phys. LVI. 429.

Adopts the chemical theory.

Moyes on the pile. Ph. M. IX. 217.

Cuthbertson on Volta's fundamental galvanic experiments. Nich. 8. II. 281.

Cuthbertson's distinction between galvanism and electricity. Ph. M. XVIII. 358. Nich. VIII. 97.

Thinks that the length of wire, ignited by galvanism, is simply as the charges; by electricity, as the square of the charge.

Cuthbertson's galvanic experiments. Nich. VIII. 205.

Gerboin's galvanic experiments. Ann. Ch. XLI. 197.

Pepys on the galvanometer. Ph. M. X. 38.

The zinc end of the pile, commonly so called, is positive.

Pepys's galvanic apparatus. Ph. M. XI. 94. XV. 94.

Pictet on some experiments of Volta. Ph. M. XI. 149.

Gilb. VIII. 166.

Gilbert observes, that a simple chain is formed by zinc, a liquid, and silver; the addition of dry metals makes no difference in its nature, so that if silver and zinc be added beyond the zinc and silver, the silver end will be the true zinc pole of the chain, which is negative, and the zinc end, or the silver pole positive, giving oxygen, while the silver end or zinc pole gives hydrogen gas.

Lüdicke on a cheap battery. Gilb. IX. 119.

Tourdes on the galvanic irritation of the

fibrine of the blood. B. Soc. Phil. n. 71. Gilb. X. 499.

Bostock on galvanism. Nich. 8. II. 296. III. 3. Gilb. XII. 476.

Note of Bonaparte's galvanic prize. Ph. M. XIII. 188. Gilb. XI. 492.

Erman's theory of the pile. Gilb. XI. 89. Journ. Phys. LIII. 121.

Erman supposes, that two heterogeneous metals in contact become electrical principally by induction; that the silver is positive where it touches the zinc, and negative on the other side; the zinc the reverse; that more alternations of dry metals have no further effect; but that a communication with a different conducting substance, on each side, favours the effect of induction; that moist conductors interposed, divide themselves by induction into different states of electricity; that the middle of a pile is the neutral point; and that a communication produces a discharge like that of a charged jar.

Sprenger on galvanism in deafness. Gilb. XI. 354, 488.

Einhof on galvanising the deaf and dumb. Gilb. XII. 230.

Parrot's galvanic theory. Gilb. XII. 49.

From a combination of induction and chemical action.

Medical galvanism. Gilb. XII. 450.

Galvanic experiments. Journ. Phys. LIV.. .LVII.

Lagrave's galvanic experiments. Journ. Phys. LVI. 361. Nich. 8. V. 62.

Compares the transmission of the galvanic fluid through water to the propagation of sound.

Wilson on the galvanic effect of minute particles of zinc and copper. Nich. 8. III. 147.

Alizeau's pile. Nat. Inst. Acc. Journ. Phys. LVII. 74.

Wilkinson's elements of galvanism. 2 v. 8. 1804. R. I.

Wilkinson on burning wire by galvanism. Nich. VII. 206.

Wilkinson on galvanism. Nich. VIII. 1, 70. IX. 175, 240.

Haüy Traité de physique. II. 1.

On galvanic apparatus. Nich. VII. 269. VIII. 79.

Experiments by Dyckhoff and others. Nich. VII. 303, 305.

Dyckhoff asserts, that the strata of a pile may be separated by bits of glass with air intervening; this Wilkinson denies. Nich. VIII. 1.

Rossi's experiments. Ph. M. XVIII. 131.

Pownall on the theory of galvanism and the Newtonian ether. Ph. M. XVIII. 155.

On the theory of galvanism. Ph. M. XVIII. 170.

Galvanic experiments. Nich. VIII. 84.

On galvanism. Nich. VIII. 171.

Thicknesse on galvanism. Nich. IX. 120.

Sylvester on the galvanic power. Nich. IX. 179.

Harrison and Gough. Nich. IX. 241.

Make the igniting power of plates as the sixth power of their diameter, from Wilkinson's experiments.

Electrical apparatus in general.

Leupold Th. Aerostat. t. 9.

E. M. Pl. VIII. Amusemens de physique.

Bohnenbergers Electrisirmachinen. Stuttg. 1784..1791.

Gütle Instrumenten kabinet. 1790.

Kunze Schauplatz der gemeinnützigen maschinen. II.

Weber Electrische versuche.

Galvanic apparatus. See Chemical Electricity.

For a cement take 7 parts lac, 4 resin, 2 amber, and 4 Venice turpentine, 12 lac, 16 resin, 1 amber, 3 Venice turpentine, 24 pitch. Kunze.

Sealing wax may be employed for varnishing glass, either by heating the glass, or by dissolving the wax in spirits: but amber varnish is better. Cavallo.

Such a varnish makes the insulating power of the glass more perfect. See Machines.

Excitation. Electrical Machines for applying Friction.

Hawksbee on a globe lined with sealing wax. Ph. tr. 1708. XXVI. 219.

Winkler Beschreibung einer electrisirmaschine. 1744.

Faure Congetture intorno alla machina elettrica. 4. Rome, 1747.

Plate machines used by Planta, 1760.

Epinasse on electrical machines. Ph. tr. 1767. 186.
_{Lines the cylinder with a resin.}

Leroy on an electrical machine for producing both species of electricity. A. P. 1772. i. 499. H. 9.

Leroy's electrical pump. A. P. 1783. 615.

Nooth on the cushion and flap. Ph. tr. 1773. 333.

Schmidt Beschreibung einer electrisirmaschine. 1778.

Langenbücher Beschreibung einer electrisirmaschine. 1778.

Ingenhousz on the plate machine. Ph. tr. 1769. 659.
_{Varnished pasteboard succeeded well in dry rooms.}

Brilhac on an electrical plate machine. Roz. XV. 377.

Bertholon's electrical machine. Roz. XVI. 74.

An electrical machine, moved by clockwork. Roz. XIX. 149.

Goth. Mag. I. i. 83.

Kohlreif on the cushion. Goth. Mag. I. iii. 101.

Rouland description des machines a taffetas. 8. Amst. 1785.

Van Marum Description d'une très grande machine electrique. 4. Haarl. 1785. R. S. Roz. XXVII. 148.

Van Marum Lettre sur une machine electrique. 4. R. S.

Van Marum Continuation d'expériences. 4. Haarl. 1787. R. S.

Van Marum description des frotteirs electriques. 4. Haarl. 1789. R. S. Roz. XXXIV. 274.
_{On a mode of applying the silk, before practised in England.}

Van Marum on the Teylerian machine. Roz. XXXVIII. 109.

Van Marum's new and simple plate machine. Roz. XXXVIII. 447.
_{Imitating Nicholson's improvements.}

Van Marum on the electrical machine. Roz. XL. 270.

Van Marum Seconde continuation. 4. Haarl. 1795. R. S.

Van Marum and Pfaff's comparison of Volta's pile with the Teylerian machine. Ph. M. XII. 161.

Prieur's extract on the Teylerian machine. Ann. Ch. XXV. 312.

Tries's claim to Van Marum's machine. Roz. XL. 116.

Leroy's electrical machine. Roz. XXIX. 129.

Nairne on his patent electrical machine. 8. Lond. 1787. R. S. Repert. VII. 380.

Seiferhelds electrisirmaschine. Nuremb. 1767.

Cavallo's remarks on the rubber and flap. Ph. tr. 1788. i.
_{Attributes the effect to a compensation.}

Saint Julien's electrical plate machine. Roz. XXXIII. 367. Fig.

*Nicholson's experiments and observations in electricity. Ph. tr. 1789. 265. Nich. I. 83.
_{The hand was the first rubber, then the simple cushion was applied, and a flap was added to it, then the rubber}

was moistened; next the amalgam was applied, and lastly Nooth invented the silk flap. The surface of a plate immediately opposite to the cushion attracts the electric fluid; nothing therefore is gained by applying a cushion to it. A piece of metal projecting forwards over the edge of the cushion of a cylinder, considerably increased the intensity of action, probably by increasing the capacity of the glass in its neighbourhood. If a piece of silk be applied closely to the cylinder, it will attract the electricity on one side, and emit it on the other, according to the direction in which the cylinder is turned: but such an arrangement is not practically advantageous. If a cylinder be well greased, so as to become opaque, and the silk flap be made semitransparent with the grease, the amalgam be then applied with leather to the cylinder, and pressed against it as long as the friction continues to increase, the action of the machine will be very powerful. When a nine inch cylinder had been thus treated, the conductor gave flashes to the table on which it stood, at the distance of 14 inches. A square foot of a jar was fully charged by the friction of 18 or 19 feet of the cylinder: the machine at Haarlem required at first the friction of 66.6 feet, and with a single cushion would have required half as much. This cylinder was equal in effect to the great Teylerian machine, which was thirty times as expensive; but afterwards Van Marum tripled the effect of the Teylerian machine.

Cuthbertson über die versuche von Deimann und Troostwyck.

Pearson's portable electrical machine. Nich. I. 506.

An electrical machine of silk. Nich. II. 420.

Fell's pocket ribbon machine. Nich. III. 4.

Grimm on a large electrical machine. Gilb. IV. 359.

Wolff's electrical machine. Nich. VII. 124.
With improved rubbers.

Galvanic batteries. See Chemical Electricity.
Gouan applied liquid mercury as a rubber.

Ingenhousz's portable machine is a varnished ribband, hung on a fixed pin or nail, and rubbed with a cat's skin: the little jar which is charged is held near the rubber, and collects negative electricity from the ribband

Lichtenberg's drum machine is of wood, covered with black woollen cloth. Gütle's electrical machine of woollen is said to be cheap and powerful.

The best cement for a cylinder consists of 5 parts of resin, 4 of bees wax, and 2 of powdered red ochre. The silken flap is made of black mode. Cavallo.

Amalgams.

Woulfe on the aurum mosaicum. Ph. tr. 1771. 114.
It was made of mercury, tin, sulfur, and muriate of ammonia.

Higgins's amalgam. Ph. tr. 1778. 861.
Four parts of mercury with one of zinc.

Kienmeyer's amalgam. Rozier XXXIII. 96.
Two parts of mercury, one of zinc, and one of tin.

Neret's amalgam consists of equal parts of tin and mercury: Cuthbertson uses mercury with tin filings and a little oil.

The amalgam of tin is made with two parts of mercury and one of tinfoil, adding a little powdered chalk. Cavallo.

For the amalgam of zinc, melt one part of zinc, and shake it in a wooden box with 4 or 5 parts of mercury, heated above the temperature of boiling water: then triturate it with a little tallow and a very little powdered whiting; and add one fourth of the amalgam of tin. Cavallo.

Electrophorus.

Wilke. Schw. Abh. 1762. XXXIX. 54, 116, 200.

Beccaria Electricitas vindex. Gräz.

Volta. Scelta di opusc. Milan. X. 37. Roz. VIII. 21. Sept. 1776. Ph. tr. 1782. Rozier, 1783. Brugnatelli bibl. fis.

Volta on the passage of electricity through imperfect conductors. Soc. Ital. V. 551.

Henley. Ph. tr. 1776. 513.

Achard A. Berl. 1776. 122.

Achard. Schr. 226.

Cavallo. Ph. tr. 1777. 116, 388.

On the electrophorus. A. Petr. I. i. H. 70.

Krafft's theory of the electrophorus. A. Petr. I. i. 154.

Ingenhousz Elements of electricity.

Ingenhousz. Ph. tr. 1778. 1027.

Socin Anfangsgründe. Han. 1778. 1792.

Pickel Experimenta physicomedica. 8. Würtzb. 1778.

Klindworth. Goth. Mag. I. ii. 35.
Obert. Goth. Mag. V. iii. 96.
Minkeler. Goth. Mag. V. iii. 110.
†*Schäffer* Abbildung des electricitätsträgers. 4. Rat.sb. 1776. R. S.
Schäffer kräfte des electrophors. 4. Rat. 1776.
Schäffers fernere versuche. Ratisb. 1777.
Adams on electricity. 8. London, 1784. 181.
Robert on the electrophorus. Roz. XXXVII. 183.
Nich. I. 355.

> The barrier, which the surface of the electrophorus presents, seems to be analogous to the operation of the galvanic battery.
> Nicholson's revolving doubler is somewhat similar in its operation to the electrophorus. See Microelectrometer.

Conductors.

Volta on a shock from a conductor. Roz. XIII. 249.
Sulla capacità dei conduttori elettrici. 4. R. S.
Nicholson. Ph. tr. 1789.

> Never uses points for a conductor, but a ball brought near to the cylinder, or the cushion without a rubber.

Coated Jars and Batteries.

See Charge.
Kleist discovered the effect of charged glass in 1745.
Needham on some experiments made at Paris. Ph. tr. 1746. XLIV. 247.

> Lemonnier discovered the permanency of the charge. Nollet gave a shock to 180 guards at once.

Dutour on charged talc. A. P. 1753. H. 76.
Wilson's experiments. Ph. tr. 1778. 995.

> Found that a point was struck at the greatest distance.

On the advantage of paper under the coating. Brooks. c. iii.

> Says, that it prevents the jars breaking.

Van Marum's battery. Gilb. I. 68.
Haldane on the force of a battery. Nich. I. 156. Gilb. III. 22.
Cuthbertson's improvement on batteries. Nich. II. 525. Gilb. III. 1.
A battery of talc. Nich. 8. V. 216.

> Robison says, that a globe is the best form for a jar.
> Partial damp is said to make a battery capable of a great intensity of charge.

Electrical Measures in general.

Achard on the force of electricity. Berl. Naturf. fr. I. 53.
Robison. Enc. Br. Suppl. Art. Electrometer.

Measures of Tension. Simple Electrometers.

Darcy's electrometer. A. P. 1749. 63. H. 7.
Richmann's electrometer. N. C. Petr. IV. 301.
Henley's quadrant electrometer. Ph. tr. 1772. 359.
Comus's electric platometer. Roz. VII. 520.
Cavallo's electrometers. Ph. tr. 1777. 388. 1780. 15.

> For the pocket, and for atmospherical observations.

Brooks's electrometer. Ph. tr. 1782. 384.

> An electrical balance.

Terry's electrometer. Roz. XXIV. 315.
An electrometer. Roz. XXV. 228.
*Coulomb's electrical balance. A. P. 1785. 569.

> Employs the torsion of a wire.

Saussure's electrometer. Voyage. III. lxxviii.
Boyer Brun's electroscope for a conductor. Roz. XXVIII. 183.
Deluc's fundamental electrometer. Idées. I. cccxcvii. Gren. I. iii. 380.
Bennet's electrometer. Ph. tr. 1787. 26. Nich. II. 438.

> Of gold leaf.

Chappe's electrometer. Roz. XXXIV. 370.
Vassalli's electrometrical experiments. M. Tur. 1790. V. 57.
Improved electrometer. Nich. I. 270.

Cadet's electrometer. Ann. Ch. XXXVII. 68. Nich. V. 31.

Maréchaux's delicate electrometer. Gilb. XV. 98.

Microelectrometers.

Condensers, Multipliers, and Galvanometers.

Volta on rendering sensible small degrees of electricity. Ph. tr. 1782. 237.

Volta on the advantage of an imperfect insulation. Roz. XXII. 325. XXIII. 381. Soc. Ital. V.

Bennet's electrometer with a condenser. Ph. tr. 1787. 32.
A plate of marble on the electrometer, and on this a small plate of metal.

Bennet's doubler of electricity. Ph. tr. 1787. 288.
Merely varnished plates laid on each other. Liable to the inconvenience of contracting a permanent charge.

Dumotiez's condenser. Roz. XXXI. 431.

Cavallo on measuring small quantities of electricity. Ph. tr. 1788. 1.
Found many accidental errors from permanent charges, even when the plates of the instruments had been untouched for a month. To illustrate this, he made experiments on the decreasing progression of the velocity with which the fluid escapes.

Cavallo's multiplier. Nich l. 394.

Cavallo's collector. Ph. tr. 1788. 255. Roz. XXXIV. 258.
Consisting of a fixed plate between two moveable ones.

Nicholson's revolving doubler. Ph. tr. 1788. 403. Nich. II. 370. IV. 95.
Some thin plates at the distance of $\frac{1}{\lambda}$ of an inch from each other had their capacity augmented 100 times. This instrument was intended for producing electricity from the charge which is almost inseparable from the plates, and usually gave a spark when turned 10 or 20 times. It pumps out positive or negative electricity from a ball into two fixed plates, by means of a revolving plate: the redundant electricity contained in either of the fixed plates is attracted to one of them by the revolving plate, connected with the ball; all the communications are then destroyed, and the revolving plate, with a charge equal and opposite to that of the first fixed plate, is brought opposite to the second, while this is connected with the ball, and acquires from the ball a charge nearly equal to that of the first plate: so that the redundant electricity of each of the fixed plates is now nearly equal to what they both contained at first, and the charge is nearly doubled by each turn.

On the doubler of electricity. Journ. Phys. XLV. (II.) 463.

A Microelectrometer. Nich. I. 16.

Read on the invention of the doubler. Nich. II. 495.

Cuthbertson on Read's condenser. Nich. Gilb. XIII. 208.

Pepys's galvanometer. Ph. M. X. 38.
Of gold leaf.

Gilbert and Bohnenberger on microelectrometers. Gilb. IX. 121, 158.

Weber's glass condenser. Gilb. XI. 344.
Indicated the electricity of ice on the Danube.

Hachette and Desormes's improved doubler. B. Soc. Phil. n. 83. Gilb. XVII. 414.

Maréchaux's electromicrometer. Gilb. XV. 98. XVI. 115.
With a screw and silver leaf.

Wilson's condenser and doubler. Nich. IX. 19.

Regulators and Dischargers.

Lane's electrometer. Ph. tr. 1767. 451.

Cuthbertson's measurement by explosion. Nich. II. 215.

Lawson's discharging electrometer. Ph. M. XI. 251.

Von Hauch's discharging electrometer. Ph. M. XI. 267. Gilb. XIV. 257.
Volta says, that Lane's electrometer agrees with Henley's in all its indications.

Distinguishers.

Chappe on a mode of distinguishing electricity. Roz. XXXIV. 62.

Nicholson on instruments for the distinction of electricity. Nich. 8. III. 121.

One from a projecting point which gives sparks at different distances, according to the kind of electricity: the other from the decomposition of water.

Cuthbertson on the distinction of electricities. Nich. 8. III. 188. Ph. M. XIX. 83.

From the heat of a candle communicated to the negative ball.

Spontaneous Electricity.

Of Inanimate Substances.

Atmospheric Electricity.

See Meteorology.

Mineral Electricity. Tourmalin and other Crystals.

Duc de la Noya Caraffa sur la tourmaline. 4. Par. 1759. M. B.

Wilson. Ph. tr. 1759. 302. 1763. 436. On some similar gems. Ph. tr. 1762. 443.

†Watson on the lyncurium. Ph. tr. 1759. 394.

Aepinus Recueil de mémoires sur la tourmaline. 8. Petersb. 1762.

Aepinus on the Brasilian emerald. N. C. Petr. XII. 351.

Bergmann. Ph. tr. 1766. 236. Schw. Abh. XXIII. 286.

Finds, that one pole of the tourmalin becomes positive by expansion, and negative by contraction, the other the reverse.

Bergmann on the electricity of Iceland crystal. Opusc. V. 366. On the tourmalin. 401.

Wilke. Schw. Abh. XXVIII. 95. XXX. 1, 105.

Franklin. A. P. 1773. H. 78.

Müller an Born. 4. Vienna, 1773.

Zallinger vom turmalin. 8. Vienna, 1779.

Gerhard. Roz. XXI. Suppl. 1782.

Delaunay Lettre sur la tourmaline. 4. R. S.

Werner in Cronstedt's mineralogy.

Haüy. A. P. 1785. 206.

On the tourmaline and on electricity as a test.

Haüy on the boracite. Ann. Ch. IX. 59. Roz. XXXVIII. 323. Gren. VII. 87.

Haüy on the electricity of some crystals. M. Inst. I. 49.

Haüy Traité de physique. I.

Haüy has observed, that electrical crystals are not symmetrically formed at the corresponding angles: thus in the borate of magnesia the 4 intire angles became negative, and the 4 truncated angles positive.

Beckmann. Erfind. 2 ed. I. 248.

Napione sul lincurio. 4. Rom. 1795. R. S.

Ritter on electrical polarity. Gilb. XV. 106.

On terrestrial electricity. Gilb. XVII. 482.

Animal Electricity.

See Chemical Electricity.

On electric fishes. Roz. Intr. II. 432.

Oseretskovsky on a preternatural electricity. A. Petr. III. i. 233.

The person was Michael Puschkin of Tobolsk; the relator was not an eye witness.

Lövens on electricity as a living force. 1779.

Geoffroy on the anatomy of electric fishes. B. Soc. Phil. n. 70. Journ. Phys. LVI. 242. Ph. M. XV. 126. Gilb. XIV. 397.

Haüy on electric animals. Traité de Phys. 41.

Raia Torpedo.

Authors on the torpedo. Krünitz. Abhandl. xvii.

Réaumur. A. P. 1714. 344. H. 19.

Templeman in Nouvelliste. 1759.

Schilling de morbo yaws. Utr. 1770.

Walsh. Ph. tr. 1773. 461. 1775. 465.

Hunter. Ph. tr. 1773. 481.

Pringle's discourse on the torpedo. 4. Lond. 1775.

†Ingenhousz. Ph. tr. 1775. 1.

*Cavendish. Ph. tr. 1776. 196.

The shock of the torpedo resembles that of a large battery weakly charged; such a shock will pass but a little way through the air. An artificial torpedo was made so as

to imitate all the effects of the natural one. One hand received almost as great a shock from it as could be obtained by both hands.
Roz. IV. 205.
Ac. Brux. III. II. 5.
Spallanzani. Goth. Mag. V. i 41.
Girardi and Walter on the torpedo. Soc. Ital. III. 553.
Bryant on the torpedo. Am. tr. II. 166.
Vassalli Eandi on the torpedo. Journ. Phys. XLIX. 69.
Nich. I. 355.

Gymnotus Electricus.

Richer. A. P. I. 116. VII. i. part 2. 92.
Duhamel Hist. Ac. Sc. 168.
Berkel Reise nach Rio de Berbice. 1680. 1689.
Allamand. Haarl. Verh. II. 372.
Gronovius. Act. Helv. IV. 26. Basle, 1760.
Musschenbr. A. P. 1760. H. 21.
Schilling. A. Berl. 1770. 68.
*Williams. Ph. tr. 1775. 94.
Garden. Ph. tr. 1775. 105.
*Hunter. Ph. tr. 1775. 395.
  Anatomical.
Ingenhousz. Phys. schr. I. 273.
Flagg. Am. tr. II. 170.
Bryant and Collins. Amer. trans. II.
Goth. Mag. V. ii. 171.
Bloch Fische. 4. Berl. 1786. II.
Fahlberg. Gilb. XIV. 416.

Silurus Electricus.

Broussonet. A. P. 1782. 692. Roz. XXVII. 139.
  After Adanson and Forskal.

Trichiurus Indicus.

Gmel. Linn. l. 1142.
Nieuhoff. It. ind. II. 270.
Raii syn. pisc. Anguilla marina.
Willughby. Ichth. app. t. 3. f. 3.

Tetrodon, as supposed.

Paterson. Ph. tr. 1786. 382.

MAGNETISM IN GENERAL.

Gilbertus de magnete. f. Lond. 1600. M. B.
Cabaei philosophia magnetica. f. Ferrar. 1629. M. B.
Kircheri magnes. 4. Cologne, 1643. M. B.
Norman's new attractive. M. B.
Ph. tr. abr. II. iv. 601. IV. 2 p. iv. 286. VI. 2 p. iv. 253. VIII. 2 p. iv. 740. X. 2 p. iv. 678.
Lister on magnetism. Birch. iv. 261.
Derham's magnetical experiments and observations. Ph. tr. 1704. XXIV. 2036.
  Some experiments on dividing magnets.
Eberhards magnetische theorie. 4. Leipz. 1720.
Dufay on the magnet. A. P. 1728. 355. 1730. 142. 1731. 417.
Musschenbroek de magnete. Diss. Phys. 1.
*Servington Savery's magnetic observations. Ph. tr. 1730. 295.
Pièces sur l'aiman. 4. Par. 1748. A. P. Prix. V.
D. and J. Bernoulli. A. P. Pr. V. xii.
Euleri nova theoria magnetis. Opusc. III.
Schwigkardi ars magnetica.
Penrose on magnetism. 4. Lond. 1753.
Déscription des courans magnetiques. 4. Strasb. 1753. Germ. Hamb. Mag. XII. i. 579.
*Aepini tentamen theoriae. 4.
Aepinus. N. C. Petr. IX. 340.
Scarella de magnete. 2 v. 4. Brescia, 1759.
Cooper's experimental magnetism. 8. 1761.
Lalande on the magnet. A. P. 1761.
Rinman Geschichte des eisens, von Georgi. iii.
Wilke Tal om magneten. 8. Stock. 1764.

Wilke über der magneten. Germ. by Gröning. 8. Leips. 1794.

Brugman de materia magnetica. 4. Franeq. 1765. R. S.

Germ. by Eschenbach. 8. Leips. 1784.

Brugmanni magnetismus. 4. Leyd. 1778.

Lovett on electricity and magnetism. 8. 1766. R. I.

*Lambert on magnetism. A. Berl. 1766. 22, 49.

Lemonnier Loix du magnétisme. 2 v. 8. Par. 1776.

Acc. A. P. 1776. H. 51.

Lacam's thoughts on magnetism. 8. R. S.

Franklin in Sigaud de la Fond Précis experimental.

Franklin on magnetism. Am. tr. III. 10.

Van Swinden Tentamen de phaenomenis magneticis, specimen 1. 4. R. S.

Gabler Theoria magnetis. 8. Ingolst. 1781.

Rittenhouse on magnetism. Amer. tr.

Adams on magnetism. 8. Lond. 1784.

Cavallo on magnetism. 8. Lond. 1787. 1800. R. I.

Cotte's magnetical observation. Roz. XXX. 349.

Peart on electricity and magnetism. 8. Gainsbor. 1791. R. S.

Dalton's meteor. obs. 61.

Walker on magnetism. 8. Lond. 1794. R. S.

Lorimer on magnetism. 4. 1795. R. I.

Kirwan on magnetism. Ir. tr. VI. 177. Gilb. VI. 391.

Magnetical observations. Gilb. III. 43. VI. 170.

Ritter on magnetic attraction. Gilb. IV. 1.

Madison on magnetism. Repert. XV. 329.

Haüy Traité de Physique. II. 58.

Theory of Magnetism.

Hausksbee on the law of magnetic attraction. Ph. tr. 1712. XXVII. 506.

Taylor. Ph. tr. 1714. XXIX. n. 344.

Musschenbroek de viribus magneticis. Ph. tr. 1725. XXXIII. 370.

Failed in the attempt to discover the law.

Knight's experiments. Ph. tr. 1747. XLIV. 656.

In favour of magnetic currents.

Euleri nova theoria magnetis. Opusc. 4. Berl. 1750. III.

Euler supposes, that the direction of the currents is regulated by a kind of valves.

Aepinus de similitudine vis electricae et magneticae. 4. Petersb. 1758. N. C. Petr. X. 296.

*Aepinus Tentamen theoriae electricitatis et magnetismi.

Aepinus's further comparison of magnetism and electricity. N. C. Petr. X. 296.

Aepinus on Mayer's theory of magnetism. N. C. Petr. XII. 325.

Cigna on the analogy between electricity and magnetism. Misc. Taur. I.

Brugmann de materia magnetica.

Krafft on the force of magnetism. C. Petr. XII. 276.

Gabler theoria magnetis.

Donndorff über electricität.

Van Swinden Recueil de mémoires sur l'analogie de l'electricité et du magnetisme. 3 v. 8. Hague, 1784.

*Coulomb on the law of the magnetic and electric forces. A. P. 1785.

Finds, that they vary as the squares of the distances inversely. A needle is urged by a constant force in the direction of the quiescent position.

Coulomb's seventh memoir. A. P. 1789. 455. Roz. XLIII. 247.

Particular consideration of the separation of a magnet.

Coulomb on the forces of needles. M. Inst. III. 176. Ph. M. XI. 183.

When the form is similar, the force is as the weight. Coulomb supposes the existence of two magnetic fluids, which are only displaced in each molecule.

Abridgment of Coulomb's theory. Journ. Phys. XLV. (II.) 448.

Silberschlag. A. Berl. 1786.
<small>Deduces magnetic attraction from currents.</small>

Rittenhouse. Am. tr. II. 178.

Haüy Theorie de l'électricité et du magnétisme.

Prévost de l'origine des forces magnétiques. 8. Genev. 1788.

Viallon's theory of magnetism. Roz. XLIII. 208.

On supposed magnetic currents. Nich. 8. I. 234.

Arnim on the theory of magnetism. Gilb. III. 48. VIII. 84.
<small>The magnetic arrangement of filings may be imitated by strewing powder on a coated plate of glass placed on two electric balls. Robison.</small>

Magnetic Substances.

Paget and Hooke on the effect of heat on the magnet. Birch. IV. 256, 264.

Musschenbroek on the Indian magnetic sand. Ph. tr. 1734. XXXVIII. 297.

Galeati on the iron found in different bodies. C. Bon. II. ii.

Arderon on giving polarity to brass. Ph. tr. 1758. 774.

Lehmann on the magnetism of copper and brass. N. C. Petr. XII. 368.

On the universality of magnetism. Brugmann by Eschenbach. Leipz. 1781.

Coulomb. A. P. 1784. 266.
<small>Found that wire, when twisted, received 9 times as much magnetic force.</small>

Coulomb on universal magnetism. B. Soc. Phil. n. 61, 63. Journ. Phys. LIV. 240, 267, 454. Journ. R. I., I. Ph. M. XII. 278. XIII. 401. Gilb. XI. 254, 367. XII. 194.
<small>A metal is affected if it contains only $\frac{1}{150000}$ part of iron.</small>

Kohl on pure cobalt. Crell. N. E. VII. 39.

Cavallo on the magnetism of various substances. Ph. tr. 1786. 62.
<small>Finds, that a smaller quantity of iron will affect the needle than can be detected by any chemical test. Some pieces of nickel were not magnetic, but they were found to contain cobalt. Some brass, but not all, becomes magnetic by hammering, and loses its power by heat; and this effect could not be produced by an artificial mixture of iron with brass.</small>

Cavallo's experiments. Ph. tr. 1787. 6.
<small>Almost all substances attracted needles floating on a very clean surface of quicksilver. The brass which was least magnetic was not rendered magnetic by hammering. Iron while dissolving in an acid, disturbed the needle 1°. Red hot iron is not attracted. This Gilbert had before observed.</small>

Brisson. A. P. 1788. 161.
<small>Cast steel is unfit for magnetic use; English and German steel best.</small>

Bennet. Ph. tr. 1792. 81.
<small>Thinks that Cavallo's experiments on solution and on hammering may be explained from the production of polarity in the substances. But is difficult to conceive, that polarity in this sense can increase the attraction.</small>

Landriani in Mayers sammlung. 8. Dresd. 1793. III. 388.

Humboldt on a magnetic serpentine. Ann. Ch. XXII. 51. Journ. Phys. XLV. (II.) 314.

Von Arnim on magnetic substances. Gilb. V. 384.
<small>With a catalogue.</small>

Young on Coulomb's experiments. Journ. R. I., I.

Carradori on Coulomb's universal magnetism. Journ. Phys. LV. 450.

Sage on the magnetism of nickel. Ph. M. XIII. 58.

Thénard on nickel. B. Soc. Phil. n. 68.

Chenevix on the magnetism of nickel. Nich. 8. III. 286. Gilb. XI. 370.

Hatchett on magnetical pyrites. Ph. tr. 1804. 315.
<small>The smallest mixture of antimony destroys the polarity of iron. M. Young.</small>

From the Journals of the Royal Institution. I. 134.
Extract from the Décade Philosophique, No. 21.

National Institute. Experiments showing that all bodies are subject to the magnetic influence, even in a degree which is capable of being measured.

These experiments were made by Mr. Coulomb, and repeated by him before the Institute. He employed all the substances that he examined in the form of a cylinder, or a small bar; he suspended them by a thread of silk in its natural state, and placed them between the opposite poles of two magnets of steel. Such a thread can scarcely support more than two or three drachms without breaking; it was therefore necessary to reduce these needles to very small dimensions. Mr. Coulomb made them about a third of an inch in length, and about a thirtieth of an inch in thickness; and those of metal only one third as thick.

In making the experiments, he placed the magnets in the same right line. Their opposite poles were separated about a quarter of an inch more than the length of the needle which was to oscillate between them. The result was, that of whatever substance the needles were formed, they always ranged themselves accurately in the direction of the magnets; and if they were deflected from this direction, they returned to it with oscillations, which were often as frequent as thirty or more in a minute. Hence, the weight and figure of the needles being given, it was easy to determine the force that produced these oscillations.

The experiments were made in succession with small plates of gold, silver, copper, lead, and tin; with little cylinders of glass, with a bit of chalk, a fragment of bone, and different kinds of wood.

In the course of his lecture on magnetism on the 30th of April, Dr. Young repeated some of these experiments with wires of different kinds: one of them was of tin, and suspended within a cylindrical glass jar by a single silk worm's thread: its oscillations were so slow as to occupy several minutes, and it was scarcely affected by turning the cross bar to which the thread was attached; so that the suspension must have been sufficiently delicate: under these circumstances the opposite poles of two strong magnets were applied close to the jar, and at the distance of about twice the length of the suspended wire: but the effect was absolutely imperceptible: in the morning indeed, there had been an appearance of oscillations occupying about a minute, and tending to the direction of the magnets, perhaps derived from some superficial particles of iron which had lost their magnetic property by oxidation in the course of the day. There must at any rate be a doubt whether the presence of a quantity of iron, too small to be ascertained by chemical tests, might not have been the cause of the effects described by Mr. Coulomb, although they indicate a force something greater, upon a rough calculation, than one 2000th of the weight of the substance. Y.

P. 217. *Note on Mr.* COULOMB's *Experiments on Magnetism.*

We find in No. 3, Tome 3, of the Bulletin de la Société Philomathique, an account of Mr. Coulomb's further experiments on magnetism. They appear to have been made with great precaution, and they tend to confirm the opinion already advanced in these Journals, p. 135, that the greater part, if not the whole, of the effect observed was owing to the presence of iron. For it appears that, according to the method employed in the purification of the metals examined, their apparent magnetic power was very materially different. Mr. Coulomb observes that, upon this foundation, we may make the action of the magnet, upon a needle thus suspended, a very useful instrument in chemical examinations; for he finds that the attractive force is directly as the quantity of iron in any mixture; and, according to its magnitude, we may estimate that quantity, when it is so small as wholly to elude all chemical tests.

Supposed Magnetism of Animals.

Schilling on the magnetism of the gymnotus electricus. A. Berl. 1770. 68.

Against Schilling. Ingenhousz Verm. schr. 271.

Spallanzani a Lucchesini. Pav. 1783.

Three essays in Van Swinden's Recueil.

Andry and Thouret. Mem. de la Soc. de Med.

Saurine on animal magnetism. Roz. XXXVI. 306.

Particular Experiments and Phenomena.

Desaguliers's experiments.

Knight's experiments. Ph. tr. 1747. XLIV. 656.

Waddel and Knight on the destruction of polarity by lightning. Ph. tr. 1749. XLVI. 111.

Colepress on heating a magnet. Ph. tr. 1667. II. 50.

Effects of iron on the needle. Ph. tr. 1685. XV. 1213.

Leeuwenhoek's magnetical experiments. Ph. tr. 1697. XIX. 512.

Ballard on the magnetism of drills. Ph. tr. 1698. 417.

Taylor's experiments. Ph. tr. 1721. XXXI. 204.

Savery's observations. Ph. tr. 1730. XXXVI. 295.

Marbel. Ph. tr. 1732. XXXVII. n. 423.

Middleton on the effect of cold on the needle. Ph. tr. 1738. XL. 310.

Eames on a plurality of poles. Ph. tr. 1738. XL. 383.

Desaguliers. Ph. tr. 1738. XL. 385. On an experiment of Dufay. 386.

A blow fixing the temporary polarity and again destroying it.

Bremond on a file made magnetic by lightning. Ph. tr. 1741. XLI. 614.

Knight's experiments. Ph. tr. 1744. XLIII. 161. 1747. XLIV. 656.

With very powerful magnets.

Aepinus on a magnetical experiment. N. C. Petr. IX. 340.

Lafollie's magnetical experiments. Roz. III. 99.

Van Swinden sur un phénomène paradoxe. Recueil. III.

Veratti's magnetical experiments. C. Bon. VI. 31.

Cavallo on magnetism as affected by effervescence. Ph. tr. 1786. 1787.

Rittenhouse's magnetical experiments. Am. tr. II. 178.

Madison's magnetical experiments. Am. tr. IV. 323.

Magnetical phenomena. Ph. M. I. 426.

Lüdicke's experiments. Gilb. XI. 114.

Ritter's experiments. Journ. Phys. LVII. 406.

Terrestrial Magnetism.

Declination, Dip, and Variation.

For particular observations, see various nautical and meteorological journals.

Gellibrand on the variation of the needle.

Petit on a terrella, and on the change of declination. Ph. tr. 1667. II. n. 28.

Declination in 1668. Ph. tr. 1668. III. 725.

Bond's prediction of the variation to 1716. Ph. tr. 1668. III. n. 40.

Makes it 9°. 17′ W. in 1716. It was actually about 10°.

Auzout on the declination at Rome in 1670. Ph. tr. 1670. V. 1184.

It was 2½°. W.

Hevelius. Ph. tr. 1670. V. 2059.

Halley. Ph. tr. 1683. XIII. 208.

Halley's hypothesis. Ph. tr. 1693. XVII. 563.

Bound with XVI. in the copy of the R. I.

Halley. Ph. tr. 1714. 165.

Heathcote. Ph. tr. 1684. XIV. 578.

In Guinea.

At Nuremberg. Ph. tr. 1685. XV. 1253.

Vallemont sur l'aimant qui s'est fait à Chartres. 12. Par. 1692. M. B.

*J. C. on the polarity of iron. Ph. tr. 1694. XVIII. 257.

Molyneaux on an error from the change of variation. Ph. tr. 1697. XIX. 625.

Ballard on the magnetism of drills. Ph. tr. 1698. XX. 417.

Cunningham on the dip. Ph. tr. 1706. XXII. 507.

Cunningham. Ph. tr. 1704. XXIV. 1639.

In China.

Ph. tr. 1700. XXII. 725.

Ships are sometimes carried into the Bristol channel instead of the British, by mistaking the variation, not by a current.

Wallis on Halley's chart. Ph. tr. 1702. XXIII. 1106.

Saunderson. Ph. tr. 1720. XXXI. 120.
In the Baltic.

Rogers and Halley. Ph. tr. 1721. XXXI. 173.

Cornwall. Ph. tr. 1722. XXXII. 55.
In the Ethiopic ocean.

†Leeuwenhoek on the magnetism of an iron cross. Ph. tr. 1722. XXXII. 72.

Graham. Ph. tr. 1724. XXXIII. 96.
Observes a diurnal change of variation.

Graham on the dip. Ph. tr. 1725. XXXIII. 332.
About 74° 40′ in 1723. Notes the frequency of vibration.

Graham. Ph. tr. 1748. XLV. 279.

Middleton. Ph. tr. 1726. XXXIV. 73. 1731. XXXVII. 71. 1736. XXXIX. 270. 1742. XLII. 157.
In Hudson's Bay.

Robin's tables from Middleton. Ph. tr. 1731. XXXVII. 69. 1733. XXXVIII. 127.

Hoxton on an agitation of the needle in a storm. Ph. tr. 1731. XXXVII. 53.

Hoxton. Ph. tr. 1739. XLI. 171.
Atlantic.

Musschenbroek. Ph. tr. 1732. XXXVII. 428.
At Utrecht.

Musschenbroek's chart for 1744. Introd. II. At the end.

On board the Hartford. Ph. tr. 1732. XXXVII. 331.

Harris. Ph. tr. 1733. XXXVIII. 75.

Elvius. Schw. Abh. 1747. 89.

Wargentin on the effect of an aurora borealis. Ph. tr. 1751. 126.

Mountaine and Dodson on the magnetic chart. Ph. tr. 1754. 875.

*Mountaine and Dodson's tables of 50 000 observations. Ph. tr. 1757. 329.

For 1700, 1710, 1720, 1730, 1744, and 1756. Conclude that no calculations can extend to all the changes.

Mountaine on maps and charts. Ph. tr. 1758. 563.

*Mountaine and Dodson's chart. R. I.

Mountaine on the variation from 1760 to 1762. Ph. tr. 1766. 216.

Williams on ascertaining the longitude by the variation. Lond. 1755. Engl. Ital.
Written by Dr. Johnson.

Euler's theory of the magnetic declination. A. Berl. 1755. 117. 1757. 175. 1766. 213.

Strömer et Zegollström de declinatione. Ups. 1755.

Euler's theory. A. Berl. 1755. 107. 1757. 175. 1766.

Canton on the diurnal variation. Ph. tr. 1759. 398.
With tables.

Mayer's theory. Gött. Anz. 1760. 633. 1762. 377. Lichtenberg in Erxleben. Mayer Op. posth.
Confused and inaccurate. Robison.

Meindert Sorrey Beschaffenheit der erdkugel aus der wirkung des magnets. 1744.

Bellin Carte des variations. Par. 1765.

Lambert. A. Berl. 1766.

Wilke's chart. Schw. Abh. XXX. 209. A. P. 1772. ii. 464.

Wilke über den magneten.

Eckeberg's observations. Schw. Abh. XXX. 238.

Mallet's observations in Lapland. Ph. tr. 1770. 363.

Cook. Ph. tr. 1771. 422.

Lemonnier. A. P. 1771. 93. H. 29. 1772. ii. 457. H. 56. 1773. 440. H. 1. 1774. 237. H. 5. On the dip. 1777. 89. H. 4.

Lemonnier Loix du magnétisme.

On the line of no declination. Lemonnier. A. P. 1777. 168.

Hutchins on the dip in the north seas. Ph. tr. 1775. 129. 1776. 179.

Douglass's observations made about 1735. Ph. tr. 1776. 18.
Known to Mountaine.

Dunn's magnetic atlas. Lond. 1776.

Legentil. A. P. 1777. 401. H. 5.

Dalrymple. Ph. tr. 1778. 389.
East Indies.

Pickersgill. Ph. tr. 1778. 1057.
Davis's straights.

Miller. Roz. XIII. 391.

Lacepède. Roz. XV. 140.

Bode Jahrbuch. 1779.

Van Swinden. S. E. VIII.
Thinks the diurnal variation owing rather to a change in the needle than in the earth, the effects in different places and with different needles varying considerably. The declination increases before an aurora borealis.

Van Swinden on the affection of the needle in the aurora borealis. A. Petr. 1780. IV. i. H. 10.

Coulomb. S. E. VIII.
Attributes the diurnal variation to the action of the sun with his atmosphere, like the aurora borealis, driving the magnetic fluid from the parts of the earth nearest to him: the action continuing in these climates an hour or two after noon, till the sun reaches the meridian of the magnetic pole.

Funcks N. und S. Erdoberflache. Leipz. 1781.
Shows the variation and the dip.

Cassini on the daily variation. Roz. XXIV. 257.

Forster in Swinburne's Travels. II.

Several observations of variation. Am. Ac. I.

Chart of the magnetic equator and meridian. A. P. 1786. 43. Journ. Phys. XLVI. 84.

Silberschlag's theory. A. Berl. 1786. 87.
Makes the lines of equal dip parallel.

Cavallo. Ph. tr. 1787. 6.
Deduces the diurnal variation from the effect of heat.

Buffon Mineralogie. V.

Cotte on the diurnal variation. Roz. XLI. 204.
Makes the needle undergo several vicissitudes in the year, becoming four times stationary. From January to March it retires from the meridian, then approaches it till May, is stationary in June, retires in July, approaches till October, and retires from it in November and December.

Churchman's magnetic atlas. R. I.

Churchman on the magnetic atlas. 4. R. I.

Dalton's meteor. observ. 61.

*Robison. Enc. Br. Art. Variation. Suppl. Art. Magnetism.

Macdonald on the diurnal variation of the needle in Sumatra. Ph. tr. 1796. 340.
The variation about 1° 8′ E. at 7 in the morning, 1° 11′ at 5 in the afternoon; diminishing again till 7 the next morning. Supposes the strongest pole to the south.

Macdonald on the variation of the needle at St. Helena. Ph. tr. 1798. 397.
Nov. 1796, the variation was 15° 48′ 34½″ W.; increasing 3′ 55″ from 6 in the morning to 8, then diminishing till 6 in the evening, and remaining stationary all night.

Haüy on natural magnets. B. Soc. Phil. n. 5. Journ. Phys. XLV. (II.) 309.

Rennel's variation chart of Africa. *Park's* travels. Zach. Ephem. IV. 192.

Harding on the variation. Ir. tr. IV. 107.
Thinks the change at Dublin is 12′ 20″ every year.

Nugent on the magnetic poles. Ph. M. V. 378.

Heller on the magnetic effects of the sun and moon. Gilb. IV. 477.

Humboldt. B. Soc. Phil. n. 37.
Found the number of vibrations in equal times at Paris 245, at Valentia 235, at Cumana 229. But what was the temperature?

Humboldt. Ph. M. XI. 355.
Finds the vanishing point of declination lat. 29°. N. long. 66° 40′ W. probably of Paris: this is further W. than in Lambert's chart in Bode. 1779.

Humboldt's letters. Ph. M. XVI. 165.

Burckhardt on the law of declination at Paris. Zach. Mon. corr. III. 161, 546. Note. Ph. M. IX.
Gives for the declination at Paris T. decl. $=.449$ (sin.

.465 gr. t) + .0425 (sin. .93 gr. t)⁴ + .0267 (sin. 1.86 gr. t)⁴ ; t being the number of years elapsed since 1668, the degrees, gr. being decimal. In 1799 the declination at Paris was 22.266°, in 1837, according to the formula, it will be a maximum at 24°. 26'. The complete period is 860 years.

On a magnetic globe floating in mercury. Ph. M. XIII. 404.

Ritter on magnetism. Gilb. XV. 206.
Supposes a lunar period.

Lalande on Churchman's north pole. Ph. M. XIV. 249.

Account of Gay Lussac and Biot's aerostatic voyage. Ph. M. XIX. 374.
They found little or no difference in the force at the height of above 4 miles.
The eruption of Hecla considerably affected the needle. Robison.

It has been observed, that the variation is certainly affected by atmospherical causes, as in the aurora borealis; but not certainly by terrestrial, and that it is fair to conclude that its cause is wholly atmospherical: the argument appears however to be a weak one.

Table of the change of Declination observed in London. Cavallo.

1576	11°	15' E.	1730	13°	0' W.
1586	11	11	1735	14	16
1612	6	10	1740	15	40
1622	6	0	1745	16	58
1633	4	5	1750	17	54
1634	4	5	1760	19	12
1657	0	0	1765	20	0
1665	1	22½ W.	1770	20	35
1666	1	35½	1774	21	3
1672	2	30	1775	21	30
1683	4	30	1780	22	10
1692	6	0	1783	22	50
1700	8	0	1790	23	34
1717	10	42	1795	23	52
1724	11	45	1800	24	7
1725	11	56			

Mean diurnal Variation, according to Canton.

Jan.	7'	8"	May	13'	0"	Sept.	11'	43"
Feb.	8	58	June	13	21	Oct.	10	36
March	11	7	July	13	14	Nov.	8	9
April	12	26	Aug.	12	19	Dec.	6	58

Progress of the diurnal Variation.

June 27, 1759.

		Decl. W.	Temperature.
Morning.	0h. 18'.	19°. 2'.	62° F.
	6 4	18 58	62
	8 30	18 55	65
	9 2	18 54	67
	10 20	18 57	69
	11 40	19 4	68½
Afternoon.	0 50	19 0	70
	1 38	19 8	70
	3 10	19 8	68
	7 20	18 59	61
	9 12	19 6	59
	11 40	18 51	57½ Canton Ph. tr. 1761.

Table of the Dip. Cavallo.

N. lat.	E. long.	N. end below.	S. lat.	W. long.	N. end below.
1776.			1776.		
53° 55'	193° 39'	69° 10'	7° 3'	33° 21'	17° 57'
49 36	233 10	72 29	11 25	34 24	9 15
	W. long.			E. long.	S. end below.
44 5	8 10	71 34			
38 53	12 1	70 30	16 45	208 12	29 28
34 57	14 8	66 12	19 28	204 11	41 0
29 18	16 7	62 17	1777.		
24 24	18 11	59 0	21 8	185 0	39 1
20 47	19 36	56 15	1774.		
15 8	23 38	51 0	35 55	18 20	45 37
12 1	23 35	48 26	1777.		
10 0	22 52	44 12	41 5	174 13	63 49
5 2	20 10	37 25	1773.		
0 3	27 38	30 3	45 47	166 18	70 5
4 40	30 34	22 15			

The mean dip observed by Nairne in London, 1772, was 72° 20'. Ph. tr. 1772. 476.

In 1576, Norman found the dip 71° 50', in 1676, Bond 73° 47', in 1720, Whiston 75° 10', in 1723, Graham 73½°, or 75°, in 1776 Cavendish makes it 72° 30': the maximum was therefore about 1720. Ph. tr. 1776. 375.

Magnetical Apparatus.

E. M. Pl. VIII. Amusemens de physique.

Artificial Magnetism.

A. P. Index. Art. Aimant.
Réaumur on making magnets. A. P. 1723.
Marcel. Ph. tr. 1732. XXXVII. 294.
Duhamel façon d'aimanter. A. P. 1735. 1745. 181. H. I.

Strength of Knight's magnets. Ph. tr. 1744. XLIII. 161.
Knight on the poles of magnets. Ph. tr. 1745. XLIII. 361.
Mitchell on artificial magnets. 8. Lond. 1750. Cambr. 1751. M. B.
Canton's method, with Folkes's report. Ph. tr. 1751. 31.
Klingenstierna et Brander de magnetismo artificiali. Stoch. 1752.
Rivière sur les aimans artificiels. Par. 1752.
Richmann on making magnets. N. C. Petr. IV. 235.
Wentz on artificial magnets. Act. Helv. II. 264.
Nebel de magnete artificiali. 4. Utr. 1756.
Antheaulme. A. P. 1753, 1761.
Antheaulme sur les aimans artificiels. Par. 1760.
Le Noble's artificial magnets. A. P. 1772. i. H. 17.
Lemonnier Loix du magnétisme.
Fothergill on Knight's machine. Ph. tr. 1776. 591.
Fuss on artificial magnets. A. Petr. II. ii. H. 35. Roz. 1782.
On artificial magnets. Roz. IX. 454.
Wilson on Knight's artificial loadstones. Ph. tr. 1779. 51.

Made of elutriated iron filings, and linseed oil.

E. M. A. VI. 694.
E. M. Physique. Art. Aimant.
Ingenhousz's paste. Verm. Schr. I. 409.
Brisson on the best steel for magnetical uses. A. P. 1788. 169. Repert. III. 276.

Cast steel bad. English or German best.

Tremery on elliptic magnets. B. Soc. Phil. n. 6.
A complex horseshoe magnet. Nich. 8. V. 216.

Sjösteen on making magnets. Gilb. XVII. 325.

Touching them in a circle.
A bar rubbed from both ends to the middle, has both ends of the same quality with the pole employed; the middle of the contrary quality.
Oil somewhat impedes the communication of magnetism. Robison.

Compasses and dipping Needles.

See Navigation.
Lahire on an annular needle. Ph. tr. 1686. XVI. 344.
Lahire's variation compass. A. P. 1716. 6.
Méan's compass. A. P. 1731. H. 92.
Buache's compass. A. P. 1732. 377.

For the dip and declination.

Quereineuf's azimuth compass. A. P. 1734. H. 105. Mach. A. VII. 3.
Middleton's azimuth compass Ph. tr. 1738. XL. 395.

With a telescope.

Lemaire's variation compass. A. P. 1747. H. 126. Mach. A. VII. 361.
Magny's compass. A. P.
Bernoulli on dipping needles. A. P. Prix. V. viii. Act. Helv. III. 233.
Trombelli and Collina on the invention of the compass. C. Bon. II. iii. 333, 372.
Knight. Ph. tr. 1749. iii.

Rhomboidal needles are bad.

*Knight's compass, with Smeaton's remarks. Ph. tr. 1750. 505, 513.
Duhamel on the improvement of the compass. A. P. 1750. 154. H. 1. 1772. ii. 44. H. 58.
Zeiher's needle and compass. N. C. Petr. VII. 309. VIII. 284.
Kotelnikow's suspension for a needle. N. C. Petr. VIII. 304.
Nairne on Mitchell's dipping needle. Ph. tr. 1772. 476.

Marine compass. A. P. 1773. 320.

Lemonnier on removing friction from compasses. A. P. 1773. 440. H. 1.

A compass. Roz. Intr. I. 422.

Lorimer's needle for the dip and the variation. Ph. tr. 1775. 72.

Cavendish. Ph. tr. 1776. 375.
<small>The needle is capable of inversion: the dipping needle on Mitchell's construction.</small>

Gaule's variation compass. A. P. 1777.

Krafft on the dipping needle. A. Petr. II. ii. 170.

Ingenhousz on suspending needles. Ph. tr. 1779. 537.
<small>Proposes to have them made hollow, so as nearly to float on a fluid, and then suspended by a magnet, with a cavity below to prevent their being shaken off.</small>

Lacépède on compasses. Roz. XV. 140.

*Van Swinden on magnetic needles. S. E. VIII. 1780.
<small>Prize memoir. Proposes flat needles, turning on a projecting point.</small>

*Coulomb on magnetic needles. S. E. IX. 1780.
<small>Prize memoir. Thinks the form of a needle of little consequence: perforating them has scarcely any effect. Divided needles act most powerfully. Found the circle of contact of the needle with its support, in a particular case, $\frac{1}{867}$ of a line, supposing it to be equally pressed, which is nearly true.</small>

Coulomb's needle suspended by a thread of silk. A. P. 1785. 560.

Coulomb's mode of measuring the dip. M. Inst. IV. 565. B. Soc. Phil. n. 31.
<small>Compares the weight required to keep the needle horizontal with the time of its horizontal vibration; and thinks that the dip may be thus determined within 10' or 12'.</small>

Coulomb. Ph. M. XV. 186.
<small>Prefers long and broad needles magnetized by Aepinus's method.</small>

Gattey on guarding needles from electricity. Roz. XVII. 296.

Rumouski on observing the dip. A. Petr. 1781. V. i. 191.

E. M. A. VI. 714. E. M. Pl. V. Marine. III. E. M. Physique. Art. Aimant. Boussole.

Degaulte sur un compass azimuthal a réflection. 8. R. S.

Cavallo. Ph. tr. 1786. 65.
<small>Recommends for delicate purposes suspension by a chain of horse hair.</small>

Cotte's variation compass. Roz. XIX. 189.

Romans's improved compass. Am. tr. II. 396. Repert. IV. 178.
<small>The box hung on a centre.</small>

Report on M'Culloch's sea compasses. Lond. 1788.

Drury on cased needles. Ir. tr. 1788. II. 119. Repert. I. 111.

Bennet's suspension of the magnetic needle. Ph. tr. 1792. 81. Repert. XII. 311.
<small>A spider's thread, which, after 18000 revolutions, showed no tendency to untwist, and broke at last.</small>

Prony's instrument for observing the variation. Journ. Phys. XLIV. (II.) 471.

Cassini's azimuth compass. M. Inst. V. 145.

Magnetical Observations.

Howard on a reversion of the needle. Ph. tr. 1676. XI. 647.

Reversion of a compass. Ph. tr. 1684. XIV. 520.

Middleton. Ph. tr. 1738. XL. 310.
<small>Found the needle affected by cold so that it could not traverse.</small>

Bouguer on marine observations of declination. A. P. Prix. II. vi.

Remark on the disturbance of the needle by the electricity of the glass. Ph. tr. 1746. XLIV. 242.
<small>The electricity may be removed by a wet finger.</small>

Waddel and Knight on the destruction of polarity by lightning. Ph. tr. 1749. XLVI. 111.

Magnetic Measures.

See Terrestrial Magnetism.
Graham. Ph. tr. 1725. XXXIII. 332.
  Observed the frequency of the vibrations of the dipping needle.
Coulomb. A. P. 1785. 578.
  Shows, that a horizontal needle is urged by a force which is constant if reduced to the direction of the meridian.
Saussure's magnetometer. Voyages. ccclv.

METEOROLOGY.

Literature of Meteorology.

Weigels Chemie. §. 398.

Meteorology in general.

Zahn on the economy of the world.
Lycosthenes on meteors.
Des Cartes Meteora. Opp. II.
Ph. tr. abr. II. i. 1. IV. 2 p. i. 1. VI. 2 p. i. 1. VIII. 2 p. i. 377. X. 2 p. i. 269.
Fritsch on meteors.
Jurin invitatio ad observationes meteorologicas. Ph. tr. 1723. XXXII. 422.
Greenwood on the method of meteorological observations. Ph. tr. 1728. XXXV. 390.
*Poleni observationes meteorologicae Patavianae. Ph. tr. 1731. 201.
Cyrilli aeris terraeque historia, 1732. Ph. tr. 1733. 184.
On the causes of a dry and wet summer. Ph. tr. 1740. 519.
  A frosty winter producing a dry summer.
Hollmann on meteorological observations. C. Gott. 1751. I. 41. And elsewhere.

Bernoulli on the atmosphere. Act. Helv. I. 33. II. 101.
Ellis on wind and weather. Ph. tr. 1755. 124.
Franklin's physical and meteorological observations, read 1756. Ph. tr. 1765. 182.
Mills's essay on the weather. 12.
Musschenbroek's cautions on observations. N. C. Petr. VIII. 367.
Richard Histoire naturelle de l'air et des météores. 10 v. 12. Par. 1770, 1771.
Lambert on meteorology. A. Berl. 1771. 60.
Lambert on meteorological observations. A. Berl. 1772. 60.
Deluc Modifications de l'atmosphère. 4. Gen. 1772. 8. Par. 1784. R. I.
Deluc Idées sur la météorologie. 2 v. 8. Lond. 1786, 1787. R. I.
Deluc on meteorology. Roz. XXXVII. 120.
Deluc's answer to Monge. Ann. Ch. VIII. 73.
Cotte Traité de météorologie. 4. Par. 1774. Suite. 2 v. 1789.
Cotte on meteorology. Roz. VII. 93.
Cotte's general results or axioms. Journ. Phys. XLIV. (I.) 231. Ph. M. VI. 146.
Note of Cotte's memoirs. Journ. Phys. XLV. (II.) 431.
Felbiger über die witterung. 4. Sagan. 1773.
Toaldo on meteorology as affecting vegetation. Roz. X. 249.
Toaldo la meteorologia applicata all' agricoltura. 8. Ven. 1786. R. S.
Toaldo Saggio meteorologico. 4. R. S.
Busch Vermischte abhandlungen. Hamb. 1777. II. 225.
Van Swinden sur les observations faites a Franéker. 8. Leyd.
Extract of a memoir of Van Swinden, by Cotte. Roz. XII. 297.
Dionis du Séjour sur les phénomènes. 8. R. S.

Gatterer's meteorological year. Commentat. Gott. 1780. III. Ph. 82.
Gatterer. Goth. Mag. I. ii. 1.
Horrebow tractatus historicometeorologicus. 4. Copenh. 1780.
Jones on the natural philosophy of the elements. 4. R. I.
Rosenthal über meteorologische beobachtungen. 4. Erf. 1781.
Ephemerides societatis meteorologicae Palatinae. 1781... Manh. B. B.
Extracts from the memoirs of the Palatine society, by Cotte. Roz. XLIII. 294. Journ. Phys. XLIV. (I.)
Monitum ad observatores societatis meteorologicae. 4. R. S.
Achard on the imperfections of meteorology. Roz. XXIII. 282.
*Hübe über die ausdünstung.
Rouland Tableau des propriétés de l'air. 8. Par. 1784. R. I.
*Sénébier on the improvement of meteorology. Roz. XXVII. 300. XXX. 177, 245, 328.
*Saussure Voyages.
Saussure Relation abregée d'un voyage à la cime du Mont Blanc. 8. Gen. R. S.
Account of Saussure's journey. Roz. XXXI. 317, 374.
Saussure's observations. Roz. XXXIV. 161.
*Saussure Hygrometrie.
Madison on meteorological observations. Am. tr. II. 123.
Pilgrams Wetterkunde. Vienna, 1788. 4.
Marsham's indications of spring. Ph. tr. 1789. 154.
Ramond Observations faites dans les Pyrénées. 8. Par. 1789. R. S.
Ramond's ascent of Mont Perdu. Nich VI. 250.

Meteorological remarks. Roz. XXXIV. 321.
Monge on the principal phenomena of meteorology. Ann. Ch. V. 1.
Garnett's collection of meteorological observations. Manch. M. IV. 234, 521.
Copland and others on the weather. Manch. M. IV. 243.
Dalton's meteorological observations and essays. 8. Lond. 1793. Rules for judging of the weather. 195.
Enc. Br. Art. Weather.
Six on meteorology. 8. 1794. R. I.
Kirwan on the weather. Ir. tr. V. 3, 31, 39.
Kirwan on the variations of the atmosphere. Ir. tr. VIII. 269.
Pouchet Meteorologie terrestre. 8. Rouen, 1797. R. S.
Lochead on the natural history of Guiana. Nich. II. 297.
Humboldt's letter from South America. Journ. Phys. XLIX. 433.
Lamarck on meteorological registers. Journ. Phys. LI. 419.
Coupé's meteorological remarks. Journ. Phys. LIII. 262.
Beddoes on prognostics of the weather. Nich. 8. I. 98.
Capper on the weather in England. Nich. 8. I. 275.
Parrot on meteorology. Gilb. X. 167.
Böckmann's meteorological remarks. Gilb. XIV. 112.
Cordier's journey to the summit of Teneriffe. Ph. M. XVII. 31.
Menzies's journey to the summit of Whararai. Journ. R. I., I. 311.
Prognostics of the weather. Nich. VII. 148.
Aerostatic voyage by Gay Lussac and Biot Ph. M. XIX. 374

Meteorological Apparatus, and Modes of Observing.

Leutmanni instrumenta meteorognostica. 8. Wittenberg, 1725.
Nollet. A. P. 1740. 385, 567. 1741. 338. H. 145.
Pickering. Ph. tr. 1744. n. 473.
*Cavendish on the meteorological instruments of the R. S. Ph. tr. 1776. 375.
Fontana's account of the Grand Duke's cabinet. Roz. IX. 41.
Changeux's meteorographic instruments. Roz. XV. 74. XVI. 325.
Hemmer Descriptio instrumentorum societatis Palatinae. 4. Manh. 1782.
Monitum ad observatores societatis Palatinae.
Rosenthal Meteorologische werkzeuge. 2 v. 8. Gotha, 1782, 1784.
Landriani Descrizione di una machina meteorologica. 4. R. S.
*Moscati's description of a meteorological observatory. Soc. Ital. V. 356.
On Lazowsky's long wire. Nich. II. 11.
Toaldo on the prognostications of animals. Ph. M. IV. 367.
Schweighäuser on the sound of a long wire. Ph. M. IX. 285.

<small>A very long wire was supposed to emit a sound upon the approach of any change of weather: it was probably from an alteration of temperature.</small>

Bossi sulla dottrina di Quatremere Disjonval. 8. Tur. 1803. R. S.
Meyer on the presensations of animals. Ph. M. XI. 211.
Nouveau traité sur les barometres. 8. Par. 1802.

Meteorological Journals.

A. P. Numerous observations may be found by the index.

Plot. Ph. tr. 1685. XV. 930.
<small>At Oxford. A barometrical diagram.</small>
Garden. Ph. tr. 1685. XV. 991.
Hillier. Ph. tr. 1697. XIX. 687.
<small>Cape Corse in Guinea.</small>
Derham. Ph. tr. 1698. XX. 41. At Upminster. 1699. XXI. 45. 1700. XXII. 527. 1703. XXIII. 1443. 1707. XXV. 2378. 1709. XXVI. 309, from Ireland†; 342. Switzerland and Upminster. 1732. XXXVII. 261. 1733. XXXVIII. 101. 1734. XXXVIII. 334, 405, 458.
Cunningham. Ph. tr. 1699. XXI. 323. 1704. XXIV. 1639.
<small>China.</small>
Townley. Ph. tr. 1699. XXI. 47. 1705. XXIV. 1877.
Locke. Ph. tr. 1705. XXIV. 1917.
Cruquius. Ph. tr. 1724. XXXIII. 4.
Middleton. Ph. tr. 1731. XXXVII. 76.
*Poleni. Ph. tr. 1731. XXXVII. 201. 1738. XL. 239.
<small>Pavia.</small>
*Musschenbroek. Ph. tr. 1732. XXXVII. 357, 428.
<small>Utrecht.</small>
Cyrilli. Ph. tr. 1733. XXXVIII. 184.
Weidler. Ph. tr. 1736. XXXIX. 238, 266.
Hadley. Ph. tr. 1738. XL. 154. Abstr. 1742. XLII. 243. Abstr.
Lynn. Ph. tr. 1741. XLI. 686.
<small>Synopsis.</small>
Revillas. Ph. tr. 1742. XLII. 193.
<small>Rome.</small>
Linings. Ph. tr. 1748. XLV. 336.
<small>South Carolina.</small>
T. Heberden. Ph. tr. 1751. 357. 1754. 617.
<small>Madeira.</small>
Watson. Ph. tr. 1753. 108.
<small>Siberia; abstract.</small>

Simon. Ph. tr. 1753. 320. 1756. 759.
Dublin.
Borlase. Ph. tr. 1763. 27. 1770. 230. 1772. 365.
Rose. Ph. tr. 1766. 291.
Quebec.
Huxham. Ph. tr. 1767. 443. Pl.
Carlyle. Ph. tr. 1768. 83.
Wolfe. Ph. tr. 1768. 151.
Warsaw.
Wargentin. Ph. tr. 1768. 152.
Stockholm.
Farr. Ph. tr. 1769. 81. 1775. 194. 1776. 367. 1777. 353. 1778. 567.
Bristol.
Miller. Ph. tr. 1769. 155. 1771. 195.
Ph. tr. 1770. 228.
At Bridgewater.
Pigott. Ph. tr. 1771. 274.
Rouen.
Barker. Ph. tr. 1772..1802.
From 1736. Lyndon.
Wollaston. Ph. tr. 1773. 67.
Cotte. S. E. 1773. 427.
From Messier, for 10 years.
*Journals kept at the house of the R. S. Ph. tr. 1775...
*Horsley. Ph. tr. 1775. 167. Abriged 1776. 354.
Barker. Ph. tr. 1775. 202.
Allahabad.
Roxburgh. Ph. tr. 1778. 180. 1780. 246.
Manuscript continuations. R. S.
Fort St. George.
Dalrymple. Ph. tr. 1778. 389.
East Indies.
Barr. Ph. tr. 1778. 560. 1780. 272.
Montreal.
M'Gouan. Ph. tr. 1778. 564.
Edinburgh.
Lloyd. Ph. tr. 1778. 571.
Leeds.

Pickersgill. Ph. tr. 1778. 1057.
Davis's Straights.
Latrobe. Ph. tr. 1779. 657. 1781. 197.
Several manuscript continuations. R. S.
Nain and Okak.
Diary kept in Hudson's bay. f. R. S.
Chandler's meteorological diary. f. R. S.
Robertson's journal kept on board the Rainbow. 4. R. S.
Schotte. Ph. tr. 1780. 478.
Senegambia.
*Ephemerides Societatis Palatinæ. Cotte's extracts. Roz.
Atkins. Ph. tr. 1784. 58.
Minehead.
At the Royal Observatory of Paris. A. P. 1784. 631.
Bent, for several years. M.S. R.S.
London.
Pearce. M. S. R. S.
Fort William.
Kirwan. Ir. tr. V. VI.
Dublin.
Observations in Greenland, Labrador, and Africa. Gilb. XII. 206.
Mourgue Essais de statistique.
Acc. Journ. Phys. LII. 118.
Several other manuscript journals. R. S.

General effects of the Sun and Moon.

Kratzenstein von dem einflusse des mondes. 8. Halle, 1746. 1771.
Lambert on the moon's influence upon the atmosphere. Act. Helv. IV. 315. A. Berl. 1771. 66.
Toaldo della vera influenza degli astri. 4. Pad. 1770. R. S.
French by Jacquin.
Toaldo Tabulae barometri aestusque maris. 4. Pad. 1773.
Toaldo Saggio meteorologico. 4. R. S.

Toaldo on the lunar influence. Roz. XIII. 442.

Toaldo Saros météorologique. 4. R. S. Roz. XXI. 176.

Toaldo's 24 aphorisms. Rozier. 1785. 388.

Toaldo's system and observations. Ph. M. III. 120. IV. 417.

Gr. Fontana on the lunisolar influence on the atmosphere. Ac. Sienn. V. 116.

Fabri Geogr. Mag. II. i. 72.

Horsley. Ph. tr. 1776. 354.

Cotte on lunar periods. Roz. XX. 249.

Cotte on the lunar period of 19 years. Roz. XXVIII. 276. XLII. 279. Journ. Phys. L. 358.

Mann on aerial tides. Roz. XXVII. 7. Ph. Mag. V. 104.

Chiminello on atmospheric tides. A. Pad. I. 195. IV. 88.

Lamarck on the lunar influence on the atmosphere. Journ. Phys. XLVI. (III.) 428. LII. 296. LIII. 277. B. Soc. Phil. n. 15. Nich. III. 488. Ph. M. IX. 373. Gilb. VI. 204.
Against Cotte.

Howard on the variation of the barometer from solar and lunar influence. Ph. M. VII. 355.
Finds a mean elevation of .1 at the quadratures.

Lamanon on atmospherical tides. Gilb. VI. 194.

Hemmer on the sun's influence upon the barometer. Ph. M. XI. 151.

Climate in general.

Halley on the heat of different latitudes. Ph. tr. 1693. XVII. 878.
From computation.

†Lahire on the thermometer covered with snow ascending in a frost. A. P. IX. 318.

Effect of the wind on the thermometer. Ph. tr. 1710. XXVII. 544. H. 13.

Mairan on the causes of heat and cold. A. P. 1719. 104. H. 3. 1721. 8. H. 16. 1765. 143. H. 1.

Mairan Recherches sur le chaud et le froid. 4. Par. 1768.

Weitbrecht on the heat of running water. C. Petr. VII. 235.

Euler on climates. C. Petr. XI. 82.
Merely mathematical; supposing the sun to cool the earth at night.

Nollet on the freezing of large rivers. A. P. 1743. 51. H. 8.

Krafft Oratio de climatibus borealibus.

Segner de calore et frigore. 4. Gött. 1746.

Ellis on the temperature of the bottom of the sea. Ph. tr. 1751. 211.

Kaestner on Halley. Hamb. Mag. II. 426.

Simpson's fluxions.

Sheldrake's causes of heat and cold. 8. Lond. 1756.

Wargentin on climate. Schw. Abh. 1757. 159.

Martine's essays.

Lomonosow on the ice in the North sea. Schw. Abh. 1763. 37.

On mean temperatures. Act. Helv. IV. 1.

Grüners Eisgebirge des Schweizerlandes. 8. Bern. 1760. 36.

Heberden on the heat at different heights. Ph. tr. 1765. 126.
Finds 1° depression for each 190 feet of height.

Barrington on the changes in the climate of Italy. Ph. tr. 1768. 58.

Douglas on the temperature of the sea at different depths. Ph. tr. 1770. 39.

Emerson's miscellanies. 490.

Williamson on the change of climate in America. Am. tr. I. 277, 336.

On climates. Roz. III. 245. IV. 174. X. 148.

Bourrit des glacières de Savoye. 8. Gen. 1773.

Bourrit des Alpes Pennines. 8. Gen. 1781. Phil. tr. 1775. 459.
    Roebuck suggests the estimation of climates by the temperature of springs.

Saussure Voyages dans les Alpes.
    Observes, that there is sometimes a sense of heat on these mountains.

Wilson on local heat. Ph. tr. 1780.

Hassenfratz on the free heat of the atmosphere. Roz. XIX. 337.

Goth. Mag. I. ii. 19.

Six on local heat. Ph. tr. 1784. 428. 1788. 103.
    In cloudy weather there is little difference in the temperature at different heights; in clear weather the lowest station is coldest at night, and hottest by day. When the heat is below 40° there is little difference in the day time. In general the difference is 1° or 2°, sometimes 4° at night. The ground is sometimes 1° or 2° colder than the air a few feet above it, and was found even 10° colder than the highest station.
    In a well at Dover, 360 feet deep, with 21 feet of water, the water was 56° at the surface, 52° in the middle, $48\frac{1}{4}°$ at the bottom, in September. At Sheerness in a well with 180 feet of water, wholly below the level of the sea, the thermometer was 51° in the middle, 56° at the bottom: but perhaps the pressure of six atmospheres disturbed the thermometer a little.

Pugh on European climates. 8. Lond. 1784. R. S.

Deluc Idées. II. dccxcvii.
    On the sense of heat upon high mountains.

Forster's works.
    Proves that ice may be formed at sea.

Kirwan's estimate of the temperature of different latitudes. 8. Lond. 1787. R. I. Fr. by Adet. 8.

Extr. Roz. XXXVII. 410.

Kirwan on the variations of the atmosphere. Extr. Ph. M. XVI. 212.
    On the heat of summers and winters.

Darwin. Ph. tr. 1788. 43.
    The air ascending from the vallies towards the hills, must expand, and thence become cooler: thus the thermometer often rises with the barometer.

Hamilton on the climate of Ireland. Ir. tr. 1788. II. 143. VI. 27. Nich. II. 381.

Morozzo on the temperature of the sea and lakes at different depths. M. Tur. 1788. IV. 309.

Guthrie on the climate of Russia. Ed. tr. II. 213.

Mann on the changes of climates. Comm. Ac. Theod. Pal. 1790. VI. 82. Gren. I. 231. Ph. M. IV. 357. V.

Mann sur les grandes gélées. 8. Ghent, 1792. R. S.

Mayer de variationibus thermometri. Op. ined. I. 1.

Toaldo on the heat of the lunar rays. C. Bon. VII. O. 9, 471.

Toaldo on climates. Ac. Pad. III. 216.

Pictet Essais de physique. I. viii.
    On the warmth of the strata of air.

Picteton mean temperatures. Roz. XLII. 78.

Williams on the use of the thermometer in sounding. 4. Philad. 1792. Am. tr. III. 82.

Dalton on climates. Meteor. observ. 118.

Cotte on temperatures. Roz. XLII. 282.

Cotte on lunar constitutions. Roz. L. 358.

*Prévost sur l'équilibre de la chaleur. Roz. XLII. 81.

Lamarck on the variations of the heavens in mean latitudes. Note. Ph. M. XV. 189.

Cassini on the equinoctial variation of temperature. Roz. XL. 295.

Rittenhouse on the temperature of the air and of the sea. Am. tr. III. 194.

Strickland on the use of thermometers in navigation. Am. tr. V. 90.

Van Swinden on hard winters. Journ. Phys. L. 277.

Playfair. Ed. tr.
    Says, that the temperature diminishes 1° for about 300 feet of elevation.

Humboldt on the temperature of the sea. B. Soc. Phil. n. 37.

Says, that the water becomes much colder in shallow places.

Prony on the declination of the columns of the Pantheon. B. Soc. Phil. n. 37.

Probably the effect of a change of temperature.

Beddoes on foretelling the temperature of summers. Nich. V. 131. Nich. 8. I. 98.

On the temperature of springs. Gilb. III. 217.

Lamarck on the climate in middle latitudes. Journ. Phys. LVI. 118. Note. Ph. M. XV. 189.

Volney on the climate and soil of America. 8. 1804. R. I.

Esmark on the height of the snow line. Ph. M. XVII. 374.

Perrin's register of the heat of the sea, in the East Indies. Nich. VIII. 131.

Cotte's general aphorisms, from Gren. III. 5. There is little variation of heat between the tropics: it becomes greater on plains than on hills: it is never so low near the sea as in inland parts: the wind has no effect on it; its maximum and minimum are about six weeks after the solstices: it varies more in summer than in winter: it is least a little before sunrise: its maxima in the sun and shade are seldom on the same day: it decreases more rapidly in the autumn than it increases in summer. A cold winter does not forebode a hot summer.

Kirwan says, that the mean heat at the sea side is $84^\circ - 53$ (sine lat.) ^{2}. From this we must deduct for elevation, 1° for each 800 feet that we ascend perpendicularly, where the declivity is about 6 feet per mile; where 7 feet, 1° for 600 feet; where 13 feet, for 500; where 15 or more, 1° for 400. For the distance from the sea, we must add 1° for each 50 miles, between 10° and 20° latitude; between 25° and 30°, 1° for 100 miles: between 30° and 35°, we must deduct 1° for 400 miles; between 35° and 70° for 150. It seldom freezes in latitudes below 35°, and seldom hails beyond 60°; between these limits it generally thaws when the sun's altitude is above 40°. The greatest cold is usually half an hour before sunrise; the greatest heat at the equator about 1 o'clock; further north it is later: in latitude 50° about half past 2. In latitudes above 48° July is warmer than August: in lower latitudes colder. At Petersburgh the greatest summer heat is usually 79°. In every habitable climate there is a heat of 60° or more, for at least 2 months.

According to Cavallo, the greatest heat of the day in July is before 2 o'clock; according to others, about half way between noon and sunset.

Particular Observations of Temperature.

Account of a frost in Somersetshire. Ph. tr. 1672. VII. 5138.

Derham on the great frost of 1708—9. Ph. tr. 1709. XXVI. 454.

Derham on a frost. Ph. tr. 1731. XXXVII. 16.

*Cossigni and Réaumur. A. P. 1733..1740.
Isle of Bourbon and Paris.

Miles. Ph. tr. 1742. XLII. 20. 1747. XLIV. 613. 1749. XLVI. 208. 1750. XLVI. 571. 1754. 507, 525. 1755. 43.

Middleton. Ph. tr. 1742. XLII. 157.

Linings. Ph. tr. 1743. XLII. 491.
In Carolina.

Arderon. Ph. tr. 1750. XLVI. 573. 1754. 507.

Stedman. Ph. tr. 1751. 4.

Demidoff. Ph. tr. 1753. 107.
In Siberia.

Trembley. Ph. tr. 1757. 148.
Hague.

Huxham. Ph. tr. 1757. 428. 1758. 523.

Smeaton. Ph. tr. 1758. 488.
Edystone and Plymouth.

Ellis. Ph. tr. 1758. 754.
In Georgia: greatest heat 105°.

Brooke. Ph. tr. 1759. 58, 70.
Maryland.

Pallas. Ph. tr. 1763. 62.
Berlin.

Howard. Ph. tr. 1764. 118.
Bedfordshire.

Martin. Ph. tr. 1764. 217.
Bengal.

Whitehurst. Ph. tr. 1767. 265.
Apr. 18, at ¼ past 9, p. m.—1° F.

Bevis and Short. Ph. tr. 1768. 54, 55.

Byres. Ph. tr. 1768. 336.
At Rome, 99°.

Watson. Ph. tr. 1771. 213.

Wilson. Ph. tr. 1771. 326.
Glasgow.

Van Swinden. Ph. tr. 1773. 89.

De Cain. S. E. 1773. 541.
On the cold in Canada from the N. W. winds.

Barker. Ph. tr. 1775. 202.
Allahabad. The heat often 109° in the shade, once 114°.

Roebuck on the heat of London and Edinburgh. Ph. tr. 1775. 459.

Roz. IV. 82.
A heat of 34¼ R. or 109° F. was fatal to more than 10000 persons at Pekin.

Brisson and Duluc. A. P. 1777. 522.
The cellar or well of the observatory varied from 9¼° to 10¼° R. or from 53° to 55½° F.

Wilson on cold at Glasgow. Ph. tr. 1780. 451.

Blagden. Ph. tr. 1781.
The mean temperature in Jamaica is about 81°.

Cullum on a hard frost 23 June 1783. Ph. tr. 1784. 416.

Cassini. A. P. 1786. 507. Roz. XXXV. 140.

Cassini on the greatest heat at Paris. M. Inst. IV. 338.
In 1701, 104° F.

Hunter. Ph. tr. 1788. 53.
Found the springs at Kingston in Jamaica, about 80°; after a gentle ascent of two miles 79°; cold spring, nearly 1400 yards above the sea, was 61¾°; the variation is 1° for 230 feet. The extremes at Kingston were 69 and 91°: the usual height in the cold season from 70° to 77°, in the hot from 85° to 90°. At Brighthelmstone the heat of a well was 50°, at Bromley, in November 49½°, and the mean between the heat in London, at sunrise and at 2 o'clock, is about 49°.2. Kirwan gives 52° for the mean heat of London. The wells at New York vary from 54° to 56°.

Heberden's table of the mean heat from 1763 to 1772. Ph. tr. 1788. 66.

P. Wilson on cold attending a hoar frost. Ed. tr. I. 146.

Pingré on some severe winters. A. P. 1789. 514.

Philotattee. *Asiatic* Mirror. Mag. 1789.
An account of the heat at Cawnpore, from 7th April to 6th May 1789. For 21 days from 14th April to 6th May, the mean heat without doors at 2, p. m. was 127°, the greatest heat, 18th April, 144°; the mean heat at night 93°: behind a tattee, or wet mat, the mean heat, at 2, was 79°, 48° lower than in the open air.

*Cotte's table of temperatures. Roz. XXXIX. 27.
Agrees in general with Kirwan. Cotte makes the mean temperature of Paris 9½° R. or 53°.4 F.

Cotte on some severe winters. Journ. Phys. XLVIII. 270.

Toaldo on the temperatures of 50 places. Roz. XXXIX. 43.

Toaldo on some sudden heats. Soc. Ital. VI. 85.

A copious table of temperatures by Heinsius. Erxleb. §. 761.
From Winkler's physik.

Rumford on the saltness of the sea. Ess. II. vi.

Manch. M. IV. 601.
The sea varies at Liverpool from 36° to 68°.

Messier on the heat of 1793. Ann. Ch. XVIII. 310.

Messier on the heat at Paris. M. Inst. IV. 501.

Manch. M. IV.
The thermometer at Kendal is about 47° at a mean. Kirwan's rules give 48½°.

Ph. M. X. 172.
The mean temperature at Columbo is 79°.5, the utmost variation 13°.

The mean of the greatest cold and heat at Paris is 54°.5.

Lalande mentions a heat of 113° in Senegal. In the summers of 1753, 1765, and 1793, it was 104° in France.

The mean temperature in London is 50°.5 from the observations of the R. S. varying in different years from 48° to 52°: the mean of the greatest cold and greatest heat is 50° or 49°.

At the equator, the line of congelation is about 15 600 feet above the sea; near the tropic, 13 430; at Teneriffe, lat. 28°, 10 000; in Auvergne, lat. 45°, 6740; lat. 51° to 54° 5800; lat. 80° n. about 1200. Bouguer says, 2434 toises in the torrid zone; in France 1500 or 1600.

Meteorological Thermometers.

See Heat.
Self registering thermometer. Leupold. Th. Aerostat. t. 23.
Van Swinden sur la comparaison des thermometres. 253.
On thermometers showing the maximum.
Lord Charles Cavendish on thermometers showing the maximum. Ph. tr. 1757. 300.
Gaussen. Roz. XVII. 61.
Six's thermometer. Ph. tr. 1782. 72.
Six on a thermometer. 8. Maidstone, 1794. R. I.
Hutchins's thermometers. Ph. tr. 1783. 303*.
Rutherford's thermometer. Ed. tr. III. 247.
Consisting of two horizontal thermometers, one of spirit, with a little cone of coloured glass within the fluid, the other of mercury, with a bit of ivory in the empty part: the one marking the greatest heat, the other the least.
Keith's self registering thermometer. Ed. tr. IV. 203. Nich. III. 264. Ph. M. II. 61. Gilb. XVII. 319.
With a float leaving a mark, or writing on a wheel.
Enc. Brit. Art. Thermometer.
Lemaistre on Six's thermometer. Gilb. II. 287.
Von Arnim's thermometrograph. Gilb. II. 289.
Crichton's self registering thermometer. Ph. M XV. 147. Gilb. XVII. 317.
A thermometer of metal showing the maximum and minimum.
A baroscope is sometimes made of a solution of 6 parts of camphor, 2 nitre, and 1 sal ammoniac, in common malt spirits; this is said to crystallize in bad weather, especially in windy weather: but it is probably more affected by cold than by wind.

Winds.

Winds in general.

Bacon de ventis. 1664. Works. III. 441.
Bohun on winds. 8. Oxf. 1671.
Acc. Ph. tr. 1672. VII. 5147.
Garden's causes of wind. Ph. tr. 1685. XV. 1148.
Morhoff Polyhistor. II. ii. c. 33.
D'Alembert sur la cause générale des vents. 4. Berl. 1747.
Acc. A. P. 1750. H. 41.
Relating to gravitation.
Musschenbroek Introductio. II. 1090.
Wargentin. Schw. Abh. 1762. 173.
Euler on the motions of fluids from heat. N. C. Petr. XI. XIII. XIV. XV.
Leipz. Samml. zur Physik. II. 575.
Coudraye Théorie des vents et des ondes. 8. Fontenay, 1786. Copenh. 1796. R. S. Par. 1802.
Ducarla on winds. Roz. XXXII. 89.
Kirwan on the variations of the atmosphere. Ir. tr.
Darwin's botanic garden. Notes.
Observations on winds. Manch. M. IV. 601.
Capper on the winds and monsoons. 4. Lond. 1801. R. S.

Regular Winds.

Garden on the cause of several winds. Ph. tr. 1685. XV. 1148.
*Halley on the trade winds, with a map. Ph. tr. 1686. XVI. 153.
*Wallis's objections to Halley. Birch. IV. 519.
*Hadley on the cause of trade winds. Ph. tr. 1735. XXXIX. 58.
On the rotatory momentum of the air.

Musschenbroek's chart of the trade winds.
  Introd. at the end.
*Semeyns Haarl. Verh. III. 183.
La Nux on the trade winds. A. P. 1760. H. 17.
Franklin. Ph. tr. 1765. 182.
  Derives the N. W. wind from the current of air descending from the upper regions: in America the N. W. wind is a land breeze.
Forrest on the monsoons. 4. Calc. 1782. B. B. 8. Lond. 1784.
  Bad theory.
Atkins. Ph. tr. 1784. 58.
  The N. W. wind prevails at Minehead.
Legentil. A. P. 1784. 480.
  The wind is inclined to W. at Paris.
On trade winds. Leipz. Mag. für Oekon. 1786. i.
*Prévost on the trade winds. Roz. XXXVIII. 365, 370.
Kirwan on the variations of the atmosphere. Extr. Ph. M. XV. 311.
  Incline to Halley's theory in preference to Hadley's.
On the monsoons at Bombay. Ph. M. XIV. 328.
Manch. M. IV. 601.
  At Liverpool the S. E. wind prevails, probably from local circumstances. In other places, S. W. or N. E. winds are most usual.

  Particulars of the trade winds, from Robertson.
  1. For 30° on each side of the equator, there is almost constantly an easterly wind in the Atlantic and Pacific oceans: it is called the trade wind: near the equator it is due east, further off it blows towards the equator, and is N. E. or S. E.
  2. Beyond 30° latitude, the wind is more uncertain.
  3. The monsoons are, perhaps erroneously, deduced from a superior current in a contrary direction.
  4. In the Atlantic, between 10° and 28° N. latitude, about 300 miles from the coast of Africa, there is a constant N. E. wind.
  5. On the American side of the Caribbee islands the N. E. wind becomes nearly E.
  6. The trade winds extend 3° or 4° further N. and S. on the W. than on the E. side of the Atlantic.
  7. Within 4° of the equator, the wind is always S. E.: it is more E. towards America, and more S. towards Africa. On the coast of Brasil, when the sun is far northwards, the S. E. becomes more S. and the N. E. more E. and the reverse when the sun is far southwards.
  8. On the coast of Guinea, for 1500 miles, from Sierra Leone to St. Thomas, the wind is always S. or S. W. probably from an inclination of the trade wind towards the land.
  9. Between lat. 4° and 10°, and between the longitudes of Cape Verd and the Cape Verd islands, there is a track of sea very liable to storms of thunder and lightning. It is called the rains. Probably there are opposite winds that meet here.
  10. In the Indian ocean, between 10° and 20° S. latitude, the wind is regularly S. E. From June to November, these winds reach to within 2° of the equator: but from December to May the wind is N. W. between lat. 3° and 10° near Madagascar, and from 2° to 12° near Sumatra.
  11. Between Sumatra and Africa, from 3° S. latitude to the coasts on the N. the monsoons blow N.E. from September to April, and S. W. from March to October: the wind is steadier, and the weather fairer in the former half year.
  12. Between Madagascar and Africa, and thence northwards to the equator, from April to October there is a S.S.W. wind, which further N. becomes W. S. W.
  13. East of Sumatra, and as far as Japan, the monsoons are N. and S. but not quite so certain as in the Arabian gulf.
  14. From New Guinea to Sumatra and Java, the monsoons are more N. W. and S. E. being on the South of the equator; they begin a month or six weeks later than in the Chinese seas.
  15. The changes of these winds are attended by calms and storms.
  16. At Liverpool the wind is said to be westerly two thirds of the year. In the south of Italy the S. E. scirocco is the most frequent.
  17. Winds passing over land become dry and dense: over the sea, warm and light.
  18. In some countries the dry winds produce dreadfully scorching effects, as the solanos in Arabia. Others, as in China, are inconvenient from their extreme moisture.

Measures of Wind.

Wren's weather clock. Birch. I. 341. Fig.
Croun's anemometer. Birch. II. 257.
Gregory on wind. Ph. tr. 1675. X. 307.
  The wind broke down an obelisc 12 feet high, 2 feet thick.

Derham on sound. Ph. tr. XXVI.

Leupold Th. aerostat. t. 18, 20, 22. Plagoscopium et plagographium. t. 39, 48, 49. Anemometers.

Bouvet's machine for measuring the force of the wind at sea. Mach. A. VI. 153.

D'ons en Bray's self registering anemometer. A. P. 1734. 123.

Wilke's anemobarometer. Schw. Abh. III. 85.

Krafft. C. Petr. XIII.

Lomonosow's anemometer. N. C. Petr. II. 128.

Smeaton. Ph. tr. 1759. 100.

Plagoscope. Emerson's mech. F. 253.

Gadolin et Hiolte de anemometro novo. Abo, 1760.

Brice on the velocity of the wind. Ph. tr. 1766. 226.

Found it 63 miles in an hour.

Bouguer Manoeuvre des vaisseaux. 151. Traité du navire. 359.

One of the best anemometers.

Nollet Art des expériences. III. 62.

Zeiher's measurement of the wind. N. C. Petr. X. 302.

Brunings on the velocity of the wind. Haarl. Verhand. XIV. 609.

Lind's portable wind gage, with a table of the wind's force. Ph. tr. 1775. 353.

An inverted siphon; the connexion is formed by a narrow tube to prevent oscillations: in frosty weather salt may be added to the water.

Stedman on the degrees of wind required for machines. Ph. tr. 1777. 493.

Heavy machines can work about 4/9 of the year.

Van Swinden sur le froid de 1776.

Lambert on observing the wind. A. Berl. 1777. 36.

Dahlberg Déscription d'un anémometre. 4. Erf. 1781. Roz. XVII. 438.

Demenge's anemometer. Roz. XV. 433.

Woltmann Theorie des hydrometrischen flügels.

Ximenes on the velocity of the wind. Goth. M. III. iii. 191.

On Knowles's machine for weighing the force of the wind. 8. R. S.

A wind fane with an index. Roz. XX. 416.

Saussure's anemometer. R. S.

Rochon Voyage à Madagascar. Par. 1791.

A wind that went 150 feet in 1″, or 102 miles in an hour.

Manch. M. IV. 602.

Hutchinson measured the velocity of the wind by running with a handkerchief, till it remained flat against a stick.

Hermans windbeobachter. Freiberg. 1793.

*Lüdicke on the ancient denominations of the winds. Hind. Arch. III. 38.

Benzenberg on wind gages. Gilb. VIII. 240. Ph. M. XIII. 194.

Garnerin went with Mr. Sowden 60 miles in ⅔ of an hour; with Mr. Locker 9 miles in ¼ of an hour.

Weatherbottle. See Meteorological thermometers.

Intensity of Wind.

Comparison of Rouse's Table, published by Smeaton, with that of Lind.

Lind's gage.	Force on a square foot in pounds av. by calculation.	Feet in 1″	Miles in 1 h.	Character.
	0.005	1.43	1	Hardly perceptible. R.
	0.020	2.93	2	Just perceptible. R.
	0.044	4.40	3	Gentle winds. R.
	0.079	5.87	4	Gentle winds. R.
	0.123	7.38	5	
0.025	0.130			A gentle wind. L.
0.050	0.260			Pleasant wind. L.
	0.492	14.67	10	Pleasant brisk gale. R.
0.10	0.521			Fresh breeze. L.
	1.107	22.00	15	Brisk gale. R.
	1.968	29.34	20	Very brisk. R.
0.5	2.604			Brisk gale. L.
	3.075	36.67	25	Very brisk. R.
	4.429	44.01	30	High wind. R.
1.0	5.208			High wind. L.
	6.027	51.34	35	
	7.873	58.68	40	Very high. R.
	9.963	66.01	45	Great storm. Derham.
2	10.416			Very high. L.
	12.300	73.35	50	Storm, or tempest. R.
3	15.625			Storm. L.
	17.715	88.02	60	Great storm. R.
4	20.833			Great storm. L.
	21.435	96.82	66	Great storm. La Condamine.
5	26.041			Very great storm. L.
	31.490	117.36	80	Hurricane. R.
6	31.250			Hurricane. L.
7	36.548			Great hurricane. L.
8	41.667			Very great hurricane. L.
9	46.875			Most violent hurricane. L.
	49.200	146.70	100	Hurricane that tears up trees and throws down buildings. R.
10	52.083			
11	57.293			
	58.450	160.00	109	Observed by Rochon.
12	62.5			

Particular Observations of Storms.

A storm at Oundle. Ph. tr. 1693. XVII. 710.

Scarburgh on a storm in Virginia. Ph. tr. 1697. XIX. 659.

Southwell on the damage done to Portland island. Ph. tr. 1697. XIX. 659.

Wallis on a storm in Northamptonshire. Ph. tr. 1698. XX. 5.

Fuller on a storm. Ph. tr. 1704. XXIV. 1530.

Salt blown 10 or 20 miles.

Derham on a storm. Ph. tr. 1704.

Leeuwenhoek on a storm. Ph. tr. 1704. XXIV. 1535.

Bridgman on a storm at Ipswich. Ph. tr. 1708. XXVI. 137.

Nelson on a storm at Colchester. Ph. tr. 1708. XXVI. 140.

Thoresby on a storm. Ph. tr. 1709. XXVI. 289. 1711. XXVII. 320. 1722. XXXII. 101.

Forth on a storm. Ph. tr. 1736. XXXIX. 288.

Degeer's explanation of a shower of insects. A. P. 1750. H. 39.

Borlase on a storm. Ph. tr. 1753. 86.

Miller on a storm in Cumberland. Ph. tr. 1757. 194.

Griffith on a storm at Oxford. Ph. tr. 1765. 273.

Particular kinds and effects of Wind.

Waterspouts. See Atmospherical Electricity.

Pliny xi. c. 103.
> Says, that waves are stilled by oil. Quoted by Cavallo.

Boyle's relations about the bottom of the sea.
> Says, that storms have little effect at 20 feet below the surface of the sea, and probably none at 30 feet.

Wright on a sand flood in Suffolk. Ph. tr. 1668. III. 722.

Templer on two hurricanes in Northamptonshire. Ph. tr. 1671. VI. 2156.

Langford on hurricanes. Ph. tr. 1698. XX. 407. Abr. II. 105.
> Thinks, that hurricanes are connected with the moon. Before a hurricane the skies appear turbulent, the sun looks red, although the hills are free from clouds or fogs. All hurricanes begin between N. and W. their course is generally opposite to that of the trade winds. Tornados come from several points.

Bocanbrey. See Waterspouts.

Derby on a whirlwind. Ph. tr. 1739. XLI. 229.

Fuller on a hurricane in Huntingdonshire. Ph. tr. 1741. XLI. 851.

Lord Lovell on a fiery whirlwind. Ph. tr. 1742. 183.
> A flash of fire, or rather more than a flash, with a smell of sulfur.

On a whirlwind. C. Bon. II. i. 453.

Henry on a stream of wind. Ph. tr. 1753. XLII.

Franklin and others on stilling waves by oil. Ph. tr. 1774. 445.
> The success was partial only, as might be expected.

Franklin. Am. tr. II.
> Says, that one side of a piece of water, 3 feet deep and 10 miles wide, has been raised 10 feet by the wind, the other being left bare.

Servières on a singular wind. Roz. XIII. Suppl. 132.

Dobson on the harmattan. Ph. tr. 1781. 46.
> An extremely dry wind in Africa, coming from the N. E. drying even potash. It generally brings a fog of some unknown nature.

On the harmattan. Goth. M. I. iv. 41.

On the Samum. Goth. M. IV. iii. 38.

Ducarla on winds cooled by evaporation. Roz. XXII. 432.

Saussure on cold winds. Nich. I. 229. Gilb. III. 201.

Dalton on bottom winds on Derwent lake. Meteor. obs. 52.
> No theory.

A violent tornado in Berwickshire. Ph. M. IV. 219.

Lamarck on a hurricane. Journ. Phys. LII. 377.

Clos on partial winds. Journ. Phys. LIV. 259.

Mitchell on a N. E. storm in America. Ph. M. XIII. 273.
> Franklin observed, that such storms generally begin to leeward; they advance 100 miles in an hour.

Currents of the Sea.

Smith's conjecture respecting an inferior current in the Straights. Ph. tr. 1684. XIV. 564.
> Says, that an inferior current was found in the Baltic so strong as to carry a boat against a superior current, by means of a bucket sunk with a cannon ball.

Ph. tr. 1700. XXII. 725.
  The entrance of ships into the Bristol channel, instead of the English, has been attributed to a current, but was supposed to be rather owing to a mistake of the variation.

Vossius on currents.

On the currents at the mouth of the Straights. Ph. tr. 1724. XXXIII. 191.
  The current runs 2 miles an hour where the breadth is 5 leagues; 1 mile, where it is 18 leagues: but at the sides there is a current outwards, especially on the south side. In 1712, Mr. L'aigle sunk a Dutch ship, laden with brandy and oil, in the middle between Tariffa and Tangier; a few days afterwards the sunk ship rose 4 leagues to the westwards: the relater was at Gibraltar at the time, and saw the brandy brought from Tangier, and conversed with the captain and other eye witnesses. The straights are unfathomable.

D. Bernoulli on the cause of currents. A. P. Prix. VII.

Belidor. Arch. hydr. II. ii. 19.

Waiz on the current at the Straights. Schw. Abh. 1775. 28.

*Peyssonnel on the currents in the West Indies and elsewhere. Ph. tr. 1756. 624.

More on the tides in the Straights. Ph. tr. 1762. 447.
  Maintains, that the currents run in contrary directions on the opposite coasts.

*Blagden on the heat of the water in the gulf stream. Ph. tr. 1781. 334.
  The stream is about 20 leagues broad, and warmer than the neighbouring water. Its heat at its commencement in the gulf of Florida is about 82°, and it loses 2° for every 3° of latitude in going northwards: it continues sensible off Nantucket.

Franklin's maritime observations. Am. tr. II. 314.
  With a chart of the gulf stream, and an account of its heat. It extends to 44° N. lat.

Pownall's hydraulic and nautical observations. 4. Lond. 1787. R. S.
  On the currents of the Atlantic.

On the agitations of Derwent water. Ph. M. XI. 163.
  Possibly from gas under the mud. But whence are the "bottom winds?"

Rennel on a current prevailing to the west of Scilly. Ph. tr. 1793. 182.
  Supposed to come out of the bay of Biscay, towards the N. W. by W. and to have been collected by the westerly winds of the Atlantic.
  Robison says, that the current at the Straights sometimes runs outwards in the middle.

Barometers.

Mercurial Barometers, and Barometers in general.

Schotti technica curiosa.

Wallis and Beale. Ph. tr. 1669. IV. 1113.

Hooke's wheel barometer. Ph. tr. 1665, 1666. I. 218.

Hooke on a barometer with spirits. Ph. tr. 1686. XVI. 241

Traité des barometres. Amst. 1686.

Derham on a wheel barometer, with a rack. Ph. tr. 1698. XX. 41.

Sturmii collegium experimentale.

Gray's microscopic barometer. Ph. tr. 1698. XX. 176.

Comparison of barometers of mercury and of water. A. P. I. 234.

Amontons on barometers. A. P. II. 23. 1704. 264, 271. H. 1. 1705. 232. H. 16. 229.

Huygens on a new barometer. A. P. X. 375. Journ. Sav. 1672. 139.

Lahire on barometers. A. P. 1706. 432.

Lahire's new barometer. A. P. 1708. 154. H. 3.

Maraldi on an irregularity of some barometers. A. P. 1706. H. 1.
  From the accidental introduction of a fluid.

Halley. Ph. tr. 1720. XXXI.
  Patrick's barometer is a tube slightly tapered without a bulb, like Bernoulli's.

Fahrenheit's new barometer. Ph. tr. 1724. XXXIII. 179.
> From the heat at which water boils. Cavallo estimates, that such a barometer will determine the density within .1 of quicksilver.

Self registering barometer. Leupold. Th. aerostaticum. t. 23.

Deslandes on a barometer which stood still for 7 months. A. P. 1726. H. 14.

Saurin on the rectification of barometers. A. P. 1727. 282.

Bülfinger on barometers. C. Petr. I. 317.

Rowning's barometer. Ph. tr. 1733. XXXVIII. 39.
> The barometer floats in a fluid, with a small prominent stem: it must therefore rise and fall very rapidly.

Middleton. Ph. tr. 1733. XXXVIII. 127.
> Commends Patrick's marine barometer.

Beighton on Orme's barometer. Ph. tr. 1738. XL. 248.
> A diagonal barometer, the mercury well boiled.

Saul on the weather glass. 8. Lond. 1730. 1748. M. B.

Ludolff's barometer scale, corrected for temperature. A. Berl. 1749. 33.

Richmann's barometers. N. C. Petr. II. 181.
> Various modes of reading off: some of them suspended siphons, nearly like Magellan's.

Nollet's observations on barometers. A. P. 1751. 275. H. 23.

Bourbon's portable barometer. A. P. 1751. H. 173.

Brisson's portable barometer. A. P. 1755. H. 140.

Recueil de pièces sur le thermomètre et sur le baromètre. 4. Basle, 1757. Act. Helv. III. 94.

Sulzer's portable barometer. Act. Helv. III. 259.

Boistissandeau's portable barometer. A. P. 1758. H. 105.

Segner Barometrum navale. Gott.

On correcting barometers for temperature. M. Taur. I.

Fitzgerald's wheel barometer. Ph. tr. 1761. 146. 1770. 74.
> With friction wheels.

Leslie on barometers. Schw. Abh. 1763. 89.

Spry on a portable barometer. Ph. tr. 1765. 83.

Deluynes on the effect of tubes of different diameters. A. P. 1768. 247. H. 10.
> On this subject see the properties of matter. Shows the great effect of boiling the mercury.

Portable barometers by Bourbon and Perica. A. P. 1771. H. 68.

Perica's barometer. Roz. XVIII. 391.

Cigna on barometer tubes. Roz. Intr. II 462.

Changeux on the barometer. Roz. IV. 85.

†Changeux's barometer. Roz. XXII. 387.
> With appendices which receive small portions of mercury, and mark the height. It is said, however, to be difficult or impossible to empty these appendices.

Deluc. Ph. tr. 1777. 401.
> Recommends siphon barometers as alone to be depended on.

Ramsden's portable barometer. Ph. tr. 1777. 658.
> Described by Roy.

Fouchy's statical barometer. A. P. 1780. 73. H. 1.

Häseler vom Ludolffischen barometer. 4. Holzmünden, 1780.

Lamanon's barometer. Roz. XIX. 3.

Magellan's barometer. Roz. XIX. 108, 194, 257, 341.

Magellan Beschreibung neuer barometer. Leipz. 1782. R. I.

E. M. A. VI. Art. Procédés. 762.

E. M. Physique. Art. Barometre.

Moscati and Landriani on the improvement of the barometer. Soc. Ital. I. 225.

Moscati Ricerche sopra il barometro. 4. R. S.

On the barometer. Roz. XXI. 436, 449.

Luz über die barometer. Leipz. 1782. R. I.

Rosenthal Meteorologishe werkzeuge.

Hurter's new barometer. Roz. XXIX. 346.
Portable.

Achard on barometrical measures. A. Berl. 1786. 3.

M'Guire's portable barometer. Ir. tr. 1787. I. 41.

M'Guire's self registering barometer. Ir. tr. IV. 141.

Adams on the barometer. London, 1790.

Adams's lect. IV. 480.
When a tube has once had mercury boiled in it, is is found, that even cold mercury will often fill it completely.

Cotte on the effect of temperature on the barometer. Roz. XLII. 441.

Austin's portable barometer. Ir. tr. IV. 99.

Barton's barometer with a wheel index. Manch. M. IV. 547.

Hamilton's portable barometer. Ir. tr. V. 95.

Beyträge zur verfertigung des barometers. Frankf. 1795.

Humboldt's portable barometer. Journ. Phys. XLVII. (IV.) 468. Ph. M. IV. 304.

Conté's portable barometer. B. Soc. Phil. n. 14.

Prony's barometrical balance. B. Soc. Phil. n. 20.

Guerin on a portable barometer. Journ. Phys. LIII. 444. Ph. M. XI. 362.

Klügel on Magellan's barometer. Hind. Arch. III. 182.

Perpetual motion by barometers. Nich. III. 126.

Keith's self registering barometer. Ed. tr. IV. 209.

Von Arnim on barometers by Prony, Conté, Humboldt, Gödeking, Brander, and Voigt. Gilb. II. 311.
Some statical, others portable.

Voigt on Haas's barometer. Gilb. IV. 456.

Müller's barometer. Gilb. V. 17.
Corrected for temperature.

R. dig's simple barometer. Gilb. VI. 445.

Wilson on increasing the sensibility of the barometer. Nich. 8. III. 21.

Schmidt on the double barometer of Huygens. Gilb. XIV. 199.
Recommends it strongly, and makes it correct itself for temperature. Without such a correction the expansion and the vapour of the spirits would produce great irregularity.

Maigné's portable barometer. Gilb. XV. 463.

A barometrical perpetual motion. Nich. IX. 212.

Rees's Cyclop. III. Plates. Pneumatics.
When the mouth of a barometer is much contracted, a friction is produced. Some preserve the surface of the reservoir level, by letting it spread on a horizontal surface; and if the surface is large enough, the method must be a good one, but the mercury ought not to be confined to a height less than one seventh of an inch.

The specific gravity of mercury, once distilled, is from 13.55 to 13.57, but Boerhaave found it after 511 distillations 14.11. The density of the mercury usually employed is 13.6.

Roy found that the expansion of 30 inches of mercury in the barometer, including the effects of its vapour, from 32° to 92°, was .1922. The results of his experiments are expressed very nearly by the formula $e = .00011182 f - .000 000 0813 f^2 - .000 000 000 07 f^3$: which gives .1920 for 92°. Some authors assert, that Roy's results are a little too great: and if any dependence can be placed on Dalton's analogies, the effect of the vapour must be extremely inconsiderable.

Statical Baroscopes, Air Barometers and Manometers.

Schotti technica curiosa. I. c. 21.

Boyle's statical baroscope. Ph. tr. 1665—6. I. 231.

Hooke on a statical barometer. Birch. III. 384, 387.

*Hooke's marine barometer. Ph. tr. 1701. XXII. 791.

Described and much commended by Halley. With a spirit thermometer and a sliding scale.

Chapelle on a barometrical fish. A. P. I. 274.

Caswell's baroscope. Ph. tr. 1704. XXIV. 1597.
A floating manometer.

Amontons's marine barometer without mercury. A. P. 1705. 49. H. 1.

Varignon's manometer. A. P. 1705. 300. H. 26.

Manometers. Leupold. Th. aerostat. t. 9.

Zeiber's marine barometer. N. C. Petr. VIII. 274.
Measuring the force by a spring.

Fouchy's dasymeter. A. P. 1780. 73. Roz. XXV. 345.
A beam resting on a curved surface, answering the purpose of Guerike's manometer, which was a thin ball supported by a bent lever balance; but perhaps no improvement.

Manometer. E. M. A. VI. 734.

Gerstner's air balance. Gren. IV. 172.

Kramp's manometer. Hind. Arch. III. 233.
Like Caswell's, an open hemisphere, to be depressed to a given mark, by weights put in a dish.

†Say's areometer, with Arnim's remarks. Gilb. II. 230.

Journ. Phys. LVI. 366.
Berger brought portions of air from different heights in well stopped bottles, and compared the quantities of mercury that was forced into them. But the method does not appear to be very accurate.

Bérard Mélanges. 163.

Davy on the manometer. Journ. R. I., I. Nich. 8. IV. 32. Gilb. XVI. 105.

On eudiometry and manometry. Gilb. XV. 61.

Variations of the Barometer in general.

*Beale on the barometer. Ph. tr. 1665—6. I. 153, 163.

Boyle on the barometer. Ph. tr. 1665—6. I. 181.

Halley. Ph. tr. 1686. XVI. 104.
The mercury is commonly low in calm weather before rain, higher in serene settled weather; lowest in high winds, even without rain; highest in E. and N. E. winds; high in calm frosty weather: it rises fast after storms of wind; it varies most in high latitudes, within the tropics very little. It has been observed by others, that N. and N. E. winds are heavier than S. and S. W., as being colder.

Lister on the barometer. Ph. tr. 1684. XIV. 790.

Leibnitz on the cause of the changes. A. P. 1711. H. 3.
Leibnitz invented a machine to illustrate the variations of the barometer by the effects of the fall of a body upon the equilibrium of a balance.

Desaguliers on the variation of the barometer. Ph. tr. 1717. XXX. 570.
In answer to Leibnitz.

Gersten de mutationibus barometri. 8. Frankf. 1733. M. B.

Acc. Ph. tr. 1733. XXXVIII. 43.

Beighton's remarks on the barometer. Ph. tr. 1738. XL. 248.

Hollmannus de differentiis altitudinum barometri. Ph. tr. 1742. XLII. 116.

Hollmannus de barometrorum cum tempestatum mutationibus consensu. Ph. tr. 1749. XLVI. 101.

On the various heights of the barometer. M. Taur. I.

C. Bon. II. i. 307, 353.

Fourcroy de Ramecourt on oscillations of the barometer. A. P. 1768. H. 36.

Beguelin. A. Berl. 1773. 47. 1774. 119.

Montaigne. Roz. II. 261.

Changeux. Roz. VII. 459.

Deluc Idées. II. 590. Modifications. I. iii. 223.

Saussure Hygrometrie. §. 294. Voyages. IV.

Lambert on the density of the air. Roz. XVIII. 126.

*Ephemerides Soc. Palat.
Toaldo on a variation of the barometer. Roz. XX. 88.
Dangos on the periodical variation of the barometer. Roz. XXX. 265.
Kirwan. Ir. tr. 1788. II. 43. Roz. XXXIX. 100.
Legentil. Voyage. I. 526.
  The barometer does not vary at Pondicherry.
Fontana delle altezze barometriche saggio analitico. 4. R. S.
Fontana on the mass of the atmosphere. Ac. Sienn. V. 76.
Cotte on the variations of the barometer in different places. Roz. XLI. 54. XLII. 340.
  At Bourdeaux and at Montmorency, 12 changes out of 19 were the same way, 7 the contrary way.
Cotte on the barometer. Ph. M. I. 208.
Franceschini on the height of the barometer. Soc. Ital. V. 294.
As. Res. IV. 195. Ed tr. IV. H. 25.
  Balfour found the barometer in April, at Calcutta, rise a little from 6 in the morning to 10, then fall till 6, rise till 10, and fall till 6 again. The difference is sometimes .1, but generally less than .05, depending probably on some reciprocation of winds.
Duc la Chapelle on the diurnal variations of the barometer. B. Soc. Phil. n. 21. Gilb. II. 361.
Pugh sur la pésanteur de l'atmosphère. 4. Rouen, 1800. R. S.
Buch on the variations of the barometer. Journ. Phys. XLIX. 85. Gilb. V. 10.
Humboldt on the barometer in South America. Ph. M. IX. 285.
  From 9 in the morning it falls till 4, then rises till 11, falls till ½ past 4, and rises till 9 again, in all weathers.
Zach Mon. corr. III. 66, 543.
  Burckhardt finds the mean height of the barometer greater by .23 when the wind is E. than when S.
Account of the diurnal variations of the barometer, from Peyrouse's Voyages. Ed. tr. V. 3.
Dalton. Manch. M. V. 666.
  Thinks that the same barometrical variations generally extend over all Europe without a day's difference. But Cotte's observations seem to be inconsistent with this opinion.

  In these climates, the barometer is generally lowest at noon and at midnight. The mean height is greatest at the equinoxes, but greater in summer than in winter. Cavallo.

  The usual scale of the barometer is, 31, very dry or hard frost; 30.5, settled fair or frost; 30, fair or frost; 29.5, changeable; 29, rain or snow; 28.5, much rain or snow; 28, stormy. Any rapid change is said to foretel bad weather.

  The diurnal variation of the barometer has been found to be more sensible at sea than on shore, especially in inland places. It is possible that currents of air from heat may be concerned in its production.

Particular Barometrical Observations.

Plot on the weather at Oxford, with a barometrical diagram. Ph. tr. 1685. XV. 930.
Beeston on the barometer in Jamaica. Ph. tr. 1696. XIX. 225.
  Variation only .3.
Cunningham on the barometer in China. Ph. tr. 1699. XXI. 323.
  Variation .6 or .7. Latitude 24° 20′.
Toaldo novae tabulae barometri aestusque maris. 4. R. S.
Roxburgh. Ph. tr. 1778. 180.
  At Fort St. George. Variation .3.
Fleuriau on the mean height of the barometer at the sea side. Journ. Phys. XLVII. (IV.) 158.
Variation at Columbo. 36. Ph. M. X. 172.
  28 i 2¼.1 Fr. or .7644.^{m}
Manch. M. V.
  The surface of the mercury moves annually about 30 inches at Kendal; in London much less.

Mean Height of the Barometer, from Erxleben and others.

Height once observed at Middlewich. Manch. M. V.	31.00
Greatest observed height. Shuckb.	30.957
Upsal	30.15
S. Carolina	30.09
Mean level of the sea. Fleuriau	30.095
Atlantic. Burckhardt	30.09
Mediterranean. Burckhardt	30.04
Mean in England and in Italy. Shuckb.	30.04
Mean level of the sea, as usually estimated	30.00
Fort St. George	30.00
Columbo. Ph. M. X.	29.98
Dover	29.90
London. R. S.	29.89

61 feet above the level of low water. The mean of any year scarcely differing 0.5.

Leyden	29.84
Kendal	29.80
Padua	29.80
Panama	29.80
Porto bello	29.80
Liverpool	29.74
Turin	29.62
Petersburg	29.57
Gottingen	29.37
Paris	29.31
Bâle	28.82
Nuremberg	28.69
Zurich	28.29
Clausthal	27.89
Chur	27.71
M. St. Gothard	23.05
Quito	21.87

Atmospherical Evaporation, or Hygrology.

Simple Evaporation. See Effects of Heat.

Halley on the evaporation of the sea. Ph. tr. 1686. XVI. 368.

Halley on the evaporation in 1693. Ph. tr. 1694. XVIII. 183.

In a place not exposed, 8 inches. Calculates, that the evaporation of the Mediterranean in a summer's day, is 5280 million tuns, and that the 9 principal rivers furnish only 1827 millions. But the experiment on evaporation was made on a surface too small for the comparison.

Lahire. A. P. IX. 315.

Hawksbee on the absorption of air by water. Ph. tr. 1707. XXV. 2412.

Leibnitz and others on vapours. M. Berol. 1710. I. 123. Op. II. ii. 82.

Desaguliers on the rise of vapours. Ph. tr. 1729. XXXVI. 6.

Makes the specific gravity of steam $\frac{1}{14000}$ from observations by Beighton and himself: or $\frac{1}{13135}$ from Nieuwentwyt's experiments on the eolipile: hence infers, that vapour in summer heat should be about $\frac{1}{2015}$ as dense as water, and should therefore float in air. But from his own experiments, the specific gravity should be above five times as great. Repertory of Arts.

Desaguliers. Ph. tr. 1742. XLII. 140.

Thinks, that vapour may be raised by an electric attraction in the air.

Hales. Veg. Stat.

Makes the annual evaporation from the earth in England 6¼ inches.

Nollet on the vapour found in the air pump. A. P. 1740. 243.

Wallerius and Ericson's experiments. Schw. Abh. 1740. 27. 1746. 3, 153. 1747. 235, 272.

Kratzenstein von dünsten und dämpfen. 8. Halle, 1744.

Krafft de vaporum generatione. 4. Tubing. 1745.

Richmann. C. Petr. XIV. 273. N. C. Petr. I. 198. II. 121.

Thinks the evaporation nearly proportionate to the temperature.

Leroy on the suspension of water. A. P. 1751. 481.

Eeles. Ph. tr. 1755. 124.

Against the existence of vesicular vapour; in favour of electrical atmospheres.

Franklin's observations, read 1756. Ph. tr. 1765. 182.

Thinks that either water or dust may be supported in the air by adhesion; that evaporation is a solution in air.

Darwin's remarks on Eeles's opinions. Ph. tr. 1757. 240.
Supposes that the particles of vapour are real steam, but incapable of communicating their heat, perhaps on account of some motion.

Hamilton on evaporation. Ph. tr. 1765. 146.
Objects both to vesicles and to fixed fire, and maintains the doctrine of solution in air.

Lambert on hygrometry, with experiments on evaporation. A. Berl. 1769. 68. 1772. 103. Roz. XVIII. 126.
Makes the quantity of vapour as the square of the density.

Lord Kames on evaporation. Ed. ess. III. 80.

Cigna on evaporation. Roz. Intr. II. 232.

Dobson on evaporation. Ph. tr. 1777. 244.
The mean annual evaporation, in an exposed situation at Liverpool, was 36.78 inches; the rain 37.43.

Fontana on evaporation in quiescent air. Roz. XIII. 22.

†Servières on the refraction of moist air. Roz. XIII. Suppl. 180.

On a phenomenon respecting ice. Roz. XIII. Suppl. 252.

Dobson on the harmattan. Ph. tr. 1781. 46.
The usual annual evaporation at Whydah is 64 inches; when the harmattan blows, it is at the rate of 133.

Achard on the cause of vapours. Rozier. XV. 463.

*Saussure Essai sur l'hygrometrie.
Saussure. Roz. XXXVI. 193.

Eason on the ascent of vapours. Manch. Mem. I. 395.
Attributes their suspension to electricity.

Williams on evaporation. Am. tr. II. 118.
Monge. A. P. 1787.
Denies the existence of vesicular vapour.

Werner on evaporation. Goth. M. VI. i. 111.
Against Deluc.

Hube über die ausdünstung. 8. Leipz. 1790.
Against Halley.

Deluc on vapours and rain. Roz. XXXVI. 276.

*Deluc on evaporation. Ph. tr. 1792. 400.
Maintains, that vapour exists in air precisely as in a vacuum, the distance at which its particles can remain without uniting with each other being determined only by the temperature, and not being affected by the interposition of air. Deluc finds that the hygrometer stands at the same height in a moist vacuum as in moist air.

Wistar on evaporation in cold air. Am. tr. III. 125. IV. 72. Repert. XIV. 375.
Volta in Gren. III. 479.
Found by many experiments, that the presence of air is indifferent to the quantity of vapour. Aug. 1795. Gilb. XII. 394.

Kirwan on the variations of the atmosphere. Ir. tr. VIII.
Extr. Ph. M. XIV. 143. Nich. 8. V. 287.
Contains much valuable matter, but the theory is complicated and improbable.

Heller on the effect of light in evaporation. Gilb. IV. 210.
Thinks it very considerable.

Effect of light in the sublimation of phosphorus. Ph. M. XI. 89.

Von Arnim on the principles of hygrology and hygrometry. Gilb. IV. 308.

Dalton on rain and evaporation. Manch. M. V. 346. Gilb. XV. 121.
Compared the rain with the quantity of water that ran out of a vessel of earth three feet deep, sunk into the ground. At Manchester, where the rain was 33.5 inches, the evaporation was 25 inches of rain, besides 5 allowed for dew. But the rain was here prevented from running off the surface of the earth, and there were probably some other causes that increased the evaporation. From the mean of many accounts of rain, which appears to be about 31 inches for all England and Wales; adding 5 inches for dew, and deducting 13 for the water carried off by rivers, we have 23 inches for the mean evaporation from the surface of England and Wales.

Dalton on the constitution of mixed gases, and on evaporation. Manch. M. V. 535. Gilb. XII. 385. Nich. VI. 257. VII. 5.
Maintains, that there is no mutual repulsion between the particles of different gases.

Dalton's elucidations of his theory of mixed gases. Nich. 8. III. 267. Ph. M. XIV. 169. Gilb. XIII. 438. Nich. VIII. 145.

Dalton's answer to Gough. Nich. IX. 89, 269.

Biot on Dalton's theory. B. Soc. Phil. n. 72.

Quotes Laplace as having compared Dalton's theory with Saussure's experiments; but Dalton had done the same. The comparison is however still imperfect.

Parrot's theory. Gilb. X. ii. XIII. 244.

Professor Parrot considers the moisture contained in air as existing in two distinct states, of chemical and of physical vapour: he thinks the chemical vapour is sustained merely by the oxygen gas contained in the air, and that it is precipitated in consequence of the diminution of the oxygen; and the physical vapour he supposes to be merely interposed between the interstices of the elastic particles of air, and retained in its situation by heat: that the chemical solution of water or ice resembles oxidation, but that no physical evaporation can take place under the freezing point. Mr. Parrot builds his theory principally on eudiometrical experiments with phosphorus, which are attended with a copious precipitation, while the absorption of oxygen seems also to be much accelerated by the presence of water; but these experiments do not appear to be, by any means, decisive in favour of Mr. Parrot's theory. The same paper contains a proposal for inoculating the clouds with thunder and lightning, by projecting a bomb to a sufficient height.

Parrot's remarks on Dalton. Gilb. XVII. 82.

Wrede's remarks on Parrot. Gilb. X. 488. XII. 319.

Böckmann's remarks on Parrot. Gilb. XI. 66.

Mitchill on vapour from cold. Gilb. XI. 474.

Sea water smokes when 25° warmer than the air: rain water when 19°.

Desormes on the water contained in gases. Gilb. XIII. 141.

Finds the quantity independent of the nature of the gas, agreeing with Deluc, Volta, and Dalton.

Henry. Ph. tr. 1803. 29. 274.

Finds, that equal volumes of the same gas, under different pressures, are absorbed by water. See Springs.

Henry on Dalton's theory of gases. Nich. VIII. 297. IX. 126.

Remarks on Dalton. *Berthollet's* chemical statics. I. 346.

Haüy Traité de physique.

Adopts Dalton's calculations, but reduces his theory to the ideas which were originally Deluc's.

Accum's apparatus for drying. Nich. VI. 212.

Gough on the solution of water in the atmosphere. Nich. VIII. 243.

Gough on Dalton's theory. Nich. IX. 52, 107, 160.

The few experiments, adduced as objections to Dalton's theory, agree, in fact, very accurately with it.

Remarks on the Quantity of Moisture contained in Air.

If we examined the progression of M. Saussure's results alone, we might conclude, that the presence of air increases the capacity of any space for vapour, nearly in the subduplicate ratio of the density, and that air of the usual density enables it to contain five times as much vapour as could remain in it when free from air. But it agrees almost as well with these experiments, and much better with those of Schmidt, to suppose that the presence of air increases the capacity of a space for moisture in the simple ratio of its density, enabling it to contain, under the common pressure, about twice as much as it could contain in its total absence. These experiments ought to be repeated, but until they are confirmed, they scarcely authorise us to reject the opinion of Deluc.

Comparison of the expansion of dry Air, and Air saturated with moisture, from Schmidt. The Barometer being at 29.84.

Temperature.	Dry Air.	Moist Air.	Elasticity of vapour.	Elasticity of steam at the same temperature.
32°	1.0000			
34¼	1.0045	1.0106	.18	.19
50	1.0357	1.0485	.37	.36
59	1.0536	1.0785	.69	.51
68	1.0715	1.1132	1.12	.68
77	1.0893	1.1528	1.65	.95
86	1.1072	1.1986	2.28	1.26
95	1.1251	1.3771	5.46	1.66
104	1.1430	1.8950	11.90	2.20
106¼	1.1474	1.9884	12.66	2.35
212	1.3574			

It is however very improbable that the expansion of moist air in high temperatures was so great as Schmidt makes it, and in the lower temperatures his experiments agree with Deluc and Dalton. Dalton says, that he found, by numerous experiments, that the expansion of moist air was exactly proportional to the effect of the elasticity of the vapour. Still, however, the best experiments on the specific gravity of steam make it not more than $\frac{1}{1600}$ as dense as water, and the specific gravity of vapour at 212°, appears from the experiments of Saussure, Schmidt, and Dalton to be about $\frac{1}{1600}$, or about $\frac{1}{100}$ at 50°, so that it is difficult to reconcile these results with the opinion of the perfect independence of vapour; unless we suppose steam to be much more expanded by heat than air. Pictet found the specific gravity of pure steam, at the common temperature of the atmosphere, about $\frac{1}{1600}$.

On Evaporation.

Dalton asserts, that the quantity of any liquid, that evaporates in a given time in the open air, is directly as the force of vapour at the same temperature, deducting only the pressure of the vapour of the same kind which is already in the atmosphere; that the atmosphere does not contribute to preserve liquidity, that it only retards evaporation a little, but does not diminish its quantity; that the evaporation of alcohol and ether requires no deduction for pressure. He found the evaporation of a disc, 3¼ inches in diameter, from 30 to 45 grains in a minute, at 212°; in a high wind it would probably have been 60 grains; at 180°, from 18 to 22; at 152°, from 8 to 12 grains, being always proportional to the elasticity of steam at the given temperature.

Hence he calculates a table for a disc of 6 inches, making 120, 154, and 189 grains the least, mean, and greatest evaporation in a minute, at 212°; taking 35, 45, and 55 as the evaporation, under similar circumstances, from his disc of 3¼ inches. But it is much simpler and more convenient to estimate the depth of the water evaporated in a day, and it happens that the column of mercury, equivalent to the elasticity of the vapour, expresses accurately enough the mean evaporation in 24 hours: for $45 \times 60 \times 24 = 64800$ grains, or 256.6 cubic inches, which would make a cylinder 30.9 inches in height, on a base 3¼ inches in diameter; and this differs only $\frac{1}{11}$ from the height of the column of mercury: we may therefore assume, that the mean daily evaporation is equal to the tabular number expressing the elasticity of the vapour; sometimes exceeding it or falling short of it about one fourth; and we may readily allow for the effect of the moisture of the atmosphere, by deducting the number corresponding to the temperature of deposition.

Mr. Dalton says, that the annual evaporation at Manchester, from a vessel kept full, was 44.4, from the ground 23.5: that the point of deposition for any time may be calculated from the evaporation, when the temperature is given. In July 1800 and 1801, the mean point of deposition was 53°, the highest 62°; in August 1800, the mean about 55°: 1801, 54.5°; in September 1801, the mean was 54°; in December, the highest 44°, the lowest 18°.

We may also infer, that at Liverpool, where Dr. Dobson found the annual evaporation from water 36.78 inches, that is, a tenth of an inch daily; the mean temperature being, according to Dr. Dobson, 54°, but more probably somewhat lower; the mean temperature at which the air began to deposit its moisture was about 7° lower than that of the air; or considering the exposed situation of the vessel, perhaps not more than 6°, so that the mean temperature of deposition was 47 or 48°. Mr. Dalton says, that the point of saturation is generally from 1 to 10° below the mean heat of the 24 hours.

Mr. Dalton found that ice lost, at 32°, 33 grains in a minute, corresponding to vapour deposited at 21.5: it was actually at 22°. Gilbert says, that Schmidt's experiments agree perfectly with Dalton's theory. Gilb. XV. 25. Lambert's experiments, reduced to English measure, give 5.95, 5.59, 3.51, 1.53, and .77, at 169°, 167°, 142°, 111°, and 84°; instead of 11.83, 11.25, 6.19, 2.68, and 1.14; which are nearly in the same proportion, although almost twice as great.

Hygrometers.

A hygrometer of transverse deal, turning a wheel. Ph. tr. 1676. XI. 647.

Conier's hygroscopes. Ph. tr. 1676. XI. 715.
Both of deal.

Gould on oil of vitriol used as a hygroscope. Ph. tr. 1684. XIV. 496.
Also on a hygroscope of lute string.

Molyneux on a hygroscope. Ph. tr. 1685. XV. 1032.
Of whipcord.

Amontons's hygrometer. A. P. II. 13.

Lahire on the abbreviation of moist ropes. A. P. IX. 157.

Leupold, Th. Aerostat. t. 13..17.

Arderon's hygroscope. Ph. tr. 1746. XLIV. 95.
A sponge counterpoised.

Arderon on the weathercord. Ph. tr. 1746. XLIV. 169.
A whipcord a little inflected, drawing transversely as it straightens itself.

Arderon's hygrometer. Ph. tr. 1646. XLIV. 184.
Of cross grained deal, acting on levers.

Ferguson's hygrometer. Ph. tr. 1764. 259.
A transverse slip of white deal, with cords and pullies: it requires to be changed every four years.

Lambert's essay on hygrometry. A. Berl. 1769. 68. 1772. 65.
With diagrams.

Smeaton's hygrometer. Ph. tr. 1771. 198.
A cord impregnated with salt.

Deluc's hygrometer. Ph. tr. 1773. 404.
A tube of ivory filled with mercury.

Deluc Idées sur la météorologie. I.

Deluc on the hygrometer. Roz. XXX. 437. XXXII. 132.

*Deluc on hygrometry. Ph. tr. 1791. 1, 389.
A transverse slip of whalebone, held by pincers, attached at one end to a thin flattened wire of silver gilt, of which the other end is fixed to a weak spring.

Lowitz's hygrometer. Gott. Mag. III. 491.

Senébier on his hygrometer. Roz. XI. 421.

Inochodzow's hygrometer. A. Petr. II. ii. 193.
A schistus which is weighed.

Copineau on the hygrometer. Roz. XV. 384.

*Saussure Essai sur l'hygrometrie. 8. Neuch. 1783. R. I.

Saussure's defence of the hair hygrometer. Roz. XXXII. 24. 98.
Says, that Deluc's hygrometer is irregular: objects to Chiminello's quill with mercury, and to Jean Baptiste's ribband.

Schreber on the oculus mundi. Naturforsch. xix. Halle, 1783.

Gedda sur les hygromètres. Copenh. 1784.

Cazalet on Casbois's hygrometer of the silk worm's intestine. Roz. XXIX. 344.
Seems to have little advantage.

Achard. A. Berl. 1786. 3.
Denies that hygrometers indicate the true quantity of vapour not precipitated.

Franklin on a hygrometer of mahogany. Am. tr. II. 51.

Krünitz Encyclopädie. XXVII.

Sir B. Thompson on the moisture absorbed by various substances. Ph. tr. 1787. 240. Repert. IV. 247.
The weight of wool was increased from 1 to 1.084 in 48 hours, in 72 to 1.163, the thermometer being at 45°, and the air saturated with moisture: of other substances examined, the most absorbent was fur, then eider down, silk, linen, and cotton: the cotton was increased to 1.943 and 1.080. Hence woollen clothes next the skin are recommended. Silver wire acquires no additional weight.

Ricke's hygrometer. Gren. I. i. 150.

Pilgrams wetterkunde.

Sage on Ricke's hygrometer. Roz. XXXIV. 58.

Geoffroy on the hair hygrometer. Roz. XXXIV. 253.

Attributes to it some irregularities.

Volta on the use of the electrometer in hygrometry. Soc. Ital. V. 551.

Ascertaining the velocity of the dissipation of electricity.

Leslie's hygrometer. Nich. III. 401. Gilb. V. 236. X. 110.

Leslie on moisture absorbed by earths and stones. Gilb. XII. 114.

Says, that rarefaction lessens the action considerably. Heated flannel dries the air very effectually.

Hochheimer's hygrometer. Ph. M. I. 367.

Weighing a plate of glass, to which the moisture is supposed to adhere.

Lüdicke on hygrometers. Gilb. I. 282. II. 70. V. 70. X. 110.

Mr. Lüdicke considers the result of his experiments as very favourable to Mr. Leslie's hygrometer. He proposes to improve it, by employing two mercurial thermometers with very fine tubes, fixed to the same support, and having their bulbs very near together: one of the tubes is to be curved; and the bulb, being first blown larger than is necessary, is to have a portion depressed, so as to form a dish for the reception of water, which it will supply for many hours, without the interruption occasioned by renewing it: the cold produced by the evaporation is then considered as the measure of the dryness of the air. It would however be easy to supply the quantity of water necessary, without giving the bulb a form so peculiar. The hair hygrometer appeared, in the comparison, to indicate the maximum of moisture too early.

Voigt's hygrometer, of a quill cut spirally. Gilb. III. 126.

Quill hygrometer. Gilb. IV. 477.

Zylius on the hygrometer, and in answer to remarks. Gilb. V. 257. VIII. 342.

Remarks in answer to Zylius. Gilb. VI. 236.

Forster's hygrometer. Ph. M. XI. 167.

From the beard of the avena sterilis.

Dalton. Manch. M. V.

Parrot on hygrometry. Gilb. XIII. 244.

Böckmann's comparison of the hygrometers of Leslie, Saussure, and Deluc. Gilb. XV. 355.

The wind affects Leslie's hygrometer very materially: the others do not agree well with each other. Deluc's seems to be a little less depressed by an elevation of temperature than Saussure's.

On the Indications of Hygrometers.

Deluc observes, that when the grass is covered with dew, the air above it is often far from the state of extreme moisture, the hygrometer standing at $50°$ or $55°$; that extreme moisture, as indicated by the hygrometer, seldom, but sometimes, exists in the open transparent air; that at great heights the air is very dry, excepting the clouds. The mean moisture in London, as indicated by Deluc's hygrometer, is $79°$, or $\frac{73}{100}$ of the extreme moisture. The whole expansion of the whalebone is about $\frac{1}{4}$.

Deluc says, that substances immersed in alcohol and ether were expanded almost as much as when immersed in water. Ph. tr. 1791. Saussure found that no vapours except that of water affected his hygrometer. Hygrometrie.

Deluc produces extreme dryness in a vessel accurately closed, with hot lime in it; extreme moisture by a wire cage covered with cloth, having a reservoir at the top to keep it moist, which is enclosed in a jar over water: here the whalebone hygrometer rises slowly but certainly to $100°$, the hair falls to $98°$.

Slips of substances cut across the grain, preserve a march more consistent with the increase of weight than threads. Glass becomes wet when Deluc's hygrometer stands at $80°$, metals and other substances, at $100°$. Coventry's hygrometer, of paper weighed, is a very delicate test.

According to Mr. Deluc, air in a vessel with water does not attain the maximum of moisture, except in very low temperatures; the whalebone hygrometer usually standing at $80°$, Saussure's at $100°$. There is generally an atmosphere of extreme moisture an inch or two above the surface of the water in a close vessel, the glass becoming clouded by the slightest change of temperature.

Deluc found the expansion of a hair corresponding to the degrees of his hygrometer thus:

15.6	at	$5°$	88.8	at	$55°$
29.4	—	10	91.6	—	60
40.9	—	15	93.8	—	65
50.5	—	20	95.6	—	70
59.2	—	25	97.2	—	75
68.8	—	30	98.0	—	80
73.0	—	35	100.0	—	85
78.3	—	40	100.6	—	90
82.1	—	45	99.2	—	95
86.1	—	50	98.3	—	100

Böckmann found $10°$ of Deluc correspond to about $32°$

of Saussure, 20° to 54°; 30° to 65°; 40° to 80°; 45° to 86°; in atmospherical observations: the greatest heights were Deluc's 56°, when Saussure's was 85°; and Saussure's 90°, when Deluc's was 48°.

Height of Deluc's hygrometer in London, from the Journal of the R. S.

	Lowest.	Highest.	Mean.
1792	40°	85°	
1793	43	85	
1794	45	89	66.8°
1795	47	92	71.8
1796	58	90	74.6
1797	60	91	79.2
1798	30	95	
1799	45	92	
1800	41	95	69.2 (not "79.2")
1801	50	95	72.5
1802	55	94	76.3
1803	58	99	79.8

It is observable, that in this table the mean height of the hygrometer was gradually increased 10° or more in three years, from 1794 to 1797, and that the same happened from 1800 to 1803, the instrument having been repaired, and a new slip probably inserted. It would therefore be adviseable that every hygrometer should be annually submitted to the tests of extreme dryness and extreme moisture, otherwise an allowance must be made for the expansion probably produced by exposure to the air, which appears to amount, in the beginning at least, to three or four degrees annually.

If we apply this correction, the mean heights will become 66.8, 67.8, 66.6, 67.2, and 69.2, 68.5, 68.3, 67.8, for the eight years that are compared, and the mean of these is 67.8. We may therefore call the mean height of the hygrometer in London 68°, or at most 70°, and not 79°. According to Deluc's comparison, this corresponds to 95.6° of Saussure's hair hygrometer; but it does not seem probable that Saussure's hygrometer would make the mean moisture of London so near the extreme, much less that it would stand above 97°, which would be inferred from 79° of Deluc.

Mr. Deluc seems to consider the weight acquired by any hygrometrical substance as the most natural test of the degree of moisture; but it does not appear that this is a very correct criterion: the proportions may vary greatly in different substances, and they certainly do vary greatly with the time of exposure. The true natural scale appears to be that which expresses the proportion of moisture in any space to that which would so far saturate it as to begin to be deposited: and Saussure's experiments show, that his hygrometer indicates this proportion in a similar manner at two different temperatures, yet not correctly with respect to either, except in particular parts of the scale. Deluc's hygrometer indicates the proportion pretty accurately through half the scale, but the mean between the height of his hygrometer and that of Saussure, agrees tolerably well throughout. It is obvious, that the height of the natural hygrometer may be found directly on Mr. Dalton's principles, by ascertaining the point of deposition, since it is expressed by the elasticity of vapour at the point of deposition divided by the elasticity at the actual temperature, or by the seventh power of the quotient of the temperatures reckoned from a point 133° below the zero of Fahrenheit; and, from the height of the natural hygrometer, we may deduce the depression necessary to produce a precipitation, by multiplying its seventh root by the temperature expressed in the same way. For Saussure's experiments on the moisture in air, the degrees of the natural scale appear to be obtained pretty correctly, by taking $2l - ll$, l being the degree of Deluc divided by 100; but this seems to make the mean moisture of London too great, since it would become .91 of the natural scale, which implies a depression of 2.4° only to produce a deposition of moisture.

Saussure found, that a cubic foot Fr. of air at 15.16° R. absorbed 11.069 gr. Fr. of moisture, expanding $\frac{1}{12}$; at 6.18°, 5.655 grains; the hair hygrometer standing at 98°; at other heights of the hygrometer, the quantities of moisture were in the proportions expressed in the table here deduced from these experiments, which consequently show the degrees of the natural hygrometer: the degrees of Deluc's hygrometer are inferred from his experiments, and to these degrees the approximation $2l - ll$ is also applied.

Saussure.	Deluc.	Mean.	Form.	Exper. at 6.18°. R.	Exper. at 15.16°. R.	Mean.
10	3.3	6.7	.065	.045	.042	.043
20	6.7	13.3	.130	.112	.099	.106
30	10.3	20.1	.195	.191	.163	.177
40	14.4	27.3	.267	.271	.233	.252
50	19.9	34.9	.358	.370	.316	.343
60	25.1	42.5	.440	.480	.423	.451
70	31.4	55.7	.530	.597	.578	.588
80	42.3	61.1	.667	.720	.726	.723
90	57.1	73.5	.812	.871	.882	.877
98	80	89.	.960	1.000	1.000	1.000

These experiments agree well enough with the formula, as far as their evidence goes, to make us adopt the expression $2l - ll = n$, and $l = 1 - \sqrt{(1-n)}$. Upon this ground the depression required for producing deposition may be calculated as in the table.

Nat. hygr. n	Form. for Deluc.	$n^{\frac{1}{2}}$	$1-n^{\frac{1}{2}}$	Depression required for deposition at 42°	52°	62°	72°	Form. 2 for Deluc.
.1	5	.7197	.2803	49	52	55	57	7
.2	10	.7946	.2054	36	38	40	42	14
.3	16	.8420	.1580	28	29	31	32	22
.4	22	.8773	.1227	21	23	24	25	30
.5	29	.9057	.0943	16	17	18	19	38
.6	37	.9296	.0704	12	13	14	14	46
.7	45	.9503	.0497	9	9	10	10	56
.8	55	.9686	.0314	5.5	5.8	6.1	6.4	70
.9	68	.9851	.0149	2.6	2.7	2.9	3.0	83
1.0	100	1.0000	.0000	0.0	0.0	0.0	0.0	100

Now, since the mean height of Deluc's hygrometer is above 70 in London, and the point of deposition cannot, in general, be supposed to be less than 5 or 6 degrees below the mean temperature, it appears that the formula for reducing Deluc's to the natural scale requires some alteration; we may therefore make it $1.5 l - 5 ll = n$, and $l = 1.5 - \sqrt{(2.25 - n)}$ whence we obtain the numbers in the last column, where 70° corresponds to a depression of about 6°, required to procure a deposition.

To raise the natural hygrometer 1°, or .01, the temperature must be depressed as many degrees as the quotient of the temperature reckoned from —133° divided by 700 n: thus, at 62°, if $n = .50$, $\frac{195}{350} = .56°$, if $n = .99$, .28°, which is nearly the difference of the depression corresponding to the different degrees of the hygrometer. For Deluc's scale the inequality is greater; a depression of .44° being required to raise the hygrometer from 50° to 51°, and of only .14° to raise it from 99° to 100°. Saussure's experiments on this subject, must, as Dalton observes, have been affected by considerable inaccuracy.

On the specific gravity of Air.

We may now attempt the solution of a problem, which is of some practical importance; that is, to determine the specific gravity of common air for any given state of the barometer, thermometer, and hygrometer. Let the height of the barometer, the temperature of the mercury being reduced, if necessary, to 32°, be b, that of Fahrenheit's thermometer, reckoned from 32°, f, the height of the point of deposition of moisture above 32° g, the specific gravity of vapour being to that of air as 1 to v, and the specific gravity of dry air to that of water, at 32°, when the barometer stands at 30, as 1 to a. Now the space occupied by the vapour will be $\frac{e}{30}$, e being $.18 + .007 g + .00019 g^2$, and the quantity of matter contained in it $\frac{e}{30 a v}$, at 32°: the remaining space being $1 - \frac{e}{30}$ will contain $\frac{b}{30 a}\left(1 - \frac{e}{30}\right)$ and the sum of these will be $\frac{b}{30 a} \cdot \left(1 - \frac{e}{30}\right) + \frac{e}{30 a v}$ which must be reduced in the ratio of 1 to $1 + .0021 f$, and will become $\frac{1}{1 + .0021 f}\left(\frac{b}{30 a} \cdot \left(1 - \frac{e}{30}\right) + \frac{e}{30 a v}\right)$. And if we employ Deluc's hygrometer, on the most probable supposition of the nature of its scale, its height in degrees divided by 100 being l, we have $e = (1.5 l - 5 ll)$. $(.18 + .007 f + .00019 f^2)$. By comparing this formula with Sir G. Shuckburgh's experiments, from which the specific gravity appears to have been $\frac{1}{815}$ when b was 30, $f = 21$, and l probably about 80°, taking $v = 1.4$ from Saussure's experiment, in which 7.5 E. grains occupied $\frac{1}{12}$ of a cubic foot, or perhaps a little more, at 66°, we have $a = 779$; and the formula becomes $\left(\frac{1}{30} b - \frac{1}{900} be + \frac{1}{42} e\right) : (779 + 1.64 f.)$ Instead of which, we may employ, in common cases, $1 : 781 + 1.64 f + .05 g + .0014 g^2$, which gives, in the circumstances of the experiment, where g is about 18, $\frac{1}{816.8}$. At 55°, with vapour deposited at 50°, the specific gravity becomes $\frac{1}{820}$, which may be assumed as the mean at the sea side for England and France: at 80°, with vapour deposited at 62°, the barometer being at 28; $\frac{1}{923}$: at 2°, when the air is dry, and the barometer at 31, $\frac{1}{703}$; so that the greatest possible variation at any one place, is nearly in the ratio of 3 to 4: and the height of the atmosphere, supposed homogeneous, is $820 \times 2.5 \times 13.6 = 27880$ feet. The weight of a cubic inch of air will be .308 grains. This estimation of the air's varying density is applicable both to barometrical measurements, and to atmospherical refraction.

Barometrical Measurements.

Hooke on the constitution of the atmosphere. 1662—3. Birch. I. 141, 181.

Hooke on the weight of air. Birch. I. 379.
Makes it $\frac{1}{713}$ as heavy as water.

Pascal de l'équilibre des liqueurs. 12. Par. 1663.

Sinclair Ars gravitatis et levitatis.

Halley on the height of the barometer at different elevations. Ph. tr. 1686. XVI. 104.
Makes the mean density of air $\frac{1}{100}$, of mercury 13.5: the height 30 at the sea; 29, 915 feet above it.

Halley's barometrical observations on Snowdon. Ph. tr. 1697. XIX. 565.
A fall of 3.8 for 3720 feet.

Halley on barometrical measurements. Ph. tr. 1720. XXXI. 116.
Proposes to employ Patrick's barometer.

Derham on the height of the barometer on the monument. Ph. tr. 1698. XX. 1.
Finds a difference of .2 in 154 feet.

Cassini on the condensation of the air. A. P. 1705. 61, 272. H. 10.

Lahire on the density of the air, and on the height of the atmosphere. A. P. 1705. 110. H. 10. 1708. 274. H. 11. 1713. 53. H. 6.

Hauksbee on the weight of the air. Ph. tr. 1706. XXV. 2221.
Found it $\frac{1}{113}$ in May, the barometer 29.7.

Maraldi. A. P. 1708. H. 26.

Scheuchzer on the expansion of the air. A. P. 1711. 154. H. 6.

Scheuchzer Experimenta barometrica de aeris elasticitate. Ph. tr. 1715. XXIX. 266.

Scheuchzer on the height of mountains. Ph. tr. 1728. XXXV. 537, 577.
Allows 73.6 feet to .1.

Varignon on the densities of the air. A. P. 1716. 107. H. 40.

Desaguliers's contrivance for taking levels. Ph. tr. 1724. XXXIII. 165.

A manometer, to be brought to a given temperature. Ph. tr. 1725. XXXIII. 201.
Some mercury, from the East Indies, was 14 times as heavy as water.

Nettleton. Ph. tr. 1725. 308.
Allows 85 feet for .1 at 30.

Celsius Experimentum in argentifodina. Ph. tr. 1725. XXXIII. 313.
Gives 105 or 112 feet for .1, Swedish measure.

Bernoulli. Act. Helv. I. 33. II. 101.

*Bouguer on the expansions of the atmosphere. A. P. 1753. 515. H. 39.

Sulzer on barometrical measurements. A. Berl. 1753. 114.

Lambert. Churbayerische Abh. III. ii. 75.

Kaestner Markscheidekunst. cciv.

*De Luc Modifications. §. 263.
Logarithms give fathoms at 39.74°; reducing for toises the air to 69.32°, the mercury to 54½°.

Deluc's barometrical observations on the depth of mines. Ph. tr. 1777. 401.

Deluc's second barometrical measurement in the Hartz. Ph. tr. 1779. 485.
Confirms his own rules.

Deluc. Roz. XLII. 264.

Deluc on refractions and expansions. Roz. XLIII. 422.

Maskelyne on Deluc's rule. Ph. tr. 1774. 158.

Horsley on Deluc's rules, with investigations. Ph. tr. 1774. 214.

Lavoisier on the weight of the air. A. P. 1774. 364.
A cubic inch weighs .49 grains. Fr.: hence a cubic inch E. .523 gr. E., which seems to be too much.

Hennert de altitudinum mensuratione. 8. Utrecht, 1776. 1788.

*Shuckburgh's observations for ascertaining the height of mountains. Ph. tr. 1777. 513.
The specific gravity of air at 53°, when the barometer is at 29.27, is $\frac{1}{837}$, consequently $\frac{1}{812}$ when the barometer is at 30°.

Barometrical experiments give $\frac{1}{777}$ and $\frac{1}{555}$. The specific gravity of mercury at 68° is 13.61. The decrease of gravity in ascending from the earth's surface produces no perceptible effect. Logarithms give fathoms at 31.24°.

*Shuckburgh's comparison of his rules with General Roy's. Ph. tr. 1778. 681.
   Thinks, that either Roy's rules or his own are sufficiently accurate.

*Roy on the measurement of heights, Ph. tr. 1777. 653.
   Finds, that logarithms give fathoms about 31.7° in England, but at Spitzbergen about 61°, and at the equator near 0°: the difference may perhaps depend on moisture: the same cause appears to require a correction for the mean height above the sea, of which a table is given, the correction for temperature being diminished about $\frac{1}{71}$ for each inch that the mean height of the barometer is below 30°. After all possible corrections, the height of Moel Eilio came out near $\frac{1}{15}$ too great: if Deluc's rules had been employed, the error would have been greater.

Chiminello on barometrical measurements. Roz. XIII. 457.

Fouchy on the weight of the air. A. P. 1780. 3.

Magellan's description of barometers.

Magellan's barometer. Roz. XIX. 108, 194, 257, 341.

Achard on measuring heights by boiling water. A. Berl. 1782. 54. Roz. XXV. 287.

Damen de montium altitudine. Hague, 1783.

Pasumot. Roz. XXIX. 13.

Trembley in Saussure Voyages. III.

Trembley's remarks on Deluc. Roz. XXXII. 87. XLII. 181.

Mayer über das höhenmessen 8. Frankf. 1787.

Mayer über die wärme in rücksicht auf dem barometer. 8. Frankf. 1796.

*Playfair. Ed. tr. I. 87.
   Accurate calculations.

Saussure on the density of the air at different heights. Roz. XXXVI. 98.

Morozzo on the constitution of the air. Soc. Ital. VI. 221.

Gerstner and Gruber on the density of the air. Roz. XLI. 110.

Robison. Enc. Br. Art. Pneumatics.

Hamilton. Ir. tr. V. 117.

Wild on the influence of the wind. Zach. Eph. IV. 385.

Laplace Exposition du système du monde.
   Follows Deluc.

Laplace Mecanique céleste. IV.

Rhode über die berechnung der berghöhen nach Laplace. Halle, 1803.

Berger's mode of bringing down air in bottles. Journ. Phys. LVI. 366.

Lambert gives $h = 10\,000 \mathrm{l}. \frac{28}{y} - \frac{43.(28-y)}{31.583-y}$ for the height in toises, y being the height of the mercury in inches Fr.

Deluc's rule is $h = 10\,000 \mathrm{l}. \frac{x}{y}\left(1+\frac{f-69.69}{484}\right)$ for toises, f being the degrees of Fahrenheit.

Maskelyne's rule deduced from Deluc's is $h = (10\,000 \mathrm{l}. \left(\frac{x}{y}\right) \mp .452 g)\left(1+\frac{f-40}{449}\right)$, g being the difference of the temperatures. Or, if we use a thermometer on which the freezing point is at 0° and the boiling point at 81.4°, for measuring the temperature of the mercury, and another with the freezing point at —9°, and the boiling point at 191° for that of the air, we shall have $h = (10000 \mathrm{l}. \left(\frac{x}{y} \mp i\right)).$ $\left(1+\frac{k+l}{1000}\right)$, i being the difference of the mercurial temperatures, and k and l the temperatures of the air.

Shuckburgh says, that for common practice, when the height is less than a mile, it is sufficient to allow 91.72 feet for every tenth of an inch of difference, adding .211 f. for each degree above 55°, and increasing the whole in the ratio of 30 inches to the mean height of the barometers. One ten thousandth may also be added for each degree of difference in the temperature.

Robison's formula is nearly similar, $h = (87 \times .21 f) \frac{30}{y} d \pm 2.83 e$; f being the mean temperature reckoned from the freezing point, y the mean height of the mercury, d the difference of the heights, in tenths, and e the difference of the temperatures. Or we may take $h = (2610 \pm 6f) d : y \pm 2.8 e$.)

It is said, that where the barometer rises or sinks in the course of the operation, the alteration is generally less at the greater height than in the proper proportion, a circumstance which adds to the difficulties.

The hygrometer might perhaps be employed in these researches with considerable advantage.

Clouds and Mists.

Bernoulli on the heights of the clouds. Act. erud. 1688. 98. Opp. I. 336.

Stirling on a darkness in America. Ph. tr. 1763. 63.

A sulfureous cloud continuing all day, on the 19th of Oct. 1762.

Meister on the form of the clouds. Gott. Mag. I. i. 38.

Marsden on a dry fog at Sumatra, killing the fish. Ph. tr. 1781. 383.

E. M. Physique. Art. Brouillard.

Deluc Idées. II.

On the mist of 1783, which affected the smell. *Gedanken* über den nebel, von Beroldingen. Brunsw. 1783. *Christ* von der merkwürdigen witterung von 1783. *Von der* entstehung des nebels. Vienna, 1783. Lausnitz *Provinzial* blätter, Görlitz, 1783. VI. *Deutscher* Mercur. Oct. 1783. *Toaldo* sulla nebbia. 1783. Goth. Mag. II. ii. *Wiedeburg* über erdbeben und nebel. 8. Jen. 1783. Cotte. Roz. XXIII. 201. Papers in Roz. XXIV. Melanderhielm. N. Schw. Abh. V. *Holm* vom erdbeben auf Island. 8. Cop. 1784. Goth. Mag. V. iii. 128. Torcia to Toaldo. Deutscher Mercur. Apr. 1784. Verdeil on the electric mists of 1783. Mem. de Lausanne. I. 110. Lamanon. Ph. M. V. 80. Hübners phys. tageb. I. i. Franklin. Manch. M. II. See Igneous Meteors.

Ducarla on parasitical clouds. Roz. XXIV. 392, 456. XXV. 31, 94.

On the attraction of mountains to mists. Roz. XXV. 303.

Saussure's cyanometer. M. Tur. 1788. IV. 409. Roz. XXXVIII. 199.

A circle of shades of blue, for estimating the colour of the sky.

Saussure's diaphanometer. M. Tur. 1788. IV. 425.

Hube über die ausdünstung.

Poissé on a mist at Maestricht. Ann. Ch. XXXIII. 217. Nich. V. 326.

Murhard on Saussure's diaphanometer, for measuring the transparency of the air. Ph. M. III. 377.

Kirwan on the variations of the atmosphere.

B. Prévost on Saussure's cyanometrical observations. Journ. Phys. LVII. 372.

L. Howard on the forms of the clouds. Ph. M. XVI. 97, 344. XVII. 11.

Dalton's correction of a mistake of Kirwan respecting the clouds. Nich. VI. 118.

It is said, that in 1791, 230 persons were drowned at Amsterdam, by falling into the canals in a great fog. Luckombe.

Dew.

A. P. II. 13. Rosée et serein.

Gersten de mutationibus barometri. 8. Frankf. 1733.

Extr. Ph. tr. 1733. XXXVIII. 43.

Some experiments on dew. Observes, that honey dew is derived from insects.

Dufay. A. P. 1736. 352.

Remarks, that metals protect glass from dew. Also wafers and paper.

Hales's vegetable statics.

Found, that 3.28 inches of dew fall annually on the earth.

Leroy. A. P. 1751. 481.

Macfait on foggy weather. Ed. ess. I. 197.

Unzer Kleine schriften. 8. Reuteln, 1766. I. 15.

Ek on dew. Roz. Intr. I. 383.

Experiments and observations on light and colours. 8. London. 1786. 78.

It is said, that dew attaches itself to the inside of a bottle partly full of water, on the side opposite to the solar light,

Hube über die ausdünstung. 211.

On honey dew. See the Authors quoted by Lichtenberg in Erxleben. §. 730.

Prieur on dew. Journ. Polyt. II. vi. 409. Ann. Ch. XXVIII. 317. Nich. IV. 86.

Hassenfratz on the evening and morning dew. Journ. de l'Ecole Polytechn. Ph. M. VII. 114.

*B. Prevost on dew. Ann. Ch. XLIV. 75. Journ. R. I., I. Nich. 8. III. 290. Gilb. XV. 485.

Most of the facts may perhaps be explained by means of Mr. Leslie's discoveries.

Dalton on rain and dew. Manch. M. V.

Makes the dew falling on grass about 5 inches annually, or somewhat less.

Account of a Memoir on Dew. By BENEDICT PRÉVOST. *Abridged from the Annales de Chimie. No.* 130. *Journ.* R. I. I. 292.

It is well known that dew is often deposited on glass, when metals in its neighbourhood remain dry; Mr. Prévost has however discovered some new and curious facts relative to this deposition. When thin plates of metal are fixed on pieces of glass, it sometimes happens that they are as much covered with dew as the glass itself: but more frequently they remain dry; and in this case they are also surrounded by a dry zone. But when the other side of the glass is exposed to dew, the part which is opposite to the metal remains perfectly dry. If the metal be again covered with glass, it will lose its effect in preventing the deposition.

These experiments may be very conveniently made on the glass of a window, when moisture is attaching itself to either of its surfaces; Mr. Prévost remarks that it often happens that dew is deposited externally, even when the air within is warmer than without. A plate of metal fixed internally on a window receives a larger quantity of moisture than the glass, while the space opposite to an external plate remains dry: and if the humidity is deposited from without, the place opposite the internal plate is also more moistened, while the external plate remains dry: and both these circumstances may happen at once with the same result. A small plate fixed externally, opposite to the middle of the internal plate, protects this part of the plate from receiving moisture, and a smaller piece of glass, fixed on the external plate, produces again a central spot of moisture on the internal one: and the same changes may be continued for a number of alternations, until the whole thickness becomes more than half an inch. Gilt paper, with its metallic surface exposed, acts as a metal, but when the paper only is exposed, it has no effect. When a plate of metal, on which moisture would have been deposited, is fixed at a small distance from the glass, the moisture is transferred to the surface of the glass immediately under it, without affecting the metal: if this plate is varnished on the surface remote from the glass, the effect remains, but if on the side next the glass, it is destroyed. The oxidation of metals renders them also unfit for the experiment. When glasses partly filled with mercury, or even with water, are exposed to the dew, it is deposited only on the parts which are above the surface of the fluid. But in all cases when the humidity is too copious, the results are confused.

In order to reduce these facts to some general laws, Mr. Prévost observes, that when the metal is placed on the warmer side of the glass, the humidity is deposited more copiously either on itself or on either surface of the glass in its neighbourhood: but that, when it is on the colder side, it neither receives humidity nor permits its deposition on the glass: that a coat of glass, or varnish, destroys the efficacy of the metal, but that an additional plate of metal restores it.

Mr. Prevost was at first disposed to attribute these phenomena to the effects of electricity, but he thinks it possible to explain them all by the action of heat only: for this purpose he assumes, first, that glass attracts humidity the more powerfully as its temperature is lower; secondly, that metals attract it but very little; thirdly, that glass exerts this attraction notwithstanding the interposition of other bodies; and fourthly, that metals give to glass, placed in their neighbourhood, the power of being heated by warm air, and being cooled by cold air, with greater rapidity; hence that the temperature of the glass approaches more nearly to that of the air on the side opposite to the metal, and attracts the humidity accordingly more or less, either to its own surface, or to that of the metal. We should indeed have expected a contrary effect; that the metal would rather have tended to communicate to the glass the temperature of the air on its own side: but granting that the assumptions of Mr. Prévost serve to generalise the facts with accuracy, their temporary utility is as great as if they were fundamentally probable. Y.

Rain in general.

Lahire on rain water. A. P. 1703. 56.
Wargentin. Schw. Abh. XXV. 3.
Leche. Schw. Abh. XXV. 16.

Schenmark. Schw. Abh. XXVI. 159.
Ulloa's voyages. II.
   It never rains in Peru, but for a part of the year the atmosphere is obscured by thick fogs, called garuas.
Franklin. 1756. Ph. tr. 1765. 182.
   Observes, that a small black cloud portends rain, denoting the beginning of a current of cold air from above.
Franklin and Percival on the difference of rain at different heights. Manch. M. II.
   No satisfactory theory.
*Heberden on the rain falling at different heights. Ph. tr. 1769. 359.
   In 1766, 12.1 inches fell at the top of Westminster abbey, below the houses, 22.6.
Barrington on the rain on mountains. Ph. tr. 1771. 294.
   Not much less than on the plains.
Dobson. Ph. tr. 1777. 255.
   Confirms Heberden's remark.
Bertholon on a cause of rain. Roz. XIV. 482.
Ducarla on rainy winds. Roz. XVIII. 446.
Deluc Idées sur la météorologie.
Deluc on vapours and rain. Roz. XXXVI. 276.
Letter to Hutton in the Monthly Review. 1789.
Chiminello on the fall of rain in different centuries. A. Sienn. VI. 1.
Hutton's theory of rain. Ed. tr. I. 41. II. 39.
   Observes, that since the capacity of air for moisture increases faster than the temperature, there must be a deposition of moisture when two saturated portions of air at different temperatures are mixed.
Libes on rain. Roz XL. 85.
Erxleben. II. 735.
   It is said, that the drops of rain, at the equator, are sometimes an inch in diameter.
Lichtenberg's remarks on rain. Gilb. II. 121.
Hassenfratz on snow and rain. Journ. Polyt. I. iv. 570. Repert. XIV. 64.
Saussure on dryness preceding rain. Gilb. I. 317. Nich. I. 51F.
Zylius on rain. Gilb. V. 257.
Kirwan on rain. Ir. tr. Nich. 8. V. 120.
   Electric theory.

Gough. Manch. M. IV
   Observes, that the quantity of rain at different heights is nearly as the height of the point of perpetual congelation above the gage.
Dalton on rain and dew. Manch M. V. 346. Nich. 8. IV. 159. Repert. ii. I. 203.
   Dalton found the rain of a gage, 50 yards high, in summer ⅓, in winter ½ as much as that of a gage below.
Howard on Hutton's theory of rain. Ph. M. XIV. 55.
   It has been remarked, that the largest quantities of rain fall on the hills, where they are the most wanted, since they soon run off, from the inclination of the ground.

Rain Gages.

Hooke's statical rain gage and register. Birch. III. 477.
Perrault. A. P. II. 25.
Leup. Th. Aerostat. t. 17, 18.
Grischow's hyetometer. M. Berl. 1734. IV. 349.
Pasumot's rain and snow gage. Roz. VIII. 43.
Landriani's chronhyometer. Soc. Ital. I. 203. Roz. XXII. 280.
   Registering the time and quantity.
Garnett on rain gages. Ir. tr. V. 357.
   Some of these gages measure the quantity by wheelwork.

Particular Registers of Rain.

See Meteorological Journals.
Townley on the rain at Townley, in Lancashire. Ph. tr. 1694. XVIII.
   The average of 15 years was 41.516.
Ph. tr. 1696. XIX. 357.
   At Gresham College.
Derham. Ph. tr. 1714. XXIX. 130.
   At Upminster.
Horsley. Ph. tr. 1723. XXXII. 328.
   In Northumberland.
Grischow. M. Berl. 1734. IV.
Linings. Ph. tr. 1745. XLIII. 380. 1753. 284.
   At Charlestown.

Hagen. Ph. tr. 1751. 360.
   At Leyden.
Byam. Ph. tr. 1755. 295.
   In Antigua.
Arderon. Ph. tr. 1763. 9.
   At Norwich.
Borlase. Ph. tr. 1764. 59.
   In Cornwall. Continued.
Barker. Ph. tr. 1771. 221.
   At Lyndon. Continued.
Hutchinson on the dryness of the year 1788. Ph. tr. 1789. 37.
A caution respecting the rain gage of the R. S. Ph tr. 1792.
Erxleben. §. 738.
   At various places.
An annual table printed by Burbage at Nottingham.
   At Exeter, Chichester, London, Diss, Chatsworth, W. Bridgford, Ferriby, Lancaster, and Kendal. It appears that December was the wettest month in 4 places; June in 2; May and November each in one, and April and December in one instance equally wetter than the rest. 1804.

Annual fall of Rain, from Erxleben, Dalton, and others.

Place	Inches
Upsal	16.7
West Bridgford, Notting.	17.0
Wittenberg	17.0
St. Petersburg	17.2
Lund	18.5
Diss, Norfolk	18.7
Upminster, Essex	19.5
Carlisle, 1 y.	20.2
Paris	20.2
Berlin	20.6
Widdrington, North. 1 y.	21.2
Rome	21.3
Edinburgh	22.0
Dublin	22.2
South Lambeth, 9 y.	22.7
London, 7 y.	23.0
Near Oundle, North. 14 y.	23.0
Lisle	24.0
Lyndon, Rutl. 21 y.	24.3
Utrecht	24.7
Haarlem	24.7
Youngsbury, Hartf. 5 y.	25.0
Kimbolton, Hunt.	25.0
Norwich, 18 y.	25.5
Fyfield, Hampsh. 7 y.	25.9
Ferriby, Yorksh.	26.6
Chichester	26.8
Ulm	27.0
Algiers	27.0
Barrowby, Yorksh. 6 y.	27.5
Chatsworth, Derbysh. 15 y.	27.8
Hague	28.4
Delft	28.6
Harderwyk	28.6
A place in Cornwall, 1 y.	29.1
Bristol, 3 y.	29.2
Bridgwater, Somers.	29.3
Abo	29.3
Leyden	30.2
Madeira	31.0
Minehead, Somers.	31.3
Dalton's mean for all England, taking first a mean of the counties	31.3
Mean of 16 places in Great Britain, Enc. Br.	32.5
Dalton's immediate mean of 32 places, mostly rainy	33.2
Manchester, 9 y.	33.0
Middleburg	33.0
Zurich	33.1
Exeter	33.2
Liverpool, 18 y.	34.4
Padua	34.5
Cotte's mean of 147 places	34.7
Sienna	35.2
Venice	36.1
Selbourne, Hampsh.	37.2
Dover, 5 y.	37.5
Lyons	39.4
Kirkmichael, Dumfr.	40.8
Ludgvan, Cornw.	41.0
Dordrecht	41.0
Townley, Lanc. 15 y.	41.3
Pisa	43.2
Lancaster, 10 y.	45.0
Waith Sutton, Westm. 5 y.	46.0
Plymouth, 2 y.	46.5
Charlestown	50.0
Garsdale, Westm. 3 y.	52.3
Fellfoot, Westm. 3 y.	55.7
Kendal, Westm. 11 y.	59.8
Kendal, in 1782	83.5
Crawshawbooth, Lanc. 2 y.	60.0
Keswick, Cumb. 7 y.	67.5
East Indies, sometimes	104.0

For rain and dew together Dalton makes the mean for England and Wales 36 inches, amounting in a year to 28 cubic miles of water.

Storms of Rain.

Ph. tr. 1698. XX. 382.
  In Yorkshire.
Derham and Leeuwenhoek. Ph. tr. 1704. XXIV. 1530, 1535.
  Chiefly wind.
Sloane. Ph. tr. 1706. XXV. 2342.
  At Denbigh.
Thoresby. Ph. tr. 1711. XXVII. 321. 1722. XXXII. 101.
  Near Halifax; fifteen persons were drowned.
Luckombe's tablet of memory.
  A flood in Spain, 1787, destroyed 2000 persons.
Campbell. Manch. M. IV. 265.
  Six inches of rain fell in a storm at Lancaster.

Snow and Hail.

Figures of snow. See Physical Optics.
Kepler on the sexangular figure of snow. *Dornav.* amphitheatr. 751.
Figures of snow. Hooke's micrographia. 88, 91.
Extr. Ph. tr. 1674. IX.
Fairfax on a hailstorm. Ph. tr. 1667. II. 481.
Grew on the nature of snow. Ph. tr. 1673. VIII. 5193.
Bartholinus de naturae mirabilibus. 4. Copenh. 1674. ii.
Acc. Ph. tr. 1674. IX.
Hailstones of more than a pound in Flanders. Ph. tr. 1693. XXIV. 858.
Halley on a hail storm. Ph. tr. 1697. XIX. 570.
On a hail storm. Ph. tr. 1697. XIX. 577, 579.
†Wallis on hail. Ph. tr. 1697. XIX. 653, 729.
Cassini on the figure of snow. A. P. II. 87. X. 25.

Hail stones weighing 1¼lb., the least two fingers thick. A. P. 1703. H. 19.
Thoresby on a hail storm. Ph. tr. 1712. XXVII. 514.
Langwith on the figures of snow. Ph. tr. 1723. XXXII. 298.
Musschenbroek on some figures of snow. Ph. tr. 1732. XXXVII. 357. Mussch. Intr. II. pl. 61.
Lulofs on the figure of snow. M. Berl. 1740. VI. 83.
Stocke nivis figurae. Ph. tr. 1742. XLII. 114.
Engelman Verhandeling over de sneewfiguren. Haarl. 1747.
Monesier sur la grêle. 4. Bourd. 1752.
*Nettis on the configuration of snow. Ph. tr. 1756. 644.
Bruni on the mass of snow that fell upon Bergamoletto. Ph. tr. 1756. 796.
Fauquier on a hail storm in Virginia. Ph. tr. 1758. 746.
Wilke on the forms of snow. Schw. Abh. 1761. 3, 89. Roz. I. 106.
  The forms are shown by freezing soap bubbles.
Messier on a number of globules passing over the sun's disc. A. P. 1777. 464. H. 3.
  Probably large hail stones.
†Chambon on hail. Roz. X. 301.
A letter on hail. Rozier. Sept. 1778.
Mongez on hail. Roz. XII. 202.
Hail stones of above two pounds. Mourgue de Montredon. A. P. 1781. 754.
  With a dry fog supposed to be volcanic.
Barberet. Acad. Dijon. I.
Pasumot on prisms of ice. Roz. XXIII. 62.
Franklin. Manch. M. II. 357.
  Suspects that hail is formed in a very cold region, high in the atmosphere. But this is not the most probable hypothesis.
Tessier's account of a hail storm extending 200 leagues. A. P. 1789. 618. 1790. 263.

Lichtenberg on hail. *N. Hannov.* Mag. Jan. 1793. Erxl. Naturl.

Thinks, that hail depends on electricity, perhaps as promoting evaporation and cold. Observes, that it very seldom hails at night; that in winter snow is much more common than hail; that it often snows or rains for some days, and then hails with thunder; and that hail often attends volcanic explosions. Most of these circumstances are easily understood, if we consider that much of the cold which congeals the hail is probably produced by evaporation.

Hassenfratz on snow and rain. Journ. Polyt. I. iv. 570. Repert. XIV. 64.

Hassenfratz on the air contained in snow. Journ. Phys. XLVIII. 375.

Hail stones of 8 pounds. Mann. Ph. M. II. 216.

Saussure on a red snow. Ph. M. III. 168.

Driessen on the congelation of snow water. Ph. M. III. 249.

Gilb. IV. 246.

Aldini attributes the form of snow to electricity. Von Arnim denies the observation on which the opinion is grounded. Gilb. V. 73.

Account of a hailstone which fell in Hungary, 1803, and which eight men could not lift. Gilb. XVI. 75.

From newspapers only.

On snow. Nich. VIII. 73.

Hailstones 14 inches in circumference are said to have fallen in Hartfordshire, 4 May, 1697; some of 23 ounces weight in the Pyrenees, 1784. In 1710 a storm of snow destroyed 7000 Swedes in their march against Drontheim.

Springs, Rivers, Lakes, and Seas: Water and Ice.

See Theory of Hydraulics, and Hydraulic Architecture.

On ebbing and flowing wells. Plin. Epist. iv. 30.

Danubius illustratus.

Boyle on the saltness of the sea. Works. III. 357.

Hydrology. Ph. tr. abr. II. ii. 257. IV. 2 p. ii. 183. VI. 2 p. ii. 163. VIII. 2 p. ii. 641. X. 2 p. ii. 567.

Vossius de Nili origine. 4. Hague, 1666. Acc. Ph. tr. 1655—6. I. 304.

Brown on the lake of Zircknitz in Carniolia. Ph. tr. IV. 1669. 1083.

A lake several miles long, which abounds with fish in the winter, but is dry from June to September, yielding grass and hay. It empties itself by a subterraneous channel.

Mariotte du mouvement des eaux. clxxix.

L'origine des fontaines. Par. 1674. Acc. Ph. tr. 1675. X.

Southwell on water. Birch. III. 196.

Valvasor on the lake of Zircknitz, with a map, Ph. tr. 1686. XVI. 411.

Young on fountains and springs. Hooke. Lect. Cutl.

Thinks they originate from the sea, since large springs are sometimes found in small islands. Hooke does not accede to the opinion.

Halley on the lake of Zircknitz. Birch. IV. 558.

Halley on the cause of springs. Ph. tr. 1692. XVII. 468.

Halley on the saltness of the sea and of lakes. Ph. tr. 1715. XXIX. 296.

Oliver on an ebbing well in Torbay. Ph. tr. 1693. XVII. 908.

Bartholinus de origine fontium. 4. Copenh. 1689.

Sedileau on Springs. A. P. 1693. 117. On the origin of rivers. X. 221.

Diodati on an inundation in Mauritius. Ph. tr. 1698. XX. 268.

Dodart on the wells at Calais, fluctuating with the tides. A. P. I. 234. H. 87.

Borelli and Lahire on reciprocating springs. A. P. II. 25.

Hearne de lacu Vettero. Ph. tr. 1705. XXIV. 1938.

Thoresby on an eruption of waters in Craven. Ph. tr. 1706. XXV. 2236.

Vallisneri Lezzione intorno alle fontane. Venice, 1715. M. B.

Robelin on wells alternating with the tides. A. P. 1717. H. 9.

Ph. tr. 1722. XXXII.
The height of the falls of Niagara is 166 feet.

Desaguliers on the rise and fall of water in ponds. Ph. tr. 1724. XXXIII. 132.
On the principle of Hero's fountain.

Gualtieri sopra le fontane. 8. Lucca, 1728. M. B.

Atwell on reciprocating springs. Ph. tr. 1732. XXXVII. 301.
On the principle of the siphon.

Hamberger et Dankwerts de fontium origine. 4. Jen. 1733.

Segner Progammata. duo. Gott. 1737.
On reciprocating springs.

On rivers. S'Gravesande. Nat. Ph. iii. c. 10.

Lucas on the cave of Killarney, which sometimes overflows with reciprocating water. Ph. tr. 1740. XLI. 360.

Marsigli Storia del mare.

Ghezzi delle fontane. 12. Ven. 1741. M. B.

Jallabert on the alternations of the lake of Geneva. A. P. 1742. H. 26.

Kühn vom ursprunge der quellen. 8. Berl. 1746.

On an inundation in Cumberland, which undermined a mountain. Ph. tr. 1750. 362.

Deparcieux on a pipe that gives more water by night than by day. A. P. 1750. H. 153. 1754. H. 33.
Probably from included air.

On springs. Belidor. Arch. hydr. II. i. 339.

Speed de aqua marina. 4. Oxf. 1755.

Guettard on the disappearance of some rivers. A. P. 1758. 271. H. 13.

Wallerius et Sv. W. de origine fontium. 1761.

Milbourne on a decrease of the river Eden. Ph. tr. 1763. 7.
Perhaps from frost.

Badialli on the mouths of rivers. C. Bon. V. ii. 99.

Barbieri on the saltness of the sea. Raccolta d'opusc. xlvii.

On the divining rod. Roz. Intr. II. 231. Montucla. Math. recr.

Baumer on springs. Roz. I. 177.

On springs. Roz. VI. 485.

Lengths and heights of rivers. Roz. VII. 292.

†Maison neuve on the saltness of the sea. Roz. XII. 392.

Rennel on the lengths of rivers. Ph. tr. 1781. 90.

Fraula on thawing. Roz. XXI. 390.

Desmarets on ice. Roz. XXII. 50, 165.

Page on the wells at Sheerness. Ph. tr. 1784. 6.
A well being dug 330 feet deep, the water rose in it to within 18 feet of the surface.

Alhut on periodical springs. Roz. XXVI. 295.

Robert and Meyerotto on the Hautes Fagnes, a marsh on an elevated plain. A. Berl. 1788. 94, 577.

Ribbach on the Hautes Fagnes. A. Berl. D. Abh. 1788. 177.

Pott on ice at the bottom of rivers. Roz. XXXIII. 59.

Besson on subaqueous ice. Roz. XXXIV. 387.

Godart on subaqueous ice. Roz. XXXV. 205.

Brunelli on the river of Amazons. C. Bon. VII. O. 39.

Rumford on the saltness of the sea. Ess. II.
Observes, that it tends to prevent the expansion of the water in cooling, and to equalise the temperature of the air, by causing the circulation of the water to continue in low temperatures.

The lake of Eichen in Baaden has some remarkable variations. Lichtenberg.

Trembley on rivers, and on the lake of Geneva. A. Berl. 1794. 3.
Baillet on waters in mines. Journ. Phys. XLVIII. 164.
Grimm and others on the origin of subterraneous water. Gilb. II. 336.
Traullé on new springs. Journ. Phys. LV. 346.
Edelbrooke on the Ganges in Bengal. As. res. VII. 1.
Cousin on the height of the Seine. M. Inst. IV. 334.
Lamarck Hydrogéologie. 8. Par. 1802. R. S.
Pearson on the wells at Brighton. Nich. 8. III. 65.
  The high water prevents the efflux of the springs, and raises the wells.
Dalton. Manch. M. V. 346. Gilb. XV. 244.
  Observes, that a foot of wet soil contains 7 inches of water, that is $\frac{7}{12}$. Thinks that the Thames carries off $\frac{1}{25}$ of the rain and dew that fall in England; other rivers 8 times as much, making together 13 inches, and leaving 23 for evaporation.
Henry. Ph. tr. 1803. 29, 274. Nich. 8. V. 229. Repert. ii. III. 255.
  Finds, that equal volumes of any gas are absorbed by water under any pressure. Hence we may understand why the water of the deepest wells contains the most air.

Sweetening Sea Water, and preserving Fresh.

Hauton. Ph. tr. 1670. V. 2048.
Lister. Ph. tr. 1685. XV. 836.
Boyle. Ph. tr. 1691. XVII. 627.
Watson. Ph. tr. 1753. 69.
Chapman. Ph. tr. 1758. 635.
On Irwin's mode of sweetening sea water. A. Gott. D. Schr. 202. Roz. XVIII. 164.
Lorgna. Soc. Ital. III. 375. V. 8.
Lorgna intorno alla dolcificazione dell acqua del mare. 4. R. S.
Bayley's machine. Repert. V. 320.

Lowitz on freshening putrid water. N. A. Petr. 1792. X. 187.
Montucla and Lalande. IV. 507.
Trotter's medical and chemical essays. 8. 1795.
  Recommends casks charged within.
Bentham's metallic tanks for preserving fresh water at sea. Repert. XVI. 238.

Atmospherical Electricity in general.

St. Gray. Ph. tr. 1735. XXXIX. 24.
  Observes, that "the electric fire (si licet magnis componere parva) seems to be of the same nature with that of thunder and lightning."
†Logan on the form of lightning. Ph. tr. 1736. XXXIX. 240.
Winkler Abhandlung von der electrischen ursprung des wetterleuchtens. 1746. Gehlers wörterb. Art. Blitz.
*Franklin's letters.
Maffei della formazione dei fulmini. 4. Verona, 1747.
Wilke. Schw. Abh. 1750. 81, 155.
Eeles on the cause of thunder. Ph. tr. 1751. 524.
Nollet and Mylius on the electricity of the clouds. Ph. tr. 1751. 553, 559.
Nollet on the effects of thunder. A. P. 1764. 408.
Watson on thunder clouds. Ph. tr. 1751. 567.
Watson on the effects of lightning. Ph. tr. 1762. 629.
Macfait on thunder. Ed. ess. I. 189.
Lemonnier on the electricity of the air. A. P. 1752. 233. H. 8.
Mazéas on the electricity of the air. Ph. tr. 1753. 377.
Birch's remark on the light seen on spear points. Ph. tr. 1754. 484.
Butschanz de fulgure et tonitru. Gotting. 1757.
Hartmann von lufterscheinungen. 8. Hanov. 1759.

Bergman on horizontal lightnings. Schw. Abh. 1760. 62.

Poncelet de la nature du tonnerre. 12. Par. 1766.

Ronayne on atmospherical electricity. Ph. tr. 1772. 137.

Cotte. A. P. 1772. i. H. 16.
_{Snow serves as a conductor in storms.}

Beccaria dell' elettricità atmosferica. 4. R. S.

Bertholon on thunder. Roz. VII. 258.

Bertholon on atmospherical electricity. Roz. XX. 224.

Bertholon de l'électricité des météores. Par. 1787.

Cavallo on the electricity of the atmosphere. Ph. tr. 1776. 407. 1777. 48.

Mako vom donner. 1778.

Reimarus vom blitze. 2 v. 8. Hamb. 1778. 1794.

Changeux on the effects of electricity on the barometer. Rozier. Apr. 1778.

Gallitzin on an electrical kite. A. Petr. II. ii. 76. Fig.
With precautions to prevent accidents.

Mourgue on thunder. Roz. XIII. Suppl. 459.

Poli sopra il tuono. 8. R. S.

Deluc Idées. II.

Deluc on lightning. Roz. XXXIX. 262.

Deluc to Lamétherie. Roz. Aug. 1790.

Deluc on lightning without thunder. Roz. Oct. 1791.

Rozier on the cause of thunder. Roz. XVI. 309.

Rozier on a phosphoric cloud. Roz. XVIII. 276.

Achard on atmospherical electricity. A. Berl. 1780. 14.

Achard on terrestrial electricity. A. Berl. 1786. 13.
In contradistinction to atmospherical.

Ducarla on rainy winds. Roz. XVIII. 446.

Ferris on ascending thunder. Roz. XXII. 197.

Electric mists of 1783. See Clouds and Mists.

Baldwin on the appearance of an electrical kite. Am. Ac. I. 257.

Diwisch Meteorologische electricität. 1786.

Oliver on lightning. Am. tr. II. 74.

Bennet's account of atmospherical electricity. Ph. tr. 1787. 288.
Finds, that a candle collects more electricity than any point.

Sénébier. Rozier. March and April 1787.

Lightning without thunder. Sénébier in Rozier. 1787. Gronau. Naturf. Fr. IX.

Bergmann on lightning. Opusc. V. 348.

Hervieu on a remarkable light in a storm. Roz. XXXIV. 386.

Aepinus's letter on atmospherical electricity. Ed. tr. II. 213.

Read's instrument for collecting atmospheric electricity. Ph. tr. 1791. 185.

Read's apparatus and journal of electricity. Ph. tr. 1792. 225.

Read's summary view of the electricity of the earth and atmosphere. Lond. 1793.

Read's meteorological journal of atmospherical electricity. Ph. tr. 1794. 185.
Finds, that out of 404 observations in a year, the air was positively electric in 241, negative in 156, and neutral in 7 only.

Read's experiments with the doubler. Ph. tr. 1794. 266.
Attributes the uncertainty of the doubler wholly to atmospheric electricity; finds all noxious and putrid exhalations, and the air of close rooms, in a negative state.

On fairy rings. Withering's bot. arr. III. 335. Monthly Mag. XV. 219. Gilb. XVII. 351.
They are formed by the agaricus orcades, or fairy ring agaric, becoming larger as the roots of the fungus spread.

Volta to Lichtenberg. Brugnatelli Bibl. fisica. Germ. *Meteorologische* briefe. Leipz. 1793.

Lampadius über electricität und wärme. 8. Berl. 1793.

Lichtenberg. Erxl. Nat.
Thinks, that thunder is less frequent but more violent in winter, because the air is less disposed to conduct.

Robison. Enc. Br. Suppl. Art. Thunder.

Toaldo on thunder. Ac. Par. III. 212.

On the clouds in a thunderstorm. Nich. I. 265.

†On fairy rings. Nich. I. 546.

Heller on the returning stroke. Gilb. II. 223.

Aldini's opinion of snow. See Snow.

Priestley on an igneous meteor. Gilb. XI. 76.
A particular kind of lightning, supposed to be about 20 miles high.

Kirwan on rain. Ir. tr. Nich. 8. V. 120.

Erman on atmospherical electricity. Gilb. XV. 385. 502.
Balitoro asserts, that lightning generally strikes the S. E. side of a house, sometimes the S. W. but never the north.

Particular Accounts of Storms.

Instances of lightning without audible thunder. Homer. Odyss. xx. 139. Virg. Georg. I. 487. Cicer. de divin. I. xviii. Hor. Od. I. 34.

Waller. Ph. tr. 1665—6. I. 222.
At Oxford.

Neale. Ph. tr. 1665—6. I. 247.

Ph. tr. 1670. V. 2084.
At Stralsund.

Kirkby. Ph. tr. 1673. VIII. 6092.
Effects on grain.

Howard. Ph. tr. 1676. XI. 647.
Effects on the compass, a complete reversion.

Ph. tr. 1696. XIX. 311.
Near Aberdeen, 4 persons killed.

Mawgridge. Ph. tr. 1697. XIX. 782.
Effects on a galley.

Thoresby. Ph. tr. 1699. XXI. 51. Ph. tr. 1700. XXII. 507.
At Leeds.

Molyneux. Ph. tr. 1708. XXVI. 36.

Chamberlayne. Ph. tr. 1712. XXVII. 528.

Wasse. Ph. tr. 1725. XXXIII. 367.
At Mixbury. Probably an igneous meteor. Mr. Jessop attributes the fairy rings to lightning.

Bocanbrey on a vortex of fire rolling on the earth. A. P. 1725. H. 5.
Seems to have been a whirlwind or dry spout.

Beard. Ph. tr. 1726. XXXIV. 118.

Davies. Ph. tr. 1730. XXXVI. 444.
In Carmarthenshire.

Cookson. Ph. tr. 1735. XXXIX. 75.
Magnetic effects.

Clark. Ph. tr. 1739. XLI. 235.

Lord Petre. Ph. tr. 1742. XLII. 136.

Ph. tr. 1745. XLIII. 447.

Miles. Ph. tr. 1748. XLV. 383. 1757. 104.

Waddel and Knight. Ph. tr. 1749. XLVI. 111.
Effects on the compass.

Chalmers on a fire ball. Ph. tr. 1750. XLVI. 366.
On board the Montague, in lat. 42° 48′, 4 Nov. 1749, a ball of fire as large as a millstone was seen rolling three or four miles along the sea with the wind; it struck the main topmast, rent the whole mainmast, and knocked down five men. It has been supposed that this was an electrical cloud.

Franklin. Ph. tr. 1751. 289.

Palmer. Ph. tr. 1751. 330.
At Southmolton.

Account of the death of Richmann. A. P. 1753. H. 78. Ph. tr. 1754. 757. 1755. 61.

Hanow Nachricht aus St. Petersburg.
Kratzenstein says, that the stroke which destroyed Richmann was not conducted by his apparatus.

Huxham. Ph. tr. 1755. 16.
At Plymouth.

Brander. Ph. tr. 1755. 298.
In Wellclose Square.

Child. Ph. tr. 1755. 309.
At Darking.

Dyer. Ph. tr. 1757. 104.
In Cornwall.

Smeaton. Ph. tr. 1759. 198.
At Lestwithiel.

Cooper. Ph. tr. 1759. 38.
> At Norwich.

Mrs. Whitfield. Ph. tr. 1759. 282.

Mountaine and Knight. Ph. tr. 1759. 286, 294.

Borlase. Ph. tr. 1762. 507.

Watson. Ph. tr. 1762. 629.
> On ships.

Bergmann. Ph. tr. 1763. 97.

Delaval. Ph. tr. 1764. 227.
> St. Bride's church.

Lawrens. Ph. tr. 1764. 235.
> Essex street.

Heberden. Ph. tr. 1764. 198.
> At S. Weald.

Veicht. Ph. tr. 1764. 284.
> On ships in the East Indies.

Paxton. Ph. tr. 1769. 79.
> Devonshire. A noise equal to 100 cannon.

Williams. Ph. tr. 1771. 71.
> Cornwall. A whole congregation, except 5 or 6, were struck senseless. Cornwall seems to be the most exposed to thunder of any county in Britain.

Henly. Ph. tr. 1772. 131.

Kirkshaw. Ph. tr. 1773. 177.
> A person struck dead in bed.

King. Ph. tr. 1773. 231.
> Wilts.

Hamilton. Ph. tr. 1773. 324.
> Lord Tylney's house at Naples.

Nicholson. Ph. tr. 1774. 350.
> A horse's ears were luminous: there was a light streaming from cloud to cloud like an aurora borealis.

Henley. Ph. tr. 1776. 463.
> A bullock was struck by lightning, which affected the skin where the hair was white: probably because the skin was here a less perfect conductor than elsewhere, and the least perfect conductors are most affected.

Cooper. Ph. tr. 1779. 160.
> On the ship Atlas.

*Brereton. Ph. tr. 1781. 42.
> East Bourne. A ball was seen to burst against the house; two persons were killed.

Roz. XVIII. 45.

Leroy. Roz. XX. 82.

Lorgna. Roz. XX. 365.

Poli sopra alcuni fulmini. 8. R. S.

Nairne on wire shortened by lightning. Ph. tr. 1783. 223.

Buissart on an ascending stroke of thunder. Roz. XXIII. 279.

Verdeil on a stroke of thunder at Lausanne. M. Laus. I. 158.

Geschichte einer ausserordentlichen begebenheit. 8. Frankf. 1785.
> Lightning without thunder.

Lee on a stroke of lightning. Am. Ac. I. 253.

Brydone on a thunder storm in Scotland. Ph. tr. 1787. 61.
> No flash appeared to strike the men, and the lowest point only of the iron of the wheels was melted.

Lord Stanhope on Mr. Brydone's account. Ph. tr. 1787. 130.
> Explains the circumstance from the effect of the returning stroke.

Lavoisier on a stroke of lightning on St. Paul's church. A. P. 1789. 613.

Hervieu on a storm. Roz. XXXIV. 386.

Klügel Beschreibung eines heftigen gewitters. 8. Halle, 1789.

Withering on some effects of lightning. Ph. tr. 1790. 293.
> A man was struck dead under a tree; a hole 2½ inches in diameter was made, and some quartzose sand and pebbles were vitrified in it.

Haldane on the cause of accidents from lightning. Nich. I. 433.

Effect of lightning. Nich. III. 432.

Lichtenberg on a thunder cloud. Ph. M. VI. 41.

Toscan on a stroke of lightning, preceded by the appearance of a globe of light on an iron bar. Gilb. XIII. 484.

Storms of thunder. Gilb. XV. 227.

Gough and Wilson on some effects of lightning. Nich. IX. 1.

Measures of Atmospherical Electricity.

Franklin's electrical kite. Ph. tr. 1751. 565.
Romas. S. E. II. 393.
Hartmann über die erforschung der electricität. 4. Hanov. 1764.
Gallitzin. A. Petr. II. ii. 76.
  A kite.
Lichtenberg's meteorological electroscope. Goth. Mag. I. i. 157.
Boyer Brun on an electroscope for a conductor. Roz. XXVIII. 133.
Read. Ph. tr. 1791. 185. 1792. 225.
Read on the electricity of the earth and atmosphere.

Preservation from Lightning, Conductors and Precautions.

Winkler de avertendi fulminis artificio. 4. Leipz. 1753.
Watson on conductors. Ph. tr. 1764. 201.
Delaval. Ph. tr. 1764. 227.
  Recommends a conductor 6 or 8 inches by ¼ for St. Bride's church.
Wilson on blunt conductors. Ph. tr. 1764. 246.
Wilson's dissent from a committee, with experiments. Ph. tr. 1773. 48, 49.
  Wilson says, that points attract discharges, which are often dangerous. A bar, near 4 inches by ½ an inch, was probably heated red hot in St. Paul's, March 1772.
Wilson's experiments in the Pantheon and elsewhere. Ph. tr. 1778. 232, 999.
  A point was struck at a greater distance than a ball.
Proposal of a committee for securing St. Paul's. Ph. tr. 1769. 160.
  Recommends 4 bars not less than an inch square, to secure the lantern.
Winn on a conductor for a ship. Ph. tr. 1770. 188.

Leroy on conductors. A. P. 1770. 53. H. 14. 1773. 599. H. S. 1790. 472, 588. Roz. XLIII. 94.
Franklin. Ed. ess. III. 129.
Franklin on electricity.
Felbiger Kunst gebaüde zu bewähren. 8. Bresl. 1771.
*Report of a committee on securing powder magazines. Ph. tr. 1773. 42. Consisting of Cavendish, Watson, Franklin, and others.
  They recommend pointed conductors; and adhere to their opinion. Ph. tr. 1778.
Henley on conductors. Ph. tr. 1774. 133.
  In favour of points.
Henley and Haffenden on a house with a conductor that was struck. Ph. tr. 1775. 336.
Henley. Ph. tr. 1777. 85.
  Observes, that lampblack and tar act as a preservative from lightning.
Tetens über die sicherung seiner person. 8. Bützow, 1774.
Guden von der sicherheit wider die donnerstrahlen. 8. Gott. 1774.
Swift on conductors. Ph. tr. 1778. 155. 1779. 454.
  In favour of points.
Papers relative to an accident at Purfleet. Ph. tr. 1778. 232.
Musgrave's dissent from the committee. Ph. tr. 1778. 801.
  Observes, that other things being equal, points are struck farther off than balls.
*Nairne's experiments in favour of pointed conductors. Ph. tr. 1778. 823.
  Says, that other things being equal, balls are struck further off than points. Thus a point, moving swiftly under a conductor, approached nearer to it without being struck than a ball. Perhaps, however, there was time for a partial discharge in silence; if so, a point must have great power in producing such a discharge.

Verhaltungsregeln bey donnerwittern, von Lichtenberg. 8. Gotha, 1778.

Rosenthal. Goth. Mag. IV. i. 1.

Reimarus von blitz ableitungen. 8. Hamb. 1778.

Reimarus on conductors. Gilb. VI. 377.

Barbier du Tinan on conductors for buildings. Roz. XIV. 17.

Latourette on conductors at Lyons. Roz. XIX. 382.

Camus on ringing bells in storms. Roz. XIX. 398.

Camus on conductors. Roz. XXII. 223.

Bartaloni on a conductor at Sienna. A. Sienn. VI. 253.

Blagden and Nairne on the accident by lightning at Heckingham. Ph. tr. 1782. 355.

There were eight pointed conductors of iron; but the communication with moisture in the earth was perhaps impared, the conductors were rusty, and perhaps they were too distant; there was at the time a very heavy rain. A woman said she saw three balls of fire strike the house. The wall was injured, and a saddle hanging in a stable was damaged.

E. M. A. V. Art. Paratonnerre.

Buissart on a multiplicity of conductors. Roz. XXI. 140.

Gallitzin and Achard on conductors. Roz. XXII. 199.

Conductors for a powder magazine. Roz. XXII. 477.

Michaelis and Lichtenberg on conductors. Roz. XXIV. 320. XXV. 297. XXVI. 101.

Showing, that the bars which were fixed on the temple of Solomon, to keep off the birds, must have served as conductors.

Landriani dell' utilità dei conduttori. 8. Milan, 1784. R. S.

Breitinger on a conductor. Roz. XXIX. 90.

Hemmer über wetterleiter. Manh. 1786. R. I.

Hemmers verhaltungsregeln. 8. Manh. 1791.

A conductor, with means for extinguishing fire. Goth. Mag. V. iv. 148.

Lord Stanhope. Ph. tr. 1787. 130.

Recommends a number of conductors not far apart.

Geanty on conductors. Roz. XXXI. 286.

Bergmann on conductors. Opusc. VI. 110.

Leipz. Samml. zur Phys. II. 583.

The church at Genoa was struck, notwitstanding a conductor.

Bonnin on conductors. Roz. XXXII. 261.

Patterson on conductors. Am. tr. III. 321. Repert. I. 114.

Employs black lead for the points.

Nicholson. Ph. tr. 1789.

Observes, that a point, projecting from a ball, only modifies its effect, and concludes, that a sharp conductor projecting from a building can seldom act as a point, especially when the cloud is negative.

Gross Ableitungskunst. Leipz. 1796.

Regnier's conductor approved. M. Inst. IV.

Haldane on conductors. Nich. Gilb. V. 115.

Wolff on conductors. Gilb. VIII. 69.

Von Arnim on conductors. Gilb. VIII. 290.

Gilbert on relief from a stroke of lightning. Ph. M. XVII. 306.

A person struck by lightning in bed at Augusta, 25 Jan. 1803, and left senseless, was recovered by some pails of cold water, which his wife threw on him.

The point of a conductor ought to be of copper, not only as being less liable to rust, but as conducting equally well with iron of twice the dimensions.

Reimarus recommends, that all the highest parts of a house should be protected by slips of lead communicating with the ground. And this method is preferred by many to a pointed conductor.

Conductors have sometimes been fixed to sticks and umbrellas, connected with a chain which is dragged along the ground, but they can afford little or no protection.

Waterspouts, perhaps of Electrical Origin, generally accompanied by Electrical Phenomena.

Mayne on a waterspout on the river at Topsham. Ph. tr. 1695. XIX. 28.

An appletree 5 inches in diameter was cut off and thrown contrarily to the direction of the spout: an anchor was also carried several feet.

Gordon on a waterspout in the Downs. Ph. tr. 1701. XXII. 805.

Delapryme on a spout. Ph. tr. 1702. XXIII. 281.

It seemed to be produced by a concourse of winds, turning like a screw, the clouds dropping down into it: it threw trees and branches about with a gyratory motion.

Delapryme on a second spout in Lincolnshire. Ph. tr. 1703. XXIII. 1331.

It was like the first, taking thatch from the houses and lead from the church: the tube seemed to fill at both ends.

*Stuart's description of waterspouts, with figures. Ph. tr. 1702. XXIII. 1077.

Some appeared to be hollow, with water ascending in them: they began from above and from below nearly at the same time.

Richardson on a fall of water from a spout. Ph. tr. 1719. XXX. 1097.

The spout does not appear to have been seen, but 10 acres of ground were destroyed, and a cavity seven feet deep was left.

Bocanbrey on a vortex of fire rolling on the earth. A. P. 1725. H. 5.

Perhaps a waterspout with some electric light.

Harris on a waterspout. Ph. tr. 1733. XXXVIII. 75.

By estimation of the distance, its thickness must have been about 60 yards, its height ¾ of a mile. It wasted first at the lower part.

Lord Lovell. Ph. tr. 1742.

A phenomena like Bocanbrey's.

Barker on a meteor like a waterspout. Ph. tr. 1749. XLVI. 248.

A black whirling cloud that carried up water, and tore off an ash 8 inches thick: it surrounded some persons like a thick mist, whirling about and dividing itself.

Ray on a waterspout in Deeping fen, Lincolnshire. Ph. tr. 1751. 477.

It was first seen moving across the land and water of the fen: it raised the dust, broke some gates, and destroyed a field of turnips: it vanished with an appearance of fire: it was accompanied by three others.

Franklin. Ph. tr. 1765. 182. Read 1756.
Franklin on electricity.

Thinks a vacuum is made by the rotatory motion of the ascending air, as when water is running through a funnel, and that the water of the sea is thus raised. But no such cause as this could do more than produce a slight rarefaction of the air, much less raise the water to above 30 or 40 feet. At the same time the force of the wind thus excited might carry up much water in detached drops, as it is really observed to exist in waterspouts.

Swinton on a meteor seen at Oxford. Ph. tr. 1761. 99.

Forster's voyage. I. 191.

Dubourdine on a waterspout seen near the Seine. A. P. 1764. H. 32.

Brisson on a waterspout. A. P. 1767. 409. H. 11.

On a terrestrial spout. Roz. VII. 70.

Butet on a terrestrial spout. Roz. VII. 334. Fig.

Mentions a fiery cloud.

Wilke. Schw. Abh. 1780.

Goth. Mag. V. iv. 90.

Oliver on waterspouts. Am. tr. II. 101.

Observes, that water may be sucked up by a quill held at some distance above it.

Perkins on waterspouts. Am. tr. II. 335.

Michaud on a waterspout. M. Tur. 1788. IV. App. 3. Roz. XXX. 284. Nich. I. 577. Gilb. VII. 49.

Spallanzani on some waterspouts. Soc. Ital. IV. 473.

Wild on a waterspout on the lake of Geneva. Journ. Phys. XLIV. (I.) 39. Gilb. VII. 70.

Baussard on a waterspout. Journ. Phys. XLVI. (III.) 346. Gilb. VII. 73.

Wolke on a waterspout. Gilb. X. 482.

Professor Wolke gives an account of a waterspout, which passed immediately over the ship, in which he was sailing, in the Gulph of Finland: it appeared to be about 25 feet in diameter, consisting of drops about the

size of a cherry; the sea was agitated round its base through a space of about 130 feet in diameter: the relater rather supposes that the water was ascending than descending.
Cavallo. III. 306.

Thinks electricity rather a consequence than a cause of waterspouts. They sometimes vanish and reappear.

Murhard on some waterspouts. Gilb. XII. 239.

Description of a Waterspout. In a letter from WILLIAM RICKETTS, *Esq. Captain in the Royal Navy, to the* RIGHT HON. SIR JOSEPH BANKS, BART. *K.B.P.R.S. Read to the Royal Society 5th May,* 1803. *From the Journals of the Royal Institution. II.* 75.

In the month of July 1800, Captain Ricketts was suddenly called on deck, on account of the rapid approach of a waterspout, among the Lipari Islands: it had the appearance of a viscid fluid, tapering in its descent, proceeding from the cloud to join the sea: it moved at the rate of about two miles an hour, with a loud sound of rain: it passed the stern of the ship, and wetted the after part of the mainsail: hence Captain Ricketts concluded that waterspouts were not continuous columns of water: and subsequent observations confirmed the opinion.

In November 1801, about twenty miles from Trieste, a waterspout was seen eight miles to the southward; round its lower extremity was a mist, about twelve feet high, nearly of the form of an Ionian capital, with very large volutes, the spout resting obliquely on its crown. At some distance from this spout, the sea began to be agitated, and a mist rose to the height of about four feet: then a projection descended from the black cloud which was impending, and met the ascending mist about twenty feet above the sea; the last ten yards of the distance were described with a very great rapidity. A cloud of a light colour appeared to ascend in this spout like quicksilver in a glass tube. The first spout then snapped at about one third of its height, the inferior part subsiding gradually, and the superior curling upwards.

Several other projections from the cloud appeared, with corresponding agitations of the water below, but not always in spots vertically under them: seven spouts in all were formed; two other projections were reabsorbed. Some of the spouts were not only oblique but curved: the ascending cloud moved most rapidly in those which were vertical; they lasted from three to five minutes, and their dissipation was attended by no fall of rain. For some days before, the weather had been very rainy with a south easterly wind; but no rain had fallen on the day of observation.

Aurora Borealis.

Account of authors. Weigels Chemie. I. 324.

M. Berl. 1710. I. 131.
Seen in 1707.

Halley. Ph. tr. 1716. XXIX. 406.
The first that he had seen.

Halley. Ph. tr. 1719. XXX. 1099.

Barrell. Ph. tr. 1717. XXX. 584.

Folkes. Ph tr. 1717. XXX. 586.

Ph. tr. 1719. XXX. 1101. In Devonshire. 1719. XXX. 1104. At Dublin.

Hearne. Ph. tr. 1719. XXX. 1107.

Percival. Ph. tr. 1720. XXXI. 21.

At Dublin. Ph. tr. 1721. XXXI. 180.

In Devonshire. Ph. tr. 1721. XXXI. 186.

Linnae regis. Ph. tr. 1723. XXXII. 300.

Burman. Ph. tr. 1724. XXXIII. 175.

Langwith, Huxham, Hallet, Halley, and Calandrini. Ph. tr. 1726. XXXIV. 132. 150.

Langwith. Ph. tr. 1727. XXXV. 301.
With a good figure.

Dobbs. Ph. tr. 1726. XXXIV. 128.

Huxham. Ph. tr. 1750. XLVI. 472.

Meyer. C. Petr. I. 351.

Derham. Ph. tr. 1727. XXXIV. 245. 1729. XXXVI. 137.

At Lynn. Ph. tr. 1727. XXXV. 253.

Restrich. Ph. tr. 1727. XXXV. 255.

Ph. tr. 1728. XXXV. 453.

Maier. C. Petr. IV. 121.

Cramer. Ph. tr. 1730. XXXVI. 279.

Hoxton on an agitation of the needle. Ph. tr. 1731. XXXVII. 53.
It lasted an hour.

Greenwood and Lewis. Ph. tr. 1731. XXXVII. 55.

Mairan Traité de l'aurore boréale. 4. Par

1733, 2. ed. 1754. A. P. 1731. Suite. 1751. Suite.

Acc. A. P. 1732. H. 1. Ph. tr. 1734. XXXVIII. 243. by Eames.

Thinks the aurora borealis about 200 leagues above the earth: in one instance, Cramer computed the height to be 160 leagues. Supposes it derived from the sun's atmosphere, extending in some directions beyond the earth's orbit; attributes the nebulae of stars and the tails of comets to a similar substance.

Mairan's explanations. A. P. 1747. 363..423. H. 32. Account. 1751. H. 40.

On Euler's system and on his own.

Mairan observed the direction of the dipping needle to the pole of the aurora borealis. M. Young.

Weidler. Ph. tr. 1734. XXXVIII. 291.

Weidler de aurora boreali. 4.

Celsius. Ph. tr. 1736. XXXIX. 241.

Short. Ph. tr. 1740. XLI. 368.

Ph. tr. 1741. XLI. 583.

Various accounts, with a good figure.

Hevelius. Ph. tr. 1741. XLI. 744.

Mortimer, Martyn, and Neve. Ph. tr. 1741. XLI. 839, 840, 843.

Martyn. Ph. tr. 1750. XLVI. 319, 345.

Nocetus de iride et aurora boreali, cum notis Boscovich. Rom. 1747.

Miles. Ph. tr. 1750. XLVI. 346.

Baker. Ph. tr. 1750. XLVI. 499.

Winkler de vi vaporum solarium in lumine boreali. 4.

Gabrius. Ph. tr. 1751. 39.

*Wargentin. Ph. tr. 1751. 126.

Observes the effect on the compass.

Wargentin's history. Schw. Abh. 1752. 169. 1753. 85.

Bartram and Franklin. Ph. tr. 1762. 474.

Franklin's works. II.

Franklin. Roz. XIII. 409.

Bergmann. Ph. tr. 1762. 479.

Bergmann. Schw. Abh. 1764. 200, 251.

On the height of the lights.

Bergmann. Opusc. V. 272.

Swinton. Ph. tr. 1764. 326, 332. 1767. 108. A luminous arch. Ph. tr. 1769. 367. 1770. 532.

Messier. Ph. tr. 1769. 86.

Wiedeburg über die nordlichter. 8. Jena, 1771. Am. tr. I. 404.

Felbiger Wie nordlichter zu beobachten. 4. Sorau, 1772.

Winn. Ph. tr. 1774. 128..

Observes, that the lights are generally followed the day after by a storm from the S. or S. W.

Hell. Ephem. Vienn. 1777.

Hüpsch Untersuchung des nordlichts. 8. Cologn, 1778.

Van Swinden. S. E. VIII. 1780. Roz. XV. 128. A. Petr. 1780. IV. i. H. 19.

Observes, that the variation of the needle increases when the aurora borealis is approaching.

Van Swinden Recueil de mémoires. Hague, 1784. III. 173.

Cavallo on an arch which lasted more than an hour, and eclipsed the stars. Ph. tr. 1781. 329.

Peyrouse de la Coudière. Goth. Mag. I. i. 10.

E. M. Physique. Art. Aurore boréale.

Wilke von den neuesten erklärungen des nordlichts. *Schwedisches* Museum. 8. Wismar, 1783. I. 31.

König. Goth. Mag. III. ii. 175.

Blagden and Gmelin. Ph. tr. 1781. 228.

Several testimonies of a rustling noise heard with these lights.

Cramer über die entstehung des nordlichts. 8. Brem. 1785.

Acc. Goth. Mag. IV. ii. 163.

Gannet. Am. Ac. I. 237.

Eggers Beschreibung von Island. 8. Copenh. 1786.

Viano. Roz. XXXIII. 153.

Ginge. Nye Samling. Copenh. III.

Hey, Wollaston, Hutchinson, Franklin, Pi-

gott and Cavendish on luminous arches. Ph. tr. 1790. 32..47, 101.
> Cavendish thinks, that the height was between 52 and 71 miles; observes, that the diffused nature of the light may make the appearance different in different places, and thus make distant observations fallacious; says, that the common aurora borealis has been supposed to consist of parallel streams.

Libes in Rozier. June 1790. Febr. 1791. XXXVIII. 191.

Lichtenberg in Erxleben.
> Compares the aurora borealis to the excitation of the tourmalin by heat.

Dalton's meteorological observations. 8. 1793. 54, 153.
> Thinks that the apparent beams of the aurora borealis are the projections of cylindrical portions of a magnetic fluid which are actually parallel to the dipping needle, and therefore appear to converge to the magnetic pole, that the light is produced by the transmission of electricity through them, which somewhat disturbs their magnetic properties. The arches are always perpendicular to the magnetic meridian, and, being more permanent in their form, afford an opportunity of determining the height, which from one observation on a base of 22 miles, appears to be about 150 miles.

Chiminello on a luminous arch. Soc. Ital. VII. 153.

Ritter on the lunar periods of the aurora borealis. Gilb. XV. 206.

Earthquakes and Agitations. In order of time.

Account of authors. Weigels Chemie. §. 369.

An earthquake in the year 17 destroyed 12 cities in Asia.

Herculaneum destroyed in 79.

Earthquakes at Antioch in 115, 458, 526, 528, 581 and 1159.

The Thames ebbed for a whole day, 1214.

St. Paul's injured in 1580.

Boyle. Ph. tr. 1665—6. I. 179.
> Near Oxford.

Pigot. Ph. tr. 1683. XIII. 311.
> At Oxford.

Lister on earthquakes. Ph. tr. 1684. XIV. 511.
> Deduces them from pyrites.

Lima nearly destroyed in 1689: a hundred thousand perished.

Hartop and Burges. Ph. tr. 1693. XVII. 827, 830.
> In Sicily.

Bonajuto. Ph. tr. 1694. XVIII. 2.
> In Sicily, 60 men killed.

Sloane. Ph. tr. 1694. XVIII. 78.
> In Peru, 1687.

Ph. tr. 1700. XXII.
> Effects on the rivers about Batavia.

Léméry. A. P. 1700. 101. H. 54.

Thoresby. Ph. tr. 1704. XXIV. 1555.

An overflow of the sea near Avranches. A. P. 1716. H. 16.

Barrel. Ph. tr. 1727. XXXV. 305.

Colman. Ph. tr. 1729. XXXVI. 124.
> At Boston.

Cyrilli historia terraemotus Neapolitani, 1733. Ph. 1731. tr. XXXVIII. 79.

Cyrilli aeris terraeque historia, 1732. Ph. tr. 1733. XXXVIII. 184.

Lewis. Ph. tr. 1733. XXXVIII. 120.

Dudley. Ph. tr. 1735. XXXIX. 63.
> In New England.

Duke of Richmond and others. Ph. tr. 1736. XXXIX. 361.
> Sussex and elsewhere.

Temple. Ph. tr. 1740. XLI. 340.
> At Naples; the shock was slight, but it was attended by a remarkable agitation of the nervous system in all who felt it. This seems to favour the supposition that electricity is concerned.

Johnson. Ph. tr. 1741. XLI. 801.
> At Scarborough.

Plant. Ph. tr. 1742. XLII. 33.
> In New England.

Ph. tr. 1742. XLII. 77.
> Leghorn.

A great earthquake at Lima in 1746.

Forster. Ph. tr. 1748. XLV. 398.
> Taunton.

A collection of 56 letters and papers relative to earthquakes in England and elsewhere, in 1750. Ph. tr. 1750. XLVI. 601.

Stukely on the causes of earthquakes. Ph. tr. 1750. XLVI. 657, 731.
Attributes them to electricity, principally from the rapidity with which they affect extensive tracts of country.

Stukely's philosophy of earthquakes. 8. Lond. 1756. M. B.

Hales on the causes of earthquakes. Ph. tr. 1750. XLVI. 669.
Thinks them sulfureous and electrical.

Tressan on the overflow of the brook Sirkes. A. P. 1750. H. 34.

Baker. Ph. tr. 1754. 564.
At York.

At Cairo 1754. Destroyed " 40 000."

Porter. Ph. tr. 1755. 115.
At Constantinople.

Accounts of the great earthquake, 1 Nov. 1755, and of the earthquakes of 9 and 18 Nov. in 49 letters. Ph. tr. 1755. 351..436.
Destroyed the city of Lisbon.

Pye. Ph. tr. 1756. 458.
Frequent at Manilla.

Whytt. Ph. tr. 1756. 501.
At Glasgow. A shower of dust in the N. Sea.

Bonnet. Ph. tr. 1756. 511.
The 14th Nov. 1755.

Allemand. Ph. tr. 1756. 512.
The 26 Dec. 1755.

Stevenson. Ph. tr. 1756. 521.
An agitation of a lake in Dumfriesshire for 4 hours. Feb. 1756.

Accounts of the irregularities of the tides in the Thames, Feb. 1756. Ph. tr. 1756. 523. 530.

Mrs. Belcher. Ph. tr. 1756. 544.
An agitation of lake Ontario, Feb. 1756.

Grovestins. Ph. tr. 1756. 544.
Hague, Feb. 1756.

Allemand. Ph. tr. 1756. 545.

Pringle. Ph. tr. 1756. 546. At Brussels. Ph. tr. 1756. 550.
Agitations.

Warren. Ph. tr. 1756. 579.

Donati. Ph. tr. 1750. 612.
At Turin.

Ph. tr. 1756. 616.
At Brigue, by the Rector of the college.

Condamine's inferences from earthquakes. Ph. tr. 1756. 622.

Prince. Ph. tr. 1756. 642.
An agitation at Ilfracombe.

Holdsworth. Ph. tr. 1756.
An agitation at Dartmouth. 643.

Vernede. Ph. tr. 1756. 663.
Maestricht.

Affleck. Ph. tr. 1756. 668.
An agitation at Antigua.

Rutherforth. Ph. tr. 1756. 681.
Agitations in Hartfordshire.

Trembley. Ph. tr. 1756. 893.

On a shock and agitations. Ed. ess. II. 423.

Hannöv. nützl. Samml. 1756. xix.
Mayer refers earthquakes to a change of the direction of gravitation.

Bertrand Recueil de traités sur les tremblemens de terre. 8. 1756. M. B.

Bertrand Mémoire sur les tremblemens de terre. 8. Hague, 1757.

Winthorp. Ph. tr. 1757. 1.
In America, 18 Nov. 1755.

An earthquake in the Azores, 1757.
Buried " 10 000" persons.

Perry. Ph. tr. 1758. 491.
In Sumatra, 1756.

Borlase. Ph. tr. 1758. 499. 1762. 418, 507.
In Cornwall.

Burrow. Ph. tr. 1758. 614.

Paderni. Ph. tr. 1758. 619.
At Herculaneum.

Peyssonel. Ph. tr. 1758. 645.

Russel. Ph. tr. 1760. 529.
In Syria.

*Michell on the cause of earthquakes. Ph. tr. 1760. 566.
Explaining the operation of subterraneous fires at different depths: and attributing the explosions to steam.

Salvador and Molloy. Ph. tr. 1761.
> At Lisbon, 30 March 1761.

Heberden. Ph. tr. 1761. 155.
> In Madeira, 31 March.

Mason. Ph. tr. 1762. 477.
> An agitation at Barbadoes, 31 March.

Weymarn. Ph. tr. 1763. 201.
> In Siberia.

Gulston, Hirst, and Verelst. Ph. tr. 1763. 251..265.
> At Chattigaan.

Saussure. A. P. 1763. H. 18.
> An elevation of waters at Geneva.

Tucker. Ph. tr. 1764. 83.
> An irregular tide at Bristol.

Ph. tr. 1765. 43.
> At Lisbon, 1764.

Bevis's history and philosophy of earthquakes. 8.

Devisme. Ph. tr. 1769. 71.
> At Macao.

Hollmann Sylloge Comm. 1.

Wark's method of measuring earthquakes. Ed. ess. III. 142. Roz. I. 376.
> By powdering the inside of a vessel partly filled with water.

A great earthquake in Guatimala. 1774.

Henry. Ph. tr. 1778. 221.
> At Manchester, 1777. It extended 140 miles: the bells tolled twice; it was observed that most noise was heard in the neighbourhood of conductors of electricity, and some shocks were felt.

At Taurir in Persia in 1780.
> Threw down 15 000 houses.

Pennant. Ph. tr. 1781. 193.
> In Wales.

Lloyd. Ph. tr. 1781. 331.
> At Hafodunos: the barometer was not affected.

Lloyd. Ph. tr. 1783. 104.
> In Wales.

*Hamilton. Ph. tr. 1783. 169.
> Calabria.

Ippolito. Ph. tr. 1783. 209.
> Calabria.

Leone Giornale de' tremuoti. 2 v. 8. Napl. 1783.

Vivenzio Storia de' tremuoti. 4. Napl. 1783. R.S.

Pira sulla causa de' tremuoti. 4. Catan. 1783.

Sarti Congeturre su i tremoti. 8. Lucc. 1783.

Dolomieu sur le tremblement de terre de 1783.

Holm vom Erdbeben auf Island. 8. Copenh. Goth. Mag. V. iii. 128.

Wiedeburg über erdbeben und nebel.

On the fog of 1783. See Clouds and Mists.

Bartels briefe über Calabrien. 2 v. Gott. 1784.

Seybold vom erdbeben. *Hübners* phys. tageb. I. ii. Salzb. 1784.

Rozier Aug. and Sept. 1785.

Williams on earthquakes. Am. Ac. I. 260.

Stephensens schilderung von Island. Alt. 1786.

More on an earthquake in the north of England. Ph. tr. 1787. 35.

Lehmann Gedanken vom erdbeben, 8. Berl. 1787.

Fleming on an agitation of Loch Tay. Ed. tr. I. 200.

†Bertholon on a paratremblement and a paravolcan. Roz. XIV. 111.
> Conductors.

Beyträge zur kenntniss beyder Sicilien. 8. Zur. 1790. II.

Voglio on an earthquake, 1779. C. Bon. VII. O. 27.

In Cuba, 1791, with a storm.
> Destroyed 3000.

Turner. Ph. tr. 1792. 283.
> Lincolnshire.

Taylor on some shocks. Ed. tr. III. 240.

An earthquake in Turkey, April 1794.
> Destroyed 6000.

Gray. Ph. M. 1796. 353.
> The 18 Nov. 1795. The extreme places affected were Leeds, Bristol, Norwich and Liverpool; the centre, Derbyshire and Leicestershire. A very dark cloud was seen before the shock, and at the moment, a blast of wind, somewhat like an explosion, was heard. Gray thinks, the causes of earthquakes sometimes subterraneous and sometimes atmospherical.

Cavanilles. Nich. III. 377. Ph. M. V. 318. Gilb. VI. 67. In Peru, 1797.

Courrejolles on earthquakes. Journ. Phys. LIV. 103. LVII. 119. Ph. M. XII. 337.

Ph. M. X. 368.
In Scotland.

Ph. M. XV. 90.
In Transylvania.

Subterraneous Fires and Volcanos.

Account of authors. Weigel Chemie.§.369. c.

Eruption of Vesuvius that destroyed Pompeii, described by Pliny. Epist.
Herculaneum was accessible by a well in 1730, its ruins having been discovered the year before.

Robinson on a rain of ashes in the gulf of Volo. Ph. tr. 1665—6. I. 377.

Eruptions of Etna. Ph. tr. 1669. IV. 909, 1028.

Borelli historia incendii Aetnaei, anni 1669. 4. Reg. Jul. 1670. M. B.

Acc. Ph. tr. 1671. VI.

On a volcano in the island of the Palma in 1677. Hooke. Lect. Cutl. 52.
Nine or ten houses were burnt, and 300 acres of land spoiled. Palma is one of the Canaries.

Paragallo Istoria del monte Vesuvio. 4. 1689. M. B.

Account of volcanos in Ternate and elsewhere. Ph. tr. 1695. XIX. 42.

Moluccan volcanos. Ph. tr. 1697. XIX. 529.

Bianchini on a fire in the Apennines. A. P. 1706. 336.
Near Firenzuola.

Valletta de incendio Vesuviano, 1707. Ph. tr. 1713. XXVIII. 22.

Berkeley on the eruptions of Vesuvius. Ph. tr. 1717. XXX. 708.

Forster on a burning island raised out of the sea near Tercera. Ph. tr. 1722. XXXII. 100.

Nesbitt on a subterraneous fire in Kent. Ph. tr. 1727. XXXV. 307.
Three acres of a marshy field were burnt by a slow and spontaneous combustion, like that of a hay rick.

Cyrillus on an eruption of Mount Vesuvius. Ph. tr. 1732. XXXVII. 336.

Prince Cassano on an eruption of Mount Vesuvius. Ph. tr. 1739. XLI. 237. Another account. 252.

*Serao on the eruption of Vesuvius in 1737. Naples.

Shepherd on the boiling of a canal. Ph. tr. 1739. XLI. 289.
Merely from inflammable air.

Histoire du mont Vésuve. 12. Par. 1741.

Supple on the eruption of Vesuvius. Ph. tr. 1751. 315. Another account. 409.

Parker on the eruption of Vesuvius. Ph. tr. 1751. 474.

Jamineau on the eruption of Vesuvius. Ph. tr. 1755. 24.

Account of an eruption of Etna. Ph. tr. 1755. 209.

Della Torre Istoria del Vesuvio. 4. Napl. 1755.

Mitchell on a shower of black dust in Zetland. 1757. 297.

Stiles and Mackinlay on an eruption of Vesuvius. Ph. tr. 1761. 39, 44.

*Hamilton on an eruption of Vesuvius. Ph. tr. 1767. 192. 1768. 1. 1769. 18. 1780. 42.

Hamilton's journey to Etna. Ph. tr. 1770. 1.

Hamilton on the soil of Naples. Ph. tr. 1771. 1.

Hamilton's letters on volcanos. Germ. 8. Frankf. 1784.

Hamilton's Campi Phlegraei, with a supplement. f. R. S.

Hamilton on the present state of Vesuvius. Ph. tr. 1786. 365.

Hamilton on the late eruption of Vesuvius. Ph. tr. 1795. 73.
With coloured plates. The eruption was as violent as any on record, excepting those of 79 and 1631. It was expected; the crater having been nearly filled; the water had also

subsided in the wells. Ashes wet with salt water were thrown out: the ashes were very thick at Taranto, 250 miles off: a stone ten feet in diameter was thrown to an immense height, and eighteen hours afterwards, a shower of stones fell at Sienna, 250 miles off. The electricity of the atmosphere was positive; there was violent lightning, with the appearance of balls of fire bursting. A stream of lava 1300 feet wide and 24 deep destroyed Torre del Greco, and covered 3000 acres of vineyards. Twenty seven ounces of ashes were deposited on a fig branch which weighed only three; the ashes appeared to be phosphoric. A mofete, or carbonic acid gas, was emitted by the earth, and destroyed vineyards; but was in one instance successfully drained off. Much sal ammoniac was sublimed. Notwithstanding these devastations, the inhabitants of Torre del Greco, 18000 in number, unanimously refused the offer of another situation for rebuilding their town.

Hamilton and others on the eruption of 1794. Gilb. V. 408. VI. 21.

Ferbers briefe aus Wälschland. 8. Prag. 1773.

Raspe Beschreibung der Niederhessischen alten vulkanen. 8. Cassel, 1774.

Mairan on the central fire. A. P. 1765. H. 13.

Catani della Vesuviana eruzzione di 1767. Catana, 1768.

Bartaloni on volcanos. Ac. Sienn. V. 301.

A volcano in Ferro broke out in 1777.
  Threw out a quantity of red water, which discoloured the sea for several leagues.

Faujas de St. Fond sur les volcans. f. Par. 1778. R. I.

Faujas de St. Fond Minéralogie des volcans. 8. Par. 1784. R. I.

†Bertholon on a paravolcan. Roz. XIV. 111.
  A conductor.

Mourgue de Montredon on hailstones supposed to be volcanic. A. P. 1781. 754.

Gioeni on a shower of ashes. Ph. tr. 1782. 1.

Gioeni Saggio di litologia Vesuviana. 8. Napl. 1790. R. S.

Ducarla on volcanic inundations. Roz. XX. 113.

Volta on terrestrial fires, and on the Pietra mala near Florence. Soc. Ital. II. 662, 900.

Dolomieu Voyage aux isles de Lipari. Germ. 8. Leipz. 1783.

Dolomieu on the antiquity of lava. Goth. Mag. III. i. 175.

Borch Briefe über Sicilien. 60.
  On the antiquity of lava.

Deluc's letters on the history of man. II.

Collini on volcanos. Germ. 4. Dresden, 1783.

Knoll über die feuerspeyenden berge. 8. Erf. 1784.

Anderson's account of Morne Garon, in St. Vincent. Ph. tr. 1785. 16. Fig.
  Probably a recent volcano.

Williams on a remarkable darkness. Am. Ac. I. 234.

Jones and Alexander on a mountain supposed volcanic. Am. Ac. I. 312, 316.

Beroldingen über die vulkane. 8. Manh. 1791.

Arduino on an ancient volcano. Soc. Ital. VI. 102.

On the origin of basaltes. Authors quoted by Lichtenberg in Erxl. §. 787.

Stanley on the hot springs in Iceland. Ed. tr. III. 127.

Three views of the Geyser. R. S.

Cassan and Rollo on a volcano in St. Lucia. Ph. M. III. 1. 256.

Holm on the eruption in Iceland, 1783. Ph. M. III. 113. See Earthquakes.

Patrin on volcanos. Gilb. V. 191.

*On the explosion of a blast furnace at Colnebrook Dale. Ph. M. XI. 92.
  A curious illustration of volcanic eruptions.

Fortis on a shower of mud at Udina. Nich. 8. V. 101. Ph. M. XVI. 374.
  Probably from dust which had been carried up.

Humboldt on mountains and volcanos. Nich. VI. 242. See Earthquakes.

  A considerable eruption of Vesuvius happened in 1804: a still greater in 1806.

Geology.
See Geography.

Goodwin sands overflowed in 1100.

Dollort sea, between Groningen and E. Friesland, formed 1277.

Irruption of the sea at Dort, 1421.
Destroyed 72 villages and 100 000 persons.

Pleurs in Italy buried by a piece of the Alps. 1618.

Mineralogy and geology. Ph. tr. abr. II. iii. 367. IV. 2 p. iii. 205. VI. 2 p. iii. 185. VIII. 2 p. iii. 655. X. 2 p. iii. 587.

Steno on a solid within a solid. Engl. Lond. 1671.
Acc. Ph. tr. 1671. VIII. 2180.

Leibnitii protogaea. Opp. II. ii. 81.

Burneti telluris theoria sacra. 4. Lond. 1681. R. I.

Whiston's new theory of the earth. 8. Camb. R. I.

Southwell on Pen park hole. Ph. tr. 1683. XIII.

Le monde naissant. 8. Utrecht, 1686.

Ray's three physicotheological discourses. 8. Lond. 1692. 1713. R. I.

Woodwardi historia naturalis telluris. 8. Lond. 1695. R. I.

Woodward's natural history of the earth. 8. Lond. 1733.

Horsham on an irruption of a bog. Ph. tr. 1697. XIX.

Keil de theoriis Burneti et Whistoni. 8. Oxf. 1698. R. I.

Lister on coal borings. Ph. tr. 1699. XXI. 73.

†Wallis on the original junction of Dover and Calais. Ph. tr. 1701. XXII. 967.

Trees found in fens. Ph. tr. 1701. XXII. 986.

Sinking of Borge, a seat in Norway, 1702.
Became a lake 100 fathoms deep.

Sherard on a new island in the Archipelago. Ph. tr. 1708. XXVI. 67.

Bourguignon on a new island near Santerini. M. Trév. Ph. tr. 1708. XXVI. 200.

Scheuchzer on the origin of mountains. A. P. 1708. H. 30.

Buttneri rudera diluvii testes. 4. Leips. 1710. M. B.

Lord Cromartie and Sloane on mosses. Ph. tr. 1711. XXVII. 296.

Goree on the new island in the Archipelago, with a figure. Ph. tr. 1711. XXVII. 353.

Derham on subterraneous trees found near the Thames. Ph. tr. 1712. XXVII. 478.

†Bishop of Clogher on the sinking of a hole. Ph. tr. 1713. XXVIII. 267.

Sachette on the earth sinking in Kent. Ph. tr. 1716. XXIX. 469.

Musgrave de Britannia olim peninsula. Ph. tr. 1717. XXX. 589.

Le Neve on the sinking of three oaks. Ph. tr. 1718. XXX. 766.

Halley on the universal deluge, read 1694. Ph. tr. 1724. XXXIII. 118.
Refers it to a comet.

†On the ground sinking in Kent. Ph. tr. 1728. XXXV. 551.

Mairan's conjectures on the diurnal motion of the earth. A. P. 1729. 41. H. 51.

Bourguet Lettres sur les sels et les cristaux. 12. Amst. 1729. M. B.

Kluvers Geologia. 4. Hamb. 1630. R. I.

Marsigli Storia del mare.

Pardines on the ground sinking at Auvergne. Ph. tr. 1739. XLI. 272.

Moro dei marini corpi che si trovano su monti. 4. Ven. 1740. M. B.

Linnaeus on the increase of the habitable globe. Am. Acad. II. 402.

Arderon on the ground sinking in Norfolk. Ph. tr. 1745. XLIII. 52.
A hole 12 feet deep, 12½ in diameter; probably undermined by water.

† Richmond on a moving moss. Ph. tr. 1745. XLIII. 282.
Manfredini on the increased depth of the sea. Comm. Bon. II. ii. i.
Krügers geschichte der erde. 8. Halle, 1746.
Sulzer vom ursprunge der berge. 4. Zur. 1746.
Sulzer's geological conjecture. A. Berl. 1762. 90.
Manfredi on the increase of the sea. C. Bon. II. ii. 1.
Buffon. Hist. nat. I.
Donati Storia dell' Adriatico. 4. Ven. 1750.
Hollmann on marine fossils. Comm. Gott. III. 285. Syll. Comm. 170.
Borlase on the changes in the Scilly isles. Ph. tr. 1753. 55.
Borlase on submarine trees in Mount's bay. Ph. tr. 1757. 51.
Three hundred yards below the present high water mark: some roots also remain in a marshy earth.
Bertrand sur les usages des montagnes. 8. Zurich, 1754. R. I.
Bertrand Recueil sur l'histoire naturelle de la terre. 4. Avignon, 1766.
Maillet Telliamed, sur la diminution de la mer. 2 v. Hague, 1755. R. I.
Browallius om wattu minskningen. 8. Stockh. 1755.
Germ. Untersuchung von der verminderung des wassers. 8. Stockh. 1756.
Matthews on the sinking of a river near Pontipool. Ph. tr. 1756. 547.
Lehmann Geschichte von Flötzgebirgen. 8. Berl. 1756.
Braun de terrae mutationibus. 4. Petersb. 1756. M. B.
Wallerius et Eckstrand de origine montium. Ups. 1758.
Wallerius et Rude de geocosmo senescente. Ups. 1758.

Wallerius et Petharlin de diluvio universali. Ups. 1761.
Wallerius et Murbert de tellure olim non fluida. 4. Ups. 1761.
Traité du deluge. 4. Bâle, 1761.
Füchsel. Act. Acad. Mogunt. II.
Raspe Specimen historiae naturalis globi. 8. Amst. 1763.
Silberschlag Theorie der erde. 8. Berl. 1764.
Silberschlags Geogenie. 3 v. 4. Berl. 1780. Beylag Gott. 1784. (Geogonie).
King on the deluge. Ph. tr. 1764. 44.
King on a descent of ground near Folkstone. Ph. tr. 1786. 220.
King's morsels of criticism.
Dalrymple on the formation of islands. Ph. tr. 1767. 394.
Abhandlung von dem ursprunge der gebirge. 8. Leipz. 1770.
Lavoisier on the nature of water. A. P. 1770. 73, 90.
Justi Geschichte des erdkörpers. 8. Berl. 1770.
Lloyd and King on Elden Hole. Ph. tr. 1771. 250.
Walker on an eruption of the Solway moss. Ph. tr. 1772. 123.
Surprised the inhabitants of 12 villages in their beds.
Ferner on the diminution of the sea. Roz. Intr. I. 5.
Beyträge zur physischen erdbeschreibung. 5 v. 8. Brandenb. 1773 .. 1785.
Collected by Otto.
Pouget on the changes upon the coasts of Languedoc. A. P. 1775. 561.
Dicquemare on the bottom of the sea. Roz. VI. 438.
Saussure on the physical geography of Italy. Roz. VII. 19.
Saussure's geological hints. Ph. M. III. 33.
Wiedeburg Neue muthmassungen. 8. Goth. 1776.

Buffon Histoire naturelle.
Pallas sur la formation des montagnes. 4. Petersb. 1777. A. Petr. I. H. 21. Remarks. Leipz. Samml. zur Physik.
Deluc Lettres sur l'histoire de la terre et de l'homme. 5 v. 8. Hague, 1779. R. I.
*Deluc's essays, xi.
Deluc's letters to Lamétherie. Roz. XXXVII. 290, 332, 441. Roz. XLI. 221. 414.
Deluc's letter in the Monthly Review enl. June 1790. 206, and II. Append.
Deluc's letters to Blumenbach. Goth. Mag. VIII. 4. IX. 1.
Christ Geschichte des Erdkörpers. 8. Frankf. 1785.
Barbieri Storia del mare. 8. Ven. 1782.
Meister Commentat. Gott. 1782. V. M. 28. 1783. VI. M. 102.
_{On mountains and on the deluge. Derived from a supposed change of the earth's axis.}
Forster on physical geography.
Fragment über die geogonie. 4. Bresl. 1783.
Strange de' monti colonnari. 4. R. S.
Recherches sur la génération des êtres organisés. 12. Par. 1784.
_{By Serain.}
On the cavern at Gailenreuth. Schr. Berl. Naturf. V. 56.
Ferber on the antiquity of the strata of the earth. N. A. Petr. 1784.
Ferber on petrefactions. A. Berl. 1790. 148.
Ferber's travels. R. I.
Darwin. Ph. tr. 1785. 5.
_{Says, that water rises highest from the lowest strata of the earth; and infers, that the strata, which are the highest in the hills, are the lowest in the plains.}
Douglas on the antiquity of the earth. 4. Lond. 1785. R. S.
Trebra vom innern der gebirge. f. Dessau, 1785.
Trebra sur l'intérieur des montagnes. Par. 1787. R. S.
Kant's theory. Berl. monatschr. 1785. i. 210.

Spallanzani's travels. R. I.
Lincoln's geological observations. Am. Ac. I. 372.
Camper on some petrefactions. Ph. tr. 1786. 443.
Whitehurst on the original state of the earth. 4. Lond. 1786. 1792. R. I.
Fossombroni on alluvions. Soc. Ital. III. 533.
Brighton blockhouse carried away by the sea in 1786.
Heidinger Eintheilung der gebirgsarten. 4. Dresden, 1787.
Limbird on a well at Boston. Ph. tr. 1787. 50.
Werner Kurze classification der gebirgsarten. 4. Dresd. 1787.
*Werner über die gänge. 12.
Werner on metallic veins. Roz. XL. 354. 469. Separate. R. I.
Theory of the earth. 8. R. S.
Lamétherie Théorie de la terre. 5 v. 8.
Lamétherie's answer to Deluc. Roz. XLI.437.
Herders ideen zur geschichte der menscheit. II.
Hutton's theory of the earth. Ed. tr. I. 209.
Hutton on some appearances near Arthur's seat. Ed. tr. II. 3.
Hutton's system. Roz. XLIII. 3.
Ousley on the moving of a bog. Ir. tr. 1788. II. 3.
Lavoisier on the strata deposited by the sea. A. P. 1789. 351.
A geological question. Roz. XXXIV. 401.
Mills on the strata in Ireland and Scotland. Ph. tr. 1790. 73.
Pini's geological essays. Soc. Ital. V. 163. VI. 389.
_{The Neptunian theory.}
Pini sopra i monti. 4. R. S.
On fossil bones. *Blumenbach* Beyträge zur naturgeschichte. 8. Gott. 1790. I. B. B.
Walch on the deluge. Blumenb. Beytr. zur naturgeschichte. I. 17. 8.
Burrows's theory. As. res. II. App.

Catcott on Penpark hole. 8. Bristol, 1792. R.S.

Dolomieu on Egypt. Roz. XLII.

Otto Naturgeschichte des meeres. 2 v. 4. Berl. 1792.

Franklin's conjecture on the earth. Am. tr. III. 1, 10. Europ. Mag. Aug. 1793. Götting. taschencalender, 1795.

Sinking of the ground in Finland, 1793.
_{A piece, of the extent of 4000 square ells, sunk 15 fathoms.}

Outram on some singular balls of limestone. Ph. tr. 1796. 350.

Account of the bones found in the caves of Bayreuth, with Hunter's observations. Ph. tr. 1794. 402.

Tait on peat mosses. Ed. tr. III. 266.

Latrobe on sand hills. Am. tr. IV. 439.

Pallas on an eruption of mud. N. A. Petr. 1794. XII. 44.

Gough on the decrease of the lakes. Manch. M. IV. 1.
Thinks that many vallies and bogs have formerly been lakes.

Beddoes on flints. Manch. M. IV. 303.

Wilse on a fall of earth in Norway. Zach. Ephem. I. 545.
With a map.

Aikin's geological observations. Nich. I. 220. III. 285.

Kirwan on the primitive state of the globe. Ir. tr. VI. 233.

*Kirwan's geological essays. 8. Lond. 1799. R. I.

Kirwan on the Huttonian theory. Ir. tr. VIII. 3. Nich. IV. 97. Gilb. VIII. 109.

Kirwan's remarks on the declivities of mountains. Ir. tr. VIII. 35. Ph. M. VIII. 29. Nich. 8. IV. 256.
Observes, that the direction of most mountains is from E. to W. that the S. and S. E. sides are steepest; and supposes that the primitive forms were traced by a current running from W. to E. and that these were modified by a current running from N. to S.

Kirwan's reply to Playfair. Ph. M. XIV. 1, 14.

Correa de Serra on a submarine forest. Ph. tr. 1799. 145.
On the east coast of England.

Bertrand on the theory of the earth. Journ. Phys. XLIX. 120. L. 88.

Lowenorn on a new island near Iceland. Ph. M. V. 286.

On a new island in the sea of Azof. Ph. M. VII. 91.

Howard's letters on the creation and deluge. Lond. 1797. R. I.

Humboldt's geological sketch of South America. Journ. Phys. LIII. 61. Ph. M. XVII. 347.

Playfair's illustration of the Huttonian theory. 8. Edinb. 1802. R. I.

Lamarck Hydrogéologie. 8. Par. 1802. R. S.

Wrede on the supposed remains of the city Vineta. Zach. Mon. corr. V. VI.

Reimarus über die bildung des erdbodens. Hamb. 1802.
Acc. Zach. Mon. corr. VII. 180.
Remarks on Deluc's opinion.

Heim on the primitive state of the earth. Zach. Mon. corr. VI. 528.

Jameson on deposits and petrefactions. Nich. 8. III. 13.

Gy's geological ideas. Journ. Phys. LVII. 109.

Hall on whinstone. Ed. tr. V. 43.

Gr. Watt on the texture of basalt. Ph. tr. 1804. 279.

Parkinson's organic remains. 4. Lond. 1804. R. I.

On a hill raised in a lake. Gilb. XVI. 384.
In a mossy soil in Holstein.

Richardson on the Huttonian theory. Ir. tr. IX. 429.

Luminous Meteors.

Account of authors. Weigel Chemie. I. 327.

Exhalations.

Spontaneous light from decomposition. See Physical Optics.

Llwyd. Ph. tr. 1694. XVIII. 49, 223.

Account of some ricks of hay burnt in December 1693, at Dolgelly, by a vapour like a weak blue flame coming from the sea.

Bianchini on a fire in the Apennines. A. P. 1706. 336.

*Derham and Beccaria on the ignis fatuus. Ph. tr. 1729. XXXVI. 204.

Derham thinks it a vapour on fire; he saw one frisking about a dead thistle, it was disturbed by the slightest motion of the air. Beccari says, that in the neighbourhood of Bologna, they sometimes divide and meet again, and give out sparks; that they are most common in rain or snow, which may perhaps be because the vapour is forced out of the earth as the water sinks into it; that they are not actually on fire, but are rather of the nature of cold phosphori; that when a horse is crossing a muddy place in hot weather, a flame often rises in his footsteps: that the meteor often appears near brooks and in clayey soils; and that one in particular seemed fixed to a certain spot, about two feet above some stones near a river, but disappeared when the observer came close to it, nearly in the same manner as a mist is seldom seen where it is very near to us.

More. Ph. tr. 1750. XLVI. 466. On the fire at Firenzuola. See Volcanos.

Shaw's travels. 4. Lond. 1754. 334.

Trebra. Deutscher Merkur. Octob. 1783.

Atmospherical Meteors and Shooting Stars.

Wallis on an igneous meteor. Ph. tr. 1677. XII. 863.

Thoresby. Ph. tr. 1711. XXVII. 322.

Halley on some extraordinary meteors. Ph. tr. 1714. XXIX. 159.

Account of a phenomenon seen in the sea. Ph. tr. 1716. XXIX. 429.

Halley on a meteor seen throughout England. Ph. tr. 1719. XXX. 978.

It exploded with a great report; it must have been 60 miles high, and have passed over 300 geographical miles in a minute.

Cotes on a great meteor. Ph. tr. 1720. XXXI. 66.

Vievar on an explosion in the air. Ph. tr. 1739. XLI. 288.

Crocker, Bevis, and Breintnall on meteors. Ph. tr. 1740. XLI. 346, 359.

Short on several meteors. Ph. tr. 1741. XLI. 625.

Lord Beauchamp, Fuller, and Gostling on a fire ball. Ph. tr. 1741. XLI. 871, 872.

Gostling. Ph. tr. 1742. XLII. 60.

Mason on a fire ball. Ph. tr. 1742. XLII. 1.

Cooke. Ph. tr. 1742. XLII. 25.

Gordon and Gostling. Ph. tr. 1742. XLII. 58, 60.

Milner. Ph. tr. 1742. XLII. 138.

A luminous track remained long after the meteor; there was also a black cloud.

Lord Lovell on a fiery whirlwind. Ph. tr. 1742. XLII. 183. See Waterspouts.

Cradock on a fiery meteor. Ph. tr. 1744. XLIII. 78.

Costard on a fiery meteor. Ph. tr. 1745. XLIII. 522.

Smith and Barker on a fire ball. Ph. tr. 1751. 1, 3.

Hirst on a fire ball. Ph. tr. 1754. 773.

Forster, Colebrooke, and Dutton. Ph. tr. 1759. 299, 301.

*Pringle on the accounts of a meteor. Ph. tr. 1759. 259.

Birch. Ph. tr. 1761. 6.

In New England.

Silberschlag Theorie der feuerkugeln von 1762. 4. Magdeb. 1764.

Winthrop. Ph. tr. 1764. 185.

Very high, as usual.

Swinton. Ph. tr. 1764. 326.

*Leroy on a meteor. A. P. 1771. 668. H. 30.

It appears to have been formed over the coasts of England: it was at first more than 18 leagues high: it described in 10″ more than 60 leagues. Does not think the appearances electric. Pringle thought they were substances revolving round the earth.

Brydone on a fiery meteor. Ph. tr. 1773. 163.

*Cavallo on a meteor seen 18 Aug. 1783, at Windsor. Ph. tr. 1784. 108.

With a figure. From the time at which the report was heard it was supposed to be 56½ miles high, 1070 yards in diameter, and over Lincolnshire.

Clapp on meteors above the atmosphere. 4. R. S.

Aubert on two meteors. Ph. tr. 1784. 112.

The first, 18 Aug. moved in a waving line, and from concurring observations seemed to be 40 or 50 miles high.

Cooper and Edgeworth on a meteor, 18 Aug. Ph. tr. 1784. 116, 118.

*Blagden on some late fiery meteors. Ph. tr. 1784. 201.

The meteor seemed to deviate to the E. and to resume its direction; its height was about 50 miles: it was observed by many persons that a whizzing was heard at the instant that it passed. It moved at least 20 miles in a second: a velocity too great for a revolving body; hence there is reason to suppose its nature electrical. More than half the igneous meteors that have been observed, have moved nearly in the direction of the magnetic meridian. The author conjectures that W. Greenland, having become more icy in the course of years, has had an effect on the distribution of the electric fluid, and the electric fluid on the place of the magnetic meridian.

Pigott on the meteor of 18 Aug. seen near York. Ph. tr. 1784. 457.

Makes its height about 41 miles, its distance about 120, S. S. E.

Bernstorff. Roz. XXIV. 112.

The 18 Aug. 1783.

Rittenhouse. Amer. tr. II.

Barletti. Soc. Ital. III. 331.

Seen 11 Sept. 1784.

Franklin. Manch. M. II. 357.

Suspects that the fog of 1783 may possibly have been produced by smoke " from the consumption by fire of some of those great burning balls or globes which we happen to meet with in our rapid course round the sun, and which are sometimes seen to kindle and be destroyed in passing our atmosphere."

Lettere fisicometeorologiche. 8. Turin, 1789.

Lüdicke on large igneous meteors. Gilb. I. 10.

Baudin. Ph. M. II. 225. Gilb. XIII. 346.

Fulda. Ph. M. III. 66.

Benzenberg and Brandes on the height of falling stars. Gilb. VI. 224. X. 242.

They were observed from a base of 46200 feet F. or 2.1 German geographical miles, 15 of which make a degree: their height was from 4 to 30 of those miles; the mean height about 11, or near 50 English miles. The velocity of two of them was from 4 to 6 miles, or about 22 English miles in a second. One was brighter than Jupiter, and was 450 miles distant.

In the second paper Dr. Benzenberg gives two instances in detail. Septem. 15. A shooting star of the fifth magnitude. Elevation of the beginning 7.7 geographical miles, of the end 8.2. Length of the path 1.5 miles. Longitude of the place of disappearance 28° 3′; Latitude 53° 22′. Observed by Brandes, in Ekwarden, and Benzenberg, in Ham, near Hamburg: length of the base 14 miles. October 3. Another of the fourth magnitude observed by the same persons. The termination 7.1 geographical miles above the earth. Longitude 27° 7′; Latitude 53° 5′. These observations show, says Dr. Benzenberg, that a long base will furnish as accurate a comparison as a shorter one; that even meteors of the fourth and fifth magnitude may be seen at places distant above fourteen geographical miles from each other; and they confirm the former observations made at Gottingen with a base of but one or two miles. Dr. Pottgiesser, in Elberfeld, forty miles distant from Hamburg, saw a meteor on the 2nd of October, in the zenith, which appears to have been the same as was seen at Hamburg in the horizon; its height is estimated at 25 German miles. It was intended to continue these observations with unremitting assiduity.

Benzenberg on the nature of falling stars. Gilb. XIV. 46.

Thinks them too numerous to be bodies revolving independently of the earth.

An igneous meteor preceded by a cloud. Gilb. XI. 478.

Hardenberg on igneous meteors. Gilb. XIII. 250.

Droysen on a meteor. Gilb. XIII. 370.

Wrede on igneous meteors. Gilb. XIV. 55. XV. 111.

A meteor seen at once in Cumana and in Germany. Gilb. XV. 109.

Account of a meteor seen 13 Nov. 1803. Nich. VI. 279.
To me this meteor appeared smaller than is represented in most of the accounts of it.

Farey on a meteor, 13 Nov. Nich. VII. 66.

Firminger on a meteor. Ph. M. XVII. 279.
With a good figure.

Prévost on a meteor. To be published, S. E.

Meteors which have fallen to the Ground.

Barham on a fiery meteor in Jamaica. Ph. tr. 1718. XXX. 837.
It struck into the earth and made several deep holes.

Halley's conjectures. Ph. tr. 1719. XXX. n. 360.

Wasse on the effects of lightning. Ph. tr. 1725. XXXIII. 367.
At Mixburg in Northamptonshire, a fire ball was seen to burst, and two holes were made about a yard deep and five inches in diameter, in a gravelly soil: an iron ball shot perpendicularly from a mortar did not make a greater impression. Mr. Wasse's nephew searched the holes, and in one he found a very hard glazed stone, ten inches long, six wide, and four thick, cracked into two pieces: a man was killed by what is called the lightning; he was much wounded, with some appearance of electric effects.

Cook on a ball of sulfur supposed to be generated in the air. Ph. tr. 1738. XL. 427.
It was found in a meadow after thunder; it was covered with crystals.

Falconet on the boetilia. *Mémoires* de l'Académie des Inscriptions. 4. Paris.

Zahn specula physicomathematicohistorica.

Gemma fisica sotterranea.

De Celis on a mass of native iron found in South America. Ph. tr. 1788. 37.
At Otumpa, in the chaco Gualamba, far from any mines or rocks; weighing about 300 quintals: supposed to be of volcanic origin. There was another piece of an arborescent form.

Account of a mass of iron in South America like the Siberian. A. P. 1787. H. 8.
Nine feet by 6, and 1 foot thick.

*Chladni on the Siberian iron. Riga, 1794. Ph. M. II. 337.

Chladni on meteoric stones. Gilb. XIII. 350.

Chladni's chronology of fallen stones. Gilb. XV. 307.
Agrees with Benzenberg, that shooting stars must be of a different nature, since these sometimes appear to ascend.

Hamilton. Ph. tr. 1795. 103.
A shower of stones fell at Sienna 18 hours after the eruption of Vesuvius.

King's remarks on stones said to have fallen from the clouds. 4. Lond. 1796.

Southey's travels.
Mentions stones that fell in Portugal, Feb. 1796.

Baudin. Ph. M. II. 225.

*Fulda on fireballs. Ph. M. III. 66, 171.

Tata on the shower of stones at Sienna. Gilb. VI. 156.

Howard on stony and metalline substances which are said to have fallen on the earth. Ph. tr. 1802. 168. Nich. 8. II. 216. Gilb. XIII. 291.

On stones that have fallen. Gilb. X. 502.

Greville on stones that have fallen in France, and a lump of iron that fell in India. Ph. tr. 1803. 200. Nich. VI. 187.

Izarn Lithologie atmosphérique. Paris, 1803. Acc. Gilb. XV. 437.

Lalande. Journ. Phys. LV. 451. Gilb. XIII. 343.

Account of a meteor that fell near the Mississippi. Ph. M. XI. 191.

Laplace's conjecture on the lunar origin of stones. Zach. Mon. corr. VI. 276. Gilb. XIII. 353.

Olbers on the fall of stones. Zach. Mon. corr. VII. 148. Gilb. XIV. 38. Ph. M. XV. 289.
Had suggested Laplace's idea in 1795.

†Patrin's remarks on Howard. Gilb. XIII. 328.

Klaproth's analysis of meteoric stones. Gilb. XIII. 337.
<small>Confirms Howard's conclusions. Finds that terrestrial native iron contains no nickel.</small>

Biot on meteoric stones. B. Soc. Phil. Gilb. XIII. 353. Ph. M. XVI. 217.

Biot on stones that fell near Aigle. B. Soc. Phil. n. 76. Nich. VI. 135. Gilb. XV. 74. XVI. 44.

Beauford. Ph. M. XIV. 148.

Salverte and Vauquelin. Ann. Ch. XLV. 62, 225. Ph. M. XV. 346, 354. Gilb. XV. 419.
<small>Vauquelin confirms Howard's conclusions.</small>

Fourcroy on the stones which fell near Aigle. Ph. M. XVI. 299.

St. Amand on stones that fell in Gascony in 1790. Gilb. XV. 429.

On a stone that fell in Provence, Oct. 1803. Gilb. XVI. 72.

Drée. Journ. Phys. LVI. 380, 405. Ph. M. XVI. 217, 289.

G. B. on the lunar origin of meteors. Nich. 8. III. 255. V. 201.

Poisson's calculations. Extr. by Biot. B. Soc. Phil. n. 71.

Ritter on the terrestrial origin of stones that have fallen. Gilb. XVI. 221.
<small>Infers it from the meteorological phenomena: observes an analogy with the aurora borealis.</small>

Lalande on stones which have fallen. Ph. M. XVII. 228.

Bourdon on a shower of stones. Ph. M. XVII. 271.

Account of a stone which fell near Glasgow. Ph. M. XVIII. 371.
<small>It was seen and heard to fall into a drain; splashed about the water and mud; penetrated 18 inches, and made a hole 15 inches in diameter; forcing its way into a sand stone rock: no warmth could however be perceived in it.</small>

From the Journals of the Royal Institution. II. 16.

It had long been conjectured by several persons in this country, that the stones said to have fallen from the air, on different parts of the earth, and lately analysed by Mr. Howard, might originally have been emitted by lunar volcanos facing the earth; and meeting with little or no resistance from the moon's atmosphere, might have risen to such a height, as to be more powerfully attracted by the earth than by the moon, and of consequence, to be compelled to continue their course, until they arrived at the confines of our atmosphere, and were again retarded by its resistance.

The idea has been lately renewed in France by Laplace; and the inflammation and combustion of the stones has been attributed to the intense heat, which must necessarily be extricated, by so great a compression of the air, as would be produced by the velocity with which these bodies must enter the atmosphere.

Mr. Biot has calculated, that an initial velocity, about five times as great as that which a cannon ball sometimes receives, would be sufficient for the projection of a body from a lunar volcano into the limits of the earth's superior attraction, which are situated at nearly one ninth of the distance of the earth from the moon.

A body, entering the atmosphere with such a velocity, would soon experience a resistance many thousand times greater than its weight, and the velocity would therefore soon be very considerably lessened. It has already been shown (Journals I. 152), that a stone of moderate dimensions could scarcely retain a velocity of above 200 feet in a second. With respect, however, to the actual probability of the stones in question having been projected from the volcanos of the moon, there will, perhaps, long be a diversity of opinions.

NATURAL HISTORY IN GENERAL.

*Account of authors. Dryander Catalogus Bibliothecae historiconaturalis Josephi Banks. 5 v. 8. Lond. 1798.

Ph. tr. and A. P. Particular references in natural history are omitted.

Bonnet sur les corps organisés. 2 v. 8. Amst. 1768.

Abrégé des transactions philosophiques. Histoire naturelle. 2 v. 8. Par. 1787.

Linnaei systema naturae. R. I.

Buffon Histoire naturelle, par Sonnini. 96 v. 8. R. I.

Shaw's naturalist's miscellany. 8. Lond. R. S.

Transactions of the Linnean society. 4. Lond. 1791... R. I.

Dictionnaire d'histoire naturelle. Par. 1803... R. I.

Density of particular Substances.

Tables of specific gravities. Ph. tr. 1685. XV. 926, 927. 1693. XVII. 694.

Ellicott on the specific gravity of diamonds. Ph. tr. 1745. XLIII. 468.

Leutmann on the specific gravity of fluids. C. Petr. V. 273.

*Davies's tables of specific gravities. Ph. tr. 1748. XLV. 418. Abr. X. 206.
Very copious, with an account of the authors.

Musschenb. Introd. II. 536.

Brisson on the specific gravities of metals. A. P. 1772. ii. 1. H. 30.

Brisson Pésanteur specifique des corps. 4. Par. 1787. R. I.

Watson on the specific gravities of salts and solutions. Ph. tr. 1770. 336.

Roy on compressed air. Ph. tr. 1777.

Kirwan on the specific gravities of saline substances. Ph. tr. 1781. 7. 1782. 179.

Kirwan's mineralogy. Ed. 2.

Gilpin on the mixtures of spirit and water. Ph. tr. 1794. 275.

Prony Architecture hydraulique.

Cavallo's Natural Philosophy. II. 74.

A Table of Specific Gravities.

Principally from Davies and Lavoisier. Davies's table is compiled with great diligence from many different authors; Lavoisier's is chiefly extracted from Brisson; it is carried to four places of decimals, but little dependence can be placed on the last.

Mineral Productions. Solids

Platina, purified	19.5000
hammered	20.3366
Platina, wire	21.0417
Platina, laminated	22.0690
Pure Gold, cast	19.2581
hammered	19.3617
Gold 22 carats fine, of the standards of London and of Paris, cast	17.4863
hammered	17.5894
French gold coin 21 11/12 carats fine, cast	17.4022
coined	17.6474
French trinket gold, 20 carats fine, cast	15.7090
hammered	15.7746
Mercury	13.5681
Lead, cast	11.3523
Litharge	6.30
Pure silver, cast	10.4743
hammered	10.5107
Parisian silver, 11 den. 10 gr. fine, cast	10.1752
hammered	10.3765
French silver coin, 10 den. 21 gr. fine, cast	10.0476
hammered	10.4077
Bismuth, cast	9.8227
Copper, cast	8.7880
wire	8.8785
Brass, cast	8.3958
Brass wire	8.5441
Cobalt, cast	7.8119
Nickel, cast	7.8070
Iron, cast	7.2070
Bar iron	7.7880
Steel, hard, not screwed	7.8163
screwed	7.8180
soft, not screwed	7.8331
screwed	7.8404
Loadstone	4.80
Haematite	4.20
Tin, cast	7.2914
screwed	7.2994
Zinc, cast	7.1908
Antimony, cast	6.7021
Glass of antimony	4.9464
Crude antimony	4.0643
Tungstein	6.0665
Arsenic, cast	5.7633
Molybdena	4.7385
Ponderous spar	4.4300
Jargon of Ceylon	4.4161
Oriental ruby	4.2833
Spinelle ruby	3.7600
Ballas ruby	3.6458
Brasilian ruby	3.5311
Pseudotopaz	4.27
Bohemian garnet	4.1881

Syrian garnet	4.0000	Jasper, red	2.6612
Sapphir of Puy	4.0769	White antique alabaster	2.7302
Oriental sapphir	3.9941	Rhombic calcarious spar	2.7151
Sapphir of Brasil	3.1307	Pyramidal calcarious spar	2.7141
Oriental topaz	4.0106	Slate	2.6718
Saxon topaz	3.5640	Pitch stone, red	2.6695
Brasillian topaz	3.5365	blackish	2.3191
Emery	4.09	yellow	2.0860
Hyacinth	3.6873	black	2.0499
Beryl, or oriental aquamarine	3.5489	Onyx pebble	2.6644
Occidental aquamarine	2.722	Transparent chalcedony	2.6640
Diamond, rose coloured	3.5310	Red Egyptian granite	2.6541
white	3.5212	Pure rock crystal	2.6530
lightest	3.501	Amorphous quartz	2.6471
Manganese, crude	3.53	Agate onyx	2.6375
Black schorl, crystallized	3.3852	Carnelian	2.6137
amorphous	2.9225	Sardonyx	2.6025
Flint glass	3.3293	Purbeck stone	2.601
White glass	2.8922	White flint	2.5941
Bottle glass	2.7325	Blackish flint	2.5817
Green glass	2.6423	Oriental agate	2.5901
Glass of St. Gobin	2.4882	Prase	2.5805
Fluor, red	3.1911	Portland stone	2.570
green	3.1817	Whetstone of Auvergne	2.5638
violet	3.1757	Red zeolithe	2.4868
blue	3.1688	Crystallized zeolithe	2.0833
white	3.1555	Millstone	2.4835
Black and white hone	3.1311	Paving stone	2.4158
White hone	2.8763	Touchstone	2.4153
Granitello	3.0626	Chinese porcelain	2.3847
Green serpentine of Dauphiné	2.9883	Porcelain of Limoges	2.3410
Green serpentine	2.8960	Porcelain of Seves	2.1457
Ophite	2.9722	Lapis obsidianus	2.3480
Green jade	2.9660	Selenite	2.322
White jade	2.9502	Sulfate of potash	2.250
Black mica	2.9004	Sulfate of soda	2.200
Basaltes, from the Giant's causeway	2.8642	Grindstone	2.1429
Basaltes from Auvergne	2.4153	Salt	2.130
White Parian marble	2.8376	Native sulfur	2.0332
Green marble	2.7417	Melted sulfur	1.9907
Red marble	2.7242	Transparent sulfur	1.950
White marble of Carrara	2.7168	Nitre	2.000
Jasponyx	2.8160	Brick	2.000
Chrysolith	2.7821	Alabaster	1.874
Chrysolith of Brasil	2.6923	Plumbago	1.86
Peruvian emerald	2.7755	Sulfate of zinc	1.850
Red porphyry	2.7651	Alum	1.720
Jasper, grey	2.7640	Borax	1.715
violet	2.7111	Sulfate of iron	1.700
yellow	2.7101	Asphaltum	1.400
brown	2.6911	Scotch coal	1.300

CATALOGUE.—NATURAL HISTORY, SPECIFIC GRAVITIES.

Newcastle coal	1.270	
Staffordshire coal	1.240	
Jet	1.238	
Ice, probably	.930	
Pumice stone	.9145	

Liquids.

Sulfuric acid,	1.8409
Ph. Lond.	1.850
Nitrous acid, Ph. Lond.	1.550
Nitric acid	1.2175
Solution of salt	1.244
Water 27, salt 10	1.240
Water 3, salt 1	1.217
Water 12, salt 1	1.060
Water of the dead sea	1.2403
Sea water	1.0263
Solution of caustic soda	1.200
Muriatic acid	1.1940
Water of the Seine, filtered	1.0015
Naphtha	.708

Substances partly Mineral. Solids.

Acetite of lead	2.700
Tartrite of antimony	2.100
Muriate of ammonia	1.400

Liquids.

Sulfuric ether	.7394
Nitric ether	.9088
Muriatic ether	.7298

Elastic Fluids.

	Kirwan.	Lavoisier. Barometer 30. Thermom. 52°.
Sulfureous acid gas	2.265	
Carbonic acid gas	1.500	.00176
Nitrous gas	1.194	
Hepatic gas	1.106	
Oxygen gas	1.103	.00137
Atmospheric air	1.000	.00128
Nitrogen gas	.985	.00120
Ammoniacal gas	.600	
Hydrogen gas	.084	.000096

Vegetable Productions.

Crystals of tartar	1.850
Extract of liquorice	1.7228
Opopanax	1.6226
White sugar	1.606
Solution of potash	1.570
Gum arabic	1.4523
Honey	1.450
Catechu	1.3980
Aloes, socotrine	1.3795
Aloes, hepatic	1.3586
Bdellium	1.3717
Myrrh	1.3600
Pomegranate tree	1.3540
Cocoa shell	1.345
Opium	1.3366
Lignum vitae	1.3330
Box, Dutch	1.328
French	.912
Asafoetida	1.3275
Tragacanth	1.3161
Ivy gum	1.2948
Scammony, from Smyrna	1.2743
from Aleppo	1.2354
Sarcocolla	1.2684
Myrrh	1.250
Guaiacum	1.2289
Gamboge	1.2210
Resin of jalap	1.2185
Galbanum	1.2120
Gum ammoniac	1.2071
Dragon's blood	1.2045
Sagapenum	1.2008
Lignum nephriticum	1.200
Ebony	1.177
Olibanum	1.1732
Heart of oak, 60 years old	1.1700
Dry oak	.932
Pitch	1.150
Copal, opaque	1.1398
transparent	1.0452
Euphorbium	1.1244
Storax	1.1098
Oil of sassafras	1.094
Benzoin	1.0924
Sandarac	1.0920
Yellow amber	1.0780
Mastic	1.0742
Yellow resin	1.0727
Frankincense	1.071
Mahogany	1.063
Acetic acid	1.0626
Oil of cinnamon	1.0439
Anime, occidental	1.0426
oriental	1.0284
Malmsey Madeira	1.0382
Oil of cloves	1.0363
Gall nuts	1.034
Elemi	1.0182
Cider	1.0181
Distilled vinegar	1.0095
Water at 60°	1.0000

CATALOGUE.—NATURAL HISTORY, SPECIFIC GRAVITIES.

Extract from Mr. Gilpin's Table. Ph. tr. 1794.

Water.	Alcohol.	at 30°.	40°.	50°.	60°.	70°.	80°.
10	0	1.00774	1.00094	1.00068	1.00000	.99894	.99759
10	1	.98804	.98795	.98745	.98654	.98527	.98367
10	2	.98108	.98033	.97920	.97771	.97596	.97385
10	3	.97635	.97472	.97284	.97074	.96836	.96568
10	4	.97200	.96967	.96708	.96437	.96143	.95826
10	5	.96719	.96434	.96126	.95804	.95469	.95111
10	6	.96209	.95879	.95534	.95181	.94813	.94431
10	7	.95681	.95328	.94958	.94579	.94193	.93785
10	8	.95173	.94802	.94414	.94018	.93616	.93201
10	9	.94675	.94295	.93897	.93493	.93076	.92646
10	10	.94222	.93827	.93419	.93002	.92580	.92142
9	10	.93741	.93341	.92919	.92499	.92069	.91622
8	10	.93191	.92783	.92358	.91933	.91493	.91046
7	10	.92563	.92151	.91723	.91287	.90847	.90385
6	10	.91847	.91428	.90997	.90549	.90104	.89639
5	10	.91023	.90596	.90160	.89707	.89252	.88781
4	10	.90054	.89617	.89174	.88720	.88254	.87776
3	10	.88921	.88481	.88030	.87569	.87105	.86622
2	10	.87585	.87134	.86676	.86208	.85736	.85248
1	10	.85957	.85507	.85042	.84568	.84092	.83603
0	10	.83896	.83445	.82977	.82500	.82023	.81530

Bourdeaux wine	.9939	Alder	.8000
Burgundy wine	.9915	Elm	.800
Liquid turpentine	.9910		to .600
Camphor	.9887	Apple tree	.7930
Oil of mint	.975	Plumb tree	.7550
Oil of nutmeg	.948		to .663
Medlar tree	.9440	Indigo	.7690
Linseed oil	.9403	Maple	.7550
Oil of caraway	.940	Cherry tree	.7150
Oil of marjoram	.940	Quince tree	.7050
Oil of spike	.936	Orange tree	.7050
Oil of rosemary	.934	Walnut	.6710
Elastic gum	.9335	Pear tree	.6610
Oil of poppy seed	.9288	Fir, yellow	.657
Olive wood	.9276	white	.569
Oil of beech mast	.9176	Male fir	.5500
Oil of almonds	.9170	Female fir	.4980
Olive oil	.9153	Cypress	.6440
Logwood	.913	Lime tree	.6040
Rape oil	.913	Filbert wood	.6000
Balsam of Tolu	.896	Arnotto	.5950
Oil of lavender	.8938	Willow	.5850
Oil of oranges	.888	Cedar	.5608
Essential oil of turpentine	.8697	Juniper wood	.556
Acetic ether	.8664	White Spanish poplar	.5294
Beech	.8520	Poplar	.3830
Ash	.8430	Sassafras wood	.482
Yew, Spanish	.8070	Cork	.2400
Dutch	.7880		

Animal Substances.

Pearl	2.750	Mare's milk	1.0346
Coral	2.680	Goat's milk	1.0341
Sheep's bone, recent	2.222	Cow's milk	1.0324
Oyster shell	2.092	Woman's milk	1.0203
Ivory	1.917	Whey of cow's milk	1.0193
Stag's horn	1.875	Wax, white	.9686
Ox's horn	1.840	yellow	.9648
Blade bone of an ox	1.656	Lard	.9478
Lac	1.1390	Spermaceti	.9433
Isinglass	1.111	Butter	.9423
Egg of a hen	1.090	Tallow	.9419
Human blood	1.053	Fat of hogs	.9368
Blood, buff coat	1.056	of veal	.9342
serum	1.028	of mutton	.9235
red globules	1.126	of beef	.9232
Ewe's milk	1.0409	Ambergrease	.9263
Asses milk	1.0355	Lamp oil	.9233
		Solution of pure ammonia	.8970

A Table of the Capacity of different Substances for Heat.

Taken principally, with corrections, from Dr. Thomson's table, which was compiled and reduced from Crawford, Kirwan, Wilke, Lavoisier, Bergmann, and others.

	Heat in equal wts.	Heat in equal volumes.
Hydrogen gas.	21.400	.0021
Oxygen gas	4.749	.0065
Kirwan	.87	
(Carbonate of ammonia	1.85)	
Atmospheric air	1.790	.0021
Varying nearly as the 8th root of the density. Y.		
Nitrogen gas	.704	.0008
Steam	1.550	.0006
Arterial blood	1.030	
Venous blood	.893	
Water	1.000	1.000
Cow's milk	1.000	1.032
Sulfuret of ammonia	.994	.813
Ice	.900	
Nitric acid	.844	
Nitrous acid	.576	.780
Sulfate of magnesia 1, water 8	.844	
Salt 1, water 8	.832	
Nitre 1, water 8	.817	
Nitre 1, water 3	.646	
Muriate of ammonia 2, water 3,	.779	
Solution of potash, sp.gr. 1.346	.759	1.022
Sulfate of iron 2, water 5	.734	
Sulfate of soda 10, water 29	.728	
Oil of olives	.710	.650
Ammonia	.708	.706
Muriatic acid, sp. gr. 1.122	.680	.763
Alum 100, water 445	.649	
Lime tree wood	.62	.253
Fir wood	.61	.27
Alcohol	.602	.504
Sulfuric acid	.597	
Kirwan	.758	
Sulfuric acid 4, water 5	.663	
Apple tree	.57	.364
Alder	.53	.256
Linseed oil	.528	.496
Oak	.51	.27
Ash	.51	.32

	Heat in equal wts.	Heat in equal vol.
Pear tree	.50	.30
Spermaceti oil	.500	
Kirwan	.399	
Beech wood	.49	.34
Oil of turpentine	.472	.468
Elm	.47	.30
Plumb tree	.44	.30
Vinegar	.387	.397
Distilled vinegar	.103	.104
Pit coal	.278	
Charcoal	.263	
Chalk	.256	
Quicklime	.22	
Water 9, quicklime 16	.335	
Agate	.195	.563
Glass, without lead	.193	
Flint glass	.174	.58
Ashes of cinders	.188	
Sulfur	.183	.364
Iron	.126	.995
Sheet iron	.110	
Rust of iron	.250	
Rust nearly freed from air	.167	
Brass	.114	.954
Copper	.112	.985
Oxid of copper	.227	
Zinc	.098	.702
Ashes of charcoal	.091	
Silver	.082	.82
Tin	.066	.49
Antimony	.064	.39
Antimony, Kirwan	.086	
White oxid of antimony washed	.227	
Oxid of antimony, nearly freed from air	.167	
Gold	.050	.95
Lead	.042	.49
Crawford	.035	
Kirwan	.050	
Bismuth	.043	.42
Mercury	.031	.42

A Comparative Table of the Physical Properties of Various Substances

Substance	Specific Gravity	Height of the modulus of elasticity, in thousands of feet	Superficial cohesion of an inch, in grains, when liquid	Lateral adhesion of a square inch, in pounds	Cohesive strength of a square inch, in thousands of pounds	Repulsive strength of a square inch, in thousands of pounds	Refractive density	Dispersive power	Colour	Melting point	Boiling point	Expansion for 1°, in millionths	Capacity for heat	Conducting power for heat	Conducting power for electricity	Extensibility	Cohesive strength of a prism a foot long, weighing 1 lb., in thousands of pounds	Refractive force according to Newton	Simple refractive power	Heat in a given measure
Water	1.000	750	2.5				1.000976	1.00		32°	212°	60	1.000		1.000			1.00	1.00	1.000
Ice	.93	850																		.840
Steam at 212°	.0004																			.0021
Hydrogen gas	.0001	90																		.0006
Nitrogen gas	.0012	3.5																		.0008
Atmospheric air	.00128	30					1.000276					2100	.704							.0021
Oxygen gas	.00137	26										2100	1.400							.0008
Carbonic acid gas	.0017	19										2100	1.600							.0006
Fir wood	.56	{28, 40}			8	6							.900							
Elm	.80	8000			13	8	1.31		Brown.											.27
Alcohol	.83	8000					1.336													.30
Ash	.84				17	7			Reddish.				.47							
Beech	.85				12	8			Whitish.				.61							
Olive oil	.92						1.37	<1	Yellowish.				.51							
White wax	.96		1.							142		580	.49				34	1.35	1.34	.320
Oak	.99								Brown.			175	.51				30			
Box	1.10				17	11	1.469		Reddish.				.71				42	1.67		.65
Solution of potash	1.39						1.535		Yellowish.							$\tfrac{1}{173}$		1.81	.51	.86
Sulfuric acid	1.84		1.9				1.542						.65			$\tfrac{1}{128}$	36	1.51	.53	.99
Ivory	1.9				16	-20	1.435		White.			570					18	.71		.95
Crown glass	1.92	9800				1	1.39					-20				$\tfrac{1}{302}$		.74		.58
Free-stone	2.5				1		1.48					200				$\tfrac{1}{1152}$ to $\tfrac{1}{176}$	1.7	.77		1.17
Plate glass	2.6		1 to 2		1		1.525	1.65					.17			$\tfrac{1}{276}$		.57	.54	.93
Flint glass	2.8						1.585	1.80					.19	(.7)		$\tfrac{1}{276}$ to $\tfrac{1}{567}$	.7	1.61		
Diamond	3.4						2.5		White.			13		(.95)	>1		.8	1.93	.63	
Zinc	7.2	2250			2.5	1			White.	700		49	.098	(.85)				.68	1.28	.70
Tin	7.3				6				Whitish.	415		42	.066	(.8)	Greatest?					.49
Iron and steel	7.8	10000		40 to 150	100	50			Grey.	1000		19	.120	1.	A million.		11 to 40			.99
Brass	8.4	5000							Greenish y.	1450		31	.114				1.7			.95
Copper	8.8	5760			36				Reddish.	1000		29	.112				8.6			.99
Silver	10.5	3240			42				White.	540		34	.082				8.4			.86
Lead	11.4				3	6			Bluish grey.	-39		48	.042				.6			.49
Mercury	13.6		17						White.	650		104	.031							.42
Gold	19.3	750			22				Yellow.	1300		25	.050				2.1			.96
Platina	22.0								White.			14								

The barometer is supposed to stand at 30 inches; Fahrenheit's thermometer at 52°. The first fifteen columns are determined by independent observations; the last five are deduced from the others by calculation. The numbers of the eighteenth are found by dividing the excess of the square of the index of refraction above unity by the specific gravity, the nineteenth simply by dividing the excess of the index: the former agreeing either with the Newtonian theory of refraction, or with the Huygenian; the latter with the Huygenian only, upon another supposition respecting the transmission of light.

General effects of Mixture.

Mixed gases. See Metereology.
Pearson. Ph. tr. 1796.
  Aristotle mentions the introsusception of tin.
Hooke on the mutual penetration of mixtures. Birch. III. 511. IV. 11.
Hauksbee's experiments on mutual penetration. Ph. tr. 1711. XXVII. 325.
Leutmann on the specific gravity of mixed metals. C. Petr. III. 138.
Gellert on the density of alloys. C. Petr. XIII. 382.
Krafft on the density of alloys. C. Petr. XIV. 252.
Kästner on the specific gravity of mixtures. N. C. Gott. 1775. VI. 102.
  A mode of comparing the curves expressive of the densities.
Achard on the bulk of solutions. A. Berl. 1785. 101.
Pouget on mixtures of alcohol and water. Ir. tr. 1789. III. 157.
*Blagden and Gilpin on the excise of spirituous liquors. Ph. tr. 1790. 321. 1792. 425. 1794. 275.
Sanmartini on the areometer. Soc. Ital. VII. 79.
Pearson on some alloys. Ph. tr. 1796. 422.
Hassenfratz on saline mixtures. Ann. Ch. XXXI. 285.
Hassenfratz on measures of spirit. Ann. Ch. Repert. XIII. 45.
Hassenfratz and von Arnim on mixtures. Gilb. IV. 364.
The alcoometrical curve. Walker's philosophy. Lect. vi.
Schlönbach on the condensation of mixtures. Gilb. XI. 175.
Hatchett on the alloys of gold. Ph. tr. 1803. 43. Nich. 8. V. 286.
Atkins on specific gravities. 4. Lond. 1803. Acc. Nich. 8. IV. 285. Ph. M. XVI. 26, 305.
  The bulk of water is diminished by the addition of $\frac{1}{74}$ of sal ammoniac: 40 parts of platina, 5 of iron make but 39 by measure. Robison. Enc. Br.

Affinities and Combinations.

The proper subject of Chemistry.

Beccaria on the internal motions of fluids. C. Bon. I. 483.
Le Sage Essai de chimie mécanique. R. S.
*Kirwan on the attractive powers of the mineral acids. Ph. tr. 1783. 15.
  Deduces a numerical measure of the elective attraction from the quantity of the substance required to neutralise the acids, and thence explains other phenomena with apparent success.
Kirwan on the real acids in salts. Ir. tr. IV. Sc. 3. VII. 163.
Elliot on affinities in alcohol. Ph. tr. 1786. 155.
Audebat on attraction acting in solution. Roz. XXXIII. 198.
Berthollet on the laws of affinity. Extr. Ann. Ch. XXXVI. 278.
Venturi on the solution of camphor in water. Ann. Ch. XXI. 262. Gilb. II. 298.
B. Prévost on spontaneous motions in mixtures. Ann. Ch. XL. 3.
Draparnaud on the mutual actions and motions of fluids. Nich. VIII. 201.
On the chemical effects of tremors. Nich. VII. 122.
  In some cases, soda and potash exchange their acids with their temperatures. Ann. Ch.

Mineralogy in General.

Ph. tr. abr. II. IV. VI. VIII. X. See Geology.

Systems.

Kirwan's mineralogy. 2 v. R. I.
Haüy on methods of mineralogy. Ann. Ch. XVIII. 225.

Philosophy of Mineralogy.

Forms of Primary Aggregation. Crystallisation.

Musschenbroek. Intr. I. pl. 1.
Baumé and Lavoisier on crystallization. Roz. I. 8, 10.
Haüy on the forms of crystals. Roz. XIX. 366. XXIV. 71. XLIII. 103. 146, 161. A. P. 1784. 273. 1785. 213. 1786. 78. 1787. 92. 1788. 13. 1789. 519. 1790. 27. Ann. Ch. III. 1. XVII. 225. Ph. M. I. 113. II. 398. Traité de physique. I.
Kästner on the fracture of crystals. Commentat. Gott. 1783. VI. M. 52.
Eason on crystallization. Manch. M. I. 29.
Wall. Manch. M. II. 419.
Says, that large crystals are formed when the liquid is much exposed to the air, and that in salt works, a little resin or oil is thrown in, in order to make the salt fine.
Antic on the crystallization of Ice. Roz. XXXIII. 56.
Regnier on the crystallization of organized bodies. Roz. XXXIII. 215.
Chaptal on the effects of air and light in crystallization. Roz. XXXIII. 297.
Dorthes on the effects of light. Ann. Ch. II. 92.
Kramp. Hind. Arch. II. 80.
Denies Haüy's principle of the decrements of crystals proceeding always according to integer numbers.
Journ. Phys. LVI. 237.
It has been asserted, that powder thrown on electric glass assumed a regular crystalline arrangement; but further experiments have confuted the assertion.
Clifford and Buée on the system of Delisle and Haüy. Nich. IX. 26. Ph. M. XIX. 159.

Haüy considers all calculations of forms of crystals as reducible to arrangements of parallelepipeds, but he more commonly refers them to three species of primitive molecules; the tetraedron, the triangular prism, and the parallelepiped, making by their combinations; first, 6 primitive forms of crystals, which are only divisible in planes parallel to their surfaces, the tetraedron, parallelepipeds, octaedrons, regular or irregular, hexaedral prisms, the dodecaedron of equal rhombi, and the dodecaedron of two hexagonal pyramids. These, as they are built up in various orders, decreasing by regular steps, which begin either at the side, or at the angles of a crystal, serving as a nucleus, form all the immense variety of crystalline figures. A dodecaedron of rhombi is sometimes composed of cubes; a dodecaedron of pentagons may be produced by the same elements with a different law of decrement: a cube is sometimes the nucleus of an octaedron of which the sides correspond to the angles of the cube.

The molecules of ice are supposed to be either cubes or tetraedrons; the diagonals of the surfaces of the calcarious rhombus, or the Iceland crystal, are as the square roots of 3 and 2, the obtuse angle of the surface $101°\ 32'\ 13''$, that of the contiguous planes $104°\ 28'\ 40''$. A. P. 1789. and Tr. Phys.

Botany in General.

Abrégé des transactions philosophiques. Botanique. 2 v. Par. 1790. R. I.
Ph. tr. abr. II. v. 623. IV. 2 p. v. 298. VI. 2 p. v. 307. VIII. 2 p. v. 747. X. 2 p. v. 699.
Linnaei philosophia botanica.
Mawe's dictionary of gardening and botany. 4. 1798. R. I.
Miller's gardener's dictionary, by Martyn. f. 1798. R. I.
Hedwig Descriptio muscorum. Leipz. R. I.
Gaertner de fructibus et seminibus. 4. Stutg. 1798. B. B.
Smith Flora Britannica. 3 v. 8. Lond. B. B.
Wildenow's introduction to botany. 8. Edinb. 1805. R. I.

Systems.

*Linnaei systema naturae. Genera plantarum. Species plantarum.

*Jussieu on the arrangement of plants. A. P. 1773. 214. H. 34. 1774. 175. H. 27.

Withering's botanical arrangement.

Lamarck on the classification of vegetables. A. P. 1785. 437.

Venténat Tableau du regne végétal selon la méthode de Jussieu. 4 v. 8. B. B.

Guiart on the method of Tournefort. Ann. Ch. XLV. 149.

Vegetable Anatomy and Physiology.

Colours of plants. Aristotle on colours. Quoted. Roz. XLI. 470.

A. P. Index. Art. Plantes.

Tonge. Ph. tr. 1669. IV. 913. 1670. V. 1165, 1168, 1199, 2067.

Beale on the seed of plants. Ph. tr. 1669. IV. 919. 1671. VI. 2143.

Willoughby. Ph. tr. 1669. IV. 963. 1670. V. 1165, 1168, 1199. 1671. VI. 2119.
Found that willows and osiers would grow when inverted.

Wray. Ph. tr. 1669. IV. 963.

Lister. Ph. tr. 1670. V. 2067. 1671. VI. 2119, 3051. 1672. VII. 5132. 1673. VIII. 6060.

Grew on the anatomy of vegetables. 12. 1671. B. B.
Acc. Ph. tr. 1671. VI. 3037.

Grew's anatomy of the trunks of plants. 8. Lond.
Acc. Ph. tr. 1675. X. 486.

Wallis. Ph. tr. 1673. VIII. 6060.

Leeuwenhoek. Ph. tr. 1676. XI. 653. 1683. XIII. 197.
Adds little to Grew and Malpighi.

Woodward. Ph. tr. 1699. XXI. 193.

Huygens on vegetation in a close bottle. A. P. I. 130.

Lahire. A. P. II. 114. 1708. 231. H. 67.

Dodart on the direction of branches. A. P. 1700. 47. H. 61.

Delapryme. Ph. tr. 1702. XXIII. 1214.

Morland. Ph. tr. 1703. XXIII. 1474.
On the use of the flower. Grew had observed the farina to be seminal; Morland supposes it to pass to the seed.

Perrault. A. P. 1709. H. 44.

Parent on the motions of plants. A. P. 1710. H. 64.

Bradley. Ph. tr. 1718. XXX. 486.

Bradley on the growth of plants. 8. 1733.

Fairchild. Ph. tr. 1724. XXXIII. 127.

Dudley. Ph. tr. 1724. XXXIII. 194.
On the multiplication of plants.

Hales's vegetable statics. 8. Lond. 1731. R. I.
Extract by Desaguliers. Ph. tr. 1727. XXXV. 264, 323.

Mairan. A. P. 1729. H. 35.
On the sensitive plant.

Nicholls. Ph. tr. 1730. XXXVI. 371.

Seba. Ph. tr. 1730. XXXVI. 441.
On vegetable preparations.

Bülfinger on the tracheae of plants. C. Petr. IV. 182.

Logan on the farina foecundans. Ph. tr. 1736. XXXIX. 192.

Dufay. A. P. 1736. 87. H. 73.
On the sensitive plant.

Duhamel and Buffon on the woody strata of trees. A. P. 1737. 121. H. 65. 1751. 23. H. 147.

*Duhamel Physique des arbres.

Klein on letters found in the middle of a beech. Ph. tr. 1739. XLI. 231.

Clark on substances found within trees. Ph. tr. 1739. XLI. 235.
A tree 13 feet in diameter.

†Baker on a perfect plant in the seed. Ph. tr. 1740. XLI. 448.

Miles on the seed of fern. Ph. tr. 1741. XLI. 770.

CATALOGUE.—NATURAL HISTORY, VEGETABLE PHYSIOLOGY.

Hollmannus de sceleto foliorum. Ph. tr. 1741. XLI. 796, 789.

Cook. Ph. tr. 1745. XLIII. 525.
Effects of the farina of a different plant.

Krafft on vegetation. N. C. Petr. II. 231.

Watson on the sex of flowers. Ph. tr. 1751. 169.

Bonnet sur l'usage des feuilles. 4. Gott. 1751. B. B.

Riville on caprification. S. E. II. 369. H. 4.

Alston on the sexes of plants. Ed. ess. I. 205.

Collet on a peat pit. Ph. tr. 1757. 109.

Pulteney on the sleep of plants. Ph. tr. 1758. 506.

Marsham on the growth of trees. Ph. tr. 1759. 7.

Marsham on the measures of trees. Ph. tr. 1797. 128.

Adanson on the motions of the tremella. A. P. 1767. 564. H. 75.

Murray on fallen leaves. N. C. Gott. 1770. II. 27.

Fordyce's elements of agriculture and vegetation. 8. 1771. 1796. R. 1.

A cross formed in the wood, and a corresponding cross in the bark, of different dimensions. A. P. 1771. 491.

Mustel. Ph. tr. 1773. 126.
Against the existence of any circulation in the sap, after Hales.

Mustel Traité de la végétation. 8.

Hunter on the heat of vegetables. Ph. tr. 1775. 446.

E. M. Forêts et Bois.

Tessier on the effects of light upon plants. A. P. 1783. 133.

Broussonet on the motions of plants, and on the hedysarum gyrans. A. P. 1784. 609.

Saussure on the electricity of vegetables. Roz. XXV. 290.

Bruce on the sensitive quality of the averrhoa carambola. Ph. tr. 1785. 356.

Percival on the perceptive power of vegetables. Manch. M. II. 114.
In favour of its existence.

Henry on the effect of fixed air on vegetation. Manch. M. II. 341.
Shows, after Percival, that it is favourable, when the plants are exposed at the same time to the atmosphere.

Bell on the physiology of plants, translated by Currie. Manch. M. II. 394.
Observes, that Hill discovered the existence of a green corona between the wood and the pith: he also asserts, that the cuticle contains vessels, which the author thinks are intended for admitting air into the tracheae. Bell thinks, that the sugar of the maple is not contained in the sap, but is derived from some proper vessels. Hope found, that the sap flowed first from the superior orifices of the lowest of several horizontal incisions. Bell concludes, that the proper juice descends, and that in its descent the wood acquires its growth. Guettard shows, that perspiration takes place from the upper surface of the leaf; and, as well as Duhamel and Bonnet, that absorption is performed by the lower surface. The motions of plants show, that they possess other powers than those of inanimate matter, and these are probably concerned in propelling the sap: for the discharge from an incision proves, that the humidity is not imbibed merely by capillary action. Bell thinks, that plants have even a degree of sensation.

Ingenhousz Nouvelles experiences. 8. Paris, 1785. R. S. Extr. Roz. XXXIV. 436.

Ingenhousz's experiments on vegetables. 8. Lond.

Ingenhousz on germination. Roz. XXVIII. 81.

Ingenhousz on the nourishment of plants. Journ. Phys. XLV. (II.) 458.

Fougeroux on the formation of the ligneous strata. A. P. 1787. 110.

Desfontaines on the irritability of the organs of plants. A. P. 1787. 468.

Desfontaines on the organization of monocotyledonous plants. M. Inst. I. 478.

Regnier on the generation of plants. Roz. XXXI. 321.

Smith on the irritability of vegetables. Ph. tr. 1788. 158.
Thinks, that they do not possess at once both irritability and spontaneous motion.

Walker on the motion of sap. Ed. tr. I. 3.
Says, that the sap ascends in the wood, and that in the spring the lower part of the bark receives it before the upper.

Mayer on the vessels of plants. A. Berl. 1788. 54.

Mayer on the impregnation of seeds. A. Berl. 1790. 61.

Kolreuter on the irritability of the stamina of the barberry. N. A. Petr. 1788. VI. 207.

St. Martin on the perspiration of plants. Esprit des Journ. Apr. 1790.

Achard on the nourishment of vegetables. A. Berl. 1790. 49.

Sénébier on the heat of vegetables. Roz. XI. 173.

Sénébier on the green matter found in water. Journ. Phys. XLVIII. 155.

Sénébier's vegetable physiology. 5 v. 8. Genev.
   Acc. Journ. Phys. LI. 354.

Hassenfratz on the nutrition of vegetables. Ann. Ch. XIII. 178.

Rossi on the fecundation of plants. Soc. Ital. VII. 369.

Tait on peat mosses. Ed. tr. III. 266.

Humboldt on the physiology of plants. 8. Leipz. 1794. Noticed. Ph. M. IX.

Knight on grafting trees. Ph. tr. 1795. 290.

Knight on fecundation. Ph. tr. 1799. 195. Nich. III. 458, 519. Ph. M. VII. 97.
Could not produce hybrid plants.

Knight on the ascent of the sap. Ph. tr. 1801. 333.

Knight on the descent of the sap. Ph. tr. 1803. 277.

Knight on the motion of the sap. Ph. tr. 1804. 183.

Correa de Serra on the fructification of submersed algae. Ph. tr. 1796. 494.

Gough on the vegetation of seeds. Manch. M. IV. 310, 488.
Showing the effect of the air on it.

Gough on the nourishment of succulent vegetables. Nich. III. 1.

Gough on the use of oxygen in vegetation. Nich. IX. 217.

Chaptal on the juices of vegetables. Ann. Ch. XXI. 284.

Peschier on the irritability of animals and plants. Journ. Phys. XLV. (II.) 343.

Hooper on the structure and economy of plants. 8. Oxf. 1797.

On the irritability of the pollen of plants. Nich. I. 471.

Delamétherie on the respiration of plants. Journ. Phys. XLVII. (IV.) 299.

Delamétherie on the irritability and organization of plants. Journ. Phys. LVI. 281, 355. LVII. 283.
With some figures.

Brugman de lolio. Journ. Phys. XLVII. (IV.) 388. Ph. M. III. 321.
Asserts, that plants excrete.

Barton on the stimulant effects of camphor. Am. tr. IV. 232.
Refreshing flowers when put into the water in which they are kept.

Fabricius on the winter sleep of animals and plants. Ph. M. III. 156.

Rafn on the physiology of plants. 8. Leips. 1798.
   Acc. B. Soc. Phil. n. 28. Ph. M. V. 233. Ph. M. IX.

Decandolle on the influence of light upon vegetables. B. Soc. Phil. n. 42. Journ. Phys. LII. 124.

Decandolle on the structure of leaves. B. Soc. Phil. n. 44. Journ. Phys. LII. 130. Ph. M. IX. 176.

Vastel on germination. Extr. B. Soc. Phil. n. 66. Ph. M. VIII. 187. Gilb. XIV. 364.

Coulomb on the circulation of sap. M. Inst. II. 246. Journ. Phys. XLIX. 392. Ph. M. VI. 310. Repert. XII. 356.

Says, that it ascends, with some air, near the axis of the tree.

*Mirbel on vegetable anatomy. B. Soc. Phil. n. 60. Journ. Phys. LII. 336... With many figures. Ph. M. XIII. 36.

Mirbel Anatomie et physiologie végétales. 2 v. 8. B. B.

Darwin's phytologia. 4. Lond. 1800. R. I.

Th. de Saussure on the influence of the soil on vegetables. Journ. Phys. LI. 9. Gilb. VI. 459.

Seems to think, that plants generate some calcarious earth.

Th. de Saussure Recherches chimiques sur la végétation. 8. Par. 1804. R. I.

Acc. B. Soc. Phil. n. 86.

Thinks, that all the solid contents are derived from the soil.

Michelotti. Ph. M. IX. 240.

Velley on the food of plants. Repert. XII. 32.

Carradori on germination in oxygen. Journ. Phys. LIII. 253.

On the effect of light on germination. Journ. Phys. LIV. 319.

Solomé on the temperature of vegetables. Ann. Ch. XL. 114.

Fairman on grafting. S. A. XX. 181. Nich. VI. 124.

Hunter on the nourishment of vegetables. Repert. ii. III. 349.

Jurine on the organization of leaves. Journ. Phys. LVI. 169. Ph. M. XVI. 3, 147.

With figures.

Edelcrantz's plaster for trees. B. Soc. Phil. n. 82.

B. Prévost on the tracheae of plants. Journ. Phys. LVII. 112.

Account of Mr. Knight's *Experiments on the descent of the Sap in Trees. From the Journals of the Royal Institution. II.* 71.

The principal object of this paper is to point out the causes of the descent of the sap from the leaves through the bark, and of the consequent formation of wood. These causes Mr. Knight supposes to be gravitation, agitation, and capillary attraction, combined with some peculiar structure of the vessels.

From experiments on vine leaves, it appears that the perspiratory vessels of the leaf are confined to its under surface: the upper part Mr. Knight considers as serving to receive the influence of light, and as probably emitting oxygen gas; and he quotes Bonnet's experiments, as showing that this surface of the leaf, when detached from the plant, is capable also of absorbing moisture.

Mr. Knight removed a portion of the bark of the branch of a vine which was in an inverted position, and he found that new bark and wood were generated at the lip of the wound which was actually uppermost; and from a comparison of this with his former experiments, he infers, that the force of gravitation is materially concerned in the circulation of the sap.

By means of bandages, Mr. Knight prevented the agitation of some young apple trees in some parts of their stems, and in particular directions, while their motion was permitted in other parts: and it was found that their growth was the most considerable in the parts, which were freely agitated, and that the diameter of the section was greater by about one sixth in the direction of the motion. Hence we may understand the greater thickness of the lower parts of the trunk, and of single trees in exposed situations, while the trees that form a wood, and shelter each other, are higher and more slender.

If a large tree has been deprived of motion, by cutting off its foliage or otherwise, its growth is promoted by removing the dry external layers of the bark, which appear to impede the motion of the sap.

Mr. Knight supposes that the expansion and contraction of the alburnum, from changes of temperature, are partly communicated to the bark, and assist in propelling its sap: but that the principal cause of this motion is gravitation, which operates more completely in the perpendicular parts of the tree, than in the horizontal branches; hence these branches are not liable to become too large for their strength, in an unfavourable position.

Leaves of the vine were succesfully grafted on the fruitstalk, the tendril, and the succulent shoot; and a branch was nourished by the leafstalk, the tendril, and the fruitstalk. The wood of a leafstalk, supporting a shoot, was deposited on the external sides of the vessels, called by Mr. Knight, central vessels, and on the medulla; but the medulla appeared to be inactive in the deposition, nor did any processes originate in it. When a bud is inserted on a stock, the new wood appears to be generated above the line of union, and to be produced by the bud.

When new bark grows over an exposed surface of alburnum, the processes called medullary, which constitute the silver grain of the wood, are seen clearly to originate in the bark, and to terminate at the lifeless surface of the alburnum.

Mr. Knight is still of opinion, that the sap acquires its power of generating wood, from its exposure to light and air in the leaves; but he thinks it possible that the young bark may in a slight degree supply the place of the leaves, when they are removed: and he concludes from some experiments, that when a small part of the wood is deprived of bark, it may be able to transmit a small quantity of sap from the leaves downwards, through its superficial parts, so that a little wood may be generated below; but that this power is confined within narrow limits.

By immersing the running roots of a potatoe in a coloured fluid, Mr. Knight traced a great number of vessels, proceeding, from the parent plant, to ramify minutely between the cortical and internal parts of the young tuber: these he supposes to convey nourishment, prepared by the leaves, for the support of the internal parts, conceiving these parts to be analogous to the alburnum of woody vegetables, which always appears to require the operation of the leaves for its complete organization.

Zoology. In General.

Ph. tr. abr. II. vi. 756. V. i. 1.
*Buffon Histoire naturelle.

Systems.

Fabricii philosophia entomologia.
Fabricii entomologia systematica.
Hunter on the identity of the wolf, jackal, and dog. Ph. tr. 1787. 253.
Pinel's classification of animals from the lower jaw. Roz. XLI. 401.
Brongniart on the classification of reptiles. B. Soc. Phil. n. 35.
Lacépède on an arrangement of birds and mammalia. M. Inst. III. 454, 469.
Dumeril on the classification of insects. B. Soc. Phil. n. 44. Journ. Phys. LI. 427.
Distinguishes the genera by the subdivisions of the tarsus.

Physiology.

Charlton Physiologia. f. 1654.
Account of 4 men that lived 24 days in a mine without food. Ph. tr. 1684. XIV. 577.
Robinson's account of Jenkins, a fisherman, aged 169. Phil. tr. 1696. XIX. 265.
Seigue on a toad found in an oak 100 years old. A. P. 1731. H. 24.
Another found in an elm 1719.
Hales's statical essays. 2 v. 8. 1731. R. I.
Miles on the globules of the blood in the water eft. Ph. tr. 1741. XLI. 725.
Jurin and Leeuwenhoek found 4 globules of the blood equal in diameter to a wire which measured $\frac{1}{240}$ inch: some were a little larger.
A capricorn beetle found in the centre of a tree. Ph. tr. 1741. XLI. 861.
Mortimer thinks it was nourished by the sap.
Papers on the fresh water polypus. Ph. tr. 1742. XLII. 281.
Maclaurin on the cells of bees. Ph. tr. 1743. XLII. 565.
Lecat Traité des sens. 8. Amst. 1744.
Douglas on the heat of animals. 8. 1747.
A case of long fasting. C. Bon. II. i. 221.
Kaan Boerhaave on the cohesion of living solids. N. C. Petr. IV. 343.
Haller Elementa physiologiae. 8 v. 4. Lausanne, 1757. M. B.
Tillet on the power of supporting heat. A. P. 1764. 186. H. 16.
Found that 130° R. or 337° F. was supported in an oven for ten minutes. Blagden says 260°.
Fontana on the laws of irritability. Ac. Sienn. III. 209.

Braun on the heat of animals. N. C. Petr. XIII. 419.

Ellis on the division of animalcules. Ph. tr. 1769. 138.

Hewson on the red particles of the blood. Ph. tr. 1773. 303.

Asserts the existence of central particles, perhaps from an optical deception. See Cavallo on factitious airs.

Macbride and Stuckey Simon on the reviviscence of snails, after being dry 15 years or more. Ph. tr. 1774. 432.

Blagden's observation in a heated room. Ph. tr. 1775. 111.

The power of bearing heat owing to life only. Hunter found a carp surrounded by water in the midst of ice. Martine found a swarm of bees at 97°. Vegetables also generate heat.

Blagden's further experiments. Ph. tr. 1775. 484.

Supported 260° with clothes, 220° without. A beef steak was dressed in 13 minutes in the same room.

Hunter on the heat of animals and vegetables. Ph. tr. 1775. 446. 1778. 7.

Amphibia are generally from 2° to 10° warmer than the surrounding medium, but not always. Trees may be cooled to 17° F. without being frozen.

Hunter on some parts of the animal economy. 4. Lond. 1786. R. S.

Hunter on the extirpation of one ovarium in a sow. Ph. tr. 1787. 233.

Seems to have reduced the numbers of the litters to ½.

Hunter on bees. Ph. tr. 1792. 128.

Dobson's experiments in a heated room. Ph. tr. 1775. 463.

At 224°.

Changeux on the experiments of Fordyce and Blagden. Roz. VII. 57.

Debraw on the sex of bees. Ph. tr. 1777. 15.

Asserts, that any female bee may be made a queen by proper food, and will then breed without any other preliminary.

Bonnet on the reproduction of the heads of snails. Roz. X. 165.

Bonnet on reproduction in lizards. Roz. X. 385.

Dicquemare. Ph. tr. 1775. 202.

The actinia may be multiplied by dividing its basis.

Polhill on Debraw's culture of bees. Ph. tr. 1778. 107.

Fontana sopra la fisica animale. 4. R. S.

Fontana sopra i globetti rossi. 8. R. S.

Crawford. Ph. tr. 1781.

Says, that venous blood drawn in the hot bath is scarlet.

Spallanzani on the reproduction of the heads of snails. Soc. Ital. I. 526. II. 506.

Spallanzani on respiration. Ph. M. XVIII. 256.

On a toad found in a hole. A. Berl. 1782. H. 13.

In a slate quarry. A fissure was found descending towards the hole.

Rigby on animal heat. 8. Lond. 1785. R. S.

Bell's arguments against the generation of cold in the human body. Manch. M. I. 1.

Explains the power of bearing heat by the frigorific effect of evaporation, joined to the small capacity of the air for heat.

White on the regeneration of animal substances. Manch. M. I. 325.

Mentions a supernumerary thumb, which was removed and grew again.

A. Fothergill on longevity. Manch. M. I. 355.

Louisa Truxo, a negress in South America, was said to be living in 1780, at the age of 175, on the authority of the newspapers only. Says that Galen lived to 140; but Blair makes him only 70. On the authority of the papers only, a Russian is said to be living at the age of 180.

Percival on the sufferings of a collier. Manch. M. II. 467.

He was 7 days without food, and died. Sir W. Hamilton mentions a girl who lived 11 days without food. Fantonus mentions a woman who ate but twice in 50 days, and then died. Men can breathe where candles will not burn.

Blumenbach's specimen of comparative physiology. C. Gott. 1785. VIII. Ph. 69. 1786. IX. 108.

Blumenbach. Ph. M. II. 251.
    Asserts the fascination of the rattlesnake, and thinks the noise is concerned in frightening birds.
Blumenbach on hereditary mutilations. Ph. M. IV. 1.
Clarke on the mortality of males. Ph. tr. 1786. 349.
    Male infants generally weigh 7¼ pounds; females 6¾. twins 11 pounds together.
Caldanii institutiones physiologicae. 8. Venice, 1786. R. S.
A case of somnambulism. M. Laus. III. 98.
Fordyce on muscular motion. Ph. tr. 1788. 23.
    Attributes it to the attraction of life.
Fordyce on digestion. 4. Lond. 1790.
Peart on animal heat. 8. Gainsborough, 1788. R. S.
Saint Julien on the heat of warm baths. Roz. XXXII. 51.
Baronio on reproduction. Soc. Ital. IV. 480.
    In warm blooded animals.
Lavoisier on respiration. A. P. 1789. 566.
Girtanner on irritability. Roz. XXXVII. 139.
Seguin on respiration and animal heat. Roz. XXXVII. 467. Ann. Ch. XXI. 225.
Priestley on respiration. Ph. tr. 1790. 106.
    Shows that some azote is absorbed.
Ferriar on the vital principle. Manch. M. III. 216.
Menzies de respiratione. 8. Edinb. 1790. Acc. Ann. Ch. VIII. 211.
    Observes, after Jurin, that about 40 cubic inches are respired at once.
Currie on the effects of cold. Ph. tr. 1792. 199.
Darwin's zoonomia. 4 v. 8. 1804. R. I.
Vauquelin on the respiration of insects. Ann. Ch. XII. 273.
Monro on the action of the muscles. Ed. tr. III. 250.

Olivi on the touch of marine worms. Soc. Ital. VII. 478.
Cruikshank and Haighton on the reproduction of nerves. Pb. tr. 1795. 177, 190.
Haighton on animal impregnation. Ph. tr. 1797. 159.
Home on muscular motion. Ph. tr. 1795. 202.
Home on the teeth of graminivorous quadrupeds. Ph. tr. 1799. 237.
Humboldt on the chemical process of vitality. Ann. Ch. XXII. 64. Nich. I. 359.
Wells on the colour of the blood. Ph. tr. 1797. 416.
    Attributes the change of colour produced by the air to the increased opacity of the lymph.
Sue on vitality. Journ. Phys. XLVI. (III.) 226.
Duméril on the smelling of insects. Extr. B. Soc. Phil. n. 5.
Cuvier on the nutrition of insects. Extr. B. Soc. Phil. n. 10. Journ. Phys. XLIX. 351.
Cuvier on the circulation in leeches. B. Soc. Phil. n. 19.
Cuvier on worms with red blood. B. Soc. Phil. n. 64.
Cuvier on the comparative anatomy of teeth. B. Soc. Phil. n. 82.
Murhard on toads found in stones. Ph. M. III.
Fabricius on the winter sleep of animals. Ph. M. III. 156.
Cavallo on the medical properties of factitious airs. 8. Lond. 1798.
    Gives an accurate account of the globules of the blood.
Léveillé on the nutrition of the foetus. Journ. Phys. XLVIII. 386.
Delamétherie on a Spaniard who supported great degrees of heat. Journ. Phys. LVII. 66. Nich. VI. 139. Ph. M. XVI. 357.
Michelotti on the action of heat upon animals. Journ. Phys. LVII. 337. Ph. M. XIX. 3.

Toplis on the fascination of snakes. Ph. M. XIX. 56.

Perrin. Nich. VIII. 131.
<small>Found a shark at 88° when the sea was at 76°.</small>

Bostock on respiration. 8. Liverpool, 1804.
<small>Calculates that 666 cubic feet of air are respired in 24 hours. Makes the whole contents of the lungs 280 cubic inches.</small>

Instances of longevity. Ph. M. XX. 373.

Cultivation of Natural Productions, including Agriculture and Horticulture.

Agricultural machines. See Mechanics, Penetration.

Tusser's 500 points. 4. Lond. 1573. B. B.

Beale. Ph. tr. 1671. VI. 2143.

Lewis on grafting roots. 1673. VIII. 60, 67.

Miller on raising exotic seeds. Ph. tr. 1728. XXXV. 485.

Ressons on grafting. A. P. 1716. 200.

Duhamel on grafting, and on the wounds of trees. A. P. 1730. 102. H. 55. 1731. 357. H. 42. 1746. 319. H. 70.

Marsham on washing fruit trees. Ph. tr. 1759. 7. 1777. 12. 1781. 449.

Fitzgerald on checking the growth of fruit trees. Ph. tr. 1761. 71.

Faignel on potatoe bread. 1761. H. 156.

Fordyce's elements of agriculture.

Dutch apparatus for cod and turbot fishery. Bailey's Mach. I. 156.

E. M. A. III. Art. Fruitier. Jardinier. VI. Art. Plantes.

Pearl Fishery. E. M. A. V. Art. Nacre et Perles.

Home's gentleman farmer. R. S.

Clarke's theory and practice of husbandry. 4. R. S.

Cazaux Art de cultiver la canne. 8. R. S.

A. Young's course of experimental agriculture. R. S.

A. Young's annals of agriculture. 8.

Sylvestre's watering carts and roller. Roz. XXXVII. 460.

Bath Society's papers. 8. Bath, 1792... R. I.

Béraud's machine for fishing coral. Roz. XLI. 21.

Cours d'architecture rurale pratique. 8. Vien. 1792. R. I.

Dutrone sur la canne au sucre. Extr. Roz. XLIII. 313.

Knight on grafting trees. Ph. tr. 1795. 290.

Kirwan on manures. Ir. tr. V. 129.

Communications to the Board of Agriculture. 4. Lond. 1797... R. I.

General Reports, printed by the Board of Agriculture. 4. R. S.

Farmer's calendar. 1801.

Mawe's dictionary of gardening.

Miller's gardener's dictionary by Martyn.

Forsyth on fruit trees. 4. Lond. 1802. R. I.

Wakefield's method of promoting vegetation by steam. Repert. XIV. 235.

On destroying insects. Ph. M. VII. 189.
<small>By hepatic solutions.</small>

Edelcrantz's plaster for trees. B. Soc. Phil. n. 82.

Dickson's practical agriculture. 2 v. 4. Lond. 1804. R. I.
<small>Thirty two million bushels of wheat are said to be produced annually in England.</small>

History of Terrestrial Physics.

Wallis on the claims of the English to the discovery of the compass. Ph. tr. 1701. XXII. 1035.

Dufay sur l'électricité. A. P. 1733. 23.

Hausen Novi profectus in historia electricitatis. 4. Leipz. 1734.

Gray. Ph. tr. 1735. XXXIX. 24.

Observes, that the electric fire seemed to be of the same nature as lightning.

Lallamand. Ph. tr. 1746. 78.
The first time he felt the shock, he lost the use of his breath for some moments. Musschenbroek says he experienced a most terrible pain.

Needham. Ph. tr. 1746. 247.
Lemonnier discovered the permanency of the electric charge, and Nollet tried its effect on 180 men at once.

Gralath's history of electricity. Danz. Gesellsch. I. 23.

Hollmann's history of attraction. C. Gott. 1754. IV. 271.

†**Watson on the lyncurium. Ph. tr. 1759. 394.**

Trombelli and Collina on the invention of the compass. C. Bon. II. iii. 333, 372.

Priestley's history of electricity.

Titius **de experimenti Lugdunensis inventore. 4. Wittemb. 1771.**

Beckmann on the shock. Erfind. 2 ed. Leips. 1783. I. 571. On the tourmalin. 248.

History of opinions respecting the elements. Roz. X. 286.

Blagden's history of the congelation of quicksilver. Ph. tr. 1783. 329.
Braun was the first that established it.

Falconer on the knowledge of the ancients. Manch. M. I. 261. III. 278.

Walker on the congelation of quicksilver in England. Ph. tr. 1789. 199.

Count Rumford's institution of a prize for discoveries on heat and light. Ph. tr. 1797. 215.
The first medal was presented to Count Rumford himself; the second to Mr. Leslie.

Gren on the history of physics, with an account of authors. Gilb. I. 167.
The Society for the Encouragement of Arts still proposes premiums for improvements in the mode of heating rooms, and for methods of sweeping chimnies by machinery.

MISCELLANEOUS PAPERS.

REPRINTED WITH CORRECTIONS.

MISCELLANEOUS PAPERS.

I. OBSERVATIONS ON VISION. BY THOMAS YOUNG.

COMMUNICATED BY RICHARD BROCKLESBY, M.D. F.R.S.

FROM THE PHILOSOPHICAL TRANSACTIONS.

Read before the ROYAL SOCIETY, *May* 30, 1793.

It is well known, that the eye, when not acted upon by any exertion of the mind, conveys a distinct impression of those objects only which are situated at a certain distance from itself; that this distance is different in different persons, and that the eye can, by the volition of the mind, be accommodated to view other objects at a much less distance: but how this accommodation is effected, has long been a matter of dispute, and has not yet been satisfactorily explained. It is equally true, and it has indeed already been observed by Dr. Porterfield, that no exertion of the mind can accommodate the eye to view objects at a distance greater than that of indolent vision, a circumstance which may easily be experienced by any person to whom this distance of indolent vision is less than infinite.

The principal parts of the eye, and of its appertenances, have been described by various authors. Winslow is generally very accurate; but Albinus, in Musschenbroek's *Introductio*, has represented several particulars more correctly. I shall suppose their account complete, except where I mention or delineate the contrary.

The first theory that I find of the accommodation of the eye is Kepler's. He supposes the ciliary processes to contract the diameter of the eye, and lengthen its axis, by a muscular power. But the ciliary processes neither appear to contain any muscular fibres, nor have they any attachment by which they can be capable of performing this action.

Descartes imagined the same contraction and elongation to be effected by a muscularity of the crystalline, of which he supposed the ciliary processes to be the tendons. He did not attempt to demonstrate this muscularity, nor did he enough consider the connexion with the ciliary processes. He says, that the lens in the mean time becomes more convex, but does not appear to attribute, in his Dioptrics, any material effect to this change: in his Treatise on Man, however, he explains the operation very minutely.

De la Hire maintains, that the eye undergoes no change, except the contraction and dilatation of the pupil. He does not attempt to confirm this opinion by mathematical demonstration; he solely rests it on an experiment, which has been shown by Dr. Porterfield and by Dr. Smith to be fallacious. Haller too has adopted this opinion, however inconsistent it seems with the known principles of optics, and with the slightest regard to hourly experience.

Dr. Pemberton supposes the crystalline to contain muscular fibres, by which one of its surfaces is flattened while the other is made more convex. But Dr. Jurin has proved that a change like this is inadequate to the effect.

Dr. Porterfield conceives, that the ciliary processes draw forwards the crystalline, and make the cornea more convex. The ciliary processes are, from their structure, attachment, and direction, utterly incapable of this action; and, by Dr. Jurin's calculations, there is not room for a sufficient motion of this kind, without a very visible increase in the length of the eye's axis; such an increase we cannot observe.

Dr. Jurin's hypothesis is, that the uvea, at its attachment to the cornea, is muscular, and that the contraction of this ring makes the cornea more convex. He says, that the fibres of this muscle may as well escape our observation, as those of the muscle of the interior ring. But if such a muscle existed, it must, to overcome the resistance of the coats, be far stronger than that which is only destined to the uvea itself; and the uvea, at this part, exhibits nothing but radiated fibres, losing themselves, before the circle of adherence to the sclerotica, in a brownish granulated substance, not unlike in appearance to capsular ligament, common to the uvea and ciliary processes, but which may be traced separately from them both. Now at the interior ring of the uvea, the appearance is not absolutely inconsistent with the presence of an annular muscle. His theory of accommodation to distant objects is ingenious, but no such accommodation takes place.

Musschenbroek conjectures, that the relaxation of the ciliary zone, so named by Zinn, which appears to be nothing but the capsule of the vitreous humour where it receives the impression of the ciliary processes, permits the coats of the eye to push forwards the crystalline and cornea. Such a voluntary relaxation is wholly without example in the animal economy, and were it to take place, the coats of the eye would not act as he imagines, nor could they so act unobserved. The contraction of the ciliary zone is equally inadequate and unnecessary.

Some have supposed the pressure of the external muscles, especially the two oblique muscles, to elongate the axis of the eye. But their action would not be sufficiently regular, nor sufficiently strong; for a much greater pressure being made on the eye than they can be supposed capable of effecting, no sensible difference is produced in the distinctness of vision.

Others say, that the muscles shorten the axis: these have still less reason on their side; since such a change would lengthen the focal distance, which in fact is longest when the eye is at rest.

Those who maintain, that the ciliary processes flatten the crystalline, are ignorant of their structure, and of the effect required:

these processes are yet more incapable of drawing back the crystalline, and such an action is equally inconsistent with observation.

Some other suppositions have also been formed by different physiologists. Zinn imagines the ciliary processes to be distended by a fluid, and to protrude the lens. Sauvages conjectures, that the ring of Petit is inflated by the electric fluid, and alters the form of the lens: Moulin, that the cornea is rendered more convex by its ligaments, which are in fact nerves: Bourdelot, that the contraction of the pupil increases the convexity of the lens. But all these opinions are liable to as strong objections as those which I have already examined.

From these considerations, and from the observations of Dr. Porterfield and others, that those who have been couched have no longer the power of accommodating the eye to different distances, I had concluded that the rays of light, emitted by objects at a small distance, could only be brought to foci on the retina by a nearer approach of the crystalline to a spherical form; and I could imagine no other power capable of producing this change than a muscularity of a part, or the whole, of its capsule.

But in closely examining, with the naked eye, in a strong light, the crystalline from an ox, turned out of its capsule, I discovered a structure, which appears to remove all the difficulties with which this branch of optics has long been obscured. On viewing it with a magnifier, this structure became more evident.

The crystalline lens of the ox is an orbicular, convex, transparent body, composed of a considerable number of similar coats, of which the exterior closely adhere to the interior. Each of these coats consists of six series of fibres, intermixed with a gelatinous substance, and attached to six lines, which have somewhat of a membranous appearance. Three of these lines or tendons are anterior, three posterior; their length is about two thirds of the semidiameter of the coat; their arrangement is that of three equal and equidistant rays, meeting in the axis of the crystalline; one of the anterior is directed towards the outer angle of the eye, and one of the posterior towards the inner angle, so that the posterior are placed opposite to the middle of the interstices of the anterior; and planes passing through each of the six, and through the axis, would mark on either surface six regular equidistant rays. The fibres arise from both sides of each line; they diverge till they reach the greatest circumference of the coat, and having passed it, they again converge, till they are attached respectively to the sides of the nearest lines of the opposite surface. The anterior or posterior portion of the six, viewed together, exhibits the appearance of three penniformiradiated muscles. The anterior lines of attachment of all the coats are situated in the same planes, and the posterior ones in the continuations of these planes beyond the axis. Such an arrangement of fibres can be accounted for on no other supposition than that of muscularity. This mass is inclosed in a strong membranous capsule, to which it is loosely connected by minute vessels and nerves; and the connexion is more observable near its greatest circumference. Between the mass and its capsule is found a considerable quantity of an aqueous fluid, the liquid of the crystalline.

I conceive, therefore, that when the will is exerted to view an object at a small distance, the influence of the mind is conveyed through the lenticular ganglion, formed from branches of the third and fifth pair of nerves, by the filaments perforating the sclerotica, to the orbiculus ciliaris, which may be considered as an annular plexus of nerves and vessels; and thence by the ciliary processes to the muscle of the crystalline, which, by the contraction of its fibres, becomes more convex, and collects the diverging rays to a focus on the retina. The disposition of fibres in each coat is admirably adapted to produce this change; for, since the least surface that can contain a given bulk is that of a sphere, the contraction of any surface must bring its contents nearer to a spherical form. The liquid of the crystalline seems to serve as a synovia in facilitating the motion, and to admit a sufficient change of the muscular part, with a smaller motion of the capsule.

It remains to be inquired, whether these fibres can produce an alteration in the form of the lens sufficiently great to account for the known effects.

In the ox's eye, the diameter of the crystalline is 700 thousandths of an inch, the axis of its anterior segment 225, of its posterior 350. In the atmosphere it collects parallel rays at the distance of 235 thousandths. From these data we find, that its ratio of refraction is as 10000 to 6574. Hauksbee makes it only as 10000 to 6832.7, but we cannot depend on his experiment, since he says, that the image of the candle, which he viewed, was enlarged and distorted: a circumstance that he does not explain, but which was evidently occasioned by the greater density of the central parts. Supposing, with Hauksbee and others, the refraction of the aqueous and vitreous humours equal to that of water, that is, as 10000 to 7465, the ratio of refraction of the crystalline in the eye will be as 10000 to 8806, and it would collect parallel rays at the distance of 1226 thousandths of an inch: but the distance of the retina from the crystalline is 550 thousandths, and that of the anterior surface of the cornea 250; hence the focal distance of the cornea and aqueous humour alone must be 2329. Now, supposing the crystalline to assume a spherical form, its diameter will be 642 thousandths, and its focal distance in the eye 926. Then, disregarding the thickness of the cornea, we find, that such an eye will collect those rays on the retina, which diverge from a point at the distance of 12 inches and 8 tenths. This is a greater change than is necessary for an ox's eye, for if it be supposed capable of distinct vision at a distance somewhat less than 12 inches, yet it probably is far short of being able to collect parallel rays. The human crystalline is susceptible of a much greater change of form.

The ciliary zone may admit of as much extension as this diminution of the diameter of the crystalline will require; and its elasticity will assist the cellular texture of the vitreous humour, and perhaps the gelatinous part of the crystalline, in restoring the indolent form.

It may be questioned, whether the retina takes any part in supplying the lens with nerves; but, from the analogy of the olfactory and auditory nerves, it seems more reasonable to suppose that the optic nerve serves no other purpose than that of conveying sensation to the brain.

Although a strong light and close examination are required, in order to see the fibres of the crystalline in its intire state, yet their direction may be demonstrated, and their attachment shown, without much difficulty. In a dead eye the radiating lines are discernible through the capsule, and sometimes the anterior ones even through the cornea and aqueous humour. When the crystalline falls, it very frequently separates as far as the centre into three portions, each having a line in its middle. If it be carefully stripped of its capsule, and the smart blast of a fine blowpipe be applied close to its surface in different parts, it will be found to crack exactly in the direction of the fibres above described, and all these cracks will be stopped as soon they reach either of the radiating lines. The application of a little ink to the crystalline is also of great use in showing the course of the fibres.

When first I observed the structure of the crystalline, I was not aware that its muscularity had ever been suspected. We have indeed seen, that Descartes supposed it to be of a muscular nature; he had, however, no accurate idea of its internal structure.

But the laborious and accurate Leeuwenhoek, by the help of his powerful microscopes, has described the course of the fibres of the crystalline, in a variety of animals; and he has also called it a muscle*; but, probably from examining only dried preparations, he has imagined, that each coat consists of circumvolutions of a single fibre, and has intirely overlooked the attachment of the fibres to lines resembling tendons. If the fibres were continued into each other in the manner that he describes, the strict analogy to muscle would be lost, and their contraction could not conveniently have that effect on the figure of the lens, which is produced by help of the tendons. Yet much anatomical merit must be allowed to the faithful description, and elegant delineation, of the crystallines of various animals, which he has given in the Philosophical Transactions. (XIV. 780, and XXIV. 1723). It appears, from his descriptions and figures, that the crystalline of hogs, dogs, and cats, resembles what I have observed in oxen, sheep, and horses; that in hares and rabbits, the radiating lines on each side, instead of three, are only two, meeting in the axis so as to form one straight line; and that in whales they are five, radiated in the same manner as where there are three. It is evident that this variety will make no material difference in the action of the muscle. I have not yet had an opportunity of examining the human crystalline, but from its readily dividing into three parts, we may infer that it is similar to that of the ox. The crystalline in fishes being nearly spherical, such a change as I attribute to the lens in quadrupeds cannot take place in that class of animals.

It has been observed that the central part of the crystalline becomes rigid by age, and this is sufficient to account for presbyopia, without any diminution of the humours; although I do not deny the existence of this diminution, as a concomitant circumstance.

I shall here beg leave to attempt the solution of some optical queries, which have not been much considered by authors.

1. Musschenbroek asks, What is the cause of the lateral radiations which seem to adhere to a candle viewed with winking eyes? I answer, the most conspicuous radiations are those which, diverging from below, form, each with a vertical line, an angle of about seven degrees; this angle is equal to that which the edges of the eyelids when closed make with a horizontal line; and the radia-

---

* Now if the cristaline humour (which I have sometimes called the crist. muscle) in our eyes, &c. Phil. Trans. XXIV. 1720.—*Crystallinum musculum*, alias *humorem crystallinum dictum, &c*, Leeuwenh. *Op. omn.* I. 102.

tions are very justly attributed by Musschenbroek to the refraction of the moisture contiguous to the eyelids. But the lateral radiations are produced by the light reflected from the eyelashes.

2. Some have inquired, Whence arises that luminous cross, which seems to proceed from the image of a candle in a looking-glass? This is produced by the direction of the friction by which the glass is commonly polished: the scratches, placed in a horizontal direction, exhibiting the perpendicular part of the cross, and the vertical scratches the horizontal part, in a manner that may easily be conceived.

3. Why do sparks appear to be emitted when the eye is rubbed or compressed in the dark? This is Musschenbroek's fourth query. When a broadish pressure, as that of the finger, is made on the opaque part of the eye in the dark, an orbicular spectrum appears on the part opposite to that which is pressed: the light of the disc is faint, that of the circumference much stronger; but when a narrow surface is applied, as that of a pin's head, or of the nail, the image is narrow and bright. This is evidently occasioned by the irritation of the retina at the part touched, referred by the mind to the place from whence light coming through the pupil would fall on this spot; the irritation is greatest where the flexure is greatest, that is, at the circumference, and sometimes at the centre, of the depressed part. But in the presence of light, whether the eye be open or closed, the circumference only will be luminous, and the disc dark; and if the eye be viewing any object at the part where the image appears, that object will be almost invisible. Hence it follows, that the tension and compression of the retina tend to destroy all the irritation, except that which is produced by its flexure; and this is so slight on the disc, that the apparent light there is fainter than that of the rays arriving at all other parts through the eyelids. This experiment demonstrates a truth, which may be inferred from many other arguments, that the supposed rectification of the inverted image on the retina does not depend on the direction of the incident rays; since the mind can refer the object to its true relative situation without any assistance from this direction. Newton, in his sixteenth query, has described this phantom as of pavonian colours, but I can distinguish no other than white; and it seems most natural that this, being the compound or average of all existing sensations of light, should be produced when nothing determines to any particular colour. This average seems to resemble the midlife form, which Sir Joshua Reynolds has elegantly insisted on in his discourses; so that perhaps some principles of beautiful contrast of colours may be drawn from hence, it being probable that those colours which together approach near to white light will have the most pleasing effect in apposition. It must be observed, that the sensation of light, from pressure of the eye, subsides almost instantly after the motion of pressure has ceased, so that the cause of the irritation of the retina is a change, and not a difference of form; and therefore the sensation of light appears to depend immediately on a minute motion of some part of the optic nerve.

If the anterior part of the eye be repeatedly pressed, so as to occasion some degree of pain, and a continued pressure be then made on the sclerotica, while an interrupted pressure is made on the cornea; we shall frequently be able to observe an appearance of luminous lines, branched, and somewhat connected with each other, darting from every part of the field of view, towards a centre a little exterior and superior to the axis of the eye. This centre corresponds to the insertion of the optic nerve, and the appearance of lines is probably occasioned by that motion of the retina which is produced by the sudden return of the circulating fluid, into the veins accompanying the ramifications of the arteria centralis, after having been detained by the pressure which is now intermitted. As such an obstruction and such a readmission must require particular circumstances, in order to be effected in a sensible degree, it may naturally be supposed that this experiment will not always easily succeed.

PLATE 1.

Explanation of the Figures.

Fig. 1. A vertical section of the ox's eye, of twice the natural size.

A. The cornea, covered by the tunica conjunctiva.
BCB. The sclerotica, covered at BB by the tunica albuginea, and tunica conjunctiva.
DD. The choroid, consisting of two laminas.
EE. The circle of adherence of the choroid and sclerotica.
FG. FG. The orbiculus ciliaris.
HI, HK. The uvea; its anterior surface the iris; its posterior surface lined with pigmentum nigrum.
IK. The pupil.
HL, HL. The ciliary processes, covered with pigmentum nigrum.
MM. The retina.
N. The aqueous humour.
O. The crystalline lens.
P. The vitreous humour.
QR, QR. The zona ciliaris.
RS, RS. The annulus mucosus.

Fig. 2. The structure of the crystalline lens, as viewed in front.
Fig. 3. A side view of the crystalline.

PLATE 1.

Fig. 1.

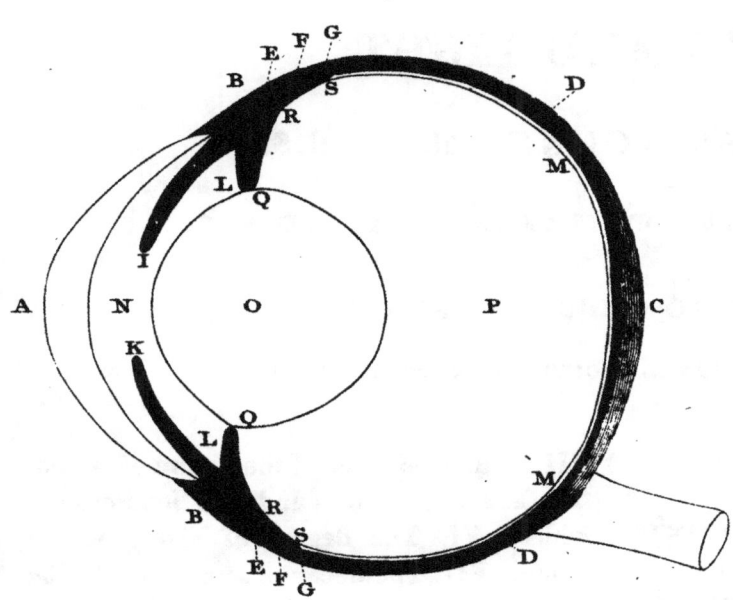

Fig. 2.

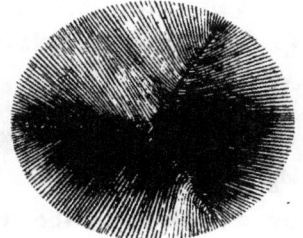

Fig. 3.

Pub. by J. Johnson, London 1 July 1806.

Joseph Skelton s.

II. OUTLINES

OF EXPERIMENTS AND INQUIRIES RESPECTING

SOUND AND LIGHT.

BY THOMAS YOUNG, M.D F.R.S.

IN A LETTER TO EDWARD WHITAKER GRAY, M.D. SEC. R.S.

FROM THE PHILOSOPHICAL TRANSACTIONS.

Read before the ROYAL SOCIETY, *January* 16, 1800.

DEAR SIR,

It has long been my intention to lay before the Royal Society a few observations on the subject of sound; and I have endeavoured to collect as much information, and to make as many experiments, connected with this inquiry, as circumstances enabled me to do; but the further I have proceeded, the more widely the prospect of what lay before me has been extended; and, as I find that the investigation, in all its magnitude, will occupy the leisure hours of some years, or perhaps of a life, I am determined, in the mean time, lest any unforeseen circumstances should prevent my continuing the pursuit, to submit to the Society some conclusions which I have already formed from the results of various experiments. Their subjects are, I. The measurement of the quantity of air discharged through an aperture. II. The determination of the direction and velocity of a stream of air proceeding from an orifice. III. Ocular evidence of the nature of sound. IV. The velocity of sound. V. Sonorous cavities. VI. The degree of divergence of sound. VII. The decay of sound. VIII. The harmonic sounds of pipes. IX. The vibrations of different elastic fluids. X. The analogy between light and sound. XI. The coalescence of musical sounds. XII. The frequency of vibrations constituting a given note. XIII. The vibrations of chords. XIV. The vibrations of rods and plates. XV. The human voice. XVI. The temperament of musical intervals.

I. *Of the Quantity of Air discharged through an Aperture.*

A piece of bladder was tied over the end of the tube of a large glass funnel, and punctured with a hot needle. The funnel was inverted in a vessel of water; and a gage, with a graduated glass tube, was so placed as to measure the pressure occasioned by the different levels of the surfaces of the water.

As the air escaped through the puncture, it was supplied by a phial of known dimensions, at equal intervals of time; and according to the frequency of this supply, the average height of the gage was such as is expressed in the first Table. It appears that the quantity of air, discharged by a given aperture, was nearly in the subduplicate ratio of the pressure. The second, third, and fourth Tables show the result of similar experiments made with some variations in the apparatus.

Table I.

A	B	C	D	E	F
.00018	.25	3.9	30.1	4.18	7.2
.001	.045	7.8	10.8	1.77	6.1
.001	.2	15.6	21.7	3.74	5.8
.001	.7	31.2	43.3	7.00	6.3
					6.3 Mean.

All numbers throughout this paper, where the contrary is not expressed, are to be understood of inches, linear, square, or cubic.

A is the area, in square inches, of an aperture nearly circular. B, the pressure in inches. C, the number of cubic inches discharged in one minute. D, is the observed velocity of the air in a second, expressed in feet. E, the square root of the height of a column of air equivalent to the pressure. F, the quotient of the two last columns.

Table II.

A	B	C	D	E	F
.07	1.	2000.	39.7	8.37	4.8
.07	2.	2900.	57.5	11.84	4.9

A is the area of the section of a tube about two inches long. B, the pressure. C, the quantity of air discharged in a minute, by estimation. D, E, and F, as in Table I.

Table III.

A	B	C	D	E	F	G
.0064	1.15	.2	46.8	9.9	3.74	2.5
.0064	10.	.45	46.8	9.9	5.61	1.8
.0064	13.5	.35	31.2	6.6	4.95	1.3
.0064	13.5	.7	46.8	9.9	7.00	1.4

A is the area of the section of a tube. B, its length. C, the pressure. D, the discharge in a minute. E, F, and G, as D, E, and F, in Table I.

Table IV.

A	B	C	D	E	F
.003	.28	46.8	21.7	4.43	4.9

A is the area of an oval aperture, formed by flattening a glass tube at the end: its diameters were .025 and .152. B, the pressure. C, the discharge. D, E, and F, as in Table I.

II. *Of the Direction and Velocity of a Stream of Air.*

An apparatus was contrived for measuring, by means of a water gage communicating with a reservoir of air, the pressure by which a current was forced from the reservoir through a cylindrical tube; and the gage was so sensible, that, a regular blast being supplied from the lungs, it showed the slight variation produced by every pulsation of the heart. The current of air issuing from the tube was directed downwards, upon a white plate, on which a scale of equal parts was engraved, and which was thinly covered with a coloured liquid; the breadth of the surface of the plate laid bare was observed at different distances from the tube, and with different degrees of pressure, care being taken that the liquid should be so shallow as to yield to the slightest impression of air. The results are collected in Tables v and vi. (Plate 2. Fig. 4..15.) In order to measure, with greater certainty and precision, the velocity of every part of the current, a second cavity, furnished with a gage, was provided, and pieces perforated with apertures of different sizes were adapted to its orifice: the axis of the current was directed as accurately as possible to the centres of these apertures, and the results of the experiments, with various pressures and distances, are inserted in Tables vii, viii, and ix. The velocity of a stream being, both according to the commonly received opinion, and to the experiments already related, nearly in the subduplicate ratio of the pressure occasioning it, it was inferred, that an equal pressure would be required to stop its progress, and that the velocity of the current, where it struck against the aperture, must be in the subduplicate ratio of the pressure marked by the gage. Having thus ascertained the velocity of the stream at different distances from the aperture, we must adopt, in order to infer from it the magnitude of the stream, some supposition respecting the mode in which its motion is retarded, and the simplest hypothesis appears to be, that the momentum of the particles contained at first in a given small length of the stream, together with that of the particles of the surrounding air, which they drag along, remains always constant, so that the area of the transverse section may be inversely as the square of the velocity; and the diameter inversely as the velocity itself; the particles of the stream occupying a section as much wider as the velocity is smaller, and carrying with them as many more particles as will require a space still larger in the same proportion. On this supposition, the ordinates of a curve may be taken reciprocally in the subduplicate ratio of the pressure marked by the second gage to that indicated by the first, at the various distances represented by the abscisses, and the solid, described by the revolution of this curve round its axis, will nearly represent the magnitude of the current in all its parts. (Plate 2. Fig. 16..26.) As the central particles must be supposed to be less impeded in their motion than the superficial ones, of course, the smaller the aperture opposed to the centre of the current, the greater the velocity ought to come out, and the ordinate of the curve the smaller; but where the aperture was not greater than that of the tube, the difference of the velocities at the same distance was scarcely perceptible. When the aperture was larger than that of the tube, if the distance was very small, of course the average velocity came out much smaller than that which was inferred from a smaller aperture; but, where the ordinate of the internal curve became nearly equal to this aperture, there was but little difference between the velocities indicated with different apertures. Indeed, in some cases, where the diameter of the aperture was a little greater than that of the stream striking on it, it appeared to indicate a greater velocity than a smaller aperture: this might have arisen in some degree from the smaller aperture not having been exactly in the centre of the current; but there is greater reason to suppose, that it was occasioned by some resistance derived from the air returning between the sides of the aperture, and the current entering it. Where this took place, the external curves, which are so constructed as that their ordinates are reciprocally in the subduplicate ratio of the pressure observed in the second cavity, with apertures equal in semidiameter to their initial ordinate, approach, for a short distance, nearer to the axis than the internal curve; after this, they continue their course very near to this curve. Hence it appears, that no observable part of the motion diverged beyond the limits of the solid which would be formed by the revolution of the internal curve, deduced from observations on a small aperture, which is seldom inclined to the axis in an angle so great as ten degrees. A similar conclusion may be made, from observing the flame of a candle subjected to the action of a blowpipe: there is no divergency beyond the narrow limits of the current; the flame, on the contrary, is every where forced by the ambient air towards the current, to supply the place of that which it has carried away by its friction. The lateral communication of motion, very ingeniously and accurately observed in water by Professor Venturi, is exactly similar to the motion here shown to take place in air; and these experiments fully justify him in rejecting the tenacity of water as its cause: no doubt it arises from the relative situation of the particles of the fluid, in the line of the current, with respect to that of the particles in the contiguous strata, which, whatever may be the supposed order of the single particles with respect to each other, must naturally lead to a communication of motion nearly in a parallel direction; and this may properly be termed friction. The lateral pressure which urges the flame of a candle towards the stream of air from a blowpipe, is probably exactly similar to that pressure which causes the inflection of a current of air near an obstacle. Mark the dimple which a slender stream of air makes on the surface of water; bring a convex body into contact with the side of the stream, and the place of the dimple will immediately show that the current is inflected towards the body; and, if the body be at liberty to move in every direction, it will be urged towards the current, in the same manner as, in Venturi's experiments, a fluid was forced up a tube inserted into the side of a pipe through which water was flowing. A similar interposition of an obstacle, in the course of the wind, is probably often the cause of smoky chimneys. One circumstance was observed in these experiments, which it is extremely difficult to explain, and which yet leads to very important consequences: it may be made distinctly perceptible to the eye, by forcing a current of smoke very gently through a fine tube. When the velocity is as small as possible, the stream proceeds for many inches without any observable dilatation; it then immediately diverges at a considerable angle into a cone, (Plate 3. Fig. 27); and, at the point of divergency, there is an audible and even visible vibration. The blowpipe also affords a method of observing this phenomenon: as far as can be judged from the motion of the flame, the current seems to make something like a revolution in the surface of the cone, but this motion is too rapid to be distinctly discerned. When the pressure is increased, the apex of the cone approaches nearer to the orifice of the tube (Fig. 28, 29); but no degree of pressure seems materially to alter its ultimate divergency. The distance of the apex from the orifice is not proportional to the diameter of the current; it rather appears to be the greater the smaller the current, and is much better defined in a small current than in a large one. Its distance in one experiment is expressed in Table x. from observations on the surface of a liquid;

in other experiments, its respective distances were sometimes considerably less with the same degrees of pressure. It may be inferred, from the numbers of Tables VII and VIII, that in several instances a greater height of the first gage produced a less height of the second: this arose from the nearer approach of the apex of the cone to the orifice of the tube, the stream losing a greater portion of its velocity by this divergence than it gained by the increase of pressure. At first sight, the form of the current bears some resemblance to the *vena contracta* of a jet of water: but Venturi has observed, that in water an increase of pressure increases, instead of diminishing, the distance of the contracted section from the orifice.

Table VI.

A	1.	2.
B	C	C
1.	.1	.1
2.	.13	
3.	.2	.2
4.	.25	.3
6.	.3	.4
7.	.35	.5
10.	.35	.6
15.	.35	.7
20.	.35	.7

Diameter of the tube, .1. A, B, and C, as in Table V.

Table V.

A.	1.	2.	3.	3.5
B.	C	C	C	C
1.	.1	.1	.1	
2.	.12	.12	.2	
3.	.17	.25	.3	
4.	.2	.4	.4	
5.	.25	.5		
6.	.30	.52		
7.	.35	.54	.5	
8.	.37	.56		
9.	.39	.58		
10.	.40	.6	.6	.5
15.		.7		
18.	.50			
20.				

The diameter of the tube .07. A is the distance of the liquid from the orifice. B, the pressure. C, the diameter of the surface of the liquid displaced.

Table VII.

A		.5	
B		.06	.15
C		D	D
.1		.083	
.2		.16	
.3		.25	.1
.4		.35	
.5		.45	
.6		.53	.2
.7		.6	
.8			.3
1.		.3	
1.2		.4	.4
1.5		.6	
2.		.67	.55
4.		1.3	.1
8.			.2
9.		.3	
14.		.5	

Diameter of the tube .06.

A is the distance of the opposite aperture, from the orifice of the tube. B, the diameter of the aperture. C, the pressure, indicated by the first gage. D, the height of the second gage.

EXPERIMENTS AND INQUIRIES

Table VIII.

A	.5				1.				2.				4.			
B	.06	.15	.3	.5	.06	.15	.3	.5	.06	.15	.3	.5	.06	.15	.3	.5
C	D	D	D	D	D	D	D	D	D	D	D	D	D	D	D	D
.1	.05	.05			.03				.017							
.2	.1	.1			.12	.08	.02		.034							
.5	.2	.22			.1	.00			.00							
1.	.32	.36	.1		.17	.1	.1	.05	.04							
2.	.52	.6	.2		.28	.22	.21	.08	.07							
3.	.8	.9	.3		.4	.36	.32	.12	.12	.1	.1					
4.	1.1	1.2	.4		.58	.52	.42	.16	.18	.15	.14					
5.		1.5	.5		.8	.68	.52	.2	.23	.2	.18	.04		.04		.05
6.		1.7	.6		1.	.83	.63	.25	.3	.25	.22	.05		.05		.06
7.		1.9	.7		1.2	1.	.75	.3	.35	.3	.26	.06		.06		.07
8.		2.1	.8		1.5	1.2	.88	.34	.4	.34	.3	.07		.07		.07
9.		2.3	.9		1.7	1.4	1.	.37	.45	.37	.34	.08		.08		.08
10.		2.6	1.		1.9	1.6	1.1	.4	.5	.4	.37	.09		.09		.09

Diameter of the tube .1. A, B, C, and D, as in Table VII.

Table IX.

A	1.15				3.3			4.
B	.15	.3	.5	1.	.06	.15	1.	.06
C	D	D	D	D	D	D	D	D
.5	.1	.1	.1					
1.	.2	.2	.2					
2.	.4	.35	.34	.13	.1	.1	.125	
3.	.6	.5	.5	.2	.15	.15	.18	.1

Diameter of the tube .3.
A, B, C, and D, as in Table VII.

Table X.

A	B
.4	6.
.8	3.
1.2	1.5
1.6	1.
2.	.5
4.	.0

A is the pressure. B, the distance of the apex of the cone from the orifice of a tube .1 in diameter.

III. *Ocular Evidence of the Nature of Sound.*

A tube about the tenth of an inch in diameter, with a lateral orifice half an inch from its end, filled rather deeper than the axis of the tube, (Fig. 30,) was inserted at the apex of a conical cavity, containing about twenty cubic inches of air, and was luted perfectly tight: by blowing through the tube, a sound nearly in unison with the tenor C was produced. By gradually increasing the capacity of the cavity as far as several gallons, with the same mouthpiece, the sound, although faint, became more and more grave, till it was no longer a musical note. Even before this period a kind of trembling was distinguishable; and this, as the cavity was still further increased, was changed into a succession of distinct puffs, like the sound produced by an explosion of air from the lips; as slow, in some instances, as 4 or 3 in a second. These were undoubtedly the single vibrations, which, when repeated with sufficient frequency, impress on the auditory nerve the sensation of a continued sound. On forcing a current of smoke through the tube, the vibratory motion of the stream, as it passed out at the lateral orifice, was evident to the eye; although, from various circumstances, the quantity and direction of its motion could not be subjected to exact mensuration. This species of sonorous cavity seems susceptible of but few harmonic sounds. It was observed, that a faint blast produced a much greater frequency of vibrations than that which was appropriate to the cavity: a circumstance similar to this obtains also in large organ pipes; but several minute observations of this kind, although they might assist in forming a theory of the origin of vibrations, or in confirming such a theory drawn from other sources, yet, as they are not alone sufficient to afford any general conclusions, are omitted at present, for the sake of brevity.

IV. *Of the Velocity of Sound.*

It has been demonstrated, by M. De la Grange and others, that any impression whatever, communicated to one particle of an elastic fluid, will be transmitted through that fluid with a uniform velocity, depending on the constitution of the fluid, without reference to any supposed laws of the continuation of that impression. Their theorem for ascertaining this velocity is the same as Newton has deduced from the hypothesis of a particular law of continuation: but it must be confessed, that the result differs somewhat too widely from experiment, to give us full confidence in the perfection of the theory. Corrected by the experiments of various observers, the velocity of any impression transmitted by the common air, may, at an average, be reckoned 1130 feet in a second.

V. *Of sonorous Cavities.*

M. De la Grange has also demonstrated, that all impressions are reflected by an obstacle terminating an elastic fluid, with the same velocity with which they arrived at that obstacle. When the walls of a passage, or of an unfurnished room, are smooth, and perfectly parallel, any explosion, or a stamping with the foot, communicates an impression to the air, which is reflected from one wall to the other, and from the second again towards the ear, nearly in the same direction with the primitive impulse: this takes place as frequently in a second, as twice the breadth of the passage is contained in 1130 feet; and the ear receives a perception of a musical sound, thus determined in its pitch by the breadth of the passage. On making the experiment, the result will be found accurately to agree with this explanation. If the sound is predetermined, and the frequency of vibrations such, that each pulse, when doubly reflected, may coincide with the subsequent pulse proceeding directly from the sounding body, the intensity of the sound will be much increased by the reflection; and also, in a less degree, if the reflected pulse coincides with the next but one, the next but two, or more, of the direct pulses. The appropriate notes of a room may readily be discovered by singing the scale in it; and they will be found to depend on the proportion of its length or breadth to 1130 feet. The sound of the stopped diapason pipes of an organ is produced in a manner somewhat similar to the note from an explosion in a passage; and that of its reed pipes to the resonance of the voice in a room: the length of the pipe in one case determining the sound; in the other, increasing its strength. The frequency of the vibrations does not at all immediately depend on the diameter of the pipe. It must be confessed, that much remains to be done in explaining the precise manner in which the vibration of the air in an organ pipe is generated. M. Daniel Bernoulli has solved several difficult problems relating to the subject: yet some of his assumptions are not only gratuitous, but contrary to matter of fact.

VI. *Of the Divergence of Sound.*

It has been generally asserted, chiefly on the authority of Newton, that if any sound be admitted through an aperture into a chamber, it will diverge from that aperture equally in all directions. The chief arguments in favour of this opinion are deduced from considering the phenomena of the pressure of fluids, and the motion of waves excited in a pool of water. But the inference seems to be too hastily drawn: there is a very material difference between impulse and pressure; and, in the case of waves of water, the moving force at each point is the power of gravity, which, acting primarily in a perpendicular direction, is only secondarily converted into a horizontal force, in the direction of the progress of the waves, being at each step disposed in some measure to spread in every direction: but the impulse, transmitted by an elastic fluid, acts primarily in the direction of its progress. It is well known, that if a person calls to another with a speaking trumpet, he points it towards the place where his hearer stands. I am assured by a very respectable Member of the Royal Society, and it was indeed long ago observed by Grimaldi, that the report of a cannon appears many times louder to a person towards whom it is fired, than to one placed in a contrary direction. It must have occurred to every one's observation, that a sound, such as that of a mill, or a fall of water, has appeared much louder after turning a corner, when the house or other obstacle no longer intervened; and it has been already remarked by Euler, on this head, that we are not acquainted with any substance perfectly impervious to sound. Many solid bodies even appear to conduct sound better than the air: as in the well known experiment of scratching a long beam with a pin; and in discovering the approach of cavalry, by applying the ear to the ground. Indeed, as Mr. Lambert has very truly asserted, the whole theory of the speaking trumpet, supported as it is by practical experience, would fall to the ground, if it were demonstrable that sound spreads equally in every direction. In windy weather it may often be observed, that the sound of a distant bell varies almost instantaneously in its strength, so as to appear at least twice as remote at one time as at another; an observation which has also occurred to another gentleman, who is uncommonly accurate in examining the phenomena of nature. Now, if sound diverged equally in all directions, the variation produced by the wind could never exceed one tenth of the apparent distance; but, on the supposition of a motion nearly rectilinear, it may easily happen that a slight change, in the direction of the wind, may convey a beam of sound, either directly or after reflection, in very different degrees of strength, to the same spot. From the experiments on the motion of a current of air, already related, it would be expected that a sound, admitted at a considerable distance from its origin through an aperture, would proceed, with an almost imperceptible increase of divergence, in the same direction; for, the actual velocity of the particles of air, in the strongest sound, is incomparably less than that of the slowest of the currents in the experiments related, where the beginning of the conical divergence took place at the greatest distance. Dr. Matthew Young has objected, not without some reason, to M. Huber, that the existence of a condensation will cause a divergence in sound: but a much greater degree of condensation must have existed in the currents described than in any sound. There is indeed one difference between a stream of air and a sound; that, in sound, the motions of different particles of air are not synchronous: but it is not demonstrable that this circumstance would affect the divergency of the motion, except at the instant of its commencement, and perhaps not even then in a material degree; for, in general, the motion is communicated with a very gradual increase of intensity, so that there is no sudden condensation nor rarefaction. The subject, however, deserves a more particular investigation; and, in order to obtain a more solid foundation for the argument, it is proposed, as soon as circumstances permit, to institute a course of experiments for ascertaining, as accurately as possible, the different strength of a sound once projected in a given direction, at different distances from the axis of its motion.

VII. *Of the Decay of Sound.*

Various opinions have been entertained respecting the decay of sound. M. De la Grange has published a calculation, by which its force is shown to decay nearly in the simple ratio of the distances; and M. Daniel Bernoulli's equations for the sounds of conical pipes lead to a similar conclusion. The same inference follows from a completion of the reasoning of Dr. Helsham, Dr. Matthew Young, and Professor Venturi. It has been very elegantly demonstrated by Maclaurin, and may also be proved in a much more simple manner, that, when motion is communicated through a series of elastic bodies increasing in magnitude, if the number of bodies be supposed infinitely great, and their difference infinitely small, the motion of the last will be to that of the first in the subduplicate ratio of their respective magnitudes; and since, in the case of concentric spherical laminae of air, the bulk increases in the duplicate ratio of the distance, the motion will in this case be directly, and the velocity inversely, as the distance. It may, however, be questioned, whether or no the strength of sound is to be considered as simply proportional to the velocity of the particles concerned in transmitting it.

VIII. *Of the harmonic Sounds of Pipes.*

In order to ascertain the velocity with which organ pipes of different lengths require to be supplied with air, according to the various appropriate sounds which they produce, a set of experiments was made, with the same mouth piece, on pipes of the same bore, and of different lengths, both stopped and open. The general result was, that a similar blast produced as nearly the same sound as the length of the pipes would permit; or at least that the exceptions, though very numerous, lay equally on each side of this conclusion. The particular results are expressed in Table xi, and in Plate 3. Fig. 31. They explain how a note may be made much louder on a wind instrument by a swell, than it can possibly be by a sudden impression of the blast. It is proposed, at a future time, to ascertain, by experiment, the actual compression of the air within the pipe under different circumstances: from some very slight trials, it seemed to be nearly in the ratio of the frequency of vibrations of each harmonic.

Table XI.

OPEN.						STOPPED.					
A	B	C	D	E	F	A	B	C	D	E	F
4.5		0.7	8.8	$\overline{\overline{d\text{※}}}$	1	4.5		0.3	1.8	$\overline{\overline{d}}$	1
	4.1	8.8			2		1.2	1.7	10.0		3
							5.0	9.0			5
9.4		0.3	0.9	$\overline{f}$	1	9.4		0.2	0.4	$\overline{f}$	1
	0.8		8.0		2			0.45	1.6		3
	2.0		18.0		3		1.1	1.6	8.5		5
	5.0	8.0	20.0		4		7.0	8.0			7
	16.5	18.0			5						
	19.0	20.0			6						
16.1		0.4	1.0	$\overline{g}$	2	16.1		0.4	0.6	$\overline{\overline{d\text{※}}}$	3
	0.8	1.0	2.2		3		0.6	0.65	1.1		5
	1.2	2.2	4.7		4		0.9	1.1	2.4		7
	2.2	4.7	11.5		5		1.6	2.4	4.9		9
	3.4		13.5		6		2.5	4.8	9.0		11
	4.0		15.0		7		6.9	7.0			13
	6.5	10.0			8						
						20.5		0.8	1.1	$\overline{\overline{c\text{※}}}$	7
							1.0	1.1	3.8		9
							1.8		3.8		11
20.5		0.6	0.8	$\overline{b}$	3		3.2	3.8	12.		17
		0.8	1.9		4			12.		o	00
	1.1	1.9	5.7		5						
	4.5	5.7			8						

A is the length of the pipe from the lateral orifice to the end. C, the pressure at which the sound began. B, its termination, by lessening the pressure; D, by increasing it. E, the note answering to the first sound produced by each pipe, according to the German method of notation. F, the number showing the place of each note in the regular series of harmonics. The diameter of the pipe was .35; the air duct of the mouth piece measured, where smallest, .25 by .035; the lateral orifice .25 by .125. The apparatus was not calculated to apply a pressure of above 22 inches. Where no number stands under C, a sudden blast was required to produce the note.

IX. *Of the Vibrations of different elastic Fluids.*

All the methods of finding the velocity of sound agree, in determining it to be, in fluids of a given elasticity, reciprocally in the subduplicate ratio of the density: hence, in pure hydrogen gas it should be $\sqrt{13} = 3.6$ times as great as in common air; and the pitch of a pipe should be a minor fourteenth higher in this fluid than in the common air. It is therefore probable, that the hydrogen gas, used in Professor Chladni's late experiments, was not quite pure. It must be observed, that in an accurate experiment of this nature, the pressure causing the blast ought to be carefully ascertained. There can be no doubt but that, in the observations of the French Academicians on the velocity of sound, which appear to have been conducted with all possible attention, the dampness and coldness of the night air must have considerably increased its density: hence, the velocity was found to be only 1109 feet in a second; while Derham's experiments, which have an equal appearance of accuracy, make it amount to 1142. Perhaps the average may, as has been already mentioned, be safely estimated at 1130. It may here be remarked, that the well known elevation of the pitch of wind instruments, in the course of playing, sometimes amounting to half a note, is not, as is commonly supposed, owing to any expansion of the instrument, for this should produce a contrary effect, but to the increased warmth of the air in the tube. Dr. Smith has made a similar observation, on the pitch of an organ in summer and winter, which he found to differ more than twice as much as the English and French experiments on the velocity of sound. Bianconi found the velocity of sound, at Bologna, to differ at different times, in the ratio of 152 to 157.

X. *Of the Analogy between Light and Sound.*

Ever since the publication of Sir Isaac Newton's incomparable writings, his doctrine of the emanation of particles of light, from lucid substances, has been almost universally admitted in this country, and but little opposed in others. Leonard Euler indeed, in several of his works, has advanced some powerful objections against it, but not sufficiently powerful to justify the dogmatical reprobation with which he treats it; and he has left that system of an ethereal vibration, which after Huygens and some others he adopted, equally liable to be attacked on many weak sides. Without pretending to decide positively on the controversy, it is conceived that some considerations may be brought forwards, which may tend to diminish the weight of objections to a theory similar to the Huygenian. There are also one or two difficulties in the Newtonian system, which have been little observed. The first is the uniform velocity with which light is supposed to be projected from all luminous bodies, in consequence of heat, or otherwise. How happens it that, whether the projecting force is the slightest transmission of electricity, the friction of two pebbles, the lowest degree of visible ignition, the white heat of a wind furnace, or the intense heat of the sun itself, these wonderful corpuscles are always propelled with one uniform velocity? For, if they differed in velocity, that difference ought to produce a different refraction. But a still more insuperable difficulty seems to occur, in the partial reflection from every refracting surface.

Why, of the same kind of rays, in every circumstance precisely similar, some should always be reflected, and others transmitted, appears in this system to be wholly inexplicable. That a medium resembling, in many properties, that which has been denominated ether, does really exist, is undeniably proved by the phenomena of electricity; and the arguments against the existence of such an ether, throughout the universe, have been pretty sufficiently answered by Euler. The rapid transmission of the electrical shock shows that the electric medium is possessed of an elasticity, as great, as is necessary to be supposed for the propagation of light. Whether the electric ether is to be considered as the same with the luminous ether, if such a fluid exists, may perhaps at some future time be discovered by experiment; hitherto I have not been able to observe that the refractive power of a fluid undergoes any change by electricity. The uniformity of the motion of light in the same medium, which is a difficulty in the Newtonian theory, favours the admission of the Huygenian; as all impressions are known to be transmitted through an elastic fluid with the same velocity. It has been already shown, that sound, in all probability, has very little tendency to diverge: in a medium so highly elastic as the luminous ether must be supposed to be, the tendency to diverge may be considered as infinitely small, and the grand objection to the system of vibration will be removed. It is not absolutely certain, that the white line visible in all directions on the edge of a knife, in the experiments of Newton and of Mr. Jordan, was not partly occasioned by the tendency of light to diverge; nor indeed has any other probable cause been yet assigned for its appearance. Euler's hypothesis, of the transmission of light by an agitation of the particles of the refracting media themselves, is liable to strong objections; according to this supposition, the refraction of the rays of light, on entering the atmosphere from the pure ether which he describes, ought to be a million times greater than it is. For explaining the phenomena of partial and total reflection, refraction, and inflection, nothing more is necessary than to suppose all refracting media to retain, by their attraction, a greater or less quantity of the luminous ether, so as to make its density greater than that which it possesses in a vacuum, without increasing its elasticity; and that light is a propagation of an impulse communicated to this ether by luminous bodies: whether this impulse is produced by a partial emanation of the ether, or by vibrations of the particles of the body, and whether these vibrations, constituting white light, are, as Euler supposed, of various and irregular magnitudes, or whether they are uniform, and comparatively large, remains to be hereafter determined; although the opinion of Euler respecting them seems to be almost the only one which is consistent with the Newtonian discoveries. Now, as the direction of an impulse, transmitted through a fluid, depends on that of the particles in synchronous motion, to which it is always perpendicular, whatever alters the direction of the pulse, will inflect the ray of light. If a small elastic body strikes against a larger one, it is well known that the smaller is reflected more or less powerfully, according to the difference of their magnitudes: thus, there is always a reflection when the rays of light pass from a rarer to a denser stratum of ether; and frequently an echo when a sound strikes against a cloud. A greater body, striking a smaller one, propels it, without losing all its motion: thus, the particles of a denser stratum of ether do not impart the whole of their motion to a rarer, but, in their effort to proceed, they are recalled by the attraction of the refracting substance with equal force; and thus a reflection is always secondarily produced, when the rays of light pass from a denser to a rarer stratum. Let AB, (Plate 4. Fig. 32,) be a ray of light falling on the reflecting surface FG; cd the direction of the vibration, pulse, impression, or condensation. When d comes to H, the impression will be, either wholly or partly, reflected with the same velocity as it arrived, and EH will be equal to DH: the angle EIH to DIH or CIF; and the angle of reflection to that of incidence. Let FG, (Fig. 33,) be a refracting surface. The portion of the pulse IE, which is travelling through the refracting medium, will move with a greater or less velocity in the subduplicate ratio of the densities, and HE will be to KI in that ratio. But HE is, to the radius IH, the sine of the angle of refraction; and KI that of the angle of incidence. This explanation of refraction is nearly the same as that of Rizzetti and Euler. The total reflection of a ray of light, by a refracting surface, is explicable in the same manner as its simple refraction: HE, (Fig. 34,) being so much longer than KI, that the ray first becomes parallel to FG, and then, having to return through an equal diversity of media, is reflected in an equal angle. When a ray of light passes near an inflecting body, surrounded, as all bodies are supposed to be, with an atmosphere of ether denser than the ether of the ambient air, the part of the ray nearest to the body is retarded, and of course the whole ray is inflected towards the body, (Fig. 35.) It has already been conjectured, that the colours of light consist in the different frequency of the vibrations of the luminous ether: the opinion is strongly confirmed, by the analogy between the colours of a thin plate and the sounds of a series of organ pipes, which, indeed, Euler adduces as an argument in favour of it, although he states the phenomena very inaccurately. The appearances of the colours of thin plates require, in the Newtonian system, a very complicated supposition, of an ether, anticipating by its motion the velocity of the corpuscles of light, and thus producing the fits of transmission and reflection; and even this supposition does not much assist the explanation. It appears, from the accurate analysis of the phenomena which Newton has given, and which has by no means been superseded by any later observations, that the same colour recurs, whenever the thickness answers to the terms of an arithmetical progression, and this effect appears to be very nearly similar to the production of the same sound, by means of a uniform blast, from organ pipes which are different multiples of the same length. The greatest difficulty in this system is, to explain the different degree of refraction of differently coloured light, and the separation of white light in refraction: yet, considering how imperfect the theory of elastic fluids still remains, it cannot be expected that every circumstance should at once be clearly elucidated. It may hereafter be considered, how far the excellent experiments of Count Rumford, which tend very greatly to weaken the evidence of the modern doctrine of heat, may be more or less favourable to one or the other system of light and colours.

XI. *Of the Coalescence of musical Sounds.*

It is surprising that so great a mathematician as Dr. Smith could have entertained, for a moment, an idea that the vibrations constituting different sounds should be able to cross each other in all directions, without affecting the same individual particles of air by their joint forces: undoubtedly they cross, without disturbing each other's progress; but this can be no otherwise effected than by each particle's partaking of both motions. If this assertion stood in need of any proof, it might be amply furnished by the phenomena of beats, and of the grave harmonics observed by Romieu and Tartini; which M. De la Grange has already considered in the same point of view. In the first place, to simplify the statement, let us suppose, what probably never precisely happens, that the particles of air, in transmitting the pulses, proceed and return with uniform motions; and, in order to represent their position to the eye, let the uniform progress of time be represented by the increase of the absciss, and the distance of the particle from its original position, by the ordinate, (Fig. 36..41). Then, by supposing any two or more vibrations in the same direction to be combined, the joint motion will be represented by the sum or difference of the ordinates. When two sounds are of equal strength, and nearly of the same pitch, as in Fig. 39, the joint vibration is alternately very weak and very strong, producing the effect denominated a beat, (Plate 5. Fig. 46, B and C); which is slower and more marked, as the sounds approach nearer to each other in frequency of vibrations; and of these beats there may happen to be several orders, according to the periodical approximations of the numbers expressing the proportions of the vibrations. The strength, or rather the momentum, of the joint sound is double that of the simple sound only at the middle of the beat, but not throughout its duration; and if we estimate the force of sound by the momentum of the particles, it may be inferred, that the strength of sound in a concert will not be in exact proportion to the number of instruments composing it. Could any method be devised for ascertaining this by experiment, it would assist in the comparison of sound with light: but the establishment of the fact would be no proof of a difference in the nature of sound and light; for there is no reason to suppose the undulations of light continuous: their intermissions may easily be a million million times greater than the duration of each parcel of undulations. In Plate 4. Fig. 36, let P and Q be the middle points of the progress or regress of a particle in two successive compound vibrations; then, CP being = PD, KR = RN, GQ = QH, and MS = SO, twice their distance, 2 RS = 2 RN + 2 NM + 2 MS = KN + NM + NM + MO = KM + NO, is equal to the sum of the distances of the corresponding parts of the simple vibrations. For instance, if the two sounds be as 80 : 81, the joint vibration will be as 80.5; the arithmetical mean between the periods of the single vibrations. The greater the difference in the pitch of two sounds, the more rapid the beats, till at last, like the distinct puffs of air in the experiments already related, they communicate the idea of a continued sound; and this is the fundamental harmonic described by Tartini. For instance, in Plate 4. Fig. 37..40, the vibrations of sounds related as 1 : 2, 4 : 5, 9 : 10, and 5 : 8, are represented; where the beats, if the sounds are not taken too grave, constitute a distinct sound, which corresponds with the time elapsing between two successive coincidences, or near approaches to coincidence; for, that such a tempered interval still produces a harmonic, appears from Plate 4. Fig. 41. But, besides this primary harmonic, a secondary note is sometimes heard, where the intermediate compound vibrations occur at a certain interval, though interruptedly; for instance, in the coalescence of two sounds related to each other, as 4 : 5, there is a recurrence of a similar state of the joint motion, nearly at the interval of $\frac{1}{5}$ of the whole period, three of the joint vibrations occupying $\frac{27}{40}$ and leaving $\frac{13}{40}$: hence, in the concord of a major third, the fourth below the key note is heard as distinctly as the double octave, as is seen in some degree in Plate 4. Fig. 38; AB being nearly two thirds of CD. If the angles of all the figures resulting from the motion thus assumed be rounded off, they will approach more nearly to a representation of the actual circumstances; but, as the laws, by which the motion of the particles of air is regulated, differ according to the different origin and nature of the sound, it is impossible to adapt a demonstration to them all: if, however, the particles be supposed to follow the law of the harmonic curve, derived from uniform circular motion, the compound vibration will be the harmonic instead of the arithmetical mean; and the secondary sound of the interrupted vibrations will be more accurately formed, and more strongly marked: thus, in the concord 4 : 5, instead of $\frac{9}{40}$ of the whole period, the compound vibration will become $\frac{2}{5}$, and three such vibrations, occupying $\frac{2}{5}$, will leave exactly $\frac{1}{5}$. (Plate 5. Fig. 44, 45.) The demonstration is deducible from the properties of the circle; and in the same manner if the sounds are related as 7 : 8, or as 5 : 7, each compound vibration will occupy $\frac{2}{15}$, or $\frac{2}{12}$; and deducting 5 or 4 vibrations from the whole period, we shall have a remainder of $\frac{1}{3}$. This explanation is satisfactory enough with regard to the concord of a major third; but the same harmonic is sometimes produced by taking the minor sixth below the key note: in this case it might be supposed that the superior octave, which usually accompanies every sound as a secondary note, supplies the place of the major third; but I have found that the experiment succeeds even with stopped pipes, which produce no octaves as harmonics. We must therefore necessarily suppose that in this case, if not in the former, the sound in question is simply produced as a grave harmonic, by the combination of some of the acute harmonics, which always accompany the primitive notes. It is remarkable, that the law, by which the motion of the particles is governed, is capable of some singular alterations by a combination of vibrations. If we add to a given sound other similar sounds, related to it in frequency as the series of odd numbers, and in strength inversely in the same ratios, we may convert the right lines indicating a uniform motion very nearly into figures of sines, and the figures of sines into right lines, as in Plate 4. Fig. 42, 43.

XII. *Of the Frequency of Vibrations constituting a given Note.*

The number of vibrations, performed by a given sound in a second, has been variously ascertained; first, by Sauveur, by a very ingenious inference from the beats of two sounds; and since, by the same observer and several others, by calculation from the weight and tension of a chord. It was thought worth while, as a confirmation, to make an experiment, suggested, but coarsely conducted, by Mersenne, on a chord 200 inches in length, stretched so loosely as to have its single vibrations visible; and, by holding a quill nearly in contact with the chord, they were made audible, and were found, in one experiment, to recur 8.3 times in a second. By lightly pressing the chord at one eighth of its length from the end, and at other shorter aliquot distances, the fundamental note was found to be one sixth of a tone higher than the respective octave of a tuning fork marked C: hence the fork was a comma and a half above the pitch assumed by Sauveur, of an imaginary C, consisting of one vibration in a second.

XIII. *Of the Vibrations of Chords.*

By a singular oversight in the demonstration of Dr. Brook Taylor, adopted as it has been by a number of later authors, it is asserted, that if a chord be once inflected into any other form than that of the harmonic curve, it will, since those parts which are without this figure are impelled towards it by an excess of force, and those within it by a deficiency, in a very short time arrive at or very near the form of this precise curve. It would be easy to prove, if this reasoning were allowed, that the form of the curve can be no other than that of the axis, since the tending force is continually impelling the chord towards this line. The case is very similar to that of the Newtonian proposition respecting sound. It may be proved, that every impulse is communicated along a tended chord with a uniform velocity; and this velocity is the same which is inferred from Dr. Taylor's theorem; just as that of sound, determined by other methods, coincides with the Newtonian result. But, although several late mathematicians have given admirable solutions of all possible cases of the problem, yet it has still been supposed, that the distinctions were too minute to be actually observed. The theorem of Euler and De la Grange, in the case where the chord is supposed to be at first at rest, is in effect this: continue the figure each way, alternately on different sides of the axis, and in contrary positions; then, from any point of the curve, take an absciss each way, in the same proportion to the length of the chord as any given portion of time bears to the time of one semivibration, and the half sum of the ordinates will be the distance of that point of the chord from the axis, at the expiration of the time given. If the initial figure of the chord be composed of two right lines, as generally happens in musical instruments and experiments, its successive forms will be such as are represented in (Plate 5. Fig. 50, 51 :) and this result is fully confirmed by experiment. Take one of the lowest strings of a square piano forte, round which a fine silvered wire is wound in a spiral form; contract the light of a window, so that, when the eye is placed in a proper position, the image of the light may appear small, bright, and well defined, on each of the convolutions of the wire. Let the chord be now made to vibrate, and the luminous point will delineate its path, like a burning coal whirled round, and will present to the eye a line of light, which, by the assistance of a microscope, may be very accurately observed. According to the different ways by which the wire is put in motion, the form of this path is no less diversified and amusing, than the multifarious forms of the quiescent lines of vibrating plates, discovered by Professor Chladni; and it is indeed in one respect even more interesting, at it appears to be more within the reach of mathematical calculation to determine it; although hitherto, excepting some slight observations of Busse and Chladni, principally on the motion of rods, nothing has been attempted on the subject. For the present purpose, the motion of the chord may be simplified, by tying a long fine thread to any part of it, and fixing this thread in a direction perpendicular to that of the chord, without drawing it so tight as to increase the tension: by these means, the vibrations are confined nearly to one plane, which scarcely ever happens when the chord vibrates at liberty. If the chord be now inflected in the middle, it will be found, by comparison with an object which marked its quiescent position, to make equal excursions on each side of the axis; and the figure which it apparently occupies will be terminated by two lines, the more luminous as they are nearer the ends. (Plate 5. Fig. 52.) But, if the chord be inflected near one of its extremities, (Fig. 53,) it will proceed but a very small distance on the opposite side of the axis, and will there form a very bright line, indicating its longer continuance in that place; yet it will return on the former side nearly to the point from whence it was let go, but will be there very faintly visible, on account of its short delay. In the middle of the chord, the excursions on each side of the axis are always equal; and, beyond the middle, the same circumstances take place as in the half where it was inflected, but on the opposite side of the axis; and this appearance continues unaltered in its proportions, as long as the chord vibrates at all: fully confirming the nonexistence of the harmonic curve, and the accuracy of the construction of Euler and De la Grange. At the same time, as Mr. Bernoulli has justly observed, since every figure may be infinitely approximated, by considering its ordinates as composed of the ordinates of an infinite number of harmonic curves of different magnitudes, it may be demonstrated, that all these constituent curves would revert to their initial state, in the same time that a similar chord bent into a harmonic curve would perform a single vibration; and this is in some respects a convenient and compendious method of considering the problem. But, when a chord vibrates freely, it never remains long in motion, without a very evident departure from the plane of the vibration; and, whether from the original obliquity of the impulse, or from an interference with the reflected vibrations of the air, or from the inequability of its own weight or flexibility, or from the immediate resistance of the particles of air in contact with it, it is thrown into a very evident rotatory motion, more or less simple and uniform according to circumstances. Some specimens of the figures of the orbits of chords are exhibited in Plate 5. Fig. 47. At the middle of the chord, its orbit has always two equal halves, but seldom at any other point. The curves of Fig. 49, are described by combining together various circular motions, supposed to be performed in aliquot parts of the primitive orbit: and some of them approach nearly to the figures actually observed. When the chord is of unequal thickness, or when it is loosely tended and forcibly inflected, the apsides and double points of the orbits have a very evident rotatory motion. The compound rotations seem to demonstrate to the eye the existence of secondary vibrations, and to account for the acute harmonic sounds which generally attend the fundamental sound. There is one fact respecting these secondary notes, which seems entirely to have escaped observation. If a chord be inflected at one half, one third, or any other aliquot part of its length, and then suddenly left at liberty, the harmonic note, which would be produced by dividing the chord at that point, is entirely lost, and is not to be distinguished during any part of the continuance of the sound. This demonstrates, that the secondary notes do not depend upon any interference of the vibrations of the air with each other, nor upon any sympathetic agitation of auditory fibres, nor upon any effect of reflected sound upon the chord, but merely upon its initial figure and motion. If it were supposed that the chord, when inflected into right lines, resolved itself necessarily into a number of secondary vibrations, according to some curves which, when properly combined, would approximate to the figure given, the supposition would indeed in some respects correspond with the phenomenon related; as the coefficients of all the curves supposed to end at the angle of inflection would vanish. But, whether we trace the constituent curves of such a figure through the various stages of their vibrations, or whether we follow the more compendious method of Euler to the same purpose, the figures resulting from this series of vibrations are in fact so simple, that it seems inconceivable how the ear should deduce the complicated idea of a number of heterogeneous vibrations, from a motion of the particles of air, which must be extremely regular, and almost uniform; a uniformity which, when proper precautions are taken, is not contradicted by examining the motion of the chord with the assistance of a powerful magnifier. This difficulty occurred very strongly to Euler: and De la Grange even suspects that there is some fallacy in the experiment, and that a musical ear judges from previous association. But, besides that these sounds are discoverable to a ear destitute of such associations, and, when the sound is produced by two strings in imperfect unison, may be verified by counting the number of their beats, the experiment already related is an undeniable proof that no fallacy of this kind exists. It must be confessed, that nothing fully satisfactory has yet occurred to account for the phenomena; but it is highly probable that the slight increase of tension produced by flexure, which is omitted in the calculations, the elasticity or inflexibility of the chord, and the unavoidable inequality of thickness of its different parts, may, by disturbing the isochronism of the subordinate vibrations, cause all that variety of sounds which is so inexplicable without them. For, when the slightest difference is introduced in the periods, there is no difficulty in conceiving how the sounds may be distinguished; and indeed, in some cases, a nice ear will discover a slight imperfection in the tune of harmonic notes: it is also often observed, in tuning an instrument, that some of the single strings produce beating sounds, which undoubtedly arise from their want of perfect uniformity: the same circumstance is the cause of the motion of the apsides, which is often observable in the rotations already described. It may be perceived that any particular harmonic is loudest, when the chord is inflected at about one third of the corresponding aliquot part from one of the extremities of that part. An observation of Dr. Wallis seems to have passed unnoticed by later writers on harmonics. He says, that if the string of a violin be struck in the middle, or at any other aliquot part, it will give either no sound at all, or a very obscure one. This is true, not of inflection, but of the motion communicated by a bow; and may be explained from the circumstance of the successive impulses, reflected from the fixed points at each end, destroying each other: an explanation nearly analogous to some observations of Dr. Matthew Young on the motion of chords. When the bow is applied not exactly at the aliquot point, but very near it, the corresponding harmonic is extremely loud; and the fundamental note, especially in the lowest harmonics, scarcely audible: the chord assumes the appearance, at the aliquot points, of as many lucid lines as correspond to the number of the harmonic, more nearly approaching to each other as the bow approaches more nearly to the point. (Plate 5. Fig. 54.) According to the various modes of applying the bow, an immense variety of figures of the orbits are produced, (Fig. 48.) more than enough to account for all the difference of tone in different performers. In experiments of this kind, a series of harmonics is frequently heard in drawing the bow across the same part of the chord: these are produced by the bow; they are however not proportionate to the whole length of the bow, but depend on the capability of the portion of the bowstring, intercepted between its end and the chord, of performing its vibrations in times which are aliquot parts of the vibration of the chord: hence we may perhaps infer, that the bow takes effect on the chord but at one instant, or for a very short time, during each fundamental vibration. In these experiments, the bow was strung with the second string of a violin.

XIV. *Of the Vibrations of Rods and Plates.*

Some experiments were made, with the assistance of a most excellent practical musician, on the various notes produced by a glass tube, an iron rod, and a wooden ruler; and, in a case where the tube was as much at liberty as possible, all the harmonics corresponding to the numbers from 1 to 13, were distinctly observed; several of them at the same time, and others by means of different blows. This result seems to differ from the calculations of Euler and Count Riccati, confirmed as they are by the repeated experiments of Professor Chladni; it is not therefore brought forward as sufficiently controverting those calculations, but as showing the propriety of an inquiry into the sources of error in such experiments. Scarcely any note could ever be heard when a rod was loosely held at its extremity; nor when it was held in the middle, and struck one seventh of the length from one end. The very ingenious method of Professor Chladni, of observing the vibrations of plates by strewing fine sand over them, and discovering the quiescent lines by the figures into which it is thrown, has hitherto been little known in this country: his treatise on the phenomena is so complete, that no other experiments of the kind were thought necessary. Glass vessels of various descriptions, whether made to sound by percussion or friction, were found to be entirely free from the usual harmonic notes; and this observation coincides with the experiments of Chladni.

XV. *Of the Human Voice.*

The human voice, which was the object

originally proposed to be illustrated by these researches, is of so complicated a nature, and so imperfectly understood, that it can be on this occasion but superficially considered. No person, unless we except M. Ferrein, has published any thing very important on the subject of the formation of the voice, before or since Dodart; his reasoning has fully shown the analogy between the voice and the *vox humana* and regal organ pipes: but his comparison with the whistle is unfortunate: nor is he more happy in his account of the falsetto. A kind of experimental analysis of the voice may be thus exhibited. By drawing in the breath, and at the same time properly contracting the larynx, a slow vibration of the ligaments of the glottis may be produced, making a distinct clicking sound: upon increasing the tension, and the velocity of the breath, this clicking is lost, and the sound becomes continuous, but of an extremely grave pitch: it may, by a good ear, be distinguished two octaves below the lowest A of a common bass voice, consisting in that case of about 26 vibrations in a second. The same sound may be raised nearly to the pitch of the common voice; but it is never smooth and clear, except perhaps in some of those persons called ventriloquists. When the pitch is raised still higher, the upper orifice of the larynx, formed by the summits of the arytaenoid cartilages and the epiglottis, seems to succeed to the office of the ligaments of the glottis, and to produce a retrograde falsetto, which is capable of a very great degree of acuteness. The same difference probably takes place between the natural voice and the common falsetto: the rimula glottidis being too long to admit of a sufficient degree of tension for very acute sounds, either the upper orifice of the larynx supplies its place, or, some other similar change is produced; hence, taking a note within the compass of either voice, it may be held, with the same expense of air, two or three times as long in a falsetto as in a natural voice; hence, too, arises the difficulty of passing smoothly from the one voice to the other. It has been remarked, that the larynx is always elevated when the sound is acute: but this elevation is only necessary in rapid transitions, as in a shake; and then probably because, by the contraction of the capacity of the trachea, an increase of the pressure of the breath can be more rapidly affected this way, than by the action of the abdominal muscles alone. The reflection of the sound, thus produced from the various parts of the cavity of the mouth and nostrils, mixing at various intervals with the portions of the vibrations directly proceeding from the larynx, must, according to the temporary form of the parts, variously affect the laws of the motion of the air in each vibration; or, according to Euler's expression, the equation of the curve conceived to correspond with this motion, and thus produce the various characters of the vowels and semivowels. The principal sounding board seems to be the bony palate: the nose, except in nasal letters, affords but little resonance; for the nasal passage may be closed, by applying the finger to the soft palate, without much altering the sound of vowels not nasal. A good ear may distinctly observe, especially in a loud bass voice, besides the fundamental note, at least four harmonic sounds, in the order of the natural numbers; and, the more reedy the tone of the voice, the more easily they are heard. Faint as they are, their origin is by no means easy to be explained. This observation is precisely confirmed, in a late dissertation of M. Knecht, published in the musical newspaper of Leipsic. Perhaps, by a close attention to the harmonics entering into the constitution of various sounds, more may be done in their analysis than could otherwise be expected.

XVI. *Of the Temperament of musical Intervals.*

It would have been extremely convenient for practical musicians, and would have saved many warm controversies among theoretical ones, if three times the ratio of 4 to 5, or four times that of 5 to 6, had been equal to the ratio of 1 to 2. As it happens to be otherwise, it has been much disputed in what intervals the imperfection should be placed. The Aristoxenians and Pythagoreans were in some sense the beginners of the controversy. Sauveur has given very comprehensive tables of a great number of systems of temperament; and his own now ranks among the many that are rejected. Dr. Smith has written a large and obscure volume, which, for every purpose but for the use of an impracticable instrument, leaves the whole subject precisely where it found it. Kirnberger, Marpurg, and other German writers, have disputed with great bitterness, almost every one for a particular method of tuning. It is not with any confidence of success, that one more attempt is made, which rests its chief claim to preference, on the similarity of its theory to the actual practice of the best instrument makers. However we estimate the degree of imperfection of two tempered concords of the same nature, it will appear, that the manner of dividing the temperament between them does not materially alter its aggregate sum; for instance, the imperfection of a comma, in a major third, occasions it to beat very nearly twice as fast as that of half a comma. If indeed the imperfection were great, it might affect an interval so materially as to destroy its character; as, in some methods of temperament, a minor third diminished by two commas approaches more nearly to the ratio 6 : 7, than to 5 : 6; but, with this limitation, the sum of harmony is nearly equal in all systems. Hence, if every one of the twelve major and minor thirds occurred equally often in the compositions which are to be performed on an instrument, it would be of no great consequence, to the sum of the imperfections, among which of the thirds they were divided: and, even in this case, the opinion of the best practical authors is, that the difference of character produced by a difference of proportions in various keys, would be of considerable advantage in the general effect of modulation. But, when it is considered, that upon an average of all the music ever composed, some particular keys occur at least twice as often as others, there seems to be a very strong additional reason for making the harmony the most perfect in those keys which are the most frequently used; since the aggregate sum of all the imperfections, which occur in playing, must by these means be diminished in the greatest possible degree, and the diversity of character at the same time preserved. Indeed, in practice, this method, under different modifications, has been almost universal; for, although many have pretended to an equal temperament, yet the methods which they have usually employed to attain it have been evidently defective. It appears to me, that every purpose may be answered, by making the third C : E too sharp by a quarter of a comma, which will not offend the nicest ear; E : G✳, and A♭ : C, equal; F✳ : A✳ too sharp by a comma; and the major thirds of all the intermediate keys more or less perfect, as they approach more or less to C in the order of modulation. The fifths are perfect enough in every system. The results of this method are shown in Table xii. In practice, nearly the same effect may be very simply produced, by tuning from C, to F, B♭, E♭, G✳, C✳, F✳, six perfect fourths; and C, G, D, A, E, B, F✳, six equally imperfect fifths. (Plate 5. Fig. 55.) If the unavoidable imperfections of the fourths be such as to incline them to sharpness, the temperament will approach more nearly to equality, which is preferable to an inaccuracy on the other side. An easy method of comparing different systems of temperament is exhibited in Plate 6. Fig. 56, which may readily be extended to all the systems that have ever been invented. For the guitar, the frets can scarcely be better fixed than according to the equal temperament.

Table xii.

A		B		C	
C	50000	1 C	+.0013487	1 A, E	−.0023603
B	53224	2 G, F	.0019006	2 D, B	.0029122
B♭	56131	3 D, B♭	.0024525	3 G, F	.0034641
A	59676	4 A, E♭	.0034641	4 C, C✳	.0044756
G✳	63148	5 E, A♭	.0044756	5 F, G✳	.0049353
G	66822	6 B, C✳	.0049353	6 B♭, E♭	.0053950
E✳	71041	7 F✳, a comma .0053950			
F	74921				
E	79752	D			
E♭	84197				
D	89304	1 E♭, G✳, C✳, F✳ — .0000000			
C✳	94723	2 F, B♭, E, B .0004597			
C	100000	3 C, G, D, A .0010116			

A shows the division of a monochord corresponding to each note, in the system proposed; B, the logarithm of the temperament of each of the major thirds; C, of the minor thirds; D, of the fifths; C and D being both negative.

Thus, Sir, I have endeavoured to advance a few steps only, in the investigation of some very obscure but interesting subjects. As far as I know, most of these observations are new; but, if they should be found to have been already made by any other person, their repetition in a connected chain of inference may still be excusable. I am persuaded also, that at least some of the positions maintained are incontrovertibly consistent with truth and nature; but, should further experiments tend to confute any opinions that I have suggested, I shall relinquish them with as much readiness, as I have long since abandoned the hypothesis, which I once took the liberty of submitting to the Royal Society, on the functions of the crystalline lens.

I am, &c.

Emanuel College, Cambridge, 8th July, 1799.

THOMAS YOUNG.

EXPLANATION OF THE FIGURES.

PLATE 2. Fig. 4..9. The section of a stream of air from a tube .07 inch in diameter, as ascertained by measuring the breadth of the impression on the surface of a liquid. The pressure, impelling the current, was in Fig. 4, 1 inch. Fig. 5, 2. Fig. 6, 3. Fig. 7, 4. Fig. 8, 7. Fig. 9, 10.

Fig. 10..15. A similar section, where the tube was .1 in diameter, compared with the section as inferred from the experiments with two gages, which is represented by a dotted line. From this comparison it appears, that where the velocity of the current was small, its central parts only displaced the liquid; and that, where it was great, it displaced, on meeting with resistance, a surface somewhat greater than its own section. The pressure was in Fig. 10, 1. Fig. 11, 2. Fig. 12, 3. Fig. 13, 4. Fig. 14, 7. Fig. 15, 10.

Fig. 16..23. A, the half section of a stream of air from a tube .1 in diameter, as inferred from experiments with two water gages. The pressure was in Fig. 16, .1. Fig. 17, .2. Fig. 18, .5. Fig. 19, 1. Fig. 20, 3. Fig. 21, 5. Fig. 22, 7. Fig. 23, 10. The fine lines, marked B, show the result of the observations with an aperture .15 in diameter opposed to the stream; C with .3; and D with .5.

Fig. 24..26. A the half section of a current from a tube .3 in diameter, with a pressure of .5, of 1, and of 3. B shows the course of a portion next the axis of the current, equal in diameter to those represented by the last figures.

PLATE 3. Fig. 27. The appearance of a stream of smoke forced very gently from a fine tube. Fig. 28 and 29, the same appearance when the pressure is gradually increased.

Fig. 30. A mouth piece for a sonorous cavity.

Fig. 31. The perpendicular lines over each division of the horizontal line show, by their length and distance from that line, the extent of pressure capable of producing, from the respective pipes, the harmonic notes indicated by the figures placed opposite the beginning of each, according to the scale of 22 inches parallel to them. The larger numbers, opposite the middle of each of these lines, show the number of vibrations of the corresponding sound in a second.

PLATE 2. Fig. 32..35. Illustrations of the affections of light.

Fig. 36. The combination of two sounds.

Fig. 37. The combination of two equal sounds constituting the interval of an octave supposing the progress and regress of the particles of air equable. Fig. 38, 39, 40, a similar representation of a major third, major tone, and minor sixth.

Fig. 41. A fourth, tempered about two commas.

Fig. 42. A vibration of a similar nature, combined with subordinate vibrations of the same kind in the ratios of 3, 5, and 7.

Fig. 43. A vibration represented by a curve of which the ordinates are the sines of circular arcs increasing uniformly, corresponding with the motion of a cycloidal pendulum, combined with similar subordinate vibrations in the ratios of 3, 5, and 7.

PLATE 5. Fig. 44. and 45. Two different positions of a major third, composed of similar vibrations, as represented by figures of sines.

Fig. 46. A contracted representation of a series of vibrations. A, a simple uniform sound. B, the beating of two equal sounds nearly in unison, as derived from rectilinear figures. C, the beats of two equal sounds, derived from figures of sines. D, a musical consonance, making by its frequent beats a fundamental harmonic. E, the imperfect beats of two unequal sounds. F, the beats of two equal sounds, supposing the strength of the sound to be as the square of the velocity: this figure agrees much better with the audible effect of a beat than the former.

Fig. 47. Various forms of the orbit of a musical chord, when inflected, and when struck.

Fig. 48. Forms of the orbit, when the sound is produced by means of a bow.

Fig. 49. Epitrochoidal curves, formed by combining a simple rotation or vibration with other subordinate rotations or vibrations.

Fig. 50 and 51. The successive forms of a tended chord, when inflected and let go, according to the construction of De la Grange and Euler.

Fig. 52. The appearance of a vibrating chord which had been inflected in the middle, the strongest lines representing the most luminous parts.

Fig. 53. The appearance of a vibrating chord, when inflected at any other point than the middle.

Fig. 54. The appearance of a chord, when put in motion by a bow applied nearly at one third of the length from its end.

Fig. 55. The method of tuning recommended for common use.

PLATE 6. Fig. 56. A comparative view of different systems of temperament. The whole circumference represents an octave. The inner circle L is divided into 30103 parts, corresponding with the logarithmical parts of an octave. The next circle R shows the magnitude of the simplest musical and other ratios. Q is divided into twelve equal parts, representing the semitones of the equal temperament described by Zarlino, differing but little from the system of Aristoxenus, and warmly recommended by Marpurg and other late writers. Y exhibits the system proposed in this paper as the most desirable; and P the practical method nearly approaching to it, which corresponds with the eleventh method in Marpurg's enumeration, except that, by beginning with C instead of B, the practical effect of the temperament is precisely inverted. This system differs little from that which was formerly proposed by Romieu. K is the system of Kirnberger and Sulzer; which is derived from one perfect third, ten perfect, and two equally imperfect fifths. M is the system of mean tones, the *sistema participato* of the old Italian writers, still frequently used in tuning organs, approved also by Dr. Smith for common use. S shows the result of all the calculations in Dr. Smith's harmonics, the system proposed for his changeable harpsichord, but neither in that nor any other form capable of practical application.

PLATE 2.

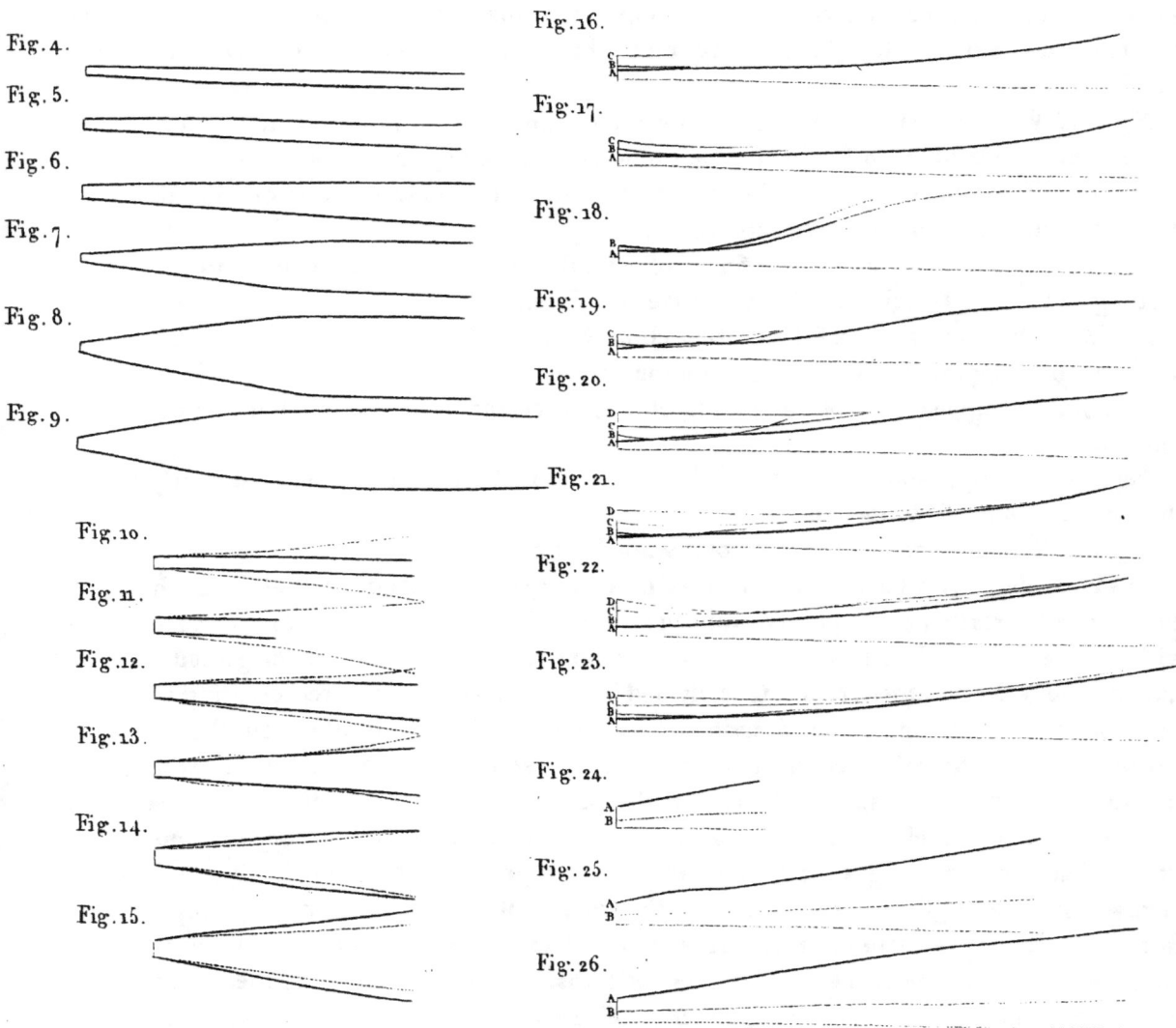

PLATE 3.

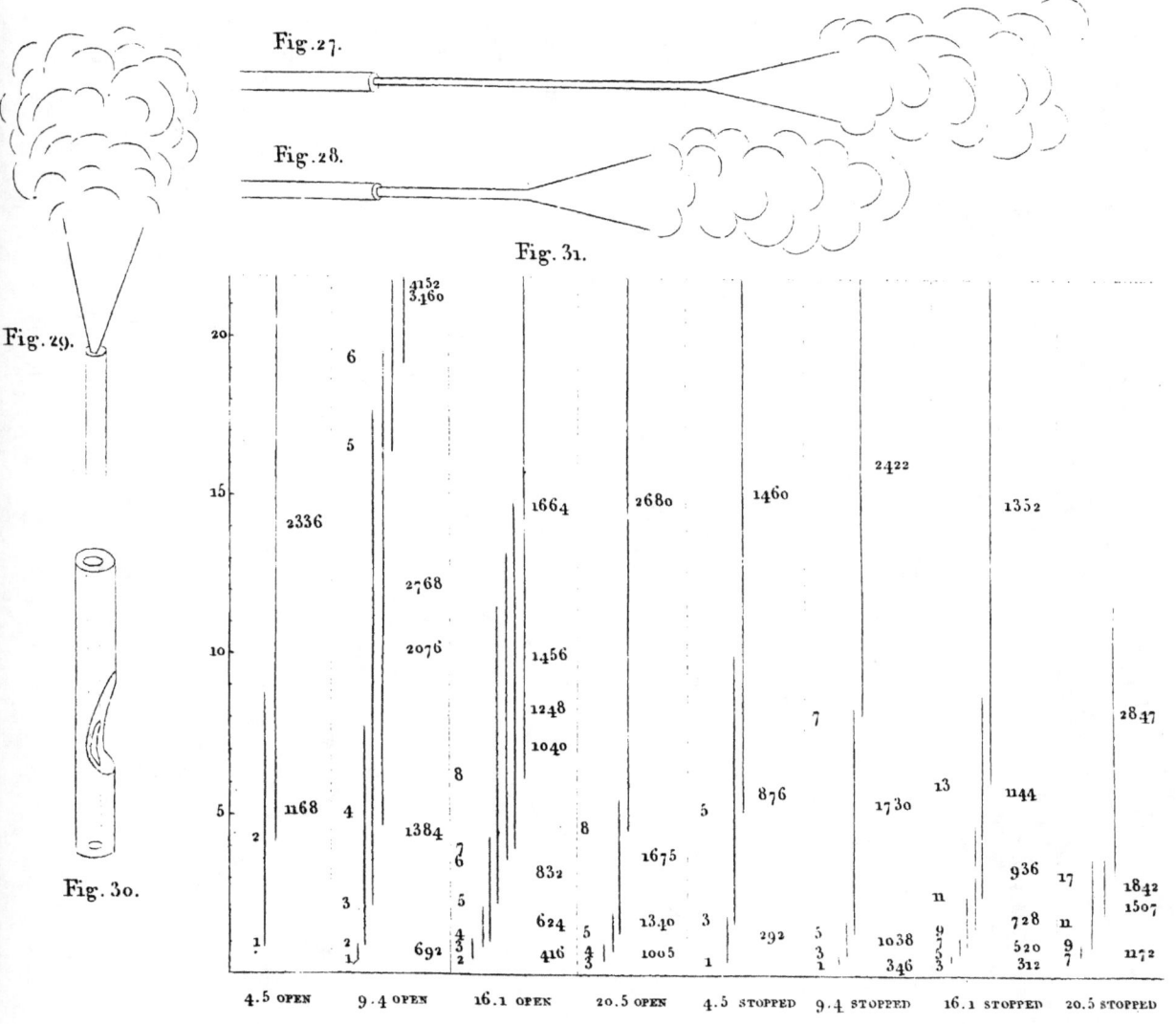

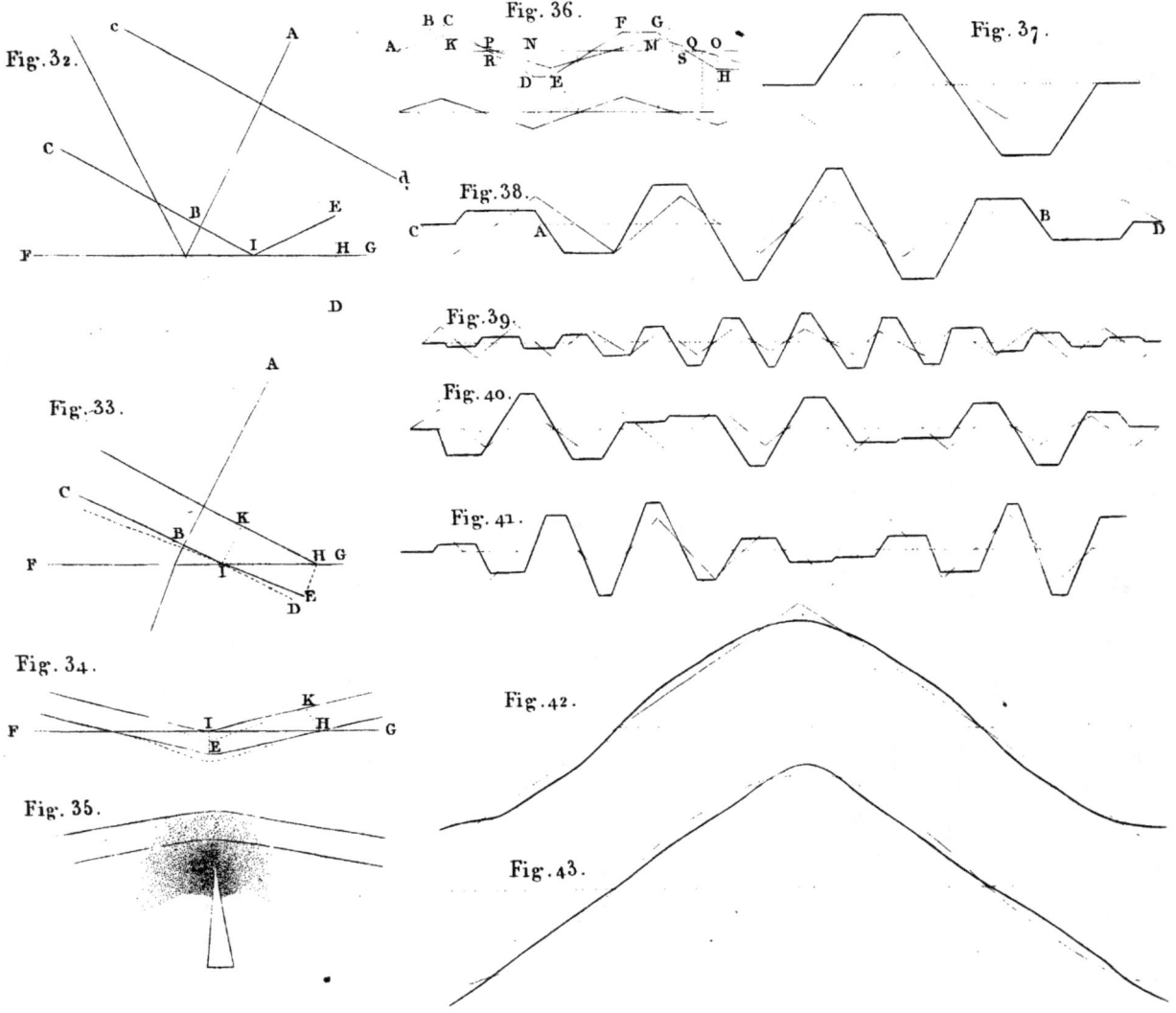

PLATE 4

III. AN ESSAY

ON

CYCLOIDAL CURVES,

WITH INTRODUCTORY OBSERVATIONS.

From the British Magazine, for April 1800.

ON MATHEMATICAL SYMBOLS.

Many of the most celebrated mathematicians of the present day have been disposed to pride themselves on the very great superiority, which they attribute to the modern methods of calculation, over those which were known to the ancients. That, in the course of so many centuries, mathematical sciences, like all others, should have been very considerably advanced, is no more than must have been expected, from the great number of persons who have employed their talents in the cultivation of those sciences. But, if we examine the matter impartially, we shall have reason to believe, not only that mathematics have been as slow in their real advancement as any other part of philosophy, but that the moderns have very frequently neglected the more essential, for frivolous and superficial advantages. To say nothing of the needless incumbrances of new methods of variations, of combinatorial analyses, and of many other similar innovations, the strong inclination which has been shown, especially on the continent, to prefer the algebraical to the geometrical form of representation, is a sufficient proof, that, instead of endeavouring to strengthen and enlighten the reasoning faculties, by accustoming them to such a consecutive train of argument as can be fully conceived by the mind, and represented with all its links by the recollection, they have only been desirous of sparing themselves as much as possible the pains of thought and labour, by a kind of mechanical abridgment, which at best only serves the office of a book of tables in facilitating computations, but which very often fails even of this end, and is, at the same time, the most circuitous and the least intelligible. These philosophers are like the young Englishman on his travels, who visits a country by driving with all possible speed from place to place by night, and refreshing his fatigues in the day time, by lounging half asleep at his hotel. Undoubtedly there are some countries through which one may reasonably wish to travel by night, and undoubtedly there are some cases where algebraical symbols are more convenient than geometrical ones: but when we see an author exerting all his ingenuity in order to avoid every idea that has the least tincture of geometry, when he obliges us to toil through immense volumes filled with all manner of literal characters, without a single diagram to diversify the prospect, we may observe with the less surprise, that such an author appears to be confused in his conception of the most elementary doctrines, and that he fancies he has made an improvement of consequence, when, in fact, he is only viewing an old object in a new disguise. It happens frequently in the description of curves, and in the solution of problems, that the geometrical construction is very simple and easy, while it almost exceeds the powers of calculus to express the curve or the locus of the equation in a manner strictly algebraical: and, indeed, the astonishing advances that were made, in a comparatively short time, by Euclid, by Apollonius, and above all, by Archimedes, are sufficient to prove, that the method of representation which they employed could not be very limited in its application: and the precision and elegance, with which the method of geometrical fluxions is treated by Newton and Maclaurin, form a strong contrast to the tedious affectation of abstraction and obscurity which unfortunately pervades the writings of many great mathematicians of a later date. It would be of inestimable advantage to the progress of all the sciences, if some diligent and judicious collector would undertake to compile a complete system of mathematics; not as an elementary treatise, nor as a mere index of reference, but to contain every proposition, with a concise demonstration, that has ever yet been communicated to the public. Until this is done, nothing is left but for every individual, who is curious in the search of geometrical knowledge, to look over all the mathematical authors, and all the literary memoirs, of the last and present centuries: for without this, he may very easily fancy he has made discoveries, when the same facts have been known and forgotten long before he existed. An instance of this has lately occurred to a young gentleman in Edinburgh, a man who certainly promises, in the course of time, to add considerably to our knowledge of the laws of nature. The tractory, tractrix, or equitangential curve, was first described by Huygens, and afterwards more fully by Mr. Bomie, (Mem. Acad. 1712,) and by Mr. Perks. (Ph. tr. XIX. n. 345, Abr. IV. 456.) Bomie and Perks have shown many remarkable properties belonging to it; and one in particular, which may be briefly demonstrated, that it is the involute of the catenaria: for since the equation of the catenaria is $zz = 2ax + xx$, we have $\dot{z}\dot{z} = a\dot{x} + \dot{x}\dot{x}$, and $\dot{x} : \dot{z} :: z : a + x$, therefore the vertex of the right angled triangle, of which the base is the evolved radius, and the hypotenuse a line parallel to the axis of the curve, describes a right line; and the perpendicular of this triangle is always $= a$, and is the constant tangent of the curve described by the evolution. Cotes has also, in his Logometria, investigated the properties of the tractrix of the circle. Bernoulli observed in 1730, that the tractrix was one of the tautochronous curves in a resisting medium. In 1736 it was the subject of a dispute between MM. Clairaut and Fontaine: it is not yet entirely forgotten on that spot of academic ground which gave birth to the discoveries of Newton; and its equation is to be found in a work no less common than Emerson's Fluxions, nearly in the same form as that which is published as new in the Philosophical Transactions for 1798. We find in the same paper a new method of dividing an elliptic area in a given ratio; but the curve which the author calls a cycloid is the companion of a trochoid, and is only a distortion of the figure by which Newton had very simply and elegantly solved the same problem. It is unnecessary to compare the attempt to demonstrate the incommensurability of an oval with the Newtonian method; since Dr. Waring's proof, deduced from the nature of the equation of limits, is decidedly more satisfactory than any other hitherto made known. On the whole, it appears that this ingenious gentleman has been somewhat unfortunate in the choice of those problems which he has selected as specimens of the elegance of the modern mode of demonstration; whether those, which he has brought forwards without proof, would have furnished him with a more favourable opportunity for the display of neatness and accuracy, may be more easily determined, whenever he may think proper to lay before the public their analysis, construction, and demonstration at full length. But, allowing the superiority of the modern calculations in many cases, their great advantage appears to be derived from the methods of series and approximations; indeed, however we may wish to adhere to the rigour of the ancient demonstrations, it is absolutely necessary for the purposes of the higher geometry to extend, in some measure, the foundations which the ancients laid in their postulates. Perhaps the most material addition may be comprehended in this form: " Let it be granted that any curve line may be drawn whenever an indefinitely great number of points may be geometrically found in, or indefinitely near to, that line." No doubt it is mathematically impossible to comply with this postulate; but it must be remembered, that it is also impossible to draw, with strictly mathematical accuracy, a right line or a circle; but in both cases we can approach sufficiently near to the truth for practice: and it appears to be more convenient to consider such curves as are thus described as belonging to geometry, than to limit the number of geometrical curves, according to Descartes, to those of which the ordinate and absciss are comparable by an algebraical equation. This postulate forms the connecting link between rational and irrational quantities, between the infinite and the indefinite, between perfect resemblance and identity; and the irrational geometry, which has long been tacitly built on it, exhibits the principal advantages of analytical calculus in a more elegant form. The groundwork of this irrational geometry is found in the method of exhaustions of Euclid and Archimedes, and it has been employed more or less generally by Descartes, Newton, Cotes, Roberval, Varignon, Delahire, Maclaurin, and many other mathematicians. In the annexed essay on cycloidal curves, the geometrical form of fluxions, or more properly speaking, the Newtonian method of ultimate ratios, has principally been adopted; and it is presumed, that by a comparison with algebraical calculations on the same subjects, the superior perspicuity and conciseness of this method will readily appear.

ON CYCLOIDAL CURVES.

DEFINITION I. When a circle is made to rotate on a rectilinear basis, the figure described on the plane of the basis by any point in the plane of the circle, is called a trochoid. A circle concentric with the generating circle, and passing through the describing point, may be called the describing circle.

DEFINITION II. If the describing point is in the circumference of the rotating circle, the two circles coincide, and the curve is called a cycloid.

DEFINITION III. If a circular basis be substituted for a rectilinear one, the trochoid will become an epitrochoid, and the cycloid an epicycloid.

SCHOLIUM 1. These terms have hitherto been too promiscuously employed; the terms cycloid and trochoid have been used indifferently; and the term epicycloid has comprehended the epitrochoid, the terms prolate and contracted being sometimes added, to imply that the describing point is within or without the generating circle. The interior epicycloid and epitrochoid may very properly be distinguished by the names hypocycloid and hypotrochoid, whenever they are the separate objects of consideration. The different species of epicycloids may be denominated according to the number of their cusps, combined with that of the entire revolutions which they comprehend: for instance, the epicycloid described by a circle on an equal basis is a simple unicuspidate epicycloid; and if the diameter of the generating circle be to that of the basis as 5 to 2, the figure will be a quintuple bicuspidate epicycloid. If the describing circle of a trochoid or cycloid be so placed as to touch the middle of the curve, and each of the ordinates parallel to the basis be diminished by the corresponding ordinate of the circle, the curve thus generated has been denominated the companion of the trochoid or cycloid, the figure of sines, and the harmonic curve.

SCHOLIUM 2. The invention of the cycloid has been attributed by Wallis, (Ph. tr. 1697, n. 229,) to Cardinal Cusanus, who wrote about the year 1450; but it seems to be at least as probable that the curve, which appears in Cusanus's figure, was meant for the semicircle employed in finding a mean proportional. Bovillus, in 1501, has a juster claim to the merit of the invention of the cycloid and trochoid, if it can be any merit to have merely imagined such curves to exist. In 1599, Galileo gave a name to the common cycloid, and attempted its quadrature, but having been accidentally misled by repeated experiments on the weight of a flat substance, cut into a cycloidal form, he fancied that the area bore an incommensurable ratio to that of the circle, and desisted from the investigation. Mersennus described the cycloid, in 1615, under the name of la trochoide, or la roulette, but he went no further. Roberval seems to have first discovered the comparative quadrature and rectification of the cycloid, and the content of a cycloidal solid, about the year 1635, but his treatise was not printed until 1695, Torricelli, in 1644, first published the quadrature and the method of drawing a tangent, both of which had been investigated by Descartes in 1639. Wallis gave, in 1670, a perfect quadrature of a portion of the cycloid. The epicycloid is said to have been invented by Roemer: its rectification and evolute were investigated by Newton in the Principia, published in 1687. In 1695 Mr. Caswell showed the perfect quadrability of a portion of the epicycloid, and Dr. Halley immediately published an extension of Caswell's discovery, together with a comparison of all epitrochoidal with circular areas. M. Varignon is also said to have reduced the rectification of the epitrochoid to that of the ellipsis, in the same year. Nicole, Delahire, Pascal, Réaumur, Maclaurin, the Bernoullis, the commentators on Newton, and many others, have contributed to the examination of cycloidal curves, both in planes and in curved surfaces; and Waring, the most profound of modern algebraists, has considerably extended his researches upon the nature of those lines which are generated by a rotatory progression of other curves. In the present essay, the most remarkable properties of cycloidal curves are deduced in a simpler and more general manner than appears to have been hitherto done, the equations of several species are investigated, and a singular property of the quadricuspidate hypocycloid is demonstrated. Those who wish for further information respecting the history of these curves, may consult either Carlo Dati's essay on the subject, or Montucla's History of the mathematics.

PROPOSITION I. THEOREM. (Plate 7. Fig. 57.) In any curve generated by the rotation of another on any basis, the right line joining the

PLATE 5.

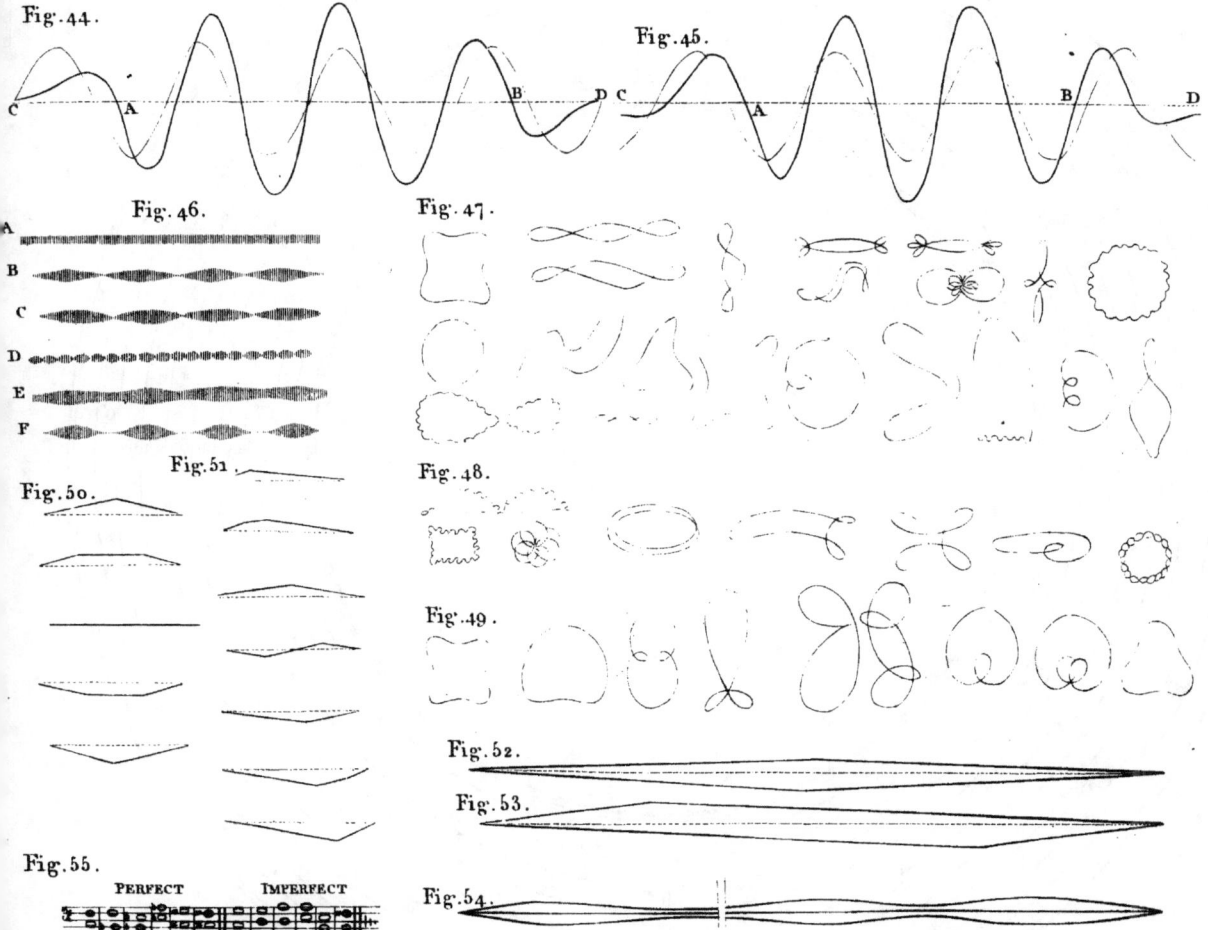

PLATE 6.

Fig. 56.

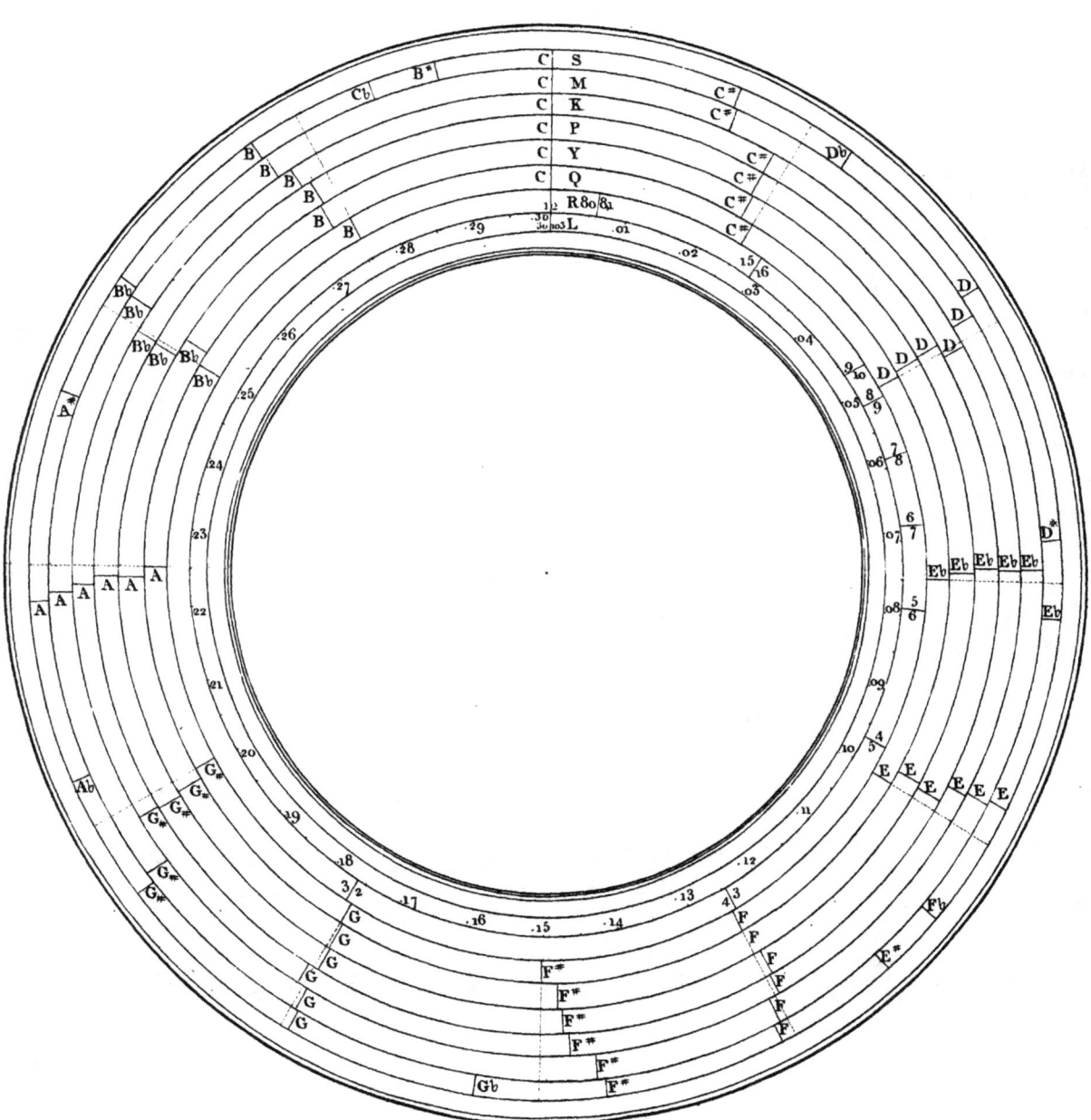

describing point, and the point of contact of the generating curve and the basis, is always perpendicular to the curve described.

It may by some be deemed sufficient to consider the generating curve as a rectilinear polygon, of an infinite number of sides; since, in this point of view, the proposition requires no further demonstration; and, indeed, Newton and others have not scrupled to take it for granted: but it is presumed, that a more rigid proof will not be considered as superfluous. Let M be the describing point, and P the point of contact: and let LO, MP, and NQ, be successive positions of the same chord of the generating curve at infinitely small distances: then it is obvious, and easily demonstrable, that the arcs OP and PQ, described by the point P of the generating curve, in its passage from O to P, and from P to Q, will be perpendicular to the basis at P, and will therefore touch each other. Let the arcs L, IMK, and N, be described with the radius PM, on the centres O, P, and Q. Then the curve described by M will touch IMK; for since O and Q lie ultimately in the same direction from P, if L be above IMK, N will also be above it, since these points must be in the circles L and N, and infinitely near to M; and if L be below IMK, N, for the same reason, must be below it; and M is common to the circle and the curve, therefore the curve touches the circle IMK at M, and is perpendicular to the radius PM.

PROPOSITION II. PROBLEM. To draw a tangent to a cycloidal curve at any given point.

On the given point, as a centre, describe a circle equal to the describing circle of the curve, and from the intersection of this circle, with the line described by the centre of the generating circle, let fall a perpendicular on the basis; the point thus found will be the point of contact, and the tangent will be perpendicular to the right line joining this point of contact and the given point, by the first proposition. It will be obvious, from inspection, which of the two intersections of the circle to be described, with the track of the centre, is to be taken as the place of that centre corresponding to the given point.

SCHOLIUM. The tangents of cycloids and epicycloids may be drawn from any given point without them by means of curves, which are described by the intersection of two lines revolving on given points, with proportionate angular velocities, and in the case of the bicuspidate epicycloid, the curve becomes an equilateral hyperbola.

PROPOSITION III. PROBLEM. (Plate 7. FIG. 58.) To find the length of an epitrochoid.

Let C be the centre of the basis VP, K that of the rotating circle PR, and of the describing circle GL, P the point of contact, and M the describing point. Then joining MXC, and supposing VX to be an element representing the motion of the point P, in either the basis or the generating circle, draw the arc MN on the centre C, and join CVN: then NM will represent the motion of the point M as far as it is produced by the revolution round the centre C: take MO to VX as GK to PK, then MO will be the motion of M arising from the revolution round K, and NO will be the element of the curve produced by the joint motion. Let CH be parallel to PM, then CX or CP : CM :: VX : MN, and PK : MK :: CP : HM :: VX : MO, therefore, CM : HM :: MN : MO, and these lines being perpendicular to CM, HM, the triangle NMO is similar to CMH, and MN : NO :: CM : CH, hence CP : CH :: VX : NO. Take PY to CP as PK to CK, then CH : CP :: PM : PY :: NO : VX. On L describe the circle PFB, and draw IMLF: let FD be perpendicular to PRB, take DE to DF as PG to PL, and E will be always in the ellipsis BEP: let AE and AF be tangents to the ellipsis and circle at E and F; then the increment of the arc BF will be to MO as PL to GL, and to VX as PL to PR. Join GM, and parallel to it draw PI; then PIL is a right angle, and ILP=AFD, and IM : IL :: PG : PL :: DE : DF, by construction; therefore the figure IPML is similar to DAEF, and as PL to PM, so is AF to AE, and so is the increment of the arc BF to that of BE; but the increment of BF is to VX as PL to PR, therefore the increment of BE is to VX as PM to PR. Now it was proved that NO : VX :: PM : PY; therefore the increment of BE is to NO as PY to PR, or as CP to 2 CK; and the whole elliptic arc BE is to the whole SM as the radius of the basis to twice the distance of the centres.

COROLLARY 1. The fluxion of every cycloidal arc is proportional to the distance of the describing point from the point of contact.

COROLLARY 2. For the epicycloid, the ellipsis coincides with its axis BP, and the arc BE with BD, which is double the versed sine of half the arc GM, in the describing or generating circle: therefore the length of the curve is to this versed sine as four times the distance of the centres to the radius of the basis.

PROPOSITION IV. PROBLEM. (Plate 7. FIG. 58, 59.) To find the centre of curvature of an epitrochoid.

Let PY be, as in the last proposition, to CP as PK to CK, and on the diameter PY describe the circle PZY, cutting PO in Z: take OW a third proportional to OZ and OP, and W will be the centre of curvature. For let QP=VX be the space described by P, while NO is described by O: it is obvious, from prop. 1. that the intersection of NA and OP must be the centre of curvature. Let $Q\Gamma$ be perpendicular to PO, and $\Gamma\Delta$ parallel to QN; then, by prop. 3, NO : VX or $QP::PO : PY$, but by similar triangles $QP : Q\Gamma::PY : PZ$; therefore NO : $Q\Gamma::PO : PZ$, and by division, NO : $\Delta O::OP : OZ$, and by similar triangles :: OW : $O\Gamma$ or OP.

COROLLARY 1. When Z coincides with O or M, OW is infinite; therefore whenever PZY intersects the describing circle, the epitrochoid will have a point of contrary flexure at the same distance from C as this intersection; and the circle PZY is given when the basis and generating circle are given, whatever the magnitude of the describing circle may be. If the basis be a straight line, PY will be equal to PK.

COROLLARY 2. By means of this proposition, we may find the curve which will produce any given curve by rolling on a given basis; or having the two curves, we may find the basis. When the basis is given, supposing NO a small portion of the given curve, of which W is the centre of curvature, VP being the circle of equal curvature with the basis at the point P, if we take OZ a third proportional to OW and OP, draw the perpendiculars PY and ZY, and take $CP-PY : PY::PY : YK$, then K will be the centre of curvature of the generating curve; for by addition $CP : PY::PK : YK$, $CP : PK::PY : YK$, and $CP : CK::PY : PK$, as before. When the basis is a right line, Y is the centre of curvature of the curve required.

SCHOLIUM. Hence we may easily find the curvature necessary in the tooth of a wheel for impelling a pallet without friction, by determining the curve which will generate, by rolling on the face of the pallet, a circle passing through the axis of the wheel; but the tooth could never be disengaged from the pallet, without an escapement introduced for the purpose.

PROPOSITION V. PROBLEM. (Plate 7. Fig. 60.) To find the evolute of an epicycloid.

In the epicycloid SM, the point M being in the circumference of PMR, PZ will be to PM in the constant ratio of PY to PR, and MZ to PM as RY to PR, and PM to MW in the same ratio; hence $PM:PW::RY : PY::CR : CP$, therefore the point W is always in a circle $PW\Xi$ of which the radius is to PK in that proportion, and which touches SP in P. On the centre C describe a circle $\Lambda\Xi\Theta$ touching $PW\Xi$ in Ξ; then, since $CR : CP::PR : P\Xi$, we have by division $CR : CP::CP : P\Xi$, and the circle $PW\Xi$ being to $\Lambda\Xi\Theta$ as PMR to SP, the arc PM being equal to SP, the similar arc PW will be equal to $\Lambda\Xi$, and taking $\Lambda\Xi\Theta=$ $PW\Xi$, $\Xi\Theta$ will be always equal to ΞW, and W in a curve ΘWS similar to SM, of which it is the evolute.

PROPOSITION VI. PROBLEM. (Plate 7. Fig. 61.) To find the area of an epitrochoid.

On the centre C describe a circle touching the epitrochoid in S, take GII to GC as PR to PC, and let the circle $G\Phi\Pi$ describe on the basis SG the epicycloid $S\Phi$. Then taking GM always to $G\Phi$ as GL to GII, M will be in the epitrochoid SM; for the angular motion of the chord $G\Phi$, is the same as that of GM in the primary epitrochoid. Let $S\Omega$ be the evolute of $S\Phi$, and $GW\Xi$ its generating circle. On diameters equal to ΞG, ΞL, and $\Xi\Pi$, describe three circles, AD, AE, and AF, touching the right line AB in A; let the angle BAD be always equal to $G\Pi\Phi$, and it is evident that AD, AE, and AF, will be equal respectively to WG, WM, and $W\Phi$. But the angular motion of WG on W being equal to the sum of the angular motions of GM on G and CG on C, is to that of AF, or of GM, or half that of KM, in the ratio of CII to CG, or CR to CP; therefore the fluxions of the areas SWG, SWM and $SW\Phi$ are to those of the segments AD, AE, and AF, in the same ratio; and that ratio being constant, the whole areas, and their differences, are also respectively to each other as CR to CP.

SCHOLIUM. The quadrable spaces of Halley are those which are comprehended between the arc of the epitrochoid, that of the describing circle, and that of a circle concentric with the basis, and cutting the describing circle at the extremities of its diameter.

PROPOSITION VII. PROBLEM. (Plate 7. Fig. 62.) To find a central equation for the epicycloid.

Let CT be perpendicular to RT, the tangent at the point M, then PMR will be a right angle, and PM parallel to CT. On the centre C describe through M the circle MNO, and let MQ be perpendicular to RO. Then the rectangle $OQN=PQR$, $OQ : PQ::QR : QN$, by addition $OQ : PQ ::OR : PN$; hence by division $OP : PQ::IR : PN$, and $PQ=\dfrac{OPN \text{ or } INP}{IR}$. But $PMq=PR \times PQ=\dfrac{PR}{IR} \times INP$: and by similar triangles $CT : CR::PM : PR$, whence $CTq=\dfrac{CRq}{PRq} \times PMq=CRq \times \dfrac{INP}{IRP}$. Let MZ and RY be tangents to SP, then $INP=MZq$, and $IRP=RYq$, $CT=CR \times \dfrac{MZ}{RY}$, and CT will be to MZ in the constant ratio of CR to RY. Putting $CP=a$, $CR=b$, $CM=z$, $CT=u$, then uu $=bb\dfrac{zz-aa}{bb-aa}$.

PLATE 7.

Fig. 57.
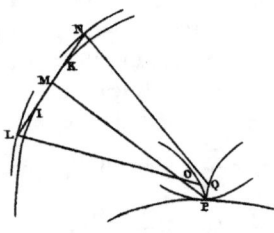

Fig. 60.
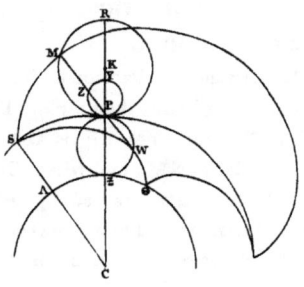

Fig. 58.
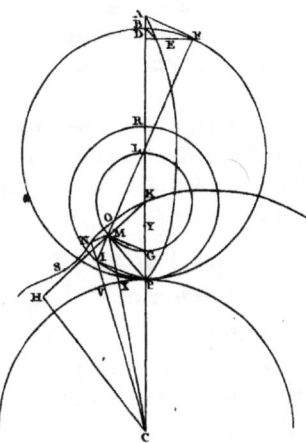

Fig. 61.
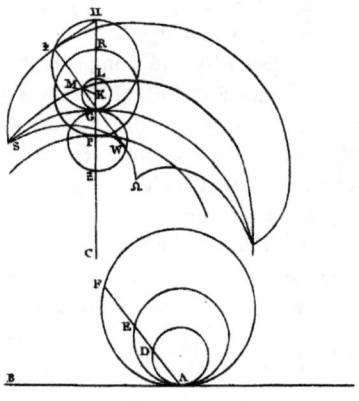

Fig. 59.
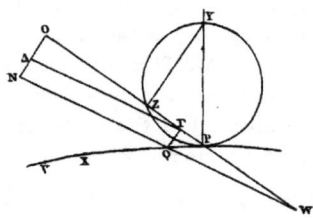

Fig. 62.
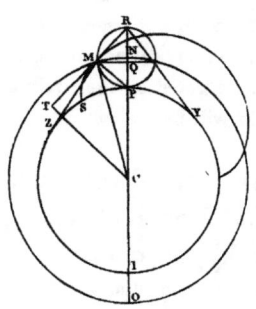

Pub. by J. Johnson, London 1 July 1800. Joseph Skelton sculp.

PROPOSITION VIII. PROBLEM. (Plate 8. Fig. 63.) To find a geometrical equation for the conchoidal epitrochoid.

Let $CP = PK$. On the centre C describe a circle equal to GM, cutting SC in Z. Join MZF, then the arc $DZ = GM$, and MZ is parallel to CK, therefore EF is also equal to DZ or GM, CF is parallel to KM, and $MF = CK$: therefore this epitrochoid is the curve named by Delahire the conchoid of a circular basis, as was first observed by Réaumur in 1708, and afterwards by Maclaurin, in 1720. Call CK, a, DE, b, ZH, x, HM, y, ZM, s; and let ZI be perpendicular to CK; then $FZ = a - s$, $CI = \frac{a-s}{2}$, and CIZ and ZHM being similar, $CZ : CI :: ZM : ZH$, or $\frac{b}{2}$: $\frac{a-s}{2} :: s : x$; hence $bx = as - ss$, $bx + ss = as$, $b^2 x^2 + 2 b x s^2 + s^4 = a^2 s^2$, and by substituting for s^2, $x^4 + 2 b x^3 - a^2 x^2 + b^2 x^2 + 2 x^2 y^2 + 2 b x y^2 + y^4 - a^2 y^2 = 0$.

COROLLARY 1. Join FN, and complete the parallelogram MFNL; then since $EF = DZ = EN$, FN is perpendicular to EK, and ML to NL, and, NL being always equal to FM or CK, L is always in a circle described on the centre N, LM a tangent to that circle, and ZM a perpendicular to that tangent drawn from the point Z.

COROLLARY 2. (Plate 8. Fig. 64.) The unicuspidate epicycloid admits of a peculiar central equation, with respect to the point S. Call SM, s, and let $ST = u$ be perpendicular to the tangent MT, then $u = \left(\frac{s^3}{2a}\right)^{\frac{1}{2}}$. For IP being half of SM, or s, $SP = \sqrt{\left(\frac{as}{2}\right)}$, and the triangles SIP and MTS being similar, $SPq : SMq :: IPq \cdot STq$, or $\frac{as}{2} : s^2 :: \frac{ss}{4} : u^2$, and $2au^2 = s^3$.

COROLLARY 3. The unicuspidate epicycloid is one of the caustics of a circle. For making the angle $CRY = MRC = \frac{1}{2} MKP = \frac{1}{4} SCP$, the triangle CRY is isosceles, and CY is constant; so that all rays in the direction of the tangent MR will be reflected by the circle QR towards Y, and consequently SM will be the caustic of a radiant point at Y.

PROPOSITION IX. PROBLEM. (Plate 8. Fig. 65.) To find a geometrical equation for the tricuspidate hypocycloid.

Let PA and MF be perpendicular to CS. Join PMB, KM, RMG, and PD. Then the angle APB is equal to the difference of APC and MPR, or to that of their complements PRM, PCA: but $PRM = \frac{1}{2} PKM = \frac{1}{3} PCA$, therefore $AP = \frac{1}{2} PCA = ADP = APS$, and the triangles APS and APB are similar and equal. Let $SC = a$, $SF = x$, $FM = y$, and $SB = r$. Then $SA : SP :: SP : SD$, and $SP = \sqrt{(ar)}$. Draw PE perpendicular to BP; then $BE = SD = 2a$, $BC = a - r$, $EC = 3a - r$, and by similar triangles, $CP : CR :: EC : CG = \frac{1}{3} EC = a - \frac{1}{3} r$; therefore $GB = \frac{2}{3} r$: but $BE : BG :: BP : BM$ or $2a : \frac{2}{3} r :: \sqrt{(ar)} : r \frac{r}{3a} \sqrt{(ar)} = BM$; again, $BP : BM ::$ BA : BF, or $\sqrt{(ar)} : \frac{r}{3a}\sqrt{(ar)} :: \frac{r}{2} : \frac{rr}{6a}$, and $SF = x = r - \frac{rr}{6a}$, $6ax = 6ar - rr$, and $r = 3a \pm \sqrt{(9aa - 6ax)}$. But $MFq = BMq - BFq$, or $y^2 = \frac{r^3}{9a} - \frac{r^4}{36aa}$, and $36 a^2 y^2 = 4ar^3 - r^4$. By adding to this the square of the former equation, and proceeding in the same manner to exterminate r, we obtain an equation of the value of x and y, which, when the surds are brought to the same side, and the square of the whole is taken, is at last reduced to $x^4 - \frac{4}{3} a x^3 + 2x^2 y^2 - 12 a x y^2 + y^4 + 12 a^2 y^2 = 0$, a regular equation of the fourth order.

SCHOLIUM. The equation of the corresponding hypotrochoids may be investigated nearly in the same manner, by dividing PR and PM in a given ratio, but the process will be somewhat more tedious.

PROPOSITION X. PROBLEM. (Plate 8. FIG. 66.) To find a geometrical equation for the bicuspidate epicycloid.

Let $CP = PR$. Join RMT, PM, PD; draw CT perpendicular to RT, TE to CR, and EG, MB, RA, to SC. Then the angle $DRP = \frac{1}{2} MKP = SCP$, and by equal triangles, $RA = CT$, and $RD = CD$, and by similar triangles $RM : RP :: RE : RT$, and $RP : RD :: RT : RC$: therefore $RM : RD :: RE : RC$, and ME is parallel to SC, and $EG = BM$. Put $CP = a$, $BC = x$, $BM = y$, $CM = s$, $CT = u$; then by prop. 7, $u^2 - \frac{4}{3} (s^2 - a^2)$; or $\frac{3}{4} u^2 = s^2 - a^2$; but $RC : CT :: CT \cdot CE :: CE : EG$, or y, hence $y = \frac{u^3}{4aa}$, $u^6 = 16a^4 y^2$, $\frac{27}{64} u^6 = \frac{7}{4} a^4 y^2 = (ss - aa)^3 = (xx + yy - aa)^3$; whence by involution the equation of the sixth order may be had at length.

COROLLARY. Since $CRM = SCR$, a ray in the direction of the tangent MR will be reflected, by a circle FR, always parallel to SC; therefore SM is the caustic of the circle FR when the incident rays are parallel to CS.

PROPOSITION XI. PROBLEM. (Plate 8. Fig. 67.) To find a geometrical equation for the quadricuspidate hypocycloid.

Let $CR = PR$, then the angle $PRM = \frac{1}{2} PKM = 2 PCS$,

RAC=ACR, RA=RC=RB=RP, AB=SC, and drawing the perpendiculars CT, TD, TE, and MF, RM=RT, AM =BT, AF=EC, FC=AE, and FM=BD. Let $SC=a$, $FC=x$, $FM=y$, $CM=s$, $CT=u$; then AB : AC :: AC : AT :: AT : AE, whence $AT=(axx)^{\frac{1}{3}}$, and in the same manner $BT=(ayy)^{\frac{1}{3}}$; and CT being a mean proportional between AT and TB, $u^2=(a^2x^2y^2)^{\frac{1}{3}}$, and $u^6=a^2x^2y^2$. But by prop. 7, $3u^2=a^2-s^2$, therefore $27a^2x^2y^2=(a^2-s^2)^3=(a^2-x^2-y^2)^3$; whence the equation may be had at length by involution. The same result may be obtained by Dr. Waring's method of reduction, from $(axx)^{\frac{1}{3}}+(ayy)^{\frac{1}{3}}=a$.

COROLLARY. Since the portion of the tangent AB intercepted between the perpendiculars AC, BC is a constant quantity, this hypocycloid may in that sense be called an equitangential curve; and the rectangular corner of a passage must be rounded off into the form of this curve, in order to admit a beam of a given length to be carried round it.

PROPOSITION XII. PROBLEM. To investigate those cases in which the general propositions either fail or require peculiar modifications.

Case 1. (Plate 8. Fig. 68.) If the generating circle be considered as infinitely small, or the basis as infinitely large, so as to become a straight line, the epicycloid will become a common cycloid, and the ratio of CP to CK in prop. 3, cor. 2, becoming that of equality, the length of the arc SM will be four times the versed sine of half PM, and VM twice the chord RM or VX, therefore the square of the arc VM is always as the absciss VZ. The evolute is an equal cycloid, and the circles in prop. 6 being as 1 to 4, the area of the cycloid is to that of its generating circle as 3 to 1. The properties of the cycloid as an isochronous and as a brachistochronous curve belong to mechanics, and it is demonstrated by writers on optics that its caustic is composed of two cycloids.

Case 2. (Plate 8. Fig. 69.) If the concentrating circle be supposed to become infinite while the base remains finite, the epicycloid will become the involute of a circle; and the fluxion of the curve being always, by prop. 3, cor. 1, to that of PM as PM to CP, its length SM will be a third proportional to IP and PM. Call CP, a, and PM, x, then the fluxion of SM is $\frac{x\dot{x}}{a}$; but the rectangle contained by half PM and the fluxion of SM is the fluxion of the area PSM, or $PSM=\int\frac{x\dot{x}}{2a}=\frac{x^3}{6a}$. The epitrochoid described by the point C of the generating plane will be the spiral of Archimedes, since CN is always equal to PM=PS=QV, and since the angular motion of CN and PM are also equal, the area $CON=PSM=\frac{x^3}{6a}$. Instead of the ellipsis of prop. 3, let PX be a parabola, of which IP is the parameter, and continuing NM to X, the arc PX will be equal to CON. For making LH=CP, it is well known that the fluxion of PX varies as XH, or as PN, which represents the fluxion of CON. For the curvature, PY, in prop. 4, becomes =CP, and the radius is a third proportional to NZ and NP.

Case 3. Supposing now the generating circle to become again finite, but to have its concavity turned towards the basis, the same curve will be described as would be described by the rotation of a third circle on the same basis in a contrary direction, and equal in diameter to the difference of those of the two first circles.

Case 4. If the circles be of the same size, with their concavities turned the same way, no curve can be described; but if the generating circle be still further lessened, a hypocycloid will be produced, of the same figure as that which would be described by a third circle equal in diameter to the difference of the two first. All the general propositions are equally applicable to hypocycloids with other epicycloids, as might easily have been understood from an inspection of the figures, if there had been room for a double series.

Case 5. (Plate 8. Fig. 70.) If the diameter of the generating circle be half that of the basis, the hypocycloid will become a right line, and the hypotrochoid an ellipsis. For since the angle PKM=2 PCS, PCM, being half PKM, coincides with PCS, and M is always in CS. Let GNL be the describing circle of the hypotrochoid, and join GNO; then NL is parallel, and ON perpendicular, to SC, and ON=HL, which is always to GO as CL to CG; therefore AN is an ellipsis: and the centre K will evidently describe a circle.

PLATE 8.

Fig. 63.
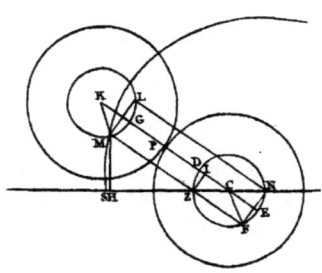

Fig. 67.
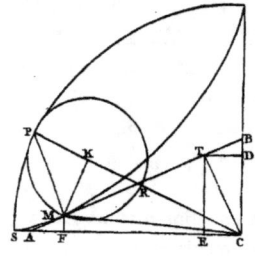

Fig. 64.
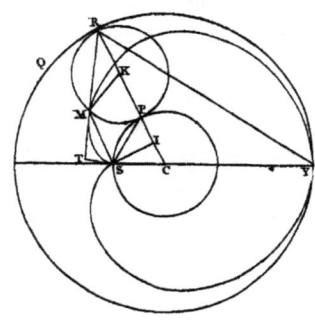

Fig. 68.
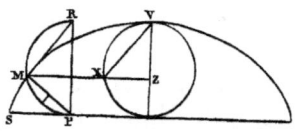

Fig. 65.
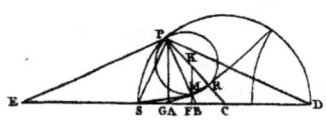

Fig. 69.
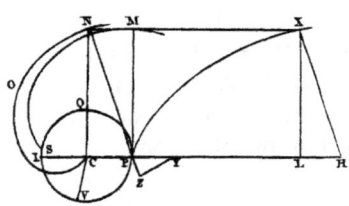

Fig. 66.
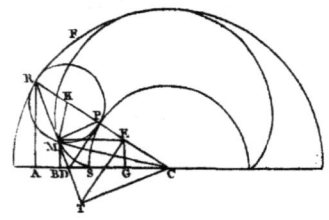

Fig. 70.
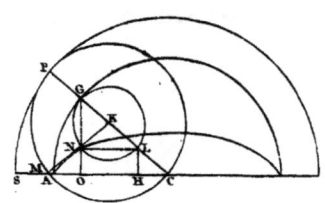

IV. AN ESSAY ON MUSIC.

From the British Magazine for October 1800.

1. OF MUSIC IN GENERAL.

THE agreeable effect of melodious sounds, not only on the human ear, but on the feelings and on the passions, is so universal and so powerful, as deservedly to excite the attention of the psychological philosopher. For what ultimate end a susceptibility for this peculiar pleasure has been implanted by nature in the mind, is not easy to be ascertained; but setting aside the well known pleasing sensation of a delicate titillation, wherever the nerves are possessed of great sensibility, and the associations of an interesting voice, giving expression to poetical and impassioned diction, it is probable that the taste for all complicated and scientific music is wholly acquired.

Music may be considered as consisting of three component parts, rhythm, melody, and harmony. Rhythm is an agreeable succession of sounds considered with respect to the time of their whole duration. Melody is an agreeable succession in respect to the pitch, or the frequency of vibrations of each sound. Harmony is an agreeable combination of several sounds at the same time. It is evident that rhythm and melody are almost inseparable; but that harmony is by no means necessary to the existence of music. In the first place, it is easy to conceive that a love of rhythm, or of the periodical recurrence of the same or similar sensations at equal intervals of time, may be derived from the habit of a certain equality and recurrence in the motions of the body, such as walking, or in children who cannot yet walk, from the passive motion of gestation; this predilection for the return of customary sensations appears to be an innate and fundamental tendency of the human system, to which physiologists and metaphysicians have been obliged ultimately to refer many properties, both of body and mind. But be this as it may, the love of rhythm, which is, perhaps, the lowest ingredient in musical taste, is, if possible, still more universal than the love of harmony and melody. Poetry, or rather metrical composition, is distinguished from prose only by the regularity of its rhythm; and the knowledge of metre and prosody, however high it may rank in the critic's estimation, is a subordinate and comparatively insignificant branch of musical science. The natural fondness for rhythm is the principal foundation of the pleasure of dancing, an amusement intimately connected with music, and no less popular. The rhythm of a musical composition is almost always at least twofold, often three or fourfold, consisting of subordinate divisions or bars, and periodical returns of larger members, either phrases or strains, containing equal numbers of those divisions. All this is perfectly natural, but perhaps, not so necessary to music as Mr. Walter Young, in his excellent essay, printed in the Edinburgh Transactions, appears to imagine; for those who are already experienced musicians are generally observed to delight in recitative, where the rhythm is almost entirely lost; and still more in fugues, where two or three series of rhythms, almost independent of each other, are carried on at the same time, one part beginning its subdivisions when another has made some progress, and a third is still to follow. But the pleasure derived from such compositions is, as Kirnberger has observed, more intellectual than sensual, arising in a great measure from the consciousness of being able to comprehend that which is " caviare to the general." Rhythm is generally marked in performance by a slight increase of force at the beginning of each subdivision or bar; sometimes, and in some instruments always, the change of sounds, in point of acuteness and gravity, or the interruption of the same sound, is a sufficient distinction; and sometimes, after the rhythm has already been firmly impressed on the mind, neither change of sound nor of strength is perpetually repeated; the imagination alone being sufficient to conceive the continuation of the rhythm: but this constitutes a kind of *tempo rubato*, where the perception of measure is intentionally weakened or suspended. The Aeolian harp pleases indeed without rhythm, but the pleasure would soon be exhausted by repetition.

The next constituent part of music is melody. Melody may in some sense be said to please on the same principle as rhythm, the partiality of the mind to a regular recurrence of intervals: for though we have it not in our power to count the single vibrations of musical sounds numerically, yet we are evidently able to compare with ease such sounds as are related to each other in the simplest numerical ratios. For instance, if a treble and a tenor voice sing the same part, there is scarcely an ear so inaccurate as not to perceive their resemblance, which is produced by the recurrence of two vibrations of the treble note at the same interval of time with one of the tenor. The same love of order may easily be extended to the comparison of fifths and fourths, where the proportions are as two to three, and as three to four. This is enough to account in some degree for the pleasure derived from melody, or the succession of sounds bearing certain proportions to each other, in respect to gravity and acuteness: besides that the same intervals, which are most melodious in succession, are found also to form the most pleasing combination of harmony when cotemporary; for since the preceding sound is very frequently continued by reflection from surrounding objects, so as to become cotemporary with the succeeding, and perhaps always remains fixed in the imagination, it is obvious that sounds, in order to be perfectly melodious, must also be harmonious. Add to this the impression generally made in infancy by the more or less melodious ditties of the nurse's voice, and the connexion of refined and chromatic melodies with the natural expression of the moans of grief, or the exclamations of joy: and from the union of all these causes it may easily be conceived from whence the love of melody, as an acquired faculty, may, without much difficulty, be derived.

The pleasure arising from harmony is not so simple and universal as that which is produced by a combination of rhythm and melody. Harmony requires for its execution and perception a greater degree of cultivation both in the performer and in the hearer than melody alone. Cotemporary sounds may, from the due proportion of the times of their vibrations, give a similar pleasure to that of melody, when the mind, considering them in succession, finds them capable of a ready comparison. But the characteristic of harmony is the regular, and at the same time diversified, motion of the air, which arises from the combined vibrations, and which appears to be well calculated to produce the pleasure that the mind derives from the perception of symmetry. In this point of view, a concord may be considered as a single sound, distinguished from a discord by a superior quality of tone; in the same manner as the tone of the harmonica is more agreeable than that of a newsman's horn, as the note of a nightingale is sweeter than that of a frog, and a smooth rich voice more pleasing than a hoarse and nasal croaking. Thus the harshness and disagreeable quality of a single sound may also, on a more nice examination, be sometimes found to consist in a want of harmonious proportion in those secondary notes, which generally enter into its composition. This quality of sound, sometimes called its tone, register, colour, or *timbre*, might be considered as a fourth component part of music; it depends on the law by which the parts of the sounding body, and the particles of the air, are governed with respect to the velocity of their progress and regress in each vibration, or in different successive vibrations. No doubt, much of the pleasure derived from music depends on it; but as it is capable of little diversity on the same instrument, it is seldom considered in treating of the theory of music. The various combinations of the stops of the organ and harpsichord, the use of the harmonics of the harp and violin, the bowing nearer to or further from the bridge, the application of muffles of various kinds, the change of the aperture of the lips in wind instruments, the choice of vowels and consonants more or less adapted to the powers of the voice; and in full pieces, the judicious introduction of different voices and instruments, as subservient to the general effect; all this relates to the quality of sound, and whoever adequately relishes the works of the great modern masters, will be fully competent to judge of its practical importance.

Be the causes what they may, natural or habitual, simple or complicated, it is certain that a very great majority of mankind experiences pleasure from music: this pleasure is a social pleasure, and, connected as it is with sentiment and passion, it is a rational pleasure. The pursuit of musical excellence, if properly conducted, amply exercises the faculties, at the same time that it forms a desirable variety, when intermixed with literary or professional employments. To call it an amusement only, betrays an ignorance of the nature and difficulty of the study; so far is the science of music from being of a light and superficial nature, that, in its whole extent, it is scarcely less intricate or more easily acquired than the most profound of the more regular occupations of the schools: and even practical perfection in music requires so much intense and laborious application, such a minute accuracy of perception, and so rapid an association of various sensitive ideas, with other ideas and mechanical motions, that it is inconceivable how men, who have no appearance of superior brilliancy in any other accomplishment, should be able to attain a conception and execution in music, which seem almost to require the faculties of a superior order of beings. An intemperate and dissipated attachment to music may indeed often be productive of evils; but probably the same individuals, who have been its victims, would have been equally idle and irregular if they had been destitute of this accomplishment. A considerable share of the pleasure of practical music arises from causes perfectly distinct from the sensual perceptions: the consciousness of having overcome difficulties, the laudable satisfaction of entertaining others, and the interest and emulation produced by a concurrence of others in the same pursuits; all these entirely outweigh the temporary amusement of the ear, and wholly remove the objection, which might be made, to the enervating effect of a continued devotion to pleasurable sensations. The ancient philosophers, with all the manliness and dignity of character to which they aspired, were not ashamed to consider music as an indispensable part of a liberal education; and Plato devotes three of the earlier years of his young citizens entirely to the study of the lyre: nor are we without examples in modern times, of philosophers, and princes, and heroes, who have excelled as much in musical performances, as in literature and in arms.

II. OF THE ORIGIN OF THE SCALE.

The first lyre, with three strings, is said to have been invented in Egypt by Hermes, under Osiris, between the years 1800 and 1500 before Christ. The second and third string were, perhaps, the octave and fifth of the first, or more probably its fifth and fourth; as it would be easy to sing the octave with the accompaniment of the primitive note only. The melody might be either always in unison with one of the strings, resembling a very simple modern bass part; or the intervals might be occasionally filled up by the voice, without accompaniment. We have, in modern music, a specimen of a pleasing air, by Rousseau, formed on three notes alone, the key note with its second and third; but there can be little doubt that the earliest melodies must have had a greater compass than this; although some suppose the three strings of the oldest lyre to have been successive notes of the scale. The trumpet is said to have been invented about the same time: a little experience might have taught the Egyptians to produce from it the octaves, the 12th, 17th, 23d, and other harmonics of the primitive sound, which are related to it in the ratio of the integers from 1 to 9, and the same sounds might have been observed by a delicate ear among the secondary notes of a long chord; and then, by descending three octaves from the 23d, and two from the 17th, they might have added to their lyre the second and major third of the principal note. But it does not appear that this method ever occurred to the ancients: they seem rather to have attended to the intervals of the notes within the octave, than to the union of similar notes in the natural harmonics; and, besides, the series of natural harmonics would never have furnished a true fourth or sixth. It is uncertain when, or by whom, the fourth string was added: but the merit of increasing the number to seven is attributed to Terpander, about the year 700 before Christ, two centuries after Homer: although some persons have asserted that he only brought the improvement from Egypt, and that Hermes was also the inventor of the lyre with seven strings. Pythagoras, or Simonides, about the year 500, added an eighth, and Timotheus a ninth string: the number was afterwards extended to two octaves; and Epigonus is said so have used a lyre of forty strings, or rather a harp, as he played without a plectrum: but the theory of the ancient music soon became more intricate than interesting. The lyre of eight strings comprehended an octave, corresponding pretty accurately with the notes of our natural scale, beginning with *e*: the key note was *a*, so that the melody appears to have borne usually a minor third, which has also been observed to be the case in the airs of most uncultivated nations; but there was a considerable diversity in the manner of tuning the lyre, according to the great variety of modes and genera that were introduced. These modes were of a nature totally different from the modern modulations into various keys, but they must have afforded a more copious fund of striking, if not of pleasing melodies, than we have at present. In some of the genera, intervals of about a quarter tone were employed; but this practice, on account of its difficulty, was soon abandoned; a difficulty which is not easily overcome by the most experienced of modern singers; although some great masters have been said to introduce a progression of quarter tones, in pathetic passages, with surprising effect. The tibia of the ancients, as it appears evidently from Theophrastus, although not from the misinterpretations of his commentators and of Pliny, had a reed mouth piece about three inches long, and therefore was more properly a clarinet than a flute; and the same performer generally played on two at once, and not in unison. Pollux, in the time of Commodus, describes, under the name of the Tyrrhene pipe, exactly such an organ as is figured by Hawkins, composed of brass tubes, and blown by bellows: nor does he mention it as a new discovery: it appears, from other authors, to have been often furnished with several registers of pipes; and it is scarcely possible that the performer, who is represented by Julian as having considerable execution, should have been contented without occasionally adding harmony to his melody. That the voice was accompanied by thorough bass on the lyre, is undeniably proved by a passage of Plato: and that the ancients had some knowledge of singing in three parts, is evident from Macrobius. Martini, who is one of the strongest opponents of that opinion, which attributes to the ancients a knowledge of counterpoint, observes, that " they allowed no concords but the octave, fourth, and fifth, or at most very rarely the third; yet they were not without a knowledge of concord of harmonious parts. It is known with certainty, that two parts, whether vocal or instrumental, or mixed, besides unison, performed at the same time the same melody, either always in octaves, or probably always in fifths, or always in fourths; which was called a symphony: perhaps also, they changed in the course of the performance from one interval to another, and this might be done by more than two parts at the same time." It is not improbable that this statement may be accurate: nor is it necessary to suppose a very exquisite and refined skill in the intricacies of composition, to produce all the effects that have with any probability been attributed to music. It is well known that Rousseau and others have maintained, that harmony is rather detrimental than advantageous to an interesting melody, in which true music consists; and it may easily be observed, that an absolute solo, whether a passage or a cadence, is universally received, even by cultivated hearers, with more attention and applause, than the richest modulations of a powerful harmony.

The minor scale being the most commonly used by the ancients, it was natural for Pope Gregory, who in the year 600 is said to have marked the notes by the Roman letters, to begin with A, the key note of that scale: although if, as there is some reason to suppose, the B was originally flat, A was not the key note, but its fifth, until the B natural was introduced, and denoted by a square b instead of a round one. By degrees the chromatic scale was filled up, and the five added intervals were denoted by the letter belonging to the note above them, with the addition of the round b, or by the note below, with the addition of four lines crossing each other, implying a half note, as composed of four commas. A simple cross would, however, at present, be much more convenient, as more readily distinguishable from the square b, which is used to signify a natural note, in opposition to these flats and sharps. This is the historical account of the origin of the scale; but, according to the modern theory and practice of music, the subject may be more easily understood, by beginning with an explanation of the major scale.

III. PRACTICAL APPLICATION OF THE SCALES.

The simplest proportions of two sounds to each other, next to unison, is when the frequency of their vibrations are related as one to two: such sounds bear a very strong resemblance to each other, and when named, they are denoted by the same letter, and are only distinguished by the appellations in alt, in altissimo, on the one side, and double, and double double, on the other. The Germans, with great propriety, make use of small letters or capitals, with one, two, or more lines over or under them. The note marked by the tenor cliff is called $\bar{c}$, the octaves above, $\bar{\bar{c}}, \bar{\bar{\bar{c}}}$, as far as six lines, which is, perhaps, the highest note used in music: the octaves below $\bar{c}$, are c, C, $\underline{C}$, $\underline{\underline{C}}$: $\underline{\underline{\underline{C}}}$ is probably not audible, vibrating but eight times in a second. C with six lines below it, would denote a sound, of which the complete vibrations should last precisely a second. The series of natural notes is this, A, B, C, D, E, F, G, A, B, c, d .. b, $\bar{c}$, $\bar{d}$ ... The subjoined table will show the absolute frequency and the dimensions of each vibration of the octaves of c, and the length of the simplest organ pipe that produces it: but, according to the different temperature of the air, and the pitch of the instruments, these numbers may vary somewhat from perfect accuracy: and it must be observed, that the usual pitch of concerts, in London, is somewhat higher than this standard; and in Germany, perhaps a little lower.

Sound moves in a second 1130 feet.		
Note.	Vibrations in a second.	Length of open pipe in feet.
C⁶	1	565.00
C⁵	2	282.50
C⁴	4	141.25
C³	8	70.62
C² audible	16	35.31
C	32	17.66
C	64	8.83
c	128	4.41
c	256	2.21
c²	512	1.10
c³	1024	.55
c⁴	2048	.28
c⁵	4096	.14
c⁶	8192	.07

(New P. Forte.)

Any sound may be assumed at pleasure for the primitive or standard note of a piece of music, and is then denominated the key note: and the idea of this note is perpetually impressed on the mind in all simple compositions, both from its frequent recurrence, and from the relation that all the other sounds bear to it. C being the key note of the scale called natural, we shall consider it as the foundation of the scale. The next in importance is the fifth, G, which, for various reasons, is intimately connected with the key note. The first reason is, that it constitutes the most perfect melody and harmony with C, since every alternate vibration of C coincides with every third of G; the second is, that an attentive ear may almost always distinguish the fifth, at least its octave, the 12th, whenever any instrument sounds C; it being one of those secondary sounds which are called natural harmonics, and which may generally be observed, in the proportion of the natural numbers, as far as twenty or more, but which have not hitherto been completely explained: thirdly, a stopped pipe, if blown forcibly, springs immediately from C to g, and an open pipe first to c, and then to g. The interval, between C and G, is most naturally divided by the note E, which answers to the number 5, when C and G are represented by 4 and 6, and which is found among the natural harmonics both of chords and pipes. These three notes constitute the harmonic triad, or common accord, in the major scale, which is the most perfect, or rather the only perfect harmony. But the intervals are still much too large for melody, and require a further subdivision; we now therefore take the fifth below instead of above the key, or its octave, the fourth above, F, which is to C as 4 to 3: this sound is no where found among the natural harmonics of C, but C is the most distinguishable of its harmonics, and therefore the relation is nearly the same. The scale is completed by filling up the perfect triads of G and F: the fifth of G furnishing D, the second of the key, which is also the ninth natural harmonic of C; the third of G, the seventh, B, which is the fifteenth harmonic of C; and the third of F being the sixth of the key, A, which is neither among the harmonics of C, nor has c among its harmonics. Hence we have a second table, in which the proportions of the length of a chord, or pipe, producing the various sounds, are detailed, and the place among the principal natural harmonics of the key annexed.

Notes.		Proportions.	Nat. harm.
Key	C	1	1
2d	D		9
3d	E		5, 10
4th	F		0, (¼)
5th	G		3, 6, 12
6th	A		0
7th	B		15
8th	c		2, 4, 8, 16

Now when two or more perfectly harmonious parts are performed together, they must necessarily be found all in the same triad, C, E, G; G, B, D: or F, A, C; and the succession of these triads, in various forms, is sufficient for the accompaniment of any simple melody. A regular melody always terminates by an ascent or descent of one degree to the key note; the last note but one must therefore be always B or D: and both of these being in the triad of G, G is called the governing note, or the dominant of C; and F, being in the same manner governed by C, is called its subdominant. And it is usual, in all regular compositions of any length, to depart for a short time from the principal harmony of the key note, and to modulate into the key of the dominant, then to return, and to modulate for a still shorter time into the subdominant, before the final close in the tonic or key note. It is necessary therefore, for greater variety, to complete the scale of the dominant, as well as that of every other note which may be occasionally introduced as a principal key note; but to do this with mathematical accuracy, in the same proportions as have been explained, would be practically impossible, and even theoretically inconvenient: hence arises the necessity of tempering some intervals, to make the others more tolerable, without too much increasing the number of sounds. It has been found sufficient in practice, to add five notes to the seven which have been enumerated; but the best proportions of these have not yet been absolutely determined: some have made all the twelve intervals equal: others have left the whole scale of C perfect: others again have taken a middle path, and have introduced a slight imperfection into this key, in order to make the neighbouring ones the less disagreeable. The least circuitous introduction of these notes is shown in the third table, together with the proportion that they bear to C when thus considered. They are denominated nearly in the German manner, the addition of the syllable "is" signifying what the English call sharp, and the French *diése*, and that of "es," flat, or *bémol*.

Notes.	Relations.	Proportions.
Fis	as 7th of G	$\frac{45}{32}$
Bes	as 4th of F	$\frac{9}{16}$
Cis	as 7th of D	$\frac{135}{128}$
Ees	as 4th of Bes	$\frac{27}{16}$
Gis	as 3d of E	$\frac{16}{15}$

But a still greater variety being required than these major scales afford, it has been found, that the interval of a fifth may be agreeably, though somewhat less harmoniously, divided, by placing the minor third below, instead of above, the major; so that C may be to E as E was to G, and consequently E to G as C was to E. The E, thus depressed to $\frac{5}{6}$, differs but by a comma, or in the ratio of 80 : 81, from the Ees found above, as the 4th of Bes; therefore the same string serves for both notes; and the scale becomes C, D, Ees, F, G, A, B, C; which is the ascending minor scale, the A and B being retained as leading best towards the key note, and the major triad of the dominant being therefore necessary to the cadence. But in descending, the triad of the subdominant F may conform to the character of the minor mode, and Aes is substituted for A; and most frequently Bes for B, as dividing the interval from C to Aes more equally and more melodiously.

Thus we have a pretty comprehensive view of the most usual practical relations of all the notes to each other. Their use as discords is somewhat more complicated, and would lead further into the science of music than is consistent with the nature of so summary a view. But it may be remarked in general, that by far the most common discord is the note which constitutes the distinction of the scale of the key from that of its dominant; for instance, F with the triad of G, which is called the accord of the flat seventh of G; and F, not being in the scale of G, is considered as a regular preparative to the final accord of C; in which that part or instrument by which the F is introduced, must necessarily descend to E, the third of the key. The second kind of discords are suspended discords, when one or more notes of any preceding accord are continued after the commencement of a different harmony in other parts of the composition. The third, which is rare, and less universally adopted, consists in an anticipation of a subordinate note of an accord which is to follow, as in the case of the added sixth of the French school. The fourth kind are passing discords, where a note, forming only a melodious step between two others, is inserted without any regard to its harmonious relations.

IV. OF THE TERMS EXPRESSIVE OF TIME.

The notation of music, as it has been established for more than two centuries, is in general admirably adapted for its purpose: but there is one great deficiency, which might very easily be remedied, and that is, the total omission of any character expressive of the absolute duration of each note, however accurately the relative value of the notes may be prescribed. It is true, some little allowance must be made for the execution of the performer, and for the habits of the audience; but this is no reason why time might not be much more accurately noted, than by the vague terms which are usually adopted. It would be easy to prefix to each movement a number, signifying how many bars are to be performed in a minute, which might at first be ascertained by the help of a stop watch, and would soon become perfectly familiar both to composers and performers, even without this assistance. According to Quanz, the number which should be substituted for *Allegro assai*, in common time, is about 40; for *Allegretto*, 20; for *Larghetto*, 10; and for *Adagio assai*, 5. But it is usual to perform modern music much more rapidly than this; or at least the style of composition is so changed, that the terms are very differently applied. An allegro, or even an allegretto, in common time, without semiquavers, is often performed as fast as 60; seldom slower than 30.

A very superficial attempt to affix a determinate meaning to the words denoting musical time, may be seen in the table subjoined; which, if it were more completely and accurately filled up, might be of considerable use to young musicians; although it will appear, from inspection of this table, that composers have hitherto employed those terms in very indefinite significations. But it must be confessed, that much latitude must necessarily be left for the ear and taste of a judicious performer, and that it is impossible for human art, to describe on paper every delicacy of finished execution.

Terms.	C	2/4	3/4	4/8	3/8
Prestissimo	As fast	as	you	can.	
Presto		100		80, H.	
Presto ma non troppo		90, H.			
Allegro assai	40, Q.	80, Pl.	70, H.		
Allegro molto		100 H.			
Allegro vivace			60, Pl.	50, Pl.	
Allegro	{ 25, Ha. 45, M. 40, 50, 60, Pl.	100, 120 H. 75, 80, Pl.	65, H.		
Allegro non troppo		60, Pl.		50, Pl.	
Allegro moderato	40, H.	70, M.			
Vivace assai		100, H.		60, H.	
Vivace			60, H.		
Spiritoso		90, H.			
Menuetto allegro molto			75, H.		
———— allegro			70, H. Pl.		
———— allegretto			55, H.		
———— moderato			50, H. M.		
Allegretto	20, Q.				45, Pl.
Allegretto grazioso	50, M.				
Moderato					
Maestoso	19			30, Pl.	
Larghetto	10, Q.				
Andante graz.				30, M.	
Andante		{ 35, H. Pl. 50, Pl.		30, M.	
And. cantab.			20, 25, M.		
Largo cant.	20, H.				
Adag. n. tr.	17, H.	27, 30, Pl.			20
Adagio	7, Cor.		14, H.	10, 12, M.	
Adagio molto	15, Scoz.			10, Pl.	

Cor. Corelli.
Ha. Handel.
Q. Quanz.
H. Haydn.
M. Mozart.
Pl. Pleyel.

If we choose to compare the time, occupied either by a bar, or by any of its parts, with the vibrations of a pendulum, we may easily do it by means of the following table, which shows the number of vibrations in a minute, corresponding to pendulums of different lengths, expressed in inches.

Length.	Vibrations.	Length.	Vibrations.
4	187	15	97
5	167	20	84
6	153	25	75
7	142	30	68
8	132	35	63
9	125	40	59
10	118	50	53
12	107	60	47

V. ON THE MECHANISM OF THE EYE.

BY

THOMAS YOUNG, M.D. F.R.S.

FROM THE PHILOSOPHICAL TRANSACTIONS.

Read before the ROYAL SOCIETY, *November* 27, 1800.

I. IN the year 1793, I had the honour of laying before the Royal Society some observations, on the faculty, by which the eye accommodates itself to the perception of objects at different distances*. The opinion which I then entertained, although it had never been placed exactly in the same light, was neither so new, nor so much forgotten, as was supposed by myself, and by most of those with whom I had any intercourse on the subject. Mr. Hunter, who had long before formed a similar opinion, was still less aware of having been anticipated in it, and was engaged, at the time of his death, in an investigation of the facts relative to it †; an investigation for which, as far as physiology was concerned, he was undoubtedly well qualified. Mr. Home, with the assistance of Mr. Ramsden, whose recent loss this Society cannot but lament, continued the inquiry which Mr. Hunter had begun; and the results of his experiments appeared very satisfactorily to confute the hypothesis of the muscularity of the crystalline lens ‡. I therefore thought it incumbent on me, to take the earliest opportunity of testifying my persuasion of the justice of Mr. Home's conclusions, which I accordingly mentioned in a Dissertation published at Gottingen in 1796 §, and also in an Essay presented last year to this Society ‖. About three months ago, I was induced to resume the subject, by perusing Dr. Porterfield's paper on the internal motions of the eye ¶; and I have very unexpectedly made some observations, which, I think I may venture to say, appear to be

---

* Phil. Trans. 1793. 169.
† Phil. Trans. 1794. 21.
‡ Phil. Trans. 1795. 1.
§ De Corporis humani Viribus conservatricibus, p. 68.
‖ Phil. Trans. 1800. 146.
¶ Edinb. Med. Essays, IV. 124.

finally conclusive in favour of my former opinion, as far as that opinion attributed to the lens a power of changing its figure. At the same time, I must remark, that every person, who has been engaged in experiments of this nature, will be aware of the extreme delicacy and precaution requisite, both in conducting them, and in drawing inferences from them; and will also readily allow, that no apology is necessary for the fallacies which have misled many others, as well as myself, in the application of those experiments to optical and physiological determinations.

II. Besides the inquiry respecting the accommodation of the eye to different distances, I shall have occasion to notice some other particulars relative to its functions; and I shall begin with a general consideration of the sense of vision. I shall then describe an instrument for readily ascertaining the focal distance of the eye; and with the assistance of this instrument, I shall investigate the dimensions and refractive powers of the human eye in its quiescent state; and the form and magnitude of the picture, which is delineated on the retina. I shall next inquire, how great are the changes which the eye admits, and what degree of alteration in its proportions will be necessary for these changes, on the various suppositions that are principally deserving of comparison. I shall proceed to relate a variety of experiments, which appear to be the most proper to decide on the truth of each of these suppositions, and to examine such arguments, as have been brought forwards, against the opinion which I shall endeavour to maintain; and I shall conclude with some anatomical illustrations of the capacity of the organs of various classes of animals, for the functions attributed to them.

III. Of all the external senses, the eye is generally supposed to be by far the best understood; yet so complicated and so diversified are its powers, that many of them have been hitherto uninvestigated: and on others, much laborious research has been spent in vain. It cannot indeed be denied, that we are capable of explaining the use and operation of its different parts, in a far more satisfactory and interesting manner than those of the ear, which is the only organ that can be strictly compared with it; since, in smelling, tasting, and feeling, the objects to be examined come, almost unprepared, into immediate contact with the extremities of the nerves; and the only difficulty is, in conceiving the nature of the effect produced by them, and of its communication to the sensorium. But the eye and the ear are merely preparatory organs, calculated for transmitting the impressions of light and sound, to the retina, and to the termination of the soft auditory nerve. In the eye, light is conveyed to the retina, without any change of the nature of its propagation: in the ear, it is very probable, that instead of the successive motion of different parts of the same elastic medium, the small bones transmit the vibrations of sound, as passive hard bodies, obeying the motions of the air nearly in their whole extent at the same instant. In the eye, we judge very precisely of the direction of light, from the part of the retina on which it impinges: in the ear, we have no other criterion than the slight difference of motion in the small bones, according to the part of the tympanum on which the sound, concentrated by different reflections, first strikes; hence, the idea of direction is necessarily very indistinct; and there is no reason to suppose, that different parts of the auditory nerve are exclusively affected by sounds in different directions. Supposing the eye capable of conveying a distinct idea of two points subtending an angle of a minute, which is, perhaps, nearly the smallest interval at which two objects can be distinguished, although a line, subtending only one tenth of a minute in breadth, may sometimes be perceived as a single object; there must, on this supposition, be about 360 thousand sentient points, for a field of view of 10 degrees in diameter, and above 60 millions for a field of 140 degrees. But, on account of the various sensibility of the retina, to be explained hereafter, it is not necessary to suppose, that there are more than 10 million sentient points, nor can there easily be less than one million: the optic nerve may, therefore, be judged to consist of several millions of distinct fibres. By a rough experiment, I find, that I can distinguish two similar sounds proceeding from points which subtend an angle of about five degrees. But the eye can discriminate, in a space subtending every way five degrees, about 90 thousand different points. Of such spaces, there are more than a thousand in a hemisphere: so that the ear can convey an impression of about a thousand different directions. The ear has not, however, in all cases, quite so nice a discrimination of the directions of sounds: the reason of this difference between the eye and ear is obvious; each point of the retina has only three principal colours to perceive, since the rest are probably composed of various proportions of these; but there being many thousands or millions of varieties of sound audible in each direction, it was impossible that the number of distinguishable directions should be very large. It is not absolutely certain, that every part of the auditory nerve is capable of receiving the impression of each of the very great diversity of tones that we can distinguish, in the same manner as each sensitive point of the retina receives a distinct impression of the colour, as well as of the strength, of the light which falls on it; although it is extremely probable, that all the different parts of the surface, exposed to the fluid of the vestibule, are more or less affected by every sound, but in different degrees and succession, according to the direction and quality of the vibration. Whether or no, strictly speaking, we can hear two sounds, or see two objects, in the same instant, cannot easily be determined; but it is sufficient, that we can do both, without the intervention of any interval of time perceptible to the mind; and indeed we could form no idea of magnitude, without a comparative, and therefore nearly cotemporary, perception of two or more parts of the same object. The extent of the field of perfect vision, for each position of the eye, is certainly not very great; although it will appear hereafter, that its refractive powers are calculated to take in a moderately distinct view of a whole hemisphere: the sense of hearing is equally perfect in almost every direction.

IV. Dr. Porterfield has applied an experiment, first made by Scheiner[*], to the determination of the focal distance of the eye; and has described, under the name of an optometer, a very excellent instrument, founded on the principle of the phenomenon[†]. But the apparatus is capable of considerable improvement; and I shall beg leave to describe an optometer, simple in its construction, and equally convenient and accurate in its application.

[*] Priestley's opt. 113.
[†] Edinb. Med. Ess. IV. 185.

Let an obstacle be interposed between a radiant point (R, Plate 15. Fig. 109,) and any refracting surface, or lens (CD), and let this obstacle be perforated at two points (A and B) only. Let the refracted rays be intercepted by a plane, so as to form an image on it. Then it is evident, that when this plane (EF) passes through the focus of refracted rays, the image formed on it will be a single point. But, if the plane be advanced forwards (to GH), or removed backwards (to IK), the small pencils, passing through the perforations, will no longer meet in a single point, but will fall on two distinct spots of the plane (G, H ; I, K :) and, in either case, form a double image of the object.

Let us now add two more radiating points, (S and T, Fig. 110,) the one nearer to the lens than the first point, the other more remote; and, when the plane, which receives the images, passes through the focus of rays coming from the first point, the images of the second and third points must both be double (*s s, t t ;*) since the plane (EF) is without the focal distance of rays coming from the furthest point, and within that of rays coming from the nearest. Upon this principle, Dr. Porterfield's optometer was founded.

But, if the three points be supposed to be joined by a line, and this line to be somewhat inclined to the axis of the lens, each point of the line, except the first point (R, Fig. 111,) will have a double image; and each pair of images, being contiguous to those of the neighbouring radiant points, will form with them two continued lines; and the images being more widely separated as the point which they represent is further from the first radiant point, the lines (*s t, s t,*) will converge on each side towards (*r*) the image of this point, and there will intersect each other.

The same happens when we look at any object through two pin holes, within the limits of the pupil. If the object be at the point of perfect vision, the image on the retina will be single ; but, in every other case, the image being double, we shall appear to see a double object : and, if we look at a line pointed nearly to the eye, it will appear as two lines, crossing each other in the point of perfect vision. For this purpose, the holes may be converted into slits, which render the images nearly as distinct, at the same time that they admit more light. The number may be increased from two to four, or more, whenever particular investigations render it necessary.

This instrument has the advantage of showing the focal distance correctly, by inspection only, without sliding the object backwards and forwards, which is an operation liable to considerable uncertainty, especially as the focus of the eye may in the mean time be changed.

The optometer may be made of a slip of card paper, or of ivory, about eight inches in length, and one in breadth, divided longitudinally by a black line, which must not be too strong: The end of the card must be cut as is shown in Plate 9. Fig. 71, in order that it may be turned up, and fixed in an inclined position by means of the shoulders: or a detached piece, nearly of this form, may be applied to the optometer, as it is here engraved (Fig. 72.). A hole about half an inch square must be made in this part ; and the sides so cut as to receive a slider of thick paper, with slits of different sizes, from a fortieth to a tenth of an inch in breadth, divided by spaces somewhat broader ; so that each observer may choose that which best suits the aperture of his pupil. In order to adapt the instrument to the use of presbyopic eyes, the other end must be furnished with a lens of four inches focal length; and a scale must be made near the line on each side of it, divided from one end into inches, and from the other according to the table here calculated, by means of which, not only diverging, but also parallel and converging rays from the lens are referred to their virtual focus. If ivory be employed, its surface must be left without any polish, otherwise the regular reflection of light will create confusion; and in this respect, paper is much preferable.

The instrument is easily applicable to the purpose of ascertaining the focal length of spectacles required for myopic or presbyopic eyes. Mr. Cary has been so good as to furnish me with the numbers and focal lengths of the glasses commonly made; and I have calculated the distances at which those numbers must be placed on the scale of the optometer, so that a presbyopic eye may be enabled to see at eight inches distance, by using the glasses of the focal length placed opposite to the nearest crossing of the lines; and a myopic eye, with parallel rays, by using the glasses indicated by the number that stands opposite their furthest crossing. It cannot be expected, that every person, on the first trial, will fix precisely upon that power which best suits the defect of his sight. Few can bring their eyes at pleasure to the state of full action, or of perfect relaxation; and a power two or three degrees lower than that which is thus ascertained, will be found sufficient for ordinary purposes. I have also added to the second table, such numbers as will point out the spectacles necessary for a presbyopic eye, to see at twelve and at eighteen inches respectively: the middle series will perhaps be the most proper for placing the numbers on the scale. The optometer should be applied to each eye; and, at the time of observing, the opposite eye should not be shut, but the instrument should be screened from its view. The place of intersection may be accurately ascertained, by means of an index sliding along the scale.

The optometer is represented in Plate 9. Fig. 72 and 73; and the manner in which the lines appear, in Fig. 74.

Table I. *For extending the scale by a lens of 4 inches focus.*

4	2.00	13	3.06	70	3.76	—40	4.44	—11	6.29
5	2.22	14	3.11	80	3.81	—35	4.51	—10	6.67
6	2.40	15	3.16	100	3.85	—30	4.62	—9.5	6.90
7	2.55	20	3.33	200	3.92	—25	4.76	—9.0	7.20
8	2.67	25	3.45	∞	4.00	—20	5.00	—8.5	7.56
9	2.77	30	3.52	—200	4.08	—15	5.45	—8.0	8.00
10	2.86	40	3.64	—100	4.17	—14	5.60		
11	2.93	50	3.70	—50	4.35	—13	5.78		
12	3.00	60	3.75	—45	4.39	—12	6.00		

Table II. *For placing the numbers indicating the focal length of convex glasses.*

Foc.	VIII.	XII.	XVIII.
00	8.00	12.00	18.00
40	10.00	17.14	32.73
36	10.28	18.00	36.00
30	10.91	20.00	45.00
28	11.20	21.00	50.40
26	11.56	22.29	58.50
24	12.00	24.00	72.00
22	12.77	26.40	99.00
20	13.33	30.00	180.00
18	14.40	36.00	∞
16	16.00	48.00	—144.00
14	18.67	84.00	— 63.00
12	24.00	∞	— 36.00
11	29.33	—132.00	— 28.29
10	40.00	— 60.00	— 22.50
9	72.00	— 36.00	— 18.00
8	∞	— 24.00	— 14.40
7	—56.00	— 16.80	— 11.45
6	—24.00	— 12.00	— 9.00
5	—13.33	— 8.57	— 5.92
4.5	—10.29	— 7.20	— 6.00
4.0	— 8.00	— 6.00	— 5.14
3.5	— 6.22	— 4.94	— 4.34
3.0	— 4.80	— 4.00	— 3.60

Table III. *For concave glasses.*

Number.	Focus.	Number.	Focus.	Number.	Focus.
1	24	8	7	15	2.75
2	18	9	6	16	2.50
3	16	0	5	17	2.25
4	12	11	4.5	18	2.00
5	10	12	4.0	19	1.75
6	9	13	3.5	20	1.50
7	8	14	3.00		

V. Being convinced of the advantage of making every observation with as little assistance as possible, I have endeavoured to confine most of my experiments to my own eyes; and I shall, in general, ground my calculations on the supposition of an eye nearly similar to my own. I shall therefore first endeavour to ascertain all its dimensions, and all its faculties.

For measuring the diameters, I fix a small key on each point of a pair of compasses; and I can venture to bring the rings into immediate contact with the sclerotica. The transverse diameter is externally 98 hundredths of an inch.

To find the axis, I turn the eye as much inwards as possible, and press one of the keys close to the sclerotica, at the external angle, till it arrives at the spot where the spectrum formed by its pressure coincides with the direction of the visual axis, and, looking in a glass, I bring the other key to the cornea. The optical axis of the eye, making allowance of three hundredths for the coats, is thus found to be 91 hundredths of an inch, from the external surface of the cornea to the retina. With an eye less prominent, this method might not have succeeded.

The vertical diameter, or rather chord, of the cornea, is 45 hundredths: its versed sine, 11 hundredths. To ascertain the versed sine, I looked with the right eye at the image of the left, in a small speculum held close to the nose, while the left eye was so averted, that the margin of the cornea appeared as a straight line, and I then compared the projection of the cornea with the image of a cancellated scale held in a proper direction behind the left eye, and close to the left temple. The horizontal chord of the cornea is nearly 49 hundredths.

Hence the radius of the cornea is 31 hundredths. It may be thought, that I assign too great a convexity to the cornea; but I have verified it by a number of concurrent observations, which will be enumerated hereafter.

The eye being directed towards its image, the projection of the margin of the sclerotica is 22 hundredths from the margin of the cornea, towards the external angle, and 27 towards the internal angle of the eye: so that the cornea has an eccentricity of one fortieth of an inch, with respect to the section of the eye perpendicular to the visual axis.

The aperture of the pupil varies from 27 to 13 hundredths; at least this is its apparent size, which must be somewhat diminished, on account of the magnifying power of the cornea, perhaps to 25 and 12. When dilated, it is nearly as eccentric as the cornea; but, when most contracted, its centre coincides with the reflection of an image from an object held immediately before the eye; and this image very nearly with the centre of the whole apparent margin of the sclerotica: so that the cornea is perpendicularly intersected by the visual axis.

My eye, in a state of relaxation, collects, to a focus on the retina, those rays which diverge vertically from an object at the distance of ten inches from the cornea, and the rays which diverge horizontally from an object at seven inches distance. For, if I hold the plane of the optometer vertically, the images of the line appear to cross at ten inches; if horizontally, at seven. The difference is expressed by a focal length of 23 inches. I have never experienced any inconvenience from this imperfection, nor did I ever discover it till I made these experiments; and I believe I can examine minute objects with as much accuracy as most of those whose eyes are differently formed. On mentioning it to Mr. Cary, he informed me that he had frequently taken notice of a similar circumstance; that many persons were obliged to hold a concave glass obliquely, in order to see with distinctness, counterbalancing, by the inclination of the glass, the too great refractive power of the eye in the direction of that inclination, and finding but little assistance from common spectacles of the same focal length. The difference is not in the cornea, for it exists when the effect of the cornea is removed, by a method to be described hereafter. The cause is, without doubt, the obliquity of the uvea, and of the crystalline lens, which is nearly parallel to it, with respect to the visual axis: this obliquity will appear, from the dimensions already given, to be about 10 degrees. Without entering into a very accurate calculation, the difference observed is found to require an inclination of about 13 degrees; and the remaining three degrees may easily be added, by the greater obliquity of the posterior surface of the crystalline opposite the pupil. There would be no difficulty in fixing the glasses of spectacles, or the concave eye glass of a telescope, in such a position as to remedy the defect.

In order to ascertain the focal distance of the lens, we must assign its probable distance from the cornea. Now the versed sine of the cornea being 11 hundredths, and the uvea being nearly flat, the anterior surface of the lens must probably be somewhat behind the chord of the cornea; but by a very inconsiderable distance, for the uvea has the substance of a thin membrane, and the lens approaches very near to it: we will therefore call this distance 12 hundredths. The axis and proportions of the lens must be estimated by comparison with anatomical observations; since they affect, in a small degree, the determination of its focal distance. M. Petit found the axis almost always about two lines, or 18 hundredths of an inch. The radius of the anterior surface was in the greatest number 3 lines, but oftener more than less. We will suppose mine to be $3\frac{1}{4}$, or nearly $\frac{3}{10}$ of an inch. The radius of the posterior surface was most frequently $2\frac{1}{2}$ lines, or $\frac{2}{9}$ of an inch*. The optical centre will be therefore $\left(\frac{18 \times 30}{30+22}=\right)$ about one tenth of an inch from the anterior surface: hence we have 22 hundredths, for the distance of the centre from the cornea. Now, taking 10 inches as the distance of the radiant point, the focus of the cornea will be 115 hundredths behind the centre of the lens. But the actual joint focus is $(91-22=)$ 69 behind the centre: hence, disregarding the thickness of the lens, its principal focal distance is 173 hundredths. For the index of its refractive power in the eye, we have $\frac{145}{133}$. Calculating upon this refractive power, with the consideration of the thickness also, we find that it requires a correction, and comes near to the ratio of 14 to 13 for the sines. It is well known that the refractive powers of the humours are equal to that of

* Mém. de l'Acad. de Paris. 1730. 6. Ed. Amst.

water; and, that the thickness of the cornea is too equable to produce any effect on the focal distance.

For determining the refractive power of the crystalline lens by a direct experiment, I made use of a method suggested to me by Dr. Wollaston. I found the refractive power of the centre of the recent human crystalline to that of water, as 21 to 20. The difference of this ratio from the ratio of 14 to 13, ascertained from calculation, is probably owing to two circumstances. The first is, that, the substance of the lens being in some degree soluble in water, a portion of the aqueous fluid within its capsule penetrates after death, so as somewhat to lessen the density. When dry, the refractive power is little inferior to that of crown glass. The second circumstance is the unequal density of the lens. The ratio of 14 to 13 is founded on the supposition of an equable density: but, the central part being the most dense, the whole acts as a lens of smaller dimensions: and it may be found by calculation (M. E. 465.) that if the central portion of a sphere be supposed of uniform density, refracting as 21 to 20, to the distance of one half of the radius, and the density of the external parts to decrease gradually, and at the surface to become equal to that of the surrounding medium, the sphere, thus constituted, will be equal in focal length to a uniform sphere of the same size, with a refraction of 16 to 15 nearly. And the effect will be nearly the same, if the central portion be supposed to be smaller than this, but the density to be somewhat greater at the surface than that of the surrounding medium, or to vary more rapidly externally than internally. Or, if a lens of equal mean dimensions, and equal focal length, with the crystalline, be supposed to consist of two segments of the external portions of such a sphere, the refractive density at the centre of this lens must be as 18 to 17. On the whole, it is probable that the refractive power of the centre of the human crystalline, in its living state, is to that of water nearly as 18 to 17; that the water, imbibed after death, reduces it to the ratio of 21 to 20; but that, on account of the unequable density of the lens, its effect in the eye is equivalent to a refraction of 14 to 13 for its whole size. Dr. Wollaston has ascertained the refraction out of air, into the centre of the recent crystalline of oxen and sheep, to be nearly as 143 to 100; into the centre of the crystalline of fish, and into the dried crystalline of sheep, as 152 to 100. Hence, the refraction of the crystalline of oxen, in water, should be as 15 to 14: but the human crystalline, when recent, is decidedly less refractive.

These considerations will explain the inconsistency of different observations on the refractive power of the crystalline; and, in particular, how the refraction which I formerly calculated, from measuring the focal length of the lens[*], is so much greater than that which is determined by other means. But, for direct experiments, Dr. Wollaston's method is exceedingly accurate.

When I look at a minute lucid point, such as the image of a candle in a small concave speculum, it appears as a radiated star, as a cross, or as an unequal line, and never as a perfect point, unless I apply a concave lens, inclined at a proper angle, to correct the unequal refraction of my eye. If I bring the point very near, it spreads into a surface nearly circular, and almost equably illuminated, except some faint lines, nearly in a

[*] Phil. Trans. 1793. 174.

radiating direction. For this purpose, the best object is a candle or a small speculum, viewed through a minute lens at some little distance, or seen by reflection in a larger lens. If any pressure has been applied to the eye, such as that of the finger keeping it shut, the sight is often confused for a short time after the removal of the finger, and the image is in this case spotty or curdled. The radiating lines are probably occasioned by some slight inequalities in the surface of the lens, which is very superficially furrowed in the direction of its fibres: the curdled appearance will be explained hereafter. When the point is further removed, the image becomes evidently oval, the vertical diameter being longest, and the lines a little more distinct than before, the light being strongest in the neighbourhood of the centre; but immediately at the centre there is a darker spot, owing to such a slight depression at the vertex as is often observable in examining the lens after death. The situation of the rays is constant, though not regular; the most conspicuous are seven or eight in number; sometimes about twenty fainter ones may be counted. Removing the point a little further, the image becomes a short vertical line; the rays that diverged horizontally being perfectly collected, while the vertical rays are still separate. In the next stage, which is the most perfect focus, the line spreads in the middle, and approaches nearly to a square, with projecting angles, but is marked with some darker lines towards the diagonals. The square then flattens into a rhombus, and the rhombus into a horizontal line unequally bright. At every greater distance, the line lengthens, and acquires also breadth, by radiations shooting out from it, but does not become a uniform surface, the central part remaining always considerably brightest, in consequence of the same flattening of the vertex which before made it faintest. Some of these figures bear a considerable analogy to the images derived from the refraction of oblique rays, and still more strongly resemble a combination of two of them in opposite directions; so as to leave no doubt, but that both surfaces of the lens are oblique to the visual axis, and cooperate in distorting the focal point. This may also be verified, by observing the image delineated by a common glass lens, when inclined to the incident rays. (Plate 12. Fig. 92. n. 28..40.)

The visual axis being fixed in any direction, I can at the same time see a luminous object placed laterally at a considerable distance from it; but in various directions the angle is very different. Upwards it extends to 50 degrees, inwards to 60, downwards to 70, and outwards to 90 degrees. These internal limits of the field of view nearly correspond with the external limits formed by the different parts of the face, when the eye is directed forwards and somewhat downwards, which is its most natural position; although the internal limits are a little more extensive than the external: and both are well calculated for enabling us to perceive, the most readily, such objects as are the most likely to concern us. Dr. Wollaston's eye has a larger field of view, both vertically and horizontally, but nearly in the same proportions, except that it extends further upwards. It is well known, that the retina advances further forwards towards the internal angle of the eye, than towards the external angle; but upwards and downwards its extent is nearly equal, and is indeed every way greater than the limits of the field of view, even if allowance is made for the refraction of the cornea only. The sensible portion seems to coincide more nearly with the painted choroid of quadrupeds: but the whole extent of perfect vision is little more than 10 degrees; or, more strictly speaking, the imperfection begins within a degree or two of the visual axis, and at the distance of 5 or 6 degrees becomes nearly stationary, until, at a still greater distance, vision is wholly extinguished. The imperfection is partly owing to the unavoidable aberration of oblique rays, but principally to the insensibility of the retina: for, if the image of the sun itself be received on a part of the retina remote from the axis, the impression will not be sufficiently strong to form a permanent spectrum, although an object of very moderate brightness will produce this effect when directly viewed. It has been said, that a faint light, like the tail of a comet, is more observable by a lateral than by a direct view. Supposing the fact certain, the reason probably is, that general masses of light and shade are more distinguishable when the parts are somewhat confused, than when the whole is rendered perfectly distinct; thus I have often observed the pattern of a paper or floor cloth to run in certain lines, when I viewed it without my glass; but these lines vanished as soon as the focus was rendered perfect. It would probably have been inconsistent with the economy of nature, to bestow a larger share of sensibility on the retina. The optic nerve is at present very large; and the delicacy of the organ renders it, even at present, very susceptible of injury from slight irritation, and very liable to inflammatory affections; and, in order to make the sight so perfect as it is, it was necessary to confine that perfection within narrow limits. The motion of the eye has a range of about 55 degrees in every direction: so that the field of perfect vision, in succession, is by this motion extended to 110 degrees.

But the whole of the retina is of such a form as to receive the most perfect image, on every part of its surface, that the state of each refracted pencil will admit; and the varying density of the crystalline renders that state more capable of delineating such a picture, than any other imaginable contrivance could have done. To illustrate this, I have constructed a diagram, representing the successive images of a distant object filling the whole extent of view, as they would be formed by the successive refractions of the different surfaces. Taking the scale of my own eye, I am obliged to substitute, for a series of objects at any indefinitely great distance, a circle of 10 inches radius; and it is most convenient to consider only those rays which pass through the anterior vertex of the lens; since the actual centre of each pencil must be in the ray which passes through the centre of the pupil, and the short distance of the vertex of the lens, from this point, will always tend to correct the unequal refraction of oblique rays. The first curve (Plate 10. Fig. 80.) is the image formed by the furthest intersection of rays refracted at the cornea; the second, the image formed by the nearest intersection; the distance, between these, shows the degree of confusion in the image; and the third curve, its brightest part. Such must be the form of the image which the cornea tends to delineate in an eye deprived of the crystalline lens; nor can any external remedy properly correct the imperfection of lateral vision. The next three curves show the images formed after the refraction at the anterior surface of the lens, distinguished in the same manner; and the three following, the result of all the successive refractions. The tenth curve is a repetition of the ninth, with a slight correction near the axis, at F, where, from the breadth of the pupil, some perpendicular rays must fall. By comparing this with the eleventh, which is the form of the retina, it will appear that nothing more is wanting for their perfect coincidence, than a moderate diminution of density in the lateral parts of the lens. If the law, by which this density varies, were more accurately ascertained, its effect on the image might easily be estimated; and probably the image, thus corrected, would approach very nearly to the form of the twelfth curve.

To find the place of the entrance of the optic nerve, I fix two candles at ten inches distance, retire sixteen feet, and direct my eye to a point four feet to the right or left of the middle of the space between them: they are then lost in a confused spot of light; but any inclination of the eye brings one or the other of them into the field of view. In Bernoulli's eye, a greater deviation was required for the direction of the axis*; and the obscured part appeared to be of greater extent. From the experiment here related, the distance of the centre of the optic nerve from the visual axis is found to be 16 hundredths of an inch; and the diameter of the most insensible part of the retina, one thirtieth of an inch. In order to ascertain the distance of the optic nerve from the point opposite to the pupil, I took the sclerotica of the human eye, divided it into segments, from the centre of the cornea towards the optic nerve, and extended it on a plane. I then measured the longest and shortest distances from the cornea to the perforation made by the nerve,

* Comm. Petrop. I. 314.

and their difference was exactly one fifth of an inch. To this we must add a fiftieth, on account of the eccentricity of the pupil in the uvea, which in the eye that I measured was not great, and the distance of the centre of the nerve from the point opposite the pupil will be 11 hundredths. Hence it appears, that the visual axis is five hundredths, or one twentieth of an inch, further from the optic nerve than the point opposite the pupil. It is possible, that this distance may be different in different eyes: in mine, the obliquity of the lens, and the eccentricity of the pupil with respect to it, will tend to throw a direct ray upon it, without much inclination of the whole eye; and it is not improbable, that the eye is also turned slightly outwards, when looking at any object before it, although the inclination is too small to be subjected to measurement.

It must also be observed, that it is very difficult to ascertain the proportions of the eye so exactly, as to determine, with certainty, the size of an image on the retina; the situation, curvature, and constitution of the lens, make so material a difference in the result, that there may possibly be an error of almost one tenth of the whole. In order, therefore, to obtain some confirmation from experiment, I placed two candles at a small distance from each other, turned the eye inwards, and applied the ring of a key so as to produce a spectrum, of which the edge coincided with the inner candle; then, fixing my eye on the outward one, I found that the spectrum advanced over two sevenths of the distance between them. Hence, the same portion of the retina that subtended an angle of seven parts at the centre of motion of the eye, subtended an angle of five at the supposed intersection of the principal rays;

(Plate 9. Fig. 75.) and the distance of this intersection from the retina was 637 thousandths. This nearly corresponds with the former calculation; nor can the distance of the centre of the optic nerve from the point of most perfect vision be, on any supposition, much less than that which is here assigned. And, in the eyes of quadrupeds, the most strongly painted part of the choroid is further from the nerve than the real axis of the eye.

I have endeavoured to express, in four figures, the form of every part of my eye, as nearly as I have been able to ascertain it; the first (Plate 11. Fig. 81.) is a vertical section; the second (Fig. 82.) a horizontal section; the third and fourth are front views, in different states of the pupil. (Fig. 83 and 84.)

Considering how little inconvenience is experienced from so material an inequality in the refraction of the lens, as I have described, we have no reason to expect a very accurate provision for correcting the aberration of the lateral rays. But, as far as can be ascertained by the optometer, the aberration arising from figure is completely corrected; since four or more images of the same line appear to meet exactly in the same point, which they would not do if the lateral rays were materially more refracted than the rays near the axis. The figure of the surfaces is sometimes, and perhaps always, more or less hyperbolical* or elliptical: in the interior laminae indeed, the solid angle of the margin is somewhat rounded off; but the weaker refractive power of the external parts must greatly tend to correct the aberration, arising from the too great curvature towards the margin of the disc. Had the refractive power been uniform, it might have collected the lateral rays of a direct pencil nearly as well; but it would have been less adapted to oblique pencils of rays: and the eye must also have been encumbered with a mass of much greater density than is now required, even for the central parts; and, if the whole lens had been smaller, it would also have admitted too little light. It is possible too, that Mr. Ramsden's observation†, on the advantage of having no reflecting surface, may be well founded: but it has not been demonstrated, that less light is lost in passing through a medium of variable density, than in a sudden transition from one part of that medium to another; although such a conclusion may certainly be inferred, from the only hypothesis which affords an explanation of the cause of a partial reflection in any case. But neither this gradation, nor any other provision, has the effect of rendering the eye perfectly achromatic. Dr. Jurin had remarked this, long ago‡, from observing the colour bordering the image of an object seen indistinctly. Dr. Wollaston pointed out to me, on the optometer, the red and blue appearance of the opposite internal angles of the crossing lines; and mentioned, at the same time, a very elegant experiment for proving the dispersive power of the eye. He looks through a prism at a small lucid point, which of course becomes a linear spectrum. But the eye cannot so adapt itself as to make the whole spectrum appear a line; for, if the focus be adapted to collect the red rays to a point, the blue will be too much refracted, and expand into a surface; and the reverse will happen if the eye be adapted to the blue rays; so that, in either case, the line will be seen as a triangular space. The observation is confirmed, by placing a small concave speculum in dif-

* Petit. Mém. de l'Acad. 1725. 20.   † Phil. Trans. 1795. 2.   ‡ Smith, c. 96.

ferent parts of a prismatic spectrum; and ascertaining the utmost distances, at which the eye can collect the rays of different colours to a focus. By these means I find, that the red rays, from a point at 12 inches distance, are as much refracted as white or yellow light at 11. The difference is equal to the refraction of a lens 132 inches in focus. But the aberration of the red rays, in a lens of crown glass, of equal mean refractive power with the eye, would be equivalent to the effect of a lens 44 inches in focus. If, therefore, we can depend upon this calculation, the dispersive power of the eye, collectively, is one third of the dispersive power of crown glass, at an equal angle of deviation. I cannot observe much aberration in the violet rays. This may be, in part, owing to their faintness; but yet I think their aberration must be less than that of the red rays. I believe it was Mr. Ramsden's opinion, that since the separation of coloured rays is only observed where there is a sudden change of density, such a body as the lens, of a density gradually varying, would have no effect whatever in separating the rays of different colours. If this hypothesis should appear to be well founded, we should be obliged to attribute the whole dispersion to the aqueous humour; and its dispersive power would be half that of crown glass, at the same deviation. But we have an instance, in the atmosphere, of a very gradual change of density; and yet Mr. Gilpin informs me, that the stars, when near the horizon, appear very evidently coloured; and Dr. Herschel has even given us the dimensions of a spectrum thus formed. At a more favourable season of the year, it would not be difficult to ascertain, by means of the optometer, the dispersive power of the eye, and of its different parts, with greater accuracy than by the experiment here related. Had the dispersive power of the whole eye been equal to that of flint glass, the distances of perfect vision would have varied from 12 inches to 7, for different rays, in the same state of the mean refractive powers.

VI. The faculty of accommodating the eye to various distances appears to exist in very different degrees in different individuals. The shortest distance of perfect vision, in my eye, is 26 tenths of an inch for horizontal, and 29 for vertical rays. This power is equivalent to the addition of a lens of 4 inches focus. Dr. Wollaston can see at seven inches, and with rays slightly converging; the difference answering to 6 inches focal length. Mr. Abernethy has perfect vision from 3 inches to 30, or a power equal to that of a lens $3\frac{1}{3}$ inches in focus. A young lady of my acquaintance can see at 2 inches and at 4; the difference being equivalent to 4 inches focus: a middle aged lady at 3 and at 4; the power of accommodation being only equal to the effect of a lens of 12 inches focus. In general, I have reason to think, that the faculty diminishes, in some measure, as persons advance in life; but some also of a middle age appear to possess it in a very small degree. I shall take the range of my own eye, as being probably about the medium, and inquire what changes will be necessary, in order to produce it; whether we suppose the radius of the cornea to be diminished, or the distance of the lens from the retina to be increased, or these two causes to act conjointly, or the figure of the lens itself to undergo an alteration.

1. We have calculated, that when the eye is in a state of relaxation, the refraction of the cornea is such as to collect rays diverging from a point ten inches distant, to

a focus at the distance of $13\frac{2}{3}$ tenths. In order that it may bring, to the same focus, rays diverging from a point distant 29 tenths, we shall find that its radius must be diminished from 31 to 25 hundredths, or very nearly in the ratio of five to four.

2. Supposing the change from perfect vision at ten inches, to perfect vision at 29 tenths, to be effected by a removal of the retina to a greater distance from the lens, this will require an elongation of 135 thousandths, or more than one seventh of the diameter of the eye. In Mr. Abernethy's eye, an elongation of 17 hundredths, or more than one sixth, is requisite.

3. If the radius of the cornea be diminished one sixteenth, or to 29 hundredths, the eye must at the same time be elongated 97 thousandths, or about one ninth of its diameter.

4. Supposing the crystalline lens to change its form; if it became a sphere, its diameter would be 28 hundredths, and, its anterior surface retaining its situation, the eye would have perfect vision at the distance of an inch and a half. This is more than double the actual change. But it is impossible to determine precisely, how great an alteration of form is necessary, without ascertaining the nature of the curves into which its surfaces may be changed. If it were always a spheroid, more or less oblate, the focal length of each surface would vary inversely as the square of the axis: but, if the surfaces became, from spherical, portions of hyperbolic conoids, or of oblong spheroids, or changed from more obtuse to more acute figures of this kind, the focal length would vary more rapidly. Disregarding the elongation of the axis, and supposing the curvature of each surface to be changed proportionally, the radius of the anterior must become about 21, and that of the posterior 15 hundredths.

VII. I shall now proceed to inquire, which of these changes takes place in nature; and I shall begin with a relation of experiments, made in order to ascertain the curvature of the cornea in all circumstances.

The method, described in Mr. Home's Croonian Lecture for 1795*, appears to be far preferable to the apparatus of the preceding year†: for a difference in the distance of two images, seen in the cornea, would be far greater, and more conspicuous, than a change of its prominency, and far less liable to be disturbed by accidental causes. It is nearly, and perhaps totally, impossible to change the focus of the eye, without some motion of its axis. The eyes sympathize perfectly with each other; and the change of focus is almost inseparable from a change of the relative situation of the optic axes; so much, that, in my eye this sympathy causes a slight imperfection of sight; for, if I direct both my eyes to the same object, even if it is beyond their furthest focus, I cannot avoid contracting, in some degree, their focal distance: now while one axis moves, it is not easy to keep the other perfectly at rest; and, besides, it is not impossible, that a change in the proportions of some eyes may render a slight alteration of the position of the axis absolutely necessary. These considerations may partly explain the trifling difference in the place of the cornea that was observed in 1794. It appears that the experiments of 1795 were made with considerable accuracy, and no doubt, with excellent instruments; and their failing to ascertain the existence of any change induced Mr. Home

* Phil. Trans. 1796. 2.   † Phil. Trans. 1795. 13.

and Mr. Ramsden to abandon, in great measure, the opinion which suggested them, and to suppose, that a change of the cornea produces only one third of the effect. Dr. Olbers, of Bremen, who in the year 1780 published a most elaborate dissertation on the internal changes of the eye[*], which he lately presented to the Royal Society, had been equally unsuccessful in his attempts to measure this change of the cornea, at the same time that his opinion was in favour of its existence.

Room was however still left for a repetition of the experiments; and I began with an apparatus nearly resembling that which Mr. Home has described. I had an excellent achromatic microscope, made by Mr. Ramsden for my friend Mr. John Ellis, of five inches focal length, magnifying about 20 times. To this I adapted a cancelled micrometer, in the focus of the eye not employed in looking through the microscope: it was a large card, divided by horizontal and vertical lines into fortieths of an inch. When the image in the microscope was compared with this scale, care was taken to place the head of the observer so that the relative motion of the image on the micrometer, caused by the unsteadiness of the optic axes, should always be in the direction of the horizontal lines, and that there could be no error from this motion, in the dimensions of the image taken vertically. I placed two candles so as to exhibit images in a vertical position in the eye of Mr. König, who had the goodness to assist me; and, having brought them into the field of the microscope, where they occupied 35 of the small divisions, I desired him to fix his eye on objects at different distances in the same direction: but I could not perceive the least variation in the distance of the images.

Finding a considerable difficulty in a proper adjustment of the microscope, and being able to depend on my naked eye in measuring distances, without an error of one 500th of an inch, I determined to make a similar experiment without any magnifying power. I constructed a divided eye glass of two portions of a lens, so small, that they passed between two images reflected from my own eye: and, looking in a glass, I brought the apparent places of the images to coincide, and then made the change requisite for viewing nearer objects; but the images still coincided. Neither could I observe any change in the images reflected from the other eye, where they could be viewed with greater convenience, as they did not interfere with the eye glass. But, not being at that time aware of the perfect sympathy of my eyes, I thought it most certain to confine my observation to the one with which I saw. I must remark that, by a little habit, I have acquired a very ready command over the accommodation of my eye, so as to be able to view an object with attention, without adjusting my eye to its distance.

I also stretched two threads, a little inclined to each other, across a ring, and divided them, by spots of ink, into equal spaces, I then fixed the ring, applied my eye close behind it, and placed two candles in proper situations before me, and a third on one side, to illuminate the threads. Then, setting a small looking glass, first at four inches distance, and next at two, I looked at the images reflected in it, and observed at what part of the threads they exactly reached across in each case; and with the same result as before.

[*] De Oculi Mutationibus internis. 4. Gotting. 1780.

I next fixed the cancellated micrometer at a proper distance, illuminated it strongly, and viewed it through a pin hole, by which means it became distinct in every state of the eye; and, looking with the other eye into a small glass, I compared the image with the micrometer, in the manner already described. I then changed the focal distance of the eye, so that the lucid points appeared to spread into surfaces, from being too remote for perfect vision; and I noted, on the scale, the distance of their centres; but that distance was invariable.

Lastly, I drew a diagonal scale, with a diamond, on a looking glass, (Plate 9. Fig. 76.) and brought the images into contact with the lines of the scale. Then, since the image of the eye occupies, on the surface of a glass, half its real dimensions, at whatever distance it is viewed, its true size is always double the measure thus obtained. I illuminated the glass strongly, and made a perforation in a narrow slip of black card, which I held between the images; and was thus enabled to compare them with the scale, although their apparent distance was double that of the scale. I viewed them in all states of the eye; but I could perceive no variation in the interval between them.

The sufficiency of these methods may be thus demonstrated. Make a pressure along the edge of the upper eyelid with any small cylinder, for instance a pencil, and the optometer will show that the focus of horizontal rays is a little elongated, while that of vertical rays is shortened; an effect which can only be owing to a change of curvature in the cornea. Not only the apparatus here described, but even the eye unassisted, will be capable of discovering a considerable change in the images reflected from the cornea, although the change be much smaller than that which is requisite for the accommodation of the eye to different distances. On the whole, I cannot hesitate to conclude, that if the radius of the cornea were diminished but one twentieth, the change would be very readily perceptible by some of the experiments related; and the whole alteration of the eye requires one fifth.

But a much more accurate and decisive experiment remains. I take, out of a small botanical microscope, a double convex lens, of eight tenths radius and focal distance, fixed in a socket one fifth of an inch in depth; securing its edges with wax, I drop into the socket a little water, nearly cold, till three fourths full, and then apply it to my eye, so that the cornea enters half way into it, and is every where in contact with the water. (Plate 9. Fig. 77). My eye immediately becomes presbyopic, and the refractive power of the lens, which is reduced by the water to a focal length of about 16 tenths, is not sufficient to supply the place of the cornea, rendered inefficacious by the intervention of the water; but the addition of another lens, of five inches and a half focus, restores my eye to its natural state, and somewhat more. I then apply the optometer, and I find the same inequality in the horizontal and vertical refractions as without the water; and I have, in both directions, a power of accommodation equivalent to a focal length of four inches, as before. At first sight indeed, the accommodation appears to be somewhat less, and only able to bring the eye from the state fitted for parallel rays to a focus at five inches distance; and this made me once imagine, that the cornea might have some slight effect in the natural state; but, considering that the artificial cornea was about a tenth of an inch before the place of the natural cornea, I calculated the effect of this difference, and found it exactly sufficient to account for the diminution of the range of vision. I cannot ascertain the distance of the glass lens from the cornea to the hundredth of an inch; but the error cannot be much greater, and it may be on either side.

After this, it is almost necessary to apologize for having stated the former experiments; but, in so delicate a subject, we cannot have too great a variety of concurring evidence.

VIII. Having satisfied myself, that the cornea is not concerned in the accommodation of the eye, my next object was, to inquire if any alteration in the length of its axis could be discovered; for this appeared to be the only possible alternative: and, considering that such a change must amount to one seventh of the diameter of the eye, I flattered myself with the expectation of submitting it to measurement. Now, if the axis of the eye were elongated one seventh, its transverse diameter must be diminished one fourteenth, and the semidiameter would be shortened a thirtieth of an inch.

I therefore placed two candles so that when the eye was turned inwards, and directed towards its own image in a glass, the light reflected from one of the candles by the sclerotica appeared upon its external margin, so as to define it distinctly by a bright line: and the image of the other candle was seen in the centre of the cornea. I then applied the double eye glass, and the scale of the looking glass, in the manner already described; but neither of them indicated any diminution of the distance, when the focal length of the eye was changed.

Another test, and a much more delicate one, was the application of the ring of a key at the external angle, when the eye was turned as much inwards as possible, and confined at the same time by a strong oval iron ring, pressed against it at the internal angle. The key was forced in as far as the sensibility of the integuments would admit, and was wedged, by a moderate pressure, between the eye and the bone. In this situation, the phantom, caused by the pressure, extended within the field of perfect vision, and was very accurately defined; nor did it, as I formerly imagined, by any means prevent a distinct perception of the objects actually seen in that direction; and a straight line, coming within the field of this oval phantom, appeared somewhat inflected towards its centre; (Plate 9. Fig. 78.) a distortion easily understood by considering the effect of the pressure on the form of the retina. Supposing now the distance between the key and the iron ring to have been, as it really was, invariable, the elongation of the eye must have been either totally or very nearly prevented; and, instead of an increase of the length of the eye's axis, the oval spot, caused by the pressure, would have spread over a space at least ten times as large as the most sensible part of the retina. But no such circumstance took place. the power of accommodation was as extensive as ever; and there was no perceptible change, either in the size or in the figure of the oval spot.

Again, since the rays which pass through the centre of the pupil, or rather through the anterior vertex of the lens, may be considered as delineating the image; and, since the divergence of these rays, with respect to each other, is but little affected by the refraction of the lens, they may still be said to diverge from the centre of the pupil; and the image of a given object on the retina must be very considerably enlarged, by the removal of the retina to a greater distance from the pupil and the lens. To ascertain the real magnitude of the image, with accuracy, is not so easy as at first sight appears; but, besides the experiment last related, which might be employed as an argument to this purpose, there are two other methods of estimating it. The first is too hazardous to be of much use; but, with proper precautions, it may be attempted. I fix my eye on a brass circle placed in the rays of the sun, and, after some time, remove it to the cancellated micrometer; then, changing the focus of my eye, while the micrometer remains at a given distance, I endeavour to discover whether there is any difference in the apparent magnitude of the spectrum on the scale; but I can discern none. I have not insisted on the attempt; especially as I have not been able to make the spectrum distinct enough without inconvenience; and no light is sufficiently strong to cause a permanent impression on any part of the retina remote from the visual axis. I therefore had recourse to another experiment. I placed two candles so as exactly to answer to the extent of the termination of the optic nerve, and, marking accurately the point to which my eye was directed, I made the utmost change in its focal length; expecting that, if there were any elongation of the axis, the external candle would appear to recede outwards upon the visible space. (Plate 9. Fig. 79.) But this did not happen: the apparent place of the obscure part was precisely the same as before. I will not undertake to say, that I could have observed a very minute difference either way: but I am persuaded, that I should have discovered an alteration of less than a tenth part of the whole.

It may be inquired, if no change in the magnitude of the image is to be expected on any other supposition; and it will appear to be possible, that the changes of curvature may be so adapted, that the magnitude of the confused image may remain perfectly constant. Indeed, to calculate from the dimensions which we have hitherto used, it would be expected that the image should be diminished about one fortieth, by the utmost increase of the convexity of the lens. But the whole depends on the situation of the refracting surfaces, and the respective increase of their curvature, which, on account of the variable density of the lens, can scarcely be estimated with sufficient accuracy. Had the pupil been placed before the cornea, the magnitude of the image must, on any supposition, have been very variable: at present, this inconvenience is avoided by the situation of the pupil; so that we have here an additional instance of the perfection of this admirable organ.

From the experiments related, it appears to be highly improbable that any material change in the length of the axis actually takes place: and it is almost impossible to conceive by what power such a change could be effected. The straight muscles, with the adipose substance lying under them, would certainly, when acting independently of the socket, tend to flatten the eye: for, since their contraction would necessarily lessen the circumference or superficies of the mass that they contain, and round off all its prominences, their attachment about the nerve and the anterior part of the eye must therefore be brought nearer together. (Plate 11. Fig. 85, 86.) Dr. Olbers compares the muscles and the eye to a cone, of which the sides are protruded, and would by contraction be brought into a straight line. But this would require a force to preserve the cornea as a fixed point, at a given distance from the origin of the muscles; a force which certainly does not exist. In the natural situation of the visual axis, the orbit being conical, the eye might be somewhat lengthened, although irregularly, by being forced further into it; but, when turned towards either side, the same action would rather shorten its axis: nor is there any thing about the human eye that could supply its place. In quadrupeds, the oblique muscles are wider than in man; and in many situations might assist in the effect. Indeed a portion of the orbicular muscle of the globe is attached so near to the nerve, that it might also cooperate in the action: and I have no reason to doubt the accuracy of Dr. Olbers, who states, that he effected a considerable elongation, by tying threads to the muscles, in the eyes of hogs and of calves; yet he does not say in what position the axis was fixed; and the flaccidity of the eye after death might render such a change very easy, as would be impossible in a living eye. Dr. Olbers also mentions an observation of Professor Wrisberg, on the eye of a man whom he believed to be destitute of the power of accommodation in his life time, and whom he found, after death, to have wanted one or more of the muscles: but this want of accommodation was not at all accurately ascertained. I measured, in the human eye, the distance of the attachment of the inferior oblique muscle from the insertion of the nerve: it was one fifth of an inch; and from the centre of vision, not a tenth of an inch; so that, although the oblique muscles do, in some positions, nearly form a part of a great circle round the eye, their action would be more fitted to flatten than to elongate it. We have therefore reason to agree with Winslow, in attributing to them the office of helping to support the eye on that side where the bones are most deficient: they seem also well calculated to prevent its being drawn too much backwards by the action of the straight muscles. And, even if there were no difficulty in supposing the muscles to elongate the eye in every position, yet at least some small difference would be expected in the extent of the change, when the eye is in different situations, at an interval of more than a right angle from each other; but the optometer shows that there is none.

Dr. Hosack alleges that he was able, by making a pressure on the eye, to accommodate it to a nearer object *: it does not appear that he made use of very accurate means for ascertaining the fact; but, if such an effect took place, the cause must have been an inflection of the cornea.

It is unnecessary to dwell on the opinion which supposes a joint operation, of changes in the curvature of the cornea, and in the length of the axis. This opinion had derived very great respectability, from the most ingenious and elegant manner in which Dr. Olbers had treated it, and from being the last result of the investigations of Mr.

* Phil. Trans. 1794. 212.

Home and Mr. Ramsden. But either of the series of experiments, which have been related, appears to be sufficient to confute it.

IX. It now remains to inquire into the pretensions of the crystalline lens to the power of altering the focal length of the eye. The grand objection, to the efficacy of a change of figure in the lens, was derived from the experiments, in which those, who have been deprived of it, have appeared to possess the faculty of accommodation.

My friend Mr. Ware, convinced as he was of the neatness and accuracy of the experiments related in the Croonian Lecture for 1795, yet could not still help imagining, from the obvious advantage all his patients found, after the extraction of the lens, in using two kinds of spectacles, that there must, in such cases, be a deficiency in that faculty. This circumstance, combined with a consideration of the directions very judiciously given by Dr. Porterfield, for ascertaining the point in question, first made me wish to repeat the experiments upon various individuals, and with the instrument which I have above described, as an improvement of Dr. Porterfield's optometer: and I must here acknowledge my great obligation to Mr. Ware, for the readiness and liberality, with which he introduced me to such of his numerous patients, as he thought most likely to furnish a satisfactory determination. It is unnecessary to enumerate every particular experiment; but the universal result is, contrarily to the expectation with which I entered on the inquiry, that, in an eye deprived of the crystalline lens, the actual focal distance is totally unchangeable. This will appear from a selection of the most decisive observations.

1. Mr. R. can read at four inches and at six only, with the same glass. He saw the double lines meeting at three inches, and always at the same point; but the cornea was somewhat irregularly prominent, and his vision not very distinct; nor had I, at the time that I saw him, a convenient apparatus.

I afterwards provided a small optometer, with a lens of less than two inches focus, adding a series of letters, not in alphabetical order, and projected into such a form as to be most legible at a small inclination. The excess of the magnifying power had the advantage of making the lines more divergent, and their crossing more conspicuous; and the letters served for more readily naming the distance of the intersection, and, at the same time, for judging of the extent of the power of distinguishing objects, too near, or too remote, for perfect vision. (Plate 11. Fig. 87.)

2. Mr. J. had not an eye very proper for the experiment; but he appeared to distinguish the letters at $2\frac{1}{4}$ inches, and at less than an inch. This at first persuaded me, that he must have a power of changing the focal distance: but I afterwards recollected that he had withdrawn his eye considerably, to look at the nearer letters, and had also partly closed his eyelids, no doubt contracting at the same time the aperture of the pupil; an action which, even in a perfect eye, always accompanies the change of focus. The slider was not applied.

3. Miss H. a young lady, of about twenty, had a very narrow pupil, and I had not an opportunity of trying the small optometer; but when she once saw an object double through the slits, no exertion could make it appear single at the same distance. She used for distant objects a glass of $4\frac{1}{2}$ inches focus; with this she could read as far off as

12 inches, and as near as five: for nearer objects she added another of equal focus, and could then read at 7 inches, and at $2\frac{1}{2}$.

4. Hanson, a carpenter, aged 63, had a cataract extracted a few years since from one eye: the pupil was clear and large, and he saw well to work with a lens of $2\frac{1}{8}$ inches focus; and could read at 8 and at 15 inches, but most conveniently at 11. With the same glass, the lines of the optometer appeared always to meet at 11 inches; but he could not perceive that they crossed, the line being too strong, and the intersection too distant.

The experiment was afterwards repeated with the small optometer: he read the letters from 2 to 3 inches; but the intersection was always at $2\frac{1}{2}$ inches. He now fully understood the circumstances that were to be noticed, and saw the crossing with perfect distinctness: at one time, he said it was a tenth of an inch nearer; but I observed that he had removed his eye two or three tenths from the glass, a circumstance which accounted for this small difference.

5. Notwithstanding Hanson's age, I consider him as a very fair subject for the experiment. But a still more unexceptionable eye was that of Mrs. Maberly. She is about 30, and had the crystalline of both eyes extracted a few years since, but sees best with her right. She walks without glasses; and, with the assistance of a lens of about four inches focus, can read and work with ease. She could distinguish the letters of the small optometer from an inch to $2\frac{1}{2}$ inches; but the intersection was invariably at the same point, about 19 tenths of an inch distant. A portion of the capsule is stretched across the pupil, and causes her to see remote objects double, when without her glasses; nor can she, by any exertion, bring the two images nearer together, although the exertion makes them more distinct, no doubt by contracting the pupil. The experiment with the optometer was conducted, in the presence of Mr. Ware, with patience and perseverance; nor was any opinion given to make her report partial.

Considering the difficulty of finding an eye perfectly suitable for the experiments, these proofs may be deemed tolerably satisfactory. But, since one positive argument will counterbalance many negative ones, provided that it be equally grounded on fact, it becomes necessary to inquire into the competency of the evidence employed to ascertain the power of accommodation, attributed, in the Croonian Lecture for 1794, to the eye of Benjamin Clerk. And it appears, that the distinction long since very properly made by Dr. Jurin, between distinct vision and perfect vision, will readily explain away the whole of that evidence.

It is obvious that vision may be made distinct to any given extent, by means of an aperture sufficiently small, provided, at the same time, that a sufficient quantity of light be left, while the refractive powers of the eye remain unchanged. And it is remarkable, that in those experiments, when the comparison with the perfect eye was made, the aperture of the imperfect eye only was very considerably reduced. Benjamin Clerk, with an aperture of $\frac{3}{40}$ of an inch, could read with the same glass at $1\frac{7}{8}$ inch, and at 7 inches*. With an equal aperture, I can read at $1\frac{1}{2}$ inch and at 30 inches: and I can retain the state of perfect relaxation, and read with the same aperture at $2\frac{1}{4}$ inches, without any real change of refractive power,

* Phil. Trans. 1795. 9.

and this is as great a difference as was observed in Benjamin Clerk's eye. It is also a fact of no small importance, that Sir Henry Englefield was much astonished, as well as the other observers, at the accuracy with which the man's eye was adjusted to the same distance, in the repeated trials that were made with it †. This circumstance alone makes it highly probable, that its perfect vision was confined within very narrow limits.

Hitherto I have endeavoured to show the inconveniences attending other suppositions, and to remove the objections to the opinion of an internal change of the figure of the lens. I shall now state two experiments, which, in the first place, come very near to a mathematical demonstration of the existence of such a change, and, in the second, explain in great measure its origin, and the manner in which it is effected.

I have already described the appearances of the imperfect image of a minute point at different distances from the eye, in a state of relaxation. For the present purpose, I will only repeat, that if the point is beyond the furthest focal distance of the eye, it assumes that appearance which is generally described by the name of a star, the central part being considerably the brightest. (Plate 12. Fig. 92. n. 36..39.) But, when the focal distance of the eye is shortened, the imperfect image is of course enlarged; and, besides this necessary consequence, the light is also very differently distributed; the central part becomes faint, and the margin strongly illuminated, so as to have almost the appearance of an oval ring. (N. 41.) If I apply the slider of the optometer, the shadows

† Phil. Trans. 1795. s.

of the slits, while the eye is relaxed, are perfectly straight, dividing the oval either way into parallel segments: (N. 42, 44.) but, when the accommodation takes place, they immediately become curved, and the more so the further they are from the centre of the image, to which their concavity is directed. (N. 43, 45.) If the point be brought much within the focal distance, the change of the eye will increase the illumination of the centre, at the expense of the margin. The same appearances are equally observable, when the effect of the cornea is removed by immersion in water; and the only imaginable way of accounting for the diversity, is to suppose the central parts of the lens to acquire a greater degree of curvature than the marginal parts. If the refraction of the lens remained the same, it is absolutely impossible that any change of the distance of the retina should produce a curvature in those shadows, which, in the relaxed state of the eye, are found to be in all parts straight; and, that neither the form nor the relative situation of the cornea is concerned, appears from the application of water already mentioned.

The truth of this explanation is fully confirmed by inspection of the optometer. When I look through four narrow slits, without exertion, the lines always appear to meet in one point: but when I make the intersection approach me, the two outer lines meet considerably beyond the inner ones, and the two lines of the same side cross each other at a still greater distance. (Plate 11. Fig. 88.)

The experiment will not succeed with every eye; nor can it be expected that such an imperfection should be universal: but one case is sufficient to establish the argument, even if no other were found. I do not however doubt, that in those who have a large pupil, and great power of changing the focus, the aberration may be very frequently observable. In Dr. Wollaston's eye, the diversity of appearance is imperceptible; but Mr. König described the intersections exactly as they appear to me, although he had received no hint of what I had observed. The lateral refraction is the most easily ascertained, by substituting for the slits a tapering piece of card, so as to cover all the central parts of the pupil, and thus determining the nearest crossing of the shadows transmitted through the marginal parts only. When the furthest intersection was at 38, I could bring it to 22 parts with two narrow slits; but with the tapered card only to 29. From these data we may determine pretty nearly, into what form the lens must be changed, supposing both the surfaces to undergo proportional alterations of curvature, and taking for granted the dimensions already laid down: for, from the lateral aberration thus given, we may find the subtangents at about one tenth of an inch from the axis; and the radius of curvature, at each vertex, is already determined to be about 21 and 15 hundredths of an inch. Hence, the anterior surface must be a portion of a hyperboloid, of which the greater axis is about 50; and the posterior surface will be nearly parabolical. In this manner, the change will be effected, without any diminution of the transverse diameter of the lens. The elongation of its axis will not exceed the fiftieth of an inch; and, on the supposition with which we set out, the protrusion will be chiefly at the posterior vertex. The form of the lens, thus changed, will be nearly that of Plate 11. Fig. 90; the relaxed state being nearly as represented in Fig. 89. Should, however, the rigidity of the internal and more refractive parts, or any other considerations, render it convenient to suppose the anterior surface more changed, it would still have room, without interfering with the uvea; or it might even force the uvea a little forwards, without any visible alteration of the external appearance of the eye.

Why, and in what cases, such an imperfection must exist in the lateral refraction, is easily understood, from the marginal attachment of the lens to its capsule. For, if the curvature at the axis be increased in any considerable degree, it cannot be continued far towards the margin, without lessening the diameter of the lens, and tearing the ramifications which enter it from the ciliary processes. Nor does there appear to be any other reason for the very observable contraction of the pupil, which always accompanies the effort to view near objects, than that by this means the lateral rays are excluded, and the indistinctness is prevented, which would have arisen from the insufficiency of their refraction.

From this investigation of the change of the figure of the lens, it appears that the action, which I formerly attributed to the external coats, cannot afford an explanation of the phenomenon. The necessary effect of such an action would be, to produce a figure approaching to that of an oblate spheroid; and, to say nothing of the inconvenience attending a diminution of the diameter of the lens, the lateral refraction would be much more increased than the central; nor would the slight change of density, at an equal distance from the axis, be at all equivalent to the increase of curvature: we must therefore suppose some different mode of action in the power producing the change. Now, whether we call the lens a muscle or not, it seems demonstrable, that such a change of figure takes place as can be produced by no external cause; and we may at least illustrate it by a comparison with the usual action of muscular fibres. A muscle never contracts, without at the same time swelling laterally, and it is of no consequence which of the effects we consider as primary. I was induced, by an occasional opacity, to give the name of membranous tendons to the radiations from the centre of the lens; but on a more accurate examination, nothing really analogous to tendon can be discovered. And, if it were supposed that the parts next the axis were throughout of a tendinous, and therefore unchangeable nature, the contraction must be principally effected by the lateral parts of the fibres; so that the coats would become thicker towards the margin, by their contraction, while the general alteration of form would require them to be thinner; and there would be a contrariety in the actions of the various parts. But, if we compare the central parts of each surface to the belly of the muscle, it is easy to conceive their thickness to be immediately increased, and to produce an immediate elongation of the axis, and an increase of the central curvature; while the lateral parts cooperate more or less, according to their distance from the centre, and in different individuals in somewhat different proportions. On this supposition, we have no longer any difficulty in attributing a power of change to the crystalline of fishes. M. Petit, in a great number of observations, uniformly found the lens of fishes more or less flattened: but, even if it were not, a slight extension of the lateral part of the superficial fibres would allow those softer coats to become thicker at each vertex, and to form the whole lens into a spheroid somewhat oblong; and here, the lens being the only agent in refraction, a less alteration than in other animals would be sufficient. It is also worthy of inquiry, whether the state of contraction may not immediately add to the refractive power. According to the old experiment, by which Dr. Goddard attempted to show that muscles become more dense as they contract, such an effect might naturally be expected. That experiment is, however, very indecisive, and the opinion is indeed generally exploded, but perhaps too hastily; and whoever shall ascertain the existence or nonexistence of such a condensation, will render essential service to physiology in general. Some interesting experiments, on this subject, have been promised to the public by a very ingenious physiologist, who has probably employed a more decisive method of investigation in his researches. Swammerdam professes to have found such a condensation in the contraction of a muscle; but it is obvious, that what he has attributed to the heart properly belonged only to the air which it contained, and one of his experiments, which was free from this source of fallacy, does not appear to have shown any satisfactory result, although conducted with some accuracy, by inclosing a muscle in a bottle filled with water, communicating with a narrow open tube [*].

Dr. Pemberton, in the year 1719, first systematically discussed the opinion of the muscularity of the crystalline lens [†]. He referred to Leeuwenhoek's microscopical observations; but he so overwhelmed his subject

---

[*] Book of Nature, II. 126, 127.

[†] De Facultate Oculi qua ad diversas rerum distantias se accommodat. L. B. 1719. Ap. Hall. Disp. Anat. IV. 301.

with intricate calculations, that few have attempted to develope it: he grounded the whole on an experiment borrowed from Barrow, which, with me, has totally failed; and I cannot but agree with Dr. Olbers in the remark, that it is easier to confute him than to understand him. He argued for a partial change of the figure of the lens; and perhaps the opinion was more just than the reasons adduced for its support. Lobé, or rather Albinus *, decidedly favours a similar theory; and suggests the analogy of the lens to the muscular parts of pellucid animals, in which he says that even the best microscopes can discover no fibres. Camper also mentions the hypothesis with considerable approbation †. Professor Reil published, in 1793, a Dissertation on the Structure of the Lens; and, in a subsequent paper, annexed to the translation of my former Essay in Professor Gren's Journal ‡, he discussed the question of its muscularity. I regret that I have not now an opportunity of referring to this publication; but I do not recollect, that Professor Reil's objections are different from those which I have already noticed.

Considering the sympathy of the crystalline lens with the uvea, and the delicate nature of the change of its figure, there is little reason to expect, that any artificial stimulus would be more successful in exciting a contractive action in the lens, than it has hitherto been in the uvea; much less would that contraction be visible without art. Soon after Mr. Hunter's death, I pursued the experiment which he had suggested, for ascertaining how far such a contraction might be observable. My apparatus (Plate 11. Fig. 91.) was executed by Mr. Jones. It consisted of a wooden vessel, blackened within, which was to be filled with cool, and then with warmer water: a plane speculum was placed under it; a perforation in the bottom was filled with a plate of glass; proper rings were fixed for the reception of the lens, or of the whole eye, and also wires for transmitting electricity: above these, a piece of ground and painted glass, for receiving the image, was supported by a bracket, which was moved by a pinion, in connexion with a scale divided into fiftieths of an inch. With this apparatus I made some experiments, assisted by Mr. Wilkinson, whose residence was near a slaughter house: but we could obtain, by this method, no satisfactory evidence of the change; nor was our expectation much disappointed. I understand also, that another gentleman, a member of this Society, was equally unsuccessful, in attempting to produce a conspicuous change in the lens by electricity.

X. In man, and in the most common quadrupeds, the structure of the lens is nearly similar. The number of radiations is of little consequence; but I find that, sometimes at least, in the human crystalline, there are ten on each side, (Plate 12. Fig. 93.) not three, as I once, perhaps from a too hasty observation, concluded *. Those who find any difficulty, in discovering the fibres, must have a sight very ill adapted to microscopical researches. I have laboured with the most obstinate perseverance to trace nerves into the lens, and I have sometimes ima-

* De quibusdam Oculi Partibus, L. B. 1746. Ap. Hall. Disp. Anat. IV. 301.
† De Oculo Humano, L. B. 1742. Ap. Hall. Disp. Anat. VII. ii. 108, 109.
‡ 1794. 352, 354.

* De Corp. Hum. Vir. Cons. 68.

gined, that I had succeeded; but I cannot positively go further than to state my full conviction of their existence, and of the precipitancy of those who have absolutely denied it. The long nerves, which are very conspicuous between the choroid and sclerotic coats, divide each into two, three, or more branches, at the spot where the ciliary zone begins, and seem indeed to furnish the choroid with some fine filaments at the same place. The branches often reunite, with a slight protuberance, that scarcely deserves the name of a ganglion: here they are tied down, and mixed with the hard whitish brown membrane, that covers the compact spongy substance, in which the vessels of the ciliary processes anastomose and subdivide. (Plate 12. Fig. 94.) The quantity of the nerves, which proceeds to the iris, appears to be considerably smaller than that which arrives at the place of division; hence there can be little doubt, that the division is calculated to supply the lens with some minute branches; and it is not improbable, from the appearance of the parts, that some fibres may pass to the cornea; although it might more naturally be expected, that the tunica conjunctiva would be supplied from without. But the subdivisions, which probably pass to the lens, enter immediately into a mixture of ligamentous substance, and of a tough brownish membrane; and I have not hitherto been able to develope them. Perhaps animals may be found, in which this substance is of a different nature; and I do not despair that, with the assistance of injections, for more readily distinguishing the blood vessels, and of an acid for whitening the nerves, it may still be possible to trace them in quadrupeds. Our inability to discover them is scarcely an argument against their existence: they must naturally be delicate and transparent; and we have an instance, in the cornea, of considerable sensibility, where no nerve has yet been traced. The capsule adheres to the ciliary substance, and the lens to the capsule, principally in two or three points; but, I confess, I have not been able to observe that these points are exactly opposite to the trunks of nerves; so that, probably, the adhesion is chiefly caused by those vessels which are sometimes seen passing to the capsule in injected eyes. We may, however, discover ramifications from some of these points, upon and within the substance of the lens, (Plate 12. Fig. 95.) generally following a direction near to that of the fibres, and sometimes proceeding from a point opposite to one of the radiating lines of the same surface. But the principal vessels of the lens appear to be derived from the central artery, by two or three branches at some little distance from the posterior vertex; which I conceive to be the cause of the frequent adhesion of a portion of a cataract to the capsule, about this point: they follow nearly the course of the radiations, and then of the fibres; but there is often a superficial subdivision of one of the radii, at the spot where one of them enters. The vessels coming from the choroid appear principally to supply a substance, hitherto unobserved, which fills up the marginal part of the capsule of the crystalline, in the form of a thin zone, and makes a slight elevation, visible even through the capsule. (Fig. 96..98.) It consists of coarser fibres than the lens, but in a direction nearly similar; they are often intermixed with small globules. In some animals, the margin of the zone is crenated, especially behind, where it is shorter: this is observable in the partridge; and, in the same bird, the whole surface of the lens is seen to be covered with points, or rather globules, arranged in regular lines, (Plate 13. Fig. 99.) so as to have somewhat the appearance of a honeycomb, but towards the vertex less uniformly disposed. This regularity is a sufficient proof that there could be no optical deception in the appearance; although it requires a good microscope to discover it distinctly; but the zone may be easily peeled off under water, and hardened in spirits. Its use is uncertain: but it may possibly secrete the liquid of the crystalline; and it as much deserves the name of a gland, as the greater part of the substances usually so denominated. In peeling it off, I have very distinctly observed ramifications, which were passing through it into the lens; (Plate 12. Fig. 97.) and indeed, it is not at all difficult to detect the vessels connecting the margin of the lens with its capsule; and it is surprising that M. Petit should have doubted of their existence. I have not yet clearly discerned this crystalline gland in the human eye; but I infer the existence of something similar to the globules, from the spotted appearance of the image of a lucid point already mentioned; for which I can no otherwise account, than by attributing it to a derangement of these particles, produced by the external force, and to an unequal impression made by them on the surface of the lens.

In birds and in fishes, the fibres of the crystalline radiate equally, becoming finer as they approach the vertex, till they are lost in a uniform substance, of the same degree of firmness, which appears to be perforated in the centre by a blood vessel. (Plate 13. Fig. 100.) In quadrupeds, the fibres at their angular meeting are certainly not continued, as Leeuwenhoek imagined, across the line of division: yet there does not appear to be any dissimilar substance interposed between them, except that very minute trunks of vessels often mark that line. But, since the whole mass of the lens, as far as it is moveable, is probably endued with a power of changing its figure, there is no need of any strength of union, or place of attachment, for the fibres, as the motion can meet with little or no resistance. Every common muscle, as soon as its contraction ceases, returns to its natural form, even without the assistance of an antagonist; and the lens itself, when taken out of the eye, in its capsule, has elasticity enough to reassume its proper figure, on the removal of a force that has compressed it. The capsule is highly elastic; and, since it is laterally fixed to the ciliary zone, it must cooperate in restoring the lens to its flattest form. If it be inquired, why the lens is not capable of becoming less convex, as well as more so, it may be answered, that the lateral parts have probably little contractive power; and if they had more, they would have no room to increase the size of the disc, which they must do, in order to shorten the axis; and the parts about the axis have no fibres so arranged as to shorten it by their own contraction.

I consider myself as being partly repaid for the labour lost in search of the nerves of the lens, by having acquired a more accurate conception of the nature and situation of the ciliary substance. It had already been observed, that in the hare and in the wolf, the ciliary processes are not attached to the capsule of the lens; and if by the ciliary processes we understand those filaments which are seen detached after tearing away the capsule, and consist of ramifying vessels, the observation is equally true of the common quadrupeds, and even of the human eye *. This remark has indeed been made by Leroi, Albinus, and others, but the circumstance is not generally understood. It is so difficult to obtain a distinct view of these bodies, undisturbed, that I am partly indebted to accident, for having been undeceived respecting them: but, having once made the observation, I have learnt to show it in an unquestionable manner. I remove the posterior hemisphere of the sclerotica, or somewhat more, and also as much as possible of the vitreous humour, introduce the point of a pair of scissors into the capsule, turn out the lens, and cut off the greater part of the posterior portion of the capsule, and of the rest of the vitreous humour. I next dissect the choroid and uvea from the sclerotica; and, dividing the anterior part of the capsule into segments from its centre, I turn them back upon the ciliary zone. The ciliary processes then appear, covered with their pigment, and perfectly distinct both from the capsule and from the uvea; (Plate 13. Fig. 101.) and the surface of the capsule is seen shining, and evidently natural, close to the base of these substances. I do not deny that the separation between the uvea and the processes, extends somewhat further back than the separation between the processes and the capsule; but the difference is inconsiderable, and, in the calf, does not amount to above half the length of the detached part. The appearance of the processes is wholly irreconcileable with muscularity; and their being considered as muscles attached to the capsule, is therefore doubly inadmissible. Their lateral union with the capsule comences at the base of their posterior smooth surface, and is continued nearly to the point where they are more intimately united with the termination of the uvea; so that, however this portion of the base of the processes were disposed to contract, it would be much too short to produce any sensible effect. What their use may be, cannot easily be determined: if it were necessary to have any peculiar organs for secretion, we might call them glands, for the percolation of the aqueous humour; but there is no reason to think them requisite for this purpose.

The marsupium nigrum of birds, and the horseshoe like appearance of the choroid of fishes, are two substances which have sometimes, with equal injustice, been termed muscular. All the apparent fibres of the marsupium nigrum are, as Haller had very truly asserted, merely duplicatures of a membrane, which, when its ends are cut off, may easily be unfolded under the microscope, with the assistance of a fine hair pencil, so as to leave no longer any suspicion of a muscular texture. The experiment related by Mr. Home *, can scarcely be deemed a very strong argument for attributing to this substance a faculty which its appearance so little authorises us to expect in it. The red substance, in the choroid of fishes, (Plate 13. Fig. 102.) is more capable of deceiving the observer; its colour gives it some little pretension, and I began to examine it with a prepossession in favour of its muscular nature. But, when we recollect the general colour of the muscles of

* Vid. Hall. Physiol. V. 432. et Duverney, ibi citat.

* Phil. Trans. 1796. 18.

fishes, the consideration of its redness will no longer have any weight. Stripped of the membrane which loosely covers its internal surface, (Fig. 103.) it seems to have transverse divisions, somewhat resembling those of muscles, and to terminate in a manner somewhat similar; (Fig. 104.) but, when viewed in a microscope, the transverse divisions appear to be cracks, and the whole mass is evidently of a uniform texture, without the least fibrous appearance: and, if a particle of any kind of muscle is compared with it, the contrast becomes very striking. Besides it is fixed down, throughout its extent, to the posterior lamina of the choroid, and has no attachment capable of directing its effect; to say nothing of the difficulty of conceiving what that effect would be. Its use must remain, in common with that of many other parts of the animal frame, entirely concealed from our curiosity.

The bony scales of the eyes of birds, which were long ago described in the Memoirs of the Academy, by Mery [*], in the Philosophical Transactions, by Mr. Ranby [†], and by Mr. Warren [‡], afterwards in two excellent Memoirs of M. Petit on the eye of the turkey and of the owl [§], and lately by Professor Blumenbach [||], Mr. Pierce Smith [¶], and Mr. Home [**], can, on any supposition, have but little concern in the accommodation of the eye to different distances: they rather seem to be necessary for the protection of that organ, large and prominent as it is, and unsupported by any strength in the orbit, against the various accidents to which the mode of life and rapid motion of those animals must expose it; and they are much less liable to fracture than an entire bony ring of the same thickness would have been. The marsupium nigrum appears to be intended to assist in giving strength to the eye, to prevent any change in the place of the lens, by external force: it is so situated as to intercept but little light, and that little is principally what would have fallen on the insertion of the optic nerve: and it seems to be too firmly tied to the lens, even to admit any considerable elongation of the axis of the eye, although it certainly would not impede a protrusion of the cornea. There is a singular observation of Poupart, respecting the eyes of insects, which requires to be mentioned here. He remarks, that the eye of the libellula is hollow; that it communicates with an air vessel placed longitudinally in the trunk of the body; and that it is capable of being inflated from this cavity: he supposes that the insect is provided with this apparatus, in order for the accommodation of its eye to the perception of objects at different distances [*]. There is no difficulty in supposing that the means of producing the change of the refractive powers of the eye, may be, in different classes of animals, as diversified as their habits, and the general conformation of their organs. But an examination of the eyes of libellulae, wasps, and lobsters, induces me not only to reject the suggestion of Poupart, but to agree with those naturalists, who have called in question the pretensions of these organs to the name usually applied to them. Cuvier has given a very fair state-

[*] II. 15.
[†] Phil. Trans. XXXIII. 223. Abr. VII. 435.
[‡] Phil. Trans. XXXIV. 113. Abr. VII. 437.
[§] Mém. de l'Acad. 1735. 163. 1736. 166. Ed. Amst.
[||] Comm. Gott. VII. 62.
[¶] Phil. Trans. 1795. 263.
[**] Phil. Trans. 1796. 14.

[*] Phil. Trans. XXII. 673. Abr. II. 762.

ment of the case, in his valuable work on comparative anatomy; and his descriptions, as well as those of Swammerdam, agree in general with what I have observed. We are prejudiced in favour of their being eyes, by their situation and general appearance. The copious supply of nerves seems to prove, at least, that they must be organs of sense. In the hermit crab, Swammerdam says, that their nerves even decussate, but this is not the case in the crawfish. The external coat is always transparent; its divisions are usually more or less lenticular. Many insects have no other organs at all resembling eyes; and when these eyes have been covered, the insects appear to have been either wholly or partially blinded*. But, on the other hand, many insects are without these eyes, and of those who have them, many have others also, more unquestionably fitted for vision. The neighbouring parts of the hard skin or shell are often equally transparent with these, when the crust lining them is removed. In the apis longicornis, the antennae, as Mr. Kirby first informed me, have somewhat of the same reticulated appearance, but not enough for the foundation of any argument respecting its use. This reticulated coat is always completely lined by an obscure and opaque mucus, which appears perfectly unfit for the transmission of light; nor is there any thing like a transparent humour in the whole structure: and the convexity of the lenticular portions is by no means sufficiently great, to bring the rays of light to a very near focus; indeed, in lobsters, the external surface is perfectly equable, and the internal surface is only divided into squares by a cancellated texture adhering to it. There is nothing in any way analogous to a retina, and there can be no formation of such an image, as is depicted in the eyes of all other animals, not excepting even the vermes: nor does there appear to be room to allow with Bidloo that there is a perforation, admitting light, under the centre of each hexagon. If they are eyes, their manner of perceiving light must rather resemble the sense of hearing than that of seeing, and they must convey but an imperfect idea of the form of objects. And it may be remarked that beetles, which have no other eyes, fly much by night, and are proverbially dull-sighted. The stemmata, which are usually 3, 6, 8, or 12 in number, have much more indisputably the appearance of eyes. In the wasp, they consist externally of a thick double convex lens, firmly fixed in the shell, perfectly transparent, and externally very hard, but internally softer; behind this appears to be a vitreous humour, and probably behind that, there is a retina. Here we must consider the crystalline lens as united to the cornea, without any uvea or aqueous humour. In the reticulated eyes, there is nothing resembling a crystalline lens. The stemmata have never any motion, but they are capable of comprehending, conjointly, a very extensive field of view; and it is possible that the posterior part of the lens may have a power of changing its convexity for the perception of objects at different distances.

XI. I shall now finally recapitulate the principal objects and results of the investigation, which I have taken the liberty of detailing so fully to the Royal Society. First, the determination of the refractive power of a variable medium, (M.E. 465.) and its application to the constitution of the crystalline lens. Secondly, the construction of an instrument for

---

* Hooke Microgr. 178.

ascertaining, upon inspection, the exact focal distance of every eye, and the remedy for its imperfections. Thirdly, to show the accurate adjustment of every part of the eye, for seeing with distinctness the greatest possible extent of objects at the same instant. Fourthly, to measure the collective dispersion of coloured rays in the eye. Fifthly, by immerging the eye in water, to demonstrate that its accommodation does not depend on any change in the curvature of the cornea. Sixthly, by confining the eye at the extremities of its axis, to prove that no material alteration of its length can take place. Seventhly, to examine what inference can be drawn from the experiments hitherto made on persons deprived of the lens; to pursue the inquiry, on the principles suggested by Dr. Porterfield; and to confirm his opinion of the utter inability of such persons to change the refractive state of the organ. Eighthly, to deduce, from the aberration of the lateral rays, a decisive argument in favour of a change in the figure of the crystalline; to ascertain, from the quantity of this aberration, the form into which the lens appears to be thrown in my own eye, and the mode by which the change must be produced in that of every other person. And I flatter myself, that I shall not be deemed too precipitate, in denominating this series of experiments satisfactorily demonstrative.

EXPLANATION OF THE FIGURES.

PLATE 9. Fig. 71. The form of the ends of the optometer, when made of card. The apertures in the shoulders are for holding a lens: the square ends turn under, and are fastened together.

Fig. 72. The scale of the optometer. The middle line is divided, from the lower end, into inches. The right hand column shows the number of a concave lens requisite for a short sighted eye; by looking through the slider, and observing the number opposite to which the intersection appears when most remote. At the other end, the middle line is graduated for extending the scale of inches, by means of a lens four inches in focus: the negative numbers implying that such rays, as proceed from them, are made to converge towards a point on the other side of the lens. The other column shows the focal length of convex glasses, required by those eyes, to which the intersection appears, when nearest, opposite to the respective places of their numbers.

Fig. 73. A side view of the optometer, half its size.

Fig. 74. The appearance of the lines through the slider.

Fig. 75. Method of measuring the magnitude of an image on the retina.

Fig. 76. Diagonal scale drawn on a looking glass.

Fig. 77. The method of applying a lens with water to the cornea.

Fig. 78. The appearance of a spectrum occasioned by pressure; and the inflection of straight lines seen within the limits of the spectrum.

Fig. 79. An illustration of the enlargement of the image, which would be the consequence of an elongation of the eye: the images of the candles, which, in one instance, fall on the insertion of the nerve, falling, in the other instance, beyond it.

PLATE 10. Fig. 80. The successive forms of the image of a large distant object, as it would be delineated by each refractive surface in the eye; to show how that form at last coincides with the retina. E G is the distance between the foci of horizontal and vertical rays in my eye.

PLATE 11. Fig. 81. Vertical section of my right eye, seen from without; twice the natural size.

Fig. 82. Horizontal section, seen from above.

Fig. 83. Front view of my left eye, when the pupil is contracted; of the natural size.

Fig. 84. The same view when the pupil is dilated.

Fig. 85. Outline of the eye and its straight muscles when at rest.

Fig. 86. Change of figure, which would be the consequence of the action of those muscles upon the eye, and upon the adipose substance behind it.

Fig. 87. Scale of the small optometer.

Fig. 88. Appearance of four images of a line seen by my eye when its focus is shortest.

Fig. 89. Outline of the lens, when relaxed; from a comparison of M. Petit's measures with the phenomena of my own eye, and on the supposition that it is found in a relaxed state after death.

Fig. 90. Outline of the lens sufficiently changed to produce the shortest focal distance.

Fig. 91. Apparatus for ascertaining the focal length of the lens in water.

PLATE 12. Fig. 92. n. 28. Various forms of the image depicted by a cylindrical pencil of rays obliquely refracted by a spherical surface, when received on planes at distances progressively greater.

Fig. 92. n. 29. Image of a minute lucid object held very near to my eye.

Fig. 92. n. 30. The same appearance when the eye has been rubbed.

Fig. 92. n. 31..37. Different forms of the image of a lucid point at greater and greater distances; the most perfect focus being like n. 33, but much smaller.

Fig. 92. n. 38. Image of a very remote point seen by my right eye.

Fig. 92. n. 39. Image of a remote point seen by my left eye; being more obtuse at one end, probably from a less obliquity of the posterior surface of the crystalline lens.

Fig. 92. n. 40. Combination of two figures similar to the fifth variety of n. 28; to imitate n. 38.

Fig. 92. n. 41. Appearance of a distant lucid point, when the eye is adapted to a very near object.

Fig. 92. n. 42, 44. Shadow of parallel wires in the image of a distant point, when the eye is relaxed.

Fig. 92. n. 43, 45. The same shadows rendered curved by a change in the figure of the crystalline lens.

Fig. 93. The order of the fibres of the human crystalline.

Fig. 94. The division of the nerves at the ciliary zone; the sclerotica being removed. One of the nerves of the uvea is seen passing forwards and subdividing. From the calf.

Fig. 95. Ramifications from the margin of the crystalline lens.

Fig. 96. The zone of the crystalline faintly seen through the capsule.

Fig. 97. The zone raised from its situation, with the ramifications passing through it into the lens.

Fig. 98. The zone of the crystalline detached.

PLATE 13. Fig. 99. The crenated zone, and the globules regularly arranged on the crystalline of the partridge.

Fig. 100. The order of the fibres in the lens of birds and fishes.

Fig. 101. The segments of the capsule of the crystalline turned back, to show the detached ciliary processes. From the calf.

Fig. 102. Part of the choroid of the cod fish, with its red substance. The central artery hangs loose from the insertion of the nerve.

Fig. 103. The membrane covering this substance internally, raised by the blowpipe.

Fig. 104. The appearance of the red substance, after the removal of the membrane.

PLATE 9.

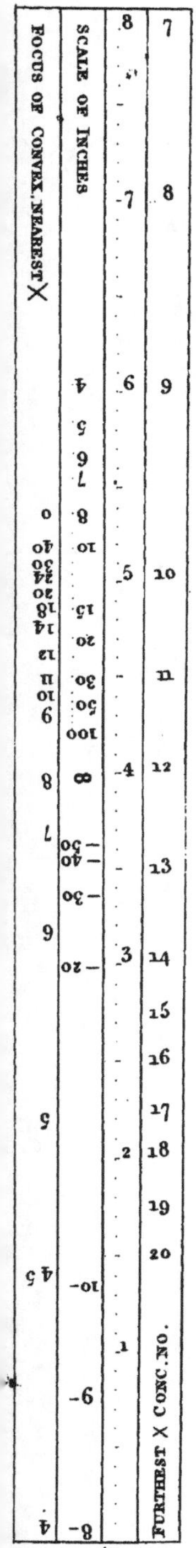

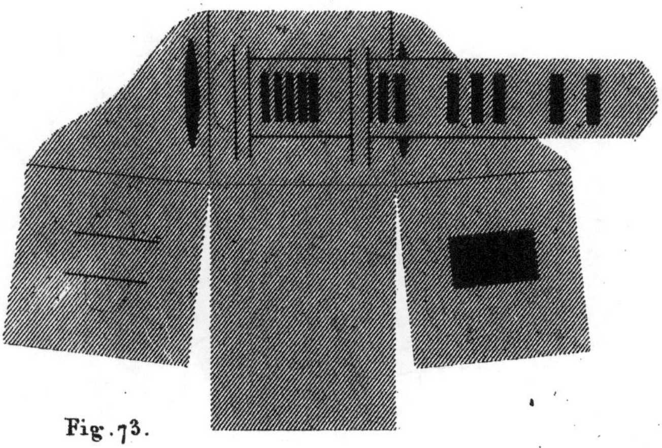

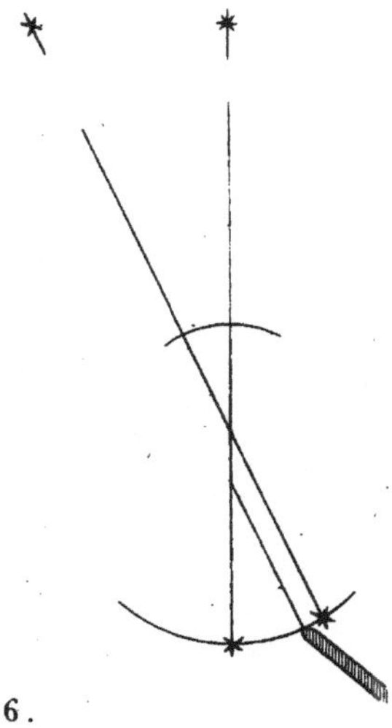

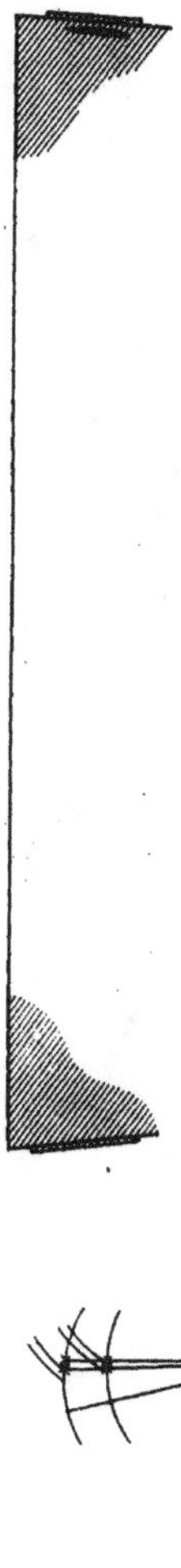

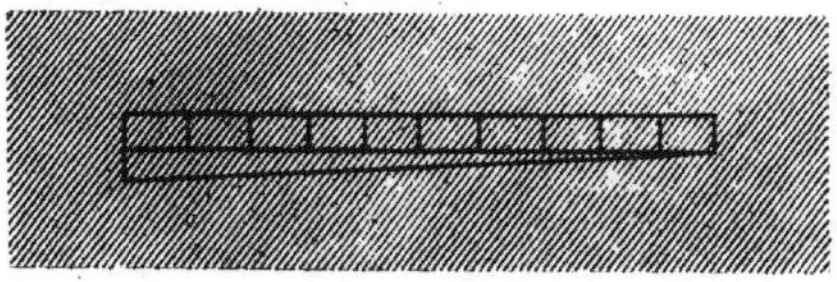

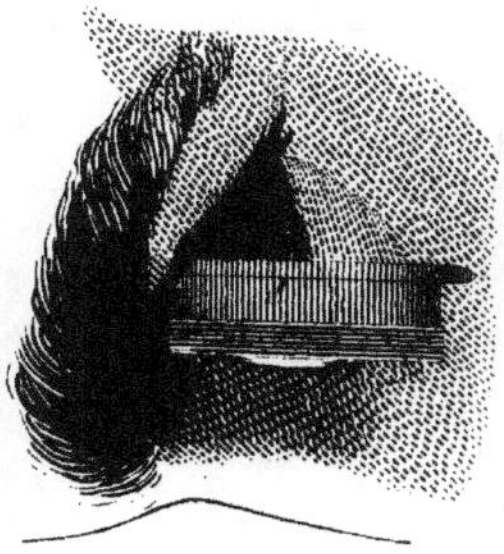

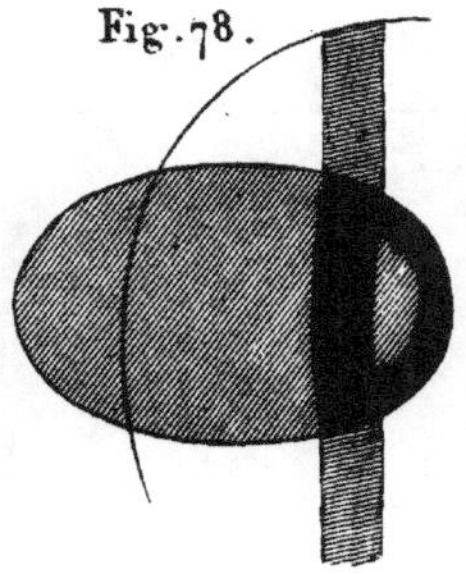

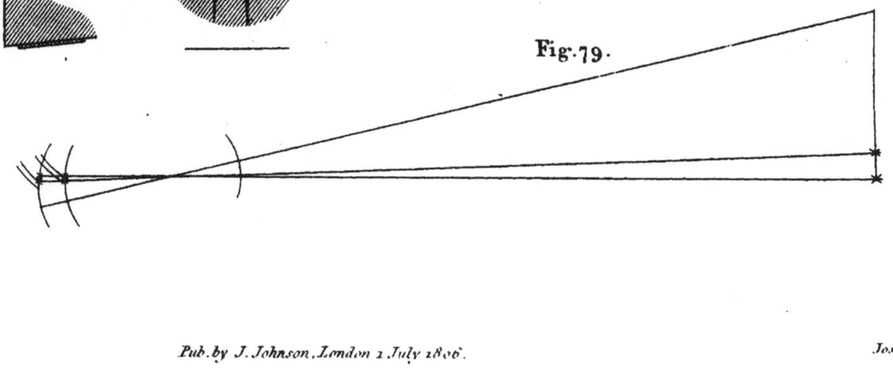

PLATE 10.

Fig. 80.

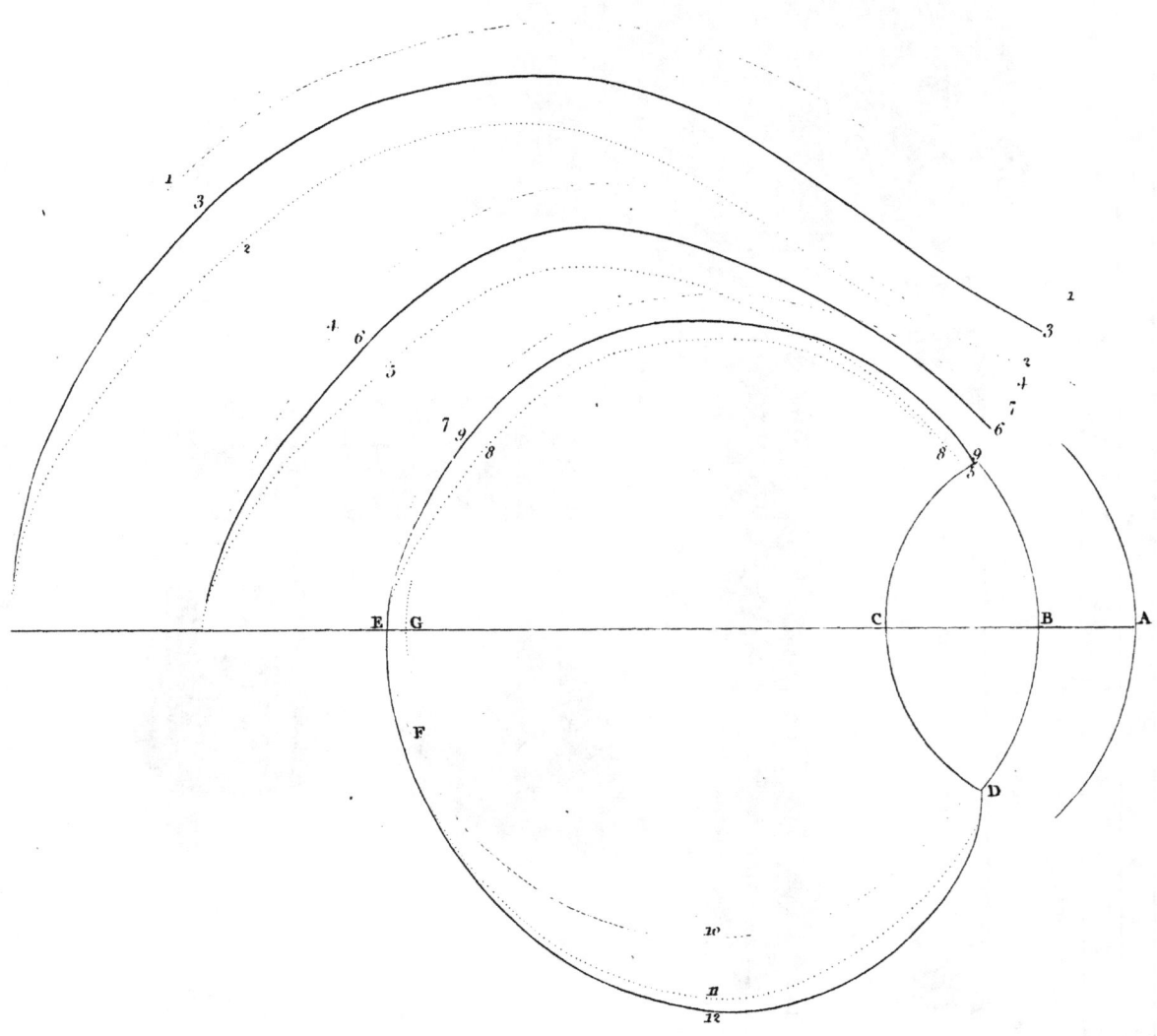

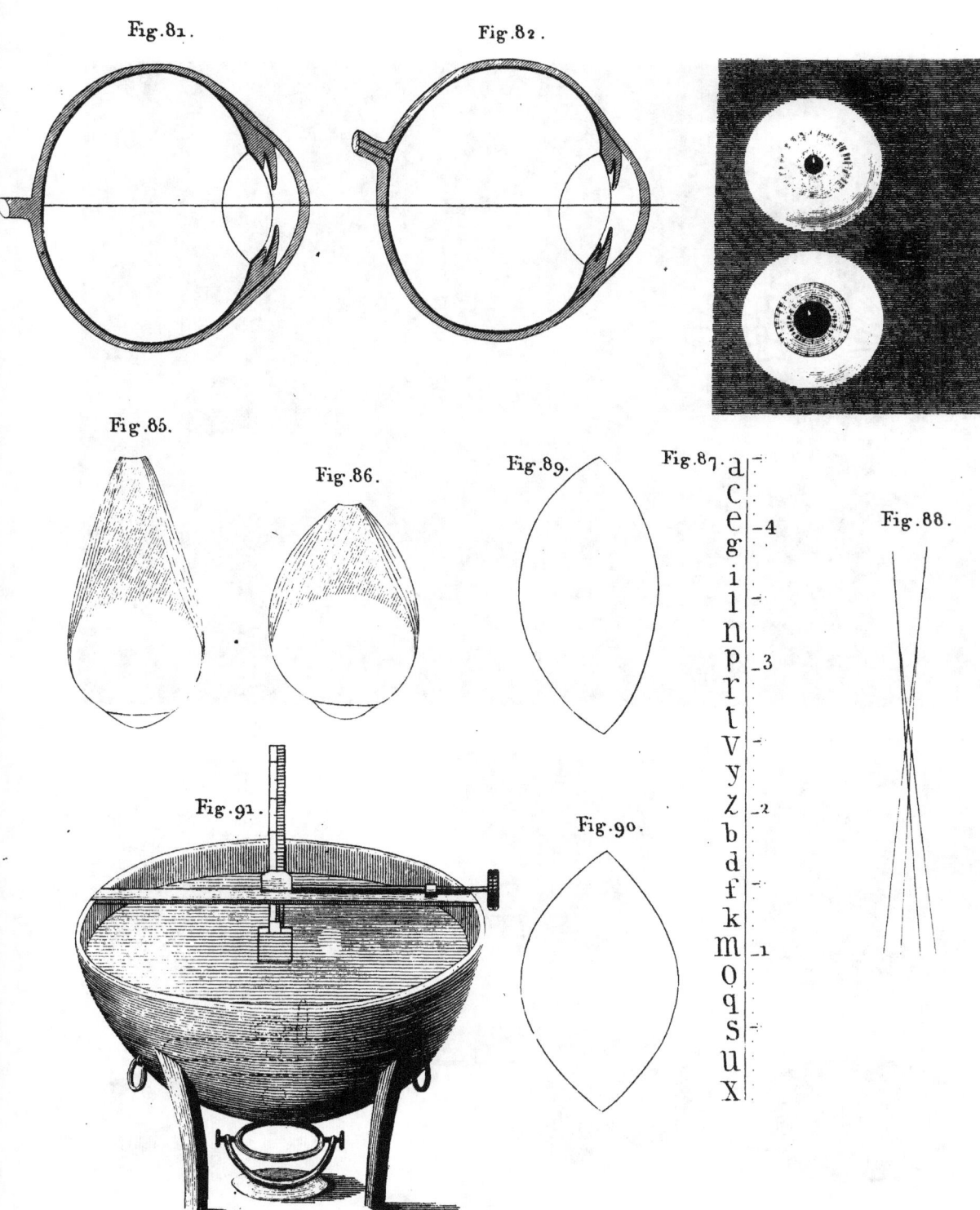

PLATE II.

PLATE 12.

Fig. 92.

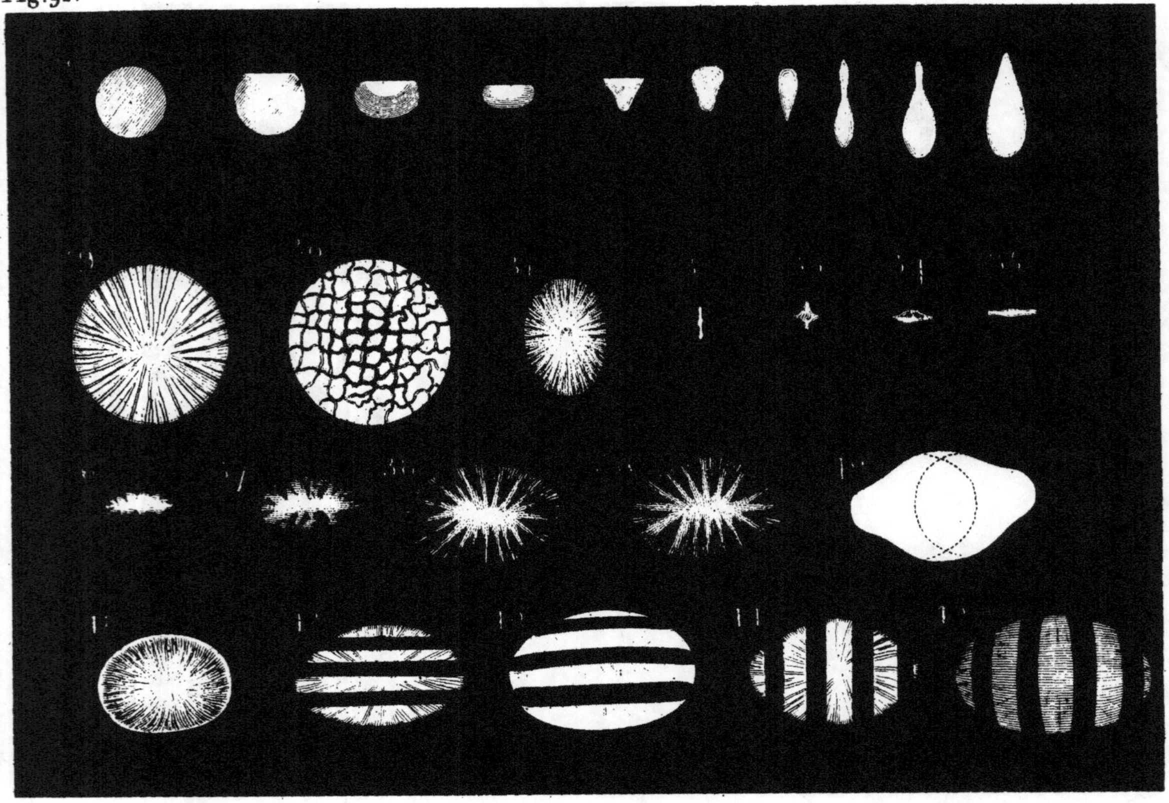

Fig. 93.

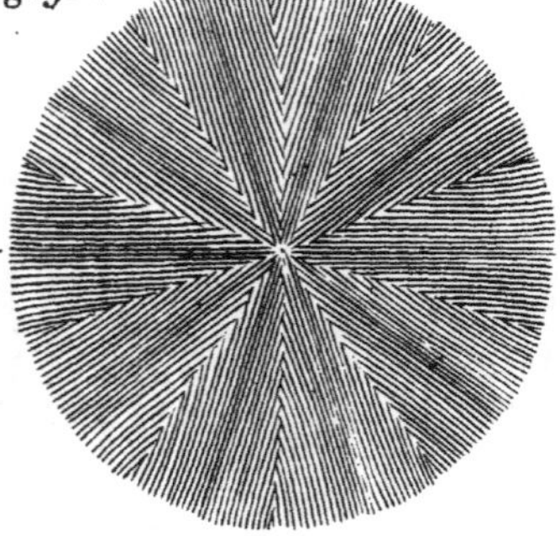

Fig. 94.

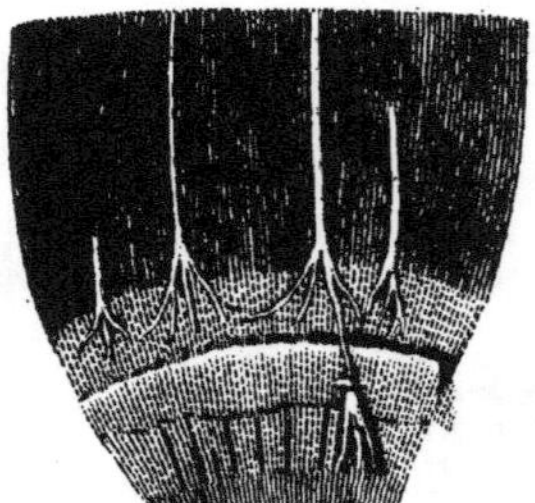

Fig. 95.

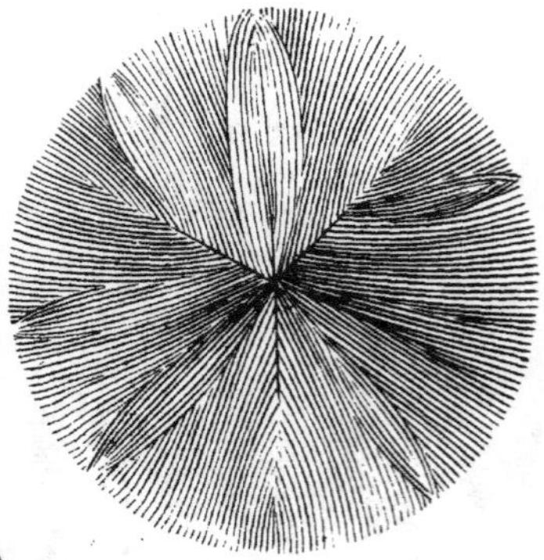

Fig. 96.

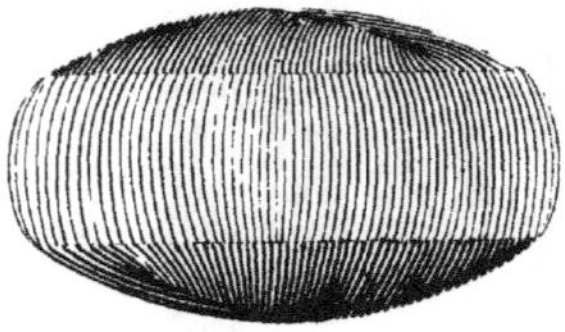

Fig. 97.

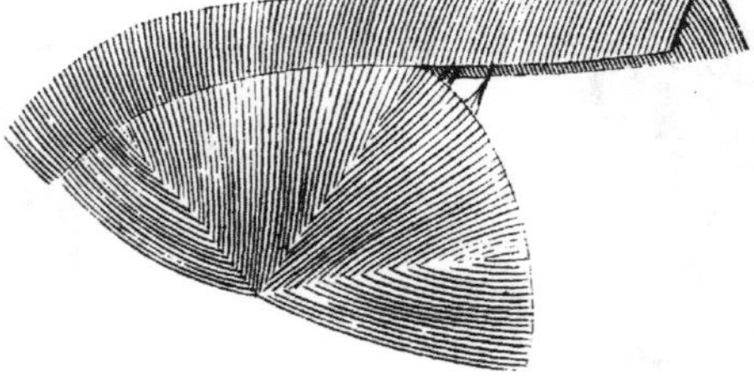

Fig. 98.

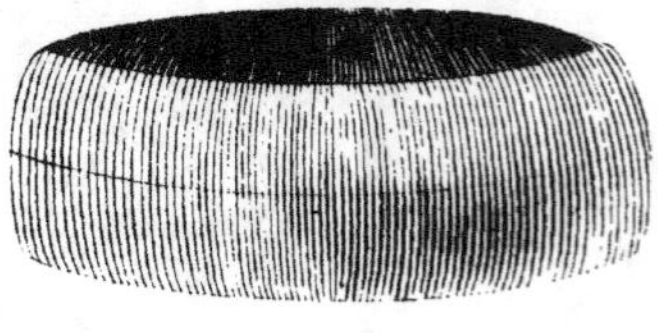

Pub. by J. Johnson London 1 July 1806.

Joseph s

PLATE 13.

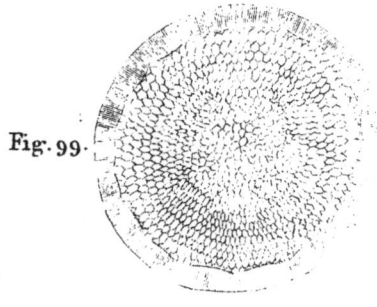

Fig. 99.

Fig. 100.

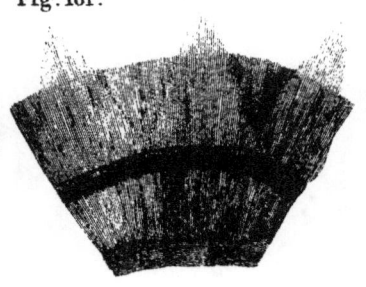

Fig. 101.

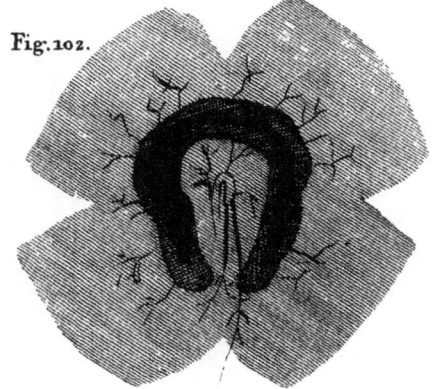

Fig. 102.

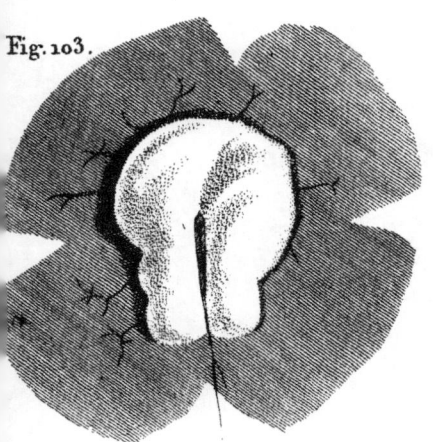

Fig. 103.

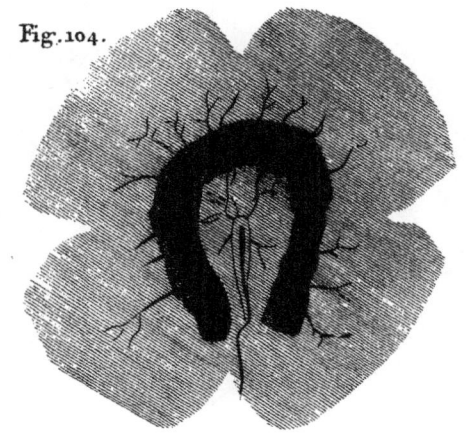

Fig. 104.

Pub. by J. Johnson London 1 July 1806.

Joseph Skelton sculp.

VI. A LETTER TO MR. NICHOLSON,

FROM THOMAS YOUNG, M.D. F.R.S.

PROFESSOR OF NATURAL PHILOSOPHY IN THE ROYAL INSTITUTION,

RESPECTING SOUND AND LIGHT,

AND IN REPLY TO SOME OBSERVATIONS OF PROFESSOR ROBISON.

From Nicholson's Journal, for August 1801.

SIR,

In the supplement of the Encyclopaedia Britannica, are inserted several excellent articles by Professor Robison, of Edinburgh: one of them appears to require some public notice on my part, and I consider your valuable Journal as the most eligible channel for such a communication, especially as you have lately done me the honour of reprinting the paper which gave rise to the Professor's animadversions. But in the first place, I shall beg leave to recall the attention of your readers, by a summary enumeration, to the principal positions which I have in that paper endeavoured to establish.

1. Sound, as transmitted through the atmosphere, consists in an undulatory motion of the particles of the air, Sect. III. This is generally admitted; but as the contrary has even very lately been asserted, it is not superfluous to have decisive evidence of the fact. Professor Robison's experiment with a stopcock furnishes an argument nearly similar.

2. A current of air, forced by a moderate pressure through a cylindrical pipe, diverges the less as its velocity is less, Sect. II.

3. At a certain point the divergency of such a current increases suddenly, and the current mixes with the surrounding air, Sect. II.

4. So far is such a motion from spreading equally in all directions, that on every side of the current the air is urged more towards it than from it, Sect. II.

5. Sound, admitted through an aperture, does not by any means diverge equally in all directions, and is probably very weak except in directions nearly rectilinear. From position 2 and 4, and from experience, Sect. VI.

6. Sound probably decays in the duplicate ratio of the distance, Sect. VII.

7. A similar blast of air produces nearly a similar sound, in organ pipes properly commensurate, Sect. VIII.

8. Light is probably the undulation of an elastic medium, Sect. X.

A. Because its velocity in the same medium is always equal.

B. Because all refractions are attended with a partial reflection.

C. Because there is no reason to expect that such a vibration should diverge equally in all directions, and because it is probable that it does diverge in a small degree in every direction.

D. Because the dispersion of differently coloured rays is no more incompatible with this system than with the common opinion, which only assigns for it the nominal cause of different elective attractions.

E. Because refraction and reflection in general are equally explicable on both suppositions.

F. Because inflection is as well, and, it may be added, even much better explained by this theory.

G. Because all the phenomena of the colours of thin plates, which are in reality totally unintelligible on the common hypothesis, admit a very complete and simple explanation by this supposition. The analogy, which is here superficially indicated, will probably soon be made public more in detail; and will also be extended to the colours of thick plates, and to the fringes produced by inflection, affording, from Newton's own elaborate experiments, a most convincing argument in favour of this system.

9. The particles of air may be jointly actuated by two or more sounds; and in this case, the several motions are to be added or subtracted, in order to find the actual joint motion, Sect. XI.

10. The grave harmonic produced by a major third is accompanied by a very audible twelfth. This circumstance is explained, and the effect of subordinate notes and subaltern stops, on the quality of sounds, is shown by figures, Sect. XI.

11. A noise returning every second, if audible, would be a C. From Sauveur; with an experiment, Sect. XII.

12. A chord retains always the form of its initial vibration. From experiments, in favour of Euler's theorem, against the simple harmonic curve, Sect. XIII.

13. The vibration of a chord is scarcely ever performed in the same plane. Its revolutions, and its subordinate vibrations, may be rendered distinctly visible under the microscope, Sect. XIII.

14. If a chord be inflected at any point of aliquot division, the harmonic secondary note corresponding to that division will not be audible; an experiment contradictory to some theories of the origin and of the inseparable nature of harmonic sounds, Sect. XIII.

15. The human voice is analogous to the organ pipe denominated from it, which consists of a tongue piece without any commensurate tube: and the falsetto is probably formed by the upper orifice of the trachea, assuming the functions of the glottis, Sect. XV.

16. A temperament of progressive imperfection is the most convenient for practical music, and is easily approximated by tuning six perfect, and six equally imperfect fifths, Sect. XVI.

From the detached nature of the subjects which I have here enumerated, and the imperfect state of those branches of the mathematics to which they refer, it would have been in vain to attempt a very perspicuous and detailed discussion of them. My researches on these subjects have been much interrupted, and probably will not be very shortly resumed; but, if they be of no further use to any person, I shall not think my labour lost; for I flatter myself that the inferences, which they have led me to draw, re-

-specting the theory of colours, will throw new light on all the most interesting parts of optics, while, by a comparison with the obvious inferences from Dr. Herschel's important discoveries, they will also lead to some material illustrations of the phenomena of heat.

I shall now trouble you with some remarks in reply to Professor Robison: the passage to which I allude is this:

"We are surprised to see this work of Dr. Smith greatly undervalued, by a most ingenious gentleman, in the Philosophical Transactions for 1800, and called a large and obscure volume, which leaves the matter just as it was, and its results useless and impracticable. We are sorry to see this: because we have great expectations from the future labours of this gentleman in the field of harmonics, and his late work is rich in refined and valuable matter. We presume humbly to recommend to him, attention to his own admonitions to a very young and ingenious gentleman, who, he thinks, proceeded too far in animadverting on the writings of Newton, Barrow, and other eminent mathematicians." Encyclop. Brit. Suppl. Art. Temperament, p. 652.

According therefore to the author of this article, I have in the first place taken the liberty of giving severe advice, to a young mathematician who had never asked it; secondly, this advice is equally applicable to my own presumption; and thirdly, Dr. Smith's treatise on harmonics is a work intitled to the highest praise.

I did, in fact, endeavour to show, that the gentleman in question had overlooked the labours of some former authors relative to his subject, but I accompanied my remarks with nothing like admonition. I have read Dr. Smith's work with attention, and I imagine, from the polite manner in which Professor Robison is pleased to speak of my essay, he will not hesitate to allow, that I have understood it. I took it up with great expectations; those expectations having been completely disappointed, I thought it right to state my cool and unprejudiced opinion of its merits, in order to prevent a similar disappointment in others. It is impossible, therefore, that an "attention" to any "admonitions" of a general nature, wherever they may be found, can influence such an opinion; and so far only as I am supposed to be an incompetent judge on the subject of harmonics, can it be asserted, that it was either blameable or superfluous for me to express that opinion. As a mathematician, and an optician, I value Dr. Smith highly, but I must still beg leave to affirm, that his whole book of harmonics contains far, far less information, than either of the articles Temperament and Trumpet, in the Supplement of the Encyclopaedia.

I do not mean to be understood, that this work is so contemptible, as not to contain the least particle of important matter; but it appears to me, that its errors counterbalance its merits. The only improvement on which Professor Robison himself seems to set a high value, is the application of the phenomena of beats to tuning an instrument: on the other hand, I conceive that the misstatement, relative to the noninterference of different sounds, is an inaccuracy which far outweighs the merit of Dr. Smith's share of that improvement. I have asserted, that Dr. Smith has written a large and obscure volume, which, for every " purpose, but for the " use of an impracticable instrument, leaves " the whole subject of temperament precisely " where it found it;" and that " the system, "proposed for his changeable harpsichord, is neither in that, nor in any other form, capable of practicable application." Professor Robison, on the contrary, says, "We do not see how it can be disputed, that Dr. Smith's theory of the beating of imperfect consonances, is one of the most important discoveries both for the practice and the science of music, that have been offered to the public. We are inclined to consider it as the most important that has been made since the days of Galileo. We are obliged to call it his discovery. Mersennus, indeed, had taken particular notice of this undulation of imperfect consonances, and had offered conjectures as to their causes; conjectures not unworthy of his great ingenuity. Mr. Sauveur also takes a still more particular notice of this phenomenon, and makes a most ingenious use of it for the solution of a very important musical problem." P. 652 and 651. Why then are we obliged to call it Dr. Smith's discovery, or indeed any discovery at all? Sauveur had already given directions for tuning an organ pipe, by means of the rapidity of its beating with others. Mém. de l'Ac. 1701. 475, ed. Amst. Dr. Smith ingeniously enough extended the method: but it appears to me, that the extension was perfectly obvious, and wholly undeserving of the name either of a discovery or of a theory. If Professor Robison thinks otherwise, there is nothing further to be said; but, in all probability, Dr. Smith considered this improvement as constituting a very small part of the merit of his treatise. No doubt an organ may be more accurately tuned by counting the beats, than by any other method, although it may be questioned, whether the advantage of counting the absolute frequency of the beats, will ever practically compensate the tediousness of the process.

It remains to be considered, whether Dr. Smith's changeable harpsichord is, or is not, an impracticable instrument; for, whatever Signor Doria might exclaim, Dr. Smith himself does not recommend his scale for common use. It is the opinion of many unprejudiced practical persons, that all occasional introduction of different semitones is perfectly impracticable; and some, who have heard the effect of Dr. Smith's instrument, have declared, that to them it was by no means agreeable. And indeed, if we pay sufficient attention to the passages and modulations of the greatest composers, we shall be convinced, that, granting all possible dexterity in the performer, it would be absolutely impracticable to adapt them to an instrument, so different from that for which they were composed, as Dr. Smith's is from the common harpsichord. It may easily be conceived, that an organ, very correctly tuned, as Mr. Watt's probably was, for a particular key, might appear " sopra modo bellissimo" in that key; but the sequel of the story shows literally what Dr. Smith has allowed, that his temperament is inapplicable to our instruments, since it was utterly impossible to sing with it in the key of Ees, or E flat, a key of exceedingly frequent occurrence. I have been informed, on the best authority, that Dr Smith restricted the organist of Trinity College to such keys and modulations, as were best suited to the system by which the organ was tuned; and that organ, as well as the instruments which were made for Dr. Smith, has long been tuned according to the more common method.

I spoke of Dr. Smith's system with flattened major thirds as of no value, not with regard to its intrinsic merits, but because it was not intended for any instrument in common use; since, in these instruments, the difficulty is not so much how to divide the imperfection among the thirds and fifths of the same scale, as to proportion properly the imperfections of the thirds of different keys. Yet I do not mean it to be understood, that I can agree to the solidity of those foundations on which Dr. Smith has built his system for a single scale: although to Stanley and to Doria it might be pleasing, because its imperfections are far too small to offend the ear. Professor Robison justly observes, that different persons differ exceedingly in their estimation of the effect of the same temperament on different concords, and that much of this arises from their different dispositions; it appears, therefore, that Dr. Smith was too precipitate in laying down his principle for the comparison of the effects of temperament.

With respect to the system which I have proposed, Professor Robison thinks, that the temperaments of several of the thirds which occur frequently are much too great. If we wish to form a judgment of any system of temperament, it must be by comparison with some other. It does not appear with what system Professor Robison would wish the comparison to be made, but he rather seems to incline to the equal temperament, although he gives directions for tuning by another. At any rate, no temperament of an interval can be said to be much too great, unless it be greater than that of the same interval in the system of equal temperament; for, if any interval be made more perfect than this, some other similar interval must be as much less perfect. In my system, the only thirds perceptibly greater than those of the equal temperament, are the major thirds on E, Aes, B, C sharp, or Cis, and Fis, and the minor on C, Cis, F, Gis, Bes, and Ees. Of these none can be said to occur frequently, except the major third on E, and the minor on C. The sixths require no separate consideration. Now, since the minor chord is intended to be less completely harmonious than the major, its character will be by no means materially impaired by this imperfection, which it would be somewhat difficult to remove. The third on E is not sharp enough to be very offensive, but in compliance with the usual practice of making this third somewhat more perfect than the intervals of Aes and C, I have, in the method recommended for common use, made it equal to the third of the equal temperament. The directions given for tuning, in § 68. and in § 80, of the article, are liable to far greater objections. For instance, the temperament of the IIIds on Aes and Fis, in the latter, is about .00880, or more than a comma and a half; which Professor Robison will readily allow to be "much too great" for any thirds; since he has asserted, with Dr. Smith and others, that the error of a comma would be intolerable. Mr. Maxwell has, however, very decidedly proved, in his Essay on Tune, that the greatest harmonists, Corelli, Tartini, and Giardini, have admitted very frequently the error of a comma, in their most refined compositions. And I have the authority of several celebrated performers on stringed and wind instruments, for asserting, that they take of choice the characteristic semitone, leading into the key note, considerably sharper than the same note is tuned on any keyed instruments, making an imperfection of nearly two commas, in the relation as third of the dominant, which is the fundamental note of the chord: while, in the mean time, our theorists have been labouring, by the most complicated contrivances, to introduce notes into keyed instruments, which shall have exactly a contrary effect, by making the ascending semitone as wide a step as possible. On asking very lately the opinion of a practical musician of great eminence, and one, who in every respect does honour to his profession, he decidedly agreed in the superiority of such a diminished semitone, and observed that the key of E derived a very elegant character from the usual method of tuning Dis as Ees, a minor third to C: hence the IIIds on Ees and G being very little tempered, the IIId on the dominant B must be about a comma and half too sharp. The fact is, that in this case, the harmony is somewhat impaired, in order to improve the melody. The semitone is considered only in its relation to the key note: the interval of 15 to 16 is far too small to be distinctly conceived as commensurate, it possesses, therefore, no melody in virtue of the perfection of its ratio; and a certain elegance of expression is added, by approaching to the natural and colloquial ascent of a voice by imperceptible degrees. It must, however, be confessed, that some excellent musicians prefer a purer harmony; and in this, as in all other matters of taste, considerable latitude must be allowed for the habits and predilections of individuals.

I am, Sir,

With great respect,

Your obedient humble servant,

No. 48, Welbeck Street,
13 July, 1801.

THOMAS YOUNG.

VII. ON THE THEORY OF LIGHT AND COLOURS.

BY

THOMAS YOUNG, M.D. F.R.S.

PROFESSOR OF NATURAL PHILOSOPHY IN THE ROYAL INSTITUTION.

FROM THE PHILOSOPHICAL TRANSACTIONS.

Read before the ROYAL SOCIETY, *November* 12, 1801.

ALTHOUGH the invention of plausible hypotheses, independent of any connexion with experimental observations, can be of very little use in the promotion of natural knowledge; yet the discovery of simple and uniform principles, by which a great number of apparently heterogeneous phenomena are reduced to coherent and universal laws, must ever be allowed to be of considerable importance towards the improvement of the human intellect; and in proportion as more and more phenomena are found to agree with any principles that are laid down, those principles must be allowed to acquire a stronger right to exchange the appellation of hypotheses for that of fundamental laws of nature.

The object of the present dissertation is not so much to propose any opinions which are absolutely new, as to refer some theories, which have been already advanced, to their original inventors; to support them by additional evidence, and to apply them to a great number of diversified facts, which have hitherto been buried in obscurity. Nor would it have been absolutely necessary, in this instance, to produce a single new experiment; for of experiments there is already an ample store, which are so much the more unexceptionable, as they must have been conducted without the least partiality for the system by which they will be explained; yet some facts, hitherto unobserved, will be brought forwards, in order to show the perfect agreement of that system with the multifarious phenomena of nature, which are connected with it.

The optical observations of Newton are yet unrivalled; and, excepting some casual inaccuracies, they only rise in our estimation, as we compare them with later attempts to improve on them. A further consideration of the colours of thin plates, as they are described in the second book of Newton's optics, has converted that prepossession which

I before entertained for the undulatory system of light, into a very strong conviction of its truth and sufficiency; a conviction which has been since most strikingly confirmed, by an analysis of the colours of striated substances. The phenomena of thin plates are indeed so singular, that their general complexion is not without great difficulty reconcileable to any theory, however complicated, that has hitherto been applied to them; and some of the principal circumstances have never been explained by the most gratuitous assumptions; but it will appear, that the minutest particulars of these phenomena are not only perfectly consistent with the theory, which will now be detailed, but that they are all necessary consequences of that theory, without any auxiliary suppositions: and this by inferences so simple, that they become particular corollaries, which scarcely require a distinct enumeration.

A more extensive examination of Newton's various writings has shown me, that he was, in reality, the first that suggested such a theory as I shall endeavour to maintain; that his own opinions varied less from this theory, than is now almost universally supposed; and that a variety of arguments have been advanced, as if to confute him, which may be found nearly in a similar form in his own works; and this, by no less a mathematician than Leonard Euler, whose system of light, as far as it is worthy of notice, either was, or might have been, wholly borrowed from Newton, Hooke, Huygens, and Malebranche.

Those who are attached, as they may be with the greatest justice, to every doctrine which is stamped with the Newtonian approbation, will probably be disposed to bestow on these considerations so much the more of their attention, as they shall appear to coincide more nearly with Newton's opinion. For this reason, after having briefly stated each particular position of my theory, I shall collect, from Newton's various writings, such passages as seem to be the most favourable to its admission; and, although I shall quote some papers which may be thought to have been partly retracted at the publication of the optics, yet I shall borrow nothing from them that can be supposed to militate against his maturer judgment.

HYPOTHESIS I. *A luminiferous Ether pervades the Universe, rare and elastic in a high degree.*

PASSAGES FROM NEWTON.

"The hypothesis certainly has a much greater affinity with his own," that is, Dr. Hooke's, "hypothesis, than he seems to be aware of; the vibrations of the ether being as useful and necessary in this, as in his." (Phil. Trans. VII. 5087. Abr. I. 145. Nov. 1672.)

"To proceed to the hypothesis: first, it is to be supposed therein, that there is an ethereal medium, much of the same constitution with air, but far rarer, subtler, and more strongly elastic.—It is not to be supposed, that this medium is one uniform matter, but compounded, partly of the main phlegmatic body of ether, partly of other various ethereal spirits, much after the manner that air is compounded of the phlegmatic body of air, intermixed with various vapours and exhalations: for the electric and magnetic effluvia, and gravitating principle, seem to argue such variety." (Birch Hist. R. S. III. 249. Dec. 1675.)

"Is not the heat (of the warm room) conveyed through the vacuum by the vibrations of a much subtiler medium than air?—And is not this medium the same with that medium by which light is refracted and reflected, and by whose vibrations light communicates heat to bodies, and is put into fits of easy reflection, and easy transmission? And do not the vibrations of this medium in hot bodies, contribute to the intenseness and duration of their heat? And do not hot bodies communicate their heat to contiguous cold ones, by the vibrations of this medium propagated from them into the cold ones? And is not this medium exceedingly more rare and subtile than the air, and exceedingly more elastic and active? And doth it not readily pervade all bodies? And is it not by its elastic force, expanded through all the heavens?—May not planets and comets, and all gross bodies, perform their motions in this ethereal medium?—And may not its resistance be so small, as to be inconsiderable? For instance, if this ether (for so I will call it) should be supposed 700 000 times more elastic than our air, and above 700 000 times more rare, its resistance would be about 600 000 000 times less than that of water. And so small a resistance would scarce make any sensible alteration in the motions of the planets, in ten thousand years. If any one would ask how a medium can be so rare, let him tell me—how an electric body can by friction emit an exhalation so rare and subtile, and yet so potent?—And how the effluvia of a magnet can pass through a plate of glass, without resistance, and yet turn a magnetic needle beyond the glass?" (Optics, Qu. 18, 22.)

HYPOTHESIS II. *Undulations are excited in this Ether whenever a Body becomes luminous.*

SCHOLIUM. I use the word undulation, in preference to vibration, because vibration is generally understood as implying a motion which is continued alternately backwards and forwards, by a combination of the momentum of the body with an accelerating force, and which is naturally more or less permanent; but an undulation is supposed to consist in a vibratory motion, transmitted successively through different parts of a medium, without any tendency in each particle to continue its motion, except in consequence of the transmission of succeeding undulations, from a distinct vibrating body; as, in the air, the vibrations of a chord produce the undulations constituting sound.

PASSAGES FROM NEWTON.

" Were I to assume an hypothesis, it should be this, if propounded more generally, so as not to determine what light is, further, than that it is something or other capable of exciting vibrations in the ether; for thus it will become so general, and comprehensive of other hypotheses, as to leave little room for new ones to be invented." (Birch, III. 249, Dec. 1675.)

" In the second place, it is to be supposed, that the ether is a vibrating medium, like air, only the vibrations far more swift and minute; those of air, made by a man's ordinary voice, succeeding one another at more than half a foot, or a foot distance; but those of ether at a less distance than the hundred thousandth part of an inch. And, as in air, the vibrations are some larger than others, but yet all equally swift, (for in a ring of bells the sound of every tone is heard at two or three miles distance, in the same order that the bells are struck,) so, I suppose, the ethereal vibrations differ in bigness, but not in swiftness. Now, these vibrations, beside their use in reflection and refraction, may be supposed the chief means by which the parts of fermenting or putrifying substances, fluid liquors, or melted, burning, or other hot bodies, continue in motion." (Birch, III. 251. Dec. 1675.)

" When a ray of light falls upon the surface of any pellucid body, and is there refracted or reflected, may not waves of vibrations, or tremors, be thereby excited in the refracting or reflecting medium?—And are not these vibrations propagated from the point of incidence to great distances? And do they not overtake the rays of light, and by overtaking them successively, do they not put them into the fits of easy reflection and easy transmission described above? (Optics, Qu. 17.)

" Light is in fits of easy reflection and easy transmission, before its incidence on transparent bodies. And probably it is put into such fits at its first emission from luminous bodies, and continues in them during all its progress." (Optics, Second Book, Part iii. Prop. 13.)

HYPOTHESIS III. *The Sensation of different Colours depends on the different frequency of Vibrations, excited by Light in the Retina.*

PASSAGES FROM NEWTON.

" The objector's hypothesis, as to the fundamental part of it, is not against me. That fundamental supposition is, that the parts of bodies, when briskly agitated, do excite vibrations in the ether, which are propagated every way from those bodies in straight lines, and cause a sensation of light, by beating and dashing against the bottom of the eye, something after the manner that vibrations in the air cause a sensation of sound, by beating against the organs of hearing. Now, the most free and natural application of this hypothesis to the solution of phenomena, I take to be this: that the agitated parts of bodies, according to their several sizes, figures, and motions, do excite vibrations in the ether of various depths or bignesses, which, being promiscuously propagated through that medium to our eyes, effect in us a sensation of light of a white colour; but if by any means those of unequal bignesses be separated from one another, the largest beget a sensation of a red colour, the least or shortest of a deep violet, and the intermediate ones of intermediate colours; much after the manner that bodies, according to their several sizes, shapes, and motions, excite vibrations in the air, of various bignesses, which, according to those bignesses, make several tones in a sound: that the largest vibrations are best able to overcome the resistance of a refracting superficies, and so break through it with least refraction; whence the vibrations of several bignesses, that is, the rays of several colours, which are blended together in light, must be parted from one another by refraction, and so cause the phenomena of prisms, and other refracting substances; and that it depends on the thickness of a thin transparent plate or bubble, whether a vibration shall be reflected at its further superficies, or transmitted; so that, according to the number of vibrations, interceding the two superficies, they may be reflected or transmitted for many successive thicknesses. And, since the vibrations which make blue and violet, are supposed shorter than those which make red and yellow, they must be reflected at a less thickness of the plate: which is sufficient to explicate all the ordinary phenomena of those plates or bubbles, and also of all natural bodies, whose parts are like so many fragments of such plates. These seem to be most plain, genuine, and necessary conditions of this hypothesis. And they agree so justly with my theory, that if the animadversor think fit to apply them, he need not, on that account, apprehend a divorce from it. But yet, how he will defend it from other difficulties, I know not." (Phil. Trans. VII. 5088. Abr. I. 145. Nov. 1672.)

"To explain colours, I suppose, that as bodies of various sizes, densities, or sensations, do, by percussion or other action, excite sounds of various tones, and consequently vibrations in the air of different bigness; so the rays of light, by impinging on the stiff refracting superficies, excite vibrations in the ether,—of various bigness; the biggest, strongest, or most potent rays, the largest vibrations; and others shorter, according to their bigness, strength, or power: and therefore the ends of the capillamenta of the optic nerve, which pave or face the retina, being such refracting superficies, when the rays impinge upon them, they must there excite these vibrations, which vibrations (like those of sound in a trunk or trumpet) will run along the aqueous pores or crystalline pith of the capillamenta, through the optic nerve into the sensorium;—and there, I suppose, affect the sense with various colours, according to their bigness and mixture; the biggest with the strongest colours, reds and yellows; the least with the weakest, blues and violets; the middle with green; and a confusion of all with white, much after the manner that, in the sense of hearing, nature makes use of aerial vibrations of several bignesses, to generate sounds of divers tones; for the analogy of nature is to be observed." (Birch. III. 262. Dec. 1675.)

" Considering the lastingness of the motions excited in the bottom of the eye by light, are they not of a vibrating nature?—Do not the most refrangible rays excite the shortest vibrations,—the least refrangible the largest? May not the harmony and discord of colours arise from the proportions of the vibrations propagated through the fibres of the optic nerve into the brain, as the harmony and discord of sounds arise from the proportions of the vibrations of the air?" (Optics, Qu. 16, 13, 14.)

SCHOLIUM. Since, for the reason here assigned by Newton, it is probable that the motion of the retina is rather of a vibratory than of an undulatory nature, the frequency of the vibrations must be dependent on the constitution of this substance. Now, as it is almost impossible to conceive each sensitive point of the retina to contain an infinite number of particles, each capable of vibrating in perfect unison with every possible undulation, it becomes necessary to suppose the number limited; for instance, to the three principal colours, red, yellow, and blue, of which the undulations are related in magnitude nearly as the numbers 8, 7, and 6; and that each of the particles is capable of being put in motion less or more forcibly, by undulations differing less or more from a perfect unison; for instance, the undulations of green light, being nearly in the ratio of $6\frac{1}{2}$, will affect equally the particles in unison with yellow and blue, and produce the same effect as a light composed of those two species: and each sensitive filament of the nerve may consist of three portions, one for each principal colour. Allowing this statement, it appears that any attempt, to produce a musical effect from colours, must be unsuccessful, or at least that nothing more than a very simple melody could be imitated by them; for the common period, which in fact constitutes the harmony of any concord, being a multiple of the periods of the single undulations, would in this case be wholly without the limits of sympathy of the retina, and would lose its effect; in the same manner as the harmony of a third or a fourth is destroyed, by depressing it to the lowest notes of the audible scale. In hearing, there seems to be no permanent vibration of any part of the organ. [See the Account of some cases of the production of colours.]

HYPOTHESIS IV. *All material Bodies are to be considered, with respect to the Phenomena of Light, as consisting of Particles so remote from each other, as to allow the ethereal Medium to pervade them with perfect freedom, and either to retain it in a state of greater density and of equal elasticity, or to constitute, together with the Medium, an Aggregate, which may be considered as denser, but not more elastic.*

It has been shown, that the three former hypotheses, which may be called essential, are literally parts of the more complicated Newtonian system. This fourth hypothesis differs in some degree from any that have been proposed by former authors, and is, in some respects, diametrically opposite to that of Newton; but, both being in themselves equally admissible, the opposition is merely accidental; and it is only to be inquired, which is the most capable of explaining the phenomena. Other suppositions might, perhaps, be substituted for this, and therefore I do not consider it as fundamental, yet it appears to be the simplest and best of any that have occurred to me.

PROPOSITION I. *All Impulses are propagated in a homogeneous elastic Medium with an equable Velocity.*

Every experiment, relative to sound, coincides with the observation already quoted from Newton, that all undulations are propagated through the air with equal velocity; and this is further confirmed by calculations. (Lagrange. Misc. Taur. I. 91. Also, much more concisely, in my Syllabus of a Course of Lectures on Natural and Experimental Philosophy, about to be published, Article 289.) It is surprising that Euler, although aware of the matter of fact, should still have maintained, that the more frequent undulations are more rapidly propagated. (Theor. mus. and Conject. phys.) It is probable, that the actual velocity of the particles of the luminiferous ether generally bears a much smaller proportion to the velocity of the undulations, than is usual in the case of sound; for light may be excited by the motion of a body moving at the rate of only one mile, in the time that light moves a hundred millions. And if our sun's light reaches some of the remotest fixed stars, the utmost absolute velocity of the particles of the ethereal medium must be reduced to less than one thousandth part of an inch in a second.

SCHOLIUM 1. It has been demonstrated, that in different mediums, the velocity varies in the subduplicate ratio of the force directly, and of the density inversely. (Misc. Taur. I. 91. Young's Syllabus, Art. 294.)

SCHOLIUM 2. It is obvious, from the phenomena of elastic bodies and of sounds, that the undulations may cross each other without interruption. But there is no necessity that the various colours of white light should intermix their undulations; for, supposing the vibrations of the retina to continue but a five hundredth of a second after their excitement, a million undulations of each of a million colours may arrive, in distinct succession, within this interval of time, and produce the same sensible effect, as if all the colours arrived precisely at the same instant.

PROPOSITION II. *An Undulation, conceived to originate from the Vibration of a single Particle, must expand through a homogeneous Medium in a spherical Form, but with different Quantities of Motion in different Parts.*

For, since every impulse, considered as positive or negative, is propagated with a constant velocity, each part of the undulation must, in equal times, have past through equal distances from the vibrating point. And, supposing the vibrating particle, in the course of its motion, to proceed forwards to a small distance in a given direction, the principal strength of the undulation will naturally be straight before it; behind it, the motion will be equal, in a contrary direction; and, at right angles to the line of vibration, the undulation will be evanescent.

Now, in order that such an undulation may continue its progress to any considerable distance, there must be, in each part of it, a tendency to preserve its own motion in a right line from the centre; for, if the excess of force at any part were communicated to the neighbouring particles, there can be no reason why it should not very soon be equalised throughout, or, in other words, become wholly extinct, since the motions in contrary directions would naturally destroy each other. The origin of sound from the vibration of a chord is evidently of this nature; on the contrary, in a circular wave of water, every part is, usually, at the same instant either elevated or depressed. It may be difficult to show mathematically the mode, in which this inequality of force is preserved: but the inference from the matter of fact appears to be unavoidable. The theory of Huygens indeed explains the circumstance in a manner tolerably satisfactory: he supposes every particle of the medium to propagate a distinct undulation in all directions; and that the general effect is only perceptible where a portion of each undulation conspires in direction at the same instant; and it is easy to show that such a general undulation, would, in all cases, proceed rectilinearly, with proportionate force; but, upon this supposition, it seems to follow, that a greater quantity of force must be lost by the divergence of the partial undulations, than appears to be consistent with the propagation of the effect to any considerable distance. Yet it is obvious, that some such limitation of the motion must naturally be expected to take place; for, if the intensity of the motion of any particular part, instead of continuing to be propagated straight forwards, were supposed to affect the intensity of a neighbouring part of the undulation, an impulse must then have travelled from an internal to an external circle, in an oblique direction, in the same time as in the direction of the radius, and consequently with a greater velocity; against the first proposition. In the case of water, the velocity is by no means so rigidly limited as in that of an elastic medium. Yet it is not necessary to suppose, nor will the phenomena of light even allow us to admit, that there is absolutely not the least lateral communication of the force of the undulation, but it appears that, in highly elastic mediums, this communication is almost insensible. In the air, if a chord be perfectly insulated, so as to propagate exactly such vibrations as have been described, they will, in fact, be much less forcible, than if the chord be placed in the neighbourhood of a sounding board, and probably in some measure, because of this lateral communication of motions of an opposite tendency. And the different intensity of different parts of the same circular undulation may be observed, by holding a common tuning fork at arm's length, while sounding, and turning it, from a plane directed to the ear, into a position perpendicular to that plane.

PROPOSITION III. *A Portion of a spherical Undulation, admitted through an Aperture into a quiescent Medium, will proceed to be further propagated rectilinearly in concentric Superficies, terminated laterally by weak and irregular Portions of newly diverging Undulations.*

At the instant of admission, the circumference of each of the undulations may be supposed to generate a partial undulation, filling up the nascent angle between the radii and the surface terminating the medium; but no sensible addition will be made to its strength by a divergence of motion from any other parts of the undulation, for want of a coincidence in time, as has already been explained with respect to the various force of a spherical undulation. If indeed the aperture bear but a small proportion to the breadth of an undulation, the newly generated undulation may nearly absorb the whole force of the portion admitted; and this is the case considered by Newton in the Principia. When an experiment is made under these circumstances in light, it is certain that, whatever may be the cause, it by no means wholly retains a rectilinear direction.

Let the concentric lines in Fig. 105. (Plate 14.) represent the contemporaneous situation of similar parts of a number of successive undulations diverging from the point A; they will also represent the successive situations of each individual undulation: let the force of each undulation be represented by the breadth of the line, and let the cone of light ABC be admitted through the aperture BC; then the principal undulations will proceed in a rectilinear direction towards GH, and the faint radiations on each side will diverge from B and C as centres, without receiving any additional force from any intermediate point D of the undulation, on account of the inequality of the lines DE and DF. But, if we allow some little lateral divergence from the extremities of the undulations, it must diminish their force, without adding materially to that of the dissipated light; and their termination, instead of the right line BG, will assume the form CH; since the loss of force must be more considerable near to C than at greater distances. This line corresponds with the boundary of the shadow in Newton's first observation, Fig. 1; and it is much more probable that such a dissipation of light was the cause of the increase of the shadow in that observation, than that it was owing to the action of an inflecting atmosphere, or of an attractive force, which must have extended a thirtieth of an inch each way in order to produce it; especially when it is considered that the shadow was not diminished by surrounding the hair with a denser medium than air, which must in all probability have weakened its attractive force, or have contracted its inflecting atmosphere. In other circumstances, the lateral divergence might appear to increase, instead of diminishing, the breadth of the beam. It is said that a beam of light, even passing through a vacuum, is visible in all directions, and if the vacuum were as perfect as it is possible to make it, the experiment would afford a strong argument against the projectile system.

The whole of the phenomena described by Grimaldi, under the very proper denomination " diffraction," afford us examples of the deviation of light from rectilinear motion, nor have we the slightest evidence that an attractive force is concerned in producing these effects; on the contrary the experiment already mentioned, in which the refractive density of the substance concerned appears to be indifferent to the result, renders the supposition of such an inflecting force extremely improbable.

As the subject of this proposition has always been esteemed the most difficult part of the undulatory system, it will be proper to examine here the objections which Newton has grounded upon it.

" To me, the fundamental supposition itself seems impossible; namely, that the waves or vibrations of any fluid can, like the rays of light, be propagated in straight lines, without a continual and very extravagant spreading and bending every way into the quiescent medium, where they are terminated by it. I mistake, if there be not both experiment and demonstration to the contrary." (Phil. Trans. VII. 5089. Abr. I. 146. Nov. 1672.)

" Motus omnis per fluidum propagatus divergit a recto tramite in spatia immota."

" Quoniam medium ibi," that is, in the middle of an undulation admitted, " densius est, quam in spatiis hinc inde, dilatabit sese tam versus spatia utrinque sita, quam versus pulsuum rariora intervalla; eoque pacto—pulsus eadem *fere* celeritate sese in medii partes quiescentes hinc inde relaxare debent;—ideoque spatium totum occupabunt.—Hoc experimur in sonis." (Princip. Lib. II. Prop. 42.)

" Are not all hypotheses erroneous, in which light is supposed to consist in pression or motion, propagated through a fluid medium?—If it consisted in pression or motion, propagated either in an instant, or in time, it would bend into the shadow. For pression or motion cannot be propagated in a fluid in right lines, beyond an obstacle which stops part of the motion, but will bend and spread every way into the quiescent medium which lies beyond the obstacle.—The waves on the surface of stagnating water, passing by the sides of a broad obstacle which stops part of them, bend afterwards, and dilate themselves gradually into the quiet water behind the obstacle. The waves, pulses, or vibrations of the air, wherein sounds consist, bend manifestly, though not so much as the waves of water. For a bell or a cannon may be heard beyond a hill, which intercepts the sight of the sounding body; and sounds are propagated as readily through crooked pipes as straight ones. But light is never known to follow crooked passages, nor to bend into the shadow. For the fixed stars, by the interposition of any of the planets, cease to be seen. And so do the parts of the sun, by the interposition of the moon, Mercury, or Venus. The rays, which pass very near to the edges of any body, are bent a little by the action of the body;—but this bending is not towards but from the shadow, and is performed only in the passage of the ray by the body, and at a very small distance from it. So soon as the ray is past the body, it goes right on." (Optics, Qu. 28.)

Now the proposition quoted from the Principia, even supposing it to be strictly demonstrated, does not directly contradict this proposition; for it does not assert that such a motion must diverge equally in all directions; and the admission of the term "almost" is sufficient to invalidate the chain of reasoning: neither can it with truth be maintained, that the parts of an elastic medium, communicating any simple motion, must propagate that motion equally in all directions. (Phil. Trans. 1800. 109..112.) All that can be inferred by reasoning is, that the marginal parts of the undulation must be somewhat weakened, and that there must be a faint divergence in every direction: but whether either of these effects might be of sufficient magnitude to be sensible, with respect to light, could not have been concluded from argument, if the affirmative had not been rendered certain by experiment.

As to the analogy with other fluids, the most natural inference from it is this: "The waves of the air, wherein sounds consist, bend manifestly, though not so much as the waves of water;" water being an inelastic, and air a moderately elastic medium: but the ether being most highly elastic, its waves bend very far less than those of the air, and therefore almost imperceptibly. Sounds are propagated through crooked passages, because their sides are capable of reflecting sound, just as light would be propagated through a bent tube, if perfectly polished within.

The light of a star is by far too weak to produce, by its faint divergence, any visible illumination of the margin of a planet eclipsing it. Such a light has, however, often been seen attached to the moon in a solar eclipse, as could not be attributed to a lunar atmosphere only. What Newton here says, of inflection, is inconsistent, as Mr. Jordan has already remarked, with some of his own experiments.

To the argument adduced by Huygens, in favour of the rectilinear propagation of undulations, Newton has made no reply; perhaps, because of his own misconception of the nature of the motions of elastic mediums, as dependent on a peculiar law of vibration, which has been corrected by later mathematicians. (Phil. Trans. 1800. 116.) On the whole, it is presumed, that this proposition may be safely admitted, as perfectly consistent with analogy and with experiment.

PROPOSITION IV. *When an Undulation arrives at a Surface which is the Limit of Mediums of different Densities, a partial Reflection takes place, proportionate in Force to the Difference of the Densities.*

This may be illustrated, if not demonstrated, by the analogy of elastic bodies of different sizes. "If a smaller elastic body strikes against a larger one, it is well known that the smaller is reflected more or less powerfully, according to the difference of their magnitudes: thus, there is always a reflection when the rays of light pass from a rarer to a denser stratum of ether; and frequently an echo when a sound strikes against a cloud. A greater body striking a smaller one, propels it, without losing all its motion: thus, the particles of a denser stratum of ether do not impart the whole of their motion to a rarer, but in their effort to proceed, they are recalled by the attraction of the refracting substance with equal force; and thus a reflection is always secondarily produced, when the rays of light pass from a denser to a rarer stratum." (Phil. Trans. 1800. 127.) But it is not necessary to suppose an attraction in the latter case, since the effort to proceed would be propagated backwards without it, and the undulation would be reversed, a rarefaction returning in place of a condensation; and this will perhaps be found most consistent with the phenomena.

PROPOSITION V. *When an Undulation is transmitted through a Surface terminating different Mediums, it proceeds in such a Direction, that the Sines of the Angles of Incidence and Refraction are in the constant Ratio of the Velocity of Propagation in the two Mediums.*

(Barrow Lect. Opt. II. 4. Huygens *de la Lum.* cap. 3. Euler *Conj. Phys.* Phil. Trans. 1800. 128. Young's Syllabus, Art. 382.)

COROLLARY 1. The same demonstration prove the equality of the angles of reflection and incidence.

SCHOLIUM. It appears from experiments on the refraction of condensed air, that the difference of the sines varies simply as the density. And the same is probably true in other similar cases.

PROPOSITION VI. *When an Undulation falls on the Surface of a rarer Medium, so obliquely that it cannot be regularly refracted, it is totally reflected, at an Angle equal to that of its Incidence.*

This phenomenon appears to favour the supposition of a gradual increase and diminution of density at the surface terminating two mediums, (Phil. Trans. 1800, 128.) although Huygens has attempted to explain it somewhat differently. The velocity, with which the successive parts of the undulation arrive at the reflecting surface, is sufficient to determine the angle of reflection; in the same manner as when a bird is swimming in a stagnant piece of water, we see a rectilinear wave diverging at a certain angle on each side. The total reflection seems to require the assistance of the particles of the rarer medium, to which the motion of the preceding portion of the undulation has been partly communicated, without being able to produce any other effect than that of urging them in the direction of the surface, and enabling them to resist the force of the direct undulation, which tends to remove them from the surface.

PROPOSITION VII. *If equidistant Undulations be supposed to pass through a Medium, of which the Parts are susceptible of permanent vibrations somewhat slower than the Undulations, their Velocity will be somewhat lessened by this vibratory Tendency; and, in the same Medium, the more, as the Undulations are more frequent.*

For, as often as the state of the undulation requires a change in the actual motion of the particle which transmits it, that change will be retarded by the propensity of the particle to continue its motion somewhat longer: and this retardation will be more frequent, and more considerable, as the difference between the periods of the undulation and of the natural vibration is greater.

COROLLARY. It was long an established opinion, that heat consists in vibrations of the particles of bodies, and is capable of being transmitted by undulations through an apparent vacuum. (Newt. Opt. Qu. 18.) This opinion has been of late very much abandoned. Count Rumford and Mr. Davy, are almost the only modern authors who have appeared to favour it; but it seems to have been rejected without any good grounds, and will probably very soon recover its popularity.

Let us suppose, that these vibrations are less frequent than those of light; all bodies therefore are liable to permanent vibrations slower than those of light; and indeed almost all are liable to luminous vibrations, either when in a state of ignition, or in the circumstances of solar phosphori; but much less easily, and in a much less degree, than to the vibrations of heat. It will follow from these suppositions, that the more frequent luminous undulations will be more retarded than the less frequent; and consequently, that blue light will be more refrangible than red, and radiant heat least of all; a consequence which coincides exactly with the highly interesting experiments of Dr. Herschel. (Phil. Trans. 1800. 284.) It may also be easily conceived, that the actual existence of a state of slower vibration may tend still more to retard the more frequent undulations, and that the refractive power of solid bodies may be sensibly increased by an increase of temperature, as it actually appears to have been in Euler's experiments. (Acad. de Berlin. 1762. 328.)

SCHOLIUM. If, notwithstanding these considerations, this proposition should appear to be insufficiently demonstrated, they must be allowed to be at least equally explanatory of the phenomena with any thing that can be advanced on the other side, from the doctrine of projectiles; since a supposed accelerating force must act in some other proportion than that of the bulk of the particles; and, if we call this an elective attraction, it is only veiling, under a chemical term, our incapacity of assigning a mechanical cause.

Mr. Short, when he found by observation the equality of the velocity of light of all colours, felt the objection so forcibly, that he immediately drew an inference from it in favour of the undulatory system. It is assumed in the proposition, that when light is dispersed by refraction, the corpuscles of the refracting substance are in a state of actual alternate motion, and contribute to its transmission; but it must be confessed, that we cannot at present form a very decided and accurate conception of the forces concerned in maintaining these corpuscular vibrations. The proposition is not advanced as adding weight to the evidence in favour of the undulatory system, but as explaining in some degree a difficulty which is common to all systems; and there is still room for other illustrations of the subject. The principal argument in confirmation of the system is built on the next proposition, which appears to be equally new and important.

PROPOSITION VIII. *When two Undulations, from different Origins, coincide either perfectly or very nearly in Direction, their joint effect is a Combination of the Motions belonging to each.*

Since every particle of the medium is affected by each undulation, wherever the directions coincide, the undulations can proceed no otherwise, than by uniting their motions, so that the joint motion may be the sum or difference of the separate motions, accordingly as similar or dissimilar parts of the undulations are coincident.

I have, on a former occasion, insisted at large on the application of this principle to harmonics; (Phil. Trans. 1800. 130.) and it will appear to be of still more extensive utility in explaining the phenomena of colours. The undulations which are now to be compared are those of equal frequency. When the two series coincide exactly in point of time, it is obvious that the united velocity of the particular motions must be greatest; and also, that it must be smallest, and, if the undulations are of equal strength, totally destroyed, when the time of the greatest direct motion, belonging to one undulation, coincides with that of the greatest retrograde motion of the other. In intermediate states, the joint undulation will be of intermediate strength; but by what laws this intermediate strength must vary, cannot be determined without further data. It is well known that a similar cause produces, in sound, that effect which is called a beat; two series of undulations of nearly equal magnitude cooperating and destroying each other alternately, as they coincide more or less perfectly in the times of performing their respective motions.

COROLLARY I. *Of the Colours of striated Surfaces.*

Boyle appears to have been the first that observed the colours of scratches on polished surfaces. Newton has not noticed them. Mazéas and Mr. Brougham have made some experiments on the subject, yet without deriving any satisfactory conclusion. But all the varieties of these colours are very easily deduced from this proposition.

Let there be, in a given plane, two reflecting points very near each other, and let the plane be so situated that the reflected image of a luminous object seen in it may appear to coincide with the points; then it is obvious that the length of the incident and reflected ray, taken together, is equal with respect to both points, considering them as capable of reflecting in all directions. Let one of the points be now depressed below the given plane; then the whole path of the light, reflected from it, will be lengthened by a line which is to the depression of the point as twice the cosine of incidence to the radius. (Plate 14. Fig. 106.)

If, therefore, equal undulations of given dimensions be reflected from two points, situated near enough to appear to the eye but as one, wherever this line is equal to half the breadth of a whole undulation, the reflection from the depressed point will so interfere with the reflection from the fixed point, that the progressive motion of the one will coincide with the retrograde motion of the other, and they will both be destroyed; but, when this line is equal to the whole breadth of an undulation, the effect will be doubled; and when to a breadth and a half, again destroyed; and thus for a considerable number of alternations; and, if the reflected undulations be of different kinds, they will be variously affected, according to their proportions to the various lengths of the line which is the difference between the lengths of their two paths, and which may be denominated the interval of retardation.

In order that the effect may be the more perceptible, a number of pairs of points must be united into two parallel lines; and, if several such pairs of lines be placed near each other, they will facilitate the observation. If one of the lines be made to revolve round the other, as an axis, the depression below the given plane will be as the sine of the inclination; and while the eye and luminous object remain fixed, the difference of the lengths of the paths will vary as this sine.

The best subjects for the experiment are

Mr. Coventry's exquisite micrometers; such of them as consist of parallel lines drawn on glass, at the distance of one five hundreth of an inch, are the most convenient. Each of these lines appears under a microscope to consist of two or more finer lines, exactly parallel, and at the distance of somewhat more than a twentieth of that of the adjacent lines. I placed one of these so as to reflect the sun's light at an angle of 45°, and fixed it in such a manner, that while it revolved round one of the lines as an axis, I could measure its angular motion; and I found, that the brightest red colour occured at the inclinations $10\frac{1}{4}°$, $20\frac{1}{4}°$, $32°$, and $45°$; of which the sines are as the numbers 1, 2, 3, and 4. At all other angles also, when the sun's light was reflected from the surface, the colour vanished with the inclination, and was equal at equal inclinations on either side.

This experiment affords a very strong confirmation of the theory. It is impossible to deduce any explanation of it from any hypothesis hitherto advanced; and I believe it would be difficult to invent any other that would account for it. There is a striking analogy between this separation of colours, and the production of a musical note by successive echos from equidistant iron palisades; which I have found to correspond pretty accurately with the known velocity of sound, and the distances of the surfaces.

It is not improbable that the colours of the integuments of some insects, and of some other natural bodies, exhibiting in different lights the most beautiful versatility, may be found to be of this description, and not to be derived from thin plates. In some cases, a single scratch or furrow may produce similar effects, by the reflections of its opposite edges.

COROLLARY II. *Of the Colours of thin Plates.*

When a beam of light falls on two parallel refracting surfaces, the partial reflections coincide perfectly in direction; and, in this case, the interval of retardation, taken between the surfaces, is to their distance as twice the cosine of the angle of refraction to the radius. For, in Plate 14. Fig. 107, drawing AB and CD perpendicular to the rays, the times of passing through BC and AD will be equal, and DE will be half the interval of retardation; but DE is to CE as the sine of DCE to the radius. Hence, in order that DE may be constant, or that the same colour may be reflected, the thickness CE must vary as the secant of the angle of refraction CED: which agrees exactly with Newton's experiments; for the correction which he has introduced is perfectly inconsiderable.

Let the medium between the surfaces be rarer than the surrounding mediums; then the impulse reflected at the second surface, meeting a subsequent undulation at the first, will render the particles of the rarer medium capable of wholly stopping the motion of the denser, and destroying the reflection, (Prop. 4.) while they themselves will be more strongly propelled than if they had been at rest; and the transmitted light will be increased. So that the colours by reflection will be destroyed, and those by transmission rendered more vivid, when the double thicknesses, or intervals of retardation, are any multiples of the whole breadths of the undulations; and at intermediate thicknesses the effects will be reversed: according to the Newtonian observations.

If the same proportions be found to hold good with respect to thin plates of a denser medium, which is indeed not improbable, it will be necessary to adopt the corrected demonstration of Prop. 4. but, at any rate, if a thin plate be interposed between a rarer and a denser medium, the colours by reflection and transmission may be expected to change places.

From Newton's measures of the thicknesses reflecting the different colours, the breadth and duration of their respective undulations may be very accurately determined. The whole visible spectrum appears to be comprised within the ratio of three to five, which is that of a major sixth in music; and the undulations of red, yellow, and blue, to be related in magnitude as the numbers 8, 7, and 6; so that the interval from red to blue is a fourth. The absolute frequency expressed in numbers is too great to be distinctly conceived, but it may be better imagined by a comparison with sound. If a chord sounding the tenor $\bar{c}$, could be continually bisected 40 times, and should then vibrate, it would afford a yellow green light: this being denoted by c, the extreme red would be $\overset{40}{a}$, and the blue $\overset{41}{d}$. The absolute length and frequency of each vibration is expressed in the table: supposing light to travel in $8\frac{1}{8}$ minutes 500 000 000 000 feet.

Colours.	Length of an Undulation in parts of an Inch, in Air.	Number of Undulations in an Inch.	Number of Undulations in a Second.	
Extreme - -	.0000266	37640	463	millions of millions.
Red - - -	.0000256	39180	482	
Intermediate - -	.0000246	40720	501	
Orange - - -	.0000240	41610	512	
Intermediate - - -	.0000235	42510	523	
Yellow - - - -	.0000227	44000	542	
Intermediate - - -	.0000219	45600	561	($=2^{16}$ nearly)
Green - - -	.0000211	47460	584	
Intermediate - - -	.0000203	49320	607	
Blue - - -	.0000196	51110	629	
Intermediate - -	.0000189	52910	652	
Indigo - - -	.0000185	54070	665	
Intermediate -	.0000181	55240	680	
Violet - - -	.0000174	57490	707	
Extreme - -	.0000167	59750	735	
Mean of all, or White	.0000225	44440	547	

SCHOLIUM. It was not till I had satisfied myself respecting all these phenomena, that I found, in Hooke's Micrographia, a passage which might have led me earlier to a similar opinion. " It is most evident, that the reflection from the under or further side of the body, is the principal cause of the production of these colours.—Let the ray fall obliquely on the thin plate, part thereof is reflected back by the first superficies,—part refracted to the second surface,—whence it is reflected and refracted again.—So that, after two refractions and one reflection, there is propagated a kind of fainter ray—," and, " by reason of the time spent in passing and repassing,—this fainter pulse comes behind the" former reflected " pulse; so that hereby (the surfaces being so near together that the eye cannot discriminate them from one,) this confused or duplicated pulse, whose strongest part precedes, and whose weakest follows, does produce on the retina, the sensation of a yellow. If these surfaces are further removed asunder, the weaker pulse may become coincident with the" reflection of the " second," or next following pulse, from the first surface, " and lagg behind that also, and be coincident with the third, fourth, fifth, sixth, seventh, or eighth—; so that, if there be a thin transparent body, that from the greatest thinness requisite to produce colours, does by degrees grow to the greatest thickness,—the colours shall be so often repeated, as the weaker pulse does lose paces with its primary or first pulse, and is coincident with a" subsequent " pulse. And this, as it is coincident, or follows from the first hypothesis, I took of colours, so upon experiment have I found it in multitudes of instances that seem to prove it." (P. 65..67.) This was printed about seven years before any of Newton's experiments were made. We are informed by Newton, that Hooke was afterwards disposed to adopt his " suggestion" of the nature of colours; and yet it does not appear that Hooke ever applied that improvement to his explanation of these phenomena, or inquired into the necessary consequence of a change of obliquity, upon his original supposition, otherwise he could not but have discovered a striking coincidence with the measures laid down by Newton from experiment. All former attempts, to explain the colours of thin plates, have either proceeded on suppositions which, like Newton's, would lead us to expect the greatest irregularities in the direction of the refracted rays; or, like Mr. Michell's, would require such effects from the change of the angle of incidence, as are contrary to the effects observed; or they are equally deficient with respect to both these circumstances, and are inconsistent with the most moderate attention to the principal phenomena.

COROLLARY III. *Of the Colours of thick Plates.*

When a beam of light passes through a refracting surface, especially if imperfectly polished, a portion of it is irregularly scattered, and makes the surface visible in all directions, but most conspicuously in directions not far distant from that of the light itself: and, if a reflecting surface be placed parallel to the refracting surface, this scattered light, as well as the principal beam, will be reflected, and there will also be a new dissipation of light, at the return of the beam through the refracting surface. These two portions of scattered light will coincide in direction; and, if the surfaces be of such a form as to collect the similar effects, will exhibit rings of colours. The interval of retardation is, here, the difference between the paths of the principal beam and of the scattered light between the two surfaces; of course, wherever the inclination of the scattered light is equal to that of the beam, although in different planes, the interval will vanish, and all the undulations will conspire. At other inclinations, the interval will be the difference of the secants from the secant of the inclination or angle of refraction of the principal beam. From these causes, all the colours of concave mirrors, observed by Newton and others, are necessary consequences: and it appears that their production, though somewhat similar, is by no means, as Newton imagined, identical with the production of those of thin plates. It is indeed surprising, that it did not occur to so accurate a reasoner, that the colours of thin plates are always lost in white light, after ten or twelve alternations, while, in this case, they are supposed to be distinguishable after many thousands.

COROLLARY IV. *Of Colours by inflection.*
Whatever may be the cause of the inflection of light passing through a small aperture, the light nearest its centre must be the least diverted, and the nearest to its sides the most: another portion of light, falling very obliquely on the margin of the aperture, will be copiously reflected in various directions; some of which will either perfectly or very nearly coincide in direction with the unreflected light, and having taken a circuitous route, will so interfere with it, as to cause an appearance of colours. The length of the two tracks will differ the less, as the direction of the reflected light has been less changed by its reflection, that is, in the light passing nearest to the margin; so that the blues will appear in the light nearest the shadow. The effect will be increased and modified, when the reflected light falls within the influence of the opposite edge, so as to interfere with the light simply inflected by that also.

On the supposition that inflection is produced by the effect of an ethereal atmosphere, varying as a given power of the distance from a centre, I have constructed a diagram, (Plate 14. Fig. 108.) with the assistance of calculations similar to those by which the effect of atmospherical refraction is determined, showing, by the two pairs of curves, the relative position of the reflected and unreflected portions of any one undulation at two successive times, and also, by shaded lines drawn across, the parts where the intervals of retardation are in arithmetical progression, and where similar colours will be exhibited at different distances from the inflecting substance. The result agrees sufficiently with the observations of Newton's third book, and with those of later writers. But I do not consider the existence of such an atmosphere as necessary to the explanation of the phenomena; the simple opinion of Grimaldi and Hooke, who supposed that inflection arises from the natural tendency of light to diverge, appearing equally probable.

PROPOSITION IX. *Radiant Light consists in Undulations of the luminiferous Ether.*

This proposition is the general conclusion from all the preceding; and it is conceived that they conspire to prove it, in as satisfactory a manner, as can possibly be expected from the nature of the subject. It is clearly granted by Newton, that there are ethereal undulations, yet he denies that they constitute light; but it is shown in the Corollaries of the last Proposition, that all cases of the increase or diminution of light are referable to an increase or diminution of such undulations, and that all the affections, to which the undulations would be liable, are distinctly visible in the phenomena of light; it may therefore be very logically inferred, that the undulations are light.

A few detached remarks will serve to obviate some objections which may be raised against this theory.

1. Newton has advanced the singular refraction of the Iceland crystal, as an argument that the particles of light must be pro-

jected corpuscles; since he thinks it probable that the different sides of these particles are differently attracted by the crystal, and since Huygens has confessed his inability to account in a satisfactory manner for all the phenomena. But contrarily to what might have been expected from Newton's usual accuracy and candour, he has laid down a new law for the refraction, without giving a reason for rejecting that of Huygens, which Mr. Haüy has found to be more accurate than Newton's; and, without attempting to deduce from his own system any explanation of the more universal and striking effects of doubling spars, he has omitted to observe, that Huygens's most elegant and ingenious theory perfectly accords with these general effects, in all particulars, and of course derives from them additional pretensions to truth: this he omits, in order to point out a difficulty, for which only a verbal solution can be found in his own theory, and which will probably long remain unexplained by any other.

2. Mr. Michell has made some experiments, which appear to show that the rays of light have an actual momentum, by means of which, a motion is produced when they fall on a thin plate of copper delicately suspended. (Priestley's Optics.) But, taking for granted the exact perpendicularity of the plate, and the absence of any ascending current of air, yet since, in every such experiment, a greater quantity of heat must be communicated to the air, at the surface on which the light falls, than at the opposite surface, the excess of expansion must necessarily produce an excess of pressure on the first surface, and a very perceptible recession of the plate in the direction of the light. Mr. Bennet has repeated the experiment, with a much more sensible apparatus, and also in the absence of air; and very justly infers, from its total failure, an argument in favour of the undulatory system of light. (Phil. Trans. 1792. 87.) For, granting the utmost imaginable subtility of the corpuscles of light, their effects might naturally be expected to bear some proportion, to the effects of the much less rapid motions of the electrical fluid, which are so easily perceptible.

3. There are some phenomena of the light of solar phosphori, which at first sight might seem to favour the corpuscular system; for instance, its remaining many months as if in a latent state, and its subsequent reemission by the action of heat. But, on further consideration, there is no difficulty in supposing the particles of the phosphori, which have been made to vibrate by the action of light, to have this action abruptly suspended by the intervention of cold, whether as contracting the bulk of the substance or otherwise; and again, after the restraint is removed, to proceed in their motion, as a spring would do, which had been held fast for a time, in an intermediate stage of its vibration; nor is it impossible that heat itself may, in some circumstances, become in a similar manner latent. (Nicholson's Journal. II. 399.) But the affections of heat may, perhaps, hereafter be rendered more intelligible to us; at present, it seems highly probable, that light differs from heat only in the frequency of its undulations or vibrations; those undulations which are within certain limits, with respect to frequency, being capable of affecting the optic nerve, and constituting light; and those which are slower, and probably stronger, constituting heat

only; that light and heat occur to us, each in two predicaments, the vibratory or permanent, and the undulatory or transient state; vibratory light being the minute motion of ignited bodies, or of solar phosphori, and undulatory or radiant light, the motion of the ethereal medium excited by these vibrations; vibratory heat being a motion to which all material substances are liable, and which is more or less permanent; and undulatory heat that motion of the same ethereal medium, which has been shown by Hoffmann, Buffon, Mr. King, and M. Pictet, to be as capable of reflection as light, and by Dr. Herschel to be capable of separate refraction. (Phil. Trans. 1800. 284.) How much more readily heat is communicated by the free access of colder substances, than either by radiation or by transmission through a quiescent medium, has been shown by the valuable experiments of Count Rumford. It is easy to conceive that some substances, permeable to light, may be unfit for the transmission of heat, in the same manner as particular substances may transmit some kinds of light, while they are opaque with respect to others.

On the whole it appears, that the few optical phenomena which admit of explanation by the corpuscular system, are equally consistent with this theory; that many others, which have long been known, but never understood, become by these means perfectly intelligible; and that several new facts are found to be thus only reducible to a perfect analogy with other facts, and to the simple principles of the undulatory system. It is presumed, that henceforth the second and third books of Newton's Optics will be considered as more fully understood than the first has hitherto been; but, if it should appear to impartial judges, that additional evidence is wanting for the establishment of the theory, it will be easy to enter more minutely into the details of various experiments, and to show the insuperable difficulties attending the Newtonian doctrines, which, without necessity, it would be tedious and invidious to enumerate. The merits of their author, in natural philosophy, are great beyond all contest or comparison; his optical discovery of the composition of white light would alone have immortalised his name; and the very arguments, which tend to overthrow his system, give the strongest proofs of the admirable accuracy of his experiments.

Sufficient and decisive as these arguments appear, it cannot be superfluous to seek for further confirmation; which may with considerable confidence be expected, from an experiment very ingeniously suggested by Professor Robison, on the refraction of the light returning to us from the opposite margins of Saturn's ring; for, on the corpuscular theory, the ring must be considerably distorted when viewed through an achromatic prism: a similar distortion ought also to be observed in the disc of Jupiter; but, if it be found that an equal deviation is produced in the whole light reflected from these planets, there can scarcely be any remaining hope to explain the affections of light, by a comparison with the motions of projectiles.

PLATE 14.

Fig. 105. The progress of a series of undulations admitted through an aperture.

Fig. 106. The difference of the paths of the light reflected from two points situated near each other.

Fig. 107. The difference of the paths of the light reflected from the opposite surfaces of a thin plate.

Fig. 108. The paths of two portions of light supposed to pass through an inflecting atmosphere.

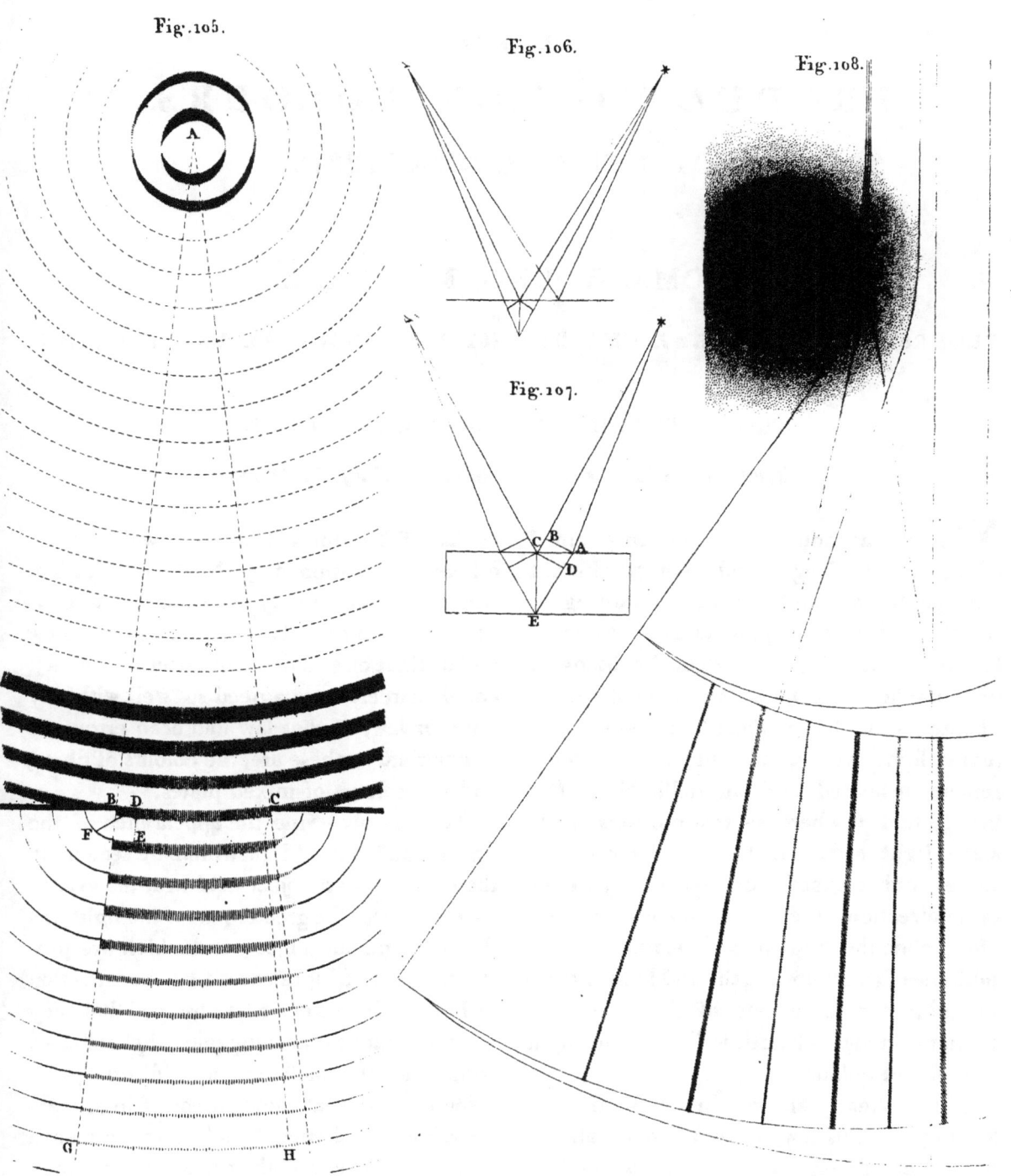

VIII. AN ACCOUNT OF SOME CASES

OF THE

PRODUCTION OF COLOURS,

NOT HITHERTO DESCRIBED.

BY

THOMAS YOUNG, M.D. F.R.S.

PROFESSOR OF NATURAL PHILOSOPHY IN THE ROYAL INSTITUTION.

FROM THE PHILOSOPHICAL TRANSACTIONS.

Read before the ROYAL SOCIETY, *July* 1, 1802.

WHATEVER opinion may be entertained of the theory of light and colours which I have lately had the honour of submitting to the Royal Society, it must at any rate be allowed, that it has given birth to the discovery of a simple and general law, capable of explaining a number of the phenomena of coloured light, which, without this law, would remain insulated and unintelligible. The law is, that " wherever two portions of the same light arrive at the eye by different routes, either exactly or very nearly in the same direction, the light becomes most intense when the difference of the routes is any multiple of a certain length, and least intense in the intermediate state of the interfering portions; and this length is different for light of different colours."

I have already shown, in detail, the sufficiency of this law, for explaining all the phenomena described in the second and third books of Newton's Optics, as well as some others not mentioned by Newton. But it is still more satisfactory to observe its conformity to other facts, which constitute new and distinct classes of phenomena, and which could scarcely have agreed so well with any anterior law, if that law had been erroneous or imaginary: these are, the colours of fibres, and the colours of mixed plates.

As I was observing the appearance of the fine parallel lines of light which are seen upon the margin of an object held near the eye, so as to intercept the greater part of the light of a distant luminous object, and which are produced by the fringes caused by the inflection of light already known, I observed that they were sometimes accompanied by coloured fringes, much broader and more distinct; and I soon found, that these broader fringes were occasioned by the accidental interposition of a hair. In order to make them more distinct,

I employed a horse hair; but they were then no longer visible. With a fibre of wool, on the contrary, they became very large and conspicuous: and, with a single silkworm's thread, their magnitude was so much increased, that two or three of them seemed to occupy the whole field of view. They appeared to extend on each side of the candle, in the same order as the colours of thin plates, seen by transmitted light. It occurred to me that their cause must be sought in the interference of two portions of light, one reflected from the fibre, the other bending round its opposite side, and at last coinciding nearly in direction with the former portion; that, accordingly as both portions deviated more from a rectilinear direction, the difference of the lengths of their paths would become gradually greater and greater, and would consequently produce the appearances of colour usual in such cases; that, supposing them to be inflected at right angles, the difference would amount nearly to the diameter of the fibre, and that this difference must consequently be smaller as the fibre became smaller; and, the number of fringes within the limits of a right angle becoming smaller, that their angular distances would consequently become greater, and the whole appearance would be dilated. It was easy to calculate, that, for the light least inflected, the difference of the paths would be to the diameter of the fibre, very nearly as the deviation of the ray, at any point, from the rectilinear direction, to its distance from the fibre.

I therefore made a rectangular hole in a card, and bent its ends so as to support a hair parallel to the sides of the hole: then, upon applying the eye near the hole, the hair of course appeared dilated by indistinct vision into a surface, of which the breadth was determined by the distance of the hair and the magnitude of the hole, independently of the temporary aperture of the pupil. When the hair approached so near to the direction of the margin of a candle that the inflected light was sufficiently copious to produce a sensible effect, the fringes began to appear; and it was easy to estimate the proportion of their breadth to the apparent breadth of the hair, across the image of which they extended. I found that six of the brightest red fringes, nearly at equal distances, occupied the whole of that image. The breadth of the aperture was $\frac{66}{1000}$, and its distance from the hair $\frac{8}{10}$, of an inch; the diameter of the hair was less than $\frac{1}{500}$ of an inch; as nearly as I could ascertain, it was $\frac{1}{600}$. Hence, we have $\frac{1}{1000}$ for the deviation of the first red fringe at the distance $\frac{8}{10}$; and, as $\frac{8}{10} : \frac{11}{1000} :: \frac{1}{600} : \frac{11}{480000}$, or $\frac{1}{43636}$ for the difference of the routes of the red light, where it was most intense. The measure deduced from Newton's experiments is $\frac{1}{39200}$. I thought this coincidence, with only an error of one ninth of so minute a quantity, sufficiently perfect to warrant completely the explanation of the phenomenon, and even to render a repetition of the experiment unnecessary; for there are several circumstances which make it difficult to calculate much more precisely what ought to be the result of the measurement.

When a number of fibres of the same kind, for instance, those of a uniform lock of wool, are held near to the eye, we see an appearance of halos surrounding a distant candle; but their brilliancy, and even their existence, depends on the uniformity of the dimensions of the fibres; and they are larger as the fibres are smaller. It is obvious that they are the immediate consequences of the coincidence of a number of fringes of the same size, which, as the fibres are arranged in all imaginable directions, must necessarily surround the luminous object at equal distances on all sides, and constitute circular fringes.

There can be little doubt that the coloured atmospherical halos are of the same kind; their appearance must depend on the existence of a number of particles of water, of equal dimensions, and in a proper position, with respect to the luminary and to the eye. As there is no natural limit to the magnitude of the spherules of water, we may expect these halos to vary without limit in their diameters; and, accordingly, Mr. Jordan has observed that their dimensions are exceedingly various, and has remarked that they frequently change during the time of observation. Mr. Jordan supposes that they depend on the joint effect of two neighbouring drops; but it has been shown that a uniformity of dimensions is necessary for their production, and no such uniformity can possibly exist in the distances of the drops from each other.

The lines, which are seen within the shadow of a hair, are produced nearly in the same manner as these colours of fibres, or rather they are the beginning of the series, derived from two portions of light inflected into the shadow, instead of one inflected and one reflected portion.

I first noticed the colours of mixed plates, in looking at a candle through two pieces of plate glass, with a little moisture between them. I observed an appearance of fringes resembling the common colours of thin plates; and, upon looking for the fringes by reflection, I found that these new fringes were always in the same direction as the other fringes, but many times larger. By examining the glasses with a magnifier, I perceived that wherever these fringes were visible, the moisture was intermixed with portions of air, producing an appearance similar to dew. I then supposed that the origin of the colours was the same as that of the colours of halos; but, on a more minute examination, I found that the magnitude of the portions of air and water was by no means uniform, and that the explanation was therefore inadmissible. It was, however, easy to find two portions of light sufficient for the production of these fringes; for, the light transmitted through the water, moving in it with a velocity different from that of the light passing through the interstices filled only with air, the two portions would interfere with each other, and produce effects of colour according to the general law. The ratio of the velocities, in water and in air, is that of 3 to 4; the fringes ought therefore to appear where the thickness is 6 times as great as that which corresponds to the same colour in the common case of thin plates; and, upon making the experiment with a plain glass and a lens slightly convex, I found the sixth dark circle actually of the same diameter as the first in the new fringes. The colours are also very easily produced, when butter or tallow is substituted for water; and the rings then become smaller, on account of the greater refractive density of the oils: but, when water is added, so as to fill up the interstices of the oil, the rings are very much enlarged; for here the difference only of the velocities in water and in oil is to be considered, and this is much smaller than the difference between air and water.

It appears to be necessary for the production of these colours, that the glasses be held nearly in a right line between the eye and the common termination of a dark and luminous object: the portion of the rings, seen on the dark ground, is then more distinct than the remaining portion; and, instead of being continuations of the rings, they exhibit every where opposite colours, so as to resemble the colours of common thin plates seen by reflection, and not by transmission.

In order to understand this circumstance, we must consider, that where a dark object (as A, Plate 15. Fig. 112.) is placed behind the glasses, the whole of the light, which comes to the eye, is either refracted through the edges of the drops, (as the rays B, C,) or reflected from the internal surface, (as D, E;) while the light, which passes through those parts of the glasses which are on the side opposite to the dark object, consists of rays refracted as before through the edges, (as F, G,) or simply passing through the fluid (as H, I.) The respective combinations of these portions of light exhibit series of colours in different orders, since the internal reflection modifies the interference of the rays on the side of the dark object, in the same manner as in the common colours of thin plates, seen by reflection. When no dark object is near, both these series of colours are produced at once; and since they are always of an opposite nature at any given thickness of a plate, they neutralise each other, and constitute white light.

In applying the general law of interference to these colours, as well as to those of thin plates already known, it is impossible to avoid a supposition, which is a part of the undulatory theory, that is, that the velocity of light is the greater, the rarer the medium; and there is also a condition annexed to this explanation of the colours of mixed plates, as as well as to that of the colours of simple thin plates, which involves another part of the same theory; that is, that where one of the portions of light has been reflected at the surface of a rarer medium, it must be supposed to be retarded one half of the appropriate interval; for instance, in the central black spot of a soap bubble, where the actual lengths of the paths very nearly coincide, but the effect is the same as if one of the portions had been so retarded as to destroy the other. From considering the nature of this circumstance, I ventured to predict, that if the two reflections were of the same kind, made at the surfaces of a thin plate, of a density intermediate between the densities of the mediums containing it, the effect would be reversed, and the central spot, instead of black, would become white; and I have now the pleasure of stating, that I have fully verified this conclusion, by interposing a drop of oil of sassafras between a prism of flint glass and a lens of crown glass: the central spot seen by reflected light was white, and surrounded by a dark ring. It was however necessary to use some force, in order to produce a contact sufficiently intimate; and the white spot differed, even at last, in the same degree from perfect whiteness, as the black spot usually does from perfect blackness. There are also some irregularities attending the phenomena exhibited in this manner by different refracting substances, especially when the reflection is total, which deserve further investigation.

The colours of mixed plates suggested to me an idea, which appears to lead to an explanation of the dispersion of colours by refraction, perhaps more simple and satisfactory than that which I advanced in the last Bakerian lecture. We may suppose that every refractive medium transmits the undulations constituting light in two separate portions, one passing through its ultimate particles, and the other through its pores: and that these portions reunite continually, after each successive separation, the one having preceded the other by a very minute but constant interval, depending on the regular arrangement of the particles of a homogeneous medium. Now, if these two portions were always equal, each point of the undulations, resulting from their reunion, would always be found half way between the places of the corresponding point in the separate portions; but, supposing the preceding portion to be the smaller, the newly combined undulation will be less advanced than if both had been equal, and the difference of its place will depend, not only on the difference of the lengths of the two routes, which will be constant for all the undulations, but also on the law and magnitude of those undulations; so that the larger undulations will be somewhat further advanced after each reunion than the smaller ones, and, the same operation recurring at every particle of the medium, the whole progress of the larger undulations will be more rapid than that of the smaller; hence the deviation, in consequence of the retardation of the motion of light in a denser medium, will of course be greater for the smaller than for the larger undulations. Assuming the law of the harmonic curve for the motions of the particles, we might without much difficulty reduce this conjecture to a comparison with experiment; but it would be necessary, in order to warrant our conclusions, to be provided with accurate measures of the refractive and dispersive powers of various substances, for rays of all descriptions.

Dr. Wollaston's very interesting observations would furnish very great assistance in this inquiry, when compared with the separation of colours by thin plates. I have repeated his experiments on the spectrum with perfect success, and have made some attempts to procure comparative measures from thin plates; and I have found that, as Sir Isaac Newton has already observed, the blue and violet light is more dispersed by refraction, than in proportion to the difference of the appropriate dimensions deduced from the phenomena of thin plates. Hence it happens, that when a line of the light, proceeding to form an image of the rings of colours of thin plates, is intercepted by a prism, and an actual picture is formed, resembling the scale delineated by Newton from theory, for estimating the colours of particles of given dimensions, the oblique spectrums, formed by the different colours of each series, are not straight, but curved, the lateral refraction of the prism separating the violet end more widely than the red. The thicknesses, corresponding to the extreme red, the line of yellow, bright green, bright blue, and extreme violet, I found to be inversely as the numbers 27, 30, 35, 40, and 45, respectively. In consequence of Dr. Wollaston's correction of the description of the prismatic spectrum, compared with these observations, it becomes necessary to modify the supposition that I advanced in the last Bakerian lecture, respecting the proportions of the sympathetic fibres of the retina; substituting red, green, and violet, for red, yellow, and blue, and the numbers 7, 6, and 5, for 8, 7, and 6.

The same prismatic analysis of the colours of thin plates appears to furnish a satisfactory explanation of the subdivision of the light of the lower part of a candle: for, in fact, the light, transmitted through every part of a thin plates is divided in a similar manner into distinct portions, increasing in number with the thickness of the plate, until they become too minute to be visible. At the thickness corresponding to the ninth or tenth portion of red light, the number of portions of different colours is five; and their proportions, as exhibited by refraction, are nearly the same as in the light of a candle, the violet being the broadest. We have only to suppose each particle of tallow to be, at its first evaporation, of such dimensions as to produce the same effect as the thin plate of air at this point, where it is about $\frac{1}{10000}$ of an inch in thickness, and to reflect, or perhaps rather to transmit, the mixed light produced by the incipient combustion around it, and we shall have a light completely resembling that which Dr. Wollaston has observed. There appears to be also a fine line of strong yellow light, separate from the general spectrum, principally derived from the most superficial combustion at the margin of the flame, and increasing in quantity as the flame ascends. This yellow light is rendered much more conspicuous by putting a few grains of salt on the wick of the candle, and it is, not improbably, always derived from some salt contained in the tallow. Similar circumstances might undoubtedly be found in other cases of the production or modification of light; and experiments upon this subject might tend greatly to establish the Newtonian opinion, that the colours of all natural bodies are similar in their origin to those of thin plates; an opinion which appears to do the highest honour to the sagacity of its author, and indeed to form a very considerable step in our advances towards an acquaintance with the intimate constitution and arrangement of material substances.

I have lately had an opportunity of confirming my former observations on the dispersive powers of the eye. I find that, at the respective distances of 10 and 15 inches, the extreme red and extreme violet rays are similarly refracted, the difference being expressed by a focal length of 30 inches. Now the interval between red and yellow is about one fourth of the whole spectrum; consequently, a focal length of 120 inches expresses a power equivalent to the dispersion of the red and yellow, and this differs but little from 132, which was the result of the observation already described. I do not know that these experiments are more accurate than the former one; but I have repeated them several times under different circumstances, and I have no doubt that the dispersion of coloured light in the human eye is nearly such as I have stated it. It may also be ascertained very accurately, by looking, through an aperture of known dimensions, at the image of a point dilated by a prism into a spectrum, and measuring the angle formed by its sides on account of the difference of refrangibility of the rays; and this method seems to indicate a greater dispersive power than the former.

IX. EXPERIMENTS AND CALCULATIONS

RELATIVE TO

PHYSICAL OPTICS.

BY

THOMAS YOUNG, M.D. F.R.S.

FROM THE PHILOSOPHICAL TRANSACTIONS.

Read before the Royal Society, November 24, 1803.

1. EXPERIMENTAL DEMONSTRATION OF THE GENERAL LAW OF THE INTERFERENCE OF LIGHT.

In making some experiments on the fringes of colours accompanying shadows, I have found so simple and so demonstrative a proof of the general law of the interference of two portions of light, which I have already endeavoured to establish, that I think it right to lay before the Royal Society a short statement of the facts, which appear to me to be thus decisive. The proposition, on which I mean to insist at present, is simply this, that fringes of colours are produced by the interference of two portions of light; and I think it will not be denied by the most prejudiced, that the assertion is proved by the experiments I am about to relate, which may be repeated with great ease, whenever the sun shines, and without any other apparatus than is at hand to every one.

Exper. 1. I made a small hole in a window shutter, and covered it with a piece of thick paper, which I perforated with a fine needle. For greater convenience of observation, I placed a small looking glass without the window shutter, in such a position as to reflect the sun's light, in a direction nearly horizontal, upon the opposite wall, and to cause the cone of diverging light to pass over a table, on which were several little screens of card paper. I brought into the sunbeam a slip of card, about one thirtieth of an inch in breadth, and observed its shadow, either on the wall, or on other cards held at different distances. Besides the fringes of colours on each side of the shadow, the shadow itself was divided by similar parallel fringes, of smaller dimensions, differing in number, according to the distance at which the shadow was observed, but leaving the middle of the shadow always white. Now these fringes were the joint effects of the portions of light passing on each side of the slip of card, and inflected, or rather diffracted, into the shadow. For, a little screen being placed either before the card, or a few inches behind it, so as either to throw the edge of its shadow on the margin of the card, or to receive on its own margin the extremity of the shadow of the card, all the fringes which had before been observed in the shadow on the wall immediately disappeared, although the light inflected on the other side was allowed to retain its course, and although this light must have undergone any modification that the proximity of the other edge of the slip of card might have been capable of occasioning. When the interposed screen was at a greater distance behind the narrow card, it was necessary to plunge it more deeply into the shadow, in order to extinguish the parallel lines; for here the light, diffracted from the edge of the object, had entered further into the shadow, in its way towards the fringes. Nor was it for want of a sufficient intensity of light, that one of the two portions was incapable of producing the fringes alone; for, when they were both uninterrupted, the lines appeared, even if the intensity was reduced to one tenth or one twentieth.

Exper. 2. The crested fringes, described by the ingenious and accurate Grimaldi, afford an elegant variation of the preceding experiment, and an interesting example of a calculation grounded on it. When a shadow is formed by an object which has a rectangular termination, besides the usual external fringes, there are two or three alternations of colours, beginning from the line which bisects the angle, disposed on each side of it, in curves, which are convex towards the bisecting line, and which converge in some degree towards it, as they become more remote from the angular point. These fringes are also the joint effect of the light which is inflected directly towards the shadow, from each of the two outlines of the object. For, if a screen be placed within a few inches of the object, so as to receive only one of the edges of the shadow, the whole of the fringes will disappear. If, on the contrary, the rectangular point of the screen be opposed to the point of the shadow, so as barely to receive the angle of the shadow on its extremity, the fringes will remain undisturbed.

II. COMPARISON OF MEASURES, DEDUCED FROM VARIOUS EXPERIMENTS.

If we now proceed to examine the dimensions of the fringes, under different circumstances, we may calculate the differences of the lengths of the paths described by the portions of light, which have thus been proved to be concerned in producing those fringes; and we shall find, that where the lengths are equal, the light always remains white; but that, where either the brightest light, or the light of any given colour, disappears and reappears, a first, a second, or a third time, the differences of the lengths of the paths of the two portions are in arithmetical progression, as nearly as we can expect experiments of this kind to agree with each other. I shall compare, in this point of view, the measures deduced from several experiments of Newton, and from some of my own.

In the eighth and ninth observations of the third book of Newton's Optics, some experiments are related, which, together with the third observation, will furnish us with the data necessary for the calculation. Two knives were placed, with their edges meeting at a very acute angle, in a beam of the sun's light, admitted through a small aperture; and the point of concourse of the two first dark lines, bordering the shadows of the respective knives, was observed at various distances. The results of six observations are expressed in the first three lines of the first Table. On the supposition that the dark line is produced by the first interference of the light reflected from the edges of the knives, with the light passing in a straight line between them, we may assign, by calculating the difference of the two paths, the interval for the first disappearance of the brightest light, as it is expressed in the fourth line. The second Table contains the results of a similar calculation, from Newton's observations on the shadow of a hair; and the third, from some experiments of my own, of the same nature; the second bright line being supposed to correspond to a double interval, the second dark line to a triple interval, and the succeeding lines to depend on a continuation of the progression. The unit of all the Tables is an inch.

TABLE I. *Obs.* 9. N.

Distance of the knives from the aperture						101.
Distances of the paper from the knives	$1\frac{1}{2}$,	$3\frac{1}{3}$,	$8\frac{3}{5}$,	32,	96,	131.
Distances between the edges of the knives, opposite to the point of concourse	.012,	.020,	.034,	.057,	.081,	.087.
Interval of disappearance	.0000122,	.0000155,	.0000182,	.0000167,	.0000166,	.0000166.

TABLE II. *Obs.* 3. N.

Breadth of the hair		$\frac{1}{280}$
Distance of the hair from the aperture		144
Distances of the scale from the aperture	150,	252.
(Breadths of the shadow	$\frac{1}{54}$,	$\frac{1}{9}$.)
Breadth between the second pair of bright lines	$\frac{2}{47}$.	$\frac{4}{47}$.
Interval of disappearance, or half the difference of the paths	.0000151,	.0000173.
Breadth between the third pair of bright lines	$\frac{4}{73}$,	$\frac{3}{16}$.
Interval of disappearance, $\frac{1}{4}$ of the difference	.0000130,	.0000143.

TABLE III. *Exper.* 3.

Breadth of the object	.434.
Distance of the object from the aperture	125.
Distance of the wall from the aperture	250.
Distance of the second pair of dark lines from each other	1.167.
Interval of disappearance, $\frac{1}{3}$ of the difference	.0000149.

Exper. 4.

Breadth of the wire	.083.
Distance of the wire from the aperture	32.
Distance of the wall from the aperture	250.
(Breadth of the shadow, by three measurements	.815, 826, or .827; mean, .823.)
Distance of the first pair of dark lines	1.165, 1.170, or 1.160; mean, 1.165.
Interval of disappearance	.0000194.
Distance of the second pair of dark lines	1.402, 1.395, or 1.400; mean, 1.399.
Interval of disappearance	.0000137.
Distance of the third pair of dark lines	1.594, 1.580, or 1.585; mean, 1.586.
Interval of disappearance	.0000128.

It appears, from five of the six observations of the first Table, in which the distance of the shadow was varied from about 3 inches to 11 feet, and the breadth of the fringes was increased in the ratio of 7 to 1, that the difference of the routes, constituting the interval of disappearance, varied but one eleventh at most; and that, in three out of the five, it agreed with the mean, either exactly, or within $\frac{1}{180}$ part. Hence we are warranted in inferring, that the interval, appropriate to the extinction of the brightest light, is either accurately or very nearly constant.

But it may be inferred, from a comparison of all the other observations, that when the obliquity of the reflection is very great, some circumstance takes place, which causes the interval thus calculated to be somewhat greater: thus, in the eleventh line of the third Table, it comes out one sixth greater than the mean of the five already mentioned. On the other hand, the mean of two of Newton's experiments and one of mine, is a result about one fourth less than the former. With respect to the nature of this circumstance, I cannot at present form a decided opinion; but I conjecture that it is a deviation of some of the light concerned, from the rectilinear direction assigned to it, arising either from its natural diffraction, by which the magnitude of the shadow is also enlarged, or from some other unknown cause. If we imagined the shadow of the wire, and the fringes nearest it, to be so contracted, that the motion of the light bounding the shadow might be rectilinear, we should thus make a sufficient compensation for this deviation; but it is difficult to point out what precise track of the light would cause it to require this correction.

The mean of the three experiments, which appear to have been least affected by this unknown deviation, gives .0000127 for the interval appropriate to the disappearance of the brightest light; and it may be inferred, that if they had been wholly exempted from its effects, the measure would have been somewhat smaller. Now the analogous interval, deduced from the experiments of Newton on thin plates, is .0000112, which is about one eighth less than the former result; and this appears to be a coincidence fully sufficient to authorise us to attribute these two classes of phenomena to the same cause. It is very easily shown, with respect to the colours of thin plates, that each kind of light disappears and reappears, where the difference of the routes of two of its portions are in arithmetical progression; and we have seen, that the same law may be in general inferred from the phenomena of diffracted light, even independently of the analogy.

The distribution of the colours is also so similar in both cases, as to point immediately to a similarity in the causes. In the thirteenth observation of the second part of the first book, Newton relates, that the interval of the glasses where the rings appeared in red light, was to the interval where they appeared in violet light, as 14 to 9; and, in the eleventh observation of the third book, that the distances between the fringes, under the same circumstances, were the 22d and 27th of an inch. Hence, deducting the breadth of the hair, and taking the squares, in order to find the relation of the difference of the routes, we have the proportion of 14 to $9\frac{1}{7}$, which scarcely differs from the proportion observed in the colours of the thin plate.

We may readily determine, from this general principle, the form of the crested fringes of Grimaldi, already described; for it will appear that, under the circumstances of the experiment related, the points in which the differences of the lengths of the paths described by the two portions of light are equal to a constant quantity, and in which, therefore, the same kinds of light ought to appear or disappear, are always found in equilateral hyperbolas, of which the axes coincide with the outlines of the shadow, and the asymptotes nearly with the diagonal line. Such, therefore, must be the direction of the fringes; and this conclusion agrees perfectly with the observation. But it must be remarked, that the parts near the outlines of the shadow are so much shaded off, as to render the character of the curve somewhat less decidedly marked where it approaches to its axis. These fringes have a slight resemblance to the hyperbolic fringes observed by Newton; but the analogy is only distant.

III. APPLICATION TO THE SUPERNUMERARY RAINBOWS.

The repetitions of colours, sometimes observed within the common rainbow, and described in the Philosophical Transactions, by Dr. Langwith and Mr. Daval, admit also a very easy and complete explanation from the same principles. Dr. Pemberton has attempted to point out an analogy between these colours and those of thin plates; but the irregular reflection from the posterior surface of the drop, to which alone he attributes the appearance, must be far too weak to produce any visible effects. In order to understand the phenomenon, we have only to attend to the two portions of light which are exhibited in the common diagrams explanatory of the rainbow, regularly reflected from the posterior surface of the drop, and crossing each other in various directions, till, at the angle of the greatest deviation, they coincide with each other, so as to produce, by the greater intensity of this redoubled light, the common rainbow of 41 degrees. Other parts of these two portions will quit the drop in directions parallel to each other; and these would exhibit a continued diffusion of fainter light, for 25° within the bright termination which forms the rainbow, but for the general law of interference, which, as in other similar cases, divides the light into concentric rings; the magnitude of these rings depending on that of the drop, according to the difference of time occupied in the passage of the two portions, which thus proceed in parallel directions to the spectator's eye, after having been differently refracted and reflected within the drop. This difference varies at first, nearly as the square of the angular distance from the primitive rainbow: and, if the first additional red be at the distance of 2° from the red of the rainbow, so as to interfere a little with the primitive violet, the fourth additional red will be at the distance of nearly 2° more; and the intermediate colours will occupy a space nearly equal to the original rainbow. In order to produce this effect, the drops must be about $\frac{1}{75}$ of an inch, or .013, in diameter: it would be sufficient if they were between $\frac{1}{70}$ and $\frac{1}{80}$. The reason, that such supernumerary colours are not often seen, must be, that it does not often happen that drops so nearly equal are found together: but, that this may sometimes happen, is not in itself at all improbable: we measure even medicines by dropping them from a phial, and it may easily be conceived that the drops, formed by natural operations, may sometimes be as uniform, as any that can be produced by art. How accurately this theory coincides with the observation, may best be determined from Dr. Langwith's own words.

"August the 21st, 1722, about half an hour past five in the evening, weather temperate, wind at north east, the appearance was as follows. The colours of the primary rainbow were as usual, only the purple very much inclining to red, and well defined: under this was an arch of green, the upper part of which inclined to a bright yellow, the lower to a more dusky green: under this were alternately two arches of reddish purple, and two of green: under all, a faint appearance of another arch of purple, which vanished and returned several times so quick, that we could not readily fix our eyes upon it. Thus the order of the colours was, I. Red, orange colour, yellow, green, light blue, deep blue, purple. II. Light green, dark green, purple. III. Green, purple. IV. Green, faint vanishing purple. You see we had here four orders of colours, and perhaps the beginning of a fifth: for I make no question but that what I call the purple, is a mixture of the purple of each of the upper series with the red of the next below it, and the green a mixture of the intermediate colours. I send you not this account barely upon the credit of my own eyes; for there was a clergyman and four other gentlemen in company, whom I desired to view the colours attentively, who all agreed, that they appeared in the manner that I have now described. There are two things which well deserve to be taken notice of, as they may perhaps direct us, in some measure, to the solution of this curious phenomenon. The first is, that the breadth of the first series so far exceeded that of any of the rest, that, as near as I could judge, it was equal to them all taken together. The second is, that I have never observed these inner orders of colours in the lower parts of the rainbow, though they have often been incomparably more vivid than the upper parts, under which the colours have appeared. I have taken notice of this so very often, that I can hardly look upon it to be accidental; and, if it should prove true in general, it will bring the disquisition into a narrow compass; for it will show that this effect depends upon some property which the drops retain, whilst they are in the upper part of the air, but lose as they come lower, and are more mixed with one another." Phil. Trans. XXXII. 243.

From a consideration of the nature of the secondary rainbow, of 54°, it may be inferred, that if any such supernumerary colours were seen attending this rainbow, they would necessarily be external to it, instead of internal: and Mr. Dicquemare has actually recorded an observation of this kind. The circles, sometimes seen encompassing the observer's shadow in a mist, are perhaps more nearly related to the common colours of thin plates as seen by reflection.

IV. ARGUMENTATIVE INFERENCE RESPECTING THE NATURE OF LIGHT.

The experiment of Grimaldi, on the crested fringes within the shadow, together with several others of his observations, equally important, has been left unnoticed by Newton. Those who are attached to the Newtonian theory of light, or to the hypotheses of modern opticians, founded on views still less enlarged, would do well to endeavour to imagine any thing like an explanation of these experiments, derived from their own doctrines; and, if they fail in the attempt, to refrain at least from idle declamation against a system, which is founded on the accuracy of its application to all these facts, and to a thousand others of a similar nature.

From the experiments and calculations which have been premised, we may be allowed to infer, that homogeneous light, at certain equal distances in the direction of its motion, is possessed of opposite qualities, capable of neutralising or destroying each other, and of extinguishing the light, where they happen to be united; that these qualities succeed each other alternately in successive concentric superficies, at distances which are constant for the same light, passing through the same medium. From the agreement of the measures, and from the similarity of the phenomena, we may conclude, that these intervals are the same as are concerned in the production of the colours of thin plates; but these are shown, by the experiments of Newton, to be the smaller, the denser the medium; and, since it may be presumed, from the impossibility of imagining any way in which their number can be changed, that it must necessarily remain unaltered in a given quantity of light, it follows of course, that light moves more slowly in a denser, than in a rarer medium: and this being granted, it must be allowed, that refraction is not the effect of an attractive force directed to a denser medium. The advocates for the projectile hypothesis of light must consider, which link in this chain of reasoning they may judge to be the most feeble; for, hitherto, I have advanced in this paper no general hypothesis whatever. But, since we know that sound diverges in concentric superficies, and that musical sounds consist of opposite qualities, capable of neutralising each other, and succeeding at certain equal intervals, which are different according to the difference of the note, we are fully authorised to conclude, that there must be some strong resemblance between the nature of sound and that of light.

I have not, in the course of these investigations, found any reason to suppose the presence of such an inflecting medium, in the neighbourhood of dense substances, as I was formerly inclined to attribute to them; and, upon considering the phenomena of the aberation of the stars, I am disposed to believe, that the luminiferous ether pervades the substance of all material bodies with little or no resistance, as freely perhaps as the wind passes through a grove of trees.

The observations on the effects of diffraction and interference may perhaps sometimes be applied to a practical purpose, in making us cautious in our conclusions respecting the appearances of minute bodies viewed in a microscope. The shadow of a fibre, however opaque, placed in a pencil of light, admitted through a small aperture, is always somewhat less dark in the middle of its breadth than in the parts on each side. A similar effect may also take place, in some degree, with respect to the image on the retina, and impress the sense with an idea of a transparency which has no real existence: and, if a small portion of light be really transmitted through the substance, this may again be destroyed by its interference with the diffracted light, and produce an appearance of partial opacity, instead of uniform semitransparency. Thus, a central dark spot, and a light spot, surrounded by a darker circle, may respectively be produced in the images of a semitransparent and an opaque corpuscle, and impress us with an idea of a complication of structure which does not exist. In order to detect the fallacy, we may make two or three fibres cross each other, and view a number of globules contiguous to each other; or we may obtain a still more effectual remedy, by changing the magnifying power; and then, if the appearance remain constant in kind and in degree, we may be assured that it truly represents the nature of the substance to be examined. It is natural to inquire whether or no the figures of the globules of blood, delineated by Mr. Hewson in the Philosophical Transactions (LXIII, for 1773,) might not in some measure have been influenced by a deception of this kind. As far as I have hitherto been able to examine the globules, with a lens of one fiftieth of an inch focus, I have found them nearly such as Mr. Hewson has described them: Mr. Cavallo has, however, published, in his essay on factitious airs, some observations which strongly confirm the suspicion of an optical fallacy, and which agree precisely with the theory here advanced.

V. REMARKS ON THE COLOURS OF NATURAL BODIES.

Exper. 5. I have already adduced, in illustration of Newton's comparison of the colours of natural bodies with those of thin plates, Dr. Wollaston's observations on the blue light of the lower part of a candle, which appears, when viewed through a prism, to be divided into five portions. I have lately observed a similar instance, still more strongly marked, in the light transmitted by the blue glass sold by the opticians. This light is separated by the prism into seven distinct portions, nearly equal in magnitude, but somewhat broader, and less accurately defined, towards the violet end of the spectrum. The first two are red, the third is yellowish green, the fourth green, the fifth blue, the sixth bluish violet, and the seventh violet. This division agrees very nearly with that of the light reflected by a plate of air $\frac{1}{6840}$ of an inch in thickness, corresponding to the 11th series of red, and the 18th of violet. A similar plate of a metallic oxid would perhaps be about $\frac{1}{15000}$ of an inch in thickness. But it must be confessed, that there are strong reasons for believing the colouring particles of natural bodies in general to be incomparably smaller than this; and it is probable that the analogy, suggested by Newton, is somewhat less close than he imagined. The light reflected by a plate of air, at any thickness nearly corresponding to the 11th red, appears to the eye to be very nearly white; but, under favourable circumstances, the 11th red and the neighbouring colours may still be distinguished. The light of some kinds of coloured glass is pure red; that of others, red with a little green: some intercept all the light, except the extreme red and the blue. In the blue light of a candle, expanded by the prism, the portions of each colour appear to be narrower, and the intervening dark spaces wider, than in the analogous spectrum derived from the light reflected from a thin plate. Perhaps their origin may have some resemblance to that of the different harmonics of a single vibrating substance. The light of burning alcohol appears to be green and violet only. The pink dye sold in the shops, which is a preparation of the carthamus, affords a good specimen of a yellow green light regularly reflected, and a crimson probably produced by transmission.

VI. EXPERIMENT ON THE DARK RAYS OF RITTER.

Exper. 6. The existence of solar rays accompanying light, more refrangible than the violet rays, and cognisable by their chemical effects, was first ascertained by Mr. Ritter: but Dr. Wollaston made the same experiments a very short time afterwards, without having been informed of what had been done on the Continent. These rays appear to extend beyond the violet rays of the prismatic spectrum, through a space nearly equal to that which is occupied by the violet. In order to complete the comparison of their properties with those of visible light, I was desirous of examining the effect of their reflection from a thin plate of air, capable of producing the well known rings of colours. For this purpose, I formed an image of the rings, by means of the solar microscope, with the apparatus which I have described in the Journals of the Royal Institution, and I threw this image on paper dipped in a solution of nitrate of silver, placed at the distance of about nine inches from the microscope. In the course of an hour, portions of three dark rings were very distinctly visible, much smaller than the brightest rings of the coloured image, and coinciding very nearly, in their dimensions, with the rings of violet light that appeared upon the interposition of violet glass. I thought the dark rings were a little smaller than the violet rings, but the difference was not sufficiently great to be accurately ascertained; it might be as much as $\frac{1}{30}$ or $\frac{1}{40}$ of the diameters, but not greater. It is the less surprising that the difference should be so small, as the dimensions of the coloured rings do not by any means vary at the violet end of the spectrum, so rapidly as at the red end. For performing this experiment with very great accuracy, a heliostate would be necessary, since the motion of the sun causes a slight change in the place of the image; and leather, impregnated with the muriate of silver, would indicate the effect with greater delicacy. The experiment, however, in its present state, is sufficient to complete the analogy of the invisible with the visible rays, and to show that they are equally liable to the general law, which is the principal subject of this paper. If we had thermometers sufficiently delicate, it is probable that we might acquire, by similar means, information still more interesting, with respect to the rays of invisible heat discovered by Dr. Herschel; but at present there is great reason to doubt of the practicability of such an experiment.

X. AN ESSAY ON THE COHESION OF FLUIDS.

BY THOMAS YOUNG, M. D. FOR. SEC. R. S.

Read December 20, 1804.

I. GENERAL PRINCIPLES.

It has already been asserted, by Mr. Monge and others, that the phenomena of capillary tubes are referable to the cohesive attraction of the superficial particles only of the fluids employed; and that the surfaces must consequently be formed into curves of the nature of lintleariae, which are supposed to be the results of a uniform tension of a surface, resisting the pressure of a fluid, either uniform, or varying according to a given law. Segner, who appears to have been the first that maintained a similar opinion, has shown in what manner the principle may be deduced from the doctrine of attraction, but his demonstration is complicated, and not perfectly satisfactory; and in applying the law to the forms of drops, he has neglected to consider the very material effects of the double curvature, which is evidently the cause of the want of a perfect coincidence of some of his experiments with his theory. Since the time of Segner, little has been done in investigating accurately and in detail the various consequences of the principle.

It will perhaps be most agreeable to the experimental philosopher, although less consistent with the strict course of logical argument, to proceed in the first place to the comparison of this theory with the phenomena, and to inquire afterwards for its foundation in the ultimate properties of matter. But it is necessary to premise one observation, which appears to be new, and which is equally consistent with theory and with experiment; that is, that for each combination of a solid and a fluid, there is an appropriate angle of contact, between the surfaces of the fluid, exposed to the air, and to the solid. This angle, for glass and water, and in all cases where a solid is perfectly wetted by a fluid, is evanescent: for glass and mercury, it is about 140°, in common temperatures, and when the mercury is moderately clean.

II. FORM OF THE SURFACE OF A FLUID.

It is well known, and it results immediately from the composition of forces, that where a line is equably distended, the force that it exerts, in a direction perpendicular to its own, is directly as its curvature; and the same is true of a surface of simple curvature; but where the curvature is double, each curvature has its appropriate effect, and the joint force must be as the sum of the curvatures in any two perpendicular directions. For this sum is equal, whatever pair of perpendicular directions may be employed, as is easily shown by calculating the versed sines of two equal arcs taken at right angles in the surface. Now when the surface of a fluid is convex externally, its tension is produced by the pressure of the particles of the fluid within it, arising from their own weight, or from that of the surrounding fluid; but when the surface is concave, the tension is employed in counteracting the pressure of the atmosphere, or where the atmosphere is excluded, the equivalent pressure arising from the weight of the particles suspended from it by means of their cohesion, in the same manner as, when water is supported by the atmospheric pressure in an inverted vessel, the outside of the vessel sustains a hydrostatic pressure proportionate to the height; and this pressure must remain unaltered, when the water, having been sufficiently boiled, is made to retain its situation for a certain time by its cohesion only, in an exhausted receiver. When, therefore, the surface of the fluid is terminated by two right lines, and has only a simple curvature, the curvature must be every where as the ordinate; and where it has a double curvature, the sum of the curvatures in the different directions must be as the ordinate. In the first case, the curve may be constructed by approximation, if we set out from a point at which it is either horizontal or vertical, and divide the height into a number of small portions, and taking the radius of each proportional to the reciprocal of the height of its middle point, above or below the general surface of the fluid, go on to add portions of circles joining each other, until they have completed as much of the curve as is required. In the second case, it is only necessary to consider the curve derived from a circular basis, which is a solid of revolution; and the centre of that circle of curvature, which is perpendicular to the section formed by a plane passing through the axis, is in the axis itself, consequently in the point where the normal of the curve intersects the axis: we must therefore here make the sum of this curvature, and that of the generating curve, always proportional to the ordinate. This may be done mechanically, by beginning at the vertex, where the two curvatures are equal, then for each succeeding portion, finding the radius of curvature, by deducting the proper reciprocal of the normal, at the beginning of the portion, from the ordinate, and taking the reciprocal of the remainder. In this case the analysis leads to fluxional equations of the second order, which appear to afford no solution by means hitherto discovered; but the cases of simple curvature may be more easily subjected to calculation: the curvature varying always as the ordinate, the curve belongs to the general description of an elastic curve.

III. ANALYSIS OF THE SIMPLEST FORMS.

Let the greatest ordinate of the curve (AB, Plate 15. Fig. 113.) be called a, the arc of the circle of curvature at the vertex (AC) z, and let us suppose, that while this circle is uniformly increased, the curve (AD) flows with an equal angular velocity, then the fluxion of the curve, being directly as the radius of curvature, will be inversely as the ordinate y, and will be expressed by $\frac{a\dot{z}}{y}$; the fluxion of the absciss will therefore be $\frac{ta\dot{z}}{ry}$, t being the cosine of the arc z, and r the radius, and the fluxion of the area will be $\frac{ta\dot{z}}{r}$. But $\frac{t\dot{z}}{r}$ is the fluxion of the sine s of the arc z in the circle to which it belongs; consequently, *the area is expressed by as, and is equal to the rectangle contained by the initial ordinate, and the sine corresponding to each point of the curve in the initial circle of curvature.* Hence it follows, that *the whole area* (ABEF or EF GH) *included by the ordinates where the curve is vertical and where it is horizontal, is equal to the rectangle contained by the ordinate and the radius of curvature.*

In order to find the ordinate y, corresponding to a given angular direction, and to a given arc z, we have $\mp \dot{y} = \frac{sa\dot{z}}{ry}$, or, since $\frac{s\dot{z}}{r}$ is the fluxion of the versed sine v, $\mp \dot{y} = \frac{a\dot{v}}{y}$, and $\mp y\dot{y} = a\dot{v}$, whence $yy = b \mp 2av$. But at the summit of the curve, when $v = 0$, $y = a$, therefore $b = aa$, and $yy = aa - 2av$; and where the curve meets the absciss, $y = 0$ and $a = 2v$. If $a = 4r$, when $y = 0$, v will be $2r$, and the curve will touch the horizontal line at an infinite distance, since its curvature must be infinitely small; if a be greater than $4r$, the least ordinate will be $\sqrt{(aa - 4ar)}$. When the curve is vertical, $v = r$, and $yy = aa - 2ar$. The rectangle, contained by the elevation above the general surface, and the diameter of the circle of curvature, which is here $2ar$, is constant in all circumstances for the same fluid, and may therefore be called the appropriate rectangle of the fluid; and when the curve is infinite, and $a = 4ar$, this rectangle is equal to $8rr$, or to $\frac{1}{2}aa$, so that r and a may be readily found from it: it is also equal to the square of the ordinate at the vertical point, where $yy = aa - 2ar$. If we describe a circle (ABCD Plate 15. Fig. 114.) of which the diameter is a, the chord of the arc of this circle (AC, AB,) corresponding in angular situation to the curve, will be equal to the ordinate (EF, GH,) at the respective point; for the versed sine in this circle will be $2v$, and the chord will be a mean proportional between a and $a - 2v$; in this case therefore, where the curve is infinite, the ordinate varies as the sine of half the angle of elevation.

For determining the absciss, it would be necessary to employ an infinite series; and the most convenient would perhaps be that which is given by Euler for the elastic curve, in the second part of the third volume of the Acta Petropolitana.

IV. APPLICATION TO THE ELEVATION OF PARTICULAR FLUIDS.

The simplest phenomena, which afford us data for determining the fundamental properties of the superficial cohesion of fluids, are their elevation and depression between plates and in capillary tubes, and their adhesion to the surfaces of solids, which are raised, in a horizontal situation, to a certain height above the general surface of the fluids. When the distance of a pair of plates, or the diameter of a tube, is very minute, the curvature may be considered as uniform, and the appropriate rectangle may readily be deduced from the elevation, recollecting that the curvature in a capillary tube is double, and the height therefore twice as great as between two plates. In the case of the elevation of a fluid in contact with a horizontal surface, the ordinate may be determined from the weight required to produce a separation; and the appropriate rectangle may be found in this manner also, the angle of contact being properly considered, in this as well as in the former case. It will appear that these experiments by no means exhibit an immediate measure of the mutual attraction of the solid and fluid, as some authors have supposed.

Sir Isaac Newton asserts, in his Queries, that water ascends between two plates of glass at the distance of one hundredth of an inch, to the height of about one inch; the product of the distance and the height being about .01; but this appears to be much too little. In the best experiment of Musschenbroek, with a tube, half of the product was .0196; in several of Weitbrecht, apparently very accurate, .0214. In Monge's experiments on plates, the product was 2.6 or 2.7 lines, or about .0210. Mr. Atwood says, that for tubes, the product is .0530, half of which is .0265. Until more accurate experiments shall have been made, we may be contented to assume .02 for the rectangle appropriate to water, and .04 for the product of the height in a tube by its bore. Hence, when the curve becomes infinite, its greatest ordinate is .2, and the height of the vertical portion, or the height of ascent against a single vertical plane, .14, or nearly one seventh of an inch.

Now when the horizontal surface of a solid is raised from a vessel of water, the surface of the water is formed into a lintearia, to which the solid is a tangent at its highest point, and if the solid be still further raised, the water will separate: the surface of the water, being horizontal at the point of contact, cannot add to the weight tending to depress the solid, which is therefore simply the hydrostatic pressure of a column of water equal in height to the elevation, in this case one fifth of an inch, and standing on the given surface. The weight of such a column will be $50\frac{1}{4}$ grains for each square inch; and in Taylor's well known experiment, the weight required was 50 grains. But, when the solid employed is small, the curvature of the horizontal section of the water, which is convex externally, will tend to counteract the vertical curvature, and to diminish the height of separation; thus, if a disc of an inch in diameter were employed, the curvature in this direction would perhaps be equivalent to the pressure of about one hundredth of an inch, and might reduce the height from .2 to about .19, and the weight in the same proportion. There is, however, as great a diversity in the results of different experiments on the force required to elevate a solid from the surface of a fluid, as in those of the experiments on capillary tubes; and indeed the sources of error appear to be here more numerous. Mr. Achard found that a disc of glass, $1\frac{1}{2}$ inch French in diameter, required, at 69° Fahrenheit, a weight of 91 French grains to raise it from the surface of water; this is only 37 English grains for each square inch; at $44\frac{1}{2}°$ the force was $\frac{1}{14}$ greater, or $39\frac{1}{2}$ grains; the difference being $\frac{1}{343}$ for each degree of Fahrenheit. It might be inferred, from these experiments, that the height of ascent in a tube of a given bore, which varies in the duplicate ratio of the height of adhesion, is diminished about $\frac{1}{180}$ for every degree of Fahrenheit that the temperature is raised above 50°; there was, however, probably some considerable source of error in Achard's experiments, for I find that this diminution does not exceed $\frac{1}{1000}$. The experiments of Mr. Dutour make the quantity of water raised equal to 44.1 grains for each square inch. Mr. Achard found the force of adhesion of sulfuric acid to glass, at 69° of Fahrenheit, 1.26, that of water being 1, hence the height was as .69 to 1, and its square as .47 to 1, which is the corresponding proportion for the ascent of the acid in a capillary tube, and which does not very materially differ from the proportion of .395 to 1, assigned by Barruel for this ascent. Musschenbroek found it .8 to 1, but his acid was probably weak. For alcohol the adhesion was as .593, the height as .715, and its square as .510: the observed proportion in a tube, according to an experiment of Musschenbroek, was about .550, according to Carré from .400 to .440. The experiments on sulfuric ether do not agree quite so well, but its quality is liable to very considerable variations. Dutour found the adhesion of alcohol .58, that of water being 1.

With respect to mercury, it has been shown by Professor Casbois of Metz, and by others, that its depression in tubes of glass depends on the imperfection of the contact, and that when it has been boiled in the tube often enough to expel all foreign particles, the surface may even become concave instead of convex, and the depression be converted into an elevation. Perhaps this change may be the effect of the commencement of a chemical action between the mercury and the component parts of the glass; but in barometers constructed according to the usual methods, the angle of the mercury will be found to differ little from 140°: and in other experiments, when proper precautions are taken, the inclination will be nearly the same. The determination of this angle is necessary for finding the appropriate rectangle for the curvature of the surface of mercury, together with the observations of the quantity of depression in tubes of a given diameter. The table published by Mr. Cavendish, from the experiments of his father, Lord Charles Cavendish, appears to be best suited for this purpose. I have constructed a diagram, according to the principles already laid down, for each case, and I find that the rectangle which agrees best with the phenomena is .01. The mean depression is always .015, divided by the diameter of the tube: in tubes less than half an inch in diameter, the curve is very nearly elliptic; and the central depression in the tube of a barometer may also be found by deducting from the corresponding mean depression the square root of one thousandth part of its diameter. There is reason to suspect a slight inaccuracy towards the middle of Lord Charles Cavendish's Table, from a comparison with the calculated mean depression, as well as from the results of the mechanical construction. The ellipsis approaching nearest to the curve may be determined by the solution of a biquadratic equation.

Diameter in inches.	Grains in an inch. C.	Mean depression by calculation. Y.	Central depression by observation. C.	Central depression by formula. Y.	Central depression by diagram. Y.	Marginal depression by diagram. Y.
.6	972	.025	.005	(.001)	.005	.066
.5	675	.030	.007	.008	.007	.067
.4	432	.037	.015	.017	.012	.069
.35	331	.043	.025	.024	.017	.072
.30	243	.050	.036	.033	.027	.079
.25	169	.060	.050	.044	.038	.086
.20	108	.075	.067	.061	.056	.096
.15	61	.100	.092	.088	.085	.116
.10	27	.150	.140	.140	.140	.161

The square root of the rectangle .01, or .1, is the ordinate where the curve would become vertical if it were continued; but in order to find the height at which the mercury adheres to a vertical surface of glass, we must diminish this ordinate in the proportion of the sine of 25° to the sine of 45°, and it will become .06, for the actual depression in this case. The elevation of the mercury that adheres to the lower horizontal surface of a piece of glass, and the thickness at which a quantity of mercury will stand when spread out on glass, supposing the angle of contact still 140°, are found, by taking the proportion of the sines of 20° and of 70° to the sine of 45°, and are therefore .0484 and .1330 respectively. If, instead of glass, we employed any surface capable of being wetted by mercury, the height of elevation would be .141, and this is the limit of the thickness of a wide surface of mercury, supported by a substance wholly incapable of attracting it. Now the hydrostatic pressure of a column of mercury .0484 in thickness, on a disc of one inch diameter, would be 131 grains; to this the surrounding elevation of the fluid will add about 11 grains for each inch of the circumference, with some deduction for the effect of the contrary curvature of the horizontal section, tending to diminish the height; and the apparent cohesion thus exhibited will be about 160 grains, which is a little more than four times as great as the apparent cohesion of glass and water. With a disc 11 lines in diameter, Mr. Dutour found it 194 French grains, which is equivalent to 152 English grains, instead of 160, for an inch; a result which is sufficient to confirm the principles of the calculation. The depth of a quantity of mercury standing on glass I have found, by actual observation, to agree precisely with this calculation. Segner says that the depth was .1358, both on glass and on paper; the difference is very trifling, but this measure is somewhat too great for glass, and too small for paper, since it appears from Dutour's experiments, that the attraction of paper to mercury is extremely weak.

If a disc of a substance capable of being wetted by mercury, an inch in diameter, were raised from its surface in a position perfectly horizontal, the apparent cohesion should be 381 grains, taking .141 as the height; and for a French circular inch, 433 grains, or 528 French grains. Now, in the experiments of Morveau, the cohesion of a circular inch of gold to the surface of mercury appeared to be 446 grains, of silver 429, of tin 418, of lead 397, of bismuth 372, of zinc 204, of copper 142, of metallic antimony 126, of iron 115, of cobalt 8: and this order is the same with that in which the metals are most easily amalgamated with mercury. It is probable that such an amalgamation actually took place in some of the experiments, and affected their results; for the process of amalgamation may often be observed to begin almost at the instant of contact of silver with mercury; and the want of perfect horizontality appears in a slight degree to have affected them all. A deviation of one fiftieth of an inch would be sufficient to have produced the difference between 446 grains and 528: and it is not impossible that all the differences, as far down as bismuth, may have been accidental. But if we suppose the gold only to have been perfectly wetted by the mercury, and all the other numbers to be in due proportions, we may find the appropriate angle for each substance, by deducting from 180°, twice the angle, of which the sine is to the radius, as the apparent cohesion of each to 446 grains; that is, for gold 1, for silver about .97, for tin .95, for lead .90, for bismuth .85, for zinc .46, for copper .32, for antimony .29, for iron .26, and for cobalt .02, neglecting the surrounding elevation, which has less effect in proportion as the surface employed is larger. Gellert found the depression of melted lead in a tube of glass multiplied by the bore equal to about .054.

It would perhaps be possible to pursue these principles so far as to determine in many cases the circumstances under which a drop of any fluid would detach itself from a given surface. But it is sufficient to infer, from the law of the superficial cohesion of fluids, that the linear dimensions of similar drops, depending from a horizontal surface, must vary precisely in the same ratio, as the heights of ascent of the respective fluids against a vertical surface, or as the square roots of the heights of ascent in a given tube; hence the magnitudes of similar drops of different fluids must vary as the cubes of the square roots of the heights of ascent in a tube. I have measured the heights of ascent of water and of diluted spirit of wine in the same tube, and I found them nearly as 100 to 64: a drop of water, falling from a large sphere of glass, weighed 1.8 grains, a drop of the spirit of wine about .85, instead of .82, which is nearly the weight that would be inferred from the consideration of the heights of ascent, combined with that of the specific gravities. We may form a conjecture respecting the probable magnitude of a drop, by inquiring what must be the circumference of the fluid, that would support by its cohesion the weight of a hemisphere depending from it: this must be the same as that of a tube, in which the fluid would rise to the height of one third of its diameter; and the square of the diameter must be three times as great as the appropriate product; or, for water .12; whence the diameter would be .35, or a little more than one third of an inch, and the weight of the hemisphere would be 2.8 grains. If more water were added internally, the cohesion would be overcome, and the drop would no longer be suspended; but it is not easy to calculate what precise quantity of water would be separated with it. The form of a bubble of air rising in water is determined by the cohesion of the internal surface of the water, exactly in the same manner as the form of a drop of water in the air. The delay of a bubble of air at the bottom of a vessel appears to be occasioned by a deficiency of the pressure of the water between the air and the vessel; it is nearly analogous to the experiment of making a piece of wood remain immersed in water, when perfectly in contact with the bottom of the vessel containing it. This experiment succeeds however far more readily with mercury, since the capillary cohesion of the mercury prevents its insinuating itself under the wood.

V. OF APPARENT ATTRACTIONS AND REPULSIONS.

The apparent attraction of two floating bodies, round both of which the fluid is raised by cohesive attraction, is produced by the excess of the atmospheric pressure on the remote sides of the solids, above its pressure on their neighbouring sides: or, if the experiments are performed in a vacuum, by the equivalent hydrostatic pressure or suction, derived from the weight and the immediate cohe-

result of their equal attractive forces bisects the whole angle formed by the lines of direction; but that the result of their repulsive forces, one of which is twice as great as the other, divides it in the ratio of one to two, forming with the former result an angle equal to one sixth of the whole; so that the addition of a third force is necessary, in order to retain these two results in equilibrium; and this force must be in a constant ratio to the evanescent angle which is the measure of the curvature, the distance of the particles being constant. The same reasoning may be applied to all the particles which are within the influence of the cohesive force: and the conclusions are equally true if the cohesion is not precisely constant, but varies less rapidly than the repulsion.

VII. COHESIVE ATTRACTION OF SOLIDS AND FLUIDS.

When the attraction of the particles of a fluid for a solid is less than their attraction for each other, there will be an equilibrium of the superficial forces, if the surface of the fluid make with that of the solid a certain angle, the versed sine of which is to the diameter, as the mutual attraction of the fluid and solid particles is to the attraction of the particles of the fluid among each other. For, when the fluid is surrounded by a vacuum or by a gas, the cohesion of its superficial particles acts with full force in producing a pressure; but when it is any where in contact with a solid substance of the same attractive power with itself, the effects of this action must be as much destroyed as if it were an internal portion of the fluid. Thus, if we imagined a cube of water to have one of its halves congealed, without any other alteration of its properties, it is evident that its form and the equilibrium of the cohesive forces would remain undisturbed: the tendency of the new angular surface of the fluid water to contract would therefore be completely destroyed by the contact of a solid of equal attractive force. If the solid were of smaller attractive force, the tendency to contract would only be proportional to the difference of the attractive forces or densities, the effect of as many of the attractive particles of the fluid being neutralised, as are equivalent to a solid of a like density or attractive power. For a similar reason, the tendency of a given fluid, to contract the sum of the surfaces of itself and a contiguous solid, will be simply as the density of the solid, or as the mutual attractive force of the solid and fluid. And it is indifferent whether we consider the pressure produced by these supposed superficial tensions, or the force acting in the direction of the surfaces to be compared. We may therefore inquire into the conditions of equilibrium of the three forces acting on the angular particles, one in the direction of the surface of the fluid only, a second in that of the common surface of the solid and fluid, and the third in that of the exposed surface of the solid. Now, supposing the angle of the fluid to be obtuse, the whole superficial cohesion of the fluid being represented by the radius, the part which acts in the direction of the surface of the solid will be proportional to the cosine of the inclination; and this force, added to the force of the solid, will be equal to the force of the common surface of the solid and fluid, or to the difference of their forces; consequently, the cosine added to twice the force of the solid, will be equal to the whole force of the fluid, or to the radius; hence the force of the solid is represented by half the difference between the cosine and the radius, or by half the versed sine; or, if the force of the fluid be represented by the diameter, the whole versed sine will indicate the force of the solid. And the same result follows when the angle of the fluid is acute. Hence we may infer, that if the solid have half the attractive force of the fluid: the surfaces will be perpendicular; and this seems in itself reasonable, since two rectangular edges of the solid are equally near to the angular particles with one of the fluid: and we may expect a fluid to rise and adhere to the surface of every solid more than half as attractive as itself; a conclusion which Clairaut has already inferred, in a different manner, from principles which he has but cursorily investigated, in his treatise on the figure of the earth.

The versed sine varies as the square of the sine of half the angle: the force must therefore be as the square of the height to which the fluid may be elevated in contact with a horizontal surface, or nearly as the square of the number of grains expressing the apparent cohesion. Thus, according to the experiments of Morveau, on the suppositions already premised, we may infer that the mutual attraction of the particles of mercury being unity, that of mercury for gold will be 1. or more, that of silver about .94, of tin .90, of lead .81, of bismuth .72, of zinc .21, of copper .10, of antimony .08, of iron .07, and of cobalt .0004. The attraction of glass for mercury will be about one sixth of the mutual attraction of the particles of mercury: but when the contact is perfect, it appears to be considerably greater.

Although the whole of this reasoning, on the attraction of solids, is to be considered rather as an approximation than as a strict demonstration, yet we are amply justified in concluding, that all the phenomena of capillary action may be accurately explained and mathematically demonstrated from the general law of the equable tension of the surface of a fluid, together with the consideration of the angle of contact appropriate to every combination of a fluid with a solid. Some anomalies, noticed by Musschenbroek and others, respecting in particular the effects of tubes of considerable lengths, have not been considered: but there is great reason to suppose, that either the want of uniformity in the bore, or some similar inaccuracy, has been the cause of these irregularities, which have by no means been sufficiently confirmed to afford an objection to any theory. The principle, which has been laid down respecting the contractile powers of the common surface of a solid and a fluid, is confirmed by an observation which I have made on the small drops of oil which form themselves on water. There is no doubt but that this cohesion is in some measure independent of the chemical affinities of the substances concerned: tallow, when solid, has a very evident attraction for the water out of which it is raised; and the same attraction must operate upon an unctuous fluid, to cause it to spread on water, the fluidity of the water allowing this powerful agent to exert itself with an unresisted velocity. An oil, which has thus been spread, is afterwards collected, by some irregularity of attraction, into thin drops, which the slightest agitation again dissipates; their surface forms a very regular curve, which terminates abruptly in a surface perfectly horizontal: now it follows from the laws of hydrostatics, that the lower surface of these drops must constitute a curve, of which the extreme inclination to the horizon is to the inclination of the upper surface, as the specific gravity of the oil to the difference between its specific gravity and that of water: consequently, since the contractile forces are held in equilibrium by a force which is perfectly horizontal, their magnitude must be in the ratio that has been already assigned; and it may be assumed as consonant both to theory and to observation, that the contractile force of the common surface of two substances, is proportional, other things being equal, to the difference of their densities. Hence, in order to explain the experiments of Boyle on the effects of a combination of fluids in capillary tubes, or any other experiments of a similar nature, we have only to apply the law of an equable tension, of which the magnitude is determined by the difference of the attractive powers of the fluids.

I shall reserve some further illustrations of this subject for a work which I have long been preparing for the press, and which I flatter myself will contain a clear and simple explanation of the most important parts of natural philosophy. I have only thought it right, in the present Paper, to lay before the Royal Society, in the shortest possible compass, the particulars of an original investigation, tending to explain some facts, and establish some analogies, which have hitherto been obscure and unintelligible.

VIII. ADDITIONAL. EXTRACTS FROM LAPLACE, WITH REMARKS.

In an essay read to the Institute of France in December 1805, and published in 1806, as a supplement to the Mécanique céleste, Mr. Laplace has advanced a theory of capillary attraction, which has led him to results nearly similar to many of those which are contained in this paper. The coincidence is indeed in some respects so striking, that it is natural, upon the first impression, to inquire whether Mr. Laplace may not be supposed either to have seen this essay, or to have read an account of its contents in some periodical publication; but upon further reflection, we cannot for a moment imagine a person of so high and so deserved a reputation as Mr. Laplace, to wish to appropriate to himself any part of the labours of others. The path which he has followed is also extremely different from that which I had taken; several of the subjects, which I had considered as belonging to the discussion, have not occurred to Mr. Laplace; and it is much more flattering than surprising, that, to an assembly of philosophers not extremely anxious to attend to the pursuits of their cotemporaries, investigations should be communicated, by the most distinguished of their members, as new and important, which had been presented, a year before, to a similar society in this country. In order to facilitate the comparison of the methods which have been adopted, I shall insert here a translation of some parts of Mr. Laplace's essay, which will also serve as an illustration of the theory advanced in this paper; and I shall add some remarks on the points in which those methods differ most.

"I have considered," says Mr. Laplace, "in the tenth book of this work, the phenomena derived from the refractive powers of transparent bodies acting on light. This force is the result of the attraction of their particles; but the law of this attraction cannot be determined by the phenomena, because they only require that it should be insensible at all sensible distances. All possible laws of attraction, which fulfil this condition, agree equally well with the different phenomena of refraction indicated by experience, the principal of which is the constant proportion of the sine of refraction to that of incidence, in the passage of a ray of light through a transparent body. It is only in this case, that this kind of attraction has been subjected to an exact analysis. I shall now submit to the consideration of mathematicians a second case, still more remarkable than the first, on account of the variety and singularity of the phenomena which depend on it, and which may be analysed with equal accuracy: this case is that of capillary action. The effects of refractive powers belong to mechanics, and in particular to the theory of projectiles; those of capillary action relate to hydrostatics, or the equilibrium of fluids, which are raised or depressed by its means, according to certain laws, which I propose to explain."

I shall here take the liberty of observing, that the arguments, which I have formerly advanced, in favour of the Huygenian theory of light, would perhaps have occasioned some little hesitation with respect to the action here supposed to be exerted by transparent bodies on light, if they had ever been so fortunate as to obtain Mr. Laplace's attention. Indeed an " attraction insensible at all sensible distances," would not explain the effects of what Newton calls inflection, which affects the rays passing at a very considerable distance, at least as much as the tenth or twentieth of an inch, on each side of an opaque substance, placed in a small pencil of light in a dark room.

"Clairaut is the first, and has hitherto remained the only person, that has subjected the phenomena of capillary tubes to a rigorous calculation, in his treatise on the figure of the earth. After having shown, by arguments which are equally applicable to all the theories which have been advanced, the inaccuracy and insufficiency of that of Jurin, he enters into an exact analysis of all the forces which can contribute to the elevation of a portion of water in a tube of glass. But his theory, although explained with all the elegance peculiar to the excellent work which contains it, leaves undetermined the law of the height of that elevation, which is found from experiment to be inversely proportional to the diameter of the tube. This great mathematician contents himself with observing, that there must be an infinite variety of laws of attraction, which, if substituted in his formulas, would afford this conclusion. The knowledge of these laws is, however, the most delicate and the most important part of the theory; it is absolutely necessary for connecting together the different phenomena of capillary action; and Clairaut would himself have been aware of this necessity, if he had wished, for example, to pass from capillary tubes to the spaces included between two parallel planes, and to deduce from calculation the equality, which is shown by experiment, between the height of ascent of a fluid in a cylindrical tube, and its height between two parallel planes, of which the distance is equal to the semidiameter of the tube; a relation which no one has yet attempted to explain. I endeavoured, long ago, to determine the laws of attraction on which these phenomena depend; some later investigations have enabled me to demonstrate, that they may all be referred to the same laws, which will account for the phenomena of refraction, that is, to such as limit the sensible effect of the attraction to an insensible distance; and from these laws, a complete theory of capillary action may be deduced."

It is true that Clairaut was the first that attempted to lay the foundation of a theory of capillary action; but he is by no means the only one that has made the attempt. Segner published, in the first volume of the Transactions of the Royal Society of Gottingen, for 1751, an essay, in which he has gone much further than Clairaut: it is true that he has made some mistakes in particular cases: but he begins, like Mr. Laplace, from the effects of an attraction insensible at all sensible distances; he has demonstrated that the curvature of each point of the surface of a fluid is always proportional to its distance above or below the general level, and he has inferred, from earlier experiments, the true magnitude of this curvature at a given height, both for water and for mercury, without material error. We shall however find, that the principles, which Clairaut, Segner, and Laplace, have successively adopted, are insufficient for explaining all the phenomena; and that it is impossible to account for them without introducing the consideration of a repulsive force; which must indeed inevitably be supposed to exist, even if its presence were not inferred from the effects of capillary action. "Attempts" have certainly been made, to explain the equality of the ascent of a fluid between the two planes, and in a tube of which the radius is equal to their distance; Mr. Leslie has made such an attempt, and with perfect success; but, if I am not mistaken, the same explanation had been given long before.

"Clairaut supposes, that a capillary tube may exert a sensible action on an infinitely narrow column of the fluid, situated in the axis of the tube. In this respect, I am obliged to differ from him, and to agree with Hauksbee, and with many other philosophers, in thinking, that capillary action, like refractive powers, and the forces of chemical affinities, is only sensible at imperceptible distances. Hauksbee has observed, that when the internal diameters of several capillary tubes are equal, the water rises in them to the same height, whether they are very thin or very thick. The cylindrical strata of glass, which are at a sensible distance from the interior surface, do not therefore contribute to the ascent of the water, although each of them, taken separately, would cause it to rise above its natural level. It is not the interposition of the strata which they surround, that prevents their action on the water; for it is natural to suppose, that the force of capillary attraction is transmitted through the substance of all material bodies, in the same manner as that of gravitation; this action is, therefore, only prevented, by the distance of the fluid from these strata; whence it follows, that the attraction of glass for water is only sensible at insensible distances.

"Proceeding upon this principle, I have investigated the action of a fluid mass, terminated by a portion of a concave or convex spherical surface, upon a fluid column within it, contained in an infinitely narrow cylindrical cavity or tube, directed towards the centre of the surface. By this action I mean the pressure, which the fluid contained in the tube would exert, in consequence of the attraction of the whole mass, upon a flat basis, situated within the tube, perpendicular to its sides, and at any sensible distance from the external surface, taking this basis for unity. I have shown that this action is either smaller or greater than if the surface were plane, accordingly as it is either concave or convex. The algebraical formula, which expresses it, consists of two terms: the first, which is much larger than the second, expresses the action of the mass supposed to be terminated by a plane surface; and I conceive that this force is the cause of the suspension of mercury in the tube of a barometer, at a height two or three times greater than that which is derived from the pressure of the atmosphere, of the refractive powers of transparent bodies, of cohesion, and of chemical affinities in general. The second term expresses that part of the attraction, which is derived from the curvature of the surface, that is, the attraction of the meniscus comprehended between that surface and the plane which touches it. This action is either added to the former, or subtracted from it, accordingly as the surface is convex or concave. It is inversely proportional to the radius of the spherical surface; and it is indeed obvious, that, the smaller the radius is, the greater is the meniscus near the point of contact. This second term expresses the cause of capillary action, which differs, in this respect, from the chemical affinities represented by the first term."

It is indeed so "obvious," that the meniscus, which constitutes the difference between a curve surface and a plane one, is inversely proportional to the radius of curvature, that the complicated calculations, which have led Mr. Laplace to this conclusion, must be considered as wholly superfluous. The attraction of the meniscus upon the evanescent column must be confined to the edge which immediately touches the column, extending only to an insensible distance on each side; and the situation of all the particles in this infinitely thin edge of the meniscus, with respect to the column, being similar, whatever the curvature may be, it is evident that their joint action must be proportional to their number, that is, to the curvature of the surface.

"From these conclusions, relating to bodies which are terminated by sensible portions of a spherical surface, I deduce this general theorem. Whenever the attractive force becomes insensible at any sensible distance, the action of a body, terminated by a curved surface, on an internal column, of infinitely small diameter, and perpendicular to the surface at any point, is equal to the half sum of the actions, which would be exerted on the same column by two spheres, having for their radii the largest and the smallest of the radii of curvature at the given point."

This theorem may be very simply inferred from the former, by considering that, according to the principle laid down in the second section of this essay, the sum of the thicknesses of the evanescent meniscoid, in any two planes passing through the axis at right angles to each other, is equal to the sum of the thicknesses of the two menisci formed by the largest and the smallest radii of curvature; consequently the sum of the whole actions of these menisci must be twice as great as the action of the meniscoid.

"By means of this theorem, and of the laws of the equilibrium of fluids, we may determine the figure which must be assumed by a gravitating fluid, inclosed in a vessel of any given form. We obtain from these principles an equation of partial differences of the second order, the integral of which cannot be found by any known method. If the figure is such, as might be formed by the revolution of a curve round an axis, the equation is reduced to common differences or fluxions, and its integral or fluent may be found very near the truth, when the surface is very small. I have shown in this manner, that, in very narrow tubes, the surface of the fluid approaches the nearer to that of a sphere, as the diameter of the tube is smaller. If these segments are similar, in different tubes of the same substance, the radii of their surfaces will be" directly "proportional to the diameters of the tubes. Now this similarity of the spherical segments will easily appear, if we consider that the distance, at which the action of the tube ceases to be sensible, is imperceptible; so that if, by means of a very powerful microscope, it were possible to make it appear equal to the thousandth part of a metre, it is probable, that the same magnifying power would augment the apparent diameter of the tube to several metres. The surface of the tube may therefore be considered as nearly plane, within the limits of a circle equal in radius to the distance at which its attraction becomes sensible; consequently the fluid within this distance, will be elevated or depressed with respect to the surface of the tube, almost precisely in the same manner as if it were perfectly plane. Beyond this distance, the fluid being subjected to no other sensible action than that of gravitation, and that of its own attraction, the surface will be very nearly that of a spherical segment, the marginal parts of which, corresponding with those of the surface of the fluid at the point which is the limit of the sphere of the sensible activity of the tube, will be inclined very nearly in the same angle to its surface, whatever its magnitude may be; hence it follows, that all these segments will be similar."

The "near approach" of the surface of a fluid in a very small tube to a portion of a sphere, is sufficiently obvious from the fundamental principle, that the curvature is proportional to the height above the general surface of the fluid; for if the diameter of the tube be small, this height will be so considerable, that its variation at any part of the concave or convex surface may be disregarded, and the curvature may consequently be considered as uniform throughout the surface. It is only upon the supposition of a surface nearly approaching to a spherical form, that Mr. Laplace has endeavoured to determine the "integral, very near the truth." He has deduced from the expression, which indicates the curvature of the surface, another which is simpler, and which might easily have been inferred at once from the uniform tension of the surface, as supporting at each point the weight of the portion of the fluid below it: he has then supposed this weight to be the same as if the surface were spherical, and has deduced from this supposition an approximate expression, for the elevation corresponding to a given angular position of the surface only. This formula is however still only applicable to those cases, in which the surface may be considered as nearly spherical; and in these it is superfluous. For example, if the surface of the mercury in a barometer be depressed one twentieth of an inch, as it actually is in a tube somewhat less than a quarter of an inch in diameter, Mr. Laplace's formula fails so completely, as to indicate a concavity instead of a convexity; for α being the reciprocal of what I have called the appropriate rectangle, and θ being 50°, the term ab^2 becomes $=4$, and makes the negative part of the formula greater than the positive. When Mr. Laplace investigates the relation of the curvature and of the marginal depression to the diameter of the tube, he simply considers the whole surface as spherical; but even on this supposition his formula is by no means the most accurate that may be found, and begins to be materially incorrect even when the diameter of the tube amounts to one fifth of an inch only. The formula, which I have already given in this paper, is sufficiently accurate, until the diameter becomes equal to half an inch; but I shall hereafter mention another, which comes much nearer to the truth in all cases.

"The comparison of these results shows the true cause of the ascent or depression of fluids in capillary tubes, which is inversely proportional to their diameters. If we imagine an infinitely narrow inverted siphon to have one of its branches placed in the axis of the tube of glass, and the other terminating in the general horizontal surface of the water in the vessel, the action of the water in the tube on the first branch of the siphon will be less, on account of the concavity of its surface, than the action of the water of the vessel on the second; the fluid must therefore ascend in the tube, in order to compensate for this difference; and, as it has been shown, that the difference of the two actions is inversely proportional to the diameter of the tube, the elevation of the fluid above the general level must follow the same law.

"If the surface of the fluid within the tube is convex, as in the case of mercury contained in a tube of glass, its action on the inverted siphon will be greater than that of the fluid in the vessel; the fluid must therefore be depressed in the tube, in proportion to the difference, that is, inversely in proportion to the diameter of the tube.

"It appears therefore, that the immediate attraction of a capillary tube has no other effect on the elevation or depression of the fluid contained in it, than so far as it determines the inclination of the first portion of the surface of the fluid, when it approaches the sides of the tube: and that the concavity or convexity of the surface, as well as the magnitude of its curvature, depends on this inclination. The friction of the fluid, against the sides of the tube, may increase or diminish a little the curvature of its surface, as we continually observe in the mercury of the barometer: and in this case, the capillary effects are increased or diminished in the same proportion. These effects are also very sensibly modified by the cooperation of the forces derived from the concavity and convexity of two different surfaces. It will appear hereafter, that water may be raised, in a given capillary tube, to a greater height above its natural level in this manner, than when the tube is immersed in a vessel filled with that fluid."

It would perhaps be more correct to say in this case "above its apparent level": for the real horizontal surface must here be considered as situated above the lower orifice of the tube, the weight of the portion of the fluid below it being as much supported by the convexity of the surface of the drop, as if it were contained in a vessel of any other kind.

"The fluxional equation of the surface of a fluid, inclosed in a capillary space of any kind, which may be referred to an axis of revolution, leads to this general result, that if a cylinder be placed within a tube, so that its axis may coincide with that of the tube, the fluid will rise in this space to the same height, as in a tube of which the radius is equal to this distance. If we suppose the radii of the tube and of the cylinder to become infinite, we obtain the case of a fluid contained between two parallel vertical planes, placed near each other. The conclusion is confirmed in this case by the experiments which were made long ago in the presence of the Royal Society of London, under the inspection of Newton, who has quoted them in his Optics; that admirable work, in which this profound genius, looking forwards beyond the state of science in his own times, has suggested a variety of original ideas, which the modern improvements of chemistry have confirmed. Mr. Haüy has been so good as to make, at my request, some experiments on the case which constitutes the opposite extreme, that is, with tubes and cylinders of a very small diameter, and he has found the conclusion as correct in this case, as in the former."

If indeed we may be allowed to place any confidence in the fundamental principle of an equable tension of the surface of the fluid, an equal length of the line of contact of the solid and fluid supporting in all cases an equal weight, these results follow of necessity, without any intricacies of calculation whatever.

"The phenomena exhibited by a drop of a fluid, moving, or suspended in equilibrium, either in a conical capillary tube, or between two planes, inclined in a small angle to each other, are extremely proper to confirm our theory. A small column of water, in a conical tube, open at both ends, and held in a horizontal position, will move towards the vertex of the cone; and it is obvious, that this must necessarily happen. In fact, the surface of the column is concave at both ends, but the radius of this curvature is smaller at the end nearer the vertex than at the opposite end; the action of the fluid upon itself is therefore less at the narrower end, consequently the column must be drawn towards this side. If the fluid employed be mercury, its surface will be convex, and the radius of curvature will still be smaller towards the vertex than towards the base of the cone; but, on account of its convexity, the action of the fluid upon itself will be greater at the narrower end, and the column must therefore move towards the wider part of the tube.

"This action may be counterbalanced by the weight of the column, so as to be held in equilibrium by it, if we incline the axis of the tube to the horizon. A very simple calculation is sufficient to demonstrate, that if the length of the column is inconsiderable, the sine of the inclination of the axis must be inversely proportional to the square of the distance of the middle of the column from the summit of the cone; and this law is equally applicable to the case of a drop of a fluid placed between two planes, which form a very small angle with each other, their horizontal margins being in contact. These results are perfectly conformable to experiment, as may be seen in the 31st query of Newton's optics. This great geometrician has endeavoured to explain them, but his explanation, compared with that which has been here advanced, serves only to show the advantages of a precise and mathematical investigation."

Mr. Laplace's superior skill in the most refined "mathematical investigations" might perhaps have enabled him to make still more essential improvements, if it had been employed on some other subjects of natural philosophy; but his explanation of these phenomena being exactly the same as that which I had already published, in an essay not containing, in its original state, any one mathematical symbol, it is obvious that the inaccuracy of Newton's reasoning did not depend upon any deficiency in his mathematical acquirements.

"It may be shown by calculation, that the sine of the inclination of the axis of the cone to the horizon will be very nearly equal to the fraction of which the denominator is the distance of the middle of the drop from the summit of the cone, and the numerator the height to which the fluid would rise in a cylindrical tube, of a diameter equal to that of the cone at the middle of the column. If the two planes, inclosing a drop of the same fluid, form with each other an angle, equal to that which is formed by the axis of the cone and its sides, the inclination of a plane, bisecting this angle, to the horizon, must be the same as that of the axis of the cone, in order that the drop may remain in equilibrium. Haukesbee has made, with very great care, an experiment of this kind, which I have compared with the theorem here laid down; and the near agreement between the experiment and the theorem is amply sufficient to confirm its truth."

If the height at which the fluid would stand, in a tube of the diameter of the upper end of the column, be h; the distance of this end from the vertex of the cone being x, and the length of the column y, the height corresponding to the remoter end will be $\frac{hx}{x+y}$, and the difference of the heights $h - \frac{hx}{x+y} = \frac{hy}{x+y}$, which must be the difference of the heights of the ends of the drop, in order that it may remain in equilibrium; but this height is to y as h to $x+y$, consequently the axis of the tube must be inclined to the horizon, in an angle, of which the sine is exactly $\frac{h}{x+y}$; the denominator being the distance of one end from the vertex, and the numerator the height at which the fluid would stand in a tube, of which the diameter is equal to that of the column at the other end.

"This theory affords us also an explanation of another remarkable phenomenon, which occurs in experiments of this nature. If a fluid be either elevated or depressed between two vertical and parallel planes, of which the lower ends are immersed in the fluid, the planes will tend to approach each other. It is shown by calculation, that if the fluid is elevated between them, each plane is subjected to a pressure, urging it towards the other plane, equal to that of a column of the same fluid, of a height equal to the half sum of the elevations of the internal and external lines of contact, of the surface of the fluid with the plane, above the general level, and standing on a base equal to a part of the plane included between these lines. If the fluid is depressed between the planes, each of them will be forced inwards, by a pressure equal to that of a column of the same fluid, of which the height is half the sum of the depressions of the lines of contact of the external and internal surfaces of the fluid with the plane, and its base the part of the plane comprehended between those lines."

In another part of his essay, Mr. Laplace asserts, that " this force increases in the inverse ratio of the distance of the planes;" if this is not an error of the press, or of the pen, it can only mean that the force increases as the distance diminishes: for the magnitude of the force is not simply in the inverse ratio of the distances, but very nearly in the inverse ratio of their squares, as I have already observed.

"Since it has been hitherto usual with natural philosophers, to consider the concavity and convexity of the surfaces of fluids in capillary spaces, as a secondary effect of capillary attraction only, and not as the principal cause of phenomena of this kind, they have not attached much importance to the determination of the curvature of these surfaces. But the theory, which has been here advanced, having shown that all these phenomena depend principally on the curvature, it becomes of consequence to examine it. Several experiments, which have been made with great accuracy by Mr. Haüy, have shown, that in capillary tubes of glass, of very small diameters, the concave surfaces of water and of oils, and the convex surfaces of mercury, differ very little from the form of a hemisphere."

Mr. Laplace informs us that M.M. Haüy and Trémery made at his request several experiments, in which the mean ascent of water, in a tube one thousandth part of a metre in diameter, was 13.57 thousandths, and that of oil of oranges 6.74. The product of the diameter and the height of ascent of water is $.039371 \times .534 = .021$ E. i., which is little more than half as much as I have assigned for this product from the best experiments of many other observers. Probably both these experiments, and those of Newton or Hauksbee, were made with tubes and plates either a little greasy, or too dry; and Mr. Haüy might be the more readily satisfied with the first results that he obtained, from finding them agree nearly with those of Newton, which Mr. Laplace wished to compare with them. These gentlemen also found the depression of mercury in a tube of the same diameter .2887 E. i., the product being .01137, instead of .015, which is the ultimate product inferred from Lord Charles Cavendish's experiments of a similar nature. The observation of Mr. Haüy, on the curvature of the surface of mercury in a tube, is also far from being accurate; Mr. Laplace himself asserts that the angular extent of the surface must fall short of that of a hemisphere more or less, accordingly as the tube has more or less attraction for the fluid; and it is easy to show that glass has a very considerable attraction for mercury. The method that I took to ascertain the angle, formed by the surface of the mercury, with the side of the tube, was to observe in what position the light reflected from it began to reach the eye, and I have every reason to think, from the comparison of a great variety of experiments of different kinds, that the angle which I have assigned is very near the truth.

I have lately repeated my calculations of the depression of mercury, in barometer tubes of considerable diameter, with great care, and by different methods. I had before formed a table, by means of diagrams, which I had actually constructed for each case, upon a sufficiently accurate approximation: I have now followed nearly the same steps in calculating, by means of tables of sines and cosines, the precise form of the surface in a variety of cases. Beginning from the vertex of the curve, I have determined the mean curvature for every small arc, from the approximate height of its middle point; calculating, with the assistance of a series of differences, the normal of the curve at each step for the same point, in order to find the transverse curvature. I have also pursued, in some cases, in order to confirm these calculations, a method totally different, finding the mass of the quantity of fluid to be supported by the tension of the surface at each concentric circle, and inferring from its magnitude the inclination of the curve to the horizon: taking the height of the external circumference of each portion, thus calculated, for the mean height; a supposition which nearly compensates for the omission of the curvature of its surface. But the accumulated effect of this curvature becomes very sensible in the vertical height of the surface, and I have therefore allowed for it, upon the supposition of a simple curvature varying with the height; but this correction, for want of including the effect of the variation of the transverse curvature, is still a little too small; the horizontal diameter of the surface, however, agrees extremely well with the former mode of calculation. In order that the results of these investigations may be the more easily compared with each other, and with experiment, I shall insert some specimens, by means of which, if it be required, the curves may be very correctly delineated.

1. Central depression .007.

FIRST METHOD, BY THE CURVATURE.

Arc.	Horizontal ordinate.	Depression.
0°	.00000	.00700
1	.02444	.00721
2	.04758	.00782
3	.06651	.00865
4	.08338	.00968
5	.09791	.01082
6	.11049	.01203
7	.12153	.01329
8	.13146	.01458
9	.14022	.01589
10	.14814	.01721
12	.16177	.01986
14	.17338	.02254
16	.18344	.02524
18	.19229	.02793
20	.20012	.03063
25	.21603	.03722
30	.22869	.04381
35	.23693	.05033
40	.24731	.05676
45	.25420	.06307
50	.25986	.06911

SECOND METHOD, BY THE TENSION.

Arc.	Horizontal ordinate.	Depression.
.00	.00000	.00700
.02	.02000	.00714
.04	.04000	.00757
.06	.05999	.00830
.08	.07997	.00939
.10	.09993	.01101
.12	.11985	.01302
.14	.13971	.01566
.16	.15948	.01909
.18	.17908	.02353
.20	.19842	.02922
.22	.21732	.03653
.24	.23550	.04530
.26	.25039	.05707
.2705	.25740	.06460

2. Central depression .05.

FIRST METHOD.

Arc.	Horizontal ordinate.	Depression.
0°	.00000	.05000
1	.00349	.05003
2	.00697	.05012
3	.01044	.05027
4	.01388	.05048
5	.01729	.05075
6	.02066	.05107
7	.02402	.05145
8	.02731	.05189
9	.03056	.05239

Arc.	Horizontal ordinate.	Depression.
10°	.03375	.05291
12	.03995	.05411
14	.04589	.05543
16	.05157	.05696
18	.05697	.05861
20	.06209	.06037
25	.07363	.06515
30	.08365	.07036
35	.09224	.07583
40	.09958	.08146
45	.10581	.08717
50	.11105	.09289

SECOND METHOD.

Arc.	Horizontal ordinate.	Depression.
.00	.00000	.05000
.01	.01000	.05025
.02	.01999	.05101
.03	.02994	.05229
.04	.03982	.05409
.05	.04961	.05644
.06	.05926	.05938
.07	.06873	.06294
.08	.07796	.06718
.09	.08688	.07212
.10	.09540	.07783
.11	.10342	.08436
.12	.11080	.09170
.1214	.11173	.09280

3. Central depression .14.

FIRST METHOD.

Arc.	Horizontal ordinate.	Depression.
0°	.00000	.14000
5	.00623	.14027
10	.01234	.14108
15	.01832	.14240
20	.02405	.14421
25	.02950	.14646
30	.03459	.14911
35	.03931	.15211
40	.04361	.15541
45	.04749	.15897
50	.05091	.16270

SECOND METHOD.

Arc.	Horizontal ordinate.	Depression.
.00	.00000	.1400
.01	.01000	.1407
.02	.01990	.1428
.03	.02950	.1464
.04	.03857	.1514
.05	.04686	.1580
.0555	.05078	.1621

For representing the depression, thus determined, in a formula capable of expressing it at once, in terms of the diameter of the tube, I have deduced an approximate determination from the supposition of a spherical surface, and corrected it, by comparison with the results of these calculations, so as to agree with them all, without an error of one two thousandth of an inch, in the most unfavourable of the five cases compared. The theorem is, first, $e = \frac{.015d}{dd + .16}$, which is nearly half the versed sine of a spherical surface, and then $f = \frac{.015}{d} - \frac{3}{4}e - 14.5 e^3$, which shows the central depression without any sensible error.

I have also found a formula, which expresses the difference between the central and marginal depression, so that an observation on the height of the barometer may be corrected, with equal accuracy, whether the elevation of the highest or lowest point of the surface has been measured, provided that the tube be of moderate dimensions. This formula is $g = \frac{5d + 100d^3}{15(5d + 100d^3) + 18}$. If d were very large, it would require some further correction, g being ultimately too great by .0069. The results of these formulas are compared, in the first of the following tables, with those of the calculations at large; and in the second, they are reduced into a form more immediately applicable to practice, and are compared also with the table published by Mr. Cavendish.

Diameter.	True central depression.	Form. 1.	True additional depression at the margin.	Form. 2.
.5197	.007	.0071	.0621	.0622
.3187	.025	.0250	.0535	.0534
.2221	.050	.0498	.0429	.0432
.1468	.090	.0905	.0313	.0311
.1018	.140	.1396	.0227	.0226

Diameter.	Observed central depression.	True central depression.	True marginal depression.
1.00		.0022	
.90		.0023	
.80		.0026	
.70		.0032	
.60	.005	.0045	.0680
.50	.007	.0074	.0691
.45		.0100	.0703
.40	.015	.0139	.0722
.35	.025	.0196	.0753
.30	.036	.0290	.0798
.25	.050	.0404	.0872
.20	.067	.0589	.0989
.15	.092	.0880	.1196
.10	.140	.1424	.1646
.05		.2964	.3083

By continuing the calculations of the figure of some of these curves to an arc of 90°, I have adapted them to the surface of water contained in a cylindrical tube; but in this case, the scale must be supposed to be augmented in the proportion of 1 to $\sqrt{2}$. The additional numbers stand thus in abstract.

1. Central depression .025.

Arc.	Horizontal ordinate.	Depression.
0°	.00000	.02500
10	.06214	.03023
20	.10280	.04097
30	.12969	.05340
40	.14793	.06606
50	.15934	.07847
60	.16768	.09039
70	.17296	.10169
80	.17580	.11228
90	.17665	.12203

2. Central depression .05.

Arc.	Horizontal ordinate.	Depression.
0°	.00000	.05000
10	.03375	.05291
20	.06209	.06037
30	.08365	.07036
40	.09958	.08146
50	.11105	.09289
60	.11991	.10414
70	.12494	.11492
80	.12769	.12518
90	.12853	.13470

3. Central depression .09.

Arc.	Horizontal ordinate.	Depression.
0°	.00000	.09000
10	.01904	.09042
20	.03662	.09366
30	.05172	.10337
40	.06397	.11192
50	.07340	.12133
60	.08022	.13106
70	.08475	.14077
80	.08727	.15017
90	.08804	.15904

Hence, for water, we have the central elevation .035355, .07071, and .12728, and the marginal elevation .17258, .19050, and .22495, in tubes of which the diameters are .49964, .36354, and .2490 respectively. The difference of the elevations is expressed nearly by $h = \frac{\sqrt{2(d+100d^4)}}{\sqrt{8+10(d+100d^4)}}$, which is correct in the extreme cases on both sides, and becomes, when d is .25, and .5, .098, and .136 respectively, instead of .0977 and .137; and when $d=1$, $h=.141$.

"Clairaut," says Mr. Laplace, "has made this singular remark; that if the law of the attraction of the matter of the tube, for the fluid, differs only in its intensity from that of the attraction of the particles of the fluid among themselves, the fluid will be elevated above the level, as long as the intensity of the first of these forces exceeds half that of the second. If it be exactly half as great, it may easily be shown, that the surface of the fluid in the tube will be horizontal, and that it will not be raised above the level. If the two forces be equal, the surface of the fluid will be concave and hemispherical, and it will be elevated within the tube. If the intensity of the attraction of the tube be wholly wanting or insensible, the surface of the fluid will be hemispherical, but it will be convex and depressed. Between these two limits, the surface will be that of a segment of a sphere, and it will be either concave or convex, accordingly as the intensity of the attraction of the matter of the tube for the fluid is greater or less, than half of that of the mutual attraction of the particles of the fluid."

These conclusions are in all probability nearly correct with respect to very small tubes; but it is remarkable that they are not fairly deducible from Mr. Laplace's principles, nor from those of Clairaut, whose steps he has followed; and that the expression, which he has derived from them, as indicating the condition of equilibrium of the surface of a fluid inclined to that of a solid, implies, by including an impossibility, that such an equilibrium cannot subsist. This equation requires that the attraction of the fluid, contained between the surface and its extreme tangent, be more than equal to the difference of the attraction of the two rectangular portions composing the flat solid, and one similar portion of the fluid, reduced only in the ratio of the sine of the angle occupied by the termination of the fluid, to the radius: but it is very evident that the action of the portion of the fluid, thus cut off by the tangent, must be utterly evanescent, in comparison with the other forces concerned, especially if we consider that the surface of the fluid, as well as that of the tube, within the distance " of the sphere of activity of the attraction" is, to use Mr. Laplace's terms, " almost absolutely plane." There can therefore be no equilibrium upon these principles, when the density of the solid is greater or less than half that of the fluid, unless the surface of the fluid have a common tangent with that of the solid: while, on the other hand, when the densities are in this proportion, the surface will remain in equilibrium in any position; the action of the fluid being always proportional to the chord of its angular extent, and composing, when combined with that of the solid, a result perpendicular to the surface. If Mr. Laplace had attempted to confirm or to confute my reasoning, respecting the mutual attractions of solids and fluids, he would probably have discovered the insufficiency of these principles, and would perhaps have been induced to admit my explanation of the foundation of the laws of superficial cohesion, as derived from the combination of an attractive with a repulsive force, varying according to a different law.

" If the intensity of the attraction of the tube for the fluid exceeds that of the attraction of the fluid for its own particles, I think it probable that, in this case, the fluid, attaching itself firmly to the tube, forms of itself an interior tube, which alone raises the fluid, so as to make its surface a concave hemisphere. It may reasonably be conjectured, that this is the case with water and with oils, in tubes of glass.

" The elevation of fluids between two vertical planes, which form very small angles with each other, and their discharge through capillary siphons, present a variety of phenomena, which are so many corollaries from my theory. On the whole, if any person will take the trouble of comparing it with the numerous experiments which have been made on capillary action, he will see that the results of these experiments, when made with proper precaution, may be deduced from it, not by vague considerations, which always leave the subject in uncertainty, but by a series of geometrical arguments, which appear to me to remove every doubt respecting the truth of the theory. I wish that this application of analytical reasoning, to one of the most curious departments of natural philosophy, may be thought interesting by mathematicians, and may induce them to make further attempts of a similar nature. Besides the advantage of adding certainty to physical sciences, such investigations tend also to the improvement of the mathematics themselves, since they frequently require the invention of new methods of calculation."

It must be confessed that, in this country, the cultivation of the higher branches of the mathematics, and the invention of new methods of calculation, cannot be too much recommended to the generality of those who apply themselves to natural philosophy; but it is equally true, on the other hand, that the first mathematicians on the continent have exerted great ingenuity in involving the plainest truths of mechanics in the intricacies of algebraical formulas, and in some instances have even lost sight of the real state of an investigation, by attending only to the symbols, which they have employed for expressing its steps.

PLATE 15.

Vol. II. p. 670.

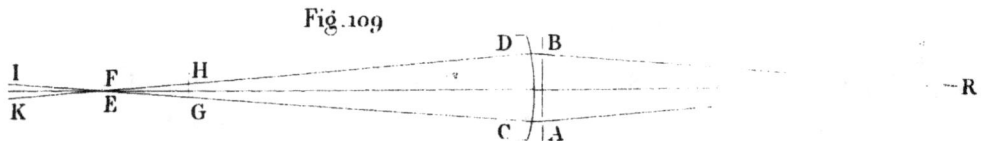

Fig. 109

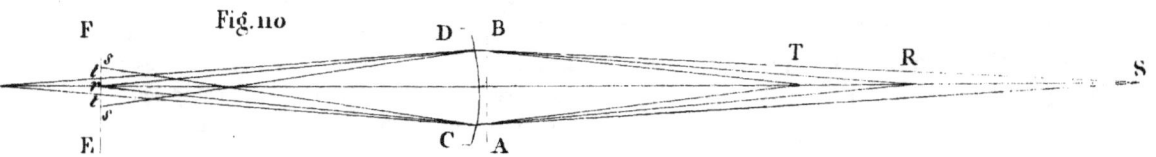

Fig. 110

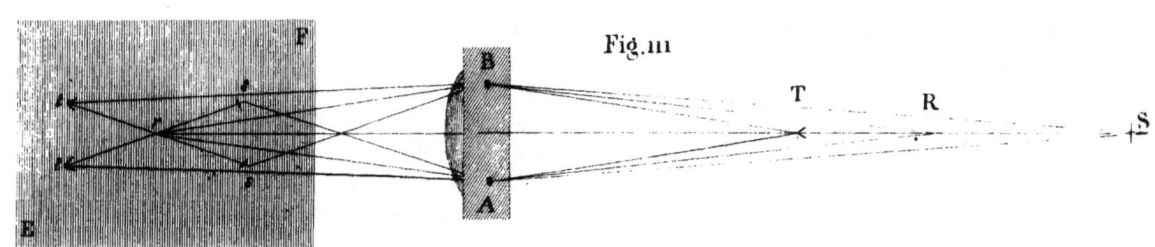

Fig. 111

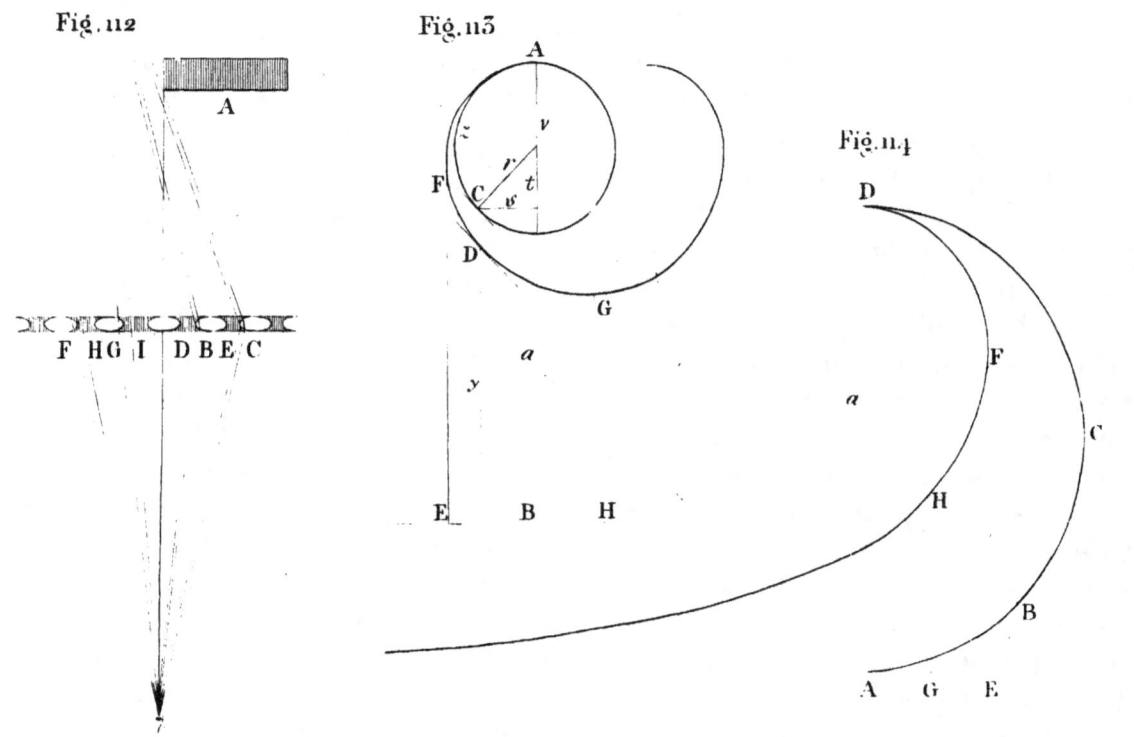

Fig. 112   Fig. 113   Fig. 114

Pub. by J. Johnson, London 1 July 1806.

ACCOUNT OF THE PROCEEDINGS OF THE ROYAL SOCIETY.

FROM NOVEMBER 1801, TO JULY 1802.

From the Journals of the Royal Institution.

The meetings of the Royal Society commenced for the season, on Thursday the 5th of November.

The Croonian lecture on muscular motion, by Everard Home, Esq. was read. Its subject was the capacity of the eye to change its focal distance, after being deprived of the crystalline lens. Mr. Home relates an experiment, where it was shown, by Dr. Young's optometer, that a person, from whose eyes the lens had been extracted, retained a greater power of accommodating it to different distances, than is found in some eyes which are entire. On repeating the experiment, the faculty appeared to be considerably diminished; a circumstance which Mr Home attributes to fatigue. The optometer was found to be much more manageable in its simple state, than with the addition of a lens; and it was singular, that this person saw distinctly from about 9 to 13 inches without the use of any glass.

On the 12th and 17th, Dr. Young's Bakerian lecture was read. The subject was the theory of light and colours. It contained an extension of the system, which the author had submitted to the Royal Society in a former paper; and its unexpected application to a great variety of phenomena, most of which had been observed by Newton, but never sufficiently explained, and others were advanced from the author's own experiments. Dr. Young first shows how little difficulty there is, for such as admit the Newtonian doctrines, to allow the truth of this theory, and how much those doctrines have been misunderstood by Euler and others. After recapitulating and extending the explanation of the more common phenomena of optics, the author enters into the detail of those applications which are the most novel and striking; by which it appears to be a general law, that, whenever two portions of the same pencil of light arrive at the same point by different routes, the production of colours depends uniformly on the difference of the length of those routes; and from this principle, the colours of striated surfaces, of thin and of thick plates, and of inflected light, are shown to be necessary consequences of the combination of undulations, in the same manner as the beating of two sounds, or the interference of the tides at sea: and all the measures, laid down by Newton, are found to agree precisely with this law. Such a coincidence Dr. Young cannot help considering as fully sufficient, to turn the scale of probability in favour of the undulatory system of light.

On the 26th, Mr. Hatchett's paper, on a new metallic substance, found in an ore from the state of Massachusets, was read. It appears to resemble in its properties the metallic acids, and, in its natural state, is combined with iron; but is distinguishable from other substances, by the orange coloured precipitate thrown down from its solution by the gallic acid, and the olive green colour of the precipitate by the prussic acid. All attempts to reduce it to the metallic form have hitherto been unsuccessful: but, from the colours of the precipitates, and from other circumstances, Mr. Hatchett thinks that its base will be found to be an acidifiable metal, and he gives it the name columbium.

On the 30th, the day of the anniversary, the Copleian medal was conferred by the council on Mr. Astley Cooper, in consequence of his success in the cure of cases of deafness, arising from obstructions of the eustachian tube, by the operation of perforating the membrane of the tympanum.

The President, in an appropriate speech, bestowed on Mr. Cooper the encomiums merited by his important improvement; and noticed, at the same time, that, in all probability, Cheselden would have been equally fortunate, had he not been prevented by popular prejudice, from trying the experiment on a condemned criminal.

The meeting of the 10th of December was occupied by an abridged translation of a pamphlet of Mr. Piazzi, on the supposed planet, which he discovered at Palermo, and which he has named Ceres Ferdinandia. Its apparent diameter was seven seconds, its distance from the sun is nearly three times that of the earth, and its period somewhat more than five years. It does not, however, appear to be by any means fully ascertained, that it deserves to be considered as a true planet. The paper was communicated by Dr. Maskelyne.

On the 17th, Mr. Home's account of the anatomy of the ornithorhynchus paradoxus was read. This singular animal appears to form a link between the mammalia and the amphibia; for while, in its general appearance, and in its sanguiferous system, it resembles the mammalia, especially some of the order of bruta, both the absence of mammae, and its internal anatomy render it probable that it is oviparous. Its teeth too, when they are found, are but four in number, and resemble the substance of horn more than of bone. Its food is unknown, but its residence is in the water. On its hind feet only, besides the five toes connected by a web, there is a detached process armed with a spur. The paper was accompanied with numerous drawings, and a dried specimen of the animal.

On the 24th, a paper on friction, by Mr. Southern, was communicated by Mr. Vince. Mr. Southern made a number of accurate experiments on the motions of large grindstones, revolving with great rapidity, and ascertained the power of friction on their axes, from the number of revolutions which they performed, when set in motion with various velocities. He considers the results as fully confirming Mr. Vince's principle, that friction is a uniformly retarding force: although the resistance of the air, and other accidental circumstances, introduced great irregularities into the experiments. He found this force equal to about one fortieth of the weight: the steel spindles running on brass, with the interposition of an unctuous substance.

The Society adjourned to Thursday the fourteenth of January.

14th January, 1802. A paper on the propriety of separating geometrical from analytical expressions. By Robert Woodhouse, M.A. of Caius College, Cambridge.

Mr. Woodhouse refers to his former communication, printed in the Philosophical Transactions in 1801, for the investigations which gave rise to the present discussion. He had there stated the frequent imperfections of geometrical analogy, when inferences are made from one figure to others of a similar kind, and had insisted on the conclusiveness of demonstrations, in which imaginary quantities are employed, when understood in their true sense. He now continues the inquiry into the distinguishing characters of geometry and algebra; and while he allows the advantage of the geometrical method, in simple cases, he gives a preference to algebraical analysis in all problems of a more complicated nature: and endeavours to add still more to the purity of the analytical representation, by banishing from it all expressions, which have any reference to geometry. The computations inserted were not capable of being read to the Society; but the author states, in the conclusion, that he has deduced, in a manner purely algebraical, the formulas for the sine in terms of the arc, for any multiple of an arc, and for other similar angular functions, which have been usually considered as most intimately connected with geometry.

21st January. A paper on the phenomena of galvanism. By George Smith Gibbes, M.D. F.R.S.

Dr. Gibbes begins with reciting some experiments on the oxidation produced during the union of tin foil with mercury, first in the air, and then under water. He assumes a different opinion from that of Dr. Wollaston, respecting the origination of electricity in chemical changes, and maintains, on the contrary, that the electrical changes are to be considered as preceding and favouring the chemical. He imagines that the simple contact of various substances produces changes of electrical equilibrium, and that the action of acids is effectual in promoting these changes, by bringing their surfaces into contact. Dr. Gibbes observes upon Dr. Wollaston's experiment of immersing zinc and silver in an acid solution, that if they are placed in two separate portions of the fluid, and the parts not immersed are brought into contact, there is no emission of gas from the silver; but that it is copiously produced when the contact takes place in the same fluid. He proceeds to relate some experiments which seem to show a difference between galvanism and electricity, particularly that galvanism does not appear to be attracted by metallic points. He also states an experiment in which a piece of paper is placed on tinfoil, and rubbed with elastic gum, and although the tinfoil is not insulated, sparks are produced on raising the paper. Dr. Gibbes concludes with some arguments against the doctrine of the decomposition of water; and advances as a probable opinion, that oxygen and hydrogen gas are composed of water as a basis, united with two other elements, which, combined, form heat.

The meetings of the 28th January, the 4th and 11th February were principally occupied by a paper on the hyperoxygenized muriatic acid, by Richard Chenevix, Esq. F.R.S.

Mr. Chenevix, after adverting to the observations of Berthollet and Mr. Hoyle, proceeds to relate a series of his own experiments, made in order to investigate minutely the composition and properties of the hyperoxygenized muriatic acid. It was already known that, in the oxygenized muriate of potash, the acid contains much more oxygen than in its separate form. Mr. Chenevix finds that the simply oxygenized acid contains, in 100 parts, 85 of common muriatic acid, and 15 of oxygen. Berthollet, from a less accurate experiment, imagined that it contained only 10 per cent of oxygen. But the hyperoxygenized acid, which is the subject of the present paper, appears to consist of 36 parts only of muriatic acid, and 64 of oxygen.

Mr. Chenevix has not succeeded in obtaining the hyperoxygenized muriatic acid in a separate state. In treating the hyperoxygenized muriate of potash with concentrated sulfuric acid, a violent explosion took place, upon the application of heat: this was avoided by adding the salt gradually to the acid, or by using the diluted acid. In the order of affinities this acid appears to stand next above the benzoic: it changes blue vegetable colours to red. When the salts formed of it are decomposed, by the addition of the sulfuric, nitric, or muriatic acids, a flash of light is observed; hence Mr. Chenevix takes occasion to question the Lavoiserian doctrine, of the light in combustion being supplied by the oxygen gas consumed: and in confirmation of his remark he observes that plants, growing in the dark, contain a great proportion of mucilage, and that mucilage burns without emitting any light. The sudden explosion of many combustible substances with hyperoxygenized muriate of potash, when thrown into an acid, led Mr. Chenevix to attempt the combustion of diamond powder in the same way: but this experiment did not succeed.

Mr. Chenevix has examined very minutely the various salts formed by this acid in combination with alkalis, earths, and metals. He finds that it has not, like some other acids, a power of carrying over a portion of silex when mixed with other earths. He combined it with metals by suspending their oxids in water, through which the gas was passed: and he found that, like the nitric acid, it contained too much oxygen to unite with the whole of the red oxid of lead exposed to it. He observes that the nitric and other acids appear to stand lower in the scale of elective attraction to the metallic oxids, in proportion as they dissolve the pure metals more readily. Mr. Chenevix unexpectedly procured the hyperoxygenized muriatic acid in submitting platina to the action of the nitromuriatic acid. Pursuing the analogy suggested by Mr. Berthollet, of the three states, of sulfur, the sulfureous, and sulfuric acid, Mr. Chenevix proposes to appropriate to the common muriatic acid, the term muriatic radical, or some equivalent denomination, and to call the acid in the two stages of oxygenization here described, the muriatous, and muriatic acid respectively.

On the 4th February, a letter from Dr. Maskelyne announced that he had observed the new planet of Mr. Piazzi passing the meridian between three and four o'clock in the morning, having about $188°\ 43'$ right ascension, and $12°\ 38'$ north declination, appearing like a star of the eighth magnitude.

Another letter, from Mr. von Zach, was read, informing the Society that he had observed this planet at Seeberg on the 7th of December, within half a degree of the place before determined in his journal. Mr. Olbers saw it at Bremen on the 2nd of January. With a power of above 120, it presented no observable disc.

On the 11th, a second letter from the Astronomer Royal informed the Society that he had repeated his observation of the new planet, so as fully to ascertain its motion. It appeared to have a visible disc when on the meridian, and viewed with a power of 50. When the air was very clear the disc was round and well defined, but somewhat smaller than that of the 34th of Virgo, a star of the 6th magnitude near it. Dr. Maskelyne observes that the smallness and roundness of the appearance of the disc of the fixed stars is a good criterion of the clearness of the air.

Another letter, from Alexander Aubert, Esq. F. R. S. was also read. Mr. Aubert discovered the planet Ceres on Sunday morning, having about $188°\ 41'$ right ascension and near $13°$ declination, its motion at present being retrograde.

On the 18th of February a letter from Mr. von Zach was read, containing a continuation of his observations on the planet Ceres, and mentioning an account from Mr. Harding that two faint spots had been seen, at the distances of 20 and 35 seconds from this planet, which it was conjectured might possibly be satellites: although the fact had not by any means been ascertained.

Dr. Herschel sent an account of the appearance of the new planet, as viewed through his telescopes. He had sought for it in vain, until he received Dr. Maskelyne's determination of its place. When viewed with powers of 600 and 1200, it could not be decidedly distinguished from a star, until it was found to change its place. Its apparent diameter was not large enough to be directly determined, but it was certainly not larger than one fourth of that of the Georgian planet, and perhaps equal only to one sixth. From a rough computation of its magnitude, Dr. Herschel concludes that its real diameter is about $\frac{1}{3}$ of that of the moon: its light is of a reddish hue.

Mr. Gilpin also gave the Society an account of observations on the 8th and 12th of February. He found the planet's right ascension change from 188° 41′ to 188° 30′, while its declination increased. Mr. Gilpin observes that its light resembles that of the planet Mars.

Thursday, 25th February. A letter from Mr. Schroeter of Lilienthal, respecting the planet Ceres Ferdinandia, informed the Society that Mr. Schroeter had observed a nebulosity round the planet, somewhat resembling that of a comet: the diameter of the true disc being 1.8″, and that of the nebula 2.6′, but the distinction was not always equally observable. Mr. Schroeter considers this body as of a hybrid nature, or a medium between a planet and a comet; but he imagines the apparent nebulosity to be owing to an atmosphere, and that, according to the different states of the atmosphere, the light reflected from the planet is either white, bluish, or reddish.

A table of observations of the same planet was also communicated by Mr. Méchain, through Sir Henry Englefield.

An account of certain stony and metalline bodies which at different times are said to have fallen on the earth, by Edward Howard, Esq. occupied the remainder of this meeting, and the principal part of the two following.

Mr. Howard begins with a historical detail of the various relations of this kind which are found on record, and particularly refers to the essays of Mr. King, and Professor Chladni, and to various authors quoted by them. But the first instances, with which chemistry has interfered, are those of a stone presented to the French Academy by the Abbé Bachelay in 1768; and another examined afterwards by Professor Barthold. The stones from Sienna in 1794; the large stone of 56lbs. weight which fell in Yorkshire in 1795, and was exhibited soon after in London; and the substances which fell at Benares in 1798, are the immediate subjects of Mr. Howard's investigation. All these agree in the general appearance of an ash grey stony substance, mixed with spangles of pyrites, and of native iron, and externally of a dark colour, covered with a semivitrified and blistered crust. The Abbé Bachelay's was supposed to contain $8\frac{1}{2}$ sulfur, 6 iron, and $55\frac{1}{2}$ earth, and some of the others were found to consist of similar ingredients. The stone, which fell near Mr. Topham's house in Yorkshire, penetrated 12 inches deep into the earth, and 6 more into a chalk rock: its fall was accompanied with noises like a discharge of artillery. A very particular and perfectly authenticated account is given, in the words of Mr. Williams, of several substances which fell about 12 miles from Benares, and penetrated some inches into the earth in several spots within the distance of 100 yards; their fall being accompanied by a very vivid light.

Mr. Howard proceeds to mention another specimen from the Museum Bornianum, now in the possession of Mr. Greville, said to have fallen in Bohemia, which agrees with the rest in its characters. A mineralogical description of these stones by the Count de Bournon is subjoined. They appear to consist principally of substances of four kinds, besides the dark crust which surrounds them; the first of these substances is in the form of dark grains, of a conchoidal fracture, from the size of a pin's head to that of a pea; the second is a kind of pyrites, the third is metallic iron, and the fourth a grey earthy substance, serving as a cement to the rest. The proportions of these substances appear to differ in some measure in the different specimens, the iron abounding most in the specimens from Yorkshire, and from Bohemia. Mr. Howard has ascertained, by a chemical analysis, that silica, iron, magnesia, sulfur, and nickel, are contained in the different parts of these substances. The globular bodies and the cementing earth each contained about 50 silex, 15 magnesia, 34 iron, and $2\frac{1}{2}$ nickel.

From 150 grains of the earthy part of the stone from Sienna, Mr. Howard obtained about 70 silica, 34 magnesia, 52 oxid of iron, and 8 oxid of nickel; the contents of the specimens from Yorkshire and from Bohemia were not materially different. Mr. Howard proceeds to inquire into the causes of the difference in the results of his analysis and those of the foreign chemists, with respect to the species of the earths. After having shown the striking analogy between these substances, and their total dissimilarity to other mineral products, Mr. Howard examines into the form and contents of various specimens of native iron: observing that Mr. Proust detected nickel in a large mass of native iron found in South America; Mr. Howard discovers a portion of the same metal in every specimen that he has examined, from different parts of the world. A description of these specimens, by the Count de Bournon, is inserted, and the large mass, discovered by Professor Pallas in Siberia, is particularly described. It is found to contain detached masses of semitransparent substances, considerably resembling some of the constituent parts of the stones from Benares. Mr. Howard does not give a decided opinion respecting the origin of all these substances, he only observes, that they agree in several remarkable properties, distinguishing them from all other bodies, that they all appear, from well authenticated accounts, to have fallen on the earth, attended in most instances by meteors or lightning, and that it is remarkable that the native iron in all the stones contains nickel, as well as the other native irons.

A letter was also read on the 11th March, from Mr. von Zach, confirming Mr. Schroeter's observation of the changeable light of the planet Ceres, which Mr. von Zach had at first attributed to the haziness of our own atmosphere, until he found that MM. Olbers and Schroeter were agreed in deriving it from a real change in the light reflected.

An Appendix to Mr. Chenevix's paper, on the Oxygenized Muriatic Acid, was read on the 18th of March.

This addition relates principally to the various muriates of mercury. It appears that Mr. Berthollet once considered the acid in corrosive sublimate as oxygenized, but he afterwards renounced that opinion; and Mr. Proust also thinks as Mr. Berthollet now does. Mr. Fourcroy still calls it a hyperoxygenized muriate of mercury; and of course supposes the excess of the oxygen in corrosive sublimate above that in calomel, to be combined with the acid, and not with the oxid. Mr. Chenevix however determines from experiment that corrosive sublimate contains no particle of hyperoxygenized muriatic acid. In 100 parts, he finds 69. of mercury, 12.3 of oxygen, and 18 of muriatic acid; but in calomel, 79, 9.5 and 11.5 respectively; so that in calomel the metal is less oxidized, and the oxid is combined with a smaller proportion of the acid. A piece of copper was found to throw down from a solution of corrosive sublimate a very pure calomel. Mr. Chenevix observes that Scheele's calomel contains a portion of subnitrate of mercury precipitated with it by the water; and that this may be avoided either by using the nitrate of mercury before it has boiled, or by adding to the dilute solution of muriate of soda, by which it is precipitated, a little muriatic acid, to engage the superfluous subnitrate. By passing a current of oxygenized muriatic acid gas through water containing red oxid of mercury, a true hyperoxygenized muriate was obtained, more soluble than corrosive sublimate, and distinguishable by its smell when decomposed; and the remaining oxid became of a dark brown colour.

The meetings of the 25th of March, and the 1st and 8th of April, were occupied by part of a paper on the corundum, by the Count de Bournon, F.R.S.

The Count de Bournon had already stated some mineralogical reasons for classing the corundum with the sapphire and other oriental gems: their affinity was afterwards confirmed by the analysis of Mr. Klaproth; yet Mr. Haüy still hesitating to admit that they ought to be placed near to each other in the system, the Count de Bournon endeavours to establish the character much more fully. He divides the specimens of corundum into two principal kinds; the one larger, less regularly formed, and generally of a greyish colour, capable of being easily reduced by fracture to a rhomboidal form: the other kind more regularly crystallized, and of more diversified colour.

The author proceeds to consider the different varieties of the corundum, first with regard to colour, which chiefly constitutes the distinctions of the sapphire, the oriental ruby, topaz, emerald, and chrysolite; and afterwards with respect to transparency, hardness, and other particulars. He observes that these stones strike fire with steel less readily than flint: that they are phosphorescent when rubbed in the dark, the ruby in particular emitting a light similar to that of red hot iron. The specific gravity varies, that of the sapphire being usually about 4.1, but most of the other varieties generally 3.9. The diversified forms of the crystals are next considered, the basis of them all being a rhomboid, contained by parallelograms, of which the angles are $96°$, and $84°$: the specimens of an original rhomboid of this kind are very rare. The derivative crystals have their angles variously replaced, the portions thus becoming more or less regularly formed pyramids.

The cohesion of these gems is next compared with their colour, and a general connexion between these qualities is found: the blue being in general the most difficultly broken. Several circumstances respecting the crystallizations are still more minutely described, and the figures to which the reflection of light is owing are particularly considered. The author observes that in order to form the appearance of the rays of a regular star, by reflection from the laminae of these gems, which has frequently given them the denomination of asterites, the best section is to make them terminate obtusely a little below the sharp angle of the rhomboid. The objections of Mr. Haüy to classing the sapphire and other oriental gems with the corundum are still further considered. An analogy to the two principal divisions of corundums into regular and irregular crystals, is shown in the forms of the feltspar, which is similarly distinguished into the very different appearances of feltspar in granite, and the crystallized adularia, besides some other similar variations. The matrix of the corundums, particularly in the Carnatic, is a rock of a loose texture, somewhat resembling sandstone in appearance, but containing small masses of a substance irregularly crystallized, which is decomposed by exposure to the air, and then appears to abound in carbonate of lime. The Count de Bournon refers, for a complete confirmation of his mineralogical opinions, to Mr. Chenevix's chemical analysis of all the substances that he has examined, which is to form a continuation of this elaborate essay.

Some observations of the place of the planet Ceres, by Professor Bode, of Berlin, were also communicated on the 8th by Dr. Herschel; and the Society adjourned to the 29th.

" *At a Meeting of the Managers of the Royal Institution of Great Britain, held at the House of the Institution, on the 5th Day of April,* 1802.

" *Resolved,* That the Resolution of the Managers of the Royal Institution, of the 31st of March, 1800, Article 4," already inserted in the Journals, " be communicated to the Royal Society; and that the Royal Society be requested to direct their Secretaries to communicate, from time to time, to the Editor of the Journals of the Royal Institution, such information respecting the papers read at the meetings of the Society, as it may be thought proper to allow to be published in those Journals."

" *At a Meeting of the Council of the Royal Society, on the* 15*th of April,* 1802.

" *Resolved,* That the Council agree to the request of the Royal Institution, as expressed in the above minute of the 5th of April, and that they thankfully accept the offer made them in the minute of the 31st of March."

In consequence of this resolution, the editors of the Journals of the Royal Institution have the privilege of inspecting all the papers communicated to the Royal Society, and of extracting from them such notices as they may think interesting to the public, without being sufficient to supersede the necessity of consulting the original memoirs, when printed in the Philosophical Transactions.

The Count de Bournon's paper, on corundum, was concluded on the 13th of May. After having considered the matrix of imperfect corundum from the peninsula of India, with the feltspar, the fibrolite, the thallite, or epidote of Haüy, the hornblende, the quartz, the talc and mica, the garnets, the zircon, and the black oxid of iron, that this matrix usually contains, some of them substances now first named, the author proceeds to the matrix of imperfect corundum from China, and from the kingdom of Ava, which is a granite rock, composed of feltspar, fibrolite, mica, and black oxid of iron, without the peculiar substance, which is the basis of the matrix of the imperfect corundum from the Carnatic: sometimes a little chlorite and thallite occur in this matrix. Next, the matrix of perfect corundum from Ceylon is investigated, but it is principally from conjecture that the author determines the spinelle ruby to be one of the substances accompanying it, since it is found in the sands, together with the corundum. The crystals of the spinelle are described as either complete tetraedons, or rhomboids, with plane angles of 60°, or dodecaedrons, or lastly tetraedral prisms terminated by pyramids: its colour is often yellowish or bluish. Its matrix is sometimes a calcarious stone, and sometimes a kind of adularia. Another substance frequently found in these sands is the tourmalin. Its primitive crystal is a very obtuse rhomboid; the solid angle being 139°; the second form is a prism, either hexaedral, enneaedral, or dodecaedral, abruptly terminated; and there are some other varieties: the colour differs very considerably in different specimens; it is sometimes yellowish, bright green, or purplish red; and sometimes the crystals are colourless. A specimen of remarkable magnitude and beauty is mentioned, which was presented to Mr. Symes by the sovereign of Ava, and placed by him in Mr. Greville's collection. The Ceylonite of Lametherie, or the pleonast of Haüy, is also found in the sands of Ceylon; it is usually of a brownish green, and it greatly resembles the spinelle, but is somewhat softer. Small crystals of zircon, with scattered fragments of some other stones, help also to compose this sand, as it is sent to Europe. Of all these substances, the spinelle is the most abundant.

It appears to be doubtful, whether or no corundum is found in any part of the world, except the East Indies; yet the Count de Bournon has reasons for thinking that it has been discovered in some of the mountains of France. But the specimens from Germany, and from Tiree, appear to have been of other descriptions. Whether or no it has been found in the neighbourhood of Philadelphia, is a disputed point. Mr. Haüy considers the specimens from the neighbourhood of Montbrison as a harder kind of feltspar: but the Count de Bournon is persuaded that they are corundums, nearly resembling the sapphire, but combined in some degree with feltspar. The emeralds found in the same place are more strongly characterized.

On the 6th of May, Dr. Herschel's observations on the two lately discovered celestial bodies were read.

Dr. Herschel begins with stating the result of his attempts to measure the diameter of the stars discovered by Piazzi and Olbers. He employed the lucid disc micrometer, which consists of an illuminated circle, viewed with one eye, while the other compares with it the magnified image formed by the telescope; and he concludes, that the apparent diameter of Ceres was .22″, and of Pallas .17″ or .13″, at the distance of nearly 1.634, and 1.187 from the earth respectively, whence the apparent diameters at the distance of the earth from the sun would be .35" and .21" or .16" respectively; and that their real diameters are about 163 and 95 or 71 English miles. There is no probability that either of these stars can have a satellite. The colour of Ceres is more ruddy than that of Pallas. They have generally more or less of a haziness, or coma, but sometimes, when the air is clear, this nebulosity scarcely exceeds the scattered light surrounding a very small star. From a view of all these circumstances, Dr. Herschel proceeds to consider the nature of the new stars. He thinks that they differ from the general character of planets, in their diminutive dimensions, in the great inclination of their orbits, in the coma surrounding them, and in the mutual proximity of their orbits: that they differ from comets in the want of eccentricity, and of a considerable nebulosity. Dr. Herschel, therefore, wishes to call them asteroids, a term which he defines as a celestial body, which moves round the sun in an orbit either little or considerably eccentric, of which the plane may be inclined to the ecliptic in any angle whatever, the motion being either direct or retrograde, and the body being surrounded or not by a considerable atmosphere, or a very small coma. This definition is intended to include such other bodies of the same kind as, Dr. Herschel supposes, will, in all probability, be hereafter discovered. Some additional observations show, that the apparent comas, surrounding Ceres and Pallas, scarcely exceed those, which are caused by aberration, round the images of minute fixed stars.

The meetings of the 20th and 27th of May were occupied by an analysis of corundum, and of some of the substances which accompany it; with observations on the affinities which the earths have been supposed to have for each other in the humid way. By Richard Chenevix, Esq. F.R.S. and M.R.I.A.

After several ineffectual attempts to procure a solution of corundum, Mr. Chenevix succeeded by means of subborate of soda, or common borax. He took 100 grains of corundum, and having pulverised it in a steel mortar, after repeatedly plunging it when red hot into cold water, he washed off by muriatic acid whatever iron might have adhered to it, and then levigated it in a mortar of agate, noting the augmentation of its weight in the operation. He exposed the powder with 200 grains of calcined borax in a crucible of platina to a violent heat; it was then boiled in the same vessel with muriatic acid, which in about 12 hours dissolved the glass. The earths were precipitated by an alkaline carbonate: and being redissolved in muriatic acid, the silica was separated by evaporation. The alumina was precipitated and redissolved by an excess of potash, and separated from it by muriate of ammoniac. The process is particularly exemplified in the instance of the sapphire, in which Mr. Chenevix found about one twentieth of its weight of silica, although Mr. Klaproth could scarcely perceive the presence of any silica. The constituent parts of many different corundums are enumerated; they all agree in the great proportion of alumina. The matrix from the peninsula of India contained silica, alumina, lime, iron, and a small quantity of manganese; the feltspar, found in it, consisted of nearly the same ingredients, with a greater preponderance of silica; but the fibrolite was remarkable for being composed almost wholly of alumina and silica, in the proportion of 3 to 2: the thallite contained, besides these two earths, considerable portions of lime and iron. The fibrolite of the matrix from China contained alumina, silica and iron. The feltspar from Ceylon differed but little from the Indian specimens. Mr. Chenevix observes that, in such analyses, crucibles of platina or silver ought to be exclusively employed: but that for boiling earths in potash, silver must be preferred, since platina is copiously dissolved by potash, its affinity with this alkali being such as to enable it to form triple salts with it, a property which the Spanish government employs for detecting platina in gold. Mr. Chenevix thinks, that the reddish colour produced in a weak solution of platina by muriate of tin, is a more delicate test of its presence. He observes, that neither potash nor soda, is, properly speaking, a fixed alkali, especially when a little water is present.

In the second part of the paper, Mr. Chenevix considers the supposed affinities of the earths for each other. He had himself maintained the existence of some of these affinities. Kirwan and Guyton had carried the opinion much further. But Mr. Darrac has combated this extension of the doctrine with considerable success, and Mr. Chenevix has repeated most of his experiments with a similar result. Dr. G. M. at Freyberg, has excited further doubts on the subject. Mr. Chenevix here enumerates the experiments of Guyton, and considers them all as inaccurate, except those which related to the solution of silica in potash, and which were not new; and even these he thinks scarcely sufficient to justify, without further examination, the conclusion of an affinity between this earth and others: and he explains Guyton's error from the impurity of his materials, especially from the presence of sulfuric acid, which Mr. Chenevix detected in the precipitates whenever they occurred. The solubility of silica in acids after the action of an alkali is, he thinks, a circumstance which has given the greatest superiority to all modern analyses; and the solution is in some measure facilitated by the presence of alumina. Alumina also appears to be capable of entering into combination with magnesia, so as no longer to be taken up by potash; and the same earth seems to promote the solution of lime in potash. So that on the whole, the existence of affinities between some of the earths appears to be established, although not to the extent supposed by MM. Kirwan and Guyton. Mr. Chenevix allows the truth of Mr. Berthollet's position respecting the effect of masses on chemical affinities, but observes, that this effect is by no means unlimited; and that the proposition, if true in its full extent, would very much increase the difficulties of chemical analyses, and lessen the important benefits which they confer on the science of mineralogy.

On the 3d of June, a description of the anatomy of the Ornithorhynchus hystrix, by Everard Home, Esq. F.R.S. was laid before the Society.

This animal has been described and figured by Dr. Shaw, under the name of myrmecophaga aculeata, but from the absence of mammae, and from its greater internal resemblance to the ornithorhynchus than to the other myrmecophagae, Mr. Home chooses to consider it as belonging to the same genus with that singular animal, although he thinks it possible that it may hereafter be found to require a distinct generic name. It is a native of New South Wales, and several specimens have been brought over in spirits: its length is about seventeen inches; it is covered with hair and with quills. Its bill somewhat resembles that of the ornithorhynchus, but wants the lateral lips. Its teeth are horny, and confined to the tongue and the palate: the hind legs are furnished with a spur. The stomach has a number of horny papillae near the pylorus: it is much larger than that of the ornithorhynchus paradoxus; and the animal appears to swallow a considerable quantity of sand with its food. The second branch of the fifth pair of nerves is extremely small, so that this species has probably no peculiar sense of feeling in its bill; that of smell appears to compensate the deficiency. The small bones of the ear are only two, corresponding to the malleus and stapes; the divisions of the cochlea are cartilaginous. The contents of the pelvis agree with those of the ornithorhynchus, in greatly resembling the class of birds. Mr. Home has examined several other species of manis and myrmecophaga, but finds that they all are furnished with mammae. The peculiar characters of the genus ornithorhynchus appear to be the spur on the hind legs, the absence of nipples, the smooth beak, and the horny teeth. From all these considerations, Mr. Home infers that the genus forms a connecting link between the mammalia, aves, and amphibia. The Society adjourned to the 17th.

On the 17th an analysis of a pulmonary calculus, by P. Crampton, Esq. was communicated by the Hon. G. Knox, F.R.S.

Mr. Crampton found in 100 parts of the pulmonary calculus that he examined, 45 of lime, 37 of carbonic acid, and 18 of animal matter and water; this was probably albumen, being coagulable in acids. He thinks it probable that this specimen may have been of a different nature from those which are described by Fourcroy, and which have been supposed to contain phosphate of lime. Mr. Crampton thinks it easier to understand how phosphate of lime might have been separated from the blood, than carbonate; but he conceives that even this may be deposited in the lungs, by a morbid process, similar to the healthy one, by which it is secreted, to form a considerable part of the bones.

The same evening a letter from Mr. Carlisle to the president was read, containing a description of two kinds of eyes observed in the Gryllus gryllotalpa; with other circumstances respecting the structure and natural history of that animal.

Mr. Carlisle first describes the eyes, commonly so called: he observes that a membrane, which appears under the microscope to be reticulated, and covered with a dark brown opaque, pulpy matter, is applied in immediate contact with all the interior surfaces of the cornea, and that behind this there is a portion of brain. It appeared, on exposing a section of the head to the direct rays of the sun, that the dark coloured substance intercepted the light almost completely. Mr. Carlisle therefore thinks that these eyes are principally subservient to measuring the intensity of light, and to denoting the illuminated and shadowed parts of objects. The stemmata, which have a greater resemblance to the eyes of quadrupeds, are two in number, situated in the summit of the head: they are pellucid, brilliant lenses, of a horny substance, $\frac{1}{50}$ of an inch in diameter: under them is found a portion of jelly, and next to this a semiopaque membrane, on which the figures of surrounding objects are painted by the lens, and may be discovered by the help of a microscope: behind it is a white mass, connected with the brain, and a branch of the bronchial tubes is so nearly in contact with it, that Mr. Carlisle thinks it may possibly affect the distance of the membrane, receiving the image, from the lens. The two setaceous projections from the tail of the insect Mr. Carlisle supposes to serve the purpose of antennae, since the insect runs backwards as readily as forwards, and never turns in its burrow: this passage is formed simply by compressing the earth, without throwing any out of it. The abdomen of the insect contains a craw, a gizzard, and a digesting stomach: it appears to live on other insects, chiefly coleopterous. The peculiar noise, caused by the friction of the upper wings against each other, which appears to be a mode of conveying intelligence between the sexes, indicates that these insects must be provided with organs of hearing. They are incapable of flying, but their wings assist them in swimming.

On the 24th of June, two communications from William Hyde Wollaston, M.D. F.R.S. were read. The first was on a method of examining refractive and dispersive powers, by prismatic reflection. It was suggested to the author by a consideration of the prismatic speculum employed by Sir Isaac Newton in his reflecting telescope. The angle, at which the total reflection of light of any kind first takes place at the surface of a rarer medium, depends on the comparative density of the two mediums in contact; and hence the measurement of this angle readily furnishes a determination of the ratio of refraction at the common surface, for the kind of light observed. Thus, by means of a triangular prism, a drop of each of two or more fluids being placed side by side on the under surface, it may easily be found, by inclining the prism more and more, which of the dark spots first disappears, and it follows that the respective fluid has the weakest refractive power. But when a solid is examined, it must in general be united by the interposition of some fluid of a higher refractive density, otherwise the contact will be too imperfect; and it is easily shown that this interposition does not affect the ultimate result. But for determining at once the numerical ratio of the sines, Dr. Wollaston has invented an apparatus, in which, by means of a rectangular prism of flint glass, the index of refraction of each substance is read off at once by a vernier, the three sides of a moveable triangle performing the operations of reduction of the ratios in a very compendious manner. In this method it is obviously unnecessary that the substances to be examined should be of any determinate form; and it s as easy to ascertain the refractive density of the most opaque as of the most transparent bodies, provided they be less refractive than the prism employed. It may also serve as a chemical test, for example in essential oils, which when adulterated are generally rendered less refractive; and a very minute quantity is sufficient for the experiment. Where the medium is of variable density, this is almost the only mode in which its refractive power can be ascertained; hence it is of singular utility in examining the refraction of the crystalline lens. (Phil. Trans. 1801. 41.) A copious table of the refractive powers of various substances is here inserted. The dispersive powers of different substances are inferred from similar observations upon the fringes which usually accompany, or rather constitute, the boundary of reflection: the author observes that they are sometimes wanting, or even reversed, when the dispersion is equal at different angles of deviation, or when it is greater even with a less deviation, as when oil of sassafras is applied to a prism of flint glass, as well as in many cases of spars with fluids. Solutions of metallic salts in general are found to be very highly dispersive: by weakening the solution till the line of separation became colourless, and then noting the refractive density, Dr. Wollaston has been able to compare the dispersive powers of several such substances with that of plate glass. He has also arranged a number of substances in a table, in the order of their dispersive powers, at a given deviation; an order materially different from that of their refractive density. A very important observation concludes this part of the essay. Dr. Wollaston observes, that by looking through a prism at a distant crevice in a window shutter, the division of the spectrum may be seen more distinctly than by any other method, and that the colours are then only four; red, yellowish green, blue, and violet, in the linear proportions of the numbers 16, 23, 36, 25; and that these proportions will be the same whatever refractive substance be employed, provided that the inclination of the prism remain unchanged. In the light of the lower part of a candle, the spectrum is distinguished by dark spaces into five distinct portions.

The second paper was on the oblique refraction of Iceland crystal. It contains a confirmation of the experiments of Huygens on this substance, with additional evidence, deduced from the superiority of Dr. Wollaston's mode of examining the powers of refraction. He observes, that Dr. Young has already applied the Huygenian theory with considerable success to the explanation of several other optical phenomena, and that it appears to be strongly supported by such a coincidence of the calculations deduced from it, with the results of these experiments, as could scarcely have happened to a false theory. Huygens supposes the undulations of light to be propagated in Iceland crystal in a spheroidal instead of a spherical form; and infers that the ratio of the sine of incidence to the oblique ordinate of refraction must be constant in any one section, but different for different planes. Dr. Wollaston observes, that, though we do not fully understand the existence of a double refraction, and are utterly at a loss to account for the phenomena occurring upon a second refraction, by another piece of the spar, yet that the oblique refraction, when considered alone, is nearly as well explained as any other optical phenomenon.

On the first of July, a paper was read, entitled, an account of some cases of the production of colours not hitherto described, by Thomas Young, M.D. F.R.S.

When a small fibre, such as a human hair, or a silkworm's thread, is held near the eye, while it is directed to a minute or distant luminous object, an appearance of parallel fringes of coloured light is produced, the colours succeeding each other in the same order as those of thin plates seen by transmitted light, and being larger and more distant as the diameter of the fibre is smaller. Dr. Young explains this circumstance from the general law of the interference of light (Syllabus, 376.); the two portions being here found in the light reflected and inflected from opposite sides of the fibre: and from a single experiment, calculated to determine the angular distance of the fringes, produced by a hair of known magnitude, he deduces a measure agreeing, within one ninth, with the dimensions of the thin plates as ascertained by Newton, and he considers this experiment both as a confirmation of Newton's measures, and of the explanation of these colours. It appears probable that the colours of all atmospherical halos are produced in a similar manner.

The colours of mixed plates constitute another new class of phenomena. When a little moisture, or oil, is scantily interposed between two pieces of glass, proper for exhibiting the common rings of colours seen by transmitted light, we may observe an appearance of other rings much larger than these, which are most conspicuous when they are placed a little out of the line joining the eye and the luminous object. These appear to originate in the interference of two portions of light, passing, the one through the particles of water or oil, the other through the air interposed, and travelling, of course, with different velocities: the explanation is confirmed by the effect of substances of different refractive densities, applied either with air intervening, or with each other, and the measures agree with the calculation.

Dr. Young observes, that he has repeated Dr. Wollaston's experiments on the division of the prismatic spectrum, with success; and thinks it probable that the separation of the bluish light of a candle, into distinct portions, is a phenomenon of the same kind, as is observable when the light transmitted through a thin plate of glass or air is analysed by means of a prism. He also adds, that he has had an opportunity of confirming his former observations upon the very low dispersive power of the human eye in its collective state.

A paper on the composition of Emery was communicated to the Society by Smithson Tennant, Esq. F.R.S. This substance has in general been considered as an ore of iron, but it appears to have very little title to that denomination. Mr. Wiegleb conceived that it consisted principally of silex, but there appears to have been some mistake with respect to the substance that he examined. Mr. Tennant finds that emery is dissolved with some difficulty in a strong heat by carbonate of soda, and after the subsidence of a little iron, the earth contained in the solution is almost purely argillaceous. This result is exactly similar to Mr. Klaproth's analysis of diamond spar or corundum. From 100 parts Mr. Tennant procured 80 of argil, 3 of silex, and 4 of iron, with an undissolved residuum of 3 parts, and a loss of 10; great care having been taken to separate the parts attracted by the magnet: some portions however contained almost one third of iron. The hardness of emery and diamond spar appears to be equal. The emery used in England is brought principally from the island of Naxos; it is imported in the form of angular blocks, incrusted with iron ore, with pyrites and mica; substances which usually accompany the corundum from China.

A catalogue of 500 new nebulae, nebulous stars, planetary nebulae, and clusters of stars, was laid before the Society, by William Herschel, LL.D. F.R.S.; and the preliminary remarks on the construction of the heavens were also read.

Dr. Herschel takes a very enlarged view of the sidereal bodies composing the universe, as far as we can conjecture their nature: and enumerates a great diversity of parts that enter into the construction of the heavens, reserving a more complete discussion of each to a future time. The first species are insulated stars; as such the author considers our sun, and all the brightest stars, which he supposes nearly out of the reach of mutual gravitation; for, stating the annual parallax of Sirius at 1″, he calculates that Sirius and the sun, if left alone, would be 33 millions of years in falling together; and that the action of the stars of the milky way, as well as others, would tend to protract this time much more. Dr. Herschel conjectures that insulated stars alone are surrounded by planets. The next are binary sidereal systems, or double stars; from the great number of these which are visible in different parts of the heavens, and the frequent apparent equality of the two stars, Dr. Herschel calculates the very great improbability, that they should be at distances from each other at all comparable to those of the insulated stars: hence he infers, that they must be subjected to mutual gravitation, and can only preserve their relative distances by a periodical revolution round a common centre. In confirmation of this inference, he promises soon to communicate a series of observations made on double stars, showing that many of them have actually changed their situation in a progressive course, the motion of some being direct, and of others retrograde. The proper motion of our sun does not appear to be of this kind, but to be rather the effect of some perturbations in the neighbouring systems. The same theory is next applied to triple, quadruple, and multiple systems of stars, and particular hypothetical cases are explained by diagrams. Some such cases, Dr. Herschel is fully persuaded, have a real existence in nature. The fourth species consists of clustering stars, and of the milky way: the stars thus disposed constitute masses, which appear brighter in the middle, and fainter towards the extremities, being perhaps collected in a spherical form. Groups of stars the author distinguishes from these by a want of apparent condensation about a centre of attraction: and clusters of stars, by a much more complete compression near such a centre, so as to exhibit a mottled lustre, almost resembling a nucleus. The eighth species consists of nebulae, which probably differ from the three last species only in being much more remote; some of them, Dr. Herschel calculates, must be at so great a distance, that the rays of light must have been nearly two millions of years in travelling from them to our system. The stellar nebulae, or stars with burs, form a distinct species. A milky nebulosity is next mentioned, which may in some cases resemble other nebulae, but in others appears to be diffused, almost like a fluid: the author is not inclined to consider it as either resembling the zodiacal light of the sun, or of a phosphorescent nature. The tenth species is denominated nebulous stars; these are stars surrounded with a nebulosity like an atmosphere, of which the magnitude must be amazingly great; for the apparent diameter of one of them, described in the catalogue, was 3′. The planetary nebulae are distinguished by their equable brightness, and circular form, while their light is still too faint to be produced by a single luminary of great dimensions. When they have bright central points, Dr. Herschel considers them as forming a twelfth species, and supposes them to be allied to the nebulous stars, which might approach to their nature, if their luminous atmospheres were very much condensed round the nucleus.

On the 8th of July, the first part of a paper on the rectification of the conic sections was laid before the society by the Rev. John Hellins, B.D. F.R.S. It contained nine theorems for the rectification of the hyperbola, by means of infinite series, one only of which had been before published, each having its particular advantages, in particular cases of the proportions of the axes and of the ordinates, so that they appear to contain a complete practical solution of this important problem, and they are illustrated by a variety of examples. The author observes that Dr. Waring's theorems, for computing the length of the curve, from ordinates referred to the asymptote, are in their present form of little use, but might easily be corrected in a manner similar to that which he has pursued. He defers, to a future opportunity, the publication of similar investigations relative to the ellipsis.

Observations on Heat, and on the action of bodies which intercept it. By Mr. Prevost, Professor of Natural Philosophy at Geneva.

This paper was read on the same evening. It consists chiefly of inferences from Dr. Herschel's important experiments on the transmission of heat by different refracting mediums, especially the different kinds of glass. Mr. Prevost sets out with the law of the interchange of heat, as ascertained by the experiments of MM. Kraft and Richmann, that while the time flows equably, the differences of the temperature of two contiguous bodies flow proportionally, or are in geometrical progression. Hence, from three observations of the actual temperature of a thermometer, at given intervals of time, we may determine the progression of the differences, and consequently the actual heat of the medium. The author applies this method to Dr. Herschel's experiments on the heat of a solar ray transmitted through different mediums, and the conclusions are very different from what we should at first sight infer: for instance, in Dr. Herschel's 24th experiment, the blue glass intercepted one tenth only of the rays of heat, and not one fourth, as the thermometer seemed to indicate. But the immediate interception must have been somewhat greater than one tenth; for a certain portion of heat, actually communicated to the glass, must have radiated afresh towards the thermometer, and contributed to produce the temperature observed; and accordingly as this circumstance took place in a greater or less degree, the thermometer must have been variously and irregularly affected. Of such an irregularity almost every one of the experiments shows evident marks, and the apparatus is not minutely enough described to furnish data for calculating its magnitude. From these principles an experiment of Mr. Pictet, on the interception of heat, is reconciled with Dr. Herschel's experiments.

In the second part of this paper, Mr. Prevost treats of the reflection of heat and of cold. He observes that Bacon suggested the inquiry respecting the concentration of invisible heat by glasses. Lambert attributed the effect of the reflection from a common fire to its invisible heat. Mr. de Saussure suggested to Mr. Pictet to confirm Lambert's suspicion by experiment, and the success is well known. His experiment on the reflection of cold Mr. Prevost has already employed in support of the opinion that the equilibrium of heat is not a quiescent equilibrium, or an equilibrium of tension, but an equilibrium of motion, where the interchanges of heat on either side are equal: and this theory has been adopted by Professor Pictet, and by other philosophers. Hence the author endeavours to deduce the law already inferred from Richmann's experiments. Mr. Prevost observes, that this theory would be equally applicable to the opinion of those who consider heat as consisting in the undulations of an elastic medium; although he thinks that opinion liable to many objections, especially on account of the resistance which the motions of the planets must suffer from it. In a note added by Dr. Young, who communicated the paper, the assertion of Newton is quoted in answer to this objection, yet Dr. Young confesses that Newton appears to have calculated erroneously: but he observes, that if the slightest difficulty of this kind should occur from astronomical considerations, it might be avoided by considering the luminiferous ether as unconcerned in the phenomena of cohesion, and then its rarity might be assumed as great as we chose to make it.

The Society adjourned to November 4.

INDEX.

The capital numerals refer to the volumes, the figures to the pages.

All proper names are inserted, except those which occur in the catalogue as the authors of essays inserted in collections of any kind. The years of the birth and death of the most eminent persons are added, where they have been ascertained, as a supplement to the chronological tables.

AARON Reschid, I. 595.
Abacus, II. 146.
Abat, II. 283.
Abbé P. II. 309.
Abduction of heat, II. 405.
Abernethy, II. 585, 586.
Aberration, II. 286.
Aberration from colour, I. 431.
Aberration of light, I. Pl. 29. II. 294, 373.
Aberration of the stars, I. 436, 462, II. 321, 344, 355, 645.
Aberrations of lenses, II. 281.
Aberrations of refraction, II. 75.
Abhandlungen der Kaiserlichen academie, II. 107.
Abrégé des transactions philosophiques, II. 106.
Absorption of air, II. 464.
Abutment of a rafter, II. 179.
Abutments, I. 163, II. 176.
Academia Caesarea, II. 107.
Academia di Siena, II. 107.
Academia Theodoropalatina, II. 109.
Academicians, I. 370.
Académie de Berlin, II. 107.
Académie de Dijon, II. 381.

Académie de Montpelier, II. 108.
Académie des Inscriptions, II. 501.
Academy del Cimento, I. 638, 749.
Academy of Brussels, II. 109.
Academy of Erfurt, II. 109.
Academy of Paris, I. 251, 357, 360, 749.
Academy of Petersburg, I. 749.
Accelerated motion, I. Pl. 1.
Accelerating forces, I. 27. II. 28, 131.
Acceleration, I. 29.
Acceleration of the moon's motion, I. 521, II. 336.
Acceleration of tides, I. 585.
Accidental colours, II. 314.
Accidental properties of matter, I. 607.
Accommodation of the eye, I. 450, II. 312, 523.
Accompaniment, I. 394, II. 566.
Account of dials at Whitehall, II. 348.
Accoutrements, II. 203.
Accum, II. 207.
Accumulation of electricity, I. 670.
Achard, I. 754, II. 112, 127, 391, 393, 401, 652, 653.

Achernar, I. 498.
Achromatic eye piece, I. 432.
Achromatic glasses, I. 431, II. 80, 323.
Achromatic lenses, II. 284.
Achromatic telescopes, I. 478, Pl. 28. II. 287.
Achromatic telescopes of one kind of glass. II. 287.
Acids, I. 678, II. 420, 510, 673.
Acre, II. 150, 151.
Acta eruditorum, II. 107.
Acta Hassiaca, II. 109.
Acta literaria Sueciae, II. 108.
Acta physicomedica, II. 107.
Acta Upsaliensia, II. 108.
Acting pump, I. Pl. 23. II. 236, 238.
Actinia, II. 517.
Action of solids on fluids, II. 669.
Actions of fluids, II. 219.
Actual focus, I. 414.
Acustics, I. 258, 367. II. 139, 264, 279.
Adair, I. 714.
Adami, II. 227.
Adams, II. 128, 144, 286, 311, 417, 437, 461.
Addition, II. 1.
Adhesion, I. 146, 152, 155 627, II. 509.

Adhesion of air, II. 381.
Adhesion of fluids, II. 652.
Adhesion of surfaces, II. 381.
Admission of heat, II. 406.
Adsiger, I. 746, 756.
Advancement of science, I. 755.
Aeolian harp, I. 383, 399, II. 274, 275, 564.
Aeolipile, II. 410.
Aepinus, I. 658, 685, 751, 756, II. 285, 417, 418, 435, 437.
Aerial excursions, II. 256.
Aerial perspective, I. 454, II. 314.
Aerial telescope, II. 286.
Aerometry, II. 387.
Aerostatic voyage, II. 447.
Aerostatation, II. To p. 256.
Aerostation, II. 256.
Affinities, II. 380, 510.
Affinities of earths, II. 677.
Africa, I. 571, II. 367.
Agaricus orcades, II. 482.
Agate, II. 184.
Agave, II. 185.
Age, II. 516.
Aggregation, I. 628, II. 511.
Agitation, I. 212, 252. II. 137, 216.
Agitation of a fluid, II. 223.
Agitation of the needle, II. 441.

Agitations, II. 490.
Agitations of chords, II. 267.
Agitations of water, II. 459.
Agnesi, II. 114.
Agricultural instruments, I. 229. II. 207.
Agriculture, II. 519.
Aigle, II. 502,
Aiman, II. 436.
Air, I. 305, II. 60, 159, 220, 238, 320, 378, 413, 464, 471, 503, 509, 511. Buoyancy of the air, I. 38. Resistance of the air, I. 38..40, 201.
Air barometers, II. 461.
Air consumed, I. 634.
Air gage, II. 236.
Air gun, I. 351. Pl. 24. II. 262, 293, 385.
Air guns, II. 253, 264.
Air holder, II. 255.
Air in water, II. 481.
Air jackets, II. 243.
Air pump, I. 271, 339, 355, Pl. 24.
Air pumps, II. 253.
Air thermometer, I. 649, Pl. 39.
Air vault, II. 253.
Air vents, I. 316.
Air vessel, I. 179, 333.
Ajutages, I. 279, II. 61, 221.
Alarm, II. 196.
Albategni, I. 595, 604. D. 928.
Albertus, I. 365.
Albinus, I. 115, II. 311, 385, 523, 597. B. 1683. D. 1771.
Alcalà, II. 364, 365.
Alcarrazas, II. 411, 412.
Alcohol, II. 401, 402, 509, 647, 653.
Alcoometrical curve, I. 510.
Aldebaran, I. 497.
Aldini, I. 677, 753, II. 419, 427.
Aldrich, II. 172.

Aldrovandus, I. 746, 748, 756, B. 1525. D. 1605.
Aleaume, II. 157.
Alembert. See Dalembert.
Ale measure, II. 150.
Aleotti, II. 224.
Aletris, II. 185.
Alexander, I. 238, 592.
Alexandre, II. 376.
Alexandria, I. 239.
Alexandrian school, I. 592.
Alexippus, II. 203.
Alfeld, II. 309.
Alfred, I. 244, II. 196.
Algae, II. 514.
Algarotti, II. 280.
Algebra, II. 113.
Algebraical curves, II. 122.
Algebraical symbols, II. 1. 555.
Algenib, I. 496.
Algol, I. 495, 496, II. 331.
Alhazen, I. 473, 483, II. 280. Fl. 1072.
Alhazen's problem, II. 281.
Aliprand, II. 154.
Alkalis, I. 678.
Allgemeines magazin, II. 109.
Allgemeines repertorium der literatur, II. 105.
Allineations, I. 496.
Alloys, II. 207, 510.
Alluvions, II. 497.
Almagest, I. 595.
Almamoun, I. 595, 604. D. 833.
Aloe, II. 185.
Alphabet, II. 275.
Alphabets, II. 143.
Alteration, I. 135, 141.
Alternate motion, I. Pl. 14.
Alternation of motion, I. 336.
Alternations of a lake, II. 480.
Altitude, I. Pl. 35. II. 365.
Altitudes, II. 355.

Altitudes of the stars, II. 355.
Alva. Duke of Alva, I. 244.
Am. Ac. II. 111.
Amalgams, II. 432.
Amazons, II. 224.
Ambuscade, II. 200.
America, II. 376, 450.
American Academy, II. 111.
American society, II. 109.
Ames, II. 217.
Amman, II. 275.
Ammersin, II. 420.
Ammonia, II. 400..402.
Amontons, I. 249, 335, 356, 366, II. 125, 165, 166, 170, 171, 261. B. 1663. D. 1705.
Amphibia, I. 735.
Amplitudes, II. 374.
Amsterdam. II. 474.
Am. tr. II. 109.
Anableps, II. 312.
Anaclastics, II. 281.
Analytical expressions. II. 672.
Anamorphosis, II. 282.
Anatomy of plants, I. 726. II. 512.
Anaxagoras, I. 744. II. 428.
Anaximander, I. 377, 743, II. 377. B. 611. D. 547. B. C.
Anaximenes, I. 743, 744, 756. D. 504. B. C.
Anchor. Weighing an anchor, I. 204.
Anchors, II. 206, 241.
Ancient arms, II. 207.
Ancient inks, II. 143.
Ancient mirror, II. 283.
Ancient music, II. 279, 566.
Anderson, II. 111, 128, 175, 260, 411.
André, I. 121.
Andromeda, I. 497.
Anemobarometer, II. 456.
Anemometer, II. 455.

Aneurisms, I. 299.
Angle, II. 9, 121.
Angles, I. 104, II. 11, 12, 145.
Anglonorman architecture, I. 254.
Angular functions, II. 672.
Angular surveying, II. 146.
Angular tables, II. 115.
Animal actions, I. 128.
Animal cotton, II. 184.
Animalcules, II. 222, 517.
Animal economy, II. 517.
Animal electricity, I. 677, II. 427, 435.
Animal force, I. 90, II. 164.
Animal heat, II. 408, 517.
Animal life, I. 733.
Animal light, I. 435.
Animal magnetism, II. 439.
Animal materials, II. 184.
Animal mechanics, II. 164.
Animal motions, I. 64.
Animals, I. 724.
Annales de chimie, II. 111.
Annales des arts, II. 111.
Annals of philosophy, II. 111.
Anne, I. 249.
Annealed wire, II. 383.
Annealing, I. 644, II. 403.
Annual parallax, II. 329, 355.
Annuities, II. 117.
Annulus mucosus, II. 530.
Anomaly, II. 340.
Anoria, I. Pl. 22.
Anstice, II. 131, 201.
Antarctic lands, II. 366.
Antares, I. 497.
Antheaulme, II. 444.
Anthelia, I. 443, II. 308.
Anthelion, II. 304, 316, 317.
Antimephitic pumps, II. 253.
Antimony, I. 686, II. 438.
Antiochus, I. 746.
Antiquity of the earth, II. 377, 497.

Anvil, I. 80.
Anvils, I. 222.
Anvil of the ear, I. 387.
A. P. II. 107.
Apennines, II. 493, 499.
A. Petr. II. 108.
Aphelia. II. 372.
Apis longicornis, II. 602.
Apocynum, II. 183.
Apogee, II. 371.
Apollodorus, I. 243. Fl. 120.
Apollonius Pergaeus, I. 240. 253, 594, 604, II. 117, 118. 121. 556. Fl. 242. B. C.
Apothecaries' grains, II. 162.
Apparent attractions, repulsions, and cohesions, I. Pl. 39. II. 655.
Apparent brightness, II. 313.
Apparent diameters of the planets, II. 372.
Apparent diameter of the sun, I. 525.
Apparent magnitude. II. 313.
Apparent motion of the sun, I. 524.
Apparent motions, I. 536.
Apparent motions of the stars, I. 523.
Appearances of comets, II. 346.
Appearances of the celestial bodies, I. 523.
Appearances of the primary planets, II. 344.
Appearances of the secondary planets, II. 344, 345.
Appearances of the stars, II. 344.
Appearances of the sun. II. 349.

Appendages to clothes. II. 189.
Appendages to mills, II. 215.
Appendages to pipes, II. 246.
Appendages to wheelwork, II. 184.
Application of hydraulic forces, II. 235.
Application of forces, II. 181.
Appropriate rectangle of a fluid, II. 651.
Approximation, II. 8, 115, 116.
Apsidal angle, II. 340.
Apsides, I. Pl. 34. II. 32.
Aquapendente, II. 310.
Aquarius, I. 504.
Aqua tinta, I. 120.
Aquatinter, II. 158.
Aqueducts, II. 235.
Aqueous humour, I. 447, II. 82, 530.
Aqueous solutions, II. 395.
Aquila, I. 497.
Arabians, I. 243, 246.
Aratus, I. 604. B. 300. B. C.
Arbogast, II. 119.
Arbuthnot, II. 147, 162.
Arc, II. 9.
Arch, I. 160, 238. See corrections. Pl. 11, II. 42.
Arches, II. 175.
Arches with halos, II. 303.
Archimedes, I. 36, 58, 65, 240, 242, 247, 248, 253, 310, 328, 329, 352, 473, 483, 567, 593, 604, Pl. 22. II. 111, 116, 118, 283, 406, 556, 557. D. 212. B. C.
Archipelago, II. 495.
Architecture, I. 157, 238, 245. II. 172. Hydraulic architecture, I. 308, 312,

II. 232. Naval architecture, II. 240.
Architecture rurale, II. 519.
Arch lute, I. 399.
Archytas, I. 239, 253. B. 442. D. 352. B. C.
Arcs, II. 122.
Arcs of circles, I. Pl. 6.
Arcturus, I. 493, 497.
Arcy. See Darcy.
Are, I. 110, II. 151.
Area of a circle, II. 17.
Area of England, II. 367. See corrections.
Areas, II. 121.
Areas of countries, II. 367.
Arena, II. 321.
Areometer, II. 231, 462, 510.
Aretin, the monk, I. 405.
Argand's lamp, II. 291.
Argo, I. 498.
Aries, I. 497, 504.
Aristarchus, I. 593, 604. Fl. 264. B. C.
Aristophanes, I. 472.
Aristoteles, II. 111.
Aristotelians, I. 16.
Aristotle, I. 7, 25, 239, 253, 352, 366, 404, 405, 407, 473, 483, 738, 744, 745, 756, II. 217, 510. B. 385. D. 322. B. C.
Aristoxenians, II. 551.
Aristoxenus, II. 554.
Aristyllus, I. 592, 604.
Arithmetic, II. 1, 115.
Arithmetical machine, II. 146.
Arithmetical progression, II. 4.
Arkwright, I. 131, 245.
Armati, II. 323.
Armillary sphere, II. 375.
Arms, II. 206.
Arnault, I. 190.

Arnold, I. 196, 200. Pl. 16. II. 194.
Arpent, II. 151.
Arrangement of particles, I. 628.
Arrangement of the stars, I. 493.
Arras, II. 264.
Arrow, I. 226.
Arrows, II. 208, 218.
Arrowsmith, I. Pl. 42. 43. II. 376.
Arsandaux, II. 195.
Arschin, II. 154.
Arsenic, I. 686.
Art de faire les ballons, II. 256.
Art de voyager dans les airs, II. 256.
Art du plombier, II. 200.
Artedi, I. 736.
Arteries, I. 291.
Articulate sounds, II. 275.
Artificial clockmaker. II. 191.
Artificial cold, II. 410. 411.
Artificial globe, I. 565.
Artificial horizon, II. 354, 355.
Artificial magnets, I. 692.
Artificial spring, II. 246.
Artillery, II. 259, 262.
Arts, II. 124.
Arts depending on extension, II. 206.
Arytaenoid cartilages, I. 387, 400.
Asbestus, II. 185, 186.
Ascending force, II. 277.
Ascending thunder, I. 482, 484.
Ascent, I. 32.
Ascent of a cannon ball, II. 260.
Ascent of a double cone, I. Pl. 3.

Ascent of a loaded cylinder, I. Pl. 3.
Ascent of balloons, II. 256.
Ascent of water, I. Pl. 39.
Ash, I. 752, II. 509.
Asiatic mirror, II. 453.
As. Res. II. 111.
Ass, I. 209, II. 279.
Asterites, II. 675.
Asterometer, II. 375.
Astle, II. 143.
Astrolabe, II. 349, 350, 377.
Astronomer Royal, I. 602.
Astronomical apparatus, II. 347.
Astronomical characters, II. 376.
Astronomical corrections, II. 371.
Astronomical dates, II. 349.
Astronomical instruments, I. 537.
Astronomical observations, II. 310, 346. 354.
Astronomical tables, II. 371.
Astronomical telescope, I. 427, II. 78, 351.
Astronomical time, I. 541.
Astronomy, I. 487, II. 324, 376. Practical astronomy, I. 536.
Astrotheology, II. 325.
Athenaeus, I. 242, 253, 746. Fl. 136.
Atkins, II. 161, 231, 313, 510.
Atmosphere, I. 272, 699, Pl. 19, 24.
Atmosphere of Jupiter, I. 588, 702. See corrections.
Atmosphere of the sun, I. 502.
Atmosphere of Venus, II. 310.

Atmospheres, II. 332.
Atmospherical electricity, II. 481.
Atmospherical evaporation, II. 464.
Atmospherical pressure, I. 273, II. 220.
Atmospherical meteors, II. 499.
Atmospherical refraction, I. 441. Pl. 29. II. 81, 299.
Atmospheric machine, I. 337.
Atmospheric tides, I. 588.
Atoms, I. 612, 744, II. 377.
Attachment of horses, I. 218.
Attalus, I. 243.
Attraction, II. 131, 377, 379, 510, 520. Magnetic attraction, II. 437.
Attraction of a hill, II. 364.
Attraction of a sphere, I. 515.
Attraction of a weight, II. 364.
Attraction of dust by electricity, II. 419.
Attraction of gravitating bodies, II. 45.
Attraction of light, II. 322, 330.
Attraction of metals for mercury, II. 659.
Attraction of moisture. I. 708.
Attraction of mountains, II. 359.
Attraction of solids, II. 339.
Attraction of spheroids, II. 359.
Attraction of stars, II. 321.
Attraction of water and oils, II. 381.
Attraction of wood, II. 381.
Attractions, II. 655.

Attractions and repulsion of electrified bodies, I. 663.
Attractions of floating bodies, I. 624, 665.
Attractions of solids and fluids, I. 621. See corrections.
Attractions of the electric fluid, I. 659.
Attrition, I. 156, II. 293.
Attrition in a vacuum, II. 425
Atwood, II. 127, 131, 177, 652.
Atwood's machine, I. 53. Pl. 1. II. 30, 131.
Aubert, II. 673.
Audible interval, II. 575.
Auger, II. 211.
Automaton, II. 374.
Automatons, II. 184.
Auriga, I. 496.
Aurora borealis, I. 687, 716, II. 441, 488.
Aurum mosaicum, II. 432.
Aurum musivum, II. 157.
Austrian measures, II. 155.
Auswahl der neuesten abhandlungen, II. 111.
Auvergne, II. 495.
Auzometer, II. 288.
Averrhoa carambola, II. 513.
Avicenna, I. 192.
Avison, II. 273.
Avoirdupois, I. 124.
Avoirdupois weight, II. 161.
Axes of an ellipsis, II. 23.
Axes of rotation, I. II. Corrections.
Axis and wheel, I. 67.
Axis and winch, I. 204.
Axles, I. 150, II. 203.
Axles of wheels, II. 201.
Azof, II. 498.
Azote, II. 518. See Nitrogen.
Azimuthal instrument, II. 349, 350.

Azimuth compass, I. Pl. 41, II. 444.
Azimuths, II. 355.
Baader, II. 251, 384.
Babylonian observations, I. 590.
Bachelay, II. 674.
Bachstrom, II. 243.
Bacon. Roger Bacon, I. 246, 253, 354, 366, 473, 483, 746, 756, II. 124, 323. B. 1214. D. 1292.
Bacon, Lord Verulam, I. 7, 16, 247, 253, 407, 598, 744, 747, 756, II. 111, 124. 681. B. 1560. D. 1626.
Bag, I. 268.
Bagatella, II. 274.
Bagging, II. 187.
Bagpipes, II. 275.
Bag pump, I. 333. Pl. 23. II. 252.
Baier, II. 325.
Bailey, II. 127.
Baillet, II. 174.
Bailly, I. 591. II. 376.
Baker, II. 121.
Bakerian lecture for 1800, II. 573.
Bakerian lecture for 1801, II. 613, 671.
Bakerian lecture for 1803, II. 639.
Balance, I. 190. Pl. 8, 9.
Balance. Hydrostatic balance, I. 308.
Balance of painters, II. 217.
Balance pump, II. 249.
Balances, I. 124, II. 159, 194.
Balance spring, I. 19.
Balance springs, II. 194. 217.
Baldwin, II. 176, 256.
Baldwin's phosphorus, II 292.

INDEX.

Bale. Society at Bale, II. 108.
Baliani, II. 221, 376.
Balista, II. 207.
Balistic machine, II. 132. 227
Balistic scale, II. 227.
Ball, II. 137.
Ball of fire, II. 483.
Ballast, I. 326. II. 199.
Balloon, I. 273, 346.
Balloons, II. 156, 256, 264.
Balls rounded, II. 210.
Bancroft, II. 322.
Bank, I. 264. II. 233.
Banking, I. 199. II. 194.
Banks, I. 318. II. 48, 142, 214.
Baratteri, II. 224.
Barbieri, II. 497.
Bark, I. 729.
Barker, II. 308.
Barker's mill, II. 237.
Bark mills, II. 213.
Barley, II. 151, 215.
Barlow, I. 124. II. 151, 161.
Barn, II. 180.
Bar of steel, II. 404.
Barometer, I. 704, 712, 748, Pl. 19. II. 69, 450, 482.
Barometers, I. 275, II. 167, 381, 448, 459. Light of barometers, II. 422.
Barometer tubes, II. 667.
Barometrical balance, II. 461.
Barometrical fish, II. 462.
Barometrical light, II. 425.
Barometrical machine, II. 251.
Barometrical measurements, II. 472.
Barometrical motion, II. 182
Barometrical observations, II. 463.
Baroscope, I. Pl. 19. II. 220, 454, 461, 462.
Barrel, II. 150, 151.
Barrel chronometer, I. 190.

Barrel organs, II. 275.
Barrels, II. 202.
Barrow, I. 248, 253, 475, 478, 483, II. 112, 113, 117, 144, 313, 597, 609, 623. B. 1630. D. 1677.
Barruel, II. 128, 653.
Bartel, II. 492.
Barthez, II. 164.
Barthold, II. 674.
Bartholin, I. 477, 483, B. 1616. D. 1680.
Bartholinus, II. 291, 337, 478, 479.
Bartoli, II. 264.
Barton, I. Pl. 4.
Barulcus, II. 198.
Basaltes, II. 494, 498.
Base measured, II. 147.
Bases measured, II. 360.
Baskets, I. 219.
Basket work, II. 188.
Bass, I. 399.
Bataafsch genootschap, II. 109.
Batavian drops, II. 403.
Batavian society, II. 109.
Bath, II. 403.
Bathing tub, II. 180.
Baths, II. 410, 411, 518.
Bath society, II. 519.
Batsha, I. 586, 605.
Batteries for electricity, II. 433.
Battering ram, I. 234.
Battery, I. 666.
Battery of charcoal, II. 428.
Battery of talc, II. 433.
Battery of Volta, I. 53. Pl. 40.
Batting cotton, II. 185.
Bauer, II. 416.
Bauhin, II. 748, 756. J. Bauhin. B. 1541. D. 1613. C. Bauhin. B. 1560. D. 1624.

Baumé, II. 231.
Bavarian Academy, II. 109
Bavarian measures, II. 148·
Baxter, II. 324.
Bayer, I. 496.
Bayreuss, II. 184.
B. B. II. 105.
Bead pump, I. 335, II. 236.
Beads, II. 157.
Beads in equilibrium, I. Pl. 11.
Beam, I. 147, 149. II. 169.
Beam compasses, I. Pl. 6. II. 144.
Beams, I. Pl. 10. II. 168. 178.
Beams in equilibrium, I. Pl. 11. II. 43.
Beams of light, II. 303.
Beams of ships, II. 241.
Bear, I. 496.
Bearing heat, II. 463.
Beating plaster, II. 213.
Beat, I. Pl. 25.
Beats, I. 390. II. 544.
Beatson, II. 239.
Beaver hats, II. 189.
Beccaria, I. 714. II. 293. 362, 415, 432, 482.
Beck, II. 416.
Becket, II. 416.
Beckmann, II. 111, 127, 141, 217.
Bédos, II. 275.
Beds, II. 179.
Beds of air, II. 221.
Beech, II. 509.
Beehives, II. 180.
Beer measure, II. 150.
Bees, II. 516, 517.
Beetle, II. 516.
Beguelin, I. 480. II. 288.
Beighton, I. 347, 357, Pl. 24.
Beitz, II. 264.
Belgrado, II. 383.
Belidor, II. 141, 219, 232, 246, 261.

Bell, I. 401. II. 268.
Bellin, II. 441.
Bellows, I. 264, 343, Pl. 24. II. 252.
Bells, II. 274, 486.
Bells of clocks, II. 194.
Beltinzoli, II. 224.
Belts, II. 189.
Belts of Saturn, II. 335.
Bemetzrieder, II. 273.
Benedetti, I. 247.
Bengal society, II. 111.
Bennet, I. 141, 142, 682, 683. Pl. 40. II. 324, 416, 630.
Bent columns and bars, I. Pl. 9.
Bentham, II. 174.
Bent lever, I. Pl. 3.
Bent lever balance, I. 120, Pl. 9, II. 160.
Bent pipes, I. 293, II. 222.
Bent sails, II. 227.
Bent straps, I. Pl. 13.
Benvenuti, II. 316.
Benzenberg, II. 284, 358, 500.
Bérard, II. 129.
Beraud, II. 417.
Berdoe, II. 416.
Bergen, II. 387.
Bergmann, I. 750, II. 112, 366, 399, 482, 508. B. 1735. D. 1784.
Bergmannisches journal, II. 263.
Berkel, II. 436.
Berkeley, II. 310.
Berlin. Académie de Berlin, II. 107. Physical society at Berlin, II. 110.
Berline, II. 202.
Berlinghieri, II. 408.
Berlinische sammlungen, II. 109.

INDEX.

Berlinisches magazin, II. 109.
Bernard, II. 152.
Bernardi, II. 244.
Bernardus, II. 147.
Bernhard, II. 222.
Bernisches magazin, II. 119.
Bernoulli, I. 60, 202, 269. 300, 350. II. 117, 140, 165, 194, 195, 261, 325, 386. D. Bernoulli, I. 250, 253, 277, 281, 379, 358, 360, 366, 384, 406, 407, 649, Pl. 20, 22, 39, II. 219, 538, 539, 547, 556, 583. B. 1700. D. 1782. Ja. Bernoulli, II. 249, 253, 357, 366, 112, 558. B.1654. D.1705. Jo. Bernoulli, I. 249, 253, 357, 359, 366, II. 45, 112, 538. B. 1667. D. 1748.
Beroldingen, II. 494.
Berthelot, II. 141.
Berthollet. II. 466, 673, 675.
Bertholon, II. 256, 482.
Berthoud, II. 202. I. 191, 195, 390.
Bertius, II. 746.
Bertrand, II. 364, 491, 496.
Betancourt Molina, II. 398, 400.
Bettesworth, II. 371.
Bevilled wheels, I. 177, Pl. 15, II. 183.
Bevis, II. 492.
Beytraege zur erdbeschreibung, II. 496.
Beytraege zur kenntniss beider Sicilien, II. 492.
Beytraege zur naturlehre, II. 127.
Beytraege zur verfertigung des barometers, II. 461.
Bezout, II. 370.
Bianchini, II. 333.

Bianconi, I. 371. II. 265, 541.
Bidloo, II. 602.
Biker, II. 402, 403.
Bikker, II. 383.
Billiard balls, I. Pl. 5. II. 138.
Billiards, I. 81. II. 137.
Bina, II. 415.
Binard, II. 201.
Binary arithmetic, II. 4.
Binding, II. 159, 184.
Binocular telescopes, II. 287.
Binomial theorem, II. 4, 114.
Bion, II. 144.
Biot, I. 365, II. 399, 405.
Biquadratic equations, II. 115.
Birch, II. 107.
Bird, I. 602, 604, II. 145, 148, 150.
Birds, I. 734, 735, II. 516, 601.
Birmingham, I. 245.
Biscop, I. 244.
Bisection, II. 11.
Bissextile, I. 539.
Bistre, I. 95.
Bito, I. 243, 253.
Black, I. 365, 652, 750, 756. B. 1728, D. 1799.
Blackened bodies, II. 406.
Blackened wire, II. 407.
Blackening rays, I. 639, II. 322.
Blackey, II. 257.
Blackfriars Bridge, I. 164, Pl. 12, 14. II. 176.
Blacksmith's work, II. 206.
Bladders of fish, II. 255.
Blair, II. 288, 376.
Blakey, II. 146, 411.
Blanchard, II. 143.
Blast furnaces, II. 253.
Blasting, I. 235. II. 216, 218.

Blasting rocks, II. 262.
Blast machine, II. 411.
Blast of air, I. 264.
Bleaching, II. 216, 321.
Bleaching of paper, II. 190.
Bleiswyck, II. 233.
Blind, II. 143, 316.
Blindness, II. 316.
Block, II. 170, 182, 436.
Blocks, I. 69, 229, Pl. 4, II. 241.
Blondeau, II. 239.
Blood, I. 733, 739, II. 517, 518, 646.
Blow, I. 80.
Blowing wheel, II. 252.
Blowpipe, II. 253, 412, 534.
Blue glass, II. 646.
Blue shadows, II. 314.
Blumenbach, II. 497, 601.
Board of agriculture, II. 519.
Board of longitude, I. 251. 602.
Board perforated, I. 145.
Boats, II. 200, 202, 240, 242.
Bob gin, II. 249.
Bode, I. 566. II. 325, 326, 335, 338, 366, 373, 676.
Bodies acting reciprocally, II. 139.
Bodies in motion, II. 140.
Body. Moveable body, I. 50.
Body colours, I. 98.
Boebert, II. 253.
Boeckmann, II. 127, 469.
Boehmische abhandlungen, II. 110.
Boetilia, II. 501.
Boerhaave, I. 751, 756. II. 105, 383. B. 1668. D. 1738.
Bogs, II. 235, 497, 498.
Bohemia, II. 110.

Bohnenberger, II. 430.
Bohun, II. 454.
Boiled water, II. 395.
Boiler, II. 258.
Boilers, II. 255, 410, 412.
Boiling, I. 641, II. 396.
Boiling of a canal, II. 493.
Boiling point, II. 509.
Boiling point of water, II. 396, 397, 400.
Boisseau, II. 152.
Bologna, II. 108.
Bolognan jars, I. 644, II. 403.
Bolognan phosphorus, I. 435.
Bolognan stone, II. 292, 293.
Bolt drawer, I. 234, II. 180. 216.
Bolter, II. 214.
Bolting mill, II. 215.
Bolts, I. 223, II. 180, 205.
Bomb, II. 262.
Bombs, II. 262, 264.
Bomie, II. 556.
Bone, II. 179.
Bones, I. 128, II. 214, 497.
Bones of the ear, I. Pl. 25.
Bonne, II. 147, 393.
Bonnet, II. 502, 513.
Bonnycastle, II. 118, 325.
Bony scales, II. 601.
Bookbinding, II. 159, 189.
Bootes, I. 497.
Borax, II. 293.
Borch, II. 494.
Borda, I. 111, 361, 366, II. 117, 150, 228, 390. B. 1733. D. 1797.
Borda's circle, II. 350.
Borders, II. 187.
Borelli, I. 128, II. 131, 136, 164, 493.
Borge, II. 495.
Boring, I. 228, 229, II. 211, 218.

INDEX.

Born, II. 111.
Boscovich, I. 457, 461, 480, 615, 751, 756. II. 126, 280, 281, 288, 294, 316, 336, 346, 362. B. 1711. D. 1787.
Bossi, II. 448.
Bossut, I. 363, II. 118, 130, 219, 227, 229, 233, 338, 377.
Bostock, II. 519.
Botany, I. 750. II. 511.
Bottom of a cistern, I. Pl. 19.
Bottom of the sea, II. 496.
Bottom winds, II. 458.
Bouguer, I. 358, 366, 437, 478, 480, 483, 531, 697, II. 239, 240, 280, 300, 344, 362, 363, 367, 370. B. 1698. D. 1758.
Boulanger, II. 415.
Boulard, II. 233.
Boulton, I. 133, 245, 338, 349, II. 259.
Bourdé de Villehuet, II. 239.
Bourdelot, II. 525.
Bourguet, II. 495.
Bournon. Count de Bournon, II. 674, 676.
Bourrit, II. 450, 451.
Bovillus, II. 558.
Bow, I. 226.
Bows, II. 208, 218.
Bowstrings, II. 186.
Bowyer, II. 217.
Box, II. 86, 509.
Boyle, I. 7, 355, 356, 366, 475, 483, 749, 756. Pl. 19. II. 112, 317, 660. B. 1627. D. 1691.
Boyle's lamp, II. 245.
Boze, II. 415.
Braccio, II. 153 .. 155.
Braces, I. 169. Pl. 13.
Brachistochronous curves, II. 133.

Brackenridge, II. 118.
Bradley, I. 436, 477, 478, 483, 506, 519, 524, 602, 604, II. 300, 329, 371, 393, 512. B. 1622. D. 1762.
Brahe. See Tycho.
Brahmins, II. 376.
Braidwood, II. 278.
Bramah, I. 222, 335.
Bramah's press, I. 263, 332, Pl. 23.
Brander, II. 159.
Brandes, II. 500.
Brass, I. 694. II. 86, 438, 509.
Brasso, II. 154.
Brass work, II. 206.
Braun, II. 394, 496.
Brazilian stone, II. 583.
Breaking clouds, II. 216.
Breaking ice, II. 216.
Breast pump, II. 250.
Breast wheel, I. 322. Pl. 22.
Breathing, II. 253.
Brehm, II. 128.
Bremisches magazin, II. 109.
Brereton, I. 714.
Brewster, II. 201.
Brice, II. 366.
Bricks, II. 174, 218.
Bricks of Babylon, II. 158.
Bridge, I. 162. Pl. 11.
Bridge of Mantes, II. 177.
Bridge of Neuilly, II. 176.
Bridge of Orleans, II. 176.
Bridge of ropes, II. 178.
Bridges, I. Pl. 14. II. 175, 234.
Bridges of boats, II. 242.
Bridgwater. Duke of Bridgwater, I. 205, 207. Pl. 17.
Briefe ueber die electricitaet, II. 416.

Briggs, I. 248, 253. B. 1561. D. 1631.
Briggs's logarithms, II. 8.
Brightness of stars, II. 326.
Brighton, II, 481, 497.
Brillat, II. 148.
Brine, II. 388.
Brisson, II. 128, 129, 503.
Bristol channel, II. 459.
Britain, II. 365.
British magazine, II. 123.
British manufactures, I. 244.
Brittle bottles, II. 403.
Brittleness, I. 142.
Broad wheels, II. 201.
Brocken, II. 319.
Bronzing, II. 157.
Brook, II. 417.
Brookes, II. 160, 366.
Broom, II. 184.
Brosses, II. 275.
Brougham, II. 296, 625.
Browallius, II. 496.
Bruchhausen, II. 127.
Bruehl, II. 192, 350.
Bruenings, II. 225.
Brugman, II. 437, 514.
Brugnatelli, II. 110, 267, 293.
Brunau, I. 356.
Brushes, II. 142, 189.
Brussels, II. 109, 269.
Buat. Chevalier du Buat, I. 292, 294, 317, 318, 364, 365, 366, II. 222, 225, 245.
Bubble, I. 621. II. 316.
Bubbles, II. 226, 655.
Buchanan, I. 131. II. 166.
Bucket revolving, I. 261.
Buckets, II. 180, 236, 248.
Buckets on a rope, II. 200.
Bucket wheel, I. 327.
Buckles, II. 189.
Buechner, II. 107.
Buerja, II. 134, 219, 279.
Buesch, II. 129, 173, 301, 446.

Buesching, II. 366.
Buettner, II. 495.
Buffon, I. 473, 637, 750, II. 324, 338, 508, 631. B 1707. D. 1788.
Buffon's mirror, II. 282.
Bugge, II. 371.
Building in water, II. 233.
Buildings, II. 174.
Bulfinger, II. 126.
Bull, I. 497.
Bullet, II. 136.
Bullet piercing a board, II. 206.
Bulletin de la société philomatique, II. 111.
Bullets, I. 351.
Bullialdus, II. 330.
Buoyancy, I. 267.
Buoyancy of cork, II. 244
Buoyancy of the air, II. 159.
Buoyant machine, II. 196 237.
Burdach, II. 264.
Burg, I. 602.
Burnet, II. 495.
Burney, II. 280.
Burning glasses, I. 423, 472 II. 284, 406.
Burning island, II. 493.
Burning mirror, I. 473. II. 282, 406.
Burning rocks, I. 235.
Burning wire, II. 430.
Burnisher, I. 119.
Burrampooter, II. 367.
Burroughs's machine, II. 284
Burrow, II. 118.
Burrows, I. 747.
Bushel, II. 151, 155.
Busse, II. 117, 547.
Butschanz, II. 481.
Button moulds, II. 189.
Buttons, II. 378.
Buttress vibrating, II. 270.
Byron, II. 143.

VOL. II.   4 T

Cabaeus, II. 224, 436.
Cabbage leaf, I. 624.
Cabinets, II. 179.
Cable, I. 148.
Cables, II. 241.
Caesar, I. 214, 353, 539, 576, 594, 604, B. 99. D. 43. B.C.
Cagnoli, II. 118.
Caille. See Lacaille.
Calabria, I. 717.
Caldani, II. 271, 518.
Calendar, I. 539, 595. II. 349.
Calendering, II. 188.
Calendering mill, I. 221.
Calender mills, II. 204.
Calibers, II. 145, 155.
Calicos, II. 188.
Calking, I. 94.
Callet, II. 117.
Caloric, I. 653. II. 384, 414.
Calorimeter, II. 408.
Caluso, II. 119.
Calvoer, II. 211.
Camden, I. 245.
Camels, II. 148, 165. Dutch camels, II. 238.
Camera lucida, I. Corrections.
Camera obscura, I. 424, Pl. 28. II. 284.
Camper, I. 117. II. 189, 597.
Camphor, II. 510, 514.
Camus, II. 129, 165, 217.
Canal, I. Pl. 21.
Canals, I. 312, 315, 354. II. 229, 234, 263.
Cancer, I. 504.
Cancrin, II. 127.
Candle, II. 482, 646.
Candles, I. 633. II. 290, 291.
Candle wicks, II. 218.
Caneparius, II. 143.

Canna, II. 153, 154.
Cannon, I. 228. II. 211, 260, 263, 621.
Cannon ball, I. 234, 306.
Canopus, I. 498.
Canterbury cathedral, I. 245.
Canton, I. 372. II. 64.
Canton's phosphorus, II. 243.
Caoutchouc, II. 142.
Capacity for electricity, II. 418.
Capacity for heat, I. 650. II. 408, 508, 509.
Capella, I. 496.
Capes, I. 571.
Capillary action, I. 621. See corrections. II. 380.
Capillary attraction, I. 299. 641.
Capillary spaces, II. 651.
Capillary tubes, I. 623, II. 419, 651, 666.
Capper, II. 454.
Capstan, I. 205, Pl. 3, 4. II. 135, 172, 196, 251.
Capricornus, I. 504.
Car, II. 201.
Carat, II. 164.
Carbine, II. 262.
Carbonic acid gas, I. 370, II. 263, 509, 513.
Carburi, II. 200.
Cardan's rules, II. 115, 124.
Carding, II. 185.
Carding silk, II. 218.
Cards for wool, II. 185.
Carisbrook castle, I. 209.
Carlisle, I. 753. II. 678.
Carney, II. 148.
Carnot, II. 118.
Carp, II. 517.
Carpenter's hammer, II. 206.

Carpentry, I. 157, 166, II. 178.
Carpets, II. 187.
Carradori, II. 384.
Carré, II. 653.
Carriages, I. Pl. 18. II. 201, 203, 291.
Carriage springs, II. 203.
Carriages united, II. 197.
Carrying, I. 132.
Cartes. See Descartes.
Cartesian devils, I. Pl. 19.
Cartesian system of weight, II. 379.
Cartesius, II. 112, 212. See Descartes.
Carthamus, II. 647.
Cartilages of the larynx, I. Pl. 26.
Carts connected, I. 219.
Cart with a crane, I. 211.
Carvings, II. 157.
Cary, II. 577, 579.
Casbois, II. 653.
Cases, II. 180.
Casks, II. 263.
Caspian sea, I. 571.
Cassegrain, I. 429, 433. II. 79.
Cassegrain's telescope, I. Pl. 28. II. 290.
Cassini, I. 44, 502, 595, 598, 604, Pl. 33. II. 299, 331, 335, 358, 362, 366. C.F. Cassini, B. 1714. D. 1784. D. Cassini, B.1625. D. 1712. J. Cassini, B. 1677. D. 1756.
Cassini's orbit, II. 340.
Cassiopeia, I. 495, 496.
Castelli, I. 354, 355, 366. II. 224. B. ab. 1575. D. 1644.
Castelli, II. 295.
Castelli's principles, II. 223.
Casting, I. 113. II. 157.

Castor, I. 500.
Casts, II. 218.
Cast steel, II. 207.
Caswell, II. 558.
Cat, II. 311, 425.
Catadioptric sector, II. 350.
Catadioptric telescope, II. 286.
Catalogue of references, I. 251. II. 87.
Catani, II. 494.
Cataract, II. 316, 598.
Cataracts, II. 222.
Catchfly, I. 724.
Catcott, II. 498.
Catenaria, I. 161. II. 135, 177, 556.
Catoptrical experiments, II. 406.
Catoptric instruments, II. 282.
Catoptric microscope, II. 285.
Catoptrics, I. 414. II. 70, 280.
Cattle mills, II. 181.
Caus, II. 247.
Causation, I. 15.
Causes materielles de l'attraction, II. 378.
Causes of colours, II. 319.
Caustic of a circle, II. 280, 561.
Caustic of a cycloid, II. 562.
Caustic of a parabola, II. 281.
Caustics, I. Pl. 28.
Caustics by refraction, II. 280.
Cavalieri, I. 36, 248, 253, 334. D. 1647.
Cavallo, I. 682, 686, 694, 714, Pl. 40. II. 129, 152, 169, 221, 246, 256, 262

INDEX.

417, 437, 452, 463, 518, 646.
Cavendish, I. 444, 575, 658, 664, 751. II. 308, 359, 418, 653, 668. Lord Charles Cavendish, II. 391, 401, 653, 666.
Cave of Killarney, II. 480.
Caverns, II. 497.
Cavities, II. 537.
Cavity of a fluid, II. 222.
Caxton, I. 247, 253.
Caylus, II. 142.
Cazaud, II. 167.
Cazeaux, II. 519.
C. Bon. II. 108.
Celestial appearances, II. 344.
Celestial globe, II. 374.
Cellio, II. 292.
Cellular pump, I. 335.
Celsius, I. 648. II. 359, 386.
Cement for electrical machines, II. 430, 432.
Cements, II. 175.
Centaur, I. 498.
Centering lenses, II. 284.
Centigramme, II. 162.
Centilitre, II. 152.
Centimetre, II. 152.
Central forces, I. Pl. 1, 2. II. 30, 132, 338.
Centre, I. 418. II. 9. Relative centre, II. 74.
Centre of a bridge, I. Pl. 14.
Centre of agitation, I. 137.
Centre of a lens, II. 73.
Centre of conversion, II. 137.
Centre of friction, II. 137.
Centre of gravity, I. 51, 61, Pl. 3. II. 39, 135, 140.
Centre of gyration, I. 84. II. 52, 137.

Centre of inertia, I. 51, Pl. 2, 3. II. 35, 36, 39, 134.
Centre of oscillation, I. 85, II. 53, 137, 227.
Centre of percussion, I. 85. II. 53, 137.
Centre of position, I. 51.
Centre of pressure, I. 266. II. 59.
Centres, II. 168, 178.
Centres of bridges, I. 171.
Centres of earth, II. 176.
Centrifugal bellows, I. Pl. 24.
Centrifugal force, I. 33, 526. II. 339.
Centrifugal pendulum, II. 194.
Centrifugal pump, I. 330, Pl. 23. II. 247, 250.
Centrifugal regulator, I. 47. II. 182.
Cepheus, I. 496.
Ceres, I. 508, 534. II. 334, 372, 673, 676.
Ceres Ferdinandia, II. 672.
Cesaris, II. 350.
Ceva, II. 145.
C. Gott. II. 108.
Chabert, II. 191.
Chaff cutter, II. 208.
Chain, I. 180, Pl. 7. II. 135, 150, 249.
Chain loaded, I. Pl. 11.
Chain pump, I. 335, Pl. 23.
Chains, I. 111. II. 155, 181, 182.
Chains and ropes, II. 196.
Chains for fusees, II. 193.
Chain shot, II. 264.
Chair, I. 171.
Chair for the deaf, II. 271.
Chair on castors, II. 201.
Chaise, II. 202.
Chaldeans, I. 590.
Chaldron, II. 151.
Chales. See Dechales.

Changes of coasts, II. 496.
Changes of colour, II. 320.
Changes of form, I. 220.
Changes of stars, II. 329.
Changes of the eye, II. 587.
Chapman, I. 364. II. 234.
Characters, II. 143, 376.
Charcoal, I. 634. II. 411, 420.
Charge, I. 665, II. 418.
Charges of guns, II. 260.
Chalk, I. 145.
Chalks, I. 94, 95.
Chambers, II. 127, 172.
Chambers of the eye, II. 311.
Chances, II. 117.
Changeable stars, I. 494. II. 330.
Change of climate, I. 692.
Change of form, as producing electricity, II. 426.
Change of latitude of the stars, II. 334.
Change of meridian, II. 341.
Change of the earth's axis, II. 359.
Change of variation, II. 440.
Charles, I. 376.
Charles II. I. 601.
Charnock, II. 240.
Charts, I. 496. II. 374.
Charybdis, II. 370.
Chase, I. 122.
Châtelet, II. 383.
Chaulnes. Duc de Chaulnes, II. 145.
Cheese, II. 216.
Cheese press, II. 204.
Chemical attractions, I. 678.
Chemical changes, as producing electricity, II. 427.

Chemical effects of electricity, I. 672. II. 423.
Chemical effects of heat, II. 403.
Chemical effects of light, II. 321.
Chemical electricity, I. 674. II. 672.
Chemical production of electricity, II. 428.
Chemistry, I. 14.
Chemists, I. 656.
Chenevix, II. 673, 676, 678.
Cherna, II. 394.
Cherubin, II. 283.
Chersiphron, I. 238.
Cheselden, II. 671.
Chesnut, II. 168.
Chiaro scuro, II. 158.
Childers, I. 133.
Childrey, I. 502.
Chiliogramme, II. 162.
Chiliolitre, II. 152.
Chiliometre, II. 152.
Chimes, II. 194, 280.
Chimney, I. 345.
Chimney pipes, I. 402, Pl. 26.
Chimnies, I. 354. II. 410, 411.
China, II. 218.
Chinese, I. 97, 118, 590. 742. II. 376.
Chinese pumps, I. 336.
Chinese weights, II. 160.
Chiron, II. 376.
Chladni, I. 373, 380, 384, 385, 406, Pl. 25. II. 49, 261, 269, 403, 501, 541, 547, 549.
Chocolate, II. 426.
Choppin, II. 151.
Chopping, II. 214.
Chord, I. Pl. 25. II. 65.
Chord, II. 9.
Chords, II. 4, 16.

Chords, II. 267.
Chords of a circle, I. 43, Pl. 2. II. 33.
Choroid, II. 530.
Choroid coat, I. 448. II. 82.
Choroid of fishes, II. 600. 606.
Christ, II. 474, 497.
Christian era, I. 539.
Christiani, II. 147, 160, 162.
Chromatic aberration, I. 432. II. 80.
Chromatic corrections, II. 286, 288.
Chromatic scale, I. 393.
Chronhyometer, II. 476.
Chronology, I. 538. II. 349, 378.
Chronology of acoustics, I. 407.
Chronology of astronomers, I. 604.
Chronology of authors on hydrodynamics, I. 366.
Chronology of mathematicians and mechanics, I. 253.
Chronology of optical authors, I. 483.
Chronology of physical authors. I. 756.
Chronometers, II. 96, 365.
Chronometer with a barrel, I. 190, Pl. 15.
Churchman, I. Pl. 41. II. 442.
Churcol, II. 380.
Churns, II. 216.
Chyle, I. 739.
Cicero, I. 596.
Cider mill, II. 214.
Cider press, II. 204.
Cieling, I. 148.
Cielings, II. 176.
Ciliary processes, II. 82, 530, 599, 605.

Ciliary zone, II. 524.
Cimabue, I. 246, 253. B. 1240, D. 1300.
Cimento. Academicians del Cimento, I. 374, 638. Academy del Cimento, II. 107.
Circle, II. 9, 121, 124. Graduated circle, I. 105.
Circle in perspective, I. Pl. 8.
Circle revolving, II. 53.
Circles, I. 101, Pl. 6. II. 15, 16, 118.
Circles with halos, II. 304.
Circular instruments, II. 350, 352.
Circular pendulum, I. 197. II. 35, 133, 216.
Circular slider, I. Pl. 7.
Circulating decimals, II. 115.
Circulation, II. 518.
Circulation of fluids, II. 405.
Circulation of the blood, I. 291, 748.
Circumference of a circle, II. 17, 121.
Circumpolar ice, II. 343.
Cisalpinus, I. 748.
Ciscar, II. 128, 239.
Cisterns, I. 313. II. 233, 245.
Clairaut, I. 250, 253, 480, 483, 513, 514, 522, 569, 621. See corrections, 754. II. 324, 338, 339, 340, 341. 359, 363, 557, 659, 661, 669, 670. B. 1712. D. 1765.
Clairaut's circle, I. 107.
Clarinet, I. 402. II. 567.
Clapp, II. 500.
Clare, II. 222.
Clark, II. 117, 130, 157.
Clarke, I. 250, 253. II. 115, 116, 231, 240, 519. B. 1675. D. 1729.

Classes of animals, I. 733.
Classes of plants, I. 730, 731.
Clavelin, II. 412.
Clavering, II. 412.
Clavichord, I. 398. II. 275.
Clavicylinder, II. 275.
Clauberg, II. 124.
Clay, II. 388.
Cleaning cloths, II. 188.
Cleaning prints, II. 142.
Clearing canals, II. 224.
Clearing harbours, II. 197.
Clearing roads, II. 204.
Clepsydras, I. 188, 353. II. 196, 217, 245.
Clerk, II. 143, 593.
Climate, II. 450.
Climate of America, II. 450.
Climates, I. 571, 696. II. Corrections.
Climbing up a steeple, II. 199.
Clock, II. 217, 359.
Clockmakers, II. 218.
Clocks, I. 189, 246. II. 191, 217.
Clods, II. 216.
Cloth, I. 186. II. 187.
Clothes, II. 189.
Clouds, II. 474.
C. L. ueber electricitaet, II. 416.
Cluster, I. 492.
Coach, I. Pl. 18. II. 201.
Coaches, II. 218.
Coach springs, I. 148. II. 168, 203.
Coal, II. 410, 412.
Coal borings, II. 495.
Coalescence of sounds, II. 544.
Coal mines, II. 211, 212, 259.
Coals, I. 124. II. 151, 167, 202, 218.

Coat, II. 189.
Coats of the eye, II. 311.
Cobalt, I. 686.
Cocheouking, I. 595, 604.
Cochlea, I. 387.
Cod fish, II. 606.
Coexistence of vibrations, II. 139.
Coffee, II. 403.
Coffee mill, II. 214.
Cogs, II. 183.
Cohesion, I. 616, 618, 655, Pl. 39. II. 174, 380, 509, 656.
Cohesion of fluids, I. 754. II. 228, 649.
Cohesion of liquids, I. 620.
Cohesion of mercury, I. 622.
Cohesion of mercury and glass, I. 626.
Cohesion of solids, I. 626.
Cohesion of water, I. 622.
Cohesion of wet plates, I. 625.
Cohesive strength, II. 49, 169.
Coining, I. 224. II. 206, 217.
Coke, II. 411.
Cold, I. 631, 638, 647. II. 383, 396, 450, 452, 518.
Cold. Artificial cold, II. 410.
Cold, as affecting the needle, II. 440.
Colden, II. 377.
Cold water, II. 394.
Cold winds, II. 458.
Cole, I. 335.
Colebrook Dale, II. 494.
Collecting heat by glasses, II. 405.
Collections, II. 105.
Collections of single authors, II. 111.
Collector, I. Pl. 40.

Collini, II 494.
Collins, II. 124.
Collision, I. 75. Pl. 5, II. 51, 52, 136, 140, 385.
Colorific rays, II. 296.
Colour, II. 509.
Coloured anthelia, II. 308.
Coloured bodies, II. 406.
Coloured fringes, I. Pl. 30.
Coloured glasses, II. 314.
Coloured rings, II. 316.
Coloured shadows, I. 455, Pl. 30. II. 314.
Colour grinders, II. 214.
Colouring, II. 143.
Colour mill, II. 215.
Colour of the air, II. 320.
Colours, I. 457, Pl. 29, 30, II. 70, 214, 280, 295, 312, 314, 318, 319, 543, 613, 616, 617, 637, 642, 671.
Colours in telescopes, II. 286.
Colours of diffracted light, I. 464.
Colours of double lights, II. 316.
Colours of fibres, II. 633, 680.
Colours of mirrors, I. Pl. 30.
Colours of mixed plates, I. 470, II. 635, 680.
Colours of natural bodies, I. 469. II. 646.
Colours of opaque bodies, II. 321.
Colours of the stars, I. 456, 490. II. 326.
Colours of thin plates, I. 468, 611.
Colours produced by friction, II. 316.
Colours round a candle, II. 316.
Columbium, II. 671.
VOL. II.

Column, I. 157, Pl. 11, II. 46.
Columnaria, I. 316, II. 246.
Column compressed, extended, and bent, I. Pl. 9.
Column crushed, I. Pl. 10.
Column of mercury, I. 626.
Columns, I. 139, II. 173. Bending of columns, II. 452.
Combination of undulations, II. 624.
Combination of vibrations, I. Pl. 25.
Combinations, II. 117. 510.
Combinations of sounds, I. 389, II. 553.
Combinations of tides, I. 584.
Combined levers, I. Pl. 3.
Comb pots, II. 185.
Combs, II. 210.
Combs of looms, II. 187.
Combustion, I. 434, 634, II. 290, 385, 408.
Comets, I. 512, 531, 721, Pl. 32, 33, II. 337, 341, 346.
Comma scapement, I. 196.
Commensurable quantities, II. 2.
Commentarii Bononiensea, II. 108.
Commentat. Gott. II. 108.
Commercial magazine, II. 111.
Commercium epistolicum, II. 124.
Commercium Norimbergense, II. 108.
Committee of the Royal Society, II. 390.
Common measure, II. 13.
Communication of electricity, II. 421.

Communication of heat, I. 635, II. 404, 465.
Communication of motion, II. 136.
Communications to the Board of Agriculture, II. 519.
Companion of a trochoid, II. 558.
Comparative anatomy of the eye, II. 311.
Comparative physiology, II. 517.
Comparative table of physical properties, II. 509.
Comparer of scales, II. 149.
Comparetti, I. 480, II. 271, 311, 317.
Comparison of heat and electricity, II. 404.
Comparison of measurements of degrees, II. 362.
Comparison of measures, II. 147.
Comparison of the English and French measures, II. 149.
Comparison of variable quantities, II. 119.
Compass, I. 689, 743, Pl. 6, II. 444, 489, 519.
Compasses, I. 101, II. 144, 145.
Compass for wheelwork, II. 183.
Compensation balances, I. Pl. 16, II. 195.
Compensations in timekeepers, II. 194.
Composite column, I. Pl. 12.
Composition, I. 392.
Composition of force, I. Pl. 3, II. 134.
Composition of motion, I. 23, Pl. 1, II. 28, 131.

Compound agitations, II. 273.
Compound bodies, II. 136.
Compound capstan, II. 197.
Compound confined motion, II. 139.
Compound interest, II. 117.
Compound microscopes, II. 78.
Compound pendulums, II. 139.
Compound rotations, II. 554.
Compound sounds, II. 273.
Compound tides, I. Pl. 38.
Compound vibrations, I. Pl. 2, II. 343.
Compressibility, I. 370, II. 378.
Compressibility of water, II. 64, 372.
Compressibility of water and mercury, I. 276.
Compression, I. 135, 136, 220, II. 204, 385.
Compression of a column, I. Pl. 9.
Compression of the air, II. 220, 408.
Concave lens, II. 72.
Concave mirror, I. 416, 471, II. 72, 282, 406.
Concavoconvex lens, I. 416.
Conchoidal epitrochoids, II. 561.
Concords, I. 391.
Condamine. See Lacondamine.
Condensation, I. 619, 632, 640, II. 385.
Condensation of mixtures, II. 510.
Condensation of the air, I. 715, II. 220, 408.
Condensed air, II. 265.

4 U

Condenser of air, I. 342. Pl. 24, II. 253, 385.
Condenser of electricity, I. 681, Pl. 40. II. 434.
Condenser of force, II. 182.
Condorcet, II. 114.
Conducting powers for electricity, I. 666, II. 419, 509.
Conducting powers for heat, I. 635, II. 404, 405, 509.
Conducting powers for magnetism, I. 686.
Conductor, I. 680.
Conductors for lightning, I. 715, II. 485.
Conductors of electrical machines, II. 433.
Conductors of electricity, II. 421.
Conductors of heat, II. 404.
Conductors of light, II. 283.
Conduit, II. 217.
Conduits, II. 245.
Cone, II. 17, 21, 45, 121, 375.
Cones at Cherbourg, II. 232.
Cones of the stars, II. 326.
Confined motion, I. 42. II. 33, 132.
Confluence of rivers, II. 224.
Confusion of colours, II. 315.
Congelation, II. 394.
Congelation from electricity, II. 423.
Congelation of quicksilver, II. 520.
Conical paradox, II. 133.
Conical pendulums, I. Pl. 2.
Conical pipes, II. 266.
Conical tube, II. 665.
Conical vessels, II. 219.
Conical wheels, I. 216, II. 201.

Conic sections, II. 121, 144.
Conjugate foci, I. 415, II. 71.
Conjunction, I. 527.
Connaissance des tems, II. 373.
Connected cylinders, II. 138.
Connected systems, II. 138.
Considerations on roads, II. 203.
Consonants, I. 401.
Consonni, II. 296.
Constellations, I. 753, Pl. 36, 37, II. 376.
Constrained revolution, II. 138.
Construction des grands globes, II. 374.
Construction d' un télescope, II. 286.
Construction of a lunar observation, II. 357.
Construction of equations, II. 121.
Construction of instruments, II. 145.
Construction of the heavens, II. 326.
Construction of thermometers, II. 398.
Contact, I. 611, II. 378.
Contact exciting electricity, II. 425.
Content of a sphere, II. 21.
Contents of the catalogue of references, II. 89.
Continents, I. 571, II. 365.
Contingencies, II. 117.
Continuation, II. 120.
Continued sounds, I. 378.
Contracting rivers, II. 234.
Contraction, I. 640.
Contraction of a stream, I. 280.
Contraction of moist ropes, II. 380.

Contraction of the earth's orbit, II. 334.
Contraction of the muscles, II. 427.
Contrate wheel, I. 177, Pl. 15.
Converging series, II. 116.
Conversion, II. 137.
Convex lens, II. 72.
Convex mirror, I. 416, II. 72.
Conveying boats, II. 235.
Conveying coals, II. 202.
Conveying heat, II. 411.
Cook, I. " 565."
Cooling, II. 386, 404, 408.
Cooling liquors, II. 411.
Cooling water, I. 746, II. 395.
Cooper, II. 436, 678.
Cooper's work, II. 180.
Copernican system, I. Pl. 38.
Copernicus, I. 596, 597, 598, 604, II. 324.
Copleian medal, I. 671.
Copper, II. 266, 509.
Copper plate printing, I. 121.
Copper plates, I. 118.
Coppersmith's work, II. 206.
Copying, I. 93, II. 143, 159.
Copying letters, I. 121.
Copying statues, I. 113.
Copying writing, II. 205.
Coquebert Montbret, II. 162.
Coral, II. 519.
Corchorus, II. 190.
Cordage, II. 186.
Cording stuffs, II. 188.
Cords, II. 186.
Corelli, II. 572, 611.
Corinthian column, I. Pl. 12.
Cork cutting, II. 208.
Corn, II. 215.

Cornea, I. 447, II. 82, 311, 530, 587.
Corner of a passage, II. 562.
Corn fan, I. 345.
Corn mills, I. 232, 233, Pl. 18, II. 107.
Cornwall, II. 484.
Coronae, I. Pl. 30, II. 317.
Coronae round a candle, II. 316.
Correction of dispersion, I. Pl. 28.
Corrections of quadrants, II. 350.
Corrections of lunar observations, II. 357.
Corrections of observations, II. 354, 355.
Corrections of timekeepers, II. 194.
Corresponding distances, II. 348.
Corundum, II. 675, 677, 680.
Cosine, II. 15.
Cosmotheoros, II. 344.
Coster, I. 246.
Cotes, I. 249, 253. II. 120, 122, 219, 287, 556, 557. B. 1682. D. 1716.
Cottages, II. 174.
Cotte, II. 391, 446, 452.
Cotton, I. 184, II. 184, 186, 218.
Cotton mill, II. 238.
Coudraye, II. 454.
Coulomb, I. 132, 133, 134, 146, 152, 154, 163, 293, 658, 682, 685, 686, 751. Pl. 40, II. 166, 241, 438.
Coulomb on friction, II. 170.
Counteraction of gravitation, I. 203.
Counterpoise for a chain, I. 210.

Counterpressure of fluids, I. 324, Pl. 21, II. 237.
Country measure, II. 150.
Courans magnetiques, II. 436.
Cours d'architecture rurale, II. 519.
Course of rivers, II. 225.
Courtivron, II. 205, 280.
Cousin, II. 119, 325.
Coventry, II. 626.
Coventry's scales, I. 112.
Covering houses, II. 179.
Cowley, II. 117, 123.
C. Petr. II. 108.
Crabtrie, II. 331.
Cracking, I. 643.
Craig, II. 120.
Crane, I. Pl. 17.
Cranes, I. 208..210, II. 198.
Cranks, I. 173, 193, 335, Pl. 14, II. 182.
Cramer, II. 489.
Crampton, II. 678.
Crape, I. 186, II. 187.
Crape micrometer, II. 289.
Crawford, I. 651, 750, II. 381, 391, 408, 508. D. 1795.
Crayons, I. 95, II. 142.
Creation, II. 498.
Credibility, II. 117.
Crell, II. 110.
Cressy, II. 263.
Crested fringes, II. 640, 643.
Creve, I. 752, II. 427.
Crichton, II. 399.
Cricoid cartilage, I. 400.
Croesus, I. 238.
Cromorn pipe, I. Pl. 26.
Croonian lecture, II. 671.
Cropping cloths, II. 188.
Crosier, I. 498.
Cross attending the moon, II. 304.
Cross bows, II. 207.

Cross hair, II. 351.
Cross stitch, II. 189.
Cross wires, II. 290.
Crotalaria, II. 185.
Crotch, II. 280.
Croune, I. 749, 756.
Crow, II. 216.
Crown, I. 497.
Crown wheel, I. 177, Pl. 15.
Croy. Duc de Croy, II. 366.
Cruikshank, I. 753.
Crushing a column, I. 145.
Crusius, II. 126.
Crutch scapement, I. 194.
Cryptogamous plants, I. 726.
Crystalline gland, II. 599.
Crystalline lens, I. 448, 451, II. 82, 311, 525, 530, 552, 592, 597, 605.
Crystalline zone, II. 605.
Crystallization, I. 628, 642, 695, 724, II. 321, 511.
Crystals, I. 445, II. 383, 511.
Ctesibius, I. 242, 253, 353, 366, 404, 407. II. 293, 385. Fl. 135. B. C.
Ctesiphon, I. 238, 253.
Cube, II. 17.
Cube in perspective, I. Pl. 8.
Cubic equations, II. 115.
Cubit, II. 152.
Cubit of the Nile, II. 148.
Cuff, II. 285.
Cuffnells, II. 241.
Culinary heat, I. 637, II. 282.
Cullen, I. 740.
Cultivation, II. 519.
Cultivator, II. 212, 213.
Cumana, II. 501.
Cumberland, II. 147.
Cumming, I. 196. Pl. 16. II. 191, 195.
Cunn, II. 117.

Cupping, I. 274.
Curr, II. 258.
Current, I. 587.
Current at the Straights, I. 708.
Current of air, II. 193.
Currents, II. 458.
Currents of air from electricity, I. 665.
Curtius, I. 238.
Curvature, II. 22, 120.
Curvature of an ellipsis, II. 23.
Curvature of an image, I. 419, 425, 429, Pl. 28. II. 76.
Curvature of a rod, I. 139.
Curvature of a spring, II. 168.
Curvature of a surface, II. 650.
Curvature of chords, II. 267.
Curvature of the earth's surface, II. 359.
Curvature of the sky, II. 313.
Curvature of the surface of a fluid, I. 621.
Curve cutting others, II. 120.
Curve described by light, II. 300.
Curved surfaces, II. 123, 227, 650.
Curve line, II. 9.
Curve of equable descent, II. 226.
Curve of equal pressure, II. 227.
Curves, II. 22, 120.
Curves of descent, II. 227.
Cusanus, II. 558.
Cushion, I. 680.
Cuthbertson, I. 342, Pl. 24, II. 254, 416, 432.
Cutlery, II. 207.

Cutting, II. 279.
Cutting cloth, II. 188.
Cutting combs, II. 210.
Cutting glass, II. 210.
Cutting instruments, I. 227, II. 207, 208.
Cutting screws, II. 210.
Cutting straw, II. 208.
Cuttle fish, I. 95.
Cuvier, II. 601.
Cyanometer, II. 474.
Cycloid, I. 44, Pl. 1, 10, II. 24, 51, 122 .. 124, 132, 226, 281, 558.
Cycloidal curves, II. 555.
Cycloidal paths, I. 527.
Cycloidal pendulum. I. 197, Pl. 2, II. 34.
Cygnus, I. 496.
Cylinder, II. 17, 40, 123. Double cylinder, I. 67.
Cylinder of an electrical machine, I. 680.
Cylinder rolling upwards, II. 134.
Cylinders, I. 228, II. 135.
Cylinder with a thread round it, II. 138, 139.
Cylinder scapement, I. 195.
Cylindrical vaulting, II. 177.
Cylindroids, II. 20, 122. See corrections.
Cymbal, I. 401.
Dakar, II. 324.
Dalby, II. 301.
Dalembert, I. 60, 250, 253, 360, 366, 406, 480, 483, II. 130, 219, 273, 322, 341, 454. B. 1717. D. 1783.
Dalibard, II. 415.
Dallebarre, II. 285.
Dalton, I. 370, 613, 632, 706 .. 708, 753, II. 266, 393, 398, 400, 409, 447, 466, 467, 470.

Damaged ships, II. 243.
Damascus sword blades, II. 207.
Damen, II. 478.
Dancing, II. 563.
Danske selskab, II. 108.
Dante, I. 746. B. 1265. D. 1321.
Danzig. Society at Danzig, II. 108.
Darcy, II. 130, 260.
Dark disc micrometer, II. 352.
Darkness, II. 474.
Dark rays, II. 647.
Darrac, II. 677.
Darwin, II. 324. R. Darwin, I. 481, II. 515, 518.
Dasymeter, II. 462.
Dates, II. 217.
Dati, II. 558.
Daubenton, II. 750, 756. B. 1716. D. 1799.
Daval, II. 643.
Davies, II. 503.
Da Vinci. See Vinci.
Davis, II. 114.
Davison, II. 114.
Davis's quadrant, II. 350.
Davy, I. 639, 653, 678, 684, 720, 752, 753, II. 623.
Dawes, II. 148.
Day, I. 525, II. 344.
Dead beat scapement, I. 195. Pl. 16, II. 193.
Dead water, I. 304, Pl. 21.
Deaf, II. 278.
Deafness, II. 271, 430, 671.
Deal, II. 86.
Debility of sight, II. 316.
Debrosses, II. 275.
Decade, II. 111.
Decagramme, II. 162.
Decametre, II. 152.
Decalitre, II. 247.
De Caus, II. 247.
Decay of light, II. 294.

Decay of sound, I. 376, II. 266, 539.
Deception of sight, II. 314.
Dechales, II. 112, 224.
Decharges, II. 264.
Decigramme, II. 162.
Decilitre, II. 152.
Decimal arithmetic, II. 4. 124.
Decimal fractions, I. 108.
Decimetre, II. 152.
Decistere, II. 152.
Declination, I. 536, 542, Pl. 35.
Declination of columns, II. 173.
Declination of falling bodies, II. 358.
Declination of the compass, I. 691, Pl. 41.
Declination in London, II. 443.
Declination of the stars, II. 344, 355.
Declivities of mountains, II. 498.
Decomposition, II. 291.
Decomposition of water, I. 672.
Decomposition with light. I. 435.
Decrement of heat, II. 404.
Decrements, II. 7.
Decremps, II. 127.
Decyphering, II. 143.
De Dominis. See Dominis.
Defects of sight, I. 450.
Definition, I. 18.
Deflective forces, I. 33.
Defondeur, I. 246.
Degaulte, II. 445.
Degeer, I. 750, 756. B. 1720. D. 1778.
Degoguet, II. 217.
Degrees, I. 104, 569, II. 358.
Degrees of a spheroid, II. 363.

Delairas, II. 128.
Delambre, II. 361.
Delarive, II. 267.
Delaunay, II. 435.
Delaval, I. 481, II. 321.
Delft ware, II. 218.
Delineator, II. 284.
Delisle, II. 324, 366, 386.
Delius, II. 211.
Della Torre, II. 493.
Deloys, II. 127.
Delta, I. 721.
Deltoid muscle, I. 128.
Deluc, I. 706, 709, 710, 750, 751, II. 128, 367, 388, 390, 391, 393, 398, 418, 446, 466, 469 .. 473, 497.
Deluc's hygrometer, I. Pl. 41.
Deluge, II. 495, 497, 498.
Déluge, II. 496.
Demetrius Phalereus, I. 592.
Democritus, I. 238, 253. 744, 745, 756. B. 470. D. 361. B. C.
Demoivre, I. 249, 253, II. 113, 117. B. 1667. D. 1754.
Demolition, I. 234, II. 216.
Denarius, II. 162.
Dendera, II. 377.
Dendrometer, I. 107, II. 156, 351.
Denebola, I. 497.
Denier, II. 161.
Denmark, II. 367. Royal Society of Denmark, I. 108.
Densities, II. 503.
Densities of the sun and planets, I. "565."
Density, I. 610.
Density of air, II. 404, 471.
Density of brine, II. 388.
Density of the atmosphere, I. Pl. 19.

Density of the earth, I. 575, II. 364.
Density of the moon, II. 336.
Density of the planets, II. 333, 339, 359, 372.
Density of water, II. 389.
Deoxidation, II. 323.
Deposition, I. 707, II. 396.
Depositions of the sea, II. 497.
Depression of liquids I. Pl. 39.
Depression of mercury, II. 381.
Depth of a river, 225, 236.
Depth of the sea, I. 579, 581, II. 255, 343.
Depth of vessels, II. 396.
Derham, I. 201. 370, II. 107, 125, 191, 325, 457, 541. B. 1657. D. 1735.
Derivations, II. 119.
Derwent lake, II. 458.
Desaguliers, I. 129, 131, 250, 253, 360, II. 126, 148, 165 .. 167, 171, 246, 414. B. 1683. D. 1742.
Design, II. 142.
Descartes, I. 29, 248, 253, 474, 475, 483, 747, 748, 756, II. 112, 272, 306, 323, 523, 527, 557, 558. B. 1596. D. 1650.
Descent, II. 181.
Descent in air, II. 226.
Descent in chords of a circle, I. 43, Pl. 2, II. 33.
Descent in curves, I. Pl. 2.
Descent in water, II. 227.
Descent of a rod on a cylinder, II. 138.
Descent of ground, II. 496.
Descent of spheroids, II. 138.

Descent of water, II. 222.
Descent on a given surface, II. 33.
Descent on elastic surfaces, II. 133.
Descent to a centre, II. 29.
Description des courans magnetiques, II. 436.
Description d'un thermometre, II. 386.
Description of curves, II. 120.
Description of equal areas, I. Pl. 1, II. 31.
Desfontaines, I. 727.
Deslandes, II. 370.
Despiles, II. 142, 217.
Deto, II. 154.
Detrusion, or distrusion, I. 135.
Deutscher Mercur. II. 474.
Deviation of light, II. 71.
Dew, II. 301, 465, 474.
De Witt, II. 204.
Diagonal, I. Pl. 1, II. 13.
Diagonal divisions, II. 155.
Diagonal scale, I. Pl. 7.
Dialling, I. 538, Pl. 35, II. 348.
Dial plate, II. 194.
Dials, II. 348, 375.
Diameter, II. 9.
Diameters of the planets, II. 372.
Diamond, I. 145, 412, II. 509.
Diamonds, II. 217, 293.
Diapason pipes, I. 402, Pl. 26.
Diaphanometer, II. 282, 474.
Diaphragms of a vessel, II. 223.
Diasporometer, II. 282.
Dibbling, II. 218.
Dickson, II. 519.
Dicquemare, II. 645.

Dictionnaire des arts et métiers, II. 141.
Dictionnaire des origines des inventions, II. 217.
Dictionnaire des sciences naturelles, II. 129.
Dictionnaire d'histoire naturelle, II. 503.
Diek, II. 284.
Dieterich, II. 325.
Differential method, II. 119.
Differential thermometer, I. 649, Pl. 39, II. 389.
Diffraction, I. 437, II. 310, 316, 621, 642.
Digester, II. 410, 412.
Digges, I. 474, II. 144.
Digging, II. 211.
Digging in water, II. 232.
Digits, I. 530.
Dijon, II. 110.
D'Inarre, II. 416.
Dikes, I. 312, II. 118, 233.
Dilatation of air, II. 408.
Dilatations of pipes, II. 299.
Diminishing friction, II. 200.
Diminution of columns, II. 173.
Diminution of degrees, II. 358.
Diminution of the sea, II. 496.
Diminution of the sun, II. 339.
Dinocrates, I. 239, 253. Fl. 300. B. C.
Diogenes Laertius, II. 216.
Dionaea, I. 724.
Dionis du Séjour, II. 337, 344, 446.
Diophantus, I. 243, 253, II. 115. Fl. 156.
Dioptrical formulae, II. 287.
Dioptric glasses, II. 281.
Dioptrics, I. 414, II. 70, 280.

Dioscorides, I. 746, 756. Fl. 23.
Dip, I. 692, Pl. 41..43, II. 299, 301, 302, 355, 440, 443.
Diplantidian telescopes, II. 351.
Dipping needle, I. 689, Pl. 41, II. 444.
Direction, II. 27.
Direction of balloons, II. 256.
Direction of motion, I. 20. Pl. 1.
Direction of sounds, II. 575.
Direction of the electric current, I. 669.
Direct motions, I. 527.
Direct tide, I. 579.
Disappearance of heat, II. 408.
Discharge of air, II. 531.
Discharge of electricity, I. 666. II. 422.
Discharge of fluids, I. 279, II. 61, 222.
Discharge of pipes, I. 293, Pl. 20. II. 222, 223, 225.
Discharger, I. Pl. 40.
Discharging electrometer, II. 434.
Discords, I. 394, II. 571.
Discourse on local motion, II. 130.
Discs of planets, I. 527.
Diseases, I. 740.
Diseases of plants, I. 730.
Disengaging horses, II. 203.
Dished wheels, I. Pl. 18.
Dispersion of light, I. 463. II. 77, 282, 287, 295, 320, 637.
Dispersion of the eye, II. 312, 313, 584, 638.
Dispersive powers, II. 298, 299, 509, 579.

Displacement of the equator, II. 342.
Dissimilitude of meridians, II. 341.
Distance, II. 9.
Distance of objects, I. 458.
Distance of the sun, deduced from the theory of gravity, II. 340.
Distances of the planets, I. 506, Pl. 32. II. 333, 372.
Distances of the satellites, II. 373.
Distances of the stars, II. 329.
Distemper, I. 95.
Distilling, II. 396, 413.
Distinctness of telescopes, II. 289.
Distinguisher of electricity, II. 434.
Distorted iris, II. 303.
Distribution of electricity, I. 661.
Distribution of magnetism, I. 688.
Distribution of pressure, I. 44, 134.
Distribution of water, II. 235, 245.
Distribution of weight, II. 211.
Disturbing force of the sun, I. 520.
Ditton, II. 119, 219, 381.
Diurnal variation, II. 442, 443.
Divergence of a stream of air, II. 534.
Divergence of light, I. 420.
Divergence of sound, I. 373. II. 265, 538.
Divergence of undulations, II. 619, 620.
Divergence of waves, I. Pl. 20.
Divided eye glass. I. 432, Pl. 28, II. 290.

Divided object glass, I. 432, II. 289.
Divided speculum, I. 433.
Dividing engine, I. 105, 112, II. 145.
Dividing stones, II. 209.
Dividing thermometers, II. 398, 399.
Diving, II. 243.
Diving bell, I. 246, 342, Pl. 24, II. 255.
Diving boat, II. 256.
Diving machine, II. 244.
Divining rod, II. 480.
Divisibility, I. 607.
Divisibility of matter, II. 378.
Division, II. 2, 3.
Division, I. 227, II. 206.
Division of a circle, II. 121.
Division of a magnet, I. 693.
Division of an angle, II. 145.
Division of labour, I. 244.
Division of the quadrant, II. 118, 145.
Division of time, II. 349.
Division without sharp instruments, II. 209.
Divisors, II. 116.
Diwisch, II. 482.
Dixon, II. 362.
Dobson, II. 467.
Docks, II. 233.
Dodart, II. 550.
Dodgson, II. 252.
Dodson, I. 749, II. 113, 117.
Dog, II. 516.
Dollond, I. 431, 478 .. 480, 483, 602, 604.
Dollort sea, II. 495.
Dolomieu, II. 492, 494.
Dome, I. 164, Pl. 12, II. 49, 175, 176.

Dominant, I. 393, II. 570.
Dominis. De Dominis, I. 474, 483, II. 280, 306. B. 1625, D. 1664.
Donati, II. 366, 496.
Donndorff, II. 416.
Door, I. 148.
Doppelmaier, II. 326, 328, 422.
Doria, II. 610, 611.
Doric column, I. Pl. 12.
Dornavius, II. 478.
Dort, II. 495.
Double axis, I. 67.
Double balance, II. 194.
Double capstan, I. Pl. 4, II. 135, 197.
Double capstan crane, II. 199.
Double concave lens, I. 416.
Double cone, I. Pl. 3, II. 133, 134, 138.
Double convex lens, I. 416.
Double curvature, II. 650.
Double images, I. 441.
Double lights, I. 464, Pl. 3, II. 316, 624, 633, 639.
Double magnifier, I. 431.
Double microscope, II. 78.
Double pen, II. 144.
Double pendulum, II. 139.
Double refraction, I. 445. Pl. 29, II. 309.
Doubler of electricity, I. 682, Pl. 40, II. 434.
Double shot, II. 263.
Double stars, I. 494, II. 328.
Double sun, II. 301, 681.
Double touch, I. 693.
Double vision, I. 453, II. 315.
Doubling, II. 186.
Doubling spar, II. 310.
Dough, II. 216.
Douglas, II. 497, 516.
Dover and Calais, II. 495.

Downs, II. 233.
Drachm, II. 101.
Drachma, II. 162.
Drag, II. 203.
Dragging hay, II. 202.
Dragon, I. 496.
Drags, II. 203.
Draining, I. 328, II. 213, 249, 250.
Drain plough, II. 212, 213.
Drains, II. 235.
Draught, I. 154, 215, II. 165, 181.
Draught of a chimney, I. 345.
Draught of carriages, II. 201.
Draughtsman's assistant, II. 142.
Drawbridge, II. 178.
Drawing, I. 93, 94, II. 142, 158.
Drawing in perspective, I. Pl. 7, 8.
Drawing off liquors, II. 251.
Drawing piles, II. 216.
Drawing ships, II. 243.
Drawing weights, II. 200.
Drawing wire, II. 205.
Dray, I. 212, II. 172, 200.
Dray cart, II. 202.
Drebel, I. 649, 747, 756. B. 1572, D. 1634.
Drebelian thermometer, II. 389.
Dresdnisches magazin, II. 109.
Dressing corn, II. 215.
Dressing hemp, II. 185.
Dressing stuffs, II. 188.
Drill, II. 211.
Drill plough, II. 212.
Driving piles, II. 206, 207.
Drop, I. 620, 624, Pl. 39, II. 380, 655, 656, 664.
Drop between plates, I. 625, II. 655.

Drop in a conical tube, II. 665.
Drop of water, II. 382, 396.
Drosera, I. 724.
Drum, I. 401, II. 268, 274.
Drum and axle, I. Pl. 3.
Dryander, II. 105.
Dryness, II. 476, 477.
Dry rot, II. 180.
Dubois, II. 416.
Ducaila, II. 375.
Ducarla, II. 384.
Duck, II. 184.
Du Crest, II. 388.
Ductility, I. 141, 629, II. 378.
Dudin, II. 159.
Dufay, I. 670, 750, 756, II. 283. B. 1698, D. 1739.
Dufresnoy, II. 142.
Dugdale, II. 233.
Duhamel, II. 107, 125, 158, 168, 179, 186 .. 189, 205 .. 208, 211, 213, 240, 242, 513. H. L. Duhamel, B. 1700, D. 1782. J. B. Duhamel, B. 1624, D. 1706.
Duillier, II. 370.
Duke of Bridgwater, II. 197.
Dulcimer, I. 398.
Dumaitz, II. 240.
Dumb, II. 278.
Dundas. Lord Dundas, II. 259.
Dunkirk, II. 233.
Dunn, II. 442.
Duodecimal arithmetic, II. 40, 116.
Duplex scapement, I. 196, Pl. 16.
Duplicate proportion, II. 125.
Duration of the world, II. 332.
Duséjour. See Dionis.
Dutch camels, II. 238.
Dutch Society, II. 109.

INDEX.

Dutch weights, II. 160.
Dutens, II. 105, 217.
Dutour, I. 480, 483, II. 417, 653, 654.
Dutrone, II. 519.
Duverney, II. 271.
Dying, II. 188.
Dynamometer, I. 127, II. 165.
Eagle, II. 311.
Ear, I. 387, Pl. 25, II. 271, 574.
Earnshaw, I. 197, 198, Pl. 16, II. 194, 195.
Earth, I. 161, 507, 720, II. 172, 220, 358, 371, 372.
Earth as a planet, II. 333.
Earthenware, I. 223, II. 217.
Earthquakes, I. 716, 717, 745, II. 490.
Earths, II. 677.
Earth's axis, II. 364. See corrections.
Earth sinking, II. 495.
Earth's motion, II. 358, 376.
Earth's radius, II. 364. See corrections.
East, I. 500.
Easter, II. 349.
Easterly wind, I. 702. See corrections.
Eastern learning, I. 236.
Ebbing well, II. 479.
Eberhard, II. 110, 126, 320, 376, 436.
Ebert, II. 127.
Ebullition, II. 396.
Eccentricities of the planets, II. 372.
Eccentric wheels, I. 178. Pl. 15.
Ecclesiastical music, I. 404.
Echo, I. 374, II. 542.
Echometer, II. 279.
Echos, II. 266.
Eckhardt, II. 211, 237.

Eckstrand, II. 496.
Eclipses, I. 528, Pl. 34. II, 345, 374.
Eclipses of Jupiter's satellites, II. 346.
Ecliptic, I. 503, 524, II. 334.
Ecole polytechnique. Eleves de l'école polytechnique, II. 280.
Economy of heat and cold, II. 410.
Economy of motion, II. 182.
Ecphantus, II. 377.
Eddies, II. 222.
Eddystone, I. 159, Pl. 11, II. 174.
Edge tools, II. 207, 208.
Edgeworth, I. 306.
Edifices of particular kinds, II. 180.
Edinburgh, II. 399. Society of Edinburgh, II. 108.
Edinburgh medical essays, II. 312.
Ed. tr. II. 109.
Edward, I. 354.
Edwards, II. 157.
Effect of a stream, II. 62.
Effect of machines, II. 54.
Effects of cold, II. 386.
Effects of heat, I. 639, II. 385, 399.
Effects of light, II. 320, 321.
Effects of machines, II. 141.
Effects of sound, I. 378, II. 269.
Effervescence, II. 440.
Eft, II. 516.
Egelin, II. 415.
Egg, I. 734.
Eggers, II. 489.
Eggs, II. 424.
Egypt, I. 236, II. 498.
Egypte, II. 111.

Egyptian measures, II. 148.
Egyptian system, I. Pl. 38.
Egyptian year, I. 539, II. 349.
Eichen, II. 480.
Eimer, II. 155.
Eintraechtige freunde, II. 111.
Eisenschmidius, II. 358.
Elastic bar, II. 48.
Elastic bodies, I. 75, II. 136.
Elastic curve, II. 136, 650.
Elastic fluids, II. 60, 260, 396.
Elastic force, II. 268.
Elastic gum, I. 142, 145, II. 246.
Elastic instruments, II. 274.
Elasticity, I. 28, 137, 628, II. 268, 379.
Elasticity of steam, II. 397, 400.
Elasticity of the air, I. Pl. 19, II. 220.
Elastic joints, II. 138.
Elastic medium, I. 654, II. 321.
Elastic pipes, I. 291.
Elastic plates, I. 385.
Elastic rings, I. 385.
Elastic rods, I. 384, II. 67, 83.
Elastic rods bent, I. Pl. 9.
Elastic springs, II. 136.
Elastic stones, II. 383.
Elastic substances, II. 46.
Elastic surfaces, II. 133.
Elden Hole, II. 496.
Elective attractions, II. 659.
Electrical apparatus, II. 430.
Electrical attraction and repulsion, I. 678, II. 419.
Electrical balance, I. 683, Pl. 40, II. 433.
Electrical crystals, II. 435.

Electrical fishes, II. 435.
Electrical forces, II. 417.
Electrical heat, II. 423.
Electrical kite, II. 482.
Electrical lamp, II. 423.
Electrical light, I. 435, 670.
Electrical machines, I. 680. Pl. 40, II. 431, 433.
Electrical mists, II. 482.
Electrical polarity, II. 419.
Electrical pressure, I. 663.
Electrical pump, II. 431.
Electrical thermometer, II. 423.
Electric current, II. 421.
Electric effluvia, II. 614.
Electric fluid, I. 659.
Electricity, I. 17, 685, 750, II. 414, 437, 465, 479, 481, 513, 519.
Electricity in equilibrium, I. 658.
Electricity in motion, I. 668.
Electricity of a compass, II. 445.
Electricity of the air, II. 481.
Electrics, I. 673, II. 419.
Electrified spheres, I. Pl. 39.
Electrometers, I. 682, Pl. 40, II. 420, 433.
Electromicrometer, II. 434.
Electrophorus, I. 680, Pl. 40, II. 432.
Electroscope, II. 433, 485.
Elements, II. 377, 520.
Elements and practice of naval architecture, II. 241.
Elements of rigging, II. 239.
Elements of the planetary motions, II. 371.
Elements of the solar system, II. 372.
Elevation of a projectile, I. 39.

Elevation of liquids, I. 622, Pl. 39, II. 651.
Elevations, I. 572, Pl. 38.
Elkington, II. 235.
Ell, II. 150, 153, 154.
Ellicott, I. 200, II. 390, 391.
Elliot, II. 271.
Ellipsis, I. 37, 47, 116, 375, Pl. 2, II. 23, 122, 562, 681.
Elliptical parallax, II. 357.
Elliptic compasses, II. 144.
Ellipticity, II. 346.
Ellipticity of the earth, I. 569, II. 360, 363.
Ellipticity of the planets, II. 372.
Elliptic motion of a pendulum, I. 47.
Elliptic orbits, I. 504. II. 31.
Elliptic spheroids, II. 339.
Elliptic vibrations, I. Pl. 2.
Ellis, II. 587.
Elm, II. 509.
Elongation, I. 527.
Elongation of Venus, I. Pl. 34.
E. M. II. 110.
E. M. A. II. 110.
Emanations of odorous bodies, II. 397.
Embankments, I. 312, Pl. 21, II. 233.
Embossing cloth, II. 188.
Embroidery, II. 189.
Emerson, II. 113, 119, 125, 130, 169, 174, 219, 370, 557. B. 1701, D. 1782.
Emery, I. 195. II. 680.
Emission of light, I. 436.
E. M. M. II. 110, 184.
Empedocles, I. 472, 483, 744, 745, 756. B. 473, D. 413. B. C.
E. M. Pl. II. 110.
Encaustic paintings, I. 97. II. 142, 180.
Enc. Br. II. 111.
Encroachments of the sea, I. 721.
Encyclopaedia Britannica, I. 60, II. 111, 607.
Encyclopédie, I. 250.
Encyclopédie methodique, II. 110.
Endless chain, II. 249.
Energy, I. 78, 225. II. 51, 52, 140.
Enfield, II. 128.
Engelman, II. 478.
Engines, II. 140.
England, II. 367, 447.
England once a peninsula, II. 495.
Englefield, I. 639. II. 269, 308, 341, 352, 373, 594, 674.
English foot, I. 111.
English philosophers, I. 7.
English standards, II. 147.
English weights, II. 100.
Engramelle, II. 275.
Engraving, I. 93, 118, 246, II. 29, 158.
Engraving plate, II. 208.
Engravings, II. 157.
Engymeter, I. 107, II. 156, 351.
Entertainment, II. 184.
Entomology, II. 516.
Eolipile, II. 257.
Epact, I. 541, II. 349.
Ephemerides academiae Caesareae, II. 107.
Ephemerides astronomicae, II. 373.
Ephemerides societatis Palatinae, II. 447.
Epicureans, I. 16, 598.
Epicurus, I. 240, 253, 604, 745, 756. B. 342, D. 270. B. C.
Epicycles, I. 594.
Epicycloid, II. 122, 247, 309, 558.
Epicycloidal surface, II. 55.
Epicycloidal teeth, I. Pl. 15.
Epicycloids, II. 344.
Epiglottis, I. 400.
Epigonus, II. 567.
Epistolae ad Velserum, II. 331.
Epitrochoid, II. 558.
Epoch, II. 349.
Epochs of planetary motions, II. 371.
Eprouvette, I. 134.
Equal areas, I. Pl. 1.
Equalisation of force, I. 193.
Equalising discharge, II. 245.
Equal quantities, II. 1, 2.
Equal temperament, II. 554.
Equal times, II. 27.
Equated clocks, I. 538, II. 194, 347.
Equation of time, I. 537, Pl. 35, II. 347.
Equations, II. 114, 121, 146.
Equations of cycloidal curves, II. 560.
Equator, II. 373.
Equatorial instruments, II. 353.
Equatorial micrometer, II. 290.
Equilateral triangle, II. 10.
Equilibrium, I. 59. Pl. 3, 8, II. 37. Hydrostatic equilibrium, II. 57. Pneumatic equilibrium, II. 60. Stability of equilibrium, I. 261.
Equilibrium of animals, I. 64.
Equilibrium of a revolving fluid, II. 339.
Equilibrium of compound bodies, II. 134.
Equilibrium of elastic bodies, II. 136.
Equilibrium of elastic substances, II. 46.
Equilibrium of electricity, I. Pl. 39.
Equilibrium of floating bodies, II. 220.
Equilibrium of fluids, I. Pl. 19.
Equilibrium of gases, I. 270.
Equilibrium of gravitating bodies, II. 339.
Equilibrium of heavy systems, II. 135.
Equilibrium of liquids, II. 219.
Equilibrium of radiant heat, I. 637.
Equilibrium of systems, II. 134.
Equilibrium of the sea, II. 342.
Equinoctial tides, I. 577, II. 370.
Equinox, I. Pl. 34.
Equisetum palustre, II. 235.
Equitangential curve, II. 556.
Eratosthenes, I. 504, 593, 604.
Erect vision, II. 313.
Erfurt, II. 109.
Eridanus, I. 498.
Eruption of a moss, II. 496.
Eruption of mud, II. 498.
Eruption of waters, II. 479.
Eruptions of volcanos, II. 492.
Erxleben, II. 110, 128.
Escapements, II. 193.
Eskinard, I. 476, II. 280, 323.

INDEX.

Essai de batir sous l'eau, II. 232.
Essay on signals, II. 143.
Essay on tune, II. 273.
Essay on windmills, II. 239.
Essays on Gothic architecture, II. 172.
Essential properties of matter, I. 605.
Estève, II. 272.
Etching, I. 119, II. 158, 218.
Ether, II. 338, 377, 400.. 402, 614.
Ether, II. 653.
Ethereal medium, I. 615, 630
Ethereal vibrations, II. 541.
Etherial vapour, II. 397.
Etna, II. 493.
Etres organisés, II. 497.
Euclid, I. 239, 253, 473, 483, II. 556, 557. Fl. 300. B. C.
Euclides, II. 117.
Eudiometry, II. 462.
Eudoxus, I. 239, 253, 604.
Euler, I. 249, 250, 253, 361, 366, 384, 406, 407, 459, 479, 480, 483, 522, 531, 602, 604, 749, 756, II. 112, 114, 119, 123, 126, 129, 165, 166, 239, 260, 265, 269, 272, 275, 288, 295, 340, 341, 373, 538, 541..543, 547..549, 550, 614, 623, 651, L. Euler, B. 1707, D. 1783. J. A. Euler, II. 236, 417, 624, 671.
Eumenes, I. 98.
Euphon, II. 275.
Evanescent quantities, II. 16
Evaporation, I. 641, 706, II. 396, 408, 412, 424, 427, 458, 464, 467.
Evaporation of ice, II. 396.
Evaporation of mercury, II. 322.

Evaporation of snow, II. 395, 396.
Evaporator, II. 411.
Evelyn, II. 158.
Evolute, II. 22.
Evolutes, II. 120.
Examen de la poudre, II. 260.
Examen des ouvrages faites pour déterminer la figure de la terre, II. 359.
Excitation, II. 421.
Excitation of electricity, I. 425.
Excitement of heat, I. 632.
Excise, II. 510.
Excretions of plants, II. 614.
Exercise, II. 181.
Exhalations, II. 499.
Exhaustion, II. 385.
Expanding fluids, II. 257.
Expanse of the universe, I. 489.
Expansible fluids, II. 379.
Expansion, I. 640. II. 385, 509.
Expansion of cold water, II. 389.
Expansion of pendulums, I. 199.
Expansion of spirits, II. 393
Expansion of the air, I. Pl. 24.
Expansion of water, II. 392
Expansions, I. 646.
Expansions of gases, II. 393
Expansions of liquids, II. 391.
Expansions of solids, II. 391
Expectations, II. 117.
Expense of gunpowder, II. 261.
Experiment on elasticity, I. 28.
Experiments and observations on light and colours, II. 321.

Experiments of the society for the advancement of naval architecture, II. 228
Experiments on magnetism, II. 439.
Explosion, II. 673.
Explosion in the air, II. 499.
Explosion of a furnace, II. 494.
Explosion of a steam engine, II. 259.
Explosion of grindstones, II. 383.
Explosions, I. 717.
Explosions of electricity, II. 422.
Explosive letters, II. 276, 277.
Exponential quantities, II. 8, 116.
Expressing a number of facts, II. 347.
Extension, I. 135, 136, 138, 222, 607, II. 205.
Extension by percussion, II. 205.
Extension of a column, I. Pl. 9.
Extension of light, II. 320.
Extension of threads, II. 168.
Extinction of fires, II. 410, 413.
Extinction of heat, II. 484.
Extinction of light, I. 464, II. 639, 642.
Extraction of roots, II. 115.
Extraction of the crystalline, II. 592.
Eyck. Van Eyck, I. 96, 246, 253. B. 1371, D. 1441.
Eye, I. 447, Pl. 30, II. 82, 311, 530, 578, 638, 680.
Eyeglasses, II. 288.
Eyepiece, I. 430, Pl. 28, II. 80, 289.

Eyes of animals, II. 311.
Eyes of birds, II. 601.
Eyes of insects, II. 601, 678.
Eytelwein, I. 365. II. 130, 148, 154, 230.
Fabre, II. 225, 250.
Fabri, II. 380.
Fabricius, I. 736, II. 331, 516.
Fabricius ab Aquapendente, II. 310.
Fabroni, I. 752.
Faculae, II. 331.
Faenza, II. 217.
Fahrenheit, I. 632, 648, II. 386.
Fair, II. 148, 160.
Fairy rings, II. 482.
Falck, II. 257.
Falconer, I. 746, II. 239.
Fall, II. 131.
Fallacy of sight, II. 313.
Fallen meteors, II. 501.
Fall in a fluid, I. 268.
Fall in air, II. 226.
Falling bodies, II. 228, 339.
Falling stars, II. 365, 500.
Falling stone, II. 358.
Fall of a heavy body, I. 30, 111.
Fall of a feather, I. 57.
Fall of bodies, II. 342.
Fall of earth, II. 498.
Fall of leaves, I. 730.
Fall of rain, II. 477.
Fallows, II. 213.
Falsetto, II. 550.
Fan for corn, I. 345, II. 215.
Fannius, I. 353, II. 160.
Fans, II. 252.
Farina, II. 512.
Farm buildings, II. 174.
Farmer's calendar, II. 519.
Fascination, II. 518, 519.
Fass, II. 155.
Fasting, II. 516.

VOL. II.

Fata Morgana, I, 441, II. 301, 314.
Faujas de St. Fond, II. 494.
Faure, II. 431.
Fecundation of plants, II. 514.
Felbiger, II. 446, 485, 489.
Felice, II. 380.
Felling timber, II. 168.
Felt, I. 186.
Felting, I. 189.
Felts, II. 189.
Fens, II. 495.
Fenwick, II. 141.
Ferber, II. 494, 497.
Fer de la Noverre, II. 234.
Ferguson, II. 112, 127, 130, 325, 416.
Fermat, I. 475, 598, II. 377.
Fern, II. 512.
Fernel, II. 360.
Fernelius, II. 363. See corrections.
Ferrein, II. 550.
Ferro, II. 494.
Ferroni, II. 116, 119.
Ferry boat, II. 242.
Fibres, II. 184, 680.
Fidler, I. Pl. 8.
Field glass, I. 430, Pl. 28.
Field of a micrometer, II. 289.
Field of view, II. 80.
Field of vision, II. 575.
Fiery meteors, II. 500.
Figure of fluids, II. 380.
Figure of gravitating bodies, II. 339.
Figure of secants, II. 374.
Figure of sines, II. 25, 122, 545, 558.
Figure of snow, II. 478.
Figure of tangents, II. 122.
Figure of the earth, I. 568, Pl. 34, II. 358.
Figures, II. 124.

Figures of the planets, II. 332.
Files, II. 207..209.
Filing, II. 210.
Filtering wells, II. 246.
Filters, II. 246.
Filter with sand, II. 246.
Finger board, II. 274.
Fir, II. 509.
Fire, I. 637, II. 175, 383.
Fire arms, II. 202, 260.
Fire balls, II. 411, 499, 501.
Fired gunpowder, II. 260.
Fire engines, I. 334, 353, Pl. 23, II. 247, 263.
Fire escapes, II. 181.
Fire in the Apennines, II. 499.
Fire ladder, II. 175.
Fire places, II. 410, 412.
Fires, II. 493.
Fires. Extinction of fires, II. 410, 413.
Fire ship, II. 242.
Fire wheel, II. 257.
Firmness, II. 383.
First movers, II. 164.
Fir wood, II. 47.
Fischer, II. 217.
Fish, II. 229, 291.
Fishery, II. 519.
Fishes, I. 304, 497, 735, II. 271, 311, 312.
Fish hooks, II. 208.
Fishing nets, II. 189.
Fissure in the moon, II. 346.
Fits of light, II. 616.
Fixed air, II. 513.
Fixed ecliptic, I. 503, Pl. 32.
Fixed fire, II. 465.
Fixed instruments, II. 352.
Fixedness, II, 396.
Fixed plane, II. 141.
Fixed stars, I. 487, Pl. 36, 37, II. 325.

Fixing instruments, II. 354.
Flageolet, I. 402.
Flails, II. 215.
Flakes of snow, I. 444.
Flame, I. 16, II. 291, 383, 419.
Flamsteed, I. 601, 604, II. 324. B. 1646, D. 1719.
Flat, II. 570.
Flat arches, II. 176.
Flaws, II. 316.
Flax, I. 183, II. 185.
Flax of New Zealand, II. 185.
Fleecy hosiery, II. 187.
Flemish weavers, I. 244.
Fletcher, II. 144, 161.
Fleurieu, II. 192.
Flexibility, II. 383.
Flexible bodies, II. 138, 267.
Flexible fibres, I. 180, II. 184.
Flexible knives, II. 208.
Flexible roads, II. 181.
Flexible threads, II. 136, 138.
Flexible vessels, I. 269.
Flexure, I. 135, 138, 145, 147, 627, 629.
Flexure in cooling, II. 404.
Flexure of a bar, II. 48.
Flexure of a column, II. 46..48.
Flexure of columns, II. 173.
Flexure of columns and bars, I. Pl. 9.
Flexure of compound bars, II. 389.
Flight of birds, II. 256.
Flint glass, II. 284.
Flints, II. 263, 498.
Floatboards, II. 236.
Floating balls, II. 382.
Floating boats, II. 243.
Floating bodies, I. 266, 624, Pl. 19, II. 59, 220, 656.
Floating bridge, II. 242.

Float regulator, II. 245.
Floodgates, I. 313, Pl. 21.
Floor, I. 148.
Floor paper, II. 190.
Floors, II. 178.
Flour, II. 215.
Flower, I. 726, II. 512.
Flue, II. 410.
Fluents, II. 120.
Fluid, I. 259.
Fluidity, II. 381, 383, 396.
Fluidity of sand, II. 220, 232.
Fluidity of sand and earth, II. 173.
Fluids, I. 257, II. 227, 405. Motions of fluids, II. 57.
Fluoric acid, I. 120.
Fluor spar, I. 486.
Flute, I. 402, II. 267, 567.
Flute pipe, I. Pl. 26.
Flute player, II. 184.
Flutes, II. 275.
Fluxion of an arc, II. 16.
Fluxion of an area, II. 22.
Fluxion of a solid, II. 20.
Fluxions, I. 249, II. 7, 119, 124.
Fly, I. 131.
Fly wheels, I. 179, II. 165, 182.
Flying, II. 164.
Focal distance, II. 315.
Foci, II. 281.
Focus, I. 414, II. 71, 283.
Focus of a lens, I. 417, II. 281.
Focus of an ellipsis, II. 23.
Focus of a sphere of variable density, II. 82.
Focus of telescopes, II. 287.
Focus of the eye, I. 450.
Fog, II. 474, 476.
Folding, II. 188.
Folkes, II. 152.
Fomalhant, I. 497.
Fondeur, I. 190.

Fontaine, II. 557.
Fontana, II. 112, 312, 463, 512.
Fontenelle, I. 249, 532, II. 217, 344.
Food of plants, II. 515.
Foot, I. 111, II. 150.
Foramen of the retina, II. 311.
Force, I. 26, 33, 79, II. 28, 129, 131, 139, 164. Accelerating force, I. 27. Centrifugal force, I. 35. Definition of force, I. 27. Deflective force, I. 33. Regulation of force, I. 91.
Force of electricity, I. 134.
Force of freezing water, II. 379.
Force of gunpowder, II. 260.
Force of horses, II. 167.
Force of light, II. 294, 618.
Force of machines, II. 141.
Force of magnetism, I. 134.
Force of mules, II. 167.
Force of steam, II. 133.
Force of water, II. 236.
Force of wind, II. 457.
Forcer for a pump, II. 251.
Forces, II. 377. Reciprocal forces, II. 37. Regulation of hydraulic forces, I. 316.
Forcing pump, I. 332, 353, Pl. 23, II. 250.
Fordyce, II. 513, 518.
Forest, II. 498.
Forfait, II. 234.
Forge, II. 205.
Forge hammer, I. Pl. 18.
Forges, I. 224, II. 252.
Forging, I. 142.
Forkel, II. 264.
Form of the earth, II. 374.
Form of the sky, I. 454.
Forms of columns, II. 173.

Forms of the planets, I. 518.
Formula for the elasticity of steam, II. 398.
Forrest, II. 455.
Forster, II. 366.
Forsyth, I. 730, II. 519.
Fortification, II. 260.
Fossil bones, II. 497.
Fossils, I. 720, II. 496.
Fossombroni, II. 146.
Fougeroux, II. 179, 180, 207.
Founderies, II. 252.
Foundery, II. 157.
Fountain of Hero, II. 337.
Fountains, II. 245, 247.
Fourcroy, I. 753, II. 179, 675, 678.
Fournier, II. 158.
Fowl, II. 279.
Fowler, II. 427.
Fraction, II. 1.
Fractions, II. 114.
Fracture, I. 135, 143, 146, II. 169.
Fracture from heat, I. 643.
Fracture of a pillar, II. 174.
Fragment ueber die geogonie, II. 497.
Frame for rectilinear motion, I. Pl. 14, II. 183.
Frame saw, I. Pl. 4.
Frame work, II. 182.
Franc, I. 124, II. 162.
France, II. 365.
Francoeur, II. 130.
François de Neufchateau, II. 213.
Franklin, I. 658, 715, 750, 754, 756, II. 112, 280, 410. B. 1706, D. 1791.
Franklin's experiment on oscillations, II. 223.
Frederic, I. 189, 596.
Freestone, II. 509.

Freezing, I. 642, 699, II. 379, 394.
Freezing mixtures, II. 410.
Freezing of acids, II. 395.
Freezing of water in pipes, II. 246.
Freezing water, II. 386.
French calendar, II. 349.
French measures, I. 111, II. 151.
French weights, I. 124, II. 160, 161.
Fresco, I. 96.
Frézier, I. 176.
Friction, I. 93, 152, 632, 667, II. 134, 137, 138, 169, 176, 200, 293, 383, 385, 414, 672. Avoiding friction, I. 203, 212.
Friction of a pallet, II. 560.
Friction of fluids, I. 292, Pl. 20, 21, II. 61, 226.
Friction of ice, I. 653.
Friction of scapements, I. 195. See corrections.
Friction of sluices, I. 314.
Friction of water, II. 227.
Friction of wheelwork, II. 55, 184.
Friction quadrant, II. 200.
Friction wheels, I. 213, Pl. 14, 18, II. 200.
Frigid zone, I. 570.
Frigorific experiments, II. 385.
Fringes, II. 189, 641.
Fringes of colours, I. 466, II. 316, 639.
Fringes of Grimaldi, II. 640.
Frisi, I. 250, II. 130, 234, 325, 338, 359.
Fritsch, II. 303, 446.
Frog, II. 312.
Froidour, II. 234.
Fromantil, II. 218.
Frontinus, II. 224.

Front view of a telescope, II. 287.
Frosts, II. 451, 452.
Fructification, II. 514.
Fry, II. 144.
Fuel, II. 385, 410.
Fulling, I. 186, II. 188.
Fulminating mercury, II. 262.
Fulton, II. 234.
Funccius, II. 264.
Functions of the eye, II. 312.
Funk, II. 127, 264, 366.
Funke, II. 326.
Funnel, II. 222.
Fur, II. 190.
Furlong, II. 150.
Furnaces, I. 346, II. 410 .. 412.
Furze, II. 233.
Fusee of a watch, I. 192, Pl 15, 16, II. 193.
Fusorius, I. 246, 253. Fl. 1450.
Fuss, II. 287.
Fust, I. 246, 253.
Fustians, II. 218.
Gabler, II. 127, 437.
Gaertner, II. 511.
Gage for wheels, II. 184.
Gages for air pumps, I. 341, Pl. 22.
Gailenreuth, II. 497.
Galen, I. 449, II. 279.
Galilean telescope, I. 428, Pl. 28, II. 78.
Galileo, I. 31, 39, 44, 192, 247, 248, 253, 274, 354, 366, 405, 407, 474, 483, 598, 604, II. 112, 558, 610. B. 1562, D. 1642.
Galley, II. 242.
Gallitzin, II. 416.
Gallon, I. 111, II. 150, 151.
Galvani, I. 677, 752, 753,

756, II. 427. B. 1737, D. 1798.
Galvanic battery, I. Pl. 40.
Galvanic circuit, I. Pl. 40.
Galvanic electricity, I. 674.
Galvanism, I. 752, II. 427, 672.
Galvanometer, II. 429, 439.
Ganges, I. 294, 295, II. 367, 481.
Gardenius, II. 427.
Garuas, II. 476.
Garnerin, I. 306, II. 256, 456.
Garnet, I. Pl. 17.
Garnet, II. 184.
Garnett, II. 112.
Garrard, II. 357.
Garsault, II. 180, 189, 203.
Gascoigne, II. 289, 291.
Gascony, II. 502.
Gases, I. 372, 613, II. 60, 221, 266, 379, 388, 409, 465.
Gasholders, II. 254.
Gasometer, I. 343, Pl. 24, II. 255.
Gates, I. 171, II. 180.
Gatterer, II. 366.
Gauger, II. 410.
Gauging, II. 156.
Gauging ships, II. 240.
Gauss, II. 121.
Gaussen, II. 388, 393, 399.
Gauze, II. 187.
Gay Lussac, I. 365. II. 393, 409.
Gedanken ueber den nebel, II. 474.
Gedanken ueber Kirnbergers temperatur, II. 273.
Gedda, II. 468.
Gehler, II. 128.
Geissler, II. 128.
Gellert, II. 655.

Gellibrand, I. 747, 756, II. 440. B. 1597, D. 1636.
Gemini, I. 504.
Gemma, I. 495, II. 501.
Gems, II. 157, 210, 675.
Gendre. See Legendre.
General physics, II. 324.
Generation of heat, II. 408.
Generation of plants, II. 513.
Geneva, I. 698.
Genevan society, II. 110.
Genista, II. 184.
Gensflich, I. 246.
Gentleman's magazine, II. 413.
Geocyclic machine, II. 375.
Geodetic calculation, II. 360.
Geoffroy, I. 750.
Geographical measurements, II. 358.
Geographisches magazin, II. 450.
Geography, I. 568, II. 346. 358, 365, 379, 496.
Geology, I. 720, II. 495.
Geometrical expressions, II. 672.
Geometrical instruments, II. 144.
Geometrical progression, II. 4.
Géométrie descriptive, II. 157.
Geometry, II. 8. 117, 555. Instrumental Geometry, I. 93.
Geometry of mechanics, I. 93.
Georgian planet, I. 501, 535, II. 335, 340, 372, 376.
Georgium sidus, II. 376.
Gerlach, II. 339, 360.
Germination, I. 726, II. 513
Gersten, II. 462.
Gerstner, I. 299, II. 225.

Geschichte einer begebenheit, II. 484.
Gesner, I. 746, 748, 756, B. 1516, D. 1565.
Gesner, II. 231.
Geyser, II. 494.
Gherli, II. 113.
Ghezzi, II. 480.
Giardini, II. 611.
Gibbes, II. 672.
Gibelin, II. 106.
Giddy, II. 397. Corrections.
Gilbert, I. 686, 747, 756, II. 111, 324, 436. B. 1540, D. 1603.
Gilbert, II. 468.
Gilding cutlery, II. 207.
Gill, II. 151.
Gilly, II. 232.
Gilpin, II. 392, 393, 585, 674.
Gilt wire, II. 378.
Gin, I. 205.
Gins, II. 198.
Gioja, II. 746, 756.
Giral, II. 176.
Girard, II. 169.
Girgenti, II. 266.
Givre, I. 711.
Glaciers, II. 405.
Glasgow, II. 502.
Glass, I. 623, II. 86, 217, 266, 509.
Glass blower, I. 264.
Glass blowing, I. 223. II. 205.
Glass chord, II. 275.
Glass drops, I. 644, II. 403.
Glass globules, II. 283, 284.
Glass houses, II. 199, 411.
Glass tubes, II. 381.
Glass vibrating, I. 385.
Glauber's salts, I. 642.
Glazier's vice, I. 222, Pl. 18, II. 205.
Glazing calicos, II. 188.

Gleichen, II. 285.
Glenie, II. 114, 260.
Globe, I. 565.
Globe of coppper, II. 374.
Globes, I. 496, II. 374.
Globes for dials, II. 348.
Globular projection, II. 376.
Globules for finding specific gravities, I. 309.
Globules for microscopes, I. 422.
Globules of the blood, II. 646.
Glories, II. 308.
Glottis, I. 400, Pl. 26, II. 550.
Gloves, II. 189.
Glow worm, II. 292.
Glue, II. 180.
Gnomonical cane, II. 348.
Gnomonics, II. 348.
Goats, II. 181.
Goddard, II. 596.
Godfrey, II. 350.
Goethe, II. 280.
Goettingisches magazin, II. 110.
Goettingische societaet. II. 108.
Goettling, II. 384.
Going fusee, with an intermediate spring, I. 193, Pl. 16.
Gold, II. 509.
Goldbeating, II. 224.
Gold debased, II. 404.
Golden number, I. 540, II. 349.
Gold leaf, I. 411. II. 205. 378.
Goldsmith, II. 127.
Goldsmiths, II. 213.
Goldsmith's work, II. 206.
Gold thread, II. 185, 205.
Gong, I. 401.
Goniometer, II. 145.
Goniometrical instruments, II. 145.

Goniometrical lines, II. 121.
Goodwin sands, II. 495.
Gordon, II. 126, 240, 617.
Gorlaeus, II. 747, 756.
Gothaisches magazin, II. 112.
Gothic arch, II. 177.
Gothic architecture, I. 166, 245.
Gothic roof, I. Pl. 12.
Gottingen. Society of Gottingen, II. 108.
Goudin, II. 120, 346.
Gough, II. 206.
Goussier, II. 127.
Governor for a steam engine, II. 133.
Governor of motion, II. 182.
Graduation, II. 145.
Grafting, I. 729, II. 514, 519.
Graham, I. 111, 195, 199, 602, 604, II. 148.
Grain, I. 124, II. 161.
Grains, II. 164.
Gramme, I. 124, II. 161, 162.
Granaries, II. 180.
Grand Duke's cabinet, II. 387.
Granite, I. 230, 231.
Graphometer, II. 145.
Grate, II. 412.
Grave harmonics, I. 391, 406, II. 544.
Gravesande. See S'Gravesande.
Gravimeter, II. 232.
Gravitating bodies, II. 45, 339.
Gravitation, I. 30, 37, 515, 518, 598, 614, 660, Pl. 34, II. 32, 137, 339, 379.
Gravitation of light, I. 460.
Gravities. Specific gravities, II. 59, 231.

Gravity, I. 745, II. 136, 338, 377.
Gray, II. 215, 414, E. W. Gray, II. 531. Stephen Gray, I. 750, 756, II. 414. D. 1736.
Grease, II. 170.
Greasing wood, II. 228.
Greathead's life boat, II. 242.
Greaves, II. 152.
Grecian year, I. 539.
Greek money, II. 160.
Greeks, I. 98, 236, 591.
Greek weights, II. 162.
Green corona of plants, II. 513.
Green matter, II. 514.
Greenwich, I. 610, II. 360.
Gregorian calendar, I. 540.
Gregorian telescope, I. 429, Pl. 28. II. 79.
Gregory, I. 476, 598, II. 118, 120, 121, 124, 128. D. Gregory, II. 280, 324. J. Gregory, II. 280. O. Gregory, II. 325, Pope Gregory, I. 404, 407, 539, II. 568.
Gren, II. 111, 128.
Grenades, II. 363.
Greville, II. 674, 676.
Grew, II. 512.
Gridiron pendulum, I. Pl. 16.
Grimaldi, I. 437, 467, 476, 483, II. 280, 319, 538, 621, 629, 640, 643.
Grinding, I. 229, II. 210, 214.
Grinding glasses, II. 283.
Grindstones, II. 210, 383.
Gripe for carriages, II. 203.
Gripe or hand, II. 181.
Grobert, II. 201.

Groignard, II. 239.
Gros, II. 161.
Gross, II. 416, 486.
Ground for etching, II. 158.
Ground sliding away, II. 176.
Groups of stars, I. 494.
Growth, I. 695.
Growth of animals, II. 424.
Growth of plants, II. 512.
Grueber, II. 296.
Gruener, II. 450.
Gryllus gryllotalpa, II. 678.
Gualtieri, II. 480.
Guden, II. 485.
Guericke, I. 274, 340, 355, 366, 749, 756, II. 220, 253. B. 1602, D. 1686.
Guetle, II. 128, 430.
Guettard, II. 513.
Guglielmini, I. 355, 366, II. 224. B. 1655, D. 1710.
Guiana, II. 447.
Guido of Arezzo, I. 405, 407. Fl. 1026.
Guitar, I. 398, II. 552.
Guldinus, I. 247.
Gulf stream, I. 587, II. 459.
Gun, I. 350, II. 262.
Gun barrels, II. 211, 262.
Gun carriage, II. 263.
Gun flints, II. 263.
Gun locks, II. 262.
Gunnery, I. 40, II. 132, 227, 259, 263.
Gunny bags, II. 190.
Gunpowder, I. 134, 349, 354, II. 167, 210, 255, 263.
Gunpowder air gun, II. 262.
Guns, II. 259.
Gunter, I. 248, 253, 747,

II. 338. B. 1581, D. 1626.
Gunter's scale, I. 107, II. 146.
Gurney, I. 143.
Gutenberg, I. 246, 253, II. 217, 218.
Guthrie, II. 366, 395.
Guyot, I. 746.
Guyton, I. 754, II. 111, 126, 169, 677, 678. See Morveau.
Gwynn, I. 335, Pl. 23.
Gymnotus electricus, I. 677, II. 436.
Gyration, II. 52, 379.
Haarlem Society, II. 109.
Haas, II. 204.
Haasius, II. 279.
Hackling, II. 185.
Hadley, I. 701, 749. D. 1744.
Hadley's instrument, II. 350.
Hadley's quadrant, I. 542, Pl. 35, II. 76, 146, 282.
Haellstroem, II. 391.
Haeseler, II. 311, 460.
Hafniensis universitas, II. 108.
Hail, II. 478.
Hailstones, II. 478.
Hair, II. 184, 484, 634.
Hair hygrometer, I. 709.
Hairs of felts, II. 190.
Hairwork, II. 188.
Hales, I. 356, II. 252, 264, 512, 516. B. 1677, D. 1761.
Haley, I. 196.
Halifax, I. 249.
Hall, I. 478, 483, II. 127, 323.
Halle, II. 141, 275.
Haller, II. 311, 516, 524.
Halley, I. 249, 490, 511, 513, 514, 522, 544, 597,

601, 690, 702, 749, 756, II. 308, 558. Corrections. B. 1660, D. 1742.
Halo, II. 303, 316.
Halos, I. 443, Pl. 29, II. 303, 635.
Hamberger, II. 126, 127, 379, 380, 480.
Hamburgisches magazin, II. 108.
Hamilton, I. 65, II. 121. Captain T. Hamilton, II. 241. Captain T. Hamilton's gage, I. 318, 319, Pl. 22. Sir W. Hamilton, I. 717, 718, 719.
Hammer, I. 80, 205.
Hammering, I. 142, 222, II. 383.
Hammering brass, I. 694.
Hammer of the ear, I. 387.
Hand, II. 150.
Handel, II. 572.
Hand, gripe, or stay, II. 181.
Hand hoe, II. 211.
Handmaid to the arts, II. 126.
Hands of timekeepers, II. 194.
Hangings, II. 179.
Hanin, I. 127.
Hannoeverische nuetzliche sammlungen, II. 491.
Hannoeverisches magazin, II. 479.
Hanow, II. 126, 403, 483.
Hanson, II. 593.
Harbours, I. 315, II. 199, 233.
Hard bodies, I. 370, II. 383.
Harding, I. 508, 603, II. 334, 673.
Hard iron, II. 403.
Hardness, II. 169, 378.
Harmattan, II. 458, 465.
Harmonica, I. 401, II. 267. 274.
Harmonic curve, II. 25, 558.

Harmonic curves combined, II. 25.
Harmonic mean, II. 6.
Harmonics, I. 258, 389.
Harmonic sliders, II. 273.
Harmonics of chords, II. 548.
Harmonics of the voice, II. 550.
Harmonic sounds, I. 380, 382, II. 539, 647.
Harmony, I. 391, II. 563.
Harmony of colours, II. 617.
Harness, I. Pl. 18, II. 188.
Harnesses, II. 203.
Harp, I. 397.
Harpoon, II. 208.
Harps, II. 275.
Harpsichord, I. 398, II. 271.
Harrington, II. 384.
Harriot, II. 166.
Harriott, II. 252.
Harris, II. 107, 266, 280.
Harris, II. 315.
Harrison, I. 196, 200, 251, 253, 602, II. 191, 375. B. 1694, D. 1776.
Harrowing, II. 212.
Harrows, II. 204.
Hartmann, II. 416, 481, 485.
Hartsoeker, II. 280.
Harvest moon, I. 530, II. 345.
Harvey, I. 748, B. 1578, D. 1657.
Hasius, II. 374.
Hassencamp, II. 376.
Hassenfratz, II. 178, 325.
Hatchett, II. 202, 671.
Hatching eggs, II. 424.
Hats, I. 187, 189, 218.
Hatton, I. 111, 191.
Haubold, II. 387.
Hauksbee, I. 296, 299, 356, 483, 749, 754, 756, II. 125, 261, 295, 300, 414, 526, 657, 666.
Hausen, II. 331, 379, 519.

Hautboy, I. 402.
Hautes Fagnes, II. 480.
Haüy, II. 129, 418, 511, 664, 666, 675, 676.
Havre, II. 233.
Hawkins, II. 280, 567.
Hawser, I. 182.
Hay, II. 202.
Haydn, II. 572.
Hayles, II. 114.
Hearing, I. 386, 388, II. 271, 574, 618.
Hearing of insects, II. 679.
Hearing trumpet, I. Pl. 25, II. 271.
Heart, I. 291, II. 221.
Heat, I. 619, 631, 667, 686, 745, 747, 750, Pl. 39, II. 257, 293, 295, 296, 379, 383, 450, 452, 465, 516, 615, 623, 631, 647, 652, 681. Capacity for heat, II. 508. Economy of heat, II. 410. Effect of heat on sound, I. 370, II. 265. Effect of heat on vibrations, I. 380. Effects of heat on the form of aggregation, II. 394. Nature of heat, I. 646, II. 413.
Heat acquired by metals, II. 405.
Heat as affecting electricity, II. 425.
Heat at different heights, II. 450.
Heat denominated latent, II. 409.
Heated room, II. 403, 517.
Heat from condensation, II. 408.
Heat from electricity, I. 671.
Heat from mirrors, I. 423.
Heating, II. 386, 404.
Heating a magnet, II. 440.
Heating by light, II. 406.
Heating rooms, II. 410, 411.

Heat of a candle, II. 406.
Heat of a pencil of rays, II. 406.
Heat of different latitudes, I. 697.
Heat of lime, II. 408.
Heat of mixtures, I. 647, II. 408.
Heat of the bottom of a vessel, II. 404.
Heat of the celestial bodies, II. 346.
Heat of the moon's rays, II. 406.
Heat of the sun, II. 501.
Heat of vegetables, II. 514, 517.
Heat producing a draught, I. 345.
Heat with compression, II. 396.
Heavels, II. 188.
Heavens, II. 313.
Heavy systems, II. 135.
Hecatare, II. 152.
Hecatogramme, II. 162.
Hecatolitre, II. 152.
Hecatometre, II. 152.
Heckingham, II. 486.
Hecla, I. 690, II. 443.
Hedwig, II. 511.
Hedysarum gyrans, II. 424, 513.
Heidmann, II. 418.
Heidinger, II. 497.
Height of mountains, I. 273.
Height of the atmosphere, II. 60.
Height of the barometer, II. 464.
Height of tides, I. 586, II. 368.
Heights, I. Pl. 38, II. 366, 367.
Heinsius, II. 335, 337.
Hejerà, II. 349.
Heliodorus, II. 280.
Heliometer, II. 351.

Helioscope, II. 351.
Heliostate, I. 425.
Hell, II. 373.
Hellins, II. 113, 681.
Hellmuth, II. 128, 325, 326.
Helsham, II. 126, 539.
Helvetica acta, II. 108.
Hemispherical counterpoise, I. 268, II. 58.
Hemmer, II. 448, 486.
Hemp, I. 182, II. 185.
Hemp for rigging, II. 241.
Hendon, II. 113.
Henley, I. 682, Pl. 40.
Hennert, II. 249, 342, 387, 472.
Henry the sixth, I. 245.
Henzion, II. 256.
Heraclides, II. 377.
Heraclitus, I. 744, 756. Fl. 506, B. C.
Herbert, II. 379, 383, 391, 416, 417.
Herculaneum, II. 498.
Hercules, I. 497.
Herder, II. 497.
Herman, II. 456.
Hermann, I. 250, 253, II. 129. B. 1678, D. 1733.
Hermes, I. 403, 590, II. 566, 567.
Hero, I. 188, 243, 253, 337, 353, 366, II. 196. Fl. 130. B. C.
Herodotus, I. 238.
Hero's clepsydra, II. 245.
Hero's cupping instrument, I. Pl. 24.
Hero's fountain, I. Pl. 23, II. 249.
Herschel, I. 428, 429, 432, 456, 481, 490, 491 .. 494, 499, 501, 507, 509, 510, 511, 516, 603, 637, 638, 698, 754, Pl. 31, 33, 39, II. 79, 282, 289, 291, 319, 326, 329,

406, 585, 609, 624, 631, 648, 673, 676, 677, 680, 681.
Hertel, II. 286.
Herz, II. 128.
Hesiod, II, 214.
Hessian academy, II. 109.
Hessian bellows, I. 345.
Hessian pump, II. 247.
Hevelius, I. 598, 604, II. 324, 335, 347.
Hewson, II. 646.
Hides, II. 208.
Hiero, I. 240, 241, 352.
Higgins, II. 175, 321, 410, 414.
High water, I. 576.
High wheels, II. 201.
Hillary, II. 383.
Hill raised, II. 498.
Hills, II. 476.
Hindenburg, II. 111, 114, 254, 388.
Hindley, II. 145.
Hindoos, II. 349, 376.
Hinge, II. 179.
Hipparchus, I. 495, 506, 519, 589, 593, 594, 604, II. 349.
Histoire de l'Académie Royale, II. 107.
Histoire de Vésuve, II. 493.
History of acoustics, II. 279.
History of astronomy, I. 589.
History of astronomy and geography, II. 376.
History of hydraulics and pneumatics, I. 352, II. 263.
History of mathematics, II. 124.
History of mechanics, I. 236, II. 216.
History of music, I. 403.
History of optics, I. 472, II. 323.

History of terrestrial physics, I. 742.
Hoar frost, I. 711.
Hobert, II. 128.
Hodometers, II. 156.
Hoe, II. 211.
Hoell, I. Pl. 23.
Hoell's machine, I. 336.
Hoesen, II. 283.
Hoesen's mirrors, II. 406.
Hoffmann, I. 637.
Hoffmann, II. 283, 631.
Hofmann, II. 125.
Hogshead, I. 124, II. 150, 151.
Holden, II. 273.
Holder, II. 275.
Holdsworth, II. 143.
Holes, II. 243.
Hollandse maatschappy te Haerlem, II. 109.
Hollmann, II. 111.
Hollow bars, II. 175.
Hollow beams, I. 140, II. 50.
Hollow bricks, II. 175.
Hollow cylinders, II. 168.
Hollow masts, I. 149.
Holm, II. 474.
Holstein, II. 498.
Home, II. 519, 573, 586, 592, 600, 601, 671, 672, 678.
Homer, II. 506.
Homogeneous medium, I. 408.
Honey dew, II. 475.
Hooke, I. 7, 100, 137, 160, 188, 190, 198, 248, 253, 268, 271, 335, 355, 356, 366, 385, 475 .. 477, 482, 483, 524, 599, 604, 748, 749, 756, Pl. 6, II. 107, 112, 124, 218, 264, 285, 317, 350, 376, 396, 614, 627, 629. B. 1635, D. 1703.

Hooke's counterpoise, I. 311, Pl. 19.
Hooke's joint, I. 173, Pl. 14, II. 182.
Hooke's lamps, II. 245.
Hooke's law, II. 221.
Hoop, I. 34, II. 180.
Hooper, II. 128, 514.
Hope, I. 728.
Hopson, II. 384.
Hop stalks, II. 218.
Horizon, I. Pl. 35, II. 354.
Horizontal moon, I. 454, Pl. 30, II. 313.
Horizontal range, I. 39, Pl. 2.
Horizontal refraction, I. 441, II. 300, 301.
Horizontal scapement, I. Pl. 16.
Horizontal surface, I. 260.
Horizontal watch, I. 195.
Horn, I. 402, II. 187.
Horn plate work, II. 206.
Horrebow, II. 447.
Horrox, I. 544.
Horse, I. 132, II. 164, 167, 279. Positions of a horse's legs, I. 48.
Horse hoc, II. 212.
Horse mill, II. 167.
Horse pump, II. 249.
Horses, I. 218, Pl. 18, II. 165, 181.
Horses falling, II. 218.
Horsley, II. 127.
Horticultural instruments, II. 20.
Horticulture, II. 519.
Hosack, II. 591.
Hosiery, II. 187, 218.
Hospital. See L'Hospital.
Hothouses, II. 412.
Hot springs, II. 494.
Hour glasses, I. 188, II. 196.
Houses, II. 175.

Howard, I. 535, 722, II. 155, 498, 502, 674.
Hoyle, II. 673.
Hube, II. 128, 465, 539.
Hubius, II. 360.
Huddart, I. 182, 183, 481, II. 187.
Huebner, II. 492.
Huepsch, II. 489.
Hugenius, II. 112.
Huilier, II. 119.
Hulk, II. 243.
Human strength, II. 165.
Human voice, I. 400, II. 266, 275.
Humboldt, I. 498, II. 514.
Humidity, I. 709.
Humming top, I. 402.
Hundred weight, II. 161.
Hunter, II. 311, 517, 573, 597.
Hunter's screw, I. 72, 208.
Hurdy gurdy, I. 399.
Huret, II. 157.
Hurricane, II. 457.
Hurricanes, II. 458.
Hutchinson, II. 239.
Huth, II. 172.
Hutton, I. 364, II. 110, 112, 113, 115, 118, 121, 128, 152, 177, 229, 322. 407.
Huygenian theory, II. 679.
Huygens, I. 190, 192, 248, 253, 277, 357, 358, 366, 443, 445, 458 .. 460, 462, 477, 479, 480, 482, 483, 492, 517, 567, 598, 604, II. 112, 136, 306, 320, 509, 541, 556, 614, 619, 622, 623, 630. B. 1629, D. 1695.
Hydra, I. 724.
Hydracontisterium, II. 247.
Hydraulic air vessels, I. 336. Pl. 23.

Hydraulic architecture, I. 308, 312, II. 232.
Hydraulic bellows, I. Pl. 24, II. 253, 254.
Hydraulic forces, I. 316, II. 235.
Hydraulic instruments, II. 245.
Hydraulic machines, I. 327, II. 245, 247, 264.
Hydraulic mean depth, II. 61.
Hydraulic measures, I. 318.
Hydraulicostatics, I. 300.
Hydraulic pendulum, II. 247.
Hydraulic pressure, I. 59, 300, 357, II. 62, 226.
Hydraulic ram, I. 337, Pl. 23, II. 249.
Hydraulics, I. 258, 277, 352, II. 60, 221, 263.
Hydraulic siphon, II. 249, 251.
Hydraulic wheels, II. 237.
Hydraulum, II. 275.
Hydrodynamic measures, II. 235.
Hydrodynamics, I. 255, II. 57, 219.
Hydrogen gas, II. 256, 265, 279, 509, 541.
Hydrographical charts, II. 374.
Hydrology, II. 342, 368, 479.
Hydrometer, I. 309. Pl. 21, II. 231. 419.
Hydrometrical fly, I. 318, Pl. 22.
Hydrostatic balance, I. 308, Pl. 21, II. 159.
Hydrostatic equilibrium, II. 57.
Hydrostatic instruments, I. 308, II. 231.
Hydrostatic lamp II. 245.

Hydrostatic machine, II. 237.
Hydrostatic paradox, I. 263.
Hydrostatic press, I. 222.
Hydrostatic pressure, I. 663.
Hydrostatics, I. 257 .. 259, Pl. 19, II. 219.
Hyetometer, II. 476.
Hygrology, II. 464.
Hygrometer, I. 709, 753, Pl. 41, II. 465, 468, 474.
Hygrometry, I. 751, II. 465, 469.
Hygroscopes, II. 468.
Hypatia, I. 352.
Hyperbola, I. 623, II. 121, 122, 123, 381, 681.
Hyperbolical logarithms, II. 8.
Hyperbolical pipes, II. 266.
Hyperbolic cylindroid, II. 122, 123.
Hyperbolic fringes, I. Pl. 30, II. 643.
Hyperbolic glasses, II. 283, 284.
Hyperbolic rainbow, II. 309.
Hyperbolic sectors, II. 119.
Hyperoxygenized muriatic acid, II. 673.
Hypocycloid, II. 122, 558, 562.
Hypotenuse, II. 13.
Hypotheses, II. 613.
Hypotheses of electricity, I. 658.
Hypotrochoid, II. 558.
Ibn Junis, I. 191, 595, 604.
Ice, I. 444, 577, 699, 746, II. 86, 216, 221, 293, 385, 394, 395, 410, 411, 479, 480, 509, 511.
Ice boat, II. 242.
Iceland, II. 498.

Iceland crystal, I. 445, 477, Pl. 29, II. 309, 435, 511, 629, 679.
Ice melted, I. 634.
Iconantidiptic telescope, II. 286, 351.
Idioelectrics. See Electrics.
Igneous meteors, I. 722, II. 499.
Ignis fatuus, I. 435, II. 499.
Ignited charcoal, II. 254.
Illumination, I. 423, II. 77, 291, 312.
Illumination of the planets, I. Pl. 34.
Illustrations of astronomy and geography, II. 374.
Image, I. 418, 422, Pl. 27, 28, II. 71, 73, 281.
Image on the retina, I. 448, Pl. 30, II. 82.
Imaginary quantities, II. 114.
Images, II. 283.
Imison, II. 129.
Immersion of thermometers, II. 388.
Impact, II. 136.
Impelling boats, II. 242.
Impelling ships, II. 242.
Impenetrability, I. 609.
Impenetrability of matter, I. 28.
Imperfections of sight, II. 315.
Impossible quantities, II. 114.
Impossible roots, II. 115.
Impregnation, II. 518.
Impregnation of seeds, II. 514.
Impulse, II. 51.
Impulse of a bullet, II. 136.
Impulse of a fluid, I. 59.
Impulse of a jet, I. 301.
Impulse of a vein, II. 227.

Impulse of fluids, II. 226.
Impulse transmitted by an elastic medium, II. 68.
Impulsion, II. 136.
Inanimate force, I. 90, II. 167.
Inarre, II. 416.
Ince, II. 179.
Inch, II. 151.
Inclination of strata, II. 354.
Inclinations, II. 118.
Inclinations of the planetary orbits, I. 504. II. 340.
Inclined float boards, II. 236.
Inclined plane, I. 42, 70, Pl. 4, 5, 17, II. 33, 42, 54.
Inclined planes, II. 138, 197.
Inclined surface, II. 138.
Inclosures, II. 180.
Incombustible houses, II. 175.
Increase of the globe, II. 495.
Increase of the sea, II. 496.
Increments, II. 7, 119.
Index, I. 99, II. Corrections.
Incommensurable quantities, II. 14.
Index of refraction, I. 412.
Index of refractive density, II. 70.
Indian cycle, II. 376.
Indian ink, I. 95, II. 143.
Indian measures, II. 148.
Indians, I. 591.
Indian weights, II. 160.
Indian zodiac, II. 376.
Indiction, II. 349.
Indigo, II. 214.
Indistinct vision, II. 316.
Indivisibles, I. 36.
Induced electricity, I. 664, II. 418.

VOL. II.

Induction, I. 15, II. 124.
Induction, II. 664.
Inelastic bodies, I. 78.
Inertia, I. 33, 51, 614, II. 130, 379.
Inevaporable fluids, II. 397.
Infants, II. 518.
Inferior tides, I. 583.
Infinite, II. 557.
Infinite quantity, II. 119.
Infinites, I. 36, II. 119.
Infinite series, II. 116.
Infinity of the stars, II. 330.
Inflammable air, II. 263.
Inflammable bodies, I. 412.
Inflammable vapours, II. 259.
Inflammation, II. 290.
Inflecting atmosphere, II. 632.
Inflection, II. 310, 317, 543, 629, 661.
Influence of light, II. 321.
Ingenhousz, II. 112, 128, 424, 432, 513.
Ingenhousz's electrical machine, II. 432.
Indian ink, I. 95.
Ink, I. 66. See corrections. II. 143, 144.
Inkstand, II. 143.
Inlaid work, II. 179.
Inlaying, II. 143.
Inquiry into the effects of heat, II. 383.
Inscription of figures, II. 118.
Insects, II. 311, 312, 382, 458, 516, 518, 519, 626, 678.
Insensibility of electricity, II. 424.
Instinct, I. 449.
Institutions de physique, II. 126.
Institut national, II. 111.

Instruments. Musical instruments, I. 397. Optical instruments, I. 420.
Instruments for observation, II. 349.
Instruments of penetration, II. 207.
Instruments subservient to music, II. 279.
Instruments subservient to seamanship, II. 244.
Insulated stars, I. 494.
Insulation, II. 419.
Integral calculus, II. 119.
Intensity of electricity, I. 683.
Intensity of light, I. 420, II. 77.
Intensity of sound, II. 265.
Interception of light, I. 409, II. 294.
Interception of sound, I. 376.
Interest, II. 117.
Interference of light, I. 464, II. 633, 639, 671.
Intermediate spring, I. 193.
Intermitting springs, I. 286.
Internal reflection, II. 296, 636.
Interpolations, II. 116, 346.
Intestines, II. 184.
Introsusception, II. 510.
Inundation, II. 370, 480.
Inundations of large rivers, I. 713.
Invalids, II. 181.
Inversable chair, II. 201.
Inversable coach, II. 201.
Inverted images, II. 301.
Inverted pump, I. 336.
Inverted rainbow, II. 309.
Inverted tide, I. 579.
Invisible girl, I. 376, II. 271.
Invisible heat, I. 654, 406.
Invisible rays, II. 296, 407.

5 A

Involute, II. 22.
Involute of a circle, II. 55, 122, 562.
Involutes of circles, I. Pl. 15.
Ionian school, I. 237.
Ionic column, I. Pl. 12.
Ireland, II. 451.
Iris, I. 447, 451, II. 311, 530.
Iris for telescopes, II. 288.
Irish academy, II. 111.
Irish car, II. 202.
Iron, I. 152, 228, 244, 685, II. 48, 169, 266, 438, 501, 509, 510.
Iron blocks, II. 177.
Iron bridges, II. 177.
Iron filings, I. 688, 693, Pl. 41.
Ironmongery, II. 179, 207.
Iron roads, II. 204.
Iron wheelways, I. 218.
Irradiation, II. 310.
Irregular refraction, II. 301.
Irrigation, II. 235, 251, 264.
Irritability, II. 518.
Irritability of plants, II. 513.
Irritation of the nerves, II. 427.
Ir. tr. II. 111.
Irvine, I. 650, 651, 750.
Island. New island, II. 495, 498.
Isochronous curves, II. 133.
Isoperimetrical problems, II. 123.
Italian school, I. 237.
Italy, II. 450, 496.
Ivory, II. 179, 209, 509.
Izarn, II. 501.
Jack, I. Pl. 17, II. 182, 198. Kitchen jack, I. 179, II. 181.
Jackal, II. 516.
Jack for pump rods, II. 199.

INDEX.

Jacket, II. 244.
Jacks for telescopes, II. 286.
Jackson, II. 158.
Jacob, II. 201.
Jacobson, II. 127.
Jacotot, II. 129.
Jacquet, II. 416.
Jacquin, II. 161.
Jallabert, II. 415.
Jamaica, I. 700.
Jamard, II. 273.
Jansen, I. 474, 483.
Jars, I. 668.
Jars for electricity, II. 433.
Jeaurat, I. 480, 483. B. 1704, D. 1803.
Jeffries, II. 210.
Jesuit, II. 157.
Jet, I. 286, Pl. 20, II. 60, 61, 247.
Jettees, II. 233.
Jet with a ball, I. 247.
Jewellery, II. 206.
Jewelling, I. 193, II. 191.
Jew's harp, I. 402.
Jib for a crane, II. 199.
Joggles, I. 168, Pl. 13.
Joiner's work, II. 178.
Jointed cart, II. 202.
Jointed work, II. 182.
Joint focus, I. 418.
Joint for steam tubes, II. 246.
Joints, I. 166.
Joints for beams, I. Pl. 13.
Joints of stones, I. Pl. 11.
Jones, II. 113, 126, 273, 447, 597.
Jordan, II. 317, 622, 635.
Journal de physique, I. 251, II. 109, 110.
Journal des savans, II. 107.
Journal polytechnique, II. 111.
Journals, I. 250, 251.

Journals of rain, II. 476.
Journals of the weather, II. 448.
Juan, I. 363, 364, 366, II. 239. B. 1713, D. 1773.
Judgment of distance, I. 453.
Juergen, I. 244, II. 218.
Juices of vegetables, II. 514.
Julian, II. 567.
Julian period, I. 541.
Julian reckoning, II. 349.
Jung, II. 124, 141.
Juno, I. 508, 534, II. 334, 372.
Jupiter, I. 508, 531, 534, 702. See corrections. Pl. 33, II. 335, 340, 372, 376.
Jupiter's satellites, I. 530, II. 346.
Jurin, I. 478, 483, 754, 756, II. 140, 524, 584, 593. B. 1680 ? D.-1750.
Jussieu, I. 732, 750, 756. B. 1699, D. 1777.
Justi, II. 141, 496.
Justus Byrgius, II. 217.
Kaestner, I. 360, II. 112, 124, 126, 134, 290, 325, 338, 361.
Kaiserliche academie, II. 107.
Kamtchatka, II. 366.
Kanne, II. 155.
Kant, II. 324, 378.
Karstens, II. 113, 127, 249.
Keel, I. 325.
Keil, II. 125, 324, 495.
Keir's lamp, I. 311.
Kellner, II. 107.
Kelly, II. 119, 371.
Kempe, I. 244.
Kempelen, I. 401.
Kent, II. 172.
Kepler, I. 36, 253, 474, 481, 483, 495, 504, 505, 597,

598, 599, 604, II. 280, 324, 332, 373, 523. B. 1571, D. 1630.
Keplerian laws, I. 504, 517, Pl. 1.
Kepler's problem, II. 340.
Kett, II. 129.
Kettle, II. 411.
Key note, I. 392.
Khell, II. 126.
Kies, II. 424.
Killarney, II. 480.
Kiln, II. 175, 411.
Kilogramme. See Chiliogramme.
Kin, II. 162.
King, I. 238. See corrections. I. 637, II. 128, 291, 501, 631.
Kingdoms of nature, I. 723.
Kingpost, I. 169, Pl. 12.
King's College Chapel, I. 245, Pl. 12.
Kiobenhavnske selskab, II. 108.
Kirb roof, I. Pl. 13. II. 42.
Kirby, II. 157, 602.
Kircher, I. 405, 407, 280, II. 272, 436. B. 1601, D. 1680.
Kirnberger, II. 273, 551, 554, 564. B. 1721, D. 1783.
Kirwan, I. 698, 700, 750, II. 392, 408, 409, 451, 452, 498, 508, 511, 677, 678. Corrections.
Kitchen range, II. 411.
Kite, I. 324, Pl. 22.
Kites, II. 227.
Klaproth, II. 675, 680.
Kleist, II. 750, 756.
Klingenstierna, I. 479, 483, II. 281, 415, 444.
Klostermann, II. 361, 363. See corrections.

Kluegel, I. 480, II. 113, 128, 130, 249, 281, 288, 375, 484.
Kluver, II. 495.
Kneading, I. 234, II. 216.
Knecht, II. 551.
Knees, II. 168.
Knife, II. 143.
Knight, I. 729, II. 377, 444, 515.
Knitting, II. 188.
Knives, I. 227, II. 207.
Knoll, II. 494.
Knowles, II. 229, 456.
Knots, II. 189.
Knox, II. 678.
Koenig, II. 587, 595.
Koenig's law, II. 140.
Koestlin, II. 424.
Komarzewski, II. 145.
Krafft, II. 307, 450, 464, 681.
Kraft, II. 126, 130.
Kramp, I. 249, II. 256, 301.
Kraschennicoff, II. 366.
Kratzenstein, I. 461, Pl. 26. II. 128, 276, 379, 417, 449, 464.
Krayenhoff, II. 424.
Krueger, II. 126, 496.
Kruenitz, II. 128, 215, 414, 416, 480.
Kunze, I. Pl. 39, II. 128, 416, 430.
Kurdwanowski, II. 294.
Labelye, II. 176.
Labillardiere, II. 185.
Laborde, II. 274.
Labour, I. 79, 90, 331, II. 165.
Labour of a man, I. 131.
Lac, II. 421.
Lacaille, II. 130, 280, 324, 363. See corrections. II. 373, 393.
Lacam, II. 437.

Lace, II. 188, 218.
Lacepede, I. 750, II. 416.
Lacondamine, II. 151, 358, 362, 363, 457.
Lacroix, II. 114, 118, 119, 120.
Ladder, II. 175.
Laertius, II. 216.
Lafaille, I. 247.
Lafond. See Sigaud.
Lagrange, I. 7, 250, 287, 406, 504, 522, II. 116, 130, 224, 537, 539, 544, 546, 547, 548, 618.
Lahire, I. 129, 249, 253, II. 307, 373, 524, 557, 558, 561. B. 1640, D. 1718.
Lahire's pump, I. 332, 348, Pl. 23.
Lake, I. 579.
Lake of Geneva, II. 480.
Lakes, II. 451, 479, 498.
Lakes of America, II. 367.
Lalande, I. 501, 540, 598, Pl. 33, II. 143, 150, 190, 214, 234, 325, 346, 371, 377, 381.
Lallamand, I. 750.
Lamarck, II. 481.
Lambert, I. 375, 406, 407, 480, 483, 491, 493, 526, 531, 637, 751, 756, II. 145, 280, 291, 295, 300, 314, 325, 387, 393, 404, 468, 473, 538, 681. B. 1728, D. 1777.
Lambton, II. 362.
Lamétherie, II. 110, 497.
Laminating, II. 188.
Laminating machine, I. 222, II. 205.
Lamp, I. Pl. 21, II. 290, 412.
Lampadius, II. 384, 417, 483.
Lampblack, II. 485.
Lamp furnace, II. 411.
Lamp micrometer, II. 290, 352.

Lamp of Amiens, II. 245.
Lamps, I. 311, II. 245.
Lampyris, II. 292.
Lamy, II. 219.
Land, I. 571.
Landaulet, II. 202.
Land breezes, I. 704.
Landen, I. 250, 353, II. 113, 116, 356. B. 1719, D. 1790.
Landriani, II. 250, 448, 486.
Lane, I. 683, Pl. 40.
Langenbuecher, II. 431.
Langez, II. 170.
Langlais, II. 263.
Langsdorf, I. 365, II. 141, 219, 225.
Languedoc, II. 231, 496.
Langwith, II. 319, 643, 644.
Lantern, II. 184, 196.
La Peyrouse, II. 185.
Laplace, I. 7, 60, 108, 110, 249, 250, 370, 407, 441, 460, 482, 505, 521, 522, 541, "565", 580, 589, 634, 652, 750, 754, 755, II. 130, 325, 363, 364, 373, 391, 393, 409, 466, 501, 660 .. 666, 669, 670.
Laplatriere, II. 187, 188, 211.
Larcher, II. 333.
Larive. See Delarive.
Larynx, I. Pl. 26, II. 550.
La Sevre, II. 384.
Last, II. 151.
Lasts, II. 189.
Latent heat, I. 652, II. 409.
Lateral adhesion, I. 140, 627.
Lateral cohesion, II. 174.
Lateral friction, II. 251.
Lateral friction of fluids, I. 297, II. 222, 223.
Lateral vibrations of rods, II. 268.
Lathe, I. 228, II. 122, 209.

Latitude, I. 536, 542, II. 364, 365.
Latitudes of stars, II. 334.
Latorre, II. 285.
Launching ships, II. 172, 240.
Laurie, I. Pl. 24.
Laurie's bellows, II. 253.
Lausanne, II. 111.
Lavoisier, I. 634, 652, 750, II. 390, 408, 503, 508. B. 1743, D. 1794.
Law of aberration, II. 294.
Law of equilibrium, II. 45.
Law of interference, II. 633.
Laws of gravitation, I. 515.
Laws of gravity, II. 338.
Laws of heat, II. 404.
Laws of mechanics, II. 140.
Laws of refraction, I. 413.
Lazowsky, II. 448.
Leach, II. 211, 234.
Lead, II. 383, 403, 509.
Leaden pipes, I. 317, II. 205, 245.
League, II. 151.
Leaky, II. 369.
Least action, II. 140.
Leather, II. 184, 189.
Leaves, I. 729, II. 513.
Lecat, II. 516.
Lecchi, II. 219, 224.
Lee, I. 244.
Leeuwenhoek, II. 112, 527, 596, 599.
Leeuwenhoek's microscopes, II. 285.
Lee way, I. 325, II. 240.
Legendre, II. 149, 360.
Legentil, II. 292.
Legs, I. Pl. 9.
Lehmann, II. 306, 492, 496.
Lehrgebaeude der optik, II. 280.
Leibnitz, I. 79, 249, 358, 475, II. 112, 377. B. 1646, D. 1716.

Leidenfrost, II. 396.
Leipziger magazin, II. 110.
Leiste, II. 254.
Lelyveld, II. 118.
Lemaire, II. 362.
Lemoine, II. 217.
Lempe, II. 141.
Lemonnier, II. 336, 370, 437, 520.
Length of a pipe, II. 569.
Length of curves, II. 121.
Length of the pendulum, II. 146, 363.
Lenoir, II. 149, 150.
Lens, I. 416, II. 72. Crystalline lens, II. 311.
Lens of least aberration, II. 281.
Lenses, I. 423, 472, Pl. 27. II. 210, 281. Grinding lenses, I. 231.
Lenses not spherical, II. 283, 284.
Leo, I. 504.
Leone, II. 492.
Leroy, II. 263, 365.
Lescailler, II. 239.
Le Sage, II. 377, 510.
Lesemelier, II. 384.
Leslie, I. 372, 636, 649, 710, 754, II. 49, 223, 231, 384, 475, 520, 662.
Leslie's discoveries, II. 407.
Leslie's hygrometer, II. 469.
Leslie's thermometer, I. Pl. 34.
Lesparat, II. 148.
Letherland, I. 195.
Lettere fisicometeorologiche, II. 500.
Letterpress, I. 122.
Letters, II. 276.
Leucippus, II. 744.
Leupold, I. 250, 253, II. 118, 125, 253, 282. D. 1727.
Leutmann, II. 448.

Level. Spirit level, I. 310.
Levelling, I. 105.
Levelling land, II. 213, 216.
Levels, I. 572, II. 353.
Lévêque, II. 370.
Lever, I. 65, Pl. 3, 4, II. 40, 134, 135, 137.
Levers, I. 173, 203, II. 54, 181, 196, 219. Hydraulic levers, II. 236.
Lever with a wheel, II. 184.
Levigating, I. 234.
Levigation, II. 213, 214.
Levity, I. 16.
Lewis, I. 210, Pl. 17.
Lexell, I. 513, II. 335.
Leyden phial, I. 666, II. 418.
L'hospital, II. 121.
L'huilier, II. 119, 123, 378.
Li, II. 153.
Libella, II. 311.
Libes, II. 129.
Libra, I. 497, 504.
Libration of the moon, I. 528, II. 345.
Lichtenberg, II. 391, 426, 486.
Lichtenberg's drum machine for electricity, II. 432.
Lichtenberg's figures, II. 419.
Lieberkuehn, II. 285.
Liebknecht, II. 366.
Liesganig, II. 362.
Life, I. 725.
Life annuities, II. 107.
Life boat, II. 242.
Life of plants, I. 730.
Litters, II. 214.
Lifting pump, I. 333, Pl. 23, II. 249.
Lifting stock, II. 196.
Light, I. 408, 457, 489, 654, 655, 745, Pl. 39, II. 70, 280, 319, 385, 397, 403, 406, 511, 513, 514, 531, 544, 607, 613, 645, 661, 671, 673, 679. Intensity of light, II. 77.
Light compared with sound, II. 541.
Light from combustion, II. 290.
Light from electricity, I. 670.
Light from friction, I. 435, II. 293.
Light house, I. Pl. 11.
Light houses, II. 174.
Light in a storm, II. 482.
Lightning, I. 713, 743, 750, II. 445, 481.
Lightning in the moon, II. 336, 345.
Lightning without thunder, II. 483.
Light of a candle, I. 438, II. 638, 646.
Light of diamonds, II. 422.
Light of electricity, II. 422.
Light of fires, II. 322.
Light of fish, II. 291.
Light of stones, II. 435, 436.
Light of the heavenly bodies, I. 531, II. 344.
Light of spirits, I. 438.
Light of the moon, II. 337.
Light of the new moon, II. 345.
Light of the sea, II. 291, 292.
Light of the stars, I. 490.
Light round the sun, II. 345.
Like causes, II. 27.
Lime, II. 175, 408.
Lime kiln, II. 209, 411, 422.
Lime mixed with gunpowder, II. 262.
Limestone, II. 498.
Lime tree bark, II. 185.
Limits of equations, II. 115.
Limperch, II. 213.
Lincoln Cathedral, I. 245.
Lind, II. 457.
Line, II. 8, 151.
Linen, II. 187, 189, 217.
Line of congelation, II. 454.
Line of draught, II. 55.
Lines, I. 100.
Lines of the third and fourth order, II. 122.
Lines or hatches, I. Pl. 6.
Link, II. 112, 150.
Linnaeus, II. 502.
Linné, I. 730, 731, 733, 736, 750, 756, II. 511. B. 1707, D. 1778.
Linnean Society, II. 503.
Linnean system, I. 730, 750.
Lintearia, I. Pl. 19.
Lion, I. 497.
Lippie, II. 151.
Liquefaction, I. 643, II. 395.
Liquid, I. 259.
Liquid adhering to a solid, I. 623.
Liquidity, I. 619.
Liquids, I. 535, 613, Pl. 39, II. 380.
Litre, II. 152.
Litron, II. 152.
Living force, II. 140.
Living under water, II. 255.
Load, II. 151.
Loaded chain, I. Pl. 11.
Loaded cylnder, I. Pl. 3.
Loaded pendulum, II. 139.
Loaded thread, II. 267.
Loaded waggon, I. Pl. 3.
Loading ships, II. 199, 243.
Loadstones, II. 444.
Lobé, II. 597.
Local heat, II. 451.
Local motion, II. 130.
Loci solidi, II. 122.
Lock, II. 179.
Lock filled from a reservoir, I. 282.
Locker, II. 456.
Lockie, II. 113.
Locks, II. 235.
Locus of right lines, II. 123.
Loevens, II. 435.
Log, I. 112, Pl. 22, II. 192, 244. Hydraulic log, I. 318.
Logarithmic circle, I. Pl. 7, II. 146.
Logarithmic curve, I. Pl. 10, II. 3.
Logarithmic tangents, II. 374.
Logarithms, I. 106, 272. See corrections, I. 598, II. 6, 9, 116, 117.
Logistic circle, II. 146.
Log glass, II. 196.
Log line, II. 218.
Lohmeier, I. 365, II. 256.
Lomonosow, II. 290.
London, I. 454, 700, II. 365.
London bridge, II. 234.
Long, II. 325.
Longevity, II. 516, 517.
Longitude, I. 251, 536, 543, 601, II. 357, 376.
Longitudes, II. 364, 365.
Longitudinal sounds, I. 380.
Longitudinal vibrations of rods, II. 269.
Long tube, II. 286.
Looking glasses, II. 210, 283, 323.
Looming, I. 441.
Looms, II. 187.
Lorgna, II. 116, 146, 225, 347, 481.

INDEX.

Lorimer, II. 437.
Lotteries, II. 117, 180.
Louis XV, I. 601.
Lovett, II. 126, 415, 437.
Lowering boats, II. 200.
Lowering weights, II. 196, 200.
Lowitz, I. Pl. 29, II. 221, 254, 374.
Low water, I. 576, II. 368.
Loxodromic circle, II. 374.
Lubinietz, II. 337.
Lucernal microscope, I. 425.
Lucid disc micrometer, I. 432, II. 352.
Luc. See Deluc.
Luckombe, II. 158, 217.
Lucretius, I. 16, 57, 240, 253, 490, 598, II. 54, 124.
Ludlam, II. 145, 347, 350.
Lullin, II. 416.
Lullin's card, II. 422.
Lulofs, II. 366.
Luminous arches, II. 489.
Luminous bodies, I. 409. II. 291.
Luminous cross, II. 527.
Luminous insects, II. 292.
Luminous meteors, II. 499.
Lunar atmosphere, II. 345, 346.
Lunar corona, II. 317.
Lunar equations, II. 341.
Lunar globe, I. 534.
Lunar heat, II. 451.
Lunar influence, II. 450.
Lunar motions, I. 519, Pl. 34, II. 340.
Lunar mountains, II. 336, 346, 358, 368.
Lunar observations, I. 544, II. 357, 365.
Lunar orbit, II. 340.

Lunar parallax, II. 341, 367, 361.
Lunar periods, II. 346, 490.
Lunar rainbow, I. 443, II. 309.
Lunar stones, II. 501.
Lunar volcanos, I. 722.
Lunar year, II. 376.
Lunes, II. 118, 123.
Lungs, II. 253.
Lute, I. 399.
Luz, II. 388, 393.
Lycopodium, I. 624.
Lycosthenes, II. 303, 446.
Lyonnet, I. 608.
Lyons, II. 119, 416.
Lyra, I. 496.
Lyre, I. 397, 403, II. 274, 566.
Maberly, II. 593.
Macclesfield, II. 300.
Mach. A. II. 107.
Machin, I. 249.
Machine for equations, II. 115.
Machine for measuring strength, I. 151.
Machinery, I. 172, Pl. 14, II. 181.
Machinery for entertainment, II. 184.
Machinery of fluids, I. 316.
Machines, I. 89, II. 141, 166. Compound machines, II. 135.
Machines approuvées, II. 107.
Machin's law, II. 132.
Machy, II. 175.
Mackay, II. 365, 371.
Mackenzie, II. 156.
Maclaurin, I. 65, 82, 250, 253, 323, 359, 360, 366, II. 113, 119, 120, 126, 140, 539, 556, 557, 558, 561. B. 1698, D. 1746.

Macrobius, I. 576, II. 567.
Madder, II. 213.
Madeira, I. 700.
Maffei, II. 481.
Magazin encyclopédique, II. 111.
Magazine pistol, II. 263.
Magdeburg hemispheres, I. 274, 630.
Magellan, II. 347, 350, 384, 460.
Magic lantern, I. 473, II. 284, 323.
Magnet, I. 690, 743, 751.
Magnetical apparatus, II. 443.
Magnetical attractions and repulsions, I. 687.
Magnetical curves, I. Pl. 41.
Magnetical effects, I. Pl. 41.
Magnetical effluvia, II. 614.
Magnetical globe, II. 443.
Magnetical measures, II. 446.
Magnetical paste, I. 693.
Magnetical substances, I. 686, II. 438.
Magnet in a globe, I. 689.
Magnetism, I. 685, II. 436.
Magnetism by induction, I. 690.
Magnetism of animals, II. 439.
Magnifier. Double magnifier, I. 431.
Magnifying powers, I. 422, II. 78, 80, 287.
Magnifying powers of telescopes, I. 427, 430.
Magnitude of the earth, II. 358.

Magnitude of the planets, I. Pl. 34.
Magnitude of the stars, I. 490, II. 329.
Magnitudes of the stars, II. 282, 352.
Magrath, II. 158.
Mahon, II. 416. See Stanhope.
Maillard, II. 257.
Maillet, II. 496.
Maintaining power, II. 192.
Mair, I. 747.
Mairan, I. 502, II. 450, 488.
Maire, I. 428.
Mako, II. 482.
Malcolm, II. 272.
Malebranche, I. 479, II. 614.
Maler, II. 127.
Mallet, II. 114, 121, 360, 363.
Malouin, II. 214.
Malta, I. 587.
Malt kiln, II. 412.
Malt mill, II. 214.
Malton, II. 157.
Mammalia, I. 734, II. 516.
Management of colours, II. 314.
Management of rivers, II. 234.
Management of timekeepers, II. 195.
Manchester, I. 245.
Manchester memoirs, II. 111.
Mandoline, I. 599.
Margin, II. 384.
Mangles, I. 221. II. 205.
Manilius, I. 604, II. 324.
Mann, II. 451.

Mannichfaltigkciten, II. 109.
Manoeuvres of ships, II. 239.
Manometers, II. 461.
Manometry, II. 462.
Mansard roof, I. Pl. 13, II. 42.
Manufactures, I. 243, II. 141, 184.
Manures, II. 519.
Maple, II. 513.
Map of the world, I. Pl. 42, 43.
Maps, II. 374.
Marat, II. 296, 384, 416.
Marble, I. 230, 231, II. 175.
Marbles, II. 210.
Marc, II. 161.
Marcellus, I. 58, 240, 242.
Marchand, II. 217.
Marchetti, II. 168.
Marc of Charlemagne, II. 161.
Marie, II. 130.
Marigni, I. 399.
Marine barometer, II. 461.
Marine fossils, II. 496.
Marine observations, II. 349.
Marine octant, I. Pl. 35.
Marine pump, II. 251.
Marine quadrants, II. 245.
Marine spencer, II. 244.
Marine surveyor, II. 244.
Marine worms, II. 518.
Mariotte, I. 355, 356, 366, 443, 444, 477. See corrections. I. 483, II. 112, 308. D. 1684.
Mariotte's theory of halos, II. 3 6.
Maritime observations, II. 239.
Maritime snrveying, II. 156.
Marius, II. 337.
Marivetz, II. 127.
Marly, II. 249, 250.
Marne, II. 384.

Marpurg, 273, 551, 554.
Marquois's scales, I. 102, Pl. 6.
Mars, I. 507, 534, Pl. 32, 33, II. 334, 372.
Marsden, II. 367.
Marsh, II. 233.
Marshes, II. 199.
Marsigli, II. 292, 365.
Martial flowers of sal ammoniac, II. 323.
Marsupium nigrum, II. 600, 601.
Martenson, II. 414.
Martin, II. 126, 157, 249, 256, 288, 292, 415.
Martine, II. 126, 386.
Martini, II. 567.
Martiniere, II. 366.
Martinique, II. 166.
Marum. See Van Marum.
Mascheroni, II. 118, 177.
Maseres, II 116.
Maskelyne, I. 493, 575, Pl. 28, II. 148, 150, 360, 363, 370, 473, 672, 674.
Mason, II. 362.
Masonry, II. 174.
Masses, I. 50.
Masses in motion, II. 134.
Masses of the planets, II. 372.
Mass of iron, II. 501.
Masts, I. 149, II. 178, 241.
Material bodies, II. 618.
Materials for building, II. 174.
Materials for manufactures, II. 184.
Mathematical machines, II. 146.
Mathematical mechanics, II. 142.
Mathematical society of Bohemia, II. 110.
Mathematical symbols, II. 555.

Mathematici veteres, I. 240, 242, II. 113.
Mathematics, II. 1, 112, 124, 130.
Matrass, II. 189.
Matrix, I. 122, II. 158.
Mattaire, II. 217.
Matter, I. 605, II. 131, 377. Impenetrability of matter, I. 28.
Matter of fire, II. 383.
Matthesius, I. 356, II. 263.
Matting, II. 188.
Maty, II. 106.
Maunoir, II. 279.
Maupertuis, I. 21, 495, II. 112, 140, 339, 362.
Maurolycus, I. 474, 483.
Mawe, II. 511.
Maxima, II. 338.
Maxima and minima, II. 172.
Maxima of curves, II. 123, 133.
Maximum, II. 8. De quibusdam maximis, II. 123.
Maximum of effect, II. 54, 140.
Maximum of heat, II. 387, 388, 389.
Maximum of labour, II. 166.
Maxwell, II. 611.
Mayer, I. 602, 749, 751, 756, II. 112, 332, 336, 341, 373, 375, 384, 393, 427, 438, 473. T. Mayer, B. 1723, D. 1762.
Mazéas, I. 480, II. 625.
M. B. Library of the British Museum.
M'Culloch, I. Pl. 41.
Mean depth, II. 61.
Mean image, II. 76.
Mean of observations, II. 116, 346, 347.
Mean tones, II. 554.
Measure. Common measure, II. 13.

Measurement of angles, II. 145.
Measurement of light, II. 282.
Measurement of refractive powers, II. 282.
Measurement of the earth, I. 593, II. 358.
Measurement of transparency, II. 282.
Measurements of degrees, I. 570.
Measure of force, I. 79, II. 139.
Measure of speech, II. 270.
Measures, II. 146, 180. Hydrodynamic measures, II. 235.
Measures of atmospherical electricity, II. 485.
Measures of heat, I. 646, II. 385.
Measures of the undulations of light, II. 640.
Measures of time, II. 196.
Measures of various countries, II. 152.
Measures of wind, II. 244, 455.
Measuring, I. 93.
Measuring a ship's way, II 244.
Measuring distances, II. 156.
Measuring earthquakes, II 492.
Measuring heat, II. 408.
Measuring heights, II. 396
Measuring instruments, I 111, II. 155.
Méchain, II. 149, 674.
Mechanical arts, II. 124.
Mechanical centres, II. 136
Mechanical curves, II. 123
Mechanical force, I. 79.
Mechanical paradox, II 184.

INDEX.

Mechanical power, I. 321, II. 137, 140.
Mechanical powers, II. 135.
Mechanics, II. 27, 129, 137, 216. History of mechanics, I. 236.
Mechanism of the eye, II. 313.
Medical electricity, II. 424.
Medical galvanism, II. 429.
Mediterranean, I. 587, 708, II. 234, 367.
Medium of sound, II. 265.
Medusae, II. 292.
Medusa's head, I. 496.
Megameter, II. 351.
Meibomius, I. 405, II. 240.
Meindert Sorrey, II. 441.
Melanderhjelm, II. 325, 362.
Mélanges de Turin, II. 109.
Melody, I. 392, II. 563.
Melody of speech, II. 276.
Melted glass, II. 396.
Melting, II. 394, 427.
Melting of ice, II. 408.
Melting point, II. 509.
Membrana pupillaris, II. 311.
Membrana tympani, II. 271.
Membranes. Vibrations of membranes, I. 381.
Mémoires de Dijon, II. 110.
Mémoires de Turin, II. 109.
Mémoires presentés, II. 107.
Mémoires sur l'Egypte, II. 111.
Memory, II. 124.
Men, II. 164.
Mendoza, II. 357.
Mendoza y Rios, II. 371.
Meniscoid, II. 663.
Meniscus, II. 662.
Meniscus lens, I. 416, II. 72.
Menkar, I. 497.
Menstrual parallax, I. 334.

Mensuration, II. 118, 156.
Menzies, II. 518.
Menzoli, II. 272.
Mercator, II. 375.
Mercurial air pump, II. 254.
Mercurial column, I. 270.
Mercurial level, II. 353.
Mercurial phosphorus, II. 422.
Mercurial pump, II. 166, 247.
Mercurial thermometer, I. 647.
Mercurial vapours, II. 252.
Mercury, the metal, I. 276, Pl. 39. II. 381, 382, 403, 461, 509, 653, 654, 659. Pressure of mercury, I. 265.
Mercury, the planet, I. 506, 532, 622, 623, II. 289, 333, 372, 659.
Meridian, I. 109, 536, Pl. 35, II. 147, 341, 354.
Meridians of Greenwich and Paris, II. 360.
Meridional line, II. 374.
Meridional parts, II. 374.
Mersenne, I. 253, 405, 407, II. 124, 264, 272, 546, 558. B. 1588, D. 1648.
Mersennus, II. 610.
Mery, II. 601.
Messenger, I. 205, II. 197.
Messier, I. Pl. 31.
Metacentre, I. 266, II. 59.
Metacentric curve, II. 241.
Metallic surface, I. 709.
Metalline thermometer, II. 386, 389.
Metals, I. 411, 678, II. 316, 654, 659.
Meteoric stones, II. 501.
Meteorographic instruments, II. 448.
Meteorological apparatus, II. 448.

Meteorological thermometers, II. 454.
Meteorologische briefe, II. 482.
Meteorology, I. 696, 753, II. 446.
Meteors, I. 721, 722, II. 499, 675.
Meto, I. 540, 592, 604.
Metre, I. 108, II. 148, 152.
Metrologie constitutionelle, II. 148.
Metrometer, II. 279.
Metternich, II. 170.
Metz, II. 155.
Mexicans, I. 97, II. 377.
Mezzotinto, I. 119.
Michael III, I. 595.
Micheli, II. 388.
Michell, I. 492, 493, 575, II. 399, 630.
Michelotti, II. 222, 223.
Microelectrometers, II. 434.
Micrometer, I. 432, Pl. 28, II. 145.
Micrometer for wires, II. 275.
Micrometers, II. 289, 351.
Micrometrical scale, I. Pl. 7.
Microscopes, I. Pl. 28, II. 78..80, 285. Double microscopes, I. 427. Simple microscopes, I. 422. Solar microscopes, I. 425.
Microscopic observations, II. 646.
Microtelescope, II. 285, 287.
Middle ages, I. 243.
Mile, II. 150, 153, 155.
Military engines, II. 207.
Military mining, II. 211, 216.
Military telescope, II. 290.
Milk, II. 180.
Milky way, I. 493, 496, Pl. 31, II. 328.

Mill, 218.
Miller, II. 511.
Milli, II. 206.
Milligramme, II. 162.
Millilitre, II. 152.
Millimetre, II. 152.
Mills, I. 232, Pl. 18, II. 167, 213, 446.
Millstones, II. 209, 214, 215.
Milner, II. 416.
Mina, II. 162.
Minasi, II. 30.
Mine, II. 152, 364.
Mineral electricity, II. 435.
Mineral materials, II. 185.
Mineralogy, I. 725, 510.
Minerals, I. 723.
Mines, II. 249, 257, 481.
Miniatures, I. 95.
Minimum, II. 8.
Minimum of action, II. 140, 377.
Minimum of vision, II. 312.
Mining, I. 229, II. 211.
Minor scale, I. 394.
Minot, II. 152.
M. Inst. II. 111.
Mirage, II. 301.
Mirbel, I. 728, II. 515.
Mirror, I. 416, Pl. 27, II. 286, 406.
Mirrors, I. 423, Pl. 28, II. 283, 287.
Miscellanea Berolinensia, II. 107.
Miscellanea curiosa, II. 107.
Miscellanea Taurinensia, II. 109.
Mississippi, II. 501.
Misterton Carr, II. 362.
Mists, I. 711, II. 474.
Mitchel, II. 444.
Mitterpachter, II. 367.
Mixed gases, I. 613, II. 221, 465.
Mixed goods, II. 218.
Mixed metals, II. 510.

Mixed oscillations, II. 139.
Mixed plates, I. 470, Pl. 30, II. 635, 680.
Mixed pump, I. 332.
Mixed semivowels, II. 276, 277.
Mixing malt, II. 216.
Mixture, I. 310, II. 510.
Mixture of colours, I. 440.
Mixtures, II. 408, 503.
Mock sun, II. 303.
Mock suns, II. 301.
Modelling, I. 113, II. 157.
Models, II. 176.
Modes of the ancients, II. 279.
Modification of hydraulic forces, II. 235.
Modification of motion, II. 181.
Modulus of elasticity, I. 137, 368, II. 46 .. 49, 84, 86, 169, 509.
Modulus of superficial cohesion, II. 381.
Modulus of tension, II. 66.
Moeris, I. 236.
Moist air, II. 471.
Moist ropes, II. 380.
Moisture, I. 707, II. 468.
Moisture contained in air, II. 466.
Moivre. See Demoivre.
Molecular attraction, II. 380.
Mole plough, II. 213.
Molières, II. 126.
Molina, II. 367.
Momentum, I. 53, 59, 220, Pl. 2, II. 36, 134.
Momentum of light, II. 322.
Momentum of water, II. 249.
Monde naissant, II. 495.
Monésier, II. 478.
Monge, I. 754, II. 157, 302, 649, 652, 656.

Monitum ad observatores meteorologicos, II. 447.
Monochord, II. 272.
Monocotyledonous plants, II. 513.
Monoculus, II. 312.
Monsoons, I. 703, Pl. 42, 43.
Mont Blanc, II. 447.
Montbret, I. 121, II. 161.
Montgolfier, I. 338, 365, Pl. 23, II. 256, 264.
Monthly magazine, II. 111.
Monthly review, II. 105.
Montpelier, I. 700.
Mont Perdu, II. 447.
Montucla, II. 124, 217, 378, 558.
Moon, I. 454, 510, 528, 533, Pl. 33, II. 294, 303, 335, 345, 449.
Moon as causing tides, II. 577.
Moonlight, II. 290.
Moons, I. 509.
Moon's age, I. 541.
Moon's appearance, II. 358.
Moon's atmosphere, II. 336.
Moon's distance, II. 337.
Moon's light, II. 280.
Moon's mass, II. 337.
Moon's motions, II. 373.
Moon's phases, I. Pl. 34.
Moon's rotation, II. 342.
Moon's surface, I. Pl. 34.
Moore, II. 371.
Moors, II. 377.
Morgan, II. 417.
Morhof, II. 105, 270.
Morne Garou, II. 494.
Moro, II. 495.
Morse, II. 366.
Mortar, I. 160.
Mortar for water, II. 232.
Mortar mill, I. 232, II. 214.
Mortars, II. 175.

Mortise, I. 168, II. 174.
Morveau, II. 111, 126, 654, 656, 659.
Mosaic work, I. 97, II. 143.
Moscati, II. 460.
Moses, I. 97.
Moss, II. 496.
Mother of pearl micrometer, II. 290.
Motion, I. 18, Pl. 1. II. 27, 129, 137, 138, 377. Composition of motion, I. 23. Confined motion, I. 42. Measure of motion, I. 79. Perpetual motion, I. 91, II. 142. Quantity of motion, I. 52. Resolution of motion, I. 25.
Motion of a rod, II. 138.
Motion of light, I. 408.
Motion of lighted wicks, II. 389.
Motion of sound, II. 265.
Motions from heat, II. 404.
Motions of a point, II. 130.
Motions of connected systems, II. 138.
Motions of plants, II. 512.
Motions of systems, II. 136.
Motions of the electric fluid, II. 421.
Motions of the stars, I. 516.
Mould board, II. 212.
Moulds, II. 404.
Moulin, II. 525.
Mountaine, I. 749, Pl. 41.
Mountainous countries, I. 712.
Mountains, I. 573, Pl. 33, II. 366, 474, 497, 498.
Mountains of Venus, II. 333.
Mourgue, II. 449.
Mouth, II. 253.

Mouths of rivers, I. 721, II. 224, 480.
Moveable body, II. 35.
Movers, II. 104.
Moving boats, II. 242.
Moving flour, II. 200.
Moving force, II. 140.
Moving forces, II. 181.
Moving globe, II. 375.
Moving ground, II. 200.
Moving media, II. 226.
Moving statues, II. 202.
Moving trees, II. 200, 202.
Mowing, II. 218.
Moxon, II. 141.
Mozart, II. 572.
M. Taur. II. 109.
M. Tur. II. 109.
Mud, II. 494, 498.
Mudge, I. 196, Pl. 16, II. 352.
Mudge's measurement of an arc, II. 362.
Mudge's scapements, II. 194.
Mueller, II. 415, 435.
Muid, II. 152.
Mulberry bark, II. 190.
Mule, II. 279.
Mules, II. 167.
Multiple arcs, II. 122.
Multiple fraction, II. 2.
Multiplication, II. 2, 3.
Multiplication of images, II. 282.
Multiplier of electricity, I. 682, Pl. 40. II. 434.
Multiplying glass, I. 416. Pl. 27.
Mural quadrant, I. Pl. 35. II. 350.
Murbert, II. 496.
Murdoch, II. 370.
Murhard, II. 105.
Muriate of lime, II. 400 .. 402.
Muriatic acid, II. 673.

Murray, II. 240.
Muscles, I. 128, 739, II. 164.
Muscles of the eye, II. 311, 591.
Muscularity of the crystalline lens, II. 525.
Muscular motion, II. 518.
Musée, II. 111.
Music, II. 272, 563. History of music, I. 403.
Musicae scriptores Meibomii, II. 272.
Musical characters, I. 121.
Musical chord, I. Pl. 25.
Musical instruments, I. 397, II. 274.
Musical notes, II. 67.
Musical pen, I. Pl. 6.
Musical sounds, I. 379.
Musical strings, II. 268.
Musical types, II. 159.
Musket ball, II. 227.
Muskets, II. 262, 264.
Muslin, II. 187, 218.
Musschenbroek, I. 152, 250, 253, 666, 750, 754, 756, II. 107, 125, 126, 168, 170, 313, 378, 390, 391, 520, 524, 527, 528, 652, 653, 659. B. 1692, D. 1761.
Mustel, II. 513.
Mutchkin, II. 151.
Mute letters, II. 276, 277.
Mutilations, II. 518.
Muys, II. 125.
Mylius, II. 336.
Myopia, II. 315.
Myopic sight, I. 452.
Myriogramme, II. 162.
Myriolitre, II. 152.
Myriometre, II. 152.
Myrmecophaga, II. 678.
Nail, I. 155, II. 150.
Nail drawer, II. 216.
Nails, II. 180, 206.

Nairne, I. 715, Pl. 40, II. 431, 443.
Nairne's machine, I. 688.
Nap, II. 188.
N. A. Petr. II. 108.
Napier, I. 247, 253, 598, 604. B. 1555, D. 1622.
Napier's logarithms, II. 8, 124.
Naples, II. 493.
Nasal semivowels, II. 276, 277.
Nasal vowels, II. 276.
Native iron, II. 501.
Nativity of Christ, I. 539.
Naturae curiosi, II. 107.
Natural history, I. 723, 745, 750, II. 502.
Natural hygrometer, I. 710.
Natural orders of plants, I. 732.
Natural philosophy, II. 105, 124.
Natural zero, I. 651, II. 389, 409.
Natur der dinge, II. 127.
Nature of colours, II. 320.
Nature of light, I. 457, II. 319.
Naturforschende freunde, II. 110.
Naturforscher, II. 107, 468.
Nauche, II. 429.
Nautical Almanac, I. 602, II. 370.
Nautical angle, II. 375.
Nautical astronomy, II. 370.
Naval architecture, II. 228, 239, 240.
Naves of wheels, II. 203.
Navigation, II. 234, 370.
N. C. Gott. II. 108.
N. C. Petr. II. 108.
Neap tide, I. 577.
Nebel, II. 444. Von der entstehung des nebels, II. 474.
Nebula, I. 492, 494, II. 328, 680.
Nebula in Orion, I. Pl. 31.
Nebulosity, I. 494.
Needle, I. 746, II. 444.
Needle floating, II. 382.
Needles, II. 189, 208, 218.
Negative electricity, I. 661.
Negative quantities, II. 1, 3.
Negativoaffirmative arithmetic, II. 115.
Neptunian theory, I. 720.
Neret's amalgam, II. 432.
Nerves, I. 739, 740, II. 164.
Nerves of the crystalline lens, II. 526.
Nerves of the eye, II. 597, 605.
Nettis, I. Pl. 29.
Neue physikalische belustigungen, II. 109.
Neufchateau, II. 213.
Neutonianismo per le donne, II. 280.
Newcastle. Duchess of Newcastle, II. 124.
Newcomen, I. 347, 357, Pl. 24.
New island, II. 498.
New river, II. 264.
New stars, II. 330.
Newton, I. 6, 7, 26, 28, 36, 37, 44, 55, 65, 83, 248, 253, 287, 357, 366, 405, .. 407, 412, 437, 439, 457, 458, 463, 466, 469, 471, 476 .. 478, 480, 482, 483, 489, 506, 522, 542, 569, 575, 586, 591, 598, 599, 601, 602, 604, 607 .. 609, 611, 614, 638, 654, 749, 756, II. 112, 121, 125, 217, 295, 296, 306, 317, 363, 376, 404, 413, 537, 538, 541, 556 .. 558, 609, 613 .. 618, 620 .. 623, 625 .. 631, 633, 634, 637, 638, 640, 641, 643, 645, 652, 657, 661, 664, 666, 671, 679. B. 1642, D. 1727.
Newton, II. 141.
Newtonian reflector, I. 429.
Newtonian rules of philosophy, I. 16.
Newtonian telescope, I. Pl. 28, II. 79.
Niagara, II. 480.
Nicetas, I. 592, 596, 604.
Nich. II. 111.
Nich. II. 8, 111.
Nicholson, I. 111, 196, 201, 227, 682, 753, Pl. 16, 33, 40, II. 128, 182, 196, 371, 607, 630. P. Nicholson, II. 172, 173, 178.
Nicholson's circle, I. 107.
Nicholson's journal, II. 111.
Nickel, I. 686, II. 438.
Nicolai, II. 114, 128.
Nicole, II. 558.
Nieuhoff, II. 436.
Nieuwentyt, II. 125.
Nieuwe Verhandelingen van het Bataafsch genootschap, II. 258.
Night, I. 525, II. 344.
Night lamp, II. 290.
Night watch, II. 192.
Nile, I. 713.
Nilometer, I. 593.
Nitocris, I. See Corrections.
Nitrate of lime, II. 292.

VOL. II.

Nitre, I. 634.
Nitrogen gas, II. 509.
Nocetus, II. 489.
Noctuary, II. 192.
Nodes, I. 504, Pl. 34, II. 340, 372.
Nodes of chords, II. 268.
Nodes of the planets, I. Pl. 32.
Nollet, I. 750, 756, II. 126, 189, 414, 520. B. 1700, D. 1770.
Nonconductors, I. 666.
Nooth, II. 432.
Norfolk, II. 495.
Noria, I. 327, Pl. 22.
Norimbergense commercium, II. 108.
Norman, II. 486.
Norske selskab, II. 109.
North, I. 500.
Northern crown, I, 497.
Northern hemisphere warmer, I. 702.
Northern lights, II. 488.
Northern passage, II. 366.
North pole, I. 687.
Norway, II. 498. Society of Norway, 109.
Norwood, I. 600, II. 362, 370, 376.
Notation of music, II. 273.
Notes of music, I. 396, II. 280.
Nourishment of plants, II. 513.
Nouvelliste, II. 435.
Noya Caraffa. Duc de la Noya Caraffa, II. 435.
Nucleus of a comet, I. 512.
Numa, I. 743.
Number, II. 1, 113.
Numbering vibrations, II. 272.
Number of the stars, I. 490, II. 326.

Numerical equations, II. 8.
Numerorum quadratorum tabula, II. 115.
Nunnez, II. 370.
Nuova raccolta, II. 222.
Nut, I. 72, Pl. 5.
Nutation, I. 506.
Nutation of the earth's axis, I. 509, II. 334.
Nutation of the moon's orbit, II. 341.
Nutrition of animals, I. 738.
Nutrition of insects, II. 518.
Oak, II. 168, 169, 509.
Oaks, II. 240.
Oars, II. 236, 242.
Oats, II. 151.
Obbiezzioni alla teoria di Newton, II. 296.
Obelisc, II. 348.
Object glasses, II. 80, 284, 286, 288.
Oblique collision, II. 136.
Oblique cylinder, II. 123.
Oblique float boards, I. 322.
Oblique forces, I. Pl. 3.
Oblique impulse, II. 226.
Oblique impulse of fluids, 303
Oblique reflection, I. 437, II. 294.
Oblique refraction, II. 605.
Oblique threads, II. 41.
Obliquity of the crystalline, II. 315.
Obliquity of the ecliptic, I. 518, 593, II. 334.
Obolus, II. 162.
Obscure heat, II. 406.
Obscure light, II. 322, 407.
Observations, II. 346, 371.
Observations dans les Pyrénées, II. 367.

Observations for finding the situations of places, II. 364.
Observations made in Cook's voyage, II. 371.
Observations of temperature, II. 452.
Observations of the earth's motion, II. 358.
Observations of the places of the planets, II. 357.
Observations of the secondary planets, II. 357.
Observations of the stars, II. 355.
Observations of the sun, II. 355.
Observations of tides, II. 368.
Observations of time, II. 348.
Observations sur les ombres colorées, II. 314.
Observations sur la physique, II. 110.
Observatories, II. 347.
Observatory, I. 148.
Observatory for meteorology, II. 448.
Observatory of Greenwich, I. 601.
Observing distances, II. 156.
Occultations, II. 310, 345.
Octave, I. 393.
Octant, I. Pl. 35.
Octants, II. 350.
Ocular music, II. 320.
Ocular spectra, I. 455, Pl. 30, II. 314.
Odorous bodies, II. 397.
Odorous emanations, II. 397.
Odours, II. 423.
Oenometer, II. 231.
Oil, II. 291, 458. Effect of oil on waves, II. 228.

Oil candle, II. 245.
Oil colours, II. 143.
Oil mill, I. 222.
Oil mills, II. 214.
Oil paint, II. 180.
Oil paintings, I. 96.
Oil press, II. 204.
Oils, II. 322.
Oil spreading on water, I. 625, II. 659.
Oil swimming on water, II. 220, 223, 381, 382.
Oily substances, I. 213.
Olbers, I. 508, 603, II. 312. 334, 586, 591, 597, 673, 675, 676. Corrections.
Old manuscripts, II. 159.
Olive oil, II. 509.
Oliver, II. 337.
Oncia, II. 154.
Opera glass, II. 78.
Ophion, II. 333.
Opposition, I. 527.
Opposition of forces, I. Pl. 3.
Optical centre, I. 418.
Optical compass, II. 350.
Optical fallacy, II. 646.
Optical instruments, I. 420, II. 76, 281.
Optical pencil, II. 287.
Optical scenery, II. 284.
Optic nerve, I. 448, 450, II. 82.
Optics, I. 259, 408, II. 280, 323.
Optometer, I. 452, II. 575, 604, 605, 671.
Opuscoli scelti, II. 110.
Oran outang, II. 279.
Orbit of the sun, I. 500.
Orbits of chords, II. 554.
Orbits of comets, I. 521, II. 341.
Orbits of the planets, II. 332, 372.
Orbits of the primary planets, II. 339.

Orbits of the secondary planets, II. 340.
Orders of architecture, I. 165.
Orders of plants, I. 732.
Ordinate of an ellipsis, II. 24.
Ordnance, II. 263.
Ore, II. 213.
Organ, I. 402, 404, II. 275, 554, 610.
Organic geometry, II. 120.
Organ pipe, II. 569.
Organ pipes, I. 385, 401, 402, Pl. 26. II. 266, 275, 537, 539.
Organs of the voice, II. 275.
Oriani, II. 300.
Orifices, II. 61.
Origine des fontaines, II. 479.
Origines des inventions, II. 217.
Orion, I. 497, II. 672.
Ornithorhynchus, II. 672.
Ornithorhynchus hystrix, II. 678.
Orreries, I. 567, II. 374.
Orthographical projection, I. 116, Pl. 8, II. 21.
Oscillation, II. 53, 137.
Oscillations, II. 194.
Oscillations of a system, II. 139.
Oscillations of a thread, II. 139.
Oscillations of floating bodies, II. 220, 223.
Oscillations of fluids, I. 287, II. 223.
Oscillations of the sea, II. 343.
Oscillations on pulleys, II. 138.
Osiris, I. 403, II. 566.
Ostrich, II. 311.
Otto, II. 367, 496, 498.

Oulton, II. 249.
Ounce, II. 161.
Oval, II. 557.
Oval dome, II. 176.
Oval lathe, II. 122, 209.
Ovarium, II. 517.
Oven, II. 403.
Ovens, II. 410, 411.
Overflowing lamp, I. Pl. 21.
Overflowing well, II. 246.
Overflow of the sea, II. 490.
Overshot wheel, I. 320, Pl. 22, II. 236.
Ovid, I. 237.
Owl, II. 312.
Oxen, II. 181.
Oxidation, II. 424, 428.
Oxid of iron, II. 211.
Oxygen, I. 434, II. 514.
Oxygen gas, I. 634, II. 292, 509.
Oyster shells, II. 293.
Packing press, II. 204.
Padlock, II. 180.
Pain, II. 178.
Painters, II. 217.
Painting, I. 454, II. 142, 217, 323.
Painting wood, II. 180.
Palatine academy, II. 109.
Palatine society, II. 447.
Palladio, I. 253, Pl. 11, II. 172. B. 1508, D. 1580.
Palladium, II. 323.
Palladius, II. 245.
Pallas, I. 508, 534, II. 334, 372, 497, 674, 676.
Pallet, II. 560. See Corrections.
Palm, II. 153.
Palmo, II. 154.
Palpable characters, II. 316.
Pan, II. 154.
Pane of glass, II. 294.
Pancirollus, II. 217.
Pangraph, II. 144.
Panorama, I. 455, II. 314.

Pantheon, I. Pl. 12, II. 452.
Pantograph, I. 103, Pl. 6, II. 144.
Pantometer, II. 144.
Pantometrum Pauccianum, II. 156.
Paper, I. 98, 187, 244, II. 143, 217, 218.
Paper hangings, II. 190.
Paper making, II. 190.
Paper mills, II. 190, 213.
Papers on naval architecture, II. 239.
Papier maché, II. 157.
Papin, I. 345, II. 141, 245, 247, 253.
Papin's digester, II. 410.
Pappus, I. 243, 253, II. 113. Pl. 383.
Papyrus, I. 98.
Parabola, I. 39, 375, Pl. 2, II. 24.
Parabolas, I. Pl. 10.
Parabolic glasses, II. 283.
Parabolic jet, I. 286.
Parabolic orbit, I. 522.
Parabolic path, II. 33.
Parachutes, I. 306, II. 256, 263.
Paradox. Hydrostatic paradox, I. 263.
Parafeu, II. 200.
Paragallo, II. 493.
Parallax, I. 542, II. 329, 355.
Parallax of a micrometer, II. 289.
Parallax of a spheroid, II. 357.
Parallax of the sun, I. 544.
Parallel circle, II. 350.
Parallelepiped, II. 18.
Parallelepipeds, II. 19.
Parallel lines, II. 9, 12, 13, 118, 158.
Parallel motion, I. Pl. 14.
Parallelogram, I. 25, II. 13, 15.

Parallel planes, II. 17.
Parallel rulers, I. 102. Pl. 14, II. 144.
Paralysis, II. 314.
Parapet, II. 174.
Paraselenes, II. 303.
Paravolcan, II. 494.
Parchment, II. 143.
Pardies, I. 357, 366, 479, II. 118, 129. B. 1636, D. 1673.
Parent, I. 249, 324, II. 129. B. 1666, D. 1716.
Parent's mill, I. 331.
Parhelia, I. 443, Pl. 29, II. 303.
Paris, I. 454, II. 360, 365.
Parisian academy, I. 249.
Park, II. 442.
Parker, I. 171, II. 175, 180.
Parker's lens, II. 407.
Parkinson, II. 130, 498.
Parrot, II. 466.
Partial differences, II. 119.
Partial electricity, I. 661.
Partial reflection, I. 461, II. 584.
Particles of light, II. 320.
Particular geography, II. 365.
Partridge, II. 605.
Pascal, I. 748, 756, II. 112, 472, 558. B. 1623, D. 1662.
Pasigraphy, II. 143.
Pasquich, II. 130.
Passage, II. 562.
Passage of heat, II. 405.
Passive strength, I. 93, Pl. 11, II. 168, 169.
Patent pipes, II. 205.
Paternoster work, I. 335.
Path of light, II. 299, 321.
Path of the centre of gravity, I. Pl. 3.
Path of the sun, I. 525.

Paths of the planets, I. Pl. 34.
Pattens, II. 189.
Patterns, II. 187.
Paucton, II. 147.
Paul, II. 279.
Paulet, II. 186, 187.
Paut, II. 190.
Pavements, II. 174.
Paving roads, II. 203.
Pear gage, I. 341, Pl. 24, II. 254.
Pearl barley, II. 215.
Pearls, II. 519.
Pearson, I. 567.
Peart, II. 417, 437, 518.
Peat borer, II. 211.
Peat mosses, II. 498, 514.
Pedestrian, I. 129.
Pedometer, II. 156.
Pegasus, I. 497, 753.
Pemberton, I. 250, 253, 599, II. 125, 319, 524, 596, 643.
Pen, I. 94.
Pencil, I. 94, 95.
Pencil of light, I. Pl. 26, II. 70.
Pencils, II. 142.
Pendulous bodies, II. 139.
Pendulum, I. 44, 107, 191, 595, Pl. 2, 5, II. 34, 146 .. 148, 216, 343, 363. Circular pendulum, I. 197.
Pendulum of two threads, II. 139.
Pendulums, I. 526, 578, II. 132, 133, 136, 194, 218, 227, 339, 358, 359, 572.
Penetrating into space, II. 330.
Penetration, I. 144, 156, 224, II. 140, 206.
Penetration of glass by water, II. 379.
Penknives, II. 207.

Pennant, I. 750, 756. B. 1726, D. 1798.
Pennington, II. 403.
Pennsylvania, II. 367.
Pennyweight, II. 161.
Penpark hole, II. 495, 498.
Penrose, II. 436.
Pens, I. 99, II. 144, 217.
Pens for lines, I. 100.
Pentrough, II. 237.
Penumbra, I. 528. II. 313.
Perambulator, II. 156.
Perception of external objects, I. 449, II. 313.
Perception of vegetables, II. 513.
Perche, II. 151.
Percussion, I. 223, II. 53, 136, 137, 140, 205.
Perez, II. 145.
Perforation in the moon, II. 335, 336.
Perforation of a jar, I. 669.
Performance of men, II. 166.
Periodical springs, II. 480.
Periodical stars, II. 331.
Periodical winds, I. 701.
Periods of sounds, II. 544.
Periods of the planets, I. 506, Pl. 32.
Periods of the satellites, II. 373.
Peripheric focus, II. 73.
Peripheric image, II. 76.
Periscopic spectacles, I. 425, II. 315.
Perkinism, II. 428.
Perks, II. 556.
Permanence of sensations, II. 455.
Permanent effects of heat and cold, II. 403.
Permeability of matter, I. 610.
Perpendicular, II. 9, 11.
Perpendicular to a plane, II. 17, 18.

Perpendicular to the meridian, II. 358.
Perpetual motion, I. 91, Pl. 6, II. 142, 238.
Perrault, I. 204, 249. B. 1613, D. 1688.
Perrault's ropes, I. 214.
Perret, II. 207, 208.
Perronet, II. 176.
Perseus, I. 496.
Persians, I. 540, 595.
Person, II. 141.
Perspective, I. 93, 114, Pl. 7, 8, II. 21, 157.
Perspective instruments, II. 257.
Perspective practique, II. 157.
Perspiration of plants, II. 514.
Perturbations, I. 518, II. 339.
Perturbations of the comets, II. 341.
Perturbations of the planets, II. 340.
Pestle, II. 214.
Petersburg, II. 246, 452. Academy of Petersburg, II. 108.
Petharlin, II. 496.
Petit, II. 383, 579, 596, 599, 601.
Petrefaction, II. 497.
Pewter ware, II. 206.
Pézénas, II. 370.
Pfaff, I. 753, II. 427.
Pfannenschmid, II. 314.
Phantasmagoria, I. 426, Pl. 28, II. 285.
Phases of planets, I. 527.
Phases of the moon, I. 528, 345.
Phenicians, I. 98.
Pherecydes, I. 237, 253. B. 600, D. 515. B. C.
Philadelphia, II. 109.

Philibert, II. 324.
Philip, III. I. 601.
Phillips, II. 234, 269.
Philo, I. 240, 243, 253, 353.
Philolaus, I. 592, 604.
Philosophical transactions, II. 105.
Philosophical transactions abridged, II. 106, 107.
Philosophizing, I. 16.
Philosophy, II. 124.
Phloscope, II. 291.
Ph. M. II. 111.
Phormium, II. 185.
Phosphorescence of vitriolated tartar, II. 293.
Phosphoric animals, II. 292.
Phosphoric cloud, II. 482.
Phosphorus, I. 634.
Phosphorus of Bologna, I. 435.
Photometers, I. 421, 699, Pl. 27, II. 282, 351.
Photometry, II. 314.
Photophorus, II. 283, 291.
Ph. tr. II. 105.
Physical astronomy, I. 488, II. 339.
Physical geography, II. 496.
Physical optics, I. 434, II. 80, after art. 460, 290, 317, 318, 639.
Physical properties, II. 509.
Physics, I. 485, II. 324, 519.
Physikalische arbeiten, II. 111.
Physikalische belustigungen, II. 108, 109.
Physiological effects of electricity, II. 424.
Physiological effects of heat, II. 403.

INDEX.

Physiology, I. 738, II. 516.
Physiology of plants, II. 512.
Pianoforte, I. 398, II. 274.
Piazzi, I. 508, 603, II. 326, 334, 347, 377, 672, 673, 676.
Picard, I. 569, 600, II. 152. D. 1682.
Pickel, II. 432.
Pictet, I. 370, 634, 635, 637, 638, 706, 751, II. 111, 148 .. 150, 283, 384, 467, 631, 681, 682.
Picture, II. 21.
Pictures, II. 142.
Pictures on a wall, II. 284.
Piderit, II. 415.
Pièces sur l'aiman, II. 436.
Piers, I. 163, 315.
Pietra mala, II. 494.
Pigment, II. 218.
Pigott, II. 270.
Pile, II. 206.
Pile engine, I. 225, Pl. 18. II. 207.
Pile of Volta, I. 676, 752.
Piles, II. 216.
Piles. See Despiles.
Pilgram, II. 447.
Pilots, II. 244.
Pin, I. 155.
Pinacographic instrument, II. Corrections.
Pincers, II. 204.
Pingré, II. 337, 365.
Pini, II. 172, 275, 497.
Pinion, I. 177, Pl. 15.
Pinions, II. 183.
Pink dye, II. 647.
Pinkerton, II. 367.
Pins, II. 189, 218.
Pint, II. 148, 150, 151.
Pipe, II. 151. Effect of a short pipe, I. 280. Vertical pipe, I. 285.
Pipemaking, II. 206.
Piper, II. 184.
Pipes, I. 293, 354, II. 205, 221, 222, 245, 246, 539.
Musical pipes, I. 379.
Pipes of lead, I. 317.
Pipes of pumps, I. 335.
Pipes of wood, II. 211.
Pira, II. 492.
Pisces, I. 504.
Pisé, I. 169, II. 175.
Pistols, II. 262.
Piston, I. Pl. 23, II. 237.
Pistons, I. 332, II. 246, 248.
Pitchers, II. 175.
Pitot, I. 318, II. 239.
Pittacus, I. 237, 253. B. 652, D. 570. B. C.
Pivots, II. 184.
Pizzati, II. 121.
Places of the planets, II. 340, 357, 372.
Places of the stars, II. 330, 355.
Plagoscope, II. 456.
Plain astronomy, I. 488.
Plane, II. 9.
Plane, II. 208.
Plane mirror, I. 415.
Plane mirrors, II. 282.
Planes, II. 17.
Planetarium, I. 567, II. 375.
Planetary aberration, II. 294.
Planetary atmospheres, II. 332.
Planetary orbit, II. 339.
Planetary worlds, I. 531, II. 346.
Planets, I. 503, Pl. 32. II. 332.
Planing, II. 209.
Planispheres, I. 566, II. 374.
Planks, I. Pl. 10.
Planoconcave lens, I. 416.
Planoconvex lens, I. 416, II. 288.
Plant, I. 726, II. 367.
Plaster, II. 175, 213, 218.
Plaster for trees, II. 515.
Plaster of Paris, I. 113.
Plat, II. 189.
Plate, II. 206, 208, 209.
Plate glass, II. 287.
Plate machine, I. 680, Pl. 40, II. 431.
Plates bandes, II. 176.
Platina, I. 610, II. 388, 509, 510.
Platina for mirrors, II. 283.
Plating mill, II. 205.
Plato, I. 239, 744, 756, II. 566, 567. B. 429, D. 348. B. C.
Platrière. See Laplatrière.
Plaw, II. 174.
Playfair, II. 498.
Pleiades, I. 497.
Plempius, I. 638.
Pleurs, II. 495.
Pleyel, II. 572.
Pliers, II. 204.
Pliny, I. 530, 576, 746, 756, II. 567. B. 24, D. 79.
Plot, II. 266.
Plotting table, II. 146.
Plough, I. Pl. 18, II. 167.
Ploughing, II. 212.
Pluche, II. 129.
Plucknett, II. 197.
Plumbery, II. 206.
Plumb line, II. 354, 359.
Plumier, II. 209.
Plunger pump, II. 249.
Plungers, I. 331, Pl. 23, II. 235.
Plurality of worlds, I. 532, II. 346.
Plush, II. 187.
Plutarch, I. 239, 240, 598, 745.
Pneumatic and hydraulic machines, II. 254.
Pneumatic apparatus, II. 254.
Pneumatic equilibrium, I. 270, Pl. 19, II. 60, 220.
Pneumatic experiments, II. 254.
Pneumatic filter, II. 246.
Pneumatic machines, I. 339, II. 252.
Pneumatics, I. 352, II. 263, 378.
Pneumatostatics, I. 258. Pl. 19, II. 220.
Po, II. 224.
Poda, II. 249.
Poetry, I. 532, II. 563.
Point, II. 3, 151. Moving point, II. 130.
Pointed instruments, II. 207.
Points, II. 118, 485.
Points in electricity, II. 422.
Point vélique, II. 240.
Polar circles, I. 570.
Polarity, I. 688, II. 439, 440. Electric polarity, II. 419.
Polarity of a balance, II. 159.
Polarity of light, II. 310.
Pole, II. 150, 203.
Poleni, I. 357, 366. B. 1683, D. 1761.
Poles, I. 570.
Pole star, I. 496, II. 354, 365.
Poli, II. 482, 484.
Polished surface, I. 412.
Polishing, I. 231, II. 210.
Polishing lenses, II. 284.
Pollen, II. 514.
Polley, II. 141.
Pollux, II. 567.
Polycrates, I. 237.
Polydorus Vergilius, II. 216.
Polygon, I. 26.
Polygonometry, II. 118.
Polygons, II. 118, 209.
Polygraph, I. 100, II. 143.
Polynomals, II. 120.
Polynomial theorem, II. 144.

VOL. II. 5 D

Polypus, II. 516.
Pompeii, II. 493.
Poncelet, II. 482.
Pondicherry, II. 301.
Ponds, II. 480.
Pont Notre Dame, II. 249.
Poppe, II. 217.
Population of England, II. 367.
Porcelain, II. 157, 206.
Porcelain thermometer, II. 388.
Pores, I. 609, II. 379.
Porisms, II. 118.
Porosity, I. 459.
Porta, II. 124.
Portable observatory, II. 353.
Portelumière, II. 283.
Porter cask, II. 233.
Porterfield, I. 452, 478, 483, II. 311, 523 .. 525, 573, 575, 592, 603.
Porters, I. 132, 210, Pl. 17, II. 166.
Portfolios, II. 143.
Port of London, II. 233.
Port of Toulon, II. 199.
Positive electricity, I. 661.
Post chaises, II. 203.
Postulates, II. 9, 10, 557.
Potash, II. 403, 509.
Potatoe, II. 292.
Potatoe bread, II. 519.
Potatoe cutter, II. 208.
Potatoe mill, II. 214.
Pottery, I. 223, II. 206, 214, 218.
Pouchet, II. 447.
Pound, I. 124, II. 161.
Pounding, II. 214.
Poupart, II. 601.
Powder, II. 259.
Powder horn, II. 262.
Powder magazine, II. 485.

Powder mill, I. 232, II. 213.
Powder proof, I. 134, II. 259, 262.
Powder thrown on glass, II. 419.
Power, II. 124. Mechanical power, I. 321.
Powers, II. 4.
Powers and products, II. 115.
Pownall, II. 459.
Practical astronomy, I. 536. II. 346.
Practical mechanics, II. 141.
Prange, II. 142, 314.
Preceptor, II. 110.
Precession of the equinoxes, I. 505, 519, II. 341, 349, 373, 374.
Preliminary mechanics, II. 142.
Premiums of the Society of Arts, II. 218, 264.
Preparation of food, II. 411.
Preparation of raw materials, II. 185.
Preparations of vegetables, II. 512.
Preponderance, I. Pl. 5, 6, II. 54.
Presbyopic sight, I. 452.
Presensations of animals, II. 448.
Preservation from lightning, II. 485.
Preservation of ships and their crews, II. 243.
Preservation of wood, II. 180.
Preserving fresh water, II. 481.
President of the R. S. II. 672.
Press. Bramah's press, I. 263, Pl. 23.

Presses, I. 220, 222, II. 204.
Pressure, I. 59, II. 37, 134. Hydraulic pressure, II. 62.
Pressure engine, II. 251.
Pressure of a fluid, I. 261.
Pressure of earth, I. 161, II. 173, 232.
Pressure of fluids, I. Pl. 19, II. 58, 222.
Pressure of running water, II. 223.
Pressure of the atmosphere, I. 273.
Pressure of the air, II. 220.
Pressure of threads, II. 41.
Pressure of water, II. 255.
Pressure on a pivot, II. 133, 139.
Prévost, I. 638, 686, 698 .. 700, 754, II. 406, 438, 681, 682. B. Prévost, I. 709.
Price, II. 117.
Priestley, I. 480, 751, II. 127, 157, 217, 280, 416, 429. B. 1733, D. 1804.
Primary mountains, I. 574.
Prime number, II. 349.
Primes, II. 116.
Principle of motion, II. 140.
Principles of mechanics, II. 137, 140.
Pringle, II. 112, 500.
Printer's grammar, II. 158.
Printing, I. 93, 118, 121, 246, II. 158, 217.
Printing from stones, I. 221.
Printing press, I. 221, II. 204.
Printing stuffs, II. 188.
Prints, II. 142.
Prism, I. 414, 416, 438, Pl. 26, 27, II. 17.

Prismatic micrometer, II. 289, 290.
Prismatic spectrum, I. Pl. 29, II. 679.
Prisms, II. 19, 20.
Prize for heat and light, II. 520.
Prize respecting heat, II. 384.
Proclus, I. 243, 253, II. 485.
Procyon, I. 497.
Product, II. 2.
Production of cold, II. 411.
Progressions, II. 4.
Progressive motion, I. 129.
Progressive motion of light, II. 294.
Projectiles, I. 33, 37, 286, Pl. 2, II. 32, 132.
Projectiles from the moon, II. 341.
Projectiles with resistance, II. 226.
Projection of a knife from a lump of snow, II. 394.
Projection of a picture, II. 21.
Projection of a sphere, I. 117, Pl. 8.
Projection of eclipses, II. 346.
Projection of light, I. 459.
Projections, II. 374.
Projections of areas, II. 118.
Projections of the sphere, II. 374.
Projections of the stars, II. 328.
Prony, I. 363, II. 114, 149, 219, 236, 360, 398.
Proofs, I. 644.
Propagation of heat in fluids, II. 405.

Propagation of heat in solids, II. 405.
Propagation of impulses, II. 618.
Propagation of light, II. 320.
Propagation of motion, II. 139.
Propagation of sound, II. 68, 264.
Propeller, II. 243.
Proper motions of the stars, I. 493, II. 330.
Properties of curves, II. 22, 120.
Properties of matter, I. 605, 660, II. 377, 607.
Prop or shore, I. 71, Pl. 5, II. 135, 212.
Proportion, II. 114.
Proportional compasses, I. 103, Pl. 6, II. 144, 217, 218.
Proportional quantities, II. 3.
Proportional scale, II. 142.
Proportions of wheels, II. 183.
Props of reservoirs, I. 313.
Prosperin, I. 513, II. 337.
Protagorides, I. 746.
Protractors, II. 145.
Proust, II. 674, 675.
Provence, II. 502.
Provinzialblaetter, II. 474.
Pruning trees, II. 208.
Prussian measures, II. 148.
Ptolemaeus, II. 324.
Ptolemaic system, I. Pl. 37.
Ptolemy, I. 473, 483, 495, 504, 530, 590, 591, 594, 595, 604, II. 349. Fl. 160.
Ptolemy Philadelphus, I. 592.
Ptolemy Soter, I. 592.

Pugh, II. 451, 463.
Pullies, I. 68, Pl. 4, II. 40, 54, 138, 170, 172, 197, 200.
Pulling up trees, II. 199.
Pulsation of heat, II. 405.
Pulsation of the air, II. 407.
Pulse, I. 291.
Pulverisation, II. 213.
Pump, I. 331, II. 166.
Pump capstan, II. 251.
Pump for fires, II. 413.
Pumping, I. 132, II. 165.
Pump rods, II. 183, 199.
Pumps, I. Pl. 23, II. 177, 236, 247.
Pupil, I. 451, II. 530.
Purfleet, II. 485.
Purifying air, II. 252.
Puschkin, II. 435.
Putrescent wood, II. 293.
Pyramid, II. 17, 45.
Pyramidical prows, II. 226.
Pyramidoidal solids, II. 20.
Pyramids, I. 593.
Pyrenees, II. 366, 367, 447.
Pyrites, II. 438.
Pyrometer for a bridge, II. 176.
Pyrometers, I. 646, II. 385.
Pythagoras, I. 236, 237, 253, 403, 404, 407, 592, 598, 604, 744, 756, II. 507. B. 568, D. 497. B. C.
Pythagoreans, II. 551.
Pythagorean system, I. Pl. 38.
Quadrangular system of wires, II. 352.
Quadrant, I. 105, II. 76, 302, 350.

Quadrant electrometer, I. 683.
Quadrant of altitude, II. 375.
Quadrant pump, II. 248.
Quadrants, I. 541, Pl. 35. II. 349.
Quadratic equations, II. 6.
Quadratrix of the hyperbola, II. 123.
Quadrature of curves, II. 120.
Quadrature of the circle, II. 124.
Quantity, II. 1, 112, 140.
Quanz, II. 571, 572.
Quarries under Paris, II. 211.
Quarry, II. 218.
Quart, II. 150, 151.
Quarter, I. 124, II. 150, 151.
Quays, I. 315.
Queen post, I. 199, Pl. 12.
Querns, II. 215.
Quicksilver, II. 380, 408.
Quiescent space, I. 20, II. 9, 27.
Quills, II. 217.
Quin, II. 231.
Quinary arithmetic, II. 116.
Raccolta di autori chi trattano del moto dell' acque, II. 222. Nuova raccolta, II. 222.
Racks, II. 181, 183.
Rackstrow, II. 324.
Radial focus, II. 73.
Radial image, II. 76.
Radiant heat, II. 322, 406.
Radiation of heat, I. 636, II. 681.
Radiations of light, II. 527.
Radical quantities, II. 115.

Radius, II. 9.
Radius of curvature, II. 22, 120.
Rafn, II. 514.
Rafter, I. 147, II. 179.
Rafters in equilibrium, I. Pl. 11.
Rag pump, II. 249.
Rags, II. 190.
Raia torpedo, II. 435.
Railing, II. 180.
Rail roads, II. 204.
Rain, I. 712, 713, II. 174, 216, 465, 475, 483.
Rainbows, I. 442, 470, Pl. 29, 30, II. 81, 303, 308, 316, 643.
Rain gages, II. 476.
Rain of ashes, II. 493.
Rain water, II. 475.
Rainy winds, II. 476.
Raisin, II. 184.
Raising a nap, II. 180.
Raising ballast, II. 199.
Raising boats, II. 200.
Raising earth, II. 199.
Raising flour, II. 199.
Raising ore, II. 200.
Raising ships, II. 199, 243.
Raising stones, II. 199.
Raising water, II. 247.
Raising weights, I. 203, II. 196.
Rameau, II. 272.
Ramelli, I. 247, 334, Pl. 23, II. 124.
Rammelsberg, I. 235.
Ramond, II. 447.
Rams, II. 205.
Ramsden, I. 105, 112, 125, 431, 433, 480, 602, 604, Pl. 7, 8, 28, II. 145, 155, 231, 285, 350, 573, 584, 585, 587, 597. B. 1730, D. 1800.
Ramsden's application of a planoconvex lens, II. 288.

Ramsgate, II. 233.
Ranby, II. 601.
Range of a cannon ball, II. 260.
Range of a projectile, I. 39, 286, II. 33.
Raper, II. 152.
Rarefaction, I. 632.
Rarefaction of air, II. 220, 253.
Rarefied air, II. 265.
Rarity of the atmosphere, II. 60.
Ras, II. 155.
Raspe, II. 494, 496.
Rasping mill, II. 215.
Rats, II. 241.
Rattlesnake, II. 518.
Raven, II. 311.
Ravenna, I. 587.
Ray, I. 748, 756, II. 436, 495. B. 1628, D. 1705.
Ray of light, I. 408, Pl. 26, II. 70.
Razors, II. 208, 209.
Razor's edge, II. 389.
Razor straps, II. 210.
Reaction, I. 55, II. 379.
Reaction of water, II. 229.
Read, I. 714, II. 482.
Reaping, II. 218.
Reaping wheelbarrow, II. 209.
Réaumur, I. 632, 648, 748, 756, II. 207, 386, 558, 561. B. 1683, D. 1757.
Reciprocal action, I. 51, 55, 56, II. 35.
Reciprocal force, I. 613, Pl. 2, II. 37.
Reciprocals of numbers, II. 4, 5.
Reciprocals of primes, II. 110.
Reciprocating springs, II. 480.
Reckoning board, II. 143.

Reckoning machines, II. 146.
Reckoning rods, II. 146.
Recoil, II. 260.
Recoiling scapements, II. 194.
Recorde, I. 473, II. 323.
Recovery of sight, II. 313.
Rectangle, II. 13.
Rectification of a curve, II. 124.
Rectification of motion, I. 174, Pl. 14, II. 182.
Rectilinear motion, I. Pl. 1.
Recueil de tables astronomiques, II. 373.
Recueil de traités sur l'électricité, II. 415.
Recurrence of sensations, II. 563.
Redern, I. 480, II. 366.
Red heat, II. 322.
Red hot ball, II. 262.
Red light, I. 465.
Red rays, II. 407.
Red sea, I. 587, II. 234, 367.
Reduction of angles, II. 146.
Reduction of observations, II. 116, 147.
Reeds, II. 185, 188.
Reel, II. 186.
Reeling, II. 186.
Rees, II. 127, 129.
References, I. 25.
Reflecting instrument, II. 282.
Reflecting instruments for angles, II. 350.
Reflecting lamps, II. 282, 290.
Reflecting level, II. 353.
Reflecting microscope, II. 79.
Reflecting surface, I. 415.
Reflecting telescope, II. 329.

Reflecting telescopes, I. 429, 431, 476.
Reflection, I. 81, 437, 460, 472, Pl. 5, 26, II. 70, 136, 543, 584, 622.
Reflection at equal angles, II. 323.
Reflection of a stone, I. 307.
Reflection of cold, I. 638.
Reflection of heat, II. 406, 631.
Reflection of invisible heat, II. 283.
Reflection of light, I. 410, II. 294, 321.
Reflection of sound, I. 374, Pl. 25.
Reflection of waves, I. 288, 375.
Refracting mediums in motion, II. 294.
Refracting telescopes, II. 286.
Refraction, I. 410, 411, 460, 472, 542, 566, Pl. 26, 29, II. 70, 287, 320, 323, 354, 465, 509, 543, 623, 660. Double refraction. II. 309.
Refraction of balls, II. 226.
Refraction of crystals, I. 445.
Refraction of the atmosphere, I. 441, II. 81.
Refractions, II. 472.
Refractio solis inoccidui, II. 302.
Refractive densities, I. 412, 421, 473, Pl. 27, II. 70, 509, 679.
Refractive force, II. 509.
Refractive powers, II. 282, 294, 296.
Refractive powers of the eye, II. 578, 604.

Refrangibility, II. 282, 320.
Refrangibility of heat, I. 638.
Refrangibility of light, II. 286.
Refrigeration, I. 698.
Regal organ pipe, I. 401, Pl. 26.
Regemotte, II. 176.
Regenerated paper, II. 190.
Register, II. 192.
Registered cordage, II. 187.
Register for a mine, II. 200.
Registers of rain, II. 476.
Regnault, II. 217.
Regnier, II. 167.
Regression of heat, II. 405.
Regulation of descent, II. 181.
Regulation of discharge, II. 245.
Regulation of force, I. 96.
Regulation of hydraulic forces, I. 316.
Regulator, I. Pl. 2, II. 182.
Regulator for a were, II. 234.
Regulators of electricity, II. 434.
Regulus, I. 497.
Reil, II. 597.
Reimarus, II. 482, 486, 498.
Relative centre of refraction, II. 74.
Relative motion, I. Pl. 1.
Relief, II. 157.
Remarks on halos, II. 306.
Remote tide, I. 579.
Removing earth, I. 219.
Removing ships, II. 243.
Removing weights, I. 203, 210, II. 200.

Renaud, I. 357, 366, II. 239. B. 1652, D. 1719.
Reneaux, II. 256.
Repeating watch, II. 192.
Repertory of arts, II. 111.
Reports on the port of London, II. 233.
Reports to the Board of Agriculture, II. 519.
Representations of the stars, II. 328.
Reproduction, I. 695, 724, II. 517.
Reptiles, II. 271, 516.
Republican calendar, I. 510.
Repulsion, I. 76, 611, 654, 655, Pl. 39, II. 377, 378.
Repulsions of floating bodies, I. 624, II. 655.
Repulsions of the electric fluid, I. 659.
Repulsive force, II. 661.
Repulsive strength, II. 49, 169.
Reservoirs, I. 312, II. 233.
Resilience, I. 143, 147, 629, II. 50.
Resingue, II. 206.
Resinous electricity, I. 670.
Resinous substances in lenses, II. 288.
Resins, II. 143.
Resistance, II. 134, 138.
Resistance of fluids, I. 293, 303, Pl. 21, II. 62, 226, 229.
Resistance of machines, II. 141.
Resistance of solids, II. 168.
Resistance of the air, I. 38, 201, 305, 341, Pl. 24, II. 194, 195.
Resistance to a globe, II. 228.

Resistance to a ship, II. 240.
Resistance to curved surfaces, II. 227.
Resistance to the tides, I. 580.
Resolution of force, II. 131.
Resolution of motion, I. 25.
Respiration, I. 739, II. 517.
Respiration of plants, II. 514.
Rest, II. 9, 129.
Result of two motions, II. 28.
Retardation, I. 29.
Retardation of the tides, II. 343.
Retarded pendulum, II. 35.
Retarding force, II. 29.
Retina, I. 448, II. 82, 311, 526, 530, 582.
Retrograde motions, I. 527.
Returning stroke, I. 713, II. 483.
Return of light, I. 412.
Reuss, II. 105.
Reversionary payments, II. 167.
Reversion of a compass, II. 445.
Reversion of series, II. 116.
Revolutions from electricity, II. 425.
Revolutions of chords, I. 383, II. 268.
Revolutions of the planets, II. 372.
Revolving doubler, I. Pl. 40.
Revolving fluid, II. 57.
Revolving globe, II. 220.

Revolving oars, II. 242.
Revolving pendulums, I. 47, Pl. 2, II. 35, 136.
Revolving stars, II. 329.
Reynolds, II. 142, 528. B. 1723, D. 1792.
Rhabdological abacus, II. 146.
Rheita, I. 428, 474, 483, Pl. 28, II. 78.
Rhemnius Fannius, II. 160.
Rhinland foot, I. 111.
Rhode, II. 473.
Rhodi, II. 280.
Rhomboid reticle, II. 351.
Rhombus, II. 352.
Rhythm, I. 392, II. 563.
R. I. Library of the Royal Institution.
Ribbon loom, II. 188.
Ribbon machine for electricity, II. 432.
Ribbons, II. 187.
Riecati, I. 384, II. 86, 549.
Riccioli, II. 324, 365.
Richard, II. 446.
Richer, II. 357.
Richmann, I. 356, 743, 749, 756, II. 391, 404, 483, 681, 682. D. 1753.
Richter, II. 127.
Ricketts, II. 488.
Riding, II. 200.
Rifle barrels, I. 40, 350, II. 262.
Rigby, II. 517.
Rigid bodies, II. 267.
Right angle, II. 9.
Right ascension, I. 536, 542.
Right ascension of the stars, II. 344.
Right ascensions, II. 349.
Right line, II. 9.
Ring, II. 189.
Ringing, I. 131, II. 165.

Ringing a magnet, I. 694.
Ringing a bell, II. 270.
Ring of Saturn, I. 511.
Rings from electricity, II. 423.
Rings of light, II. 647.
Rings of the planets, II. 333, 346.
Rinman, II. 141, 436.
Rittenhouse, II. 390.
Ritter, I. 437, 481, 639, 753, II. 323, 647.
Rise and fall of the tides, I. 583.
Rising and setting, I. 566.
Risner, II. 280.
River, II. 62.
River of Amazons, II. 224, 370, 480.
Rivers, I. 292, 312, 572, 721, II. 224, 234, 366, 479. Tides of rivers, I. 582.
Rivière, II. 444.
Rizzetti, II. 201, 320, 543.
Road. Circular road, I. 48.
Road harrow, II. 203.
Road plough, II. 203.
Roads, II. 203, 218.
Robert, II. 256.
Robertson, I. 427, II. 121, 144, 146, 256, 370, 455.
Roberval, I. 508, II. 557, 558.
Robins, I. 40, 360, 364, 366, II. 112, 361, 393. B. 1707, D. 1751.
Robison, I. 28, 41, 131, 132, 146, 250, 253, 293, 331, 363, 365, 372, 611, 658, 694, 751, II. 128, 159, 166, 169, 223, 225, 227, 229, 247, 253, 259, 275, 286, 342, 349, 363, 377,

397, 400, 409, 438, 443, 444, 459, 473, 607, 609, 610, 631. B. 1739, D. 1804.
Rochfort, II. 250.
Rochon, I. 121, II. 295, 456, 457.
Rock crystal, II. 290, 309, 310.
Rockets, II. 146, 263.
Rod, II. 150.
Rods, I. 111, Pl. 9, 14, II. 155, 181. Sounds of rods, I. 184.
Rods suspended, II. 182.
Roeding, II. 370.
Roehl, II. 325, 356.
Roemer, I. 436, 477, 483, II. 558. B. 1644, D. 1710.
Roesler, II. 346.
Rohault, II. 125.
Rohr, II. 105.
Roller, I. Pl. 17.
Roller pump, I. 334, Pl. 23.
Rollers, I. 213, II. 182, 200, 204, 212.
Rollin, II. 217.
Rolling, I. Pl. 2.
Rolling clock, II. 191.
Rolling figures, II. 24.
Rolling press, II. 204.
Roman buildings, II. 175.
Roman foot, II. 147.
Roman money, II. 160.
Roman ounce, II. 160.
Romans, I. 118, 244.
Roman year, I. 539.
Rome, I. 700.
Romieu, I. 406, 407, II. 544.
Romme, I. 364, II. 229, 239, 241.
Rood, II. 151.
Roof, I. 72, 169, Pl. 5. II. 42.
Roofs, I. Pl. 13, II. 178.

Room, II. 537.
Root cutter, II. 208.
Rooting up trees, II. 200.
Roots of equations, II. 114, 146.
Rope and pulley, II. 166.
Rope crane, II. 198.
Rope making, I. 181, II. 186.
Rope pump, I. 327, Pl. 21. II. 251.
Ropes, I. 183, II. 168, 170, 171, 178, 181, 186.
Ropes for towing, II. 243.
Rose, II. 414.
Rosenberg, II. 417.
Rosenthal, II. 127, 391, 447, 448.
Rosetta, I. 721.
Rosnier, I. 365, II. 256.
Rot, II. 180.
Rotation, I. 42, 81, 85. Corrections. II. 52, 137. Corrections.
Rotation of balls, II. 260.
Rotation of billiard balls, I. Pl. 5.
Rotation of the earth, I. 525, 702, II. 334, 341.
Rotation of the moon, I. 511, 521.
Rotation of the planets, I. 505, II. 333, 341, 372.
Rotation of the sun, I. 500.
Rotation of tubes, II. 386.
Rotation of stars, II. 331.
Rotations of chords, II. 546.
Rotation with progression, II. 138.
Rotation with resistance, II. 138.
Rotatory motion, I. Pl. 5, II. 182.
Rotatory power, I. 83, Pl. 2, II. 52, 137.
Rotatory power of a stream, II. 63, 238.

Rotatory pump, I. 330, II. 250.
Rotatory saw, II. 210.
Rotolo, II. 162.
Rotten wood, II. 292, 293.
Rotterdam, II. 109.
Roubo, II. 179, 202.
Rouland, II. 431, 447.
Rouse, II. 457.
Rousseau, II. 273, 566, 567.
Rowe, II. 119.
Rowing, I. 131, II. 165, 242.
Rowning, II. 127.
Roy, II. 148, 155, 221, 362, 363, 367, 368, 390, 391, 393.
Royal Institution, I. 251, 755, II. 676. Objects of the Royal Institution, I. 1.
Royal Society, I. 7, 248, 249, 749, II. 105, 671, 676.
Roy's expansions of mercury, II. 461.
Rozier, II. 107, 109.
R. S. Library of the Royal Society.
Rudder, I. 325.
Rudders, I. 150, II. 241.
Rude, II. 496.
Rudiments of ancient architecture, II. 172.
Rudolph, I. 597.
Rulers, I. 100.
Rules, II. 144.
Rules of philosophy, I. 16.
Ruling, II. 143.
Ruling machine, I. 119, II. 158.
Rumford. Count Rumford, I. 350, 364, 632, 633, 635, 652, 757, Pl. 27, II. 112, 169, 261, 294, 520, 543, 623, 631.
Running, I. 130, Pl. 9.

Rupert. Prince Rupert, I. 335. Prince Rupert's drops, I. 644.
Rupture, II. 168.
Rupture of a pillar, II. 174.
Rush work, II. 188.
Russel, I. 534, II. 142, 336.
Russia, II. 366, 451.
Russian stoves, II. 411.
Rust, II. 207.
Rutherford, I. 697.
Rutherford's thermometer, I. Pl. 41.
Rutherforth, II. 126.
Ruts, II. 202, 204.
S. A. II. 110.
Sacks, II. 188.
Saddle, II. 203.
Saddlery, II. 203.
Safety valve, II. 259.
Sagittae, II. 25.
Sagittarius, I. 504.
Sail, I. Pl. 22, II. 240.
Sailing carriages, II. 201.
Sailing chariots, II. 238.
Sailmaker's assistant, II. 241.
Sails, II. 238, 241.
Saint Auban, II. 260.
Saint Fond, II. 256.
Saint Lucia, II. 494.
Saint Paul's cathedral, I. 165.
Saint Pierre, 1. 601, II. 128.
Saint Vincent, II. 494.
Sal ammoniac, II. 510.
Salinas, II. 272.
Salmon, II. 200, 272.
Salt marsh, II. 235.
Saltness, II. 479.
Saltpetre, II. 261.
Salts, II. 673.
Salt works, II. 411, 511.
Saluces, II. 261.

Sammlung die baukunst betreffend, II. 173.
Sammlungen zur physik, II. 110.
Samum, II. 458.
Sanctorius, I. 192, 247, 253. B. 1561, D. 1636.
Sand, II. 173.
Sand flood, II. 458.
Sand glasses, II. 196.
Sand hills, II. 498.
Santerini, II. 495.
Sap, I. 729, II. 513, 514.
Sapphire, II. 675.
Saracens, I. 189, 245, 246.
Sarepta, II. 263.
Saros, I. 590.
Saros météorologique, II. 450.
Sarti, II. 492.
Sashes, II. 179.
Satellites, I. 509, 511, Pl. 33, II. 335, 373.
Satellites of Jupiter, II. 337.
Satellites of Saturn, II. 337, 341.
Satellites of the Georgian planet, II. 337.
Satellitian instrument, II. 375.
Saturn, I. 508, 535, Pl. 33, II. 335, 340, 372.
Saturn's ring, I. 598, II. 345, 371, 631.
Saul, II. 460.
Saunders, II. 174.
Saunderson, II. 113.
Saussure, I. 637, 706, 709, 710, 751, II. 366, 393, 416, 447, 466 .. 471. Theodore de Saussure, II. 515.
Sauvages, II. 525.
Sauveur, I. 405, 407, II. 545, 546, 610.
Sauveur's pitch, II. 273.

Saverien, II. 126.
Savery, I. 346, 356, 366, Pl. 24, II. 264. Servington Savery, II. 289.
Saving lives, II. 244.
Saving ships, II. 243.
Saving water, II. 234.
Saw, I. Pl. 4.
Sawing, I. 229, II. 210.
Sawing mill, II. 210.
Saws, II. 207.
Sawyer, II. 165.
Scaffolding, II. 199.
Scale in music, II. 566.
Scalene cone, II. 21.
Scale of heat, I. 646.
Scale of musical notes, I. 392.
Scales, II. 155.
Scales of thermometers, II. 398.
Scales vibrating, II. 139.
Scaliger, I. 541.
Scapement, I. 193.
Scapements, I. Pl. 16, II. 193.
Scape wheel, II. 194.
Scaphander, II. 244.
Scarella, II. 436.
Scarfing, I. 167, Pl. 13.
Scarificator, II. 212.
Scarpa, II. 271.
Scavenger's carts, II. 202.
Scelta di opuscoli, II. 110.
Schaeffer, I. 247, 253, II. 433.
Schaffhausen, II. 178.
Scheele, I. 751, II. 384, 675. B. 1742, D. 1786.
Scheibel, II. 105.
Scheiner, I. 474, 483, II. 310, 331, 575. B. 1573, D. 1650.
Schemnitz, I. 336, Pl. 23, II. 249, 251, 385.
Scherfer, II. 287.

Scheuchzer, II. 125.
Schilling, II. 435, 439.
Schmid, II. 325.
Schmidt, II. 393, 398, 400, 418, 431, 467, 468.
Schober, II. 170, 230.
Schott, I. 355, II. 124, 144, 219.
Schroeter, I. 507, Pl. 33, II. 325, 332, 333, 335, 336, 674, 675.
Schubert, II. 340.
Schulze, II. 165, 166.
Schurer, II. 127.
Schw. Abh. II. 108.
Schwedische Academie, II. 108.
Schwedisches Museum, II. 489.
Schwigkard, II. 436.
Scientific dialogues, II. 129.
Scilly, II. 496.
Scissors, II. 207, 217.
Sclerotica, II. 82, 530.
Scorpio, I. 497, 504.
Scotch measures, II. 147, 151.
Scotiography, II. 144.
Scotland, II. 367.
Screen of glass, I. 637.
Screw, I. 72, 155, Pl. 5. II. 42, 123, 135.
Screw micrometer, II. 289.
Screw of Archimedes, I. 328, Pl. 22, II. 248.
Screws, I. 208, II. 145, 197, 209.
Scruple, II. 161.
Sculling, I. 132.
Sculpture, I. 93, II. 157.
Scylla, II. 370.
Scythes, II. 208.
S. E. II. 107.
Sea, I. 571, 579, 699, II. 450, 452, 496.
Sea breezes, I. 704.

Sea charts, II. 374.
Sea gage, II. 244.
Seal, II. 312.
Sealing wax, II. 421.
Seal skins, II. 190.
Seamanship, I. 324, II. 239.
Seas, II. 479.
Seasons, I. 525, Pl. 34, II. 344.
Sea water, II. 292, 394, 481.
Sebastian's machine, II. 132.
Secant, II. 15.
Secants, I. 106.
Secondary mountains, I. 574.
Secondary planets, II. 335, 340.
Secondat, II. 415.
Second fluxion, II. 22.
Section of a canal, I. Pl. 21.
Sections of plants, II. 286.
Sector, I. 104, Pl. 7, II. 193.
Secular equations, II. 341.
Secular variations, II. 340.
Security from fire, II. 175.
Sedan chairs, II. 200.
Segment, II. 9.
Segner, I. 754, II. 126, 236, 320, 325, 386, 406, 450, 460, 480, 649, 654, 661.
Segner's machine, II. 237.
Seguin, I. 750, II. 384.
Seiferheld, II. 431.
Seine, II. 234, 481.
Self registering thermometers, I. 697.
Sembrador, II. 212.
Semifluids, II. 220, 232, 383.
Semimaterial existences, I. 610.
Semiramis, I. Corrections.

Semitone, I. 393, II. 612.
Semivowels, I. 400, II. 276, 277.
Semple, II. 232.
Sénébier, II. 112, 127, 321, 514.
Seneca, I. 238, 253, 472, 576, II. 124, 337. B. 8, D. 65.
Senegal, II. 453.
Senguerd, II. 125, 253.
Sennert, II. 124.
Sensation, I. 725.
Sensation of colours, I. 439.
Sensation of light, I. 409.
Sensation of sight, II. 312.
Senses, I. 738.
Sensibility of the retina, I. 450.
Sensible effects of electricity, I. 672.
Sensible effects of the celestial motions, I. 528.
Sensitive plant, II. 512.
Sentinel register, II. 192.
Sepia, II. 313.
Septier, II. 152.
Serain, II. 497.
Serao, II. 493.
Serein, I. 711.
Serenus, II. 121.
Serge, II. 385.
Series of eclipses, I. 529.
Series of rods, I. Pl. 14.
Serpent, I. 402.
Serpentarius, I. 495, 497.
Serpentine, II. 488.
Serpents, I. 735.
Serrati, II. 128.
Serson's top, II. 137.
Serum, II. 180.
Servetus, I. 748.
Servière, I. Pl. 23, II. 125.
Setting wheat, II. 212.
Severn, II. 370.
Sewing, II. 189.

Sex of bees, II. 517.
Sex of flowers, II. 513.
Sextant, II. 351.
Seyffer, II. 309.
S'Gravesande, I. 250, 253, II. 125, 219. B. 1688, D. 1742.
Shadow, I. 467, Pl. 30, II. 348, 641.
Shadow of a spheroid, II. 346.
Shadows, II. 313.
Shake, II. 550.
Shag, II. 187, 188.
Shark, II. 519.
Sharp, II. 570.
Sharp instruments, II. 209.
Shaw, I. 724, II. 499, 503, 678.
Shearing cloths, II. 188.
Shears, II. 199, 208.
Sheathing, II. 240, 241.
Sheffield, I. 245.
Shehallion, I. 575, II. 364.
Sheldrake, II. 450.
Sherwin, II. 117.
Shining, II. 414.
Ship, I. 148, 325, Pl. 22, II. 182, 241.
Ship bolt drawer, II. 216.
Ship building, II. 239.
Shipley church, II. 266.
Ships, I. 304, II. 172, 242, 263.
Ship's pumps, II. 236, 251.
Ship's sails, I. 359.
Ship's stove, II. 411.
Ship's way, I. Pl. 22, II. 156.
Shock of electricity, II. 494, 520.
Shoes, II. 189.
Shooting a rope, II. 243.
Shooting stars, I. 721, II. 499.
Shore, I. Pl. 5.
Shores or props, II. 135.

Short, I. 502, II. 624.
Shortest descent, II. 133.
Shortest roads, II. 203.
Short hand, II. 143.
Shot, I. 351, II. 262.
Shower bellows, I. 344, Pl. 24, II. 255.
Shower of ashes, II. 494.
Shower of dust, II. 493.
Shower of insects, II. 458.
Shower of mud, II. 494.
Showers of stones, I. 719. II. 501.
Shrinkage, II. 390.
Shroud, I. 182.
Shuckburgh, II. 148, 149, 152, 161, 367, 391, 393, 398, 471, 473.
Shut pipes, II. 266.
Shuttles, II. 188.
Shwanpan, II. 146.
Sicard, II. 278.
Sickingen, II. 168.
Sidereal day, I. 537.
Sidereal revolutions, II. 372.
Sienna, II. 501, 674.
Sieve of Eratosthenes, II. 115.
Sieves, II. 188, 215.
Sigaud de la Fond, II. 127, 416, 437.
Sight, II. 312.
Sights, II. 286, 323.
Signals, II. 143.
Signal trumpet, II. 275.
Signs of the ecliptic, I. 504.
Signs of the zodiac, I. 589.
Silberschlag, II. 127, 141, 225, 496, 499.
Silk, I. 184, II. 184, 217.
Silk plant, II. 185.
Silk strings, II. 275.
Silkworms, II. 184.

Silkworm's thread, I. 134, II. 378.
Silurus electricus, II. 436.
Silver, II. 266, 509.
Silver leaf, II. 205.
Silver plate, II. 209.
Silver thread, II. 205.
Similar solids, II. 17.
Similar triangles, II. 14, 15.
Simonides, I. 403, 407, II. 567. B. 579, D. 469, B. C.
Simple fraction, II. 1.
Simple machines, II. 141.
Simple sounds, I. 378.
Simpson, I. 250, 253, 478, 483, 700, II. 113, 117, 118. B. 1711, D. 1761.
Simson, II. 113, 117, 121.
Sine, II. 15, 672.
Sine of an angle, I. 106.
Sines, II. 122. Sums of sines, II. 16.
Singing birds, II. 279.
Single authors, II. 111.
Single vision, I. 453, II. 313.
Sinking of earth, II. 495.
Sinking of ground, II. 498.
Siphon, I. 282, II. 196, 221, 238, 245, 251, 380.
Siphon of Hero, I. 188.
Siphons, I. 316.
Sirius, I. 492, 493, 497, II. 330, 680.
Sisson, I. 602, II. 148.
Sistema participato, II. 554.
Situations of places, II. 364.
Six, I. 701, II. 447.
Six's thermometer, I. 696, Pl. 41, II. 388.
Sixth in music, II. 571.
Size, I. 96, 187, II. 187.
Size for cotton, II. 185.

Sky, I. 454, Pl. 30, II. 313.
Slate, II. 175, 209.
Slating, II. 179.
Sleep, II. 518.
Slicing tallow, II. 209.
Slicing turnips, II. 208, 209.
Slider pump, I. 334, Pl. 23.
Sliding rule, I. Pl. 7.
Sling, I. 33, 226.
Slitting mill, I. 227, Pl. 18. II. 208, 209, 218.
Sloughing, I. 730.
Sluice, I. Pl. 21.
Sluice board, II. 199.
Sluice gates, II. 180.
Sluices, I. 313, II. 233.
Slusius, II. 114.
Small, II. 377.
Smeaton, I. 69, 79, 84, 158, 160, 168, 207, 250, 253, 315, 323, 340, 361, 366, Pl. 11, II. 128, 167, 233, 390, 391, 457. B. 1724, D. 1792.
Smeaton's blocks, I. Pl. 4.
Smelling of insects, II. 518.
Smith, I. 429, 478, 483, II. 79, 272, 273, 280, 511, 524, 541, 544, 551, 554, 609 .. 611. D. 1768.
Smith, II, 367. Pierce Smith, II. 601.
Smith's microscope, I. Pl. 28.
Smith's work, II. 178.
Smoke, I. 453, II. 258, 411, 534, 553.
Smoke jack, I. 324, II. 410, 411.
Smoky chimnies, I. 346, II. 410.
Snails, II. 312, 517.
Snellius, I. 474, 483, II. 323, 363. B. 1591, D. 1626.
Snow, I. 444, Pl. 29, II. 305, 306, 394, 420, 476, 478, 479, 482.
Snow line, II. 452.
Snow plough, II. 212.
Snuff boxes, II. 180, 209.
Snuff mills, II. 213.
Snuff press, II. 204.
Società Italiana, II. 110.
Societas Palatina, II. 447.
Société d'agriculture du département de la Seine, II. 251.
Société de Lausanne, II. 111.
Société philomatique, II. 111.
Society for the encouragement of arts, I. 250, II. 110, 218, 520.
Socin, II. 416.
Soda, II. 403.
Soft iron, II. 403.
Softness, I. 629.
Soil, II. 515.
Solar altitudes, II. 349, 356.
Solar and culinary heat, I. 637.
Solar and lunar years, II. 340.
Solar atmosphere, I. Pl. 31.
Solar clocks, II. 347, 374.
Solar cycle, II. 349.
Solar day, I. 537.
Solar light, II. 291, 322.
Solar microscope, I. 425, Pl. 28, II. 284 .. 286, 317.
Solar phosphori, I. 435, II. 292, 323, 630.
Solar spots, II. 376.
Solar system, I. 499, Pl. 32, II. 372.
Solar tides, I. 584.
Solar time, II. 347.
Soldering glass, II. 283.
Soldner, II. 398.
Solid, II. 8.
Solid angle, II. 17.
Solidity, I. 627, II. 383.
Solid of greatest attraction, II. 339.
Solid of least resistance, II. 226 .. 228.
Solid of revolution, II. 17.
Solids, I. 613, II. 123, 156, 658.
Solomon, II. 486.
Solstice, II. 539, Pl. 34, II. 356.
Solution of iron filings, I. 694.
Solutions, II. 403, 510.
Solway moss, II. 496.
Somnambulism, II. 518.
Son, II. 185.
Sonde, II. 151.
Somometer, II. 279.
Sonorous cavities, II. 537.
Sosigenes, I. 594, 604.
Sothic period, I. 590.
Sound, I. 367, 655, II. 65, 222, 264, 409, 531, 607.
Sound from hydrogen gas, II. 267.
Sounding, II. 244.
Sound in gases, II. 265.
Sounding board, I. 656.
Sounding line, II. 156.
Sound in water, II. 271.
Sound in wood, II. 265.
Sound of lead, II. 383.
Sounds of chords, II. 549.
Sounds of cylinders, II. 268.
Sounds of gases, II. 267.
Sounds of rods, I. 406.
Sources of heat, I. 631.
Sources of heat and cold, II. 385.
Sources of light, I. 434, II. 290.
Sources of motion, I. 90, 131, 164.
Sources of sound, I. 378, II. 266.
Sous, II. 162.
South, I. 500.
South America, I. 571, II. 447, 498.
Southern, II. 256, 672.
Southey, II. 501.
South pole, I. 687.
South Seas, II. 275.
Sowden, II. 456.
Sowing, II. 212.
Space, I. 20, 489, II. 8, 117.
Spade, II. 166.
Spallanzani, I. 750, 756, II. 439, 497. B. 1729, D. 1799.
Spark, I. 169, Pl. 40, II. 420.
Sparks from rubbing the eye, II. 528.
Sparks of electricity, II. 423.
Spasmodic action, II. 314.
Speaking trumpet, I. 375, Pl. 25, II. 279.
Spear points, II. 481.
Specific gravities, I. 310, II. 59, 231, 382, 388, 503. Table of specific gravities, II. 503 .. 507.
Specific gravities of gases, I. 372.
Specific gravity, II. 403, 509, 510.
Specific gravity of air, II. 221, 471.
Specific gravity of men, II. 244.
Specific heat, II. 408, 508.
Specimens of sounds, II. 277, 278.
Spectacles, II. 315, 323.
Spectre, II. 314.
Spectrum, I. 438, Pl. 29, II. 296, 321, 604, 637, 679.

Speculum, II. 282.
Speculum metal, II. 283.
Speculum musicum, II. 272.
Speech, II. 275.
Speed, II. 480.
Speer, II. 232.
Speer's hydrometer, II. 390.
Spencer, II. 244.
Sphere, I. 117, II. 17, 21, 123, 229, 339, 376. Attraction of a sphere, II. 45.
Sphere charged with electricity, I. 662.
Sphere covered by a fluid, II. 220.
Sphere of paper, II. 376.
Spheres, I. 515, II. 209.
Spheres connected, I. 662.
Spherical motion, II. 138.
Spherical segments, II. 281, 313.
Spherical surfaces, II. 71, 120.
Spherical triangles, II. 135.
Spherical trigonometry, II. 119.
Spherical vortex, II. 226.
Sphericity, II. 342.
Spheroid, I. 577.
Spheroidal navigation, II. 371.
Spheroidal trigonometry, II. 119, 359.
Spheroids, II. 138, 339, 359.
Spherometer, II. 284.
Spica Virginis, I. 497.
Spiders, II. 184.
Spider's thread, I. 134.
Spider's web, I. 141, II. 352, 378.
Spina, II. 323.
Spinet, I. 398.
Spinners, II. 218.
Spinning, I. 181, II. 185, 186.
Spinning machine, II. 186.

Spinning wheel, I. 244, II. 186, 218.
Spiral, II. 122.
Spiral compasses, II. 144.
Spiral mill, II. 236.
Spiral of Archimedes, II. 562.
Spiral orbit, II. 32.
Spiral pipe, II. 238.
Spiral pipes, I. 328.
Spiral pump, I. 329, Pl. 22, II. 248.
Spiral spring, II. 139.
Spiral vibrations of rods, II. 269.
Spirit, I. 716.
Spirit level, I. 310, Pl. 21.
Spirit levels, II. 353.
Spirit of wine, I. 372, II. 382.
Spirit thermometer, I. 647, II. 390.
Spiritual substances, I. 610.
Spirituous liquors, II. 510.
Splitting hides, II. 208.
Sponge, I. 625.
Spontaneous combustions, II. 385.
Spontaneous electricity, II. 435.
Spontaneous light, II. 291.
Spoon for earth, II. 216.
Spoon wheels, II. 236.
Spots of the sun, I. 501, Pl. 31, II. 331.
Spoules, II. 186.
Spout, II. 487.
Spouting fluids, II. 222, 223.
Sprat, II. 107.
Spring, I. Pl. 2, 10, II. 139, 217, 377.
Spring of a coach, I. 148.
Spring of the air, II. 220, 253.

Springs, I. 179, 217, II. 131, 168, 182, 194, 203, 245, 383.
Springs of water, I. 286, Pl. 20, II. 451, 452, 479.
Spring steelyard, I. 127, Pl. 9, II. 160.
Spring temper, II. 403.
Spring tides, I. 577, 585.
Spur wheel, I. 177, Pl. 15.
Square, II. 13.
Square of the velocity, II. 140.
Squares, I. 102.
Squinting, II. 315.
Stability of a balance, I. Pl. 8.
Stability of a wedge, I. 155.
Stability of equilibrium, I. 62, 261, Pl. 3, II. 40.
Stability of floating bodies, I. 267, Pl. 19, II. 59.
Stability of fluids, I. Pl. 19.
Stability of ships, I. 326, II. 240.
Stables, II. 174.
Stacada, I. 401.
Stadium, I. 593, II. 152.
Stahl, I. 751, 756. B. 1660, D. 1734.
Staiolo, II. 154.
Staircase, II. 174.
Stairs, II. 165.
Stalkart, II. 240.
Stampers, II. 184, 190, 205.
Stamping, I. 224.
Standard measures, I. 107, II. 146.
Standard pendulum, II. 147.
Standard weights, I. 124, II. 160.

Stanhope, I. 67, 329, 658, 664. See Mahon.
Staple, II. 179.
Star Lyra, I. Pl. 31.
Stars, I. 487, Pl. 36, 37, II. 325, 342, 355, 680. Effect of the stars on light, II. 303.
Stars visible in London, II. 327.
Statical baroscopes, I. Pl. 19, II. 220, 461.
Statical engine, II. 237.
Statical lamp, II. 245.
Statics, I. 93, 123, II. 159.
Statics of fluids, I. 308.
Statics of semifluids, II. 220.
Stationary planets, I. Pl. 34.
Station pointer, II. 145.
Statique, II. 129.
Statt'er, II. 127.
Statuary's compass, I. Pl. 7.
Stay, II. 181.
Steam, I. 271, 619, II. 200, 386, 394, 397, 404, 464, 509, 519. Warming by steam, II. 410.
Steam air pump, II. 259.
Steam boat, I. Pl. 29, II. 243, 259.
Steam engine, I. 48, 133, 346, 361, 362, Pl. 24, II. 133, 165, 167, 257, 263.
Steam regulator, II. 258.
Steam thermometer, II. 389.
Steam tubes, II. 246.
Steatite, II. 157.
Steel, I, 227, 685, II. 86, 169, 207, 403, 438, 509.
Steele, II. 273.
Steelyards, I. 126, Pl. 8, 9, II. 160.
Steelyard with a crane, II. 210.

Stemmata, II. 602.
Stenciling, I. 94.
Steno, II. 495.
Stephensen, II. 492.
Stere, II. 152.
Stereographical projection, I. 117, Pl. 8, II. 22, 375.
Stereotomy, II. 123.
Stereotype printing, I. 122, II. 158.
Stevin, I. 366, II. 134.
Stevinus, I. 247, 253. D. 1633.
Stewart, II. 113, 118, 340.
Stick broken by a blow, I. 86.
Stiffness, I. 139, 629, II. 49, 383.
Stiffness of a cylinder, II. 83.
Stile, I. 98.
Stipa, II. 185.
Stirling, II. 119.
Stirrup, I. 387, II. 203.
Stockholm. Academy at Stockholm, II. 108.
Stocking loom, II. 188.
Stockings, I. 244, II. 218.
Stodart, I. 227.
Stone, I. 151, II. 48, 161.
Stone bullets, II. 218.
Stone cutting, I. 229, 230, II. 208.
Stone gatherer, II. 200.
Stone quarries, II. 209.
Stones, II. 168.
Stones fallen, I. 722, II. 501, 674.
Stones joined, I. Pl. 11.
Stopcocks, I. 317, Pl. 21. II. 246.
Stopping holes, II. 243.
Stopping horses, II. 203.
Storms, II. 457.
Storms of rain, II. 478.
Stoves, II. 253, 410, 412.

Strabo, I. 576.
Strada, II. 247.
Straight line, II. 9.
Straights, II. 458, 459.
Straights of Dover, II. 495.
Strain, I. 169.
Strain on a bar, II. 44.
Strain on a plate, II. 84.
Strains of carpentry, II. 176.
Stralsundisches magazin, II. 109.
Strand, I. 182.
Strange, II. 497.
Strap, I. 168.
Strap on a wheel, II. 183.
Straps for beams, I. Pl. 13.
Straps for wheels, I. Pl. 15.
Strata, II. 354.
Straw, II. 185, 208.
Straw paper, II. 190.
Straw plat, II. 189.
Straw work, II. 188.
Stream, I. 321, II. 9, 63.
Stream bellows, II. 255.
Stream of a fluid, I. Pl. 20.
Stream of air, I. Pl. 21, II. 532, 553.
Stream of electricity, I. 670.
Stream of wind, II, 458.
Streams of air from electricity, I. 655, II. 424.
Streams crossing, II. 222.
Strength, I. 143, 144, 629, II. 49, 164, 168, 169, 380, 509.
Strength in resisting the pressure of a fluid, II. 84.
Strength of a column, I. Pl. 10, II. 85, 86.
Strength of a tube, II. 84.
Strength of different substances, I. 151.
Strength of elastic substances, II. 46.

Strength of flood gates, I. 312, II. 84.
Strength of gems, II. 675.
Strength of ice, II. 396.
Strength of joints, I. Pl. 13.
Strength of materials, I. Pl. 11.
Strength of muscles, I. 128.
Strength of ropes, I. 183.
Strength of wires, II. 169.
Striated surfaces, II. 625.
Striking a magnet, I. 694.
Striking part, I. 202.
Stringed instruments, II. 274.
String of baskets, I. 219.
Stripes of colours, I. 465, Pl. 30.
Stroemer, II. 441.
Strohmeyer, II. 387.
Stroke, II. 137.
Stroke of a bullet, II. 206.
Stroke of lightning, II. 484.
Strongest column, II. 51.
Strongest forms, I. 149, 150, Pl. 10, II. 173.
Structure of the eye, II. 311.
Structure of wheels, II. 183.
Structures of particular kinds, II. 174.
Stuart, II. 172.
Stuccos, II. 175.
Stukely, II. 491.
Sturm, II. 113, 125.
Sturmius, II. 309.
Subaqueous buildings, II. 232.
Subaqueous ice, II. 480.
Subcontrary section, II. 21.
Subdominant, I. 393, II. 570.
Sublimation, II. 396.
Sublimation of mercury, II. 397.
Submarine apparatus, II. 255.

Submarine forest, II. 498.
Submarine mountains, II. 366.
Submarine navigation, II. 243.
Submarine trees, II. 496.
Submarine vessels, II. 256.
Subterraneous fires, I. 717, II. 493.
Subterraneous work, II. 211.
Subtraction, II. 1.
Succulent vegetables, II. 514.
Sucking, II. 253.
Sucking and forcing pump, I. 333.
Sucking pump, I. 332, Pl. 23.
Suckow, II. 126.
Suction, I. 274.
Sue, II. 429.
Suessmilch, II. 380.
Suez, II. 367.
Sugar cane, II. 519.
Sugar mill, I. 221, Pl. 18.
Sugar mills, II. 165, 205.
Sulfate of lime, II. 310.
Sulfate of potash, II. 293.
Sulfate of soda, I. 642.
Sulfur, II. 310, 414, 501.
Sulfuric acid, I. 678, II. 403, 509, 653.
Sulfurets, I. 678.
Sulzer, II. 273, 496, 554.
Summer, I. 525, 700.
Summers, II. 452.
Sun, I. 454, 499, II. 303, 331, 355, 371, 372.
Sun and moon, II. 449.
Sun and planet wheel, I. 178.
Sun glasses, II. 289.
Sunk bottles, II. 255.
Sunk roof, II. 179.
Sun's atmosphere, II. 332.
Sun's distance, II. 356.

Sun's motion, I. 517, II. 330.
Sun's parallax, I. 514, II. 356.
Sun's path, I. Pl. 34.
Sun's place, II. 341.
Sums of progressions, II. 4.
Sun's rays, I. 415, 647, 697.
Sun's spots, I. Pl. 31.
Sun's transit, II. 348.
Superficial adhesion, II. 382.
Superficial cohesion, I. 620.
Superior tides, I. 583.
Supernumerary rainbows, I. 470, Pl. 30, II. 316, 643.
Support, I. Pl. 3.
Support for a telescope, II. 289.
Support for balances, II. 159.
Support for lenses, II. 284.
Supports for clocks, I. 202, II. 195.
Surds, II. 115.
Suremain Misséry, II. 264.
Surface, II. 8.
Surface of a fluid, I. 260.
Surface of a liquid, I. 620.
Surface of a sphere, II. 21.
Surfaces, II. 268.
Surfaces admitting heat, II. 407.
Surfaces of fluids, I. Pl. 39, II. 220, 381, 649, 667.
Surface of the sea, I. 568.
Surging the messenger, II. 197.
Surveying, II. 146, 156.
Surveys, II. 358.
Survivorships, II. 117.
Surya Siddhanta, II. 377.
Suspended body, II. 137.
Suspended scaffolding, II. 199.
Suspending ships, II. 243.
Suspension, I. 42.

Suspension for a clock, II. 195.
Suspension of a weight, I. Pl. 3.
Suspension of carriages, II. 203.
Suspension of quicksilver, II. 380.
Susurrant letters, II. 276, 277.
Sutton, II. 257.
Svanberg, II. 362.
Swammerdam, II. 596, 602.
Swan, I. 496.
Sward cutter, II. 208.
Swedenberg, II. 254.
Swedish measures, II. 147.
Sweeping chimnies, II. 411.
Sweetening sea water, II. 487.
Swig, I. 70, Pl. 4, II. 197.
Swiftest descent, I. 40, II. 34, 132.
Swimming, II. 164, 243.
Swinden. See Van Swinden.
Swinging of a ship, II. 240.
Swinging troughs, II. 248.
Switzer, II. 219.
Sword cutlery, II. 207.
Swords, II. 207.
Symbols, II. 376.
Symes, II. 676.
Symington, I. 322, Pl. 24.
Symington's steam boat, II. 259.
Sympathetic sounds, I. 386, II. 270.
Sympathy of chords, II. 271.
Sympathy of clocks, I. 202, II. 195.
Sympathy of pipes, II. 271.
Synchronous tide, I. 579.
Synesius, II. 350.
Synthetical order, I. 9.
Syntractories, II. 123.
Syrinx, I. 402.
System of Ptolemy, I. 594.

System of the world, II. 338, 339.
System of wires, II. 352.
Systems of stars, II. 328.
Systems of the world, I. Pl. 38.
Table of conductors and nonconductors, II. 421.
Table of excitation, II. 426.
Table of heights, II. 367.
Table of the effects of heat, II. 399.
Table of thermometers, II. 399.
Table of refractive powers, II. 296.
Table of wind, II. 457.
Tables, II. 113.
Tables for correcting refraction and parallax, II. 371.
Tables for the nautical almanac, II. 370.
Tables of logarithms, II. 117.
Tables of measures, II. 148.
Tables of specific gravities and capacities for heat, II. 503.
Tables of the places of the heavenly bodies, II. 373.
Tablets, II. 143.
Tabor and pipe, II. 275.
Tachygraphy, II. 143.
Tackle, I. Pl. 4, 17, II. 197.
Tails of comets, I. 512, Pl. 33, II. 337.
Tajo, II. 243.
Talc, II. 419, 433.
Tallow, II. 170, 209, 291, 659.
Tamburine, I. 401.
Tangencies, II. 118.
Tangent, I. Pl. 1, II. 15.
Tangent of an ellipsis, II. 23.

Tangents, I. 106, II. 120. Inverse method of tangents, II. 123.
Tanks, II. 481.
Tap, II. 246.
Tapestry, II. 187.
Taranto, II. 493.
Tarif, II. 146.
Tarquin, I. 237.
Tarred ropes, II. 171.
Tartalea, I. 247, 253. D. 1557.
Tartini, I. 406, II. 273, 544.
Tatham, II. 177, 234, 235.
Tattee, II. 453.
Taurus, I. 504.
Tautochronous curves, II. 133.
Taylor, I. 405 .. 407, 478, 483, 754, II. 117, 119, 157, 546, 652.
Teaching the deaf, II. 278.
Teazles, II. 188.
Technology, II. 141.
Teeth, II. 518.
Teeth of wheels, I. 176, Pl. 15, II. 55, 56, 183.
Teichmeyer, II. 126.
Telegraph, I. 100, Pl. 6. II. 143, 144.
Telescope, I. 473, II. 323.
Telescope of forty feet, II. 287.
Telescopes, I. 427, . 433, Pl. 28, II. 78 .. 80, 199, 286, 315.
Telescopic level, II. 286.
Telescopic sights, II. 286, 323, 351.
Temper, I. 142.
Temperament, I. 395, Pl. 25, II. 272, 554, 610.
Temperate zones, I. 570.
Temperature, I. 696, II. 450, 461.
Temperature of a bridge, II. 176.

Temperature of condensed air, II. 408.
Temperatute of running water, I. 299.
Temperature of vegetables, II. 515.
Temperature of water, II. 223.
Temperatures, II. 394, 397, 399.
Tempering instruments, II. 207.
Tempering of metals, I. 644.
Tempering steel, II. 403.
Temper of iron, I. 627.
Temple of Solomon, II. 486.
Tempo rubato, II. 564.
Tenacity, I. 629.
Teneriffe, I. 700, II. 365, 447.
Tennant, II. 680.
Tennis, II. 132, 180.
Tenon, I. 168.
Tension of a pendulum, II. 133.
Tensions of cords, II. 200.
Tents, II. 180.
Tenuity of light, II. 320.
Tercera, II. 493.
Tertiary mountains, I. 574.
Ternate, II. 493.
Terpander, I. 403, 407, II. 566.
Terrella, or magnet in a globe, I. 689.
Terrestrial electricity, II. 419.
Terrestrial fires, II. 494.
Terrestrial heat, II. 406.
Terrestrial magnetism, I. 689, II. 440.
Terrestrial physics, II. 519.
Terrestrial refraction, I. 442, II. 300.

VOL. II.

Terzi, II. 264.
Testimony, II. 117.
Tetens, II. 381, 485.
Tetrodon, II. 436.
Textures not woven, II. 188.
Teylerian machine, II. 432.
Teylerian museum, I. 680.
Thales, I. 236 .. 239, 253, 592, 604, 743, 744, 756. B. 636. D. 546. B. C.
Thawing, I. 699, II. 394, 480.
Theatres, II. 174, 290.
Theodolite, I. 105, II. 352.
Theon, I. 604.
Theophrastus, I. 745, 756, II. 567. B. 373, D. 288. B. C.
Theorems. General theorems, II. 114.
Theories of light, I. 457.
Theory of electricity, I. 658, II. 417.
Theory of machines, II. 141.
Theory of music, II. 272.
Theory of optics, I. 408.
Theory of the earth, II. 497.
Theory of the tides, II. 342, 343.
Thermolamp, II. 291.
Thermometers, I. 647, 696, 747, II. 385, 451, 454.
Thermometrical power, II. 167.
Thermoscope, I. Pl. 39, II. 386.
Theuth, I. 236.
Thévenot, II. 244.
Thicknesse, II. 143.
Thick plates, I. 471, Pl. 30, II. 316, 628.
Thin plates, I. 468, Pl. 30, II. 316, 320, 647.

Thistle cutter, II. 208.
Thomson, II. 408, 508.
Thorowgood, II. 193.
Thoth, I. 236.
Thoughts on gravitation, II. 380.
Thouvenel, II. 261.
Thread, II. 186, 218.
Three bodies, II. 131, 139, 338.
Threshing, II. 214, 218.
Threshing machines, I. 232, II. 215, 216, 218.
Threshing mill, I. Pl. 18.
Throwing a stone, I. 226.
Throwing wheels, I. 327, Pl. 22, II. 250.
Thrust of arches, II. 176.
Thrust of earth, II. 173, 232.
Thunder, I. 713, II. 479, 481.
Thunderstorm, I. 714, II. 483.
Thyreoid cartilage, I. 400.
Tibiae, I. 404, II. 567.
Tide, II. 167, 196.
Tide machine, I. 337.
Tide mills, II. 236.
Tides, I. 576, Pl. 38, II. 341, 342, 368, 491.
Tides in the atmosphere, II. 450.
Tides of lakes, II. 343.
Tides of the Atlantic, I. 580.
Tie beam, I. 169.
Tielen, II. 141.
Tiles, II. 174.
Tiling, II. 179.
Tillet, II. 161.
Tilloch, II. 111.
Timber, II. 168.
Timber carriage, II. 202.
Timber in a ship, II. 241.
Timbers, II. 178.
Time, I. 22, 188, 537, II. 131, 347.

5 G

Time at sea, II. 348.
Time in music, II. 571.
Timekeepers, I. 188, 602, II. 191.
Time pieces, II. 191.
Timocharis, I. 506, 592, 593, 604.
Timotheus, II. 567.
Tin, II. 266, 403, 509.
Tin plate work, II. 206.
Tint, I. Pl. 6.
Titius, II. 127, 387, 520.
Titubation of the earth, II. 358.
Toad in an oak, II. 516.
Toaldo, II. 370, 446, 449, 450, 474.
Tobacco pipes, II. 266.
Tobacco press, II. 204.
Toise, II. 151.
Ton, I. 124, II. 151, 152.
Tone of sound, II. 565.
Tongs or grapples, II. 199.
Tongue, II. 278, 279.
Tonnage, II. 156.
Tools, II. 180.
Tooth of a wheel, II. 560.
Top, II. 137, 354.
Topham, I. 129.
Topham, II. 674.
Torelli, II. 157.
Tornados, II. 458.
Torpedo, I. 677, II. 435.
Torre del Greco, II. 493.
Torrents, II. 225.
Torricelli, I. 274, 354, 355, 366, 748, 756, II. 558. B. 1608, D. 1647.
Torricellian vacuum, I. 339.
Torricellius, II. 112.
Torrid zone, I. 570.
Torsion, I. 135, 140, II. 168, 383.
Tortoise, II. 312.
Tortoise shell, II. 179.

Total reflection, I. 413, 461, II. 296.
Tottering equilibrium, I. Pl. 3.
Touch hole, II. 260.
Toughness, I. 142, 629, II. 49.
Toughness of fibres, II. 185.
Toulon, II. 233.
Tourmalin, I. 674, II. 435.
Tourmalins, II. 323.
Tournefort, I. 748, 756. B. 1656, D. 1708.
Towing, II. 243.
Tozzetti, II. 107.
Trabuco, II. 155.
Trachea, I. 400.
Tracheae of birds, II. 279.
Tracheae of plants, I. 512.
Track of light, II. 281.
Traction, II. 55.
Tracts on wet docks, II. 233.
Tractors, II. 428.
Tractory, II. 121, 123, 226, 556.
Tractrix, II. 123, 556.
Trade winds, I. 701, 749, Pl. 42, 43, II. 454. Corrections.
Train of light, II. 303.
Traité des barometres, II. 459.
Traité d'optique, II. 280.
Traité du déluge, II. 496.
Traité sur les barometres, II. 448.
Trajectories, II. 132.
Tralles, II. 367.
Transferring pictures, II. 142.
Transformation of series, II. 116.
Transit circle, I. Pl. 35, II. 352.
Transit instruments, I. 541, Pl. 35, II. 348, 352, 354.

Transit of Mercury, II. 289.
Transit of the moon, II. 357.
Transit of Venus, II. 355.
Transits, II. 352, 365.
Transmission of heat, II. 407.
Transmission of impulses, II. 618.
Transmission of light, II. 321.
Transparency, II. 282.
Transparent mediums, II. 70.
Transplanting turnips, II. 212.
Transverse strain, I. 169.
Traps for drains, II. 235, 246.
Trarer, II. 310.
Treatise on gunpower, II. 260.
Trebra, II. 497.
Tree aloe, II. 185.
Trees, II. 199.
Trees electrified, II. 424.
Trembley, II. 119, 324.
Tremery, II. 666.
Tremors, II. 414, 510.
Trenches, II. 211.
Trenching plough, II. 212.
Tressan, II. 416.
Trevithick, I. 336, 349, II. 259.
Triad, I. 393.
Triangle, II. 9 .. 16, 145.
Triangle, an instrument, To I. 401.
Triangle representing forces, I. Pl. 3.
Triangles, II. 118.
Triangular compasses, I. 102, Pl. 6, II. 144.
Triangular framing, II. 241.
Trichiurus Indicus, II. 436.
Trichurus, I. 724.
Trigonometrical instrument, II. 145.

Trigonometry, II. 118.
Triple stars, I. 494.
Tripoli, II. 210.
Trisection of an angle, II. 145.
Trithemius, I. 189.
Trituration, I. 232, II. 213.
Trochi, II. Corrections.
Trochoid, I. 24, Pl. 1. II. 558.
Trombone, I. 402.
Trone pound, II. 161.
Tronthiemske selskab, II. 109.
Troostwyck, II. 419, 424.
Tropical year, I. 538.
Tropical revolutions, II. 372.
Tropics, I. 570.
Trotter, II. 481.
Troughton, I. Pl. 7, 8, II. 148, 149, 161, 351, 391.
Troy weight, II. 161.
Trudaine's lens, II. 284, 406.
Trumpet, I. 402, II. 260, 275, 566.
Trumpet Marigni, I. 399, Pl. 25, II. 267.
Trumpet marine, II. 274.
Tubes, I. 140, II. 50.
Tull, II. 212.
Tumbler, II. 257.
Tumbling figures, II. 184.
Tun, I. 124, II. 151.
Tunica albuginea, II. 530.
Tunica conjunctiva, II. 530.
Tuning, II. 554.
Tuning fork, I. 401, 656, II. 620.
Tunnel, II. 212.
Turf, II. 211.
Turin. Society of Turin, II. 109.
Turkey, II. 312.
Turner, II. 127, 235.
Turnery, II. 180.

Turning bridges, II. 178.
Turning parapet, II. 174.
Turnips, II. 208, 209, 212.
Turnor, II. 217.
Tuscan column, I. Pl. 12.
Tusser, II. 519.
Twilight, I. 526, 566, Pl. 34, II. 344.
Twilight of Venus, II. 333.
Twinkling, I. 490.
Twinkling of the stars, II. 331.
Twins, I. 497.
Twisted ropes, I. 70.
Twisted wire, II. 383.
Twisting, I. 134, 181, II. 186.
Twitching wool, II. 185.
Tycho Brahe, I. 596, 597, 604, II. 324. B. 1546, D. 1601.
Tychonic system, I. Pl. 38.
Tympanum, I. 387.
Type metal, I. 122, II. 158.
Typography, II. 158.
Types, II. 158.
Tyrrhene pipe, II. 567.
Ubaldi, I. 247.
Udina, II. 494.
Ulloa, I. 363, 511, II. 308, 346. B. 1716, D. 1795.
Ultimate ratios, II. 16, 551.
Ulugh Beigh, I. 595, 596, 604.
Umbrella, I. 375.
Umbrellas, II. 180.
Unannealed glass, II. 403.
Unctuous substances, II. 171.
Undershot wheel, I. 321 Pl. 22.
Undulations, II. 615.
Undulations of light, I. 465 II. 627, 632, 640.
Undulatory system of light II. 70.
Unequal balance, I. Pl. 8.
Unger, II. 279.

Union, I. 627, II. 377.
Union of flexible fibres, I. 180, II. 184.
Union of lights, I. 464.
Unit, II. 1.
Unit of measures, II. 146.
Universal measure, II. 146.
Unloading ships, II. 199, 243.
Unlocking horses, II. 203.
Unrolling books, II. 159.
Unterberger, II. 113.
Untersuchungen vom meere, II. 292.
Unusual refraction, II. 302.
Unzer, II. 474.
Upholstery, II. 179.
Upsal. Academy at Upsal, II. 108.
Uranometer, II. 353.
Uranus, I. 509.
Ursprung der gebirge, II. 496.
Uvea, I. 447, II. 82, 311, 530.
Vacuum, II. 377, 396, 420, 423.
Valenciennes, II. 157.
Valentin, II. 326.
Valerius, I. 247, 253.
Vallancey, II. 234.
Vallemont, II. 440.
Vallies, II. 498.
Vallisneri, II. 480.
Valsalva, II. 271.
Valve of a pump, II. 252.
Valves, I. 317, Pl. 21. II. 246.
Valves of canals, I. 315.
Vandelli, I. 364.
Vandermonde, II. 273.
Vanderzyl, II. 126.
Vanes, II. 236.
Van Eyck. See Eyck.
Vanishing point, II. 21.
Van Marum, I. 680, II. 400, 416, 431.

Van Swinden, II. 128, 365, 380, 388, 394, 437, 446, 489.
Vapour, I. 706, 711, II. 396, 420, 426, 464.
Vapour baths, II. 410.
Vapours, I. 271, 714, II. 60, 252, 388, 427, 476.
Vapours negatively electrical, I. 674.
Vara, II. 153, 154.
Varenius, II. 224, 365.
Variable pendulums, II. 133.
Variable quantities, II. 7, 119.
Variation, II. 365, 440.
Variation chart, I. Pl. 41..43.
Variation in London and in the West Indies, I. 691.
Variation of curvature, II. 120.
Variation of gravity, II. 359.
Variation of the barometer, II. 462.
Variation of the compass, I. 690, 747, 749, Pl. 41.
Variation of the declination, or change of variation, II. 691.
Variation of the moon, II. 341.
Variations, II. 66, 119.
Variations of temperature, I. 698.
Variations of the tides, II. 342.
Variations of triangles, II. 119.
Varignon, II. 129, 557, 558.
Varnish, II. 158, 180.
Varnish for electrical machines, II. 430.
Varnish microscopes, II. 286.

Varnish of silk, II. 185.
Varro, I. 98.
Vaults, II. 176.
Vausenville, II. 128.
Vega, II. 113, 117, 152, 162, 163.
Vegetable anatomy, I. 726, II. 512.
Vegetable materials, II. 184.
Vegetable physiology, II. 512.
Vegetables, I. 723.
Vegetation, II. 323, 424, 512.
Velocities, II. 7.
Velocities of the planets, I. Pl. 32.
Velocity, I. 29, 320, II. 29. Effect of velocity in overcoming strength, I. 144.
Velocity and force, II. 139.
Velocity due to a height, I. 32.
Velocity of a blast, I. 344.
Velocity of air, II. 223.
Velocity of a jet, II. 60.
Velocity of an impulse, I. 144.
Velocity of descent, I. 43.
Velocity of electricity, I. 668.
Velocity of fluids, I. 279, II. 235.
Velocity of friction, I. 633.
Velocity of light, I. 436, II. 293, 320.
Velocity of radiant heat, II. 407.
Velocity of rivers, II. 225.
Velocity of ships, II. 241.
Velocity of sound, II. 68, 69, 264, 537.
Velocity of water wheels, II. 237.
Velocity of waves, II. 64, 224.

Velocity producing fracture, II. 169.
Velser, II. 331.
Velveret, II. 187.
Vena contracta, I. Pl. 20, II. 223, 535.
Venetian painting, II. 143.
Venloo, II. 264.
Venténat, II. 512.
Ventilation, I. 344.
Ventilation by heat, II. 257.
Ventilators, II. 264.
Ventilators simply mechanical, II. 252.
Ventriloquism, II. 276.
Ventriloquists, II. 550.
Venturi, I. 281, 297, 328, Pl. 20, II. 223, 531, 534, 539.
Venus, I. 507, 527, 531, 532, 544, Pl. 33, II. 310, 333, 340, 344, 372, 374, 378.
Vera, I. Pl. 22.
Vera's rope machine, II. 250.
Veratti, II. 415.
Verdries, II. 125.
Vergilius, II. 216.
Vermes, I. 737.
Vernier, I. 105, Pl. 7, II. 218.
Verniers, II. 352.
Verona, II. 110.
Verschock, II. 154.
Versed sine, II. 15.
Vertical gnomon, II. 348.
Vertical pipe, I. 285, Pl. 20, II. 223.
Vesicles in the atmosphere, II. 306.
Vesicular vapour, II. 464.
Vessel, I. 325.
Vessels of plants, I. 727, II. 514.
Vessels of the crystalline lens, II. 598.

Vestibule, I. 387.
Vesuvius, I. 718, 719, II. 493, 494.
Viallon, II. 250.
Vibrating chord, I. Pl. 25.
Vibrations, I. 379, Pl. 25, II. 132, 377, 553, 554, 615.
Vibrations from elasticity, II. 268.
Vibrations making musical notes, II. 67.
Vibrations of a board, II. 226.
Vibrations of a chord, II. 65, 66.
Vibrations of a cylinder, II. 85.
Vibrations of an elastic rod, II. 84.
Vibrations of chords, I. 381.
Vibrations of different fluids, II. 541.
Vibrations of fluids, I. 287, II. 266.
Vibrations of heat, I. 654.
Vibrations of magnets, II. 442.
Vibrations of pendulums, II. 572.
Vibrations of plates, II. 268.
Vibrations of rods, II. 67, 266.
Vibrations of solids, II. 267.
Vibrations of sounding bodies, I. 191.
Vibrations of sounds, II. 264.
Vibrations of springs, II. 139.
Vibrations of the air, II. 536.
Vices, I. 222, II. 204.
Vielle, I. 399, II. 274.
Vienna weights, II. 161.
Vignettes, II. 158.

Vilette's mirror, II. 282.
Villehuet, II. 239.
Vince, I. 65, 152, 481, II. 121, 128, 229, 325, 347, 672.
Vinci. Da Vinci, I. 247, 253, II. 142, 217, 218. B. 1445, D. 1520.
Viola di gamba, I. 399.
Violin, I. 399.
Violins, II. 274.
Violoncello, I, 399.
Viper, I. 735.
Virgo, I. 497, II. 504.
Virtual focus, I. 414.
Virtual image, I. 422, Pl. 27.
Virtual velocities, I. 73, II. 45, 57, 140.
Viscosity, I. 629.
Visible interval, II. 575.
Vision, I. 447, II. 280, 310, 523, 574.
Vision of infants, II. 312.
Vitality, II. 518.
Vital principle, II. 518.
Vitellio, I. 473, 483. Fl. 1269.
Vitreous electricity, I. 670.
Vitreous humour, I. 448, II. 82, 311, 315, 530.
Vitriolated tartar, II. 293.
Vitruve, II. 141.
Vitruvius, I. 188, 243, 253, 352, 353, 366, Pl. 22, II. 141. Fl. 15. B. C.
Vitruvius Britannicus, II. 172.
Vivenzio, II. 492.
Viviani, II. 122.
Vliessingen, II. 109.
Voice, I. 400, Pl. 26, II. 275.
Voices of animals, II. 279.
Voigt, II. 384.
Volatilisation, II. 396.

Volcanic inundations, II. 494.
Volcanos, II. 716, II. 493.
Volcanos in the moon, I. 533, II. 336.
Volcanos in the sun, II. 331.
Volition, II. 725.
Volney, II. 452.
Volta, I. 674, 677, 678, 683, 706, 720, 751 .. 753, Pl. 40.
Voltaire, I. 253, II. 126, B. 1694, D. 1778.
Voluntaries, II. 279.
Vortex, II. 221, 226.
Vortex of fire, II. 483.
Vortices, II. 338, 340, 376, 377, 379.
Vossius, II. 112.
Vowels, I. 400, II. 276, 550.
Vox humana pipe, I. 401, Pl. 26.
Vox oculis subjecta, II. 278.
Voyage pour éprouver les montres de Leroy, II. 192.
Vulcanian theory, I. 720.
Waggon, II. 201, 202.
Waggon mill, II. 182.
Waggon overturning, I. Pl. 3.
Walking, I. Pl. 9.
Wain, I. 496.
Waiz, II. 415.
Wales, II. 365, 367.
Walker, II. 121, 128, 437.
Walking, I. 129, II. 164.
Walking wheels, I. 208, 336, II. 181, 199.
Wall, I. 159.
Waller, II. 107.
Wallerius, II. 480, 496.
Wallingford, I. 189, 246, 253. Fl. 1326.
Wallis, I. 36, 248, 253, 405, 407, II. 112, 124, 549, 558. B. 1616, D. 1713.

Wallot, II. 334.
Walls, II. 173.
Walter of Coventry, I. 245 253. Fl. 1213.
Ware, II. 592, 593.
Waring, I. 250, 253, II. 113, 114, 122, 557, 558, 681.
Warlike machines, II. 207.
Warm baths, II. 518.
Warming by steam, II. 410.
Warming rooms, II. 411.
Warping, II. 187.
Warren, II. 601.
Washing machine, II. 216.
Washing mill, II. 213.
Washing trees, II. 519.
Waste of light, II. 321.
Waste water, II. 252.
Watch, II. 244.
Watches, I. 251, II. 191, 217, 218, 370.
Watchman, II. 192.
Watch scapements, I. Pl. 26.
Watch springs, II. 207.
Water, I. 276, 372, 412, 619, 622, II. 479, 496, 509, 673. Decomposition of water, II. 423. Force of water, II. 236.
Water bellows, II. 254.
Watercock, II. 246.
Water colours, I. 95.
Water courses, II. 225.
Water in air, I. 710.
Watering, II. 249.
Watering gardens, II. 251.
Water lens, II. 284.
Water level, II. 353.
Water mill, I. 133.
Water mills, II. 167, 236.
Water pipes, I. 316, Pl. 21, II. 245, 480.
Waterpoise, II. 231.
Waterproof cloth, II. 188, 382.

Water screw, I. 329, Pl. 22, II. 250.
Water shovel, II. 248.
Water snail, I. 328.
Water spouts, I. 716, II. 486.
Water wheels, I. 302, 320. 361, Pl. 22, II. 236.
Water whimsey, I. 205, II. 250.
Watson, II. 131.
Watt, I. 48, 66, 131, 245, 250, 346, 348, 361 .. 363, Pl. 24, II. 259, 409, 610.
Wave, II, 63.
Waves, I. 287, Pl. 20, II. 221, 222, 224, 458, 621. Combinations of waves, I. 290.
Wax, II. 291, 509.
Wax candle, I. 634.
Wax casts, II. 157.
Way, II. 151.
Waywiser for a ship, II. 244.
Weak sight, II. 316.
Wearmouth bridge, II. 177.
Wears. See Weres.
Weather, I. 705, II. 447.
Weather boards, II. 180.
Weather bottle, II. 456.
Weather clock, II. 455.
Weather cord, II. 468.
Weatherglass, II. 460.
Weavers, II. 217.
Weaver's alarm, II. 196.
Weaving, I. 185, II. 187.
Weber, II. 384, 416, 425, 430.
Wedge, I. 71, 155, Pl. 4, II. 42, 135, 197, 209, 210.
Wedge moving in water, I. 303.

Wedges for stones, I. Pl. 11.
Wedgwood, I. 250, 253, 648, II. 218, 390, 399. D. 1795.
Weeds, II. 208.
Weidler, I. 511, II. 304, 324, 489.
Weigel, II. 105, 281.
Weighing, I. 123.
Weighing machines, I. 126, Pl. 9, II. 159.
Weighing money, II. 159.
Weighing ships, II. 243.
Weight, I. 16, Pl. 3, II. 379.
Weight in air, I. 38.
Weight of air, II. 221, 472.
Weight of animals, I. 152.
Weight of a vibrating chord, II. 268.
Weight of heat, II. 414.
Weight of water, II. 161, 386.
Weight on a bar, II. 44.
Weights, II. 159, 160, 196.
Weights, ancient and modern, II. 162.
Weights of clocks, I. 179.
Weissken, II. 279.
Weitbrecht, II. 652.
Welding steel, II. 207.
Well, II. 497.
Wells, II. 313, 479.
Were, I. 295, II. 62.
Weres, II. 222, 223, 234.
Werneburg, II. 116.
Werner, II. 497.
Wesley, II. 415.
West, I. 500.
Westerly winds, I. 703.
Westfeld, II. 320.
Westgarth, I. 336.
Westminster abbey, I. 245.

Westminster bridge, II. 176, 234.
Wet docks, II. 233.
Wet leather, I. 630.
Wet ropes, II. 171.
Wex, II. 250.
Whale, I. 497.
Whalebone, II. 209, 469.
Whalebone hygrometer, I. 709.
Whales, II. 207, 311.
Whararai, II. 447.
Wheat, I. 124, II. 151, 167.
Wheel, I. Pl. 1, 14.
Wheel and axis, I. 67, Pl. 3, II. 40, 196.
Wheel barometer, II. 459.
Wheelbarrows, II. 166, 202.
Wheel boats, II. 242.
Wheel carriages, I. 214, Pl. 18, II. 201.
Wheel cutting machine, I. 178.
Wheelcutter, I. Pl. 15, II. 210.
Wheel of Orfyreus, I. Pl. 6.
Wheels, I. 213, 216, II. 54, 181, 183.
Wheels and pinions, I. 67.
Wheels of timekeepers, II. 193.
Wheels with straps, I. Pl. 15.
Wheel thermometer, II. 388.
Wheelways of iron, I. 218.
Wheelwork, I. 175, II. 55, 183.
Whetstones, II. 210.
Whimsey, I. 205, II. 250.
Whinstone, II. 498.
Whip, I. 227.
Whips, II. 189.

Whirling table, I. 34, 261, Pl. 1.
Whirlpool, I. 285.
Whirlwind, II. 458, 499.
Whispering gallery, I. 376.
Whispering letters, II. 276, 277.
Whistling, I. 402.
Whiston, II. 125, 495.
Whitehead, II. 350.
Whiteburst, I. 111, 189, 338, II. 146, 253, 497.
White lead, II. 180, 214.
White light, I. 437, II. 296.
White lights, II. 146.
White's crane, I. 209, Pl. 17.
Whizzing of a meteor, II. 265.
Whole number, II. 1.
Whydah, II. 465.
Wiebeking, II. 232.
Wideburg, II. 285.
Wiedeburg, II. 337, 366, 474, 489, 496.
Wiegleb, II. 127, 264, 680.
Wildenow, II. 511.
Wilfrid, I. 244, 253.
Wilke, I. 750, 751, 756, II. 426, 436, 508.
Wilkins, I. 253, 365, II. 129. B. 1614, D. 1672.
Wilkinson, II. 366.
Wilkinson, II. 419, 430, 597.
William of Sens, I. 245.
William IV, I. 596, 604.
Williams, II. 361, 441, 674.
Willich, II. 111, 129.
Willughby, I. 748, 756, II. 486. B. 1635, D. 1672.
Wilson, I. 501, 715, Pl. 31, II. 285, 293, 415.

Winch, I 131, 174, 204, Pl. 3, II. 140, 165, 166, 181, 182.
Winches, II. 182.
Wind, I. 324, 705, II. 167, 221, 226, 238, 244, 450, 463.
Wind and water, I. 363.
Wind fane, II. 456.
Wind gages, I. 319, II. 456.
Winding, II. 185, 186.
Wind instruments, II. 275, 539.
Windlass, II. 165.
Windmills, I. 133, 323, 354, 359, Pl. 22, II. 167, 212, 213, 238, 249, 263.
Windows, II. 174, 179, 253.
Windpipes, II. 279.
Winds, I. 696, 701, II. 454.
Windsails, II. 252.
Wine casks, II. 233.
Wine press, II. 204.
Winkler, I. 750, II. 126, 265, 380, 383, 414, 418, 431, 481, 485, 489. B. 1703, D. 1770.
Winnowing machine, II. 215, 216, 252.
Winslow, II. 523, 591.
Winter, I. 525, 700.
Winter sleep, II. 514, 518.
Wire, I. 244, II. 86, 217, 378, 383, 387.
Wire cloth, II. 187.
Wire drawing, I. 223, II. 205.
Wire for pinions, II. 183.

Wire gratings, II. 189.
Wires shortened by electricity, II. 423.
Wirtz, I. 329, Pl. 22.
Withering, II. 512.
Witsen, II. 240.
Wolf, II. 516.
Wolff, II. 125.
Wolff, II. 128.
Wolfius, II. 220.
Wollaston. Dr. Wollaston, I. 421, 425, 437, 438, 442, 444, 445, 480, 639, 753, Pl. 27, 29, 39, Corrections, II. 224, 307, 319, 348, 580, 581, 584, 585, 595, 637, 638, 647, 672, 679, 680. Rev. F. Wollaston, I. Pl. 35, II. 326.
Wollaston on horizontal refraction, and on the dip, II. 302.
Woltmann, I. Pl. 22, II. 232, 236.
Wood, I. 151, II. 48, 169, 180, 231, 266, 411.
Wood cuts, I. 118, II. 218.
Wooden bridges, I. 171, Pl. 14, II. 178.
Wooden springs, II. 182.
Woodhouse, II. 111, 612.
Wood shining, II. 292.
Woodstock park, II. 266.
Wood and mercury, II. 555.
Woodward, II. 332, 495.
Woody strata, II. 512.
Wool, I. 185, II. 184, 218.

Wool combing, II. 185.
Woollen clothes, II. 468.
Woollen manufactures, I. 244, II. 217.
Wootz, II. 207.
Worcester. Marquis of Worcester, I. 346, 356, 366, II. 124. D. 1667.
Working stones, II. 208.
Work of a labourer, I. 331.
Works of single authors, II. 111.
Worms, II. 240, 518.
Worsteds, II. 425.
Wounds of trees, II. 510.
Woven rope, II. 187.
Wren, I. 248, 255, 599, 602. B. 1632, D. 1723.
Writing, I. 93, 97.
Wright, II. 249, 325.
Wrisberg, II. 591.
Writing, II. 143.
Writing music, II. 279.
Writing voluntaries, II. 279.
Wunsch, I. 373.
Wurm, II. 335.
Wynn, II. 166.
Ximenes, II. 168, 222.
Yard, II. 148, 150.
Year, II. 376.
Yoke, II. 203.
Yoke of land, II. 155.
York minster, I. 245.
Young. A. Young, II. 519. M. Young, I. 281, II. 129, 259, 264, 438, 489, 539, 549. T. Young, II.

438, 671, 679, 680, 682. Walter Young, II. 564.
Yvette, II. 234.
Zach, II. 325, 333, 373, 673, 675.
Zahn, II. 303, 311, 446, 501.
Zallinger, II. 435.
Zarlino, II. 272, 554.
Zealand Society, II. 109.
Zeeuwsch genootschap, II. 109.
Zeiher, II. 287, 295.
Zenith sectors, I. 541, Pl. 35, II. 352.
Zephyr, II. 253.
Zero, I. 654. Natural zero, II. 409.
Ziegler, II. 410.
Zigzag, II. 248.
Zimmermann, II. 326, 379.
Zinc, II. 180, 509.
Zinn, II. 311, 524, 525.
Zircknitz, II. 479.
Zodiac, II. 376.
Zodiacal light, I. 502, Pl. 31, II. 303, 332.
Zona ciliaris, II. 550.
Zone of the crystalline, II. 605.
Zones, I. 570.
Zoology, II. 516.
Zucchius, I. 481, II. 280.
Zuliani, II. 140, 228.
Zurich. Society at Zurich, II. 109.
Zuyderzee, I. 721.

THE END.

William Savage, Printer, Bedford Bury.